A Checklist of Canadian Literature
and Background Materials
1628-1960

A CHECKLIST OF

Canadian Literature

AND BACKGROUND MATERIALS

1628-1960

In two parts: first, a comprehensive list of the books which
constitute Canadian literature written in English; and second,
a selective list of other books by Canadian authors which
reveal the backgrounds of that literature

Second edition, revised and enlarged

REGINALD EYRE WATTERS

The Royal Military College of Canada

UNIVERSITY OF TORONTO PRESS

First edition 1959
© University of Toronto Press 1959
Reprinted 1960, 1966
Second edition 1972
© University of Toronto Press 1972
Toronto and Buffalo

Printed in Canada

ISBN 0-8020-1866-1
Microfiche ISBN 0-8020-0197-1
LC 72-80713

To the memory of
Professor A.S.P. Woodhouse
1895-1964
Teacher, colleague, friend

FOREWORD TO THE FIRST EDITION

When the Humanities Research Council of Canada received its first grant from the Rockefeller Foundation, it determined to put a part of its funds into an effort to foster comparative studies of culture and letters in Canada and other members of the British Commonwealth, and first of Australia, in the belief that a comparison of what happened to the British tradition when set down on two such different frontiers could hardly fail to yield interesting results. It was soon discovered, however, that while Australia had Edmund Miller's bibliography, *Australian Literature,* Canada lacked a comparable instrument of research altogether; and the Council decided that before any effective work could be done a checklist of English-Canadian writings must be provided. Accordingly, it invited Dr. R.E. Watters of the University of British Columbia to undertake the task. Though the Council was able to promise no more than the defraying of actual expenses, and could not even guarantee publication of his results, he heroically undertook the task, which he has now brought to completion. As Dr. Watters explains in his preface, he has conformed to the desires of the Council and has produced a work differing in scope and character from Miller's *Australian Literature* in two respects. It casts a wider net by going beyond belles-lettres to include a selection of writings illustrating historical and social background. It makes no attempt to record full bibliographical detail, but is frankly a checklist of Canadian writings in English from the beginning to 1950, designed to furnish a starting point for, and to give practical aid to, further research.

It was the hope of the Council that the study of Canadian culture and letters would itself benefit greatly from the plan of comparative examination; and even from this preliminary effort the benefit to Canadian studies will be immense: for Dr. Watters' work is the indispensable instrument for further exploration in the Canadian field, and for the writing of the literary history of Canada now being planned.

On behalf of the Humanities Research Council, I would express gratitude to Dr. Watters for his devoted labours, to the Rockfeller Foundation for the support that has made these labours possible, and to the University of Toronto Press for its very generous grant in aid of publication.

A.S.P. WOODHOUSE
Chairman, Humanities Research Council of Canada

University College
Toronto
9 October 1958

PREFACE

This revised and enlarged *Checklist of Canadian Literature* attempts to provide as complete a record as possible of the separately published works that constitute the literature of English-speaking Canada up to 1960. Its purpose is to stimulate interest and suggest research in our literary culture, to reveal individual figures and areas of investigation rich in published material, and to facilitate the finding of the books concerned. Background materials are included because the cultural soil must be known if a nation's belles-lettres are to be adequately studied or fully appreciated.

Part I of the *Checklist* attempts to record all known titles in the recognized forms of poetry, fiction, and drama that were produced by English-speaking Canadians.[1] The titles and accompanying information had to be obtained from the entries of the various library catalogues searched, and not from actual examination of the books themselves. Therefore, no attempt whatever was made to apply any qualitative evaluation of these writings. The *Checklist* is simply an inventory of what Canadians are known to have published, together with some locations where the publications can be found. Separation of the bad from the excellent, the trivial from the important, can come only from those who carefully examine and appraise the books listed here. It is to be hoped that among the thousands of forgotten or overlooked books many more of significant worth may be found to exist than Canadians at present may expect.

Part II of the *Checklist* does not aim at the same completeness. It is a more or less selective listing of books by Canadians which seem likely to be of value to anyone studying the literature or culture of Canada. Here are included books in such categories as biography, literary criticism, scholarship, local history, religion, and so forth. Books in more general categories with less immediate relationship to literature — such as military, economic, or constitutional history, and writings in law, commerce, or the sciences — have been omitted.

The inadequacies of Part II, in both the original (1959) edition and this revision, are readily acknowledged. I had hoped — too optimistically, it is true — that during the dozen years following the first appearance of the *Checklist* properly qualified persons would have produced checklists or bibliographies in the various categories of Part II, and thereby rendered unnecessary the entire section. Although this has not yet happened, excellent beginnings have been made. Raymond Tanghe's *Bibliography of Canadian Bibliographies* (1960), together with its *Supplements* and the second edition edited by Douglas Lochhead (1972) — not to mention *On Canadian Literature 1806–1960* (1966), co-authored by the present compiler and Inglis Freeman Bell — make unnecessary the retention of a "Bibliography" section in

---

[1] The title of earliest date is *Quodlibets Lately Come Over from New Britaniola, Old NewFound-Land. ...* This is a collection of epigrams and verses by Robert Hayman, printed in London in 1628.

this revision. Similarly, the "Education" section has been dropped because of the appearance of such works as *A Bibliography of Higher Education in Canada* (1960) by Robin Harris and Arthur Tremblay, with its supplements (1965, 1971). Eventually, if not quite yet, the multiplication of such works as Bruce Peel's *A Bibliography of the Prairie Provinces to 1953* (1956), *Supplement* (1963), William F.E. Morley's *The Atlantic Provinces* (1967), and André Beaulieu's *La Province de Québec* (1971), written in collaboration with Benoit Bernier and Agathe Garon — the first three volumes of a projected series of bibliographies of Canadian local histories — may also render superfluous the "Local History" section of the present *Checklist.* Meanwhile, literary scholars awaiting more of such specialized compilations may perhaps still find useful the material provided here in Part II. (The "Miscellaneous" section of the original edition has also been eliminated. Enough information was found about each title to permit it to be either re-classified or dropped as irrelevant to the intention of the *Checklist.*)

To the best of my knowledge, all of the approximately 16,000 books[2] listed in both parts of the *Checklist* are by Canadian authors, some 7,000 of whom are represented here. The definition of "Canadian author" was, however, deliberately left very broad. In dealing with thousands of authors it seemed wiser to include persons whose claims might be rather weak than to attempt an impracticable strictness. Decisions based on place of birth, length of residence in Canada, whether certain books were written in or out of Canada, or reflected early Canadian environment, and so on, may be very appealing in theory, but their application poses staggering problems. The extreme difficulty of discovering enough biographical or other information — even dates of birth or death — about authors of limited production or small reputation to make such decisions possible can be appreciated only when it is experienced. Of course, the great majority of the authors listed could, if required, conform to stringent definitions. However, it should be understood that Canadian birth alone was not considered a sufficient claim for persons who left Canada in early childhood and apparently never returned. On the other hand, persons who came to Canada in maturity to reside here and then commenced or continued as authors are normally included, whether or not in later life they left the country. Authors who might be termed tourists or visitors (whether in private or official capacity) are excluded. To be sure, exceptions exist to all working principles and must remain until much more information about our authors becomes generally available. Definitions that can be applied only to well-known persons are obviously useless to screen others whose lives might be parallel but about whom almost nothing can be found. To exclude the known and include the unknown solves no problems, even though in practice this result may have been inadvertently achieved all too often. In previous compilations of a

---

[2]This revised and expanded edition includes up to 4,000 more titles than the original edition. Between twenty and twenty-five per cent of these are titles published before 1951; the rest have dates up to 1960.

somewhat similar nature but different purpose (e.g., *The Canadian Catalogue of Books ... with Imprint 1921–1949,* the *Check List of Canadian Imprints 1900–1925,* and the National Library's *Canadiana*), books by Canadians, about Canada, or printed in Canada were combined, sometimes without national identification of the authors. A great many names and titles found in these lists do not appear in this *Checklist* simply because investigation revealed them not to be Canadian even by loose definition. No doubt the decisions made about various individual authors will often be considered arbitrary, but in the absence of wider agreement the contrary decisions would have been regarded by other critics as no less arbitrary.

Separate publication was a requirement for each work listed. A minimum of 8 or 9 pages was also required, although some items of fewer pages, mostly poetry, were included for reasons that seemed sufficient to override this principle of minimum length. Offprints of periodical articles, even when separately bound or catalogued in libraries, were excluded. Consequently, the "Transactions" and similar publications of the numerous societies are not listed.[3] Sometimes, of course, material that first appeared in a periodical was also published independently under the same or a different title. These items were listed if they met the requirement of minimum length.

Canadian bibliography is complicated by facts of publication which are relatively unusual elsewhere. For instance, a novel by a Canadian may appear with a New York imprint or a London imprint or a Canadian imprint, or with two or even all three different imprints. The copy bearing the Canadian imprint may actually have been printed in England by the English publisher, and may therefore have the same pagination as the English imprint, whereas the American imprint may have 15 or 30 more or fewer pages. Or the Canadian and American imprints may have the same pagination, with the English imprint being different. Sometimes all three imprints have slightly different pagination, and occasionally different copyright dates. Whenever it seemed clear that the same work was involved, the existence of these variant imprints was not normally indicated in this *Checklist*, since for nearly all purposes it would make little or no difference to a reader whether he reads an American edition of 198 pages or an English or Canadian edition of 204 pages. The imprint with earliest copyright date, when located in a library, is regularly preferred in almost all circumstances — and when a change of title is known the change is also recorded. Canadian imprints were regarded without prejudice either for or against. However, because of the availability and up-to-date excellence of the printed catalogues of the British Museum Library and the Library of Congress, the *Checklist* undoubtedly contains a high proportion of British and American imprints of Canadian books, and thereby probably creates a misleading impression about Canadian publishing quite unwarranted by the actual facts.

[3] A very useful project for some future bibliographer would be a combined index of all the papers and reports printed in the Transactions and Proceedings of Canada's many historical and literary societies.

Another result of the disregarding of different imprints should also be stated. Out of five library locations which follow a title, all but one library may have copies with a different imprint and pagination, or a later date. To connect each library with its specific holding would have demanded labour and apparatus incommensurate with the immediate purpose of the *Checklist.*

For the works published between 1950 and 1960 the various cumulative volumes of *Canadiana* were the usual source of the bibliographical data given here. For the vast majority of the pre-1950 titles the information was obtained from library catalogue entries, either as filmed by the National Library or filed as print-outs, photo-copies, etc., in the Union Catalogue in Ottawa. Libraries are by no means uniform about the information provided on their catalogue cards. For instance, pagination and the names of printers or publishers are sometimes omitted. Direct inquiry would almost always elicit the desired information, but the burden of correspondence was too great to remedy all such incompleteness. Minor differences in pagination as recorded from library to library were disregarded, because the main purpose in supplying pagination — to distinguish between slight pamphlets and substantial volumes — was not affected.

The towns or cities given as places of publication are in Canada unless otherwise indicated — except for well-known cities in Great Britain and the United States; "London, Ont." is so identified. Unless confusion was probable between towns of the same name in different provinces, no provincial designation was considered necessary. For clarity and practical convenience, and in accord with the official preference of the Post Office, "Saint John" is the form used for the New Brunswick city as a place of publication, regardless of whether or not the form "St. John" was employed by the printers. If the form "St. John" appeared in the *title* of the book, however, the *Checklist* also uses "St. John" in recording the title, while adhering to "Saint John" for place of publication. The Newfoundland capital is always given as "St. John's," while the third city of this trio is given as "St. John, Que."

Most of the location symbols used to indicate libraries are those created by the bibliographic staff of the National Library for use in the Union Catalogue of Canadian Libraries.[4] Other symbols, also explained in the list of abbreviations, were

---

[4]Since the original compilation of this *Checklist* some important library changes have occurred which are, from my point of view, rather unfortunate. Many of the titles with the location-symbol OOP (Library of Parliament) have been transferred to the National Library, which uses OONL as symbol. The same kind of transfer has recently occurred in Toronto, with many, if not most, of the Toronto Public Library (OTP) holdings being taken over by the Metropolitan Toronto Library Board, whose symbol is OTMCL. Finally, the symbol NSHPL is now being used not to indicate just a holding by the Nova Scotia Provincial Library itself, but rather a listing in the Nova Scotia Union Catalogue maintained there to record the holdings of some forty libraries in the province. Entries in the Union Catalogue in Ottawa do not yet record these transfers and changes. For me or my assistants to recheck in person all titles with OOP, OTP, or NSHPL locations was simply impossible - and not really necessary. Persons wishing to examine at first hand any particular book associated here with one of these location symbols will surely be given all possible help by the reference staffs of the libraries concerned.

required for titles not located in any of the libraries searched. For nearly every such title the source was a book-seller's catalogue or a bibliography or reference book, such as Tod and Cordingley's *A Check-List of Canadian Imprints 1900–1925* or Morgan's *Canadian Men and Women of the Time.* Non-biographical compilations of more general character, such as the *English Catalogue, American Catalogue,* or *Cumulative Book Index,* although frequently consulted were not systematically checked, because the main effort had to be expended on discovering information sufficient to determine Canadian authorship and on titles that could be located in libraries. Otherwise it would have been all too easy to group together titles by two authors of the same name, only one of whom was a Canadian. The unlocated titles included here are offered in the hope that their being listed may lead to acquisition of the actual books by libraries or collectors. Any compiler of a checklist who includes unlocated titles incurs the risk of offering possibly "phantom" titles of non-existent books. However, to me, the risk has seemed somewhat vindicated by the fact that a great many titles unlocated in the original edition have subsequently been located for this revised edition. Another fact may also be mentioned: the vast improvement in the Canadiana holdings of our major libraries during the past decade or so can readily be verified by the greatly increased number of locations recorded in this revision.

However, users of the *Checklist* are asked to remember that only rarely is more than one sample location given for each of four areas in Canada: the Maritimes, Quebec, Ontario, the west. A book might be owned by every major library in Ontario, for instance, but have its title associated here with only one library in that province. Location symbols, therefore, are no reliable indication of the prevalence or scarcity of any book.

No locations at all are provided for titles published between 1951 and 1960 inclusive. The simple reason is that all or nearly all of these are held by the National Library and can probably also be found in those university libraries which have consistently and energetically been adding steadily to their Canadiana collections during the past twenty years.

The classification of titles into the various categories will, it is hoped, be recognized for the tentative effort it is. Despite the risks of making grotesque errors when the books themselves could not be examined, the attempt seemed well worth while. Library call-numbers were, of course, the principal source of information - but disagreement was not infrequently found, with a title classified as fiction in one library, biography in another, and travel and description in a third. In such an event, the practice in the *Checklist* was to follow the decision of the majority of the libraries holding the book or the more authoritative of two. When possible, such books were of course examined. No perfect solution, however, could be discovered for border-line cases, such as the character sketches and familiar essays and fictional satires of writers like Stephen Leacock, or books of miscellaneous prose generally, even though the makeshift category of "Poetry and Prose" might serve for

xiv   A CHECKLIST OF CANADIAN LITERATURE

combinations of these two forms. The Author Index is designed to enable any reader to compile for himself the complete canon of any author's publications which come within the scope of the *Checklist*. By subsequently examining the books themselves, he can achieve more precise classifications. Plans for considerably more extensive classifications within this *Checklist* were eventually abandoned with reluctance simply because they could not be achieved by available methods. For instance, the complete separation of juvenile from adult fiction would have been a desirable accomplishment, and grouping local history by region or community, and biography by subject, would be more useful than arranging simply by author - but such divisions would be possible only by actual examination of the books, since not all library catalogue entries attempt to give the information which would be needed.

The Index of Anonymous Titles is partly intended to lead a reader with the actual book in hand to discover the name of the author if that is known, just as the inclusion of initials and pseudonyms in the Author Index, with cross-references to the real name when it is known, is intended to serve a similar purpose. Sometimes the anonymity or pseudonymity was broken by the compiler or his assistants through examination of biographical books; more often, perhaps, the real author was uncovered by finding that one or two libraries attributed the title to him, even though in other libraries the real authorship apparently remained unknown. In this way the *Checklist* should serve as a kind of clearing-house for such information. If a descriptive term such as "Backwoodsman" or "A Manitoba Lady" was used on a title-page instead of a proper name, the work was considered to be pseudonymous rather than anonymous and is to be found by looking under "Backwoodsman" or "Manitoba Lady" in the Author Index. Books published with initials instead of names may also be found through the Author Index, with the last initial regarded as the name. Thus, a book whose author designated himself "A.B.C." would be found under "C., A.B."

In the world of bibliography perfect accuracy and total inclusiveness, however ardently desired and pursued, have apparently seldom if ever been achieved. Users of this book, therefore, are cordially urged to send corrections and additions to the compiler or to the University of Toronto Press.

I welcome the present opportunity of here recording manifold acknowledgements:

The project of compiling *A Checklist of Canadian Literature...* was originally conceived by a committee of the Humanities Research Council of Canada headed by the late Professor A.S.P. Woodhouse.[5] To him I shall always remain deeply indebted on many counts.

My preface to the original edition mentioned the names of some of the scores of persons who contibuted advice, information, and effort, or assisted in other ways

---

[5]The foreword written by Professor Woodhouse for the original edition is reprinted on a previous page.

towards its preparation. I would here like to reiterate my most sincere thanks to them and to those left unnamed, for only upon the foundation which they helped to build could this revised and enlarged edition be constructed.

Although perhaps fewer persons were directly involved in preparing this revision, their assistance was equally indispensable. Again I received encouragement and generous help from librarians across the country, whose answers to my letters enabled me to re-classify correctly titles about which I had enquired and complete entries in which some bibliographical data were missing. Again I was provided with working facilities and staff assistance by Miss Martha Shepard of the National Library while working with the Union Catalogue in Ottawa. Other librarians whose contributions were especially valuable included Mr. Inglis F. Bell, Associate Librarian, University of British Columbia; Miss N.V. Gregg, Head of the Reference Department, Harriet Irving Library, University of New Brunswick; and Dr. Douglas Lochhead, Librarian of Massey College, Toronto. Each of these, by making available to me the results of a search of their library's card catalogue for titles given in the original *Checklist,* has saved me countless hours in my attempt to provide an increased number of present locations. Similar help was afforded me by the staff of the Library of the University of Western Ontario.

My colleague, Dr. George Parker, not only searched the new series of British Museum printed catalogues for locations and additional titles and transcribed for me the results of his previous search of the catalogues of the University of Toronto libraries, but also solved some puzzles by direct investigation at Toronto and at the British Museum. Also to be thanked is Elizabeth McGaw, whose accurate typing in recording some thousands of new entries was indispensable. Thanks to the support of a grant to the Royal Military College by the Defence Research Board, I was able to enlist the help of Mrs. Molly McClung (now Dr. McClung) in the summer of 1971, when I was incorporating and consolidating the added material with that of the original edition, filling gaps in entries, checking and rechecking, and preparing the final master-copy. Because of her interest and efficiency the work proceeded more expeditiously than I had dared to hope. Credit is also due to my wife Beth, who has lived with the *Checklist* since its inception, has transcribed data from film and cards, has read proof, has stood for what must have seemed interminable hours before the long lines of Union Catalogue drawers in the National Library extracting information, and is still cheerful, as I write this, about the proofreading of this revised edition yet to come.

Finally, among individuals whose correspondence or conversation has been especially helpful, I wish to thank, however inadequately, the following: Dr. Fred Cogswell, Mr. T.B. Higginson, Mr. R.D. Hilton Smith, Dr. Carl F. Klinck, Mr. William F.E. Morley, Mr. Edward Phelps, and Dr. Gordon Roper.

To the Canada Council I am particularly indebted for the award of a Senior Fellowship for 1967-68, which enabled me to devote a full year to planning this revised edition and accomplishing a major part of the task. I wish also to express my appreciation to the Royal Military College of Canada, which granted me leave of absence for that year and has since provided me with essential secretarial and other facilities.

To the staff of the University of Toronto Press, and in particular to Miss Jean Jamieson and Miss Jean Wilson, who provided editorial supervision and readied the master-copy for the printers, I am deeply obligated. Their unstinted professional assistance has been invaluable in reducing the number of inconsistencies and errors.

Perhaps my heaviest obligations, nevertheless, are still to those predecessors, known and unknown, upon whose earlier work this *Checklist* is built. Such pioneers in Canadian biography and bibliography as Henry J. Morgan, C.C. James, W. Stewart Wallace, Marie Tremaine, and many others are here saluted. I wish also to express my indebtedness to Dr. Jean Lunn and her assistants for their invaluable compilation, the National Library's *Canadiana* volumes. The host of anonymous cataloguers responsible for the cards in all the library collections searched, including those compiling the Union Catalogue at the National Library in Ottawa, and especially those who produced the monumental printed catalogues of the British Museum and the Library of Congress, are here being collectively thanked once again. Without their careful skills and prodigious labours the *Checklist of Canadian Literature* simply could not have existed. My sincere hope is that the work done here will, in turn, be of use to them or their successors, as well as to readers and students of Canadian literature and its backgrounds.

This book has been published with the help of a grant from the Humanities Research Council of Canada, using funds provided by the Canada Council.

R.E.W.

Kingston, Ontario
15 September 1971

SYMBOLS AND ABBREVIATIONS

(A symbol used to indicate a library location, but which is not included in this list, may be found in *Symbols of Canadian Libraries,* 4th ed., 1968, National Library of Canada.)

AC	Alberta: Calgary Public Library
ACG	Alberta: Glenbow Foundation, Calgary
ACU	Alberta: University of Calgary
Adelphi	Divers catalogues issued by The Adelphi Book Shop, Victoria, B.C.
AE	Alberta: Edmonton Public Library
AEP	Alberta: Provincial Library, Edmonton
AEU	Alberta: University of Alberta, Edmonton
Allibone: Supp	*A Critical Dictionary of English Literature and British and American Authors. ...* By S. Austin Allibone. With Supplement in 2v by John Foster Kirk. (Philadelphia, Lippincott, 1891)
AmCat	*American Catalogue of Books,* 1861–1910; also its predecessor Roorbach's *Bibliotheca Americana,* 1820–1861
Amtmann	Divers Canadiana catalogues issued by Bernard Amtmann, Bookseller, Montreal
BCF	*A Bibliography of Canadian Fiction* (English). By Lewis E. Horning and Lawrence J. Burpee. (Toronto, Briggs, 1904)
BibC	*Bibliotheca Canadensis; or, A Manual of Canadian Literature.* By Henry J. Morgan. (Ottawa, Desbarats, 1867)
BKO	British Columbia: Okanagan Regional Library, Kelowna
BM	British Museum, London. Printed Catalogues, 1881–1900; 1900–1905; 1959–1966
Brown U	Harris Poetry Collection, Brown University, Providence, R.I.
BVa	British Columbia: Vancouver Public Library
BVaS	British Columbia: Simon Fraser University, Burnaby
BVaU	British Columbia: University of British Columbia, Vancouver

BVi British Columbia: Victoria Public Library

BViP British Columbia: Provincial Library, Victoria

BViPA British Columbia: Provincial Archives, Victoria

BViV British Columbia: University of Victoria

CAAE Canadian Association for Adult Education, Commission for Continuous Learning. "A Selective Bibliography of Canadian Plays" (1957)

CanLit *Canadian Literature,* ed. by George Woodcock, 1959–. [a continuing serial]

CAR *The Canadian Annual Review of Public Affairs,* 1901–1938. Ed. by J. Castell Hopkins [*et al.*]. (Toronto, Canadian Review Co., 1903–)

CBI *Cumulative Book Index,* 1928– [a continuing serial]; also its predecessor *The United States Catalogue,* 1912–1928

CC *Canadian Catalogue of Books Published in Canada, about Canada, as well as Those Written by Canadians* [with Imprints 1921–1949]. (Toronto, Public Libraries, 1923–1950)

CCJ *A Bibliography of Canadian Poetry (English).* By Charles C. James. (Toronto, Briggs, 1899)

CT *Canadian Novelists 1920–1945.* By Clara Thomas. (Toronto, Longmans, 1946)

CWW *The Canadian Who's Who.* Ed. by Charles G.D. Roberts and Arthur L. Tunnell [*et al.*]. (Toronto, Trans-Canada Press, 1936–). [A continuing serial. Figures following the letters abbreviate the year of issue of the volume referred to.]

DCB *The Dictionary of Canadian Biography.* By W. Stewart Wallace. 2nd ed. in 2v. (Toronto, Macmillan, 1945)

Dionne *Inventaire chronologique,* 4v, by Narcisse E. Dionne. Quebec, 1905–1909

Dora Hood Divers Canadiana catalogues issued by the Dora Hood Bookstore, Toronto

EngCat *The English Catalogue of Books,* 1801–. [a continuing serial]

Haight *Canadian Catalogue of Books* [1791–1895]. By W.R. Haight. (Toronto, Haight, 1896). Also the Supplements covering 1896–1897 and 1898–1904

LC Library of Congress, Washington, D.C. Printed Catalogues with supplements

Matthews *Canadian Diaries and Autobiographies,* by William Matthews. Berkeley, U. of California Press, 1950

MBC   Manitoba: Brandon University

MOR   *The Canadian Men and Women of the Time. A Handbook of Canadian Biography.* By Henry J. Morgan. (Toronto, Briggs, 1898). Rev. and enl. ed.: Toronto, Briggs, 1912. [Figures following the letters abbreviate the date of the 1898 or 1912 edition.]

MW   Manitoba: Winnipeg Public Library

MWP   Manitoba: Provincial Library, Winnipeg

MWU   Manitoba: University of Manitoba, Winnipeg

MWUC   Manitoba: University of Winnipeg (formerly United College)

NBB   *New Brunswick Bibliography.* ... By William G. McFarlane. (Saint John, Sun Print., 1895)

NBFL   New Brunswick: Legislative Library, Fredericton

NBFU   New Brunswick: University of New Brunswick, Fredericton

NBS   New Brunswick: Saint John Regional Library

NBSaM   New Brunswick: Mount Allison University, Sackville

NBSM   New Brunswick: New Brunswick Museum, Saint John

NBSU   New Brunswick: University of New Brunswick in Saint John

NfSA   Newfoundland: Provincial Archives, St. John's

NfSG   Newfoundland: Gosling Memorial Library, St. John's

NfSL   Newfoundland: Legislative Library, St. John's

NfSM   Newfoundland: Memorial University, St. John's

NSH   Nova Scotia: Halifax Memorial Library

NSHA   Nova Scotia: Canada Fisheries Research Board, Halifax

NSHD   Nova Scotia: Dalhousie University, Halifax

NSHK   Nova Scotia: University of King's College, Halifax

NSHL   Nova Scotia: Legislative Library, Halifax

NSHP   Nova Scotia: Public Archives, Halifax

NSHPL*   Nova Scotia Public Library, Halifax

NSWA   Nova Scotia: Acadia University, Wolfville

OH   Ontario: Hamilton Provincial Library

OHM   Ontario: McMaster University, Hamilton

OKQ   Ontario: Queen's University, Kingston

OKR   Ontario: Royal Military College of Canada, Kingston

* See footnote 4 on page xii.

OL   Ontario: London Public Library

OLU   Ontario: University of Western Ontario, London

OOA   Ontario: Public Archives Library, Ottawa

OOC   Ontario: Ottawa Public Library

OOCC   Ontario: Carleton College [now Carleton University] , Ottawa

OODF   Ontario: Library, Department of Forestry and Rural Development, Ottawa

OOGB   Ontario: Geographical Bureau Library, Ottawa

OOL   Ontario: Department of Labour, Ottawa

OOND   Department of National Defence, Administration Branch, Interservice Reference Library, Ottawa

OONL   Ontario: National Library of Canada, Ottawa

OONM   Ontario: National Museum, Ottawa

OOP*   Ontario: Library of Parliament, Ottawa

OORD   Ontario: Department of Indian Affairs and Northern Development Library, Ottawa

OOS   Ontario: Dominion Bureau of Statistics, Ottawa

OOSJ   Ontario: Scolasticat St.-Joseph, Ottawa

OOSU   Ontario: St. Paul University, Ottawa

OOT   Ontario: Department of Transport

OOU   Ontario: University of Ottawa, Ottawa

OPAL   Ontario: Lakehead University, Port Arthur

OSu   Ontario: Laurentian University, Sudbury

OTAr   Ontario: Ontario Archives, Toronto

OTK   Ontario: Knox College Library, University of Toronto

OTL   Ontario: Legislative Library, Toronto

OTMC   Ontario: Massey College, University of Toronto

OTP*   Ontario: Toronto Public Library

OTTC   Ontario: University of Trinity College, Toronto

OTU   Ontario: University of Toronto, Toronto

OTUV   Ontario: Victoria University, Toronto

OTW   Ontario: Wycliffe College, Toronto

OTY   Ontario: York University, Toronto

OWA   Ontario: University of Windsor (formerly Assumption University)

* See footnote 4 on page xii.

OWtL Ontario: Waterloo Lutheran University

OWtU Ontario: University of Waterloo

Patrick cat Divers catalogues issued by Joseph Patrick, book dealer, Toronto

PC Prince Edward Island: Prince Edward Island Libraries, Charlottetown

PCL Prince Edward Island: Legislative and Public Library, Charlottetown

Peel *A Bibliography of the Prairie Provinces to 1953.* Comp. by Bruce Braden Peel. (Toronto, University of Toronto Press, 1956.) [Supplement, 1963.]

Phelps *A Bibliography of Lambton County and the City of Sarnia, Ontario,* by Edward Phelps. University of Western Ontario Library Bulletin Series, No. 8 (March 1970)

QMBM Quebec: Bibliothèque de la Ville de Montréal

QMG Quebec: Sir George Williams University, Montreal

QMJ Quebec: Jewish Public Library, Montreal

QML Quebec: Loyola College, Montreal

QMM Quebec: McGill University, Montreal

QMSS Quebec: Bibliothèque nationale du Québec (formerly Bibliothèque Saint-Sulpice), Montreal

QMU Quebec: Université de Montréal

QQ Quebec: Bibliothèque municipale, Quebec

QQL Quebec: Législature de la Province de Québec, Quebec

QSherU Quebec: Université de Sherbrooke

RES Royal Empire Society, London. Subject Catalogue of the library, vol. 3: Canada, etc. (London, the Society, 1932)

Rhod *Canadian Literature in English,* by Vernon Blair Rhodenizer. Montreal, Quality Press, 1965. Also the *Index* compiled by Lois Mary Thierman. Edmonton, La Survivance Print., [1968?]

Ryerson Impt *The Ryerson Imprint.* By W. Stewart Wallace. (Toronto, Ryerson, 1954)

S&T *A Bibliography of Canadiana.* ... Ed. by Frances M. Staton and Marie Tremaine. (Toronto, Public Library, 1934). [Also Supplement, 1959.]

SR Saskatchewan: Regina Public Library

SRL Saskatchewan: Legislative Library, Regina

SRP   Saskatchewan: Saskatchewan Provincial Library, Regina

SS   Saskatchewan: Saskatoon Public Library

SSU   Saskatchewan: University of Saskatchewan, Saskatoon

T&C   *A Check-List of Canadian Imprints 1900–1925.* By Dorothea D. Tod and Audrey M. Cordingley. (Ottawa, King's Printer, 1952)

Tremaine   *A Bibliography of Canadian Imprints, 1751–1800.* Comp. by Marie Tremaine. (Toronto, University of Toronto Press, 1952)

UTQ   *University of Toronto Quarterly,* "Letters in Canada" issues, 1936–. [An annual survey which began with the year 1935; included a checklist.]

CONTENTS

PART I

POETRY

POETRY

Chapbooks, individual works, collections, anthologies

Abbott, F.W.
VAGRANT VERSES FROM A BLUENOSE PEN. [Liverpool, N.S.?], n.p., [1914]. 8p
  [NSWA

Abbott, Frederick
BOY TALKS TO GOD. A Serious Fantasy. Boston, Humphries, 1940. 51p [LC
LIFE'S AN OPPORTUNITY, AND OTHER INSPIRATIONAL VERSE. Boston, Humphries,
  1943. 63p [LC
LOLLYPOP TREE, AND OTHER CHILD VERSE. Boston, Humphries, 1940. 85p [CBI
SOME LEGENDS, AND OTHER VERSE. New York, Harrison, 1938. 127p [LC

Abell, Walter Halsey, 1897–1956
ETERNAL SPRINGTIME. A Love Cycle. Yellow Springs, Kahoe & Spieth, 1927. 75p
  [LC

Abraham, Dorothy E., 1894–
BOOK OF REMEMBRANCE. Victoria, Author, [1941?]. 31p [BVi

Acadia University
SONGS OF ACADIA COLLEGE. Wolfville, 1907. 91p [NSWA

Acorn, Milton, 1923–
THE BRAIN'S THE TARGET. Toronto, Ryerson, 1960. 16p
IN LOVE AND ANGER. Montreal, Author, 1956. 20p

Acklom, George Morebye, 1870–
MARGARET. An Idyll. Portland, Smith & Sale, 1898. 104p [NSHD OTUV
WINTER VIGIL. New York, Vinal, 1928. 30p [LC NSHD

Acland, Peregrine Palmer, 1892–1963
THE REVEILLE OF ROMANCE. N.p., 1914. 4p [OTU

Adams, Levi –1832
THE CHARIVARI; OR, CANADIAN POETICS. A Tale after the manner of Beppo.
  [Anon] Montreal, 1824. 48p [Attributed to Adams by C.F. Klinck in
  Dalhousie Review, V.40] [BVaU NSHPL OTP QMU
JEAN BAPTISTE. A Poetic Olio in II Cantos. Montreal, 1825. 34p [OLU
TALES OF CHIVALRY AND ROMANCE. [Anon] Edinburgh, Robertson; London,
  Baldwin, Cradock & Joy, 1826. 306p [Attributed to Adams by C.F. Klinck in
  Dalhousie Review, V.40] [BM

Adams, Mary Electa, 1823–1898

FROM DISTANT SHORES. Poems. [Toronto, 1898?] 23p [OTP

Adams, Myrtle (Reynolds), 1889–

MORNING ON MY STREET. Toronto, Ryerson, 1958. 12p
REMEMBER TOGETHER. Toronto, Ryerson, 1955. 12p
TO ANY SPRING. Toronto, Ryerson, 1960. 12p

Adams, Norman Edgar, 1904–

BANFF NATIONAL PARK. A Poem. Calgary, Author, 1960. 4p
CALGARY. A Poem. Forest Lawn, Alta., Author, 1958. 8p
CALGARY'S GREAT STAMPEDE SHOW. A Poem. Forest Lawn, Alta., Author, 1959.
  4p

Adams, R.F.

POEMS OF THE CANADIAN WEST. Vancouver, Evans & Hastings, 1919. 86p [BM
  BVaU OTP

Adams, Robert Chamblet, 1839–

THE HISTORY OF ENGLAND IN RHYME. Boston, Lothrop, 1880. 30p [An
  illustrated ed. pub. 1889. 78p] [LC OLU OOU
THE HISTORY OF THE UNITED STATES IN RHYME. Boston, Lothrop, 1884.
  72p [Later pub. as ILLUSTRATED HISTORY OF THE UNION IN RHYME, rev.
  by Herbert Heywood. Boston, Thayer, 1891. 156p] [Brown U LC OLU
ON BOARD THE "ROCKET." Boston, Lothrop, 1879. 335p [Contains sailors'
  songs with music.] [BVaU LC

Ager, Paul R.

LIFE THOUGHTS. Toronto, Briggs, 1912. 36p [BVaU NSHPL OTP
SOME THOUGHTS IN VERSE. London, Stockwell, 1921. 16p [BM

Aikins, Charles Carroll Colby, 1888–

POEMS. Boston, Sherman French, 1917. 36p [BVaU LC NBFU OKQ

Aimsfeld [pseud]

THE HOWLS OF A DINGO. Australian Bush Rhymes. Victoria, Diggon-Hibben, 1919.
  48p [BVaU

Aitken, Melita

THE MAPLE GROVE AND OTHER POEMS. Toronto, Warwick & Rutter, 1920. 61p
  [NBFU OTP

Aldwinckle, Eric, 1909–

TWO FABLES. Toronto, Toronto Theosophical Society, 1950. 27p [OONL

Alexander, Bertha M.

THE HIGHWAY AND OTHER POEMS. 2nd ed. St. John's Nfld., Evening Telegram,
  [1952?]. 31p [1st ed.: Vancouver, [1950?].]

Alexander, Rev. James Lynne, 1800–1879

A DAY AT NIAGARA IN THE YEAR 1825. Revived, Revised, and Annotated by his great-grandson, Richard Lonton Denison. Toronto, 1952. 28p [mimeographed]

ONTARIO'S OLDEST POEM: A DAY AT NIAGARA IN THE YEAR 1825. By the Rev. James Lynne Alexander. Revived, Revised and Annotated by his Great-Grandson, Richard Lonton Denison. Toronto, 1952. 15p [A reprint of the following title.]

WONDERS OF THE WEST; or, A Day at the Falls of Niagara, in 1825. A Poem. By a Canadian [pseud]. York, Fothergill, 1825. 46p [OTP

Alexander-Armstrong, J.

SONGS OF THE NEW WORLD. Toronto, Imrie, 1896. 74p [BM OTUV

Allan, Mrs. Ethel Stilwell, 1883–

TO YOU. By Ethel Stilwell [pseud]. Toronto, Author, 1926. [OKQ

Allan, Eva Valentine

VERSES. ... Ottawa, 1904. 26p [Brown U

Allan, Mrs. Marguerite Buller

THE RHYME GARDEN. London, Lane, 1917. 64p [BM LC

Allan, Peter John, 1825–1848

THE POETICAL REMAINS OF PETER JOHN ALLAN, ESQ., LATE OF FREDERICTON, NEW BRUNSWICK. Ed. by Rev. Henry Christmas. London, Smith Elder, 1853. xxiv + 171p [BM BVaU NBFU OLU

Allen, Egbert Chesley, 1882–1947

OUR NORTHERN YEAR. Stories and Songs of the Canadian Seasons. ... Toronto, Ryerson, 1937. 119p [NBFU OTU

POEMS. ... N.p., Author, 1945. 36p [NSHPL

Allen, Favia Gordon

ECHOES FROM LOVE'S MONUMENT. Epic Poem. Yarmouth, Davis, 1912. 18p [NSHPL

AN IDYLL REVERIE, MY PARADISE I'LL SEEK AND OTHER POEMS. 1912. [Rhod p872

Allen, Grant, 1848–1899

THE LOWER SLOPES. Reminiscences of Excursions Round the Base of Helicon. London, Mathews & Lane, 1894. 79p [BM LC NBFU OTU

Allen, Jacob D.

THE MUSINGS OF UNCLE JAKE. London, Ont., 1866. 208p [OLU

POEMS. London, Ont., Advertiser, 1869. 240p [Brown U OTU

Allen, James A.

MAPLE LEAVES. A Collection of Verse. London, Stockwell, 1938. 79p [BM BVaU OOP

Allen, Rev. John Slater, 1841–1923

FROM APOLLYONVILLE TO THE HOLY CITY. A Poem. Halifax, Wesleyan Office, 1880. 302p [LC NSHD OKQ

Allen, Joseph Antisell, 1814–1900

THE CHURCH OF THE POPE, AND PRIMITIVE CHRISTIANITY. Kingston, British Whig, [1891]. 103p [OTUV

DAY-DREAMS BY A BUTTERFLY. In Nine Parts. Kingston, Creighton, 1854. 156p [BM BVaU LC OTP

THE LAMBDA-NU TERCENTENARY POEM ON SHAKESPEARE. Stratford-upon-Avon, Morgan, 1864. 46p [BM OTUV

Alline, Rev. Henry, 1748–1784

HYMNS AND SPIRITUAL SONGS. Stonington-Port, Conn., Turnbull, 1802. 281p [Same title pub. at Boston in 1784 and at Dover, N.H., in 1795 and 1798.] [BM NBFU

Allison, Dorothea

A FAIRY'S GARLAND OF B.C. FLOWERS. Vernon, B.C., Vernon News, n.d. 31p [BViPA

Allison, Mary Gertrude (Mother Agatha)

AN OLD SONG IN NEW METERS. By M.G.A. Toronto, Longmans, 1923. [T&C

Allison, William Talbot, 1874–1941

THE AMBER ARMY, AND OTHER POEMS. Toronto, Briggs, 1909. 85p [BM BVaU NBFU OKQ

Alpha Arts and Letters Society, Hamilton

THE GOOD SHIP "FUN." Hamilton, Davis-Lisson, 1935. 32p [CC

Amoss, Harry [Harold Edwin], 1880–

CHURCHILL AND OTHER POEMS. Toronto, Ryerson, 1957. 34p

PRAYER OF THE GOOD TROUPER, AND OTHER POEMS. Toronto, Ryerson, 1933. 88p [BVaU LC OTU

SUNDAY-MONDAY. Selected Poems. Toronto, Ryerson, 1947. 56p [BVaU NBFU OKQ

Anderson, Agnes Nicholson

FROM TOWERING HEIGHTS. 4th ed. Victoria, Diggon-Hibben, 1952. 33p

Anderson, Alvah John

A BOOK OF POEMS. [Saskatoon, 1939?]. 93p [SSU

Anderson, Annie M.

A CHAPBOOK. [Poems by six students and one graduate of the University of British Columbia.] By Abbie M. Anderson, Geoffrey Bruun, Geoffrey Coope, Sallee Murphy, Alfred Rive, Lionel Stevenson, Dorothy H. Walsh. Vancouver, priv. print., 1922. 28p [BVaU OTP

Anderson, Rev. David
POEMS. Toronto, Author, 1930. 24p [Brown U

Anderson, Rev. Duncan, 1828—1903
LAYS OF CANADA, AND OTHER POEMS. Montreal, Lovell, 1890. 115p [BVaU LC NSHD OKQ

Anderson, Mrs. Helen B., 1865—
UNDER COUNTRY SKIES. Toronto, Writers' Studio, 1933. 32p [Brown U

Anderson, James, 1838?—1923
SAWNEY'S LETTERS; or Cariboo Rhymes. Barkerville, B.C., Cariboo Sentinel, 1868. 4p [Enlarged ed., Barkerville, Cariboo Sentinel, 1869. Also, under title SAWNEY'S LETTERS AND CARIBOO RHYMES, Toronto, Johnston, 1895. 49p. Repub. in 1950 and 1962.] [BVaU BViPA NBFU OTU

Anderson, Patrick, 1915—
THE COLOUR AS NAKED. Toronto, McClelland, 1953. 93p
A TENT FOR APRIL. Montreal, First Statement, 1945. 28p [BVaU LC OTU
THE WHITE CENTRE. Toronto, Ryerson, 1946. 72p [BVaU LC MWU NSHD OKQ QMM

Anderson, Robert Stuart Guthrie
THE YOUNG MINISTER AND OTHER POEMS. By R.S.G.A. [pseud]. Toronto, Westminster, n.d. 10p [Cover title: "KIRK FOLK"] [BVaS NBFU OTU

Anderson, Robert Thompson, 1880—
CANADIAN BORN AND OTHER WESTERN VERSE. Edmonton, Esdaile, 1913. 100p [BM BVaU
THE OLD TIMER, AND OTHER POEMS. Edmonton, Edmonton Print., 1909. 103p [BM BVaU OTU
TROOPERS IN FRANCE. Edmonton, Coles Print., 1932. 122p [BViPA

Anderson, Mrs. Violet Louise, 1906—
THE LEDGE. Toronto, Emblem Books, 1957. 15p

Andress, Clara E.
COMMONPLACE SKETCHES. Sudbury, Author, 1938. 25p [Brown U OTU

Andrews, Frederick
VALOUR AND FAITH. Ilfracombe, Devon, Stockwell, 1958. 80p

Andrews, William Darling, 1853—1903
THE LIFEBOAT AND OTHER POEMS. Toronto, Briggs, [1888]. 64p [Same title: Toronto, Briggs, n.d. (1887?). 32p] [BVaU LC NBFU OKQ QMSS

Angus, Frances Ramsay
AS WE ARE. Boston, Humphries, 1940. 107p [LC NSHD OKQ QMM

Angus, Marion Isabel (Hand), 1902—1951
FRAGRANT WISDOM. Vancouver, Vancouver Bindery, 1931. 63p [BVaU NBFU
   OTP
SEA MIST AND OTHER POEMS. N.p., [1926?]. 24p [BViPA OKQ

Angus, Mary
CHRISTMAS GREETINGS TO THE CHILDREN YOUNG AND OLD FROM THE FISH,
   INSECTS AND BIRDS. N.p., 1946. 13p [QMU

Anonymous
AN ADDRESS TO THE LIEGE MEN OF EVERY BRITISH COLONY. Kingston, Herald,
   1822. 13p [OTU QMSS
CANADA. A Satire. By One of her Sons. N.p., [18—?]. 24p [OTU
CANADIAN CANTICLES [A Collection of 127 Poems]. Toronto, Musson, [1912?].
   114p [BVaU NBFU OTUV
THE CANADIAN TEMPERANCE MINSTREL. Being a Collection of Hymns, Songs,
   and Poetry, Selected and Original. Montreal, Campbell, 1842. 108p [OOP
THE CARLETON ELECTION; or, The Tale of a Bytown Ram. An Epic Poem. In Ten
   Cantos. [Ottawa?], Author, 1832. 38p [OOA
CURIOUS FACTS. Toronto, 1895. 124p [CCJ
A FEW HYMNS. N.p., 1906. 24p [QMU
GEMS FROM CANADIAN AUTHORS. Toronto, Bryce, 1888. 12p [OONL
A GLIMPSE AT TORONTO IN THE 20TH CENTURY, WITH A RETROSPECTIVE GLANCE.
   Toronto, 1875. 14p [OTUV
HUNTING ADVENTURES IN UTOPIA. Toronto, 1880. 30p [CCJ
HYMNS FOR SPECIAL SERVICES. Ottawa, Hunter Rose, 1868. 16p [QMU
JOHNNY CRAPAUD. A Legend of Bygone Days. After the late Thomas Ingoldsby,
   Esq. Toronto, Sylvester Blowhole, 1851. 12p [NSHP
LINES COMMEMORATIVE OF THE AWFUL CONFLAGRATION OF ST. ROCH'S.
   Quebec, 1845. 11p [QMU
"LOVE, A LA MODE": A SLIGHT SLAP AT THE NEAT LITTLE ELOPEMENT AT
   TORONTO. A Very Moral Dissertation. London, Ont., n.p., 1863. 39p [OTU
THE MAPLE LEAF; or, Canadian Annual. A Literary Souvenir. ... Toronto,
   Rowsell, 1847—1849. 3v [BVaU OOP OTP
THE NEW-BRUNSWICK TEMPERANCE SONGSTER. A Collection of Songs and Hymns
   Original and Selected. Respectfully Dedicated to the Several Total Abstinence
   Societies throughout the British Provinces. By a member of the "Saint John
   Temperance Association Choir." Saint John, McMillan, 1848. 180p [OTP
NO SECT IN HEAVEN. Saint John, 1868. [LHC, p118
POESIE'S DREAM. Part 1st and 2nd. Rose Glen and other Poems. Halifax, J. Howe,
   1835. 72p [NSHPL
POETS FOR PEACE. A Collection of Poems, by British Columbia Poets, intended to
   express a Position of Non-neutrality on the Matter of the Testing of Thermo-

nuclear Weapons and the Preservation of Peace. Vancouver, 1960. 33p
[mimeographed]
PRO AND CON. A Satirico-Political Dialogue in Familiar Rhyme. Quebec, 1828.
12p [OTP QMSS
THE PROVOST'S KINDERGARTEN. Being the Dinner of the Year of One-ty Four at
the St. Charles Grill. ... 1910. Toronto, n.d. 12p [Adelphi cat. no. 58
RAISE THE FLAG, AND OTHER PATRIOTIC CANADIAN SONGS AND POEMS. Toronto,
Rose, 1891. 63p [BM Brown U NSHD OTU
THROUGH THE YEAR WITH CANADIAN POETS. Gananoque, Ont., Hilda M. Ridley,
1960. 29p (Carillon Poetry Chap-Books)
WAIFS FROM THE HEDGES AND HIGHWAYS. V. 1 [Montreal], Anon. Pub. Co.,
1903. 98p [OTP

Appleton, Lydia Ann
MISCELLANEOUS POEMS, MORAL AND RELIGIOUS. Written on Various Occasions.
Toronto, "Watchman," 1850. 92p [OTUV

Apps-Brown, Minnie (Poole), 1866—1948
THAT WORLD OF MY OWN. Paris, Ont., Pickell, 1949. 36p

Archibald, Alexander Kent, 1803—
POEMS. Boston, Wiley, 1848. 200p [BM BVaU LC NSHD

Archibald, Ernest
THOUGHTS OF A RAMBLING MUSE. Halifax, Imperial, 1948. 181p [Brown U

Arion (pseud)
ALPHONZO STILLETTO'S POETIZATION OF THE INCIPIENT STAGE OF THE GREAT
PACIFIC SCANDAL AND OF THE CELEBRATED SPEECH OF LORD DUFFERIN IN
REPLY TO A HEALTH TOAST AT A DINNER GIVEN BY THE HALIFAX CLUB. By
Arion [pseud]. Montreal, "Witness" Print., 1874. 29p [Brown U BVaU OTU

Armour, Edward Douglas, 1851—1922
ECHOES FROM HORACE IN ENGLISH VERSE. Toronto, U. of Toronto Press, 1922.
100p [BM OTU
LAW LYRICS. Toronto, Canada Law Book, 1918. 39p [BM BVaU LC NBFU
OTU QMM

Armstrong, Clara
MY ROSARY OF FRIENDSHIPS AND OTHER POEMS. Montreal, Witness Press, 1936.
31p [OTU
STARS OF HAPPINESS. Abbey, Sask., Author, 1938. 23p [CC

Armstrong, Joseph H., 1867—1891
LYRICS, IDYLS AND FRAGMENTS. Ed. by Norman De Lagutry. New York,
Publishers' Print. Co., 1892. 111p [LC NSHPL OTP
SONGS OF A PAGAN. 1889 [Rhod p897

Ascher, Isidore Gordon, 1835–1914
COLLECTED POEMS. London, Elliot Stock, 1929. 300p [BM
ONE HUNDRED AND FIVE SONNETS. Oxford, Blackwell, 1912. 117p [BM LC
VOICES FROM THE HEARTH. A Collection of Verses. By "Isidore." Isidore G.
   Ascher. Montreal, Lovell, 1863. 168p [BVaU LC NBFU OKQ QMU

Ashmead, Henry A.
POEMS FROM THE PRESS. Patriotic, Descriptive, Sentimental and Humorous.
   Toronto, Hunter Rose, 1916. 179p [Brown U BVaU NBFU OOP

Athena (pseud)
IN MY CORNER. By Athena [pseud]. London, Stockwell, 1926. 15p [BM

Atkin, Grace Murray, 1891–
FLOWERS OF THE WIND. New York, Kennerley, 1919. 58p [BVaU LC

Attfield, Mrs. Hilda Mary, 1900–
ECHOES OF WAR AND OTHER VERSE. Ilfracombe, Devon, Stockwell, 1944. 46p
   [BM LC OTP

Austin, Rev. Benjamin Fish, 1850–1932
THE DAWN OF A NEW ERA. The Ideal State in the Light of Mental Science. By
   Hedwig S. Albarus [pseud]. Toronto, Austin, 1903. 23p [OPAL

Austin, Lilian Edna
ETCHINGS OF FENELON FALLS. Boston, Meador, 1931. 64p [LC OTU

Avison, Margaret Kirkland, 1918–
WINTER SUN. Toronto, U. of Toronto Press, 1960. 89p

Awde, Robert
CANADA: PRESENT AND FUTURE. A Patriotic Poem. ... Toronto, 1889. 3p [OTU
JUBILEE, PATRIOTIC, AND OTHER POEMS. Toronto, Briggs, 1887. 50p [BVaU
   NBFU OKQ
WAITING AT TABLE. Poems and Songs. London, Author, 1865. 143p [BM OTU

Ayscough, Florence (Wheelock), 1878–1942
FIR-FLOWER TABLETS. Poems. Translated from the Chinese by Florence Ayscough.
   ... English Versions by Amy Lowell. Boston, Houghton, 1921. xcv + 227p [BM
   BVaU OTU QMM

B., P.
SONGS FROM A CANADIAN HOMESTEAD. Morland, Amersham, Bucks., 1923. 28p
   [BViPA

B., P.J.
PENCILLINGS BY THE WAY, during a Vacation Visit in Chebucto. By a Student who
   is a Native of Halifax. P.J.B. Montreal, Lovell, 1868. 24p [Brown U NSHD OTU

Bagg, Stanley Clark, 1820—
LEISURE MOMENTS. A Few Poems. By Stella [pseud]. Montreal, Rose, 1871
   24p [QMM

Bailey, Alfred Goldsworthy, 1905—
BORDER RIVER. Toronto, McClelland, 1952. 61p [BVaU NBFU OTP
SONGS OF THE SAGUENAY AND OTHER POEMS. Quebec, Chronicle-Telegraph,
   1927. 34p [BVaU NBFU OKQ QMM
TÂO. Toronto, Ryerson, 1930. 8p [BVaU NBSaM OTU QMM

Bailey, George Taylor, 1887—
POEMS OF LIFE. Toronto, Warwick Bros., 1925. 128p [BVaU NSHD OTU
   QMBM

Baillie, Oliver E.
ON ACTIVE SERVICE. N.p., [1915?]. 7p [Same title, with different estimated
   dates, and pagination given as "19", "[24]", and "2 v. in 1".] [Amtmann cat.
   149 BVaU OONL OTP

Bain, Ebenezer, 1838?—
RAMBLINGS IN RHYMELAND. War Poems, Songs and Other Verse, Sentimental,
   Humorous, Philosophical. Montreal, Author, 1918. 101p [BM BVaU NSHD
   OTU QMM

Bainbridge, Edith
POEMS. Toronto, Author, 1943. 16p [OTU

Baker, Henry
TRANSLATIONS AND CHOICE PIECES FROM SOME OF THE BEST FRENCH AND
   GERMAN AUTHORS. Montreal, Lovell, 1867. 286p [OTP

Baker, Ida Emma (Fitch), 1858—1948
AT EVENTIDE. Toronto, Presbyterian Pub., 1943. 48p [BVaU LC OTU
BY LAMPLIGHT. Toronto, Author, 1936. 50p [BVaU NBFU OTU
GLEAMS OF IMMORTALITY. Toronto, Ross Press, n.d. 16p [OTU
NAME ABOVE EVERY NAME. Toronto, Author, 1941. [CC
SELECTED POEMS. With an intro. by Ray Palmer Baker. Toronto, Ryerson, 1951.
   82p

Baker, Maude E.
PEN SYMPHONIES. Halifax, Allen, n.d. 27p [OTUV

Baker, Ray Palmer, 1883—
CROYNAN HALL, THE MAID OF THE MASK, A TALE OF ROTHENBURG. Toronto,
   Briggs, 1908. 100p [BVaU NBFU OKQ QMM
A TALE OF ROTHENBURG AND OTHER POEMS. Toronto, Haynes, 1906. 24p
   [BVaU NBFU OTP

Baker, William King

COLLECTED SHORTER POEMS. London, Routledge, 1927. 300p [BM NSHD
   OTU QMM

A FOREST IDYLL AND OTHER POEMS. London, Baker, 1916. 107p [BM

GABRIEL LAJEUNESSE. ... London, Routledge, 1923. 52p [BM NSHD OTU QMSS

THE LOYALISTS. London, Routledge, 1921. 149p [BM LC NBFU

PENN, THE STATESMAN AND GULIELMA. A Quaker Idyll. Edinburgh, Oliphants,
   [1918]. 327p [BM LC OLU

A QUAKER APOSTLE: IN MEMORIAM, JOHN T. DORLAND. London, Baker, 1916. [BM

Baldwin, Harry, 1883–1953

WHICH CODE? Ottawa, Author, 1949. 100p [AEU OOP

Baldwyn, Augusta, 1821?–1884

POEMS. Montreal, Lovell, 1859. 163p [BVaU OKQ QMM

Ball, Mrs. Helen

THE MOMENT SNARED. Toronto, Author, 1952. 32p

THESE THINGS LINGER. Toronto, Author, 1946. 23p [BVaU OTP

Ball, Nellie (Martin), 1882–1950

SELECTED POEMS OF NELLIE BALL. With an intro. by Luella Carlyle Thomson.
   Toronto, Crucible Press, 1951. 16p

Ballantyne, Lereine (Hoffman), 1891–1962

FIRELIGHT FANCIES. Toronto, McClelland, 1926. 40p [BVaU NSHD OTP

Bannatyne, William

POEMS AND SONGS ON VARIOUS SUBJECTS. Toronto, Campbell, 1875. 198p
   [BVaU OTU

Bannerman, Frances (Jones), 1855–

MILESTONES. A Collection of Verses. London, Richards, 1899. 197p [BM

Bannon, Richard Valentine, 1900–

EASTLAND ECHOES. Toronto, Macmillan, 1937. 44p [Brown U BVaU OTUV

Barbeau, Charles Marius, 1883–1969

COME A-SINGING! Canadian Folk-songs. By Marius Barbeau, Arthur Lismer,
   [and] Arthur Bourinot. Ottawa, King's Printer, 1947. 59p [BVaU LC
   NSHD OKQ QMM

FOLK-SONGS OF FRENCH CANADA. Ed. by ——. Trans. by Edward Sapir.
   New Haven, Yale U. Press, 1925. 216p [BM BVaU LC NBFU OTU QMM

FOLK SONGS OF OLD QUEBEC. Trans. by Regina Lenore Shoolman. Ottawa,
   National Museum, 1935. 72p [BM BVaU LC NSWA OKQ QMM

Barclay, Charles A.

DAWN, EAST AND WEST. A Canadian Political Sketch. Toronto, Sovereign,
   1914. 63p [BVaU NBFU OTU

Barnard, Sylvia, 1937—
THE TIMELESS FOREST. Toronto, Contact Press, 1959. 45p

Barnes, F.H.
POEMS. By F.H.B. Toronto, Briggs, 1912. 88p [BM OKQ

Barrett, Ena Constance, 1894—1967
LILTS OF NEWFOUNDLAND. 2nd ed., with Additional Lilts. Curling, Nfld.,
 Western Star Press, 1931. 39p [NfSM
MAYFLOWERS AND ROSES. A Bouquet of Verse. Curling, Nfld., Barrett's Print.
 Shop, 1946. 119p [NfSM OTP
RAINBOW LYRICS. London, Erskine MacDonald, n.d. 104p [NBSaM

Barrington, Gwenyth, 1901—
WAR, WORDS, AND THE WASTEBASKET. N.p., [1942?]. 19p [LC

Bartole, Genevieve
FIGURE IN THE RAIN. Toronto, Ryerson, 1948. 7p [BVaU NBSaM OKQ

Barton, J. King
NOTHING TO YOU; or, Mind Your Own Business. In Answer to "Nothings" in
 General and "Nothing to Wear" [by William Allen Butler] in Particular.
 By Knot-Rab [pseud]. New York, Wiley, 1857. 68p [BM LC OLU

Bate, Fanny
GEMS OF HOPE. In Memory of the Faithful Departed. Selected and Arranged
 by ——. Toronto, Briggs, 1896. 280p [BM OLU

Bates, Ronald Gordon Nudell, 1924—
THE WANDERING WORLD. Toronto, Macmillan, 1959. 60p

Battersby, Mrs. H.S. —1887?
HOME LYRICS. A Book of Poems. V. II. Toronto, Hunter Rose, 1887. 143p
 [HOME LYRICS, V. I is stated to have been published in 1876. Nothing else
 discovered about it.] [Brown U BVaU OLU

Baubie, William Edward
FRENCH-CANADIAN VERSE. Written and Illus. by ——. Chicago, Lakeside
 Press, 1917. 74p [BVaU LC OTP

Bayer, Mary Elizabeth
FACES OF LOVE. Toronto, Ryerson, 1959. 12p
OF DIVERSE THINGS. Toronto, Ryerson, 1957. 12p
THE SILVER SWAN. An Epithalamion. Toronto, Ryerson, 1960. 8p

Bayley, Cornwall, 1784—1807
CANADA. A Descriptive Poem. Written at Quebec, 1805. With Satires —
 Imitations — and Sonnets. [Anon] [Quebec], John Neilson, [1806]. 52p
 [OTP

Bayley, Robert Charleton, 1913–

A BAKER'S DOZEN. A Sheaf of Thirteen Occasional Poems. Moncton, priv. print., n.d. 16p [BVaU NBFU OTU

SEVEN SONGS IN THE MAJOR AND MINOR. Moncton, Imprimerie Acadienne, [1949?]. 10p [NBFU OKQ

VISIONS FUGITIVE. ... Fredericton, Ubsdell Print., 1946. 16p [BM BVaU NBFU OKQ

Baylis, Samuel Mathewson, 1854–1941

ECHOES OF THE GREAT WAR 1914–1918. Montreal, Witness Press, 1919. 32p [BM LC NSHD OTU QMM

Baynes, O'Hara

A CLOSE CALL. N.p., [1918?]. 9p [NSWA OTUV

Beattie, Jessie Louise, 1896–

BLOWN LEAVES. Toronto, Ryerson, 1929. 24p [BVaU NBFU
SHIFTING SAILS. Toronto, Ryerson, 1931. 24p [OKQ

Beattie, John McNab, 1916–

POEMS AND BALLADS OF THE OTTAWA VALLEY. By Mac Beattie [pseud]. Arnprior, Ont., Arnprior Press, 1960. 59p

Beattie, Kim, 1900–

"AND YOU!" Toronto, Macmillan, 1929. 91p [BVaU OTP

Beattie, William

ODES OF APPRECIATION OF ROBERT BURNS. N.p., n.d. 32p [Odes dated 1909–1916.] [OTK QMU

Beck, George Fairley

DAYBREAK. A Poem. Toronto, 1873. 13p [OTP

Beck, Roland Stanley

THE FLASK OF LOVE AND OTHER POEMS. By Roland St. Anbeck [pseud]. Vancouver, Sun Pub., 1926. 61p [BVaU

Bedell, Laura Amelia (Whitemarsh), 1875–1971

ALWAYS THE TIDES. Picton, Picton Gazette, 1964. 131p
BLUE HARBOUR. Picton, Author, 1947. 80p [BVaU NBSaM OTU
FROM DAWN TO DUSK. Bloomfield, Ont., Author, 1944. 71p [OTP
SPUN LACE. Toronto, Writers' Studio, 1933. 30p [AEU Brown U OTP

Bedford-Jones, Henry James O'Brien, 1887–1949

THE MISSION AND THE MAN. The Story of San Juan Capistrano. Pasadena, San Pasqual Press, 1939. 40p [LC

Beeman, Herbert, –1931

FOR OUR BUREAU. Being the Bureau Ballads contributed to Volumes One and

Two of "Via Vancouver," the Journal of the Foreign Trade Bureau of the
Vancouver Board of Trade. Vancouver, Cowan Brookhouse, 1924. 63p
[BVaU OTU QMU
VANCOUVER, THE HALFWAY HOUSE OF THE EMPIRE. Vancouver, Pacific Printers,
1929. 12p [BViPA
SOME ADVENTURES OF MR. SURELOCK KEYS, HITHERTO UNRECORDED. ... Point
Grey, B.C., Kerrisdale Kronickle, 1913. 15p [BVaU

Belcher, Alexander Emerson, 1844–1926
POEMS AND PATRIOTIC VERSES. N.p., n.d. [1916]. 8p [QMU

Belcher, Antoine L.
WOODLAND GNOMES. Vancouver, Evergreen Press, 1957. 32p

Belcher, Beaufort
RADICAL RICIDULE. Toronto, Macdonald Galleries, 1935. 78p [BVaU OTP

Bell, John Allison
CHEBUCTO AND OTHER POEMS. ... Halifax, Bowes, 1890. 53p [NSHD

Bell, William Aitchison, 1847–1915
POEMS ON VARIOUS OCCASIONS. With a Biographical Sketch. Toronto, Best,
1927. 59p [BVaU OKQ

Bellmore, Euphemia
BOOK OF POEMS. 8th ed. Toronto, Dudley & Burns, 1874. 27p [Brown U
BVaU OTUV

Benedict, Charles Julius Ernest Leslie, 1868–
CRUELTY. Montreal, Author, 1930. 16p [BVaU
LIFE AND THE LAND WE LOVE. Montreal, Author, 1932. 104p [BM BVaU
THE RETURN. Montreal, Author, 1932. 7p [BM BVaU
SEMPER EADEM. Montreal, Author, 1932. 4p [BVaU
WESTMOUNT IN SONG AND STORY. Westmount, Westmount News, 1933.
99p [BVaU QMM

Bengough, John Wilson, 1851–1923
IN MANY KEYS. A Book of Verse. Toronto, Briggs, 1902. 237p [BM BVaU
NBFU OKQ QMM
MOTLEY. Verses Grave and Gay. Toronto, Briggs, 1895. 172p [BVaU LC
NSHD OKQ QMM

Bennett, Dorothy R.
SPRINGTIME AND OTHER POEMS. London, Stockwell, 1933. 15p [BM

Bennett, Ethel Hume (Patterson), 1881–
NEW HARVESTING. Contemporary Canadian Poetry, 1918–1938. Chosen by
——. Toronto, Macmillan, 1938. 198p [BM BVaU LC NSHD OKQ QMM

Bennett, Rev. James, 1817–1901
SONG OF THE FLOWERING GIRLS. THE LARK AND THE REAPERS. AN ELEGY
ON THAT PIOUS DOG HECTOR. CONSCIENCE. Saint John, 1900. 8p [OTP

Bennett, Owen J.
CLOTH OF GOLD AND OTHER POEMS. Vancouver, Wrigley Print., 1950.
11 + 57p [BVaU

Benson, Mrs. Irene Chapman
JOURNEY INTO YESTERDAY. Toronto, Ryerson, 1943. 10p [BVaU LC
NBFU OKQ QMM

Benson, Mary Josephine (Trotter), 1887–
MY POCKET BERYL. Toronto, McClelland, 1921. 127p [BM BVaU NSHD
OKQ

Benson, Nathaniel Anketell Michael, 1903–1966
DOLLARD. A Tale in Verse. Toronto, Nelson, 1933. 44p [BVaU LC NBFU
OKQ QMM
THE GLOWING YEARS. Toronto, Nelson, 1937. 137p [BVaU NSHD OKQ
MODERN CANADIAN POETRY. Ed. by ——. Ottawa, Graphic, 1930. 227p
[BM BVaU LC NSHD OTU QMM
ODE ON THE DEATH OF GEORGE V. Toronto, Ryerson, 1936. 4p [BM LC
NSHD OKQ
POEMS. Toronto, Robertson, 1927. 43p [BVaU NBFU OKQ QMM
TWENTY AND AFTER. Toronto, Ryerson, 1927. 20p [BVaU NBSaM
OKQ QMM
THE WANDERER, A NARRATIVE POEM ... AND OTHER POEMS. Toronto,
Ryerson, 1930. 31p [Sequel to TWENTY AND AFTER.] [BVaU NBSaM
OKQ QMM

Bentley, E.
EPISTLES AND POEMS. [Toronto? 1896?]. 31p [OTUV

Bentley, Eliza
PRECIOUS STONES FOR ZION'S WALLS. A Record of Personal Experience in
Things connected with the Kingdom of God on Earth. Toronto, Briggs,
1897. 440p [BM Brown U OTU

Bentley, Mrs. Verna Bessie, 1904–
IN HER MIND CARRYING. By Verna Loveday Harden [pseud]. Toronto,
Ryerson, 1959. 12p
POSTLUDE TO AN ERA. By Verna Loveday Harden [pseud]. Toronto, Crucible
Press, 1940. 26p [LC
WHEN THIS TIDE EBBS. By Verna Loveday Harden [pseud]. Toronto, Ryerson,
1946. 8p [LC MWU NBSaM OKQ

Bernhardt, Clara Mae, 1911–
FAR HORIZON. Preston, Ont., Author, 1941. 32p [AEU LC OONL
HIDDEN MUSIC. Galt, Galt Print., 1948. 38p [NBFU
NIN NAUNANIMIN: A Sonnet Sequence, by Clara Bernhardt; KYNDILL, by
   Lillian Collier Gray; DRUID'S DREAM, by Wallace Havelock Robb; MEADOW-
   LONG DAY, by Dorothy Murray Sliter; BLUE INK, by Gertrude Bowen
   Webster. Belleville, Intelligencer, 1939. 47p [Brown U NBFU
SILENT RHYTHM. Preston, Ont., Author, 1938. 40p [Brown U MW

Berridge, Amelia
THOUGHTS IN ST. MARK'S AND OTHER POEMS. Ilfracombe, Devon, Stockwell,
   [1954]. 46p

Berry, Mrs. Nora, 1907–
A BOUQUET OF VERSES. By Jane Cadmore [pseud]. Kingston, 1954. 70p
   [Another ed., noted as "Slightly Revised," same date, same pagination.]

Bertram, W.E.
SELECTED POEMS. N.p., 1930. 32p [QMU

Betts, Craven Langstroth, 1853–1941
A GARLAND OF SONNETS ... in Praise of the Poets. ... New York, Mansfield
   & Wessels, 1899. 7 + xxxiiip [BVaU LC NBFU OTU
THE PERFUME-HOLDER. A Persian Love Poem. New York, Saalfield & Fitch,
   1891. 49p [BVaU LC NBFU OTU
SELECTED POEMS OF CRAVEN LANGSTROTH BETTS. New York, Associated
   Authors & Compilers, 1916. 353p [LC NBFU
SONGS FROM BERANGER. Trans. in the Original Metres. New York, Stokes,
   1888. 253p [BM LC
THE TWO CAPTAINS: AT LONGWOOD, AT TRAFALGAR. New York, Watts,
   1921. 16p [BM LC NBFU OKQ

Betts, Mary
DREAMS. N.p., n.d. 33p [UTQ'37

Bevan, Molly
"CHRISTMAS AGAIN" AND OTHER POEMS. Montreal, 1923. 18p [QMSS
GIFTS OF THE YEAR AND OTHER POEMS. Toronto, Macmillan, 1927. 67p
   [BVaU NBFU OTU QMM

Bevans, Mrs. Florence Edith
ROGUE'S GALLERY OF PUPS. By Jemima Remington [pseud]. London,
   Stockwell, 1938. 43p [BM
WHERE PUSSYWILLOWS DIP AND OTHER POEMS. By Jemima Remington [pseud].
   Toronto, Author, 1936. 32p [BVaU OTU

Bevis, Henry
CANADIAN AUTUMN AND OTHER POEMS. [Gloucester, Minchin & Gibbs, 1925].
37p [BM OTP

Bezanger, Gilbert
OUTLAW LYRICS. Montreal, Pelletier, n.d. 62p [BVaU OKQ

Biggs, Alfred
SONGS OF LIMEHOUSE AND OTHER VERSE. Gardenvale, Que., Garden City
Press, 1939. 52p [OTU

Bigney, Mark Frederick, 1817–1886
THE FOREST PILGRIM AND OTHER POEMS. New Orleans, Gresham, 1867. 258p
[LC

Bigsby, Bernard
COLLECTED VERSE. Poems of Personal and Family Interest. New York, Rowland
& Ives, 1916. 166p [LC
MINNOWS FROM BRENCHLEY BROOK. Ed. by ——. London, Barrett, 1861. 24p
[BM OTMC

Bird, Ashmore H.
WRITTEN THOUGHTS. Victoria, Colonist, 1925. 38p [AEU BVaU

Birney, Earle, 1904–
DAVID AND OTHER POEMS. Toronto, Ryerson, 1942. 40p [BVaU LC
NSHD OKQ QMM
NOW IS TIME. Poems. Toronto, Ryerson, 1945. 56p [BVaU LC NBFU OKQ
QMM
THE STRAIT OF ANIAN. Selected Poems. Toronto, Ryerson, 1948. 84p [BVaU
LC NSHD MWU OTU
TRIAL OF A CITY AND OTHER VERSE. Toronto, Ryerson, 1952. 71p
20TH CENTURY CANADIAN POETRY. An Anthology with Intro. and Notes.
Ed. by ——. Toronto, Ryerson, 1953. 169p

Bishop, Mrs. Celia Maria Colpitts, 1879–
MEMORIES IN RHYMES DOWN IN THE MARITIMES. Moncton, Author, 1952. 82p

Bishop, M. Blanche, 1864–1917
TIDAL YEARS AND OTHER POEMS. Memorial Edition. Wolfville, N.S., Kentville
Pub. Co., 1929. 66p [Brown U NSHD

Bishop, Mary (Davidson), 1905–1957
IN HEAVEN'S VIEW. A Selection of the Verse of ——. Hounslow, Middlesex, Cedar
Press, 1958. xiv + 46p

Bishop, Mrs. Vivien Oonah de Blois, 1889–
VARIED VERSE. By V.O. de B. [pseud]. Victoria, Author, 1957. 46p
[mimeographed]

Bjarnason, Paul
ODES AND ECHOES. Vancouver, Author, 1954. 186p

Black, Hibbert Crane
ANONYMOUS POEMS. [Anon] Amherst, N.S., Gazette Power Print., 1889. 54p
[NSWA
RANDOM POEMS. Sackville, Tribune Press, 1909. 85p [OTU NBSaM

Black, Vera
POEMS. Ste Agathe des Monts, Que., Author, 1939. 47p [OTU

Blackadder, Edward, 1869–1922
FANCIES OF BOYHOOD. A Series of Poems, Original and Translated. Halifax,
Nova Scotia Print., 1890. 73p [BVaU OTP
POEMS: SONNETS, LYRICS, AND MISCELLANEOUS. Halifax, Nova Scotia Print.,
1895. 34p [OTUV

Black-Myers, Mrs. Mabel
SONGS FROM NOVA SCOTIA. N.p., 1957. 48p (Carillon Poetry Chap-Books)

Blair, Duncan Black, 1815–1891
THE PSALMS OF THE APOCALYPSE. New Glasgow, Mackenzie, 1893. 14p [NSWA

Blair, John Jr.
COLLECTION OF RHYMES &c. [Parkhill, Ont., Gazette Print., 18—?] 157p
[Various paging.] [OH
POEMS SERIOUS, SENTIMENTAL, PATRIOTIC, AND HUMOROUS. St. Catharines,
Ont., Meek, 1875. 132p [BVaU NBFU OKQ

Blake, Samuel Verschoyle, 1868–
HER SOLDIER DEAD, AND OTHER VERSE. ... Toronto, [1914?]. 16p [Brown U
BVaU OTU

Blennerhasset, Margaret (Agnew), 1778?–1842
THE WIDOW OF THE ROCK AND OTHER POEMS. By a Lady [pseud]. Montreal,
Sparhawk, 1824. 192p [BM LC NSHD OTP QMM

Blewett, Jean (McKishnie), 1862–1934
THE CORNFLOWER AND OTHER POEMS. Toronto, Briggs, 1906. 256p [BM
BVaU NSHD OKQ QMM
HEART SONGS. Toronto, Morang, 1897. 264p [BM BVaU OTP
JEAN BLEWETT'S POEMS. Toronto, McClelland, 1922. 259p [BM BVaU
NSHD OKQ

Bliss, William Blowers, 1795–1874
TRANSLATIONS FROM CATULLUS, HORACE, ETC. Halifax, Author, 1872. 70p
[NSHD

Blomfield, Mary Diamond
A LOYALIST SEQUENCE. A Book of Verse on Loyalist and Patriotic Themes.
Toronto, Ontario Press, 1924. 31p [OTP

Boa, Myrtle J., 1891–
IDYLLS OF OUR ISLAND. Montreal, Witness Press, [1923]. 28p [BM BVaU
QMM
RAINBOW RHYMES OF THE TIMES. Westmount, Que., Westmount News, 1933.
63p [Brown U

Boag, John H.
VICTORY VERSE. London, Lutterworth Press, 1941. 54p [BM BVaU LC

Boak, Ethel Lawson
ESCAPE. Victoria, Diggon-Hibben, n.d. 15p [AEU NSWA

Bolton, B. Frank
THE ROUT OF THE MUSES. A Political Poem. N.p., n.d. 24p [BVaU NBFU OPAL
QMU

Bolton, Margaret
A ROBIN CALLS AND OTHER POEMS. Toronto, Wilson Press, 1946. 32p [BVaU

Bonis, Rev. Robert Raynes, 1906–
OUT IN THE WILDERNESS AND OTHER POEMS. Minden, Ont., Echo Press, 1933.
41p [Brown U OTU

Boone, W.T.
D'ARCY DUNN, OR THE HAUNTED CHURCH; AND OTHER POEMS. Windsor,
N.S., New Book Pub. Library, 1867. 106p [NSHD NSWA

Boreham, Margaret Bossance
LITTLE WHITE BOATS. London, Stockwell, [1935?]. 72p [Brown U NBSaM
NEW SONGS. N.p., n.d. 12p [AEU NBSaM OPAL QMU
SONGS OF THE ROAD. N.p., n.d. 10p [NBSaM

Borrett, William Coates, 1894–
TALES TOLD IN RHYME, "THE FUSILIER" AND OTHERS. ... Halifax, Imperial
Pub. Co., 1950. 138p [NSHD

Borthwick, Rev. John Douglas, 1832–1912
THE HARP OF CANAAN; or, Selections from the Best Poets on Biblical Subjects.
Ed. by ——. Montreal, Worthington, 1866. 269p [Also: Montreal, Desbarats,
1871. 192p] [BVaU NBFU OTUV
POEMS AND SONGS ON THE SOUTH AFRICAN WAR. An Anthology from England,
Africa, Australia, United States, but Chiefly Canada. Collected by ——. Montreal,
[Gazette Pub. Co.], 1901. 215p [BVaU LC NSHD OTU

Boswell, R.
NORA. A Romance of the Great War. London, Stockwell, [1933?]. 64p [AEU

Boultbee, Horatio Clarence
LONGER POEMS. Toronto, T.H. Best, 1953. 149p
THE OXFORD LISTS AND OTHER POEMS. Toronto, Oxford U. Press, 1931. 44p
[BM BVaU NBFU OTP

Bourinot, Arthur Stanley, 1893–1969
CANADA AT DIEPPE. Toronto, Ryerson, 1942. 16p [LC NBFU OTP
THE COLLECTED POEMS. ... Toronto, Ryerson, 1947. 222p [BVaU LC MWU
NSHD OTP
DISCOVERY. Toronto, Ryerson, 1940. 11p [BVaU LC NBSaM OTU QMM
ELEVEN POEMS. Ottawa, Author, 1937. 9p [BM BVaU NSHD OTP
EVERYTHING ON EARTH MUST DIE. Ottawa, Author, 1955. 3p
FIVE POEMS. Toronto, Ryerson, 1943. 8p [LC NSHD OTP
A GATHERING. Poems. Ottawa, Author, 1958. 14p
LA SALLE. Written on ... the 250th Anniversary. ... Ottawa, Author, 1937. 4p [Rev.
version later pub. in RHYMES OF THE FRENCH REGIME.] [BM NSHD OKQ QMM
LAURENTIAN LYRICS AND OTHER POEMS. Toronto, Copp Clark, 1915. 30p [BM
BVaU NSHD OTU QMM
LINES FROM DEEPWOOD. Toronto, Heaton Print., 1946. 8p [OTP
LYRICS FROM THE HILLS. Ottawa, Hope, 1923. 40p [BM BVaU LC NSHD
OKQ QMM
MORE LINES FROM DEEPWOOD. [Toronto, Shepard Print., 1949]. 16p [BVaU
NBFU OKQ
NINE POEMS. Toronto, Ryerson, 1944. 12p [NSHD OTP
OTTAWA LYRICS, AND VERSES FOR CHILDREN. Ottawa, Graphic, 1929. 71p
[BVaU NSHD OTU QMM
PATTERING FEET. A Book of Childhood Verses. Ottawa, Graphic, 1925. 77p
[BM BVaU LC NBFU OKQ
POEMS. Toronto, Best, 1921. 47p [BM BVaU LC NSHD OKQ QMM
RHYMES OF THE FRENCH REGIME. Toronto, Nelson, 1937. 44p [BVaU LC
NSHD OKQ QMM
SELECTED POEMS (1915–1935). With a Note by Sir Andrew Macphail. Toronto,
Macmillan, 1935. 90p [BVaU LC NSHD OKQ QMM
SONNETS IN MEMORY OF MY MOTHER. Ottawa, Hope, [1931]. 18p [OTP NSHD
TEN NARRATIVE POEMS. Ottawa, Author, 1955. 32p
THIS GREEN EARTH. Gananoque, Ont., 1953. 52p
THE TREASURERS OF THE SNOW. Toronto, Ryerson, 1950. 16p [NBSaM OTP
TOM THOMSON AND OTHER POEMS. Toronto, Ryerson, 1954. 10p
TRUE HARVEST. Poems. Toronto, Ryerson, 1945. 56p [BVaU LC NSHD OTU
QM
UNDER THE SUN. Poems. Toronto, Macmillan, 1939. 69p [BVaU LC MWU
NSHD OKQ QMM
WHAT FAR KINGDOM. Poems. Toronto, Ryerson, 1941. 66p [BVaU LC NSHD
OTU QMM

Bourke, David Dominick, 1845–1921

THE NARROW DELL. A Story in Verse, and Other Poems. Ed. and completed by his daughter, Julia Bourke. New York, Exposition Press. 1955. 190p

Boutilier, Daniel William, 1897–1957

ROCKIN' CHAIR RHYMES. [Amherst, N.S.?], Author, [1954?]. 48p

Bowden, Ernest J.

OUR DESTINY AND OTHER POEMS. Toronto, Briggs, 1911. 111p [BM BVaU OKQ

Bowen, Minnie Hallowell

ADORATION. Poems. Sherbrooke, Que., n.d. 16p [Brown U

THE CANADIAN NAVY. [Anon] N.p., n.d. 7p [OONL

INNKEEPER OF BETHLEHEM. Sherbrooke, Que., Page-Sangster Print., 1937. 15p [OTU

RED FLOWER OF LIFE. Poems. Sherbrooke, Que., Page Print., [193–?]. 17p [Brown U

THE STORY OF THE LONE PINE. Sherbrooke, Que., Page Print., 1921. 7p [BM OTP

Bowen, Mrs. Minnie Henrietta Bethune, 1861–

WINNOWAIA. By M.H. Bowen. With a Foreword by Frank Oliver Call. Sherbrooke, Que., Page-Sangster Print., 1935. 39p [OKQ QMU

Bowes, Carleton Frederick, –1962

IDYLLS OF ACADIE AND OTHER POEMS. [Halifax?], 1924. 24p [Brown U NSHPL

MISCELLANEOUS VERSE. Halifax, Author, 1921. 30p [BVaU NSWA

Bowles, Walter

VERSE AND VERSE. Toronto, Ryerson, 1956. 56p

Bowman, Anne

RHYMES FROM THE SHADOWS. Guelph, n.d. 15p [Adelphi cat. 58

Bowman, Ariel

HOURS OF CHILDHOOD, AND OTHER POEMS. [Anon] Montreal, A. Bowman, 1820. 94p [OTUV QMSS

Bowman, Louise (Morey), 1882–1944

CHARACTERS IN CADENCE. Toronto, Macmillan, 1938. 91p [BM BVaU NBFU OTUV QMM

DREAM TAPESTRIES. Toronto, Macmillan, 1924. 91p [BM BVaU LC NBFU OKQ QMM

MOONLIGHT AND COMMON DAY. Toronto, Macmillan, 1922. 63p [BM BVaU NBFU OLU QMM

Box, William McNab
FORTY POEMS. London, Chester & Lang, 1944. 49p [BM LC
NATURE'S BYWAYS. Toronto, Crucible Press, 1941. 10p [LC OTP

Boyd, Adam
FRASER CANYON AND OTHER POEMS. Victoria, Diggon-Hibben, 1946. 20p
[BViPA

Boyd, Ann
SPRING MAGIC. Toronto, Ryerson, 1931. 16p [OKQ

Boyd, Edna Alice
SCRIBBLINGS. Toronto, Author, [1933?]. 39p [OTU

Boyd, John, 1864–1933
THE DEATH OF DOLLARD AND OTHER POEMS. Montreal, Author, 1914. 64p
[BVaU OOP QMM

Boyle, Charles Frederick, 1911–1966
EXCUSE FOR FUTILITY. Toronto, Ryerson, 1939. 8p [BVaU NBSaM OKQ
QMM
PRAYERS AT A HIGH ALTAR. Toronto, Ryerson, 1942. 14p [NBFU
STARS BEFORE THE WIND. Toronto, Ryerson, 1937. 8p [BVaU NBSaM OKQ
QMM

Boyle, David, 1842–1911
UNCLE JIM'S CANADIAN NURSERY RHYMES. For Family and Kindergarten Use.
[Anon] Toronto, Musson, 1908. 83p [OTP

Boyne, Edward
[POEMS] COMPOSED BY BLIND POET BOYNE. Toronto, [1896?]. 47p [OKQ

Bradford, John Locke
THE BLIND SOLDIER AND OTHER POEMS. Halifax, Imperial Pub., 1921. 32p
[Brown U
DAD AND THE LONG TREK. Wolfville, N.S., Davidson, 1943. 40p [NSHD

Brack, Jessie (Wanless), 1826–
"DREAMS OF HOME" AND OTHER POEMS. Toronto, 1911. 32p [OTP

Bradbury, Fred G.R.
LIGHTS AND SHADOWS OF LANDSCAPE AND LIFE. Songs, Poems, and Rhymes.
N.p., Author, 1932. 95p [AEU OOP
PEN PICTURES FROM NATURE'S ART GALLERIES. N.p., n.d. 79p [AEU

Bradshaw, B. Maude
POETRY FOR EVERY MONTH. Toronto, Educational Book, 1930. 128p [CC

Bradshaw, Thecla Jean (Robbins)
MOBILES. Toronto, Ryerson, 1955. 16p

Bramley-Moore, Alfred Arthur, 1881—
POEMS ON THE GOSPEL. Montreal, Chapman, 1923. 94p [BM Brown U
BVaU NBFU OOP

Brannen, Sterling, 1888—1953
SNACKS. A Collection of Original Verse, Epigrams, Paragraphs. Fredericton,
Author, [1947?]. [BVaU NBFU

Breakenridge, John, 1820—1854
THE CRUSADES AND OTHER POEMS. Kingston, Rowlands, 1846. 327p [BM
BVaU LC OTP

Breckenridge, Rev. James, —1879
POEMS. Toronto, Dredge, 1860. 256p [OTP

Breeze, James T.
THE ASSASSINATION OF PRESIDENT LINCOLN. A Poem. Belleville, Bell, 1865.
8p [Bound with MEMORIES OF MY YOUTH. ... See below.]
THE BEAUTIES OF BELLEVILLE. [Anon] Belleville, 1864. 20p [OKQ
CANADIAN POEMS. Port Hope, "British Canadian" Office, 1866. 16p [OKQ
THE DOMINION OF CANADA. The Great Institution of Our Country. A Poem on
the Grand Trunk Railway. Montreal, 1867. 24p [OTP QMSS
THE FENIAN RAID!! THE QUEEN'S OWN! Poems on the Events of the Hour.
Napanee, "Weekly Express," 1866. 6p [QMSS
THE GLORY OF THE AGE, THE ATLANTIC CABLE. A Poem on the Wondrous
Achievements of Science. Ottawa, Citizen, 1866. 16p [NSWA
THE GREAT THEME OF THE AGE. A Poem on the Confederation of the British
American Provinces. Ottawa, "Daily Citizen," 1866. 23p [QMBM
THE MARTYRED PRESIDENT. 3rd ed. Montreal, 1867. 8p [CCJ
MEMORIES OF MY YOUTH. A Collection of Poems. Napanee, Kennedy, 1865.
32p [OTP
ORIGINAL CANADIAN LITERATURE. The Miscellaneous Works of the Canadian
Poet, J.T. Breeze. Brockville, O'Brien, 1868. 16p [OTP
A POEM OF WELCOME TO HER ROYAL HIGHNESS THE PRINCESS LOUISE ... with
A POEM ON THE WRECK OF THE STEAMER "WAUBUNO". ... Collingwood,
"Bulletin," 1879. 8p [OTP
THE POET'S GLANCE OF KINGSTON SCENES. Picton, 1864. 24p [CCJ
THE POET'S MEMENTO OF PICTON. A Poem on the Scenery, Institutions,
Ministers, Literary and Public Men of the Town. Picton, "North American,"
1865. 24p [OTUV
THE POET'S RAMBLES THROUGH TORONTO. ... Toronto, Guardian, 1864. 24p
[OTP
TO MY BROTHER IN HEAVEN. THE BETHANY FAMILY. ABRAHAM LINCOLN IN
HEAVEN. N.p., [18—?]. 16p [OTP

Bresnahan, Mrs. Jessie M.
POEMS OF THE PEACE RIVER COUNTRY AND OTHERS. Ilfracombe, Devon,
Stockwell, 1960. 71p

Brewer, Alice
SPRING IN SAVARY. Toronto, Ryerson, 1926. 16p [BVaU NBSaM OKQ

Brewster, Elizabeth Winnifred, 1922—
EAST COAST. Toronto, Ryerson, 1951. 8p
LILLOOET. Toronto, Ryerson, 1954. 28p
ROADS AND OTHER POEMS. Toronto, Ryerson, 1957. 12p

Breyfogle, W.R.
AUTUMN LEAVES AND OTHER VERSE. Peterborough, Ont., Author, 1936. 58p
[NSHPL
DRIFTWOOD AND OTHER VERSE. Peterborough, Ont., Author, 1938. 42p [NSWA
IN LILAC TIME AND OTHER RHYME. Peterborough, Author, 1934. 56p [BVaU
NSWA OPeT

Brichan, Wellington, 1812—1880?
THE WIFE, OR THE WUDDY, AND OTHER POEMS AND SONGS. Sarnia, Observer
Steam Job Press, 1876. 106p [Phelps p89

Brindle, Walter, 1869?—
FRANCE AND FLANDERS. Four Years Experience Told in Poem & Story. By
Sapper W. Brindle. Saint John, Smith, 1919. 84p [Brown U NBFU

British Columbia, University of. Student Publications Board
CHAPBOOK. Vancouver, Boyd, 1931. 22p [BVaU

Broadfoot, Samuel Rupert
CANADA, THE LAND OF PROMISE, AND OTHER POEMS. Woodstock, Sentinel-
Review Press, 1916. 51p [2nd ed.: Same publisher, s.d. 101p] [BM BVaU
NBFU OTP QMSS
HOLIDAYING IN CANADA ON THE OTTAWA RIVER. Ottawa, Author, 1941. 203p
[NBFU OOA

Brooke, Frances (Moore), 1724—1789
VIRGINIA. A Tragedy. With Odes, Pastorals, and Translations. London, Author,
1756. 159p [BM

Brooke, John
POEMS. Toronto, Hunter Rose, 1882. 84p [BVaU NBFU OTU QMM

Brooks, Anne Sutherland
BLUE DUSK AND OTHER POEMS. By Anne Sutherland. [Toronto], Livingstone,
[1934]. 63p [AEU Brown U OTP
I MET SOME LITTLE PEOPLE. Toronto, Ryerson, 1941. 55p [BVaU NSHD OTP

LITTLE SONGS FOR SALE. By Anne Sutherland. Toronto, Ryerson, 1928. 24p
[NBFU OKQ

A RIBBAND OF BLUE. By Anne Sutherland. Guelph, Author, 1929. 31p [AEU
OTU

THE SUNNE-BEAM STAIRE. Guelph, Author, 1930. 38p [AEU

WITHIN A WICKET GATE. 2nd ed. By Anne Sutherland. Toronto, Ryerson, 1927.
24p [NBFU OKQ

Brooks, Lillie A. (Macmillan), 1874–

THE BAND OF PURPLE. A Collection of Canadian Poems. Ed. by ——.
Toronto, Oxford U. Press, 1915. 19p [BM BVaU NBFU OTU

CHRISTMAS SONGS. N.p., n.d. 8p [OKQ

THE FORTY-EIGHTH HIGHLANDERS. [1915]. [BM

THE LAND OF THE NORTHERN MEN. Toronto, Ryerson, 1924. 55p [BVaU
NBFU OKQ QMBM

Brown, Audrey Alexandra, 1904–

ALL FOOLS DAY. Toronto, Ryerson, 1948. 56p [Brown U BVaU LC NBFU
OTP

CHALLENGE TO TIME AND DEATH. Toronto, Macmillan, 1943. 55p [BVaU LC
NSHD OTP

A DRYAD IN NANAIMO. Toronto, Macmillan, 1931. 70p [New ed., together
with eleven new poems: Toronto, Macmillan, 1934. 120p] [BM BVaU LC
NSHD OTU QMM

THE TREE OF RESURRECTION AND OTHER POEMS. Toronto, Macmillan, 1937.
151p [BM BVaU LC NSHD OKQ QMM

V-E DAY. Toronto, Ryerson, 1947. 5p [BVaU LC NBSaM OKQ

Brown, Edward Killoran, 1905–1951

SELECTED POEMS OF DUNCAN CAMPBELL SCOTT. With a memoir by ——.
Toronto, Ryerson, 1951. 176p

Brown, Frank S., –1915

CONTINGENT DITTIES AND OTHER SOLDIER SONGS OF THE GREAT WAR. By
Frank S. Brown, Sergeant, P.P.C.L.I. (The Pats). Ed. by Holbrook Jackson.
London, Low Marston, 1915. 79p [BM Brown U BVaU LC NBFU

Brown, J.

RIVULET. A Collection of Hymns and Temperance Songs, for Bands of Hope
and Temperance Meetings. Comp. by ——. Halifax, Messenger Print.,
[1876]. 8p [NSHD

Brown, James N.J.

PROSPECTOR'S TRAIL. [Vancouver?], Author, 1941. 64p [BVaU

Brown, Jessie Findlay

UP CAME THE MOON. Oshawa, Ont., Mundy-Goodfellow, 1936. 79p [Brown U
BVaU NBFU OTU

Brown, John Henry, 1859–1946
POEMS. Lyrical and Dramatic. Ottawa, Durie, 1892. 204p [BM BVaU LC
  NSHD OTU QMM

Brown, Margaret H., 1887–
THE AWAKENING. Shanghai, Author, 1933. 29p [AEU OTUV QMG

Browne, H.F.
THE STRANGE ADVENTURES OF A CARP. By "Norroy" [pseud]. London, Dean,
  1884. 19p [BM
A TALE OF A WHALE. Written and Illus. by "Norroy" [pseud]. London,
  Dean, 1884. 19p [BM LC

Browne, Thaddeus A.
THE BELGIAN MOTHER AND BALLADS OF BATTLE TIME. Toronto, Macmillan,
  1917. 105p [BM Brown U BVaU NBFU OTU
A TRIBUTE TO SIR WILFRID LAURIER, PREMIER OF CANADA, 1896–1911. IN
  MEMORIAM. [A Poem. With Portraits.] Ottawa, Modern Press, 1919. 39p
  [BM NBSaM OTP QQL
THE WHITE PLAGUE, AND OTHER POEMS. Toronto, Briggs, 1909. 75p [BM
  Brown U BVaU NSHD OTU

Browning, Samuel
POEMS. V. I. London, Green, 1846. 320p [V. II, THE HISTORY OF JOSEPH AND
  OTHER POEMS, not published (?); cf. Announcement Prefixed.] [BM LC QMSS

Brownlow, Edward Burrough, 1857–1895
ORPHEUS AND OTHER POEMS. Montreal, Pen and Pencil Club, 1896. 96p [BM
  BVaU MWU NBFU OTU QMM

Bruce, Charles Tory, 1906–1971
THE FLOWING SUMMER. Toronto, Ryerson, 1947. 31p [BVaU LC NSHD OTP
GREY SHIP MOVING. Toronto, Ryerson, 1945. 34p [BM BVaU LC MWU
  NSHD OTU QMM
THE MULGRAVE ROAD. Toronto, Macmillan, 1951. 39p
PERSONAL NOTE. Toronto, Ryerson, 1941. 8p [BVaU NBFU OTU QMM
TOMORROW'S TIDE. Toronto, Macmillan, 1932. 28p [BVaU NBFU OOCC
WILD APPLES. Sackville, N.B., Tribune Press, 1927. 23p [NSHD OKQ

Bruce, Mary
MAN IS A CREATOR. N.p., Author, 1940. 34p [OTU QMU

Brundle, John, 1882–
ACROSS THE ARCTIC SEAS. From the pen of John, a Suffolk Herd Boy [pseud].
  Roche's Point, Ont., Author, 1951. 79p
BROMESWELL, MY SUFFOLK HOME. A Pastoral of My Child and Boyhood. From the
  pen of John, a Suffolk Herd Boy [pseud]. Roche's Point, Ont., Author, 1952. 31p
CULLED SELECTIONS OF THE MIND. From the pen of John, a Suffolk Herd Boy
  [pseud]. Roche's Point, Ont., Author, 1957. 24p

THE FORSAKEN PLOT IN THE LITTLE CHURCHYARD. From the pen of John, a Suffolk Herd Boy [pseud]. Roche's Point, Ont., Author, 1950. 32p [Brown U BVaU OTU

THE GINK. Roche's Point, Ont., Author, 1954. 3p

THE GIRL WHO DIED OF A BROKEN HEART. From the pen of John, a Suffolk Herd Boy [pseud]. Roche's Point, Ont., Author, 1941. 33p [Brown U LC OTU

THE GREAT ANTARTIC [sic] CALL. From the pen of John, a Suffolk Herd Boy [pseud]. Roche's Point, Ont., Author, 1954. 32p

LAURA, THE HEROINE OF BEAVER DAM, JUNE 24TH 1813. From the pen of John, a Suffolk Herd Boy [pseud]. Roche's Point, Ont., Author, 1949. 40p [Brown U BVaU OTU

THE LITTLE ROSEBUD. From the pen of John, a Suffolk Herd Boy [pseud]. Roche's Point, Ont., Author, 1958. 14p

OFF BOSTON LIGHT, JUNE 1, 1813. From the pen of John, a Suffolk Herd Boy [pseud]. Roche's Point, Ont., Author, 1945. 20p [BVaU OTP

THE SIX PIECES. Words and Music. Roche's Point, Ont., Author, 1946. 16p [BVaU OTU

SONGS, SPIRITUAL AND OTHERWISE. Words and Music. Roche's Point, Ont., Author, 1941. 19p [Brown U BVaU OTU

SUNDAY PICKINGS OF THE MIND. From the pen of John, a Suffolk Herd Boy [pseud]. Roche's Point, Ont., Author, 1941. 22p [Brown U OTU

TWO CAROLS. Roche's Point, Ont., Author, 1954. 4p

THE UNNAMED MAID OF LYME. From the pen of John, a Suffolk Herd Boy [pseud]. Toronto, McLean, 1939. 20p [Brown U BVaU LC OTU

THE WOMAN OF THE UNBEATEN TRAIL, NANCY HANKS, 1782–1818. Roche's Point, Ont., Author, 1940. 8p [Brown U OTU

YE SAILORS OF THE ISLAND RACE. ... Roche's Point, Ont., Author, 1956. 10p [Refers to Admiral Robert Blake and Admiral Lord Nelson.]

Bruun, Arthur Geoffrey, 1898–

MAGIC CASEMENTS AND OTHER VERSES. Vancouver, Author, 1922. 9p [BVaU

Brymner, Douglas, 1823–1902

THE TWO MONGRELS. A Modern Eclogue. By Tumas Treddles [pseud]. Toronto, Hunter Rose, 1876. 7p [OTP

Bucham, Mary A.

MEMORIES, AND OTHER POEMS. Toronto, Briggs, 1905. 87p [BM BVaU OKQ

Buchanan, Mrs. Mary

COUNTRY BREEZES FROM BREEZY BRAE. Thornbury, Ont., Beaver Valley Pub., n.d. 174p [OTUV

Buck, Alanson L.

THE OUTLAW AND OTHER POEMS. Toronto, Briggs, 1913. 161p [BM Brown U NBFU OLU SSU

Buck, Annie Lucinda (Myers), 1865–
MY LOVE'S GARDEN AND OTHER POEMS. London, Stockwell, [1922?]. 19p
  [OONL
POETICAL PAMPHLETS. N.p., n.d. [Contains autobiography.] [OLU

Buck, James A.
THE SAVIOUR'S SECOND COMING. The Great Mystery of Babylon Unravelled.
  The Great Judgement Day at Hand. ... [Anon] Belleville, 1884. 27p [Brown U

Buckley, Beatrice Barron
SONGS OF WEENY GOPHER. Toronto, Macmillan, 1941. 61p [OONL OTP

Buckley, Joan
BLUE STEEPLES. Vancouver, Clarke & Stuart, 1942. 21p [BVaU NBFU OKQ
GREEN FLAME. Toronto, Crucible Press, 1940. 22p [BVaU LC NBFU OTP
SPRING AFTER WAR. Langley Prairie, B.C., Advance Press, 1946. 24p [Brown U
  BVaU
WESTERN SUNFLOWERS. An Anthology of British Columbian Verse. Langley
  Prairie, B.C., Author, 1946. 33p [BVaU OKQ

Bullen, John Ravener, 1886–1927
WHITE FIRE. Athol, Mass., Recluse Press, 1927. 86p [LC

Bullock, Rev. William, 1797–1874
SONGS OF THE CHURCH. Halifax, Clapp, 1854. 235p [Also: London, 1855.]
  [BM NSHD OTP

Bunner, Freda Helen (Newton), 1904–
ORPHAN AND OTHER POEMS. Toronto, Ryerson, 1956. 8p

Burchell, M. Edith
RHYMES AND CHIMES. N.p., [1927?]. 14p [NSHP OONL QMU

Burns, Elizabeth Rollit
LITTLE CANADIANS. ... [Montreal], Desbarats, [1899]. 40p [BM BViP OTUV

Burns, Malcolm, 1887–
GOLDEN GLEAMS. Vancouver, Rose, Cowan & Latta, 1936. 93p [BVaU OLU

Burpee, Lawrence Johnstone, 1873–1946
A CENTURY OF CANADIAN SONNETS. An Anthology. Ed. by ——. Toronto,
  Musson, 1910. 112p [BVaU NBFU OTU QMM
FLOWERS FROM A CANADIAN GARDEN. Selected and ed. by ——. Toronto,
  Musson, [1909?]. 112p [BVaU NBFU OKQ QMM
SONGS OF FRENCH CANADA. Trans., selected, and arranged by ——. Toronto,
  Musson, 1909. 88p [BVaU OKQ QMM

Burr, Everett Harold, 1894–1931
RICH MAN, POOR MAN. Toronto, Ryerson, 1932. 8p [BVaU NBSaM OTU QMM

Burtis, William Richard M., 1818–1882
THE NEW DOMINION. A Poem. Saint John, McMillan, 1867. 16p [Brown U
  NBFU

Burton, Violet, 1894–
NO STONE TO THROW, AND OTHER POEMS. London, Stockwell, 1935. 12p [CC

Burwell, Rev. Adam Hood, 1790–1849
SUMMER EVENING CONTEMPLATIONS. Montreal, Lovell, 1849. 12p [BM

Buschlen, John Preston, 1888–
THE WORLD WAR. Poems. Toronto, Hollingsworth & Buschlen, [1914]. 19p
  [ACU BM BVaU OTU

Butchart, Reuben, 1863–1963
THE LYRIC FLUTE, AND OTHER POEMS. Toronto, Macmillan, 1928. 78p
  [Brown U BVaU LC NBFU OTU

Butcher, Albert Edward Valentine
POEMS. Ilfracombe, Devon, Stockwell, 1959. 17p
THE SAGA OF THE NANCY, AND OTHER POEMS. Ilfracombe, Devon, Stockwell,
  1960. 32p

Butcher, John H., 1879?–
THE FARMER POET. A Book of Homespun Poetry. N.p., 1953. 88p

Butler, Ethel H.
LITTLE THUNDER'S WOOING. A Legend of the Blomidon and Glooscap Country.
  Port Royal, N.S., Abanaki Press, 1950. 16p [Brown U BVaU

Butler, J. Edward P., 1902–
THE HOUND OF EARTH. A Selection of Poems. Newcastle, N.B., Union Advocate,
  1937. 16p [NBFU
RECOLLECTED IN TRANQUILLITY. A Selection of Poems. Chatham, N.B., priv.
  print., 1956. 40p

Butler, Martin, 1857–
MAPLE LEAVES AND HEMLOCK BRANCHES. A Collection of Poems. Fredericton,
  "Gleaner," 1889. 60p [146p?] [NBFU OTP QMM
PATRIOTIC AND PERSONAL POEMS. Fredericton, Journal Office, 1898. 146p
  [NBFU OTU

Byrnes, John Maclay
THE PATHS TO YESTERDAY. Memories of Old St. John's, Newfoundland.
  Including a number of typical Newfoundland Poems, each from the gifted
  pen of a Terra Novian. Boston, Meador, 1931. 235p [BVaU LC OTU

C., A.P.
EXTRACTS AND HYMNS. Brockville, Merrill, n.d. [187–?] 16p [Amtmann
cat. 140

Cain, Sydney C.
PRAIRIE FAIRIES AND OTHER VERSES. Regina, Leader, n.d. 30p [BViPA

Calder, Robert McLean
A BERWICKSHIRE BARD. The Songs and Poems of Robert McLean Calder.
Edited, with Introductory Memoir by W.S. Crockett. Paisley, J. & R. Parlane,
1897. 306p [BM
HAME SANGS. London, King, 1887. 140p [OTUV

Caldwell, James Ernest, 1862–1954
THE CASTLE ON THE HILL. Ottawa, Thorburn, 1899. 30p [OTUV
SONGS OF THE PINES. Toronto, Briggs, 1895. 142p [BVaU LC NSHD
OTUV QMM

Call, Frank Oliver, 1878–1956
ACANTHUS AND WILD GRAPE. Toronto, McClelland, [1920]. 80p [BM BVaU
LC NSHD OKQ QMM
BLUE HOMESPUN. Toronto, Ryerson, 1924. 43p [BM BVaU LC NSHD OTU
IN A BELGIAN GARDEN, AND OTHER POEMS. London, MacDonald, 1917. 45p
[BM BVaU NBFU OKQ
SIMPLES, CURTAINS, BURNED FORESTS, THE CATHEDRAL BUILDERS. N.p., n.d.
4p [OONL
SONNETS FOR YOUTH. Toronto, Ryerson, 1944. 8p [BVaU LC NSHD OTP

Callaghan, Francis, 1902?–
THE REED AND THE CROSS. Toronto, Ryerson, 1923. 51p [BM BVaU LC
NSHD OKQ QMM

Callan, Richard
CHAINS OF HARMONY. Atlanta, Ga., Banner Press, Emory University, 1939.
67p [BVaU LC OTUV

Calvert, William Dobree
YPNOS. Toronto, Crucible Press, 1941. 56p [V.1] [BVaU LC OKQ
YPNOS. [North Vancouver], Author, 1942–44. [V.2–4] [BViPA

Cameron, Rev. Charles Innes, 1837–1879
POEMS AND HYMNS. Geelong, Australia, Purdie, 1870. 119p [Also: Toronto,
Robinson, 1879. 60p] [BVaU LC NSHD OTP QMM

Cameron, Elizabeth
SONGS THAT THE WIND HAS SUNG. Lakefield, Ont., The News, [1926?]. 26p
[Brown U OTU

Cameron, Fred J.

THE HERMIT OF CHOKECHERRY CREEK, AND OTHER POEMS. Edmonton, Institute of Applied Arts, 1950. 113p [AEU Brown U

Cameron, George Frederick, 1854—1885

LYRICS ON FREEDOM, LOVE AND DEATH. Ed. by his brother Charles J. Cameron. Boston, Moore; Kingston, Shannon, 1887. 296p [BM BVaU LC NSHD OKQ QMM

Cameron, Hugh Duncan, 1833—

THE GARLAND. A Collection of Songs and Lyrics, Original and Selected, for Schools and Colleges. Goderich, 1865. 120p [CCJ Rhod.

Cameron, Jean

CHAPBOOK. [Poems by members of the Letters Club of the University of British Columbia. ...] By Jean Cameron, Carol Coates, Roy Daniells, James Dunn, Ronald Grantham, Lionel Haweis, Jeanne Lakeman-Shaw, Frances Lucas, Betty Moore, R.A. Pilkington, Vernon van Sickle, Frank Wilson. Vancouver, priv. print., 1931. 24p [BVaU

Cameron, William Bleasdell, 1862—1951

THE YARN OF THE HOWLING GALE. (An Alberta Barque with a Bad Bight). [Anon] Athabasca, Alta., Cameron Shipyards, 1938. 12p [A satire aimed at the Social Credit party. Attributed to William Bleasdell Cameron.] [AEU

Campbell, Amy E.

HEART FORGET-ME-NOTS. Toronto, Briggs, 1910. 80p [BM BVaU NBFU OTU

Campbell, Arthur

SONGS OF THE PINEWOODS. London, Cox, 1894. 90p [BM OTUV QMM

Campbell, Austin, 1884—

... THEY SHALL BUILD ANEW. Toronto, Ryerson, 1944. 7p [BVaU LC NBFU OTU

Campbell, Charles

CANADA. A Metrical Story. Toronto, Briggs, 1897. 32p [BM BVaU LC NSHD OTUV

Campbell, H.

CHRIST'S COMING DAY. A Rhapsody on the Apocalypse. New York, Our Hope Pub. Co., 1938. 68p [CC

Campbell, John Lorne, 1906—

A COLLECTION OF FOLK-SONGS AND MUSIC MADE IN NOVA SCOTIA. [Dublin?], 1947. 59p [LC

HIGHLAND SONGS OF THE FORTY-FIVE. Ed. and Trans. ... by ——. Edinburgh, Grant, 1933. xxxvi+327p [LC OTU QMM

Campbell, John Robert Lamont, −1959

THE GARDEN OF THOUGHTS. Charlottetown, Author, n.d. 20p [QMU
GOLDEN MOMENTS COINED IN THE MINT OF TIME. By John of the Lilacs [pseud].
Sackville, N.B., Tribune Press, 1947. 322p [OOP OTU

Campbell, [Miss] M.A.

POSTHUMOUS POEMS. Woodstock, Ont., 1865. 26p [OOP

Campbell, Marjorie (Freeman), 1896−

HIGH ON A HILL. Toronto, Ryerson, 1949. 16p [BVaU NBSaM OTP
MERRY-GO-ROUND. Toronto, Ryerson, 1946. 16p [BVaU LC NBSaM OKQ
PORTS OF CALL. Toronto, Ryerson, 1960. 56p

Campbell, Ralph J., 1904−1936

LOCAL LYRICS. Halifax, Allen, [192−?]. 35p [Brown U

Campbell, Wilfred, 1858−1918

ATLANTEAN LYRICS. [Two Poems.] N.p., Author, [1913?]. 3p [NSWA OTP
BEYOND THE HILLS OF DREAM. Boston, Houghton, 1899. 137p [BM BVaU
LC NSHD OTU QMM
THE COLLECTED POEMS OF WILFRED CAMPBELL. New York, Revell, 1905.
354p. [Also: Toronto, Briggs, 1905, under title of THE POEMS OF WILFRED
CAMPBELL (*q.v.*).] [BM LC NBFU OTU
DECEMBER LYRICS. Ottawa, 1913. 2p [OTU
DEPARTURE. Ottawa, 1899. 2p [NBFU OTU
THE DISCOVERERS. A Poem ... issued for the New Year, 1905. [Ottawa, 1904?]
3p [NBFU OTP QMU
THE DREAD VOYAGE. Poems. Toronto, Briggs, 1893. 190p [BVaU NSHD OTU
QMM
LAKE LYRICS AND OTHER POEMS. Saint John, McMillan, 1889. 160p [BVaU
LC NSHD OKQ QMM
LANGEMARCK, AND OTHER WAR POEMS. With intro. by Rev. Dr. Herridge.
Ottawa, St. Andrew's Church, [1917]. 14p [NBFU
THE LYRE DEGENERATE. A Poem ... issued for the New Year, 1904. [Ottawa,
1903?]. 3p [NBFU OLU QMG
LYRICS OF IRON AND MIST. Ottawa, Author, 1916. 4p [NBFU
LYRICS OF THE DREAD REDOUBT. Ottawa, Author, 1917. 3p [NBFU
NIGHT. THE HOUSE OF DREAMS. Two Poems. ... Issued Privately to ...
Friends for the New Year, 1903. N.p., 1903. 3p [OKQ
THE OXFORD BOOK OF CANADIAN VERSE. Chosen by ——. Toronto, Oxford U.
Press, 1913. 343p [BM BVaU LC NSHD
POEMS OF LOYALTY BY BRITISH AND CANADIAN AUTHORS. Selected by ——.
London, Nelson, 1913. 99p [BM BVaU NBFU OTU
THE POEMS OF WILFRED CAMPBELL. Toronto, Briggs, 1905. 354p [BM BVaU
NBFU OKQ QMM

THE POETICAL WORKS OF WILFRED CAMPBELL. Ed. with a Memoir by W.J.
  Sykes. London, Hodder, 1923. xxii + 363p [BM BVaU LC NSHD OTU
  QMM
REQUIEM. EDWARD THE PEACE MAKER. [Ottawa, Author, 1910]. 3p [BVaU
  NBFU OTU
SAGAS OF VASTER BRITAIN. Poems of the Race, the Empire and the Divinity of
  Man. Toronto, Musson, 1914. 163p [BM BVaU NSHD OTP
A SHEAF OF WINTER LYRICS. Ottawa, Author, [1906]. 4p [BVaU OTU QMM
SNOWFLAKES AND SUNBEAMS. St. Stephen, St. Croix Courier, 1888. 36p [OTP
THE VANGUARD. A Poem ... issued Privately to his Friends for the New Year, 1901.
  Ottawa, Author, [1900?]. 4p [AEU NBFU OLU QMU
WAR LYRICS. Ottawa, Author, 1915. 4p [NBFU

Campbell, William M.
ZORRA. Boston, Sherman, 1915. 74p [BM OTL

Campbell, Zola Isabell (Campbell), 1880–1967
A TALE OF THE EARLY YEARS. Edmonton, n.d. 16p [Describes early days of
  South Edmonton (Strathcona).] [BViPA Peel

Canadian Authors' Association. Calgary Branch
CANADIAN POEMS. Calgary, the Branch, 1937. 46p [AEU Brown U OTU
COLLECTED POEMS. Calgary, McAra, 1934. 39p [BVa

Canadian Authors' Association. Edmonton Branch
ALBERTA POETRY YEAR BOOK, 1930. Edmonton, the Branch, 1931. [Also
  issued in subsequent years.] [OTU QMM
ALBERTA POETRY YEAR BOOK [21st]. [Edmonton], Edmonton Branch,
  Canadian Authors Association, [1950]. 62p [OONL

Canadian Authors' Association. Manitoba Branch
MANITOBA POETRY CHAPBOOK, 1933. Winnipeg, Israelite Press, 1933. 32p
  [BViP OKQ OTP

Canadian Authors' Association. Montreal Branch
MONTREAL IN VERSE. An Anthology of English Poetry by Montreal Poets.
  Ed. by Leo Cox. Montreal, Poetry Group of the Montreal Branch, 1942.
  48p [LC NBFU OKQ QMM
POETRY YEAR-BOOK, 1925. Montreal, the Branch, 1925. [Also issued in
  subsequent years.] [BVaU LC NBFU OTU QMM

Canadian Authors' Association. Nova Scotia Branch
AN ACADIAN SHEAF. Selections from Current Nova Scotian Poetry. Halifax,
  Macnab, 1934–35. 2v [NSHD OTU QMM

Canadian Authors' Association. Ottawa Branch
PROFILE. A Chapbook of Canadian Verse. Ottawa, the Branch, 1946. 47p
  [BVaU OTP

Canadian Authors' Association. Saskatchewan Branch
SASKATCHEWAN. Her Infinite Variety. [Regina, Leader Pub. Co., 1924].
88p [BVaU LC OKQ
SASKATCHEWAN POETRY YEAR-BOOK, 1935. Regina, Western, 1935. 38p
[Also issued in subsequent years. Title varies.] [BM Brown U LC OTU

Canadian Authors' Association. Toronto Branch
VOICES OF VICTORY. Representative Poetry of Canada in War-time. Toronto,
Macmillan, 1941. 97p [BVaU OTP

Canadian Authors' Association. Victoria and Islands Branch
VICTORIA POETRY CHAPBOOK. A Year Book. Victoria, Clarke Print., 1935.
26p [Also issued in subsequent years—5 vols. to 1942.] [BViPA OTU
VICTORIA POETRY CHAP-BOOK, 1935—42. Victoria, the Branch, 1942. 26p
[Brown U BVaU LC NSHD

Canadian Authors' Association. Windsor Branch
BORDER VOICES. Ed. by Carl Eayrs. Windsor, Ont., the Branch, 1946. 48p
[OOP

Canadian Expeditionary Force
O CANADA! A Medley of Stories, Verse, Pictures and Music Contributed by
Members of the Canadian Expeditionary Force. London, Simpkin; Hamilton,
Kent, [1916]. 95p [BM NSHD OKQ

Canadian Soldier-Poets
RHYME AND REASON. A Souvenir Volume of Verse by Canadian Soldier-Poets.
With Compliments of the *Maple Leaf,* Italy. Foreword by C.W. Gilchrist.
Rome, 1945. 63p [NBFU

Card, Dorothy Edith
PRAIRIE HARVEST AND OTHER POEMS. New York, Vantage Press, 1954. 48p

Carlon, J.
THE CRUCIFIX. Poems and Songs. [Peterborough?], n.p., n.d. 29p [OTP

Carman, Bliss, 1861—1929
"AN OPEN LETTER" FROM BLISS CARMAN. Boston, Small Maynard, [1920].
17p [BVaU LC NBFU OKQ
APRIL AIRS. Toronto, McClelland, 1922. [Publisher's dummy copy made up of
miscellaneous unconsecutive pages.] [OONL
APRIL AIRS. A Book of New England Lyrics. Boston, Small Maynard, 1916.
77p [BM BVaU LC NSHD OTP
AT MICHAELMAS. A Lyric. Wolfville, Acadian Press, 1895. 11p [NSHD OKQ
BALLADS AND LYRICS. London, Bullen, 1902. 79p [A different selection
from the following title.] [BM NBFU OKQ

BALLADS AND LYRICS. Toronto, McClelland, 1923. 293p [A different selection from the one pub. under same title in 1902.] [BM BVaU NSHD OKQ QMM

BALLADS OF LOST HAVEN. A Book of the Sea. Boston, Lamson Wolffe, 1897. 117p [BM BVaU LC MWU NSHD OKQ

BEHIND THE ARRAS. A Book of the Unseen. Boston, Lamson Wolffe, 1895. 102p [BVaU LC MWU NSHD OTU QMM

BLISS CARMAN'S POEMS. Toronto, McClelland, 1931. 546p [BM BVaU LC NBFU OTU QMBM

BY THE AURELIAN WALL, AND OTHER ELEGIES. Boston, Lamson Wolffe, 1898. 132p [BM BVaU LC NSHD OKQ

CHRISTMAS EVE AT S. KAVIN'S. New York, Kimball, 1901. 15p [BVaU LC NBFU OKQ

CORONATION ODE. Boston, Page, 1902. 12p [BM LC NBFU OKQ

CORYDON. A Trilogy in Commemoration of Matthew Arnold. ... Fredericton, MacNutt, 1898. 15p [NBFU

ECHOES FROM VAGABONDIA. Boston, Small Maynard, 1912. 65p [BM BVaU LC NBFU OKQ

ECHOES FROM VAGABONDIA. Toronto, McClelland, [1922]. [Publisher's dummy copy made up of miscellaneous unconsecutive pages.] [BM OONL

FAR HORIZONS. Boston, Small Maynard, 1925. 85p [BM BVaU LC NSHD OTU QMM

FLOWER OF THE ROSE. By Louis Norman [pseud]. Cambridge, Mass., 1938. 4p [First pub. under pseud. of Louis Norman. New York, Primrose Bindery, 1892.] [NSHD OTU

FOUR SONNETS. Boston, Small Maynard, 1916. 4p [BVaU NBFU OKQ

... FROM THE GREEN BOOK OF THE BARDS. Boston, Page, 1903. 137p [BVaU LC NSHD OKQ

... FROM THE BOOK OF MYTHS. Boston, Page, 1902. 88p [BVaU LC NBFU OTU

... FROM THE BOOK OF VALENTINES. Boston, Page, 1905. 103p [BVaU LC NBFU OTU

THE GATE OF PEACE. A Poem. New York, Village Press, 1907. 14p [NBFU OKQ

THE GIRL IN THE POSTER. For a Design by Miss Ethel Reed. [Springfield, Mass.], Wayside Press, 1897. 9p [LC NSHD OKQ

THE GREEN BOOK OF THE BARDS. Cambridge, Mass., University Press, 1898. 12p [NBFU OKQ

LAST SONGS FROM VAGABONDIA. Toronto, McClelland, [1922]. [Publisher's dummy copy made up of miscellaneous unconsecutive pages.] [BM OONL

LAST SONGS FROM VAGABONDIA. By Bliss Carman and Richard Hovey. Boston, Small Maynard, 1901. 79p [BM BVaU LC NBFU OKQ

LATER POEMS. With an Appreciation by R.H. Hathaway. Toronto, McClelland, [1921]. xxix + 203p [BM BVaU LC NBFU OKQ QMM

LOW TIDE ON GRAND PRE. By Bliss Carmen [sic]. Toronto, Copp Clark, [1899].

13 leaves (Canadian Series of Booklets) [Unauthorized publication] [BVaU
LC NSHD OKQ

LOW TIDE ON GRAND PRE. A Book of Lyrics. New York, Webster, 1893. 120p
[Numerous later editions.] [BM BVaU LC NBFU OTU QMM

THE MAN OF THE MARNE, AND OTHER POEMS. By B.C. and M.P.K. New
Canaan, Conn., Ponus Press, 1918. 26p [LC NBFU OKQ

MORE SONGS FROM VAGABONDIA. Toronto, McClelland, [1922]. [Publisher's
dummy made up of miscellaneous unconsecutive pages] [BM OONL

MORE SONGS FROM VAGABONDIA. By Bliss Carman and Richard Hovey.
Boston, Copeland & Day, 1896. 72p [BM BVaU LC NSHD OKQ

THE MUSIC OF EARTH. With foreword and notes by Lorne Pierce. Toronto,
Ryerson, 1931. 45p [BM BVaU LC NBSaM OTP QMM

ODE ON THE CORONATION OF KING EDWARD. Boston, Page, 1902. 34p
[BVaU LC NSHD OTU QMM

OUR CANADIAN LITERATURE. Representative Verse (English). Chosen by Bliss
Carman and Lorne Pierce. Toronto, Ryerson, 1925. 361p [Rev. ed., 1935,
with French poems added. Rev. and enl. ed., with V.B. Rhodenizer:
CANADIAN POETRY IN ENGLISH. Toronto, Ryerson, 1954. xxxvi + 456p]
[BVaU LC NBFU OTU QMM

THE PATH TO SANKOTY. [Siasconset, Mass.], The Gift Shop, 1908. 4p [LC
OKQ

A PAINTER'S HOLIDAY, AND OTHER POEMS. New York, F.F. Sherman, 1911.
43p [BVaU LC NBFU OKQ

PIPES OF PAN. Containing "From the Book of Myths," "From the Green Book
of the Bards," "Songs of the Sea Children," "Songs from a Northern Garden,"
"From the Book of Valentines." Boston, Page, 1902–1905. 5v [The
volumes were later bound as one and so published. Numerous editions. First
Canadian ed.: Toronto, Ryerson, 1942.] [BM BVaU LC NBFU OKQ

POEMS. New York, Scott-Thaw; London, Murray, 1904. 2v [BM BVaU LC
NBFU OKQ

THE PRINCESS OF THE TOWER; THE WISE MEN FROM THE EAST; TO THE WINGED
VICTORY. New York, Village Press, 1906. 18p [LC NBFU OKQ

THE ROUGH RIDER, AND OTHER POEMS. New York, Kennerley, 1909. 78p
[BM BVaU LC NBFU OKQ

SAINT KAVIN. A Ballad. [Cambridge, Mass., Author], 1894. 9p [NBFU OKQ

SANCTUARY, SUNSHINE HOUSE SONNETS. New York, Dodd Mead, 1929. 55p
[BVaU LC NSHD OKQ

A SEAMARK. A Threnody for Robert Louis Stevenson. Boston, Copeland &
Day, 1895. 10p [BVaU LC NSHD OTU QMM

SELECTED POEMS. Ed. and with an intro. by Lorne Pierce. Toronto, McClelland,
1954. 119p

... SONGS FROM A NORTHERN GARDEN. Boston, Page, 1904. 121p [BM
BVaU LC OTU QMM

SONGS FROM VAGABONDIA. Toronto, McClelland, [1922]. [Publisher's dummy made up of miscellaneous consecutive pages] [BM OONL

SONGS FROM VAGABONDIA. By Bliss Carman and Richard Hovey. Boston, Copeland & Day, 1894. 54p [1st ed.] [BM BVaU LC NSHD OKQ

SONGS FROM VAGABONDIA; MORE SONGS FROM VAGABONDIA; LAST SONGS FROM VAGABONDIA. By Bliss Carman and Richard Hovey. Boston, Small Maynard, [1911]. 3v in 1. [LC OLU QMSS

... SONGS OF THE SEA CHILDREN. Boston, Page, 1904. 182p [BM BVaU LC NBFU OKQ

SAPPHO. Lyrics. With Excerpts from a Literal Rendering by H.T. Wharton. [N.p., Author, 1902]. 8p [NBFU OKQ

SAPPHO. One Hundred Lyrics. With an intro. by Charles G.D. Roberts. Boston, Page, 1904. 130p [Numerous later editions.] [BM BVaU LC NBFU OTU QMM

TO A CHICKADEE. (Sierra Madre Mountains, California). Palo Alto, Calif., Yerba Buena Press, 1933. 7p [NBFU OKQ

THE VENGEANCE OF NOEL BRASSARD. A Tale of the Acadian Expulsion. Cambridge, Mass., Bradley, 1899 [mis-dated MDCCCCXIX]. 23p [BVaU NBFU OKQ QMM

A VISION OF SAPPHO. [New York], Author, 1903. 7p [NBFU OKQ

A WINTER HOLIDAY [AND OTHER POEMS]. Boston, Small Maynard, 1899. 43p [BVaU LC NBFU OKQ

WILD GARDEN. New York, Dodd Mead, 1929. 76p [BM BVaU LC NSHD OTU QMM

THE WORD AT ST. KAVIN'S. Nelson, N.H., Monadnock Press, 1903. 28p [BM BVaU LC NSHD OKQ

YOUTH IN THE AIR. A Poem. Palo Alto, Calif., Yerba Buena Press, 1932. 4p [LC NBFU OKQ

Carnochan, Janet, 1839–1926

FORT GEORGE'S LONELY SYCAMORE. A Reminiscence of Niagara. N.p., n.d. 4p [QMU

Carpenter, Edmund Snow, 1922–

ANERCA. [Eskimo Poems.] Ed. by ——. Toronto, Dent, 1959. 45p

Carsley, Sara Elizabeth (Keatley), 1887–

ALCHEMY AND OTHER POEMS. Toronto, Macmillan, 1935. 61p [BVaU NBFU OKQ

THE ARTISAN. Toronto, Ryerson, 1941. 8p [BVaU LC NBSaM OTU QMM

Carter, Eldon

RHYMES OF A CANADIAN IN FRANCE. London, Stockwell, [1938]. 24p [BM Brown U

Carter, Ross L.
RAMBLING RHYMES. Edmonton, Douglas Print., n.d. [Peel Supp

Cartwright, Rev. Conway Edward, 1837–1920
LENA. A Legend of Niagara and Other Poems. Dublin, McGee, 1860. 72p
[BVaU OOP

Cartwright, George, 1739–1819
LABRADOR. A Poetical Epistle. [1792]. St. John's, Nfld.,Withers, 1882. 18p
[A reprint.] [NSHP OTP

Cary, Thomas, 1751–1823
ABRAM'S PLAINS. A Poem. ... Quebec, Author, 1789. 20p [QMBM

Casey, Rev. David A., 1886–
AT THE GATE OF THE TEMPLE. Toronto, Briggs, 1914. 72p [BM Brown U
OTUV
LEAVES ON THE WIND. Toronto, McClelland, 1919. 91p [BM BVaU OTP

Casey, Michael Thomas, 1900–1938
... SONNETS AND SEQUENCE. Toronto, Ryerson, 1938. 11p [BVaU LC
NBSaM OTP

Caswell, Edward Samuel, 1861–1938
CANADIAN SINGERS AND THEIR SONGS. A Collection of Portraits and Autograph
Poems. Toronto, Briggs, 1902. 45p [Later editions much enlarged, *e.g.*,
Toronto, McClelland, 1925. 268p] [BM BVaU LC NSHD OTU QMBM

Catley, Elaine Maud (Clark), 1889–
CANADA CALLING. Calgary, Author, 1938. 31p [AEU NBSaM
ECSTASY AND OTHER POEMS. Toronto, Ryerson, 1927. 8p [BVaU NBSaM
OTP QMM
LIGHT AND OTHER POEMS. Calgary, Author, 1960. 32p
STAR DUST AND OTHER POEMS. Calgary, Author, [1927]. 30p [ACG OKQ
QMM

Cattapani, Henrietta (Gardner)
SONGS OF SENTIMENT. N.p., 1909. 154p [BM BVaU OKQ

Caustick, Christopher (pseud)
THE OUTLINES OF A SPEECH TO BE DELIVERED ON THE HUSTINGS, AT THE
NEXT GENERAL ELECTION FOR THE PROVINCE OF NOVA SCOTIA. By
Christopher Caustick, Esq. Saint John, G.W. Day, 1853. 32p [NSWA OTP

Cawdell, James Martin, 1781?–1842
THE WANDERING RHYMER. A Fragment, with Other Poetical Trifles. [Anon]
York, Gazette, 1826. 22p [OTP

Cawthorpe. Margaret A.
LYRICS FROM THE WESTLAND. Toronto, Briggs, 1912. 90p [BM BVaU NBFU OKQ

Chalmers, Monica Roberts
AND IN THE TIME OF HARVEST. Toronto, Ryerson, 1945. 12p [BVaU NBSaM OTP

Chamberlain, Alexander Francis, 1865–1914
AN ODE ON THE QUEEN'S BIRTHDAY. Toronto, 1891. 12p [OTP
POEMS. Boston, Badger, 1904. 77p [AEU LC

Chambers, Catherine (Mintie) Wilkinson, 1881–
POTLUCK POEMS. By Kay Wilkinson. [Vancouver, 1951.] 32p [Mimeographed.
Also pub. with slip mounted on cover changing title to TRINKET & TREASURE.
Poems.]

Chandler, Amos Henry, 1837–
LYRICS, SONGS AND SONNETS. By Amos Chandler and Charles Pelham Mulvany.
Toronto, Hunter Rose, 1880. 232p [BVaU LC MWU NBFU OKQ

Chandler, Mrs. Mary Rena
NEIGHBOUR LORE. Wolfville, Davidson, 1931. 54p [Brown U BVaU

Chant, Joseph Horatio, 1837–1928
GLEAMS OF SUNSHINE. Optimistic Poems. Toronto, Briggs, 1915. 189p
[BM BVaU Brown U OTP

Chaplein, R.A.
POETRY OF THE HEART; or, Thoughts from the Soul. Together with Verses
on various Subjects. Saint John, McMillan, 1872. 130p [AEU NBFU OTP

Chapman, Edward John, 1821–1904
A DRAMA OF TWO LIVES; THE SNAKE-WITCH; A CANADIAN SUMMER-NIGHT;
AND OTHER POEMS. London, Kegan Paul, 1899. 97p [A DRAMA OF TWO
LIVES also privately printed at Toronto, earlier.] [BM BVaU LC NBFU OKQ
EAST AND WEST. A Summer's Idleness. By E.J.C. Toronto, Trout, 1887.
18p [OTU
A MEMORY. By E.J.C. Toronto, Lovell, 1874. 7p [OONL QMU
A SEQUEL TO "CHRISTABEL." By "L" [pseud]. N.p., 1899. 23p [Pseu-
donymous review of his own poem, "The Snake-Witch."] [OTU
A SONG OF CHARITY. By E.J.C. Toronto, Armour, 1857. 80p [Also:
London, Pickering, 1858. 98p] [BM BVaU LC NBFU OKQ

Cherrington, Joseph Henry, 1895–
PORTRAITS IN RHYME. New York, Vantage Press, 1959. 73p

Chestnut, Robert Henry, 1884–
RAMBLING RHYMES OF THE SEA, THE FOREST, THE COAST, THE MISSIONS. ...
Pertaining to the British Columbia Coast. Vancouver, Clarke & Stuart, 1933.
76p [BVaU NBFU

Chicanot, Eugene Louis
HOMESTEAD RHYMES. N.p., n.d. 77p [QMU
RHYMES OF THE MINER. An Anthology of Canadian Mining Verse. Comp.
and Ed. by ——. Gardenvale, Federal Publications, 1937. 222p [BM
BVaU NBFU OTU QMM

Child, Philip, 1898–
THE VICTORIAN HOUSE AND OTHER POEMS. Toronto, Ryerson, 1951. 54p
[BVaU NBFU OTP

Chilton, Robert S.
POEMS. Goderich, McGillicuddy, 1885. 70p [OTUV

Chilton, Mrs. Vina Bruce
A FEW MORE DAWNS. Toronto, Copp Clark, 1952. 50p

Chipman, Hamilton Borradaile, 1885–
MERI-KA-CHAK–HIS MESSAGE. Winnipeg, Manitoba Co-operative Conference,
[1930?]. 77p [QMU

Chipman, Warwick Fielding, 1880–1967
THE AMBER VALLEY. Poems. Toronto, Gundy, [1915]. 93p [BM BVaU OTUV
BEYOND THE ROAD'S END. Toronto, Dent, [1929]. 40p [BM BVaU QMM

Chisholm, Thomas, 1842–
DIALOGUES ON ENGLISH HISTORY, AND THE HISTORY OF ENGLAND IN ONE
HUNDRED LINES. Toronto, Briggs, 1903. 67 + 3p [BM Brown U OTU

Christie, E. Copeland
IN MANY MOODS. N.p., n.d. 13p [OTUV

Churchill, Asa Gildersleeve
A DIRECTORY OF THE BUSINESS MEN OF SUNDRIDGE. Huntsville, Forester
Office, 1885. 13p [Brown U
POETICAL DIRECTORY OF THE TOWN OF LINDSAY AND BUSINESS MEN OF THE
SURROUNDING COUNTRY. Lindsay, Canadian Post, 1873. 30p [OTUV

Churchill, Lavern
POINTS ON THE COMPAS. Volume A. Toronto, McClelland, 1922. 59p [BM
BVaU NBFU OOP QMM

Clark, Daniel, 1835–1912
SELECTIONS FROM SCOTTISH CANADIAN POETS. ... With an intro. by ——.

Toronto, Imrie, Graham, 1900. 314p ["Vol. I" stamped on spine, but apparently no further volumes were published.] [BM BVaU OKQ

Clark, Jeremiah Simpson, 1872–1950

THE ACADIAN EXILE, AND SEA SHELL ESSAYS. Charlottetown, Irwin, 1902. 59p [BM OLU QMM

Clark, Mary Elizabeth

WARTIME AND OTHER POEMS. N.p., n.d. 24p [NSWA

Clarke, George Frederick, 1883–

... THE SAINT JOHN AND OTHER POEMS. Toronto, Ryerson, 1933. 14p [BVaU NBSaM OKQ

Clarke, George Herbert, 1873–1953

AT THE SHRINE, AND OTHER POEMS. Cincinnati, Stewart & Kidd, 1914. 146p [LC NBFU OKQ

HALT AND PARLEY AND OTHER POEMS. Toronto, Macmillan, 1934. 30p [BM BVaU LC NBFU OTU

THE HASTING DAY. Poems. Toronto, Dent, 1930. 99p [Same title: Toronto, Ryerson, 1933. 100p] [BM BVaU NBFU OTU QMM

HYMN TO THE SPIRIT ETERNAL. Toronto, Macmillan, 1937. 4p [BVaU NSHD OKQ

McMASTER UNIVERSITY, 1890 – 1940. Commemoration Ode. Toronto, Macmillan, 1940. 4p [OKQ

THE NEW TREASURY OF WAR POETRY. Poems of the Second World War. ... Ed. with intro. and notes by ——. Boston, Houghton, 1943. 285p [BM BVaU LC NBFU OTU QMM

ODE ON THE BURIAL OF KING GEORGE THE FIFTH. Toronto, Macmillan, 1935. [OTU

ODE ON THE ROYAL VISIT TO CANADA. Toronto, Macmillan, 1939. 4p [BVaU NSHD OTU

SELECTED POEMS. Ed. by George Whalley. Toronto, Ryerson, 1954. xxvi + 54p

THREE LYRIC SONGS. London, Harris, 1937. 11p [UTQ'38

A TREASURY OF WAR POETRY. British and American Poems of the World War, 1914–1917. Ed. with intro. and notes by ——. Boston, Houghton, 1917. xxx + 280p [BM LC NBFU OTU QMM

A TREASURY OF WAR POETRY. British and American Poems of the World War, 1914–1919. 2nd series. Ed. with intro. and notes by ——. Boston, Houghton, 1919. xxxvii + 361p [BViP LC OKQ

WARFARINGS. Chicago, Windsor & Kenfield, 1901. 94p [LC NBFU OKQ

Clarke, Henriette (Burchell)

LITTLE TOWNS. Philadelphia, Poetry Publishers, 1934. 40p [BVaU LC OTU

UNSEEN BLOSSOMS, AND OTHER POEMS. New York, Exposition Press, 1951. 62p

Clarke, J.
POEMS. Vancouver, Clarke, 1922. 19p [BVaU

Clarke, James Paton, 1807?–1877
CANADIAN CHURCH PSALMODY. Consisting of Psalm Tunes, Chants, Anthems, with Introductory Lessons and Exercises in Sacred Music. Ed. by ——. Toronto, Rowsell, 1845. 108p [OTU QMBM
LAYS OF THE MAPLE LEAF; or, Songs of Canada. The Poetry from the Canadian Annual, the Music composed by ——. Toronto, Author, n.d. 30p [OTP

Clarke, Katherine A.
GLEANINGS FROM MY PORTFOLIO. Original Poems. Toronto, 1894. 75p [Brown U BVaU OTU
LYRICAL ECHOES. Toronto, Briggs, 1899. 157p [BM BVaU OTUV

Clarke, Mrs. Phyllis Comyn
FROM THE CANADIAN PRAIRIES AND OTHER SONNETS. London, Cranton, 1940. 29p [BM BVaU LC OTP

Clarke, Violet Alice
THE VISION OF DEMOCRACY AND OTHER POEMS. Toronto, Ryerson, 1919. 180p [BM BVaU NBFU OKQ

Clarke, Mrs. W.N.
THE NEW SONG, AND OTHER POEMS. Toronto, 1883. [CCJ

Clarkin, Mrs. Lucy Gertrude
POEMS. Charlottetown, Irwin Print., 1947. 120p [Brown U
WAY O' DREAMS. Charlottetown, Dillon & Coyle, [1922?]. 78p [NBFU

Clement, Claude
THOUGHTS IN VERSE. By Claude Clement and Others, Who saw the Doings at Y——ville. [Toronto?], 1855. 12p [Brown U

Cleveland, Rev. Edward, 1804–1886
BIBLE SKETCHES (A CONNECTED SERIES); or, The Stream of Time. A Poem. Boston, Mudge, 1875. 300p [LC QMM

Clinch, Rev. Joseph Hart, –1884
EPISTOLA POETICA AD FAMILIARUM. ... Olicanae, Bowes, 1864. 17p [NSHK
THE CAPTIVITY IN BABYLON AND OTHER POEMS. Boston, Burns, 1840. 115p [LC NSHK

Coates, Carol
FANCY FREE. Toronto, Ryerson, 1939. 15p [BVaU NBSaM OKQ
INVITATION TO MOOD. Toronto, Ryerson, 1949. 54p [BVaU LC NBFU OTUV
THE RETURN AND SELECTED POEMS. Toronto, Caronell Press, 1941. 34p [Brown U BVaU

Coburn, Rev. David E., 1870–

AGAPE. The Story of Jesus as Portrayed in the New Testament. London, Stockwell, 1936. 206p [BVa LC NBFU

ALWAYS REJOICING. Meditation. N.p., priv. print., 1946. 80p [NBSaM

BALLADS OF YESTERDAY AND TODAY. N.p., priv. print., 1937. 24p [NBSaM

BEULAH LAND. N.p., priv. print., 1949. 40p [NBSaM

THE BIRTH OF CANADA. N.p., priv. print., 1949. 62p [NBSaM

THE BOOK OF BOOKS. The Bible. N.p., priv. print., 1950. 39p [NBSaM

THE CENTURIES. N.p., priv. print., 1949. 105p [NBSaM OONL

THE CHRISTIAN. N.p., priv. print., 1949. 24p [NBSaM

A CHRISTMAS PAGEANT. [Poems]. N.p., priv. print., n.d. 10p [Bound with SONGS OF THE SIMPLE LIFE and LET THERE BE LIGHT.] [NBSaM

THE CHURCH. N.p., priv. print., 1948. 100p [NBSaM

EASTER SONGS. N.p., priv. print., 1948. 7p [NBSaM

THE GOLD SEEKERS. N.p., priv. print., 1937. 22p [NBSaM

THE HARP OF ISRAEL ON ENGLISH STRINGS. ["An attempt to express the Psalms in English verse."] N.p., priv. print., 1937. 219p [NBSaM

IN ACADIE. N.p., Author, n.d. 40p [NBFU

IN 1880 A.D. N.p., n.d. [Contains "We can't Have Everything," 24p, and "Keswick Ridge in 1880," 46p] [OONL

IN FAITH'S BRIGHT GLOW. Long Reach, N.B., Author, 1958. 80p [NBFU

THE ISLE OF SAINTS. N.p., priv. print., 1949. 16p [NBSaM

LET THERE BE LIGHT. ... Books 1-3. N.p., priv. print., n.d. [Bound with A CHRISTMAS PAGEANT and SONGS OF THE SIMPLE LIFE.] [NBSaM

LIFE SONGS. N.p., n.d. 16p [NSWA

LOOKING UPWARDS. Meditations. N.p., priv. print., 1947. 80p [NBSaM

MAH ENOSH AND OTHER POEMS. N.p., priv. print., 1937. 56p [NBSaM

MEDITATIONS. N.p., priv. print., 1948. 80p [NBSaM

MEDITATIONS. Man and his Needs. N.p., priv. print., 1948. 32p [NBSaM

MEDITATIONS 1950. N.p., priv. print., 1950. 120p [NBSaM

MID THINGS INVISIBLE. N.p., priv. print., 1948. unpaged. [NBSaM

A MISSION TO THE NATION, AND OTHER POEMS. Long Reach, N.B., Author, 1957. 1v (various paging) [NBFU

THE OUTLOOK, 1950. N.p., priv. print., 1950. 24p [NBSaM

A PILGRIM'S SONGS. N.p., priv. print., 1949. 2v [NBSaM

PSALMS OF LIFE. Long Reach, N.B., Author, 1958. 40p [NBFU

REVERIES OF A COMMON FELLOW. N.p., priv. print., 1948. 56p [NBSaM

THE SHADOW OF DEATH. N.p., priv. print., 1940–1945. 6v [NBSaM OONL

THE SHINING WAY. N.p., n.d. 16p [NBSaM

SONGS FROM CANADA. N.p., priv. print., 1948. 40p [NBSaM OONL

SONGS OF THE SIMPLE LIFE. N.p., priv. print., n.d. 19p [Bound with A CHRISTMAS PAGEANT and LET THERE BE LIGHT.] [NBSaM

THE UNFOLDING MYSTERY. Long Reach, N.B., Author, n.d. 8p [NBFU

THE VIRGIN MARY. N.p., n.d. 6p [NBSaM

WAYSIDE SONGS. N.p., priv. print., 1949. 24p [NBSaM OONL

WE CAN'T HAVE EVERYTHING. N.p., Author, n.d. 46p [NBFU OONL

WILD FLOWERS. Long Reach., N.B., Author, 1958. 16p [NBFU

"WITH PSALMS AND HYMNS AND SPIRITUAL SONGS." N.p., priv. print., 1945.
78p [NBSaM

WOLFE AND MONTCALM, AND OTHER POEMS. N.p., Author, n.d. 61p [NBFU
OONL

YESTERDAY AND TODAY BALLADS. N.p., n.d. 211p [OONL

Cochrane, E.G.

EBLANA; or, Dublin Doings. A Poem in Twelve Cantos. Quebec, 1846. 124p
[CCJ

Cochrane, Hugh

IDEAL, AND OTHER POEMS. Montreal, Waters, 1890. 12p [OTUV QMBM

RHYME AND ROUNDELAY. Montreal, Drysdale, [18—?]. 18p [OTP

ROUNDELS. Montreal, 1891. 12p [QMBM

Cockin, Hereward Kirby, 1854—1917

THE HAPPY FAMILY; or, Deacon Brown's Dream; and, THE LORD MAYOR OF
YORK AND HIS BROTHER NED. By Hereward [pseud]. Toronto, Clougher,
n.d. 16p [BVaU OTUV

GENTLEMAN DICK O' THE GREYS, AND OTHER POEMS. Toronto, Robinson,
1889. 119p [3rd ed.: Toronto, Robinson, [1889]. 126p] [BVaU NSHD
OTP

Cockings, George, —1802

THE AMERICAN WAR. A Poem in Six Books. In which the Names of the
Officers who have Distinguished Themselves, during the War, are Intro-
duced. London, Richardson, 1781. 181p [BM LC

ARTS, MANUFACTURES, AND COMMERCE: A Poem. London, Author, 1769.
36p [BM

BENEVOLENCE AND GRATITUDE: A Poem. London, Author, 1772. 44p [BM

POEMS ON SEVERAL SUBJECTS. London, Author, 1772. 42p [BM

WAR. An Heroic Poem. From the Taking of Minorca by the French, to the
Raising of the Siege of Quebec, by General Murray. London Printed;
Portsmouth, N.H., Reprinted and Sold by Daniel Fowle, 1762. 26p [LC

WAR. An Heroic Poem, from the Taking of Minorca by the French, to the
Reduction of Havannah by the Earl of Albemarle, Sir George Pocock. ...
The 2nd ed. to the Raising the Siege of Quebec. With large Amendments
and Additions by the Author. Boston, Adams, 1762. 190 + 46p
["Britannia's Call to her Brave Troops and Hardy Tars" and other poems.
46p at end.] [BM BVaU LC

Cody, Hiram Alfred, 1872–1948

SONGS OF A BLUENOSE. Toronto, McClelland, 1925. 111p [BVaU NSHD OOP

Coghill, Linnie Allen

REVERIES. Kingsville, Ont., Author, 1937. 38p [UTQ'38

Cogswell, Charles

AMBITION'S DREAM. In two fyttes. New & rev. ed. London, Griffith & Farren, 1878. 92p [NSHD

Cogswell, Frederick William, 1917–

DESCENT FROM EDEN. Toronto, Ryerson, 1959. ix + 38p

THE HALOED TREE. Toronto, Ryerson, 1956. 16p

LOST DIMENSION. Dulwich Village, Eng., Outposts Publications, 1960. 12p

THE STUNTED STRONG. Fredericton, U. of New Brunswick, 1954. 16p

THE TESTAMENT OF CRESSEID. By Robert Henryson [1430?–1506?] Trans. by ——. Toronto, Ryerson, 1957. 24p

Cohen, Leonard Norman, 1934–

LET US COMPARE MYTHOLOGIES. Toronto, Contact Press, 1956. 79p

Cole, Harriet, 1841–1882

SONGS FROM THE VALLEY; or The Valley of Vision and Other Poems. Halifax, Messenger Print., 1879. [NSHD gives pagination as 19p, NSWA as 94p] [NSHD NSWA

Coleman, H. Bromley

O DELILAH! A Chap Book of "Silhouettes." London, Giraffe Press, 1928. [BM

VAGABOND THOUGHTS IN RHYTHM. Vancouver, Boyd, 1923. 56p [BVaU OKQ

Coleman, Helena Jane, 1860–1953

MARCHING MEN–WAR VERSES. Toronto, Dent, 1917. 40p [BM BVaU NSHD OKQ

SONGS. Being a Selection of Earlier Sonnets and Lyrics. Toronto, Ryerson, 1937. 24p [NBSaM OKQ QMM

SONGS AND SONNETS. Toronto, Briggs, 1906. 158p [BM BVaU NBFU OTP

Coleman, Herbert Thomas John, 1872–

COCKLE-SHELL AND SANDAL-SHOON. Toronto, Ryerson, 1927. 24p [BVaU NBSaM OKQ

THE FAR HILLS AND OTHER POEMS. Toronto, Ryerson, 1958. 48p

PATRICIA ANN. The Story of a Doll. Toronto, Dent, 1936. 63p [QMSS

THE POET CONFIDES. Toronto, Ryerson, 1928. 24p [BVaU NBSaM OTP

A RHYME FOR A PENNY. Toronto, Macmillan, 1929. 49p [BVaU LC OTU

Coleman, Mary Garland (King)

TAPESTRY. Sidney, B.C., The Review, 1949. 12p [BViP

Coleman, Rev. Oliver, 1875–
FOR XMAS AND THE NEW YEAR. London, Stockwell, 1938. 16p [BM BVaU

Colgan, John C.
THE POEMS OF JOHN C. COLGAN. Toronto, Hunter Rose, 1873. 197p [BVaU
OKQ

Collie, Michael John, 1929–
POEMS. Toronto, Ryerson, 1959. 20p
SKIRMISH WITH FACT. Toronto, Ryerson, 1960. 24p

Collin, William Edwin, 1893–
MONSERRAT AND OTHER POEMS. Toronto, Ryerson, 1930. 11p [BVaU
NBFU OKQ

Collins, Alice Helen (Roger), –1955
FRIENDS AND OTHER VERSES. N.p., n.p., [192–?]. 20p [BVaU OTP
GREEN SHUTTERS AND OTHER THOUGHTS. [Walkerton], Gazette, 1935. 47p
[OTP
THE HILL OF JOY AND OTHER VERSES. [Elora, Express, 1929?]. 12p [AEU
NBFU QMSS
THE KEY OF GOLD AND OTHER THOUGHTS. Walkerton, Telescope, n.d. 72p
[OKQ QMSS
LOOK UP! Walkerton, Herald-Times, 1939. 16p [OTU
REALLY TRUE AND OTHER VERSES. Tavistock, Ont., Gazette, 1924. 22p
[BVaU QMSS
THE STAR. N.p., n.d. 12p [NBFU OONL QMSS
THIS TINY BOOK. Silhouettes by Helen A. Roger Collins; Verses by Alice H. Roger
Collins. Elora, Express, 1928. 23p [Brown U
THOUGHTS. [Toronto, Hunter Rose], 1920. 30p [BVaU OTP
WINGED WORDS. Walkerton, Herald-Times, 1938. 36p [NBFU

Collins, Burton L., 1880–
BIRDS UNCAGED AND OTHER POEMS. New York, Abbey Press, 1901. 143p [AEU
OTU QMU

Collins, Herbert Eugene
PETALS FROM THE FLOWER OF SONG. Campbell, Calif., Keesling Press, 1934.
95p [Also: same title, without place or publisher, dated 1916. 26p] [BM
BVaU LC OTU

Colman, Mary Elizabeth, 1895–
FOR THIS FREEDOM TOO. Toronto, Ryerson, 1942. 16p [BVaU LC NBSaM OTU
THE IMMIGRANTS. Toronto, Ryerson, 1929. 8p [BVaU NBSaM OKQ

Colombo, John Robert, 1936–
FIRE ESCAPES, FIRE ESC, FIRE. Toronto, Hawkshead Press, 1959. 4p (Bagatelle
series, no. 2)

FRAGMENTS. Kitchener, priv. print., 1957. 11p

THE IMPRESSION OF BEAUTY. Toronto, Hawkshead Press, 1959. 1p (Bagatelle no. 4)

IN THE STREETS. By Ruta Ginsberg [pseud]. Kitchener, Hawkshead Press, [1959?] 2p

POEMS AND OTHER POEMS. Toronto, Hawkshead Press, 1959. 8p (Bagatelle no. 6)

POEMS TO BE SOLD FOR BREAD. Toronto, Hawkshead Press, 1959. 4p (Bagatelle no. 3)

RUBATO. New Poems by Young Canadian Poets. Ed. by ———. Toronto, Purple Partridge Press, 1958. 28p [Poems by 10 students of the University of Toronto.]

TEN POEMS. By —— and Others. Ed. by ———. Toronto, Editor, 1959. 10p

THIS CITADEL IN TIME. Kitchener, Hawkshead Press, 1958. 12p

THIS IS THE WORK ENTITLED CANADA. Toronto, Purple Partridge Press, 1959. 4p

THIS STUDIED SELF. Kitchener, Hawkshead Press, 1958. 16p

TWO POEMS. Toronto, Hawkshead Press, 1959. 4p (Bagatelle no. 1)

VARIATIONS. Kitchener, Hawkshead Press, 1958. 18p

THE VARSITY CHAPBOOK. Ed. by———. Toronto, Ryerson, 1959. 28p

Colquhoun, Kathryn E.

THE BATTLE OF ST. JULIEN, AND OTHER POEMS. Toronto, Ryerson, 1928. 8p [BVaU NBSaM OTP

THE NET OF DREAMS. New York, Harrison, 1942. 31p [BVaU NSHD OTU

Commander, Kingsmill

VIKINGS OF THE STARS. New York, Vinal, 1928. 97p [LC OKQ

Commercial Traveller, A

"THAT MOST PERSISTENT BEGGAR." With Apologies to Mr. Rudyard Kipling. By a Commercial Traveller [pseud]. St. Catharines, Ont., Pacard, 1900. 10p [NBFU OOP

Complin, Margaret (Robertson), −1951

FOR REMEMBRANCE. Regina, Author, 1944. 21p [OTP

WINGED MOCCASINS TO WINGED WORDS. Regina, Author, [1937?]. 23p [BViPA OTP

Conklin, William J., 1906−

FOR THE INFINITE. Toronto, Ryerson, 1960. 8p

WIND-BLOWN LEAVES. N.p., 1951. 18p (Carillon Poetry Chap-Books)

Connor, Fredric Jarrett, 1920−

GALARIAN. By Fredric Jarrett [pseud]. Montreal, Hart Severance, 1953. 128p

LYRICS CANADIENNES. Pt. I. By Fredric Jarrett [pseud]. Shawbridge, Que., Hart Severance, 1947. 20p [BVaU Brown U NSHD OTP

Conron, Joy Linton
SHADOWS ON THE WALL. Poems. Toronto, Author, 1950. 20p [OONL

Contact Press
POETS 56. Ten Younger English Canadians. Toronto, Contact Press, 1956.
51p [mimeographed]

Conybeare, Charles Frederick Pringle, 1860–1927
LYRICS FROM THE WEST. Toronto, Briggs, 1907. 77p [BM BVaU OTP
VAHNFRIED. London, Kegan Paul, 1902. 196p [AEU BM OLU

Cook, Evelyn M., 1918–
FRAGMENT. Islington, Ont., Author, n.d. 12p [CC
HARVEST. Islington, Ont., Author, n.d. 12p [CC
SOLILOQUY. Islington, Ont., Author, n.d. 12p [CC

Cook, Merrill H.
SHORE LINES AND SAND SONGS. Toronto, Beacon Press, 1937. 19p [OLU
THE STUMPS AND OTHER MUSINGS. Toronto, Author, 1940. 21p [AEU
WEEDS AND CREEDS. Toronto, Author, 1938. 19p [SRU

Coombs, William Gordon, 1884–
POEMS TRUE TO LIFE. Worcester, Eng., Littlebury, 1958. 109p

Copeland, John Morison, 1878–
SIR TOBY'S LAMPOONS AND LAMENTS. Toronto, Sovereign Press, 1933. 112 p
[Brown U BVaU OTP

Copway, George, 1818–1863
THE OJIBWAY CONQUEST. A Tale of the Northwest. By Kah-ge-ga-gah-bowh.
New York, Author, 1850. 91p [BM OTP

Cormack, Barbara (Villy), 1903–
RUTH. A Tale of New Beginnings. Edmonton, Author, 1948. 23p [BVaU
SEEDTIME AND HARVEST. Toronto, Ryerson, 1942. 7p [AEU BVaU NBSaM
OKQ QMM

Cosens, Abner
WAR RHYMES. By Wayfarer [pseud]. Wingham, Ont., Advance Print., [1919?].
92p [Brown U

Couch, Ankrem
JUVENILE POEMS. Toronto, Bell & Co., 1877. 56p [OLU
POEMS. Brooklyn, Webb & Phelps, 1884. 52p [OTP
ROGUES' HOLLOW. A Satire. Toronto, Author, 1879. 29p [OTP

Coughlin, Dennis
VILLAGE SCENES. A Canadian Poem. Ottawa, Woodburn, 1889. 22p [OONL

Coulby, Margaret Evelyn, 1924–
THE BITTER FRUIT, AND OTHER POEMS. Toronto, Ryerson, 1948. 8p [BVaU
  NBSaM OKQ

Coulter, John William, 1888–
THE BLOSSOMING THORN. Toronto, Ryerson, 1946. 54p [BVaU MWU
  NSHD OKQ QMM

Cowan, Annie Ironside (Simpson), 1859–
VANCOUVER ISLAND AND OTHER POEMS. N.p., Author, n.d. 15p [BViPA

Cowan, Thomas Goudie, 1896–
TOMMY ONE AND TOMMY TWO. Vancouver, priv. print., 1951. 71p

Cowdell, Thomas Daniel
THE NOVA SCOTIA MINSTREL. 3rd ed. Dublin, Dugdale, Keene, and Cutler,
  1817. 150p [Rev. and enl. ed. of work first published under title: A POETICAL
  JOURNAL OF A TOUR FROM BRITISH NORTH AMERICA TO ENGLAND, WALES AND
  IRELAND. ... Dublin, Wilkinson & Courtney, 1809. 76p] [BM LC NSHD OTP
A POETICAL ACCOUNT OF THE AMERICAN CAMPAIGNS OF 1812 and 1813. By an
  Acadian [pseud]. Dedicated to the People of Canada, by the publisher. Halifax,
  Howe, 1815. 139p [NSHD OTU

Cowherd, Thomas
THE EMIGRANT MECHANIC, AND OTHER TALES IN VERSE. Together with Numerous
  Songs upon Canadian Subjects by the Brantford Tinsmith Rhymer. Jackson,
  Mich., Daily Citizen Book & Job Print., 1884. 319p [Also: Brantford, Author,
  1884. 319p] [BVaU OTP QMM

Cowles, Nellie Campbell
VERSES BY THE WAYSIDE. Toronto, Musson, 1910. 128p [BM Brown U

Cox, Edward
THOUGHTS BY THE WAY. Toronto, Robinson, 1886. 63p [OKQ

Cox, Geoffrey Warburton
WHAT-NOTS. Toronto, Ryerson, 1927. 20p [BVaU NBSaM OKQ

Cox, Leonard (Leo), 1898–
NORTH STAR. Toronto, Macmillan, 1941. 56p [BVaU LC NSHD OTUV QMM
RIVER WITHOUT END. Toronto, Ryerson, 1937. 16p [BVaU NBSaM OKQ
SHEEP-FOLD. Toronto, Ryerson, 1926. 8p [BVaU NBSaM OKQ
THE WIND IN THE FIELD. Toronto, Ryerson, 1932. 32p [BVaU NBSaM OKQ

Craig, Martha
LEGENDS OF THE NORTH LAND. N.p., [19–?]. 23p [OTP

Crawford, Alexander Wellington, 1866–1933
POEMS OF YESTERDAY. Toronto, Ryerson, 1924. 54p [BVaU NSHD OTP

Crawford, George Johnson Adair, 1858–1915
LOCAL AND OTHER RHYMES. Petrolia, Ont., Advertiser Pub. House, 1908. 39p
[OLU

Crawford, Isabell C.
THE REDMAN'S PRAYER AND OTHER POEMS. Kamloops, B.C., Sentinel, 1929.
48p [BVaU QMBM

Crawford, Isabella Valancy, 1850–1887
THE COLLECTED POEMS. Ed. by J.W. Garvin. Toronto, Briggs, 1905. 309p
[BM BVaU LC NSHD OKQ
OLD SPOOKSES' PASS, MALCOLM'S KATIE, AND OTHER POEMS. Toronto, Bain,
1884. 224p [BM BVaU MWU NBFU OKQ QMM

Crawford, Mrs. John
SONGS OF ALL SEASONS, CLIMES, AND TIMES. A Motley Jingle of Jumbled Rhymes.
Toronto, Rose, 1890. 117p [BVaU NBFU OKQ

Creed, Gavin L.
BARDS IN BATTLE DRESS. Ed. by ——. 1944. [Rhod p958
FOR FREEDOM. Toronto, Dent, 1942. 60p [BM BVaU LC OTU

Creighton, Alan B., 1903–
CROSS-COUNTRY. Toronto, Macmillan, 1939. 68p [NBFU OLU QMM
EARTH CALL. A Book of Poems. Toronto, Macmillan, 1936. 67p [BVaU NBFU
OKQ QMM
A NEW CANADIAN ANTHOLOGY. Ed. by Alan Creighton. Assisted by Hilda M.
Ridley. Toronto, Crucible Press, 1938. 236p [BVaU LC OKQ

Creighton, Helen, 1899–
SONGS AND BALLADS FROM NOVA SCOTIA. Collected by ——. Toronto, Dent.
1932. 333p [BM BVaU NBFU OTU
TRADITIONAL SONGS FROM NOVA SCOTIA. Collected by Helen Creighton and
Doreen H. Senior. Toronto, Ryerson, 1950. 284p [Includes music] [BVaU
NSHD OTU
TWELVE FOLK SONGS FROM NOVA SCOTIA. Collected by Helen Creighton and
D.H. Senior. London, Novello, 1940. 41p [OTU

Crofton, Arthur M.
RAGNAROK. A Vision of the Last Great Day. Sydney, N.S., Author, 1919. 37p
[BM BVaU

Crofton, Francis Blake, 1841–1912
SOMBRE TINTS. Halifax, Imperial Pub., 1904. 18p [BM BVaU NSHD OKQ

Cumberland, Robert William, 1895–
VERSE AND TRANSLATION. Kingston, Jackson Press, 1925. 50p [NSHD OTU

Cuming, Thomas Grant Austin, 1890–
SPECKLED THOUGHTS AND OTHER THINKING. By Tag-a-long, Thomas G.A. Cuming. Smith's Cove, N.S., Author, 1959. 67p

Cumming, Robert Dalziel, 1871–
PAUL PERO. Toronto, Ryerson, 1928. 30p [BVaU NBSaM OKQ QMM
SONGS OF A SICK TUM TUM. By Skookum Chuck [pseud]. New York, Totem, 1912. 105p [BVaU

Cummings, Virginia (MacDonald)
THE MIRACLE OF DOGWOOD, AND OTHER POEMS. Vancouver, Author, 1946. 16p [BVaU OTP

Cumpston, William Henry
GLIMMERINGS OF TRUTH; Being a Collection of Poems. Hull, H. Brown; London, Simpkin Marshall, 1887. 107p [BM
POEMS FOR THE TIME. Montreal, Howard Print., 1915. 27p [BM Brown U BVaU NBFU

Cunningham, Willis W., 1867–
ANVIL WHISPERS. N.p., n.d. 91p [BVaU NBFU OTP

Currie, George Graham, 1867–1926
EPITAPHS, EPIGRAMS, AND OTHER EPHEMERA. Jacksonville, Fla., Drew Press, 1912. 244p [LC
HOW I ONCE FELT. Songs of Love and Travel. Montreal, Lovell, 1893. 142p [BVaU NBFU OKQ QMU
IN THE OTHER MAN'S PLACE. Some Latter Day Tragedies in Verse. Jacksonville, Fla., Drew Press, 1911. 194p [LC
SONGS OF FLORIDA AND OTHER VERSE. New York, J.T. White, 1922. 298p [LC
SONNETS AND LOVE SONGS. Jacksonville, Fla., Drew Press, 1911. 200p [LC

Currie, John Allister, 1868–1931
A QUARTETTE OF LOVERS. Toronto, Williamson, 1892. 65p [NBFU OTP

Currie, Margaret (Gill), 1843–
GABRIEL WEST AND OTHER POEMS. Fredericton, Cropley, 1866. 127p [BVaU NBFU OTUV
JOHN SAINT JOHN AND ANNA GREY. A Romance of Old New Brunswick. Toronto, Briggs, 1897. 128p [BM BVaU NBFU OTU QMM

Curzon, Mrs. Sarah Anne, 1833–1898
LAURA SECORD, THE HEROINE OF 1812. A Drama; And Other Poems. Toronto, Robinson, 1887. 215p [BM BVaU LC MWU NSHD OTU QMM

Cuthbertson, Ethel Imrie
MISCELLANEOUS POEMS. Vancouver, Ward, Ellwood, & Pound, 1914. 14p [BVaU

POEMS OF PROGRESS OR PROHIBITION. Vancouver, Ward, Ellwood, & Pound, n.d. 12p [BVaU

Dagger, Gordon, 1888–
THE PROSPECTOR AND OTHER POEMS. New York, Harrison, 1942. 61p [BVaU OKQ

Dakin, Laurence B., 1904–
THE DREAM OF ABARIS, AND OTHER POEMS. Paris, Obelisk Press, 1933. 78p [BM
THE HOUSE OF ORSEOLI. [A Poem.] Manchester, N.H., Falmouth Press, 1952. 98p
POEMS. Paris, Obelisk Press, 1932. 55p [BM LC
SONNETS AND LYRICS. Paris, Obelisk Press, 1935. 59p [BM
SORROWS OF THE HOPEFUL ["A Prose Poem"]. London, 1936. 15p [BM
THE TOWER OF LIFE. Portland, Me., Falmouth Book House, 1946. 101p [BM
NSHD

Dalton, Annie Charlotte (Armitage), 1865–1938
THE AMBER-RIDERS. Toronto, Ryerson, 1929. 109p [BVaU NBFU OKQ
THE CALL OF THE CARILLON. Vancouver, Wrigley, [193-?] 16p [BVaU NBFU OKQ
A CHRISTMAS CAROL FOR ALL GOOD SOLDIERS AND SAILORS. Vancouver, Clarke
& Stuart, 1914. 7p [BVaU OKQ
THE EAR TRUMPET. Toronto, Ryerson, 1926. 8p [BVaU NBFU OKQ
FLAME AND ADVENTURE. Toronto, Macmillan, 1924. 73p [BVaU LC NSHD
OKQ
LILLIES AND LEOPARDS. Toronto, Ryerson, 1935. 68p [BVaU NSHD OOP
THE MARRIAGE OF MUSIC. Vancouver, Evans & Hastings, 1910. 71p [2nd ed.,
with additional poems. London, E. Macdonald, 1915. 92p] [BM BVaU NBFU
OKQ
THE NEIGHING NORTH. Toronto, Ryerson, 1931. 80p [BVaU NBFU OKQ
THE SILENT ZONE. [Vancouver, Cowan & Brookhouse, 1926]. 111p [BVaU
NBFU OOP
SONGS AND CAROLS. Vancouver, priv. print., 1925, 16p [BVaU NBFU OKQ
A SOUVENIR OF VANCOUVER. Vancouver, priv. print., 1906 12p [BM OKQ

Daniel, Charles T.
WILLIAM AND ANNE; or, A Tale of Love and War. Guelph, The Herald, 1864. 112p
[OLU

Daniells, Roy, 1902–
DEEPER INTO THE FOREST. Toronto, McClelland, 1948. 76p [BVaU OKQ

Darby, Ray
THE ADVENTURES OF GLEN ALAN. Regina, School Aids, n.d. 1v [unpaged] [AEU
OOMAH. With Pictures by John Phillips. Winnipeg, Contemporary Pub., 1945.
39p [ACG
PETER SMITH AND THE SKY-PEOPLE. Regina, School Aids, 1944. 1v [unpaged] [AEU

Darling, Elizabeth

SPARE MOMENTS. A Little Book of Poems. [Kingston, Whig Steam Presses], n.d. 25p [OTU

Darling, Rev. William Stewart, 1818–1886

THE EMIGRANTS. A Tale of the Backwoods of Canada. Toronto, Lovell & Gibson, 1863. 40p [LC

Darnell, Rev. Henry Faulkner, 1831–1915

KINDESLIEBE. A Romance of Fatherland. Philadelphia, MacCall, 1891. 188p [NSHD OTU

SONGS BY THE WAY. A Collection of original Poems for the Comfort and Encouragement of Christian Pilgrims. Montreal, Lovell, 1862. 185p [BVaU LC NBFU OKQ

SONGS OF THE SEASONS. Avon, N.Y., 1886. 57p [Patrick cat. 30

VERSES IN MEMORY OF THE RIGHT REV. G.J. MOUNTAIN. St. John's, Que., 1863. 7p [CCJ

Date, Henry Harrington, –1905

SONG OF THE U.E. LOYALIST AND YORK PIONEER. N.p., 1895. 16p [BVaU OTUV

David, Joan Eira

IN HOLLY TIME. [Toronto? 1937?]. 30p [Brown U

Davidson, Fisher, 1912–

DOMINION AND OTHER POEMS. Toronto, Author, 1948. 45p [BVaU LC NBFU OKQ

MISTS OF QUEBEC. Ten Poems. Montreal, Quality Press, 1960. 11p

TWO SONNETS FOR A CENTENARY: William Lyon Mackenzie, 1838–1938; Durham, 1839–1939. Welland, Ont., Author, 1939. 4p [OTU

Davidson, Frederick

CAPTURED FANCIES. Toronto, [Printer's Guild], 1942. 122p [LC

Davidson, Judson France

THE ANACREONTEA, AND PRINCIPAL REMAINS OF ANACREON OF TAOS, in English Verse. With an Essay, Notes, and Additional Poems by ——. Ed. by Frederick J.A. Davidson. Toronto, Dent, 1915. 212p [BM OTU

A LAPFUL OF LYRICS AND MERRY MUSE-WHANGS. By Judson France [pseud]. Toronto, Imrie & Graham, 1885. 32p [Brown U OOP

R.R.R. MUSE WHANGS. Poems Amorous, Bacchanalian, Political, Memorial, Humorous, and Miscellaneous. By Judson France [pseud]. Toronto, Sign o' the Will-o'-the Wisp, 1887. 104p [BVa OTUV QMM

Davidson, Kathleen

SEVEN SHEAVES. By Kathleen Davidson, Amy Downey, Kathleen Dupuis, Borgny Eileraas, Lois Borland, Myra Smith, Jean Sibbald. Saskatoon, 1945.

38p ["Dedicated to The Sheaf" — the Univ. of Sask. campus newspaper.]
[SSU

Davidson, True, 1901–
MUSES OF THE MODERN DAY AND OTHER DAYS. Toronto, Dent, 1931. 131p
[BVaU NBFU OTU QMU

Davies, Hilda A.
OVERGROWN TRAILS AND OTHER POEMS. By Tanis [pseud]. Calgary, Dichmont,
1932. 18p [ACG

Davin, Nicholas Flood, 1843–1901
ALBUM VERSES AND OTHER POEMS. Ottawa, MacLean Roger, 1882. 32p [BM
LC OTUV
EOS: AN EPIC OF THE DAWN, AND OTHER POEMS. Regina, Leader Co., 1889.
141p [BM BVaU LC NSHD OKQ SSU
EOS: A PRAIRIE DREAM, AND OTHER POEMS. Ottawa, Citizen Print., 1884. 36p
[BM OTU

Davis, Alastair Jeffreys
THE CHILDREN'S HOUR. Eton, Spottiswoode, 1938. 63p [BM

Davis, Allan Ross, 1858–1933
CANADA'S POLITICAL STRUGGLES. Toronto, 1925. 4p [Amtmann cat. 151

Davis, Ella M.
GIFT BOOK OF SONNETS AND BIRTHSTONE RONDOLETTES. Regina, Author, 1946.
12p [BVaU OTU

Davis, Stuart, 1921–
SONGS BY "STU" DAVIS. A Collection of Original Western and Folk Songs Com-
posed and Sung by "Canada's Cowboy Troubador." Folio no. 3. Toronto,
Canadian Music Sales Corp., 1953. 40p

Davison, Leslie Loring, 1871–1889
STRAY LEAVES FROM THE "BOOK OF WONDERS." Ed. by Ben Zeene [pseud].
Wolfville, Davison, 1890. 72p [NSHD OTUV

Davison, R.E.
A ROMANCE OF THE WEST. A Tale of the Iroquois and Delaware Indians.
Winnipeg, Winnipeg Print., n.d. 27p [BVaU MWP QMU

Dawson, Rev. Aeneas MacDonell, 1810–1894
DOMINION DAY, CARACTACUS, MALCOLM & MARGARET. Poems. Ottawa, Mitchell,
1886. 62p [LC NSHD OTU QMM
LAMENT FOR THE RIGHT REVEREND JAMES GILLIS, D.D., BISHOP OF EDINBURGH
... and Other Poems. Ottawa, Bell & Woodburn, 1864. 57p [Brown U OTUV
THE LAST DEFENDER OF JERUSALEM. ... Ottawa, Free Press, 1882. 16p [BM
BVaU NSHD OTP

LINES ON THE MASSACRE OF OSZMINIA (LITHUANIA). Glasgow, 1844. [OOP
[THREE POEMS, WRITTEN DURING 1866. Ottawa?, n.p., 1866?. 11p] [No cover,
no t.p.] [NSHP
ZENOBIA, QUEEN OF PALMYRA. A Poem. Ottawa, Mitchell, 1883. 108p [BM
BVaU LC NSHD OTUV

Dawson, Cristall
POEMS. Toronto, 1924. 29p [OOP

Dawson, Julia
THE CHANGING YEAR, AND OTHER POEMS. Toronto, Mundy-Goodfellow Print.,
1937. 68p [AEU Brown U OTUV

Dawson, Samuel Edward, 1833—1916
CHAMPLAIN. Montreal, Author, 1890. 8p [OTUV

Day, Alfred Ernest, 1875—
THE KINGDOM SONG. A Group of Little Poems with Airs. Made by Evan Reay
[pseud]. Toronto, Ryerson, 1931. 16p [BVaU LC OKQ

Dean, Louis Mitchell
DRIFTED LEAVES. Aylmer, Ont., Express, 1946. 48p [UTQ'48

Dean, T.C.
T.C. DEAN'S POEMS. Being a Collection from the Magazines with some that will
first see the Light in this Volume. Trenton, Ont., Courier Book Office, 1879.
16p [Patrick cat. 30

Dear, Allan
CANADIAN SONG LYRICS. Comp. by ——. Winnipeg, Canada Pub. Co., 1940.
61p [CC

Delafosse, Frederick Montague, 1860—1950
A DREAM AND AN ALLEGORY. N.p., n.p. 1944. 27p [OTU
VERSES GRAVE AND GAY. Peterborough, Author, 1937. 70p [OKQ

De Mille, James, 1833—1880
BEHIND THE VEIL. A Poem. Halifax, Allen, 1893. 30p [BVaU NSHD OKQ

Dermot, Walter H.
THE AUTUMN WREATH. A Poem. Ottawa, Hunter Rose, 1869. 14p [NBFU OTU
QMSS

Des Brisay, Margaret Elizabeth
MEMORIALS OF MARGARET ELIZABETH, ONLY DAUGHTER OF REV. ALBERT DES
BRISAY, of the Province of New Brunswick. By a friend. ... New York, Carlton
& Phillips, 1856. 236p [Brown U

Devine, Frederick
THEY TURNED HER OUT IN THE STREET AND OTHER POEMS. Saint John, N.B.
Globe Pub., 1914. 62p [NBFU QMBM

Devine, Thomas Godfrey, 1875–
MADAWASKA. Boston, Badger, 1912. 55p [LC OTU

Dewart, Rev. Edward Hartley, 1828–1903
ADDITIONAL POEMS. N.p., [1892?]. pp257-268. (cover title) [paged to follow
text of SONGS OF LIFE] [OKQ
SELECTIONS FROM CANADIAN POETS. With Occasional Critical and Biographical
Notes. Ed. by ——. Montreal, Lovell, 1864. 304p [BM BVaU LC MWU
NSHD OKQ
SONGS OF LIFE. A Collection of Poems. Toronto, Dudley & Burns, 1869. 256p
[BVaU LC MWU NBFU OTU QMM

Dewing, Winifred F.
POEMS. N.p., n.d. 24p [OKQ

DeWolfe, Cecil Edgar
A LITTLE BOOK OF LYRIC VERSE. Windsor, N.S., [1916?]. [Rhod p879

Dick, Alexander
SPLORES OF A HALLOWEEN TWENTY YEARS AGO. Woodstock, Warwick, 1867.
22p [OTP

Dickie, Charles Herbert, 1859–
RHYME ... AND REASON. West Vancouver, Author, 1945. 47p [BVaU

Dickie, Donalda James, 1883–
THE CANADIAN POETRY BOOK. A Book of Modern Verse. Comp. by ——.
Toronto, Dent, [1924]. 111p [BViP OPAL QMU

Dickson, Stephen, 1761?–
THE UNION OF TASTE AND SCIENCE. A Poem. To which are subjoined a few
Elucidating Notes. Quebec, Neilson, 1799. 17p [Facsimile reprint: Toronto,
Bibliog. Soc. of Canada, 1952.] [NBFU OTU QMBM

Diespecker, Richard E. Alan, 1907–
BETWEEN TWO FURIOUS OCEANS, AND OTHER POEMS. Toronto, Oxford U. Press,
1944. 91p [BVaU LC NBFU OTP
PRAYER FOR VICTORY. Post-War Thoughts by a Soldier [pseud]. Montreal,
Woodward Press, 1943. 8p [Brown U
THREE WINDOWS WEST. Toronto, Dent, 1956. xv + 160p

Dingwall, M.M.
NOW THAT I'M FIFTY. Edmonton, Author, 1949. 19p [UTQ'51

Dixon, Benjamin Homer, 1819–1899?

GOLDEN MOMENTS. Comp. by B.H.D. Toronto, Chewett, 1865. 153p [The 2nd ed. of his SELECTED HYMNS] [NBFU OTP

SELECTED HYMNS. Comp. by B.H.D. Toronto, Chewett, 1863. 114p [OTUV

Dixon, George

THE BARD OF WAR. A Poetical Series in which the Author proposes to treat of the Russian, Persian and China Wars. Also the Rebellion of British India and the Civil War in America from 1861 to 1865, to conclude with the true Fenian Episode and Fall of Republics. Saint John, Chubb, 1868. [CCJ NBB

Dobell, Curzon

LOVE LYRICS AND REBEL RHYMES. New York, Exposition Press, 1954. 96p

Dole, William Peters, 1825–

CARMEN ACADIUM. Ode for the Jubilee Year of the Reign of Queen Victoria. Saint John, 1887. 11p [CCJ

OUR COUNTRY. By W.P. Dole, James Hannay, and H.L. Spencer, Saint John, 1889. [CCJ

Dollard, Rev. James Bernard, 1872–1946

THE BELLS OF OLD QUEBEC, AND OTHER POEMS OF NEW FRANCE. Toronto, Extension Print., 1920. 59p [Brown U OTU

IRISH LYRICS AND BALLADS. New York, Kenedy, 1917. 131p [BVaU LC NBFU OTU QMM

IRISH MIST & SUNSHINE. A Book of Ballads. Toronto, Blake, 1901. 89p [Another ed.: Toronto, Blake, 1902. 144p] [BVaU LC NBFU OTU

POEMS. Toronto, Catholic Church Extension Society, 1910. 148p [BM BVaU OTP

Donald, Rev. Andrew, 1806–

POEMS. Campbell Settlement, Sussex, N.B., Printed by L.M. Donald, 1876. 20p [Brown U NBFU

Dorey, Mrs. Alice Ann

LIGHT AND SHADOW. Toronto, Ryerson, 1949. 25p [Brown U BVaU OTU

Dorland, Ella Wilson, 1878–

GLEN ECHOES. By E. Dee [pseud]. St. Catharines, Ont., Author, 1941. 59p [UTQ'42

GLEN IDYLLS. St. Catharines, Ont., Author, 1938. 47p [OTU

Dorman, Robert, 1883–

THOUGHTS OF A RESTLESS MIND. Ottawa, Author, 1956. 40p

Dorsey, J. Leo M.

STAIR BUILDING. Poems. N.p., [1943?]. 32p [OTP

Doucet, Rev. Stanislaus J., 1847–1925?
EMMANUEL THE LIVING BREAD. A Religious Poem. By Monsignor Doucet.
Chatham, N.B., 1922. 16p [Amtmann cat. 221
THE SOUL. A Philosophic Poem. Saint John, McMillan, 1917. 23p [2nd ed.:
Chatham, N.B., 1923. 32p] [Brown U NBFU OTU

Dougall, Lily, 1858–1923
ARCADES AMBO. Verses by Lily Dougall ... and Gilbert Sheldon. Oxford, Blackwell,
1919. 63p [LC QMM

Doughty, Arthur George, 1860–1936
HELEN AND APHRODITE. [Priv. printed]. [CCJ
NUGAE CANORAE. By A.G.D. Portland, Smith & Sale, 1897. 69p [OTUV
ROSE LEAVES. A Collection of Simple Verses Written on Various Occasions.
London, Moring, 1894. 80p [BM BVaU OTUV QMM
THE SONG STORY OF A FRANCESCO AND BEATRICE. [Priv. printed, 1896?]. [CCJ

Douglas, Gilean
NOW THE GREEN WORD. Mill Valley, Calif., Wings Press, 1952. 56p
THE PATTERN SET. Montreal, priv. print., 1958. 20p
POETIC PLUSH. Dallas, Tex., Story Book Press, 1953. 40p

Douglas, Robert W., –1931
LOVE SONGS OF SCOTLAND; JEWELS OF THE TENDER PASSION. ... Selected and Ed.
by ——. New York, New Amsterdam Book Co., 1901. 214p [BVaU LC OTUV

Dowhan, Stanley J., 1917–
THE LEAVES ARE SCATTERED. Ed. by M.F. Liddell. London, British Authors'
Press, 1944. 39p [BM LC OKQ

Downes, Gwladys Violet
LOST DIVER. Fredericton, U. of New Brunswick, 1955. 16p

Dowsett, Frank Martin, 1897–
SONNETS OF A SEEKER. Toronto, Author, 1954. 18p

Dowson, Eric Arthur
COUNTRY PLACES AND OTHER POEMS. Ilfracombe, Devon, Stockwell, 1957. 64p

Doyle, Gerald Stanley, 1892–1956
OLD TIME POETRY AND SONGS OF NEWFOUNDLAND. St. John's, Author, 1940.
80p [NFSM OONL
OLD TIME SONGS OF NEWFOUNDLAND. St. John's, Nfld., Manning & Rabbitts,
1927. 71p [3rd ed., 1955. 88p] [BViP LC NSHD OTU

Drayton, Geoffrey, 1924–
THREE MERIDIANS. Toronto, Ryerson, 1950. 8p [BVaU NBSaM OTU

Drew, Mabel Ellen
TIME IS THE MEASURE. Toronto, Crucible Press, 1950. 26p [Brown U OONL

Drummond, Frank S., 1873–
POEMS. N.p., 1931. 83p [OTP
THE "ROYAL SAUVAGE" AND OTHER SKETCHES. Toronto, Gilchrist-Wright, 1930.
   8p [OTP
SKETCHES. Toronto, Hunter Rose, 1929. 19p [OTP

Drummond, William Henry, 1854–1907
COMPLETE POEMS. With an intro. by Louis Fréchette and an appreciation by Neil
   Munro. Toronto, McClelland, 1926. 34 + 450p [BM BVi OTU QMM
THE GREAT FIGHT. Poems and Sketches. With a Biographical Sketch. ... New York
   & London, Putnam, 1908. 158p [BVaU LC NSHD OTU QMM
THE HABITANT, AND OTHER FRENCH-CANADIAN POEMS. New York, Putnam,
   1897. 137p [BVaU LC NSHD OTU QMM
HABITANT POEMS. Intro. by Arthur L. Phelps. Toronto, McClelland, 1959. 111p
   [New Canadian Library, no. 11]
JOHNNIE COURTEAU, AND OTHER POEMS. New York, Putnam, 1901. 161p [BM
   BVaU LC NSHD OTU QMM
PHIL-O-RUM'S CANOE, AND MADELEINE VERCHERES. Two Poems. New York,
   Putnam, 1898. 12p [BVaU MWU NSHD OKQ QMM
THE POETICAL WORKS OF WILLIAM HENRY DRUMMOND. With an intro. by Louis
   Fréchette. New York, Putnam, 1912. 449p [BVaU LC NSHD OTUV
THE VOYAGEUR AND OTHER POEMS. New York, Putnam, 1905. 142p [BM
   BVaU LC NSHD OTU QMM

Drury, Susie
MAPLE LEAVES. By Susie D. [pseud]. London, Ont., Daily Free Press, 1871.
   200p [BVaU NBFU OKQ

Duddridge, Hugh, 1872–
SEEN FROM MY SEEDER STEP. A Volunteer Crop of Verse from a Saskatchewan
   Farm. Prince Albert, Sask., Author, 1950. 73p [OONL SSU

Dudek, Louis, 1918–
CANADIAN POEMS, 1850–1952. Ed. by Louis Dudek and Irving Layton. 2nd ed.
   Toronto, Contact Press, 1952. 127p [Also: 2nd ed., rev., 160p]
CERBERUS. Poems by Louis Dudek, Irving Layton, Raymond Souster. Toronto,
   Contact Press, [1952]. 98p
EAST OF THE CITY. Poems. Toronto, Ryerson, 1946. 51p [BVaU LC MWU
   NBFU OKQ
EN MEXICO. Toronto, Contact Press, 1958. 78p
EUROPE. Toronto, Laocoön (Contact) Press, 1954. 139p
LAUGHING STALKS. Toronto, Contact Press, 1958. 113p

THE SEARCHING IMAGE. Toronto, Ryerson, 1952. 12p

THE TRANSPARENT SEA. Toronto, Contact Press, 1956. 114p

TWENTY-FOUR POEMS. Toronto, Contact Press, 1952. 24p

UNIT OF FIVE. Poems by Louis Dudek, Ronald Hambleton, P.K. Page, Raymond Souster, James Wreford. Ed. by Ronald Hambleton. Toronto, Ryerson, 1944. 87p [BVaU LC MWU NSHD OTU QMM

Dumbrille, Dorothy, 1898—

LAST LEAVE, AND OTHER POEMS. Toronto, Ryerson, 1942. 16p [BVaU LC NBFU

STAIRWAY TO THE STARS. Toronto, Allen, 1946. 72p [BVaU NBFU OKQ QMM

WATCH THE SUN RISE! A Collection of Poems. Alexandria, Ont., Author, 1943. 47p [BVaU LC NBFU OTP

WE COME! WE COME! Toronto, Crucible Press, 1941. 46p [LC OKQ

Duncan, Eric, 1858—1944

THE RICH FISHERMAN, AND OTHER SKETCHES. Toronto, Macmillan, 1932. 113p [BVaU NBFU OTU

THE RICH FISHERMAN, AND OTHER TALES. London, Century, 1910. 99p [BM BVaU

RURAL RHYMES, AND THE SHEEP THIEF. Toronto, Briggs, 1896. 64p [BM BVaU OTUV QMM

Duncan, Nora M. (Dann), 1881—

DOWN TO THE SEA. North Vancouver, North Shore Press, 1936. 35p [BVaU

THE HEROINE OF MOODYVILLE. An Epic of Burrard Inlet. N.p., n.d. 4p [BViPA

RAINBOW REVERIES. North Vancouver, North Shore Press, 1934. 85p [BVaU OOP

Dunlap, Louie Spencer

REMEMBRANCE. Toronto, [Noble Scott Ltd?], 1924. 68p [QMU

Dunn, Mrs. C.A.

FUGITIVE PIECES. Woodstock, Ont., Author, 1867. 94p [BVaU OTP

Dunn, Marcia (Christoforides), 1910—

THE BALLAD OF A BATHURST BOY, 1874—1956. Fredericton, University Press of N.B., 1956. 21p [About Sir James Dunn.]

Dunning, Elsa

HERITAGE. Toronto, Crucible Press, 1941. 24p (Carillon Poetry Chap-Books) [AEU NBSaM OTP

UNREAPED CORNERS. N.p., n.d. 31p [QMU

Dunsmore, J.M.

SONGS OF DISCOVERY AND EXPLORATION. Toronto, 1938. 29p [Adelphi cat. 41A

Durand, Evelyn, 1870–1900

ELISE LE BEAU, A Dramatic Idyll; and Lyrics and Sonnets. ... Ed. with a memoir by Laura B. Durand. Toronto, U. of Toronto Press, 1921. 27 + 168p [BM BVaU NBFU OTP

Durie, Mrs. Anna

WOLFE AND OTHER POEMS. Toronto, College Print., 1929. 10p [NBFU OTU

OUR ABSENT HERO. Poems in Loving Memory of Captain William Arthur Peel Durie, 58th Battalion, C.E.F. Toronto, Ryerson, 1920. 113p [BM BVaU OTUV QMM

Durkin, Douglas Leader, 1884–1968

THE FIGHTING MEN OF CANADA. Toronto, McClelland, 1918. 85p [BM BVaU LC NSHD OKQ

Durrant, Louisa

TWELVE TIMES SEVEN AND OTHER POEMS. Ilfracombe, Devon, Stockwell, 1957. 79p

Duvar, John Hunter-, 1830–1899

JOHN A' VAR. His Lays. [Priv. print.] [CCJ

Dyas de Lom, Elizabeth English, –1912

POEMS. Toronto, 1911. 42p [Brown U BVaU

Dyde, Samuel Walters, 1862–1947

FROM MY GALLERY. Kingston, Author, n.d. 31p [OKQ

THE HIGHWAY. Kingston, Jackson Press, 1928. 15p [OKQ

WAR VERSES. Kingston, Jackson Press, 1924. 25p [LC OKQ

A YEAR. Kingston, Jackson Press, 1927. 8p [OKQ

Dyer, Mary Sparks

SPIRES ALOFT. Galt, Galt Printers, [1938?]. 39p [Brown U NBFU

Dyer, W.E.

ECHOES FROM A SUNDAY-SCHOOL. Toronto, Briggs, 1890. 120p [OONL

Dynes, Violet E.

AGATES IN THE SAND. Vancouver, Sun, 1944. 64p [AEU BVaS

Dysart, Arthur L.

POEMS AND LYRICS. Fredericton, Clark, 1909. 83p [NBFU OTL

Earle, Kathleen

SPINDRIFT. Toronto, Crucible Press, 1941. 22p [NBSaM OTP

Eassie, Robert M.

ODES TO TRIFLES, AND OTHER RHYMES. London, Lane, 1917. 118p [BM BVaU LC OTU

Easton, C.T.
SONGS OF FOREST AND STREAM. N.p., Rod and Gun Press, 1912. 38p
[PCL

Eaton, Arthur Wentworth Hamilton, 1849–1937
ACADIAN BALLADS AND DE SOTO'S LAST DREAM. New York, Whittaker,
1905. 107p [BM BVaU LC NSHD OTU
ACADIAN BALLADS AND LYRICS IN MANY MOODS. Collected Poems. Toronto,
McClelland, 1930. 240p [BVaU LC NSHD OLU
ACADIAN LEGENDS AND LYRICS. London, White & Allen, 1889. 148p
[BVaU LC NSHD OKQ
THE LOTUS OF THE NILE, AND OTHER POEMS. New York, Whittaker, 1907.
110p [BM BVaU LC NSHD OTU
POEMS OF THE CHRISTIAN YEAR. New York, Whittaker, 1905. 97p [BM
LC NSHD OTP

Eaton, Evelyn Sybil Mary, 1902–
BIRDS BEFORE DAWN. Toronto, Ryerson, 1942. 12p [BVaU LC NSHD
OTU QMM
THE HOURS OF ISIS. London, Barkerville, 1928. 89p [BM
THE INTERPRETER. [Poems.] London, Selwyn & Blount, 1925. 61p [BM
STOLEN HOURS. London, Selwyn & Blount, 1923. 43p [BM OONL

Eaton, Oliver Mowat
SYNCHRONISMS OF AN HOUR, AND OTHER POEMS. N.p., 1895. 107p [Also:
Brockville, 1897] [OTUV

Eayrs, Carl
BORDER VOICES. A Collection of Poems. Ed. by ——. Windsor, Ont.,
Canadian Authors Assoc., 1946. 48p [OOP

Ebbs-Canavan, Frances A. (Sweeney)
HARVEST OF DREAMS. Toronto, Ryerson, 1935. 12p [BVaU NBSaM
OKQ
THE TALE OF A BELGIAN HARE. By Frances Ebbs-Canavan and Lillian Clarke
Sweeney. Victoria, Diggon-Hibben, 1945. 7p [BM BVaU

Eby, Oscar S.
RED CHALK TALKS. Kitchener, 1922. 32p [Brown U BVaU

Edelstein, Hyman, 1889–1957
ALL QUIET IN CANADA – AND WHY. "Cpl. Ray's" pen-and-camera Pictures
of the War (1939–44), with Verse Comment and Later Poems. Ottawa,
Tower Books, 1944. 42p [LC OKQ
CANADIAN LYRICS AND OTHER POEMS. Toronto, Briggs, 1916. 63p [Enl.
ed.: Montreal, Belles Lettres Pub., 1921. 64p] [BM BVaU NSHD OTU
QMM

FROM JUDEAN VINEYARDS. Poems. Montreal, 1914. 60p [OTU
"HE SHALL ROLL THEIR STONES AWAY." Including "Invocation" from
    an Epic Poem on the R.C.M.P. Ottawa, Tower Books, 1957. 12p
LAST MATHEMATICIAN. Toronto, Ryerson, 1949. 11p [BVaU NBSaM
    OTP
LATTER ROSE. Poems. Ottawa, Belles Lettres Pub., 1924. 59p [BVaU
    NSHD OTU QMM
PINE AND PALM. Poems. Montreal, Capitol Print., 1927. 26p [BVaU
    QMM
POEMS. 3rd ed. Montreal, Belles Lettres Pub., 1922. 64p [QMM
SELECTED POEMS. Ottawa, Overbrook, 1931. 158p [BVaU OOP QMM
SPIRIT OF ISRAEL. Toronto, Ryerson, 1942. 8p [BVaU LC NBSaM
    OTP QMM
SPIRIT OF ISRAEL AND OTHER POEMS. Toronto, Ryerson, 1950. 67p
    [BVaU NBFU OTP

Edgar, Florence Hester (Hayes), 1874?–1944
A LEGACY OF LYRICS. Toronto, U. of Toronto Press, 1946. 111p [BVaU
    LC OTUV QMM
OUT OF THE INFINITE. By Florence H. Edgar and William Wilkie Edgar.
    N.p., n.d. 12p [OKQ

Edgar, James David, 1841–1899
THIS CANADA OF OURS, AND OTHER POEMS. Toronto, Briggs, 1893. 64p
    [BM BVaU LC MWU NSHD OKQ
THE WHITE STONE CANOE. A Legend of the Ottawas. Toronto, Toronto
    News, 1885. 27p [BVaU NBFU OTU QMM

Edgar, Mary Susanne, 1889–
WOOD-FIRE AND CANDLE-LIGHT. Toronto, Macmillan, 1945. 121p [AEU
    LC NBFU OTP

Edgar, Oscar Pelham, 1871–1948
POEMS. N.p., n.d. 32p [OOP

Edgar, William Wilkie
DUETS IN VERSE, FRENCH AND ENGLISH. [French] by Marie Sylvia and
    [trans. into English] by W.W. Edgar. Ottawa, Graphic, 1929. 81p
    [BVaU OTU QMM

Edwards, George
POEMS. Clarence, Ont., 1867. 50p [CCJ

Edwards, Henry Arthur, 1905–
STAR SHINE AND MOON LIGHT. Vancouver, Author, 1947. 20p [BVaU OKQ
"WHITE MAGIC" AND OTHER POEMS. Vancouver, Author, 1948. 20p [OKQ

Edwards, Lydia Agnes
HOW CANADIANS MOURNED FOR THEIR QUEEN. Tributes of Loyalty and Love in Memory of Queen Victoria. Comp. by ——. Truro, N.S., News Pub. Co., 1901 51p [NSHD OTP

Edwards, Mary Frances, 1913–
AFTER DUSK. Toronto, Author, 1942. 31p [LC

Eggleston, Wilfrid, 1901–
PRAIRIE MOONLIGHT AND OTHER LYRICS. Toronto, Author, 1927. 23p [OKQ SSU

Elder, Robert
THE BRAVIES. Boston, Meador, 1933. 61p [LC

Ellenbogen, George, 1934–
WINDS OF UNREASON. Toronto, Contact Press, 1957. 87p

Ellice, Edward, 1781–1863
THE BOOK-KEEPER; and A Translation from the German of Schiller. By Mercator [pseud]. Montreal, Dawson, 1868. 61p [OTL

Elliott, Albert E.
POEMS OF COMFORT. Out of the Shadows and Into the Sunshine. By Albert E. Eliott [sic]. Toronto, McClelland, 1948. 63 + 58p [BVaU OTP QMU

Elliott, James (See p217.)

Elliott, Robert, 1858–1902
POEMS. Ed. by John Dearness and Frank Lawson. Published under the Auspices of the Baconian Club, London. London, Ont., Lawson & Jones, 1904. 105p [BM Brown U BVaU OTU

Ellis, W.A.
WAR WARBLINGS OF A BRITISH TAR. Vancouver, Terminal City Press, n.d. 33p [BVaU QMU

Ellis, William Hodgson, 1845–1921
WAYSIDE WEEDS. Toronto, Dent, 1914. 70p [BVaU LC NBFU OTU

Ells, Willard W.
ORIGINAL POEMS. Kentville, N.S., "New Star," 1890. 24p [BVaU

Ellwood, Thomas
NIGHT OF DOOM. Halifax, Howe & Sons, 1865. 28p [NSHD

Elmore, Blanche
POEMS. Detroit, Wilson-Smith, [18–?]. 20p [OTP
POEMS. [1st Ser.?] Toronto, 1894. 22p [BVaU OTU
POEMS. Toronto, Ellis, 1895. 22p [BVaU OTV QMU

POEMS. [2nd Ser.?] Toronto, Ellis, 1896. 23p [OTP
POEMS. 3rd Series. Toronto, Ellis, 1897. 23p [BVaU OKQ
POEMS. [4th Ser.] Toronto, Imrie Graham, 1898. 23p [BVaU OTUV
POEMS. [5th Ser.] Toronto, Douglas Bros., 1899. 22p [OTP

Elsom, Albin Edmund, 1889—
JUBILEE RHYMES. Moose Jaw, Sask., Author, 1955. 32p

Elsom, Margaret
PLEASANT PATHS. Toronto, Crucible Press, 1946. 18p [BVaU NBSaM
THIS HOUR. Woodstock, Ont., Author, 1945. 13p [CC

Elson, John Mebourne, 1880—
RIDERS OF THE DAWN. Toronto, Macmillan, 1934. 33p [BVaU LC
 NBFU OKQ

Emberson, Frederick C., —1913
GOLD AND SILVER. The Best Twenty Poems and Thoughts Extant. Selected
 with some Approach to Analytical Certainty. By F.C. Emberson and Maud
 Ogilvy. Montreal, Drysdale, n.d. 94p [QMM

Emerson, Nan (MacPherson)
WIND SONG AND OTHER VERSE. Winnipeg, Author, 1957. 128p

Ernst, Howard Sheldon
"LOOKING UP." Weston, Ont., Author, 1940. 22p [OTU

Errol, Constance
BY LOST LAGOON. [Vancouver, 1927?] , 23p [BVaU NBFU

Este, C.H. Douglas
LOWLY SONGS. Montreal, Witness, 1916. 35p [BM
LYRICS OF AN OPTIMIST. Montreal, 1917. 62p [BM

Evans, Allen Roy, 1885—
BITTER SWEET. Vancouver, Wrigley, 1933. 71p [BVaU

Evans, Rev. Richard C., 1861—
THE SONGS, POEMS, NOTES AND CORRESPONDENCE OF BISHOP R.C. EVANS,
 and Some Addresses Presented to him from many Parts of the World. London,
 Ont., 1918. 208p [Brown U BVaU OLU

Evans, Robert
TABOR MELODIES. Toronto, Rose, 1878. 125p [BVaU NBFU OKQ QMM

Evans, Walter Norton, 1836—1896
CARTIER AND HOCHELAGA. MAISONNEUVE AND VILLE-MARIE. Two Poems of
 Montreal. Montreal, Drysdale, 1895. 28p [BM LC OLU QMM
MOUNT ROYAL. Montreal, Robinson, 1886. 27p [Same title: Illus. by Elizabeth
 Warren and A.B. Clarkson. Montreal, 1893. 66p] [BVaU NSHD OTP QMM

Everson, Ronald Gilmour, 1903–
A LATTICE FOR MOMOS. Toronto, Contact Press, 1958. 58p
THREE DOZEN POEMS. Montreal, Cambridge Press, 1957. 51p

Ewach, Honoré, 1900–
UKRAINIAN SONGS AND LYRICS. A Short Anthology of Ukrainian Poetry.
   Trans. and ed. by ——. Winnipeg, Ukrainian Pub. Co., 1933. 77p [BM
   BVaU OTU

Ezra, Isaac Ben, 1896–
THE GOLDEN KERNEL AND OTHER POEMS. Toronto, Derby Pub. Co., 1951.
   xiii + 115p
THE LEGEND OF THE FOUR AND OTHER POEMS. Philadelphia, Dorrance, 1954.
   136p

F., T.D.J.
CHRIST ENTERING JERUSALEM. Winnipeg, 1911. 11p [Amtmann cat. 151

Fairbairn, Helen, 1864–
FROM DAWN TO DUSK. Verses. Toronto, U. of Toronto Press, 1945. 50p
   [BM BVa OTU QMM

Fairbanks, Cassie
THE LONE HOUSE. A Poem Partly Founded on Fact. Halifax, Bowes, 1859.
   16p [NSHD OTP

Fairweather, George Edwin
ROTHESAY, AND OTHER VERSES. N.p., 1896. 12p [OTUV
THE STONE CHURCH BELL, AND OTHER POEMS. Saint John, Barnes, 1895.
   60p [BVaU NBFU OTP

Farley, Judith Julia
AN HISTORICAL POEM, THE SAINT LAWRENCE RIVER. Quebec, Daily Telegraph
   Print., 1906. 11p [OTU QMSS

Farley, Tom, 1917–
IT WAS A PLANE. Toronto, Ryerson, 1952. 12p

Farmer, Broadus Baxter
SONGS OF THE ISLAND, AND OTHER POEMS. N.p., n.d. 7p [OTU

Farmer, Thomas Devey Jermyn
SHRINES OLD AND NEW, AND OTHER POEMS. Toronto, Briggs, 1913. 258p
   [BM BVaU OTU
WHERE THE RIVERS MEET. A Retrospect and a Contrast. Winnipeg, 1911. 23p
   [ACG OH

Farrill, Mrs. Caroline Grant

SOME MORNING SOON. Toronto, Crucible Press, 1941. 20p [LC

Faulkner, Rhoda Ann (Page), 1826–1863

WILD NOTES FROM THE BACK WOODS. By R.A.P. [Ed. with intro. by Edwin C. Guillet, 12 April 1942, unpub.] Cobourg, "Star," 1850. 62p [OTP

Faulkner, Sarah E. (Sherwood), 1853–

SEA MURMURS AND WOODLAND SONGS. Toronto, Briggs, 1903. 111p [BM BVaU NBFU OKQ

Fenerty, Charles

BETULA NIGRA. A Poem. By Charles Fennerty [sic]. Halifax, Cunnabell, 1855. 12p [NSHD

ESSAY ON PROGRESS. Halifax, Bowes, 1866. 12p [NSHD

HID TREASURE; or, The Labours of a Deacon, and Other Poems. Manuscript. 81p [NSHD

Fenton, Frederick B.

POEMS OF PEACE AND WAR. London, Heath Cranton, 1916. 27p [BM OTU

Ferguson, Rose

MAPLE LEAVES AND SNOWFLAKES. Toronto, Briggs, 1913. 72p [BM OKQ

Ferne, Doris Maud (Napper), 1896–

EBB TIDE. Toronto, Ryerson, 1941. 8p [BVaU NBSaM OTU QMM

PASCHAL LAMB, AND OTHER POEMS. Toronto, Macmillan, 1946. 39p [BM BVaU LC NBFU OKQ

Fewster, Ernest Philip, 1868–1947

THE IMMORTAL DWELLER. Vancouver, Murphy & Chapman, 1938. 66p [BVaU NSHD OKQ

LITANY BEFORE THE DAWN OF FIRE. Toronto, Ryerson, 1942. 10p [BVaU LC NBSaM OTU QMM

REJOICE, O MY HEART. Vancouver, Grace Fewster, 1949. 68p [BVaU NBFU OKQ QMM

WHITE DESIRE. Ottawa, Overbrook, 1930. 54p [BVaU NSHD OKQ

THE WIND AND THE SEA. Poems. Vancouver, Poetry Soc., 1946. 113p [BVaU OKQ

Fiamengo, Marya Ekaterina, 1926–

THE QUALITY OF HALVES AND OTHER POEMS. Vancouver, Klanak Press, 1958. 41p

Field, George Blackstone, 1883–1952

ECHOES FROM YPRES. New Westminster, B.C., priv. print., 1954. 45p

RHYMES OF THE SURVEY AND FRONTIER. Toronto, Briggs, 1911. 77p [AEU BM BVaU NBFU OKQ

Finch, Robert Duer Claydon, 1900–
ACIS IN OXFORD, AND OTHER POEMS. Toronto, U. of Toronto Press, 1961.
46p [Earlier ed. priv. print. at New Bodleian, Oxford, 1959.]
NEW PROVINCES. Poems of Several Authors. [Ed. by F.R. Scott.] Toronto,
Macmillan, 1936. 77p [Contains poems by Finch and Others.] [BVaU
NBFU OKQ QMM
POEMS. Toronto, Oxford, 1946. 51p [BM BVaU LC MWU NBFU OTU QMM
THE STRENGTH OF THE HILLS. Toronto, McClelland, 1948. 132p [BVaU
MWU NBFU OKQ

Finnigan, Joan, 1925–
THROUGH THE GLASS, DARKLY. Toronto, Ryerson, 1957. 12p

Firth, Mrs. Rose Lyle, 1893–
STRANGE ROADS. Vancouver, Author, 1940. 56p [BVaU OKQ
STRANGE ROADS. II. Vancouver, Author, 1955. 55p

Fischer, William Joseph, 1879–1921
SONGS OF THE WAYSIDE. Boston, Badger, 1903. 85p [OTUV
THE TOILER AND OTHER POEMS. Toronto, Briggs, 1907. 167p [BM BVaU
NBFU OKQ

Fisher, Peter, 1782–1848
THE LAY OF THE WILDERNESS. A Poem in Five Cantos. By a Native of New
Brunswick [pseud]. Saint John, Chubb, 1833. 165p [NSHP

Fishpool, John Foster, 1885–
SPARKS FROM THE ANVIL. St. Thomas, Ont., Municipal World, 1935. 47p
[Brown U

Fitzgerald, Desmond, 1915–
THE SYMPHONY OF THE STARS. By Daryl Gerald [pseud]. London, Ont.,
Crucible Press, 1939. 11p [OTP

Fleck, Widow [Mrs. John Fleming?]
POEMS ON VARIOUS SUBJECTS. By Widow Fleck. Montreal, 1833. 12p [CCJ

Fleming, Ann (Cuthbert) (Knight), –1860
HOME. A Poem. By Ann Cuthbert Knight. Edinburgh, 1815. 98p [CCJ
A YEAR IN CANADA, AND OTHER POEMS. By Ann Cuthbert Knight. Edinburgh,
Doig & Stirling, 1816. 126p [BM OTP QMSS

Fleming, Rev. Everett Samuel James, 1895–
BIBLE STORY POEMS. Old Friends in New Attire. Sidney, B.C., 1949. 28p
[BVaU OTUV
THE FORBIDDEN PLATEAU; OR, THE GREAT BETRAYAL. A Legend of Vancouver
Island. Campbell River, B.C., Author, 1959. 8p

THE GREAT WHITE ROCK. A Legend of Semiahmoo Bay. Sidney, B.C., Author, 1950. 5p [OONL

THE JERICHO ROAD AND OTHER BIBLE STORY POEMS. Sidney, B.C., Author, 1949. 28p [QMU

LOGS FOR THE FIRE. Campbell River, B.C., Author, 1959. 49p

MY NURSE AND OTHER POEMS. Sidney, B.C., Author, 1951. 24p

A POCKETFUL OF LAUGHING GAS AND OTHER POEMS FOR FUN. New Westminster, B.C., Author, 1945. 33p [BVaU OTUV

SOURDOUGH AND GOLD DUST. New Westminster, B.C., Author, 1954. 15p

WHITHER AND WHY. Sidney, B.C., Author, 1949. 22p [BVaU OTU

Fletcher, Edward Taylor, 1816?–1897

THE LOST ISLAND (Atlantis). A Poem. Ottawa, Bureau, 1889. 24p [BM BVaU LC NSHP OKQ

NESTORIUS. A Phantasy. By E.T.F. Ottawa, Bureau, 1892. 23p [BM OTU QMM

Fletcher, Mrs. Elizabeth, 1879–

POEMS. Guelph, Author, [1933?]. 28p [OKQ

Fletcher, Mary E., 1874–1929

CRUSTULA JURIS. Being a Collection of Leading Cases on Contract Done into Verse. By Mary E. Fletcher and Bernard Wallace Russell. Toronto, Carswell, [1913]. 62p [BVaU NBFU OTU

Fletcher, Olive H.

SONGS OF OUR EMPIRE'S WAR AND PRAISEWORTHY ALLIES. Schumacher, Ont., Author, 1944. 96p [OOP

Flint, Annie Johnson, 1866–1932

BY THE WAY. ... [Verses.] Toronto, Evangelical Pub., 1920. 48p [BM

FLINT'S BEST-LOVED POEMS. Toronto, Evangelical Pub., 1948. 141p [Adelphi cat. 68

OUT OF DOORS. Nature Songs. Toronto, Evangelical Pub., 1920. 56p [BM OTU QMU

POEMS. Vol. I. Toronto, Evangelical Pub., 1944. 142p [AEP

POEMS. Vol. II. Toronto, Evangelical Pub., 1948. 141p [BM

SONGS OF FAITH AND COMFORT. Toronto, Evangelical Pub., 1919. 56p [BM

SONGS OF THE BLESSED HOPE. Toronto, Evangelical Pub., n.d. 47p [QMU

Flood, John N., 1893–

THE SAGA OF THE CARIBBEAN CRUISE OF M.V. AROSA SUN, FEBRUARY 1956. Saint John, Author, n.d. 8p [A diary in rhyme, addressed to the author's daughter.]

Flood, Robert William, 1877–

BITS O'RHYME TO PASS THE TIME. Vancouver, Wrigley Print Co., 1954. 26p

ROUGH TIMES AND OTHER RHYMES. Vancouver, Murphy Chapman, 1941. 31p [BVaU

Foran, Ethel Ursula
POEMS. A Few Blossoms from the Garden of my Dreams. Montreal, Beauchemin, 1922. 128p [BM BVaU NSHD OOP QMM

Foran, Joseph Kearney, 1857–1931
POEMS AND CANADIAN LYRICS. Montreal, Sadlier, 1895. 244p [BVaU LC NBFU OTU QMM

Foran, Michael McKeon, 1898–
NIGHT FLIGHT ... AND OTHER POEMS. London, Ont., Young Press, 1945. 46p [BVaU OTU
THIS IS MY WORST. A Collection of Humorous Verse. Toronto, Author, 1955. 54p

Ford, Robert Arthur Douglas, 1915–
A WINDOW ON THE NORTH. Toronto, Ryerson, 1956. 48p

Forsyth, William Langdon
ZEBUNISA, AND OTHER POEMS. By Sauda [pseud]. Montreal, 1873. 99p [BVa LC OTUV

Fortner, Dora Pearl, 1894–
DAYDREAMS. N.p., 1957. 20p (Carillon Poetry Chap-Books)
FLIGHTS OF FANCY. Poems. N.p., 1955. 20p (Carillon Poetry Chap-Books)

Found, Lillian (Redmond), 1878–
BANNER IN THE SKY, AND OTHER POEMS. Ottawa, Author, 1945. 38p [Brown U
WHAT MATTER WHAT WAY. Ottawa, Le Droit, 1950. 36p [OONL

Fowke, Edith Margaret (Fulton)
CANADA'S STORY IN SONG. By Edith Fowke and Alan Mills [pseud of Albert Miller.] Piano accompaniments by Helmut Blume. Toronto, Gage, 1960. x + 230p
FOLKSONGS OF CANADA. Ed. by ——. Waterloo, Ont., Waterloo Music Co., 1954. 198p
SONGS OF WORK AND FREEDOM. By Edith Fowke and Joe Glazer. Music arrangements: Kenneth Bray. Chicago, Roosevelt University, Labor Education Division, 1960. 208p

Fox, Annie Marion
QUESTING AND OTHER POEMS. Toronto, Author, 1935. 16p [OTU
WINGED WORDS. Toronto, Livingstone, 1930. 32p [BVaU OTP

Fox, Marion Wathen, 1871–1956
SILHOUETTES OF THE FOREST. Saint John, Barnes Hopkins, [194–?]. 21p [NBFL

Fox, William Sherwood, 1878–1967
ON FRIENDSHIP. Toronto, Ryerson, 1953. 17p

Frame, Margaret Fulton

PHANTOM CARAVAN. Selected and Arranged by Charles Clay. Ottawa, Tower Books, 1947. 48p [BVaU NBFU OLU

Fraser, Alexander Louis, 1870–1954

AFTERMATH. Saint John, Globe, 1919. 55p [BVaU NBFU OKQ
AT LIFE'S WINDOWS. Saint John, Globe, 1910. 67p [NBFU OKQ
BY COBEQUID BAY. Toronto, Ryerson, 1927. 12p [BVaU NBSaM OKQ QMM
BY EASTERN WINDOWS. Saint John, Globe, 1933. 109p [NBFU OTU
THE DRAINED CUP AND OTHER POEMS. Saint John, Globe, 1925. 46p [BVaU NBFU OKQ
FOR THINKING HEARTS. Toronto, H.M. Ridley, 1954. 20p (Carillon Poetry Chap-Books)
FUGITIVES. Saint John, Globe, 1912. 79p [NBFU QMM
GOD'S WEALTH, AND OTHER POEMS. Saint John, Globe, 1922. 42p [NBFU OKQ
HALIFAX, 1749–1949. Halifax, MacCurdy, 1949. 16p [Brown U NBFU
THE INDIAN BRIDE. A War Legend. Saint John, Globe, 1915. 16p [NBFU OKQ
MOOSE RIVER MINES, AND OTHER POEMS. Toronto, Crucible Press, 1949. 20p [NBFU OTUV
PEOPLE OF THE STREET AND OTHER POEMS. Saint John, Globe, 1929. 85p [NSHD OKQ
RUTH AND OTHER POEMS. Toronto, Crucible Press, 1946. 22p [BVaU NSHD OTP QMM
SONNETS AND OTHER VERSES. Saint John, Globe, 1909. 62p [BVaU LC NSHD OTUV QMM

Fraser, Dawn

SONGS OF SIBERIA AND RHYMES OF THE ROAD. Glace Bay, N.S., Eastern Pub., [1919?]. 229p [BM OLU

Fraser, Donald Andrew, 1875–1948

CENTENARY. A Collection of Verses arranged in Celebration of the One Hundredth Birthday of the City of Victoria, B.C., 1843–1943. Victoria, Diggon-Hibben, 1943. 39p [BVaU OKQ
MY NUGGET-POKE. A Selection of Sonnets and Other Short Poems. Victoria, Author, n.d. 108p [BVaU OKQ
PEBBLES AND SHELLS. A Book of Verses. Toronto, Briggs, 1909. 172p [BM BVaU NSHD OLU
THE THREE KINGS, AND OTHER VERSES FOR CHILDREN. Victoria, Cusack, 1922. 64p [BVaU OKQ

Fraser, Hermia (Harris), 1902–

THE ARROW-MAKER'S DAUGHTER AND OTHER HAIDA CHANTS. Toronto, Ryerson, 1957. 16p

SONGS OF THE WESTERN ISLANDS. Toronto, Ryerson, 1945. 10p [BVaU NBSaM OTU

Fraser, James MacDonell, 1882–
SEASONAL SONGS INCLUDING "WE SHALL REMEMBER THEM." Comp. by ——. Picton, Ont., Gazette, 1935. 16p [NSHD OTU

Fraser, John, 1820–1899
A TALE OF THE SEA, AND OTHER POEMS. Montreal, Dawson, 1870. 87p [BVaU NSHD OKQ QMM

Freebairn, Adam L., 1881–
KOOTENAI BROWN AND OTHER WESTERN POEMS. Pincher Creek, Alta., Author, [194–?]. 32p [AEU OTU
THE MOUNTAIN HEIGHTS AND OTHER POEMS. [Pincher Creek, Alta.], n.d. 24p [ACG OTU
MY SON AND OTHER POEMS. Pincher Creek, Alta., Author, [194–?]. 30p [ACG
RHYMES FROM THE FOOTHILLS. [Pincher Creek, Alta.], n.d. 31p [ACG OTU

French, Jane E.L.
POEMS AND LYRICS. Victoria, Victoria Print., [1923]. 96p [BM BVaU OOP

Freund, Philip, 1909–
PRIVATE SPEECH. London, Allen, 1950. 358p [BM LC

Frisch, Anthony John, 1921–
THE HOUSE. New Poems, in English, French, German. Hull, Que., Ivy Pub. Co., 1950. 32p [BVaU NBFU OLU QMM
POEMS. Toronto, Ryerson, 1954. 22p
THIRD POEMS. Hull, Que., Ivy Pub. Co., 1951. 28p
THOUGH I SPEAK. Poems. Montreal, Ivy Pub. Co., 1949. 31p [BVaU NBFU OKQ

Frost, George
MAN AND NATURE; or, Evening Thoughts in Poetry. Saint John, Barnes, 1874. 75p [Brown U OTU

Fry, Alice
THE RUBY BOOK OF REMEMBRANCE. Toronto, Crucible Press, 1947. 23p [Brown U

Fuller, Ada Elizabeth
A ROMANCE OF DREAM VALLEY. [A Poem.] Canada, 1921. [BM
SUNSHINE AND SHADOW. Poems. Niagara Falls, Ont., 1919. 64p [BM Brown U OTU

Fuller, William Henry
YE BALLAD OF LYTTEL JOHN A. [MOR'98

Fulton, S.O.
RED TARN; or, The Vision of the Lake. A Thrilling Temperance Poem in Fourteen
Cantos. Amherst, N.S., Gazette, 1873. 156p [NSHD

Fulton, Sadie E.
POEMS. Montreal, 1890. 10p [Brown U OLU

Funk, I.J.
THE ROCK CALLED HADES. London, Stockwell, [194–?]. 79p [OOP

Fyles, Thomas W., 1832–
POEMS. Toronto, Briggs, 1907. 111p [BM BVaU NBFU OTUV

Gahan, James Joseph, 1851–
CANADA. Quebec, Delisle, 1877. 21p [OTP
THE IMMACULATE MARY, AND OTHER POEMS. Quebec, Barrow, n.d. 24p
[QMSS
VIVIAN. A Tale of Chateau Richer. Toronto, Boyle, 1880. 24p [NSHD OTP

Galloway, Andrew Strome Ayees, 1915–
THE YEW TREE BALLAD, AND OTHER POEMS. Aylmer, Ont., Barnecott & Monteith,
1936. 48p [Brown U

Galloway, Christian F.J.
PEACE RIVER, AND OTHER VERSE. London, Mitre Press, 1953. 59p

Garbutt, Mrs. Elizabeth, 1887–
MT. EISENHOWER AND OTHER POEMS. Calgary, Dominion Text Book Co., 1946.
40p [ACU NBSaM

Gardiner, Lue (Gillmor)
RHYMES FROM RANGES. Edmonton, Author, 1942. 30p [CC
RHYMES FROM THE NORTHWEST. Edmonton, Author, 1940. 39p [ACG OONL

Gardner-Smith, E.
THE CALL OF THE WEST AND OTHER POEMS. Calgary, Burnand, [1928?]. 32p
[ACG OKQ

Garrett, Mrs. Florence Pearl, 1883–
LIFE'S GLEANINGS. Winnipeg, Wallingford, 1937. 36p [Brown U BVaU
MEMORIES. Winnipeg, Author, 1936. 28p [CC
THE WHISPERING LEAVES. Winnipeg, Author, 1936. 32p [CC

Garrett, Rev. John C.
THE CENTENNIAL. A Poem Written on the Centenary of St. Mark's Church,
Niagara, Ont., (1792–1892). N.p., 1892. 24p [OTU

Garvey, Michael
VOTIVE LIGHTS, INCENSE AND MELODY. Toronto, Author, 1926. 61p [OTP

Garvin, John William, 1859–1935
CANADIAN POEMS OF THE GREAT WAR. Chosen and ed. by ——. Toronto,
   McClelland, 1918. 256p [BVaU LC NSHD OKQ
CANADIAN POETS. Ed. by ——. Toronto, McClelland, 1916. 471p [Rev. ed.:
   Toronto, McClelland, 1926. 536p [BM BVaU LC NBFU OTU QMM
CANADIAN POETS AND POETRY. Chosen and ed. by ——. Toronto, McClelland,
   1916. 471p. [BVaU LC OTUV QMM
CANADIAN VERSE FOR BOYS AND GIRLS. Ed. by ——. Toronto, Nelson, 1930.
   215p [BVaU NBFU OTUV QMM
CAP AND BELLS. An Anthology of Light Verse by Canadian Poets. Chosen
   by ——. Toronto, Ryerson, 1936. 105p [BM BVaU LC NBFU OTU

Gay, James, 1810–1891
CANADA'S POET; YOURS ALWAY JAMES GAY. Poet Laureate of Canada and Master
   of All Poets, this Day. ... London, Field & Tuer, 1884. 87 + 15p [BM BVaU
   LC NSHD OKQ
POEMS BY JAMES GAY, POET LAUREATE OF CANADA, MASTER OF ALL POETS.
   Written while Crossing the Sea in 1882. Guelph, Author, 1883. 18p [W.A.
   Deacon, THE FOUR JAMESES, *q.v.*

Gerrard, George
THE CONSOLATION. A Poem. Toronto, Hunter Rose, 1881. 64p [BVaU NBFU
   OTU QMM

Ghent, Percy Parker, 1888–1952
VAGRANT RHYMES. Sundridge Village, Ont., Harper, 1935. 21p [OTP

Gibbon, John Murray, 1875–1952
BALLADS OF B.C. Toronto, Thompson, n.d. 19p [BViPA
CANADA IN SONG. With Musical Arrangements by L.R. Bell. Toronto, Thompson,
   1941. 27p [CC
CANADIAN CADENCES. Toronto, Ryerson, 1947. 16p [BVaU NSHD OLU
A CANADIAN CALENDAR. Ste Anne de Bellevue, Que., Canadian Bookman, 1919.
   15p [BM BVaU OKQ
CANADIAN FOLKSONGS (OLD AND NEW). Selected and trans. by ——. Toronto,
   Dent, 1927. 105p [Rev. and enl. ed.: Toronto, Dent, 1949. 114p] [BVaU
   NSWA OTU
FRENCH CANADIAN FOLK SONGS; FRENCH AND ENGLISH TEXTS. English trans-
   lation by J. Murray Gibbon. Arranged for chorus of men's voices by Ernest
   MacMillan. Boston, Boston Music Co., 1928. 4v [NSHD
NEW WORLD BALLADS. Toronto, Ryerson, 1939. 177p [BVaU LC NBFU OTP
   QMM
NORTHLAND SONGS. Toronto, Thompson, 1936. 4v [BVa LC OTP

PIONEER SONGS OF CANADA. Musical Arrangements by Irvin Cooper. Toronto, Thompson, 1941. 28p [BVaU

PRINCE CHARLIE AND FLORA. A Scottish Ballad Opera. Libretto by ——. Toronto, Dent, 1929. [32p [OTU

Gibson, George Herbert Rae, 1881–1932

IRONBARK CHIPS AND STOCKWHIP CRACKS. Melbourne, Australia, [1893]. 219p [QMM

IRONBARK SPLINTERS FROM THE AUSTRALIAN BUSH. 2nd ed. London, Werner Laurie, [191–?]. 167p [BVi OTP

SOUTHERLY BUSTERS. In Verse. By Ironbark [pseud]. Sydney, Australia, J. Sands, n.d. 15 + 210p [BM

Gibson, J.E.

YOU'LL HATE ME FOR THIS. A Book of Impromptu Verse. Vancouver, Wrigley, 1946. 92p [BVaU OONL

Gill, Frank P.

RHAPSODY. Songs and Lyrics. Calgary, Star Print., [1928?]. 46p [BVaU OTU

Gillespie, George W.

MISCELLANEOUS POEMS. Toronto, Author, 1843. 152p [OTP

Gillespy, William, 1824–1886

FUGITIVE POETRY. Hamilton, 1846. 100p [CCJ

Gillies, Rev. Archibald C., 1834–1887

DAILY MEDITATIONS. A Collection of Poems. Kingston, 1860. 96p [CCJ

Gillis, James Donald, 1870–

THE GREAT ELECTION. [Cape Breton], North Sydney Herald, [1915?]. 43p [NSHD OTUV

Gillmore, E.T.B.

MAPLE LEAVES IN KHAKI–The Blooding of the Whelps, and Other Verses. Ottawa, Taylor & Clarke, [1901?]. 16p [NSHD OTP

Gilmour, Lucy C.

SCRAPS OF VERSE. From a Shut-In. Charlottetown, Maritime Stationers, 1912. 35p [OONL

Gilpin, Lois A. (Hunter), 1876–

THE ARBUTUS TREE. Vancouver, Clarke & Stuart, [1955?]. 40p

EASTER SUNDAY, EARLY, AND OTHER POEMS. Vancouver, Vancouver Stationers, 1935. 18p [Brown U BVaU

Girling, T.A.

THE SALIENT AND OTHER POEMS. London, Palmer & Hayward, 1918. 51p [2nd ed., 1918. 65p] [BVaU LC

Glassco, John, 1909–
THE DEFICIT MADE FLESH. Toronto, McClelland, 1958. 64p

Gleave, Thomas Barwell
BECKONING HILLS. Toronto, Kirkby, 1949. 47p [Brown U
BEYOND OUR WALLS. Toronto, Kirkby, 1946. 48p [OTP
COME REST AWHILE. Toronto, Kirkby, 1948. 47p [Brown U BVaU OTU
ENCHANTED BY-WAYS. Toronto, Kirkby, 1947. 55p [Brown U OTUV
HERE'S TO HAPPINESS. Toronto, Kirkby, 1945. 48p [Brown U OTU
THE MYSTIC CAVE. Twelve Original Fairy Tales in Verse. Montreal, Richardson
   etc., n.d. 40p [OTU
VISTAS GRAVE AND GAY. Toronto, Kirkby, 1944. 48p [BVaU OTP

Glendinning, Alexander
RHYMES. ... V. I London, Ont., Free Press Print., 1871. 240p [BVaU NBFU
OKQ

Goddard, Evelyn
POEMS ON THE DOGWOOD, B.C.'S FLORAL EMBLEM. By Cowichan poets. Selected
   by ——. Duncan, B.C., Cowichan Leader, 1958. 12p

Godfrey, Mrs. Norah, –1948?
CAVALCADE. Toronto, Ryerson, 1946. 16p [BVaU LC MWU NBSaM OTP

Goldberg, Nathan Ralph, 1919–
COFFEE AND BITTERS. By Nathan Ralph [pseud]. Toronto, Macmillan, 1947.
   37p [BM BVaU LC NBFU OTP
TWELVE POEMS. By Nathan Ralph [pseud]. Toronto, Ryerson, 1941. 8p
   [BVaU LC NBSaM OTP QMM

Goldsmith, Oliver, 1794–1861
THE MANUSCRIPT BOOK OF OLIVER GOLDSMITH. ... Description and comment by
   E. Cockburn Kyte. Toronto, Bibliographical Society of Canada, 1950. 4 + 9p
   [OONL
THE RISING VILLAGE. A Poem. London, Sharpe, 1825. 48p [BM NSHD
THE RISING VILLAGE, with Other Poems. By Oliver Goldsmith, a Descendant of
   the Author of "The Deserted Village." Saint John, M'Millan, 1834. 144p
   [BM BVaU LC MWU NSHD OKQ

Goodchild, Roland
THISTLEDOWN. Occasional Verses. London, Stockwell, 1917. 48p [BM

Gooderham, Grace A.
FRIENDLY FEET. N.p., Author, [192–?]. 16p [Brown U

Gooderham, Mary W.
COMPANION BOOK TO A CHRISTMAS GARLAND. Being Hymns for Christmas,
   Eighteen Hundred and Ninety-nine to Christmas, Nineteen Hundred and
   Ten. Toronto, [1910?]. 11p [Brown U BVaU

Goodley, Margaret
SIFTING STARDUST. Oshawa, Author, 1939. 44p [UTQ'40

Gordon, Alexander McGregor Rose, 1846–1898
HOCH DER KAISER. Myself and God. By A. McGregor Rose (A.M.R. Gordon).
  Pictures by Jessie A. Walker. New York, Abbey Press, 1900. 31p [Brown U
  LC OTU
POEMS. By A. McGregor Rose [pseud]. Collected and Ed. with a Life of the Author
  by Robert Dey. Manchester, Heywood, n.d. 168p [OTUV
SIR WILFRID'S PROGRESS THROUGH ENGLAND AND FRANCE IN THE JUBILEE
  YEAR. Montreal, Sterling, 1897. 19p [OTUV

Gordon, Alfred, 1888–
DANDELION. A Tale for Children. N.p., priv. print., n.d. 4p [NBFU
IN PROPHESY (A RECESSIONAL), AND SONNETS OF THE EUROPEAN WAR. Montreal,
  Author, 1914. 16p [BM Brown U BVaU NBFU OTU
POEMS. Toronto, Musson, 1915. 120p [BM BVaU NBFU OTU
VIMY RIDGE AND NEW POEMS. Toronto, Dent, 1918. 64p [BVaU NSHD OTU

Gordon, Huntly K., 1895–1949
VERSES AND SKETCHES. Toronto, U. of Toronto Press, 1952. 33p

Gordon, John R., 1889–
RHYMES OF THE RANGE. Calgary, Author, 1952. 11p

Gordon, Robert Kay, 1887–
A CANADIAN CHILD'S A B C. Toronto, Dent, 1931. 56p [Brown U BVaU OTUV

Gould, Alice Kathryn
BY THE RIDEAU. A Tale of Smiths Falls in Song and Story. [Smith Falls],
  Record-News, 1935. 32p [OTU

Gould, Mona Helen (McTavish), 1908–
GOSSIP! Verse. Toronto, Gossip, 1949. 48p [UTQ'50
I RUN WITH THE FOX. Toronto, Macmillan, 1946. 30p [BVaU NBFU OTP
TASTING THE EARTH. Toronto, Macmillan, 1943. 44p [BVaU LC NBFU OTP

Gowman, Henry
PICKLE CROW AND OTHER POEMS. Toronto, Hilda M. Ridley, 1951. 18p (Carillon
  Poetry Chap-Books)

Grace, Edith Jayne
GEMS OF WISDOM. Ilfracombe, Devon, Stockwell, 1957. 16p

Graham, Alexander, fl. 1840–1873
LEISURE HOUR MUSINGS. Peterborough, 1873. 256p [OTUV

Graham, Hannah Isabel
BE OF GOOD CHEER. Toronto, Allen, 1939. 106p [BM BVaU OTP

BEN ONA AND THE CHRISTMAS CAROL. Toronto, Ryerson, 1931. 16p [BVaU OTP

SAINT IGNACE AND OTHER POEMS. Toronto, Ryerson, 1934. 15p [BVaU OTU

A SONG OF DECEMBER AND OTHER POEMS. Toronto, Briggs, 1904. 19p [BM BVaU OTP

Graham, Janet (Pollock), 1880–

FROM HILL AND DELL. Little Nature Sketches of the Ottawa Valley. Lachute, Que., Watchman, 1940. 56p [LC OTU QMM

Grant, Francis Wylie, 1904–

SPINDRIFT. A Booklet of Maritime Rhymes. [Wallace, N.S.?] Author, 1957. 60p

Grant, Mrs. J.P.

STRAY LEAVES. A Collection of Poems. Montreal, Lovell, 1865. 166p [BVaU LC NBFU OTU QMM

Grant, James Miller, 1853–1940

CANADA, MY HOME. N.p., Author, 1901. 5p [BM NSHD OTUV

CANADA, MY HOME, AND OTHER POEMS. By Grant Balfour [pseud]. Toronto, Musson, 1910. 88p [Another ed., 1925] [BVaU NBFU OTU QMM

CANADA THE FREE. [A Poem]. By Grant Balfour [pseud]. N.p., 1908. s. sh. folio [BM

MY MOTHERLAND. By Grant Balfour [psued]. N.p., 1904 13p [BM OTP

ON STRIKE TILL THREE. By Grant Balfour [pseud]. Toronto, Briggs, 1913. 15p [BM BVaU NBFU OKQ

Grant, William Ewart

LEAVES OF EMPIRE. Toronto, Ryerson, 1919. 58p [BVaU OKQ

Grantham, Ronald, 1910–

NEW EARTH. Vancouver, Boyd, 1931. 22p [BVaU NBFU OTP

Gray, Alice Rowan

KENILWORTH AND OTHER POEMS. Winnipeg, Peerless, 1934. 44p [BViV MWP

Gray, Rev. Archibald

SHADES OF THE HAMLET, AND OTHER POEMS. Woburn, Mass., Fowle, 1852. 57p [NSHD

Gray, Francis William, 1877–1958

CHRISTMAS REMEMBRANCES, 1953. Victoria, Author, 1953. 24p

MUSINGS OF A MARITIME MINER, IN WAR AND PEACE. ... Sydney, N.S., Author, 1940. 26p [BVaU NSHD

Gray, J.H. Gresham

JINGLES OF A JESTER. By Gresham Gray. 1st ed. [Victoria], 1951 [c1950]. 160p

RHYMES WITHOUT REASON. By Gresham Gray. [Victoria], J.H. Gray, [1951].
216p

Gray, James Martin, 1930–
POEMS. Edinburgh, Serif Books, 1958. 46p

Gray, Mrs. Lillian Collier
GRAY ACRES. Toronto, Crucible Press, 1944. 32p [OTP

Gray, Nelson Cockburn
NEW PATRIOTIC POEMS. Montreal, Nova Co., 1908. 12p [NSWA OPAL

Grayson, Ethel Kirk, 1890–
BEGGAR'S VELVET. Toronto, Ryerson, 1948. 42p [BVaU MWU NBFU OTP
QMBM

Greaves, Arthur
BUBBLES FROM THE DEEP. Sonnets and Other Poems, Dramatic and Personal.
Philadelphia, Author, 1873. 194p [LC OTP

Green, E.
DEVIL'S DRIFT. Winnipeg, Author, 1932. 30p [CC

Green, James Albert
VERSES OF THE CANADIAN NORTHLAND. [Cincinnati, 1920.] 22p [OWA

Greene, Charles Johnson
CANADA-LAND. ... Lyrics of a Group of Ten Original Songs. Vancouver, Campbell,
[1948?]. 10p [BVaU

Gregory, Alice
PARK HILL. An Historical Poem. Toronto, 1928. 8p [Amtmann cat. 152

Grier, Eldon, 1917–
A MORNING FROM SCRAPS. Montreal, n.d. 22p
THE RING OF ICE. Poems. Montreal, Cambridge Press, 1957. 101p

Grier, Rose J.E., 1832–1920
ALLEVIATIONS. Toronto, Brown Searle, 1905. 60p [BM NBFU OTUV

Griffin, Edith May
RAMBLING WITH EDITH GRIFFIN. Sarnia, priv. print., [1946?]. 42p [Phelps

Griffin, Frederick, 1798–1879
THE DESTINY OF MAN, THE STORM KING, AND OTHER POEMS. 2nd ed. London,
Trübner, 1883. 103p [1st ed.: London, 1872.] [BM
THE WORLD UNDER GLASS. London, 1879. [BM

Griffiths, Thomas George, 1888–
THE DREAMER AND OTHER POEMS. Toronto, United Church Pub. House, 1932.
8p [OKQ

Grigg, B.W.A.
THE LILIES AND OTHER POEMS. N.p., n.d. 15p [NSWA

Grigg, Richard
INGERSOLL RHYMINGS. Ingersoll, Oxford Tribune, 1894. 106p [OTUV

Grigsby, Joan S., 1909–
LANTERNS BY THE LAKE. London, Kegan Paul, 1929. 136p [BM OKQ
THE ORCHID DOOR, ANCIENT KOREAN POEMS. Collected and Done into English
Verse. Kobe, Thompson, 1935. 105p [BVa LC

Groom, I. Sutherland
QUEENS AND OTHERS. Toronto, Ryerson, 1955. 16p

Grote, George Whitfield
ODE ON THE CORONATION OF KING EDWARD VII, 1902. Toronto, Author, 1902.
23p [BM OKQ

Groves, Edith (Lelean), 1870–1931
EVERYDAY CHILDREN, A BOOK OF POEMS. With ... a Biographical Sketch of the
Author by Helen Macmurchy. ... Toronto, Committee in Charge ... Groves
Memorial Fund, 1932. 155p [Brown U BVaU OLU
THE KINGDOM OF CHILDHOOD. Toronto, Warwick & Rutter, 1925. 106p
[Brown U BVaU OTU
WE ARE SEVEN. ... Songs for Children and Grown-Ups. Music by B.L. Tamblyn.
Toronto, 1927. 20p [Adelphi cat. 55A

Guerin, Mrs. Agnes Carter, 1850–
WOVEN THOUGHTS. By Mrs. R.C. Guerin. Toronto, Briggs, 1904. 101p [BM
BVaU OTU

Guise, Mary Ellen
PENNIES ON MY PALM. Toronto, Ryerson, 1931. 8p [BVaU NBFU OKQ

Gunn, Garrioch
WHITE LAURUSTINE. Poems. Toronto, Macmillan, 1914. 132p [BVaU OKQ

Gunn, John M.
A CHRISTMAS MESSAGE, AND SOME BITS OF VERSE. London, Ont., Talbot, 1923.
23p [OTP

Gunne, A. Evelyn
THE SILVER TRAIL. Poems. Boston, Badger, 1906. 110p [BViPA LC NBFU
THE SPIRIT OF THE NORTH, AND OTHER POEMS. Toronto, Imrie, 1900. 41p
[BM OTUV

Gunter, Lillian Forbes
LOVING MEMORIES, AND OTHER POEMS. Regina Leader Pub. Co., 1922. 45p
[BM QMU

Gurney, F.C.

SOUL SO DARK, AND OTHER POEMS. Didsbury, Alta., 1942. 86p [OONL

Gustafson, Ralph Barker, 1909–

ANTHOLOGY OF CANADIAN POETRY (English). Comp. by ——. Harmondsworth, Middlesex, Eng., Penguin Books, 1942. 123p [BM BVaU LC NSHD OLU

EPITHALAMIUM IN TIME OF WAR. New York, Author, 1941. 11p [BVaU NBFU OKQ

FLIGHT INTO DARKNESS. Poems. New York, Pantheon, 1946. 96p [Earlier ed., 1944.] [BVaU LC NBFU OTU QMM

THE GOLDEN CHALICE. London, Nicholson & Watson, 1935. 105p [BM NSHD OTU QMM

A LITTLE ANTHOLOGY OF CANADIAN POETS. Ed. by ——. Norfolk, Conn., New Directions, 1943. 26p [BVaU LC MWU OTP

LYRICS UNROMANTIC. New York, 1942. 19p [BVaU NBFU OKQ

THE PENGUIN BOOK OF CANADIAN VERSE. Ed. with an intro. and notes by ——. Harmondsworth, Middlesex, Penguin Books, 1958. 255p

RIVER AMONG ROCKS. Toronto, McClelland, 1960. 1v [unpaged].

ROCKY MOUNTAIN POEMS. Vancouver, Klanak Press, 1960. 36p

Guthrie, James C., 1898–

FOOTSTEPS ON THE WATER. Toronto, Hunter Rose, 1930. 164p [Brown U

Guthrie, Norman Gregor, 1877–1929

FLAKE AND PETAL. Toronto, Musson, 1928. 83p [BVaU NSHD OTP

FLOWER AND FLAME. By John Crichton [pseud]. Toronto, Ryerson, 1924. 74p [BVaU NBFU OTP QMM

PILLAR OF SMOKE. By John Crichton [pseud]. Toronto, Musson, 1925. 90p [BVaU NBFU OTP

A VISTA. Poems. By John Crichton [pseud]. Montreal, Chapman, 1921. 85p [BM BVaU NBFU QMM

Gutteridge, Donald George, 1937–

THE BROODING SKY. Poems. London, Ont., Author, 1960. 20p

Gwilt, Fanny G.

CONSTANCE. A Lay of the Olden Time. By Maple Leaf [pseud]. Montreal, Lovell, 1874. 50p [BVaU LC NBFU OTP QMM

H., A.L.O.

GREETINGS FROM MAYFLOWER LAND. Halifax, [1896?]. [unpaged] [NSWA

Hackett, John A.

RHYMES OF THE NORTH, AND OTHER RHYMES. Victoria, Diggon, 1924. 66p [BVaU

Hagarty, John Hawkins, 1816–1900
A LEGEND OF MARATHON. By an Ontario Judge [pseud]. [Toronto, Author, 1888]. 36p [OTUV QMM
POEMS. N.p., priv. print., 1902. 77p [BVaU NBFU OTU

Hagerman, Jessie Sills
EUGENIA RECITES. Recitations from Canadian Verse. Ed. by ——. Toronto, Crucible Press, 1940. 60p [LC OKQ

Haliburton, Ida Mae (Siddall), 1879–
SHINING HOURS. Toronto, Ryerson, 1958. xii + 83p

Haliburton, Robert Grant, 1831–1901
VOICES FROM THE STREET. A Series of Poems. Halifax, priv. print., n.d. 20p [CCJ

Hall, Charles Frederick
POEMS. Truro, N.S., Cosmocrat Press, 1890. 41p [NSHPL NSWA

Hall, Emma L.
THE GESTE OF JANUS THE JONGLEUR. By Yvonne St. Claire [pseud]. N.p., n.d. 4p [OKQ]
THE OCEAN'S ORATORIO. By Yvonne St. Claire [pseud]. Toronto, Author, n.d. 4p [Reprinted and enl.: Toronto, Author, 1937.] [NSHD OKQ
THE SCENTED GARDEN. By Yvonne St. Claire [pseud]. Toronto, Author, 1936. 24p [NBFU OKQ
SONGS OF A YOUNG COUNTRY. By Yvonne St. Claire [pseud]. Toronto, Author, 1935. 15p [BVaU NBFU OKQ
THE SOUL'S INQUIRY. By Yvonne St. Claire [pseud]. Toronto, Author, 1939. 4p [OTUV

Hallett, M.E.
SUNSHINE & SHADOW. Victoria, Diggons, 1924. 28p [QMU

Halliburton, Brenton, 1775–1860
REFLECTIONS ON PASSING EVENTS. Written prior to the Termination of the late War with Russia. [With notes.] By an Octogenarian [pseud]. Halifax, Bowes, 1856. 24p [NSHD

Halpin, Barney
PULPIT POUNDING BILL. Black Diamond, Alta., [1938?]. [Peel Supp

Hambleton, Ronald, 1917–
OBJECT AND EVENT. Toronto, Ryerson, 1953. 38p
UNIT OF FIVE. Poems by Louis Dudek, Ronald Hambleton, P.K. Page, Raymond Souster, James Wreford. Ed. by ——. Toronto, Ryerson, 1944. 87p [BVaU LC MWU NBFU OTU QMM

Hamilton, Hans Patrick, 1889–

CANDLESTICKS. The Golden Candlesticks and Light. London, The Art Store, 1926. 47p [LC

CARMEL. ... London, The Art Store, 1926. 22p [LC

THE GOLDEN CANDLESTICKS, AND OTHER POEMS. Guelph, Gummer Press, 1926. 48p [Also pub. under the title CANDLESTICKS.] [LC

THINGS THAT MIGHT HAVE BEEN. London, The Art Store, 1926. 23p [BVaU LC

WAVES FROM THE SEA. London, The Art Store, 1926. 23p [LC

Hamilton, Margaret Mildred, 1905–

RHYTHMIC REVERIES ROUND THE YEAR. Fredericton, Brunswick Press, 1956. 45p

Hamilton, Pierce Stevens, 1826–1893

THE FEAST OF ST. ANNE, AND OTHER POEMS. Halifax, Burgoyne, 1878. 151p [2nd ed.: Montreal, Lovell, 1890. 165p] [BVaU NSHD OTP

Hamlyn, Harvey

ONE HUNDRED FAMOUS LOVE LYRICS. Collected by ——. New York, Sully & Co., 1926. xiv + 142p [LC NBSaM

TO MY PAL. Comp. by ——. Toronto, Ryerson, 1927. 95p [OTP

Hammond, George Arthur

EIGHTEEN BASIC QUESTIONS. Also "An Inquiry." Kingsclear, N.B., Lahstok Pub., 1900–1905. 12 + 36p [NSWA

FINAL [VARIOUS POEMS]. Kingsclear, N.B. Author, 1908. [Various pagings] [NSWA

THE HARP. York County, N.B., Author, 1869. 300p [OTUV

AN INQUIRY. "In a Moment–in the Twinkling of an Eye." Kingsclear, N.B., Lahstok Rustic Press, 1900. 36p [NSHPL

THE PILLAR OF WITNESS. Kingsclear, N.B., Lahstok Pub., 1899. 52p [OTUV

QUEEN VICTORIA'S OLIVE TREE, AND OTHER POEMS. London, Robert Banks, n.d. 82p [OTUV

RAYON. An Idyllic Vagary. Kingsclear, N.B., Lahstok Pub., 1901. 34p [NSWA OTUV

THE RECLUSE, AND OTHER POEMS. Kingsclear, N.B., Lahstok Pub., 1893. 10p [NSWA OTUV

A SERENADE. Lahstok, N.B., Rural Press, 1888. 102p [OTP

THE STORK, FLYING EASTWARD. [Kingsclear, N.B.] Rural Press, 1887. 56p [NSWA OTUV

A TRIAD. Lahstok, N.B., Rural Press, 1887. 3 parts in one. [Pt. 1: The Lake of Tears, an Allegory; Various Poems. Pt. 2: On the Strand, a Fable; Golden Circle Dirges. Pt. 3: Knud Iverson, a Dramatic Sketch; Twilight Cimmerian; Autumnal Musings; The Loiterer, a Fragment.] [OTP

Hannay, James, 1842–1910
BALLADS OF ACADIA. Saint John, Bowes, 1909. 47p [BVaU NBFU OTU
THE MAIDEN'S SACRIFICE. Saint John, 1909. 7p [Brown U BVaU NBFU OTU

Hansberger, Clara
LIGHTED LANTERNS. By Clara Hansberger, Evangeline Chapman, Alma Golling
  Barker [and others]. Moose Jaw, Mrs. G.C. Barker, [1943?]. 22p [Brown U
  OTU

Hardy, Edwin Austin, 1867–1952
SELECTIONS FROM THE CANADIAN POETS. Ed. by ———. Toronto, Morang, 1906.
  128p [Another ed.: Toronto, Macmillan, 1920. 128p] [BM BVaU NSHD
  OTP

Hargadon, Michael A., 1888–
AMONG THE MOUNTAINS. Montreal, Southam Press, 1925. 31p [OTP
IRISH AND CANADIAN POEMS. Montreal, Modern Print., 1921. 74p [BM BVaU
  OTP
A LOVELY HOME. [Verses.] Dublin & London, Maunsel, 1915. 75p [BM

Harlton, W.D.
A POEM ON GEOGRAPHY. Toronto, n.p., 1891. 16p [OTU

Harper, Alice, 1883–1935
COLOURED SAND. Vancouver, Mrs. E.E. Harper, [1938?]. 31p [BVaU

Harper, Constance Ward
THE MOON-MAN AND THE FAIRIES. Vancouver, Sun Pub. Co., n.d. 32p [BVaU
PATRIOTIC AND OTHER POEMS. Vancouver, Thomson, 1916. 64p [BM BVaU
  OTUV

Harper, John Murdoch, 1845–1919
THE ANNALS OF THE WAR. Illus. by a Selection of Historical Ballads. Toronto,
  Musson, 1913. 268p [BVaU LC NSHD OLU
THE BATTLE OF THE PLAINS. Quebec, 1895. 46p [BVaU NSWA OTUV
SACRAMENT SUNDAY. Montreal, 1894. 15p [CCJ
TRANSLATIONS IN VERSE FROM HOMER AND VIRGIL. Montreal, Dawson Bros.,
  1888. [Patrick cat. 30
WOLFE AND MONTCALM. Toronto, Copp Clark, n.d. 20p [NSHD OTUV

Harrington, Dorothy
LITTLE THINGS. Kitchener, Author, n.d. 22p [UTQ'46

Harrington, Michael Francis, 1916–
NEWFOUNDLAND TAPESTRY. Dallas, Tex., Kaleidograph Press, 1943. 80p [LC
POEMS OF NEWFOUNDLAND. This Volume Contains The Prize-Winning Poems in
  The O'Leary Newfoundland Poetry Award 1944–1952. Ed. by ———. St. John's,
  F.M. O'Leary, 1953. xix + 118p
THE SEA IS OUR DOORWAY. Toronto, Ryerson, 1947. 8p [BVaU NBFU OKQ

Harris, Lawren Stewart, 1885–1970
CONTRASTS. A Book of Verse. Toronto, McClelland, 1922. 125p [BM BVaU NSHD OKQ

Harris, Robert, 1849–1919
VERSES BY THE WAY. From an Artist's Sketch Book. Charlottetown, 1920. 89p [BVaU NBFU QMM

Harris, William Critchlow
OCCASIONAL POEMS. EARLY AND LATE. Charlottetown, Examiner, 1915. 69p [BVaU

Harrison, Edna Kent
THE LAMP, AND OTHER VERSE. London, Stockwell, [1929?]. 16p [Brown U NSHD OTU

Harrison, Elizabeth
A WHIP FOR TIME. Toronto, Macmillan, 1947. 28p [BVaU LC MWU OTP

Harrison, Stanley Gordon, 1889–
GENTLEMEN, –THE HORSE! Lexington, Ky., Thoroughbred Press, 1951. 88p
OMAR OF THE TURF. Lexington, Ky., Thoroughbred Press, 1950. 6p [OONL
SONGS OF THE PRAIRIE AND THE C.E.F. London, Macdonald, 1919. 72p [BM BVaU OTL

Harrison, Susie Frances (Riley), 1859–1935
THE CANADIAN BIRTHDAY BOOK. Comp. by Seranus [pseud]. Toronto, Blackett Robinson, 1887. 415p [BVaU NBFU OTP
FOUR BALLADS AND A PLAY. By Seranus [pseud]. N.p., 1933. 18p [OTP
IN NORTHERN SKIES, AND OTHER POEMS. By Seranus [pseud]. [Toronto? 1912?] 20p [OKQ
LATER POEMS AND NEW VILLANELLES. Toronto, Ryerson, 1928. 16p [BVaU NBSaM OTP
PENELOPE AND OTHER POEMS. By Seranus [pseud]. N.p., [19–?] 16p [OTP
PINE, ROSE AND FLEUR DE LIS. Toronto, Hart, 1891. 208p [BVaU LC NSHD OTP
SONG OF WELCOME IN HONOUR OF HIS EXCELLENCY, THE MARQUIS OF LANS-DOWNE, GOVERNOR-GENERAL OF CANADA. Written and Composed by Seranus [pseud]. Ottawa, Free Press, 1883. 8p [Brown U
SONGS OF LOVE AND LABOR. By Seranus [pseud]. Toronto, Author, [1925?]. 20p [BVaU NBFU OTP

Harshaw, Augusta F.
LAYS OF THE FIRESIDE. A Collection of Poems. Toronto, Musson, 1905. 90p [BVaU OTUV

Harvey, Emeline Daggett
MOODS AND TENSES. Chicago, priv. print., 1923. 53p [LC

Harvey, Peggy, 1884—
A WHIMSICAL VANCOUVERITE. N.p., n.p., [1936?]. 32p [BVaU

Harvey, William Earl, 1898—
BALLADS OF BATTLE. Vancouver, Roedde, 1941. 83p [BVaU LC OOP
BALLADS OF THE WEST. Vancouver, Pacific Print., 1920. 94p [BM BVaU OTU
SONGS OF AMERICA. Portland, Ore., Ryder, 1928. 66p [LC
SONGS OF THE WEST. St. Paul, Minn., Author, 1927. 68p [BVa LC

Haskins, James, 1805—1845
THE POETICAL WORKS OF JAMES HASKINS. Ed. by Henry Baldwin. Hartford,
   Parsons, 1848. 320p [BVaU OTP

Hatheway, Warren Franklin, 1850—1923
GOD AND THE DOUBTER. Saint John, Ellis Robertson, n.d. 19p [NBFU

Hatt, Daniel Elisha, 1869—1942
THE ALL SEASON RECITER. With Selections for Special Church Occasions.
   Toronto, Musson, 1924. 79p [AEU OTP
DIGBY CHICKENS.... By D.E.H. [pseud]. Digby, N.S., Courier Print., n.d. 18p
   [NBSaM
OKANAGAN. N.p., Vernon Press, n.d. 20p [BVaU NBSaM
OUTDOOR VERSE. ... Seattle, Teller Pub. Co., n.d. 64p [AEU BViPA
RANDOM RHYMES. Being a Collection of Dialect and Other Pieces. Summerland,
   B.C., Review, 1915. 39p [BM BVaU NSHPL
RELIGIOUS LYRICS. Vancouver, Wilson Bible & Tract Depot, n.d. 29p [BViPA
   NBFU OPAL QMU
SITKA SPRUCE. Songs of Queen Charlotte Islands. Thurston Harbour, B.C., Latta
   Co., 1918. 51p [BM BVaU NBFU OTUV

Hatzan, Alexander Leon, 1864—
MAM'SELLE L'ANGE VOX[!]; or, The Lady with the Angel Voice. A Poem Story
   of Love, Travel and Adventure. Niagara Falls, Mohawk Book, 1932. 177p
   [BM BVaU LC QMSS

Haughton, William
SILVICOLA; or, Songs from the Backwoods. Viroqua, Casson, 1878. 100p [OTUV

Haultain, Theodore Arnold, 1857—1941
VERSICULI. Toronto, Author, 1893. 32p [BVaU OTP

Haverson, James Percival, 1880—
SOUR SONNETS OF A SOREHEAD, AND OTHER SONGS OF THE STREET. Toronto,
   McLeod Allen, 1908. 62p [BM BVaU LC OTU QMSS

Haweis, Lionel Thomas Joy, 1870–1942

LITTLE LANTERNS. ... [Series 1] . Vancouver, Citizen Print., 1918. [64p]
[Printed on one side of page only.] [BVaU
LITTLE LANTERNS. ... [Series 2] . Vancouver, Citizen Print., 1924. [63p]
[Printed on one side of page only.] [BVaU NBFU
TSOQALEM. A Weird Indian Tale of the Cowichan Monster. A Ballad.
Vancouver, Citizen Print., 1918. 66p [BVaU NBFU OTP

Hawley, William Fitz, 1804–1855

QUEBEC, THE HARP, AND OTHER POEMS. Montreal, Herald and New Gazette,
1829. 172p [BVaU LC OTU QMM
THE UNKNOWN; or, Lays of the Forest. Montreal, Hoisington, 1831. 240p [BM
BVaU LC OKQ

Hayes, Catherine E. (Simpson), 1852–1943

DERBY DAY IN THE YUKON, AND OTHER POEMS OF THE NORTHLAND. By Yukon
Bill [pseud] . Toronto, Musson, 1910. 128p [BVaU OKQ QMM

Hayman, Robert, 1579?–1631?

QUODLIBETS LATELY COME OVER FROM NEW BRITANIOLA, OLD NEWFOUND-LAND.
EPIGRAMS, AND OTHER SMALL PARCELS, BOTH MORALL AND DIVINE. ... By
R.H., Sometimes Governour of the Plantation. ... London, Mitchell, 1628. 64p
[BM LC NBFU

Haynes, James

POEMS. Quebec, Hunter Rose, 1864. 152p [BVaU LC NSHD OLU QMBM

Haynes, Laura E. (Nixon), 1876–

COMING MY WAY? Ed. and Selected by Carl Eayrs. Ottawa, Tower Books, 1948.
99p [OOP
LANTERNS IN THE DUSK. St. Catharines, Falcon Print., 1944. 22p [OTP
PIONEERS. St. Catharines, Print. Shop, 1938. 48p [OTP
WHEN YOU AND I REMEMBER. N.p., n.d. 20p [OTP

Hayward, Mrs. Caroline

THE BATTLES OF THE CRIMEA, WITH OTHER POEMS. By Mrs. Alfred Hayward.
Port Hope, Ansley, 1855. 67p [BM BVaU OTP

Hazel, Emily, 1882–1955

THE BEAUTY OF THE EARTH AND OTHER POEMS. Ottawa, Author, 1952. 12p
FROM A HOSPITAL WINDOW. Ottawa, Author, 1950. 12p [OONL
HAPPY THOUGHTS AND OTHER POEMS. With A Children's Section. Ottawa,
Author, 1954. 18p
LOVELY BLOSSOMS AND OTHER POEMS. With a Children's Section. Ottawa,
Author, 1954. 24p
SIMPLE JOYS AND OTHER POEMS. Ottawa, Author, 1951. 12p

Hazelton, Mrs. Ruth Cleaves
MINT AND WILLOW. ... Toronto, Ryerson, 1952. 12p

Hazlemere, Robert
"GLORY AND LOVELINESS HAVE PASSED AWAY." A Choric Ode. Vancouver,
1928. 2p [OKQ
STARRY EARTH. A Book of Poems and Lyrics. Toronto, McClelland, 1929.
80p [BVaU NSHD QMBM

Hazlewood, Hetty
A GARLAND GATHERED AT MORN. A Collection of Short Poems. Toronto,
Hunter, 1871. 79p [BVaU OKQ

Heath, John, 1917–1951
APHRODITE. Toronto, Ryerson, 1958. 24p

Heaton, Hugh
THE STORY OF ALBERT THE CAMEL'S SON. Toronto, Heaton, 1936. 39p [BM
THE STORY OF MADAM HEN AND LITTLE HORACE. Toronto, Heaton, 1935. 37p
[BM BVaU LC NBFU OONL

Heavysege, Charles, 1816–1876
THE DARK HUNTSMAN (A Dream). Montreal, Witness Press, 1864. 8p [A poem
with same title pub. in *The Canadian Monthly & National Review*, 10:134-135
(Aug. 1876).] [OONL
JEPHTHAH'S DAUGHTER [and Twenty Sonnets]. Montreal, Dawson, 1865. 74p
[BM BVaU MWU NSHD OKQ
THE OWL. Montreal, 1864. 4p [CCJ
THE REVOLT OF TARTARUS. A Poem. [Anon] Liverpool, Hamilton, 1852.
[Also: Montreal, 1853.] [BM BVaU
SONNETS. By the Author of THE REVOLT OF TARTARUS. Montreal, Rose, 1855.
61p [OLU

Hedges, Doris (Ryde), 1900–
CRISIS. Toronto, Ryerson, 1947. 8p [BVaU MWU NBFU OKQ
THE DREAM IS CERTAIN. Boston, Christopher Pub. Hse., 1954. 32p
THE FLOWER IN THE DUSK. Toronto, Ryerson, 1946. 8p [BVaU LC MWU
NBSaM OKQ
WORDS ON A PAGE, AND OTHER POEMS. Toronto, Ryerson, 1949. 42p [BVaU
LC OTP

Heffernan, W.E.
NOVA SCOTIA: WARBLINGS OF THE WILDWOOD. Springhill, N.S., Jones, 1906.
218p [BVaU

Hemsley, Stuart Davidson, 1905–
BEASTLY BALLADS. By Stuart Davidson Hemsley and James Simpkins. Toronto,
Burns & MacEachern, 1954. 61p

Henderson, Christine Margaret (Lighthall), 1868–1968

THE BLUE JAY'S MESSAGE, AND OTHER POEMS. Montreal, Author, 1934. 8p [BVaU

OUR VOLUNTEERS, AND OTHER POEMS. Montreal, Author, 1940. 8p [CC

SHIP'S WAKE AND ROAD'S LURE. Montreal, Lovell, 1937. 102p [BVaU NBFU OTU QMM

THOUGHTFUL PETIE'S ADVENTURES, AND OTHER POEMS. New York, Banner, 1939. 42p [OTU

THE UNWELCOME GUEST, AND OTHER POEMS. Montreal, Author, [1931?]. 8p [CC

Henderson, Edith Beatrice

OUTWARD BOUND. Toronto, Ryerson, 1930. 8p [BVaU NBSaM OKQ

Henderson, W.R., 1876–

HENDY'S NORTHERN SPASMS. Flin Flon, Man., Flin Flon Miner, 1931. 25p [MWP

Henry, Eileen Cameron, 1908?–

SEA-WOMAN AND OTHER POEMS. Toronto, Ryerson, 1945. 8p [BVaU LC NBSaM OTP

Henry, James

SONGS BY THE WAY. Montreal, "Witness," 1892. 159p [BVaU NSHD

Henry, Marion Kathleen (Waddell), 1893–

CENTAURS OF THE WIND. Toronto, Ryerson, 1956. 12p

Henry, Mrs. P.A.

SELECTIONS FROM THE WRITINGS OF MRS. P.A. HENRY. Bowmanville, n.d. 13p [OTUV

Hensley, Sophia Margaret (Almon), 1866–

THE HEART OF A WOMAN [Poems]. By Almon Hensley. London, Putman, 1906. 175p [BM LC

POEMS. (For Private Circulation). By Sophie M. Almon. Windsor, N.S., Anslow, 1889. 18p [BVaU NSHD OTU

THE WAY OF A WOMAN, AND OTHER POEMS. By Sophia Margeretta Hensley. San Diego, Canterbury Co., 1928. 112p [LC NSHPL

A WOMAN'S LOVE LETTERS [Poems]. By Sophie M. Almon-Hensley. New York, Tait, 1895. 82p [LC NSHPL OTUV QMM

Herbert, George

MISCELLANEOUS POEMS AND SONGS. [Fredericton?], Author, 1885. 32p [OTUV

Herbert, Sarah, 1824–1844

THE AEOLIAN HARP; or, Miscellaneous Poems. By Sarah Herbert and Mary E. Herbert. Halifax, Fuller, 1857. 237p [BM BVaU NSHD OTP

Herbin, John Frederic, 1860–1923
CANADA AND OTHER POEMS. Windsor, N.S., Anslow, 1891. 12p [BVaU NSHD OTP
THE MARSHLANDS. A Souvenir in Song of the Land of Evangeline. Windsor, N.S., Anslow, 1893. 33p [BVaU NSHD OTUV
THE MARSHLANDS, AND THE TRAIL OF THE TIDE. Toronto, Briggs, 1899. 99p [3rd ed.: Toronto, Briggs, 1909. 124p] [BM BVaU NSHD OKQ

Herriman, Dorothy Choate, 1901–
MATER SILVA. With Decorations by the Author. Toronto, McClelland, 1929. 72p [BVaU NBFU OTUV

Herron, David Henry
HABITANT NUGGETS. Cobalt, Daily Nugget Print., 1910. 64p [NBFU
HABITANT NUGGETS. Cobalt, Dailly Nugget Print., [192–?]. 33p [BM Brown U OOP

Hezzelwood, Oliver, 1861–1933
IN THE ESTUARY, AND OTHER POEMS. Toronto, Davis, 1933. 79p [BVaU OTP
POEMS. And a Play: "The Invisible Urge." Toronto, Ontario Press, 1926. 168p [BVaU OKQ QMM

Hibbert, William, 1901?–
OUT OF THE PIT. Drumheller, Alta., Drumheller Mail, 1948. 116p [AC

Hickson, A. Beatrice
POEMS, 1916. By A.B.H. N.p., 1916. 18p [BM Brown U NSHD

Higginson, Thomas, 1794–1884
POETICAL WORKS. Vankleek Hill, Ont., Otto, 1888. [Bound with writings of Thomas H. Higginson (Persolus) entitled THE LITERARY WORKS OF T.H. HIGGINSON] 2v in 1. [BVaU NSWA OTU QMM

Higginson, Thomas Boyd, 1912–
JUVENILIA. London, Mitre Press, [1960?]. 31p

Higinbotham, John David, 1864–1961
FOOTHILL AND PRAIRIE MEMORIES. A Group of Poems. N.p., n.d. 32p [ACG OKQ

Hill, Thomas, –1860
THE CONSTITUTIONAL LYRIST. Fredericton, "Loyalist" Office, 1845. 240p [CCJ NBB

Hiltz, W.W.
MORE VERSES. Toronto, [Regal Stationery], 1931. 45p [BVaU OTU QMU
VERSES OF A CONVALESCENT. Toronto, 1929. 45p [Brown U BVaU NBFU OTUV

Hindley, Rev. John Ingham, 1842—
INDIAN LEGENDS: Nanabush, the Objibbeway Saviour; Moosh-kuh-ung, or The
Flood. [Barrie? Ont.] , 1885. 22p [BVaU LC OLU

Hine, William Daryl, 1936—
THE CARNAL AND THE CRANE. Toronto, Contact Press, 1957. 50p
THE DEVIL'S PICTURE BOOK. Poems. New York, Abelard-Schuman, 1960. 31p
FIVE POEMS, 1954. Toronto, 1954. 13p (Emblem Books)

Hodgins, James Cobourg, 1866—1953
FUGITIVES. Toronto, Rose, 1891. 16p [OTUV
A SHEAF OF SONNETS. Philadelphia, Franklin Print., 1896. 22p [BVaU LC

Hodgson, Alice Muriel (Neve)
SOME GOLDEN MEMORIES. Lachute, Watchman Print., 1944. 71p [AEU QMU

Hoey, Willa
A BOOK OF VERSES. Toronto, Garden City Press, 1931. 15p [OTU

Hogan, Anastasia
SELECTION OF POEMS. St. John's, Nfld., Milligan, n.d. 146p [NSfG OTP

Hogarth, Thomas William
BULL TERRIER DOGGEREL. Galashiels, Scot., Walker, 1937. 30p [BM LC

Hogg, James, 1800—1866
POEMS. Religious, Moral and Sentimental. Saint John, Chubb, 1825. 228p
[NBFU OTP

Holland, Norah Mary, 1876—1925
SPUN-YARN AND SPINDRIFT. Toronto, Dent, 1918. 96p [BM BVaU NBFU
OKQ QMM
WHEN HALF GODS GO, AND OTHER POEMS. Toronto, Macmillan, 1924. 124p
[BVaU LC NSHD OKQ QMM

Holman, Carrie Ellen, 1877—
IN THE DAY OF BATTLE. Poems of the Great War. Comp. by ——. Toronto,
Briggs, 1916. 166p [3rd ed.: 1918. 224p (Contains first pub. of McCrae's
"In Flanders Fields").] [LC NBFU OTU

Holmes, Vincent, 1929—
QUIET ENTRY. Victoria, B.C., Author, 1956. 7p

Honohan, Laura M.
POEMS. N.p., n.d. [c1945?]. 244p [Adelphi cat. 68

Hood, Robert Allison, 1880—1958
BALLADS OF THE PACIFIC NORTH-WEST. Toronto, Ryerson, 1946. 170p [BVaU
LC NBFU OKQ QMM

BY SHORE AND TRAIL IN STANLEY PARK. ... Toronto, McClelland, 1929. 156p
[BVaU NSHD OTP
VIGNETTES OF VANCOUVER. Vancouver, Education Services, 1954. ix + 84p

Hooke, Alfred John, 1905–
A TRIBUTE TO HON. E.C. MANNING ON THE OCCASION OF HIS 50TH BIRTHDAY
PARTY, SEPTEMBER 30TH, 1958. ... Edmonton, Alberta Social Credit League,
1958. 4p

Hooker, Rev. LeRoy, 1840–1906
STANLEY. A Christmas Ballad by Jason and Boaz. Toronto, 1882. 14p [CCJ

Hoople, Carrie (Munson)
ALONG THE WAY WITH PEN AND PENCIL. New York, Grafton Press, 1909. 213p
[LC OTUV

Hope, M.L.
FRAGMENTS. Toronto, Briggs, 1911. 32p [BM BVaU
INDIAN AND OTHER TALES. Toronto, Briggs, 1911. 21p [BM BVaU OKQ

Hopkins, Elizabeth Nuttall
THOUGHTS IN VERSE. With a preface by Professor William Clark. Toronto, Briggs,
1906. 54p [BM Brown U BVaU OTP

Hopper, Clara
THE EMIGRANT'S STONE, AND OTHER POEMS. Toronto, Ryerson, 1932. 8p
[BVaU NBSaM OKQ QMM

Horan, John William, 1908–
SONGS OF THE NORTH. Stories in Verse of Life Down under the Midnight Sun of
North Western Canada. Edmonton, Nor'West Miner, 1940. 40p [2nd ed.:
Edmonton, Sterling, 1942. 54p] [OKQ QMM
YELLOWKNIFE; " 'Til the Ice-Worms Nest Again." With Selected Poems taken
from "Songs of the North." Edmonton, Northgate Books, 1947. 47p [BVaU
OTU QMBM

Horne, Winnifred Alice
POEMS. Ottawa, 1960. 23p

Hornsell, William
THE ICE-BOUND SHIP, and THE DREAM. By W.H. [pseud]. Montreal, Rose, 1860.
48p [OTP

Hornyansky, Michael Sands, 1927–
THE QUEEN OF SHEBA. The Newdigate Prize Poem, 1951. Oxford, Blackwell,
1951. 13p

Hosie, John, 1880—1934
THE ARBUTUS TREE, AND OTHER POEMS. Toronto, Ryerson, 1929. 8p [BVaU
NBSaM OKQ QMM

Houghton, Frank Llewellyn, 1897—
QUARTERDECK DITTIES. By Deadlight [pseud]. Printed for Private Circulation
only. Ottawa, Author, 1948. 30p [OONL

Houghton, Levi
MY TRIP THROUGH THE ROCKIES. [verses and illustrations.] Victoria, 1917.
n.p. [BM
VERSES ON EVERYDAY LIFE. Written Chiefly by Request, in the Calgary General
Hospital. By a Calgary Old-Timer. ... N.p., n. pub., [1916?]. 20p [Enlarged
ed., Victoria, 1918. 31p] [AEU BM BVaU
VICTORIA THE BEAUTIFUL. [verses and illustrations.] Victoria, 1917. n.p.
[BM BViPA

Houliston, George B.
POEMS. ... Three Rivers, Que., [1889?]. 12p [Brown U

Howard, Blanche Muirhead
REACH FOR A STAR. Toronto, Ryerson, 1951. 10p

Howard, Dorothy
AS THE RIVER RUNS. Toronto, Ryerson, 1947. 8p [BVaU NBFU OTU
A CHILD CAME LAUGHING. N.p., [194—?]. 20p [OKQ
WHEN I TURN HOME. Toronto, Ryerson, 1945. 8p [BVaU LC OTP

Howard, Hilda (Glynn), 1887—
ALONG THE ROAD TO HAZELTON. By H. Glynn-Ward [pseud]. London, Mitre
Press, 1960. 56p
THE PIONEERS AND OTHER POEMS. By H. Glynn-Ward [pseud]. Toronto,
Ryerson, 1940. 12p [BVaU LC NBSaM OTP QMM

Howe, Joseph, 1804—1873
THE MAY-FLOWER OF NOVA SCOTIA. Halifax, June 8, 1840. Halifax, Nova
Scotia Philanthropic Soc., 1840. 1p [NSHD
A POEM ON THE SAME SUBJECT. [Sable Island]. Halifax, Wesleyan Conference
Steam Press, 1858. [Bound with SABLE ISLAND (pp.31-34), by John Bernard
Gilpin, q.v.] [BM LC NSWA OTP QMM

Howey, William, 1883—
CALIFORNIA CAROLS. Toronto, 1927. 111p [Brown U BVaU OTU
CANADIAN CAROLS. Toronto, Ryerson, 1926. 117p [BVaU OTP
CAROLS AND CAMEOS. ... Toronto, Ryerson, 1927. 124p [BVaU LC NBFU
OKQ

A VISIT TO FAIRYLAND, AND LEGENDS OF NATURE. Toronto, Ryerson, 1928. 125p [BVaU OTU

Howley, Rev. Michael Francis, 1843–1914
POEMS AND OTHER VERSES. New York, Fisher, 1903. 122p [OOSU QMM

Howse, Beulah Virginia, 1905–
POEM PICTURES OF CANADA. Ilfracombe, Devon, Stockwell, 1956. 46p

Howson, George J.
A COLLECTION OF ORIGINAL ACROSTICS ON LADIES' CHRISTIAN NAMES. Toronto, Hunter Rose, 1888. [OONL

Hudson, Dunbar Hibbard
SONGS OF A CHEERFUL WAYFARER. Toronto, Author, 1926. 124p [BVaU

Hudson, Reba Marguerite
BRIEF FOR BEAUTY. Toronto, Macmillan, 1946. 28p [BM BVaU LC OTP

Hughes, Aubrey Dean
ARGOSIES AT DAWN. Toronto, Ryerson, 1931. 8p [BVaU NBSaM OKQ

Hughes, James Laughlin, 1846–1935
CHESTER HUGHES. N.p., n.d. 15p [Poems by J.L. Hughes in memory of his son.] [OTU
THE CHILD'S PARADISE. Stories and Musings for Parents and Teachers. Toronto, Ryerson, 1919. 127p [BM BVaU NBFU OTU
GOD MADE THEM GOOD. True Stories of the So-called "Bad." Toronto, Allen, 1922. 127p [OKQ QMU
IN NATURE'S TEMPLE SHRINES. Toronto, Allen, 1921. 127p [BVaU NSHD OTP QMBM
LIFE'S GLORIES. Toronto, Gundy, 1926. 292p [Also: Boston, Stratford, 1929. 365p] [BVaU LC OTP
LOVE MEMORIES. Toronto, Warwick, 1919. 127p [BVaU
MY SUNSHINE BOOK. Toronto, Allen, 1923. 127p [BVaU OKQ QMM
NEW SONGS OF GLADNESS. N.p., 1916. 64p [BVaU OTP QMM
RAINBOWS ON WAR CLOUDS. Syracuse, Bradeen, 1919. 112p [BVaU LC NBFU OKQ
SONGS OF GLADNESS. N.p., 1914. 32p [Also: same title, dated 1915, unpaged.] [AEU OTP QMU
SONGS OF GLADNESS AND GROWTH. Toronto, Briggs, 1916. 247p [BM BVaU NSHD OKQ
SONGS OF LIFE AND GROWTH. N.p., 1912. 32p [BVaU OTU
STORIES AND MUSINGS. Toronto, Briggs, 1917. 99p [BM BVaU LC OKQ

Hughes, Robert, 1882—
RHYMES–FOR THE TIMES–AND OTHER TIMES. Toronto, Author, [195–?]. 76p

Humphrey, Mrs. Muriel Miller
TWENTY SONNETS. Toronto, Ryerson, 1932. 11p [BVaU NSHD OKQ QMM

Hunt, Anna Rebecca (Gale)
IN BOHEMIA AND OTHER STUDIES FOR POEMS. By Mrs. T. Sterry Hunt ("Cana-
dienne"). Toronto, Briggs, 1900. 189p [Rev. ed.: 1905. 173p] [BM BVaU
OKQ QMM
STUDIES FOR POEMS. By Claude Berwick [pseud]. Boston, Marvin, n.d. 146p
[BVaU QMSS

Hunter, Alexander Jardine, 1868–1940
THE KOBZAR OF THE UKRAINE. Being Select Poems of Taras Shevchenko done
into English Verse with Biographical Fragments by Alexander Jardine Hunter.
Teulon, Man., Hunter, 1922. 144p [BM Brown U BVaU

Hunter, D.J.
HELLO, FELLOWS! HAVE YOU READ MY RHYMES? ... They're Different. "A
Tussle" with the Bulls and Bears in the Stock Market Arena rippled into Raw,
Rough and Ripping Rhymes, specially rhythm'd for Unsophisticated and
Hardboiled Male and Female Speculators. ... Toronto, Hunter-Rose, 1933.
57p [BVaU OTU

Husband, Mrs. S. Berthe, 1891—
ALTAR FLOWERS. London, Ont., Author, 1936. 32p [OLU

Hutchinson, Rev. Daniel Falloon
SATISFACTION OF JUSTICE. A Poem. Kingston, 1851. 50p [CCJ

Hutchison, Thomas
MASONIC AND MISCELLANEOUS POEMS. North Vancouver, Author, 1932. 46p
[BVaU

Huxtable, Horace L.
THE FOUNTAIN. A Dramatic Fantasy. Toronto, Ryerson, 1929. 12p [BVaU
NBSaM OKQ QMM

Hynes, Marie J. McGee
THE BARD'S MINSTRELSY. Toronto, Mission Press, 1951. 24p

Imrie, John, 1846–1902
A BOUQUET OF SONNETS FOR THOUGHTFUL MOMENTS. Toronto, Imrie &
Graham, [18—?]. 32p [OTP
NEW POEMS. Toronto, 1900. 100p [T&C

SACRED SONGS, SONNETS AND MISCELLANEOUS POEMS. Toronto, Imrie & Graham, 1886. 210p [Several later editions.] [BVaU MWU NSHD OKQ

A SELECTION OF READINGS AND SONGS FROM THE WORKS OF JOHN IMRIE. 4th ed. Toronto, Imrie & Graham, 1899. 96p [BM Brown U OTUV

SONGS AND MISCELLANEOUS POEMS. Toronto, Imrie & Graham, 1891. 348p [5th ed.: Toronto, 1906.] [BM BVaU LC OTP

Ingersoll, William Ernest

THE AIR VOYAGER. Boston, Badger, 1902. [AmCat

Ingraham, Mary (Kinley), 1874–1949

A MONTH OF DREAMS. Wolfville, N.S., Author, 1932. [unpaged] [NSWA

Innes, John, 1864–1941

TRAGEDY OF THE SWAY-BACKED PINTO. Vancouver, Paton, 1920. 24p [BM BVaU OKQ

Inness, Capt. W.A.

RHYMES OF THE R.N.C.V.R., AND OTHER VERSES. Halifax, Weeks, 1919. 63p [BM OOP

Isard, Mrs. Elizabeth Anne

WAYSIDE SONGS. Newmarket, Ont., Era, 1896. 224p [BM BVaU OKQ

Isles-Brown, Mrs. Esme

TWELVE POEMS. Toronto, Ryerson, 1927. 8p [BVaU NBSaM OKQ

Ivey, John F.

THE FIELDS OF YESTERDAY. Cobourg, 1935. 76p [Brown U OTU

Jack, Annie L. (Hayr), 1839–1912

BELATED VIOLETS. N.p., n.d. 4p [OTUV

RHYME-THOUGHTS FOR A CANADIAN YEAR. Toronto, Briggs, 1904. 12p [BM BVaU OTP

Jackson, Isa Grindlay

BALLADES AND BITS. Toronto, Ryerson, 1937. 54p [BVaU OTP

Jackson, Katherine H. (McDonald)

SUMMER SONGS IN IDLENESSE. Toronto, Briggs, 1903. 71p [BVaU NBFU OTUV

Jacobs, Rev. Peter, 1808–1858

A COLLECTION OF OJIBWAY HYMNS. Trans. by ——. Ed. by the Rev. John Jacobs. Sarnia, Sarnia Canadian, 1886. 191p [BVaU NSWA OTP

Jacombe, Grace M.

CHALK DUST. Ottawa, Tower Books, 1950. 40p [OONL

Jakeway, Charles Edwin, 1847–1906
THE LION AND THE LILIES, A TALE OF THE CONQUEST, AND OTHER POEMS.
  Toronto, Briggs, 1897. 278p [BM BVaU NBFU OTU QMM

James, William T., 1861–
RHYMES AFLOAT AND AFIELD. Toronto, James, 1891. 144p [BVaU NBFU
  OKQ

Jameson, Edward A.
POEMS. Toronto, Hilda M. Ridley, 1951. 18p (Carillon Poetry Chap-Books)

Janes, Lemuel Willey, 1889–
ADVENTURES IN VERSE. N.p., 1932. 52p [OTU
SEA MOODS AND OTHER POEMS. [Montreal? 1936?]. 15p [Brown U
WHEN SHADOWS FALL. [Montreal?], Author, 1937. 16p [Brown U OONL
WHISPERING WINDS. N.p., [193–?]. 12p [MWU OONL

Jaques, Edna, 1891–
AUNT HATTIE'S PLACE. Toronto, Allen, 1941. 80p [BM BVaU LC NBFU OTU
BACKDOOR NEIGHBORS. Toronto, Allen, 1946. 80p [BVaU OTP
BESIDE STILL WATERS. Toronto, Allen, 1939. 88p [BVaU LC OTP
BRITONS AWAKE. Toronto, Allen, 1940. 19p [BM BVaU NBFU OTU
DREAMS IN YOUR HEART. Toronto, Allen, 1937. 78p [BM BVaU NBFU OTP
DRIFTING SOIL. Moose Jaw, "Times," 1935. 19p [Earlier ed., 1934.] [Brown U
FIRESIDE POEMS. Toronto, Allen, 1950. 88p [BVaU OTP
THE GOLDEN ROAD. Toronto, Allen, 1953. 86p
HILLS OF HOME. Toronto, Allen, 1948. 80p [BVaU OTP
MY KITCHEN WINDOW. Toronto, Allen, 1935. 83p [BM BVaU LC NBFU OTU
ROSES IN DECEMBER. Toronto, Allen, 1944. 86p [BVaU LC OTP
WIDE HORIZONS. Moose Jaw, "Times," 1935. 20p [Earlier ed., 1934.] [BVaU

Jardine (pseud)
THOUGHTS OF HAPPY BOYHOOD. Saint John, McMillan, 1902. 121p [NBFU

Jarvis, Charlotte (Beaumont), 1803–1875
LEAVES FROM ROSEDALE. Toronto, Briggs, 1905. 132p [BM BVaU NBFU
  OTP

Jefferson, Marie Neilson
WILD WATERS AND PINE. Sketches in Verse of the St. Maurice Valley. Three
  Rivers, 1938. 34p [Brown U OTU

Jefferson, Robert, 1856–
SASKATCHEWAN VERSE. Battleford, Sask., Battleford Press, [1930?]. 108p
  [BVaU OKQ SSU

Jenkins, Mariel
BEAUTY FOR ASHES. Toronto, Crucible Press, 1943. 40p [LC OTP
LAKE ON THE MOUNTAIN. Toronto, Author, 1937. 20p [OKQ

Jenkins, Robert Smith, 1870—1931
CANADIAN POEMS. The Poetical Works of ——. Ed. by Mrs. R.S. Jenkins.
Toronto, McClelland, 1939. 285p [BM BVaU LC NBFU OTP
POEMS OF THE NEW CENTURY. First Series. Minor Lyric and Narrative Poems.
Toronto, Briggs, 1903. 173p [BM BVaU LC NSHD OTP QMM

Jennings, Clotilda, —1895
LINDEN RHYMES. By Maude [pseud]. Halifax, Fuller, 1854. 152p [BVaU
NSHD OTP
NORTH MOUNTAIN, NEAR GRAND-PRE. By Mileta [pseud]. [N.p.?], 1883. [CCJ

Jenns, Eustace Alvenley
EVENING TO MORNING, AND OTHER POEMS. Victoria, Hibben, 1880. 33p [BVaU
ORPHEUS AND EURYDICE, AND OTHER POEMS. Vancouver, News-Advertiser,
1910. 110p [Brown U BVaU

Jerdon, Gertrude
FLOWERING THORNS. London, Nisbet, 1886. 63p [BM BVaU OTUV

Jerningham, Rosa (Bell) and John
MRS. JERNINGHAM'S JOURNAL; AND JOHN JERNINGHAM'S JOURNAL. Toronto,
Canadian News, 1871. 192p [NSWA OWtU

Johnson, Albert Edward, 1902?—
THE CROWN AND THE LAUREL. Oxford, G. Ronald, 1953. 34p
IN A SUMMER SEASON. Syracuse, Syracuse U. Bookstore, 1927. 47p [BVaU LC
OKQ
POEMS. Syracuse, Syracuse U. Bookstore, 1925. 48p [BVaU LC OKQ
POEMS. New York, Syracuse U. Bookstore, 1925. 4p [OKQ
WHEN THOU HAST SHUT THE DOOR. Portland, Falmouth, 1939. 49p [LC
A WINNIPEG CHAPBOOK. Winnipeg, Veteran Press, 1923. 13p [BVaU NBFU
OKQ

Johnson, Charles H.
THE STORY THAT NEVER GROWS OLD. Wolfville, N.S., Davidson, 1944. 76p [OTP

Johnson, Charles Nelson, 1860—
POEMS OF THE FARM AND OTHER POEMS. Chicago, Daniels, 1901. 75p [LC

Johnson, Emily Pauline, 1862—1913
"AND HE SAID, 'FIGHT ON'." Toronto, Musson, 1913. 6p [OONL
CANADIAN BORN. Toronto, Morang, 1903. 67p [BM BVaU NBFU OTP
FLINT AND FEATHER. With short Biographical Sketch. ... Toronto, Musson,
[1912]. 156p [Various later eds.] [BVaU NSHD OKQ QMM
FLINT AND FEATHER. Complete Poems. With Intro. by Theordore Watts-Dunton
and a Biographical Sketch of the Author. Toronto, Musson, [1924]. 176p
[BVaU NSHD OTP QMM
IN THE SHADOWS. Gouverneur, N.Y., priv. print., 1898. 4p [NBFU

LEGEND OF SIWASH ROCK. Vancouver, Vancouver Business & Professional Women's Club, 1952. 8p

OJISTOH. Illustrated Indian Woman Monologue. New York, Werner, 1911. 39p [LC

"WHEN GEORGE WAS KING," AND OTHER POEMS. Brockville, "Times," 1908. 11p [BVaU NSHD OTP

THE WHITE WAMPUM. London, Lane, 1895. 88p [BVaU LC NBFU OKQ QMM

Johnson, Frank

LASHED TO THE MIZZEN; or, A Night off the Cape. Montreal, Lovell, 1872. 19p [First pub. in 1867?–*cf.* BCF. London ed., 1877.] [BM BVaU QMSS

Johnson, Garland

FROM CHILDHOOD TO WOMANHOOD IN ONTARIO. Toronto, Best Print., 1936. 27p [AEU OTUV QMU

Johnson, George Washington, 1839–1917

MAPLE LEAVES. Hamilton, Author, 1864. 202p [BVaU OTP

SUMMARY OF CANADIAN HISTORY IN RHYME. Toronto, Educational Pub. Co., 1908. 15p [Brown U BVaU OONL

Johnson, Helen Mar, 1834–1863

POEMS. Boston, Himes, 1855. 249p [OONL

Johnson, Mrs. Herrick

THE SHADOW OF THE ROCK AND THE VOICE IN THE TWILIGHT. [Two Poems.] Toronto, Hart & Rawlinson, n.d. 14p [QMU

Johnston, Albert Richard, 1917–

FOLK SONGS OF CANADA. Arr. by Richard Johnston. Ed. by Gordon Hallett. [Piano solo ed.] Waterloo, Ont., Waterloo Music. Co., 1957. 24p

Johnston, George Benson, 1913–

THE CRUISING AUK. Toronto, Oxford U. Press, 1959. 72p

Johnston, Katherine Leila

OVER THE THRESHOLD AND OTHER POEMS. ... Toronto, Ryerson, 1922. 53p [BM BVaU NBFU OTP

Johnston, Rev. Minton C.

THE STILL SMALL VOICE. Montreal, Author, 1938. 16p [OTU

Johnston, Thomas

CANADIAN AND SCOTTISH SONGS AND POEMS. Calgary, Author, 1920. 149p [BViPA

Johnston, William, 1840–1917

CANADIAN MELODIES AND MISCELLANEOUS POEMS. Stratford, Ont., Beacon, 1909. 212p [Brown U BVaU OTU

Johnston-Smith, Frederick James
THE UNION JACK. What It is and What It Means. With Twelve Lyrics. Toronto, n.d.
38p [Brown U

Johnstone, Rev. John
A VISION OF IMMANUEL. Toronto, Briggs, 1906. 65p [BVaU NSHD OTUV

Jones, Douglas Gordon, 1929–
FROST ON THE SUN. Toronto, Contact Press, 1957. 46p

Jones, Ellen Lavinia (Clutterbuck), 1888–
CAROLS OLD AND NEW. [Calgary?], 1939. [Rhod p926

Jones, James Edmund, 1866–1939
CAMP-FIRE CHORUSES. Songs Old and New that Everyone can Sing. Comp. by ——.
Toronto, Oxford, 1916. 133p [BM BVaU NBFU OTU
THE LAST SUPPER AND GETHSEMANE. In Two Parts. Toronto, My Friends' Book
& Gift Shop, 1927. 67p [OLU

Jones, K.L.
MEETING OF THE WATERS. Kingston, n.d. [Rhod p868

Jones, Lily Edwards
WOODLAND SONGS. Hamilton, Hamilton Typesetting, 1936. 96p [BVaU OH

Jones, William Griffith, 1914–
JINGLES FROM THE JONESES. Ponoka, Alta., Herald, 1952. 52p

Joseph, Alexander Callow, 1886–1958
BANG. Explosions in Verse. By Al Pat [pseud]. With Reprints from his Last Book
RHYMES OF AN OLD WAR HORSE. Trenton, Ont., Author, 1944. 64p [OTP
RHYMES OF AN OLD WAR HORSE. By Al Pat [pseud]. 1938 Canadian Corps
Reunion ed. Toronto, Author, 1938. 31p [2nd ed., Toronto, Southam, 1955.
40p] [OTUV
ROGER. ... A Collection of Verse & Yarns from "The Troops." By Al Pat [pseud].
Toronto, Author, 1946–1947. 2 parts. [OTP

Joussaye, Marie
SELECTIONS FROM ANGLO-SAXON SONGS. Dawson, Dawson News. Pub., [1920?].
56p [NSWA OONL
THE SONGS THAT QUINTE SANG. Belleville, Sun, 1895. 91p [BVaU NBFU OTP
QMM

Joy, G.F.
PRAIRIE CHICKENS. In Memoriam G.E.S. By Chanticleer [pseud]. London, Stockwell, 1908. 32p [OONL

Joynes, Agnes
THE SHEPHERD OF THE HILLS. Toronto, Ryerson, 1926. 8p [BM BVaU NBSaM
OTP QMM

Judge, May Edith Perceval

THE BLUE-WALLED VALLEY. Toronto, Ryerson, 1929. 8p [BVaU NBFU OKQ QMM

KINDREDSHIP AND OTHER POEMS. Vancouver, Clarke & Stuart, 1944. 30 p [BVaU OKQ

THE WAY TO FAIRYLAND, AND OTHER RHYMES. Toronto, Ryerson, 1931. 16p [BVaU NBFU OKQ QMM

Julien, Henri Octave, 1852–1908

SONGS OF THE BY-TOWN COONS. [Anon] Montreal, Montreal Star, [1899?]. 26p [OTU

Kaye, Leslie Lonker, 1936–

THE McGILL CHAPBOOK. Ed. by ——. Toronto, Ryerson, 1959. 28p

Kearney, W.D.

AN EPIC POEM ENTITLED "THE OPEN HAND." An Indian Tale of Maine and New Brunswick, Founded on Historical Facts and Sustained by Tradition. Presque Isle, Me., Gilman, 1864. 58p [Reprinted under title: THE OPEN HAND. An Epic Poem dealing with the Early Settlement of Maine and New Brunswick. ... Hartland, N.B., Stevens, 1920. 58p [BVaU LC NBFU OTP

Kearns, Rose Anne (or, Anne Rose)

LYRICS, GRAVE AND GAY. Little Poems for Many Moods. N.p., Seagers Press, 1943. 36p [OKQ

LYRICS OF LOVE AND LAUGHTER. Toronto, 1933. 30p [Brown U OTUV

Keating, James W.

AN EPIC POEM: THE NORTON HOUSE. St. Catharines, March 3rd, 1886. St. Catharines, Sherwood, 1886. 14p [AEU

Kelland, Otto Paul, 1904–

ANCHOR WATCH. Newfoundland Stories in Verse. St. John's, 1960. 123p

Kelley, Frank Mortimore, 1875–

FIREWEED. With the Season's Greetings. N.p., Author, [1945?]. 12p [AEU OPAL

Kemp, Ernest Arthur, 1888–

FROM SEA TO SEA. Poems. Ilfracombe, Devon, Stockwell, 1959. 47p

Kennedy, A. Allison

WISPS. Lyrics and other Verse. Toronto, Burns & MacEachern, 1956. 70p

Kennedy, Leo, 1907–

NEW PROVINCES. Poems of Several Authors. [Ed. by F.R. Scott.] Toronto Macmillan, 1936. 77p [Contains poems by Kennedy and others.] [BVaU NBFU OKQ

THE SHROUDING. Poems. Toronto, Macmillan, 1933. 59p [BM BVaU LC OKQ QMM

Kent, Thomas
THE HARP OF PROPHECY. London, Ont., Author, 1910. 39p [OTP QMU

Kenvyn, Ronald
WATERFRONT WAILS, AND OTHER VERSES. Vancouver, Cowan & Brookhouse, 1918. 44p [BM BVaU

Keogh, W.O.
POEMS OF A CANADIAN PIONEER FAMILY [by Mary Nolan (Brown) Keogh (Mrs. T.A.), Alice B. Keogh, and Lucius R. Keogh]. Comp. by ——. [Anon] N.p., [1921?]. 120p [BM BVaU OKQ

Keough, Walter James, 1881—
THE GREAT WHITE BANNER. Saint John, Barnes, 1913. 100p [BM Brown U LC NBFU

Kern, Julia Ann (Pegg)
GLOWING EMBERS. ... Vancouver, Wrigley, [1935?]. 16p [BViPA

Kernighan, Robert Kirkland, 1857—1926
THE KHAN'S BOOK OF VERSE. [Anon] Toronto, Evening Telegram, 1925. 197p [BVaU OKQ
THE KHAN'S KANTICLES. Hamilton, Spectator, 1896. 240p [BM BVaU NBFU OKQ QMM
THE MEN OF THE NORTHERN ZONE. Hamilton, Duncan, n.d. 10p [NBFU
WAR POEMS. By The Khan [pseud]. Dundas, R. W. Karch, 1916. 31p [BM BVaU OTU QMU

Kerr, Estelle Muriel, 1879—1971
THE ISLAND. Rhymes and Sketches. Toronto, Print Craft, [19—?]. 22p [OTP QMU
LITTLE SAM IN VOLENDAM. Rhymes and Pictures. New York, Moffat Yard, 1908. 32p [LC

Kerr, J. George
"SINGING FOR JESUS" AND OTHER POEMS. Woodstock, Ont., 1891. 51p [Adelphi cat. 64

Kerr, William Henry Corrie, —1891
EDWARD HANLAN. A Lay of Young Canada. Toronto, Belfords Clarke, 1879. 29p [Commemorates Hanlan's winning of sculling championship in 1879.] [OTP

Kerrigan, Hilda Mary, 1911—
ENCHANTMENT. Poems. Author, 1950. 12p [OONL

FAIR WINDS. Ottawa, Author, 1953. 10p
PLEASANT PATHWAYS. Ottawa, Author, 1958. 18p [Also: 1959, 22p]

Kerry, Esther Wilson
HE IS A CANADIAN, AND OTHER VERSE. Montreal, Regal Press, 1919. 31p [BM
  BVaU LC OTP

Kester, Mary Sparks
ROAD O'DREAMS. Poems. Elmira, Ont., Elmira Print., 1922. 31p [BVaU OLU

Ketchum, William Quintard, 1898–
REQUIESCANT AND OTHER POEMS. Toronto, 1919. 35p [BM BVaU OOP

Kidd, Adam, 1802–1831
THE HURON CHIEF, AND OTHER POEMS. Montreal, Herald & New Gazette, 1830.
  216p [BM BVaU LC OKQ QMM

Kidd, Thomas, 1846–1930
HISTORY OF LULU ISLAND, AND OCCASIONAL POEMS. Vancouver, Wrigley Print.,
  1927. 247p [On cover: HISTORY OF RICHMOND MUNICIPALITY.] [BVaU

Killingsworth, J. Alexander
ROSES AND THORNS. St. Thomas, Author, 1921. 62p [BM
SPARKS AND CINDERS. St. Thomas, Journal Press, 1913. 146p [BM BVaU OTU

King, Amabel (Reeves), 1899–
THE NEW CRUSADERS AND OTHER POEMS. Toronto, Macmillan, 1943. 66p
  [BVaU LC OTP
VOICES OF VICTORY. Representative Poetry of Canada in Wartime. Comp. by —
  Toronto, Macmillan, 1942. xii + 97p [BVaU NSHPL

King, Benjamin Franklin, 1857–1894
BEN KING'S VERSE. Toronto, McClelland, 1923. 238p [BM BVaU NBFU

King, Rev. John Harry
THE HERO OF THE DRAMA OF GENESIS. An Epic of Sacred Story. Halifax, Nova
  Scotia Print., 1895. 72p [BVaU NSHD OOP

King, William James, 1879–
FOR YOU, MY DEAR. "Life's Varied Moods." Montreal, Author, 1938. 78p [OLU
  QMM
ROMANCE THRO' MORE THAN FORTY YEARS. Montreal, Author, 1944. 51p
  [OTP

Kingsley, Mary
HOMELY POEMS OF HUMBLE FORM. N.p., n.d. 30p [OPAL QMU

Kingsley, Roland Edward, 1882–
RHYMES OF BREVITY FOR TIMES OF LEVITY. Montreal, Author, 1937. 48p [OTU

Kingsmill, Col. William, 1794–1876
A STORY OF THE OLD MARINE. Guelph, 1869. 24p [Story of Cordingley, survivor of the Battles of the Nile and Trafalgar, living near Toronto, aged 106.] [BVaU OTU

Kingston, George Allen, 1870–1943
CHAMPLAIN AND D'ARONTAL. A Story in Verse. Toronto, Author, 1932. 11p [OTU
FROM LAND TO LINDBERGH. A Tale of Revolutionary Times with a 1932 Sequel. Toronto, Author, 1932. 12p [AEU OH
LEGENDARY LYRICS. Picton, Gazette, 1938. 117p [BVaU NBFU OTP
ON TO THE BAY. Toronto, Author, 1932. 7p [CC
RT. HON. SIR GILBERT PARKER, BART., DECEASED. A Tribute in Blank Verse. Toronto, Author, 1932. [CBI

Kinnear, Caroline A.
THE HOME TRAIL AND OTHER VERSES. Kamloops, Sentinel, 1938. 22p [BViPA OTU

Kinney, Edwin Enoch
WESTWARD AND OTHER POEMS. Vancouver, Chalmers, 1923. 75p [BVaU

Kirby, William, 1817–1906
CANADIAN IDYLLS. 2nd ed. Welland, 1894. 175p [1st ed., limited to 200 copies: Welland, 1884.] [BVaU LC NBFU OKQ
CANADIAN IDYLLS ... Interlude Second: The Harvest Moon. ... Toronto, Hunter Rose, 1883. 24p [Included in CANADIAN IDYLLS (1894).] [OTP
CANADIAN IDYLLS. Pontiac and Bushy Run. Niagara, Author, 1887. 44p [Included in CANADIAN IDYLLS (1894).] [OTP
CANADIAN IDYLLS. The Queen's Birthday. Toronto, Hunter Rose, 1881. 16p [Included in CANADIAN IDYLLS (1894).] [OTP
CANADIAN IDYLLS. ... The Queen's Birthday; Interlude First: The Bells of Kirby Wiske, and the Lord's Supper in the Wilderness. Toronto, Rose Belford, 1882. 22p [OTP
CANADIAN IDYLLS. Number IV: Spring, Stony Creek. Toronto, Briggs, 1880. 30p [Included in CANADIAN IDYLLS (1894).] [OOP
THE HUNGRY YEAR. Toronto, Methodist Book, 1878. 15p [Reprinted as "Autumn Poem" in CANADIAN IDYLLS (1894).] [OTP
THE U.E. A Tale of Upper Canada in XII Cantos. [Anon] Niagara, "Mail," 1859. 178p [BM BVaU NBFU OKQ

Kirkconnell, Watson, 1895–
CANADA TO ICELAND. ... Lindsay, Warder Press, 1930. 7p [Brown U
CANADIAN OVERTONES. An Anthology of Canadian Poetry written originally in Icelandic, Swedish, Hungarian, Italian, Greek, and Ukrainian, and now Translated. ... Winnipeg, Columbia Press, 1935. 104p [LC MWU NBFU OTU QMM

THE ETERNAL QUEST. Winnipeg, Columbia Press, 1934. 135p [BVaU NBFU OTP QMM

EUROPEAN ELEGIES. One Hundred Poems Chosen and Translated from European Literature in Fifty Languages. Ottawa, Graphic, 1928. 166p [BVaU NSHD OKQ QMM

THE FLYING BULL AND OTHER TALES. London, Oxford U. Press, 1940. 189p [Also: Toronto, Clarke Irwin, 1956.] [BVaU LC MWU NSHD OTP

A GOLDEN TREASURY OF POLISH LYRICS. Selected and Rendered into English. Winnipeg, Polish Press, 1936. 109p [BM BVaU OKQ QMM

A LITTLE TREASURY OF HUNGARIAN VERSE. Ed. and Trans. by ——. Washington, D.C., American Hungarian Federation, 1947. 55p [BM BVaU OTU QMM

LYRA SACRA. Four Occasional Hymns. Winnipeg, Author, 1939. 7p [CC

THE MAGYAR MUSE. An Anthology of Hungarian Poetry, 1400–1932. Ed. and Trans. by ——. Winnipeg, Kanadai Magyar Ujság Press, 1933. 222p [BM BVaU LC NSHD OTU QMM

MANITOBA SYMPHONY. N.p. [1937?]. 9p [OKQ

THE NORTH AMERICAN BOOK OF ICELANDIC VERSE. New York, Carrier & Isles, 1930. 228p [BM BVaU LC NSHD OKQ QMM

THE PATH OF DEMOS. [Winnipeg], n.d. 5p [NSHPL

THE QUEBEC TRADITION. An Anthology of French-Canadian Prose and Verse. Selected by Séraphin Marion and Translated into English by ——. Montreal, Les Editions Lumen, 1946. 245p [French and English on opposite pages.] [NBFU OTU

THE TIDE OF LIFE AND OTHER POEMS. Ottawa, Ariston Publishers, 1930. 79p [BVaU NSHD OTU QMM

WESTERN IDYLL. Hamilton, Author, 1940. 10p [OTU

Kirkpatrick, Mrs. Helen, 1877–
BOOK OF POEMS. By Gemmill [pseud]. Winnipeg, Evans Print., 1937. 31p [AEU
RAMBLINGS IN VERSE. By Gemmill [pseud]. Winnipeg, Evans Print., 1949. 59p [Brown U

Kirkwood, Kenneth Porter, 1899–
ABSTRACTIONS. ["Prose Poems."] Tokyo, Meiji Press, 1937. 93p [OTU
IN GARDENS OF PROSERPINE. Tokyo, Taiheiyosha Press, 1930. 27p [BM LC
LYRICS AND SONNETS. Tokyo, Author, 1934. 165p [BM OTP
POEMS. Tokyo, Author, [1930–32]. 76p [Contents: In Gardens of Proserpine; Travel Dust; Song in my Heart.] [QMM
SONG IN MY HEART. Tokyo, Author, 1932. 76 p [BM LC OTU
TIME'S TAVERN. Tokyo, Meiji Press, 1937. 158p [QMM
TRAVEL DUST. Tokyo, Author, 1932. 90p [BM LC OTU

Klein, Abraham Moses, 1909–
HATH NOT A JEW. New York, Behrman's Jewish Book House, 1940. 116p [BVaU LC MWU NSHD OTU QMM

THE HITLERIAD. New York, New Directions, 1944. 30p [BVaU LC MWU NSHD OTU QMM

HUIT POEMS CANADIENS (EN ANGLAIS). Montreal, Author, 1948. 16p [OKQ QMBM

NEW PROVINCES. Poems of Several Authors. [Ed. by F.R. Scott.] Toronto, Macmillan, 1936. 77p [Contains poems by Klein and others.] [BVaU NBFU OKQ

POEMS. Philadelphia, Jewish Pub. Soc., 1944. 82p [BVaU NBFU OTU

THE ROCKING CHAIR AND OTHER POEMS. Toronto, Ryerson, 1948. 56p [BVaU LC MWU NSHD OTU QMM

SEVEN POEMS. Montreal, Author, 1947. 8p [OTU QMBM

Kmietowicz, Frank Andrews, 1912–

REJOICE WE CONQUER. By Frank Andrews [pseud]. Toronto, New Line Fraternity, 1960. 59p

Knapp, M. Emma

LYRICS OF THE PAST, AND OTHER POEMS. ... Saint John, McMillan, 1872. 160p [Brown U NSHD

Knatchbull-Hugessen, Kenneth Wyndham, 1925–1942

JEUNESSE, AND OTHER POEMS. With an Introductory Memoir by his Father. Montreal, Southam Press, 1944. 47p [BVaU NBFU OTUV

Knight, Dorothy W., 1881–

OTHER VERSES (1893). N.p., n.d. 29p [Also bound with VERSES, below.] [NSWA

VERSES. By Dorothy Knight, Eleven Years Old. With a Preface by her Father. Brockville, priv. print., 1892. 41p [Cover title: ECHOES FROM THE THOUSAND ISLANDS.] [BVaU NSWA OKQ

THE VISION OF THE SEASONS AND OTHER VERSES. Montreal, Drysdale, 1898. 68p [BM BVaU NSHPL OKQ QMM

Knight, Fulton Stanley, 1883–

HORS D'OEUVRES. A Little Offering to whet the Appetite, a Tid-bit to roll under the Tongue and, as a Connoisseur, to titillate pleasurably the Senses. V. 1; Christmas 1960. Meaford, Ont., Knight Press, [1960?]. 28p

Knight, George

JOY OF LIVING, AND OTHER VERSES. Toronto, Dent, 1948. 66p [OTU QMM

Knight, Rev. Matthew Richey, 1854–

POEMS OF TEN YEARS, 1877–1887. Halifax, Macgregor & Knight, 1887. 143p [BVaU NSHD OTP

Knister, Raymond, 1900–1932

COLLECTED POEMS OF RAYMOND KNISTER. Ed. with a memoir by Dorothy Livesay. Toronto, Ryerson, 1949. 45p [BVaU NBFU OTP

Korn, Rachel H.

BASHERTKEIT (KISMET) POEMS 1928–1948. Montreal, Canadian Jewish Congress, 1949. 116p [Brown U

Laborde, Margaret Faith, 1897–

POEMS FOR CHILDREN. Brantford, Author, 1933. 47p [CC

Lacey, Gladys Margaret

ON REEDS FROM NISO'S STREAM. Boston, Humphries, 1947. 88p [LC OTP

Lady, A (pseud)

A POEM ON THE THREE-FOLD ESSENCE OF GOD. By a Lady [pseud]. Montreal, Starke, [18—?]. 16p [OTP

Laidlaw, Thomas, 1825–1902

IN THE LONG AGO; or, The Days of the Cattle Bell. N.p., [18—?]. 7p [OTP
THE OLD CONCESSION ROAD. Guelph, Mercury Press, 1892. 54p [Same title: Guelph, Turnbull, 1899. 69p] [OTP
SPRIGS O' HEATHER FOR SCOTTISH GATHERINGS. Guelph, Mercury Press, [18—?]. 28p [OTP

Lamb, Elkin

EXCEPT IT DIE. Toronto, Rous & Mann, 1945. 45p [OTP
THINGS NEW AND OLD. [Anon] Toronto, Rous & Mann, 1945. 22p [Brown U

Lambert, Gertrude M.

RHYMES AT RANDOM. Vancouver, Ernest Church, 1939. 16p [OTU

Lambie, Alexander, 1870–

WHEN POLLY WENT AWAY. A Book of Rhyme for Sleepy Time. Vancouver, Williamson, 1917. 26p [BVaU

Lampman, Archibald, 1861–1899

ALCYONE. Ottawa, Ogilvy, 1899. 110p [NBFU OKQ
AMONG THE MILLET, AND OTHER·POEMS. Ottawa, Durie, 1888. 151p [BM BVaU LC MWU NSHD OKQ QMM
AT THE LONG SAULT AND OTHER NEW POEMS. Foreword by Duncan Campbell Scott, introduction by E.K. Brown. Toronto, Ryerson, 1943. 45p [BVaU NSHD OKQ
HAPPINESS. A Preachment ... carrying to you the Best Wishes of the Ryerson Press, Christmas, 1925. Toronto, Ryerson, 1925. 15p [BVaU NBFU OTP
LITTLE BOOK, THY PAGES STIR. An Autograph Poem. [facsim.] Toronto, Ryerson, 1923. 3p [BVaU LC NBFU OTP
LYRICS OF EARTH. Boston, Copeland & Day, 1895. 56p [BVaU LC NSHD OKQ

LYRICS OF EARTH. Sonnets and Ballads. With an intro. by D.C. Scott. Toronto, Musson, 1925. 276p [BVaU NSHD OKQ QMM

THE POEMS OF ARCHIBALD LAMPMAN. Ed. with a memoir by Duncan Campbell Scott. Toronto, Morang, 1900. 473p [BM BVaU LC NSHD OKQ QMM

SELECTED POEMS OF ARCHIBALD LAMPMAN. Chosen with a memoir by Duncan Campbell Scott. Toronto, Ryerson, 1947. 176p [LC MWU NBFU OTP QMM

THESE POEMS. By Archibald Lampman and Duncan Campbell Scott. N.p., 1897. 6p [NBFU OKQ

TWO POEMS. By Archibald Lampman and Duncan Campbell Scott ... issued to their Friends at Christmastide, 1896. N.p., 1896. 3p [NBFU OKQ

Lancaster, William

THE CHRIST. A Poem. Toronto, Guardian, 1873. 30p [OTUV

Lande, Lawrence Montague, 1906–

BABBLINGS AND RANDOM VERSE. Montreal, priv. print., 1952. 51p

EXPENDABLE, AND OTHER POEMS. Montreal, priv. print., 1960. 33p

RESPONSE TO PRECIOUS MOMENTS. Montreal, Author, 1959. 53p

RESPONSE. With an intro. by Edgar A. Collard. Enl. ed. Montreal, Author, 1960. 89p

Lane, Wilmot Burkmar, 1872–

THE CLOSED BOOK (An Epic of the Soul's Quest). Toronto, Macmillan, 1943. 42p [BVaU LC NSHD OTP

QUINTE SONGS AND SONNETS. Toronto, Ryerson, 1925. 91p [BVaU NBFU OTP

Lang, Christopher D.

RHYMES OF A PROPER ROUGHNECK. Winnipeg, Jackson Trade Pub. Co., 1935. 47p [UTQ

Lang, Sidney Edward, 1864–

THE STORY OF PHILOSOPHY IN VERSE. A Handbook for Amateurs. Toronto, Macmillan, 1934. 101p [BVaU LC

Langford, Dorothy J.

HEAVENLY TREASURE. Toronto, Evangelical Pub., 1948. 40p [AEU NSHP

Langford, Walter Frederick, 1898–

NORTHERN MEDLEY. An Anthology of Canadian Verse. Ed. by ——. Toronto, Longmans, [1954]. 95p

Langlands, Katharine Louise, 1913–

MEMORIES. Huntsville, Ont., Author, 1937. 28p [OTU

Lanigan, George Thomas, 1846–1886

NATIONAL BALLADS OF CANADA. Imitated and Trans. from the Originals by "Allid" [pseud]. Montreal, Lovell, 1865. 15p [BM OTP

SOME EARLY TRANSLATIONS OF GEO. T. LANIGAN. N.p., [1922?]. 12p [OTP

Lanigan, John Alphonsus, 1854—1919
LEISURE HOURS. A Selection of Short Poems and Miscellaneous Scraps. 2nd ed.
Buffalo, Author, 1870. 108p [1st ed., 1869.] [BVaU LC NSHD QMM
WOODLAND RAMBLES. Poems. Buffalo, Peter Paul Book Co., 1894. 153p [LC
NSHD

Larkin, Sarah Elizabeth, 1896—
RADISSON. Trois-Rivières, Les Editions du Bien Public, 1938. 147p [LC OTU
QMBM
THREE RIVERS. A Tale of New France. New York, Putnam, 1934. 93p [BM
BVaU LC NBFU OTP QMBM
THE TREVALS. A Tale of Quebec. Montreal, Renouf, 1936. 147p [BVaU LC
OLU QMBM

Larsen, Thorleif, 1887—1960
SOME UNDERGRADUATE POEMS. [Anon] [An Anthology ed. and copyrighted by
Thorleif Larsen.] Toronto, Briggs, 1905. 72p [BVaU OTU

Laskey, John K.
LEISURE HOURS. A Collection of Original Poems. Saint John, Durant, 1838. 71p
[NBSaM
MARS HILL AND OTHER POEMS. Saint John, 1838. 70p [CCJ NBB

Laurence, Frances Elsie (Fry), 1893—
THE BAND PLAYS A MARCH, AND OTHER POEMS. [Edson, Alta.], Author, 1936.
66p [BVaU OKQ
REARGUARD AND OTHER POEMS. Toronto, Ryerson, 1944. 10p [BVaU LC
NSHD OTP
XII POEMS. Toronto, Ryerson, 1929. 8p [BVaU NBSaM OKQ QMM

Lauriston, Victor, 1881—
MAPLE LAND. 1905. [MOR'12

Lauzon, Edythe Morahan-de
ANGEL'S SONGS FROM THE GOLDEN CITY OF THE BLESSED. Montreal, Urquhart,
1918. 311p [BVaU LC OTP

Lawson, Francis Edgar, 1861—1911
SONGS OF FRANK LAWSON. Toronto, Briggs, 1912. 90p [AEU NBFU OLU
QMU

Lawson, James Reid, 1820—1891
SONGS OF ZION. Saint John, n.d. 32p [CCJ

Lawson, Jessie (Kerr), 1838—1917
LAYS AND LYRICS. Toronto, Briggs, 1913. 123p [BM BVaU NBFU OTP QMU

Lawson, Mary Jane (Katzmann), 1828—1890
FRANKINCENSE AND MYRRH. Selections from the Poems of the late Mrs. William Lawson (M.J.K.L.). Selected and ed. by Harry Piers and Constance Fairbanks. Halifax, Morton, 1893. 152p [BVaU NSHD OLU

Lawson, Thomas
THE POETICAL WORKS OF THOMAS LAWSON. Halifax, Holloway, 1888. 44p [NSHD OTUV

Layton, Irving, 1912—
THE BLACK HUNTSMEN. Montreal, First Statement Press, 1951. 56p
THE BLUE PROPELLER. Montreal, Contact Press, 1955. 50p
THE BULL CALF AND OTHER POEMS. Toronto, Contact Press, 1956. 49p
CERBERUS. Poems by Louis Dudek, Irving Layton, Raymond Souster. Toronto, Contact Press, [1952]. 98p
THE COLD GREEN ELEMENT. Toronto, Contact Press, 1955. 56p
HERE AND NOW. Montreal, First Statement Press, 1945. 44p [BVaU MWU NBFU OKQ QMM
THE IMPROVED BINOCULARS. Selected Poems. Highlands, N.C., J. Williams, 1956. 106p [2nd ed., 1957. 139p]
IN THE MIDST OF MY FEVER. Palma de Mallorca, Spain, Divers Press, 1954. 39p
A LAUGHTER IN THE MIND. Highlands, N.C., J. Williams, 1958. 54p
A LAUGHTER IN THE MIND. 2nd print., with 20 additional poems. Montreal, Editions d'Orphée, 1959. 97p [1st ed.: Highlands, N.C., J. Williams, 1958.]
THE LONG PEA SHOOTER. Montreal, Laocoön Press, 1954. 68p
LOVE THE CONQUEROR WORM. Toronto, Contact Press, 1953. 49p
MUSIC ON A KAZOO. Toronto, Contact Press, 1956. 59p
A RED CARPET FOR THE SUN. Toronto, McClelland, 1959. 240p

Lazechko-Haas, Myra
VIEWPOINT. Toronto, Ryerson, 1952. 12p

Leacock, Stephen Butler, 1869—1944
HELLEMENTS OF HICKONOMICS, IN HICCOUGHS OF VERSE DONE IN OUR SOCIAL PLANNING MILL. New York, Dodd Mead, 1936. 84p [BM BVaU LC NSHD OTU
THE MARIONETTE'S CALENDAR, 1916. Rhymes by Stephen Leacock; drawings by A.H. Fish. London, Lane, 1915. 14p [BM BVaU OTU

Leaver, Harold R.
THE MYSTERY OF JOHN JASPER. Edmonton, Capital City Press, 1925. 76p [An attempted completion of Dickens' *The Mystery of Edwin Drood.*] [BVaU NSHD OKQ

LeClaire, Gordon, 1905—
CARPENTER'S APPRENTICE AND OTHER POEMS. Toronto, Ryerson, 1957. 24p
DUST INTO FLAME. 1943. [Rhod. p938-9

INTIMATE MOMENTS. Random Runinations Expressed in Verse. Chicago, André, 1934. 19p [LC

SONNETS TO THE STARS, AND OTHER POEMS. Boston, Meador, 1936. 76p [OTU

STAR-HAUNTED. New York, Harrison, 1937. 95p [LC OTU QMM

THOUGH QUICK SOULS BLEED. New York, Banner Press, 1939. 122p [BVaU LC OTU QMM

Ledingham, Mary

SUCH THORNS AS PIERCE MY HEART. New York, Fortuny's, [1939?]. 62p [BVa OTUV

Lee, Joseph, 1876–

BALLADS OF BATTLE. Toronto, Gundy, 1916. 101p [BVaU NSHD OTP

Lee, Sophia Victoria (Gilbert)

WAYSIDE ECHOES. Poems. Toronto, Briggs, 1894. 179p [LC OKQ

Lefevre, Lily Alice (Cooke), –1938

A GARDEN BY THE SEA, AND OTHER POEMS. London, Humphreys, 1921. 128p [BVaU NSHD OKQ

THE LIONS' GATE AND OTHER VERSES. Victoria, Province Pub. Co., 1895. 95p [BVaU NBFU OKQ QMM

THE LIONS' GATE AND THE BEAVER AND THE EMPRESS. N.p., 1903. 9p [Same title: Vancouver, Thomson, 1933. 17p] [BVaU OTP

Leggett, William Martin, 1813–1863

THE FOREST WREATH. A Collection of Lyrics. Saint John, Durant & Sancton, 1833. 191p [NSHD OTP

Lehigh, M. Stanley

TRAIL OF THE SERPENT, RHYMES, AND MADRIGALS. Brockville, Recorder Print., 1905. 73p [BM

VICTOR AND OTHER POEMS. Brockville, Recorder Print., 1901. 69p [BM OTUV QMM

YOUTHFUL FANCIES, AND IONE. Brockville, Recorder Print., 1897. 95p [AEU OTUV

Leichliter, G.A.

SONGS TO MEN AND NATURE. Toronto, Standard Pub., n.d. 30p [NBSaM

Leland, S.P.

POEMS. Montreal, Dawson Bros., [1865]. [Priv. info.

LeMoine, James MacPherson, 1825–1912

THE LEGENDARY LORE OF THE LOWER ST. LAWRENCE. Quebec, Mercury Office, 1862. 33p [BM NSHP OTUV

Leonard, Mrs. Carrie
GEMS FOR THE HOME CIRCLE. Original Poems. London, Ont., Cameron, 1869.
150p [OTP

Lepage, John, −1885
THE ISLAND MINSTREL. A Collection of the Poetical Writings of John LePage.
Charlottetown, Haszard, 1860. 242p [OLU QMBM
THE ISLAND MINSTREL. A Collection of Some of the Poetical Writings of John
LePage. Vol. II. Charlottetown, Bremner, 1867. 219p [BVaU NSHD
OOP QMM

Le Pan, Douglas Valentine, 1914−
THE WOUNDED PRINCE AND OTHER POEMS. London, Chatto & Windus, 1948.
39p [BM BVaU LC MWU NBFU OTP
THE NET AND THE SWORD. London, Chatto & Windus, 1953. 56p

Leprohon, Rosanna Eleanor (Mullins), 1829−1879
THE POETICAL WORKS OF MRS. LEPROHON (Miss R.E. Mullins). Montreal, Lovell,
1881. 228p [BVaU LC NBFU OKQ

Le Scrivinir, Robert
DO FLOWERS BLOOM FOR LOVE, AND OTHER POEMS. Toronto, Print-craft Ltd.,
[193−?] 21p [Brown U

Leslie, Kenneth, 1892−
BY STUBBORN STARS, AND OTHER POEMS. Toronto, Ryerson, 1938. 64p
[BVaU LC NBFU OTP QMM
LOWLANDS LOW. Poems. [Halifax, McCurdy, 1935.] 47p [BVaU QMM
SUCH A DIN! Poems. Halifax, n.d. 45p [BVaU QMM
WINDWARD ROCK. Poems. New York, Macmillan, 1934. 61p [BM LC NBFU
QMM

Leslie, Mary, 1842−1920
HISTORICAL SKETCHES OF SCOTLAND IN PROSE AND VERSE. ... Being an Account
of the Kings and Queens of Scotland from the Reign of Fergus the First to
Victoria. ... Toronto, Bryant, [1905?]. 174p [BM BVaU OTP
RHYMES OF THE KINGS AND QUEENS OF ENGLAND. Being an Account of the
Rulers of England from the Norman Conquest to the Reign of Victoria. Toronto,
Briggs, 1896. 177p [BM BVaU OTP

Leveridge, Lilian, 1879−1953
THE BLOSSOM TRAIL. Toronto, Ryerson, 1932. 30p [BVaU NBSaM OTP QMM
A BREATH OF THE WOODS. Toronto, Ryerson, 1926. 24p [BVaU NBSaM OKQ
QMM
THE HERO SONGS OF CANADA. Toronto, Canadian Magazine, 1927. 23p [BVaU
NBFU OKQ

LYRICS AND SONNETS. Toronto, Ryerson, 1939. 32p [BVaU NSHD OKQ

OVER THE HILLS OF HOME, AND OTHER POEMS. New York, Dutton, 1918. 89p
[Same title: Toronto, McClelland, 1918. 64p] [BM BVaU LC NSHD OKQ QMM

Levine, Albert Norman, 1923—

MYSSIUM. Toronto, Ryerson, 1948. 8p [BVaU NBSaM OKQ

THE TIGHT-ROPE WALKER. London, Totem Press, 1950. 30p [BM BVaU OTP

Lewis, Charles Edward

BRIAR-WREATHES [sic]. London, Eyre & Spottiswoode, 1899. 22p [BM LC

Lewis, Fred

IMMORTALITY. Winnipeg, Author, 1944. 28p [OTP

Lewis, Lydia T.

LOVE SONGS AND OTHER LYRICS. By Lesbia [pseud]. Ottawa, Hope, 1922. 40p
[BM BVaU OOP

ROSES FOR LOVE. A Miscellany in Verse. London, Stockwell, 1933. 94p [BM

Lewis, Ray

THE CUP OF CIVILIZATION. From "Songs of the Universe." Ed. by Isadore Bern-
stein. Flushing, N.Y., McConnell, n.d. 8p [OKQ

SONGS OF EARTH. New York, Boni, 1917. 121p [AEU NBFU OTP

Lewis, Richard G.

VERSE AND REVERSE. Hamilton, Luday Studios, 1936. 50p [OPAL

Lewis, Susan Victoire

COLLECTED VERSE OF SUSAN VICTOIRE LEWIS. Ottawa, Ru-Mi-Lou Books, 1929.
96p [BVaU NBFU OKQ

Lighthall, William Douw, 1857—1954

CANADIAN POEMS AND LAYS. Selections of Native Verse. ... Arranged and Ed.
by ——. London, Scott, 1893. xxxii + 276p [BM BVaU LC NBFU OKQ
QMM

CANADIAN POEMS AND SONGS. See SONGS OF THE GREAT DOMINION.

CANADIAN POETS OF THE GREAT WAR. Ottawa, Royal Society, n.d. 24p [OTP
QMM

THE LAND OF MANITOU. Montreal, Desbarats, 1916. 18p [BM BVaU LC NSHD
OTU QMM

OLD MEASURES. Collected Verse. Montreal, Chapman, 1922. 140p [BVaU NBFU
OTP QMM

SONGS OF THE GREAT DOMINION. Voices from the Forests and Waters, the Settlements and Cities of Canada. Selected and ed. by ——. London, Scott, 1889.
xxxvii + 465p [Also pub. under title: CANADIAN SONGS AND POEMS. London,
Scott, 1892. 465p [BM BVaU LC NSHD OKQ

THOUGHTS, MOODS AND IDEALS. Crimes of Leisure. With Appendix. Montreal, Witness, 1887. 24p [Also a supplement in 1895.] [BVaU NSHD OTP QMM

Lindsell, Gerald Charles Huntingdon, 1883–
THE GREY GEESE. Toronto, Apted, 1931. 18p [OTP

Linnell, John Stainforth
YOUTH AND OTHER POEMS. Toronto, Macmillan, 1929. 76p [BM Brown U BVaU OOU

Liston, James Knox, fl. 1843–1868
NIAGARA FALLS. A Poem in Three Cantos. Toronto, Lawrence, 1843. 100p [BM BVaU LC OTP QMBM
POETRY FOR THE DOMINION OF CANADA. Consisting of Songs of the Canadian Winter, Songs of the Morning Stars, Shouts of the Sons of God, The Antemundane State. Toronto, Adam Stevenson, 1868. 96p [BVaU LC NBFU OTP QMM

Litster, Thomas Harkness, 1859–1943
SONGS IN YOUR HEART AND MINE. Toronto, McClelland, 1917. 142p [BM BVaU NBFU OKQ

Little, David Fleming, –1881
POEMS. Halifax, Nova Scotia Print., 1881. 101p [BVaU NSHD OTP

Little, Jean
"IT'S A WONDERFUL WORLD." Guelph, Author, 1947. 30p [Adelphi cat. 55

Little, Robert D., 1888–
RHYME AND REASON. Richmond Hill, Ont., Author, 1946. 58p [OTU

Lively, Gerald J.
THE PLEA OF THE WEST AND OTHER POEMS. London, Stewart, 1913. 24p [AEU QMSS

Livesay, Dorothy, 1909–
CALL MY PEOPLE HOME. Toronto, Ryerson, 1950. 24p [BVaU NBFU OTP
DAY AND NIGHT. Poems. Toronto, Ryerson, 1944. 48p [BVa MWU NBFU OTP QMM
GREEN PITCHER. Toronto, Macmillan, 1928. 16p [BVaU NBFU OTP
NEW POEMS. Toronto, Emblem Books, 1955. 15p
POEMS FOR PEOPLE. Toronto, Ryerson, 1947. 40p [BM BVaU NBFU OTP
SELECTED POEMS, 1926-1956. With an intro. by Desmond Pacey. Toronto, Ryerson, 1957. xxii + 82p
SIGNPOST. Toronto, Macmillan, 1932. 61p [BM BVaU LC NBFU OTP

Livesay, Florence Hamilton (Randal), 1874–1953
SHEPHERD'S PURSE. Toronto, Macmillan, 1923. 67p [BM BVaU NSHD OTP QMM

SONGS OF UKRAINIA. With Ruthenian Poems. Trans. by ——. London, Dent, 1916. 175p [BM BVaU LC NBFU OTP QMM

Livingston, Irvin Stanley, 1909—
FLAX AFIRE. New York, Pageant Press, 1953. 69p

Livingston, Kay
ACA NADA. Toronto, Copp Clark, n.d. 16p [NSWA OONL

Livingston, Stuart, 1865—1923
IN VARIOUS MOODS. Poems. Toronto, Briggs, 1894. 100p [BVaU LC NBFU OTP

Lloyd, Cecil Richard Francis, 1884—1938
LANDFALL. The Collected Poems of Cecil Francis Lloyd. Toronto, Ryerson, 1935. 47p [BVaU NBFU OTP QMM
LEAVES OF THE SYBIL. [Winnipeg, Author], 1927. 45p [Also: Toronto, Hunter Rose, 1928. 47p] [BM LC NSHD OKQ QMM
ROSEMARY AND RUE. Winnipeg, Stovel, 1929. 16p [BM OKQ QMM
VESPER BELLS. Toronto, Hunter Rose, 1929. 19p [BVaU OTP

Lloyd, Rev. William, 1884—
MORN MIST AND OTHER POEMS. Ilfracombe, Devon, Stockwell, 1960. 38p

Llwyd, Rev. John Plummer Derwent, 1861—1933
POEMS OF NATURE, CHILDHOOD, AND RELIGION. Toronto, Macmillan, 1928. 64p [NSHD

Lobb, Roy Leonard, 1888—
PLAIN-FOLKS. A Book of Friendly Verse. Beatty, Sask., Author, 1949. 146p [Brown U OTU
WHERE ARE YOU GOING? Spiritual poems. New York, Greenwich Book Pub., 1959. 64p

Lochhead, Douglas Grant, 1922—
THE HEART IS FIRE. Toronto, Ryerson, 1959. 12p
IT IS ALL AROUND. Toronto, Ryerson, 1960. 24p
AN OLD WOMAN LOOKS OUT ON GABARUS BAY REMEMBERING HISTORY, JUNE 8, 1958. Halifax, Three Fathom Press, 1959. 4p

Lockerby, Elizabeth N.
OAK LEAVES. ... Halifax, Macnab, 1869. 57p [NSHD
THE WILD BRIER; or, Lays by an Untaught Minstrel. ... By E.N.L. Charlottetown, Bremner, 1866. 196p [BVaU NSHP OTP

Lockhart, Rev. Arthur John, 1850—1926
BESIDE THE NARRAGUAGUS, AND OTHER POEMS. Buffalo, Peter Paul Book Co., 1895. 112p [BVaU LC OKQ QMM

THE BIRDS OF THE CROSS, AND OTHER POEMS. Winterport, Longee, 1909. 239p
[LC OKQ
THE HARP OF ACADIA. An Anthology ... of [Maritime] Authors. Ed by ——. N.p.,
1923. 2v [NSWA
THE MASQUE OF MINSTRELS AND OTHER PIECES. Chiefly in Verse. By Two
Brothers. Bangor, Burr, 1887. 361p [Pub. jointly with his brother Burton
Wellesley Lockhart.] [LC NBFU OKQ QMM

Lockhart, Olive Octavia (Moores), 1900–
ST. AIDAN'S AND OTHER POEMS. Victoria, B.C., St. Aidan's United Church, 1956.
24p

Logan, John Daniel, 1869–1929
CHRISTOBEL. A Trifoliate Coronal of Sonnets to the Ideal Incarnate. By Aloysius
Novicius [pseud]. [Priv. print.], [19—?]. 4p [NBFU OTP
CONFESSIO AMANTIS. An Epistle in Verse to Welcome Rt. Rev. Monsignor William
Foley. ... Halifax, Author, 1926. 8p [NBFU
FROM THE SOUL'S OBSERVATORY; or, Songs of the Spirit at Vesper-rise. ... Five
Poems. ... Halifax, Author, 1921. 8p [BVaU NBFU OTP
INSULTERS OF DEATH, AND OTHER POEMS OF THE GREAT DEPARTURE. With a
Prose Preachment entitled "The Fatal Paradox and Sin of Sorrow for the Dead."
Halifax, Davidson, 1916. 37p [NBFU OTP
THE LITTLE BLUE GHOST. An Easter Madrigal. With the Lost Love Letters of a
Florian Apostate. ... Halifax, Allen, 1922. 23p [BVaU NBFU OOP
LUX IGNATIANA. An Inaugural Ode composed for ... the Inauguration of the Rev.
William M. Magee, S.J., as President of Marquette University. ... Milwaukee,
Marquette U. Press, 1928. 12p [NBFU
MATER CORONATA. An Ode with Lyrical Interlude. ... Halifax, Dalhousie Alumni
Assoc., 1924. 11p [NBFU OKQ
MORE TINY TOWN TALES. ... Poems for Tiny Tots. Halifax, Author, 1924. 10p
[NBFU
THE NEW APOCALYPSE, AND OTHER POEMS OF DAYS AND DEEDS IN FRANCE.
With an essay ... "The New Atonement of the Living Dead." Halifax, Allen,
1919. 39p [BVaU NBFU OTU
PICTOU POETS. A Treasury of Verse in Gaelic and English. Selected ... by ——.
With an intro. by ... George Geddie Patterson. Pictou, N.S., Advocate Press,
1923. 48p [OOP
PRELUDES, SONNETS AND OTHER VERSES. With an Epistle in Criticism and an
Essay entitled "The Rhythmical Dummy; a Recipe for Verse-makers." Toronto,
Briggs, 1906. 68p [BM BVaU NSHD OTP
A ROSARY OF RENUNCIATION. Six Sestets. With a Little Prose Homily on Mystical
Union with the Ideal Beauty. Halifax, Author, 1925. 7p [NBFU
THE SINGING SILENCE. An Elegy in Memory of the late Monsignor William Foley.
[Milwaukee], Author, 1927. 4p [NBFU

SONGS OF THE MAKERS OF CANADA AND OTHER HOMELAND LYRICS. Toronto, Briggs, 1911. 64p [BVaU NBFU OTP

TINY TOWN TALES. Three Poems. Halifax, Author, 1923. 6p [NBFU

TWILIGHT LITANIES, AND OTHER POEMS FROM THE IVORY TOWER. Halifax, Allen, 1920. 92p [BM BVaU NBFU OOP

TWO POEMS. ... Halifax, Author, 1921. 4p [NBFU OKQ

Logan, John Edward, 1852–1915

A CRY FROM THE SASKATCHEWAN. [Anon] Montreal, Robinson, 1885. 13p [BVaU

VERSES. Montreal, Pen and Pencil Club. 1916. 129p [BM BVaU NSHD OTP

London, Ont. Writers' Club, Poetry Group

LONDON POETRY GROUP OFFERS A SELECTION OF POEMS. London, Ont., 1953. 43p [A continuing series.]

Lorimer, John G., 1807–1897

THE RECLUSE OF NEW BRUNSWICK; or, The Hermit of Point Lepreaux. Saint John, Shives, 1842. 24p [CCJ NBB

Lort, Ross Anthony, 1889–

ALL CREATURES GREAT AND SMALL. Vancouver, Bradbury, 1931. 255p [BVaU

Loucks, Vera Agnes (Morden), 1904–

ESSENCE OF LIVING. Fort St. John, B.C., Alaska Highway News, 1956. 22p

Love, Mrs. Georgina A.

HILLS AND HIGHWAYS. Poetry of Life. Toronto, Merchants Press, [1948?]. 40p [CC OPAL

Lovell, Kathleen Frances (Ramsay), 1926–

MY THOUGHTS. Ilfracombe, Devon, Stockwell, 1957. 56p

Lovell, R.G.

DREAMS IN LAMPLIGHT. London, Ont., Hunter, 1940. 33p [OLU

PEACE AND WAR. Foleyet, Ont., Crucible Press, 1950. 28p [UTQ'51

TWISTED GOLD. Toronto, Crucible Press, 1944. 20p [Brown U NBSaM OLU

Lover of Truth, A (pseud)

ALLAN GRAY AND HIS DOUBTS; or, Rhyme and Reason for the Young. ... Halifax, Nova Scotia Print., 1881. 112p [BVaU NSHD

THE POEM: NO SECT IN HEAVEN! And a Reply to the Same in Poetry. Saint John, "News" Office, 1868. 16p [NBFU

Loverove, A.G.

POEMS BY A DOUKHOBOR. N.p., [193–?]. 16p [SSU

Low, May (Austin), 1863–

CONFESSION, AND OTHER VERSES. Boston, Sherman French, 1909. 47p [LC NSHD OTU QMU

Low, Mildred, —1963
IF I FORGET THEE. ... Souvenir of the Centenary of Ottawa, Capital of Canada,
1826–1926. Ottawa, 1926. 16p [Brown U
VICTORY OR DEATH AND OTHER POEMS. London, Robert Scott, 1916. 20p [BM

Lowrey, David
FLORENCE. Toronto, 1904. 29p [Brown U BVaU
IN HADES. Toronto, Author, 1906. 16p [BM BVaU OTUV

Lowry-Calder, Sarah Isabell
POEMS. Ottawa, Ru-Mi-Lou Books, 1928. 202p [OONL QMU

Lowther, Armstrong John, 1880–1948
POEMS. By Laird [pseud]. Vancouver, Clarke & Stuart, [1946?]. 91p [BVaU

Lund, Charles Edward, 1850–
MISCELLANEOUS VERSE. Readings, Recitations, Songs and Hymns. (Enl. ed.)
Toronto, Best, 1926. 126p [1st ed., 1912.] [BM NBFU OTUV

Luxton, Mary Clendinning O'Donnell (Martin), 1879–
VIGNETTES. Poems. Victoria, Author, 1954. 35p
VIGNETTES IN VERSE. Victoria, Diggon, 1952. 16p

Lynch, Norman C.
THE SUNSET TRAIL AND OTHER POEMS. Montreal, Regnault, 1928. 51p [QMSS

Lytle, Mrs. W.J.A.
IN STORM AND SUNSHINE. By Beryl Berney [pseud]. London, Stockwell, 1936.
19p [BM

M., A.
NIAGARA. A Poem. By A.M. New York, Seymour, 1822. 24p [OTP

M., F.
ASTRAY. By F.M. Toronto, Chewett & Co., n.d. 8p [NSWA

McArthur, Peter, 1866–1924
FIVE SONNETS. New York, American Lithograph, 1899. 8p [LC
LINES. New York, priv. print., 1901. 28p [NBFU OTU
THE PRODIGAL, AND OTHER POEMS. New York, Kennerley, 1907. 64p [BVaU
LC NBFU OKQ

MacBride, Morrison Mann, 1877–1938
SELECTED POEMS FROM THE PEN OF THE HONOURABLE MORRISON MANN MAC-
BRIDE. V. I. Brantford, Mercantile Press, 1938. 149p [Brown U BVaU OTL

McBride, Robert
THE CANADIAN ORANGE MINSTREL FOR 1860. Contains Nine New and Original

Songs, Mostly all of them Showing some Wrong that affects the Order or the True Course of Protestant Loyalty to the British Crown. London, Ont., Free Press Print., 1860. 13p [OTP

THE CANADIAN ORANGE MINSTREL FOR 1870. Written for the Purpose of Keeping in Rememberance the Dark Doings and Designs of Popery in this Country. An Antidote for Pamphile Lemay's Songs, &c. Toronto, Stewart, 1870. 13p [OTP

POEMS SATIRICAL AND SENTIMENTAL ON MANY SUBJECTS CONNECTED WITH CANADA. London, Ont., Dawson, 1869. 302p [Earlier ed.: London, Author, 1858. 78p [BVaU OTP QMM

McCaig, Donald, 1832–1905

MILESTONE MOODS AND MEMORIES. Poems and Songs. Toronto, Hunter Rose, 1894. 132p [BVaU NBFU OTP

McCall, Oswald Walter Samuel, 1885–

IN SUCH A NIGHT AS THIS. Toronto, Musson, 1947. 204p [BM BVa LC

McCallum, John

PATRIOTIC ODES. Kingston, n.d. 16p [OLU

McCarroll, James, 1815–1896

MADELINE, AND OTHER POEMS. Intro. by Charles Lotin Hildreth. Chicago, Belford Clarke, 1889. 325p [BVaU LC OTUV

McCausland, Margaret

POSIES FOR FOLLY. Child Verse. St. Thomas, Ont., "Municipal World," 1910. [BM

McCawley, Stuart

A BOOK OF SONGS AND "COME-ALL-YE'S" OF CAPE BRETON AND NEWFOUNDLAND. Collected by ——. Glace Bay, N.S., Brodie, 1929. 64p [BVa NSHPL OKQ

RHYMES OF A ROUGHNECK. Glace Bay, N.S., Brodie Print., n.d. 24p [NSHK

McClelland, Lily Coulter

GEMS OF PRAISE. Saskatoon, 1950. 47p [SSU

McColl, Carrie Wetmore

APPLE BLOSSOMS. ... Toronto, Ryerson, 1920. 73p [BM NSHD OOP

MacColl, Evan, 1808–1898

THE ENGLISH POETICAL WORKS OF EVAN MACCOLL. ... With a Biographical Sketch of the Author by A. MacKenzie. ... Toronto, Hunter Rose, 1883. 360p [Other editions, with some variation in contents: "Second Canadian Edition," Toronto, Hunter Rose, 1885. 351p; Montreal, Drysdale, 1887. 338p; "Fourth Canadian Edition," Kingston, British Whig, 1888. 332p] [BVaU LC NSHD OTP QMSS

THE MOUNTAIN MINSTREL; or, Poems and Songs in English. 2nd ed., enl. Edinburgh, M'Lachlan & Stewart, 1838. 232p [BM OTP

McColl, Hugh
THE DAY OF JUDGMENT AND OTHER POEMS. Translated from the Gaelic of Dugald
Buchanan and Peter Grant. To which is Prefixed a Sketch of the Life of Dugald
Buchanan. ... Strathroy, Ont., Age Book & Job Office, 1870. 72p [OTU

MacColl, Mary Jemima, 1847–
BIDE A WEE, AND OTHER POEMS. Buffalo, Peter Paul, 1880. 103p [Also: Toronto,
Rose Pub., 1882. 113p] [BVaU NBFU OTP

McCollum, Alma Frances, 1879–1906
FLOWER LEGENDS AND OTHER POEMS. Toronto, Briggs, 1902. 116p [BM BVaU
LC NBFU OTP

McComb, James
POEMS OF FAITH, HOPE & LOVE. Vancouver, Clarke & Stuart, 1936. 16p [CC

MacConnell, H.B.
WHERE DUTY LEADS. Toronto, Briggs, 1916. 71p [BM BVaU OKQ

MacCormack, Franklyn
WHY I LOVE YOU, AND OTHER POEMS, FROM MY OLD BOOK OF MEMORIES.
Toronto, Winston, 1948. 245p [BM

McCoy, Charlotte
SING A SONG OF CANADA. By Charlotte McCoy and Anne S. Brooks. With Music
by Ada T. Kent. Toronto, Nelson, 1937. 32p [UTQ

McCrae, John, 1872–1918
IN FLANDERS FIELDS AND OTHER POEMS. With an Essay in Character by Sir
Andrew Macphail. Toronto, Briggs, 1919. 141p [BM BVaU LC NBFU OTP

McCrossan, Charles Wesley
CANADIAN HEART SONGS. Toronto, Briggs, 1912. 163p [BM BVaU NBFU
OKQ

McCuaig, William Wilberforce
SONGS OF A SHANTY-MAN, AND OTHER "DIALECT" POEMS OF FRENCH-CANADIAN
LIFE. Toronto, Musson, [1913]. 91p [BVaU OTP QMSS

McCulloch, Mercy Emma (Powell)
RHYMING THROUGH THE YEARS. Toronto, Ryerson, 1951. 125p

McCullough, Mary Eleanor, 1915–1942
THE SKY WAS MY FRIEND. Songs of the Ottawa Valley. Ottawa, Le Droit, 1942.
48p [BVaU NSHD OTP

McCully, Laura Elizabeth, 1886–1924
BIRDS OF DAWN, AND OTHER LYRICS. [Toronto], 1919. 28p [BM BVaU NBFU
MARY MAGDALENE AND OTHER POEMS. Toronto, Macmillan, 1914. 99p [BM
BVaU NBFU OTP

McDavitt, Alice Pyne

HOMESTEADER AND OTHER POEMS. New York, Cosmopolitan, 1913. 80p [OTL

Macdonald, Agnes (Foley)

ONCE AND AGAIN. Port Royal, N.S., Abanaki Press, 1951. 25p

MacDonald, Ann Celestine (Rock), 1876–1960

CARILLON PEACE TOWER, OTTAWA AND OTHER POEMS. Ottawa, Flora Printers, 1955. 36p

McDonald, D.A.

THOUGHTS OF A CONVICT. By Ex-Convict No. 1999, Kingston Penitentiary [pseud]. N.p., [1934?]. 32p [Brown U

McDonald, Rev. Donald, 1783–1867

SPIRITUAL HYMNS. Charlottetown, 1835. [Another ed., 1840.] [DCB

Macdonald, Rev. Donald

HYMNS FOR PRACTICE. Not to be Used in the Solemn Worship of the Sanctuary. By Rev. Donald Macdonald and Elders. Charlottetown, Haszard & Moore, 1894. 238p [Brown U OLU

McDonald, Donald

MONEY TALKS. Letters to the Sarnia Canadian Observer on Hard Times and Their Cure. Camlachie, Ont., Author, 1931. 32p [New ed., 1932. 68p] [BVaU

MacDonald, Goodridge, 1897–

ARMAGEDDON AND OTHER POEMS. N.p., Author, [1917?]. 8p [NBFU
BEGGAR MAKES MUSIC. Toronto, Ryerson, 1950. 11p [BVaU NBFU OTP
COMPASS READING AND OTHERS. Toronto, Ryerson, 1955. 11p
THE DYING GENERAL, AND OTHER POEMS. Toronto, Ryerson, 1946. 8p [BVaU LC NBSaM OTP
RECENT POEMS. Toronto, Ryerson, 1957. 12p
TWENTY-FOUR POEMS. London, Poets' and Painters' Press, 1958. 31p

Macdonald, James Edward Hervey, 1874–1932

VILLAGE & FIELDS. A Few Country Poems. Thornhill, Ont., Woodchuck Press, 1933. 13p [OTP
MY HIGH HORSE. A Mountain Memory. Thornhill, Woodchuck Press, [193–?]. 6p [BVaU OTP
WEST BY EAST AND OTHER POEMS. Toronto, Ryerson, 1933. 37p [BVaU LC NBFU OTP QMM
A WORD TO US ALL. Being a Message for Canadians. ... Toronto, Ryerson, 1945. 8p [NBFU OTP

MacDonald, Jane Elizabeth Gostwycke (Roberts), 1864–1922

DREAM VERSES, AND OTHERS. Toronto, Copp Clark, 1906. 122p [BVaU LC NBFU OTUV
POEMS. Fredericton, Author, 1885. 16p [BVaU NBFU OOP

Macdonald, John James, 1849–

AN IDEAL COURTSHIP. By James MacRae [pseud]. Toronto, Ryerson, 1923. 43p
[BM OKQ

POEMS. Written by John J. Macdonald, a Native of County Glengarry. N.p.,
[1877?]. 64p [QMSS

Macdonald, M.C.

NO TAX ON THE PERICRANIUM. Toronto, Smithers & Bonelli, 1938. 48p [OLU

McDonald, Ruth M. (Gulley), 1912–

PRAIRIE SILHOUETTES. A Chap-Book of Verse. Edmonton, Author, 1960. 12p

MacDonald, Robert Gear, 1874–1943

FROM THE ISLE OF AVALON. London, Morland, 1908. 53p [BM

MacDonald, Wilson Pugsley, 1880–1967

ARMAND DUSSAULT, AND OTHER POEMS. Buffalo, Broadway Press, 1946. 46p
4th ed. [First ed. published in Toronto in 1933 with title: PAUL MARCHAND
AND OTHER POEMS, *q.v.* Second ed. rev. and third ed. pub. in Toronto by S.J.R.
Saunders, 1935, 1940, with title QUINTRAINS OF "CALLANDER" AND OTHER
POEMS, *q.v.* 5th and 6th printings, 1948 and 1958, had title: ARMAND
DUSSAULT. ...] [BM BVaU NBFU OKQ QMG

CAW-CAW BALLADS. Toronto, MacDonald, 1930. 44p [Also: Buffalo, N.Y.,
Broadway Press, 1958 (8th printing). 47p] [BVaU LC NBFU OKQ

COMBER COVE. Toronto, Saunders, 1937. 91p [BVaU LC NBFU OTP

A FLAGON OF BEAUTY. Toronto, Pine Tree Pub. Co., 1931. 217p [Also: Buffalo,
N.Y., Broadway Press, 1958 (6th printing). 233p] [BM BVaU LC NBFU OTP

THE GIRL BEHIND THE MAN BEHIND THE GUN. [Verses.] Victoria, Lane & Son,
[1915]. 1p [BM BViPA

GREATER POEMS OF THE BIBLE. Metrical Versions, Biblical Forms, and Original
Poems. Toronto, Macmillan, 1943. 277p [BVaU NBFU OKQ

THE LYRIC YEAR. Poems and Pen-work by ——. Toronto, Ryerson, 1952. 53p
[BVaU NBFU OTP

THE MIRACLE SONGS OF JESUS. Toronto, Author, 1921. 12p [Not the same book
as the following title.] [BVa NBFU OONL QMG

THE MIRACLE SONGS OF JESUS. Toronto, Ryerson, 1921. 26p [BM BVaU LC
NBFU OTP QMBM

AN ODE ON THE DIAMOND JUBILEE OF CONFEDERATION. Toronto, Warwick,
[1927]. 14p [BVaU NBFU OTP

OLD SAMUEL CASHSWIGGER. Willowdale, Ont., Author, 1958. 3p

OUT OF THE WILDERNESS. Ottawa, Graphic, 1926. 209p [9th printing: Toronto,
Ryerson, 1957.] [BVaU LC NBFU

PAUL MARCHAND, AND OTHER POEMS. Toronto, Pine Tree Pub. Co., 1933. 46p
BVaU LC NBFU OKQ

PUGWASH. Toronto, Pine Tree Pub. Co., 1957. 15p

QUINTRAINS OF "CALLANDER" AND OTHER POEMS. Toronto, Saunders, 1935.
46p [Includes PAUL MARCHAND, first pub. in 1933.] [BVaU NBFU
SONG OF THE PRAIRIE LAND, AND OTHER POEMS. Toronto, McClelland, 1918.
144p [Same title: Toronto, Ryerson, [1923]. 155p] [BM BVaU LC NBFU
OKQ
THE SONG OF THE UNDERTOW AND OTHER POEMS. Toronto, Saunders, 1935.
175p [Also: Buffalo, Broadway Press, 1935. 175p] [BVaU LC NBFU OTP

McDonnell, William, 1814–1900
CLEOPA. Lindsay, "Watchman," [18—?]. 17p [OTP
FATHER AMBROSE. Lindsay, "Watchman," [18—?]. 12p [OTUV
MANITA. A Poem. ... Being an Indian Legend of Sturgeon Point, Ontario. ...
[Lindsay?], [18—?]. 29p [BVaU OTP

McDougald, Annie (Bethune)
CANADA'S CORONATION CAVALCADE, 1910–1937. Westmount, Que., Author,
1937. 27p [QMBM
SONGS OF OUR MAPLE SAPLINGS. Toronto, Musson, 1917. 13p [BM NBFU
OTP QMSS

Macdougall, Beatrice
LIFT UP YOUR HEARTS. Montreal, Author, 1931. 47p [OTP

McDougall, Joseph Easton, 1901–
BLIND FIDDLER. Toronto, Ryerson, 1936. 17p [NBSaM OTU QMM
IF YOU KNOW WHAT I MEAN. Toronto, Macmillan, 1929. 91p [BVaU LC OTU

McDougall, Margaret (Dixon), 1826–1898
VERSES AND RHYMES BY THE WAY. By Nora Pembroke [pseud]. Pembroke,
Mitchell, 1880. 180p [BVaU OTP QMM

McElheran, Irene Beatrice (Brock), 1879–1955
MESSAGES. Toronto, Nelson, 1932. 12p [OONL

McElhinney, Mark Gamble, 1867–
MORNING IN THE MARSH. Poems for Lovers of the Great Outdoors. Ottawa,
Graphic, 1927. 61p [BVaU NBFU OTP QMM

McEown, Frank
VANCOUVER. Words and Melody. Vancouver, 1925. 4p [Adelphi cat. 45

McEvoy, Bernard, 1842–1932
AWAY FROM NEWSPAPERDOM, AND OTHER POEMS. Toronto, Morang, 1897. 144p
[BM BVaU NBFU OTP QMSS
ELVIRA AND FERNANDO, AND OTHER SELECTIONS. Toronto, Oxford U. Press,
1927. 150p [BVaU NBFU OKQ
THE FEAST OF THE DEAD. Toronto, Brown-Searle, 1899. 8p [BVaU NBFU OTP
THE RHYME OF THE STREET CAR. Vancouver, Author, 1926. 7p [BVaU

VERSES FOR MY FRIENDS. Vancouver, Cowan Brookhouse, 1923. 209p [Reprints most of the verses in AWAY FROM NEWSPAPERDOM.] [BM BVaU LC OTP

McFadden, Mrs. Isobel
LIGHT UPON THE HILLS. Toronto, Author, 1948. 26p [Brown U BVaU OTUV
REWARD AND OTHER POEMS. Toronto, Ryerson, 1939. 8p [BVaU NBSaM OTP

Macfarlane, John, 1857–1914
THE CORONATION ODE. 1902. [MOR'12
THE HARP OF THE SCOTTISH COVENANT. Poems, Songs and Ballads. Ed. by ——.
 Paisley, 1895. 341p [BM OTU QMM
HEATHER AND HAREBELL. Songs and Lyrics. Montreal, Drysdale, 1891. 62p
 [BVaU OTP QMSS
SONGS OF THE THISTLE AND MAPLE. Toronto, Briggs, 1913. 103p [BM BVaU
 OTP QMM
WITHIN THE NIGHT, AND OTHER LYRICS. Toronto, Hart, 1892. [CCJ

Macfie, Archibald
THE FARMER AND HIS SON. A Dialogue. Chatham, Planet Print., 1888. 28p [OTP

McGaffey, Ernest, 1861–
WAR LYRICS FROM BRITISH COLUMBIA. ... In Aid of the Red Cross Society.
 [Victoria?], 1915. 8p [BVaU NSWA OPAL QMU

McGee, Mrs. Rosa Bateman
SONGS FOR SIGHS. ... Peterborough, Dawe's Print., [194–?]. 22p [Brown U

McGee, Thomas D'Arcy, 1825–1868
CANADIAN BALLADS, AND OCCASIONAL VERSES. Montreal, Lovell, 1858. 124p
 [BM BVaU LC NBFU OTP QMSS
THE POEMS OF THOMAS D'ARCY MCGEE. With copious notes ... and biographical
 sketch by Mrs. J. Sadlier. New York, Sadlier & Co., 1869. 612p [BM BVaU
 LC NSHD OTP QMSS

MacGeorge, David, 1845–
BUBBLES FROM THE BOILER ROOM. Galt, Reformer Press, 1910. 197p [BVaU
 OTU
ORIGINAL POEMS. Galt, Reformer Press, 1904. 145p [BM BVaU OTP QMBM

MacGeorge, Rev. Robert Jackson, 1811?–1884
THE CANADIAN CHRISTIAN OFFERING. Ed. by ——. Toronto, Trinity Church
 Office, 1848. 102p [NSHD OTP QMM

McGillicuddy, Owen Ernest, 1887–1954
THE LITTLE MARSHAL AND OTHER POEMS. Toronto, Goodchild, 1918. 48p
 [BVaU OTP QMSS

MacGowan, James Alexander

MAPLE UNDERWOOD, RUDELY CUT BY A YOUTHFUL BEAVER. A Collection of Infant Verse. Toronto, Hunter Rose, 1884. 61p [Brown U

MacGregor, R. Aldine

PATRICIA HERALD VERSE. Sioux Lookout, Ont., Patricia Herald, n.d. [c1927]. 17p [OTU

Machar, Agnes Maule, 1837–1927

"THE CLIFF" TO "THE ISLANDS". ... Gananoque, 1891. 9p [NSHD

EASTER POEMS: Easter Lilies, by Agnes Maule Machar; An Easter Poem, by Mrs. L.C. Whiton. Boston, Lothrop, 1889. 11p [LC

LAYS OF THE "TRUE NORTH," AND OTHER CANADIAN POEMS. London, Elliot Stock, 1899. 243p [2nd and enl. ed.: London, Elliot Stock, 1902. 260p] [BM BVaU LC NBFU OTP QMM

THE THOUSAND ISLANDS. Toronto, Ryerson, 1935. 16p [A posthumous pub.] [BVaU NBSaM OTP

MacInnes, Thomas Robert Edward, 1867–1951

COMPLETE POEMS OF TOM MACINNES. Toronto, Ryerson, 1923. 298p [BM BVaU NSHD OTP

THE FOOL OF JOY. Toronto, McClelland, 1918. 83p [BM BVaU NBFU OTP

FOR THE CROWNING OF THE KING, JUNE 26TH, 1902. An Ode. N.p., [1902]. 10p [BViPA OTP

HIGH LOW ALONG. A Didactic Poem. Vancouver, Clarke & Stuart, 1934. 68p [BVaU LC NBFU OKQ

IN AMBER LANDS. Poems. New York, Broadway Pub., 1910. 202p [BVaU LC NBFU OKQ

IN THE OLD OF MY AGE. A New Book of Rhymes. Toronto, Ryerson, 1947. 55p [BVaU LC MWU NSHD OTP QMBM

LONESOME BAR, A ROMANCE OF THE LOST, AND OTHER POEMS. Montreal, Desbarats, 1909. 205p [2nd ed. of A ROMANCE OF THE LOST, *q.v.*] [BVaU NSHD OKQ

RHYMES OF A ROUNDER. New York, Broadway Pub., 1913. 79p [Same title: Vancouver, Sasamat Pub. Co., 1935. 136p] [BVaU LC NBFU OTP

A ROMANCE OF THE LOST. Montreal, Desbarats, 1908. 175p [BM BVaU NSHD OTP

ROUNDABOUT RHYMES. ... A Foreword by Charles G.D. Roberts. Toronto, Ryerson, 1923. 80p [BM BVaU NBFU OTP

McInnis, Edgar Wardell, 1899–

BYRON. [Newdigate Prize Poem, 1925.] Oxford, Blackwell, 1925. 15p [NBFU OKQ

POEMS WRITTEN AT "THE FRONT." Charlottetown, Irwin, 1918. 17p [BM NBFU OTP

THE ROAD TO ARRAS. Charlottetown, Irwin, 1920. 31p [NBFU

MacIntosh, Claire (Harris), 1882–
ATTUNE WITH SPRING IN ACADIE. New York, Putnam, 1931. 106p [BM LC
NSHD OTP
PHANTOM PIRATES. Halifax, Imperial Pub. Co., 1941. 47p [LC NBFU OTP
THE SPIRIT OF THE BLUENOSE, AND OTHER POEMS. Halifax, Imperial Press, 1951.
43p

McIntosh, Duncan
THE TRAVELLER'S COMPANION. [Glasgow, Pickering & Inglis], 1924. 342p
[BVaU NBFU OTP QMU
VERSES FROM MY DIARY. ... Glasgow, McIntyre, 1907. 160p [OLU

McIntyre, James, 1827–1906
MUSINGS ON THE BANKS OF CANADIAN THAMES. Including Poems on Local,
Canadian and British Subjects, and Lines on the Great Poets of England,
Ireland, Scotland and America, with a Glance at the Wars in Victoria's Reign.
Ingersoll, Ont., Rowland, 1884. 128p [BVaU OTP QMM
POEMS OF JAMES MCINTYRE. ... Ingersoll, Ont., Chronicle, 1889. 198p [BVaU
LC OTP QMM

MacIntyre, John Horton, 1863–
ACORNS AND AGATES. By Mack [pseud]. London, Ont., 1931. 57p [OOP
LOWLY LIVES, WITH LOFTY LONGINGS AND OTHER POEMS. London, Ont.,
Hunter, 1935. 165p [BVaU OLU
FOREGLEAMS OF THE DAWNING. By Mack [pseud]. London, Ont., Author,
1940. 73p [Brown U
MAPLE LEAVES AND SPRIGS O' HEATHER. By Mack [pseud]. Toronto, Ryerson,
1925. 170p [BVaU OTP QMM
ODES AT EVENTIDE. London, Ont., Author, 1939. 149p [AEU OL

MacIver, Iver Donald, 1910–
THE VACANT HOUSE AND OTHER VERSE. Wolfville, N.S., Davidson, 1937. 16p
[NSHD OKQ

Mackay, Angus, 1865–1923
BY TRENCH AND TRAIL IN SONG AND STORY. By Angus Mackay (Oscar Dhu). ...
Seattle and Vancouver, Mackay Print., 1918. 144p [BViPA LC
DONALD MORRISON, THE CANADIAN OUTLAW. A Tale of the Scottish Pioneers.
By Oscar Dhu [pseud]. N.p., 1892. 118p [AEU NSWA OTP QMU

MacKay, Isabel Ecclestone (Macpherson), 1875–1928
BETWEEN THE LIGHTS. Toronto, Briggs, 1904. 65p [BM BVaU NBFU OTP
THE COMPLETE POEMS OF ISABEL ECCLESTONE MACKAY. Toronto, McClelland,
1930. 345p [BM BVaU LC NBFU OTP
FIRES OF DRIFTWOOD. Toronto, McClelland, 1922. 139p [BM BVaU NBFU
OTP
PANSIES FOR THOUGHTS. N.p., n.d. 16p [BVaU

THE SHINING SHIP AND OTHER VERSE FOR CHILDREN. Toronto, McClelland, 1918. 82p [New and enl. ed.: Toronto, McClelland, 1929. 174p] [BVaU NBFU OTP

Mackay, J.

QUEBEC HILL; or, Canadian Scenery. A Poem in Two Parts. London, Blackader, 1797. 34p [BM LC OTP

Mackay, Mrs. Jean C.

THE REDMAN'S SHRINE. Toronto, Crucible Press, 1941. 32p [LC

McKay, John George, 1886–1923

APRES LA GUERRE. Ed., with a Memoir ... by Neilson Campbell Hannay. ... Boston, Fort Hill Press, 1925. 100p [BM BVaU LC NSHD OTUV QMM

MacKay, Louis Alexander, 1901–

THE ILL-TEMPERED LOVER, AND OTHER POEMS. Toronto, Macmillan, 1948. 72p [BVaU LC NBFU OTP QMM
VIPER'S BUGLOSS. By John Smalacombe [pseud]. Toronto, Ryerson, 1938. 7p [BVa NBSaM OKQ QMM

McKellar, Duncan

POEMS. Toronto, Allen, 1922. 63p [NBFU OKQ

MacKenzie, D.E.

RHYMES FROM THE ROCKS. Halifax, Mission Press, 1946. 37p [NBSaM

McKenzie, Ethel (O'Neil)

SECRET SNOW. Philadelphia, Swain, 1932. 178p [LC NBFU OOP QMM

Mackenzie, George Allan

"IN THAT NEW WORLD WHICH IS THE OLD." Poems of the New Life. Toronto, Musson, [1914?]. 95p [BVaU NBFU OKQ
MALCOLM. A Story of the Day-Spring. Toronto, Rowsell & Hutchison, 1887. 39p [AEU LC OTP
MALCOLM AND OTHER POEMS. Toronto, Haynes Press, 1912. 41p [BVaU OTUV QMSS
SIX LYRICS OF THE HIGHER LIFE. Toronto, [Haynes?], 1913. 6p [BVaU OTU
SONG OFFERINGS FROM INDIA. Selections from the Poems of Rabindranath Tagore of Bengal, rendered into English. Toronto, Author, 1913. 6p [NBFU OTU
SONGS IN THE NIGHT WATCHES. N.p., 1926. 13p [BViP NSWA QMU
SONGS OF THE INNER LIFE. [Anon] Toronto, Author, 1900. 24p [NSWA OTP
VIA CRUCIS. N.p., 1924. 15p [QMU

Mackenzie, James Bovell, 1851–1919

ALFRED THE GREAT AND OTHER POEMS. Toronto, Imrie, 1902. 95p [BVaU NBFU OTP

CLIVE, BARON PLASSEY. A Lay of Empire; and Other Poems. Toronto, Rous
& Mann, 1912. 63p [BVaU OTP

McKenzie, Marjorie
GRAPHITE AND GALENA. Kingston, Jackson Press, 1927. 27p [BVaU

McKenzie, Rev. William Patrick, 1861–1942
THE AULD FOWK. Some Verses in Scots. Toronto, Ryerson, 1930. 16p [BVaU
NBFU OTP

BITS O' VERSE IN SCOTS. Toronto, Ryerson, 1927. 16p [BVaU NBFU OKQ

FIELDS OF BLOOM. Cambridge, Mass., Cambridge Tribune, 1930. 44p [BVaU LC

FOWLS O' THE AIR AND OTHER VERSES IN SCOTS. Toronto, Ryerson, 1928. 16p
[BVaU NBSaM OKQ

HEARTSEASE HYMNS, AND OTHER VERSES. Toronto, Tyrrell, 1896. 44p [CCJ
lists an earlier ed.: Toronto, 1895. 44p; later editions: Cambridge, 1901.
53p; Chicago, 1938. 44p] [BM BVaU LC NSHD OTP QMM

PRELUDE POEMS FOR THE NEW DAY. By W.P.M. Chicago, Associated Authors,
1942. 63p [LC OKQ

A SONG OF TRUST AND OTHER THOUGHTS IN VERSE. Toronto, Hart, 1887. 42p
[LC

SONGS OF THE HUMAN. Toronto, Hart, 1892. 132p [BVaU OTP

THE SOWER, AND OTHER POEMS. Cambridge, Mass., Author, 1903. 56p
[Later ed.: Cambridge, Tribune Press, 1928. 44p] [LC OKQ

VOICES AND UNDERTONES IN SONG AND POEM. Toronto, Hart, 1889. 156p
[BVaU LC OOC QMM

Mackenzie, William Roy, 1882–1957
BALLADS AND SEA SONGS FROM NOVA SCOTIA. Ed. by ——. Cambridge,
Mass., Harvard U. Press, 1928. 421p [AEU NBFU OLU

THE QUEST OF THE BALLAD. Princeton, N.J., Princeton U. Press, 1919. 247p
[BVi NBFU OTP QMG

MacKeracher, Rev. William Mackay, 1871–1913
CANADA, MY LAND, AND OTHER COMPOSITIONS IN VERSE. Toronto, Briggs,
1908. 66p [BM BVaU NBFU OTP

JEAN BATEESE AT THE CARNIVAL. Toronto, Briggs, 1909. 15p [BM OTP

SONGS OF A SOPHOMORE. By W.M.M. Montreal, 1892. 24p [CCJ

SONNETS AND OTHER VERSE. Toronto, Briggs, 1909. 80p [BM NBFU OTP
QMM

VACATION VERSE. By W.M.M. Montreal, Witness, 1891. 23p [OTU

VERSES OF FEELING AND FANCY. Montreal, Drysdale, 1890. 96p [BVaU
OTP QMBM

McKibbin, Isabel Reid
CHRISTMAS CRACKERS, AND OTHER RHYMES. London, Stockwell, 1933.
46p [BM

Mackie, Mrs. Delia Elizabeth
MY SHIPS COME A-SAILING. Ottawa, Legge Press, 1954. 26p

McKillop, Archibald
THE FLOOD OF DEATH; or, The Malt that Lay in the House that Jack Built.
  Toronto, Dudley & Burns, 1875. 24p [OTP
TEMPERANCE ODES, AND MISCELLANEOUS POEMS. Quebec, Thomson, 1860.
  96p [BVaU OTP

McKinnell, Mrs. George
COUCHICHING CAROLS. [Anon] Orillia, 1889. 51p [Brown U BVaU OTUV

MacKinnon, Cecilia
FOUNTAINS OF ORDUNNA. Boston, Brimmer Press. 1923. 72p [AEU NBSaM
  OOP

MacKinnon, Rev. Murdoch Charles, 1889–1956
CHRIST IN KHAKI AND SACRED SONG. [Perth, Ont., Author, 1930?] [8]p
  [OTUV
FROM THE WINEPRESS. Toronto, Ryerson, 1933. 20p [BVaU NBSaM OTP

MacKinnon, Mrs. Una H. Morris
TIDES OF THE MISSIQUASH. ... Halifax, Weeks Print. Co., [192–?]. 32p
  [NSHD

McKinnon, Rev. William Charles, –1862
BATTLE OF THE NILE. A Poem in Four Cantos. ... [Contains also "The Steep of
  Fame," a poem; its sequel "Life"; and "An Elegy to the shade of Thomas
  Campbell. ..."] Sydney, N.S., Kuhn, 1844. 75p [NSHD

MacKnight, Samuel John
ATAVAR OF PEACE AND OTHER POEMS. Boston, Shawmut Steam Print., 1896.
  16p [NSHD
LYRIC AND OTHER POEMS. Halifax, Bowes, 1892. 28p [BVaU NSHD OTP
  QMBM

MacLachlan, Alan
RHYMES OF A MONTREALER. Montreal, Author, 1942. 60p [NBFU OTU QMU

McLachlan, Alexander, 1818–1896
THE EMIGRANT, AND OTHER POEMS. Toronto, Rollo & Adam, 1861. 236p
  [BM BVaU NBFU OTP
LYRICS. Toronto, Armour, 1858. 151p [BVaU MWU NBFU OTP QMBM
POEMS. [Chiefly in the Scottish Dialect.] Toronto, Geikie, 1856. 192p [BVaU
  NBFU OTP
POEMS AND SONGS. Toronto, Hunter Rose, 1874. 223p [BM BVaU LC
  MWU NBFU OTP QMSS

THE POETICAL WORKS OF ALEXANDER MCLACHLAN. ... Toronto, Briggs, 1900.
424p [BVaU NBFU OTP
THE SPIRIT OF LOVE, AND OTHER POEMS. Toronto, Cleland, 1846. 36p [OTP

McLachlan, James
INHUMANITY. A Poem in Three Parts. Montreal, Lovell, 1868. 40p [NSHD
OTP QMSS

McLaren, Mrs. Floris Clark, 1904—
FROZEN FIRE. Toronto, Macmillan, 1937. 39p [BVaU NBFU OTU QMM

MacLaren, Ian
A RESENTMENT IN RELIEF. Ilfracombe, Devon, Stockwell, 1957. 31p

McLaughlin, Angus
POEMS THAT WILL INTEREST EVERYBODY. N.p., Author, 1912. 30p [NSWA
OONL
SELECTED POEMS. N.p., n.d. 78p [BVaU OONL QMSS
TITANIC. N.p., Author, [1912?]. 44p [QMU

McLean, Adele Peters
POEMS, LEGENDS AND LETTERS. Toronto, Musson, [19—?]. 128p [BM
BVaU OTP QMBM

MacLean, Alexander Henry, 1916—
POEMS. ["ca 1939"] [Rhod p947

Maclean, B.C.
SONNETS. Montreal, 1900. 8p [OTP QMSS

MacLean, Rev. D.
POEMS AND HYMNS. Charlottetown, Haszard & Moore, 1902. 172p [QMM

MacLean, Kate (Seymour)
ADVENT DAYS AND POEMS OF REMEMBRANCE. Kingston, Jackson Press, 1902.
28p [Brown U BVaU
THE COMING OF THE PRINCESS, AND OTHER POEMS. Toronto, Hunter Rose,
1881. 175p [BVaU OTP QMM
FROM THE BALCONY, AND OTHER POEMS. Kingston, Jackson Press, 1904.
32p [Brown U OLU

McLeish, John Alexander Buchanan, 1892—
NOT WITHOUT BEAUTY. Montreal, Lovell, 1940. 7p [Same title: Toronto,
Ryerson, 1948. 8p] [BVaU MWU NBFU OTP
ODE IN A WINTER EVENING, AND OTHER POEMS. Montreal, Lovell, 1938. 40p
[OTU QMM

McLennan, William, 1856—1904
SONGS OF OLD CANADA. Trans. by ——. Montreal, Dawson, 1886. 83p
[BM BVaU LC NSHD OKQ

MacLeod, Audrey
FAGGOTS FOR THE FIRE. Toronto, Nelson, 1933. 114p [OKQ

MacLeod, Calum Iain Nicholson, 1913–
AN t-EILTHIREACH. Original Gaelic Poems and Melodies. Sydney, N.S., Author, 1952. 43p

McLeod, Carroll W.
DAT H'AMPIRE H'AIR TRAIN PLAN. Toronto, Heaton Print., 1943. 85p [BVa LC OTP QMM
THE PATH OF THE "PROP." Quebec, Le Soleil, 1935. 61p [OWtL QMG

MacLeod, Elizabeth Susan (MacQueen), 1842–1939
CAROLS OF CANADA. ... Charlottetown, Coombs, 1893. 198p [2nd ed., 1899. 230p] [BVaU LC NBFU OTP
FOR THE FLAG; or, Lays and Incidents of the South African War. Charlottetown, Irwin, 1901. 185p [BM BVa OTP

MacLeod, Euphemia
MY ROSE AND OTHER POEMS. Boston, The Four Seas Co., 1919. 100p [BVi LC NSHPL OONL
SEANCES WITH CARLYLE. Boston, The Four Seas Co., 1919. 88p [LC NSHPL OH

MacLeod, Margaret (Arnett), 1877–1966
SONGS OF OLD MANITOBA. With Airs, French and English Words, and Introductions. Toronto, Ryerson, 1959. x + 93p

McMartin, L.E.
A BOOK OF VERSES, GAY AND SOMBRE. By Pendragon [pseud]. Toronto, Sovereign Press, 1936. 66p [BVaU OTL

McMaster, Bryce
COLLECTED POEMS. Oxford, Blackwell, 1947. 122p [BM LC
SHORT POEMS. By Clansman [pseud]. London, Kegan Paul, 1908. 47p [BM
THE STRANGER, AND OTHER POEMS. London, Arnold, 1923. 79p [BM OKQ
A TRIBUTE. [In verse]. By Clansman [pseud]. 1911. [BM

McMaster University, Members and Associates of
THE TOWER. An Anthology of Poems. [A continuing publication.] Hamilton, McMaster University, 1952–.

McMaster University Monthly
POEMS SELECTED FROM "THE McMASTER UNIVERSITY MONTHLY." Toronto, Briggs, 1894. 76p [OKQ

MacMechan, Archibald McKellar, 1862–1933
LATE HARVEST. Toronto, Ryerson, 1934. 54p [BVaU NSHD OKQ QMM

THREE SEA SONGS. (Nova Scotia Chapbook). Halifax, Marshall, 1919. 10p
[BVaU NBFU OKQ

McMeekan, John Murray
A RHYME OF ROUYN. Rouyn, Que., Author, 1941. [CC

Macmillan, Lachlan, 1878–
"VERSES FROM A SURGEON'S DIARY." Vancouver, Author, 1956. 2v

McMillan, Sophia Louise
MANITOBA'S VISION AND OTHER POEMS. [Winnipeg?], n.d. 58p [MWP OONL

Macmurray, Rev. Thomas James, 1852–
THE LEGEND OF DELAWARE VALLEY AND OTHER POEMS. Toronto, Briggs,
1887. 132p [BVaU NSHD OTU

McMurray, William
[TWO POEMS: LABRADOR; ADVICE TO A MARRIED LADY.] Quebec, Moore, 1790.
16p [Title supplied by Tremaine. No copy known to exist now.] [Tremaine
Cdn Imprints

McNab, B.A.
CONFISCATION. Being the Tale of a "Kicker" and a Calf. [Anon] Malagash,
N.S., Author, 1920. 4p [NSWA

McNair, Rev. John
THE SONGS OF HEBREW HISTORY. [N.p., 1902?] 94p [NSWA OTU

McNaughton, Harry P.
SHADOW LIGHTS OF SHAMSHUIPO. A Rhyming Picture of the Yesteryears.
Winnipeg, Author, 1944. 74p [OONL

Macnaughton, Isabel Christie
WOOD FIRES. New Ed., containing Three Additional Poems, also a Fantasy.
Oliver, B.C., Chronicle, 1948. 34p [First pub. in 1942.] [BVaU OTUV

MacNeill, A.D., –1895?
WOODLANDS AND OTHER RHYMES. Orangedale, N.S., Author, [1898?].
40p [NSHD OKQ

McNeill, Kate
POEMS. Vancouver, Evans & Hastings, 1918. 128p [BM BVaU NBFU OOP

McNeilly, Jean
POEMS FROM THE PRAIRIES. London, Stockwell, 1939. 24p [BM BViPA

McNichol, Vera Luella (Ernst), 1910–
BIBLE STORIES IN VERSE. [Kitchener, Dixon Press, 1957.] 2v
SUNSHINE AND AFTERGLOW. [Toronto, Livingstone Press, 1956.] 96p

MacNiven, Mrs. C., 1823—1865
AILEEN. A Poem. Ingersoll, 1865. 52p [BibC CCJ

MacNiven, Hope
THE BARD OF CLUTHA AND OTHER POEMS. Ingersoll, Gurnett, 1875. 82p
[BVaU OTP QMBM

Macphail, Andrew, 1864—1938
THE BOOK OF SORROW. Ed. by ——. London, Oxford U. Press, 1916. 500p
[BM BVaU LC NSHD OTU QMM

Macpherson, (Jean) Jay, 1931—
THE BOATMAN. Toronto, Oxford U. Press, 1957. x + 70p
A DRY LIGHT & THE DARK AIR. Toronto, Hawkshead Press, 1959. 4p
NINETEEN POEMS. Deya, Mallorca, Spain, Robert Graves Seizin Press, 1952. 9p
O EARTH RETURN. Toronto, 1954. 9p (Emblem Books)

McPherson, John, 1817—1845
POEMS, DESCRIPTIVE AND MORAL. With an introductory memoir by J.S.
   Thompson. Halifax, Chamberlain, 1862. 46 + 252p [BVaU NBFU OTP
THE PRAISE OF WATER. A Prize Poem. Halifax, Croskill, 1843. 16p [NSHP

McQuarrie, Nora
RAINBOW OF VERSE. Powell River, B.C., Town Crier, 1945. 74p [UTQ'46

MacQueen, Thomas, 1803—1861
THE EXILE. A Poem. Glasgow, Duncan, 1836. 166p [BM OTP
MY GLOAMING AMUSEMENTS. A Variety of Poems on Several Serious and
   Entertaining Subjects. Beith, Scotland, 1831. [BM
THE MOORLAND MINSTREL. Glasgow, Muir Gowans & Co., 1841. 214p
   2nd ed. [1st ed. in 1840] [BM OLU

McRobbie, Kenneth Alan, 1929—
EYES WITHOUT A FACE. Toronto, Gallery Editions, 1960. 58p

Magaret, Helene
THE TRUMPETING CRANE. New York, Farrar & Rinehart, 1934. 156p [NBFU

Main, Robert, 1873—1957
"HAPPY HOURS" FOR BOYS AND GIRLS. Nelson, B.C., Daily News, 1948. 23p
   [BVaU
POEMS. Toronto, Heaton, 1944. 57p [BVaU OTU

Mair, Charles, 1838—1927
DREAMLAND AND OTHER POEMS. Montreal, Dawson, 1868. 151p [BM BVaU
   LC NBFU OOC QMBM
TECUMSEH, A DRAMA (2nd ed.) AND CANADIAN POEMS. Toronto, Briggs, 1901.
   276p [BM BVaU OTP QMM

Maitland, Mary A. (Davidson), 1839–1919
AUTUMN LEAVES. Toronto, Briggs, 1907. 16p [BM OTUV
GOD SPEED THE TRUE. A Little Volume of Cheerful Canadian Verse. Toronto, Hunter Rose, 1919. 87p [Brown U

Major, J.C.
THE RED RIVER EXPEDITION. Winnipeg, P.G. Laurie 'News Letter Office,' 1870. 28p [Reprinted in Bibliog. Soc. of Canada's Facsimile Series, no. 3, Toronto, 1953.] [AEU NSHPL OKQ QQLA

Major, Marie Austen, 1903–
ROSES WITH THE THRONG. Manchester, Granite State Press, 1937. 90p [LC

Mandel, Elias Wolf, 1922–
FUSELI POEMS. Toronto, Contact Press, 1960. 66p
TRIO. First Poems. By Gael Turnbull, Phyllis Webb and E.W. Mandel. Toronto, Contact Press, 1954. 89p

Manners, Robert Rutland
PASCO, A CUBAN TALE, AND OTHER POEMS. With an essay on music appended. Cambridge, Mass., Riverside Press, 1877. 170p [Rev. ed. pub. under title: CUBA, AND OTHER VERSE. Toronto, Briggs, 1898. 155p] [BM BVaU OTUV QMBM

Manning, Frederick Charles, 1895–1917
POEMS. N.p., priv. print., [1920?]. 35p [BVaU NSHD OTP

Manning, James Harold, 1897–1924
COURCELETTE, AND OTHER POEMS. Saint John, McMillan, 1925. 106p [BVaU NBFU OTU QMM

Marcus, Rev. Moses
THE TEAR OF SYMPATHY, OR POETIC EFFUSIONS. Hallowell, Ont., Wilson, 1834. 120p [Brown U

Marham, Rose Etheridge
FALLEN ROSE LEAVES, GATHERED AND PRESSED. Toronto, Briggs, [1889?] 96p [Another ed., 1907.] [BVaU OTUV QMM

Marquis, Thomas Guthrie, 1864–1936
THE CATHEDRAL. A Poem. Toronto, Ryerson, 1924. 10p [NBFU OLU
THE CATHEDRAL AND OTHER POEMS. With a Foreword by Sir Charles G.D. Roberts. Toronto, Musson, 1936. 53p [BVaU NBFU OTP QMSS

Marriott, Anne, 1913–
CALLING ADVENTURERS! Toronto, Ryerson, 1941. 8p [BVaU NBFU OTP
SALT MARSH. Toronto, Ryerson, 1942. 16p [BVaU LC NBFU OTP QMM
SANDSTONE, AND OTHER POEMS. Toronto, Ryerson, 1945. 42p [BVaU LC MWU NBFU OTP

THE WIND OUR ENEMY. Toronto, Ryerson, 1939. 8p [BVaU NBSaM OKQ QMBM

Mars, P.C.
THE CALL OF TERRA NOVA. Newfoundland, 1924. 83p [Brown U BVaU

Marsden, Rev. Joshua, 1777–1837
AMUSEMENTS OF A MISSION; or, Poems, Moral, Religious and Descriptive, Interspersed with Anecdotes. Written during a Residence Abroad. By J.M. 2nd ed. London, Blanchard, 1818. 123p [BM OTP
THE BACKSLIDER. A Descriptive Moral Poem in Four Books. Plymouth-Dock, Johns, 1815. 64p [BM NSHD OTP
LEISURE HOURS; or, Poems, Moral, Religious & Descriptive. New York, Paul & Thomas, 1812. 160p [LC
THE MISSION. A Poem. Plymouth-Dock, Johns, 1816. 39p [BM
POEMS ON METHODISM: Embracing The Conference, or Sketches of Wesleyan Methodism. Philadelphia, Sorin & Ball, 1848. 156p [LC

Marshall, Emily Marguerite
IN LOVING MEMORY. Toronto, Best Print., 1938. 44p [OTP
"THE LADY OF MYSTERY" AND OTHER POEMS. Toronto, Beaver Print., [194–?]. 191p [Brown U BVaU QMU
THE LEGEND OF LOVESICK LAKE AND OTHER POEMS. Toronto, Warwick, 1925. 117p [BVaU NBFU OTU QMU
A ROMANCE OF THE MALIBU HILLS. New York, Vantage Press, 1958. 45p [NBFU

Marshall, John George, 1786–1880
REFLECTIONS DURING MY VISIT TO MY NATIVE PLACE. Halifax, Wesleyan Office, 1881. 22p [NSHP

Marshall, William Edward, 1859–1923
A BOOK OF VERSE. Bridgewater, Cragg, 1908. 126p [NSHD OTU
BROOKFIELD AND OTHER VERSE. Montreal, Lovell, 1919. 201p [BVaU NSHD OTU QMM
A LEGEND OF VENICE. Told in Rhymes. Bridgewater, Bulletin Press, 1907. 30p [NSWA

Martin, Alfred Tobias John
MARTIN'S ADDRESS TO MERCURY. Quebec, 1837. 7p [OTP

Martin, George, 1822–1900
MARGUERITE, or, The Isle of Demons; and Other Poems. Montreal, Dawson, 1887. 285p [BVaU NSHD OTP QMSS

Martin, Martha, 1875–
CAUGHT IN FLIGHT. Poems. New York, Vechten Waring, 1931. 103p [LC QMSS

CHAUTAUQUA GREETS YOU! New York, Gotham Press, 1940. 38p [LC QMSS
COME INTO MY GARDEN. A Collection of Flower and Tree Poems. New York,
Beekman Hill Press, 1935. 61p [QMBM
NATURE LYRICS AND OTHER POEMS. Boston, Badger, 1907. 89p [LC QMM
OUT OF THE SHADOWS, AND OTHER POEMS. New York, Beekman Hill Press,
1937. 78p [LC QMSS
POEMS. With The Birth of a Poem. New York, Gotham Press, 1941. 46p
[BVaU LC QMSS
POEM – ANECDOTES OF CHILD-MUSICIANS. New York, Beekman Hill Press,
1934. 50p [QMM
POEM-MINIATURES. Montreal, Guertin, 1899. 61p [BM
POETS' PILGRIMAGE. New York, Beekman Hill Press, 1938. 60p [BVaU LC
NBFU OTU QMSS
THE WEED'S PHILOSOPHY AND OTHER POEMS. Montreal, 1913. 43p [BVaU
NSWA QMM

Martin, William Henry
SONGS BY THE WAY. Toronto, Crucible Press, 1941. 30p [Brown U OTUV

Martley, John
SONGS OF THE CASCADES. Pt. I. By Erl Viking [pseud]. London, Cox, 1894.
192p [BM BVaU

Marty, Aletta Elise, 1866–1929
CREATIVE YOUNG CANADA. Collection of Verse, Drawings, and Musical
Compositions, by Young Canadians from Seven to Twenty years of age.
Toronto, Dent, 1928. 143p [Brown U BVaU OTUV

Mary Francis of Jesus, Sister, 1878–
GREY DAYS AND GOLD. By Miriam [pseud]. Victoria, Sisters of St. Ann, 1933.
149p [Brown U BViPA

Mason, Rev. George
LO – THE POOR INDIAN. Prize Poem. Victoria, Rose, 1875. 8p [BViPA
ODE ON THE LOSS OF THE STEAMSHIP "PACIFIC," NOVEMBER 4TH, 1875.
Nanaimo, B.C., Free Press, 1875. 4p [BVaU

Mason, Guy Montague, 1893–1954
THE CRY OF INSURGENT YOUTH. Toronto, Ryerson, 1927. 16p [BVaU
NBFU OTP
SPENDTHRIFTS. Toronto, Ryerson, 1928. 12p [BVaU NBFU OTP

Mason, Harold Campbell, 1895–
THREE THINGS ONLY. Toronto, Nelson, [1953?]. 75p

Massey, Gwendolen May (Merrin), 1907–
LEGEND AND OTHER POEMS. By Gwendolen Merrin. Toronto, Ryerson, 1944. 12p
[BVaU LC NSHD OTU QMM

SYMPHONY AND OTHER POEMS. By Gwendolen M. Merrin. Toronto, Author, 1935. 15p [BVaU NBFU OTP

Matheson, Charles Winfield, 1878–
POETICAL WORKS. N.p., n.d. 248 leaves [NSHD

Matheson, Daniel C.
POEMS. Hullcar, B.C., 1909. 11p [BM

Matheson, Duncan M.
CHEBUCTO, AND OTHER POEMS. ... Halifax, 1917. 125p [2nd ed.: Halifax, 1919. 152p] [Brown U NSHD OTU

Matheson, Mary Mackenzie (Nasmyth), 1885–
AUTUMN AFFLUENCE. Toronto, Ryerson, 1960. 8p
DESTINY AND OTHER POEMS. Toronto, Ryerson, 1928. 8p [BVaU NBFU OKQ
THE FRIENDLY HEART AND OTHER POEMS. [Toronto, priv. print., 1955]. 33p
I SEEK MY WAY. Toronto, Ryerson, 1949. 26p [BVaU
JOY AND OTHER POEMS. N.p., n.d. 20p [AEU BViPA QMU
LET'S LAUGH A LITTLE. By Merry Matheson. Vancouver, Halsall Print., [1957?]. 38p
MAGIC HILL AND OTHER POEMS. Toronto, Ryerson, 1929. 18p [BVaU NBFU OTP QMM
"THE MOVING FINGER" AND OTHER POEMS. Vancouver, Clarke & Stuart, 1944. 48p [BVaU OTP
OUT OF THE DUSK. Toronto, Ryerson, 1941. 8p [BVaU LC NSHD OTP QMM
SHINING WINGS. Vancouver, Wrigley, n.d. 36p [BVaU OTUV
SMILING THROUGH. Vancouver, Wrigley, 1934. 16p [OKQ
TO A PRAIRIE ROSE AND OTHER POEMS. Vancouver, Clarke & Stuart, 1933. 28p [BVaU
THE URGE DIVINE, AND OTHER POEMS. Toronto, Ryerson, n.d. 33p [BVa
WORSHIP, AND OTHER POEMS. N.p., n.d. 21p [OKQ

Mathieson, Hugh
THE BACKWASH OF HELL, AND FIFTY OTHER POEMS AND SONGS. Montreal, 1928. 62p [Brown U

Matthews, Richard F., 1832–
POEMS. London, Ont., Dawson, 1866. 68p [BVaU NSHD OTP

Maunsell, H. Wakefield
THESE WALLS. Toronto, Crucible Press, 1945. 22p [BViPA OTU

Maura, Sister (née Mary Power), 1881–1957
BREATH OF THE SPIRIT. Toronto, Macmillan, 1937. 35p [Brown U NSHD OOP

INITIATE THE HEART. New York, Macmillan, 1946. 46p [LC
RHYME AND RHYTHM. Toronto, Ryerson, 1932. 11p [BVaU NBFU OTU QMM
RHYTHM POEMS. Toronto, Ryerson, 1944. 8p [BVaU LC NSHD OTP
THE ROSARY IN TERZA RIMA. Toronto, Dent, 1941. 30p [BVaU LC OTU QMM
A SHEAF OF SONGS BY SISTER MAURA. Lower Granville, N.S., Abanaki Press, 1948.
24p [Brown U BVaU NBFU OTU

Mawle, William Waddy, 1902–
RANDOM RHYME AND VARIED VERSE. Victoria, Author, 1959. 97p

Maxwell, Lilian Mary (Beckwith), 1877–1956
THE RIVER ST. JOHN AND ITS POETS. 2nd printing, enl. Sackville, N.B., Tribune
Press, 1947. 85p [1st ed.: Fredericton, Author, 1946. 64p] [BVaU NBFU
OTP QMSS

May, Roberta E.
SCATTERED SEEDS. Ilfracombe, Devon, Stockwell, 1952. 31p

May, Sydney
PRAIRIE FAIRIES AND OTHER VERSES. Calgary, Author, 1932. [CC

Mayne, Daniel Haydn
POEMS AND FRAGMENTS. Toronto, Coates, 1838. 126p [OTP

Meek, Kenneth, 1908–
A CAROL OF THANKS. Part Song for Female Voices. New York, Gray, 1946.
[CC

Mellor, Violet
ISLAND LIGHT. From A COLLECTION OF POEMS, by ——. Toronto, Aberdeen
Press, 1953. 8p

Melville, Tom ("Scotty")
BARBED WIRE BALLADS. Regina, School Aids Pub. Co., 1945. 61p [BVaU
OTP

Menzies, Alfred
BEAUTY AND HUMILITY. Winnipeg, 1933. 89p [OONL

Menzies, George, 1796?–1847
THE POSTHUMOUS WORKS OF THE LATE GEORGE MENZIES. Being a Collection of
Poems, Sonnets, &c. &c. Written at Various Times when the Author was
connected with the Provincial Press. Woodstock, Ont., Douglass, 1850. 95p
[OTP

Merkel, Andrew Doane, 1884–1954
THE ORDER OF GOOD CHEER. A Narrative Poem. Halifax, Imperial Pub. Co., 1944.
46p [Same title, with drawings ... by Robert Chambers: Lower Granville, N.S.,
Abanaki Press, 1946. xix + 102p] [BVaU LC NBFU OTU

TALLAHASSEE. A Ballad of Nova Scotia in the Sixties. Halifax, Imperial Pub. Co., 1945. 103p [BVaU LC NBFU OTP QMM

Merkley, George E., 1865–1904?

CANADIAN MELODIES AND POEMS. Toronto, Hart & Riddell, 1893. 104p [BVaU NBFU OTP QMM

Merner, F.

TRUE CANADIANISM. An Appeal. 4th ed., rev. and enl. N.p., n.d. 16p [AEU OPAL

Merrill, Anne

SONGS OF SHERBROOKE. Sherbrooke, Que., Page-Sangster, 1932. 73p [BVaU OKQ QMM

VERSE. Goffstown, N.H., Gibbs & Brown, 1941. 16p [LC

Merrill, Helen M.

SANDPIPERS AND OTHER POEMS. Toronto, priv. print., 1915. 7p [NBFU OTU

Meyers, Leonard William, 1917–

WHEN WORDS COLLIDE. San Antonio, Tex., Naylor Co., 1960. 48p

Michie, A.R.

LYRICS AND POEMS. ... Toronto, Briggs, 1912. 112p [BM Brown U BVaU OLU

Middleton, Clara J. (Russell) Jackson, 1872?–1955

GREEN FIELDS AFAR. Memories of Alberta Days. By Clara and J.E. Middleton. Toronto, Ryerson, 1947. 61p [BVaU NBFU OTP

Middleton, Helen E.

DRUMBEATS THROUGH YOUR DREAMS. Saint John, Author, 1945. 40p [Brown U BVaU NBFU

Middleton, Jesse Edgar, 1872–1960

SEA DOGS AND MEN AT ARMS. A Canadian Book of Songs. Toronto, McClelland, 1918. 104p [BM BVaU LC NBFU OTP QMM

Mildmay, Rev. Aubrey Neville St. John, 1865–

HORAE MEDITERRANEAE. [Selected Passages of English verse, with Greek and Latin Renderings and Some Original Poems by the Author.] London, Baxter, 1947. 71p [BM

IN THE WAITING TIME OF WAR, AND OTHER POEMS. London, Swan Sonnenschein, 1900. 39p [BM BVaU

SEA-ROOM. A Vancouver Empire Song. Toronto, Briggs, 1910. 9p [BM Brown U BVaU OTUV

Miller, Ewart

OVER THE WHEEL. Toronto, Author, 1940. 25p [LC OTU

Miller, Margaret Gertrude (Lang), 1869–
GLEANINGS ALONG THE HIGHWAYS. A Collection of Poems. Hamilton, Davis-Lisson, 1934. 349p [Brown U OLU

Miller, P. Florence
IN CARIBOU LAND. Intro. by E.J. Pratt. Toronto, Ryerson, 1929. 64p [BVaU OKQ QMBM

Miller, Peter, 1920–
MEDITATION AT NOON. Toronto, Contact Press, 1958. 101p
SONATA FOR FROG AND MAN. Toronto, Contact Press, 1959. 82p

Miller, Roscoe R.
ELIXIR OF MORALE. Toronto, Standard Pub., 1943. 104p [BVaU LC OTP QMM

Milligan, James Lewis, 1876–
THE BECKONING SKYLINE AND OTHER POEMS. Toronto, McClelland, 1920. 111p [BM BVaU NBFU OTU QMM
CHRISTMAS. Eight Poems. Toronto, Gothic Press, [1925?]. 10p [BVaU OKQ
A CLOCK IN A BASSINET. A Ballad of Love and Time. Toronto, Ryerson, 1938. 8p [BVaU OTL
SILURIA AND OTHER POEMS. Toronto, Ryerson, 1947. 24p [BVaU OTP
SONGS IN TIME'S DESPITE. London, Griffiths, 1910. 64p [BM BVaU LC OKQ
THEY SHALL RETURN AND OTHER POEMS. Toronto, Forward Pub. Co., 1943. 16p [BVaU OTP

Milliken, Lorene Frances (Ritz)
MANITOBA LANDSCAPE. N.p., 1954. 8p (Carillon Poetry Chap-Books)
A MORNING MOOD. Gananoque, Ont., Hilda M. Ridley, 1953. 12p (Carillon Poetry Chap-Books)
MY SOUL SINGS. N.p., 1955. 8p (Carillon Poetry Chap-Books)
PRINCESS OF AUNE. [Winnipeg, Author,] 1956. 10p (Carillon Poetry Chap-Books)
WHITE ORCHIDS. Gananoque, Ont., Hilda M. Ridley, 1952. 12p (Carillon Poetry Chap-Books)

Mills, David, 1831–1903
POEMS WRITTEN AT SPARE MOMENTS. Ottawa, Crain, 1901. 79p [BM Brown U OTU

Mills, Phebe A.
VESPER CHIMES. Halifax, Macnab, 1872. 122p [BVaU NSHD OOP

Minto, Charles
THE HOWES O' BUCHAN, AND FAR AWA', WITH OTHER POEMS. Montreal, priv. print., 1896. 173p [BM OTP QMSS

Mitchell, John, 1882–1951
THE WATER-DRINKER. By Patrick Slater [pseud]. Toronto, Allen, 1937. 148p
[BVaU OTP

Mitchell, John Hanlon, 1897–1953
OTHER SONGS. By John Hanlon [pseud]. Toronto, Ryerson, 1927. 32p [BVaU
NBSaM OTP QMM
SONGS. By John Hanlon [pseud]. Toronto, Ryerson, 1927. 24p [BVaU LC NBFU
OTU QMM

Mitchell, Ronald Elwy
DAN OWEN AND THE ANGEL JOE. ... New York, Harper, 1948. 250p [BM LC
DEEP WATERS. London, Gollancz, 1937. 286p [BM LC

Mocket, John
A FEW THOUGHTS JOTTED DOWN IN RHYME TO WHILE AWAY A LITTLE TIME.
N.p., n.d. [Amtmann cat. 250

Moffatt, Gertrude (MacGregor), 1884–1923
A BOOK OF VERSES. With an intro. by Bernard K. Sandwell. Toronto, Macmillan,
1924. 139p [Reprinted: Toronto, Book Society of Can., 1950. 139p] [BVaU
NSHD OTP

Moffatt, Warneford
NEW CANADIAN POEMS. Composed at Various Times. ... Toronto, Briggs, 1914.
105p [Brown U
AN ODE ON THE CANADIAN SOLDIERS WHO FELL NEAR YPRES, WITH OTHER
POEMS. London, Simpkin, 1916. 31p [BVaU OTU

Molesworth, Eva Sarah, –1944
A GARDEN IN ANTRIM. Toronto, Briggs, 1908. 10p [BM OTU

Monckton, Geoffrey F.
LOVERS OF ENGLAND. London, Vickery, 1921. 55p [BM

Monk, Samuel Cornwallis, 1814–1888
THE SAGUENAY. An Unpublished Poem. [Anon] Montreal, priv. print., 1860.
[OOP
THE ROMAN CONQUEST. A Manuscript Poem. [Anon] N.p., priv. print., 1870.
62p [OOA

Montgomery, Lucy Maud, 1874–1942
THE WATCHMAN AND OTHER POEMS. Toronto, McClelland, 1916. 159p [BM
BVaU LC NBFU OTU QMM

Montreal, Que. Women's Art Society
POEMS ON PEACE, From Among Those Submitted in Competition. Montreal, the
Society, [1931?]. 6p [CC

Moodie, Marion Elizabeth, 1867–
SONGS OF THE WEST. Toronto, Briggs, 1904. 8p [AEU BM OTP QMU
SONGS OF THE WEST AND OTHER POEMS. Toronto, Ryerson, 1934. 23p [BVaU
NBSaM OTP QMM

Moodie, Susanna (Strickland), 1803–1885
ENTHUSIASM AND OTHER POEMS. London, Smith Elder, 1831. 214p [BM
NSHPL OTP QMM

Moody, Irene Helen (Hawkins), –1958
ALWAYS THE BUBBLES BREAK. Toronto, Macmillan, 1947. 39p [BVaU LC
NBFU OTP
ATTAR OF SONG AND OTHER POEMS. Toronto, Macmillan, 1936. 71p [BM BVaU
NBFU OTP QMBM
LAVA. Toronto, Macmillan, 1940. 96p [BVaU LC NBFU OKQ
WRAITHS. Toronto, Macmillan, 1934. 66p [BM BVaU NBFU OTL QMBM

Mooney, Hugh R., 1914–
CLIPPED WINGS. Victoria, Quality Printers, 1946. 88p [BVa

Moore, Charles Ed [Edward?], [Editor?]
THE POETIC GLOBE. Poems. Toronto, 1887. [OOP

Moore, Francis, 1870–
MEDITATIONS IN RHYME OF THINGS MATERIAL, MORAL, AND MYSTIC. By F.R.M.
Collingwood, Ont., Enterprise Bulletin, 1942–49. [Four pamphlets bound
together.] [QMM

Moore, Helen, –1941
HELEN'S POEMS. [Anon] Collected by Anna M. Walker. Stanger, Alta., 1944.
39p [OPAL

Moore, James Mavor, 1919–
AND WHAT DO *YOU* DO? A Short Guide to the Trades and Professions. London,
Toronto, Dent, 1960. 57p

Moore, Philip Hooper, 1879–1961
ROSSIGNOL RHYMES. 1929. White Point Beach, N.S., Rossignol Press, [1930?].
164p [NSHD OTU
SMOKE SCREEN. Bridgewater, N.S., Bulletin Press, 1944. 78p [OTP

Moore, S.
POEMS. Montreal, Lovell, 1887. 315p [BVaU OTP QMSS

Moore, William Wallace
RANDOM RHYMES. Toronto, Hunter Rose, 1885. 224p [BVaU OTUV

Moose Jaw, Sask. Prairie Poetry Club
THE CRESCENT MOON. A Magazine of Original Verse by Canadian Prairie Writers.
... Moose Jaw, Crescent Press, 1934–35. 2 issues. [UTQ

Moose Jaw, Sask. Writers' Club
CHRISTMAS, 1940. Moose Jaw, the Club, 1940. 32p [OTU
CHRISTMAS, 1942. Moose Jaw, the Club, 1942. 24p [SSU
OUR AUTUMN OFFERINGS. [Moose Jaw, the Club, 1944?]. 23p [SSU
PRAIRIE POEMS. Moose Jaw, the Club, 1943. 24p [Brown U SSU
VERSES FOR YOU. Moose Jaw, the Club, 1941. 35p [Brown U

Morant, Mollie (Wylde)
THE SINGING GYPSY. Toronto, Ryerson, 1941. 8p [BVaU NBSaM OTP QMM

Morden, Charles Draper
UNIVERSUS. ... Ottawa, Author, 1911. 55p [BM Brown U BVaU OTU

More, Amelia
GLORY GEMS. Orillia, Gospel Light, 1893. 48p [Amtmann cat. 151

Morgan, Mary, 1856?—
ECHOES FROM THE SOLITUDES. London, Allen, 1901. 95p [BM NSWA OTUV
QMM
GLIMPSES INTO THE LETTERS OF A WANDERER, including Poems & Translations.
London, Mathews, 1914. 66p [BM
HALF-SILENT FELLOWSHIPS. Edinburgh, Foulis, 1909. 104p [BM BVaU OLU
QMM
MARGUERITES. London, Haas, 1898. 71p [BM
POEMS AND TRANSLATIONS. Montreal, Robinson, 1887. 195p [Cf. WOOD NOTES
IN THE GLOAMING, *below*] [BVaU NBFU OTP QMM
SEEDS FROM THE GARDEN OF THE WORLD. Edinburgh, Foulis, 1904. 208p [BM
SONNETS FROM SWITZERLAND. 1896. [MOR'98
TRAUMEREIEN. [MOR'12
WOODNOTES IN THE GLOAMING. Poems and Translations. Boston, Cupples, 1889
[AmCat

Morgan, Mary Ellen (O'Brien)
IN OUR HOUSE. By Nana [pseud]. Victoria, B.C. 1958. 54p

Morgan, Mrs. Seraph A.C.
SCRAPS OF SONG FROM LA RIVIERE AUX BROCHETS. St. John, Que., Author,
n.d. 51p

Morgan-Powell, Samuel, 1898—
DOWN THE YEARS. Toronto, Macmillan, 1938. 90p [BVaU NBFU OTP QMM

Morison, Mrs. J.A.
MY SOLDIER BOY AND OTHER POEMS. Toronto, Copp Clark, 1916. [CAR

Morley, Edna Lillian, 1891—
SONGS OF FREEDOM. Milverton, Ont., Sun, [1940?]. 8p [Brown U OTUV
VERSES. Milverton, Ont., Author, 1938. 42p [OTU
WATCHWORDS OF LIBERTY. Toronto, Crucible Press, 1942. 28p [LC OTU

Morris, Frank
A MASTER MIND. "Thou madest him lower than the angels." Port Hope, Ont.,
  Author, 1906. 16p [OTU

Morris, Maria
METRICAL MUSINGS. By M. and C.M. Morris [of Halifax]. New York, Craighead,
  1856. 188p [NSHD

Morris, Melba, 1909–
ON WINGS OF THOUGHT. Owen Sound, Bates Advt. & Print., 1936. 38p [Brown U
  MWU
THROUGH CASEMENT WINDOWS. Owen Sound, Bates Advt. and Print., 1935. 38p
  [UTQ

Morrison, Llewellyn A.
HEART BELLS. London, Ont., Lawson & Jones, 1899. 303p [BVaU OTP

Morrison, Sara Moore
SCENES AND HOURS. Toronto, Crucible Press, 1945. 40p [CC

Morse, William Inglis, 1874–1952
ACADIAN LAYS AND OTHER VERSE. Toronto, Briggs, 1908. 65p [BVaU NBFU
  OTP
THE LADY LATOUR. With Picture Poses Appended for those who Journey. Toronto,
  Ryerson, 1920. 91p [BM BVaU NBFU OOP QMM
THE NARROWING PATH, 1901–1920. London, priv. print., 1933. 80p [BVaU
  NBFU OTU QMM

Morse-Farnum, Mrs. H.I.
POEMS AND THOUGHTS TERSELY TOLD. ... N.p., 1910. 48p [Brown U

Mortimer, John
DAY DREAMS OF A PIONEER, AND OTHER POEMS. Toronto, Briggs, 1911. 64p
  [BM Brown U BVaU OLU

Morton, Irene (Elder), 1849–1923
IDYLLS OF THE DANE. Boston, Gorham, 1916. 106p [LC

Morton, James [of H.M. Customs, Nova Scotia]
IRELAND: A Poem. Dublin, Milliken, 1846. 95p [BM

Morton, James [of Victoria, B.C.], **1870?–1967**
THE CHURCHILL TREE. Songs of War and Peace. Victoria, Diggon-Hibben, 1945.
  44p [BVaU OTP
HERESIES AND OTHER POEMS. Victoria, Author, 1937. 64p [BVaU OTU

Moscovitch, Henry, 1941–
THE SERPENT INK. Toronto, Contact Press, 1956. 35p

Mounfield, William M.
LINES OF A LUNGER. [Hamilton?], n.p. 1917. 21p [NBFU

Mountain, Mrs. Annie
THE LEGEND OF ST. HELIER. Jersey, LeFeuvre, 1863. 16p [NSHP
OLD AND NEW SARUM; ADDISON'S BIRTHPLACE AND STONEHENGE. Salisbury,
England, Brown & Co., 1862. 26p [Selected from WILTSHIRE BALLADS.]
[AEU QMU
"A WREATH OF RUE," FOR LENT, AND THE SACRED LAKE. Toronto, Rowsell &
Hutchison, 1873. 49p [BVaU OTP

Mountain, Rev. George Jehoshaphat, 1789–1863
SONGS OF THE WILDERNESS. Being a Collection of Poems written in 1844. London,
Rivington, 1846. 155p [BM BVaU LC NBFU OTP QMM

Mountcastle, Clara H., 1837–
IS MARRIAGE A FAILURE? LOST! AND MANY GEMS OF VERSE. Toronto, Imrie &
Graham, 1899. 64p [BM OTP
THE MISSION OF LOVE, LOST, AND OTHER POEMS. With Songs and Valentines.
By Caris Sima [pseud]. Toronto, Hunter, 1882. 200p [BVaU LC NBFU OKQ

Mowat, Grace Helen, 1875–1964
FUNNY FABLES OF FUNDY. Ottawa, Ru-Mi-Lou Books, 1928. 79p [BVaU
NBFU OOP QMBM

Moyer, W.A.E.
SOME RHYMING RAMBLINGS. St. Catharines, Author, 1942. 14p [CC

Moyse, Charles Ebenezer, 1852–1924
ELLA LEE. Glimpses of Child Life. London, Mathews, 1910. 43p [BM OONL
QMM
THE LURE OF EARTH, AND OTHER POEMS. London, 1911. 71p [BM OONL QMM

Muchall, Mary Elizabeth Jane (Traill), 1841–1892
STEP BY STEP; or, The Shadow on a Canadian Home. ... A Story in Two Parts: ...
"The Beginning" ... "And the End." Toronto, Rowsell & Hutchison, 1876.
59p [BVaU NSHD OTP
THE STOLEN SKATES. A Canadian Tale. By Mrs. Muchall. Toronto, James
Campbell, n.d. [187–?]. 45p [Patrick cat. 39

Mullane, George, 1850–1938
VICTOR HUGO'S DAUGHTER AND OCCASIONAL VERSE. Halifax, 1923. 32p [OTU

Mulliss, William, 1876?–1932
MORE "WORDS, WORDS, WORDS." Montreal, Southam Press, 1931. 13p [OTP
"WORDS, WORDS, WORDS." Montreal, Southam Press, 1927. 26p [BVaU OTP

Mulock, Edith
VOICES OF THE DUSK. Toronto, Oxford U. Press, 1934. 32p [LC OTU

Mulvenna, Robert D.
HAPPY DAYS. A Salute to Toronto on its 125th Anniversary. Toronto, [1960?].
14p
THE OLD HOME TOWN. Toronto, Author, [1945?]. 11p [OTUV

Muncaster, Eric, 1889–
"GENTLEMEN, THE KING!" AND OTHER THOUGHTS. Montreal, Author, 1934. 60p
[Brown U OTUV

Munday, Albert R.
LOVER LYRICS, AND OTHERS. Toronto, Briggs, 1916. 51p [BM BVaU OKQ

Munday, Rupert
WITHIN THE TAVERN CAUGHT. Foleyet, Ont., Crucible Press, 1950. 40p [BVa

Munn, George
PATRIOTIC AND OTHER POEMS. Toronto, Imrie & Graham, 1900. 128p [BM
BVaU NSHD OKQ

Munro, Mrs. Elizabeth V., 1900–
BRICKS WITHOUT STRAW. Saint John, Wayside Press, 1934. 19p [AEU NBSaM

Munro, W.D.
MIRROR AND REFLECTIONS. Victoria, Diggon-Hibben, 1942. 21p [OKQ

Munro, William
MANITOULIN ECHOES FROM BLUFF, DALE, LAKE AND STREAM, IN VERSE. Gore
Bay, Ont., Recorder Press, [19—?]. 53p [OTP

Murdoch, Robert, 1836–
A COMPLETE WORK OF ROBERT MURDOCH. ... Containing his Poems, Songs, Toasts
and Epigrams. With a Sketch of the Life of the Poet. Halifax, Macnab, 1890.
149p [BVaU NSHD OTU

Murdock, William, 1823–1887?
DISCURSORY RUMINATIONS, A FIRESIDE DRAMA, Etc., Etc. Saint John, Chubb,
1876. 233p [BVaU NBFU OTP QMBM
POEMS AND SONGS. Saint John, Barnes, 1860. 152p [2nd ed., enl. and improved:
Saint John, McMillan, 1872. 232p] [BVaU MWU NSHD OTP QMM

Murphy, J.A.
SONGS OF THE EVENING. A Volume of Original Verse. Ottawa, Mortimer, 1896.
18p [OTP

Murphy, James, 1867–1931
MURPHY'S SEALERS' SONG BOOK. Comp. by ——. St. John's, Telegram Print., 1905.
28p [NfSM
CORONATION SONG BOOK OF NEWFOUNDLAND. Comp. by ——. St. John's,
Murphy, 1911. 12p [NfSG

OLD SONGS OF NEWFOUNDLAND. Comp. by ——. St. John's, 1912. 11p [NfSM
SONGS AND BALLADS OF NEWFOUNDLAND, ANCIENT AND MODERN. St. John's,
Milligan, 1902. 90p [NBSaM
SONGS OF OUR LAND. "Old Home Week" Souvenir. Comp. by ——. St. John's,
Telegram Print., 1904. 89p [NfSG
SONGS SUNG BY OLD-TIME SEALERS OF MANY YEARS AGO. Comp. by ——. St.
John's, 1925. 20p [NfSM
SONGS THEIR FATHERS SUNG. For Fishermen. Old Time Ditties. Comp. by ——. St.
John's, Murphy, 1923. 17p [NfSM OTUV

Murphy, Louise
SWEET CANADA. Twelve Bird Songs and a Round. Toronto, Longmans, 1923.
[BVa

Murray, George, 1830—1910
HOW CANADA WAS SAVED. ... Toronto, Copp Clark, 1874. 17p [NSHD
MEN AND WOMEN MERELY PLAYERS. Drawings by R.G. Mathews; Verses by
George Murray. Montreal, Renaissance Press, 1903. 21p [QMM
POEMS. Ed. with a memoir by John Reade. Montreal, O'Connor, 1912. 236p [BM
BVaU NSHD OTP QMM
VERSES & VERSIONS. Montreal, Brown, 1891. 403p [BVaU LC OTP QMM

Murray, Rev. John Clark, 1836—1917
EPIMETHEUS [a Poem], to my students. Montreal, 1897. 12p [BVaU OTP QMM

Mutter, Mrs. Jean
MUD-PUP. A Sequence in Light Verse. Victoria, Diggon-Hibben, 1944. 30p [BVaU
OTP

Myers-Funnell, Rozelle V.
A BOOKLET OF VERSE. A Jubilee Offering. Ottawa, Birkett, 1897. 25p [BM OOP

Nairn, Robert, 1854—1937
VERSES, HUMOROUS AND PATHETIC. Rat Portage, News Pub. Co., 1900. 47p
[OKQ

Napier, Nina (Marwick), 1900—
LIBRARY LEVITY. Seattle, McCaffrey, 1946. 38p [2nd ed., enl., 1952. 47p]
[BVaU LC OTP

Nash, Arthur Charles, 1878—
BUDS AND BLOSSOMS. Vancouver, Clarke & Stuart, 1960. 60p
THE DRAMA OF DUNQUERQUE. Vancouver, Storer, 1941. 38p [BVa LC OTP
LYRICS OF LIFE. Vancouver, Storer, 1941. 64p [BVa LC OTP
MEMORIES IN MELODY. Toronto, Ryerson, 1920. 86p [BM BVaU OTP
AN ODE TO CANADA AND OTHER POEMS. Toronto, Briggs, 1910. 60p [Reprinted:
Vancouver, Clarke & Stuart, 1958.] [BM BVaU OOP

REVERIES IN MELODY. New York, Exposition Press, 1957. 63p
RUTH AND OTHER POEMS. Vernon, B.C., News Print., 1910. 33p [BViP
THE SOJOURNER. Vancouver, Storer, 1943. 64p [BVa LC OTP
SONGS OF THE SEASONS. Vancouver, Dunsmuir Print., 1944. 40p [BVaU LC
OTP

Nasir, George
FIFTEEN POEMS. Winnipeg, Dahl Co., 1948. 15p [NBFU OKQ
NEW POEMS. Winnipeg, Dahl Co., 1949. 8p [OKQ

Nealis, Jean Elizabeth U. (Wilkenson), 1842–
DRIFT. Montreal, Sadlier, 1884. 98p [NBFU OTP

Nease, Lilla Stewart (Dunlap), 1858–
PASTURES NEW. By Lilla Stewart Nease and Henry Roche. Picton, Times Pub. Co.,
1935. 24p [UTQ

Needler, George Henry, 1866–1962
THE BATTLEFORD COLUMN. Versified Memories of a Queen's Own Corporal in the
Northwest Rebellion, 1885. Montreal, Prov. Pub. Co., 1948. 92p [Also:
Montreal, Provincial Pub. Co., 1957.] [BVaU NBFU OTP
THE NIBELUNGLEID. Trans. into Rhymed English Verse in the Metre of the Original.
New York, Holt, 1904. 349p [NBFU OTU

Neilan, William Sydney
THROUGH WAYSIDE GARDENS. A Collection of Verses. Montreal, Renouf, 1931.
114p [BVaU OTP QMBM

Nelson, Edwin G.
RAISE THE FLAG AND OTHER PATRIOTIC CANADIAN SONGS AND POEMS. 1891.
[Rhod p858

Nelson, H.M.
PROMOTION BALLADS, AND OTHERS ABOUT THE INVINCIBLE NOTHING. Toronto,
Briggs, 1914. 74p [2nd ed., rev., 1915. 99p] [BM BVaU OTP

Nelson, V.H.
THE NEW BRUNSWICK MINSTREL. Saint John, n.d. [CCJ NBB

New Frontiers
THE STONE, THE AXE, THE SWORD, AND OTHER CANADIAN POEMS. Toronto, New
Frontiers, 1955. 32p [Selections from the poems of Alexander McLachlan,
Isabella Valancy Crawford, Archibald Lampman, and Peter McArthur.]

Newell, Rev. John Robert, 1853–1912
POEMS AND SONGS. Boston, Badger, 1904. 136p [BVa LC OTU
THE TIMES, AND OTHER POEMS. Toronto, Hunter, 1881. 151p [BVaU NBFU
OKQ

Newson, William Victor, 1877–1931?
A VALE IN LUXOR. Intro. note by Nellie L. McClung. Toronto, Ryerson, 1926.
  12p [BVaU NBSaM OTP
WAIFS OF THE MIND. Toronto, Ryerson, 1927. 30p [BVaU NBFU OKQ

Newton, John
THE EMIGRANT AND OTHER PIECES. Hamilton, Robertson, 1846. 48p [OTP

Nicholl, M.A.
LAYS FROM THE WEST. By "Stella" —M.A. Nicholl. Winnipeg, Manitoba Free
  Press, 1884. 103p [BVaU OTU

Nichols, J. Arthur
AROUND HOME. By Art Nichols. Windsor, Curtis, 1937. 48p [AEU OH QMU
FIRE-SIDE FANCIES. Chatham, Planet Press, 1925. 111p [OKQ

Nichols, Mrs. Ruby
SONGS FROM THEN AND NOW. Toronto, Ryerson, 1947. 7p [BVaU MWU
  NBFU OTU
SYMPHONY. Toronto, Ryerson, 1956. 12p

Nickerson, Moses Hardy, 1846–1943
CAROLS OF THE COAST. Songs, Ballads, and Legends, Original and Translated.
  Halifax, Nova Scotia Print., 1892. 288p [BVaU NSHD OTP
SONGS OF SUMMERLAND, AND OTHER POEMS. To which are added "Rhymin'
  Remarks on Men and Things," by Thomas Cod. Boston, Nickerson, 1927. 212p
  [LC OTP

Nicolls, Minnie P.
IDEALS. Vancouver, Evans & Hastings, 1904. 48p [BVaU

Nightingale, Winnifred M., 1902–
HUMBLY YOURS. Guelph, Author, 1935. 24p [OTU

Niven, Frederick John, 1878–1944
A LOVER OF THE LAND, AND OTHER POEMS. New York, Boni, 1925. 72p [BM
  BVaU LC NBFU OKQ
MAPLE LEAF SONGS. London, Sidgwick & Jackson, 1917. 44p [BM BVaU OTP

Nixon, John Eric, 1897–
MORRISON'S PLACE AND OTHER POEMS. Regina, Commercial Print., [194–?].
  39p [Peel Adelphi
SELECTED POEMS. Toronto, Crucible Press, 1945. 46p [BVaU OKQ

Nixon, Marian Essley
FOUR WISHES, AND OTHER POEMS. London, Stockwell, 1933. 64p [BM

Nobody Knows Who (pseud)
POEMS. By Nobody Knows Who [pseud]. Southampton, Forbes & Pittman, 1857.
  134p [BVaU

Noel, Garet (pseud?)
THE SONG OF NIAGARA. By "Garet Noel." Toronto, Copp Clark, n.d. 12p
  [NSHD OTUV

Norcross, Rene
THE UP AND UP. Vancouver, City Museum, 1949. 8p [BM BVaU NBFU

Norman, Dorothy, 1905—
DUALITIES. New York, priv. print., 1933. 114p [LC

North, John
TALE OF THE DAYS OF HI YU BILL AND ITS ROYAL COMMISSION. As told by Isaac,
  the Moosehide Chief. Arranged by John North. Toronto, Moore Print-Shop,
  1908. 30p [BM BVaU OKQ

North, Peter Robert, 1894—
HARSHLY THE RAIN FELL. Toronto, Author, 1950. 12p [Brown U OONL

Norton, Mrs. Mary
THE MINISTRY OF FLOWERS AND OTHER POEMS.By Mrs. Norton. ... Toronto,
  Briggs, 1890. 110p [BVaU NBFU OTP

Norwood, Rev. Robert Winkworth, 1874—1932
BILL BORAM. New York, Doran, 1921. 96p [BVaU LC NSHD OKQ
HIS LADY OF THE SONNETS. Boston, Sherman French, 1915. 85p [BVaU LC
  NSHD OKQ QMM
ISSA. New York, Scribner, 1931. 95p [BVaU LC NSHD OKQ
THE MODERNISTS. New York, Doran, 1918. 146p [BVaU LC NSHD OKQ
MOTHER AND SON. New York, Doran, 1925. 72p [BVaU LC NSHD OKQ
THE PIPER AND THE REED. New York, Doran, 1917. 119p [BVaU LC NSHD
  OKQ

Nott, Edward Vernon, 1878—
THE BALLAD OF THE SOUL'S DESIRE. London, Greening, 1903. 124p [BM OTUV
CLEOPATRA WITH ANTHONY. London, Greening, 1904. [BM
THE JOURNEY'S END, AND OTHER VERSE. London, Greening, 1904. 98p [BM
SUMMER DAYS AND OTHER VERSES. London, Greening, 1906. 95p [BM

Nova Scotia. Poetry Society
NOVA SCOTIA BOOK OF VERSE. Halifax, the Society, [1949—51?]. 2v [NBFU
  OTP

Nova-Scotian, A (1827) (pseud)
HENRY. A Poem in Two Cantos. By a Nova-Scotian [pseud]. Halifax, Cunnabell,
  1827. 22p [NSHP

Nowlan, Alden A., 1933—
A DARKNESS IN THE EARTH. Eureka, Calif., Hearse Press, [1959?]. 16p
THE ROSE AND THE PURITAN. Fredericton, U. of New Brunswick, 1958. 16p

Obodiac, Stanlee, 1922–
THE SOUL SPEAKS. Yorkton, Redeemer's Voice, 1950. 63p [Brown U OONL

O'Brian, Grace (Williams)
AT THE TOP OF THE HILL. Toronto, Dent, 1928. 86p [BM OTL

O'Brien, Rev. Cornelius, 1843–1906
AMINTA. A Modern Life Drama. New York, Appleton, 1890. 187p [BM BVaU LC NSHD OOU QMM

O'Byrne, Michael Cyprian
NYSSIA. An Old World Story. Toronto, Ellis, 1905. 85p [NSWA

Odell, Jonathan, 1737–1818
THE AMERICAN TIMES. A Satire in Three Parts. ... By Camillo Querno [pseud], Poet-Laureate to the Congress. London, Richardson, 1780. 40p [Attributed to Odell, but his authorship has been questioned. See *American Literature* 2: 79–82 (March 1930).] [BM BVaU LC OTU
THE LOYAL VERSES OF JOSEPH STANSBURY AND DOCTOR JONATHAN ODELL. ... Ed. by Winthrop Sargent. Albany, N.Y., Munsell, 1860. 199p [BVaU LC NBFU OLU
THE LOYALIST POETRY OF THE REVOLUTION. Ed. by Winthrop Sargent. Philadelphia, Collins, 1857. 218p [Poems by Odell included.] [BVaU LC OTU

Ogden, H.G.
BALLADS OF CORNER BROOK. ... St. John's, Nfld., 1925. 47p [Brown U BVaU

Ogilvy, Maud
A CHRISTMAS SONG, AND OTHER VERSES. [1913]. 8 leaves. [BVaU

O'Grady, Standish, fl. 1793–1841
THE EMIGRANT. A Poem in Four Cantos. Montreal, Lovell, 1841. 204p [BVaU OTP

O'Hagan, Thomas, 1855–1939
COLLECTED POEMS. Toronto, McClelland, 1922. 178p [BM BVaU LC NBFU OTP
A GATE OF FLOWERS, AND OTHER POEMS. Toronto, Briggs, 1887. 64p [BVaU LC NBFU OTU QMM
IN DREAMLAND, AND OTHER POEMS. Toronto, Williamson, 1893. 84p [BM BVaU LC NBFU OTP
IN THE HEART OF THE MEADOW AND OTHER POEMS. Toronto, Briggs, 1914. 47p [BM BVaU LC OTP
SONGS OF HEROIC DAYS. Toronto, Briggs, 1916. 44p [BM BVaU NBFU OTU QMSS
SONGS OF THE SETTLEMENT, AND OTHER POEMS. Toronto, Briggs, 1899. 70p [BM BVaU LC OTP
THE TIDE OF LOVE. Toronto, Ryerson, 1928. 8p [BVaU NBFU OTU QMM

Okanagan Historical Society
SONGS OF THE OKANAGAN. Vernon, B.C., the Society, 1944. 31p [BViPA OOA

Old Presbyterian, An
POETRY BY AN OLD PRESBYTERIAN. [Anon] Glencoe, Transcript Presses, 1902.
[Phelps

Old Resident Of New Brunswick, An
SOLITUDE AND OTHER POEMS. By an Old Resident of New Brunswick [pseud].
1842. 24p [OKQ

Olivers, Thomas
DESCRIPTIVE AND PLAINTIVE ELEGY ON THE DEATH OF THE LATE REV. JOHN
WESLEY. Lunenburg, N.S., Moody, 1837. 12p [NSHD

O'Malley, Rev. Andrew, 1863–1921
JOAN OF ARC. Barrie, Author, 1920. 110p [OTU
SONNETS OF A RECLUSE. Toronto, Register Extension Print., 1915. 100p
[V. II and V. III were pub. at Barrie by Gazette Print., no dates. Pagination in
each was also 100p.] [BVaU QMU
THE WRECK OF THE TITANIC. Toronto, Blake, 1912. 38p [NSWA OTP

O'Neill, Rev. Arthur Barry, 1858–
BETWEEN WHILES. Akron, Ohio, McBride, 1899. 189p [LC

Ontario. Women's Liberal Association
HEARTS OF GOLD. Being Chronicles of Heroism in Canadian History. Toronto,
Globe, 1915. 30p [LC NBFU OTU QMU

Orford, McLeod
INVERHURON AND OTHER POEMS. Toronto, Hilda M. Ridley, 1951. 20p
(Carillon Poetry Chap-Book)

Oria (pseud)
IVY LEAVES FROM THE OLD HOMESTEAD. By Oria [pseud]. Halifax, Bowes, 1854.
154p [NSHP

Ormsby, Ïërne
EGYPT'S GOLD. [Poems.] Bradford, Beamsley House, 1933. 36p [BM

Osborn, Edith Margaret (Camp), 1902–
FROSTY-MOON AND OTHER POEMS. By Margot Osborn. Toronto, Ryerson, 1946.
8p [BVaU LC NBSaM OTP

Osborne, Marian (Francis), 1871–1931
FLIGHT COMMANDER STORK, AND OTHER VERSE. Toronto, Macmillan, 1925.
48p [BM BVaU OKQ
POEMS. London, Chiswick Press, 1914. 84p [BM BVaU NBFU OTU QMM
THE SONG OF ISRAFEL AND OTHER POEMS. Toronto, Macmillan, 1923. 67p [BM
BVaU NBFU OTP

Osler, Annie F.

THOUGHTS IN VERSE. Toronto, Tyrrell, 1911. 69p [OTU QMBM

Ostenso, Martha, 1900–1963

IN A FAR LAND. Poems. New York, Dodd Mead, 1942. 70p [Earlier ed.: New York, Seltzer, 1924.] [BVaU LC NBFU OTU QMM

Outram, Richard Daley, 1930–

EIGHT POEMS. Toronto, Tortoise Press, 1959. 8p

P., T.W.

THE POLITICIAN. Toronto, Rose, 1888. 31p [QMU

Pacey, Desmond, 1917–

THE COW WITH THE MUSICAL MOO, AND OTHER VERSES FOR CHILDREN. Fredericton, Brunswick Press, 1952. 26p

HIPPITY HOBO AND THE BEE AND OTHER VERSES FOR CHILDREN. Fredericton, Brunswick Press, 1952. 26p

Pagdin, Thomas, 1868–

POEMS. Ilfracombe, Devon, Stockwell, 1958. 62p

Page, Patricia Kathleen, 1916–

AS TEN AS TWENTY. Toronto, Ryerson, 1946. 43p [BVaU MWU NBFU OTP

THE METAL AND THE FLOWER. Toronto, McClelland, 1954. 64p

UNIT OF FIVE. Poems by Louis Dudek, Ronald Hambleton, P.K. Page, Raymond Souster, James Wreford. Ed. by Ronald Hambleton. Toronto, Ryerson, 1944. 87p [BVaU LC MWU NSHD OTU QMM

Painter, Mrs. Ann

THE WIDOW JUSTIFIED; or, The Age of Wonders. A Satirical Poem. To which is added THE FAIR; or, Waterdown Annual Show; also THE QUEEN OF MAGIC INVENTIONS. A Comic Song. Hamilton, Gillespy-Robertson, 1858. 47p [OTUV

Palmer, David, 1789–1866

NEW BRUNSWICK AND OTHER POEMS. Saint John, McMillan, 1869. 171p [BVaU NBFU OTU

Palmer, Lizzie (Estabrooks)

SELECTED POEMS. Fredericton, Reporter, 1889. 40p [NBFU

Parham, Charles J.

LYRICAL TRANSLATIONS. From the Languages of Oc, Italian, Spanish, Portuguese and Provincial Dialects. ... Ottawa, 1887. 88p [Brown U OOP

Parke, Shubael

THE SMUGGLER. A Poem. Hamilton, 1852. 76p [BibC CCJ

Parker, Gilbert, 1862–1932
EMBERS. Being a Book of Verses. Plymouth, Brendon, 1908. 197p [Also pub. with A LOVER'S DIARY. 2v in 1. New York, Scribner, 1913.] [BM BVaU NBFU OTP
EMBERS; A LOVER'S DIARY. New York, Scribner, 1913. [2v in 1]. 261p [BVa OKQ
A LOVER'S DIARY. Songs in Sequence. Chicago, Stone & Kimball, 1894. 147p [Also: Toronto, Copp Clark, 1898.] [BVaU LC NBFU OTP QMU

Parker, Hedley S.V.
MIRAMICHI POET. Six Poems. Ed. with a memoir and notes by Louise Manny. Saint John, New Brunswick Museum, 1947. 20p [BVaU NBFU

Parker, Mayne Leonard, 1892–
SHADOWS LAY NORTH. By Len Parker. Dallas, Texas, Story Book Press, 1955. 74p

Parker, William Frederick, 1860–1918
FRONDOLEER. By Spatha [pseud]. [Davenport, Iowa?], Globe, 1878. 38p [LC
NORMEELYON. Florence, Neb., 1883. 27p [LC
POEMS. [Davenport, Iowa?], Globe, 1880. 46p [LC

Parkinson, Amy, 1859?–1938
BEST. The Story of the Messenger Hours, with Some of the Thoughts they have Brought. Toronto, Briggs, 1902. 43p [BM BVaU NBFU OTP
IN HIS KEEPING. Words of Sustaining from the Source of All Strength; with Kindred Thoughts in Verse. Toronto, Upper Canada Tract Society, n.d. 33p [BM OPAL
LOVE THROUGH ALL. A VOICE FROM A SICK ROOM. THOUGHTS FOR EACH DAY. Toronto, Endeavor Herald, 1893. 36p [OTP

Parsons, Richard Augustus, 1893–
REFLECTIONS. St. John's, Newfoundland Academy of Art, 1954. 52p
REFLECTIONS, BOOKS I & II. Toronto, Pub. for the Author by Ryerson Press, 1958. 117p [Bk. I first pub. by Newfoundland Academy of Art, 1954.]
THE VILLAGE POLITICIANS. St. John's, Newfoundland Academy of Art, 1960. 133p

Partridge, Thomas Jefferson, 1860–
ANNAPOLIS ROYAL AND OTHER POEMS. Halifax, [1921?]. 33p [NSWA OTUV
LOUISBURG, AMERICA'S FIRST FIELD. Cambridge, Mass., Powell, 1931. 70p [NSHD
POEMS. Gloucester, Mass., H.C. Lantz, n.d. 71p [OONL

Pasmore, Malvina (Copp)
GREEN LEAVES. Montreal, Witness Press, 1937. 45p [Brown U BVaU OLU QMU
SAINT JOAN. London, Burns Oates, 1926. 20p [AEU BM

THIS LIFE OF OURS. London, Werner Laurie, 1925.

YOU AND I. London, Phillimore, 1928. 73p [BM NBSaM

Paterson, A.O.

CANADA, STORY IN VERSE. [Victoria, Diggon-Hibben, 1942.] 12p [Also eds. in 1943, 1947.] [BVaU

DREAM OF NOEL. By A.O.P. Victoria, Author, 1945. 12p [BVaU

Paton, James Morton, 1863–

LIVING POETRY. Ed. by ——. Toronto, Ryerson, 1942. 122p [BVaU LC OOP

Patterson, Henry

SONGS IN TRAVEL. Montreal, Lovell, 1872. 186p [BVaU OTP QMBM

Payne, Mabel Lucy (Formby), 1886–

MOON IN THE AFTERNOON, AND OTHER POEMS. Mayne Island, B.C., and Vancouver, the Author, 1955. 31p

Peace, Mrs. N.S.

THE CONVICT SHIP, AND OTHER POEMS. Greenock, Baird, 1850. 264p [BM OTUV

Peacock, Annie Louisa, 1873–1957

ERE SUNRISE. N.p., 1956. 12p (Carillon Poetry Chap-Books)

Peacock, Harold

ROUGH RHYMES OF A CANADIAN SOLDIER. Birmingham, Eng., Allday Ltd., [19—?]. 48p [OTUV

Pearce, Peggy

REVERIES. St. Thomas, 1934. 23p [OKQ

WAYSIDE GRASSES. Toronto, Ryerson, 1935. 10p [BVaU NBSaM OTP QMM

Pearce, S. Moore

AMERICANADA. Poems. Ilfracombe, Devon, Stockwell, 1960. 79p

Pearce, Theodocia, 1894–1925?

LIGHTS FROM LITTLE LANTERNS. New York, Lawren, 1926. 77p [BVa NSHD OTP

Pearson, J.J.

POEMS. Toronto, Briggs, 1913. 107p [BM BVaU OKQ

Peck, Nellie M.

NIGHT FLOWERING STOCK 1942–1944. Poems. By N.M.P. Montreal, Gazette Print., 1945. 102p [NBSU OTU

Pecknold, Dorothy Martin, 1893–

THOUGHTS ... AND BY-GONE MEMORIES. Port Alice, B.C., Author, 1950. 32p [BVaU OONL

Peddel, Nicholas
HOME SWEET HOME. Newfoundland Poems. N.p., 1904. 36p [Brown U OLU

Pegley, Charles Edward
THE FOUR HORSEMEN, AND OTHER VERSE. Sandwich, Border Cities Star Print.,
1923. [BM
SHADOWS AND OTHER POEMS. Windsor, Author, 1926. 48p [AEU

Pellerin, Mrs. Maude Gage, 1884–
THE SONGS OF OLD QUEBEC. Lennoxville, Press, 1949. 52p [OONL

Penman, Rev. Archibald D., 1882–
MIRACLE MEDITATIONS AND SONG SERVICES FROM SCRIPTURES. Poem. New
York, Comet Press, 1957. 83p

Pennington, Richard, 1904–
BISCAY BALLADS. By David Peterley [pseud]. Montreal, Redpath Press, 1958.
17p

Penny, Arthur Guy, 1886–1963
ECHOING LAUGHTER. Verses Selected From "Penny-A-Liner's" Column, "Lines-
O-Type," in the Quebec *Chronicle-Telegraph*. Quebec, Chronicle-Telegraph Print.
Co., 1954. 98p
THE KING'S CONSCIENCE AND VARIOUS VERSE. Quebec, Chronicle-Telegraph,
1925. 101p [BVaU NBFU OTU QMSS
"MIXTURE, AS BEFORE." Further Echoes From "Penny-a-Liner's" Column,
"Lines-o-type," in the Quebec *Chronicle-Telegraph*. Quebec, Chronicle-Telegraph
Print. Co., 1955. 114p
RHYMES FOR CHRISTMAS AND OTHER OCCASIONS, 1904–1954. Quebec, Chronicle-
Telegraph Print. Co., 1956. 82p

Perigoe, Harvey
THE GENIUS AND NELSON, AND OTHER POEMS. Feversham, Ont., Author, [1902].
64p [BM OTUV

Perry, Martha Eugenie
CANTEEN. Victoria, Clarke, 1944. 20p [BVaU OTP
GREEN TIMBERS AND OTHER POEMS. Toronto, Ryerson, 1955. 57p
HEARING A FAR CALL. Toronto, Ryerson, 1943. 12p [BVaU LC NBSaM OTP
QMM
HERO IN ERMINE AND OTHER POEMS. Victoria, Clarke, 1939. 32p [BVaU NBFU
QMM
SONG IN THE SILENCE, AND OTHER POEMS. Toronto, Ryerson, 1947. 16p [BVaU
LC MWU NBSaM OKQ

Pettit, Phyllis Adye
PROMISE. Narrative and Other Poems. Toronto, Crucible Press, 1943. 36p [LC

Phelps, Arthur Leonard, 1887–1970
A BOBCAYGEON CHAPBOOK. Lindsay, Ont., Author, 1922. 8p [NBFU OKQ
POEMS. Mount Vernon, Iowa, Cornell College English Club, 1921. 17p [NBFU
   OKQ

Philips, Frederic
JOTTINGS BY THE WAY. 1909. [CAR
VERSE FROM A WESTERN ISLE. Victoria, Cusack, 1909. 49p [BM Brown U
   BVaU NSHD OTP

Phillipps-Wolley, Clive Oldnall, 1854–1918
IN MEMORY OF OUR DEAD AT MODDER RIVER FEB. 21, 1900. Victoria, 1900.
   6p [BViPA
OUR TESTAMENT. [Anon] Victoria, 1900. 6p [OTP
SONGS FROM A YOUNG MAN'S LAND. Toronto, Allen, 1917. 160p [A re-issue
   of SONGS OF AN ENGLISH ESAU, and other verse.] [BM BVaU NSHD OTP
   QMBM
SONGS OF AN ENGLISH ESAU. Toronto, Morang, 1902. 133p [BM BVaU OTP

Phillips, Mrs. Adria C.
SONGS OF THE AVON. Toronto, Crucible Press, 1948. 28p [Brown U

Phillips, Mrs. Bluebell Stewart, 1904–
FREEDOM'S HOPE AND OTHER VERSE. Point Claire, Que., 1942. 19p [Brown U

Phillips, William Rupert
FAR AWAY FIELDS ARE GREEN. Niagara, Ont., 1941. 28p [Brown U
THE RAINBOW OF NIAGARA FALLS, AND OTHER POEMS. Niagara Falls, Ont.,
   Lindsay Press, 1940. 32p [QMU

Pickel, Enid M., –1956
PRAIRIE SKYLINE. By Enid and Vestal Pickel. Regina, priv. print., 1949. 40p
   [BVaU

Pickthall, Marjorie Lowry Christie, 1883–1922
THE COMPLETE POEMS OF MARJORIE PICKTHALL. Toronto, McClelland, 1927.
   250p [Several later editions.] [BM BVaU MWU NBFU OKQ QMM
THE DRIFT OF PINIONS. Montreal, University Magazine, 1913. 94p [BM BVaU
   NBFU OTP QMM
THE LAMP OF POOR SOULS, AND OTHER POEMS. New York, Lane, 1916. 140p
   [Includes contents of THE DRIFT OF PINIONS.] [BM BVaU LC NBFU OTP
   QMM
LITTLE SONGS. Toronto, McClelland, 1925. 87p [BM BVaU NBFU OTP
   QMM
MARY TIRED. London, Stonebridge Press, 1922. 4p [OKQ

THE NAIAD AND FIVE OTHER POEMS. [Anon] Toronto, Ryerson, 1931. 11p [Poems chosen by Lorne Pierce from a hitherto undiscovered MS book, and printed for a few friends. Only 14 copies printed.] [BM NBFU OTP

THE SELECTED POEMS OF MARJORIE PICKTHALL. Ed. and with an intro. by Lorne Pierce. Toronto, McClelland, 1957. 104p

TWO POEMS. [Contents: "Ebb Tide"; "Vision."] Toronto, Ryerson, 1923. 5p [BM OKQ

THE WOODCARVER'S WIFE, AND LATER POEMS. Toronto, McClelland, 1922. 105p [BM BVaU NBFU OTP QMM

Pierce, H.A.

POEMS. N.p., Author, 1896. 16p [OTUV

Pierce, Harriet (Singleton)

AN EASTERN WINDOW: A BOOK OF DAYS. Collected by Lorne Pierce, and made into a Scrap-Book before his Mother's Death. Toronto, United Church, 1938. 20p [NBFU

Piers, Constance (Fairbanks), 1866–1939

CHRISTMAS PIE. Selections from Verses Written for Private Greeting Cards and Calendars. Halifax, 1938. 18p [NSHD

Pike, Mrs. Annie Margaret

AN ARAB CHIEF, AND OTHER PLAYTIME VERSES. Vancouver, McBeath Spedding, 1923. 32p [BM BVaU LC

PHELIM THE BLIND AND OTHER VERSES. London, Headley, [1913?]. 31p [BM BVaU

PLAYTIME RHYMES. London, Headley, 1907. 47p [BM BVaU

SILVER BELLS AND COCKLE SHELLS. London, Merton, 1926. 114p [BM BVa

Pincock, Jenny (O'Hara), 1890–1948

HIDDEN SPRINGS: A Narrative Poem of Old Upper Canada; and Other Poems. Waterloo, Ont., Mrs. F.J.T. Maines, 1949. 66p [OLU

Pleiter, Mrs. Derk (Neisje), 1885–1967

REVERIES IN VERSE. Corunna, Ont., Author, [c1966]. 36p [Earlier ed., London, Ont., n.d. 31p] [Phelps p101

Poetry Society, England. Nova Scotia Centre

NOVA SCOTIA BOOK OF VERSE. V. 1. 1949. Halifax, 1949. 61p [A continuing pub. Various pagings]

Pollard, William Correll, 1878–

POEMS. London, Stockwell, 1936. 35p [OTP

Polley, Lucy (Mrs. Alvin Polley)

AUNT JUDITH'S RHYMES. 1912, [Rhod p877

Pollock, J.E.
LORENZO, AND OTHER POEMS. Toronto, Briggs, 1883. 117p [BVaU OTP

Poole, Thomas Wesley, 1831?–1905
THE POLITICIAN. By T.W.P. [pseud]. Toronto, Rose Pub. Co., 1888. 31p
[Patrick cat. 30

Pooley, W.J.
FAIR DEVON AND OTHER POEMS. Merritt, B.C., Author, n.d. 18p [mimeo-
graphed]. [Also same title: [Victoria?], 1948. 4th ed. 12p] [BViPA

Pope, William, fl. 1848
REMINISCENCES OF PRINCE EDWARD ISLAND, IN AN HISTORICAL AND DESCRIP-
TIVE POEM. With Explanatory Notes Addressed to the Hon. Joseph Pope.
Liverpool, Dunsford, 1848. 38p [BVaU OTUV

Porter, James
THE BONFIRE. A Poem. Victoria, Author, 1908. 6p [BViPA
1608: QUEBEC TERCENTENARY: 1908. A Poem. Victoria, Author, 1908. 7p
[BViPA

Porter, John Elmoran
FURROW IN THE DUNES. By Jacke E. Porter. New York, Harrison, 1942. 63p [LC
A NOVA SCOTIAN SINGS. Yarmouth, N.S., Davis, [1958?]. 20p
THE STOPPER'S OUT. By Jacke E. Porter. Yarmouth, N.S., Davis, 1934. 47p
[MWU NSHPL QMU

Porter, Rev. William Henry, 1840–1928
CANADIAN SCENES AND OTHER POEMS. Toronto, Briggs, 1907. 112p [BM BVaU
NSHD OKQ QMU
GATHERED LILIES. Poems of Sympathy and Comfort for the Bereaved.
[Brantford, Expositor, n.d.] 16p [NSHPL
GLIMPSES OF CANADA. Acrostics. N.p., n.d. [1901?]. 38p [Adelphi cat. 41A
OUR LORD'S PRAYER IN GETHSEMANE. N.p., n.d. 32p [NSHPL
THE YEAR ROUND. Original Poems. ... London, Ont., Knowles, 1888. 29p [OLU

Potter, Frank G.
ALL CANADIAN POEMS. Original, Patriotic and Spiritual; written in Nova Scotia,
Alberta, and British Columbia. Kentville, N.S., Kentville Pub. Co., 1936–38.
47p [NBFU OTP

Poynter, Mary Augusta (Dickinson)
ALONG THE WINDING ROAD. New York, Revell, 1925. 98p [LC OTU

Pratt, Edwin John, 1883–1964
BEHIND THE LOG. Toronto, Macmillan, 1947. 47p [BM BVaU LC MWU
NBFU OTP QMM

BREBEUF AND HIS BRETHREN. Toronto, Macmillan, 1940. 65p [BVaU LC NSHD OTP

COLLECTED POEMS. Toronto, Macmillan, 1944. 314p [BM BVaU LC NSHD OTP QMM

COLLECTED POEMS. 2nd ed. Ed. with an intro. by Northrop Frye. Toronto, Macmillan, 1958. xxviii + 395p

DUNKIRK. Toronto, Macmillan, 1941. 13p [BVaU LC MWU NSHD OTP

THE FABLE OF THE GOAT AND OTHER POEMS. Toronto, Macmillan, 1937. 47p [BVaU LC NBFU OTP QMM

THE IRON DOOR. An Ode. Toronto, Macmillan, 1927. 30p [BM BVaU NBFU OTP QMM

MAGIC IN EVERYTHING. Toronto, Macmillan, 1955. 6p

MANY MOODS. Toronto, Macmillan, 1932. 53p [BM BVaU LC NSHD OTU QMM

NEW PROVINCES. Poems of Several Authors. [Ed. by F.R. Scott.] Toronto, Macmillan, 1936. 77p [Contains poems by Pratt and others.] [BVaU NBFU OKQ

NEWFOUNDLAND VERSE. Toronto, Ryerson, 1923. 140p [BM BVaU NBFU OTP QMM

RACHEL. A Sea Story of Newfoundland in Verse. [Anon] New York, priv. print., 1917. 15p [NfSM OTU

THE ROOSEVELT AND THE ANTINOE. New York, Macmillan, 1930. 44p [BM BVaU LC NBFU OTP QMM

STILL LIFE AND OTHER VERSE. Toronto, Macmillan, 1943. 40p [BVaU LC NBFU OTP QMM

TEN SELECTED POEMS. With Notes. Toronto, Macmillan, 1947. 149p [BVaU OTP

THEY ARE RETURNING. Toronto, Macmillan, 1945. 15p [BVaU LC NBFU OTP QMM

THE TITANIC. Toronto, Macmillan, 1935. 42p [BM BVaU NSHD OTP QMM

TITANS. London, Macmillan, 1926. 67p [BM BVaU LC NBFU OTU QMM

TOWARDS THE LAST SPIKE. A Verse Panorma of the Struggle to Build the First Canadian Transcontinental from the Time of the Proposed Terms of Union with British Columbia (1870) to the Hammering of the Last Spike in the Eagle Pass (1885). Toronto, Macmillan, 1952. 53p

VERSES OF THE SEA. With an intro. by Charles G.D. Roberts. Toronto, Macmillan, 1930. 97p [BVaU NBFU OKQ

THE WITCHES BREW. London, Selwyn & Blount, 1925. 32p [BM BVaU NBFU OTP QMSS

Pratt, Lenore Alexandra (Tucker), 1901—
BIRCH LIGHT. Toronto, Ryerson, 1956. 15p

MIDWINTER THAW. Toronto, Ryerson, 1948. 12p [BVaU NBSaM OTP

Prentice Boy, A
DERRY HARMONIST. By "A Prentice Boy" [pseud]. Ottawa, 1861. [CCJ

Prescott, Henrietta, −1875
POEMS, WRITTEN IN NEWFOUNDLAND. London, Saunders & Otley, 1839. 311p
[BM LC NSHD OTP QMSS

Price, Bertha Maud (Weston), 1872−1955
LEGENDS OF THE LAKES. A Tribute to the Lakes of the Eastern Townships.
Sherbrooke, Que., Author, 1923. 43p [Rev. ed. pub. under title: LEGENDS
OF OUR LAKES AND RIVERS. Massawippi, Que., Author, 1937. 58p] [BM
BVaU OTP QMM
OUT OF DOORS IN CANADA. Poems. Sherbrooke, Que., Page Print., 1927. 14p
[QQL

Priestley, Norman Flaxman, 1884−1958
SUMMER FEVER AND OTHER VERSES. Calgary, 1945. 24p [Peel Supp.

Prince, Sadie O., 1861−1905
POEMS. Toronto, Briggs; Montreal, Coates, 1890. 179p [BVaU NSHD OOP

Procter, John James, 1838−1910
THE BLACK HAWK, STANDARD BEARER, AND OTHER POEMS. St. John, Que.,
News Print., 1883. 144p [OTP QMSS
VOICES OF THE NIGHT, AND OTHER POEMS. Montreal, Lovell, 1861. 118p [BM
BVaU OTP QMSS

Protestant, A (pseud)
RHYMES FOR THE TIMES. Original Poems on Popery, Slavery, and Intemperance.
By a Protestant [pseud]. Montreal, 1857. 119p [Brown U BVaU OTU

Prower, Nelson, 1856−
SONNETS AND OTHER VERSES. Vancouver, Wrigley, 1935. 29p [CC
VARIOUS VERSES. By William Frederick Harvey, M.A., Nelson Prower, M.A., and
the Rev. R.C. Fillingham, B.A. London, Hayman, Christy & Lilly, 1893. 88p
[BM

Prowse, Mrs. I.S.
THE BURNING FOREST. A Tale of New Brunswick. 1830. [Lit Hist p116
POEMS. London, Smith Elder, 1830. 183p [BM NSHD

Purdy, Alfred Wellington, 1918−
THE CRAFTE SO LONGE TO LERNE. Toronto, Ryerson, 1959. 23p
EMU, REMEMBER! Fredericton, U. of New Brunswick, 1956. 16p
THE ENCHANTED ECHO. Vancouver, Clarke & Stuart, 1944. 62p [Brown U
BVaU NBFU
PRESSED ON SAND. Toronto, Ryerson, 1955. 16p

Quest, R.E. (pseud)
WANDERINGS. By R.E. Quest [pseud]. Montreal, Renouf, 1960. 122p

Raby, Mary C.
BEAUTY WALKS THE EARTH. Toronto, Crucible Press, 1941. 15p [Brown U
OTU

Ragg, Alban E.
POEMS BY A BUSINESS MAN, A.E.R. [pseud]. Toronto, Brown-Searle, 1901. 21p
[Copyright was issued to "William Tyrrell," *q.v.*] [BM BVaU OKQ

Ramage, Kate Douglas
VASHTI, AND OTHER POEMS. Montreal, Lovell, 1884. 90p [OTUV

Ramsay, Andrew John, 1849?–1907
THE CANADIAN LYRE. By J.R. Ramsay [pseud]. Hamilton, Donnelley, 1859.
126p [BVaU OTP QMBM
I SHALL NOT TELL [and Other Poems]. By A. Ramsay. New York, [c1880]. [CCJ
MURIEL THE FOUNDLING, AND OTHER ORIGINAL POEMS. By Andrew Ramsay.
Toronto, Hovey, 1886. 288p [BVaU NBFU OTP
WIN-ON-AH; or, The Forest Light, and Other Poems. By J.R. Ramsay [pseud].
Toronto, Adam Stevenson, 1869. 98p [BVaU NBFU OTP

Rand, Rev. Silas Tertius, 1810–1889
THE DYING INDIAN'S DREAM. A Poem. Halifax, Nova Scotia Print., 1872.
15p [3rd ed. rev. with some additional Latin poems: Windsor, N.S., Knowles,
1881. 28p] [BM BVaU NSHP OTP
HYMNI RECENTES LATINI. Translationes et Originales. Halifax, Selden, 1888.
168p [English and Latin versions on facing pages.] [BVaU NBFU OTP QMU

Rand, Theodore Harding, 1835–1900
AT MINAS BASIN, AND OTHER POEMS. Toronto, Briggs; Montreal, Coates, 1897.
173p [2nd ed., 1898. 206p] [BM BVaU NBFU OTP QMM
SONG WAVES. Toronto, Briggs, 1900. 121p [BM BVaU NBFU OTP
A TREASURY OF CANADIAN VERSE. Ed. by ——. Toronto, Briggs, 1900. 412p
[Also an ed. in 1924.] [BM BVaU LC NBFU OTP QMM

Rashley, Richard Ernest, 1909–
MOON LAKE AND OTHER POEMS. Toronto, Ryerson, 1959. 10p
PORTRAIT, AND OTHER POEMS. Toronto, Ryerson, 1953. 8p
VOYAGEUR, AND OTHER POEMS. Toronto, Ryerson, 1946. 16p [BVaU LC
NBSaM OTP

Ratcliffe, Walter A., 1865–
LAURIER AND VICTORY! A Souvenir of the Campaign of 1896. Toronto, Ellis,
1896. 17p [OTU

MORNING SONGS IN THE NIGHT. Toronto, Briggs; Montreal, Coates, 1897. 151p [BM BVaU OTU QMM

Ray, Evan
THE KINGDOM OF SONG. A Group of Little Poems, with Airs. Toronto, Ryerson, 1931. [Ryerson Impt

Read, Mrs. Jane B.
POEMS FOR YOUNG PEOPLE, EMBRACING TEMPERANCE AND RELIGION. Brantford, Stewart & Mathison, 1871. 16p [OTP
POEMS ON MORAL AND RELIGIOUS SUBJECTS. Brantford, Daily Courier, 1872. 16p [OTP

Reade, Mrs. Frances Lawson
POEMS FROM ARABESQUE. By Yolande Langworthy [pseud]. New York, Black, 1930. 94p [LC

Reade, John, 1837–1919
MADELEINE DE VERCHERES. Toronto, Copp Clark, n.d. 19p [NSHD OTUV
THE PROPHECY OF MERLIN AND OTHER POEMS. Montreal, Dawson, 1870. 237p [BVaU LC NSHD OTP QMM

Reade, Robert Cyrus, 1884–
THE '05 STORY. Verses. Toronto, U. of Toronto Press, 1955. 12p [Written for the Jubilee Reunion Dinner of the class of 1905 of University College, U. of Toronto, held May 25, 1955.]

Reaney, James Crerar, 1926–
THE RED HEART. Toronto, McClelland, 1949. 73p [MWU NBFU OTP
A SUIT OF NETTLES. Toronto, Macmillan, 1958. x + 54p

Recoskie, Rose Mary
ORCHIDS TO LADY MARIA. New York, Pageant Press, 1953. 46p
PETALS OF FLOWERS. Poems. New York, Exposition Press, 1952. 56p

Redpath, Beatrice Constance (Peterson), –1937
DRAWN SHUTTERS. London, Lane, 1916. 96p [BM BVaU LC NBFU QMM
WHITE LILAC AND OTHER POEMS. London, Lane, 1922. 80p [BM BVaU NBFU OTP QMM

Redwing (pseud)
ELMO, THE STORY OF A CANADIAN GIRL, AND OTHER POEMS. By Redwing [pseud]. N.p., n.d. 12p [OPAL

Reed, Wilfred Joseph, 1911–
THE CITY BY THE SEA, AND OTHER IMAGINATIVE STORIES. Vancouver, Wrigley, 1936. 133p [BVaU

THE EMPIRE OF THE NORTH AND OTHER IMAGINATIVE STORIES OF THE PAST AND
FUTURE. Vancouver, Wrigley, 1935. 129p [BVaU OTP QMBM
STORIES OF TRAVEL. Vancouver, Wrigley, 1935. 126p [BVaU

Reeder, Will
GEMS FROM WILL REEDER'S NOTE BOOK. Vol. 1: Vancouver, 1941; Vol. 3:
Vancouver, 1949. [BViPA

Reid, Lionel Meredith, 1900–
RHYMES AND FANCIES, BY A BOY. Boston, Badger, 1913. 47p [Written when
author was a schoolboy at Campbellford and Toronto.] [OTP

Reid, Robert, 1850–1922
KEN YE THE LAND? By Rob Wanlock [pseud]. Outremont, Que., 1894. 2p
[Patrick cat. 30
POEMS, SONGS AND SONNETS. Paisley and London, Gardiner, 1894. 264p [BM
BVaU LC OTU QMM
A SONG OF CANADA. Montreal, 1896. 3p [Patrick cat. 30

Reid, Robert Scott, 1924–
DANDELION BOUQUET. Clarionette Rhymes Collected from the 1959 Issues of the
Kindersley *Clarion*. Kindersley, Sask., Clarion, [1960?]. 39p

Renison, Rev. Robert John, 1875–1957
A SUMMER ODYSSEY. Toronto, Rous & Mann, 1938. 7p [UTQ

Rennie, Doris Victoria, 1903–
DAWN'S AWAKENING. Poems. Ilfracombe, Devon, Stockwell, 1956. 15p

Reynolds, Ella Julia
SAMSON IN HADES. Toronto, Ryerson, 1957. 15p

Rhodenizer, Vernon Blair, 1886–1968
CANADA FOR MAN AND OTHER POEMS. Montreal, Quality Press, 1958. 16p

Rhynas, Mrs. Margaret, 1878–
A BOUQUET OF REMEMBERINGS. N.p., n.d. 15p [NBSaM
LITTLE STARS ON CHRISTMAS SKIES. [Burlington, Ont., Author, 1935.] 20p
[NBSaM OPAL
SILVER BELLS OF MEMORY. Burlington, Ont., Author, 1938. 29p [OTU

Rice, William, 1817–
POEMS. Toronto, Rowsell & Hutchinson, 1898. 22p [BVaU OTP

Richan, Sarah (Hopkins), 1871–
THE UNRESTING SEA. An Anthology comp. by ——. Kentville, N.S., Kentville
Pub. Co., 1950. 41p [OONL

Richardson, John, 1796–1852

KENSINGTON GARDENS IN 1830. A Satirical Trifle. By the Author of ECARTE.
London, Marsh & Miller, 1830. 32p [Reprinted by the Bibliographical Society
of Canada, Facsimile Series No. 6, Toronto, 1957.] [BM BVaU NBFU OTU

TECUMSEH; or, The Warrior of the West. A Poem in Four Cantos, with Notes.
By an English Officer [pseud]. London, Glynn, 1828. 135p [Republished by
Richardson in abridged form in his *New Era*, Brockville, V. 2, 1842. 16p] [BM
NBFU OKQ

Richardson, Martha E.

SONNET REVERIES. Montreal, Witness Press, 1908. 22p [BM QMU

Richey, Rev. James Arminius

FRAGMENTS AND VERSES. Halifax, Bowes & Sons, 1869. 94p [NSHD OLU

MORE HALF-HOURS; or, a Second and Enlarged Edition of FRAGMENTS AND
VERSES. Halifax, Author, 1877. 108p [NSWA OLU

POEMS. By J.A.R. Montreal, 1867. [OOP

POEMS, DEVOTIONAL AND MISCELLANEOUS. Halifax, Author, 1886. 180p [2nd
ed. of VERSES, DEVOTIONAL AND MISCELLANEOUS.] [BVaU OTP

A SERIES OF POEMS. By J.A.R. Montreal, Wilson, 1857. 46p [BVaU NSHD
OTP QMSS

VERSES, DEVOTIONAL AND MISCELLANEOUS. Halifax, Theakston, 1882. 164p
[BM NSHD OTP

Riddehough, Geoffrey Blundell

THE PROPHET'S MAN. Toronto, Ryerson, 1926. 12p [BVaU NBSaM OTU QMM

Ridley, Hilda M., –1960

A NEW CANADIAN ANTHOLOGY. Edited by Alan Creighton ... assisted by Hilda M.
Ridley. Toronto, Crucible Press, 1938. 236p [BVaU LC OTU

Ridley, Laura Adelaide, –1953

CHRISTMAS EVE AND OTHER POEMS. Toronto, Crucible Press, 1943. 16p [BVaU
OTP

Rigby, Carle Almond

VICTORY AND OTHER POEMS. Yarmouth, N.S., 1946. 30p [NBSaM OLU QMU

Ripley, Anne

EN ROUTE. Nelson, Daily News Print., 1945. 18p [OTP

Ritchie, Cicero Theodore, 1914–

SPRIGS OF BALSAM. Upsalquitch, N.B., Author, 1942. 15p [NSHD

Ritchie, Eliza, 1850–1933

IN THE GLOAMING. Halifax, Weeks Pub. Co., 1935. 23p [NSHD

SONGS OF THE MARITIMES. An Anthology of the Poetry of the Maritime Provinces
of Canada. Toronto, McClelland, 1931. 213p [BM BVaU NSHD OTP QMM

Robb, Wallace Havelock, 1888–

AN ABBEY DAWN POEM. Kingston, Author, 1944. 8p [QMU

A DAY AT ABBEY DAWN. By Charles Honce and Wallace Havelock Robb. Mt.
Vernon, N.Y., Golden Eagle Press, n.d. 12p [OTU

THE DOOR OF DAWN. New York, Poets' Press, 1937. 96p [LC OTU QMM

ELEGY. Kingston, Author, 1952. 3p

A FAR BELL CALLING. A Selection of Bell Poems in a Pastoral Mood and
Morningsong From the Works of Wallace Havelock Robb. 2nd ed. Kingston,
Abbey Dawn Press, 1956. 12p

INDIAN CHRISTMAS CAROL. Kingston, Abbey Dawn, 1940. 16p [LC OTU QMM

THE QUILL AND THE CANDLE. Poems of Birdland in Canada. Toronto, Ryerson,
1927. 54p [BVaU OORD QMM

SAID SIR JOHN MACDONALD, "THAT'S THE LAW"; or, Ballad of the High-Stepping
Bays (*circa* 1842). Kingston, Author, 1957. 5p

TECUMTHA: SHAWNEE CHIEFTAIN–ASTRAL AVATAR. Kingston, Abbey Dawn
Press, 1958. xiii + 223p

Robbins, Ronald Cynewulf, 1915–

OUT OF SOLITUDE. London, Linden Press, 1959. 47p

Roberts, Charles George Douglas, 1860–1943

AUTOTOCHTHON. Windsor, N.S., Author, 1889. 4p [NBFU OTU

AVE. An Ode for the Centenary of the Birth of P.B. Shelley, 4th August, 1792.
Toronto, Williamson, 1892. 27p [BVaU LC NBFU OTU

BE QUIET WIND; UNSAID. [Two Poems.] Toronto, Author, 1929. 2p [BVaU

THE BOOK OF THE NATIVE. Toronto, Copp Clark, 1896. 156p [BM BVaU LC
NBFU OTU QMSS

THE BOOK OF THE ROSE. Boston, Page, 1903. 83p [BM BVaU LC NBFU OTU
QMM

CANADA SPEAKS OF BRITAIN AND OTHER POEMS OF THE WAR. Toronto, Ryerson,
1941. 15p [LC NSHD OTU QMM

FLYING COLOURS. An Anthology. Ed. by ——. Toronto, Ryerson, 1942. 126p
[BVaU LC NBFU OTU

THE ICEBERG AND OTHER POEMS. Toronto, Ryerson, 1934. 31p [BVaU LC
NSHD OTU QMBM

IN DIVERS TONES. Boston, Lothrop, 1886. 134p [BM BVaU LC NBFU OTP
QMM

LATER POEMS. [Fredericton], Author, 1881. 8p [OTP

LATER POEMS. ... In September; Before the Breath of Storm; Actaeon; A Ballad
of Philomela; In the Afternoon; Lotos. [Fredericton], Crockett, [1882]. 13p
[OTP

NEW POEMS. London, Constable, 1919. 44p [BM BVaU NBFU OKQ

NEW YORK NOCTURNES AND OTHER POEMS. Boston, Lamson Wolffe, 1898. 84p
[BM BVaU LC NSHD OLU QMM

NORTHLAND LYRICS. By William Carman Roberts, Theodore Roberts, and
Elizabeth Roberts MacDonald. Selected and arranged by ——. Boston, Small
Maynard, 1899. 86p [BM BVaU LC NBFU OKQ

ORION, AND OTHER POEMS. Philadelphia, Lippincott, 1880. 113p [BM BVaU
LC NBFU OTU QMM

POEMS. New York, Silver Burdett, 1901. 222p [BM BVaU LC NSHD OTU
QMM

POEMS. ... New Complete Edition. Boston, Page, 1907. 257p [BVaU LC NSHD
OOU

POEMS OF WILD LIFE. Selected and ed. by ——. London, Scott, 1888. 238p [BM
BVaU LC NSHD OTU QMM

SELECTED POEMS. Ed. with an intro. by Desmond Pacey. Toronto, Ryerson,
1956. xxv + 100p

SELECTED POEMS OF SIR CHARLES G.D. ROBERTS. Toronto, Ryerson, 1936.
188p [BM BVaU LC NSHD OTU

SONGS OF THE COMMON DAY, AND AVE: AN ODE FOR THE SHELLEY CENTENARY.
Toronto, Briggs, 1893. 126p [BM BVaU NSHD OTP

THE SWEET O' THE YEAR AND OTHER POEMS. Toronto, Ryerson, 1925. 8p
[BVaU NBSaM OTU QMM

TWILIGHT OVER SHAUGAMAUK, AND THREE OTHER POEMS. Toronto, Ryerson,
1937. 10p [BVaU NBFU OTP

THE VAGRANT OF TIME. Toronto, Ryerson, 1927. 46p [Another ed. containing
"These Three Score Years": Toronto, Ryerson, 1927. 63p] [BVaU NBFU
OTP QMM

Roberts, Dorothy Mary Gostwick, 1906–

DAZZLE. By Dorothy Roberts. Toronto, Ryerson, 1957. 12p

IN STAR AND STALK. By Dorothy Roberts. Toronto, Emblem Books, 1959. 14p

SONGS FOR SWIFT FEET. By Gostwick Roberts. Toronto, Ryerson, 1927. 8p
[BVaU NBFU OTP QMM

Roberts, Frank Calvin, 1861–

DAT RIVAAR METABATCHUAN, AND OTHER OUTDOOR VERSE. Philadelphia,
Burbank, 1924. 65p [Brown U LC

Roberts, Lloyd, 1884–1966

ALONG THE OTTAWA. A Book of Lyrics. Toronto, Dent, 1927. 92p [BM BVaU
NBFU OTU QMM

BOOK OF POEMS. Toronto, Goodchild, 1919. [CAR

ENGLAND OVER SEAS. London, Matthews, 1914. 56p [BM LC NBFU OKQ

I SING OF LIFE. Selected Poems. Toronto, Ryerson, 1937. 99p [BVaU LC
NBFU OTP

Roberts, Theodore Goodridge, 1877–1953

THE LEATHER BOTTLE. Toronto, Ryerson, 1934. 87p [BVaU LC NBFU OTU
QMM

THE LOST SHIPMATE. Toronto, Ryerson, 1926. 14p [BVaU NBFU OTP QMM
NORTHLAND LYRICS. By William Carman Roberts, Theodore Roberts, and
  Elizabeth Roberts MacDonald. Selected and Arranged by Charles G.D. Roberts.
  Boston, Small Maynard, 1899. 86p [BM BVaU LC OKQ
SEVEN POEMS. Fredericton, Author, 1925. 11p [BVaU

Roberts, William Carman
NORTHLAND LYRICS. By William Carman Roberts, Theodore Roberts, and
  Elizabeth Roberts MacDonald. Selected and Arranged by Charles G.D. Roberts.
  Boston, Small Maynard, 1899. 86p [BM BVaU LC NBFU OKQ

Robertson, John
WARBLINGS AND WAILINGS OF LEISURE HOURS. By Scotus [pseud]. Three
  Rivers, Que., Author, 1859. 78p [OTP

Robertson, John Charles, 1864—1956
LATIN SONGS NEW AND OLD. Selected and written by ——. Toronto, U. of
  Toronto Press, 1934. 64p [Rev. and enl.: Toronto, 1937.] [LC OTP

Robertson, John Wilson
WOOD-NOTES WILD. By John Wilson (Bard O' Glen Eerie) [pseud]. 2nd & enl.
  ed. Toronto, Briggs, 1912. 200p [First ed.: Fort William, 1903. 24p] [BM
  BVaU OKQ

Robeson, Ephraim, 1862—1951
POETICAL MUSINGS. [3rd ed. rev. and enl.] Athens, Ont., Standard Pub. House,
  1947. 46p [OKQ

Robinson, Mrs. F. Maud
SONGS FROM SISSIBOO HILL. ... Toronto, Livingstone Press, 1934. 24p [NBFU

Robinson, Harold.
PRAIRIE DAYS AND OTHER VERSES. Winnipeg, Hull Print., [1935?]. 67p [BViPA

Robinson, Hazel Alberta, 1913—1955
POEMS. N.p. [19—?]. 40p [OKQ
POEMS AND A PLAY. Toronto, Ryerson, 1955. 39p [Radio play, "This Perilous
  Dream," presented on the CBC, Nov. 11, 1949.]

Robinson, Helen Templeton Douglas, 1877—1956
THE CALL OF LIFE. Boston, Humphries, 1957. 60p
SKY WAYS. Boston, Humphries, 1943. 48p [OTP
CANDLE AND CUP. A Collection of some of H.T.D. Robinson's Most Popular
  Published Lines. Toronto, Crucible Press, 1941. 20p [LC OTP

Robinson, Jessie M.
ALPHA AND OMEGA. London, Stockwell, 1932. 46p [BM
CAROLS FOR CHRISTMAS. London, Stockwell, 1926 [BM

THE EMPIRE CALL; or, The Line that Belts the World. Toronto, priv. print., 1901. [Rhod. p869

Roddick, Amy (Redpath), −1954

THE ARMISTICE, AND OTHER POEMS. Montreal, Dougall, 1919. 60p [BVaU OTP QMM

THE BIRTH OF MONTREAL (A Chronicle Play), AND OTHER POEMS. Montreal, Dougall, 1921. 174p [BM BVaU NSHD OTP QMM

ENGLAND'S OLDEST COLONY. Montreal, Author, 1940. 4p [OTU

THE FLAG, AND OTHER POEMS. Montreal, Dougall, 1918. 47p [BM BVaU NSHD OTU QMM

FROM MONTREAL ELSEWHERE. Poems. Montreal, Dougall, 1929. 80p [BVaU NSHD OTU QMM

I TRAVEL TO THE POETS' MART. Montreal, Dougall, 1936. 52p [BVaU LC OTP QMM

THE IROQUOIS ENJOY A PERFECT DAY; A CHANCE MEETING; AND OTHER POEMS. Montreal, Dougall, 1939. 64p [BVaU LC OTU QMM

THE ROMANCE OF A PRINCESS; A COMEDY; AND OTHER POEMS. Montreal, Dougall, 1922. 94p [BM BVaU LC OTP QMM

THE TOMAHAWK, A PLAYLET; AND OTHER POEMS. Montreal, Dougall, 1938. 76p [BVaU LC OTU QMM

WAITING'S WEDDING, AND OTHER POEMS. Montreal, Dougall, 1941. 62p [BVaU LC OTU QMM

Rodgers, Robert Wylie

DRY BELT JINGLES. Cabin Lake, Alta., [193−?]. 12p [ACG

DRY BELT GINGLES [sic]. No. 2. Cabin Lake, Alta., [1948?]. 8p [ACG

Rody, Margaret Ellen Vance (Strain), 1882−

BEAUTY AND THOUGHT IN VERSE. Vancouver, Capitol, 1942. 54p [BVaU

GLEANINGS. Kamsack, Sask., Kamsack Times, [1931]. 47p [Same title: New York, Poets' Press, 1942. 32p] [BVaU BViPA CC

Rogers, Amos Robert, 1927−

THE WHITE MONUMENT. Toronto, Ryerson, 1955. 13p

Rogers, Charles Gordon

BALLADS O' BARLEYCORN. Ottawa, Graphic, 1925. 164p [BVaU OTU QMBM

GOVERNMENT CLERKS. A Book of Ballads. New York, Kellogg, 1902. 39p [BM LC OOP

Rogers, Thomas George, 1877−1961?

THOUGHTS IN VERSE. N.p., [1959?]. 18p

Rogerson, Isabella (Whiteford)

POEMS. By Isabella Whiteford. Belfast, 1860. 297p [BVaU

THE VICTORIAN TRIUMPH AND OTHER POEMS. Toronto, Briggs, 1898. 232p [OTP

Rooke, Archibald Gordon, 1885–
GOLDEN GLEAMS. North Vancouver, Review Press, 1933. 15p [BVaU
PATRIOTIC PARADE AND PARODIES WITH A PUNCH. Mother Goose Up to the
Minute. Priv. print., 1941. 17p [BViPA

Rooker-Clark, May
LATE BLOSSOMS. London, Stockwell, 1940. 24p [OKQ

Rorison, Jean (Kilby)
IN MY GARDEN. Toronto, Ryerson, 1929. 8p [BVaU NBFU OTP QMM

Rose, George MacLean, 1829–1898
LIGHT FOR THE TEMPERANCE PLATFORM. A Collection of Readings, Recitations
and Dialogues. ... Toronto, Hunter Rose, 1876. Pt. II. 120p [OTP QMU

Rose, Harry
RHYMES OF A ROVER. Toronto, Rose, 1933. 22p [OTU

Ross, Alexander, 1783–1856
SELMA: A Tale of the Sixth Crusade. By A. Ross. London, 1839. [BM

Ross, Allan, 1833–
POEMS. Treherne, Man., Treherne Times, 1907. 182p [BVaU OTP

Ross, Henry
NORMAN HAZARD; or, The Fur Trader's Story. Stanbridge East, 1905. 16p
[OTP

Ross, James Alway, 1869–1945
CANADA FIRST AND OTHER POEMS. Toronto, McClelland, 1920. 111p [BM
Brown U BVaU OTU
THE SINGER AND HIS SONG, AND OTHER POEMS. Ottawa, Tower Books, 1950.
79p [BVaU OONL

Ross, Malcolm Mackenzie, 1911–
POETS OF THE CONFEDERATION. Charles G.D. Roberts, Bliss Carman, Archibald
Lampman, Duncan Campbell Scott. Ed. and with an intro. by ——. Toronto,
McClelland, 1960. xiv + 130p [New Canadian Library Original, No. 01]

Ross, William Wrightson Eustace, 1894–1966
EXPERIMENT: 1923-29. By W.W.E. Ross. Toronto, Contact Press, 1952. 23p
[mimeographed]
LACONICS. By E.R. [pseud]. Ottawa, Overbrook Press, 1930. 92p [BVaU
Brown U
SONNETS. By E.R. [pseud]. Toronto, Heaton Pub. Co., 1932. 72p [BVaU OTU

Rowan, Alice Margaret
POEMS. With foreword by the Rev. Robert C. Johnstone. Winnipeg, Lasker,
1925. 27p [OTP

Rowley, William Philip

A CARAVAN OF THOUGHTS. Toronto, Author, 1940. 24p [mimeographed] [CC

IN SUBJECT MOOD. Trio of Poems. Toronto, Author, 1941. 16p [CC

Roy, George Ross, 1924–

THE CITY. A Prose Poem. Strasbourg (France), Imprimerie régionale Strasbourg, 1956. 4p

TWELVE MODERN FRENCH CANADIAN POETS. Translated by G.R. Roy, with French text. Toronto, Ryerson, 1958. xi + 99p

Roy, Rev. James, 1834–1922

LET DOWN THE NETS, AND OTHER VERSES. Ottawa, 1902. 43p [OTU Royal Empire Society

Roy, James Alexander, 1884–

CHRIST IN THE STRAND AND OTHER POEMS. Kingston, Jackson, 1922. 68p [OTU QMM

Royal, Charles Elliott

ROYAL RHYMES AND ROMANCES. Vancouver, International Pub. Co., 1919. 64p [BVaU

THE TRAIL OF A SOURDOUGH. Rhymes and Ballads. Toronto, McClelland, 1919. 168p [BM BVaU QMM

Ruark, Fletcher, 1880–1952

JECILA AND OTHER POEMS. Windsor, Ont., Curtis, 1934. 78p [BVaU LC OTP QMM

MOSAIC, AND OTHER POEMS. Windsor, Ont., Curtis, 1948. 157p [OTP QMM

POEMS. Windsor, Ont., Curtis, 1931. 79p [BVaU LC OTU QMM

RED WIND, AND OTHER POEMS. New York, Avon House, 1940. 64p [BVaU LC OTP QMM

THE SOUTHLAND AND OTHER POEMS. 1920.

Rumsey, John

CURIAE CANADENSES; or, The Canadian Law Courts. A Poem. By Plinius Secundus [pseud]. Toronto, Rowsell, 1843. 126p [BVaU LC OTP

Russell, Euphemia

BOOK OF POEMS. 4th ed. Toronto, Stewart, 1872. 30p [Apparently first pub. as: POETRY. Toronto, 1869. 23p —See CCJ.] [OTP

Russell, Foster Meharry, 1907–

BRAIDS OF BEAUTY. Cobourg, Ont., Sentinel-Star, 1960. 149p

Russell, Margaret (Clarke), 1875–

HOUSEWORK POEMS. Toronto, My Friends' Little Book Shop, 1923. [BM

THE NAUGHTY SUN AND OTHER VERSE. London, Stockwell, 1931. 32p [BM

THE SILLY MOON AND OTHER VERSE. London, Stockwell, 1935. 48p [BM
  Brown U
STARS. A Fairy Tale. London, Ont., Players' Craft Press, 1928. 63p [NBFU OLU

Ruttan, Kate (McIntyre)
RHYMES, RIGHT OR WRONG, OF RAINY RIVER. I.O.O.F. and Masonic Madrigals
  by McIntyre [pseud]. Orillia, Times Print., 1926. 182p [Brown U

Ryan, F.B.
THE SPIRIT'S LAMENT; or, The Wrongs of Ireland. A Poem. Montreal, 1847.
  194p [BVaU

Ryan, Mary Anne (McIver), 1839—1919
POEMS. Ottawa, Taylor, 1869. 176p [BVaU NSHD OTP QMBM

Ryan, William Thomas Carroll, 1839—1910
OSCAR, AND OTHER POEMS. By Carroll Ryan. Hamilton, Franklin, 1857.
  120p [BVaU OTU
PICTURE POEMS. By Carroll Ryan. 1884. [CCJ MOR'98
POEMS, SONGS, BALLADS. By Carroll Ryan. Montreal, Lovell, 1903. 223p
  [BM BVaU OOP QMM
SONGS OF A WANDERER. By Carroll Ryan. Ottawa, Desbarats, 1867. 289p
  [BM BVaU NSHD OTU QMM

S., G.A.
"PREPARE!" An Appeal to Britons. By G.A.S. [pseud]. Toronto, [1911?].
  22p [Brown U OTU

Sabiston, M.
GRENADA AND OTHER POEMS. London, Tinsley, 1876. xxii + 202p [BM OLU

Sadler, Mrs. Violet T., —1958?
HARBOUR BELL RECITER. Vancouver, Greetings, n.d. 122p [BVaU
SUNLIGHT AND SHADOWS. Poems. Vancouver, O. Smith Print., 1958. 40p

Sage, Donalda Margaret (MacKinnon)
FRAGMENTS OF FANTASY. By Nelda MacKinnon Sage. Toronto, Ryerson,
  1928. 8p [BVaU NBFU OKQ QMM
TOP O' THE WORLD. By Nelda MacKinnon Sage. Toronto, Dent. 1929. 94p
  [BM BVaU OKQ

Sahagian, Y.S.
ECHOES PENNED FOR YOUNG LADIES AND YOUNG LADS. Hamilton, Spectator
  Print., 1914. 27p [OH

St. Clare, Reginald
TRANSATLANTIC SKETCHES FROM LIFE. A Satire. Hamilton, Lyght, [18—?].
  46p [OTP

St. George, V.J.
TO A SOLDIER OF BRITISH COLUMBIA. ... Victoria, Quality Press, n.d. 11p
  [BVaU

St. John, Charles Henry
CORPORAL DAY. Boston, Badger, 1904. 47p [LC
THE DAWN OF FREEDOM. Boston, Badger, 1904. 156p [LC
POEMS. Boston, 1859. 144p [OOP

Salter, John
THE POETICAL WORKS. Comprising Metrical Sketches on the Functions of the
  Brain, and Other Pieces. Halifax, Cunnabell, 1852. 116p [NSHPL

Salverson, Laura (Goodman), 1890–1970
WAYSIDE GLEAMS. Toronto, McClelland, 1925. 97p [BVaU NBFU OTP QMM

Samson, Solomon, 1885–1957
A GLIMPSE OF NEWFOUNDLAND (AS IT WAS AND AS IT IS) IN POETRY AND
  PICTURES. All Edited, Arranged, Illustrated and Set with Pictures appropriate
  to the Poems, by Robert Saunders. Poole, Eng., J. Looker, 1960. xv + 80p

Sandercock, W. Clark, −1938
THE DANCE IN THE BUFFALO SKULL AND OTHER POEMS. Toronto, Saunders,
  1935. 156p [BVaU OTU

Sanders, Robert Walter, 1876–
HELP FOR MOTHERS AND FOR OTHERS, RHYMES. Greenville, S.C., 1922. 35p
  [LC
UP INTO THE HILLS AND OTHER POEMS. Niagara Falls, Ont., Slingerland, 1939.
  24p [2nd & enl. ed.: St. Catharines, Author, 1958. 60p] [OTP

Sanderson, Camilla
GOOD MORNING. Toronto, Briggs, 1918. 53p [BVaU
IF I COULD SING. Toronto, Briggs, 1913. 12p [BM OTU

Sanderson, Rev. Joseph Edward, 1830–1913
FORESTS. A Canadian Pastoral. Toronto, Briggs, 1906. 12p [BVaU OTUV

Sanford, Melissa T.
ORIGINAL FABLES AND RIDDLES IN RHYME. With Other Poems. By Melissa T.
  and Edwin L. Sanford. Montreal, Drysdale, 1888. 57p [OTP

Sangster, Charles, 1822–1893
HESPERUS, AND OTHER POEMS AND LYRICS. Montreal, Lovell, 1860. 186p
  [BM BVaU LC MWU NBFU OTP QMM
... OUR NORLAND. ... Toronto, Copp Clark, [1896?]. 14p [Brown U NSHD OOP
THE ST. LAWRENCE AND THE SAGUENAY, AND OTHER POEMS. Kingston,
  Creighton & Duff, 1856. 262p [BVaU LC NBFU OTP QMM

Sarson, H. Smalley
FROM FIELD AND HOSPITAL. London, E. Macdonald, 1916. 24p [BM

Saskatchewan Poetry Society, Regina
THE SASKATCHEWAN POETRY BOOK. Regina, the Society, 1952. 44p

Saskatchewan, University of. Writers' Club.
STUDENT VERSES. Saskatoon, the Club, 1927—. [Issued from time to time over a decade or more.] [CC

Saskatchewan. Western Producer.
AN ANTHOLOGY OF Y.C. VERSE. A Volume of Selections from the Verse contributed by the Young Co-operators and published in the Western Producer from 1932 to 1936. Saskatoon, Western Producer, 1937. 75p [Brown U SSU

Saturday Night (Toronto)
POEMS FOR THE INTERIM. A Selection of Twenty-four Poems by Nineteen Canadian Authors. Published during 1945—46 in "Saturday Night." Toronto, Saturday Night, 1946. 24p [BVaU NBFU QMM

Saunders, Daisy L.
CHURNINGS FROM A PRAIRIE KITCHEN. Toronto, Hunter Rose, 1926. 83p [Brown U QMM SSU

Saunders, Thomas A., 1909—
THE DEVIL AND CAL McCABE; OR, THE TALE OF THE COWMAN'S CORNS. A Story in Verse. Toronto, Ryerson, 1960. 26p
HORIZONTAL WORLD. Toronto, Ryerson, 1951. 41p
SCRUB OAK. Toronto, Ryerson, 1949. 12p [BVaU NBSaM OTP
SOMETHING OF A YOUNG WORLD'S DYING. Toronto, Ryerson, 1958. 20p

Sauvey, Katherine Isobelle (McKowen), 1863?—1944
GRIST FOR THE MILL. Toronto, Crucible Press, 1941. 18p [NBSaM OTP

Savage, Rocke
PRAIRIE TRAILS. A Book of Verse. London, Stockwell, 1939. 122p [BM OTU

Sawdon, Mrs. Edna Johnston
DREAM VALLEY. Winnipeg, Canada Music Pub. Co., 1940. 210p [CC

Sawtell, Mrs. M. Ethelind
THE MOURNER'S TRIBUTE; or, Effusions of Melancholy Hours. Montreal, Armour & Ramsay, 1840. 271p [BM BVaU OTP QMM

Saw-Waw-Goosh, or The Yellow Fox
A MONTH IN THE MARSH. By Saw-Waw-Goosh, or The Yellow Fox. Chatham, Ont., Thompson, 1860. 32p [OTP

Scaife, Arthur Hodgkin

THE SOLILOQUY OF A SHADOW-SHAPE ON A HOLIDAY FROM HADES, etc. [An Imitation of the Rubaiyat of Omar Khayyam]. London, Karslake, 1900. [BM

Scharfe, Ruth Elva, 1917–

A SCRAPBOOK OF VERSE. Ottawa, Author, 1960. 20p

Schofield, Bob

MARILYN – QUEEN OF THE LAKE. And other Lyrics. Ilfracombe, Devon, Stockwell, 1957. 24p

Schooley, Mary (Rice)

SINCERE DESIRES. Vancouver, Wrigley, 1936. 27p [Brown U BVaU

Schrum, Hazel (Keenan), 1915–

GOLDEN DAWN VERSES. Sudbury, Author, [1960?]. 16p

Schull, Joseph, 1910–

I, JONES, SOLDIER. Toronto, Macmillan, 1944. 62p [BVaU NBFU OTU
THE LEGEND OF GHOST LAGOON. Toronto, Macmillan, 1937. 178p [Brown U BVaU NBFU OOP

Scott, Archibald

DESULTORY POEMS. Hampton, N.B., 1880. 60p [NBFU OTP

Scott, Duncan Campbell, 1862–1947

AT SCARBORO' BEACH. N.p., priv. print., n.d. 2p [NBFU
BEAUTY AND LIFE. Toronto, McClelland, 1921. 96p [BM BVaU NBFU OTP QMM
BYRON ON WORDSWORTH. Being Discovered Stanzas of Don Juan. N.p., priv. print., [1924?]. 4p [OKQ
THE GREEN CLOISTER. Later Poems. Toronto, McClelland, 1935. 96p [BVaU LC NBFU OTP
LABOR AND THE ANGEL. Boston, Copeland & Day, 1898. 59p [BVaU LC NBFU OTU QMM
LINES IN MEMORY OF EDMUND MORRIS. N.p., 1915. 14p [BM NBFU OTU
LUNDY'S LANE AND OTHER POEMS. New York, Doran, 1916. 194p [BVaU LC NBFU OTP QMM
THE MAGIC HOUSE AND OTHER POEMS. Ottawa, Durie, 1893. 95p [BM BVaU MWU NBFU OTP QMM
NEW WORLD LYRICS AND BALLADS. Toronto, Morang, 1905. 66p [BM BVaU LC NBFU OTP QMM
THE POEMS OF DUNCAN CAMPBELL SCOTT. Toronto, McClelland, 1926. 341p [BM BVaU NBFU OKQ QMM
REALITY. N.p., n.d. 4p [NBFU
SELECTED POEMS OF DUNCAN CAMPBELL SCOTT. With a memoir by E.K. Brown. Toronto, Ryerson, 1951. 176p

TO THE CANADIAN MOTHERS, AND THREE OTHER POEMS. N.p., priv. print.,
1917. 14p [BVaU NBFU OKQ

VIA BOREALIS. Toronto, Tyrrell, 1906. 21p [BM BVaU NBFU OTP QMM

Scott, Elise Aylen, 1904–

ROSES OF SHADOW. By Elise Aylen [pseud]. With a foreword by Duncan
Campbell Scott. Toronto, Macmillan, 1930. 56p [BVaU NBFU OKQ QMM

Scott, Francis Reginald, 1899–

THE BLASTED PINE. An Anthology of Satire, Invective and Disrespectful Verse,
Chiefly by Canadian Writers. Selected and arr. and with an intro. by F.R.
Scott and A.J.M. Smith. Toronto, Macmillan, 1957. xix + 138p

EVENTS AND SIGNALS. Toronto, Ryerson, 1954. 58p

THE EYE OF THE NEEDLE. Satires, Sorties, Sundries. Montreal, Contact Press,
1957. 71p

NEW PROVINCES. Poems of Several Authors. [Ed. by ——.] Toronto, Macmillan,
1936. 77p [Contains poems by Finch, Kennedy, Klein, Pratt, F.R. Scott
and A.J.M. Smith.] [BVaU NBFU OKQ

OVERTURE. Poems. Toronto, Ryerson, 1945. 79p [BVaU MWU NBFU OKQ
QMM

Scott, Rev. Frederick George, 1861–1944

COLLECTED POEMS. Vancouver, Clarke & Stuart, 1934. 199p [BM BVaU LC
NSHD OTP QMM

THE GATES OF TIME, AND OTHER POEMS. London, Bagster, 1915. 149p [AEU
BM NBFU QMG

A HYMN OF EMPIRE, AND OTHER POEMS. Toronto, Briggs, 1906. 55p [BM
BVaU NBFU OTP QMM

IN SUN AND SHADE. A Book of Verse. Quebec, Dussault & Proulx, 1926.
38p [BM BVaU NBFU OKQ QMSS

IN THE BATTLE SILENCES. Poems Written at the Front. London, Constable,
1916. 33p [BM BVaU LC NBFU OTP QMM

MY LATTICE AND OTHER POEMS. Toronto, Briggs, 1894. 108p [BVaU LC
MWU NBFU OTP QMM

LIFT UP YOUR HEARTS. Toronto, Ryerson, 1941. 23p [BVaU NBFU OTP

NEW POEMS. Quebec, Lafrance, 1929. 39p [BM BVaU LC OTU QMM

POEMS. London, Constable, 1910. 297p [BM BVaU LC NBFU OTP QMM

POEMS. London, S.P.C.K., 1936. 322p [BM OTU QMM

POEMS OLD AND NEW. Toronto, Briggs, 1900. 154p [BM BVaU LC NBFU
OTP QMM

SELECTED POEMS. Quebec, Robitaille, 1933. 118p [BM BVaU NSHD OTP
QMM

THE SOUL'S QUEST. A Poem. Market End, Coggeshall, Essex, Edwin Potter,
1886. 11p [Amtmann cat. 248

THE SOUL'S QUEST AND OTHER POEMS. London, Kegan Paul, 1888. 123p
[BM BVaU NBFU OTP QMM

THE UNNAMED LAKE AND OTHER POEMS. Toronto, Briggs, 1897. 48p
[BM BVaU LC MWU NBFU OTP

Scott, George
BALLADS OF DISARMAMENT AND OTHER POEMS. Saint John, Globe Pub.,
1923. 60p [NBFU

Scott, J. Donald
FIRST BORN. ... Toronto, 1931. 36p [Brown U OTU

Scott, Leslie (Grant)
THE LIGHT OF GENIUS, THE MYSTIC, AND OTHER POEMS. Toronto, Briggs,
1912. 38p [BM BVaU OTU

Scott, Mary Zillah
POEMS. Vancouver, Author, 1946. 28p [BViPA

Scribble, Sam (pseud)
THE KING OF THE BEAVERS. Montreal, 1865. 20p [OOP
ORPHEUS AND EURYDICE. A Classical Extravaganza. Montreal, 1866. 25p
[OOP

Scriven, Joseph Medlicott, 1819–1886
HYMNS AND OTHER VERSES. Peterborough, Stephens, 1869. 112p [OTU
WHAT A FRIEND WE HAVE IN JESUS, AND OTHER HYMNS. With a Sketch of the
Author by James Cleland. Port Hope, Williamson, 1895. 30p [NSWA OTUV

Sedgewick, Garnett Gladwin, 1882–1949
THE GRAVEYARD BY THE SEA. Vancouver, Author, 1938. 26p [Text of Paul
Valéry's "Le Cimetière Marin"] [OTU

Sella, Ernestine E.
PALM ROOM BALLADS. By Ernestine [pseud]. N.p., 1913. 62p [BM Brown U

Selle, Leonard Saville George, 1910–
MOMENTS, AND OTHER POEMS. Fraserdale, Ont., Author, 1951. 30p (Carillon
Poetry Chap-Books)
ONCE UPON A RHYME. Reflections in Light Verse. North Bay, Ont., Northland
Printers, 1955. 52p

Selwyn, Cecil Edward
PRAIRIE PATCHWORK; or, Western Poems for Western People. Winnipeg, Stovel,
1910. 96p [BM BVaU OTP
REGIMENTAL DITTIES. ... Winnipeg, Author, 1914. 31p [BM
RHYMING SNAPSHOTS OF AN IDLE FELLOW. Toronto, Ryerson, 1924. 132p
[BVaU NBFU OKQ

Sepass, Khalserten, 1841–1943 [Indian Chief]
THE SONGS OF Y-AIL-MIHTH. Trans. by Mrs. C.L. Street; ed. by Eloise Street.
Vancouver, Indian Time, 1955. 76p

Service, Robert William, 1874–1958

BALLADS OF A BOHEMIAN. New York, Barse, 1921. 220p [BM BVaU LC
NBFU OTU QMM

BALLADS OF A CHEECHAKO. Toronto, Briggs, 1909. 137p [Many later editions
by many publishers.] [BM BVaU NBFU OTP QMM

BAR-ROOM BALLADS. A Book of Verse. New York, Dodd Mead, 1940. 169p
[Also: London, Benn, 1940. 206p] [BM BVaU LC NBFU OTU QMM

CAROLS OF AN OLD CODGER. Verse. London, Benn, 1954. 198p

COLLECTED VERSE. London, Benn, 1930. [Various pagings] [BM BVa LC
NBFU OTP

THE COMPLETE POEMS. New York, Dodd Mead, 1940. 735p [BVaU NBFU OTU

THE COMPLETE POEMS. New York, Dodd Mead, 1942. [1032p] [Various
pagings] [LC NBFU OOU

COMPLETE POETICAL WORKS. New York, Barse, 1921. [855p] [Various
pagings] [Reprinted as: COLLECTED VERSE. London, Benn, 1930; and
COMPLETE POEMS. New York, Dodd Mead, 1933.] [BM BVa LC NBFU OTP

LYRICS OF A LOW BROW. New York, Dodd Mead, 1951. 182p

MORE COLLECTED VERSE. London, Benn, 1955. 1v [Various pagings]

RHYME AND ROMANCE. A Robert Service Anthology. London, Benn, 1958.
320 + 191 + 336 + 232p [Contents: THE TRAIL OF '98; SONGS OF A SUN-
LOVER; THE HOUSE OF FEAR; RHYMES OF A REBEL.]

RHYMES FOR MY RAGS. A Verse Book. London, Benn, 1956. 191p

RHYMES OF A REBEL. New York, Dodd Mead, 1952. 213p [Also: London,
Benn, 1952. 232p]

THE RHYMES OF A RED-CROSS MAN. London, Unwin, 1916. 192p [BM
BVaU LC NBFU OTP QMM

RHYMES OF A ROLLING STONE. Toronto, Briggs, 1912. 195p [BM BVaU
LC NBFU OTP QMM

RHYMES OF A ROUGHNECK. New York, Dodd Mead, 1950. 207p [BM BVaU
LC NBFU OTP

SELECTED POEMS BY ROBERT SERVICE. With Some Account of his Life and
Experiences. London, Unwin, 1917. 28p [BM BVaU

THE SHOOTING OF DAN McGREW, AND OTHER VERSES. New York, Barse &
Hopkins, 1920. [BM

SONGS FOR MY SUPPER. Verse. London, Benn, 1953. 207p

SONGS OF A SOURDOUGH. Toronto, Briggs, 1907. 116p [Many later editions.]
[BM BVaU LC NSHD OTP QMM

SONGS OF A SUN-LOVER. London, Benn, 1949. 191p [BM BVaU LC OTP

SONGS OF THE HIGH NORTH. London, Benn, 1958. 126p

THE SPELL OF THE YUKON AND OTHER VERSES. New York, Barse, 1907. 126p
[BVaU LC OTU QMM

TWENTY BATH-TUB BALLADS. London, Francis, Day & Hunter, 1939. 48p
[LC

Sewell, (Henry) Fane, −1944
THE KING, CANADA AND EMPIRE. By Fane Sewell. Toronto, Briggs, 1910.
20p [BM BVaU OTP

Shackleton, Helen
SAUCY AGAIN. Verses. Toronto, Macmillan, 1937. 49p [BM LC OOP
SAUCY AND ALL. Verses. Toronto, Macmillan, 1929. 48p [BM OTMC

Shannon, William
THE DOMINION ORANGE HARMONIST. ... Toronto, Maclear, 1876. 394p
[OLU OTP
THE UNITED EMPIRE MINSTREL. A Selection of the Best National, Constitu-
tional and Loyal Orange Songs and Poems, etc. etc. Toronto, Rowsell, 1852.
292p [OONL

Sharkey, Hugh Francis Xavier
AN ANVIL OF THE CROSS. [Vancouver, Author, 1934.] 141p [BVaU OWA
THE LOOM OF THE FAIRIES. N.p., [1929?]. 71p [OWA

Sharland, Rose E.
BALLADS OF OLD BRISTOL. Bristol, Arrowsmith, 1914. 69p [BM
EXMOOR LYRICS, AND OTHER VERSES. Bristol, Arrowsmith, 1910. 66p [BM
MAPLE LEAF MEN, AND OTHER WAR GLEANINGS. Toronto, Musson, [1916?].
88p [BM OTP QMU
VOICES OF DAWN OVER THE HILLS. Bristol, Arrowsmith, 1912. 77p [BM BVaU

Sharman, Mrs. Lyon, 1872−
THE SEA WALL, AND OTHER VERSE. Toronto, Macmillan, 1925. 79p [BVaU
NBFU OTP QMM
TOWN AND FOREST. Toronto, Macmillan, 1942. 73p [LC NBFU OTU

Shaw, Mrs. Amanda
THE WONDROUS HUSH. New York, Revell, 1931. 48p [BVaU LC OTP

Shaw, Bill
RHYMES OF THE R.C.A.F. Aylmer, Ont., Author, 1942. [CC

Sheard, Virna (Stanton), 1865?−1943
THE BALLAD OF THE QUEST. Toronto, McClelland, 1922. 52p [BVaU LC
NBFU OTP
CANDLE-FLAME [and Other Poems]. Toronto, McClelland, 1926. 79p [BVaU
NBFU OTP QMM
CARRY ON! Toronto, Warwick & Rutter, 1917. 23p [BM BVaU NBFU OTU
FAIRY DOORS. Toronto, McClelland, 1932. 76p [BVaU OTP
LEAVES IN THE WIND. Toronto, Ryerson, 1938. 55p [BVaU NBFU OTP
THE MIRACLE AND OTHER POEMS. Toronto, Dent, 1913. 111p [BM BVaU
NBFU OTU QMSS

Sheldon-Williams, Ralf Frederic Lardy
TO FRANCE. N.p., 1917. 8p [Adelphi cat. 92

Shepard, Fred Scott
NATURE'S CATHEDRAL AND OTHER POEMS. Toronto, Evangelical Pub., n.d. 14p
[OONL

Shepminster, John
THE IRON PONY, AND OTHER RHYMES, HUMOROUS AND SATIRICAL. Toronto,
Author, 1884. 33p [OTP

Sherk, Florence Nightingale (Horner), 1859–
THE WORKSHOPS AND OTHER POEMS. Fort William, Times-Journal, 1919. 65p
[BVaU OTP

Sherman, Francis Joseph, 1871–1926
A CANADIAN CALENDAR: XII LYRICS. Havana, Author, 1900. 23p [NBFU
THE COMPLETE POEMS OF FRANCIS SHERMAN. Ed. with a memoir by Lorne
Pierce. Toronto, Ryerson, 1935. 178p [BVaU NBFU OTP QMM
THE DESERTED CITY. Stray Sonnets by F.S. Rescued for the Few who Love
them, by H.D. N.p., priv. print., 1899. 12p [NBFU OONL
IN MEMORABILIS MORTIS. Cambridge, Mass., University Press, Author, 1896.
10p [BVaU NBFU OTP
MATINS. Boston, Copeland & Day, 1896. 58p [BM BVaU NBFU OKQ
A PRELUDE. Fredericton, priv. print., 1897. 10p [NBFU OTP

Sherwood, Harold
A WELCOME TO ALBERT, PRINCE OF WALES, AND OTHER POEMS. Toronto,
Lovell & Gibson, 1860. 49p [BVaU OTP

Sherwood, William Albert, 1859–1919
LAYS, LYRICS AND LEGENDS. Toronto, Hunter Rose, 1914. 152p [BVaU
NBFU OTP

Shiels, Andrew, 1793–1879
DUPES AND DEMAGOGUES. A Souvenir. By "Albyn" [pseud]. Halifax, n.p.,
1879. 40p [NSHD
EYE TO THE ERMINE. A Dream. By "Albyn" [pseud]. Halifax, Bowes, 1871.
20p [NSHD
JOHN WALKER'S COURTSHIP. A Legend of Lauderdale. By Albyn [pseud].
Halifax, Bowes, 1877. 32p [NSHD
THE LATE HONOURABLE SIMON BRADSTREET ROBIE. By Albyn [pseud].
[For the *Halifax Sun,* Jan. 7, 1858.] [Halifax?], 1858. 1p [NSHP
LETTER TO ELIZA. By Albyn [pseud]. Halifax, MacNab, 1869. 43p [NSHD
MY MOTHER. In Memoriam. By Albyn [pseud]. Halifax, Bowes, 1868. 10p
[NSHD

THE PREFACE. A Poem of the Period. By Albyn [pseud]. Halifax, Bowes, 1876. 55p [NSHP

RETRIBUTION. A Literary Contribution to the Nova Scotia Department of the Philadelphi Exhibition. By Albyn [pseud]. Halifax, MacNab, 1875. 21p [NSHD

RUSTICATING IN REALITY. A Pierian Paraphrase. By Albyn [pseud]. Halifax, Bowes, 1873. 30p [NSHD

SABBATH IN DARTMOUTH. By Albyn [pseud]. Halifax, Bowes, 1870. 15p [NSHP

THE WATER LILY. A Poem. By Albyn [pseud]. Halifax, Bowes, 1852. 32p [BM NSHP

THE WITCH OF THE WESTCOT. A Tale of Nova Scotia in 3 Cantos. And other Waste Leaves of Literature. Halifax, Howe, 1831. 213p [BVaU NSHP OTP

Shoolman, Regina Lenore, 1909–

UNCERTAIN GLORY. Toronto, Ryerson, 1932. 8p [BVaU NBFU OTP QMM

Shortt, Prescott (pseud)

SONGS FROM THE SILENCE. Toronto, Crucible Press, 1941. 22p [OTU

Shute, Evan Vere, 1905–

ANATOMY CLASS. By Vere Jameson [pseud]. London, Ont., Author, 1953. 59p

BLUEBIRD. By Vere Jameson [pseud]. London, Ont., Author, 1954. 47p

HASTY PUDDING. By Vere Jameson [pseud]. London, Ont., Hunter Print., 1951. 102p

HEIRLOOMS. By Vere Jameson [pseud]. London, Ont., Hunter Print., 1956. 59p

HY–BRASIL. By Vere Jameson [pseud]. London, Ont., Author, 1952. 49p

MOTHS AFTER MIDNIGHT. By Vere Jameson [pseud]. Toronto, Ryerson, 1945. 14p [BVaU LC NBFU OKQ QMU

OMAR FROM NISHAPUR. By Vere Jameson [pseud]. London, Ont., Author, 1948. 36p [BVaU NBFU OKQ

SKY PAINTER. By Vere Jameson [pseud]. London, Ont., Author, 1950. 94p [OTU

THE SULTAN OF JOBAT [and Other Poems]. By Vere Jameson [pseud]. London, Ont., Author, 1947. 50p [BVaU NBFU OKQ

WHERE THE HERON STANDS. By Vere Jameson [pseud]. N.p., Author, 1949. 113p [NSHPL OKQ

Sigurdson, A.S.

PENCIL STUB STANZAS. A Book of Light Verse. Vancouver, Author, 1950. 91p [BVa OONL

Silcox, Ethel Audrey (Smith), –1944

EARTHBOUND, AND OTHER POEMS. Toronto, Ryerson, 1932. 8p [BVaU NBFU OTP

BEGINNINGS IN SONG. By E.A.S.S. Newport, R.I., Milne, 1918. 10p [LC NBFU

Silverman, Harold S.

TWENTY-TWO IMPROVISATIONS. Toronto, Author, 1940. 22p [BVaU

Simcox, J.P.
IF HITLER WON, AND OTHER VERSES. Killam, Alta., 1941. 26p [Amtmann

Simpson, Andrew R.
MISCELLANEOUS POEMS. London, Ont., Advertiser, 1906. 148p [BM BVaU
   OTU

Sims, Frederick L.H.
DRINK AND DRUDGERY. Two Social Sins. Toronto, Author, 1900. 29p [OKQ

Simson, Letitia F.
FLOWERS OF THE YEAR, AND OTHER POEMS. Saint John, McMillan, 1869. 103p
   [BVaU NBFU OTU QMSS

Sinclair, Rev. Alexander Maclean, 1840–1924
CLARSACH NA COILLE. A Collection of Gaelic Poetry. Glasgow, Sinclair, 1881.
   345p [NBFU OTU
COMHCHRUINNEACHADH CHLINN-A-BHAIRD. The Glenbard Collection of Gaelic
   Poetry. Charlottetown, Haszard & Moore, 1890. 434p [OTP
THE GAELIC BARDS FROM 1411 TO 1715. Ed. by ——. Charlottetown, Haszard &
   Moore, 1890. 216p [NSHD OTP
THE GAELIC BARDS FROM 1715–1765. Ed. by ——. Charlottetown, Haszard &
   Moore, 1892. 260p [OTU
NA BAIRD LEATHANACH. The Maclean Bards. V. 2. Charlottetown, Haszard &
   Moore, 1900. 176p [OTU
ORAIN LE IAIN LOM MAC-DHOMHNAILL. Poems by John Lom Macdonald.
   Ed. by ——. Antigonish, The Casket, 1895. 127p [OTU

Sinclair, Rev. Lawrence
ADDITIONAL WRITINGS. Huntsville, Ont., Author, 1929. 12p [NSHK
IMPERIAL AND OTHER POETICAL WRITINGS. London, Stacey, [1925]. 140p
   [OONL

Singer, James C.
POEMS. Toronto, Thompson Bros., 1929. 47p [BVaU OTP

Sivell, Rhoda (Cosgrave), 1874? –
VOICES FROM THE RANGE. Toronto, T. Eaton Co., 1911. 43p [Another ed.,
   Toronto, Briggs, 1912. 102p] [BM BVaU OKQ SSU

Skeats, Wilfred S.
THE SONG OF THE EXILE. A Canadian Epic. Visions and Miscellaneous Poems.
   Toronto, Hart & Co., 1891. 160p [BVaU NSHD OTP

Skelton, Robin, 1925–
PATMOS AND OTHER POEMS. London, Routledge, [1955]. x + 76p
THIRD DAY LUCKY. Toronto, Oxford U. Press, 1958. 71p

Skene, James H.
JUST A FEW THOUGHTS. Poems of Peace, Faith and Hope. Stratford, Ont., B—H Press, 1939. 23p [Amtmann cat. 141

Skimings, Eloise A.
GOLDEN LEAVES. Goderich, Signal, 1904. 346p [BVaU OTU

Skinner, Constance Lindsay, 1879? —1939
SONGS OF THE COAST DWELLERS. New York, Coward-McCann, 1930. 85p [BVaU LC NBFU OTP

Slack, Crawford Chelson, 1855—1929
VILLAGE VERSE STORIES, AND OTHER POEMS. Athens, Ont., "Reporter," n.d. 126p [OTUV

Slader (*i.e.* Sladen), Arthur
THE CONFLAGRATIONS. Comprising Two Poems. ... First, The Burning Boat—A Serio-Satiric Poem on the Destruction by Fire of the Steamer "Royal Tar." ... Second, The Burning City—A Descriptive Poem in Commemoration of the Lamentable Fire ... in the City of St. John, N.B. ... 1837. Saint John, Observer Office, 1837. 32p [NSHP OTP

Sliter, Dorothy Browning (Murray)
HIGH WIND. Toronto, Crucible Press, 1944. 32p [OTP

Small, Mercator
THE BOOKKEEPER and a Metrical Translation of "The Song of the Bell" from the German of Schiller. Montreal, 1868. [OOP

Small, Watten
POEMS AND SONNETS. Saint John, Day, 1866. 76p [NBSaM

Smellie, George, 1811—1896
THE SEA. Sketches of a Voyage to Hudson's Bay. ... By The Scald [pseud]. London, Hope, 1855. 195p [OTP

Smillie, J.
RUSTIC RHYMES. Brussels, Ont., "Post," 1894. 43p [OTUV

Smith, Anna Beatrice, 1904—1936
WATER FROM THE ROCK. By Anna Beatrice Smith (Imogen Carroll). Ed. by Dr. Mabel Cartwright. Toronto, Macmillan, 1937. 60p [BM BVaU OKQ QMSS

Smith, Arthur James Marshall, 1902—
THE BLASTED PINE. An Anthology of Satire, Invective and Disrespectful Verse, Chiefly by Canadian Writers. Selected and arr. and with an intro. by F.R. Scott and A.J.M. Smith. Toronto, Macmillan, 1957. xix + 138p

THE BOOK OF CANADIAN POETRY. A Critical and Historical Anthology. Ed. with
an intro. and notes by ——. Chicago, U. of Chicago Press, 1943. 452p [Rev. and
enl. ed.: Toronto, Gage, 1948. 487p; 3rd ed., rev. and enl., 1957. xxv + 532p]
[BM BVaU LC NBFU OTP QMM

NEW PROVINCES. Poems of Several Authors. [Ed. by F.R. Scott.] Toronto,
Macmillan, 1936. 77p [Contains poems by Smith and others.] [BVaU NBFU
OKQ

NEWS OF THE PHOENIX AND OTHER POEMS. Toronto, Ryerson, 1943. 42p [BVaU
MWU NBFU OTP QMM

THE OXFORD BOOK OF CANADIAN VERSE IN ENGLISH AND FRENCH. Chosen and
with intro. by ——. Toronto, Oxford U. Press, 1960. lvi + 445p

A SORT OF ECSTASY. Poems, New and Selected. East Lansing, Mich., Michigan
State College Press; Toronto, Ryerson, 1954. 55p

THE WORLDLY MUSE. An Anthology of Serious Light Verse. Ed. by ——. New
York, Abelard Press, 1951. 388p

Smith, F. Percy
SONGS OF THE SAGUENAY. Arvida, Que., n.d. 28p [Brown U

Smith, Goldwin, 1823–1910
BAY LEAVES. Translations from the Latin Poets. Toronto, Blackett Robinson,
1890. 115p [Also: New York, Macmillan, 1893. 89p] [BM BVaU LC MWU
NBFU OTP QMU

Smith, Gordon Stace, 1886–
IN THE KOOTENAY AND OTHER VERSES. London, Mitre, 1931. 75p [BM BVaU
POEMS AND A REVERIE. Toronto, Weaver, 1940. 32p [OTP

Smith, Jennie Nelson
ISLE OF PAISLEY. New York, Vinal, 1928. 102p [LC NSHD OTP
MOOR-MISTS. Halifax, Royal Print., 1925. 128p [NSHD OTP

Smith, Kay, 1911–
FOOTNOTE TO THE LORD'S PRAYER, AND OTHER POEMS. Montreal, First
Statement Press, 1951. 36p

Smith, Lyman Cyrus, 1850–1928
A BLOSSOM OF THE SEA, AND OTHER POEMS. Wilmington, Ind., New Amstel, 1910.
218p [LC NBFU OTP QMM
MABEL GRAY AND OTHER POEMS. Toronto, Briggs, 1896. 131p [Another ed.,
1897. 120p] [BM BVaU LC OTP
WAR POEMS. Kingston, British Whig, 1918. [7]p [OOC

Smith, Martin F., 1840–
A BOOK OF CANADIAN AND AMERICAN POEMS. Hamilton, Donnelly & Lawson,
1863. 316p [OTP

Smith, Mary Barry
JUBILEE POEM. Saint John, "Globe," 1887. [CCJ

Smith, Mary Irene (Doherty), 1928–
SONGS OF THE ATHABASKA. Regina, 1960 [c 1949]. 65p

Smith, Norma Ethel, –1948
BELTHOR, THE SHEPHERD OF BETHLEHEM. Halifax, McAlpine, n.d. [12]p [OTUV
THE HILL AND FAR AWAY. Halifax, Imperial Pub. Co., 1948. 60p [NSWA

Smith, Rev. Oswald Jeffrey, 1889–
MALCOLM AND MARIE. A Romance of the Russian Revolution. London, Stockwell, 1932. 64p [AEU BM
POEMS OF A LIFETIME. Wheaton, Ill., Van Kampen, [1954]. 192p [Later ed., London, Marshall, Morgan & Scott, 1965. 224p] [AEU OTU
SONGS IN THE NIGHT. Toronto, Alliance Tabernacle, 1922. 95p [Amtmann cat. 151
SONGS OF THE SPIRIT. Toronto, Tabernacle Pubs., 1932. 32p [Amtmann cat. 151
VOICES OF HOPE. Toronto, 1919. 133p [Adelphi cat. 55A

Smith, Rev. William Wye, 1827–1917
ALAZON, AND OTHER POEMS. Including many of the Fugitive Pieces of Rusticus [pseud]. Toronto, Scobie, 1850. 125p [BVaU OTP
THE POEMS OF WILLIAM WYE SMITH. Toronto, Dudley Burns, 1888. 265p [BM BVaU LC OTP QMM
THE SELECTED POEMS OF WILLIAM WYE SMITH. Toronto, Briggs, 1908. 230p [BM BVaU NBFU OTP QMM

Smyth, John, –1852
SELECT POEMS. Toronto, 1841. 32p [OTP
A SMALL SPECIMEN OF THE GENIUS OF CANADA WEST, AND THE WONDERS OF THE WORLD. Toronto, Coates, 1845. 34p [OTP

Smythe, Albert Ernest Stafford, 1861–1947
THE GARDEN OF THE SUN. With an introduction by "A.E." (George Russell). Toronto, Macmillan, 1923. 81p [BM BVaU NBFU OTP QMM
POEMS GRAVE AND GAY. Toronto, Imrie & Graham, 1891. 184p [BM BVaU OTP
THE STORY OF ARMAND VILLIERS. Being Crusts and Crumbs for Christmas, 1916. N.p., [1916]. 14p [NBFU

Snook, Percy
RHYMES OF THE TRAIL. By a Canadian Pioneer (Percy Snook). London, Erskine Macdonald, 1923. 63p [BM Brown U

Snow, Victoria (Langton), 1864–
SPARKS FROM A KITCHEN FIRE. Toronto, Nelson, 1935. 143p [OTU

Snyder, Joseph A.
POEMS. Ilfracombe, Devon, Stockwell, 1956. 64p

Snyder, Olive Anderson
LITTLE TOWNS. N.p. [Elora, Ont.?], n.d. 25p [OTP
PICTURES ... AND OTHER POEMS. [Elora, Ont.], Express Print., n.d. 22p [OTUV
SONGS OF THE MONTH, AND OTHER POEMS. [Elora, Ont.], Express Print., n.d.
25p [OTP

Sollows, Atlanta Sara, 1889–1954
CLIMB THE RIGGING. Toronto, Crucible Press, 1944. 52p [BVaU NBFU OTP

Souster, Raymond, 1921–
CERBERUS. Poems by Louis Dudek, Irving Layton, and Raymond Souster.
Toronto, Contact Press, [1952]. 98p
CITY HALL STREET. Toronto, Ryerson, 1951. 8p
CREPE-HANGER'S CARNIVAL. Selected Poems, 1955–58. Toronto, Contact Press,
1958. 65p [mimeographed]
A DREAM THAT IS DYING. Poems. Toronto, Contact Press, n.d. 27p
FOR WHAT TIME SLAYS. Poems. Toronto, Author, 1955. 24p [mimeographed]
GO TO SLEEP, WORLD. Toronto, Ryerson, 1947. 59p [MWU NBFU OTP
QMM
SELECTED POEMS. Chosen by Louis Dudek. Toronto, Contact Press, 1956. 135p
SHAKE HANDS WITH THE HANGMAN. Poems 1940–1952. Toronto, Contact Press,
1953. 24p
UNIT OF FIVE. Poems by Louis Dudek, Ronald Hambleton, P.K. Page, Raymond
Souster, James Wreford. Ed. by Ronald Hambleton. Toronto, Ryerson, 1944.
87p [BVaU LC MWU NSHD OTU QMM
WALKING DEATH. Poems. Toronto, Contact Press, 1954. 24p
WHEN WE ARE YOUNG. Montreal, First Statement Press, 1946. 28p [BVaU
MWU NBFU OTP QMM

Sparrow, Charles, 1877–
POEMS OF MEMORY AND ENVIRONMENT. Toronto, Briggs, 1908. 32p [Brown U
BVaU OTU

Spears, Heather, 1934–
ASYLUM POEMS AND OTHERS. Toronto, Emblem Books, 1958. 15p

Spedon, Andrew Learmont, 1831–1884
THE CANADIAN MINSTREL. Montreal, Mitchell & Wilson, 1870. 112p [LC NSHD
OTP
THE WOODLAND WARBLER. A Volume of English and Scottish Poems and Songs.
Montreal, Becket, 1857. 136p [OTP

Spence, Francis Stephens, 1850–1917
CANADA. Toronto, Copp Clark, [1912?]. 27p [Brown U BVaU NSWA OTUV

Spencer, Agnes
THE LOGS' LAMENT. N.p., "Dorset Farm," 1898. 14p [OTUV

Spencer, Hiram Ladd, 1829–1915
THE FUGITIVES. A Sheaf of Verses. [With an Introductory Sketch of the Author by A.M. Belding.] Saint John, Bowes, 1909. 173p [BM BVaU NBFU OTP QMU
POEMS. Boston, Phillips Sampson, 1850. 95p [BM LC NSWA
A SONG OF THE YEARS, AND A MEMORY OF ACADIA. Saint John, 1889. 19p [LC NSWA OTP

Spiers, William
THE FINAL CRISIS. A Poem. [Anon] Toronto, 1882. 23p [Brown U

Spreckley, R.O.
"OLD QUEBEC" AND OTHER VERSE. Godalming, Eng., Craddock, 1919. [BM

Sproule, Dorothy (Corrigan), 1877–1963
BREAD AND ROSES. Montreal, Woodward Press, 1937. 48p [BVaU OKQ QMM
THE CLOUD AND THE FIRE. Montreal, Author, 1940. 40p [BVaU OTU QMM
EARTH AND STARS. Montreal, Mercury Press, 1935. 46p [OTP
THE GOLD OF DAWN. Poems. New York, Harrison, 1938. 109p [BVaU LC OTU QMM
THE GOLDEN GOAL. Montreal, Mercury Press, 1933. 42p [QMM
THE MYSTIC STAR. Montreal, Mercury Press, 1931. 32p [BVaU OTP
POEMS OF LIFE. ... With an intro. by Lloyd C. Douglas. Montreal, Mercury Press, 1931. 32p [BVaU OTP QMM
THE SILVER CLOUD. Montreal, de la Salle Print., 1942. 35p [BVaU QMM OLU

Squire, Ada A.
ACROSS THE SEA. London, Ont., "Advertiser," 1892. 51p [OTUV

Srzentich, Mirko, 1934–
HOT ALPHABET. ... By Mike Strong [pseud]. Toronto, Hawkshead Press, 1960. 8p

Stafford, Rev. Ezra Adams, 1839–1891
RECREATIONS. Toronto, Briggs, 1883. 96p [BVaU LC OTP

Stafford, Ezra Hurlburt, 1865–
A CHRISTMAS CANTICLE, SAINTS' DAY BALLADS, AND SUNDRY OTHER MEASURES. Toronto, Bryant Press, 1895. 20p [OTP

THE DAUGHTER OF THE REPUBLIC. Montego Bay, Jamaica, St. James Press,
1927. 62p [BM OTP
THE ORANGE GROVE AND OTHER POEMS OF THE JAMAICA PEASANTRY. Montego
Bay, Jamaica, St. James Press, 1927. 62p [BM OTP

Stancliff, Isabella Morison, 1891–
– AND SINCE. By Ella Stancliff. Powell River, B.C., Town Crier Press, 1937.
24p [CC
JUST ONE YEAR. By Ella Stancliff. Powell River, B.C., Town Crier, 1936. 20p
[BVaU

Stanford, Joseph Hunt, 1871–1935
MIRIAM AND OTHER POEMS. Toronto, Briggs, 1908. 55p [BVaU OKQ

Stansbury, Joseph, 1740–1809
THE LOYAL VERSES OF JOSEPH STANSBURY AND DOCTOR JONATHAN ODELL. ...
Ed. by Winthrop Sargent. Albany, N.Y., Munsell, 1860. 199p [BVaU LC
NBFU OLU

Stark, James
DESTINY OF CANADA. Toronto, Imrie & Graham, 1892. 31p [OTP

Starke, Richard Griffin, 1831–1909
THE LORD OF LANORAIE. A Canadian Legend. Montreal, Lovell, 1898. 92p
[BM BVaU LC NBFU OTP QMM

Stead, Robert James Campbell, 1880–1959
THE EMPIRE BUILDERS AND OTHER POEMS. Toronto, Briggs, 1908. 100p
[Several later editions.] [BM BVaU NSHD OTP QMM
KITCHENER AND OTHER POEMS. Toronto, Musson, 1917. 161p [BM BVaU
LC NBFU OTP QMM
PRAIRIE BORN AND OTHER POEMS. Toronto, Briggs, 1911. 95p [BM BVaU
NSHD OLU
SONGS OF THE PRAIRIE. Toronto, Briggs, 1911. 96p [BM BVaU OKQ
WHY DON'T THEY CHEER? Poems. London, Unwin, 1918. 166p [BM BVaU LC
LC OTP

Steele, Harwood Elmes Robert, 1897–
CLEARED FOR ACTION. By Howard Steele [pseud]. London, Fisher Unwin,
1914. 166p [BM BViP MWU OH

Steiner, Florence B., 1877–1946
TOY BALLOONS. Verses for Children. Toronto, Ryerson, 1934. 62p [Brown U
BVaU NBFU OOP
TOY SHIPS. Poems for Children. Ottawa, Graphic, 1926. 63p [OKQ

Stenning, Annie A.
THE NEVER NEVER ROAD. Montreal, Renouf, 1923. 15p [BM

Stephen, Alexander Maitland, 1882–1942

BROWN EARTH AND BUNCH GRASS. Vancouver, Wrigley Print., 1931. 133p
[BVaU OKQ QMM

THE GOLDEN TREASURY OF CANADIAN VERSE. Chosen by ——. Toronto, Dent,
1928. 146p [BVaU NBFU OKQ QMM

THE LAND OF SINGING WATERS. London, Dent, 1927. 189p [BM BVaU LC
NSHD OTP QMM

LORDS OF THE AIR. Poems of the Present War. Vancouver, Author, 1940. 16p
[BVaU LC OKQ

THE ROSARY OF PAN. Toronto, McClelland, 1923. 137p [BM BVaU NBFU
OTP QMM

VERENDRYE. A Poem of the New World. Toronto, Dent, 1935. 66p [BVaU
LC NBFU OKQ

Stephens, William A., 1809–1891

THE CENTENNIAL. An International Poem. Toronto, 1878. 72p [Brown U
BVaU

HAMILTON, AND OTHER POEMS. Toronto, Rogers & Thompson, 1840. 180p
[2nd ed., 1871. 410p] [BVaU NSHD OTP QMM

A POETICAL GEOGRAPHY, AND RHYMING RULES FOR SPELLING. Toronto,
Brewer McPhail, 1848. 36p [OTP

Stevens, George Roy, 1895–

TRAVELOGUE. Montreal, Southam Print., 1959. 43p

Stevens, W.H.

MOODS AND SEASONS; OR, MULTUM-IN-PARVO. Toronto, Anderson-Kew, 1904.
N.p. [OTUV

Stevens, Winifred Mary (Hird), 1882–1934

GOLD DUST. New Westminster, B.C., Author, 1930. 32p [BVaU

THE VIKING'S BRIDE. Toronto, Ryerson, 1929. 8p [BVaU NBFU OKQ QMM

Stevenson, Lionel, 1902–

A CHAPBOOK. By Lionel Stevenson ... [and Others]. Vancouver, priv. print.,
1922. 28p [BVaU NBFU

A POOL OF STARS. Toronto, Ryerson, 1926. 16p [BVaU NBSaM OKQ QMM

THE ROSE OF THE SEA. Toronto, Ryerson, 1932. 12p [BVaU NBSaM OTP
QMM

Stevenson, Orlando John, 1869–1950

FIFTY-FOUR NARRATIVE POEMS. Ed. by ——. Toronto, Copp Clark, 1933.
241 p [NBSM

A GROUP OF POEMS. Guelph, Author, 1944. 18p [BVaU NBFU OTP

... SEVEN POEMS. ... With Annotations by ——. Toronto, Copp Clark, 1933.
90p [OLU

THE UNCONQUERABLE NORTH, AND OTHER POEMS. Toronto, Macmillan, 1938. 79p [BVaU LC OTP

Stewart, Alexander Charles, 1867–1944
THE BEAVER, AND OTHER ODDS AND ENDS. Toronto, Hunter Rose, 1918. 108p [BVaU NSHD OLU QMM

DUST AND ASHES (Chiefly). [Toronto], Author, 1910. 188p [BVaU NSHD OTP QMM

THE PENSIONERS. A Poem. Toronto, Rose Pub. Co., 1890. 16p [OTP

THE POETICAL WORKS OF ALEXANDER CHAS. STEWART. Toronto, Hunter Rose, 1890. 189p [BVaU OTP

THE SHELL, WITH FRAGMENTS AND REVERBERATIONS. Toronto, Briggs, 1917. 69p [BVaU OTUV

Stewart, Charles
THE HARP OF STRATHNAVER, A LAY OF THE SCOTTISH HIGHLAND EVICTIONS—AND OTHER POEMS. Buffalo, Peter Paul, [18—?]. 89p [Also: Galt, Ont., 1884. 89p] [CCJ OTP

Stewart, Thomas Brown Phillips, 1864–1892
POEMS. By Phillips Stewart. London, Kegan Paul, 1887. 89p [BM NBFU OTP QMM

Stickle, Charles Harris
POEMS OF A GREAT RANGE. Toronto, Author, 1901. [T&C

Stilson, Dorothy Elizabeth
CHRISTMAS EVERY DAY. San Gabriel, Calif., Willing Pub. Co., 1949. 64p [AEU

Stitt, James Herbert, 1891–1958
SONGS FOR REMEMBRANCE. Ottawa, priv. print., 1959. 10p

Stockton, Noel, 1917–
FAMILY VERSE AND OTHER SELECTED POEMS. Bracebridge, Ont., Herald-Gazette Office, 1958. 41p

Stone, Clement R.
VANCOUVER VISTAS. Vancouver, Author, 1936. 24p [BVa OKQ

Story, Duncan Albert, 1853–
WHERE THE TIDES EBB AND FLOW. Montreal, Gazette Print., 1932. 72p [BVaU OLU QMSS

Strachan, Ada M.
HEPATICAS IN SPRING. [Toronto?], Author, 1935. 23p [Brown U

Strachan, Jessie
POEMS AND SCOTCH PROSE. Bluevale, Ont., Author, 1935. 40p [UTQ'37

Strachan, Richard
GLIMPSES OF GLORY; or, Incentives to Holy Living. An Antidote to Weariness in Well-Doing, and Comfort for the Afflicted and Bereaved. Ed. by Zethar [pseud]. Toronto, Briggs, 1890. 138p [Brown U

Strangways, Britton, 1863–
THE MORNING GOETH FORTH AND OTHER POEMS. Toronto, Ontario Press, 1924. 95p [BVaU LC OOP

Straton, Barry, 1854–1901
THE BUILDING OF THE BRIDGE. An Idyl of the River St. John. Saint John, McMillan, 1887. 19p [NSWA
LAYS OF LOVE, AND MISCELLANEOUS POEMS. Saint John, McMillan, 1884. 80p [BVaU NSHD OTP QMM

Stringer, Arthur John Arbuthnot, 1874–1950
DARK SOIL. Indianapolis, Bobbs-Merrill, 1933. 123p [BM BVaU LC OLU
EPIGRAMS. London, Ont., Warren, 1896. 42p [OTP
HEPHAESTUS; PERSEPHONE AT ENNA; AND SAPPHO IN LEUCADIA. Toronto, Methodist Book, 1903. 43p [BM BVaU NBFU OTU
IRISH POEMS. New York, Kennerley, 1911. 110p [Another ed., under title OUT OF ERIN, pub. in 1930.] [BM BVaU LC NBFU OTU
THE KING WHO LOVED OLD CLOTHES, AND OTHER IRISH POEMS. New York, Bobbs-Merrill, 1941. 105p [BM LC MWU OLU
NEW YORK NOCTURNES. Toronto, Ryerson, 1948. 12p [BVaU MWU NBFU OTP
THE OLD WOMAN REMEMBERS, AND OTHER IRISH POEMS. Indianapolis, Bobbs-Merrill, 1938. 57p [BM BVaU LC OLU
OPEN WATER. New York, Lane, 1914. 132p [BM BVaU LC OTU
OUT OF ERIN (SONGS IN EXILE). Indianapolis, Bobbs-Merrill, 1930. 155p [Pub. in 1911 as IRISH POEMS.] [BVaU LC NSHD OLU QMM
PAULINE, AND OTHER POEMS. London, Ont., Warren, 1895. 64p [OTU
SAPPHO IN LEUCADIA. Boston, Little Brown, 1907. 264p [Extract from THE WOMAN IN THE RAIN AND OTHER POEMS.] [LC NBFU
SHADOWED VICTORY. Indianapolis, Bobbs-Merrill, 1943. 78p [BM BVaU LC NBFU OTU
WATCHERS OF TWILIGHT, AND OTHER POEMS. London, Ont., Warren, 1894. 43p [BVaU NBFU OTP
A WOMAN AT DUSK, AND OTHER POEMS. Indianapolis, Bobbs-Merrill, 1928. 154p [BM BVaU LC NSHD OTU QMBM
THE WOMAN IN THE RAIN, AND OTHER POEMS. Boston, Little Brown, 1907. 264p [Also: Toronto, McClelland, 1949. 264p] [BVaU LC NBFU OTU QMM

Stuart, Mabel L.
ROSES OF FRANCE AND OTHER POEMS. Toronto, Warwick, 1919. 16p [NSHPL OONL

Stuart, Mary F.
WAYSIDE POEMS. By Slinfold [pseud]. Fort William, Author, 1939. 98p [BVaU

Sturrock, W.
A MILITARY MITE TO THE MOUNTAIN OF LITERATURE; or, The Rhymes of a Red
  Coat [pseud]. Quebec, Middleton & Dawson, 1858. 142p [BVaU OTL
  QMBM

Sullivan, Alan, 1868–1947
VENICE AND OTHER VERSE. Toronto, Bryant, 1893. 48p [NSWA OTP
THE WHITE CANOE AND OTHER VERSE. Toronto, Bryant, 1891. 30p [OTP

Summerss, George, 1834–
BIRD OF THE BUSH. A Collection of Poems [with Autobiographical Sketch].
  Toronto, Hunter Rose, 1908. 240p [BVaU OKQ
POEMS. N.p., [1880?]. 84p [BVaU NSHD OTP

Sutherland, Alexander Hugh, 1870–1952
EARLE, AND OTHER POEMS. Victoria, Quality Press, n.d. 28p [BViPA
MANITOBA MEMORIES. Winnipeg, Stovel Co., [1928?]. 35p [A 1912 imprint is
  listed in BM.] [BM BViPA NBFU OTP
OUR KING AND QUEEN. N.p., n.pub., n.d. 4p [BViPA
THE PASSING OF AEGEUS. A Greek Epic. [Anon] Victoria, Clarke, n.d. 11p
  [BViPA
STAR-DUST. Astronomical Poems. Victoria, Clarke, 1943. 18p [BVaU

Sutherland, John, 1919–1956
OTHER CANADIANS. An Anthology of the New Poetry in Canada, 1940–1946.
  Ed. by ——. Montreal, First Statement Press, 1947. 113p [BVaU LC NSHD
  OTP QMM

Swaan, William
SONGS OF THE SOUTH SEAS. Winnipeg, Hull Print., 1949. 52p [UTQ'50

Swanson, Robert E.
BUNKHOUSE BALLADS. Book 3. Toronto, Allen, 1945. 58p [BVaU LC
RHYMES OF A HAYWIRE HOOKER. By Robert E. Swanson and Seattle Red [pseud].
  Vancouver, Lumberman Print., 1953. 68p
RHYMES OF A LUMBERJACK. A Second Book of Verse. Toronto, Allen, 1943. 94p
  [BVaU LC OTP QMSS
RHYMES OF A WESTERN LOGGER. Vancouver, Lumberman Print., 1942. 56p
  [Other later editions.] [BVaU LC NBFU
RHYMES OF A WESTERN RAMBLER. Vancouver, Author, 1942. 48p [mimeo-
  graphed] [Adelphi cat. 64

Swanson, William J., 1862–
NORTH COUNTRY RHYMES. Desbarats, Ont., 1938. 41p [Brown U OTU

Swart, George G.
THE BOOK OF LIFE EVERLASTING EXPLAINING THE CHART, THE ETERNAL WHEEL OF LIFE EVERLASTING. ... Kitchener, Ont., n.d. 32p [Adelphi cat. 55A

Swart, Morley Lewis, 1879—
WAR-TIME MELODIES, AND OTHER SONGS. London, Ont., Advertiser, 1904. 91p [OLU

Swayze, James Frederick, 1907—1967
AND SEE PENELOPE PLAIN. Toronto, Ryerson, 1958. 16p
IN THE EGYPTIAN GALLERY. Toronto, Ryerson, 1960. 12p

Sweeney, John, 1864—
SONGS AND VERSES OF A PEACE RIVER PIONEER. Peace River, Record-Gazette, [194—?]. 36p [AEU

Sweeny, Robert, —1840
ODDS AND ENDS: ORIGINAL AND TRANSLATED. New York, Magarey, 1826. 156p [Same title: Montreal, Starke, 1836. 188p] [LC OTP
REMNANTS. By the Author of "Odds and Ends" [pseud]. Montreal, Starke, 1835. 64p [OTP

Swift, Sherman Charles, 1879—1947
"TREASURE TROVE" AND OTHER POEMS. Toronto, U. of Toronto Press, 1911. 53p [BM BVaU OTP

Swire, Frederick
SHORT POEMS AND OTHER WRITINGS. London, Ont., Vivian, 1877. 109p [OTP

Sykes, Mrs. Eileen
THE GAY GARLAND. New York, Pageant Press, 1954. 53p

Symons, Frank Stewart, 1887—
POEMS. [Montreal?], 1948. 46p [OONL QMU
WORLD SO FULL. Montreal, Gazette Print., 1952. 112p

Tait, Robert Holland
"THE TRAIL OF THE CARIBOU." The Royal Newfoundland Regiment, 1914—1918. Boston, Newfoundland Pub. Co., 1933. 65p [A verse history.] [Brown U OTU

Talbot, Thomas (fl. 1844—82)
THE ENCHIRIDION OF EPICTETUS, AND THE GOLDEN VERSES OF PYTHAGORAS, TRANSLATED. ... Together with some Original Poems. London, Sampson, 1881. 244p [An earlier ed.: Montreal, 1872.] [BM

THE EXILE, AND OTHER VERSES. Together with Translations from some of the Greek and Latin Poets. London, Low Marston, 1879. 246p [BM OLU

Tamblyn, Bertha Louise
HOLLY TIME SONGS. Fifteen Original Christmas Songs for Children and Grown-ups ... music by Bertha Louise Tamblyn. Toronto, Thompson, 1938. 32p [OTP

Taylor, Alastair MacDonald
FIRE-MIST. Los Angeles, O.D.S. Print. Co., 1936. 31p [BM LC OOP

Taylor, Archibald M'Alpine
BOYHOOD HOURS. A Collection of Simple Poems, Songs and Odes. Toronto, Hunter Rose, 1881. 178p [BVaU LC NBFU OKQ

Taylor, Frances Beatrice, 1891–
THE SONG OF KORTHAN. New York, Revell, 1923. 30p [LC
WHITE WINDS OF DAWN. Toronto, McClelland, 1924. 128p [BVaU NBFU OTU QMM

Taylor, Gertrude Emilie (Bartlett), 1876–
THE WHITE BIRD AND OTHER POEMS. Toronto, Macmillan, 1932. 57p [BVaU NBFU OTP

Taylor, Helen B.
VANCOUVER AND OTHER POEMS. Vancouver, Author, [1944?]. 26p [BViPA

Taylor, Lilian (Fortier), 1889–
MAGIC WINDOWS. [Hollyburn, B.C.], Author, [1946]. 34p [BViPA
WHITE MISTS OF ACADIE. Wolfville, Acadian Print., 1934. [2nd ed.: Kentville, Kentville Press, 1935. 20p] [Brown U NSHD

Taylor, Mabel Cecilia (Ryan)
MY CHRISTMAS TREE. Moose Jaw, Author, 1944. 68p [OTP

Taylor, Phena Catherine
"THE GATEWAY OF THE NORTH." Vancouver, Capitol Print., n.d. 55p [BViPA

Taylor, Wardlaw
FRUSTA. St. Andrews, N.B., Beacon, n.d. 18p [NBS

Taylor, William Henry
CANADIAN SEASONS. ... With a Medley of Reveries in Verse and Prose and Other Curios. Toronto, Miln-Bingham Printers, 1913. 150p [BM BVaU OKQ

Tebbs, Rev. George William, 1873–
SUNNY MEMORIES. By Old Man Sunshine [pseud]. [Hamilton?], Author, 1934–35. 86p [OPAL

Telford, William, 1828–1895
THE POEMS OF WILLIAM TELFORD ... Bard of Peterborough St. Andrew's Society.
Peterborough, Stratton, 1887. 156p [BVaU OTP QMM NBFU

Tener, John Frost
CALLING ALL FREE MEN. Vancouver, Murphy & Chapman, 1941. 34p [BVaU
LC

Tenny, W.H.F.
COMPANIONSHIP AND THE CROWD AND OTHER POEMS. Toronto, Ryerson, 1925.
8p [BVaU NBSaM OTU QMM
SONGS OF THE NORTH, AND OTHER POEMS. Toronto, Ryerson, 1923. 143p
[2nd ed., enl., 1924.] [BM BVaU NBFU OTU QMM

Thayers, M.J. (Shaw)
BUDS AND BLOSSOMS. Toronto, McLean, 1894. 192p [BVaU NBFU OKQ
A WREATH OF WILD FLOWERS. Toronto, Morton, 1877. 79p [OTP

Thomas, A. Vernon, 1876–1950
MAIN STREET. Manitoba's Historic Highway. A Panorama of Buffalo, Indians,
Explorers ... Portrayed in Verse. ... [Winnipeg?], n.p., [193–?]. 15p [MWP

Thomas, Edgar James, 1881–
THREE POEMS. [Jubilee Ode, Christmas Carol, New Year Wassail]. [? Winnipeg,
193–] 7p [Adelphi cat. 33-A
A WREATH OF PRAIRIE FLOWERS FOR A QUEEN. Winnipeg, Author, 1953. 8p

Thomas, Hartley Munro, 1896–
SONGS OF AN AIRMAN, AND OTHER POEMS. With an introduction by S.W. Dyde,
Principal of Queen's Theological College, Kingston, Ont. Toronto, McClelland,
1918. 101p [BM BVaU LC NSHD OKQ

Thomas, Mrs. L. Burns
STRAY LEAVES. Vancouver, n.p., [1916?]. 48p [BVaU OTP

Thompson, Andrew Thorburn, 1870–1938?
THE CANADIAN KNIGHTS ENTERTAINMENT. N.p., 1918. 11p [BM OTU
THE ODYSSEY OF THE GENTLEMEN ADVENTURERS TRAVELLING INTO THE
BRAZILS. ... Ottawa, priv. print., 1928. 46p [BVaU OOU QMU

Thompson, Blanche Jennings, 1887–
A GLIMPSE INTO MY GARDEN. Short Poems by Thornapple [pseud]. Thorold,
Ont., Thorold Post Print., 1903. 100p [BM Brown U BVaU OTUV

Thompson, Claude Willett
VAGRANT VERSES. Quebec, Telegraph Pub. Co., 1926. 35p [NBFU

Thompson, Dorothy (Burr), 1900–
SWANS AND AMBER. Some Early Greek Lyrics, Freely Translated and Adapted.
Toronto, U. of Toronto Press, 1948. xii + 193p [BVaU OTU NBSaM MWU

Thompson, Ida Isabella Margaret (Clarke), 1881–
OUT OF THE NORTH WITH DRUMS AND OTHER POEMS. N.p., n.d. 3p [QMU
PRAIRIE JUNE AND OTHER POEMS. N.p., n.d. 41p [BVaU

Thompson, John Sparrow
SCRIPTURE SKETCHES. Halifax, Cunnabell, 1829. 280p [NSHD

Thomson, Mrs. Annie Laurence, 1837?–1926
A LITTLE BOOK OF VERSE. Bexhill-on-Sea, Parsons, 1914. 73p [BVaU NSHD

Thomson, Edward William, 1849–1924
THE MANY-MANSIONED HOUSE, AND OTHER POEMS. Toronto, Briggs, 1909. 151p
   [BM BVaU NBFU OTU QMM
PETER OTTAWA. Toronto, 1905. 16p [NBFU OKQ
THIS IS OF AUCASSIN AND NICOLETTE. ... Verse Translation. Boston, Copeland,
   1896. 78p [BM LC
WHEN LINCOLN DIED, AND OTHER POEMS. Boston, Houghton, 1909. 146p
   [According to QMM, this is another ed. of THE MANY-MANSIONED HOUSE. ...]
   [BM LC NBFU OLU QMM

Thomson, John Stuart, 1869–1950
A DAY'S SONG. Toronto, Briggs, 1900. 124p [BM BVaU NBFU OKQ QMM
ESTABELLE AND OTHER VERSE. Toronto, Briggs, 1897. 113p [BM BVaU OTP
   QMM
EULALINE. New York, 1899. 9p [Brown U

Thomson, Robert Burns, 1847–1922
THE POEMS OF ROBERT BURNS THOMSON. Winnipeg, Wallingford, 1936. 387p
   [BM LC OOP

Thomson, Theresa Emily (Meeres)
MYTH AND MONUMENT. By Theresa E. & Don W. Thomson. Toronto, Ryerson,
   1957. 16p
RIVER & REALM. By Theresa E. & Don W. Thomson. Toronto, Ryerson, 1959.
   14p
SILVER LIGHT. By Theresa E. and Don W. Thomson. Toronto, Ryerson, 1955.
   13p
SILVER SHADOWS. Toronto, Ryerson, 1951. 8p

Thomson, Wilson
THE SHIFTBOSS, AND OTHER POEMS. Timmins, Ont., Author, [1943?]. 23p [LC

Thow, William, 1896–
A CAST OF REVERIES. Montreal, 1956. 71p
MORE ODD MEASURES. Toronto, Ryerson, 1937. 12p [BVaU NSHD OTP QMM
ODD MEASURES. Toronto, Ryerson, 1936. 11p [Same title: Montreal, Author,
   1959. 46p] [BVaU NBSaM OTU QMM
POET AND SALESMAN. Toronto, Ryerson, 1939. 16p [BVaU NSHD OTP QMM

A SORT OF SENTIMENT. Montreal, 1953. 75p

TALES OF A SONGSMITH. Montreal, 1951. 130p [Reprinted 1961.]

VERSES OF A VAGRANT. Toronto, Best, 1929. 173p [BVaU OTU QMSS

Tilden, Vera Willis

LINES BY VERA WILLIS TILDEN. ... [London, Ont.?], Author, [1946?]. 65p
[LC

NOSEGAY OF SONG. Blenheim, Ont., News Tribune, 1946. 31p [LC OTP

Tobin, Anastasia Bertille, 1888–

AUTUMN IN KING'S COVE AND OTHER POEMS. King's Cove, Bonavista Bay, Nfld.,
Author, 1951. 50p

Todd, Maude Pepper

IN A GARDEN OF YESTERDAY. Toronto, Ryerson, 1925. 12p [OKQ

Todd, Robert Henry, 1877–

CHEER-UP VERSES AND RANDOM RHYMES. Brampton, Charters, 1931. 191p
[OTU

Tolchard, John T.

A WEB OF DREAMS. Toronto, Ryerson, 1933. 32p [OPAL

Tolcher, H.

POEMS. Calgary, Gibson, 1896–98. 3v [43, 90, 29p]. [OTUV

Tolkien, J. Kenneth

THE INN OF GAHNOBWAY. Montreal, Benallack Litho. Co., 1903. 177p [BVaU
OTUV QMSS

Toll, Ellsworth R.

SELECTED POEMS. N.p., n.p., 1943. 76p [OTUV

Tolmie, Margaret (Duncan), 1886–

"DEAR CANADA WE SING TO THEE" AND OTHER POEMS. Sarnia, Frontier Print.,
1946. 32p [BVaU OKQ

Tooth, Arthur, 1914–1942

FLIGHT'S END. ... New York, Exposition Press, 1947. 45p [Brown U LC

Toots (pseud)

THE TWO ELDERS, AND THE SEQUEL, THE MEAL CLUB PLOT. By Toots [pseud].
Toronto, Citizen Office, 1856. 15p [BVaU OTP

Toronto, Ont. Danforth Technical School

ZEPHYRS. A Collection of Poetry and Art, the Work of Students of Danforth
Technical School. Toronto, Tech Tatler Pub., 1936. 44p [UTQ'37

Toronto, Ont. Jarvis Collegiate Institute. Poetry Club
CARAVAN. A Book of Verse. Toronto, College Press, 1930. 30p [Also in 1931.
31p] [CC

Toronto Tandem Club
PROCEEDINGS OF THE TORONTO TANDEM CLUB, 1839, 1840, 1841. [Anon]
Toronto, Rowsell, 1841. 66p [BM BVaU

Toronto Women's Press Club
VERSE AND REVERSE. By Members of the Toronto Women's Press Club. Toronto,
Goodchild, 1921, 1922. 47p [BVaU NBFU OKQ
CANADIAN DAYS. Selections for Every Day in the Year from the Works of Canadian
Authors. Toronto, Musson, [1911]. 168p [BVaU LC NBFU OTU

Torville, Charles Hollis, 1888–
POEMS. [Vancouver?], Author, n.d. 24p [BVaU

Tovell, Rev. Isaac, 1845–
GOLDEN WEDDING DAY; or, Semi-Centennial Pulpit and Pew of Richmond St.
Methodist Church, Toronto. Toronto, Briggs, 1884. 48p [OTP
THE OLD FRAME CHURCH, AND THE FRIENDS OF YORE. St. Catharines, Author,
1890. n.p. [OTUV

Towriss, Mrs. Louise Yates, 1877–1942
CHORDS AND ECHOES. Athens, Ont., Author, 1940. 24p [CC
A HOUSE OF MEMORIES. Athens, Ont., Athens Reporter Presses, 1935. 39p [OKQ

Tracy, Neil, 1905–
THE RAIN IT RAINETH. Sherbrooke, Que., La Tribune, 1938. 30p [NBFU

Tranter, Mrs. Gladdis Joy, 1902–
A SOLDIER'S LEGACY. Toronto, Ambassador Books, 1944. 85p [BVaU LC OTP
QMM
WINGED WORDS. Winnipeg, Wallingford Press, 1935. 20p [MWP

Treleaven, A.E.L.
GUELPH'S 50TH ANNIVERSARY. A Poem. Guelph, Herald Steam Print., 1877.
4p [Brown U

Trott, James Charles
A COLLECTION OF POEMS AND SONGS. Halifax, "Guardian," 1895. 196p [BM
BVaU

Trotter, Bernard Freeman, 1890–1917
A CANADIAN TWILIGHT, AND OTHER POEMS OF WAR AND OF PEACE. Toronto,
McClelland, 1917. 127p [BM BVaU LC NSHD OTU QMM

Tuck, Clyde Edwin
VOICES IN THE WIND. Boston, Christopher Pub. House, 1950. 94p [LC

Tucker, James Alexander, 1872–1903
POEMS. With a prefatory memoir by Arthur Stringer. Toronto, Briggs, 1904. 133p [BM BVaU LC NBFU OTU QMM

Tucker, Norman
NARRATIVE POEMS. Vernon, B.C., News Print., 1927. 111p [BVaU OTU

Tucker, Rev. William Bowman, 1859–1934
LAURENTIAN TALES. Montreal, Southam, 1922. 275p [BM BVaU NBFU OTU QMM
SONGS OF THE WAYSIDE. Montreal, Lovell, 1918. 192p [BM BVaU NBFU OTU QMM
THE SPRINGS OF THE PISGAH HILLS AND OTHER POEMS. [MOR'12

Tudor-Hart, Edith
SONGS OF THE SHADOWS. London, Fowler Wright, 1927. 128p [BM BVaU
VISTAS OF OUR LADY. ... London, Fowler Wright, n.d. 57p [BM

Tunstall, C.A.
COLLECTED POEMS OF C.A. TUNSTALL, M.D., Class Poet, McGill Medical Faculty, 1891. ... Montreal, 1891. 6p [Brown U

Tupper, Charles Andrew
THE GLEAMING EDGE. With a Foreword by Theodore Goodridge Roberts. Tweed, Ont., Valley Press, 1947. 39p [OTP
PRELUDE TO SONG. Toronto, Crucible Press, 1941. 20p [LC OTP QMM

Tupper, Kathryn (Munro)
FORFEIT AND OTHER POEMS. By Kathryn Munro. Toronto, Ryerson, 1926. 8p [BVaU NBFU OTP
NEW MOON. By Kathryn Munro. Toronto, Nelson, 1938. 125p-[BVaU NBFU OTP
TANAGER FEATHER. By Kathryn Munro. Toronto, Ryerson, 1950. 12p [BVaU NBFU OTP
UNDER THE MAPLE. By Kathryn Munro. Toronto, Ryerson, 1930. 23p [BVaU NBFU OTP

Tuque-Rouge (pseud)
"MAMMA'S JOY" AND "PAPA'S PEARL"; or, Canada's Winter Carnival. By Tuque Rouge [pseud]. [Montreal, 1885?]. 12p + 12p [QMSS

Turnbull, Gael, 1928–
TRIO. First Poems. By Gael Turnbull, Phyllis Webb and E.W. Mandel. Toronto, Contact Press, 1954. 89p

BJARNI SPIKE-HELGI'S SON, AND OTHER POEMS. Ashland, Mass., Origin Press, 1956. 32p

Turner, Jack
BUDDY'S BLIGHTY AND OTHER VERSES FROM THE TRENCHES. Halifax, Imperial Pub., 1917. 29p [Another ed., Boston, Small Maynard, 1918. 106p] [BM OOP

Tweedale, Bernard
SOME VERSES AND DRAMATIC PIECES. Vancouver, 1914. 35p [BVaU

Twomlow-Britt, Joseph, 1914–
ACTION STATIONS! New York, Harrison, 1946. 45p [LC OTP
THE SONG OF THE SEA. Dallas, Kaleidograph Press, 1939. 39p [LC

Tyndall, W.J.
DE LUCKY GARCON AND OTHER FRENCH CANADIAN POEMS. Ottawa, Author, [1922?]. 94p [BM BVaU OTP

Tyrrell, William, 1816–1904
POEMS BY A BUSINESS MAN. Toronto, 1901. [Possibly same as item listed for Alban E. Ragg, *q.v.*] [T&C

Uncle Albert (pseud)
POEMS. Commemorating construction of the Alaska Highway. N.p., ("printed in Canada"), n.d. 61p [Adelphi cat. 41A

Uren, Alfred Ernest, 1881–
BOB AND BILL SEE CANADA. A Travel Story in Rhyme for Boys and Girls. Toronto, Musson, 1919. 94p [Another ed., 1926.] [BM BVa OTU

Urquhart, William T.
POEMS. Montreal, 1868. 36p [CCJ

Urwick, Hilary
21 POEMS. London, Fortune Press, 1944. 29p [BM LC

Vance, S.C.
RURAL RHYMES. Truro, Daily News Print., [18—?]. 36p [NSHD OTP

Vancouver Poetry Society
A BOOK OF DAYS, 1916–46. Toronto, Ryerson, 1946. 93p [BVaU OTP
FULL TIDE. A Magazine of Poetry. [A 12-page mimeographed pamphlet issued annually, 1936–50.] [BVaU OKQ
THE V.P.S. CHAPBOOK. Vancouver, Sign of the Raven, 1925. 22p [Poems by Ernest Fewster, A.M. Stephen, and H. Bromley Coleman.] [BVaU NBFU

Vancouver Poetry Writers' Group
POEMS. West Vancouver, Mrs. Lewis, 1938. 36p [BVa OKQ
POEMS ... 1929–30. Vancouver, priv. print., 1930. 28p [BVaU OTP
POEMS ... 1931–1933. Vancouver, the Group, 1933. 38p [BVaU OTP
POEMS ... 1933–34. Vancouver, Commonwealth Press, 1934. 39p [BVaU OTP
VERSES ... 1928–1929. Vancouver, Mrs. Moody, 1929. 29p [OTP

Veazey, Mary Emma, 1871–
THE MARITIMER AND OTHER POEMS. Toronto, Crucible Press, 1941. 24p [LC
  NBFU OTU
MY SHIPS OF YESTERDAY AND OTHER POEMS. Toronto, Ryerson, 1935. 12p
  [Brown U NBFU
PATRIOTIC POEMS. 1916.

Vidal, James Henry, 1864–1960
ROMANCE OF AMBITION. White Rock, B.C., Author, 1945. 14p [Phelps p105
WORLD WAR I EPIC. A Story in Verse. White Rock, B.C., Author, n.d. 20p [AEU

Viets, Rev. Roger, 1738–1811
ANNAPOLIS-ROYAL. [A Poem]. [Anon] Halifax, Henry, 1788. 7p [Attributed
  to Roger Viets.] [Tremaine: Cdn Imprints NBFU

W., R.
BUD O' THE BUSH; or, The Beauty of Mysteries. N.p., 1924. 36p [OKQ

W., W.W.
A POEM ON THE TIMES, SHOWING FORTH THE VIRTUES OF LINCOLN, MCCLELLAN,
  AND FREMONT. By W.W.W. Toronto, "Merchants" Press, [1864?]. 40p [OTP

Waddell, Jean (Percival), 1867–
CANDLED BY STARS. Toronto, Ryerson, 1944. 52p [BVaU LC NSHD OTP
  QMM
DOWN AISLES OF CALM. Toronto, Ryerson, 1934. 71p [BVaU OTP QMM
A HARP IN THE WIND. Toronto, Ryerson, 1938. 65p [BVaU OTP QMM

Waddington, John Frushard
CANADA AND OTHER POEMS. London, Heath, [1918?]. 100p [BM OKQ

Waddington, Miriam (Dworkin), 1917–
GREEN WORLD. Montreal, First Statement, 1945. 28p [BVaU MWU NBFU
  OTP QMM
THE SEASON'S LOVERS. Toronto, Ryerson, 1958. 56p
THE SECOND SILENCE. Toronto, Ryerson, 1955. 57p

Wade, H. Gerald, 1875—
AN ACADIAN SINGER, FRANCIS SHERMAN. 2nd ed. Winnipeg, Stovel, 1930. 20p
[1st ed., same year.] [NSHD OTP QMM

Waight, Quentin, 1894—
PRELUDE TO GLORY. [Poems and a Play.] Seattle, Superior Pub. Co., 1951.
xiv + 166p [Includes a one-act play.]

Wain, Walter Everard, 1904—
MURMURINGS OF A SOJOURNER. Vancouver, Author, 1959. 59p [mimeographed]

Wales, Julia Grace, 1881—
ARGENTEIUL LYRICS. By Julia Grace Wales, Anna Letitia Wales, Emma Theodosia
Wales. Lachute, Que., Watchman, 1935. 41p [Brown U

Walker, (Sergeant) Alexander, fl. 1848—1867
THE KNAPSACK. A Collection of Fugitive Poems. By a Soldier [pseud]. Kingston,
Creighton, 1853. 132p [OTP

Walker, Annie Louisa (Mrs Henry Coghill), 1836—1907
LEAVES FROM THE BACKWOODS. [Anon] Montreal, Lovell, 1861. 174p [2nd
ed., 1862.] [BM BVaU OKQ QMM
OAK AND MAPLE. English and Canadian Verses. By Mrs. Harry Coghill. London,
Paul, 1890. 114p [BM OOP

Wallace, Horatio, 1866—
POEMS AND SONGS OF LIFE. London, Wright & Brown, 1935. 96p [Brown U
BVaU OLU
THE SONG OF THE MADNESS OF THE CHILDREN OF ODIN, AND OTHER POEMS,
1914—1917. Winnipeg, Columbia Press, 1917. 30p [BM OKQ

Wallace, Joseph S., 1890—
THE GOLDEN LEGEND. Moscow, Foreign Languages Pub. House, 1958. 98p
[Compiler's intro., commentary, and notes in Russian by I.L. Armand.]
HI, SISTER, HI, BROTHER! Toronto, New Frontiers, 1956. 36p
NIGHT IS ENDED. Thoughts in Lyric. Winnipeg, Contemporary Publishers, 1942.
[BVa LC MWP NBFU OTP

Wallace, Rev. Michael A., —1892
HYMNS OF THE CHURCH, THE NATIVITY, AND OTHER POEMS. Portland, Me.,
Sanborn & Carter, 1853. 321p [LC NSHD OTP

Wallis, Katherine Elizabeth, 1861—1957
CHIPS FROM THE BLOCK. Poems. New York, Exposition Press, 1955. 56p

Walsh, Lillian Crewe, 1883—
WELCOME TO CAPE BRETON, THE HIGHLANDS OF CANADA. A Collection of Verse.
Glace Bay, N.S., priv. print., 1955. 16p

Walsh, Marie

SMILE. Poems. Ilfracombe, Devon, Stockwell, 1957. 12p

Walters, Annie Godfrey (Lewis), 1898–

THIS IS ANNIE. Woodstock, Ont., Author, 1959. 64p

Walton, George, 1897–

THE WAYWARD QUEEN. Toronto, Contact Press, 1959. 64p

Wanklyne, Hazel

THE FLOWER WITHIN. Montreal, priv. print., 1936. 16p [OTP

Wanless, Andrew, 1824–1898

POEMS AND SONGS, MAISTLY SCOTCH. Detroit, Wanless, 1873. 192p ["2nd. ed.
to which is Added a Number of New Pieces never before Published"; 1st ed.,
1872.] [BVaU LC NBFU OLU QMM

SCOTCH AND CANADIAN RHYMES AND SONGS. Toronto, Thompson, 1857. 84p
[BVaU OTP

Ward, Burnett A.

VEREY LIGHTS FROM THE LISTENING POST. By Flare-Pistol Pete [B.A. Ward].
Vancouver, Commonwealth Press, 1935. 64p [BVaU

Ward, J.G.

THE SPRING OF LIFE. A Didactic Poem in Four Books. Montreal, Author, 1834.
228p [BVaU OTP

Ward, James Edward, 1883–1958

INDIAN SUMMER AND OTHER POEMS. Toronto, Macmillan, 1933. 79p [BVaU
NBFU OKQ

... THIS ENGLAND. Toronto, Longmans, 1942. 48p [BVaU LC NBFU OTP
QMM

Warman, Cy, 1855–1914

DAYS REMEMBERED. ... New Glasgow, Mackenzie, 1899. 14p [NSHD

MOUNTAIN MELODIES. Denver, Colo., 1892. 63p [LC

OL' QUEBEC. Toronto, McLeod & Allen, 1908. 15p [BVaU QMSS

SONGS OF CY WARMAN. Boston, Rand Avery, 1911. 177p [BM BVaU LC OLU
QMM

Warmington, Mrs. M.

MISCELLANEOUS POEMS. Drayton, [Ont.?], n.d. 52p [OTUV

Warner, Ernest Albert, 1884–1957

CRUMBLES. Being a Collection of Verses, Written at Various Times and Upon
Different Themes. Burks Falls, Ont., [Arrow, 1928]. [24p] [Priv. info.

Warnock, Amelia Beers (Mrs. John Garvin), 1878–1956

THE FLUTE AND OTHER POEMS. By Katherine Hale [pseud]. Toronto, Ryerson, 1950. 16p [BVaU NBSaM OKQ

GREY KNITTING AND OTHER POEMS. By Katherine Hale [pseud]. Toronto, Briggs, 1914. 15p [BM BVaU NSHD OKQ

THE ISLAND, AND OTHER POEMS. By Katherine Hale [pseud]. Toronto, Author, 1934. 96p [NBFU OKQ QMM

MORNING IN THE WEST. A Book of Verse. By Katherine Hale [pseud]. Toronto, Ryerson, 1923. 68p [BM BVaU NSHD OTUV QMM

THE NEW JOAN AND OTHER POEMS. By Katherine Hale [pseud]. Toronto, McClelland, 1917. 19p [BM BVaU NBFU OKQ

THE WHITE COMRADE AND OTHER POEMS. By Katherine Hale [pseud]. Toronto, McClelland, 1916. 23p [BM BVaU NBFU OKQ

Warr, Bertram Howard, 1883–

IN QUEST OF BEAUTY. Selected Poems. Foleyet, Ont., Crucible Press, 1950. 40p [OONL

Warr, Bertram J., 1917–1943

YET A LITTLE ONWARDS. Resurgam Younger Poets No. 3. London, Favil Press, [1941?]. 5p [BM

Warren, G.B.

FOR THE SCEPTRE OF THE SEA. London, John Long, 1916. 62p [BM BVaU OH

THE LAST WEST AND PAOLO'S VIRGINIA. Vancouver, Evans & Hastings, 1919. 45p [BM Brown U BVaU OOP

Warren, Hugh L.

RHYMES OF A NORTHLAND. Toronto, Goodchild, 1920. 63p [BVaU NSHD OOP

Warren, Mrs. Sara Evangeline Matheson

PRAIRIE PANELS. Vauxhall, Alta., Author, 1950. 22p [OONL

SONGS OF THE ISLAND. Vauxhall, Alta., Author, 1951. 24p

Waterman, Guy Victor, 1902–1944

WORK UNFINISHED. Biographical Note by Angeline Waterman. Collected Work. Ottawa, Tower, 1947. 36p [OONL

Waters, Francis Lealy Dominick, 1857–

EIGHT BELLS. Sailor's Snug Harbor Yarns and Ballads. By Frank Waters. New York, Appleton, 1927. 151p [BM LC

THE MUSICIAN. A Legend of the Hartz Mountains. By Frank Waters. Boston, Badger, 1903. 88p [LC NSHD

THE WATER LILY. An Oriental Fairy Tale. By Frank Waters. Ottawa, Durie, 1888. 87p [BM BVaU NBFU OTP QMM

Watson, Albert Durrant, 1859–1926

THE DREAM OF GOD. A Poem. Toronto, Author, 1922. 42p [BM BVaU OKQ

HEART OF THE HILLS. Toronto, McClelland, 1917. 117p [BM BVaU OTU QMM
LOVE AND THE UNIVERSE, THE IMMORTALS AND OTHER POEMS. Toronto, Macmillan, 1913. 191p [BM BVaU NSHD OTU QMM
THE POETICAL WORKS OF ALBERT DURRANT WATSON. Toronto, Ryerson, 1924. 342p [BVaU NBFU OTP
THE WING OF THE WILD BIRD, AND OTHER POEMS. Toronto, Briggs, 1908. 125p [BVaU NBFU OTU QMM
WOMAN. A Poem. Toronto, Ryerson, 1923. 64p [BM BVaU NBFU OTP

Watson, Elizabeth C.
THE METROPOLITAN MOTHER GOOSE. Ottawa, Metropolitan Insurance Co., n.d. 10p [Amtmann cat. 141

Watson, Isabella B.
WAR TIME POEMS AND HEART SONGS. Toronto, Briggs, 1918. 123p [BM BVaU OOP

Watson, James Wreford, 1915—
OF TIME AND THE LOVER. By James Wreford [pseud]. Toronto, McClelland, 1950. 92p [BVaU NBFU OTP
UNIT OF FIVE. Poems by Louis Dudek, Ronald Hambleton, P.K. Page, Raymond Souster, James Wreford [pseud]. Ed. by Ronald Hambleton. Toronto, Ryerson, 1944. 87p [BVaU LC MWU NBFU OTU QMM

Watson, John L.
OCCUPANTS OF THE OLD GRAVEYARD; and Miscellaneous Poems and Songs. Brampton, Conservator Print., 1918. 131p [OTU

Watson, Robert, 1882—1948
CANADA'S FUR-BEARERS [Little Nature Studies in Verse]. Ottawa, Graphic, 1925. 48p [Same title: Winnipeg, Author, 1925. 32p] [BVaU OTP QMM
DREAMS OF FORT GARRY. An Epic Poem on the Life and Times of the Early Settlers of Western Canada. With Woodcuts. ... Winnipeg, Stovel, 1931. 63p [BVaU QMM
THE MAD MINSTREL. Toronto, Ryerson, 1923. 128p [BM BVaU LC OTP QMM

Watson, Samuel James, 1837—1881
THE LEGEND OF THE ROSES—A POEM; RAVLAN—A DRAMA. Toronto, Hunter Rose, 1876. 228p [BVaU NBFU OTU QMM

Watson, Thomas, 1857—1937
CANADIAN CRYSTALS. Poems. Toronto, Briggs, 1901. 160p [BM BVaU NBFU OKQ
LOVING HEARTS AND HAPPY HOMES. Toronto, Standard, n.d. 27p [OONL

Watson, Wilfred, 1911—
FRIDAY'S CHILD. London, Faber & Faber, 1955. 56p

Watt, Alexander, 1890–
BLESSED BE HE. A Tribute to Alexander Watt. Kitchener, Hawkshead Press, 1958.
4 + 6p

Watt, David H.
POEMS ON THE MANITOBA SCHOOL QUESTION. Toronto, Stewart Pub. Co., 1895.
23p [BM MWP OTP

Watt, (Ernest) Frederick Balmer, 1901–
BOY BLUE'S VERSES. Edmonton, Author, 1918. 16p [BVaU OKQ
LANDFALL. Toronto, Macmillan, 1946. 59p [BM Brown U BVaU OTU
VAGRANT. Toronto, Ryerson, 1927. 20p [BVaU NBSaM OKQ QMM
WHO DARE TO LIVE. Toronto, Macmillan, 1943. 68p [BM BVaU OTP QMM

Weaver, R.A.
REFLECTIONS. A Collection of Poems. Cranberry Lake, B.C., Author, 1945. 36p
[UTQ'47

Webb, Phyllis, 1927–
EVEN YOUR RIGHT EYE. Toronto, McClelland, 1956. 64p
TRIO. First Poems. By Gael Turnbull, Phyllis Webb and E.W. Mandel. Toronto,
Contact Press, 1954. 89p

Webber, George
THE LAST OF THE ABORIGINES. A Poem in Four Cantos. St. John's. [BibC

Webber, William Lester, 1882–
SKOOKUM WA-WA. "Good Talk." Vancouver, Lumberman Print., 1945. 94p
[BVaU

Weber, Manasseh, 1872–1957
SUCH WAS LIFE. Calgary, 1956. 72p [Rhymed history of Didsbury, Alta.]

Webling, Peggy
VERSES TO MEN. London, Author, 1920. 46p [BM

Webling, Walter Hastings, 1866–
FORE! Brantford, Ont., Author, 1907. 9p [OTUV
FORE! "A Few More Golf Shots." Brantford, Ont., Author, 1908. [BM
FORE: THE CALL OF THE LINKS. New York, Caldwell, 1909. 73p [AEU
GOLF, IN VERSE AND REVERSE. Brantford, Harley Print., 1924. [20]p [AEU
OONL
LOCKER-ROOM BALLADS. Toronto, Gundy, 1925. 95p [BM BVaU LC NBFU
OTU
"ON AND OFF THE LINKS." Hamilton, Davis Print., 1921. 20p [NBSaM

Webster, Joseph H.
THE ACADIAN MINSTREL. Comp. by ——. Halifax, MacKinlay, 1860. 114p
[NSWA

Wees, Frances Shelley (Johnson), 1902–
POEMS. Poems. Printed for her Friends. [Toronto?], 1936. 16p [BVaU OSUL

Weir, Arthur, 1864–1902
FLEUR DE LYS AND OTHER POEMS. Montreal, Renouf, 1887. 147p [BVaU OLU
QMM
THE ROMANCE OF SIR RICHARD, SONNETS AND OTHER POEMS. Montreal, Drys-
dale, 1890. 121p [BVaU OLU QMM
THE SNOWFLAKE, AND OTHER POEMS. Montreal, Lovell, 1897. 144p [BM
BVaU LC NBFU OLU QMM

Weir, Robert Stanley, 1856–1926
AFTER YPRES, AND OTHER VERSE. Toronto, Musson, 1917. 47p [BM BVaU
LC OTU QMSS
POEMS, EARLY AND LATE. Toronto, Oxford U. Press, 1922. 63p [BVaU OTU
QMM

Wellband, Florence, 1907–1933
SCENTED PETALS. Vancouver, Clarke & Stuart, 1933. 40p [Brown U BVaU

Wensley, Amelia
AT SUMMER'S END. Toronto, Ryerson, 1941. 8p [BVaU NBSaM OTP

Wesleyan Minister, A
SACRED POETRY. By a Wesleyan Minister. N.B., Sentinel Office, 1840. 24p
[NSHD

West, Gilbert Ashton, 1883–
KOOTENAY KUTS. Including "The Cherry Picker" and Other Jingles. A Small
Collection Of Rhymes and Reasonings Of A Rambling Rancher. 2nd ed. Nelson,
B.C., Nelson Daily News, 1953. 28p
KOOTENAY KUTS AND OTHER JINGLES. By Kap-o-Kaslo [pseud]. Kaslo, B.C.,
Author, 1929. 24p [BVaU

West, Paul Noden, 1930–
THE SPELLBOUND HORSES. Toronto, Ryerson, 1960. 16p

Westacott, Florence Elizabeth
"THE CITY DWELLER" AND OTHER POEMS. ... Toronto, Sovereign Press, 1935.
40p [BVaU NBFU OTP

Westaway, John
THE JOHN WESTAWAY SOCIETY SONGS. Vancouver, n.d. 65p [Adelphi cat. 61

Wetherald, Agnes Ethelwyn, 1857–1940
THE GARDEN OF THE HEART. A Garland of Verses. By Ethelwyn Wetherald and
Others. Boston, Badger, 1903. 16p [NBFU
THE HOUSE OF THE TREES AND OTHER POEMS. Boston, Lamson Wolfe, 1895.
94p [BVaU LC NBFU OTP

THE LAST ROBIN. Lyrics and Sonnets. Toronto, Briggs, 1907. 193p [BM BVaU OKQ

LYRICS AND SONNETS. Toronto, Nelson, 1931. 304p [BM BVaU NBFU OKQ

POEMS, LYRICS, AND SONNETS. Toronto, Musson, n.d. 193p [BVaU OTUV

THE RADIANT ROAD [and Other Poems]. Boston, Badger, 1904. 43p [BVaU LC OTP

TANGLED IN STARS. Poems. Boston, Badger, 1902. 45p [LC NBFU OTP

TREE-TOP MORNINGS. Boston, Cornhill, 1921. 65p [BVaU LC NBFU OKQ

Wetherell, James Elgin, 1851–1940

AESOP IN VERSE. Toronto, Macmillan, 1926. xvi + 199p [BVaU OLU

LATER CANADIAN POEMS. Ed. by ——. Toronto, Copp Clark, 1893. 187p [BVaU NSHD OTU QMM

LATER ENGLISH POEMS, 1901–1922. Ed. by ——. Toronto, McClelland, 1922. 208p [NSHD OTU

POEMS OF THE LOVE OF COUNTRY. Selected and ed. by ——. Toronto, Morang, 1905. 144p [BVaU NBFU OTU

Whalley, George, 1915–

NO MAN AN ISLAND. Toronto, Clarke Irwin, 1948. 72p [BVaU LC NBFU OTP QMM

POEMS 1939–1944. Toronto, Ryerson, 1946. 16p [BVaU NBSaM OKQ

Wharton, Lewis, 1885–

SONGS OF CARTHAGE AND OTHER POEMS. Ottawa, Overbrook Press, 1930. 61p [BM BVaU LC OTP

Wheeler, Julia A.

WAYS OF PLEASANTNESS. Knowlton, Que., Smith, 1942. 55p [OTP QMM

Whelan, Michael

THE CALL OF CHRIST, AND OTHER POEMS. Chatham, N.B., "Gazette" Office, 1922. 24p [NBFU OTUV

THE GREAT MIRAMICHI FIRE OF 1825 IN STORY AND SONG. With Other Poems. [Chatham, N.B.], 1925. 24p [NBFU OTUV

THE PIONEERS, AND OTHER POEMS. Newcastle, N.B., "Union Advocate," 1917. 16p [OTUV

QUEEN OF THE NORTH, AND OTHER SONGS AND SONNETS. Newcastle, N.B., 1914. 36p [NBFU OTUV

THE SACRED SILENCE, AND OTHER POEMS. Chatham, N.B., Gazette Press, [1925?]. 8p [Brown U NBFU

White, Isaac S.

FIVE WAR POEMS. A Memento of this Great, Most Cruel and Atrocious War. Winnipeg, Author, 1915. 23p [BM MWP

MANITOBA MUSES; or, Gentle Joseph and Other Poems. Toronto, Bryant, 1912. 327p [BM BVaU OOP

White, Samuel Alexander, 1885–1956
THE DAUGHTERS OF CONTENT, AND OTHER POEMS. London, Stockwell, 1921.
16p [BM

White, Vine B.
SONGS FOR YOU. Toronto, McClelland, 1917. 93p [BM Brown U OTU

White, William Thomas, 1866–1955
THE BATTLE OF BRITAIN, AND OTHER POEMS. Montreal, Author, 1945. 60p
[BVaU LC NSHD OOP QMM
ESSAYS OF FRANCIS BACON, LORD VERULAM, PARAPHRASED IN BLANK VERSE.
Montreal, Author, 1945. 54p [BVaU NBFU OTUV

Whitehouse, Francis Cecil, 1879–
CANADIAN AND OTHER POEMS. Toronto, Ryerson, 1934. 122p [BM BVaU OTP
QMM
THE COQUIHALLA WRECK AND OTHER POEMS. Toronto, Ryerson, 1932. 18p
[BVaU NBSaM OTP QMM
THE DREAMERS. N.p., Author, 1936. 19p [A supplement to CANADIAN AND
OTHER POEMS.] [BM BVaU OTU
REBELS AND OTHER LOVE POEMS. By Ramon Francisco [pseud]. Ottawa, Graphic,
1929. 93p [BM BVaU OTP
SONGS OF THE SERVICE. [Toronto?], 1916. 16p [BM

Whitell, Evelyn
HEALING POEMS. Vancouver, Caxton Press, 19——. 16p [BViPA
LIFE'S GREATEST ADVENTURE. Vancouver, Caxton Press, n.d. 8p [BViPA

Whiting, Lilian B.
CANADIAN WILD FLOWERS. [Ottawa?], 1952. 33p
NORTH OF THE BORDER UP CANADA WAY. [Ottawa?], 1951. 41p

Whitman, Howard Murray
COME WALK WITH ME–AND OTHER VERSE. Philadelphia, Dorrance, 1938. 54p
[LC OTP

Whitman, James, fl. 1858–1885
CANADA. A Ballad in Three Parts. Halifax, Smith, 1885. 23p [NSHD OTP

Whitnall, Samuel Ernest, 1876–
JOKINGS APART. With a Poem of Farewell to the Author, by Stephen Leacock.
Oxford, Alden Press, 1950 [c1951]. 143p [OONL

Whylock, R.M.
COSMIC ORATORY. By Regis [pseud]. Toronto, Ryerson, 1929. 8p [BVaU
NBSaM OTU QMM

Whyte, James C.
A MEDLEY OF POEMS, HYMNS AND SONGS. Hanover, Ont., Post Print., n.d. 116p
  [BVaU OOP

Whyte, Thomas Henry
POETICAL INSPIRATION. ... Toronto, Rowen Press, 1934. 40p [Brown U

Whyte-Edgar, Mrs. C.M., 1869—1948
A WREATH OF CANADIAN SONG. Containing Biographical Sketches and Numerous
  Selections from Deceased Canadian Poets. Toronto, Briggs, 1910. 284p [BM
  BVaU NBFU OTU

Wickenden, Alfred Ahier, 1886—
UP TRAIL. Philadelphia, Poetry Publishers, 1937. 78p [LC QMM

Wickenden, Helen (Slack), 1887—
A QUEBEC BOUQUET. Boston, Stratford, 1930. 35p [BVaU LC

Wicksteed, Gustavus William, 1799—1898
THE EXCOMMUNICATED. An Episode in the History of Canada and the British
  Flag. N.p., n.d. 10p [Parallel text in French by Louis Frechette] [QMU
WAIFS IN VERSE. Montreal, Lovell, 1878. 137p [2nd ed., Ottawa, Bureau, 1887.
  165p] [BM BVaU LC NSHD OKQ

Wigle, Rev. Hamilton A., 1858—1934
LEAVES, ORIGINAL POEMS. Halifax, Book Room, [1915?]. 16p [Brown U
POETRY FOR PULPIT AND PLATFORM. Toronto, Briggs, 1911. 160p [BM BVaU
THE VETERAN AND OTHER POEMS. Toronto, Briggs, 1910. 88p [BM BVaU OTP

Wilbee, (Sergeant) Arthur Frank, 1894—
GEMS FROM THE GARDEN. White Rock, B.C., White Rock Printers, 1959. 44p
SOUVENIRS. Vancouver, Author, 1941. 48p [BVaU OKQ

Wilcox, Noel H.
THE PIPER OF DREAMS. [Halifax?], Author, 1927. 31p [NSHD OKQ
SILVER ARROWS. ... Halifax, Weeks Print., 1930. 30p [NSHD

Wilkins, Caroline M.
POEMS. N.p., Author, 1926. 95p [BVaU OPAL QMU

Wilkins, Harriet Annie, 1829—1888
THE ACACIA. By Harriet Annie [pseud]. Hamilton, "Spectator," 1863. 200p
  [1st ed.: Hamilton, 1860. 120p—OLU.] [BVaU NSHD OKQ
AUTUMN LEAVES. By Harriet Annie [pseud]. Hamilton, "Spectator," 1869. 87p
  [BVaU OTP QMM
THE HOLLY BRANCH. By Harriet Annie [pseud]. Hamilton, "Spectator," 1851.
  140p [BVaU OTP

VICTOR ROY. A Masonic Poem. Hamilton, "Spectator," 1882. 128p [BVaU OKQ
WAYSIDE FLOWERS. Toronto, Hunter Rose, 1876. 255p [BVaU LC OTP QMM

Wilkinson, Anne Cochran (Boyd), 1910–1961
COUNTERPOINT TO SLEEP. Montreal, First Statement Press, 1951. 36p
THE HANGMAN TIES THE HOLLY. Toronto, Macmillan, 1955. 57p

Wilkinson, Caroline Eleanor (Carter), –1949
POEMS THAT APPEAL. Niagara Falls, Ont., Leslie, 1928. 100p [Brown U BVaU

Wilkinson, John Richardson, –1908
CANADIAN BATTLEFIELDS AND OTHER POEMS. Toronto, Briggs, 1899. 292p
[2nd ed., rev. and enl., 1901. 309p] [BM BVaU LC OKQ

Willerton, Irene
SO LITTLE MAKES ME GLAD. Victoria, [1938?]. 28p [BVaU

Willey, Christina
POEMS OF CHRISTINA WILLEY. Toronto, Weaver, 1928. 22p [OKQ

Williamson, Alexander Johnston, 1796?–1870
DEVOTIONAL POEMS. Toronto, Rogers & Thompson, 1840. 24p [OTP
ORIGINAL POEMS ON VARIOUS SUBJECTS. ... Toronto, Coates, 1836. 151p [OTP
THERE IS A GOD. With Other Poems. Toronto, Lawrence, 1839. 24p [OTUV

Williamson, Lydia (Buckland), 1860–1952
DUET FOR CELLO AND DRUM. By Richard Scrace [pseud] and O.T.G. Williamson.
Toronto, Southam Press, 1947. 45p [OTP

Wills, Percy Edward, 1898–
RAMBLING RHYMES FROM THE GRAVEYARD. Port Alberni, B.C., West Coast
Printers, 1933. 32p [BVaU

Willsher, E. Ann
STANLEY PARK, VANCOUVER, B.C.: Spring, Summer, Autumn, Winter. Four
Poems. Vancouver, Clarke & Stuart, 1944. 18p [BViPA OTP

Willson, David, 1778?–1866
HYMNS AND PRAYERS FOR THE CHILDREN OF SHARON. Newmarket, 1846. 108p
[Another ed., 1849. 207p] [CCJ OLU
HYMNS OF PRAISE. Containing Doctrine and Prayer. ... Newmarket, Porter, 1853.
320p [OTP

Willson, (Henry) Beckles, 1869–1942
HEARTACHE IN CANAAN, AND OTHER POEMS. Oxford, Shakespeare Head Press,
1938. 93p [BM Brown U BVaU OTU

Wilson, Alice Elizabeth, 1897–1934
MY SANCTUARY GARDEN. ... Toronto, McClelland, 1937. 96p [Brown U BVaU
OLU

Wilson, Anne Elizabeth, 1901–1946
EAGER FOOTSTEPS. Toronto, Musson, 1924. 47p [BM BVaU OKQ

Wilson, Daniel, 1816–1892
ANE AULD PROPHECIE. London, Jack, 1849. 12p [OTU
THE QUEEN'S CHOIR. A Revery in Roslin Woods. By D.W. [pseud]. Edinburgh,
  priv. print. [Thomas Nelson], 1853. 24p [BM OTU
SPRING WILD FLOWERS. London, Nelson, 1875. 243p [Original ed. pub. earlier
  under pseud. of Wil. D'Leina, Esq.] [BM OTUV

Wilson, Estelle Hollister
ROSEMARY AND RUE. Montreal, Renouf, 1914. 91p [BVaU NSHD

Wilson, Mrs. Mabel May, 1899–
IN FRIENDSHIP'S NAME. Moose Jaw, Author, 1952. 31p

Wilson, Milton Thomas, 1923–
RECENT CANADIAN VERSE. Selected and ed. by ——. Kingston, Jackson Press,
  1959. 44p

Wilson, William Shire
SELECT PATHETIC AND THRILLING POEMS. Pamphlet Form. Hamilton, Author,
  1914. 8p [BM OKQ

Wilton, Margaret Harvey, 1902–
PAGEANTRY OF DAYS. Toronto, Author, 1940. 15p [NBFU OKQ
WITH THE BEAUTY OF THAT HOUR. Toronto, Author, 1950. 24p [OKQ

Windross, T.B.
GATES OF GLORY AND OTHER POEMS. Ottawa, Tower Books, 1949. 42p [BVaU

Wingfield, Alexander Hamilton, 1828–1896
THE CENTENNIAL. An International Poem. Toronto, 1878. 310p [OONL
POEMS AND SONGS, IN SCOTCH AND ENGLISH. Hamilton, "Times," 1873. 255p
  [BVaU MWU OKQ

Winkel, William C.
PETALS FROM FLORAVALE. N.p., 1944. 18p [Adelphi Cat. 33A

Winkler, George E.
LONELY TRAILS. By the Prospector [pseud]. Victoria, Victoria Print., [1935].
  170p [BVaU
SONGS UNBIDDEN. Victoria, Victoria Print., [1920]. 170p [BVaU

Winlow, Alice Maud (Dudley), 1885–
POEMS OF ARMAGEDDON. By A.M.W. and E.P.F. [Ernest Philip Fewster?] Vancouver, Sun Pub. Co., 1914. 24p [BVaU

Winnipeg, Man. Poetry Society
PRIZE POEMS. 1942 Competition. [Winnipeg, the Society, 1942.] 14p [BVaU MWU OTU

Winspear, Alban Dewes, 1899–
THE ROMAN POET OF SCIENCE. Lucretius. De rerum natura. Set in English verse by ——. New York, Harbor Press, 1956. xx + 299p

Wise, William H., –1949
OF FOUR AND FORTY YEARS. Toronto, Author, 1935. 59p [OTU

Withrow, Oswald Charles Joseph, 1878–1946
POEMS FROM PRISON. Toronto, Author, 1937. 48p [BVaU OTP

Wood, Mrs. Alexandrina Gertrude, 1881–
A HANDFUL OF LILACS AND OTHER POEMS. By Gertrude Wood. N.p., 1946. 32p [SSU
THROUGH THE YEAR WITH GERTRUDE WOOD. Aneroid, Sask., News Magnet Press, 1950. 27p [Brown U OONL SSU

Wood, Harold Samuel, 1903–
CHUCKLES FROM HOME. Toronto, Reliance, 1930. 69p [BVaU LC OTP
WHY SHOULD WE FIGHT FOR ENGLAND? Toronto, McClelland, 1941. 12p [UTQ'42
YOUR HOME AND MINE. Toronto, Musson, 1932. 95p [BVaU OTP NBFU QMM

Woodcock, George, 1912–
THE CENTRE CANNOT HOLD. London, Routledge, 1943. 44p [BM LC
IMAGINE THE SOUTH. Pasadena, Cal., priv. print., 1947. 40p [BVaU LC
THE WHITE ISLAND. London, Fortune, 1940. 39p [BM LC OTU

Woodley, Elsie Caroline, 1909–
BITTERSWEET. Toronto, Ryerson, 1930. 8p [BVaU NBSaM OTU QMM

Woodman, Mary A.L., 1880–
PEN PICTURES OF NOVA SCOTIA, BERMUDA, JAMAICA. Wolfville, N.S., Author, 1959. 30p
PEN PICTURES OF OUR VALLEY. Published in Honour of Twenty-Fifth Anniversary of Apple Blossom Festival, Also for Benefit of Those Unable to Visit Our Valley. Wolfville, N.S., Author, 1957. 21p

Woodrow, Constance (Davies), 1899–1937
CAPTIVE AND OTHER POEMS. Toronto, Author, 1930. 4p [Adelphi cat. 41A
THE CAPTIVE GYPSY. Introductory note by Charles G.D. Roberts. Toronto, Ryerson, 1926. 20p [Also: Toronto, Balk-Preston, 1928. 34p] [BVaU NBSaM OTP QMM
THE CELTIC HEART. Toronto, Ryerson, 1929. 69p [BVaU LC NBFU OKQ
IMMORTALITY. Toronto, Balk-Preston, 1928. Broadside. [NBFU OKQ

PIERRETTE TO PIERROT. A Group of Love Lyrics. Toronto, Tower Print., 1929. 4p [BViPA NBFU OKQ
SELECTIONS FROM "SONNETS TO GABRIEL." Toronto, Author, 1931. 4p [NBFU OTU

Wordon, Harry, 1935? –
A BARD IN EXILE. Poems. Ottawa, Clementson Co., 1960 [c1959]. 52p

Worfolk, Estelle Jean
WAYSIDE REVERIES. Montreal, Menu Print. Service, 1939. 60p [BVaU

Wraith, W.J.
THE WANDERING JEW AND OTHER POEMS. By Walter Alexander [pseud].
Lucknow, Ont., Sentinel Presses, 1917. 100p [Brown U BVaU OTU

Wrigglesworth, Lewis John, 1882–1956
POETICAL WRITINGS OF LEW WRIGGLESWORTH. [Calgary?], n.d. 32p [ACG

Wright, Alice E.
COMFORT AND OTHER POEMS. Toronto, Goodchild, 1924. 63p [Brown U BVaU

Wright, Arthur Walker, 1855–1944
VERSES, VERSIONS, AND VERSICLES. Mount Forest, Author, 1907. 52p [Adelphi cat. 33A

Wright, Daisy (McLeod)
LITTLE JOHN BULL. Boston, Gorham, 1915. 60p [LC

Wright, Evelyn Rose (Foster), 1897–
RHYMES FOR A RAINY DAY. Fredericton, Brunswick Press, 1955. 25p

Wright, Frederick, 1810–1878
LAYS OF A PILGRIM. Brockville, Wylie, 1864. xii + 142p [OTP
WAY-SIDE PENCILLINGS. Ogdensburg, N.Y., Hitchcock, Tillotson & Haddock, 1855. 200p [OTP

Wright, George A.
LIFE LINES. Brockville, Recorder Print., 1944. 32p [OTL

Wright, Geraldine
THE SKATER, AND OTHER POEMS. Vancouver, Author, 1948. 10p [BVaU

Wright, Mrs. Grace Armstrong, 1901–
THE BIRTH OF SCOUTING, AND OTHER POEMS. N.p., 1958. 46p (Carillon Poetry Chap-Books)

Wright, Laura Moore, 1892–
VICTORY VERSES. ... Shaunavan, Sask., Author, 1942. 36p [Brown U BVaU OTU

Wright, Robert Walter, 1852–1938
AMONG THE IMMORTALS. Songs and Sonnets from the Hebrew. Toronto, Briggs, 1906. 238p [BVaU OKQ

THE DREAM OF COLUMBUS. A Poem. Toronto, Briggs, 1894. 64p [BVaU OTUV

Writers' Craft Club, Carillon Group
A SHEAF OF VERSE. By Members of the Carillon Group of the Writers' Craft Club. Toronto, Ryerson, 1929. 20p [BVaU NBFU QMM

Wrong, Harold Verschoyle, 1891–1916
VERSES. Oxford, [Blackwell?], 1922. 31p [OPAL

Wyle, Florence, 1881–1968
POEMS. Toronto, Ryerson, 1959. 16p

Wylie, David, 1811–1891
METRICAL WAIFS FROM THE THOUSAND ISLANDS. Brockville, "Recorder," 1869. 62p [BVaU OKQ

Wyllie, Evelyn
TWILIGHT MUSINGS. Victoria, Diggon's, 1928. 31p [BViPA

Yarker, Margaret G.
ECHOES OF EMPIRE. Toronto, Briggs, 1900. 32p [BVaU OTUV

Yeoman, Eric McKay, 1885–1909
POEMS. Toronto, 1910. 22p [QMM

Yorke, W. Milton
TALES OF THE PORCUPINE TRAILS. Toronto, Musson, 1911. 108p [BM BVaU OKQ

Young, Rev. Egerton Ryerson, 1869–
THE BELLS OF CHRISTMAS. Toronto, Briggs, n.d. 14p [OKQ

Young, Flornie (Baxter)
SONGS FROM KAWARTHA. New York, Vantage Press, 1959. 221p

Young, Thomas Frederick, –1940
CANADA, AND OTHER POEMS. Toronto, Hunter Rose, 1887. 117p [BVaU NBFU OTP

Yule, Pamelia S. (Vining), 1825? –1897
THE NAMES OF JESUS. A Poem. By Pamelia S. Vining. N.p., 1866. 11p [OTP

POEMS OF THE HEART AND HOME. By Mrs. J.C. Yule. Toronto, Bengough & Moore, 1881. 220p [BVaU NBFU OKQ QMM

Zemke, Paul H.
PRIVATE REFLECTIONS. With Cartoons by Len Norris. Toronto, Classic, 1946.
44p [CC

Elliott, James
ORIGINAL LYRICS. By a Canadian Rhymer [pseud]. Toronto, Author, 1856.
66p [OTP OTUV
OUR TRAVELLER WITH THE VALISE. Toronto, Bengough, Moore & Bengough,
1882. 22p [OTP
PENCIL SKETCHES? CITY OF GOSHEN? INDIANA. By Pat Prodpen [pseud].
N.p., n.d. 42p [OTP
THE PEREGRINATIONS OF PAT PRODPEN, THE POET POEM PEDDLER OF PARRY
SOUND [pseud]. Being Part Second of OUR TRAVELLER WITH THE VALISE.
Toronto, 1882. 32p [OTP
POEMS AND PEN PICTURES. By Pat Prodpen [pseud]. N.p., n.d. [c1883]. 29p
[Brown U BVaU OTP
POEMS AND PEN PICTURES. V. 2. By Pat Prodpen [pseud]. N.p., n.d. [1884].
47p [OTP

POETRY AND PROSE

Mixed anthologies and collections, and books in which both forms are employed by the same author

Allen, Egbert Chesley, 1882–1947
OUR NORTHERN YEAR. Stories and Songs of the Canadian Seasons. Toronto, Ryerson, 1937. 119p [AEU NBFU OTU

Anonymous
LESSONS ON BIRD PROTECTION. Ottawa, Dominion Parks Branch, Dept. of the Interior, 1922. 15p [QMU
THE PILGRIM'S ANNUAL. A Book of Folly and Wisdom Compiled by an Average Man. Cranbrook, B.C., 1916. 52p [Preface signed "W.H.B."] [BVaU
REMINISCENCES OF A SOLDIER. Consisting of Poems, Fragments, and Short Prose Pieces. Toronto, Rogers Thompson, 1843. 120p [BVaU NSWA OTP
THE VARSITY BOOK, PROSE AND POETRY. Toronto, Varsity Pub. Co., 1885. 200p [An assortment of pieces by such persons as W.H. Blake, W.W. Campbell, T.A. Haultain, M. Hutton, F.H. Sykes, A. MacMechan, and others.] [BVaU OKQ

Armstrong, Janet M.
RHYMES AND RAMBLES. Guelph, Guelph Pub., 1935. 31p [MWU OONL

Audette, Adalard
A FEW VERSES AND A BRIEF HISTORY OF THE CANADIANS ON THE SOMME AND VIMY RIDGE IN THE 1914 – WORLD WAR – 1918. London [Ont.?], Talbot & Co., 1919. 32p [OPAL
VERSES AND HISTORY OF THE GREAT WAR 1914. [Ottawa, Le Courrier Fédéral], 1919. 32p [OTP
VERSES WRITTEN IN THE TRENCHES. N.p., n.d. 21p [NSWA QMU

Austin, Rev. Benjamin Fish, 1850–1932
THE MISSION OF SPIRITUALISM AND ORIGINAL POEMS. Toronto, Austin Pub. Co., [1902?]. 32p [NBFU OPAL QMU

Avery, Mrs. Geneva
GARNERED GRAIN. [Toronto?], Colonist Print. & Pub., [1944?]. 69p [Phelps p88

Baker, Henry
LE SOUVENIR: TRANSLATIONS AND CHOICE PIECES FROM SOME OF THE BEST

FRENCH AND GERMAN AUTHORS. Ed. by ——. Montreal, Lovell, 1867.
288p [OTP

Ball, John Bernard, 1911–
AHOY FOR ETERNITY AND NATIONAL CREDIT. Regina, Ball Pub., 1956. 113p
OUR ISLAND UNIVERSE AND POETRY SELECTIONS. Regina, Author, 1955. 96p

Baulch, S. Fred
THE BRAUNDS OF BUCKS. Containing some Account of the Lives saved during a
Series of Years by Means of a small Boat only in Bideford Bay. With a Copy of
Verses. Toronto, Sovereign Press, 1889. 8p [NSWA QMU

Baylis, Samuel Mathewson, 1854–1941
AT THE SIGN OF THE BEAVER. Northland Stories and Stanzas. Toronto, Briggs,
1897. 225p [Also: Toronto, Briggs, 1907.] [BM BVaU NSHD OKQ QMM
CAMP AND LAMP. Rambles in Realms of Sport, Story, Song. Montreal, Drysdale,
1897. 316p [BM BVaU NBFU OTU QMM

Belding, Albert Martin, 1859–1937?
A HEART-BROKEN CORONER, AND OTHER WONDERS. By A.M. Belding and
H.A. Woodworth. Saint John, Sun Print., 1895. 80p [BVaU NSHD OLU

Bird, William Richard, 1891–
ATLANTIC ANTHOLOGY. Ed. by —— and Alec Lucas. Toronto, McClelland,
1959. 310p

Birney, Earle, 1904–
NEW VOICES. Canadian University Writing of 1956. Comp. by ——. Toronto,
Dent, 1956. 184p

Broadus, Edmund Kemper, 1876–1936
A BOOK OF CANADIAN PROSE AND VERSE. Comp. and ed. by —— and Eleanor
Hammond Broadus. Toronto, Macmillan, 1923. 390p [New and completely
rev. with additions: Toronto, Macmillan, 1934. 415p] [BM BVaU LC
MWU NSHD OKQ QMM

Brooker, Bertram, 1888–1955
YEARBOOK OF THE ARTS IN CANADA, 1936. Ed. by ——. Toronto, Macmillan,
1936. 256p [BM BVi NBFU OKQ

Brundle, John, 1882–
THE RAPE OF SNAKE ISLAND INDIAN RESERVE BY THE DEPARTMENT OF
INDIAN AFFAIRS, OTTAWA, AND THE TOWNSHIP OF NORTH GWILLIMBURY,
ONTARIO. Roche's Point, Ont., Author, 1952. 44p

Burns, David
RANDOM WRITINGS. Brooklin, Author, 1916. 96p [QMU

Burpee, Lawrence Johnstone, 1873–1946
HUMOUR OF THE NORTH. Selected and arranged by ——. Toronto, Musson, 1912. 104p [BVaU LC NSHD OTP

Burr, Rev. W.K.
LEAVES FROM MY PORTFOLIO. Belleville, Daily Ontario, 1880. 255p [OTUV

Byrne, Peter, 1929–
ONCE AND SOME WORDS BETWEEN THE MINUTES. Montreal, Editions Quartz, 1960. 1v [unpaged]

Canadian Expeditionary Force
O CANADA! A Medley of Stories, Verse, Pictures and Music Contributed by Members of the Canadian Expeditionary Force. London, Simpkin; Hamilton, Kent, [1916]. 95p [BM BVaU NSHD OKQ

Canadian Grenadier Guards
A BRIEF OUTLINE OF THE STORY OF THE CANADIAN GRENADIER GUARDS. ... Told in an Anthology of Verse and Prose. Comp. by an Officer of the Guards. Montreal, for private circ'n, 1926. 76p [NSHPL

Cawdell, James Martin, 1781?–1842
THE ROSEHARP; for Beauty, Loyalty and Song. [Toronto, 1835]. 8p [Purports to be the introductory number of the organ of the Roseharp Patriotic Academy, but appears to have been written entirely by Cawdell.] [OTP

Chandler, E.
A FEW THINGS IN VERSE AND PROSE. Montreal, Lovell, 1877. 124p [BVaU QMU

Chapman, Edmar
BATCHAWANA ECHOES. Tales of the Trails, in Verse and Prose. N.p., Author, n.d. 41p [OKQ

Charland, Gustave-Marquis
FACTS AND FANCIES. By Gustave-Marquis Charland and Dorothy Lovell Charland. Sherbrooke, Tribune, 1943. 404p [Bk. I (Travels) ... by G.M.C. Bk. II (Poetry and Prose) by D.L.C.] [BVaU LC OTU QMM

Coates, George Reed, 1876–1898
SONNETS, POEMS, SKETCHES. [Toronto, n.p., 1898] [76p] [BVaU NBFU OLU

Coleman, Edmund T.
PRIZE ESSAY AND POEM OF THE LITERARY INSTITUTE, VICTORIA, V.I. On the Beauties of the Scenery as Surveyed from Beacon Hill. [Poem by W.H. Parsons.] Victoria, McMillan, 1868. 15p [BViPA

Cook, Merrill H.
MARGARET OF THE MOHAWKS. Story and Verse. Toronto, Beacon Press,
n.d. 25p [NBSaM OTU

Cross, Ethelbert F.H., 1872–
FIRE AND FROST. Stories, Dialogues, Satires, Essays, Poems. ... Toronto,
Bryant, 1898. 239p [BM BVaU MWU NBFU OTU QMM

Currie, George Graham, 1867–1926
SONNETS AND LOVE SONGS, AND IRENE, A MEMOIR. West Palm Beach, Fla.,
Dean Pub. Co., 1901. 263p [LC

Davidson, Rev. G.F.
NEPTUNE'S CAVE. A Fish Story in Three Slices. Toronto, Oxford Press, 1901.
38p [AEU NBSaM

Dawson, Rev. Aeneas MacDonell, 1810–1894
OUR STRENGTH AND THEIR STRENGTH. The North West Territory and other
papers chiefly relating to the Dominion of Canada. Ottawa, Times Office,
1870. 326p [Also contains 80p of poems and lectures on the poets of Canada.]
[BM BVaU LC NSWA OTU SSU

Dewart, Rev. Edward Hartley, 1828–1903
THE CANADIAN SPEAKER AND ELOCUTIONARY READER. Comprising a Choice
Selection of Orations, Dialogues and Poetry. ... Ed. and comp. by ——.
Toronto, Miller, 1868. 326p [BVaU LC OKQ

Diespecker, Richard E. Alan, 1907–
WHISPERS FROM THE WILD. [Victoria? 1924?] 31p [BVaU

Douglas, Mia Farquharson (Mrs. D.H.)
MIGNONETTE. Priv. print., 1939. 30p [QMU

Duncan, Jessie
BYWAYS OF LIFE. Being Travel Talks, Poems, and a Biblical Drama, "Athaliah."
N.p., n.d. 165p [NBFU

Dunlap, David Alexander, 1863–1924
SHAHWANDAHGOOZE DAYS. N.p., Author, 1917. 76p [BVa OTU QMU

Edgar, Mary Susanne, 1889–
UNDER OPEN SKIES. Toronto, Clarke Irwin, 1955. xiv + 167p

Edmonton, Alta. Words Unlimited Writers Group
ALBERTA SPEAKS. Edmonton, the Group, 1957. 48p [A continuing serial.
Various pagings.]

Edwards, William, 1810–1881
CORRESPONDENCE AND PAPERS ON VARIOUS SUBJECTS. ... Together with a
  sketch of his life, compiled and arranged by his brother, James Edwards.
  Peterborough, Examiner Steam Press, 1882. 170p [OLU OTP

Ells, Sidney Clarke, 1878–
NORTHLAND TRAILS. Toronto, Garden City Press, 1938. 189p [New and rev.
  ed.: Toronto, Burns & MacEachern, 1956. 229p] [BM BVaU OTP

Emberson, Frederick C., –1913
HASH (Wholesale to Boarding Houses). Montreal, Drysdale, n.d. 61p [OOP
THE YARN OF THE LOVE-SICK JAP. Montreal, Drysdale, n.d. 126p [BVaU
  OOP QMSS
YARN OF THE LOVE SICK PARSEE. Montreal, Drysdale, [1897?]. 126p [BVaU
  OTU QMM

Fairbairn, Mrs. Christabel
VERSES AND PROSE. N.p., F.P. Fairbairn, 1939. 25p [QMU

Fairley, Margaret Adele (Keeling), 1885–1968
SPIRIT OF CANADIAN DEMOCRACY. A Collection of Canadian Writings from the
  Beginnings to the Present Day. Toronto, Progress Books, 1945. 319p [BVaU
  LC MWU NBFU OKQ

Farmer, Thomas Devey Jermyn
THE GREAT POETS OF ITALY, in Prose and Verse. ... Toronto, Briggs, 1916.
  283p [BM BVaU NBFU OTU

Fletcher, Beatrice Ellen
UPS AND DOWNS. Prose and Verse. Ilfracombe, Devon, Stockwell, 1952. 80p

Fletcher, Mary E., 1874–1929
POETRY AND PROSE. With an intro. by Archibald MacMechan. Toronto,
  Ryerson, 1930. 46p [BVaU NSHD OKQ

Foran, Ethel Ursula
SPRINGTIME FANCIES. Montreal, Gazette, 1935. 159p [BVaU LC NSHD
  OLU QMM

Foran, Joseph Kearney, 1857–1931
A GARLAND. Lectures and Poems. 1857–1931. Montreal, Gazette, 1931. 251p
  [BVaU LC NBFU OTU QMM

Frame, Elizabeth, 1820–1913
DESCRIPTIVE SKETCHES OF NOVA SCOTIA. In Prose and Verse. By a Nova
  Scotian [pseud]. Halifax, MacKinlay, 1864. 242p [BVaU NSWA OTP
  QMM

French, Donald Graham, 1873–1945
STANDARD CANADIAN RECITER. A Book of the Best Readings and Recitations from Canadian Literature. Comp by ——. Toronto, McClelland, 1918. 348p [BVa NSHD OTP

Frisch, Anthony John, 1921–
FIRST FLOWERING. A Selection of Prose and Poetry by the Youth of Canada. Ed. by ——. Toronto, Kingswood House, 1956. 210p

Garvie, Alexander Rae, 1839–1875
THISTLEDOWN. Miscellanies in Prose and Verse. With an intro. by G. Stewart. Toronto, Hunter Rose, 1875. 274p [BVaU NBFU OTU

Gibson, Mary Stewart (Durie), 1875–1911
STORIES AND VERSES. By Mary Stewart Durie. Toronto, Briggs, 1912. 168p [BM BVaU OTU

Gill, Robert
VERSES WITH A SKETCH IN DRAMATIC FORM, Written for his Family and Friends; and Addresses delivered on Various Occasions. Toronto, priv. print., 1927. 83p [Brown U OTU

Gillis, James Donald, 1870–
A MARITIMES LIFE. N.p., n.d. 126p [NSHD OTU
THE PIE SOCIAL. A Modern Romance. N.p., n.d. 74p [AEU NSHD OTU

Goulding, Dorothy Jane, 1923–
DOROTHY JANE'S BOOK. Songs and Stories from Kindergarten of the Air. Toronto, Dent, 1949. 90p [AEU MWU OH

Graham, Janet (Pollock), 1880–
AUNT JEAN'S CHRISTMAS PROGRAMME. Lachute, Que., Watchman, 1933. 30p [Contains poems as well as "dialogues" and plays.] [NSHPL

Gustafson, Ralph Barker, 1909–
CANADIAN ACCENT. A Collection of Stories and Poems. Ed. by ——. Harmondsworth, Middlesex, Eng., Penguin Books, 1944. 144p [BVaU LC MWU OTP

Halldorsson, Albert Laurence, 1925–
WINGS OF THE WIND. A Selection of Poems and Essays in Continuous Form. Winnipeg, Columbia Press, 1948. 80p [BViPA OTP

Halliburton, Brenton, 1775–1860
JOHN BULL AND HIS CALVES. Reflections on Passing Events. [Halifax?], priv. print., [1864?]. 47p [Separate issue of the appendix to G.W. Hill's MEMOIR OF SIR BRENTON HALLIBURTON, *q.v.*] [NSHD OTP QMSS

Hardy, William George, 1896–
THE ALBERTA GOLDEN JUBILEE ANTHOLOGY. Ed. by ——. Toronto, McClelland, 1955. 471p

Harper, John Murdoch, 1845–1919
SACRAMENT SUNDAY, AND BELLS OF KARTDALE. Toronto, Musson, n.d. 101p [BVaU NBFU OONL

Hatheway, Warren Franklin, 1850–1923
WHY FRANCE LOST CANADA, AND OTHER ESSAYS AND POEMS. Toronto, Briggs, 1915. 210p [BVaU LC NBFU OTP

Hayes, Catherine E. (Simpson), 1852–1943
PRAIRIE POT-POURRI. By Mary Markwell [pseud]. Winnipeg, Stovel, 1895. 186p [BM OTP QMM SSU

Heighington, Wilfrid, 1897–1945
WHEREAS AND WHATNOT. Toronto, Macmillan, 1934. 152p [BVaU LC OTP

Henderson, Christine Margaret (Lighthall), 1868–1968
ENGLAND REMEMBERED. Montreal, Lovell, 1944. 47p [BVaU NSWA OTP QMM

Henderson, J. Duff
ALVIRA alias ORCA. The Nineteenth Century Story. [Also some Poems and some Dramas.] Toronto, Hunter Rose, 1899. 279p [BCF OTP

Herbert, Mary E.
FLOWERS BY THE WAYSIDE. A Miscellany of Prose and Verse. ... Halifax, Citizen Office, 1865. 78p [NSHD

Higginson, Thomas H., 1829–1868
THE LITERARY WORKS OF T.H. HIGGINSON (Persolus). Vankleek Hill, Ont., Otto, 1888. [Bound with separately titled POETICAL WORKS, by Thomas Higginson.] 2v in 1 [BVaU OTU QMM

Hopper, Alfred E., 1870–
COMPOSITE CARGO. A Unique Collection of Poems and Prose Pieces. Ottawa, Tower Books, 1948. 43p [BViPA

Howe, Joseph, 1804–1873
POEMS AND ESSAYS. Montreal, Lovell, 1874. 341p [BVaU LC MWU NBFU OTU QMM

Hunt, William Edward
POEMS AND PASTELS. Toronto, Briggs, 1896. 137p [BM BVaU NBFU OKQ QMM

Jamieson, Nina (Moore), 1885–1932
THE CATTLE IN THE STALL. Sketches and Poems. ... Toronto, Garden City
Press, 1932. 194p [BVaU LC NBFU OTU QMBM

Jennings, Clotilda, –1895
THE WHITE ROSE IN ACADIA, and AUTUMN IN NOVA SCOTIA. A Prize Tale and
Poems. By Maude [pseud]. Halifax, Bowes, 1855. 36p [NSHD

Johnson, Frank
THE VILLAGE OF MERROW. Its Past and Present. Montreal, Lovell, 1876.
208p [BM BVaU LC NBFU OTP QMM

Johnson, Helen Mar, 1834–1863
CANADIAN WILD FLOWERS. Selections from the Writings of Miss Helen M.
Johnson, of Magog, P.Q., Canada. With a Sketch of her Life by Rev. J.M.
Orrock. ... Boston, Orrock, 1884. 200p [BVaU LC OTP

Johnston, Mabel Annesley (Sullivan), 1870–1945
A CANADIAN BOOK OF MONTHS, VERSE AND PROSE. By Susanne Marny [pseud].
Toronto, Briggs, 1908. 96p [BM BVaU OTP

Joseph, Alexander Callow, 1886–1958
THE ROVIN' PIGEON. With Verse, Yarns, Humor, Short Stories, etc. from
D.V.A. Hospital Patients across Canada. By Al Pat [pseud]. Toronto, 1948–54.
Pts. 1–7. [Unbound. Pagination and cover titles vary.] [OTP

Kendrick, William K.F.
CANADIAN STORIES IN PROSE AND VERSE. Toronto, Clarke Irwin, 1932. 130p
[Rev. ed., 1936.] [OOP OTU

Kidner, Frank, 1853–1924
"PI." A Compilation of Odds and Ends Relating to Workers in Sanctum and
Newsroom, culled from the Scrapbook of a Compositor. [Anon] Hamilton,
Griffin & Kidner, 1890. 216p [BVa OKQ QMU

King, Carlyle Albert, 1907–
SASKATCHEWAN HARVEST. A Golden Jubilee Selection of Song and Story.
Ed. by ——. Toronto, McClelland, 1955. 224p.

Klinck, Carl Frederick, 1908–
CANADIAN ANTHOLOGY. Ed. by —— and R.E. Watters. Toronto, Gage, 1955.
xvi + 558p

Layton, Irving, 1912–
NOW IS THE PLACE. Stories and Poems. Montreal, First Statement Press, 1948.
57p [BVaU LC NBFU OKQ QMM

Leckie, Rev. Neil MacMillan
ANY WELL THAT SPRINGS. Toronto, Ryerson, 1956. 89p

Leitch, Patrick Joseph, 1847—1905
POEMS AND LECTURES. Montreal, Pelletier, 1901. 116p [BM BVaU OTU QMSS

Lockhart, Rev. Arthur John, 1850—1926
THE PAPERS OF PASTOR FELIX (Arthur John Lockhart). Toronto, Briggs, 1903.
386p [BVaU LC NSHD OKQ QMSS

MacCulloh, Lewis Luke
THE SCRIBBLER. A Series of Essays published in Montreal on Literary, Critical,
Satirical, Moral, and Local Subjects. Interspersed with Pieces of Poetry. Montreal,
Lane, 1822. 8v [NSWA QMSS

Macdonald, John James, 1849—
POEMS AND ESSAYS. Ottawa, Ru-Mi-Lou Books, 1928. 132p [BVaU OOP QMM

Macdonald, William Livingstone
GLIMPSES OF LIFE. Poems and Prose of Inspiration and Education. Toronto, Ontario
Pub. Co., 1936. 139p [OODF

MacGeorge, Rev. Robert Jackson, 1811?—1884
TALES, SKETCHES AND LYRICS. Toronto, Armour, 1858. 269p [BVaU NBFU
OTP QMM

MacGowan, James Alexander
THROUGH THE TWILIGHT. Poems and Essays. Toronto, Rowsell, 1893. 59p
[OTUV

McGregor, J. Herrick
THE WISDOM OF WALOOPI. Letchworth, Herts., Garden City, [1913?]. 250p
[Reprintings from the Victoria "Times" and "Colonist."] [BM BVaU LC OLU

MacKenzie, Evan James, 1869?—
A VETERAN OF THE FIRST WORLD WAR TELLS HIS STORY. Victoria, [1954?]. 46p

MacLennan, Catherine Mae
RAMBLING ROUND STANLEY PARK. Vancouver, Wrigley, 1935. 47p [BVaU OTU

McLeod, Murdoch
LIFE ON THE ALGOMA FARM. [Vancouver, Author, 1954.] 82p [mimeographed]
POEMS AND STORIES FROM RAMBLES AROUND BRITISH COLUMBIA, FOR B.C.
CENTENNIAL YEAR 1958. [Vancouver, Author, 1958?] 82p [mimeographed]
TALES OF THE B.C. TRAILS, 1959. [Vancouver, Author, 1959?] 82p [mimeo-
graphed]

Mair, Charles, 1838—1927.
TECUMSEH, A DRAMA AND CANADIAN POEMS; DREAMLAND AND OTHER POEMS;

THE AMERICAN BISON; MEMOIRS AND REMINISCENCES. With intro. by Robert Norwood. Toronto, Radisson Society, 1926. 72 + 470p [BM BVaU NBFU OTP QMM

Marsden, Rev. Joshua, 1777—1837
THE NARRATIVE OF A MISSION to Nova Scotia, New Brunswick, and the Somers Islands; with a Tour to Lake Ontario. To which is added, THE MISSION, An Original Poem. ... Plymouth-dock, Johns, 1816. 289p [2nd ed., 1827.] [BM BVaU LC NSWA OTP QMSS

Mason, Harold Campbell, 1895—
BITS O' BRONZE. Toronto, Allen, 1921. 119p [BM BVaU NSHD OOP

Merrill, Helen M.
PICTURESQUE PRINCE EDWARD COUNTY. Picton, Ont., Gazette, 1892. 128p [BVaU OTP QMSS

Mildmay, Rev. Aubrey Neville St. John, 1865—
VIGNETTES. [In Verse and Prose.] London, Elliot Stock, 1894. 89p [BM

Milliken, Lorene Frances (Ritz)
NEW POEMS AND PROSE PIECES. Winnipeg, Author, 1960 [c 1958]. 68p

Moore, Frederick William Louis
MUSIC——EVERYWHERE. A Message over the Air to Young Canada. ... Victoria, Diggon-Hibben, [1934?]. 35p [BViPA NBFU

Morrison, Dorothy, 1909—
THE PRAIRIE LILY. Regina, School Aids, 1948. 40p [OH SRL

Morse, Charles, 1860—1945
APICES JURIS, and Other Legal Essays in Prose and Verse. Toronto, Canada Law Book Co., 1906. 356p [BM BVaU LC OTP

Munro, Bruce Weston, 1860—1900?
GROANS AND GRINS OF ONE WHO SURVIVED. Toronto, Warwick, 1889. 385p [BVaU LC NSHD OTMC

Murdoch, Beamish, 1800—1876
CELEBRATION OF THE CENTENERY [sic] ANNIVERSARY OF THE SETTLEMENT OF THE CITY OF HALIFAX. Oration by Beamish Murdoch; Poem by Joseph Howe. Halifax, 1849. 12p [NSWA

Nairn, Robert, 1854—1937
POEMS AND ADDRESSES. Toronto, Briggs, 1912. 80p [BM OTUV

Nelson, George Edmondson, 1902—
CAVALCADE OF THE NORTH. An Entertaining Collection of Distinguished Writing

by Canadian Authors. Ed. by ——. Garden City, N.Y., Doubleday, 1958. 640p

Nobile, Achilles Alexander, 1833—

GEMS OF FOREIGN POETRY ... TRANSLATED INTO ENGLISH PROSE. New York, 1888. 32p [French, Italian, and Spanish.] [LC

MISCELLANEOUS POEMS, TRANSLATED INTO ENGLISH PROSE. Toronto, Williams, 1883. 116p [Earlier ed.: Paris, 1881. 62p] [BVaU LC NSHD QMM

MISCELLANEOUS WORKS OF SIGNOR A.A. NOBILE. Novels, Translations, Lectures. San Francisco, Patterson, 1894. 160p [On cover: v.1.] [No more published?] [LC

Orrock, Rev. J.M., 1830—

THE ARMY OF THE GREAT KING. Short Sermons on Short Texts; Miscellaneous Pieces, and Poetic Musings. Boston, Himes, 1855. 224p [LC

Oxley, James Macdonald, 1855—1907

A CHRISTMAS PORTFOLIO. Contributed to by Canadian Authors and Artists. [Ed. by ——.] London, Ont., Y.W.C.A., [1903]. 110p [BM NBFU OTP

Palmer, George

"STAND TO." By 2571 [pseud]. Calgary, Hynd, 1919. 76p [BM BVaU NBFU OTP

Parker, Gilbert, 1862—1932

THE WORKS OF GILBERT PARKER. Imperial ed. New York, Scribner, 1912—23. 23v [BM BVaU LC NBFU OTU QMM

Pendle, Walter Henry, 1889—

POEMS, SHORT TALES, PHANTASIES. Vancouver, 1951. 97p

Penman, Rev. Archibald D., 1882—

THE COMINGS OF CHRIST, PAST AND FUTURE (POEMS, SONGS AND TRIBUTES). Ilfracombe, Devon, Stockwell, 1956. 139p

Peterson, Flora (Culp)

LIFE AND SHE. Boston, Christopher Pub. House, 1960. 166p

Phillips, John Arthur, 1842—1907

THOMPSON'S TURKEY, AND OTHER CHRISTMAS TALES, POEMS. Montreal, Lovell, 1873. 256p [BVaU OTP QMSS

Porter, Rev. William Henry, 1840—1928

CONVERSE WITH THE KING. [Brantford, Expositor, 1892.] 240p [NSHPL OTUV

Ramsay, Andrew John, 1849?–1907
ONE QUIET DAY. A Book of Prose and Poetry. By J.R. Ramsay [pseud].
  Hamilton, Lancefield, 1873. 191p [BVaU MWU NSHD OTP

Regina College Writers' Club
TUESDAY NIGHT, 1935. Regina, Western Printers, 1935. 32p [CC

Richardson, Bond & Wright Limited
ONE HUNDRED CHIN LIFTERS ON OUR 100TH YEAR, 1853–1953. Montreal, the
  Company, 1953. ix + 132p

Rickard, Thomas Arthur, 1864–1953
AUTUMN LEAVES. Vancouver, Wrigley, 1948. 194p [BViPA OTU

Ridley, Hilda M., –1960
CANADIAN BIRTHDAY BOOK. Ed. by ——. London, Davis, 1934. 99p [BM

Robins, John Daniel, 1884–1952
A POCKETFUL OF CANADA. Ed. by ——. Toronto, Collins, 1946. 430p [BVaU
  LC NBFU OTP QMM

Rogers, Thomas George, 1877–1961?
THE LIFE BEYOND. Thoughts by a Layman, in Prose and Verse, Concerning the
  Life to Come. Toronto, Author, 1960. 71p

Rorke, Louise Richardson, –1949
SOME CANADIAN CHRISTMASES IN PROSE AND VERSE. N.p., n.d. 6p [NBS

Ross, George William, 1841–1914
PATRIOTIC RECITATIONS AND ARBOR DAY EXERCISES. Comp. by ——. Toronto,
  Warwick, 1893. 374p [Poems, Speeches, etc., principally by Canadian authors.]
  [BVaU NSHD OTP QMM

Rutherford, John
CHARLIE CHATTERTON. A Montreal Story. With Canadian and Other Poems.
  Montreal, Lovell, 1868. 144p [BVaU NBFU OTP QMM

Ryan, Norman J.
"RED" RYAN'S RHYMES AND EPISODES. Hamilton, n.d. 92p [Brown U OOP

Scott, Duncan Campbell, 1862–1947
THE CIRCLE OF AFFECTION, and Other Pieces in Prose and Verse. Toronto,
  McClelland, 1947. 237p [BVaU NBFU OTP

Seymour, Rev. James Cooke, 1839–1902
HUMOR, PITH AND PATHOS. Readings and Recitations. Toronto, Briggs, 1887.
  [Ryerson Impt.

Sheldrake, Sparham, 1851–1903
CURIOUS FACTS. Prose and Verse. By Sparham Sheldrake ("Sigma"). Toronto,
Williamson, 1895. 123p [OTP

Shute, Evan Vere, 1905–
WHERE THE HERON STANDS. By Vere Jameson [pseud]. [London, Ont.?],
Author, 1949. 113p [OKQ

Simpson, John, 1807–1878
THE CANADIAN FORGET ME NOT FOR MDCCCXXXVII. Ed. by ——. Niagara,
Sewell, 1837. 157p [BVaU LC OTP

Smyth, John, –1852
A SMALL SPECIMEN OF THE GENIUS OF CANADA WEST. ... Toronto, Coates, 1845.
34p [OTP

Snell, Miss M.S., 1841–
ESSAYS, SHORT STORIES AND POEMS. Including a Sketch of the Author's Life.
Chatham, Ont., Banner Steam Print., 1881. 162p [BVaU OLU

Snider, John H.
SCRIBBLINGS OF A SCRIBE. By Taylor C. Knight [pseud]. Dryden, Ont., Observer,
1946. 74p [BVaU OKQ

Stead, Robert James Campbell, 1880–1959
THE MAPLE'S PRAISE OF FRANKLIN DELANO ROOSEVELT 1882–1945. Ed. by ——.
Ottawa, Tower Books, 1945. 18p [OTU QMU

Stephen, Alexander Maitland, 1882–1942
THE VOICE OF CANADA. Canadian Prose and Poetry. Selected by ——. Toronto,
Dent, 1926. 144p [BM BVaU LC NSHD OTP

Stephens, William A., 1809–1891
HAMILTON AND OTHER POEMS AND LECTURES. 2nd ed. Toronto, Lovell, 1871.
410p [BVa MWU OKQ

Stevenson, Orlando John, 1869–1950.
REMINISCENCES. Guelph, n.p., 1951. 32p

Stewart, George, 1848–1906
STEWART'S LITERARY QUARTERLY MAGAZINE. Devoted to Light and Entertaining
Literature. Ed. by ——. Saint John, n.p., 1867–72. 5v [NSWA

Stone, Phil
"GOLD IN THE BRASS." A Collection. Toronto, Author, 1938. 35p [OTU

Strong, William
THE NEW HEAVEN. Letters, Editorials, and Poems. London, Friars Print. Assoc.,
1902. 110p [Brown U BVaU OTUV

Sutherland, Alexander Hugh, 1870–1952
THE SELKIRK SETTLEMENT ON THE RED RIVER. Victoria, Author, 1938. 61p
  [Brown U BViPA
VICTORIA, B.C. Victoria, Clarke Print. Co., n.d. 30p [BViV NBFU

Swift, Sherman Charles, 1879–1947
THE VOYAGES OF JACQUES CARTIER IN PROSE AND VERSE. Sonnets by S.C. Swift,
  Prose Sketches by T.G. Marquis. Toronto, Allen, 1934. 79p [BM BVaU LC
  OKQ QMM

Tennyson, Bertram, –1903?
THE LAND OF NAPIOA and Other Essays in Prose and Verse. Moosomin, N.W.T.,
  Spectator Print., 1896. 163p [BM BVaU OOP

Toronto, University of
VARSITY BOOK, PROSE AND POETRY. Toronto, Varsity Pub., 1885. 200p [OTU

Toronto Art Students' League
A CALENDAR FOR 1895–1896. With some Selections from Canadian Writers.
  Toronto, the League, 1895–6. 2v [NBFU

Waid, J.B., 1804–
VARIETY, POETRY AND PROSE. By the Bard of Niagara [pseud]. Montreal, Lovell,
  1872. 254p [BVaU LC NBFU OKQ QMM

Walters, Harry Macdonald
CIVIL SERVICE JINGLES, AND OTHER THINGS. Ottawa, Lowe-Martin, 1911. 71p
  [BVaU OOP

Wanless, Andrew, 1824–1898
SKETCHES AND ANECDOTES. Detroit, Author, 1891. 300p [BVaU LC OLU

Warman, Cy, 1855–1914
TALES OF AN ENGINEER, with Rhymes of the Rail. New York, 1895. 242p
  [BVaU LC OLU

Watson, Albert Durrant, 1859–1926
OUR CANADIAN LITERATURE. Representative Prose and Verse. Chosen by Albert
  Durrant Watson and Lorne Albert Pierce. Toronto, Ryerson, 1922. 309p [Also:
  Toronto, Ryerson, 1923. 443p] [BVaU NSHD OTP QMM

Watters, Reginald Eyre, 1912–
BRITISH COLUMBIA. A Centennial Anthology. Toronto, McClelland, 1958.
  xvi + 576p

CANADIAN ANTHOLOGY. Ed. by C.F. Klinck and R.E. Watters. Toronto, Gage, 1955. xvi + 558p

Weber, Ephraim, 1870–1956
MUSINGS BY THE WAY. N.p., n.d. 33p

Webling, Lucy
POEMS AND STORIES. By Lucy Webling and Peggy Webling. Toronto, McLean, [18—?]. 150p [BVaU NBFU

Wetherell, James Elgin, 1851–1940
THE GREAT WAR IN VERSE AND PROSE. Selected and ed. by ——. Toronto, Wilgress, 1919. 160p [BM BVaU OTU

Wicksteed, Gustavus William, 1799–1898
WAIFS IN VERSE AND PROSE. Ottawa, Bureau, 1891. 260p [Another ed., 1891; also an 1894 ed. with addenda paged 261-328.] [BVaU LC OLU QMM

Wigmore, Annie
DREAMS OF THE FIRST AND TWENTIETH CENTURY. Toronto, Hunter Rose, 1898. 94p [OTP QMU

Willis, John Howard
SCRAPS AND SKETCHES; or, The Album of a Literary Lounger [pseud]. Montreal, Cunningham, 1831. 246p [OTP QMSS

Woodrow, Constance (Davies), 1899–1937
THE CHILDREN'S CARAVAN. Toronto, Balk-Preston, 1928. 40p [NBFU OTU

Wootton, Wilfrid Shakespeare, 1910–
THE SINGING WATERS OF BRITISH COLUMBIA. Vancouver, Author, 1953. 31p

Wylie, David, 1811–1891
RECOLLECTIONS OF A CONVICT, and Miscellaneous Pieces. By Y-le [pseud]. Montreal, Chalmers, 1847. 197p [BVaU OTU QMSS

FICTION

Novels, collected short stories, anthologies (juvenile fiction included)

Abbott, Rev. Joseph, 1789–1863
PHILIP MUSGRAVE; or, Memoirs of a Church of England Missionary in the North
American Colonies. Ed. by ——. London, Murray, 1846. 158p [Fictional
presentation of MEMORANDA material; *q.v.* below, p. 949.] [BM BVaU NSWA
OTP

Acklom, Rauff de Ryther Daun, 1900–
CONVENIENT SEASON. By David J. Manners [pseud]. New York, Dutton, 1941.
281p [LC NBFU OTMC
UNDER RUNNING LAUGHTER. By David J. Manners [pseud]. New York, Dutton,
1943. 315p [LC NBFU OTU

Acland, Baldwyn John Dyke, 1883–
FILIBUSTER. A Novel of Adventure. By B. Dyke Acland. London, Hodder, 1929.
320p [BM LC NBFU OTMC
PEREGRINE. A Novel. By B. Dyke Acland. London, Hodder, 1930. 320p [BM
BVaU LC NBFU
STICKY FINGERS. London, Hodder, 1932. 316p [BM
SUNDOWN. By Dyke Acland. London, Hodder, 1931. 320p [Pub. in the U.S. as
GRAND OLD MAN. New York, McBride, 1931. 277p] [BM BVaU LC OTMC
THE THIRTY THIEVES. By B. Dyke Acland. London, Hodder, 1930. 310p [BM
LC NBFU

Acland, Eric
DRUMS OF NIAGARA. An Adventure Story of Early Canada. Toronto, Nelson,
1953. 226p

Acland, Peregrine Palmer, 1892–1963
ALL ELSE IS FOLLY. Toronto, McClelland, 1929. 345p [English ed., subtitled
"A Tale of War and Passion. ... With a ... Foreword by Ford Madox Ford."
London, Constable, 1929. 273p] [BM BVaU NBFU OTMC QMM

Adam, Graeme Mercer, 1839–1912
AN ALGONQUIN MAIDEN. A Romance of the Early Days of Upper Canada. By
G. Mercer Adam and A. Ethelwyn Wetherald. Montreal, Lovell, 1887. 240p
[BM BVaU LC NBFU OTP QMM

Adams, Isabel

THE DUMB MAN. New York, Appleton, 1933. 279p [BM BVaU LC OOP

HEART OF THE WOODS. A Story of Life among the Habitants in the Laurentian Foot-hills. New York, Century, 1928. 365p [BM BVaU LC NBFU OTMC QMM

Adams, Percy Miller, 1894–

LIFE ON THE HEAD END. New York, Vantage Press, 1956. 192p

Adshead, Herbert Bealey, 1862–1932

PIONEER TALES AND OTHER HUMAN STORIES. Calgary, Alberta Job Press, 1929. 70p [AC OTMC

Algie, James, 1857–1928

BERGEN WORTH. By Wallace Lloyd [pseud]. London, Fisher Unwin, 1901. 276p [BM BVaU

HOUSES OF GLASS. A Philosophical Romance. By Wallace Lloyd [pseud]. New York, Dillingham, 1898. 398p [BM LC OTU

THE SWORD OF GLENVOHR. By Wallace Lloyd [pseud]. Toronto, [19—?]. [T&C

Allen, Barney, 1902–

THE GYNECOLOGIST. Toronto, Rock Pub., 1949. 58p [LC

THEY HAVE BODIES. A Realistic Novel in Eleven Chapters and Three Acts. New York, Macaulay, 1929. 279p [LC NBFU

TORONTO DOCTOR. Toronto, Rock Pub., 1949. 390p [BVaU LC NBFU OKQ

Allen, Grant, 1848–1899

AN AFRICAN MILLIONAIRE. London, Richards, 1897. 317p [BM BVaU OTU

AN ARMY DOCTOR'S ROMANCE. New York, Tuck, 1893. 93p [BM LC

AT MARKET VALUE. Chicago, Neely, 1894. 329p [BM BVaU LC OTU

BABYLON. By Cecil Power [pseud]. New York, Munro, 1885. 310p [BM BVaU LC NBFU OTU

THE BACKSLIDER. New York, Lewis Scribner, 1901. 380p [10 stories] [LC

THE BECKONING HAND AND OTHER STORIES. London, Chatto, 1887. 341p [BM OTU

BLOOD ROYAL. New York, Cassell, 1892. 276p [BM BVaU LC OTU

A BRIDE FROM THE DESERT. New York, Fenno, 1896. 192p [3 stories] [LC OTMC

THE BRITISH BARBARIANS. New York, Putnam, 1895. 281p [BM BVaU LC OTU

THE CRUISE OF THE ALBATROSS; or When was Wednesday the Tenth? A Story of the South Pacific. Boston, Lothrop, 1898. 121p [AEU LC NBFU OTU

THE DEVIL'S DIE. London, Chatto, 1888. 3v [BM OTU

DR. PALLISER'S PATIENT. London, Mullen, 1889. 152p [BM

THE DUCHESS OF POWYSLAND. London, Chatto, 1892. 3v [BM OTU

DUMARESQ'S DAUGHTER. New York, Harper, 1891. 297p [BM BVaU LC NBFU OTU

FOR MAMIE'S SAKE. A Tale of Love and Dynamite. New York, Munro, 1886. 295p [BM LC OTMC

THE GREAT TABOO. London, Chatto, 1890. 280p [BM LC OTMC

HILDA WADE. New York, Putnam, 1900. 383p [BM BVaU LC OTU

IN ALL SHADES. London, Chatto, 1886. 3v [BM BVaU OTU

THE INCIDENTAL BISHOP. New York, Appleton, 1898. 306p [BM LC OTU

IVAN GREET'S MASTERPIECE. London, Chatto, 1893. 330p [BM OTU

THE JAWS OF DEATH. London, Simpkin, 1889. 110p [BM OTU

KALEE'S SHRINE. By Grant Allen ... and May Coates. Bristol, Arrowsmith, 1886. 196p [LC OTU

LINNET. London, Richards, 1898. 394p [BM LC OTU

MICHAEL'S CRAG. Chicago, Rand McNally, 1893. 242p [BM BVaU LC NBFU OTU

MISS CAYLEY'S ADVENTURES. New York, Putnam, 1899. 344p [BM BVaU LC NBFU OTU

MOORLAND IDYLLS. London, Chatto, 1896. 257p [BM

PHILISTIA. ... By Cecil Power [pseud]. New York, Munro, 1884. 254p [BM LC OTMC

RECALLED TO LIFE. New York, Holt, 1891. 230p [BM LC

ROSALBA. The Story of Her Development. By Olive Pratt Rayner [pseud]. New York, Putnam, 1899. 396p [BM LC

THE SCALLYWAG. New York, Cassell, 1893. 437p [BM LC OTU

SIR THEODORE'S GUEST, AND OTHER STORIES. Bristol, Arrowsmith, 1902. 316p [BM

A SPLENDID SIN. London, White, 1896. 228p [BM LC

STRANGE STORIES. London, Chatto, 1884. 356p [BM BVaU OTU

THE TENTS OF SHEM. A Novel. London, Chatto, 1889. 3v [BM BVaU LC OTU

A TERRIBLE INHERITANCE. New York, Crowell, [18—?]. 57p [LC OTU

THIS MORTAL COIL. A Novel. London, Chatto, 1888. 3v [BM NBFU OTU

TOM, UNLIMITED. A Story for Children. By Martin Leach Warborough [pseud]. London, Richards, 1897. 250p [BM

TWELVE TALES. London, Richards, 1899. 351p [BM BVaU LC OTMC

THE TYPEWRITER GIRL. By Olive Pratt Rayner [pseud]. London, Pearson, 1897. 261p [Same title: By Grant Allen. New York, Street & Smith, 1900.] [BM LC OTU

UNDER SEALED ORDERS. In Two Parts. ... New York, Collier, 1894. 470p [BM LC OTU

WEDNESDAY THE TENTH. A Tale of the South Pacific. Boston, Lothrop, 1890. 131p [Same as THE CRUISE OF THE ALBATROSS, q.v.] [BVaU NSHD OONL

WHAT'S BRED IN THE BONE. £1000 prize novel. London, "Tit-Bits," 1891. 414p [BM BVaU LC NBFU OTMC

THE WHITE MAN'S FOOT. ... London, Hatchards, 1888. 216p [BM OTU
THE WOMAN WHO DID. Boston, Roberts, 1895. 223p [Repub. with intro. by
   Ernest Boyd. Boston, Little Brown, 1926. xv + 223p] [BM BVaU LC NBFU
   OTU

Allen, Joseph
THE MAKING OF A CANADIAN. Newark, N.J., Allen Pub., 1918. 383p [LC BVaU
   OTP

Allen, Ralph, 1913–1966
THE CHARTERED LIBERTINE. Toronto, Macmillan, 1954. 270p
HOME MADE BANNERS. Toronto, Longmans, 1946. 256p [BVaU LC NBFU
   OTU
PEACE RIVER COUNTRY. London, Hodder, 1958. 191p

Allison, Dorothea
MERRY BELLS; or, Tales of the Okanagan Fairies. Comp. by ——. Vernon, B.C.,
   Vernon News, 1945. 25p [BKO

Alloway, Mary H. (Wilson), 1848–1919
CROSSED SWORDS. A Canadian-American Tale of Love and Valor. By Mrs. Clement
   Alloway. Toronto, Briggs, 1912. 391p [BM BVaU NBFU OTMC QMM

Amy, William Lacey, –1962
THE BEAST. By Luke Allan [pseud]. Boston, Small Maynard, 1924. 335p [BM
   BVaU LC OTMC
BEHIND THE WIRE FENCE. By Luke Allan [pseud]. London, Arrowsmith, 1935.
   287p [BM OONL
BEYOND THE LOCKED DOOR. By Luke Allan [pseud]. London, Jenkins, 1938.
   286p [BM
THE BLACK OPAL. By Luke Allan [pseud]. London, Arrowsmith, 1935. 288p
   [BM OONL
BLUE PETE AND THE KID. By Luke Allan [pseud]. London, Jenkins, 1953. 190p
BLUE PETE AND THE PINTO. By Luke Allan [pseud]. London, Jenkins, 1948.
   192p [BM
BLUE PETE AT BAY. By Luke Allan [pseud]. London, Jenkins, 1951 [1952]. 190p
BLUE PETE BREAKS THE RULES. By Luke Allan [pseud]. London, Jenkins, 1943.
   187p [ACU
BLUE PETE: DETECTIVE. By Luke Allan [pseud]. London, Jenkins, 1928. 312p
   [BM LC OTUV SRL
BLUE PETE: HALF BREED. By Luke Allan [pseud]. London, Jenkins, 1921. 256p
   [BM BVaU LC OTMC
BLUE PETE, HORSE THIEF. A Mounted Police Story. By Luke Allan [pseud].
   London, Jenkins, 1938. 283p [AEU BM
BLUE PETE IN THE BADLANDS. By Luke Allan [pseud]. London, Jenkins, 1954.
   173p

BLUE PETE, INDIAN SCOUT. By Luke Allan [pseud]. London, Jenkins, 1950. 221p
[BM OONL

BLUE PETE, OUTLAW. By Luke Allan [pseud]. London, Jenkins, 1944. 192p [BM

BLUE PETE PAYS A DEBT. By Luke Allan [pseud]. Toronto, Longmans, 1942.
288p [ACU BM

BLUE PETE: REBEL. By Luke Allan [pseud]. London, Jenkins, 1940. 286p [ACU
BM OTU

BLUE PETE RIDES THE FOOTHILLS. By Luke Allan [pseud]. London, Jenkins,
1953. 188p

BLUE PETE TO THE RESCUE. By Luke Allan [pseud]. London, Jenkins, 1947.
196p [BM

BLUE PETE, UNOFFICIALLY. By Luke Allan [pseud]. London, Jenkins, 1949.
224p [BM

BLUE PETE WORKS ALONE. By Luke Allan [pseud]. London, Jenkins, 1948. 240p
[BM

BLUE PETE'S DILEMMA. By Luke Allan [pseud]. London, Jenkins, 1945. 190p
[BM

BLUE PETE'S VENDETTA. By Luke Allan [pseud]. London, Jenkins, 1947. 186p
[BM

THE BLUE WOLF. A Tale of the Cypress Hills. London, Hodder, 1913. 311p [ACU
BM OTP

CASE OF THE OPEN DRAWER. By Luke Allan [pseud]. London, Arrowsmith, 1936.
288p [BM

THE DARK SPOT. By Luke Allan [pseud]. London, Arrowsmith, 1932. 295p
[BM

THE END OF THE TRAIL. By Luke Allan [pseud]. London, Arrowsmith, 1931.
311p [BM OONL

FIVE FOR ONE. By Luke Allan [pseud]. Bristol, Arrowsmith, [1934]. 288p [BM
NBFU OONL

THE FOURTH DAGGER. London, Arrowsmith, 1932. 287p [BM NBFU OTMC

THE GHOST MURDER. By Luke Allan [pseud]. London, Jenkins, 1937. 316p
[BM OTU

JUNGLE CRIME. By Luke Allan [pseud]. London, Arrowsmith, 1931. 318p [BM

THE LONE TRAIL. By Luke Allan [pseud]. London, Jenkins, 1921. 312p [BM
OTUV

THE MAN ON THE TWENTY-FOURTH FLOOR. By Luke Allan [pseud]. London,
Jenkins, 1937. 312p [BM OTU

THE MANY-COLOURED THREAD. By Lacey Amy. Toronto, Longmans, 1932.
311p [BM NBFU OTUV

THE MASKED STRANGER. By Luke Allan [pseud]. London, Arrowsmith, 1930.
287p [BM

MURDER AT MIDNIGHT. By Luke Allan [pseud]. London, Arrowsmith, 1930.
288p [BM LC

MURDER AT THE CLUB. By Luke Allan [pseud]. Bristol, Arrowsmith, 1933. 288p [BM OONL

THE PACE. By Luke Allan [pseud]. London, Hutchinson, 1926. 282p [BM LC

THE RETURN OF BLUE PETE. By Luke Allan [pseud]. London, Jenkins, 1922. 312p [BM BVaU LC NBFU OTMC

SCOTLAND YARD TAKES A HOLIDAY. London, Arrowsmith, 1937. 288p [BM

THE SIRE. By Luke Allan [pseud]. London, Hutchinson, 1927. 288p [BM BVaU LC OPAL

THE TENDERFOOT. By Luke Allan [pseud]. London, Jenkins, 1939. 286p [BM NBFU OTU

THE VENGEANCE OF BLUE PETE. A Mounted Police Story. By Luke Allan [pseud]. London, Jenkins, 1939. 284p [BM OTU

THE TRAITOR. London, Arrowsmith, 1933. 288p [BM

THE WESTERNER. By Luke Allan [pseud]. London, Jenkins, 1923. 304p [BM NBFU

THE WHITE CAMEL. By Lacey Amy. London, Jarrolds, 1926. 318p [BM LC

Anderson, Clara (Rothwell), —1958

JOHN MATHESON. A Wholesome Human Story of Canadian Rural Life. Toronto, Ryerson, 1923. 346p [BM NBFU OKQ QMM

Anderson, Margaret Pauline, 1870—

LEONA CLINCH; or, Lord Kendale's Repentance. Saint John, Barnes, 1907. 338p [BM

Annett, Ronald Ross, 1895—

ESPECIALLY BABE. Toronto, Ryerson, 1942. 263p [LC NBFU OTU

Anonymous

THE ADOPTED DAUGHTER; or, The Trials of Sabra. A Tale of Real Life. Ogdensburgh, N.Y., Hitchcock, 1858. 199p [3rd ed., rev.: Montreal, Lovell, 1863. 196p. Also a 4th ed., 1873.] [BVaU NSHPL OHM OTP QMU

ELLEN MASON. Or, Principle and Prejudice. Toronto, James Campbell, n.d. [Also: Edinburgh, Gall & Inglis; London, Houlston & Wright, [1862]. 111p [OTP

ELSPETH SUTHERLAND; or, The Effects of Faith. Toronto, n.d. 48p [BCF

HOUSE OF THE GALLERY, 2d Session, 3d Parliament. Official Correspondence between the Hon. the First Minister of Duffy, and His Exalted Majesty Night Blooming Ceres, Monarch of the Moon ... relative to the Construction of the Imperial, Lunar, Grand, Mid-air, Lunatic Governmental Railway. ... Ottawa, Citizen, 1875. 14p [NSHP OTU

THE HUNTED OUTLAW; or, Donald Morrison the Canadian Rob Roy. Montreal, Montreal News, 1889. 98p [OTP

NEWS FROM THE INVISIBLE WORLD; or, Interesting Anecdotes of the Dead. Halifax, Nicholson, 1840. 627p [OTP

"OUR SWELL." Chatham, Ont., Planet Steam Print., 1881. 36p [NSHP OTP

THE PRINCE AND THE PROTEGE. A Tale of the Early History of Nova Scotia.
  Halifax, Croskill, 1844. [Prize story, "Morning Post" competition.] 15p [NSHP
SIR PETER PETTYSHAM. A Satirical Story of Canadian Life. Montreal, Canadian
  Railway News Co., 1882. 42p [NSWA QMSS
TRUE CANADIAN DETECTIVE STORIES. Toronto, Howard Pub., 1944. 127p [NBFU
WARS OF THE GULLS. An Historical Romance in Three Chapters. New York,
  Dramatic Repertory, Shakespeare Gallery, 1812. 36p [Reprinted for C.L.
  Woodward, New York, 1880.] [LC OOND
THE YOUNG CANADIAN. A True Story. London, J. Groom, [1855?]. 32p [BM

Appleby, M.
TOLD BY THE INNKEEPER. Ed. by ——. London, Old Royalty Book Pubs., n.d.
  143p [BVaU

Archibald, Edith Jessie (Mortimer), 1854–1938
GUFSHATHI AND HERRIAMAN. A Missionary Story. Saint John, n.d. 82p [NSWA
THE TOKEN. A Tale of Cape Breton Island. ... Toronto, Ryerson, 1930. 315p
  [BM BVaU NSHD OKQ QMM

Ardagh, Alice Maud, 1866–1936
FOR ME TO LIVE. Chicago, Bible Institute Colportage Assoc., 1936. 208p [LC
TANGLED ENDS. By "Espérance" [pseud]. Toronto, Briggs, 1888. 148p [OTU

Armbrest, Duncan
THE BEECH WOODS. How the Neighbours Learned the Many Secrets of a Canadian
  Wood. Toronto, Briggs, 1916. 120p [BM OTU

Armitage, John, 1885?–
WING PO. A Romance of Modern China. By Hin Me Geong [pseud]. Toronto,
  Macmillan, 1929. 323p [BVaU NBFU OTMC

Armour, Agatha, –1891 (Mrs. John G. Thompson)
LADY ROSAMOND'S SECRET. A Romance of Fredericton. Saint John, Telegraph,
  1878. 146p [NBFU OTU
MARGUERITE VERNE; or, Scenes from Canadian Life. Saint John, Telegraph, 1886.
  324p [NSHD
MARION WILBURN. Saint John, Telegraph, n.d. [NBB
SYLVIA LEIGH; or, The Heiress of Glenmarle. Saint John, Telegraph, 1880. [BCF

Armsmith, Catherine
FAIRY TALES OF KOOTENAY. London, Stockwell, 1929. 80p [BM BVaU OTMC

Armstrong, Matt
TURTLE RIVER FILLY. Garden City, N.Y., Doubleday, 1950. 213p [OONL

Armstrong, Rinaldo William
RIVERS RUN TO THE SEA. Toronto, Ryerson, 1936. 288p [BM BVaU LC NBFU
  OTMC

Arnold, Gertrude
SISTER ANNE! SISTER ANNE! Toronto, McClelland, 1920. 235p [BM BVaU NBFU

Arthur, Sidney
A MAN'S WORTH. A Canadian College Romance. Toronto, Hunter Rose, 1926. 294p [AEU OH QQL

Ascher, Isidore Gordon, 1835–1914
THE DOOM OF DESTINY. London, Diprose & Bateman, 1895. 174p [BM
AN ODD MAN'S STORY. London, Elliot Stock, 1889. 207p [BM NSWA OONL
A SOCIAL UPHEAVAL. London, Greening, 1898. 304p [BM

Ashtalcovitch, Michael K.
WHAT IS FEAR? Toronto, Author, 1945. 403p [CC

Ashworth, Edward Montague
LA ROUX. By Johnston Abbott [pseud]. Toronto, Macmillan, 1924. 348p [BVaU LC NBFU OTMC
THE SEIGNEURS OF LA SAULAYE. Gentlemen Adventurers of New France. ... By Johnston Abbott [pseud]. Toronto, Macmillan, 1928. 379p [BVaU LC NBFU OTP

Atkin, Grace Murray, 1891–
THE CAPTIVE HERD. Toronto, McClelland, 1922. 311p [BM BVaU LC OTMC
THE NEW WORLD. Toronto, McClelland, 1921. 285p [BVaU LC OTMC QMM
A SHADOW FALLS. Toronto, Ryerson, 1954. 186p
THAT WHICH IS PASSED. New York, Crowell, 1923. 334p [LC NBFU OTMC

Atlee, Benge, 1890–
BLACK FEATHER. New York, Scribner, 1939. 345p [LC NBFU OTMC

Austin, Rev. Benjamin Fish, 1850–1932
CHRIST OR BARABBAS. A Psychic Novel. Los Angeles, Austin Print., 1921. 142p [LC OLU
THE MYSTERY OF ASHTON HALL. By Benjamin Nitsua [pseud]. Rochester, New York, Austin, 1910. 321p [BM LC OTMC

Austin, Lilian Edna
SHUDDERS. Boston, Meador, 1931. 61p [LC

Ayscough, Florence (Wheelock), 1878–1942
THE AUTOBIOGRAPHY OF A CHINESE DOG. Ed. by his Missuss. ... Boston, Houghton, 1926. 105p [BM LC QMM

B., H.H.
THE LAST OF THE ERIES; or, A Tale of Canada. By H.H.B. Simcoe, Author, 1849.
224p [NSWA OLU

Babcock, John Pease, 1855–1936
PEACE RIVER JOE. The Prize Winning Story of the I.O.D.E. 1924 Competition.
Victoria, B.C., Litchfield's, 1924. 24p [BVaU OTMC

Bacchus, Noel, 1888–
YOU'VE GOT TO SHOW ME, AND OTHER STORIES. New York, Pageant, 1953. 117p

Baird, Mrs. C.A.
A FRAGMENT OF ONTARIO'S SCOTT ACT; or, A Ruined Life. By a "W.C.T.U."
[Mrs. Dewolf of Hamilton, Ont.]. LAWYER ROBERT STREIGHTON'S DISCOVERY
AT A MINERAL SPRING. By Carleton [pseud–Mrs. C.A. Baird]. Boston, Barta,
1893. 85p [OH

Baird, Rev. Frank, 1870–1951
PARSON JOHN OF THE LABRADOR. London, R.T.S., 1924. 246p [BM NBFU
ROB MACNAB. A Story of Old Pictou. ... Halifax, Royal Print., 1923. 250p
[BVaU NSHD OTMC
ROGER DAVIS, LOYALIST. London, R.T.S., 1907. 191p [BM NBFU OTMC

Baird, Irene
HE RIDES THE SKY. Toronto, Macmillan, 1941. 241p [BVaU NSHD OTMC QMM
JOHN. Philadelphia, Lippincott, 1937. 235p [BM BVaU LC NBFU OTMC
QMM
WASTE HERITAGE. Toronto, Macmillan, 1939. 329p [BVaU LC NBFU OTMC
QMM

Baker, Ida Emma (Fitch), 1858–1948
PRESSED DOWN AND RUNNING OVER. Toronto, Author, 1939. 26p [OTU

Baldwin, Harold, 1888–
PELICANS IN THE SKY. A Novel. London, Murray, 1934. 311p [BM

Ball, Augustus Harry, 1873–
ROVERS OF THE VALLEY. Toronto, Dent, 1928. 248p [BM OTMC

Ball, Derrick
THE BURLESQUE VOYAGE. London, Davies, 1953. 281p

Ballantyne, Lereine (Hoffman), 1891–1962
SPIRIT FIRE. A Story of the Petun Indians. New York, Revell, 1932. 188p [LC
NBFU OTMC

Bambrick, Winifred
CONTINENTAL REVUE. London, Faber, 1946. 352p [BM BVaU LC NBFU
OTMC QMM

Banks, William, 185-?—1920
WILLIAM ADOLPHUS TURNPIKE. Toronto, Dent, 1913. 260p [BM BVaU OTMC

Banwell, Selwyn, 1880—
THE LOYALIST. Toronto, Rous & Mann, 1934. 31p [BVaU NBFU OKQ QMBM

Barbeau, Charles Marius, 1883—1969
THE DOWNFALL OF TEMLAHAM. Toronto, Macmillan, 1928. 253p [BM BVaU
LC NBFU OTMC QMM
THE GOLDEN PHOENIX AND OTHER FRENCH-CANADIAN FAIRY TALES. By Marius
Barbeau, retold by Michael Hornyansky. Toronto, Oxford U. Press, 1958. 144p
THE INDIAN SPEAKS. By Marius Barbeau and Grace Melvin. Toronto, Macmillan,
1943. 117p [BVaU LC NSHD OKQ
MOUNTAIN CLOUD. Toronto, Macmillan, 1944. 300p [BM BVaU LC NSHD
OKQ QMM
THE TREE OF DREAMS. Toronto, Oxford U. Press, 1955. ix + 112p [Legends and
sketches of folk personalities.]

Barnard, Leslie Gordon, 1890—1961
THE IMMORTAL CHILD. A Christmas Letter to an Unknown Friend. Montreal,
Author, 1941. 24p [BVaU NBFU OTMC QMM
JANCIS. Toronto, Macmillan, 1935. 245p [Also: London, Dickson, 1936. 245p]
[BM BVaU NBFU OTU QMM
ONE GENERATION AWAY. Montreal, Dodd-Simpson, 1931. 438p [BVaU LC
NBFU OTMC QMM
SO NEAR IS GRANDEUR. Toronto, Macmillan, 1945. 207p [BVaU NBFU OTMC
QMM

Barrington, Gwenyth, 1901—
WOMEN WITHOUT MONEY. Woman's Private Life with the Dollar. Toronto, Longmans, 1947. 156p [AEP OOP PC

Barry, Lily Emily Frances, 1863?—1955
IN THE PATHS OF PEACE. Montreal, Canada Engraving, 1901. 310p [BM OTMC
QMM

Bartley, E.T.
LILIAN'S RETROSPECT. Toronto, Hunter Rose, 1877. 142p [BVaU OTMC

Barton, J. King
IO. A Tale of the Ancient Fane. By K. Barton. New York, Appleton, 1851. 251p
[BM LC

Batson, Alfred, 1900—
AFRICAN INTRIGUE. New York, Garden City Pub. Co., 1933. 307p [AEP BVa
LC NSHPL

Baubie, William Edward
THE MAN CONDEMNED. Written and illus. by ——. Boston, Stratford, 1936. 350p
[LC QMSS

Baxter, Arthur Beverley, 1891–1964
THE BLOWER OF BUBBLES. London, Chalmers, 1919. 262p [BM BVaU LC
NBFU OTMC QMM
THE PARTS MEN PLAY. New York, Appleton, 1920. 330p [BM BVaU LC NBFU
OTMC QMM

Bayley, Mrs. Diana
EMPLOYMENT THE TRUE SOURCE OF HAPPINESS; or, The Good Uncle and Aunt.
London, Harris, 1825. 147p [BM
IMPROVEMENT; or, A Visit to Grandmama. London, Arnold, 1832. viii + 172p
[Adelphi
SCENES AT HOME AND ABROAD. By Mrs. Henry Bayley. London, Stokes, 1827.
115p [BM
TALES OF THE HEATH. ... London, Harris, 1825. 228p [BM

Beames, John, 1889–
AN ARMY WITHOUT BANNERS. Toronto, McClelland, 1930. 301p [BM BVaU
LC NBFU OTP
DUKE. London, Benn, 1933. 287p [BM OTP
GATEWAY. London, Benn, 1932. 253p [BM NBFU OTP

Beardsley, Charles E.
THE VICTIMS OF TYRANNY. A Tale. Buffalo, 1847. 2v [OONL OTP

Beaton, Maude Pettit (Hill), 1877–
KEEP YOUR QUILT, MARY ANN. New York, Margent Press, 1944. 249p [NBFU
OTMC QMSS
RING IN THE GRASS. New York, Margent Press, 1946. 202p [LC OTU

Beattie, Earle James, 1916–
THE DAY SLIPPERY RAN AWAY. Toronto, McClelland, 1959. 32p

Beattie, Jeann, 1922–
BEHOLD THE HOUR. Toronto, Ryerson, 1959, [c1957]. 309p
BLAZE OF NOON. Toronto, Ryerson, 1950. 353p [BVaU NBFU OTMC

Beattie, Jessie Louise, 1896–
HILL-TOP. A Tale of Ontario Rural Life. Toronto, Macmillan, 1935. 276p [LC
NBFU OTMC
THE SPLIT IN THE SKY. Toronto, Ryerson, 1960. xii + 214p
THREE MEASURES. Toronto, Macmillan, 1938. 295p [NBFU OTMC

Beaugrand, Honoré, 1849–1906

LA CHASSE-GALERIE, AND OTHER CANADIAN STORIES. Montreal, Pelletier, 1900. 101p [BVaU LC OTU

Beavan, John

LITTLE INDIAN CAMEOS. Stories of Canadian Indians. Ilfracombe, Devon, Stockwell, 1942. 208p [BM

Beavon, Eric A., 1898–

SINDIGA THE SAVAGE. A Tale of the Wilds. New York, Harper, 1931. 292p [BM LC

Bech, Birger

FIVE YEARS IN A SAILOR'S LIFE. Toronto, Queen City Pub., 1886. 72p [BVaU OTP

THE UNKNOWN. Toronto, Queen City Pub., 1887. 92p [OTP

Beck, Lily Adams (Moresby), –1931

ANNE BOLEYN. By E. Barrington [pseud]. Garden City, Doubleday, 1932. 396p [BM BVaU LC NBFU OTMC QMM

CAPTAIN JAVA. By Louis Moresby [pseud]. Garden City, Doubleday, 1928. 368p [BM BVaU LC NBFU OTMC

THE CHASTE DIANA. By E. Barrington [pseud]. New York, Dodd Mead, 1923. 325p [BM BVaU LC NBFU OTMC

THE CROWNED LOVERS. The True Romance of Charles the First and his Queen. By E. Barrington [pseud]. London, Cassell, 1935. 191p [BM LC

THE DIVINE LADY. A Romance of Nelson and Emma Hamilton. By E. Barrington [pseud]. New York, Dodd Mead, 1924. 417p [BM BVaU LC NBFU OTMC

DREAM TEA. London, Benn, 1934. 285p [BM LC NBFU OOP

DREAMS AND DELIGHTS. New York, Dodd Mead, 1926. 317p [BM BVaU LC NBFU OTMC

THE DUEL OF THE QUEENS. A Romance of Mary, Queen of Scotland. By E. Barrington [pseud]. Garden City, Doubleday, 1930. 387p [BM BVaU LC NBFU OTMC QMM

THE EMPRESS OF HEARTS. By E. Barrington [pseud]. New York, Dodd Mead, 1928. 300p [BM BVaU LC NBFU OTMC QMM

THE EXQUISITE PERDITA. By E. Barrington [pseud]. New York, Dodd Mead, 1926. 377p [BM BVaU LC NBFU OTMC QMM

THE GALLANTS. By E. Barrington [pseud]. Boston, Atlantic Monthly, 1924. 308p [BM BVaU LC NBFU OTMC QMM

THE GARDEN OF VISION. New York, Cosmopolitan Book, 1929. 421p [BM LC NBFU OTMC QMM

GLORIOUS APOLLO. By E. Barrington [pseud]. New York, Dodd Mead, 1925. 371p [BM BVaU LC NSHD OTMC

THE GLORY OF EGYPT. ... By L. Moresby [pseud]. London, Nelson, 1926. 281p
[BM LC NBFU OTMC

THE GRACES. London, Cassell, 1934. 308p [BM NBFU

THE GREAT ROMANTIC. Being an Interpretation of Mr. Sam. Pepys and Elizabeth
his Wife. By E. Barrington [pseud]. Garden City, Doubleday, 1933. 339p [BM
BVaU LC NBFU OTMC

THE HOUSE OF FULFILMENT. ... New York, Cosmopolitan Book, 1927. 342p
[BM BVaU LC NBFU OTMC

THE IRISH BEAUTIES. By E. Barrington [pseud]. Garden City, Doubleday, 1931.
310p [BM BVaU LC NBFU OTMC QMM

THE JOYOUS STORY OF ASTRID. New York, Cosmopolitan Book, 1931. 283p
[LC NBFU

THE KEY OF DREAMS. New York, Dodd Mead, 1922. 351p [BM BVaU LC
NBFU QMM

"THE LADIES!" A Shining Constellation of Wit and Beauty. By E. Barrington
[pseud]. Boston, Atlantic Monthly, 1922. 286p [BM BVaU LC NBFU
OTMC QMM

THE LAUGHING QUEEN. By E. Barrington [pseud]. New York, Dodd Mead, 1929.
307p [BM BVaU LC NSHD OTMC QMM

THE NINTH VIBRATION, AND OTHER STORIES. New York, Dodd Mead, 1922.
313p [BM BVaU LC NSHD OTMC QMM

THE OPENERS OF THE GATE. Stories of the Occult. New York, Cosmopolitan
Book, 1930. 368p [BVaU LC NBFU OLU QMM

THE PERFUME OF THE RAINBOW, AND OTHER STORIES. New York, Dodd Mead,
1923. 324p [BM BVaU LC NBFU OTMC

RUBIES. By Louis Moresby [pseud]. New York, Doran, 1927. 287p [BM BViP
LC NBFU

THE THUNDERER. A Romance of Napoleon and Josephine. By E. Barrington
[pseud]. New York, Dodd Mead, 1927. 333p [BM BVaU LC NBFU OTMC
QMM

THE TREASURE OF HO. New York, Dodd Mead, 1924. 303p [BM BVaU LC
NSHD QMM

THE WAY OF STARS. A Romance of Reincarnation. New York, Dodd Mead,
1925. 408p [BM BVaU LC NSHD OTMC

THE WOOING OF THE QUEENS. By E. Barrington [pseud]. London, Cassell, 1934.
279p [BM OTMC

Bedford-Jones, Henry James O'Brien, 1887–1949

AGAINST THE TIDE. By John Wycliffe [pseud]. New York, Dodd Mead, 1924.
279p [LC NBFU

THE BLACK BULL. New York, Putnam, 1926. 344p [LC NBFU OTMC

THE BREEZE IN THE MOONLIGHT. The Second Book of Genius. By Hao Ch'iu
Chuan. Translated ... by George Soulié de Morant, and done into English by
H. Bedford-Jones. New York, Putnam, 1926. 371p [BM LC

THE CALIFORNIA TRAIL. New York, Phoenix Press, 1948. 255p [LC
THE CONQUEST. New York, Cook, 1914. 95p [BVaU LC
THE CROSS AND THE HAMMER. A Tale of the Days of the Vikings. Elgin, Ill.,
   Cook, 1912. 95p [LC NSHPL
CYRANO. New York, Putnam, 1930. 344p [LC NBFU OTP
D'ARTAGNAN. The Sequel to *The Three Musketeers*. ... Augmenting and Incorporat-
   ing a Fragmentary Manuscript by Alexander Dumas. New York, Covici Friede,
   1928. 311p [LC NBFU OTMC
D'ARTAGNAN'S LETTER. By M.&H. Bedford-Jones. New York, Covici Friede,
   1931. 244p [LC NBFU
DRUMS OF DAMBALA. New York, Covici Friede, 1932. 295p [BM LC NBFU
   OTMC
FAR HORIZONS. London, Hurst & Blackett, 1925. 287p [BM OTP
FLAMEHAIR THE SKALD. A Tale of the Days of Hardrede. Chicago, McClurg, 1913.
   310p [LC
THE HAZARDS OF SMITH. London, Hurst & Blackett, 1924. 306p [BM OTP
JOHN BARRY. By Donald F. Bedford [jt. pseud. for Donald Friede, Kenneth
   Fearing, and Henry Bedford-Jones]. New York, Creative Age, 1947. 418p
   [BVa LC PC
THE KING'S PARDON. New York, Covici Friede, 1933. 281p [LC NBFU
THE KING'S PASSPORT. New York, Putnam, 1928. 336p [BM LC NBFU OTMC
MALAY GOLD. Toronto, Harlequin Books, 1953. 128p
THE MARDI GRAS MYSTERY. Garden City, Doubleday, 1921. 313p [LC NBFU
THE MESA TRAIL. Garden City, Doubleday, 1920. 244p [BM LC NBFU OTMC
RODOMONT. A Romance of Mont St. Michel in the Days of Louis XIV. New York,
   Putnam, 1926. 335p [BM LC NBFU OTMC
SAINT MICHAEL'S GOLD. New York, Putnam, 1926. 314p [BM LC NBFU
THE SHADOW. New York, Fiction League, 1930. 322p [BM BVaU LC NBFU
   OTMC
THE STAR WOMAN. New York, Dodd Mead, 1924. 293p [BM LC NBFU OTMC
THE TRAIL OF THE SHADOW. London, Hurst & Blackett, 1924. 286p [BM OTP

Begg, Alexander, 1839—1897
"DOT IT DOWN." A Story of Life in the Northwest. Toronto, Hunter Rose, 1871.
   381p [BVaU LC NSHD OTMC QMM
WRECKS IN THE SEA OF LIFE. New York, Lovell, 1884. 348p [LC

Belaney, George Stansfeld, 1888—1938
THE ADVENTURES OF SAJO AND HER BEAVER PEOPLE. By Grey Owl [pseud].
   Toronto, Macmillan, 1935. 256p [*Cf.* also: SAJO AND THE BEAVER PEOPLE. ...
   New York, Scribner, 1936. 187p] [BM BVaU LC NBFU OTMC
BEAVERS. Pages from the Writings of Grey Owl. Edited by E.E. Reynolds.
   Cambridge, University Press, 1940. 127p [BM

THE TREE. By Wa-sha-quon-asin (Grey Owl) [pseud]. Toronto, Macmillan, 1937. 62p [BM NBFU OTMC

Belcher, Edward, 1799–1877
HORATIO HOWARD BRENTON. A Naval Novel. London, Hurst & Blackett, 1856. 3v [BM

Bell, Frederick McKelvey, 1878–1931
A ROMANCE OF THE HALIFAX DISASTER. Halifax, Royal Print., 1918. 76p [NBFU OTU

Bell, Jessie Mary Eleanor (Roberts), 1901–
THE BLACK TOTEM. Toronto, Ryerson, 1960. 180p

Bemister, Margaret, 1877–
INDIAN LEGENDS. Stories of America before Columbus. New York, Macmillan, 1914. 187p [LC
STORIES FROM PRAIRIE AND MOUNTAIN. Toronto, Copp Clark, 1909. 114p [BM
THIRTY INDIAN LEGENDS. Toronto, Macmillan, 1912. 182p [BM OTMC

Bending, Frederick J., 1883–1954
THE SHADOW'S EDGE. Toronto, Hodder, 1922. 288p [BM OOP

Bennett, Ethel Hume (Patterson), 1881–
CAMP CONQUEROR. Boston, Houghton, 1928. 281p [BVa LC
CAMP KEN-JOCKETY. Boston, Houghton, 1923. 311p [BVa LC OTMC
JUDY OF YORK HILL. By Ethel Hume. Boston, Houghton, 1922. 281p [LC
JUDY'S PERFECT YEAR. Boston, Houghton, 1925. 288p [BM BVa LC
A TREASURE SHIP OF OLD QUEBEC. New York, Dodd Mead, 1936. 266p [BM BVaU LC OTMC

Bennett, Ethel Mary (Granger)
LAND FOR THEIR INHERITANCE. Toronto, Ryerson, 1955. 317p
SHORT OF THE GLORY. Toronto, Ryerson, 1960. 333p
A STRAW IN THE WIND. Toronto, Ryerson, 1958. 281p

Beresford-Howe, Constance Elizabeth, 1922–
THE INVISIBLE GATE. New York, Dodd Mead, 1949. 241p [BM LC NBFU
MY LADY GREENSLEEVES. New York, Ballantine Books, 1955. 217p
OF THIS DAY'S JOURNEY. New York, Dodd Mead, 1947. 240p [BM LC NBFU OTMC QMBM
THE UNREASONING HEART. New York, Dodd Mead, 1946. 236p [BM BVaU NBFU OTMC QMBM

Bernhardt, Clara Mae, 1911–
OPEN WINDOWS. Grand Rapids, Mich., Eerdmans Pub. Co., 1947. 167p [LC OTU
SONG OF ZION. Grand Rapids, Mich., Eerdmans Pub. Co., 1944. 185p [LC OTU

Bevans, Mrs. Florence Edith
PERCIVAL PLAIN DOG. By Jemima Remington [pseud]. Toronto, "The Humane Pleader," 1924. 68p [QMSS

Beynon, Frances Marion
ALETA DEY. A Novel. London, Daniel, 1919. 255p [BM OTMC

Beynon, Marie Edith
SAINTS, SINNERS AND QUEER PEOPLE. Novelettes and Short Stories. New York, Weed, 1897. 341p [LC

Bhatia, Jamuna (Huband), 1919—
ALIEN THERE IS NONE. By J. Rana [pseud]. London, Hodder, 1959. 256p

Bice, Clare, 1909—
ACROSS CANADA. Stories of Canadian Children. New York, Macmillan, 1949. 119p [BVaU LC NBFU OTMC
THE GREAT ISLAND. A Story of Mystery In Newfoundland. Toronto, Macmillan, 1954. 103p
JORY'S COVE. A Story of Nova Scotia. New York, Macmillan, 1941. 104p [BVaU LC OLU

Bigman, Sidney, 1919—
SECOND SIGHT. A Novel. New York, McKay Co., 1959. 219p
WITHIN THESE BOUNDARIES. A Novel. London, Secker & Warburg, 1959. 219p

Bigsby, Bernard
"THAT BOWL OF PUNCH!" What It Did, and How It Did It. Six Christmas Stories. ... Toronto, Hunter Rose, 1872. 51p [BVaU OTP

Billett, Mrs. Mabel Broughton, 1892—
CALAMITY HOUSE. A Mystery Novel. London, Hutchinson, 1927. 288p [BM
THE ROBOT DETECTIVE. London, Hutchinson, 1932. 288p [BM LC NBFU OTP
THE SHADOW OF THE STEPPE. London, Hutchinson, 1930. 288p [BM LC OTP
THE SMOOTH SILENCE. Toronto, Ryerson, 1936. [CC

Bilsky, Eva, —1952
TUCK-A-BED TALES. By Aunt Eva [pseud]. Montreal, Mercury, 1945. 38p [OONL
WHAT HAPPENED AFTER? Some Familiar Fairy Tales Continued. By Aunt Eva [pseud]. Montreal, Mercury, 1941. 63p [OONL

Bird, William Richard, 1891—
HERE STAYS GOOD YORKSHIRE. Toronto, Ryerson, 1945. 332p [BVaU LC NBFU OKQ QMM
JUDGMENT GLEN. Toronto, Ryerson, 1947. 315p [BVaU NBFU OTMC
MAID OF THE MARSHES. Amherst, N.S., Author, 1935. 198p [NSHD OTMC QMBM

THE PASSIONATE PILGRIM. Toronto, Ryerson, 1949. 324p [BVaU NBFU OTMC QMM

PRIVATE TIMOTHY FERGUS CLANCY. Ottawa, Graphic, 1930. 325p [BVaU OTU

THE SHY YORKSHIREMAN. A Novel. Toronto, Ryerson, 1955. 253p

SO MUCH TO RECORD. Toronto, Ryerson, 1951. 317p

SUNRISE FOR PETER, AND OTHER STORIES. Toronto, Ryerson, 1946. 224p
 [BVaU LC NSHD OTU

TO LOVE AND TO CHERISH. Toronto, Ryerson, 1953. 309p

TRISTRAM'S SALVATION. A Novel. Toronto, Ryerson, 1957. 254p

Birney, Earle, 1904—

DOWN THE LONG TABLE. Toronto, McClelland, 1955. 298p

THE KOOTENAY HIGHLANDER. London, Landsborough Publications, 1960
 [c1958]. 253p [Same as TURVEY, *q.v.*]

TURVEY. A Military Picaresque. Toronto, McClelland, 1949. 288p [BVaU LC NBFU OKQ QMM

Bishop, Leslie Gurney, 1908—

PAPER KINGDOM. London, Heinemann, 1936. 278p [BM LC

Bjarnason, Bogi

ANDROCLES, JUNIOR. Treherne, Man., The Times, 1930. 26p [CC

CIRCUMSTANTIAL EVIDENCE. N.p., n.d. 48p [MWP

SANS THE GRANDE PASSION. Treherne, Man., The Times, 1935. 122p [MWP

Blachford, Lt. Col.

THE ULTIMATUM. A Short Tale with a Long Moral. London, Ont., 1867. 32p
 [OLU

Black, Edith Ferguson, 1857—

ALLAN RUTHVEN, KNIGHT. London, R.T.S., 1907. 304p [BM

A BEAUTIFUL POSSIBILITY. Philadelphia, Union Press, 1904. 330p [BM LC

A PRINCESS IN CALICO. London, R.T.S., 1903. 140p [BM

Black, Martha Louise (Munger), 1866—1957

A KLONDIKE CHRISTMAS TALE. Whitehorse, Author, n.d. 11p [OTU

Blackburn, Kathleen

THE DAGMAR WHO LOVED. New York, Broadway Pub. Co., 1904. 212p [LC

Blackburn, Victoria Grace, —1928

THE MAN CHILD. By Fan-Fan [pseud]. Ottawa, Graphic, 1930. 274p [BVaU OTMC QMM

Blake, Cameron

ONLY MEN ON BOARD. London, Hodder, 1933. 316p [BM

SET STORMY. London, Hodder, 1931. 314p [BM NBFU

Blanchard, Henry Percy, 1862–
AFTER THE CATACLYSM. A Romance of the Age to Come. New York, Cochrane, 1909. 136p [LC

Blewett, Jean (McKishnie), 1862–1934
HEART STORIES. Toronto, Warwick & Rutter, 1919. 29p [BVaU OLU

Blondal, Patricia (Jenkins), 1927?–1959
A CANDLE TO LIGHT THE SUN. A Novel. Toronto, McClelland, 1960. 316p

Bloomfield, Leonard, 1887–
SACRED STORIES OF THE SWEET GRASS CREE. Ottawa, (Nat. Museum of Canada, Bull. 60), 1930. 346p [In Cree and English.] [BVaU NSHPL OLU QMU

Boag, Mrs. Isabel
CHIMNEYS. London, Heath Cranton, 1934. 291p [BM OTP

Bodsworth, Fred, 1918–
LAST OF THE CURLEWS. New York, Dodd Mead, 1955. 128p
THE STRANGE ONE. New York, Dodd Mead, 1959. 400p

Boggs, Helen
ACORN LEAVES. A Series of Canadian Tales. By Nell Gwynne [pseud]. Toronto, Copp Clark, 1873. 215p [BVaU OTMC QMM
WHEN THE SHADOWS FLEE AWAY. A Story of Canadian Society. By Bernard [pseud]. Montreal, Lovell, 1891. 272p [OTU

Boniface, Father, 1880–
THE UNKNOWN HERO OF VERLEBURG. An Historical Novel. Quebec, Franciscan Missionary Press, 1923. 253p [OONL

Bonner, Margerie
HORSE IN THE SKY. New York, Scribner, 1947. 189p [BVaU LC NBFU OTMC
THE LAST TWIST OF THE KNIFE. New York, Scribner, 1946. 190p [LC
THE SHAPES THAT CREEP. New York, Scribner, 1945. 216p [BVaU LC OTMC

Bonner, Mary Graham, 1890–
RAINBOW AT NIGHT. New York, Furman, 1936. 319p [LC OLU PC

Boothe, Stella, and Carter, Olive I.
MARY GAY STORIES. Toronto, Educational Book Co., 1930. 119p [BM

Borneman, Ernst Wilhelm Julius, 1915–
THE FACE ON THE CUTTING-ROOM FLOOR. By Cameron MacCabe [pseud]. London, Gollancz, 1937. 320p [BM LC
LOVE STORY. London, Jarrolds, 1941. 192p [BM OTMC
TOMORROW IS NOW. The Adventures of Welfare Willy in Search of a Soul. London, Spearman, 1959. 205p
TREMOLO. New York, Harper, 1948. 224p [BM LC NBFU OTU

Borrett, William Coates, 1894–
DOWN EAST. Another Cargo of Tales Told under the Old Town Clock. Halifax,
 Imperial Pub. Co., 1945. 232p [BVaU LC NSHD OTMC
DOWN TO THE SEA AGAIN, WITH TALES TOLD UNDER THE OLD TOWN CLOCK.
 Halifax, Imperial Pub. Co., 1947. 221p [AEU NSWA OONL QQL
EAST COAST PORT, and Other Tales Told under the Old Town Clock. Halifax,
 Imperial Pub. Co., 1944. 237p [BVaU LC NBFU OTMC
HISTORIC HALIFAX. Tales Told under the Old Town Clock. Toronto, Ryerson,
 1948. 234p [BVaU OTU QMM
MORE TALES TOLD UNDER THE OLD TOWN CLOCK. Halifax, Imperial Pub. Co.,
 1943. 233p [BVaU LC OTU QMM
TALES RETOLD UNDER THE OLD TOWN CLOCK. Toronto, Reryson, 1957.
 xii + 212p
TALES TOLD UNDER THE OLD TOWN CLOCK. Halifax, Imperial Pub. Co., 1942.
 196p [BVaU LC NBFU OTMC QMM

Bossin, Hye
A TATTLER'S TALES OF TORONTO. Toronto, Handy Library, 1940. 64p [OTU

Boswell, R.
MERCY'S HERO. London, Stockwell, 1933. 79p [BM OTP

Bottomley, Kate Madeline (Barry), 1865–
THE DOCTOR'S DAUGHTER. By "Vera" [pseud]. Ottawa, Woodburn, 1885. 242p
 [NBFU assigns this book to WALTER, William Wilfred (Vera, pseud), 1869–]
 [NBFU OTMC
HONOR EDGEWORTH; or, Ottawa's Present Tense. By "Vera" [pseud]. Ottawa,
 Woodburn, 1882. 337p [BVaU NSHD OTMC

Bourinot, John George, 1837–1902
SEA, FOREST, AND PRAIRIE. ... Montreal, 1893. 323p [RES

Boyle, David, 1842–1911
THE UPS AND DOWNS OF NO. 7 REXVILLE. Being a Full, True and Correct Account
 of what Happened in the said School Section during a period of Twelve Months.
 ... By an Old Maid. N.p., n.d. 106p [BVaU OTP

Boyle, Joyce, 1901–
MUSKOKA HOLIDAY. Toronto, Macmillan, 1953. 216p
THE STONE COTTAGE MYSTERY. Toronto, Macmillan, 1958. 151p

Brandon, Captain (?Roy Victor?)
A RIVER OF GOLD. Tales of the Rocky Mountains. By Captain Brandon. Plymouth,
 W. Brendon, 1927. 155p [BM BVaU OTP

Bridle, Augustus, 1869–1952
HANSEN. A Novel of Canadianization. Toronto, Macmillan, 1924. 368p [BM
 BVaU NSHD OTMC QMM

Brillant, J. Maurice
VISION OF MURDER. New York, Comet Press, 1954. 136p

Brockie, William (pseud)
TALES OF THE MOUNTED. By William Brockie [pseud]. Toronto, Ryerson, 1949. 182p [OTU

Brodie, Alfred E.
THE FRONT MAN. Toronto, Maclean, 1935. 154p [NBFU OTMC QMM

Brodie, Ethel Mary
THE ROSE-COLORED WORLD, AND OTHER FANTASIES. New York, Metropolitan Press, 1910. 279p [LC

Brooke, Frances (Moore), 1724–1789
THE EXCURSION. London, Cadell, 1777. 2v [BM OTU
THE HISTORY OF EMILY MONTAGUE. By the Author of "Lady Julia Mandeville." London, Dodsley, 1769. 4v [Several later editions. Canadian ed.: With intro. and notes by Lawrence J. Burpee, and appendix by F.P. Grove. Ottawa, Graphic, 1931. 333p] [BM BVaU NSHD OKQ QMM
THE HISTORY OF LADY JULIA MANDEVILLE. By the translator of "Lady Catesby's Letters" [pseud]. 7th ed. ... London, Dodsley, 1782. 2v [First pub. 1763.] [BM BVaU OKQ QMM

Brooker, Bertram, 1888–1955
THE ROBBER. A Tale of the Time of the Herods. New York, Duell Sloan, 1949. 307p [BVaU LC NBFU OTMC
THE TANGLED MIRACLE. A Mortimer Hood Mystery. By Huxley Herne [pseud]. Toronto, Nelson, 1936. 300p [BM
THINK OF THE EARTH. Toronto, Nelson, 1936. 288p [BM BVaU LC NBFU OTU

Brooks, Mrs. Annie Elston
THE HEIRESS OF MYRTLE GROVE. An English Tale. By a Montreal Lady, A.E.B. [pseud]. Montreal, Lovell, 1870. 200p [BVaU NBFU OTU

Brown, Mrs. Ellen V., 1900–
SEDGEWICK MANOR. New York, Pageant Press, 1951. 200p

Brown, Margaret Adeline (Porter), 1867–
MY LADY OF THE SNOWS. Toronto, Briggs, 1908. 518p [BM BVaU NSHD OTMC

Brown, W.H.
SHE MIGHT HAVE DONE BETTER. A Novel. St. Johns, Que., The News, 1877. 2v [BVaU OKQ

Brown, William McEvery, —1935
THE QUEEN'S BUSH. A Tale of the Early Days of Bruce County. London, Bale &
  Danielsson, 1932. 295p [BM BVaU NBFU OTP

Browne, Marion, 1912—
GREATER LOVE. Ilfracombe, Devon, Stockwell, 1957. 416p

Bruce, Charles Tory, 1906—1971
THE CHANNEL SHORE. Toronto, Macmillan, 1954. 398p
THE TOWNSHIP OF TIME. A Chronicle. Toronto, Macmillan, 1959. 234p

Bruce, Eva
CALL HER ROSIE. New York, Ives Washburn, 1942. 300p [BM BVaU OTMC

Bruce, Muriel
MUKARA. A Novel. New York, Henkle, 1930. 278p [LC NBFU OTMC

Brundle, John, 1882—
THE FORSAKEN PLOT IN THE LITTLE CHURCHYARD. From the Pen of John, A
  Suffolk Herd Boy. Roche's Point, Ont., Author, 1950. 32p [OONL

Buchan, John Stuart, 1852—
A BIT OF ATLANTIS. By Douglas Erskine [pseud]. Montreal, Chapman, 1900.
  197p [BM BVaU OTMC QMBM

Buckler, Ernest, 1908—
THE MOUNTAIN AND THE VALLEY. New York, Holt, 1952. 373p

Buell, John Edward, 1927—
THE PYX. A Novel. New York, Farrar Straus, 1959. 174p

Burch, E.T.
"SO, I SAID TO THE COLONEL." Toronto, Ryerson, 1941. 72p [AEP OTMC
  ·OTUV

Burkholder, Mabel Grace (Clare), 1881—
BEFORE THE WHITE MAN CAME. Indian Legends and Stories. Toronto, McClelland,
  1923. 318p [BM BVaU NBFU OTMC QMM
THE COURSE OF IMPATIENCE CARNINGHAM. Toronto, Musson, 1911. 327p [AEU
  LC NBFU OTMC
THE SHIELD OF HONOR. Elgin, Ill., Cook, 1929. 76p [LC

Burnham, John Hampden, 1860—1940
ADELINE GRAY. A Tale. New York, Wynkoop & Hollenbeck, 1894. 155p [LC
JACK RALSTON; or, The Outbreak of the Nauscopees. A Tale of Life in the Far
  North-East of Canada. Edinburgh, Nelson, 1901. 448p [BM BVaU OTMC
MARCELLE. An Historical Novel. Toronto, Briggs, 1905. 409p [BM BVaU
  OTMC

Burton, Alice Elizabeth, 1908—

CLING TO HER, WAITING. London, Dakers, 1939. 269p [BM LC

FORTNIGHT IN FRASCATI. By Susan Alice Kerby [pseud]. London, Dakers, 1940. 285p [BM LC

FORTUNE'S GIFT. By Susan Kerby [pseud]. New York, Dodd Mead, 1947. 372p [Same as MANY STRANGE BIRDS, *q.v.*] [BVaU QMM

GONE TO GRASS. By Susan Alice Kerby [pseud]. London, Hutchinson, 1948. 224p [BM

MISS CARTER AND THE IFRIT. By Susan Alice Kerby [pseud]. London, Hutchinson, 1945. 160p [BM LC

MR. KRONION. A Novel. By Susan Alice Kerby [pseud]. London, Laurie, 1949. 223p [BM OLU QMM

MANY STANGE BIRDS. By Susan Alice Kerby [pseud]. London, Hutchinson, 1947. 223p [Same as FORTUNE'S GIFT, *q.v.*] [BM QMM

THE ROARING DOVE. By Susan Kerby [pseud]. New York, Dodd Mead, 1948. 260p [BVaU LC QMM

Buschlen, John Preston, 1888—

BEHIND THE WICKET. Short Stories Relating to Life in the Canadian Banks. Toronto, Briggs, 1914. 264p [BM BVaU NBFU OTMC

A CANADIAN BANKCLERK. Toronto, Briggs, 1913. 366p [BM BVaU NBFU OTMC

CURTAIN OF LIFE. By Jack Preston [pseud] and Jesse Lasky, Jr. New York, Macaulay, 1934. 244p [LC

THE DRUMMER. Toronto, Ansell Pub. Co., 1915. 330p [BM BVaU LC NBFU OTMC

FINDING HIS BALANCE; or, The Bank Clerk Who Came Back. By Jack Preston [pseud]. Toronto, Stevenson & Hevey, 1915. 366p [OTMC QMM

HEIL! HOLLYWOOD. By Jack Preston [pseud]. Chicago, Reilly & Lee, 1939. 344p [BVaU LC

NOT ASHAMED. A Romance of the Tropics. By Jack Preston [pseud]. New York, Sears, 1934. 319p [BM LC

PETER BOSTEN. A Story about Realities. By John Preston [pseud]. Lamoni, Ia., Herald, 1915. 352p [LC

SCREEN STAR. By Jack Preston [pseud]. Garden City, Doubleday, 1932. 308p [BM LC

Butcher, Margaret

COMET'S HAIR. London, Skeffington, 1939. 256p [BM

DESTINY ON DEMAND. London, Skeffington, 1938. 288p [BM

HOGDOWN FARM MYSTERY. London, Skeffington, 1950. 221p [BM OTMC

VACANT POSSESION. A Novel. London, Skeffington, 1940. 256p [BM OTMC

Butler, Suzanne, 1919—

MY PRIDE, MY FOLLY. Boston, Little Brown, 1953. 311p

PORTRAIT OF PETER WEST. Boston, Little Brown, 1958. 291p
VALE OF TYRANNY. Boston, Little Brown, 1954. 266p

Butler, William Francis, 1838—1910
RED CLOUD. A Tale of the Great Prairie. ... London, Low & Marston, 1882. 327p
[Also new ed.: Toronto, Musson, 1927. 332p] [BM BVaU LC NBFU OTMC
QMM

Byerly, Alpheus Edward, 1894—1960
JANET CAMPBELL. A Tale of Upper Canada. Guelph, Guelph Pub. Co., 1935. 21p
[BVaU OTU

Byers, Donald A., 1925—
FOREVER GREEN. New Toronto, Goodyear Tire, 1957. 19p

C., W.A.
MICK TRACY, THE IRISH SCRIPTURE READER; or, The Martyred Convert and the
Priest. A Tale of Facts. By W.A.C. [pseud]. London, Frome, 1863. [Other eds.:
London, Book Society, 1862. 355p; Philadelphia, 1867; and London, Partridge,
1870.] [BM EngCat OTMC
TIM DOOLAN, THE IRISH EMIGRANT. Being a Full and Particular Account of his
Reasons for Emigrating—his Passage across the Atlantic—his Arrival in New York—
his Brief Sojourn in the United States, and his Further Emigration to Canada. By
the Author of MICK TRACY [pseud]. London, Partridge, [1869]. 362p [At
the end of prefatory note author locates himself in "Canada West."] [Another
ed.: London, Partridge, 1879.] [BVaU EngCat OTMC

Caden, José-Jean-Marie-Désiré, 1910—
A MOTHER CHEATS ALTARS. A Novel. New York, Greenwich Book Publishers,
1959. 168p

Cahill, James
THE BLACK PIRATE. London, Lutterworth, 1946. 128p [BM
FLYING WITH THE MOUNTIES. London, Black, 1937. 248p [BM BVaU NBFU
OTMC
M'BONGA'S TREK. London, Lutterworth, 1947. 127p [BM OHM
THE PILOT OF INDIAN LEAP. London, Oxford U. Press, 1939. 288p [BM NBFU

Callaghan, Morley Edward, 1903—
A BROKEN JOURNEY. New York, Scribner, 1932. 270p [BVaU LC NBFU
OTMC QMM
IT'S NEVER OVER. New York, Scribner, 1930. 225p [BVaU LC NBFU OTMC
QMM
THE LOVED AND THE LOST. A Novel. Toronto, Macmillan, 1951. 234p
LUKE BALDWIN'S VOW. Philadelphia, Winston, [1948]. 187p [BM BVaU LC
NBFU OTU QMM

THE MANY COLOURED COAT. Toronto, Macmillan, 1960. 318p

MORE JOY IN HEAVEN. New York, Random House, 1937. 278p [Also, with intro. by Hugo McPherson: Toronto, McClelland, 1960. x + 159p] [BVaU LC NBFU OTMC

A NATIVE ARGOSY. New York, Scribner, 1929. 371p [BM BVaU LC NBFU OTMC QMM

NO MAN'S MEAT. Paris [France], E.W. Titus, 1931. 42p [AEU OLU OTU

NOW THAT APRIL'S HERE, AND OTHER STORIES. New York, Random House, 1936. 316p [BVaU LC NBFU OTMC QMM

STORIES. Toronto, Macmillan, 1959. xi + 364p

STRANGE FUGITIVE. New York, Scribner, 1928. 264p [BM BVaU LC NBFU OTMC QMM

SUCH IS MY BELOVED. New York, Scribner, 1934. 288p [Also, with intro. by Malcolm Ross: Toronto, McClelland, 1957. xiii + 144p] [BM BVaU LC NBFU OTU QMM

THEY SHALL INHERIT THE EARTH. Toronto, Macmillan, 1935. 337p [BM BVaU LC NBFU OTMC QMM

THE VARSITY STORY. Toronto, Macmillan, 1948. 172p [BVaU NBFU OTMC QMM

Cameron, Rev. Charles J.

SEA, FOREST, AND PRAIRIE. Being Stories of Life and Adventure in Canada Past and Present. By Boys and Girls in Canada's Schools. [Ed. by ——.] Montreal, Dougall, 1893. 323p [OTMC QMSS

Cameron, Daniel George, 1856–

TWIGS FROM THE OAK, AND OTHER TREES. Regina, Commercial Print., 1933. 283p [BVaU OTMC

Cameron, Edward Robert, 1857–1931

MEMOIRS OF RALPH VANSITTART, A MEMBER OF THE PARLIAMENT OF CANADA, 1861–1867. Toronto, Musson, 1902. 229p [Another ed.: Toronto, Musson, 1924.] [BM BVaU LC NSWA OTMC

Cameron, John Alexander Hugh, 1878–

A COLONEL FROM WYOMING. New York, Christian Press, 1907. 364p [BM BVaU LC OOP

THE WOMAN HATER. New York, Christian Press, 1912. 297p [BM BVaU LC OTMC

Campbell, Arthur

THE COMBAT. A Tragedy of the Countryside. London, Long, 1908. 388p [BM OOP

THE MYSTERY OF MARTHA WARNE. A Tale of Montreal. Montreal, Robinson, 1888. 151p [OOP

A RIDE IN MOROCCO, AND OTHER SKETCHES. Toronto, Briggs, 1897. 305p [BM
LC NSHD

Campbell, Austin, 1884–
THE ROCK OF BABYLON. Ottawa, Graphic, 1931. 354p [BVaU NBFU OTMC
QMM

Campbell, Basil Berridge, 1889–
TONY. A Truly, Truly Story, or Something of that Sort. Toronto, Ryerson, 1934.
113p [OKQ

Campbell, Mrs. Dorothy de Brissac
THE BRAVE LITTLE PEOPLE. Toronto, Ryerson, 1933. 141p [OTMC

Campbell, Grace MacLennan (Grant), 1895–1963
FRESH WIND BLOWING. Toronto, Collins, 1947. 233p [BVaU LC NBFU OTMC
QMM
THE HIGHER HILL. Toronto, Collins, 1944. 319p [BVaU LC NBFU OTMC
QMM
THORN-APPLE TREE. Toronto, Collins, 1942. 230p [BVaU LC NBFU OTMC
QMM
TORBEG. Toronto, Collins, 1953. 311p
THE TOWER AND THE TOWN. Toronto, Collins, 1950. 342p [BVaU LC NBFU
OTMC

Campbell, Mrs. Isabella, 1830–1887
THE INNER LIFE. By Mrs. Campbell. Quebec, Hunter Rose, 1862. 32p [QMSS

Campbell, Rev. John, 1840–1904
TWO KNAPSACKS. A Novel of Canadian Summer Life. By J. Cawdor Bell [pseud].
Toronto, Williamson, [1892]. 419p [BVaU OKQ

Campbell, Margaret Elizabeth (Baird), 1912–
DEATH AND LILACS. By Fred Bayard [pseud–i.e., Margaret Elizabeth Campbell
and Johanna Frederika Jansen]. New York, Phoenix, [1948]. 256p [BM LC

Campbell, Mrs. Mary Helen
SUNDAYS IN YOHO. Twelve Stories for Children and their Friends. Ed. by ——.
Montreal, Drysdale, 1884. 272p [OTU

Campbell, Wilfred, 1858–1918
A BEAUTIFUL REBEL. A Romance of Upper Canada in Eighteen Hundred and
Twelve. Toronto, Westminster, 1909. 317p [BM BVaU LC OTMC
IAN OF THE ORCADES; or, The Armourer of Girnigoe. London, Oliphant, 1906.
320p [BM BVaU LC NBFU OTMC

Canadian Great War Veteran (pseud)
THE PRINCE. A Canadian Great War Veteran's Stories, chiefly concerning his

Alberta Range Horse, as related to his Grandson, Christmas Day, 1950. Edmonton, Imperial Pub., 1950. 63p [ACG

Canadian Magazine, Toronto

SELECTED SHORT STORIES. A Collection of Notable Short Stories by Canadian Writers First Published in the *Canadian Magazine*. Toronto, MacLean, 1936. 246p [Another collection pub. under same title, 1937. Also 246p] [BVaU NBFU OTP QMBM

SEVEN SEA STORIES. From the *Canadian Magazine*. Toronto, Excelsior Pub. Co., 1935. 127p [OTMC

STORIES IN MANY MOODS. A Collection of Notable Short Stories by Canadian Writers First Published in the *Canadian Magazine*. Toronto, MacLean, 1935. 126p [BVaU NBFU OTU

Carey, Douglas

THE RAVEN'S FEATHERS. Ottawa, Graphic, 1930. 322p [NBFU OTP QMM

THE SCORPION. A Limehouse Mystery. Ottawa, Graphic, 1931. 312p [BVaU NBFU OTMC

Carleton, Veros (pseud)

THE HOUSE OF TEMPTATION. Ottawa, Graphic, 1931. 354p [BVaU NBFU OTMC

Carman, Albert Richardson, 1865–1939

THE PENSIONNAIRES. The Story of an American Girl who took a Voice to Europe and Found—Many Things. Boston, Turner, 1903. 314p [BM BVaU LC OTMC

THE PREPARATION OF RYERSON EMBURY. A Purpose. London, Unwin, 1900. 248p [BM BVaU OTMC

Carmichael, Alfred

INDIAN LEGENDS OF VANCOUVER ISLAND. Text by ——. Toronto, Musson, 1922. 97p [BM BVaU LC NSWA OTMC QMM

Caron, Maurice B.

THE CURE OF ST. MICHAEL. London, Hodder, 1925. 284p [BM QMM

Carr, Amy

THE SWINGING PENDULUM. Ottawa, Ru-Mi-Lou Books, 1928. 188p [BVaU OLU

Carr, Kate

CUPID AND THE CANDIDATE. Toronto, Briggs, 1906. 243p [BM

Carroll, Rev. John, 1809–1884

THE SCHOOL OF THE PROPHETS; or, Father McRorey's Class and Squire Firstman's Kitchen Fire. A Fiction founded on Facts. First Series. Toronto, Burrage & Magurn, 1876. 264p ["Second Series," apparently also in 1876; 264p] [BVaU LC NBFU OTMC QMM

Carruthers, Janet Anne, 1890–1957
THE FOREST IS MY KINGDOM. London, Oxford U. Press, 1952. 231p

Carter, Dyson, 1910–
FATHERLESS SONS. A Novel. Toronto, Progress Books, 1955. 480p
NIGHT OF FLAME. Toronto, McLeod, 1942. 337p [Reprinted, under
   pseudonym of Warren Desmond: New York, New Am. Library, 1949. 192p]
   [BM LC NBFU OTMC
TOMORROW IS WITH US. A Novel. Toronto, Progress Books, [1950]. 235p
   [BVaU

Casey, Roy S.
THE HAPPY FAMILY. Vancouver, Wrigley, n.d. 269p [BVaU OTMC

Caswell, H.S.
STORIES AND SKETCHES. Montreal, Lovell, 1872. 179p [BVaU QMSS

Catley, Harry
GATE AND GAITERS. A Book of Naval Humour and Anecdotes. By Chief Petty
   Officer Harry Catley, Gunner's Mate. Toronto, Author, 1949. 322p [OTP

Cautley, Helen
THE PUSSIOS AND THE PURR. New York, Carrier, 1929. 80p [CBI

Chalmers, Audrey (McEvers), 1899–
HIGH SMOKE. New York, Viking Press, 1950. 224p [OONL

Chambers, Mrs. Ada Pierce
IN AN ANATOLIAN VALLEY. Toronto, Ryerson, 1955. 251p

Chapin, Gardner B.
TALES OF THE ST. LAWRENCE. Montreal, Lovell, 1873. 382p [BVaU OTU

Chapman, Ethel M.
GOD'S GREEN COUNTRY. A Novel of Canadian Rural Life. Toronto, Ryerson,
   1922. 287p [BM NBFU OTMC
THE HOMESTEADERS. Toronto, Ryerson, 1936. 252p [BM NBFU OTMC
WITH FLAME OF FREEDOM. Toronto, Allen, 1938. 243p [BVaU NBFU
   OTMC

Charach, Paul
POWER OF A WOMAN. Winnipeg, Author, 1949. 104p [OTP

Charlton, Margaret Ridley, 1858–1931
IN THE DAYS OF SIR WALTER RALEIGH. Montreal, 1900. [BCF
WITH PRINTLESS FOOT. By Margaret Ridley Charlton and C.A. Frazer. Montreal,
   Sabiston, 1894. 82p [NSWA OLU
A WONDER WEB OF STORIES. By Margaret Ridley Charlton and C.A. Frazer.
   Montreal, Grafton & Sons, 1892. 187p [OTMC

Cheetham, William
LIGHTS AND SHADOWS OF CLERICAL LIFE.   Montreal, Lovell, 1879.   310p
   [BVaU OTU

Cheney, Harriet Vaughan (Foster), 1815–
A PEEP AT THE PILGRIMS IN SIXTEEN HUNDRED THIRTY SIX. A Tale of Olden
   Times. By the Author of Divers Unfinished Manuscripts, &c. [pseud].
   Boston, Wells & Lilly, 1824. 2v [Another ed.: Boston, Phillips Sampson,
   1850. 463p] [BM LC
THE RIVALS OF ACADIA. An Old Story of the New World. [Anon] Boston,
   Wells & Lilly, 1827. 271p [LC

Chetwynd, Ralph, 1899–1957
HEIFER DUST INN. By R. Chetwynd and N. Burris. Lillooet, B.C., Lillooet
   Pub., 1941. 99p [OTU

Child, Philip, 1898–
BLOW WIND–COME WRACK. London, Jarrolds, 1945. 192p [Announced as
   by John Wentworth (pseud).] [BM CBI
DAY OF WRATH. Toronto, Ryerson, 1945. 274p [BVaU LC NSHD OKQ
GOD'S SPARROWS. London, Butterworth, 1937. 319p [BM LC NBFU OTU
MR. AMES AGAINST TIME. Toronto, Ryerson, 1949. 244p [BVaU LC NSHD
   OTU
THE VILLAGE OF SOULS. London, Butterworth, 1933. 315p [New ed.:
   Toronto, Ryerson, 1948. 294p] [BM BVaU LC NSHD OTU

Chisholm, Arthur Murray, 1872–1960
BLACK POWDER DAN. London, Hodder, 1925. 319p [BM OTMC
THE BOSS OF WIND RIVER. Garden City, Doubleday, 1911. 340p [LC NBFU
   OTMC
THE LAND OF BIG RIVERS. A Story of the Northwest. New York, Chelsea
   House, 1924. 305p [BM BVaU LC NBFU OTMC
THE LAND OF STRONG MEN. New York, Fly, 1919. 432p [LC NBFU OTMC
PRECIOUS WATERS. Garden City, Doubleday, 1913. 422p [BM LC NBFU OTU
PROSPECTIN' FOOLS. London, Hodder, 1927. 320p [BM NBFU OTU
RED. London, Hodder, 1927. 320p [BM
RED BILL. New York, Burt, 1929. 308p [BVaU NBFU OTMC
THE RED-HEADED KIDS. An Adventure Story. New York, Chelsea House,
   1925. 320p [BVaU LC NBFU OTMC
THE RED HEADS. London, Hodder, 1926. 312p [BM
WHEN STUART CAME TO SITKUM. A Western Story. New York, Chelsea House,
   1924. 320p [LC NBFU OTMC
YELLOW HORSE. A Western Story. London, Hodder, 1926. 311p [BM LC
   NBFU OTMC

Choquet, Joseph P.
UNDER CANADIAN SKIES. A French-Canadian Historical Romance. Providence, R.I., Oxford Press, 1922. 311p [BVaU NBFU OTU

Christie, Annie Rothwell (Fowler), 1837–1927
LOVED I NOT HONOUR MORE. By Annie Rothwell [pseud]. Toronto, Hunter Rose, 1887. 150p [OOP

Christie, Robert Cleland Hamilton, 1917–
INHERIT THE NIGHT. New York, Farrar, 1949. 409p [BM BVaU OOP
THE TREMBLING LAND. Garden City, N.Y., Doubleday, 1959. 288p

Chute, Arthur Hunt, 1890–1929
THE CRESTED SEAS. New York, Sears, 1928. 258p [BM LC NBFU
FAR GOLD. New York, Sears, 1927. 307p [BM BVaU LC NBFU OTMC
THE MUTINY OF THE FLYING SPRAY. New York, Sears, 1927. 308p [BM BVaU LC NBFU OTMC QMM

Clark, Catherine Anthony (Smith), 1892–
THE GOLDEN PINE CONE. Toronto, Macmillan, 1950. 181p [NBFU OTMC
THE ONE-WINGED DRAGON. Toronto, Macmillan, 1955. 271p
THE SILVER MAN. Toronto, Macmillan, 1958. 231p
THE SUN HORSE. Toronto, Macmillan, 1951. 209p

Clark, Daniel, 1835–1912
JOSIAH GARTH. A Novel Dealing with the Rebellion of 1837. Toronto, n.d. [DCB MOR'12
PEN PHOTOGRAPHS OF CELEBRATED MEN AND NOTED PLACES ... GHOSTS AND THEIR RELATIONS. Tales, Sketches, Essays, etc. Toronto, Flint Morton, 1873. 321p [BVaU OTMC QMSS

Clarke, George Frederick, 1883–
THE ADVENTURES OF JIMMY-WHY. Fredericton, Brunswick Press, 1954. 91p
THE BEST ONE THING. London, Mills & Boon, 1926. 255p [BM LC NBFU OTP
CHRIS IN CANADA. London, Blackie, 1925. 224p [BVaU NBFU OTMC
DAVID CAMERON'S ADVENTURES. ... London, Blackie, [1950]. 237p [BM NBFU OONL
THE MAGIC ROAD. London, Mills & Boon, 1925. 272p [BM LC NBFU OKQ
NOEL AND JIMMY-WHY. Fredericton, Brunswick Press, 1959. 97p
RETURN TO ACADIA. An Historical Romance of the Eighteenth Century in What was Later to be New Brunswick. Fredericton, Brunswick Press, 1952. 251p
THETIS SAXON. Toronto, Longmans, 1927. 286p [BM BVaU NBFU OTP QMM

Clay, Charles, 1906—

FUR TRADE APPRENTICE. London, Oxford U. Press, 1940. 360p [LC OTMC

MUSKRAT MAN. Toronto, Ryerson, 1946. 283p [BVaU LC NBFU MW
OTMC QMM

PHANTOM FUR THIEVES. Toronto, Ryerson, 1944. 248p [BVaU OTMC QMM

SWAMPY CREE LEGENDS. Being Twenty Folk Tales from the Annals of a
Primitive, Mysterious, Fast-disappearing Canadian Race. As told to Charles
Clay—by Kuskapatchees, the Smokey One. Toronto, Macmillan, 1938.
95p [BM BVaU LC OTU QMM SSU

A TRULY REMARKABLE EXPERIENCE. N.p., 1936. 4p [OTU

YOUNG VOYAGEUR. London, Oxford U. Press, 1938. 409p [BVaU NBFU
OLU

Claxton, Lilian

IN HIGH SECURITY AND OTHER STORIES. Kingston, Daily News Office, n.d.
68p [OTMC

Clayton, Rev. F.H.

SCENES AND INCIDENTS IN IRISH LIFE. By an Irishman [pseud]. Montreal, Lovell,
1884. 340p [BVaU QMBM

Cleaver, Solomon, 1855—1939

JEAN VAL JEAN. As told by ——. Toronto, Clarke Irwin, 1935. 119p [OTMC

Clemo, Ebenezer, 1831?—1860

CANADIAN HOMES; or, The Mystery Solved. A Christmas Tale. By Maple Knot
[pseud]. Montreal, Lovell, 1858. 136p [OTMC QMM

THE LIFE AND ADVENTURES OF SIMON SEEK; or, Canada in all Shapes. By
Maple Knot [pseud]. Montreal, Lovell, 1858. 179p [OTP

Clint, Mabel Brown, 1874—1939

UNDER THE KING'S BASTION. A Romance of Quebec. By Harold Saxon
[pseud]. Quebec, Carrel, [1902?]. 217p [NSHD OTMC QMSS

Clout, John Allbuary, 1894—

A CARAVAN TO CAMUL. By John Clou [pseud]. Indianapolis, Bobbs-Merrill,
1954. 383p [Also pub. as: THE GOLDEN BLADE. Abridged ed. Toronto,
Graphic Books, 1955. 317p]

Coates, Carol

SHANLING; or, The Tale of the Celestial Tea-Pot. A Christmas Fantasy. Oakville,
Ont., Barber, 1944. 13p [BM OKQ

Coates, Taylor, 1903—

DYSMAS THE THIEF. New York, Vantage Press, 1959. 292p

Cobb, Humphrey, 1899–

PATHS OF GLORY. New York, Viking, 1935. 266p [BM BVaU LC NBFU OTU QMM

Coburn, Kathleen Hazel, 1905–

THE GRANDMOTHERS. ... Toronto, Oxford U. Press, 1949. 233p [BM BVaU LC NBFU OTMC

Cockburn, Russell R.

MALLY. Story of a Dog. Toronto, Macmillan, 1939. 248p [BM BVaU NBFU OTU

Cody, Hiram Alfred, 1872–1948

THE CHIEF OF THE RANGES. A Tale of the Yukon. Toronto, Briggs, 1913. 303p [BM BVaU LC NBFU OTMC

THE CRIMSON SIGN. Toronto, McClelland, 1935. 306p [NBFU OTMC

THE FIGHTING-SLOGAN. Toronto, McClelland, 1926. 285p [BM BVaU LC NBFU OTMC

FIGHTING STARS. Toronto, McClelland, 1927. 272p [BM BVaU LC NSHD OTMC

THE FOURTH WATCH. Toronto, Briggs, 1911. 313p [BM BVaU LC NBFU OTMC

THE FRONTIERSMAN. A Tale of the Yukon. Toronto, Briggs, 1910. 342p [BM BVaU LC NBFU OTMC

THE GIRL AT BULLET LAKE. Toronto, McClelland, 1933. 304p [BVaU NBFU OTMC

GLEN OF THE HIGH NORTH. Toronto, McClelland, 1920. 288p [BM BVaU LC NBFU OTMC QMM

IF ANY MAN SIN. Toronto, Briggs, 1915. 309p [BM BVaU LC NBFU OTMC

JESS OF THE REBEL TRAIL. Toronto, McClelland, 1921. 277p [BM BVaU LC NBFU OTMC

THE KING'S ARROW. A Tale of the United Empire Loyalists. Toronto, McClelland, 1922. 280p [BM BVaU LC NBFU OTMC

THE LONG PATROL. A Tale of the Mounted Police. Toronto, Briggs, 1912. 310p [BM BVaU LC NBFU OTMC QMBM

THE MASTER REVENGE. Toronto, McClelland, 1924. 298p [BM BVaU LC NBFU OTMC

THE RED RANGER. Toronto, McClelland, 1931. 293p [BVaU NBFU OTMC

THE RIVER FURY. Toronto, McClelland, 1930. 305p [BVaU NBFU OTMC

ROD OF THE LONE PATROL. Toronto, McClelland, 1916. 348p [BVaU LC NBFU OTMC

STORM KING BANNER. Toronto, McClelland, 1937. 304p [BVaU NBFU OTMC

THE STUMBLING SHEPHERD. Toronto, McClelland, 1929. 301p [BVaU NBFU OTMC

THE TOUCH OF ABNER. Toronto, McClelland, 1919. 310p [BVa LC NSHD OTMC

THE TRAIL OF THE GOLDEN HORN. Toronto, McClelland, 1923. 296p [BM BVaU LC NBFU OTMC

UNDER SEALED ORDERS. Toronto, McClelland, 1917. 318p [BVaU LC NBFU OTMC

THE UNKNOWN WRESTLER. Toronto, McClelland, 1918. 308p [BM BVaU LC NBFU OTMC

Coleman, Helena Jane, 1860–1953

SHEILA AND OTHERS. The Simple Annals of an Unromantic Household. By Winifred Cotter [pseud]. Toronto, Dent, 1921. [Also: New York, Dutton, 1920. 196p] [CC LC

Colfer, Rebecca B.

STRAY LEAVES FROM THE DRAMA OF EVERYDAY LIFE. ... By "R" [pseud]. Montreal, Lovell, 1878. 193p [BVaU NBFU OTMC QMSS

Collins, Joseph Edmund, 1855–1892

ANNETTE THE METIS SPY; A HEROINE OF THE N.W. REBELLION. [Nancy, the Lightkeeper's Daughter]. Toronto, Rose, 1886. 155p [NSHPL OTP QMG SSU

THE FOUR CANADIAN HIGHWAYMEN; or, The Robbers of Markham Swamp. Toronto, Rose, 1886. 158p [OTU

THE STORY OF A GREENLAND GIRL. Toronto, 1884. [BCF NBB

THE STORY OF LOUIS RIEL, THE REBEL CHIEF. Toronto, Rose, 1885. 176p [Also: Toronto, Robertson, [1885]. 192p] [BVaU NBFU OLU SSU

Collins, Ruth M.

HORACE, THE HOUND THAT HOWLED. New York, Dodd Mead, 1951. 64p

Colman, Louis

LUMBER. Boston, Little Brown, 1931. 296p [BM LC OTP

Colter, Mrs. Hattie E.

A GENTLE BENEFACTRESS. By Mrs. J.J. Colter. Boston, Lothrop, 1892. 329p [BM LC

HAROLD BOWDOIN'S INVESTMENT. London, Stockwell, 1904. 171p [BM NBS

IN THE HEART OF THE HILLS; or, The Little Preacher of the Pacific Slope. Edinburgh, Oliphant, 1898. 203p [BM

THE MASTER OF DEEPLAWN. Philadelphia, Am. Baptist Pub. Soc., 1895. 352p [LC NBS

MEDOLINE SELWYN'S WORK. By Mrs. J.J. Colter. Boston, Bradley, 1889. 395p [LC

MILDRED KENT'S HERO. Boston, Bradley, 1889. [BCF MOR'12

ONE QUIET LIFE. By Mrs. J.J. Colter. Boston, Lothrop, 1876. [AmCat

ROBBIE MEREDITH. By Mrs. J.J. Colter. Boston, Lothrop, 1876. [AmCat

Conger, Janet C.
A DAUGHTER OF ST. PETER'S. New York, Lovell, 1889. 196p [BVaU LC
  OTMC

Conibear, Frank
DEVIL DOG. New York, Sloane, 1954. 214p
WATER TRIO. By Frank Conibear and J.L. Blundell. London, Davies, 1948.
  278p [BViP OTMC

Conibear, Kenneth, 1907–
HUSKY. The Story of Cap. By Frank and Kenneth Conibear. London, Davies,
  1940. 241p [BM BViPA NBFU OTU
NORTH LAND FOOTPRINTS; or, Lives on Little Bent Tree Lake. London,
  Dickson, 1936. 339p [BM BVaU NBFU OTMC
NORTHWARD TO EDEN. London, Davies, 1938. 403p [BM LC NBFU OTU
  QMM

Cook, Lyn, 1918–
THE BELLS ON FINLAND STREET. Toronto, Macmillan, 1950. 197p [BVaU
  NBFU OTMC QMBM
JADY AND THE GENERAL. Toronto, Macmillan, 1955. 242p
THE LITTLE MAGIC FIDDLER. Toronto, Macmillan, 1951. 252p
PEGEEN AND THE PILGRIM. Toronto, Macmillan, 1957. 248p
REBEL ON THE TRAIL. Toronto, Macmillan, 1953. 247p

Cook, Marjorie Grant
ANOTHER WAY OF LOVE. London, Heinemann, 1923. 320p [BM NBFU OOP
DEAR EMILY. By Caroline Seaford [pseud]. London, Gollancz, 1938. 304p
  [BM QMM
GLORY JAM. By Caroline Seaford [pseud]. London, Gollancz, 1934. 328p
  [BM NBFU OOP QMM
LATCHKEY LADIES. By Marjorie Grant [pseud]. London, Heinemann, 1921.
  310p [BM OOP QMM
MORE THAN KIND. By Caroline Seaford [pseud]. London, Gollancz, 1935.
  287p [BM OOP QMM
THEY GREW IN BEAUTY. A Novel. By Caroline Seaford [pseud]. London,
  Cape, 1946. 290p [BM NBFU QMM
VELVET DEER. By Caroline Seaford [pseud]. London, Dickson, 1937. 240p
  [BM NBFU

Cooke, Henry Robswood
ALTURLIE. London, Hodder, 1925. 320p [BM
BUCCANEERS' ISLAND. ... London, Long, 1913. 256p [BM
OUTLAWED. A Tale of Culloden. London, Hodder, 1924. 318p [BM
  BVaU OTMC

Cooke, Ronald John Victor, 1913–
ALGONQUIN ADVENTURE. Toronto, Ryerson, 1958. 138p
THE HOUSE ON CRAIG STREET. Winnipeg, Harlequin Books, 1949. 190p
[OTMC
THE MAYOR OF COTE ST. PAUL. Toronto, Harlequin Books, 1950. 157p
[OTMC

Coombs, Francis Lovell, 1876–
THE LOST TRAIN AND OTHER TALES ... OF YOUNG CANADIAN RAILROADERS.
V. 1. Ottawa, Mortimer, 1933. [At the head of title: "The Railroad Scouts
Series." May be same as following title.] [Amtmann cat. 149
THE RACE FOR YELLOW CREEK. And other Tales of Adventure and Ingenuity
of a Group of Young Canadian Railroaders. Ottawa, Mortimer, [1933].
149p [BVaU
YOUNG CRUSOES OF THE SKY. New York, Century, 1911. 380p [BM LC
THE YOUNG RAILROADERS. Tales of Adventure and Ingenuity. New York,
Century, 1910. 380p [BM LC

Cooney, Percival John, 1871–1932
THE DONS OF THE OLD PUEBLO. Chicago, Rand McNally, 1914. 439p [BM
BVaU LC OTMC
KINSMEN. A Story of the Ottawa Valley. Toronto, Gundy, 1916. 366p
[Also: Toronto, McClelland, 1929.] [BVaU NSHD OTMC

Copland, John A., 1863–
ESCULAPIUS. Harriston, Ont. [BCF
A METEOR KING. Harriston, Ont., Harriston Tribune, 1899. 122p [BM OTMC

Corbett, Sidney, 1891–
THE CRUISE OF THE GULL-FLIGHT. New York, Longmans, 1937. 367p [BM
LC NBFU OTMC
THE GULL-FLIGHT SAILS AGAIN. Toronto, Longmans, 1939. 328p [BM LC
NBFU OOP

Coristine, Alwyn
THE SORRY CAVALIER. London, Stockwell, 1933. 285p [BM OTP

Cormack, Barbara (Villy), 1903–
THE HOUSE. Toronto, Ryerson, 1955. 255p
LOCAL RAG. Toronto, Ryerson, 1951. 234p

Cornell, Beaumont Sandfield, 1892–1958
LANTERN MARSH. Toronto, Ryerson, 1923. 399p [BM BVaU NBFU OTMC
RENAISSANCE. A Novel. Toronto, Macmillan, 1922. 278p [NSHD OKQ

Cornell, Hughes
KENELM'S DESIRE. Toronto, Musson, 1906. 388p [BVaU OTMC

Cornish, John, 1914—
OLGA. Toronto, Macmillan, 1959. 174p
THE PROVINCIALS. Toronto, McClelland, 1951. 258p

Cosier, C.H.T.
THE MIGHTY MILLSTONE. A Scientific-Religious Novel. London, Stockwell,
1938. 288p [BM

Costain, Thomas Bertram, 1885—1965
BELOW THE SALT. A Novel. Garden City, N.Y., Doubleday, 1957. 480p
THE BLACK ROSE. Garden City, Doubleday, 1945. 403p [BM BVaU LC
NBFU OTMC
THE DARKNESS AND THE DAWN. A Novel. Garden City, N.Y., Doubleday,
1959. 478p
FOR MY GREAT FOLLY. A Novel. New York, Putnam, 1942. 504p [BM
LC OTMC
HIGH TOWERS. Toronto, McClelland, 1949. 403p [BM BVaU LC NBFU OTMC
THE MISSISSIPPI BUBBLE. New York, Random House, 1955. 185p
THE MONEYMAN. New York, Doubleday, 1947. 434p [BM BVaU LC NBFU
OTMC
RIDE WITH ME. New York, Doubleday, 1944. 595p [BVaU NBFU OTMC
QMM
THE SILVER CHALICE. A Novel. Garden City, Doubleday, 1952. 533p
SON OF A HUNDRED KINGS. A Novel of the Nineties. Garden City, Doubleday,
1950. 465p [BVaU LC NBFU OTMC
STORIES TO REMEMBER. Selected by Thomas B. Costain and John Beecroft.
Garden City, N.Y., Doubleday, 1956. 2v
THE TONTINE. A Novel. Garden City, N.Y., Doubleday, 1955. 2v

Coulter, John William, 1888—
TURF SMOKE. A Fable of Two Countries. Toronto, Ryerson, 1945. 187p
[BVaU NBFU OTMC QMM

Cousins, Olive Evelyn Joy, 1894—
THE CORMAC TREASURE. London, Stockwell, 1941. 320p [BM BVa LC
QMM

Covey, Mrs. Elizabeth (Rockfort), 1873—
COMRADES TWO. [A Tale of the Qu'Appelle Valley]. By Elizabeth Fremantle
[pseud]. London, Heinemann, 1907. 254p [Also: Toronto, Musson, [1907?]
254p] [AEU BVaU OTMC
THE ONE, AND I. By Elizabeth Fremantle [pseud]. Philadelphia, Jacobs,
[1908]. 319p [Same as COMRADES TWO.] [LC OTMC

Cowan, Charles L.
SANDY'S SON. Toronto, Poole, 1931. 288p [BVaU NBFU OTP

Cowan, Hugh, 1870–1943
LA CLOCHE. The Story of Hector MacLeod and his Misadventures in the
Georgian Bay and the La Cloche Districts. Toronto, Algonquin Hist. Soc.,
1928. 327p [BVaU NBFU OTP

Cox, Corolyn
STAND BY. New York, Harper, 1925. 351p [BM LC

Craig, John Ernest, 1921–
THE LONG RETURN. Toronto, McClelland, 1959. 255p
WAGONS WEST. London, Dent, 1956. 128p [First pub.: Toronto, Dent,
1955.]

Craig, Hamilton
A HAZARD AT HANSARD. (The Speech from the Throne, Ottawa, fourth
August, 2014). London, Stockwell, 1925. 31p [BM NSHD OTU

Craig, Mary Coad, 1871–
THE TWO DECANTERS. Written for his Wife by Duncan Clark, M.D. [pseud]
Ed. by ——. Ottawa, Graphic, 1930. 301p [NBFU OTMC QMM

Crawford, Isabell C.
THE TAPESTRY OF TIME. Boston, Christopher, 1927. 365p [BViPA LC

Creal, Margaret
A LESSON IN LOVE. A Novel. New York, Simon & Schuster, 1957. 281p

Creighton, Luella Sanders (Bruce), 1901–
HIGH BRIGHT BUGGY WHEELS. Toronto, McClelland, 1951. 352p
TURN EAST, TURN WEST. New York, Dodd Mead, 1954. 373p

Crisp, William George, 1904–
WHITE GOLD IN THE CASSIAR. London, Dent, 1955. 221p

Crofton, Francis Blake, 1841–1912
THE BEWILDERED QUERISTS AND OTHER NONSENSE. New York, Putnam, 1875.
127p [LC NSHD OTP ·
HAIRBREADTH ESCAPES OF MAJOR MENDAX. A Personal Narrative.
Philadelphia, Hubbard, 1889. 236p [NSHD OTU
THE MAJOR'S BIG-TALK STORIES. London, Warne, 1881. 152p [BM NSHD

Cropp, Marjorie Elizabeth, 1903–
TREMENDOUS ADVENTURE OF THE PEACE FAIRY. Regina, School Aids and
Text Book Pub. Co., 1945. [unpaged] [ACU

Crozier, Rev. Hugh Gibson, 1873–
DAVID THE THEOLOGUE. Ilfracombe, Devon, Stockwell, 1954. 163p

Cummins, John S.
ALTHAM. A Tale of the Sea. London, Saunders & Otley, 1849. 2v [BM OTP

Cunningham, Louis Arthur, 1900–1954
AIRMAIL TO EDEN. London, Jenkins, 1954. 188p
DISCORDS OF THE DEEP. London, Quality Press, 1938. 255p [BM OTU
EVERGREEN COTTAGE. New York, Arcadia House, 1949. 256p [LC
FOG OVER FUNDY. Philadelphia, Penn. Pub. Co., 1936. 303p [LC NBFU
OTMC
THE FOREST GATE. Hanley, Eng., Locker, 1947. 160p [BM
KEY TO ROMANCE. New York, Arcadia House, 1954. 224p
THE KING'S FOOL. Ottawa, Graphic, 1931. 281p [BVaU LC NBFU OTMC
QMM
THE LILY POOL. New York, Arcadia House, 1955. 223p
MARIONETTE. Philadelphia, Penn. Pub. Co., 1941. 303p [LC NBFU OTU
MEG SHANNON. New York, Arcadia House, 1956. 222p
MOON OVER ACADIE. Philadelphia, Penn. Pub. Co., 1937. 310p [LC NBFU
OTMC
OF THESE THREE LOVES. Philadelphia, Penn. Pub. Co., 1939. 302p [LC OTU
SHOULD THY LOVE DIE. London, Jenkins, 1954. 192p
THE SIGN OF THE BURNING SHIP. Philadelphia, Penn. Pub. Co., 1940. 290p
[LC NBFU OTMC
STARS OVER SEVEN OAKS. New York, Arcadia House, 1957. 220p
A SUNLIT GROVE. New York, Arcadia House, 1959. 220p
SWEET CONSTANCY. London, Jenkins, 1955. 190p
THIS THING CALLED LOVE. New York, Carrier, 1929. 311p [BVaU LC NBFU
OTMC QMM
VALLEY OF THE STARS. Philadelphia, Penn. Pub. Co., 1938. 305p [LC NBFU
OOP
TIDES OF THE TANTRAMAR. Philadelphia, Penn. Pub. Co., 1935. 313p [BVaU
LC NBFU OTMC
THE WANDERING HEART. New York, Gramercy Pub. Co., 1947. 253p [LC
OTMC
WHISPER TO THE STARS. New York, Arcadia House, 1958. 222p
YOU ARE THE DREAM. New York, Arcadia House, 1957. 220p
YVON TREMBLAY. An Acadian Idyll. Ottawa, Graphic, 1927. 284p [BVaU
NBFU OTMC

Cunningham, Michael, 1910–
THE BISHOP FINDS A WAY. New York, Farrar, Straus & Young, 1955. 213p

Cureton, Stephen
PERSEVERANCE WINS. The Career of a Travelling Correspondent. Toronto,
Clougher, 1880. 269p [OOP

Curran, James Watson, 1865–1952
WOLVES DON'T BITE. Sault Ste. Marie, Daily Star, 1940. 225p [OTU

Cushing, Eliza Lanesford (Foster), 1794—

SARATOGA. A Tale of the Revolution. [Anon] Boston, Cummings, 1824. 2v
[LC

YORKTOWN. An Historical Romance. ... [Anon] Boston, Wells & Lilly, 1826. 2v
[LC

Cushing, Enid Louise

BLOOD ON MY RUG. New York, Arcadia House, 1956. 223p

THE GIRL WHO BOUGHT A DREAM. By Mabel Louise Dawson [pseud]. New York,
Arcadia House, 1957. 220p

MURDER'S NO PICNIC. New York, Arcadia House, 1953. 220p

MURDER WITHOUT REGRET. New York, Arcadia House, 1954. 221p

THE UNEXPECTED CORPSE. New York, Arcadia House, 1957. 223p

Daem, Mary (Bannerman), 1914—

LUCKY LURE AT ARROW POINT. London, Abelard-Schuman, 1959. 126p

THE WHISTLING MOUNTAIN. Toronto, Abelard-Schuman, 1960. 154p

Dale, Mrs. R.J.

TO THE GREATER GLORY. By V.V. Vinton [pseud]. London, Cape, 1939. 224p
[BM OTU QMM

Dalgarno, Agnes

THUNDER IN THE SKY. Ilfracombe, Devon, Stockwell, 1958. 34p

Dalziel, David

JEWS AND GENTILES; or, Life in Sittsville. Toronto, Author, 1898. 174p [OOP

A PARODY ON PATIENCE. N.p., n.d. 48p [OTP

Dancey, Stanley Nelson, 1885—

THE FAITH OF A BELGIAN. A Romance of the Great War. Ottawa, Dadson Merrill,
1916. 325p [BM OONL

Darnell, Rev. Henry Faulkner, 1831—1915

THE CRAZE OF CHRISTIAN ENGLEHART. New York, Appleton, 1890. 264p [LC

THE CROSS ROADS. An Allegory. ... Manchester, Eng., Simms, 1856. 40p [OLU

FLOSSY; or, A Child of the People. Buffalo, Darnell, 1889. [Sequel to PHILIP
HAZELBROOK. ...] [AmCat

PHILIP HAZELBROOK; or, The Junior Curate. Buffalo, Sherrill, 1886. [AmCat

Davidson, Fisher, 1912—

PRINCIPAL BOY. Boston, Humphries, 1953. 38p

Davies, Blodwen, 1897—1966

RUFFLES AND RAPIERS. Toronto, Ryerson, 1930. 124p [BVaU NBFU OTU

Davies, Robertson, 1913—

LEAVEN OF MALICE. Toronto, Clarke Irwin, 1954. 312p

A MIXTURE OF FRAILTIES. Toronto, Macmillan, 1958. 379p

TEMPEST-TOST. Toronto, Clarke Irwin, 1951. 376p

Davis, Allan Ross, 1858–1933
THE OLD LOYALIST. A Story of United Empire Loyalist Descendants in Canada.
   Toronto, Briggs, 1908. 367p [BM BVaU NBFU OKQ

Davis, Harold Lenoir, 1896–
WINDS OF MORNING. Toronto, McLeod, 1952. 344p

Davison, Frank Cyril Shaw, 1893–1944?
HARE AND TORTOISE. By Pierre Coalfleet [pseud]. Toronto, McClelland, 1925.
   255p [BM BVaU LC NBFU OTMC
MEANWHILE. By Pierre Coalfleet [pseud]. New York, Duffield, 1927. 360p
   [BVaU NBFU QMM
SIDONIE. By Pierre Coalfleet [pseud]. London, Collins, [1921]. 273p [BM
   NBFU
SOLO. By Pierre Coalfleet [pseud]. New York, Putnam, 1924. 351p [BM BVaU
   LC NBFU OTMC

Day, Frank Parker, 1881–1950
JOHN PAUL'S ROCK. New York, Minton Balch, 1932. 242p [LC NBFU OTP
RIVER OF STRANGERS. Garden City, Doubleday, 1926. 237p [BM BVaU LC
   NSHD OTP
ROCKBOUND. Garden City, Doubleday, 1928. 292p [BM LC NSHD OTP

Deacon, W.F.
THE AUTHOR; or, Sketches from Life. Saint John, 1866. 64p [BCF
MURDER WILL OUT; or, Confessions of a Village Apothecary. [BCF

Deane, Aubrey
ANNETTE. A Tale. With a Memoir of the Author by T.N. Talfourd. London,
   Colborn, 1852. 3v [OTMC
THE STREET RIVER TRAGEDY. [BCF

Deans, Dorothea
PETALS IN PASSING. Owen Sound, Fleming, 1929. 22p [BVaU OONL

Delafosse, Frederick Montague, 1860–1950
ENGLISH BLOODS. By Roger Vardon [pseud]. Ottawa, Graphic, 1930. 227p [BM
   BVaU OTP QMM

De La Roche, Mazo, 1879–1961
BESIDE A NORMAN TOWER. London, Macmillan, 1934. 229p [BM BVaU LC
   NBFU OTMC QMM
BILL AND COO. Toronto, Macmillan, 1958. 40p
A BOY IN THE HOUSE. London, Macmillan, 1952. 124p
A BOY IN THE HOUSE AND OTHER STORIES. Boston, Little Brown, 1952. 244p
THE BUILDING OF JALNA. Boston, Little Brown, 1944. 366p [BM BVaU LC
   NBFU OTMC

CENTENARY AT JALNA. Toronto, Macmillan, 1958. 302p

DELIGHT. New York, Macmillan, 1926. 232p [BM BVaU LC NBFU OTMC QMM

EXPLORERS OF THE DAWN. New York, Knopf, 1922. 292p [BM BVaU LC NBFU OTMC

FINCH'S FORTUNE. London, Macmillan, 1931. 399p [BM BVaU LC NBFU OTU QMM

GROWTH OF A MAN. Boston, Little Brown, 1938. 380p [BVaU LC NBFU OTU QMM

JALNA. Boston, Little Brown, 1927. 347p [BVaU LC NSHD OTU

LARK ASCENDING. Boston, Little Brown, 1932. 301p [BM BVaU NBFU OTU QMM

MARY WAKEFIELD. Boston, Little Brown, 1949. 337p [BM BVaU LC NBFU OTU QMM

THE MASTER OF JALNA. Toronto, Macmillan, 1933. 331p [BM BVaU LC NBFU OTU QMM

MORNING AT JALNA. London, Macmillan, 1960. 263p

POSSESSION. New York, Macmillan, 1923. 289p [BM BVaU LC NSHD OTU QMM

RENNY'S DAUGHTER. Boston, Little Brown, 1951. 376p

RETURN TO JALNA. Boston, Little Brown, 1946. 462p [BM BVaU LC NBFU OTMC QMM

THE SACRED BULLOCK, AND OTHER STORIES OF ANIMALS. London, Macmillan, 1939. 221p [BM BVaU LC NBFU OTMC QMM

THE SONG OF LAMBERT. Toronto, Macmillan, 1955. 51p

THE THUNDER OF NEW WINGS. Boston, Little Brown, 1932. 279p [A novel serialized in a magazine and printed in a few copies "that it might be protected from pirating"—letter from author.] [OKQ

THE TWO SAPLINGS. London, Macmillan, 1942. 214p [BM BVaU LC NBFU OTMC QMM

VARIABLE WINDS AT JALNA. Toronto, Macmillan, 1954. 359p

THE VERY HOUSE. London, Macmillan, 1937. 257p [BM BVaU LC NBFU OTMC QMM

WAKEFIELD'S COURSE. Boston, Little Brown, 1941. 406p [BM BVaU LC NSHD OTMC QMM

THE WHITEOAK BROTHERS, JALNA——1923. Toronto, Macmillan, 1953. 307p

WHITEOAK CHRONICLES. [Contains *Young Renny, Jalna, Whiteoaks, Finch's Fortune, The Master of Jalna, Whiteoak Harvest.*] London, Macmillan, 1940. 1390p [BM OTMC

WHITEOAK HARVEST. Boston, Little Brown, 1936. 378p [BM BVaU LC NBFU OTMC QMM

WHITEOAK HERITAGE. Boston, Little Brown, 1940. 325p [BM BVaU LC NBFU OTMC QMM

WHITEOAKS OF JALNA. Boston, Little Brown, 1929. 423p [BM BVaU LC MWU NSHD OTP

YOUNG RENNY. Toronto, Macmillan, 1935. 277p [BM BVaU NBFU OTMC QMM

De Long, Rev. A.M.
A WOLF IN SHEEP'S CLOTHING. Toronto, Briggs, 1905. 163p [BM

De Mille, James, 1833–1880
Besides titles which follow, the following untraced titles have been attributed to De Mille by either BCF or NBB, or both:

ASHDOD WEBSTER AND HIS STARRING TOUR
THE SOLDIER AND THE SPY [1869? 1865?]
THE ARKANSAS RANGER [1869? 1865?]

(The last two also are mentioned in Allibone Supp.)

THE AMERICAN BARON. New York, Harper, 1872. 132p [BVaU LC NSHD OTMC

AMONG THE BRIGANDS. Boston, Lee & Shepard, 1871. 328p (Young Dodge Club Series) [BVaU NSHD OTMC

ANDY O'HARA; or, The Child of Promise. [Anon] New York, Carlton & Porter, 1861. [AmCat

THE BABES IN THE WOOD. A Tragic Comedy. A Tale of the Italian Revolution of 1848. Boston, Gill, 1875. 142p [BVaU LC NSHD

THE "B.O.W.C." [Brethren of the White Cross]. A Book for Boys. By the author of THE DODGE CLUB, etc. [pseud]. Boston, Lee & Shepard, 1869. 322p [BVaU NSHD OKQ

THE BOYS OF GRAND PRÉ SCHOOL. Boston, Lee & Shepard, 1870. 348p (B.O.W.C. Series) [BVaU NSHD OKQ

A CASTLE IN SPAIN. A Novel. New York, Harper, 1883. 183p [BM BVaU NSHD OTU

A COMEDY OF TERRORS. Boston, Osgood, 1872. 152p [BM BVaU LC OKQ

CORD AND CREESE. A Novel. New York, Harper, 1869. 305p [BM BVaU LC NSHD OKQ

THE CRYPTOGRAM. A Novel. New York, Harper, 1871. 261p [BVaU NSHD OKQ

THE DODGE CLUB; or, Italy in 1859. New York, Harper, 1869. 133p [BVaU NSHD OKQ QMM

THE DODGE CLUB ABROAD. New York, Harper, 1868. [Same as preceding title?]

FIRE IN THE WOODS. Boston, Lee & Shepard, 1872. 323p (B.O.W.C. Series) [BM BVaU NSHD OKQ

HELENA'S HOUSEHOLD. A Tale of Rome in the First Century. [Anon] New York, Carter, 1867. 422p [First pub. in 1858?—see Allibone Supp.] [BM NSHD OKQ

JOHN WHEELER'S TWO UNCLES; or, Launching into Life. [Anon] New York, Carlton & Porter, [1860?]. [AmCat

THE LADY OF THE ICE. A Novel. New York, Appleton, 1870. 146p [BVaU
NSHD OTMC

THE LILY AND THE CROSS. A Tale of Acadia. Boston, Lee & Shepard, 1874. 264p
[BVaU LC NSHD OTU

THE LIVING LINK. A Novel. New York, Harper, 1874. 171p [BVaU LC NSHD
OTMC

LOST IN THE FOG. Boston, Lee & Shepard, [1870]. 316p (B.O.W.C. Series)
[BVaU NBFU OTU

THE MARTYR OF THE CATACOMBS. A Tale of Ancient Rome. [Anon] New York,
Carlton & Porter, 1865. 202p [First pub. in 1858?—see Allibone Supp.]
[AmCat

OLD GARTH. A Story of Sicily. New York, Munro, 1883. 52p [BVaU LC NSWA

AN OPEN QUESTION. A Novel. New York, Appleton, 1873. 233p [BVaU NSHD

PICKED UP ADRIFT. Boston, Lee & Shepard, 1872. 335p (B.O.W.C. Series)
[NBFU OKQ

THE SEVEN HILLS. Boston, Lee & Shepard, 1873. 331p (Young Dodge Club
Series) [BVaU NSHD

A STRANGE MANUSCRIPT FOUND IN A COPPER CYLINDER. [Anon] New York,
Harper, 1888. 291p [Also: Toronto, Macmillan, 1910]. [BM BVaU LC
NSHD OKQ

THE TREASURE OF THE SEAS. Boston, Lee & Shepard, 1873. 336p (B.O.W.C.
Series) [BM BVaU NSHD OKQ

THE WINGED LION; or, Stories of Venice. New York, Dillingham, 1877. 323p
(Young Dodge Club Series) [BVaU LC NSHD OTU

Denison, Merrill, 1893–

BOOBS IN THE WOODS. Sixteen Sketches. ... Ottawa, Graphic, 1927. 204p [BVaU
NBFU OTMC QMM

Denison, Muriel (Goggin), –1954

HAPPY TRAMP. The Story of a Little Girl and her Old English Sheep Dog. New
York, Dodd Mead, 1942. 260p [BM BVa LC OOP

SUSANNAH. A Little Girl with the Mounties. New York, Dodd Mead, 1936. 299p
[LC NBFU OTMC SRL

SUSANNAH AT BOARDING SCHOOL. New York, Dodd Mead, 1938. 344p [BM
LC NBFU OTMC

SUSANNAH OF THE MOUNTIES. A Canadian Story of the Nineties. London, Dent,
1938. 280p [Same as SUSANNAH. A Little Girl. ...] [BM OTMC

SUSANNAH OF THE YUKON. New York, Dodd Mead, 1937. 343p [BM LC
NBFU OTMC

SUSANNAH RIDES AGAIN. New York, Dodd Mead, 1940. 329p [BM NBFU
OTMC

Dennis, June (pseud)

A MIKE FOR MARION. By June Dennis [pseud]. Toronto, Longmans, 1952. 200p

Dent, John Charles, 1841—1888
THE GERRARD STREET MYSTERY, AND OTHER WEIRD TALES. Toronto, Rose, 1888. 206p [BVaU MWU NBFU OTMC QMM

Dent, Walter Redvers, 1900—
SHOW ME DEATH! Toronto, Macmillan, 1930. 375p [BM BVaU LC NBFU OTMC

Deprend, Jeffrey
EMBERS. Chicago, Wallace, 1919. 340p [BM LC OTMC
THE GOLDEN POPPY. Chicago, Wallace, 1922. 313p [LC NBFU

Devine, Rev. Edward James, 1860—1927
THE TRAINING OF SILAS. New York, Benziger, 1906. 322p [LC NSHD OKQ

Dewdney, Selwyn Harrington, 1909—
WIND WITHOUT RAIN. Toronto, Copp Clark, 1946. 506p [BVaU NSHD OTMC

Dickie, Donalda James, 1883—
THE BOOK OF NEW CANADIANS. Toronto, Dent, 1930. 158p [NBFU
SENT TO COVENTRY. Toronto, Dent, 1929. [BM

Dickie, Francis Joseph, 1890—
HUNTERS OF THE WILD. London, Lutterworth, 1937. 125p [BM BVaU
THE MASTER BREED. Toronto, McClelland, 1923. 272p [BVaU LC NBFU OTMC
UMINGMUK OF THE BARRENS. Toronto, Musson, 1927. 278p [BM BVaU NBFU QMM

Dickson, Mrs. Emma Wells
MISS DEXIE. A Romance of the Provinces. By Stanford Eveleth [pseud].
Toronto, Briggs, 1895. 426p [OLU

Dickson, Gordon Rupert, 1923—
SECRET UNDER THE SEA. New York, Holt Rinehart, 1960. 121p

Dickson, Lovat, 1902—
OUT OF THE WEST LAND. Toronto, Collins, 1944. 446p [BM BVaU LC NBFU OTMC

Diesel, Gladys Cynthia Rebecca (Shope), 1907—
THE LEGEND OF OWL HOOT HILL. Edmonton, Author, 1957. 8p

Diespecker, Richard E. Alan, 1907—
ELIZABETH. Toronto, Dent, 1950. 170p [BVaU NBFU OTMC
REBOUND. Toronto, Harlequin Books, 1953. 224p

Dix, Maurice Buxton, 1889—
BEACONS OF DEATH. London, Ward Lock, 1937. 288p [BM LC NBFU OLU

THE DARTMOOR MYSTERY. London, Ward Lock, 1935. 320p [BM
EMILY COULTON DIES. London, Ward Lock, 1936. 286p [BM LC NBFU
THE FIXER. London, Ward Lock, 1936. 318p [BM
THE FLAME OF THE KHAN. London, Ward Lock, 1934. 256p [BM LC OTMC
THE FLEETWOOD MANSIONS MYSTERY. London, Ward Lock, 1934. 317p [BM
   LC
THE GOLDEN FLUID. London, Ward Lock, 1935. 319p [BM OTMC
THE KIDNAPPED SCIENTIST. An Adventure of the Trio of Mount Street. London,
   Ward Lock, 1937. 287p [BM LC
LADY RICHLY LEFT. London, Staples, 1951. 264p
THE MASINGLEE MURDERS. London, Hale, 1947. 174p [BM
MURDER AT GRASSMERE ABBEY. London, Ward Lock, [1933]. 320p [BM LC
MURDER STRIKES TWICE. London, Ward Lock, 1939. 285p [BM LC
NIGHT ASSASSIN. London, Hale, 1941. 248p [BM
PROLOGUE TO MURDER. London, Ward Lock, 1938. 303p [BM
THIRD DEGREE. London, Gramol, 1936. 48p [BM
THIS IS MY MURDER. London, Ward Lock, 1938. 288p [BM LC
THE TREASURE OF SCARLAND. London, Ward Lock, 1936. 256p [BM LC
TWISTED EVIDENCE. London, Ward Lock, 1933. 256p [BM LC

Dobbin, Mrs.
"THOS." A Simple Canadian Story. By George Graham [pseud]. Montreal,
   Lovell, 1878. 160p [LC OTMC

Dolen, G.
THE DREAMER OF POND LAND AND OTHER STORIES. Toronto, W.M.S. of United
   Church, n.d. 80p [BVaU

Dollard, Rev. James Bernard, 1872–1946
THE GAELS OF MOONDHARRIG; or, The Modern Fianna. Dublin, Sealy, Bryers,
   1907. 124p [BM

Donovan, Edward Joseph, 1904–
ADVENTURE ON GHOST RIVER. New York, Duell Sloan, 1960. 150p

Donovan, Peter, 1884–
LATE SPRING. London, Hodder, 1930. 352p [BM NBFU OTMC

Dougall, Lily, 1858–1923
BEGGARS ALL. A Novel. London, Longmans, 1891. 461p [BM LC NBFU
   OTMC QMM
A DOZEN WAYS OF LOVE. London, Black, 1897. 370p [BM QMM
THE EARTHLY PURGATORY. London, Hutchinson, 1904. 345p [Pub. in the
   U.S. as THE SUMMIT HOUSE MYSTERY; or, The Earthly Purgatory. New York,
   Funk & Wagnalls, 1905. 339p] [BM LC OOP QMM
THE MADONNA OF A DAY. New York, Appleton, 1895. 271p [BM BVaU LC
   OTMC QMM

THE MERMAID. A Love Tale. New York, Appleton, 1895. 290p [BM BVaU
OOP QMM

THE MORMON PROPHET. New York, Appleton, 1899. 427p [BM LC QMM

PATHS OF THE RIGHTEOUS. London, Macmillan, 1908. 441p [BM LC NSHD
QMM

A QUESTION OF FAITH. Boston, Houghton, 1895. 290p [BM LC OOP QMM

THE SPANISH DOWRY. A Romance. London, Hutchinson, 1906. 312p [BM BVaU
OOP QMM

WHAT NECESSITY KNOWS. New York, Longmans, 1893. 445p [BM BVaU
NBFU OOP QMM

YOUNG LOVE. London, Black, 1904. 179p [BM QMM

THE ZEIT-GEIST. New York, Appleton, 1895. 184p [BM LC NBFU QMM

Dow, Lawrence T., −1956
THE LONESOME DOLL. By Larry Lawrence [pseud]. [Halifax, Patterson-Dow,
1955.] 20p

Draper, Blanche A., 1893−
THE GREAT AWAKENING. New York, Vantage Press, 1953. 177p

Drummond, May Isobel (Harvey)
THE STORY OF QUAMIN. A Tale of the Tropics. New York, London, Putnam, 1911.
313p [BM LC NSWA

Duff, Emma Lorne, −1935
A CARGO OF STORIES FOR CHILDREN. Toronto, McClelland, 1929. 259p [3rd
ed., rev. and enl., 1931.] [BViV

Duff, Louis Blake, 1878−1959
A SHEPHERD'S CROOK ON THE HILLS OF ST. JOHNS. Welland, Ont., priv. print.,
1952. 5p

Duffield, Dorothy Dean·(Tate), 1893−
ARKADY. By Anne Duffield [pseud]. London, Cassell, 1948. 247p [BM

BELOVED ENEMY. By Anne Duffield [pseud]. London, Cassell, 1950. 223p [BM

A BEVY OF MAIDS. By Anne Duffield [pseud]. London, Cassell, 1941. 254p [BM

BITTER RAPTURE. By Anne Duffield [pseud]. London, Cassell, 1937. 324p [BM
LC

BRIEF RAPTURE. By Anne Duffield [pseud]. New York, Arcadia House, 1938.
288p [LC

BUBBLING SPRINGS. By Anne Duffield [pseud]. London, Cassell, 1940. 316p
[BM LC

CASTLE IN SPAIN. By Anne Duffield [pseud]. London, Cassell, 1958. 217p

COME BACK MIRANDA. By Anne Duffield [pseud]. London, Cassell, 1955. 215p

DESERT MOON. A Novel. By Anne Duffield [pseud]. London, Cassell, 1939. 298p
[BM LC PC

THE DRAGON'S TAIL. By Anne Duffield [pseud]. London, Cassell, 1938. 293p
[BM LC

DUSTY DAWN. By Anne Duffield [pseud]. London, Cassell, 1949. 214p [BM

ENCHANTMENT. By Anne Duffield [pseud]. New York, Hillman-Curl, 1937. 320p
[LC

FALSE STAR. By Anne Duffield [pseud]. New York, Arcadia House, 1939. 285p
[LC

FIAMETTA. By Anne Duffield [pseud]. London, Cassell, 1956. 216p

FLAMING FELICIA. By Anne Duffield [pseud]. London, Cassell, 1934. 336p
[BM LC

FLEETING SHADOWS. By Anne Duffield [pseud]. London, Cassell, 1934. 366p
[BM LC

FOREVER TOMORROW. By Anne Duffield [pseud]. London, Cassell, 1946. 235p
[BM

GAY FIESTA. By Anne Duffield [pseud]. London, Cassell, 1938. 285p [LC

GLITTERING HEIGHTS. By Anne Duffield [pseud]. London, Cassell, 1936. 314p
[BM LC

GOLDEN HORIZONS. By Anne Duffield [pseud]. London, Cassell, 1935. 378p
[BM LC

THE GOLDEN SUMMER. By Anne Duffield [pseud]. London, Cassell, 1954. 213p

THE GRAND DUCHESS. By Anne Duffield [pseud]. London, Cassell, 1954. 213p

GRECIAN RHAPSODY. By Anne Duffield [pseud]. London, Cassell, 1938. 279p
[BM LC OONL

HARBOUR LIGHTS. By Anne Duffield [pseud]. London, Cassell, 1953. 223p

HIGH HEAVEN. By Anne Duffield [pseud]. London, Cassell, 1939. 271p [BM LC
NBS

THE HOUSE ON THE NILE. By Anne Duffield [pseud]. London, Cassell, 1937.
363p [BM LC

THE INSCRUTABLE NYMPH. By Anne Duffield [pseud]. London, Cassell, 1942.
268p [BM LC OONL

KAREN'S MEMORY. By Anne Duffield [pseud]. New York, Arcadia House, 1939.
304p [BM LC OONL

THE LACQUER COUCH. By Anne Duffield [pseud]. London, Murray, 1929. 352p
[BM NBS

LANTERN-LIGHT. By Anne Duffield [pseud]. London, Cassell, 1933. 367p [BM
LC

THE LONELY BRIDE. By Anne Duffield [pseud]. New York, Arcadia House, 1947.
272p [LC

LOVABLE STRANGER. By Anne Duffield [pseud]. Philadelphia, Macrae, 1949.
256p [NBS

LOVE DEFERRED. By Anne Duffield [pseud]. Philadelphia, Macrae, 1951. 253p

LOVE'S MEMORY. By Anne Duffield [pseud]. New York, Arcadia House, 1936.
320p [LC

MISS MAYHEW AND MING YUN. A Story of East and West. By Anne Duffield [pseud]. New York, Stokes, 1928. 311p [LC QMBM

MOON OVER STAMBOUL. By Anne Duffield [pseud]. London, Cassell, 1936. 384p [BM LC

OLD GLORY. By Anne Duffield [pseud]. London, Cassell, 1942. 272p [BM LC

OUT OF THE SHADOWS. By Anne Duffield [pseud]. London, Cassell, 1944. 255p [BM LC

PARADISE. By Anne Duffield [pseud]. London, Cassell, 1936. 378p [BM LC

PASSIONATE INTERLUDE. By Anne Duffield [pseud]. London, Murray, 1931. 331p [BM LC

PHANTASY. By Anne Duffield [pseud]. London, Cassell, 1932. 345p [BM LC

PREDESTINED. By Anne Duffield [pseud]. London, Murray, 1929. 336p [BM

REPENT AT LEISURE. By Anne Duffield [pseud]. London, Cassell, 1945. 267p [BM LC

THE SHADOW OF THE PINES. By Anne Duffield [pseud]. London, Cassell, 1940. 282p [BM LC

SILVER PEAKS. By Anne Duffield [pseud]. London, Cassell, 1941. 312p [BM LC

SONG OF THE MOCKINGBIRD. By Anne Duffield [pseud]. London, Cassell, 1946. 287p [BM NBS

STAMBOUL LOVE. By Anne Duffield [pseud]. New York, Knopf, 1934. 406p [LC

THE STORY OF YUKU. By Dorothy Dean Tate. Toronto, Briggs, 1910. 240p [BM BVaU LC OTMC

SUGAR ISLAND. By Anne Duffield [pseud]. London, Cassell, 1951. 222p

SUNRISE. By Anne Duffield [pseud]. London, Cassell, 1943. 287p [BM LC PC

THE SWEEPING TIDE. By Anne Duffield [pseud]. London, Cassell, 1940. 288p [BM LC PC

TAFFY CAME TO CAIRO. By Anne Duffield [pseud]. London, Cassell, 1944. 171p [BM LC

TOMORROW IS THEIRS. By Anne Duffield [pseud]. London, Cassell, 1951. 232p

TURN TO THE SUN. By Anne Duffield [pseud]. New York, Arcadia House, 1944. 352p [LC

VIOLETTA. By Anne Duffield [pseud]. London, Cassell, 1960. 253p

WILD MEMORY. By Anne Duffield [pseud]. London, Cassell, 1935. 378p [BM LC

Duley, Margaret, 1896?–1968

COLD PASTORAL. London, Hutchinson, 1939. 336p [BM OTU

THE EYES OF THE GULL. London, Barker, 1936. 200p [BM OTU

GREEN AFTERNOON. London, Methuen, 1944. 252p [BM

HIGHWAY TO VALOUR. Toronto, Macmillan, 1941. 324p [Also: London, Methuen, 1943.] [BM BVaU NBFU OKQ

NOVELTY ON EARTH. Toronto, Macmillan, 1942. 300p [OTMC

Dumbrille, Dorothy, 1898–

ALL THIS DIFFERENCE. Toronto, Progress Books, 1945. 208p [BVaU NBFU OTMC QMM

DEEP DOORWAYS. A Story of Life in Canada between Two Wars. Toronto, Allen, 1947. 277p [BVaU NBFU OTMC QMBM

Duncan, Norman, 1871–1916

THE ADVENTURES OF BILLY TOPSAIL. A Story for Boys. New York, Revell, 1906. 331p [BM BVaU LC NBFU OTMC

BATTLES ROYAL DOWN NORTH. New York, Revell, 1918. 269p [BVaU LC OTMC QMM

THE BEST OF A BAD JOB. A Hearty Tale of the Sea. Toronto, Frowde, 1912. 204p [BVaU LC NBFU OKQ

BILLY TOPSAIL AND COMPANY. A Story for Boys. New York, Revell, 1910. 318p [BVaU LC OTMC

BILLY TOPSAIL, M.D. A Tale of Adventure with Doctor Luke of the Labrador. New York, Revell, 1916. 317p [BM BVaU LC NBFU OTMC

THE BIRD STORE MAN. An Old Fashioned Story. New York, Revell, 1914. 136p [BVaU LC NBFU OTMC

CHRISTMAS EVE AT SWAMP'S END. New York, Revell, 1915. 32p [BVaU LC NBFU OKQ

CHRISTMAS EVE AT TOPMAST TICKLE. [A Selection from DOCTOR LUKE OF THE LABRADOR with Additions.] New York, Revell, 1910. 32p [NBFU OKQ

THE CRUISE OF THE SHINING LIGHT. New York, Harper, 1907. 343p [BM BVaU LC NBFU OTMC

DOCTOR LUKE OF THE LABRADOR. New York, Revell, 1904. 327p [BM BVaU LC NBFU OTMC QMM

EVERY MAN FOR HIMSELF. New York, Harper, 1908. 304p [BM BVaU LC NBFU OTMC

FINDING HIS SOUL. New York, Harper, 1913. 61p [BM LC NBFU OTMC

HARBOUR TALES DOWN NORTH. New York, Revell, 1918. 282p [BVaU NSHD OTMC QMM

THE MEASURE OF A MAN. A Tale of the Big Woods. New York, Revell, 1911. 356p [BM BVaU LC NBFU OTMC

THE MOTHER. New York, Revell, 1905. 220p [BM BVaU LC NBFU OTMC

THE SOUL OF THE STREET. Correlated Stories of the New York Syrian Quarter. New York, McClure Phillips, 1900. 168p [BM LC NBFU OLU

THE SUITABLE CHILD. New York, Revell, 1909. 96p [BM BVaU LC NBFU OTMC

THE WAY OF THE SEA. New York, McClure Phillips, 1903. 332p [BM BVaU LC NBFU OKQ

Duncan, Sara Jeannette (Mrs. Everard Cotes), 1861–1922

AN AMERICAN GIRL IN LONDON. London, Chatto, 1891. 321p [BM BVaU LC NSHD OTMC

THE BURNT OFFERING. London, Methuen, 1909. 320p [BM BVaU LC NSHD OTU

THE CONSORT. London, Stanley Paul, 1912. 344p [BM MWU OTMC

COUSIN CINDERELLA. A Canadian Girl in London. Toronto, Macmillan, 1908. 365p [BM BVaU LC NBFU OTMC

A DAUGHTER OF TO-DAY. New York, Appleton, 1894. 392p [BM LC NBFU OTMC

THE GOLD CURE. A Novel. London, Hutchinson, 1924. 286p [BM

HILDA. A Story of Calcutta. New York, Stokes, 1898. 317p [Same as THE PATH OF A STAR, *q.v.*] [LC OLU

HIS HONOUR AND A LADY. Toronto, Rose, 1896. 321p [BM BVaU LC NBFU OTMC

HIS ROYAL HAPPINESS. New York, Appleton, 1914. 377p [BM BVaU LC NBFU OTMC

THE IMPERIALIST. Toronto, Copp Clark, 1904. 472p [Also: New York, Appleton, 1904. 476p] [BVaU LC NBFU OTMC

THE PATH OF A STAR. London, Methuen, 1899. 311p [Same as HILDA, *q.v.*] [BM BVaU NBFU OTMC

THE POOL IN THE DESERT. New York, Appleton, 1903. 318p [AEU BM LC OTMC

SET IN AUTHORITY. London, Constable, 1906. 344p [BM BVaU LC NSHD OTMC

THE SIMPLE ADVENTURES OF A MEMSAHIB. New York, Appleton, 1893. 311p [BM BVaU LC NSHD OTMC

THE STORY OF SONNY SAHIB. London, Macmillan, 1894. 114p [BM BVa LC NBFU OTMC OOP

THOSE DELIGHTFUL AMERICANS. New York, Appleton, 1902. 352p [BM BVaU LC NSHD OTU

TITLE CLEAR. A Novel. London, Hutchinson, [1922]. 288p [BM BVaU

VERNON'S AUNT. Being the Oriental Experiences of Miss Lavinia Moffatt. London, Chatto, 1894. 200p [BM LC NBFU OTMC

A VOYAGE OF CONSOLATION. ... A Sequel to ... AN AMERICAN GIRL IN LONDON. London, Methuen, 1898. 318p [BM BVaU LC NBFU OTMC

Dunham, Bertha Mabel, 1881−1957
KRISTLI'S TREES. Toronto, McClelland, 1948. 198p [BVaU LC NBFU OLU

TOWARD SODOM. Toronto, Macmillan, 1927. 336p [BVaU LC NSHD OTU

THE TRAIL OF THE CONESTOGA. With a foreword by W.L. Mackenzie King. Toronto, Macmillan, 1924. 341p [Another ed.: Toronto, McClelland, 1942.] [BVaU LC NBFU OTMC

THE TRAIL OF THE KING'S MEN. Toronto, Ryerson, 1931. 314p [BM BVaU NBFU OTMC

Dunlop, James Donald
FOREST LILY. A Novel. New York, Neely, 1898. 366p [LC

Dunlop, William, 1792−1848
TWO AND TWENTY YEARS AGO. A Tale of the Canadian Rebellion. By a Backwoods-

man [pseud]. Toronto, Cleland's Print., 1859. 112p [Attributed to Dunlop by F.S.L. Ford. Reprinted with some changes and expansion by Sarah Anne Curzon as a serial in the *Dominion Illustrated* between Oct. 12, 1889 and Jan. 18, 1890 under the title: "In the Thick of It; a Tale of 'Thirty-Seven.'"] [OKQ

Durie, Mrs. Anna
JOHN DANGERFIELD'S STRANGE RE-APPEARANCE. Toronto, Best, 1933. 404p [BVaU NBFU OTP

Durkin, Douglas Leader, 1884–1968
THE HEART OF CHERRY MCBAIN. Toronto, Musson, 1919. 325p [BM BVaU NBFU OTMC
THE LOBSTICK TRAIL. Toronto, Musson, 1921. 334p [BM BVaU NSHD OTMC
THE MAGPIE. Toronto, Hodder, 1923. 330p [BM BVaU NBFU OTMC
MR. GRUMBLE SITS UP. New York, Liveright, 1930. 232p [BVaU LC NBFU OOP

Duvar, John Hunter-, 1830–1899
ANNALS OF THE COURT OF OBERON. Extracted from the Records. ... London, Digby Long, 1895. 246p [BM

Dyer, Mary Sparks
THROUGH THAT BRIGHT WOOD. Galt, Galt Printers, [19—?]. 39p [OLU

E., J.
THE OLD AND THE NEW HOME. A Canadian Tale. By J.E. Toronto, Campbell, 1870. 144p [BM OTP

Earl, Lawrence, 1915–
THE FROZEN JUNGLE. Toronto, McClelland, 1955. 244p

Earle, Kathleen.
LOSTWOOD LODGE. Toronto, Ryerson; Edinburgh, Blackwood, 1954. 352p

East, Henry Mortimer
THE LIFE OF "DOC" SHEPPARD; or, The Adventures of a Push-Cart. By Tamen Reysh [pseud]. Toronto, Johnston & Johnston, 1881. 62p [BVaU OTU

Eaton, Arthur Wentworth Hamilton, 1849–1937
TALES OF A GARRISON TOWN. By Arthur Wentworth Eaton and Craven Langstroth Betts. New York, Merrill, 1892. 250p [BM BVaU LC OTU

Eaton, Edith Maud, 1867–1914
MRS. SPRING FRAGRANCE. By Sui Sin Far (Edith Eaton). Chicago, McClurg, 1912. 347p [LC

Eaton, Evelyn Sybil Mary, 1902–
CANADIAN CIRCUS. London, Nelson, 1939. 240p [BM LC NBFU OTU
DESIRE–SPANISH VERSION. London, Chapman & Hall, 1932. 284p [BM LC
NBFU
THE ENCIRCLING MIST. London, Selwyn & Blount, 1925. 131p [BM LC
FLIGHT. London, Gollancz, 1954. 207p
GIVE ME YOUR GOLDEN HAND. New York, Farrar Straus, 1951. 309p
HEART IN PILGRIMAGE. By Evelyn Eaton and Edward Roberts Moore. New York,
Harper, 1948. 273p [BM LC NBFU OTMC QMM
IN WHAT TORN SHIP. New York, Harper, 1944. 263p [BM LC NBFU OTMC
QMM
JOHN–FILM STAR. A Novel for Boys. London, Nelson, 1937. 246p [BM LC
MY MORTAL SIGHT. New York, Random House, 1959. 211p
PRAY TO THE EARTH. Boston, Houghton, 1938. 237p [BM LC NBFU OTMC
QUIETLY MY CAPTAIN WAITS. New York, Harper, 1940. 365p [BM BVaU LC
NSHD OKQ
RESTLESS ARE THE SAILS. New York, Harper, 1941. 348p [BM BVaU LC
NSHD OTMC QMM
THE SEA IS SO WIDE. New York, Harper, 1943. 281p [BM BVaU LC NBFU
OTMC QMM
SUMMER DUST. London, Bles, 1936. 288p [BM LC NBFU

Eaton, Oliver Mowat
RODNEY AND FRANCES. A Tale of Divine and Human Love. Kingston, British
Whig, 1901. 38p [BM OTL

Eaton, Sara Lucretia (Sneath), 1928–
INDIAN PRINCESS. Leeds, E.J. Arnold, 1953. 128p
MOCCASIN AND CROSS. Toronto, Copp Clark, 1959. 181p

Eayrs, Hugh Smithurst, 1894–1940
THE AMATEUR DIPLOMAT. By Hugh S. Eayrs and T.B. Costain. London, Hodder,
1917. 313p [BM BVaU

Edelstein, Hyman, 1889–1957
CRYING LAUGHING. Montreal, Century Pub., 1939. 126p [BVaU NBFU OKQ
THE HIGHER LOYALTY. By Don Synge [pseud]. Ottawa, Tower Books, 1946.
241p [LC NBFU OKQ

Edmund, Henry
BEAVER LODGE. A Story of Frontier Settlement in Northern Saskatchewan.
Toronto, United Church, 1930. 75p [OTMC

Edwards, Charles Austin McNally, 1917–
SON OF THE MOHAWKS. Toronto, Ryerson, 1954. 188p

Edwards, Lois (Jennings)
MY HEART IN HIDING. New York, Morrow, 1951. 248p

Edwards, Phil
THE DELINQUENCY OF JOHN MEREDITH. Toronto, 1910. 224p [Adelphi cat. 60

Edwards, Robert Chambers, 1864—1922
BOB EDWARDS' SUMMER ANNUAL. Series 1 to 5. Toronto, Musson, 1920—24.
    [ACG BVaU OKQ

Eggleston, Magdelana (Raskevich), 1907—
MOUNTAIN SHADOWS. London, Heinemann; Toronto, British Book Service,
    1955. 254p

Eggleston, Wilfrid, 1901—
THE HIGH PLAINS. Toronto, Macmillan, 1938. 267p [BVaU OTU QMM SSU

Eliot, Elinor Marsden
MY CANADA. Toronto, Hodder, 1915. 269p [BM BVaU OTMC

Elliott, Andrew Jackson, 1899—
THE AGING NYMPH. Toronto, Collins, 1948. 252p [BVaU NBFU OTMC QMM

Elliott, Thomas Rose
HUGH LAYAL. A Romance of the Up Country. Toronto, Macmillan, 1927. 263p
    [BVaU LC NBFU OTP QMM

Elson, John Mebourne, 1880—
THE SCARLET SASH. A Romance of the Old Niagara Frontier. Toronto, Dent,
    1925. 308p [BM BVaU LC NSHD OTP

Embree, Beatrice Minnie, 1886—
THE GIRLS OF MISS CLEVELAND'S. Toronto, Musson, 1920. 180p [BM BVaU
    NBFU OTMC

English, Anastasia Mary, 1864—1959
ONLY A FISHERMAN'S DAUGHTER. By Maria [pseud]. St. John's, Manning &
    Rabbotts, 1899. 209p [NfSM NSHPL
"THE QUEEN OF FAIRY DELL" AND OTHER TALES. By Maria [pseud]. St. John's,
    Evening Herald Office, 1912. 164p [NfSM

English, Arthur
OGYGIA. A Tale of Old Newfoundland. Ottawa, Ru-mi-lou Books, [1930]. 278p
    [NfSG OTU
THE VANISHED RACE. Montreal, Garand, 1927. 154p [BVaU MWU OOP

Estey, Emma Louisa (Spurden), 1861—
THREE LITTLE GIRLS AND THEIR MOTTO. By E.L.S.E. Philadelphia, Am. Baptist
    Pub. Soc., 1893. 200p [LC

WALTER HARLEY'S CONQUEST. By E.L.S.E. Philadelphia, Am. Baptist Pub. Soc., 1889. 240p [LC

Eustace, Cecil John, 1903–
DAMAGED LIVES. [Novel Adaptation from a Columbia Pictures Scenario.] New York, Putnam, 1934. 221p [BM
THE SCARLET GENTLEMAN. Toronto, Macmillan, 1927. 286p [BM LC NBFU

Evans, Allen Roy, 1885–
ALL IN A TWILIGHT. Garden City, Doubleday, 1944. 214p [BM BVaU LC NBFU OTU
DREAM OUT OF THE DUST. A Tale of the Canadian Prairies. London, Ward Lock, 1956. 206p
NORTHWARD HO! London, Home & Van Thall, 1947. 220p [BM BVaU NBFU OTMC
REINDEER TREK. New York, Coward-McCann, 1935. 269p [Also pub. as: MEAT: A Tale of the Reindeer Trek (1929–1935). London, Hurst & Blackett, 1935. 288p] [BM BVaU LC NBFU OTMC

Evans, Hubert Reginald, 1892–
DERRY, AIREDALE OF THE FRONTIER. New York, Dodd Mead, 1928. 253p [BVa LC OTMC
DERRY, OF TOTEM CREEK. New York, Dodd Mead, 1930. 252p [BVaU LC OTMC
DERRY'S PARTNER. New York, Dodd Mead, 1929. 268p [BVa LC OTMC
FOREST FRIENDS. Stories of Animals, Fish and Birds, West of the Rockies. Philadelphia, Judson, 1926. 218p [BM LC
MIST ON THE RIVER. A Novel. Toronto, Copp Clark, 1954. 282p
MOUNTAIN DOG. Philadelphia, Westminster Press, 1956. 168p
THE NEW FRONT LINE. Toronto, Macmillan, 1927. 291p [BVaU OTMC QMM
THE SILENT CALL. New York, Dodd Mead, 1930. 248p [BVa LC

F., Miss E.
NOTHING LIKE BLACK ON WHITE. By Miss E.F. Ottawa, Maclean Roger, 1878. 158p [OTMC

Fairchild, George Moore, 1854–1912
THE MAID OF THE MOUNTAIN. Toronto, Rous & Mann, 1932. [BM BVaU NBFU OTMC
A RIDICULOUS COURTING, and Other Stories of French Canada. Chicago, Donnelley, 1900. 261p [BVaU LC NBFU OTMC

Falkner, Frederick Benjamin, 1902–
THE AQUALUNG TWINS AND THE 'IRON CRAB.' Toronto, Dent, 1959. 188p
THE AQUALUNG TWINS FIND CHINESE TREASURE. Toronto, Dent, 1956. 167p

Farran, Roy Alexander St. Thomas Aquinas, 1921–
THE DAY AFTER TOMORROW. London, Panther Books, 1959. 158p [Earlier ed.:
London, Collins, 1956.]
THE SEARCH. London, Collins, 1958. 253p

Faughnan, Thomas, *fl.* 1835–1883
THE YOUNG HUSSAR; or, Lady Iris's Adventure. A Story of Love and War. Picton,
Ont., Author, 1890. 484p [BVaU NSHD OTP

Fenety, George Edward, 1812–1899
THE LADY AND THE DRESSMAKER; or, A Peep at Fashionable Folly. By a Bluenose
[pseud]. Halifax, Author, 1842. 24p [Also bound with a continuation added
to make a total of 136p] [BVaU NSHP

Fennell, Irene
GHOST LIGHT. New York, Pegasus Pub. Co., 1939. 154p [NBFU OTU

Ferguson, Ida May
TISAB TING; or, The Electrical Kiss. By Dyjan Fergus [pseud]. Toronto, Hunter
Rose, 1896. 300p [BM BVaU NSHD OOP

Fewster, Edna Lysle.
LENGTHENING SHADOWS. A Novel. New York, Pageant Press, 1957. 94p

Field, Bradda, 1904–
BRIDE OF GLORY. Being the Strange Story of Emy Lyon. New York, Greystone,
1942. 963p [Pub. in England as: MILEDI. Being the Strange Story of Emy Lyon.
London, Constable, 1942. 979p] [BM BVaU LC NBFU OTMC
THE EARTHEN LOT. New York, Harcourt, 1928. 400p [BM BVaU LC NBFU
GRAND HARBOUR. London, Constable, 1934. 400p [BM LC NBFU
SMALL TOWN. London, Constable, 1931. 310p [BVaU LC NBFU OTU

Findlay, David Kilpatrick, 1901–
SEARCH FOR AMELIA. Philadelphia, Lippincott, 1958. 256p

Fischer, William Joseph, 1879–1921
CHILD OF DESTINY. Toronto, Briggs, 1908. 272p [BM OTMC
WINONA AND OTHER STORIES. St. Louis, Mo., Herder, 1906. 219p [OTMC

Fisher, Olive Margaret, 1889–
TOTEM, TIPI AND TUMPLINE. Stories of Canadian Indians. By Olive M. Fisher and
Clara L. Tyner. Toronto, Dent, 1955. xi + 264p

Flatt, Mrs. Olive Augusta, 1884–
GRANDMA'S SHORT STORIES. Hamilton, Davis-Lisson, 1951. 95p

Flatt, W.D.
THE MAKING OF A MAN. Toronto, Briggs, 1918. 154p [BM BVaU NBFU OTMC

Fleet, William Henry

HOW I CAME TO BE GOVERNOR OF THE ISLAND OF CACONA. By The Hon. Francis Thistleton [pseud]. Montreal, etc., Ramsay, etc., 1852. 220p [BVaU OTP QMM

Fleming, May Agnes (Early), 1840–1880

THE ACTRESS' DAUGHTER. New York, Carleton, 1886. 394p [BM LC NBS

THE BARONET'S BRIDE; or, A Woman's Vengeance. Ed. by W.J. Benners, Jr. New York, Munro, 1892. 250p [LC

CARRIED BY STORM. New York, Carleton, 1880. 440p [Also: New York, Dillingham, 1907. 398p] [LC NBFU OTMC

A CHANGED HEART. A Novel. New York, Carleton, 1881. [Later ed.: New York, Dillingham, 1897. 480p] [AmCat OTU

THE DARK SECRET; or, The Mystery of Fontelle Hall. New York, Hurst, 1875. 361p [AEU NBFU

EDITH PERCIVAL. A Novel. New York, Dillingham, 1893. 330p [First pub. in 1860?–BCF] [LC

ERMINIE; or, The Gipsy's Vow. A Tale of Love and Vengeance. New York, Brady, 1863. [Probably same as: GYPSY QUEEN'S VOW. New York, Beadle, 1870.] [AmCat

ESTELLA'S HUSBAND; or, Thrice Lost, Thrice Won. New York, Munro, 1891. 291p [Later pub. under title: THRICE LOST, THRICE WON.] [LC OTU

FATED TO MARRY; [and] A NIGHT OF TERROR; [and] KATHLEEN. New York, Ogilvie, 1881. [AmCat

THE GHOST OF RIVERDALE HAL. New York, Lupton, 1895. 62p [LC

GUY EARLSCOURT'S WIFE. A Novel. New York, Carleton, [1872?]. [Later ed.: New York, Dillingham, 1900. 484p] [LC NBFU

THE GYPSY QUEEN'S VOW. New York, Hurst, 1875. 399p [NBFU

THE HEIR OF CHARLTON; A Story of Shaddeck Light. New York, Dillingham, 1905. 396p [First pub., 1878] [AmCat LC NBFU OKQ

THE HEIRESS OF GLEN GOWER; or, The Hidden Crime. Ed. by W.J. Benners, Jr. New York, Munro, 1892. 251p [LC

KATE DANTON; or, Captain Danton's Daughters. New York, Carleton, 1876. 436p [LC OTMC QMBM

LA MASQUE; or, The Midnight Queen. New York, Brady, 1863. [Later pub. as: THE MIDNIGHT QUEEN. New York, Dillingham, 1888. 396p] [BM LC NSHD OTMC

LADY EVELYN; or, The Lord of Royal Rest. New York, Street & Smith, 1899. 262p [LC

LOST FOR A WOMAN. A Novel. New York, Carleton, 1880. 456p [LC NBFU OTMC

A MAD MARRIAGE. A Novel. New York, Carleton, 1875. 459p [BM LC NBFU

MAGDALEN'S VOW. Ed. by W.J. Benners, Jr. New York, Munro, 1893. 286p [LC OTU

MARRIED FOR MONEY, AND OTHER STORIES. New York, Ogilvie, 1891. 246p
[LC

MAUDE PERCY'S SECRET. A Novel. New York, Carleton, 1884. 432p [LC

NORINE'S REVENGE, [and] SIR NOEL'S HEIR. New York, Dillingham, 1888. 402p
[First pub. in 1875?–BCF] [LC NBFU

ONE NIGHT'S MYSTERY. New York, Carleton, [1876?]. [Later ed.: New York,
Dillingham, 1897. 443p] [AmCat NBFU

PATRICIA KEMBLEY. A Novel. Toronto, Rose Belford, 1882. 479p [OTMC

A PRETTY GOVERNESS, AND OTHER STORIES. New York, Ogilvie, 1891. 218p
[LC

PRIDE AND PASSION. A Novel. New York, Carleton, 1882. 416p [LC

THE SECRET SORROW. New York, Ogilvie, 1883. 341p [LC

SHARING HER CRIME. A Novel. New York, Carleton, 1883. 384p [LC

SHE MIGHT HAVE DONE BETTER. A Novel. Toronto, Rose Pub. Co., n.d. 240p
[OH

SILENT AND TRUE; or, A Little Queen. New York, Carleton, 1877. 460p [LC
NBFU

SIR NOEL'S HEIR. A Novel. New York, Lupton, 1892. 123p [See also under
NORINE'S REVENGE.] [LC NBS

THE SISTERS OF TORWOOD. A Novel. New York, Dillingham, 1898. 316p
[Earlier ed.: London, Henderson, 1890.] [BM BVaU LC

SYBIL CAMPBELL; or, The Queen of the Isle. New York, Brady, 1863. 151p [Also
pub. as: AN AWFUL MYSTERY. New York, Beadle, 1875; and as: THE QUEEN OF
THE ISLE. New York, Dillingham, 1886. 400p –LC] [BM LC OTU

A TERRIBLE SECRET. New York, Carleton, [1874?]. [Later ed.: New York,
Dillingham, 1897. 410p] [AmCat NBFU

THE THREE COUSINS, [and] ONE SUMMER MONTH. New York, Ogilvie, 1881.
[AmCat

THE TWIN SISTERS; or, The Wronged Wife's Hate. New York, Starr, 1869. [Also
pub. under title: THE RIVAL BROTHERS; or, The Wronged Wife's Hate. New
York, Beadle, 1875. 224p] [AmCat NBFL

UNCLE FRED'S VISIT AND HOW IT ENDED. London, Mowbray, [1888]. 51p [BM

THE UNSEEN BRIDEGROOM; or, Wedded for a Week. Ed. by W.J. Benners, Jr.
New York, Munro, 1892. 217p [LC

VICTORIA; or, The Heiress of Castle Cliffe. New York, Brady, 1864. 124p [Later
pub. under title: UNMASKED; or, The Heiress of Castle Cliffe. New York, Beadle,
1870.] [BM LC OTU

THE VIRGINIA HEIRESS. New York, Street & Smith, 1888. 239p [LC OTU

WEDDED FOR PIQUE. A Novel. New York, Dillingham, 1897. 302p [LC NBFL

WHO WINS? or, The Secret of Monkswood Waste. New York, Munro, 1895. 225p
[LC OTU

A WIFE'S TRAGEDY. A Novel. New York, Carleton, 1881. 431p [Also: Toronto,
Rose Belford, 1881. 297p] [LC OTMC

A WONDERFUL WOMAN. A Novel. New York, Dillingham, 1888. [First pub. in
1873? Also: Toronto, J. Ross Robertson, 1881. 109p; and New York,
Dillingham, 1901. 544p] [AmCat LC NSHD OTMC

A WRONGED WIFE. New York, Dillingham, 1883. [Same as THE TWIN SISTERS?]
[AmCat

Flewellyn, Julia (Colliton), 1850–

FORGOTTEN CHILDREN. Anderson, Ind., Gospel Trumpet Co., 1929. 189p [LC
HILL-CREST. Toronto, Cooper, 1894. 269p [Also: Boston, Arena, 1895. 304p]
[LC OTMC

Floroff, Peter C.N.

THE FAWN. New York, Vantage Press, 1958. 115p

Foley, Pearl Beatrix, –1953

THE GIFT OF THE GODS. Toronto, Allen, 1921. 279p [BM LC NBFU OTMC
THE GNOME MINE MYSTERY. A Northern Ontario Mining Story. By Paul de Mar
[pseud]. London, Hamilton, 1933. 255p [BM BVaU NBFU
THE OCTAGON CRYSTAL. New York, Carrier, 1929. 265p [BM LC NBFU
OTMC
THE YELLOW CIRCLE. Philadelphia, Lippincott, 1937. 315p [BM LC NBFU
OTMC

Fontaine, Robert Louis, 1911–1965

THE HAPPY TIME. New York, Simon & Schuster, 1945. 269p [BM BVaU NBFU
OTU
MY UNCLE LOUIS. New York, Toronto, McGraw-Hill, 1953. 294p

Footner, Hulbert, 1879–1944

THE ALMOST PERFECT MURDER. Philadelphia, Lippincott, 1937. 319p [BM LC
NBFU OTMC
ANTENNAE. New York, Doran, 1926. 350p [Same as RICH MAN, POOR MAN, *q.v.*]
[LC NBFU
ANYBODY'S PEARLS. Garden City, Doubleday, 1930. 325p [BM LC NBFU
OTMC
A BACKWOODS PRINCESS. New York, Doran, 1926. 320p [BM BVaU LC NBFU
OOP
CAP'N SUE. London, Hodder, 1927. 320p [BM LC NBFU
THE CASUAL MURDERER. Philadelphia, Lippincott, 1937. 337p [BM LC NBFU
OTMC
THE CHASE OF THE "LINDA BELLE." London, Hodder, 1925. 320p [BM
COUNTRY LOVE, ETC. London, Hodder, 1922. 319p [BM
DANGEROUS CARGO. New York, Harper, 1934. 339p [BM BVaU LC OTMC
THE DARK SHIPS. New York, Harper, 1937. 384p [BM LC NBFU OTMC
DEAD MAN'S HAT. New York, Harper, 1932. 299p [BM BVaU LC NBFU
THE DEATH OF A CELEBRITY. New York, Harper, 1938. 278p [BM LC OOP

DEATH OF A SABOTEUR. New York, Harper, 1943. 282p [BM LC OTMC

THE DEAVES AFFAIR. Toronto, McClelland, 1922. 319p [BM BVaU LC NBFU OTMC

THE DOCTOR WHO HELD HANDS. A Madame Storey Novel. Garden City, Doubleday, 1929. 310p [BM BVaU LC NBFU OTMC

EASY TO KILL. New York, Harper, 1931. 312p [BM BVaU LC OTMC

THE FOLDED PAPER MYSTERY. London, Collins, 1930. 250p [See THE MYSTERY OF THE FOLDED PAPER, below.] [BM

THE FUGITIVE SLEUTH. London, Hodder, 1918. 268p [BM SSU

THE FUR BRINGERS. A Story of the Canadian Northwest. New York, McCann, 1920. 313p [BM BVaU LC NBFU OTMC

THE HOUSE WITH THE BLUE DOOR. New York, Harper, 1942. 280p [BM NBFU OOP

THE HUNTRESS. New York, McCann, 1922. 312p [BM BVa LC NBFU

ISLAND OF FEAR. London, Cassell, 1936. 287p [BM LC NBFU OOP

JACK CHANTY. A Story of Athabasca. Garden City, Doubleday, 1913. 337p [BVaU LC NBFU OTMC QMM

MADAME STOREY. New York, Doran, 1926. 341p [Cf. THE KIDNAPPING OF MADAME STOREY AND OTHER STORIES. London, Collins, 1936. 284p] [BM LC NBFU OTMC

MORE THAN BREAD. Philadelphia, Lippincott, 1938. 365p [BM LC NBFU OTMC

MURDER IN THE SUN. London, Collins, 1938. 252p [BM

THE MURDER OF A BAD MAN. New York, Harper, 1936. 306p [BM LC OOP

MURDER RUNS IN THE FAMILY. New York, Harper, 1934. 258p [BM LC NBFU OOP

THE MURDER THAT HAD EVERYTHING. New York, Harper, 1939. 307p [BM LC OTMC

MURDERER'S VANITY. New York, Harper, 1940. 306p [BM LC NBFU

THE MYSTERY OF THE FOLDED PAPER. New York, Harper, 1930. 350p [BVaU LC NBFU OTU

THE NATION'S MISSING GUEST. New York, Harper, 1939. 270p [BM LC NBFU OOP

A NEW GIRL IN TOWN. London, Hodder, 1927. 327p [BM

THE NEW MADE GRAVE. London, Collins, 1935. 284p [BM LC

ON SWAN RIVER. London, Hodder, 1919. 314p [BM NBFU

THE OBEAH MURDERS. New York, Harper, 1937. 279p [LC

OFFICER! Toronto, McClelland, 1924. 279p [BM LC OTP

ORCHIDS TO MURDER. New York, Harper, 1945. 244p [BM BVaU NBFU OTMC

THE OWL TAXI. New York, Doran, 1921. 309p [BM BVaU LC OTMC

THE QUEEN OF CLUBS. New York, Doran, 1927. 313p [BM BVaU NBFU OTMC

THE RAMSHACKLE HOUSE. New York, Doran, 1922. 311p [BM LC OTP

RICH MAN, POOR MAN. London, Faber, 1928. 286p [Same as ANTENNAE,*q.v.*]
[BM

THE RING OF EYES. London, Collins, 1933. 252p [BM LC NBFU

ROGER MANION'S GIRL. New York, Harper, 1935. 303p [BM

SCARRED JUNGLE. New York, Harper, 1935. 303p [BM LC NBFU OTMC

THE SEALED VALLEY. Toronto, Musson, 1914. 356p [BM BViPA LC OTMC

A SELF-MADE THIEF. Garden City, Doubleday, 1929. 285p [LC OTMC

THE SHANTY SLED. New York, Doran, 1926. 294p [BM BVaU LC NBFU OTP

SINFULLY RICH. New York, Harper, 1940. 348p [BM BVaU LC NBFU OTMC

THE SUBSTITUTE MILLIONAIRE. New York, Doran, 1919. 350p [BM LC OTMC

THIEVES WIT. An Everyday Detective Story. New York, Doran, 1918. 345p [BM
LC OTMC

TORTUOUS TRAILS. [Detective Stories.] London, Collins, 1937. 283p [BM

TRIAL BY WATER. New York, Farrar & Rinehart, 1931. 321p [BM LC NBFU
OOP

TWO ON THE TRAIL. A Story of the Far Northwest. Garden City, Doubleday, 1911.
349p [BM BVaU LC OTMC

THE UNDER DOGS. New York, Doran, 1925. 325p [BM LC NBFU OTP

UNNEUTRAL MURDER. New York, Harper, 1944. 254p [BM LC NBFU OTMC

THE VELVET HAND. New Madame Storey Mysteries. Garden City, Doubleday,
1928. 333p [BM BVaU LC OTMC

THE VIPER. London, Collins, 1930. 245p [BM BVaU OTMC

THE WHIP-POOR-WILL MYSTERY. New York, Harper, 1935. 338p [BM LC OOP

WHO KILLED THE HUSBAND? New York, Harper, 1941. 208p [BM LC OTMC

THE WILD BIRD. New York, Doran, 1923. 282p [BM BVaU LC OTMC

THE WOMAN FROM "OUTSIDE." New York, McCann, 1921. 268p [LC OTMC

Ford, John David, 1912–

FEAST OF THE MIDNIGHT SUN. A Story of the Canadian Arctic. New York,
Greenwich Book Pub., 1958. 94p

Forrest, Edmund William, –1880

NED FORTESCUE; or, Roughing it through Life. A Story founded on Fact. Ottawa,
Hunter, 1869. 232p [2nd ed.: Montreal, Author, 1871. 365p] [BVaU NBFU
OTMC

VELLENAUX. A Novel. Saint John, "Daily News," 1870. 262p [BVaU NSHD
OTMC

Forster, Agnes J.

DOORS AWAITING. New York, Ryerson, 1940. 245p [NBFU OTU

Fortier, Cora B.

UNKNOWN FAIRIES OF CANADA. Twelve Fairy Stories. By Maxine [pseud].
Toronto, Macmillan, 1926. 90p [NBFU OTU

Fox, Marion Wathen, 1871–1956
MIDGET STORIES FOR BUSY PEOPLE. No. 1. Saint John, Barnes Hopkins, 1954.
16p

Frame, Elizabeth, 1820–1913
THE TWILIGHT OF FAITH. Toronto, 1872. 128p [Earlier ed.: Boston, 1871.]
[BM NSHP

Frank, Mrs. M.J.
THE BROCK FAMILY. By A.L.O.M. (A Lady of Manitoba) [pseud]. Toronto,
Briggs, 1890. 263p [OTU

Fraser, Annie Ermatinger, –1930
THE DRUM OF LANORAYE. A Narrative of the Days of Talon, the Great Intendant.
Toronto, Ryerson, 1932. 308p [BVaU NBFU OTMC QMM

Fraser, Francess Jane (Williams), 1922–
THE BEAR WHO STOLE THE CHINOOK, AND OTHER STORIES. By Frances Fraser.
Toronto, Macmillan, 1959. 72p

Fraser, Thurlow, 1869–1926
THE CALL OF THE EAST. A Romance of Far Formosa. Toronto, Briggs, 1914.
351p [BVaU LC OTMC

Fraser, William Alexander, 1859–1933
THE BLOOD LILIES. New York, Scribner, 1903. 262p [BM BVaU NBFU OTMC
BRAVE HEARTS. New York, Scribner, 1904. 307p [BM BVaU LC OTMC
BULLDOG CARNEY. Toronto, McClelland, 1919. 306p [BM BVaU LC NBFU
OTMC
CASTE. New York, Doran, 1922. 274p [BM BVaU LC NBFU OTMC
DELILAH PLAYS THE PONIES. Toronto, Musson, 1927. 319p [BVaU NBFU
OTMC QMM
THE EYE OF A GOD AND OTHER TALES OF EAST AND WEST. New York,
Doubleday, 1899. 260p [BVaU LC MWU OTMC QMM
THE LONE FURROW. New York, Appleton, 1907. 354p [BM BVaU LC NBFU
OTMC
MOOSWA & OTHERS OF THE BOUNDARIES. New York, Scribner, 1900. 260p
[Also later eds.: Toronto, Ryerson.] [BM BVaU LC OKQ
THE OUTCASTS. Toronto, Briggs, 1901. 137p [BVaU LC NSHD OKQ
RED MEEKINS. New York, Doran, 1921. 297p [BVaU LC NBFU OTMC
THE SA'-ZADA TALES. New York, Scribner, 1905. 231p [BM BVaU LC NSHD
OTMC
THIRTEEN MEN. New York, Appleton, 1906. 305p [BM LC OTMC QMM
THOROUGHBREDS. New York, McClure, 1902. 405p [BM BVaU LC NBFU
OKQ
THE THREE SAPPHIRES. New York, Doran, 1918. 321p [BVaU LC NBFU
OTMC

Fraser, William Ross, 1908–
A WHITE STONE. A Novel. New York, Philosophical Library, 1955. 188p

Frazer, Miss C.A.
ATMA. A Romance. By A.C.F. [pseud]. Montreal, Lovell, 1891. 143p [BVaU
LC NBFU OKQ

Frechette, Annie Thomas (Howells)
THE FARM'S LITTLE PEOPLE. Sequel to ON GRANDFATHER'S FARM. Philadelphia,
Am. Baptist Pub., 1897. 107p [LC OOP
ON GRANDFATHER'S FARM. Philadelphia, Am. Baptist Soc., 1897. 85p [LC OOP
REUBEN DALE. 1873. [BCF

Freedman, Frank, 1917–
THIS SIDE OF HOLMAN'S HILL. London, Secker & Warburg, 1957. 197p

Freeman, John Dolliver, 1864–1943
KENNEDY'S SECOND BEST. A Story of the Great Northwest. Toronto, McClelland,
1926. 302p [BM BVaU NBFU OTMC

French, John McLean, 1863–1940
THE TRAIL OF DESTINY. A Romance of the Canadian Bush. New York, Burt,
1924. 317p [BViV OH

French, Maida (Parlow)
ALL THIS TO KEEP. Toronto, Collins, 1947. 354p [BVaU LC NBFU OTMC
BOUGHS BEND OVER. Toronto, McClelland, 1943. 246p [BVaU LC NBFU
OKQ QMM

Freund, Philip, 1909–
BOOK OF KINGS. A Novel. New York, Pilgrim, 1938. 254p [LC
THE DARK SHORE. A Novel. New York, Ives Washburn, 1941. 296p [BM LC
NBFU OTMC
DREAMS OF YOUTH. New York, Pilgrim, 1938. 234p [LC NBFU
EASTER ISLAND. New York, Beechhurst, 1947. 221p [LC NBFU
EDWARD ZOLTAN. New York, Beechhurst, 1946. 200p [BVaU LC OTMC
THE EVENING HERON. New York, Pilgrim, 1937. 218p [BM LC NBFU OTMC
A MAN OF TASTE, AND OTHER STORIES. New York, Beechhurst, 1949. 357p
[BVaU LC NBFU
THE MERRY COMMUNIST. New York, Pilgrim, 1934. 116p [LC NBFU
THE SNOW AND OTHER STORIES. New York, Pilgrim, 1935. 226p [LC NBFU
STEPHANIE'S SON. A Novel. New York, Beechhurst, 1947. 373p [LC OTMC
THREE EXOTIC TALES. New York, Pilgrim, 1945. 239p [LC NBFU
THE YOUNG GREEK AND THE CREOLE, AND OTHER STORIES. New York, Pilgrim,
1944. 271p [LC NBFU
THE ZOLTANS. New York, Beechhurst, 1948. 3v [Includes BOOK OF KINGS,
EDWARD ZOLTAN, STEPHANIE'S SON.] [BVaU LC NBFU

Frost, J.W.
BROKEN SHACKLES. The Story of a Fugitive Slave. By Glenelg [pseud]. Toronto, Briggs, 1889. 304p [BCF OTMC

Fry, Pamela
HARSH EVIDENCE. London, Wingate, 1953. 172p
THE WATCHING CAT. London, Davies, 1960. 223p

Fuller, James William, 1871–
IZOLDA. A Magyar Romance. New York, Abbey, 1902. 228p [LC OLU

Furse, Barbara Ross
CROCODILE TEARS. London, Long, 1935. 287p [BM OTU

Fytche, Maria Amelia, 1844–1927
KERCHIEFS TO HUNT SOULS. A Novel. Boston, Arena, 1895. 290p [BM LC
THE RIVAL FORTS; or, The Velvet Siege of Beauséjour. Halifax, A. McNeil, 1907. 369p [NBFU OOP

G., E.A.
A SUMMER HOLIDAY. By E.A.G. Toronto, Briggs, 1887. 38p [Haight Pt I

Gagnieur, Elizabeth
BACK IN THE FIFTIES; or, Winnings and Weedings. A Tale of Tractarian Times. By Elizabeth Gagnieur (Alba). Montreal, Sadlier, 1907. 437p [OOP

Galbraith, John
IN THE NEW CAPITAL; or, The City of Ottawa in 1999. Toronto, Toronto News, 1897. 151p [BM OTU

Gale, James Scarth, 1863–1937
KOREAN SKETCHES. Toronto, Revell, 1899. 256p [BM LC NBFU
THE VANGUARD. A Tale of Korea. Toronto, Revell, 1904. 320p [BM LC

Gallant, Mavis, 1922–
GREEN WATER, GREEN SKY. Boston, Houghton, 1959. 154p
THE OTHER PARIS. Stories. Boston, Houghton, 1956. 240p

Galloway, Christian F.J.
THE EXPLOITS OF LANCELOT. [A Tale.] London, Stockwell, 1924. 35p [BM

Gamble, Henry Elliot
D'ARCY. A Romantic Thriller. Toronto, Ryerson, 1947. 131p [OTMC

Ganong, Joan
ANGIE AND THE ARAB. Fredericton, Brunswick Press, 1957. 56p

Gardner, Elizabeth Mary (Vidal), 1857–1932

CHARACTERISTIC CONVERSATIONS OF CURLY KATE. Toronto, Briggs, 1907. 47p
[Phelps p92

Gardner, Mrs. Elsie Bell

MAXIE, AN ADORABLE GIRL; or, Her Adventures in the British West Indies. New
York, Cupples, 1932. 207p [LC

MAXIE AT BRINKSOME HALL; or, Strange Adventures with her Chums. New York,
Cupples, 1934. 212p [LC

MAXIE AND HER ADVENTURES IN SPAIN; or, The Rescue of a Royalist. New York,
Cupples, 1936. 205p [LC

MAXIE AND THE GOLDEN BIRD. New York, Cupples, 1939. 210p [LC

MAXIE IN THE JUNGLE; or, The Temple of the Incas. New York, Cupples, 1937.
209p [LC

MAXIE IN VENEZUELA; or, The Clue to the Diamond Mine. New York, Cupples,
1932. 200p [LC

MAXIE SEARCHING FOR HER PARENTS; or, The Mystery in Australian Waters. New
York, Cupples, 1932. 204p [LC

Garner, Hugh, 1913–

CABBAGETOWN. Toronto, Collins, 1950. 160p [NBFU OLU

PRESENT RECKONING. Toronto, Collins, 1951. 158p

STORM BELOW. Toronto, Collins, 1949. 227p [BVaU NBFU OTMC QMM

WASTE NO TEARS. By Jarvis Warwick [pseud]. New Toronto, Export Pub.
Enterprises, 1951. [Priv. info.

THE YELLOW SWEATER, AND OTHER STORIES. Toronto, Collins, 1952. 238p

Garrioch, Rev. Alfred Campbell, 1848–1934

THE FAR AND FURRY NORTH. A Story of Love and Travel in the Days of the
Hudson's Bay Co. Winnipeg, Douglass McIntyre, 1925. 238p [BVaU NBFU
OTMC QMBM SSU

Genest, Frank Devlin, 1894–1944

THE LETTERS OF SI WHIFFLETREE, FRESHMAN. With a preface by Stephen
Leacock. Montreal, 1921. 69p [BM BVaU NBFU OTMC

Gibbon, John Murray, 1875–1952

THE CONQUERING HERO. Toronto, Gundy, 1920. 288p [BM BVaU NSHD
OTMC QMM

DRUMS AFAR. An International Romance. London, Lane, 1918. 352p [BM
BVaU NBFU OTMC QMM

EYES OF A GYPSY. Toronto, Macmillan, 1926. 255p [BM BVaU NBFU OTMC

HEARTS AND FACES. The Adventure of a Soul. Toronto, Gundy, 1916. 352p [BM
BVaU NBFU OTU

PAGAN LOVE. Toronto, McClelland, 1922. 310p [BVaU NBFU OTU QMM

THE TRUE ANNALS OF FAIRYLAND IN THE REIGN OF KING COLE. Ed. by ——.
London, Dent, 1909. 338p [BVaU LC NBFU OTMC

Gibbons, Charles Harrison, 1869—
A SOURDOUGH SAMARITAN. Toronto, Hodder, 1923. 320p [BVaU NBFU OOP

Gibbs, Willa, 1917—
THE DEAN. London, Hodder, 1957. 190p [Same as ALL THE GOLDEN DOORS.
New York, Appleton, 1957.]
SIMON OF LEICESTER. London, Hodder, 1960. 313p
THE TWO DOCTORS. A Novel. London, Hodder, 1959. 222p [Pub. in U.S. as
THE DEDICATED, New York, Morrow, 1960. 224p]

Gill, Rev. Edward Anthony Wharton, 1858—1944
AN IRISHMAN'S LUCK. A Tale of Manitoba. Toronto, Musson, 1914. [Also: Lon-
don, Hodder, 1914. 310p] [BM OOP
LOVE IN MANITOBA. London, Swift, 1911. 315p [Also: Toronto, Musson, 1912.]
[BM BVaU OOP
A MANITOBA CHORE BOY. The Experiences of a Young Emigrant Told from his
Letters. London, Religious Tract Soc., 1912. 83p [BM BVaU OTU SSU

Gill, T.M.
THE HEART OF LUNENBURG. By Sabattis [pseud]. Levis, Que., Author, 1930.
96p [OTP
THE LURE OF THE CITY. By Sabattis [pseud]. Sackville, N.B., Tribune Press, n.d.
129p [OTU

Gillen, Mollie (Woolnough)
A STAR OF DEATH. London, Bles, 1960. 255p

Gillese, John Patrick, 1926—
KIRBY'S GANDER. Toronto, Ryerson, 1957. ix + 212p

Gillis, James Donald, 1870—
A MARITIMES LIFE. A Romance: The Life of Kalby MacKee. Melrose Hill,
Inverness Co., N.S., Author, n.d. 126p [mimeographed]
THE PIE SOCIAL. A Modern Romance. Melrose Hill, Inverness Co., N.S., Author,
n.d. 74p [mimeographed]

Ginsburg, Bere Joseph, 1894—
GENERATION PASSETH ... GENERATION COMETH. Toronto, Ryerson, 1960. 215p

Glasier, Alfred A.
THE IRVING CLUB AMONG THE WHITE HILLS. Saint John, Godard, 1877. 113p
[NSWA OONL

Glassco, John, 1909—
UNDER THE BIRCH. The Story of an English Governess. By Miles Underwood

[pseud]. Paris, France, Ophelia Press, 1965. 187p [First pub. in 1960, with title: THE ENGLISH GOVERNESS.]

Glay, George Albert, 1905?—
BEGGARS MIGHT RIDE. New York, Appleton, 1951. 341p
GINA. New York, Pellegrini, 1948. 378p [BM LC

Glendinning, Margarite
GERTIE, THE HORSE WHO THOUGHT AND THOUGHT. New York, Whittlesey House, 1951. 88p

Godfrey, Denis, 1912—
THE BRIDGE OF FIRE. London, Cape, 1954. 285p
WHEN KINGS ARE ARMING. Toronto, Clarke Irwin, 1951. 224p

Godfrey, J.J.
SHAVINGS. A Semi-Legal Medley. Pt. 1. Toronto, Poole, 1907. 46p [BM BVaU LC OTUV

Gomery, Percy, 1881—1960
CURVE, GO SLOW. A Romance of the Pacific Coast. Ottawa, Graphic, 1927. 333p [BVaU NBFU OTU QMM
END OF THE CIRCLE. Toronto, Macmillan, 1929. 266p [BVaU NBFU OTMC

Goosequill (pseud)
AS OTHERS SEE US. Being the Diary of a Canadian Debutante. By "Goosequill" [pseud]. Toronto, Macmillan, 1915. 299p [BM BVaU NSWA OLU

Gordon, Charles G. William, 1899—
GRINGO. Garden City, Doubleday, 1930. 355p [LC NBFU

Gordon, Rev. Charles William, 1860—1937
THE ARM OF GOLD. By Ralph Connor [pseud]. New York, Dodd Mead, 1932. 314p [BM BVaU LC NBFU OTMC
BEYOND THE MARSHES. By Ralph Connor [pseud]. Toronto, Westminster, 1898. 19p [BM BVaU LC NSHD OTMC
BLACK ROCK. A Tale of the Selkirks. By Ralph Connor [pseud]. Toronto, Westminster, 1898. 327p [BM BVaU LC NBFU OTMC QMM
BREAKING THE RECORD. By Ralph Connor [pseud]. New York, Revell, 1904. 31p [LC NBFU OKQ
CORPORAL CAMERON OF THE NORTH WEST MOUNTED POLICE. A Tale of the Macleod Trail. By Ralph Connor [pseud]. New York, Hodder, 1912. 454p [BM BVaU LC NSHD OTMC QMM
THE DOCTOR. A Tale of the Rockies. By Ralph Connor [pseud]. Toronto, Westminster, 1906. 399p [Pub. in England under title: THE DOCTOR OF CROW'S NEST. London, Hodder, 1906. 399p] [BM BVaU LC NBFU OTMC QMM

THE FOREIGNER. A Tale of Saskatchewan. By Ralph Connor [pseud]. Toronto, Westminster, 1909. 384p [Also as: THE SETTLER. A Tale of Saskatchewan. London, Hodder. 1909. 307p] [BM BVaU LC NSHD OTMC

THE FRIENDLY FOUR, AND OTHER STORIES. By Ralph Connor [pseud]. New York, Doran, 1926. 275p [BM BVaU LC NBFU OTMC QMM

THE GASPARDS OF PINE CROFT. A Romance of the Windermere. By Ralph Connor [pseud]. Toronto, McClelland, 1923. 318p [BM BVaU LC NBFU OTMC QMM

THE GAY CRUSADER. A Romance of Quebec. By Ralph Connor [pseud]. New York, Dodd Mead, 1936. 376p [BVaU LC NBFU OTMC

THE GIRL FROM GLENGARRY. By Ralph Connor [pseud]. New York, Dodd Mead, 1933. 312p [Also as: THE GLENGARRY GIRL. London, Lane, 1934. 341p [BM BVaU LC NBFU OTMC

GLENGARRY SCHOOL DAYS. A Story of Early Days in Glengarry. By Ralph Connor [pseud]. Chicago, Revell, 1902. 340p [Also as: GLENGARRY DAYS. London, Hodder, 1902. 252p] [BM BVaU LC NBFU OTU QMM

GWEN. An Idyll of the Canyon. By Ralph Connor [pseud]. New York, Revell, 1904. 94p [Reprinting of chapters 9–13 of THE SKY PILOT.] [BM BVaU LC NBFU OTMC

GWEN'S CANYON. By Ralph Connor [pseud]. Toronto, Westminster, 1898. 30p [BM

HE DWELT AMONG US. By Ralph Connor [pseud]. New York, Revell, 1936. 174p [BM BVaU LC NBFU OTMC

THE MAJOR. By Ralph Connor [pseud]. Toronto, McClelland, 1917. 383p [BM BVaU LC NBFU OTMC

THE MAN FROM GLENGARRY. A Tale of the Ottawa. By Ralph Connor [pseud]. Toronto, Westminster, 1901. 473p [Also, with intro. by S.R. Beharriell: Toronto, McClelland, 1960. xiii + 289p] [BM BVaU LC NBFU OTU QMM

MICHAEL McGRATH, POSTMASTER. London, Sharpe, 1900. 42p [BM

THE PATROL OF THE SUN DANCE TRAIL. By Ralph Connor [pseud]. New York, Doran, 1914. 363p [BM BVaU LC NBFU OTU

THE PILOT AT SWAN CREEK [and Other Stories]. London, Hodder, 1905. 184p [BM BVaU NBFU OKQ

THE PROSPECTOR. A Tale of the Crow's Nest Pass. By Ralph Connor [pseud]. New York, Revell, 1904. 401p [BM BVaU LC NBFU OKQ

THE REBEL LOYALIST. By Ralph Connor [pseud]. Toronto, McClelland, 1935. 328p [BM BVaU LC NBFU OTMC

THE ROCK AND THE RIVER. A Romance of Quebec. By Ralph Connor [pseud]. New York, Dodd Mead, 1931. 377p [BM BVaU LC NSHD OKQ

THE RUNNER. A Romance of the Niagaras. By Ralph Connor [pseud]. Garden City, Doubleday, 1929. 481p [BM BVaU LC NBFU OTMC

THE SKY PILOT. A Tale of the Foothills. By Ralph Connor [pseud]. Chicago, Revell, 1899. 300p [BM BVaU LC NBFU OKQ

THE SKY PILOT IN NO MAN'S LAND. By Ralph Connor [pseud]. Toronto,
McClelland, 1919. 349p [BM BVaU LC NBFU OTMC QMM

THE SWAN CREEK BLIZZARD. By Ralph Connor [pseud]. New York, Revell,
1904. 29p [*Cf.* THE PILOT AT SWAN CREEK..., above.] [LC NBFU OTMC

TO HIM THAT HATH. A Novel of the West of Today. By Ralph Connor [pseud].
New York, Doran, 1921. 291p [BM BVaU LC NBFU OTMC

TORCHES THROUGH THE BUSH. A Tale of Glengarry. By Ralph Connor [pseud].
New York, Dodd Mead, 1934. 300p [BM BVaU LC NBFU OTMC QMM

TREADING THE WINEPRESS. By Ralph Connor [pseud]. Toronto, McClelland,
1925. 394p [BM BVaU LC NBFU OTMC QMM

Gordon, Mrs. Charlotte

RED GOLD. A True Story of an Englishwoman's Development in the West.
Vancouver, McBeath & Campbell, 1928. 265p [BVaU NBFU OTMC

Gordon, Robert Kay, 1887–

IN THE GRIP OF THE BARREN LANDS. By Norman Blake [pseud–i.e., R.K.
Gordon and Heber Carss Jamieson]. London, Blackie, 1927. 208p [BM
NBFU OTU

THREE AGAINST THE GANG. By Norman Blake [pseud–see under previous
title]. London, Blackie, 1929. 207p [BM OTP

Goumois, Maurice-Marc-Albert de, 1896–

A WORLD GOES BY. A Novel. New York, Pageant Press, 1956. 285p

Gourlay, John Edgar Reginald, 1854–

THE NECKLACE OF PANDURA. By Reginald Gourlay. New York, Broadway
Pub., 1907. 121p [LC

Gouzenko, Igor, 1919–

THE FALL OF A TITAN. A Novel. Trans. from the Russian by Mervyn Black.
London, Cassell, 1954. 680p

Govan, Margaret Kilgour Livingston, 1904–

ISLAND HIDEAWAY. Toronto, Dent, 1957. 183p

THE TRAIL OF THE BROKEN SNOW-SHOE. London, Toronto, Dent, 1956. 159p

THE TRAIL OF THE RED CANOE. Toronto, Dent, 1954. 179p

Graham, Angus A., 1867–

NAPOLEON TREMBLAY. London, Hale, 1939. 336p [BM LC NBFU OTU

Graham, Charles Ross, 1920–

THE BODY ON MOUNT ROYAL. By David Montrose [pseud]. Toronto, Harlequin
Books, 1953. 189p

THE CRIME ON COTE DES NEIGES. By David Montrose [pseud]. Toronto,
Collins, 1951. 160p

Graham, Gwethalyn, 1913–1965

EARTH AND HIGH HEAVEN. Philadelphia, Lippincott, 1944. 288p [Also, with
intro. by Eli Mandel: Toronto, McClelland, 1960. xi + 254p] [BM BVaU
NBFU OTMC QMM

SWISS SONATA. London, Cape, 1938. 383p [BM BVaU LC NBFU OTU

Graham, Janet (Pollock), 1880–

THE ENCHANTED WOOD. New York, Pageant Press, 1954. 102p

Graham, Rosemary Margaret

MUSTARD AND COMPANY. London, Dent, 1960. 150p

Grahame, Gordon Hill, 1889?–

ANTOINE, THE FEARLESS. Toronto, Ryerson, 1935. 288p [BM NBFU OTU

THE BOND TRIUMPHANT. Toronto, Hodder, 1923. 321p [BM BVaU LC
NSHD OTU QMM

THE GENTLEMAN. London, Melrose, [1934?]. 288p [BM NBFU OKQ

THE GOLDEN GALLEONS OF CARIBEE. London, Hodder, 1925. 288p [BM
BVaU NBFU OTMC

LARRY; or, The Avenging Terrors. Toronto, Musson, 1923. 311p [BM NBFU
OTMC

MAPLE LEAF HOLIDAY. Akron, Ohio, Saalfield Pub. Co., 1948. 92p [LC

THE VOODOO STONE. Toronto, Ryerson, 1935. 254p [BM BVa NBFU OTMC

Grainger, Martin Allerdale, 1874–1941

WOODSMEN OF THE WEST. Toronto, Musson, 1908. 206p [BM BVaU LC
NBFU OTMC

Grant, Mrs. Hilda Kay, 1910–

DOVE COTTAGE. By Jan Hilliard [pseud]. London, New York, Abelard-Schuman,
1958. 192p

THE JAMESON GIRLS. By Jan Hilliard [pseud]. Toronto, Nelson, Foster &
Scott, 1956. 240p

MIRANDA. A Novel By Jan Hilliard [pseud]. New York, Abelard-Schuman,
1960. 247p

A VIEW OF THE TOWN. By Jan Hilliard [pseud]. New York, Abelard-Schuman,
1954. 269p

Grant, James Miller, 1853–1940

THE FAIRY SCHOOL OF CASTLE FRANK. By Grant Balfour [pseud]. Toronto,
Poole, 1899. 89p [BM OTP

THE MOTHER OF ST. NICHOLAS (SANTA CLAUS). A Story of Duty and Peril.
By Grant Balfour [pseud]. Toronto, Poole, 1899. 91p [BM OTP

ON GOLDEN WINGS THROUGH WONDERLAND. By Grant Balfour [pseud].
Toronto, McClelland, 1927. 269p [LC OTU QMM

Grant, Minnie Caroline (Robinson), −1923
SCENES IN HAWAII; or, Life in the Sandwich Islands. By Mrs. W. Forsyth
Grant. Toronto, Hart, 1888. 203p [BVaU LC

Gray, Archie William, 1896−
THE TOWERS OF ST. ELOI. Rodney, Ont., Gray, 1933. 273p [NBFU OTP

Gray, John Morgan, 1907−
ONE-EYED TRAPPER. Toronto, Macmillan, 1941. 256p [BM BVaU NBFU
OOP

Grayson, Ethel Kirk, 1890−
APPLES OF THE MOON. Toronto, Allen, 1933. 416p [BM NBFU OTU
FIRES IN THE VINE. Toronto, Macmillan, 1942. 497p [BVaU LC NBFU OTU
WILLOW SMOKE. New York, Vinal, 1928. 343p [BVaU LC NBFU OTMC

Green, Henry Gordon, 1912−
THE PRAYING MANTIS. A Novel. Fredericton, Brunswick Press, 1953. 309p

Greene, Harry Irving, 1868−
BARBARA OF THE SNOWS. New York, Moffatt Yard, 1911. 358p [Also:
Toronto, Musson, 1924. 358p] [BM LC OTMC
YOZONDE OF THE WILDERNESS. Toronto, McLeod, 1910. 167p [BVaU LC
OTMC

Greene, Marion, 1900−
CANAL BOY. Toronto, Macmillan, 1959. 152p
DOWN RIVER LIES THE WORLD. Toronto, Ryerson, 1946. 176p [BM BVaU
LC NBFU OTMC QMM

Greenough, William Parker
THE CRUISE OF A WOMAN HATER. By G. de Montauban [pseud]. Boston,
Ticknor, 1887. 280p [LC

Greenwood, A.E.
THE LIGHT AND THE LURE. By Marx Hawthorne [pseud]. Toronto, Carswell,
1897. 104p [BM OTP

Gregory, Claudius Jabez, 1889−1944
FORGOTTEN MEN. Hamilton, Davis-Lisson, 1933. 441p [BVaU LC NBFU
OTMC
SOLOMON LEVI. New York, Kyle & Hovendon, 1935. 400p [BM LC NBFU
OTMC
VALERIE HATHAWAY. Toronto, McClelland, 1933. 415p [BVaU LC NBFU
OTMC

Grenfell, Wilfred Thomason, 1865−1940
DEEDS OF DARING. Selected from NORTHERN NEIGHBOURS and LABRADOR
DAYS. London, Hodder, 1934. 127p [BM NSHPL QMBM

DOWN NORTH ON THE LABRADOR. New York, Revell, 1911. 229p [BM BVaU LC NSWA OTMC QMM

DOWN TO THE SEA. Yarns from Labrador. New York, Revell, 1910. 226p [BM BVaU LC OTMC QMM

THE HARVEST OF THE SEA. A Tale of Both Sides of the Atlantic. New York, Revell, 1905. 162p [BM BVaU LC NSHD OTU QMM

LABRADOR DAYS. Tales of the Sea Toilers. Boston, Houghton, 1919. 230p [BM BVaU LC OTMC

NORTHERN NEIGHBORS. Stories of the Labrador People. Boston, Houghton, 1923. 332p [BM BVaU LC NSHD OTMC

OFF THE ROCKS. Stories of the Deep-Sea Fisherfolk of Labrador. Philadelphia, Sunday School Times, 1906. 203p [BM BVaU LC OTU

TALES OF THE LABRADOR. Boston, Houghton, 1916. 239p [BM BVaU LC NBFU OTMC QMM

THAT CHRISTMAS IN PEACE HAVEN. Boston, Houghton, 1923. 55p [One of the stories in TALES OF THE LABRADOR.] [NfSM

Grey, Francis William, 1860–1939

THE CURE OF ST. PHILIPPE. A Story of French-Canadian Politics. London, Ont., Digby Long, 1899. 313p [BM OTP

Griffin, George H.

LEGENDS OF THE EVERGREEN COAST. Vancouver, Clarke & Stuart, 1934. 141p [BVaU NBFU

Griffin, Watson, 1860–1952

THE GULF OF YEARS. Toronto, Point Publishers, 1927. 407p [BM BVaU NSHD OKQ QMM

TWOK. A Novel. Hamilton, Griffin & Kidner, 1887. 236p [Contains also "Who is Santa Claus?"] [BVaU NSHD OTMC QMM

Griffith, J.W.

HELP IN THE DISTANCE. A New Dominion Story. Elora, Ont., Author, 1868. 67p [OTP

Grodenk (pseud)

MY OWN STORY. A Canadian Christmas Tale. Toronto, A.S. Irving, 1869. 144p [OONL OTP

Grove, Frederick Philip, 1879–1948

CONSIDER HER WAYS. Toronto, Macmillan, 1947. 298p [BVaU LC NSHD OTMC

FRUITS OF THE EARTH. Toronto, Dent, 1933. 335p [BM BVaU LC NSHD OTU QMM

THE MASTER OF THE MILL. Toronto, Macmillan, 1944. 393p [BVaU LC NSHD OTMC QMM

OUR DAILY BREAD. A Novel. New York, Macmillan, 1928. 390p [BM BVaU LC NBFU OKQ

A SEARCH FOR AMERICA. Ottawa, Graphic, 1927. 448p [BVaU LC MWU NSHD OKQ

SETTLERS OF THE MARSH. New York, Doran, 1925. 341p [BVaU LC MWU NSHD OTP QMM

TWO GENERATIONS. A Story of Present-Day Ontario. Toronto, Ryerson, 1939. 261p [BVaU LC NSHD OKQ

THE YOKE OF LIFE. Toronto, Macmillan, 1930. 355p [BVaU LC NSHD OKQ

Grove, Miss

LITTLE GRACE; or, Scenes in Nova-Scotia. By Miss Grove. Halifax, Mackenzie, 1846. 178p [OTP

Grover, Lucius Halen, 1866–

FIVE SHORT STORIES FOR CHILDREN. By "Uncle Dudley," the Kiddies' Friend. Edmonton, Western Veteran Pub., n.d. 24p [BVaU

THE GOLDEN RULE. ... Sandwich, B.C., Author, 1920. 41p

VIVETTE. Courtenay, B.C., Comox Argus, 1920. 43p [AEU BVaU OTMC

Guelton, Mrs. Elizabeth

THE STORY OF PETER, A CANADIAN CAT. A Humane Story. Toronto, Briggs, 1904. 24p [BCF

Guest, Flora (Bigelow)

THE JEWELLED BALL. Montreal, Cambridge Corp., 1908. 326p [BVaU NBFU OOP

Guiton, Helen

A COUNTRY LOVER. A Canadian Idyll. Toronto, Dent, 1948. 255p [BVaU NBFU OTMC QMM

Gurd, Mrs. Mabel Hodgson, –1920?

A BIT OF A DRIFTER, AND OTHER STORIES. Montreal, Chapman, 1921. 191p [BVaU NBFU

Guttormsson, Ragnhildur (Johnson), 1886–

IAN OF RED RIVER. Toronto, Ryerson, 1959. 129p

Hagell, Edward Fredric, 1895–

WHEN THE GRASS WAS FREE. Toronto, Ryerson, 1954. x + 127p

Haig-Brown, Roderick Langmere, 1908–

KI-YU. A Story of Panthers. Boston, Houghton, 1934. 213p [Also pub. under title: PANTHER. London, Cape, 1934. 257p] [BM BVaU LC NBFU OTU QMM

MOUNTED POLICE PATROL. New York, Morrow, 1954. 248p

ON THE HIGHEST HILL. New York, Morrow, 1949. 319p [BM BVaU LC NBFU OTU QMM

PANTHER. See under KI-YU.

SALTWATER SUMMER. New York, Morrow, 1947. 256p [BM BVaU LC NBFU OTU

STARBUCK VALLEY WINTER. New York, Morrow, 1943. 310p [BM BVaU LC NBFU OTU QMM

THE TALL TREES FALL. See under TIMBER.

TIMBER. A Novel of Pacific Coast Loggers. New York, Morrow, 1942. 410p [Also pub. under title: THE TALL TREES FALL. London, Collins, 1943. 288p] [BM BVaU LC NBFU OTUV QMM

Hailey, Arthur, 1920—

THE FINAL DIAGNOSIS. A Novel. Garden City, N.Y., Doubleday, 1959. 319p

FLIGHT INTO DANGER. A Novel of Suspense. By John Castle [pseud] & Arthur Hailey. London, Souvenir Press, 1958. 162p [John Castle, pseud. of Ronald Charles Payne and John William Garrod.]

RUNWAY ZERO-EIGHT. Montreal, Bantam Books, 1960. 120p [Same as FLIGHT INTO DANGER, *q.v.*]

Hale, Charles Maynard, 1889—

DESTINY ISLAND. London, Cassell, 1939. 280p [BM NBFU

REDEMPTION ISLAND. By Charles M. Hale and Evan John [pseud]. New York, Morrow, 1928. 309p [BM LC NBFU

Haley, Mildred C. (Rogers), 1890?—

THE TANGLES AT TALKINGTON. Toronto, Hunter Rose, 1925. [CC

Haliburton, Thomas Chandler, 1796—1865

THE ATTACHE; or, Sam Slick in England. By the author of THE CLOCKMAKER; or, Sayings and Doings of Sam Slick [pseud]. [First series.] London, Bentley, 1843. 2v [BM BVaU NSHD OTP

THE ATTACHE; or, Sam Slick in England. By the Author of the THE CLOCKMAKER; or, Sayings and Doings of Sam Slick [pseud]. [Second series.] London, Bentley, 1844. 2v [BM BVaU NSHD OTU QMM

THE BUBBLES OF CANADA. By the Author of THE CLOCKMAKER. ... London, Bentley, 1839. 332p [BM BVaU LC NSWA OKQ

THE CLOCKMAKER; or, The Sayings and Doings of Samuel Slick, of Slickville, [Anon] [First series.] Halifax, Joseph Howe, 1836. 221p [Also: Philadelphia, Cary, Lea & Blanchard, 1837. 218p; and many later editions.] [BVaU LC OKQ

THE CLOCKMAKER; or, The Sayings and Doings of Samuel Slick, of Slickville. [First series.] Intro. by Robert L. McDougall. Toronto, McClelland, 1958. xvi + 156p [New Canadian Library Series, No. 6]

THE CLOCKMAKER; or, The Sayings and Doings of Samuel Slick, of Slickville. [Anon] [First—Third Series.] London, Bentley, 1837—40. 3v [BM BVa LC NSHD OKQ

THE CLOCKMAKER; or, The Sayings and Doings of Samuel Slick, of Slickville.
[Anon] Second Series. London, Bentley, 1838. 378p [Many later editions.]
[BM BVaU LC NBFU OKQ

THE CLOCKMAKER; or, The Sayings and Doings of Samuel Slick, of Slickville.
[Anon] Third series. London, Bentley, 1840. [Also: Philadelphia, Lea, &
Blanchard, 1840. 215p; and many later editions.] [BM BVaU LC NBFU OTU

FRAGMENTS FROM SAM SLICK. Selected and arranged by Lawrence J. Burpee.
Toronto, Musson, 1909. 91p [BVaU NBFU OTU

JUDGE HALIBURTON'S YANKEE STORIES. Philadelphia, Lindsay & Blakiston, 1846.
2v in 1. [Same as THE CLOCKMAKER, First and Second Series. See Chittick
p659.] [BVaU NBFU OTP

THE LETTER BAG OF THE GREAT WESTERN; or, Life in a Steamer. ... By the
Author of "The Sayings and Doings of Samuel Slick." London, Bentley, 1840.
323p [Also: Halifax, Howe, 1840. 189p] [BM BVaU LC NSHD OKQ

NATURE AND HUMAN NATURE. By the Author of "Sam Slick the Clockmaker" ...
[pseud]. London, Hurst & Blackett, 1855. 2v [BM BVaU LC NSHD OKQ

THE OLD JUDGE; or, Life in a Colony. By the Author of "Sam Slick, the Clockmaker" ... [pseud]. London, Colburn, 1849. 2v [Also: New York, Stringer &
Townsend, 1849. 2v in 1. 239p] [BM BVaU NSHD OKQ

SAM SLICK. Ed. with a critical estimate and a bibliography, by Ray Palmer Baker.
Toronto, McClelland, 1923. 420p [BM BVaU LC NSHD OTU

SAM SLICK IN SEARCH OF A WIFE. See under SAM SLICK'S WISE SAWS. ...

SAM SLICK THE CLOCKMAKER. His Sayings and Doings. With an intro. by E.A.
Baker. London, Routledge, 1904. xvi + 435p [OTMC OTUV [Same title,
but with an intro. by T.G. Marquis: Toronto, Musson, n.d. "Centenary Edition"
[1936]. xxii + 425p] [OONL OTMC

SAM SLICK'S WISE SAWS AND MODERN INSTANCES; or, What He Said, Did, or
Invented. ... London, Hurst & Blackett, 1853. 2v [Also pub. under title:
WISE SAWS; or, Sam Slick in Search of a Wife. New York, Dick & Fitzgerald,
1855.] [BM BVaU LC NSHD OTMC

THE SAYINGS AND DOINGS OF SAMUEL SLICK ESQ., TOGETHER WITH HIS OPINION
ON MATRIMONY. New York, Dick & Fitzgerald, n.d. 263p [Same as THE
CLOCKMAKER, third series?] [BVaU OTMC QMM

THE SEASON TICKET. ... [Anon] London, Bentley, 1860. 376p [BM BVaU LC
NSHD OKQ

SELECTIONS FROM SAM SLICK (JUDGE HALIBURTON). Ed. by Paul A.W. Wallace.
Toronto, Ryerson, 1923. 150p [BM BVaU OTU QMM

TRAITS OF AMERICAN HUMOR, BY NATIVE AUTHORS. Ed. and adapted by the
author of "Sam Slick." London, Colburn, 1852. 3v [BM BVaU LC NSHD
OKQ

YANKEE YARNS AND YANKEE LETTERS. Philadelphia, Peterson Bros., [1852?].
189p [OTU QMSS

Hall, Emma L.
THE ASS HE RODE. By Yvonne St. Claire [pseud]. Toronto, Author, 1937. 10p
[NBFU OTU
THE ASS HE RODE. THE OCEAN'S ORATORIO. THE SCENTED GARDEN. SONGS OF A
YOUNG COUNTRY. By Yvonne St. Claire [pseud]. N.p., n.d. 4v in 1. [QMM
CLAUDIA. A Story of the Early Church. By Yvonne St. Claire [pseud]. N.p., n.d.
11p [OKQ
THE FLIGHT INTO EGYPT. By Yvonne St. Claire [pseud]. N.p., n.d. 8p [OTUV
THE PILLOW. A Story suggested by New Testament Incidents. By Yvonne
St. Claire [pseud]. Toronto, Industrial and Educational Pub. Co., n.d. 32p
[OTU
SPLENDID DAWN. By Yvonne St. Claire [pseud]. London, Epworth Press, 1949.
141p [OKQ
THE VEIL. A Story of the First Century. By Yvonne St. Claire [pseud]. Toronto,
Thorn Press, 1938. 79p [AEU OTMC

Hall, Ethel May
SEELING THE NEEDY FOR A PAIR OF SHOES, AND OTHER STORIES. London, Ont.,
Franks, 1944. 72p [BVaU OLU

Hallam, Douglas, 1883–1948
THE SPIDER WEB. The Romance of a Flying Boat. By P.I.X. [pseud]. Edinburgh,
Blackwood, 1919. 278p [OTU

Halldorsson, Albert Laurence, 1925–
FRUITS OF THE VALLEY. An Historic [sic] Novel. Winnipeg, Author, 1950. 128p
[MWU OONL

Ham, George Henry, 1847–1926
THE FLITTING OF THE GODS. An Authentic Account of the Great Trek from Mount
Olympus to the Canadian Rockies. Toronto, Mail Job Print., 1906. 20p [NSWA

Hambleton, John O. ("Jack"), 1901–1961
ABITIBI ADVENTURE. Toronto, Longmans, 1950. 173p [BM BVaU NBFU
OTMC
CHARTER PILOT. A Bill Hanson Story. Toronto, Longmans, 1952. 216p
CUB REPORTER. Toronto, Longmans, 1951. 231p
FIRE IN THE VALLEY. Toronto, Longmans, 1960. 156p
FOREST RANGER. Toronto, Longmans, 1948. 226p [BM BVaU OOP QMM
TEMAGAMI GUIDE. Toronto, Longmans, 1954. 167p
WINGS OVER LABRADOR. Toronto, Longmans, 1957. 167p
WOLVERINE. Toronto, Longmans, 1954. 184p
YOUNG BUSH PILOT. Toronto, Longmans, 1949. 200p [BVaU NBFU OOP

Hambleton, Ronald, 1917–
EVERY MAN IS AN ISLAND. London, Hutchinson, 1959. 245p

Hamilton, Leslie, 1899–
CHERCHEZ LA FEMME? Hamilton, Beaver, 1941. 190p [OOP
RENDEZVOUS IN VIENNA. Hamilton, Beaver, 1941. 188p [OTU

Hango, Mrs. Angéline Rose, 1882–
TRUTHFULLY YOURS. Toronto, Oxford U. Press, 1948. 144p [BVaU NBFU
OTU QMM

Hanson, Nell
WINDS OF PITY. London, Murray, 1935. 332p [BM LC

Hardy, William George, 1896–
ABRAHAM, PRINCE OF UR. See under FATHER ABRAHAM.
ALL THE TRUMPETS SOUNDED. A Novel based on the Life of Moses. New York,
Coward McCann, 1942. 501p [BM BVaU NBFU OTMC
THE CITY OF LIBERTINES. Toronto, McClelland, 1957. 437p
FATHER ABRAHAM. London, Lovat Dickson, 1935. 416p [Pub. in the U.S. under
title: ABRAHAM, PRINCE OF UR. New York, Dodd Mead, 1935. 376p] [BM
BVaU NBFU OTMC
TURN BACK THE RIVER. New York, Dodd Mead, 1938. 385p [BM BVaU LC
NBFU OTU
THE UNFULFILLED. Toronto, McClelland, 1951. 334p

Harlaw, John
GLENLYON. A Story of Scotch and Canadian Romance. London, Stockwell,
[1936]. 135p [BVaU NBFU OKQ

Harold, Rev. P.J.
IRENE OF CORINTH. An Historic Romance of the First Century. Toronto, Hunter
Rose, 1884. 298p [LC NSHD OLU

Harper, John Murdoch, 1845–1919
THE LITTLE SERGEANT; or, Le Service et les Amours. Quebec, Quebec News Co.,
[1905?]. 214p [OTMC
OUR JEAMES. [Attributed to Harper in Morgan, *Canadian Men and Women ...*
1912. *Cf.* item listed below under HENDERSON, J. MURDOCH. "Henderson was
the maiden name of Harper's mother."]

Harrington, Evelyn (Davis), 1911–
OOTOOK, YOUNG ESKIMO GIRL. New York, Abelard-Schuman; Toronto, Nelson,
1956. 127p
STORMY SUMMER. New York, Abelard-Schuman; Toronto, Nelson, 1956. 190p

Harris, Mrs. Carrie Jenkins, –1903
CYRIL WHYMAN'S MISTAKE. Toronto, Bryce, 1894. 124p [OONL
FAITH AND FRIENDS. ... Windsor, N.S., Anslow, 1895. 43p [NSHP

A MODERN EVANGELINE. Windsor, N.S., Anslow, 1896. 120p [NSWA QQL
MR. PERKINS OF NOVA SCOTIA; or, The European Adventures of a Would-be
Aristocrat. Windsor, N.S., Anslow, 1891. 170p [NBSaM
A ROMANTIC ROMANCE. Windsor, N.S. Anslow, 1893. 153p [NSHP OONL

Harris, Christie Lucy (Irwin), 1907—
CARIBOO TRAIL. Toronto, Longmans, 1957. 188p

Harrison, Charles Yale, 1898—1954
A CHILD IS BORN. New York, Cape & Smith, 1931. 236p [LC NBFU OTMC
GENERALS DIE IN BED. London, Douglas, 1930. 269p [BM BVaU LC NBFU
OTP
MEET ME ON THE BARRICADES. A Novel. New York, Scribner, 1938. 206p [BM
LC NBFU OTMC
NOBODY'S FOOL. A Novel. New York, Holt, 1948. 300p [BM BVaU LC NBFU
OTMC
THERE ARE VICTORIES. New York, Covici Friede, 1938. 320p [LC NBFU OTMC

Harrison, Susie Frances (Riley), 1859—1935
CROWDED OUT AND OTHER SKETCHES. By Seranus [pseud]. Ottawa, Evening
Journal, 1886. 165p [BVaU NBFU OTP QMSS
THE FOREST OF BOURG-MARIE. London, Arnold, 1898. 306p [BVaU NBFU OKQ
RINGFIELD. A Novel. By Seranus [pseud]. Toronto, Musson, 1914. 311p [NBFU
OKQ

Hart, Adolphus Mordecai, 1813—1879
LIFE IN THE FAR WEST; or, The Comical, Quizzical, and Tragical Adventures of a
Hoosier. Cincinnati, Pearsons, [1860?]. 131p [LC

Hart, Julia Catherine (Beckwith), 1796—1867
ST. URSULA'S CONVENT; or, The Nun of Canada. Containing Scenes from Real Life.
Kingston, Thomson, 1824. 2v [BVaU LC NBFU OTP
TONNEWONTE; or, The Adopted Son of America. A Tale, Containing Scenes from
Real Life. By an American [pseud]. Watertown, N.Y., Adams, 1825. 2v in 1
(275p) [Also with imprint: Exeter, Meder, 1831. 312p] [BVaU LC OTP

Hart, Percy William Edward, 1870—
JASON–NOVA SCOTIA. Founded upon a Romantic Legend of my Native Land.
New York, Bibelot Bros., 1903. 238p [BM BVaU LC NSHD OOP
LONG LIFE & HAPPY. A Narratale. New York, Bibelot Bros., 1932. 256p [LC
YARNS. The Ludovic Zam Affair. New York, Bibelot Bros., 1901. 272p [LC
NSHD

Harvey, Emeline Daggett
GOLD DUST. Chicago, Lotus Pub. Co., 1892. 257p [LC OTMC

Harvey, William Earl, 1898—
THE PSYCHOLOGICAL KINGDOM. St. Paul, Minn., Review Pub., 1927. 106p [LC

Hayes, Catherine E. (Simpson), 1852–1943
"AWEEMA." An Indian Story of a Christmas Tryst in the Early Days. By Mary
Markwell [pseud]. Winnipeg, Hart, 1906. 61p [BVaU OTP SSU

Hayes, John Francis, 1904–
BUCKSKIN COLONIST. Toronto, Copp Clark, 1947. 251p [BM BVaU OTU
QMBM
BUGLES IN THE HILLS. Toronto, Copp Clark, 1955. 312p
THE DANGEROUS COVE. A Story of Early Days in Newfoundland. Toronto, Copp
Clark, 1957. 265p
A LAND DIVIDED. Toronto, Copp Clark, 1951. 285p
QUEST IN THE CARIBOO. Toronto, Copp Clark, 1960. 240p
REBELS RIDE AT NIGHT. Toronto, Copp Clark, 1953. 286p
TREASON AT YORK. Toronto, Copp Clark, 1949. 314p [BVaU OTMC

Heathcote, Mrs. Edmund
THE ADMIRAL'S NIECE; or, A Tale of Nova Scotia. London, Newby, 1858. 2v in 1.
[BM BVaU QMBM

Heaton, Hugh
THE STORY OF PROFESSOR PORKY. Toronto, Heaton, 1937. 34p [BM

Heavysege, Charles, 1816–1876
THE ADVOCATE. A Novel. Montreal, Worthington, 1865. 125p [BVaU LC
NSHD OTMC QMSS

Hedges, Doris (Ryde), 1900–
DUMB SPIRIT. A Novel of Montreal. London, Barker, 1952. 224p
ELIXIR. London, Barker, 1954. 191p
ROBIN. New York, Vantage Press, 1957. 176p

Heeney, Rev. William Bertal, 1873–1955
D'ARCY CONYERS. Toronto, Hodder, 1922. 229p [BM NBFU OTMC
PICKANOCK. A Tale. London, Lane, 1912. 288p [BM BVaU NBFU OTMC

Heighington, Wilfrid, 1897–1945
THE CANNON'S MOUTH. Toronto, Bryant Press, 1943. 368p [NSHD OTU

Heming, Arthur Henry Howard, 1870–1940
THE LIVING FOREST. Toronto, Gundy, 1925. 268p [BM BVaU LC OKQ QMM
THE LIVING FOREST; Two Boys in the Canadian Woods. Garden City, Doubleday,
1935. 268p [LC NBFU OTMC
SPIRIT LAKE. London, Macmillan, 1907. 335p [Also: Toronto, Musson, 1923.
280p] [BM BVaU LC NSHD OKQ

Henderson, J. Murdoch [pseud? See note above under Harper, John Murdoch.]
THE CHRONICLES OF KARTDALE. Our Jeames. Ed. by ——. Montreal, Drysdale,
1896. 343p [BM OTP QMM

Henry, Edwin Arthur, 1866–
LITTLE FOXES. Stories for Boys and Girls. New York, Fleming Revell, 1922. 160p
[BM LC OTMC

Henry, Vera (Johnson)
A LUCKY NUMBER. Philadelphia, Lippincott, 1957. 243p

Henshaw, Julia Wilmotte (Henderson), 1869–1937
HYPNOTIZED; or, The Experiment of Sir Hugh Galbraith. A Romance. Toronto,
Ontario Pub. Co., 1898. 285p [BM OOP
WHY NOT, SWEETHEART? Toronto, Morang, 1901. 246p [BM BVaU NSHD
OTMC

Hensley, Sophia Margaret (Almon), 1866–
LOVE & COMPANY, LIMITED. By J. Try-Davies [pseud] and Mary Woolson.
Montreal, Foster Brown, 1901. 114p [BM NSHPL OTP
A SEMI-DETACHED HOUSE AND OTHER STORIES. By J. Try-Davies [pseud].
Montreal, Lovell, 1900. 164p [BM BVaU NSHPL OTMC QMBM

Herapath, Theodora, 1889–
THE MIGHT-HAVE-BEENS. By Anne Capelle [pseud]. London, Melrose, 1936. 288p
[BM CC

Herbert, George
GERALD FITZGERALD. A Novel. London, Newby, 1858. 3v [BM OLU

Herbert, Mary E.
BELINDA DALTON; or, Scenes in the Life of a Halifax Belle. Halifax, 1859. 60p
[OONL OLU NSHD
WOMAN AS SHE SHOULD BE; or, Agnes Wiltshire. Halifax, Author, 1861. 145p
[BVaU NBFU OTP
A YOUNG MAN'S CHOICE. ... Halifax, Citizen, 1869. 43p [NSHD

Herbert, Sarah, 1824–1844
AGNES MAILARD. A Temperance Tale. Halifax, n.d. [BibC

Herbin, John Frederic, 1860–1923
THE HEIR TO GRAND-PRE. Toronto, Briggs, 1907. 155p [BM BVaU NSWA
OKQ QMBM
JEN OF THE MARSHES. Boston, Cornhill, 1921. 349p [BVaU LC NSHD OTMC

Herman, Alan, 1916–
THIS TIME A BETTER EARTH. A Novel. By Ted Allan [pseud]. New York, Morrow,
1939. 279p [BM LC NBFU OOP

Herring, Frances Elizabeth (Clarke), 1851–1916
ENA. London, Griffiths, 1913. 187p [BM BVaU LC NBFU
THE GOLD MINERS. A Sequel to ON THE PATHLESS WEST. London, Griffiths,
1914. 120p [BM BVaU LC

NAN AND OTHER PIONEER WOMEN OF THE WEST. London, Griffiths, 1913. 171p
[BM BVaU LC

Hewitt, Foster William 1902–
ALONG OLYMPIC ROAD. Toronto, Ryerson, 1951. 142p

Hickey, Rev. David
WILLIAM AND MARY. A Tale of the Siege of Louisburg, 1745. Toronto, Briggs,
1884. 317p [BVaU NSHD OTP

Hickman, William Albert, 1875–1957?
CANADIAN NIGHTS. Toronto, McClelland, 1914. 365p [BVaU LC NBFU OTMC
THE SACRIFICE OF THE SHANNON. Toronto, Briggs, 1903. 323p [BVaU LC
NSHD OKQ QMM
AN UNOFFICIAL LOVE-STORY. New York, Century, 1909. 141p [BM BVaU LC
NSWA OTMC

Hiebert, Paul Gerhardt, 1892–
SARAH BINKS. Toronto, Oxford U. Press, 1947. 182p [BVaU LC NSHD OKQ
QMM SSU

Higgins, David Williams, 1834–1917
THE MYSTIC SPRING, and Other Tales of Western Life. Toronto, Briggs, 1904.
407p [New and rev. ed.: New York, Broadway Pub., 1908. 312p] [BM BVaU
LC NSHD OTP
THE PASSING OF A RACE and More Tales of Western Life. Toronto, Briggs, 1905.
304p [BM BVaU LC OKQ

Hilts, Rev. Joseph Henry, 1819–1903
AMONG THE FOREST TREES; or, How the Bushman Family Got their Homes.
Toronto, Briggs, 1888. 380p [BM BVaU OTU
CLOTHED WITH THE SUN; or, From Olivet to the Gates of Glory. Toronto, Briggs,
1891. 408p [OTMC

Hodgins, James Cobourg, 1866–1953
THE WILDERNESS CAMPERS. Toronto, Musson, 1921. 265p [BM NBFU OOP

Hodgins, Samuel Raymond Norris, 1895–
THE PARSLEYS & THE SAGE. Toronto, Ryerson, 1952. 153p
WHY DON'T YOU GET MARRIED. A Hodge-Podge of Sketches, a Few Wise, Many
Witty, and all Wholesome. Toronto, McClelland, 1923. 270p [BVaU LC
OTMC QMSS

Hodgson, John C.J., 1892–
LION AND LILY. A Story of New France. Montreal, Renouf, 1935. 281p [NBFU
OKQ QMM

Holliday, Joseph, 1910–
DALE OF THE MOUNTED. Toronto, Allen, 1951. 150p

DALE OF THE MOUNTED, ATLANTIC ASSIGNMENT. Toronto, Allen, 1956. 158p
DALE OF THE MOUNTED, ATOMIC PLOT. Toronto, Allen, 1959. 158p
DALE OF THE MOUNTED, DEW LINE DUTY. Toronto, Allen, 1957. 158p
DALE OF THE MOUNTED IN NEWFOUNDLAND. Toronto, Allen, 1955. 160p
DALE OF THE MOUNTED IN THE ARCTIC. Toronto, Allen, 1953. 156p
DALE OF THE MOUNTED ON THE WEST COAST. Toronto, Allen, 1954. 156p
DALE OF THE MOUNTED: PURSUIT ON THE ST. LAWRENCE. Toronto, Allen, 1960.
  160p
DALE OF THE MOUNTED: SUB HUNT. Toronto, Allen, 1958. 160p
OIL TRAILS IN HEADLESS VALLEY. Toronto, Longmans, 1954. 157p

Holmes, Abraham S., 1809–1908
BELINDA; or, The Rivals. A Tale of Real Life. By A.S.H. Detroit, Bagg & Harmon,
  1843. 104p [BVaU NBFU OLU

Hood, Robert Allison, 1880–1958
THE CASE OF KINNEAR. Toronto, Macmillan, 1942. 329p [BVaU NBFU OTMC
THE CHIVALRY OF KEITH LEICESTER. A Romance of British Columbia. Toronto,
  McClelland, 1918. 339p [BVaU LC NBFU OTMC
THE QUEST OF ALISTAIR. Toronto, McClelland, 1921. 328p [BM BVaU LC
  NBFU OTMC

Hooke, Hilda Mary, 1898–
THUNDER IN THE MOUNTAINS. Legends of Canada. Toronto, Oxford U. Press,
  1947. 223p [BVaU LC NBFU OTMC QMM

Hooker, Rev. LeRoy, 1840–1906
BALDOON. [A Story]. Chicago, Rand McNally, 1899. 278p [BM LC OTU
ENOCH, THE PHILISTINE. A Traditional Romance of Philistia, Egypt, and the Great
  Pyramid. New York, Rand McNally, 1898. 250p [BM LC
ME AN' TEDDY. By Me. Ed. by ——. Chicago, Conkey, 1906. 87p [BM LC

Hope, Ethel Penman, –1958
DR. PAUL. Toronto, McClelland, 1918. 235p [LC OOP
EYES OF THE LAW. Toronto, McClelland, 1920. 236p [BM OTMC
A HILLSIDE CHRISTMAS. The Story of a Smiling Heart. Toronto, McClelland,
  1917. 17p [BM OONL
THE WAYS OF THE HEART. Toronto, Musson, 1910. 265p [BM OTMC

Horn, Harold (pseud)
MORTIMER'S GOLD. By Harold Horn [pseud]. Toronto, Hodder, 1922. 315p
  [BM NBFU OOU

Horner, Leslie
FAMOUS CANADIAN STORIES RE-TOLD FOR CHILDREN. Ed. by D.G. French.
  Toronto, McClelland, 1923. 348p [BM BVa NSHD OTMC

Horsfield, Richard Edward, 1895–
THE LEASES OF DEATH. By M.B. Gaunt [pseud]. London, Long, 1937. 288p [BM LC

Hoskin, Mary
THE LITTLE GREEN GLOVE AND OTHER STORIES. Toronto, Extension Print., 1920. 221p [BVaU OTMC OTUV

Houghton, Frank Llewellyn, 1897–
THE BLUE CIRCLE GANG. A Canadian Adventure Story. Toronto, Nelson, 1949. 191p [BViPA NSHPL OTP
THE CAVE AT CORMORANT POINT. A Canadian Navy Adventure. Toronto, Nelson, [1950?]. 169p [NBFU OONL

Howard, Rev. Allen Leslie, 1875?–
THE MAGNIFICENT EUGENIC; or, "Give me Joseph." Brampton, Charters, 1933. 283p [NBFU

Howard, Florence Ruth, 1902–
GREEN ENTRY. New York, Morrow, 1940. 274p [BM LC
SAILMAKER. A Novel. New York, Morrow, 1948. 222p [BVaU LC
VIEW FROM A WINDOW. A Novel. New York, Morrow, 1942. 341p [BM BVaU LC

Howard, Hilda (Glynn), 1887–
THE WRITING ON THE WALL. By H. Glynn-Ward [pseud]. Vancouver, Sun Pub. Co., 1922. 326p [BVaU NBFU OTMC

Howarth, David
THE VALLEY OF GOLD. A Tale of the Saskatchewan. New York, Revell, 1921. 272p [BVaU LC NBFU OKQ

Howe, Joseph, 1804–1873
THE LORD OF THE BEDCHAMBER. A Political Lampoon. [BCF

Huddleston, Mrs. George Croft
BLUEBELL. A Novel. Toronto, Belford, 1875. 315p [Also: London, 1875. 3v] [BM BVaU NBFU OTU
MISS TODD'S DREAM. ... London, Ward & Downey, 1889. 160p [BM

Hughes, Isabelle Grace (Bragg), 1912–
LORENA TELFORTH. London, Davies, 1952. 255p [NBFU
SERPENT'S TOOTH. Toronto, Collins, 1947. 342p [BVaU OTU QMM
TIME IN AMBUSH. Toronto, Collins, 1949. 257p [BVaU NBFU OTU
THE WISE BROTHER. Toronto, Ryerson, 1954. 272p

Hunt, Anna Rebecca (Gale)
AFTER MANY DAYS. An Anglo-American Romance. By Canadienne [pseud]. London, Kegan Paul, 1914. 404p [BM QMSS

DISTURBERS. By William Henry Williamsonn and "Canadienne" [pseud]. London, Laurie, 1914. 316p [BM

Hunt, Katherine Chandler, 1909–
MURDER IS MY SHADOW. New York, Macmillan, 1959. 151p

Hunter, Alfred Taylour, 1867–
STORIES TOLD OUT OF LODGE. Toronto, Carswell, 1898. 216p [OTU

Hunter, Francis James, 1853–1938
COLONEL GASCOIGNE, V.C. A Story of Travel, Adventure, and Love. [Montreal?], n.p., n.d. 274p [BViPA OTMC QMSS

Hunter, James Hogg, 1890–
BANNERS OF BLOOD. Toronto, Evangelical Pub., 1947. 228p [BVaU NBFU OTMC

HOW SLEEP THE BRAVE! A Novel of 17th Century Scotland. Toronto, Evangelical Pub., 1955. 256p

THE MYSTERY OF MAR SABA. Toronto, Evangelical Pub., 1940. 414p [BVaU NBFU OTU

UNCLE JIM'S STORIES FROM NATURE'S WONDERLAND. Grand Rapids, Mich., Zondervan, 1953. 71p [BM LC

Huntington, Lucius Seth, 1827–1886
PROFESSOR CONANT. A Story of English and American Social and Political Life. Toronto, Rose, 1884. 291p [BVaU LC NSHD OTU QMM

Hutchison, Bruce, 1901–
THE HOLLOW MEN. A Novel. Toronto, Longmans, 1944. 278p [BVaU LC OTMC QMM

Hutchison, Margaret
TAMARAC. Toronto, Macmillan, 1957. 282p

Huyghue, Douglas S.
ARGIMOU. A Legend of the Micmac. By Eugene [pseud]. Halifax, Courier, 1847. 72p [NSHP

NOMADS OF THE WEST; or, Ellen Clayton. London, Bentley, 1850. 3v [BM LC OTU

Hyde, Laurence.
SOUTHERN CROSS. A Novel of the South Seas, Told in Wood Engravings. With a Review of Stories in Pictures from Earliest Times. Intro. by Rockwell Kent. Los Angeles, Ward Ritchie Press, 1951. 255p [Also: Toronto, McClelland, 1951.]

Iles, George, 1852–1942
CANADIAN STORIES. Together with Choosing Books ... and Jottings from a Notebook. Montreal, Author, 1918. 184p [BVaU NSHD OTU QMM

Ingaldson, Violet Paula (Paulson)
COLD ADVENTURE. Toronto, Copp Clark, 1959. 168p

Ingersoll, William Ernest
DAISY HERSELF. Toronto, Musson, 1920. 320p [BM BVaU NBFU OTMC
THE ROAD THAT LED HOME. A Romance of Plow-Land. With some Passages from the Lives of Henry Nicol, Philosopher of Islay; Ernie Bedford, Pedagogue. ... New York, Harper, 1918. 307p [BM BVaU LC NBFU

Innis, Mary E. (Quayle), 1899–1972
STAND ON A RAINBOW. Toronto, Collins, 1943. 290p [BVaU LC NBFU OKQ QMM

Inskipp, M.
MONSOON MAGIC. London, Unwin, 1927. 288p [BM NBFU QMM

Irwin, Grace Lillian, 1907–
ANDREW CONNINGTON. Toronto, McClelland, 1954. 248p
LEAST OF ALL SAINTS. Toronto, McClelland, 1952. 302p
IN LITTLE PLACE. A Novel. Toronto, Ryerson, 1959. 216p

Israel, Charles Edward, 1920–
HOW MANY ANGELS. A Novel. Toronto, Macmillan, 1956. 329p

Jack, Annie L. (Hayr), 1839–1912
THE LITTLE ORGANIST OF ST. JEROME and Other Stories of Work and Experience. Toronto, Briggs, 1902. 91p [BM BVaU NSHD OTMC QMBM

Jack, Isaac Allen, 1843–1903
THE MEMOIRS OF A CANADIAN SECRETARY. A Posthumous Paper. [Anon] Toronto, 1928. 42p [Edited by Ephraim Davis.] [The Toronto imprint and date are fictitious. Actually pub. at Saint John, about 1883. *Cf.* DCB.] [NBFU OTP

Jacob, Fred, 1882–1926
DAY BEFORE YESTERDAY. A Novel. Toronto, Macmillan, 1925. 319p [BVaU LC NBFU OTMC
PEEVEE. A Novel. Toronto, Macmillan, 1928. 400p [BVaU LC NBFU OTMC QMM

James, George Moffat, 1867–
STANDING BEFORE KINGS. Belleville, James Texts, 1924. 258p [NBFU OTP

Jamieson, Heber Carss, 1879–1962

IN THE GRIP OF THE BARREN LANDS. By Norman Blake [pseud–i.e., Robert Kay Gordon and H.C. Jamieson]. London, Blackie, 1927. 208p [BM NBFU OTU

THREE AGAINST THE GANG. By Norman Blake [pseud–see under previous title]. London, Blackie, 1929. 207p [BM OTP

Jamieson, Nina (Moore), 1885–1932

THE HICKORY STICK. A Romance of the School in the Cedars. Toronto, McClelland, 1921. 343p [BM NBFU OTMC

Janes, Lemuel Willey, 1889–

THE TREASURY OF NEWFOUNDLAND STORIES. Ed. by ——. St. John's, Maple Leaf Mills, n.d. 158p [NfSM OOP

Janes, Percy

SO YOUNG AND BEAUTIFUL. Ilfracombe, Devon, Stockwell, 1958. 342p

Jarvis, Thomas Stinson, 1854–1926

DR. PERDUE. Chicago, Laird & Lee, 1892. 397p [LC

GEOFFREY HAMPSTEAD. A Novel. New York, Appleton, 1890. 378p [BM LC NBFU OTMC

SHE LIVED IN NEW YORK. A Novel. New York, Judge Pub., 1894. 304p [LC

Jarvis, William Henry Pope, 1876–1944

THE GREAT GOLD RUSH. A Tale of the Klondike. Toronto, Macmillan, 1913. 335p [BM BVaU OTU QMBM

THE LETTERS OF A REMITTANCE MAN TO HIS MOTHER. Toronto, Musson, [1909?]. 122p [BM BVaU NSHD OTP SSU

TRAILS AND TALES IN COBALT. Toronto, Briggs, 1908. 157p [BM BVaU OTU

Jasinskas, Jonas, 1907–

A KISS IN THE DARK. By J. Jasmin [pseud]. Trans. from the Lithuanian by Milton Stark. Chicago, International Press, 1954. 150p [Previously pub. in Lithuania in 1937.]

Jenkins, Charles Christopher, 1882–1943

THE REIGN OF BRASS. A Romance of Two Epochs. Toronto, Ryerson, 1927. 318p [BM NBFU

THE TIMBER PIRATE. New York, Doran, 1922. 318p [BM BVaU LC NBFU OTMC

Jenkins, Robert Smith, 1870–1931

THE HEIR FROM NEW YORK. Toronto, Standard Book, 1911. 362p [BM OTU

Jennings, Clotilda, –1895

ISABEL LEICESTER. A Romance. By Maude Alma [pseud]. Hamilton, Spectator, 1874. 182p [OH OTP

Jerdon, Gertrude
CHANGING PLACES; or, Wilton Fairlegh in Animal Land. London, Partridge, 1886.
144p [BM
KEYHOLE COUNTRY. A Story about Things You would Certainly See if You Went
through the Keyhole. London, Sampson Low, 1885. 133p [BM

Jetna (pseud)
JOHN ANDERSON, MY JO. Toronto, Poole, n.d. 57p [OTMC

Johnson, Charles Nelson, 1860–
THE HERMIT OF THE NONQUON. Chicago, Rand McNally, 1893. 235p [LC

Johnson, Emily Pauline, 1862–1913
THE LEGEND OF THE CHUCK OLUK. Abbreviated from LEGENDS OF VANCOUVER.
Vancouver, Handicrafts Guild, n.d. 8p [BVaU
LEGENDS OF VANCOUVER. Vancouver, Thompson Stationery Co., 1911. 89p
[Various later editions with different paging and place of publication.] [BM
BVaU BViPA LC NSHD OTU QMM
THE MOCCASIN MAKER. With introduction by Sir Gilbert Parker, and appreciation
by Charles Mair. Toronto, Briggs, 1913. 248p [BM BVaU NBFU OTMC QMM
THE SHAGGANAPPI. With introduction by Ernest Thompson Seton. Toronto,
Briggs, 1912. 257p [BM BVaU NSHD OTU QMM

Johnson, Frank
GILES AND JANEY; or, The Kindly Gentleman. A Canadian Tale. Montreal, Lovell,
1867. 11p [OTP

Johnson, George Washington, 1839–1917
THE BELLE OF BLADEN'S BROOK. A Novel. Cleveland, 1865. 200p [BCF BibC
THE MENTE'S SECRET; or, The Vengeance of Madra. A Novel. Cleveland, 1864.
180p [BCF BibC

Johnson, Natalie Gordon (Wilson)
PASSION FRUIT. London, Mitre, 1942. 191p [BM

Johnson, Walter Seely, 1880–
PASTOR INVICTUS; or, Rebellion in St. Eustache. A Story of Quebec Province.
Montreal, Quality Press, 1931. 78p [BVaU NBFU OTP QMM

Johnston, Mabel Annesley (Sullivan), 1870–1945
TALES OF OLD TORONTO. ... By Suzanne Marny [pseud]. Toronto, Briggs, 1909.
166p [BM BVaU OTU QMM

Johnston, Maysie F.
BEAUTY NOT COMPLETE. Toronto, Nelson, 1936. 350p [BM

Jones, Alice, 1853–1933
BUBBLES WE BUY. Boston, Turner, 1903. 409p [Pub. in England under title:

ISABEL BRODERICK. Bubbles We Buy. London, Lane, 1904. 410p] [BM LC NBFU OOP

FLAME OF FROST. New York, Appleton, 1914. 316p [BM LC NBFU

GABRIEL PRAED'S CASTLE. Boston, Turner, 1904. 380p [BM LC NSHD OOP

MARCUS HOLBEACH'S DAUGHTER. New York, Appleton, 1912. 331p [BM LC OTU

THE NIGHT HAWK. A Romance of the '60's. By Alix John [pseud]. New York, Stokes, 1901. 378p [BM LC

Jones, Mrs. Nancy, 1890–1959

THE STARS MAKE ROOM. A Novel. Toronto, Ryerson, 1957. 302p

Jones, Susan (Morrow), 1864?–1926

THE CAREER OF MRS. OSBORNE. By Carleton-Milecete [pseud]. New York, Smart Set Pub., 1903. 211p [LC OTMC

A DETACHED PIRATE. The Romance of Gay Vandeleur. By Helen Milecete [pseud]. Boston, Little Brown, 1903. 347p [Also: London, Greening, 1900. 232p] [BM LC OTMC

THE FOREST RUNNER. By S. Carleton [pseud]. London, Melrose, 1925. 268p [BM

A GIRL OF THE NORTH. A Story of London and Canada. By Helen Milecete [pseud]. London, Greening, 1900. 330p [BM OTMC

THE LA CHANCE MINE MYSTERY. By S. Carleton [pseud]. Boston, Little Brown, 1920. 304p [BM LC

THE MICMAC. By S. Carleton [pseud]. New York, Holt, 1904. 234p [BM LC OTMC

OUT OF DROWNING VALLEY. By S. Carleton Jones [pseud]. New York, Holt, 1910. 315p [LC

Jordan, John, 1920–

THE YOUNGER ONES. New York, Pageant Press, 1952. 217p

Jordan, Mary V.

NOW AND FOREVER. Toronto, Ryerson, 1945. 240p [LC OTMC

Keirstead, Burton Seely, 1907–

THE BROWNSVILLE MURDERS. By B.S. Keirstead and D. Frederick Campbell. New York, Macmillan, 1933. 275p [LC NBFU OTMC

Kelly, Judith Sage, 1908–

A DIPLOMATIC INCIDENT. Boston, Houghton, 1949. 277p [BM LC OTMC

IT WON'T BE FLOWERS. London, Harper, 1936. 272p [LC OTMC

MARRIAGE IS A PRIVATE AFFAIR. New York, Harper, 1941. 359p [BM LC OTMC

Kelly, Sidney James, 1892–

THE END OF BONDAGE. A Novel. Vancouver, Author, 1943. 178p [BVaU

Kendall, Ralph Selwood, 1878–

BENTON OF THE ROYAL MOUNTED. A Tale of the Royal Northwest Mounted
Police. New York, Lane, 1918. 318p [BM LC NBFU OTMC

THE LUCK OF THE MOUNTED. A Tale of the Royal Northwest Mounted Police.
New York, Lane, 1920. 312p [BM BVaU LC NSHD OTMC QMM

Kendall, Rev. Sidney C.

AMONG THE LAURENTIANS. A Camping Story. Toronto, Briggs, 1885. 139p
[BM BVaU OTU QMM

THE LADY OF MARK. ... New York, Abbey, 1901. 151p [LC

THE SOUNDINGS OF HELL. Los Angeles, 1903. 162p [LC

Kennedy, Howard Angus, 1861–1938

THE NEW WORLD FAIRY BOOK. New York, Dutton, 1904. 354p [Also pub. as
THE CANADIAN FAIRY BOOK. Toronto, Dent, 1927. 354p] [BM LC OTMC

PROFESSOR BLACKIE, HIS SAYINGS AND DOINGS. London, Clarke, 1895. 344p
[BM OTU QMM

THE RED MAN'S WONDER BOOK. [Indian Legends.] New York, Dutton, 1931.
366p [BVaU LC OTMC QMM

UNSOUGHT ADVENTURE. Montreal, Carrier, 1929. 320p [BM BVaU LC NBFU
OKQ QMM

Kennedy, James B.

AFLOAT FOR ETERNITY; or, A Pilgrim's Progress for the Times. Toronto, Briggs,
1893. 190p [NSHD

Kennedy, John de Navarre, 1888–

CRIME IN REVERSE. Toronto, Nelson, 1939. 345p [BM LC NBFU OTMC

IN THE SHADOW OF THE CHEKA. Toronto, Nelson, 1935. 320p [LC NBFU
OTMC

THE RAIN OF DEATH. Toronto, Nelson, 1945. 324p [BM BVaU NBFU OTMC

Kennedy, Roderick Stuart, 1889–1953

THE ROAD SOUTH. Toronto, Ambassador Books, 1947. 266p [BVaU NBFU
OTMC QMM

Kent, Agnes Scott

DAVID. A Jewish Lad's Conversion to Christianity. Toronto, Evangelical Pub.,
1926. 52p [OTMC

RACHEL. Toronto, Evangelical Pub., 1930. 223p [LC OTMC

ZONYA, DAUGHTER OF ABRAHAM. The Story of her Quest for Light. Toronto,
Evangelical Pub., 1938. 314p [LC OTMC AEU

Kent, Madeleine Fabiola

THE CORSAIR. A Biographical Novel of Jean Lafitte, Hero of the Battle of New
Orleans. Garden City, N.Y., Doubleday, 1955. 299p

Kerr, Illingworth Holey, 1905—
GAY DOGS AND DARK HORSES. Toronto, Dent, 1946. 372p [BVaU NBFU OTMC SSU

Kerr, William Hastings, 1826—1888
THE ADDRESS OF THE HON. JOHN THORN TO THE FREE AND ENLIGHTENED ELECTORS OF SPLASHVILLE CENTRE, AS ORIGINALLY COMPOSED AND WRITTEN. N.p., n.d. 5p [Amtmann

Kidd, Henry George, 1878—
BEN HALLEY'S CREW. A Tale of the Woods and River. Sherbrooke, Page Print., 1923. 404p [BM BVaU LC OOP QMSS

Kilpatrick, Dorothy Hamilton
THE ROMANCE OF PRINCE RAMA, AND OTHER INDIAN TALES. Toronto, World Friendship, 1926. 153p [BVaU OTMC

King, Basil, 1859—1928
THE BREAK OF DAY. A Novel. London, Harper, 1930. 346p [BVaU LC NBFU OTMC

THE CITY OF COMRADES. New York, Harper, 1919. 405p [BM BVaU LC NSHD OTMC QMM

THE DUST FLOWER. New York, Harper, 1922. 349p [BM BVaU NBFU OTMC QMM

THE EMPTY SACK. New York, Harper, 1921. 445p [BVaU LC NBFU OTMC QMM

THE GIANT'S STRENGTH. New York, Harper, 1907. 341p [BM BVaU LC OTMC

GOING WEST. New York, Harper, 1919. 48p [LC NBFU OTP

GRISELDA. Chicago, Stone, 1900. 333p [LC

THE HAPPY ISLES. New York, Harper, 1923. 485p [BM BVaU LC NSHD OTMC QMM

THE HIGH FORFEIT. A Novel. New York, Harper, 1925. 340p [BM BVaU LC NBFU OTMC QMM

THE HIGH HEART. New York, Grosset & Dunlap, 1917. 419p [BVaU LC NBFU OTMC

IN THE GARDEN OF CHARITY. New York, Harper, 1903. 319p [BM BVaU LC NBFU OTMC

THE INNER SHRINE. A Novel of Today. [Anon] New York, Harper, 1909. 355p [BM BVaU LC NBFU OTMC QMM

LET NOT MAN PUT ASUNDER. A Novel. New York, Harper, 1901. 424p [BM BVaU LC NBFU OTMC

THE LETTER OF THE CONTRACT. New York, Harper, 1914. 209p [BM BVaU LC NBFU OTMC

THE LIFTED VEIL. New York, Harper, 1917. 340p [BM BVaU LC NBFU OTMC QMM

PLUCK. A Novel. New York, Harper, 1928. 323p [BVaU LC NBFU OTMC

SATAN AS LIGHTNING. A Novel. New York, Harper, 1929. 280p [LC NBFU OTMC

THE SIDE OF THE ANGELS. A Novel. New York, Burt, 1916. 394p [BM BVaU LC NBFU OTMC

THE SPREADING DAWN. Stories of the Great Transition. New York, Harper, 1927. 316p [BM BVaU LC NBFU OTMC QMM

THE STEPS OF HONOR. New York, Harper, 1904. 285p [BM BVaU LC NBFU

THE STREET CALLED STRAIGHT. A Novel. By the Author of THE INNER SHRINE [pseud]. London, Harper, 1912. 414p [BM BVaU LC NBFU OTMC QMM

THE THREAD OF FLAME. New York, Harper, 1920. 350p [LC NBFU OTMC QMM

THE WAY HOME. A Novel. New York, Burt, 1913. 546p [BM BVaU LC OTMC QMM

THE WILD OLIVE. A Novel. By the Author of THE INNER SHRINE [pseud]. New York, Harper, 1910. 346p [BM BVaU LC NBFU OTMC

King, Violet May
BETTER HARVEST. Toronto, Dent, 1945. 366p [BVaU NBFU OTMC

Kingsley, Harold
THE FIFTH GOD. London, Selwyn & Blount, 1928. 301p [BM LC
KONG. New York, Dodd Mead, 1927. 309p [BM LC NBFU QMSS

Kirby, William, 1817–1906
THE GOLDEN DOG (LE CHIEN D'OR). A Legend of Quebec. Montreal, Lovell, 1877. 678p [BVaU NSHD OTP QMBM

THE GOLDEN DOG. ... A Romance of the Days of Louis Quinze in Quebec. "Authorized edition." Boston, Page, 1896. 624p [Numerous later editions.] [BM BVaU NSHD OTU QMM

THE GOLDEN DOG (LE CHIEN D'OR). A Romance of Old Quebec. Shortened ed., with an intro. by E.C. Woodley. Toronto, Macmillan, 1931. 227p [BVaU MWU NBSaM OONL

Kiriak, Illia, 1888–1955
SONS OF THE SOIL. Toronto, Ryerson, 1959. 303p

Kirk, Abdier
THE TWO SPIRITS. A Tale, written in Imitation of the German. Halifax, 1843. 46p [NSHP

Kirkconnell, Watson, 1895–
TITUS THE TOAD. London, Oxford U. Press, 1939. 60p [BVa OTU

Kirkpatrick, Ernest Stanley, 1871–
TALES OF THE ST. JOHN RIVER AND OTHER STORIES. Toronto, Briggs, 1904. 132p [BM BVaU LC NSHD OTU

Klanak Press

KLANAK ISLANDS. A Collection of Short Stories by Henry Kreisel and Others. Vancouver, Klanak Press, 1959. 79p

Klein, Abraham Moses, 1909–

THE SECOND SCROLL. New York, Knopf, 1951. 198p

Knister, Raymond, 1900–1932

CANADIAN SHORT STORIES. Ed. by ——. Toronto, Macmillan, 1928. 340p [BM ˉ BVaU LC NSHD OKQ QMM

MY STAR PREDOMINANT. Toronto, Ryerson, 1934. 319p [BM BVaU NBFU OTU

WHITE NARCISSUS. A Novel. New York, Harcourt, 1929. 250p [BM BVaU LC NBFU OKQ QMM

Knowles, Robert Edward, 1868–1946

THE ATTIC GUEST. A Novel. Toronto, Revell, 1909. 402p [BM BVaU LC NBFU OTU QMM

THE DAWN AT SHANTY BAY. Toronto, Revell, 1907. 156p [BM BVaU LC NBFU OTU QMM

THE HANDICAP. A Novel of Pioneer Days. Toronto, Revell, 1910. 386p [BM BVaU LC NBFU OTU QMM

ST. CUTHBERT'S. A Novel. Toronto, Revell, 1905. 339p [Pub. in England as ST. CUTHBERT'S OF THE WEST] [BM BVaU LC NBFU OTU

THE SINGER OF THE KOOTENAY. A Tale of Today. Toronto, Revell, 1911. 368p [BM BVaU LC NBFU OTU

THE UNDERTOW. A Tale of Both Sides of the Sea. Toronto, Revell, 1906. 403p [New ed.: Toronto, McClelland, 1935.] [BM BVaU LC NBFU OTU

THE WEB OF TIME. Toronto, Revell, 1908. 415p [BM BVaU LC OKQ

Knox, Alexander, 1907–

BRIDE OF QUIETNESS. Toronto, Macmillan, 1933. 302p [BM LC NBFU OTU

Knox, Jean

A MODERN LEGEND. N.p., 1916. 28p [OOP

Knox, Olive Elsie (Robinson)

BLACK FALCON. Toronto, Ryerson, 1954. 192p

BY PADDLE AND SADDLE. Toronto, Macmillan, 1943. 270p [BM BVaU LC OTU

RED RIVER SHADOWS. Toronto, Macmillan, 1948. 303p [BM BVaU NBFU OTU

THE YOUNG SURVEYOR. Toronto, Ryerson, 1956. 164p

Ko-Ko (pseud)

SOCIETY TYPES. Toronto, Morang, 1899. 108p [OOP

Kreisel, Henry, 1922–

THE RICH MAN. A Novel. Toronto, McClelland, 1948. 263p [BM BVaU NBFU OTU QMM

Kristofferson, Mrs. Kristine Benson
TANYA. Toronto, Ryerson, 1951. 250p

Kyle, "Tom" E.
THE INVESTIGATOR (copyrighted). Founded upon Actual Facts. Toronto, Investigator Pub., 1930. 42p [BVaU

Lacroix, Henry Olivier, 1826–1897
THE UN-PACIFIC SCANDAL AT THE CUSTOM-HOUSE OF MONTREAL. ... Montreal, Lacroix, 1873. 16p [NSHD OTU QMSS

Laing, Nora
DESERT SHIPS. London, Skeffington, 1936. 288p [BM

Lambert, Richard Stanton, 1894–
THE INNOCENCE OF EDMUND GALLEY. London, Newnes, [1936]. 209p [BViP LC MW OTP
NORTH FOR ADVENTURE. [Fictionized account of Samuel Hearne's search for the Coppermine River, 1769–1772.] Toronto, McClelland, 1952. 208p

Lambie, Alexander, 1870–
A STRANGER IN OUR MIDST, and Some Western Fables. [Anon] Vancouver, Author, [1934?]. 189p [BM BVaU NBFU OTMC

Lambkin, Amelia MacMillan
BUCKSKIN AND ERMINE. Cedar Rapids, Iowa, Torch Press, 1928. 170p [OOP

L'Ami, Charles E.
THE GREEN MADONNA. Philadelphia, Westminster Press, 1952. 302p

Lancefield, Richard Thomas, 1854–1911
NO LAGGARDS WE. [Anon] Hamilton, Author, n.d. 84p [OTP
TIM AND MRS. TIM. A Story for the "Club" and "Society" Man and the "New Woman." Toronto, Toronto News Co., 1897. 145p [BM LC OTMC

Lane, Edward
THE FUGITIVES; or, A Trip to Canada. An Interesting Tale, Chiefly Founded on Facts, Interspersed with Observations on the Manners, Customs, etc., of the Colonists and Indians. London, Effingham Wilson, 1830. 496p [BM BVaU OTP

Langford, Robert John Spinluff, 1887–
HOW I WON THE WAR, by Wellington Marlborough Wolseley Smythe. As told to ——. Toronto, Copp Clark, 1940. 96p [OTU

Lanigan, George Thomas, 1846–1886
FABLES. By George Washington Aesop [pseud] and Bret Harte. ... London, Hamilton, 1882. 54p [A pirated edition, with three fables by Bret Harte.] [BM LC

FABLES. Taken "Anywhere, anywhere, out of the World." By G. Washington Aesop [pseud]. New York, The World, 1878. 52p [BM LC

Lanigan, Richard

THEY TWO; or, Phases of Life in Eastern Canada Fifty Years Ago. Written in 1875 by an Ex-Journalist [pseud]. Montreal, Lovell, 1888. 164p [BVaU NSHD OOP QMBM

Laskey, John K.

ALETHES; or, The Roman Exile. Saint John, Shives, 1840. 155p [NBSaM

Late Physician, A (pseud)

THE RUINED MERCHANT; GRAVE DOINGS; THE STATESMAN; THE THUNDERSTRUCK; and THE BOXER. By a Late Physician [pseud]. Toronto, Brewer McPhail, 1849. 319p [OTP

Lauder, Mrs. Maria Elise Turner

AT LAST. A Novel. Toronto, Briggs, 1893. 310p [BVaU LC OTP

LEGENDS AND TALES OF THE HARZ MOUNTAINS, NORTH GERMANY. By Toofie Lauder [pseud]. London, Hodder, 1881. 259p [BM BVaU LC OTU QMM

Laurence, Frances Elsie (Fry), 1893–

HALF A GIPSY. By Christine Field [pseud]. London, Melrose, 1916. 348p [BM LC

Laurence, Margaret (Wemyss), 1926–

THIS SIDE JORDAN. Toronto, McClelland, 1960. xi + 281p

Lauriston, Victor, 1881–

INGLORIOUS MILTON. An Unconventional Biography. Chatham, Tiny Tree Club, 1934. 408p [BVaU LC NSHD OTMC QMM

THE TWENTY-FIRST BURR. New York, Doran, 1922. 292p [BVaU LC NBFU OTMC

Laut, Agnes Christina, 1871–1936

THE FREEBOOTERS OF THE WILDERNESS. Toronto, Musson, 1910. 443p [BM BVaU LC OTMC

HERALDS OF EMPIRE. Being the Story of one Ramsay Stanhope, Lieutenant to Pierre Radisson in the Northwest Fur Trade. Toronto, Briggs, 1902. 372p [BM BVaU LC NSHD OKQ

THE NEW DAWN. New York, Moffat Yard, 1913. 542p [LC NBFU OTMC

LORDS OF THE NORTH. A Romance of the North-west. ... Toronto, Briggs, 1900. 442p [BM BVaU LC NSHD OKQ

THE QUENCHLESS LIGHT. New York, Appleton, 1924. 290p [BM BVaU LC NBFU OTMC

Lauzon, Edythe Morahan-de

FROM THE KINGDOM OF THE STARS. The Vision of John Hilary, a Prince of Abyssinia. Montreal, Urquhart, 1922. 410p [LC NBFU OTMC

Lawrence, W.H.C.

THE STORM OF '92. A Grandfather's Tale Told in 1932. [Anon] Toronto, Sheppard, 1889. 71p [BVaU OTU

Lawson, Jessie (Kerr), 1838–1917

THE CURSE THAT CAME HOME. Edinburgh, Oliphant, 1894. 256p [BM

DOCTOR BRUNO'S WIFE. A Toronto Society Story. London, Simkin Marshall, 1893. 208p [BM OTU

EUPHIE LYN; or, The Fishers of Old Inweerie. Edinburgh, Oliphant, 1893. 256p [BM OTU

A FAIR REBEL. London, Simkin Marshall, 1899. 96p [EngCat

THE HARVEST OF MOLOCH. A Story of Today. Toronto, Poole, 1908. 320p [BM BVaU NSHD OTMC

MISS NERO. London, Simkin Marshall, 1899. 94p [EngCat

A VAIN SACRIFICE. A Novel. Edinburgh, Oliphant, 1892. 221p [BM

WILLIAM MARAH. London, Simkin Marshall, 1900. 94p [EngCat

Layhew, Mrs. Jane

R_x FOR MURDER. Philadelphia, Lippincott, 1946. 252p [BM LC OTU

Leacock, Stephen Butler, 1869–1944

AFTERNOONS IN UTOPIA. Tales of the New Time. Toronto, Macmillan, 1932. 240p [BM BVaU OTU

ARCADIAN ADVENTURES WITH THE IDLE RICH. London, Lane, 1914. 310p [Also: with an intro. by Ralph L. Curry. Toronto, McClelland, 1959. vii-xi + 157p] [BM BVaU LC NBFU OKQ

BEHIND THE BEYOND, AND OTHER CONTRIBUTIONS TO HUMAN KNOWLEDGE. London, Lane, 1913. 195p [BM BVaU LC NBFU OKQ

THE BEST OF LEACOCK. *See* THE BODLEY HEAD LEACOCK.

THE BODLEY HEAD LEACOCK. Ed. with an intro. by J.B. Priestley. London, Bodley Head, 1957. 464p [Canadian ed., (Toronto, McClelland, 1957), has title: THE BEST OF LEACOCK.]

COLLEGE DAYS. New York, Dodd Mead, 1923. 169p [BM BVaU LC NBFU OTU

THE DRY PICKWICK AND OTHER INCONGRUITES. London, Lane, 1932. 271p [BM BVaU LC NBFU OTU

FRENZIED FICTION. London, Lane, 1918. 240p [BM BVaU LC NSHD OKQ

FUNNY PIECES. A Book of Random Sketches. New York, Dodd Mead, 1936. 292p [BM BVaU LC OTU QMM

FURTHER FOOLISHNESS. Sketches and Satires on the Follies of the Day. London, Lane, 1916. 312p [BM BVaU LC NBFU OKQ

THE GARDEN OF FOLLY. Toronto, Gundy, 1924. 282p [BM BVaU NSHD OKQ

HAPPY STORIES, JUST TO LAUGH AT. New York, Dodd Mead, 1943. 240p [BM BVaU LC NSHD OTU QMM

HERE ARE MY LECTURES AND STORIES. New York, Dodd Mead, 1937. 251p [BM BVa LC OTU QMM

THE HOHENZOLLERNS IN AMERICA. With the Bolsheviks in Berlin and Other Impossibilities. London, Lane, 1919. 269p [BM BVaU LC NSHD OKQ

THE IRON MAN & THE TIN WOMAN. With Other Such Futurities. A Book of Little Sketches of Today and To-morrow. New York, Dodd Mead, 1929. 309p [BM BVaU LC NSHD OTU QMM

LAST LEAVES. Toronto, McClelland, 1945. 213p [BM BVaU LC NSHD OTU

LAUGH PARADE. A New Collection of the Wit and Humor of Stephen Leacock. New York, Dodd Mead, 1940. 326p [BM BVaU LC NBFU OTU QMM

LAUGH WITH LEACOCK. An Anthology of the Best Works of Stephen Leacock. New York, Dodd Mead, 1930. 339p [BVaU LC NBFU OTU

THE LEACOCK BOOK. Being Selections from the Works of Stephen Leacock. Arranged with an intro. by Ben Travers. London, Lane, 1930. 248p [BM BVaU

THE LEACOCK ROUNDABOUT. A Treasury of the Best Works of Stephen Leacock. New York, Dodd Mead, 1946. 422p [BVaU LC OTU QMM

LITERARY LAPSES. A Book of Sketches. Montreal, Gazette Print., 1910. 125p [Many later editions. Also: with an intro. by Robertson Davies. Toronto, McClelland, 1957. xi + 146p] [BM BVaU NBFU OTMC QMM

MEMORIES OF CHRISTMAS. Toronto, Bush, 1943. 29p [Two Christmas essays. ... selected from MY REMARKABLE UNCLE.] [OTP

THE METHODS OF MR. SELLYER. A Book Store Study. New York, Lane, 1914. 37p [Written for Convention of American Booksellers' Assoc., May 14, 1914.] [BVaU NBFU OLU

MODEL MEMOIRS AND OTHER SKETCHES FROM SIMPLE TO SERIOUS. New York, Dodd Mead, 1938. 316p [BM BVaU LC NBFU OKQ QMM

MOONBEAMS FROM THE LARGER LUNACY. New York, Lane, 1915. 282p [BVaU LC NBFU OKQ

MY REMARKABLE UNCLE AND OTHER SKETCHES. New York, Dodd Mead, 1942. 313p [BM BVaU LC NSHD OKQ QMM

NONSENSE NOVELS. London, Lane, 1911. 230p [BM BVaU LC NSHD OKQ

OVER THE FOOTLIGHTS, AND OTHER FANCIES. London, Lane, 1923. 278p [BM BVaU LC NSHD OKQ QMM

THE PERFECT SALESMAN. Ed. by E.V. Knox. New York, McBride, 1934. 151p [Also pub. under title: STEPHEN LEACOCK. London, Methuen, 1934. 151p] [BVa LC NBFU OTU QMM

SHORT CIRCUITS. Toronto, Macmillan, 1928. 336p [BM BVaU LC NBFU OTU QMM

STEPHEN LEACOCK. London, Methuen, 1934. 151p [See THE PERFECT SALESMAN.] [BM

STEPHEN LEACOCK'S LAUGH PARADE. New York, Dodd Mead, 1940. 326p [See LAUGH PARADE.]

SUNSHINE SKETCHES OF A LITTLE TOWN. London, Lane, 1912. 264p [Many later editions. Also: with an intro. by Malcolm Ross. Toronto, McClelland, 1960. iii + 153p] [BVaU LC OKQ QMM

THE UNICORN LEACOCK. Ed. by James Reeves. London, Hutchinson, 1960. 191p
WET WIT AND DRY HUMOUR. Distilled from the Pages of ——. New York, Dodd
   Mead, 1931. 260p [BVaU LC OTU
WINNOWED WISDOM. A New Book of Humour. New York, Dodd Mead, 1926.
   288p [BM BVaU LC NBFU OTU
WINSOME WINNIE, AND OTHER NEW NONSENSE NOVELS. London, Lane, 1920.
   243p [BM BVaU LC NBFU OKQ

Lean, Mary
JOAN OF GLEN GARLAND. A Canadian Girl Guide Story. Toronto, Upper Canada
   Tract Soc., 1934. 286p [BM OTP

Leavitt, Lydia (Brown)
BOHEMIAN SOCIETY. Brockville, Brockville Times, [1884?]. 65p [BVaU LC
   OTMC QMM
WISE OR OTHER WISE. By Lydia and Thaddeus Leavitt. Toronto, Wells, 1898. 64p
   [OTU

Leavitt, Thaddeus W.H., 1844?–1909
KAFFIR, KANGAROO, KLONDYKE. Tales of the Gold Fields. Toronto, Browne,
   1898. 86p [OTU
THE WITCH OF PLUM HOLLOW. Toronto, Wells, 1892. 254p [LC OTU

Lemieux, Kenneth
HICKORY HOUSE. By Kenneth Orvis [pseud]. Toronto, Harlequin Books, 1956.
   160p

LeMoine, James MacPherson, 1825–1912
THE LEGENDS OF THE ST. LAWRENCE. Told during a Cruise of the Yacht *Hirondelle*
   from Montreal to Gaspé. Quebec, Holiwell, 1898. 203p [BM BVaU NSWA
   OTU QMM

Leonard, Grace Emma (Pettingell)
THE CANADIAN FAMILY ROBINSON. A Modern Tale of the Shipwreck and Subse-
   quent Adventures of a Family. Toronto, Upper Canada Tract.Soc., 1935. 254p
   [Also: Fredericton, U. Press of New Brunswick, [1955]. 254p [BM NBFU
   OTMC

Leonard, May, 1862–
TRIXIE'S INHERITANCE; or, Which Shall Win? Saint John, Daily Telegraph, 1886.
   50p [OTP
ZOE; or, Some Day. Saint John, Day, 1888. 87p [NSWA

Leprohon, Rosanna Eleanor (Mullins), 1829–1879
ANTOINETTE DE MIRECOURT; or, Secret Marrying and Secret Sorrowing. A Cana-
   dian Tale. Montreal, Lovell, 1864. 369p [French trans. by J.A. Genand pub. at
   Montreal in 1865. 342p] [BVaU NBFU OTMC

ARMAND DURAND; or, A Promise Fulfilled. Montreal, Lovell, 1868. 77p [Also pub. in French.] [BM BVaU OTU QMM

CLIVE WESTON'S WEDDING ANNIVERSARY. Montreal, 1872. [BCF DCB

LE MANOIR DE VILLERAI. Un Roman Canadien. Traduit de l'Anglais. Montreal, Beauchemin & Valois, 1884. 383p [The English original appeared in the *Family Herald,* Montreal, 1859. The French translation by E.L. De Bellefeuille first appeared in Montreal, 1861. 405p] [BM BVaU NBFU OTP

The following six novels were pub. only in serial form (see BCF BibC DCB):

CLARENCE FITZ-CLARENCE. 1851.

EVA HUNTINGDON. A Tale. 1850.

EVELEEN O'DONNELL. 1859.

FLORENCE FITZ-HARDINGE. 1849.

IDA BERESFORD. 1848.

MY VISIT TO FAIRVIEW VILLA.

LeRossignol, James Edward, 1866–

THE BEAUPORT ROAD. Tales of Old Quebec. Toronto, McClelland, 1928. 291p [BVaU NSHD OTU QMM

THE FLYING CANOE (La Chasse Galerie). Toronto, McClelland, 1929. 302p [BVaU NSHD OTP QMM

THE HABITANT-MERCHANT. Toronto, Macmillan, 1939. 258p [BVaU NSHD OTU QMM

JEAN BAPTISTE. A Story of French Canada. Toronto, Dent, 1915. 269p [BM BVaU LC NSHD OTU QMM

LITTLE STORIES OF QUEBEC. Toronto, Briggs, 1908. 170p [BVaU LC NBFU OTU QMM

Leslie, Edwin

KNIGHTS WHO FOUGHT THE DRAGON. Philadelphia, Sunday School Times, 1906. 207p [BM LC OOP

Leslie, Mary, 1842–1920

THE CROMABOO MAIL CARRIER. A Canadian Love Story. By James Thomas Jones [pseud]. Guelph, Hacking, 1878. 296p [BVaU LC OTP

Lesperance, John Talon, 1838–1891

THE BASTONNAIS. Tale of the American Invasion of Canada in 1775–76. Toronto, Belford, 1877. 359p [Also pub. in French: Montreal, 1896.] [BM BVaU LC NSHP OKQ

TUQUE BLEUE. A Christmas Snowshoe Sketch. Montreal, Dawson, 1882. 35p [BVaU NSHD OTMC QMM

Levesque, Paul, 1913–

PLAYING WITH MURDER. By Will U. Lovitt [pseud]. New York, Greenwich Book Publishers, 1960. 69p

Levine, Albert Norman, 1923–
THE ANGLED ROAD. Toronto, McClelland, 1952. 158p

Lewis, Josephine
AS THE ROWANS GO GAY. Glasgow, Scot., W. MacLellan, 1952. 322p
SANTA CLAUS AND JACK FROST. Story for Children. London, Stockwell, 1935.
   80p [CC

Liddle, Beatrice Boles
THREE INTERESTING STORIES: ... Glorified Wilderness ...; Path of Earthly Stars ...;
   Seaward Deluge. ... Calgary, Albertan Job Press, 1946. 54p [LC QMBM

Lighthall, William Douw, 1857–1954
THE FALSE CHEVALIER; or, The Lifeguard of Marie Antoinette. Montreal, Grafton,
   1898. 328p [BM BVaU NBFU OTU QMM
HIAWATHA THE HOCHELAGAN. An Aboriginal Romance. Montreal, 1906. 200p
   [T&C
THE MASTER OF LIFE. A Romance of the Five Nations. ... Toronto, Musson, 1908.
   262p [BM BVaU LC NSHD OKQ QMM
THE YOUNG SEIGNEUR; or, Nation-Making. A Romance. By Wilfrid Chateauclair
   [pseud]. Montreal, Drysdale, 1888. 200p [BM BVaU NSHD OTU QMM

Lindsay, Robert Howard, 1910–
FOWL MURDER. Mystery of Between the Lines. Boston, Little Brown, 1941. 285p
   [LC

Livesay, Florence Hamilton (Randal), 1874–1953
SAVOUR OF SALT. Toronto, Dent, 1927. 277p [BM BVaU NBFU OTP QMM

Livingston, Stuart, 1865–1923
THE HISTORY OF PROFESSOR PAUL. A Novel. Toronto and Hamilton, Hunter &
   Grant, [1889]. 102p [BVaU

Lizars, Robina, –1918
COMMITTED TO HIS CHARGE. A Canadian Chronicle. By R. and K.M. Lizars.
   Toronto, Morang, 1900. 312p [BM BVaU NBFU OTMC

Lloyd-Owen, Frances
THE CALL OF THE COUGAR. London, Harrap, 1941. 256p [BM
THE GNOME'S KITCHEN. A Story of Woodland Animals. London, Harrap, 1937.
   254p [BM BVaU
JOE & PINTO. London, Harrap, 1937. 250p [BM BVa

Logan, Annie Robertson (Macfarlane), –1933
THE CHILDREN OF THE HEARTH. New York, 1891. [BCF

Long, Morden Heaton, 1886–
KNIGHTS ERRANT OF THE WILDERNESS. Toronto, Macmillan, 1925. 223p [BM
   BVaU LC NBFU OTP

Loomer, Leslie Oran, 1878—

THE PROPHET. A Story of the Two Kingdoms of Ancient Palestine. Windsor, N.S. Anslow, 1911. 171p [BM NSHPL OONL

Louth, Cyril E., 1906?—1956

BUT FOR THE GRACE OF GOD. New York, Pageant Press, 1956. 112p

Low, May (Austin), 1863—

DEVICES AND DESIRES. Montreal, 1892. [MOR'12

Lowrey, Harold C., 1886—

INDIAN GOLD. Toronto, Musson, 1929. 244p [BVaU NBFU OTMC

YOUNG CANADA BOYS WITH THE S.O.S. ON THE FRONTIER. Toronto, Allen, 1918. 202p [OONL

Lowry, Malcolm, 1909—1957

ULTRAMARINE. London, Cape, 1933. 276p [Rev. ed., Toronto, Clarke Irwin, 1962. 203p] [BM BVaU NBFU OTU

UNDER THE VOLCANO. New York, Reynal, 1947. 375p [BM BVaU LC NBFU OTU QMSS

Lund, Captain T.

IN THE SNOW. A Romance of the Canadian Backwoods. Toronto, Musson, n.d. 247p [ACG BM OONL

THE LONE TRAIL OMNIBUS. London, Werner Laurie, 1936. 702p [Contains: "Weston of the Royal North-West Mounted Police," "Up North," and "The Murder of Dave Brandon."] [BM

THE MURDER OF DAVE BRANDON. London, Werner Laurie, 1931. 244p [BM BViPA OONL

ROBBERY AT PORTAGE BEND. A Story of the Royal North-West Mounted Police. London, Werner Laurie, 1933. 252p [BM BViPA OTU

STEELE BEY'S REVENGE. London, Werner Laurie, 1934. 249p [BM

UP NORTH. A Tale from Northern Canada. London, Werner Laurie, 1929. 253p [BM OONL

THE VANISHED PROSPECTOR. A Story from Northern Canada. London, Werner Laurie, 1937. 285p [BM BViPA OONL

WESTON OF THE ROYAL NORTH-WEST MOUNTED POLICE. London, Werner Laurie, 1928. 252p [BM BViPA OOP

Lyle-Smythe, Alan, 1914—

ALIEN VIRUS. By Alan Caillou [pseud]. London, Davies, 1957. 249p

THE MINDANAO PEARL. By Alan Caillou [pseud]. London, Davies, 1959. 221p

THE PLOTTERS. By Alan Caillou [pseud]. London, Davies, 1960. 285p

Lysenko, Vera

WESTERLY WILD. Toronto, Ryerson, 1956. 284p

YELLOW BOOTS. Toronto, Ryerson, 1954. 314p

McAlister, Lottie (Plewes), 1865–
CLIPPED WINGS. Toronto, Briggs, 1899. 186p [BM BVaU NSHD OTU

McAlpine, Mrs. Jennie
PAMELA OF ECHO GLEN. New York, Pageant Press, 1954. 118p

McArthur, Peter, 1866–1924
THE GHOST AND THE BURGLAR. New York, McArthur & Ryder, 1905. 24p
THE PEACEMAKERS. New York, McArthur & Ryder, 1905. 24p

Macbeth, Madge Hamilton (Lyons), 1878–1965
THE GREAT FRIGHT, ONESIPHORE OUR NEIGHBOR. By Madge Macbeth and A.B.
   Conway [pseud]. New York & Montreal, Carrier, 1929. 326p [Pub. in England
   as: BEGGAR YOUR NEIGHBOUR. London, Paul & Co., 1929.] [BM BVaU LC
   NBFU OKQ
THE KINDER BEES. By Gilbert Knox [pseud]. London, Lovat Dickson, 1935.
   316p [BM NBFU OTMC
KLEATH. Boston, Small Maynard, 1917. 386p [BM BVaU LC NBFU OOP
THE LAND OF AFTERNOON. A Satire. By Gilbert Knox [pseud]. Ottawa, Graphic,
   1924. 352p [BVaU LC NSHD OTU
THE LONG DAY. By W.S. Dill [pseud]. Ottawa, Graphic, 1926. 232p [BVaU
   NBFU OTU
LOST. A Cavalier. London, Allen, 1947. 242p [BM OOP
THE PATTERSON LIMIT. Toronto, Hodder, 1923. 320p [BM NBFU OTU
SHACKLES. Ottawa, Graphic, 1926. 324p [BVaU LC NBFU OTU
SHREDS OF CIRCUMSTANCE. London, Allen, 1947. 365p [BM NBFU OOP
   QMBM
WINGS IN THE WEST. London, Hamilton, [1937?]. 320p [BM OTU
THE WINNING GAME. New York, Broadway Pub., 1910. 242p [LC

McCarroll, James, 1815–1896
RIDGEWAY. An Historical Romance of the Fenian Invasion of Canada. By Scian
   Dubh [pseud]. Buffalo, McCarroll, 1868. 262p [BVaU OTP

McCaughey, Lloyd
MODERN SHORTS. By Lloyd McCaughey, Yarker Banks, and Leslie Hamilton.
   Hamilton, Beaver Pubs., 1941. 188p [OTU

McCawley, Stuart
CAPE BRETON HUMOR. Glace Bay, N.S., Brodie Print., 1929. 64p [NSHPL

McClintock, Gray
ITINERANTS OF THE TIMBER LANDS. New York, Crowell, 1934. 285p [LC
   NBFU
THE WOLVES ARE RUNNING. A Novel. London, Blackie, 1934. 216p [BM
THE WOLVES AT COOKING LAKE AND OTHER STORIES. Albany, Lyon, 1932.
   224p [BViPA LC

McClung, Nellie Letitia (Mooney), 1873–1951

ALL WE LIKE SHEEP AND OTHER STORIES. Toronto, Allen, 1926. 261p [BM
BVaU NBFU OTMC

BE GOOD TO YOURSELF. A Book of Short Stories. Toronto, Allen, 1930. 179p
[BVaU NBFU OTMC

THE BEAUTY OF MARTHA. London, Hutchinson, 1923. 288p [BM

THE BLACK CREEK STOPPING-HOUSE AND OTHER STORIES. Toronto, Briggs,
1912. 224p [BM BVaU NBFU OTP SSU

FLOWERS FOR THE LIVING. A Book of Short Stories. Toronto, Allen, 1931.
212p [BVaU NBFU OTU

LEAVES FROM LANTERN LANE. Toronto, Allen, 1936. 199p [BM BVaU NBFU
OTMC

MORE LEAVES FROM LANTERN LANE. Toronto, Allen, 1937. 201p [BVaU
NBFU OTU

PAINTED FIRES. New York, Dodd Mead, 1925. 316p [BM BVaU LC NBFU
OTU

PURPLE SPRINGS. Toronto, Allen, 1921. 335p [BM BVaU LC NBFU OTU
QMSS

THE SECOND CHANCE. New York, Doubleday, 1910. 369p [BM BVaU LC
NBFU OKQ

SOWING SEEDS IN DANNY. New York, Doubleday, 1908. 313p [BM BVaU LC
NBFU OKQ

WHEN CHRISTMAS CROSSED "THE PEACE." Toronto, Allen, 1923. 149p [BM
BVaU NBFU OLU

McCourt, Edward Alexander, 1907–1972

THE FLAMING HOUR. Toronto, Ryerson, 1947. 170p [BVaU NBFU OTU
QMBM

HOME IS THE STRANGER. Toronto, Macmillan, 1950. 268p [BM BVaU NBFU
OTU

MUSIC AT THE CLOSE. Toronto, Ryerson, 1947. 228p [BVaU NBFU OTU

WALK THROUGH THE VALLEY. Toronto, McClelland, 1958. 222p

THE WOODEN SWORD. Toronto, McClelland, 1956. 255p

McCowan, Daniel, 1882–1956

HILL-TOP TALES. ... Toronto, Macmillan, 1948. 266p [BVaU LC NBFU OTP

MacCrimmon, Harriet M.

THIS IS MY COUNTRY AND OTHER STORIES. Ilfracombe, Devon, Stockwell, 1952.
23p

McCulloch, John Herries, 1892–

BACK ROAD TO GLORY. London, Hurst & Blackett, 1944. 168p [BM

DARK ACRES. Edinburgh, Moray Press, 1935. 318p [BM NBFU SSU

THE MEN OF KILDONAN. A Romance of the Selkirk Settlers. Toronto, McClelland, 1926. 276p [BM BVaU LC NSHD OKQ QMM

THE SPLENDID RENEGADE. New York, Coward McCann, 1928. 373p [LC NSHD OOP

TEN DAY TRAIL. Edinburgh, Moray Press, 1936. 301p [BM NBFU OOP

McCulloch, Rev. Thomas, 1776–1843

COLONIAL GLEANINGS ... WILLIAM AND MELVILLE. ... Edinburgh, Oliphant, 1826. 144p [Two novels bound together.] [NSHD

LETTERS OF MEPHIBOSHETH STEPSURE [pseud]. Halifax, Blackader, 1860 [actually 1862]. 143p [Reprinted from the *Acadian Recorder* of the years 1821 and 1822.] [NBFU NSHP [Also as THE STEPSURE LETTERS, with an intro. by Northrop Frye. New Canadian Library, Toronto, McClelland, 1960. 143p]

Macdonald, Flora

MARY MELVILLE, THE PSYCHIC. Toronto, Austin, 1900. 267p [BM LC OTU

MacDonald, Jane Elizabeth Gostwycke (Roberts), 1864–1922

OUR LITTLE CANADIAN COUSIN. 1. The Maritime Provinces. Boston, Page, 1904. 129p [LC NBFU OKQ

MacDonald, John Arthur, 1912–

DARKLY THE RIVER FLOWS. A Novel of Family Life. Toronto, Longmans, 1945. 201p [Winner of Longmans Green $1000 prize award.] [BVaU LC NBFU OTP QMM

MacDonald, John Geddie

THE CROSS HANGS LOW. New York, Pageant Press, 1952. 185p

MacDonald, Marianne, 1934–

BLACK BASS ROCK. Toronto, Macmillan, 1952. 223p

SMUGGLERS COVE. Toronto, Macmillan, 1955. 208p

THE TREASURE OF UR. Toronto, Macmillan, 1958. 222p

Macdonald, Zillah Katherine, 1885–

A CAP FOR CORRINE. New York, Messner, 1952. 184p

FIREMAN FOR A DAY. New York, Messner, 1952. 62p

MYSTERY OF THE PIPER'S GHOST. Philadelphia, Winston, 1954. ix + 178p

NURSE FAIRCHILD'S DECISION. Montreal, Bantam Books, 1957. 152p [First pub. New York, Messner, 1952, under title: A CAP FOR CORRINE.]

NURSE TODD'S STRANGE SUMMER. By Zillah K. Macdonald and Vivian J. Ahl. New York, Messner, 1960. 192p

ROSEMARY WINS HER CAP. By Zillah K. Macdonald with Josie Johnston [pseud]. New York, J. Messner, 1955. 192p

ROXANNE, INDUSTRIAL NURSE. By Zillah K. Macdonald with Josie Johnston [pseud]. New York, J. Messner, 1957. 192p

A TUGBOAT TOOTS FOR TERRY. New York, Messner, 1953. 63p

Macdonell, Blanche Lucile, 1853–1924
DIANE OF VILLE MARIE. A Romance of French Canada. Toronto, Briggs, 1898.
251p [BM BVaU NBFU OTU QMM

McDonnell, William, 1814–1900
EXETER HALL. A Theological Romance. New York, American News Co., 1869.
186p [LC OTMC
FAMILY CREEDS. A Romance. Toronto, Belfords & Clarke, 1879. 468p [LC OTU
THE HEATHENS OF THE HEATH. New York, Bennett, 1874. 498p [BVaU OTU
REMINISCENCES OF A PREACHER. [A Theological Romance.] Boston, Mendum,
1887. 232p [LC

McDougall, Colin Malcolm, 1917–
EXECUTION. Toronto, Macmillan, 1958. 227p

McDougall, E. Jean (Taylor)
THE LILY OF FORT GARRY. By Jane Rolyat [pseud]. Toronto, Dent, 1930. 287p
[BM BVaU NBFU OTP
WILDERNESS WALLS. By Jane Rolyat [pseud]. Toronto, Dent, 1933. 268p [BM
BVaU NSHD OTP

McDougall, Rev. John, 1842–1917
"WA-PEE MOOS-TOOCH"; or, "White Buffalo." A Tale of Life in Canada's Great
West. Calgary, Herald, 1908. 336p [BM BVaU OKQ SSU

McDougall, Margaret (Dixon), 1826–1898
THE DAYS OF A LIFE. By Norah [pseud]. Almonte, Ont., Templeman, 1883.
438p [LC OTU
THE LADY OF THE BEACON OF ARAHEERA. A Chronicle of Innishowen. Ed. by
Paul Peppergrass [pseud]. Quebec, Corey, 1857. 187p [BCF OTP

McDowell, Franklin Davey, 1898–1965
THE CHAMPLAIN ROAD. Toronto, Macmillan, 1939. 421p [Huronian ed.:
Toronto, Macmillan, 1949. 338p] [BM BVaU LC NBFU OKQ QMM
FORGES OF FREEDOM. Toronto, Macmillan, 1943. 542p [BM BVaU LC NBFU
OKQ

McEwen, Rev. J.D.
SANDY McDONALD IN BRAZIL. Sherbrooke, P.Q., Page Print., 1921. 123p [OONL
QMSS

McEwen, Jessie Evelyn, 1911–
THE BLUE FLY CARAVAN. By Agnes Fisher [pseud]. Toronto, Nelson, 1932. 148p
[BVaU OTMC
THE FAIRIES OF THE GLEN. By Agnes Fisher [pseud]. New York, Nelson, 1943.
40p [LC
THE LITTLE YELLOW HOUSE. Toronto, Ryerson, 1953. 249p

ONCE UPON A TIME. By Agnes Fisher [pseud]. New York, Nelson, 1943. 302p
[LC

TALTREES. Toronto, Ryerson, 1949. 221p [BVaU NBFU OTMC QMM

MacFarlan, Allan Andrew, 1899–
CAMPFIRE ADVENTURE STORIES. New York, Association Press, 1952. 225p

McFarlane, Arthur Emerson, 1876–1945
BEHIND THE BOLTED DOOR? New York, Dodd Mead, 1916. 342p [BM BVaU LC
GREAT BEAR ISLAND. A Boy's Story of Adventure and Discovery. Boston, Little
    Brown, 1911. 290p [LC
REDNEY McGAW. A Story of the Big Show and the Cheerful Spirit. Boston, Little
    Brown, 1909. 268p [LC OTU

McFarlane, Leslie, 1902–
THE MURDER TREE. New York, Dutton, 1931. 275p [BM LC OTMC
STREETS OF SHADOW. New York, Dutton, 1930. 287p [BM LC

MacGeorge, David, 1845–
THE DOCTOR'S DAUGHTER. Galt, Jaffray Bros., 1905. 102p [BM BVaU OTP

MacGillivray, Miss Carrie Holmes, –1949
THE SHADOW OF TRADITION. A Tale of Old Glengarry. Ottawa, Graphic, 1927.
    303p [Later ed.: Toronto, McClelland, 1945. 327p] [BVaU NBFU OTU
    QMBM

McGillivray, James
THE FRONTIER RIDERS. Toronto, Musson, 1925. [Also: London, Hodder, 1925.
    320p] [BM

MacGregor, Mary Esther (Miller), 1876–1961
AS A WATERED GARDEN. By Marian Keith [pseud]. Toronto, McClelland, 1946.
    298p [BVaU NBFU OTMC
THE BELLS OF ST. STEPHEN'S. By Marian Keith [pseud]. New York, Doran, 1922.
    336p [BM BVaU LC NBFU OTMC
BOY OF NAZARETH. By Marian Keith [pseud]. New York, Abingdon-Cokesbury,
    1950. 158p [LC
DUNCAN POLITE. The Watchman of Glenoro. By Marian Keith [pseud]. New York,
    Revell, 1905. 306p [BM BVaU LC NBFU OTMC QMM
THE END OF THE RAINBOW. By Marian Keith [pseud]. New York, Hodder, 1913.
    352p [BM LC NBFU OTMC
THE FOREST BARRIER. A Novel of Pioneer Days. By Marian Keith [pseud].
    Toronto, McClelland, 1930. 308p [NBFU OTP
A GENTLEMAN ADVENTURER. A Story of the Hudson's Bay Company. By Marian
    Keith [pseud]. New York, Doran, 1924. 301p [BM BVaU LC NBFU OTMC
THE GRAND LADY. By Marian Keith [pseud]. Toronto, McClelland, 1960. 222p

IN ORCHARD GLEN. By Marian Keith [pseud]. Toronto, McClelland, 1918. 274p [BVaU LC OTMC

LILACS IN THE DOORYARD. By Marian Keith [pseud]. Toronto, McClelland, 1952. 256p

LITTLE MISS MELODY. By Marian Keith [pseud]. Toronto, McClelland, 1921. 302p [BM BVaU LC OTMC QMM

'LIZABETH OF THE DALE. By Marian Keith [pseud]. Toronto, Westminster, 1910. 434p [BM BVaU LC NBFU OTMC

THE SILVER MAPLE. A Story of Upper Canada. By Marian Keith [pseud]. New York, Revell, 1906. 357p [BM BVaU LC NBFU OTMC

TREASURE VALLEY. By Marian Keith [pseud]. New York, Doran, 1908. 384p [BM BVaU NBFU OTMC QMM

UNDER THE GREY OLIVES. By Marian Keith [pseud]. Toronto, McClelland, 1927. 175p [BVaU LC NBFU OTMC

YONDER SHINING LIGHT. By Marian Keith [pseud]. Toronto, McClelland, 1948. 278p [Sequel to AS A WATERED GARDEN.] [BVaU NBFU OTMC

McGuirl, Charles

"MIKE," THE STRAY DOG. Willowdale, Ont., Author, 1952. 186p [First pub. in 1947 in *Canadian Teacher*.]

Machar, Agnes Maule, 1837–1927

DOWN THE RIVER TO THE SEA. New York, Home Book Co., 1894. 279p [BVaU NSHP OTP

FOR KING AND COUNTRY. A Story of 1812. By A.M.M. Toronto, Adam & Stevenson, 1874. 265p [BVaU NBFU OTP QMSS

THE HEIR OF FAIRMOUNT GRANGE. London, Digby Long, [1895?]. 196p [BM NBFU OONL

KATIE JOHNSTONE'S CROSS. A Canadian Tale. By A.M.M. Toronto, Campbell, 1870. 207p [BM BVaU OTP QMSS

LOST AND WON. [No further information found.] [BCF MOR'12

LUCY RAYMOND; or, The Children's Watchword. By the Author of "Katie John-stone's Cross" [pseud]. Toronto, Campbell, [1902?]. 214p [OONL

MARJORIE'S CANADIAN WINTER. A Story of the Northern Lights. Boston, Loth-rop, 1892. 375p [Also: Toronto, Briggs, 1906. 375p] [BVaU NBFU OKQ

THE QUEST OF THE FATAL RIVER. 1904. [No further information found.] [CAR

ROLAND GRAEME, KNIGHT. A Novel of our Times. Montreal, Drysdale, 1892. 285p [Also: Toronto, Briggs, 1906. 285p] [LC NSHD OKQ QMM

McIlwraith, Jean Newton, 1859–1938

THE CURIOUS CAREER OF RODERICK CAMPBELL. Boston, Houghton, 1901. 287p [BM BVaU LC NBFU OTU

A DIANA OF QUEBEC. Toronto, Bell & Cockburn, 1912. 316p [BM BVaU NBFU OTU QMSS

KINSMEN AT WAR. Ottawa, Graphic, 1927. 289p [BM BVaU NBFU OTU

THE LITTLE ADMIRAL. Toronto, Hodder, 1924. 288p [NBFU OTMC

THE MAKING OF MARY. By Jean Forsyth [pseud]. New York, Cassell, 1895. 173p [BM LC

McInnes, Graham Campbell, 1912–

LOST ISLAND. An Adventure. Toronto, Macmillan, 1954. ix + 229p

SUSHILA. A Novel. New York, Putnam, 1957. 315p

MacInnes, Thomas Robert Edward, 1867–1951

CHINOOK DAYS. Vancouver, Sun Co., 1926. 206p [BVaU NBFU OTP

MacIntyre, Mary

SKIPPY AND OTHERS. Toronto, Macmillan, 1943. 131p [OOP

Mack, Elsie Frances (Wilson), 1909–1967

THE BLUE LOCKET. By Frances Sarah Moore [pseud]. New York, Bouregy & Curl, 1951. 254p

DEBORAH. New York, Bouregy & Curl, 1951. 254p

THE DISPUTED BARRIER. New York, Arcadia House, 1947. 256p [LC

THE ELOPEMENT. New York, Bouregy & Curl, 1952. 256p

THE ENCHANTED HIGHWAY. New York, Bouregy & Curl, 1951. 254p

FAIR IS MY LOVE. By Frances Sarah Moore [pseud]. New York, Avalon Books, 1950. 252p [BM LC OONL

FIREWEED. By Frances Sarah Moore [pseud]. New York, Arcadia House, 1945. 256p [LC

GILDED CHALLENGE. By Frances Sarah Moore [pseud]. New York, Avalon Books, 1950. 256p [BM LC OONL

GROUND MIST. By Frances Sarah Moore [pseud]. New York, Arcadia House, 1946. 272p [LC

THE HEART DIVIDED. By Frances Sarah Moore [pseud]. New York, Arcadia House, 1946. 256p [LC

HIDDEN BOUNDARY. By Frances Sarah Moore [pseud]. New York, Bouregy & Curl, 1952. 254p

LEGACY OF LOVE. By Frances Sarah Moore [pseud]. New York, Avalon Books, 1957. 220p

LOVE SHOULD BE LAUGHTER. By Frances Sarah Moore [pseud]. New York, Curl, 1947. 256p [BM LC

MAGIC IS FRAGILE. New York, Bouregy & Curl, 1952. 256p

MINE TO LOVE. New York, Avalon Books, 1950. 256p [LC OONL

OBBLIGATO. By Frances Sarah Moore [pseud]. New York, Bouregy & Curl, 1952. 253p

OF ALL OUR YESTERDAYS. By Frances Sarah Moore [pseud]. New York, Arcadia House, 1945. 272p [LC

THE QUEST. New York, Bouregy & Curl, 1953. 256p

THE RIGHT GIRL. By Frances Sarah Moore [pseud]. New York, Avalon Books, 1956. 224p

THE STORM. By Frances Sarah Moore [pseud]. New York, Bouregy & Curl, 1951. 256p

MacKay, Isabel Ecclestone (Macpherson), 1875–1928

BLENCARROW. A Novel. Toronto, Allen, 1926. 307p [BM BVaU LC NBFU OTMC QMM

THE HOUSE OF WINDOWS. London, Cassell, 1912. 338p [BM BVaU NBFU OTMC

INDIAN NIGHTS. Toronto, McClelland, 1930. 198p [BM BVaU LC NSHD OKQ

MISS WITTERLY'S CHINA. Toronto, Women's Missionary Soc. of the Methodist Church, Canada, n.d. 11p [Short story reprinted from the *Endeavour Herald,* Toronto] [BVaU

MIST OF MORNING. Toronto, McClelland, 1919. 407p [BM BVaU LC NBFU OTMC

UP THE HILL AND OVER. New York, Doran, 1917. 363p [BVaU LC NBFU OTMC

THE WINDOW GAZER. Toronto, McClelland, 1921. 308p [BM BVaU NBFU OKQ

McKechnie, Neil Kenneth, 1873–1951

THE HEIR OF ALL THE AGES. The Family Tree of Mr. Smith. Indianapolis, Bobbs-Merrill, 1926. 200p [BM LC NBFU

THE SADDLEROOM MURDER. Philadelphia, 1937. 307p [LC NBFU

McKelvie, Bruce Alistair, 1889–1960

THE BLACK CANYON. A Story of '58. London, Dent, 1927. 173p [BVaU NBFU OTMC

HULDOWGET. A Story of the North Pacific Coast. Toronto, Dent, 1926. 221p [BVaU NSHD OTMC

LEGENDS OF STANLEY PARK. N.p., n.pub., [1941?]. 20p [BVaU

PELTS AND POWDER. A Story of the West Coast in the Making. ... Toronto, Dent, 1929. 238p [BVaU NBFU OTMC

MacKenzie, Donald, 1908–

DANGEROUS SILENCE. London, Collins, 1960. 192p

THE JURYMAN. London, Elek Books, 1957. 204p

NOWHERE TO GO. London, Elek Books, 1956. 207p [American ed.: Boston, Houghton, 1957. 250p]

THE SCENT OF DANGER. London, Collins, 1958. 192p

McKibbin, Rev. Archibald, 1863–1925

THE OLD ORCHARD. By Mack Cloie [pseud]. Toronto, Briggs, 1903. 323p [BM BVaU OTU

THE PANCAKE PREACHER. By Mack Cloie [pseud]. Toronto, Briggs, 1906. 450p [BM OLU

A WEE SCOTCH TOON. [No further information found.] [MOR'12

McKim, Audrey, 1909–

ANDY AND THE GOPHER. Boston, Little Brown, 1959. 119p

HERE COMES DIRK. Toronto, Oxford U. Press, 1951. 145p

LEXY O'CONNOR Toronto, McClelland, 1953. 262p

McKinley, Mabel (Burns)

THREE BOYS ON THE YANGTSE. House-boating in China. Toronto, McClelland, 1929. 252p [OTP

MacKinnon, Lilian (Vaux), 1879–

MIRIAM OF QUEEN'S. Toronto, McClelland, 1921. 310p [BM BVaU LC NBFU OTMC

McKinnon, Rev. William Charles, –1862

FRANCES; or, Pirate Cove. A Legend of Cape Breton. Halifax, British North American, 1851. 42p [NSHD

ST. CASTINE. A Legend of Cape Breton. Sydney, N.S., Cape Breton Herald, 1850. 72p [NSHP OOP

ST. GEORGE; or, The Canadian League. A Tale of the Outbreak in 1837. Halifax, Fuller, 1852. 2v [LC NSHP OOP

McKishnie, Archibald P., 1875–1946

BIG JOHN WALLACE. A Romance of the Early Canadian Pioneers. Toronto, Massey-Harris Press, 1922. 47p [BVaU NBFU OTP

BRAINS, LIMITED. Toronto, Allen, 1925. 287p [BM NBFU OOP

DWELLERS OF THE MARSH REALM. Chicago, Donohue, 1937. 79p [BVaU LC NBFU OTMC

GAFF LINKUM. A Tale of Talbotville. Toronto, Briggs, 1907. 255p [BM LC NBFU OKQ

LOVE OF THE WILD. Toronto, McLeod & Allen, 1910. 327p [BVaU LC NBFU OTMC QMM

MATES OF THE TANGLE. Toronto, Musson, 1924. 247p [BVaU LC NBFU OTMC

OPENWAY. Toronto, Musson, 1922. 233p [BM BVaU NSHD OTMC

A SON OF COURAGE. Toronto, Allen, 1920. 284p [BM BVaU LC NBFU OTMC

WILLOW, THE WISP. Toronto, Allen, 1918. 308p [BVaU LC NBFU OTMC QMM

McKnight, J.L.
VAGRANT. A Landsman's Log Book. Saint John, McMillan, 1888. [BCF NBB

McKowan, Evah May (Cartwright), 1885–
GRAYDON OF THE WINDERMERE. Toronto, McClelland, 1920. 310p [BVaU
LC NBFU OTMC
JANET OF KOOTENAY. Life, Love and Laughter in an Arcady of the West. Toronto,
McClelland, 1919. 279p [BVaU LC NBFU OTMC

McLaren, Margaret
CHETIGNE ISLAND. A Novel. West Chezzetcook, N.S., Author, [1916?]. 86p
[BVaU NSHD OTU

MacLean, Annie Marion, –1934
"CHEERO!" New York, Woman's Press, 1918. 93p [LC
OUR NEIGHBOURS. New York, Macmillan, 1922. 288p [LC NSWA

Maclean, Charles Sutherland, 1915–
THE HEAVENS ARE NOT TOO HIGH. London, Kimber, 1957. 282p

Maclean, Rev. John, 1851–1928
THE HERO OF THE SASKATCHEWAN. Barrie, Ont., 1891. 49p [OKQ

MacLennan, Hugh, 1907–
BAROMETER RISING. New York, Duell Sloan, 1941. 326p [Also, with an intro. by
Hugo McPherson. Toronto, McClelland, 1958. xv + 219p] [BM BVaU LC
NSHD OTU QMM
EACH MAN'S SON. Toronto, Macmillan, 1951. 244p
THE PRECIPICE. Toronto, Collins, 1948. 372p [BM BVaU LC NBFU OTU
QMM
TWO SOLITUDES. New York, Duell Sloan, 1945. 370p [Also: Toronto, Macmillan,
1957.] [BM BVaU LC NBFU OTU
THE WATCH THAT ENDS THE NIGHT. Toronto, Macmillan, 1959. 373p

McLennan, William, 1856–1904
AS TOLD TO HIS GRACE, AND OTHER STORIES. Ste. Philomène, 1891. 132p [QMM
IN OLD FRANCE AND NEW. New York, Harper, 1899. 319p [LC NBFU OTU
QMM
THE SPAN O' LIFE. A Tale of Louisbourg & Quebec. By William McLennan and
J.N. McIlwraith. ... New York, Harper, 1899. 307p [BM BVaU LC NBFU
OTU QMM
SPANISH JOHN. Being a Memoir, now First Published in Complete Form, of the
Early Life and Adventures of Colonel John McDonnell, known as "Spanish John".
... New York, Harper, 1898. 271p [BM BVaU LC NSHD OTU QMSS

McLeod, Arthur James, 1836–
THE NOTARY OF GRAND PRE. A Historic Tale of Acadia. Boston, Author, 1901.
152p [BVaU NBFU OTP QMSS

MacLeod, Elizabeth Susan (MacQueen), 1842–1939
DONALDA. A Scottish-Canadian Story. Toronto, Briggs, 1905. 281p [Cover title: DONALDA; or, "Canada's Countess"] [BM NBFU OTU

McMahon, W.F.
"PRIZE PAPERS," SATIRICAL. ... Hamilton, McKay Print., [18—?]. 191p [BVaU NSHD OTP

MacMillan, Anne (Morton), 1893–
LEVKO. Toronto, Longmans, 1956. 159p
MOUNTIE PATROL. Toronto, Longmans, 1960. 160p
PERKY IN EVER, EVER LAND. By Anne MacMillan and Marion McVeety. Regina, School Aids and Text Book Pub., Co., 1954. 198p
PRINCE OF THE PLAINS. Regina, School Aids and Text Book Pub. Co., 1952. 204p

Macmillan, Cyrus, 1880–1953
CANADIAN FAIRY TALES. Toronto, Gundy, 1922. 203p [Same title: London, Lane, 1928. 234p] [BM BVaU LC NBFU OTU QMSS
CANADIAN WONDER TALES. Toronto, Gundy, 1918. 199p [Same title: London, Lane, 1918. 240p] [BM BVaU LC NBFU OTU
GLOOSKAP'S COUNTRY AND OTHER INDIAN TALES. Toronto, Oxford U. Press, 1955. 273p ["The stories in this collection were first published by John Lane, The Bodley Head, Limited in *Canadian Wonder Tales* (1918) and *Canadian Fairy Tales* (1922)."]

MacMillan, Don A.
RINK RAT. Toronto, Dent, 1949. 248p [NBFU OLU

MacMillan, William, 1890–
ARCTIC ADVENTURE. New York, Mill, 1945. 192p [LC OORD
DARK TREASURE. New York, Mill, 1943. 254p [BM LC
MYSTERY SHIP. New York, Mill, 1944. 185p [LC
NORTHLAND STORIES. Tales of Trapping Life in the Canadian Wilderness. New York, Peltries Pub. Co., 1922. 95p [LC
RED-LEG MORGAN. London, Harrap, 1936. 256p [BM

McNamee, James
FLORENCIA BAY. Toronto, McClelland, 1960. 204p

McNaughton, Rev. Duncan
THE WIFE OF FAIRBANK ON KIRKS AND MINISTERS. Toronto, Press of the Canada Presbyterian, 1893. 432p [LC OTP

MacNaughton, Eleanor (Le Sueur), 1846–
A LITTLE LOVING LIFE. 1892. [MOR'12
THE MEADOWHURST CHILDREN AND OTHER TALES. Franklin, Ohio, Editor Pub. Co., 1898. [AmCat MOR'12

McNeill, James, 1925–

THE SUNKEN CITY AND OTHER TALES FROM ROUND THE WORLD. Toronto, Oxford U. Press, 1959. 160p

McNider, Stanley

JUAN HALLADO. 1885. [BCF

Macphail, Andrew, 1864–1938

THE VINE OF SIBMAH. A Relation of the Puritans. London, Macmillan, 1906. 432p [BM LC OTU

McPhedran, Marie (Green), 1904–

DAVID AND THE WHITE CAT. ... New York, Aladdin Books, 1950. 47p [BM LC OONL

GOLDEN NORTH. Toronto, Macmillan, 1948. 192p [BVaU LC NBFU OTU QMM

Macpherson, Charlotte Holt (Gethings), fl. 1828–1890

TRUE STORIES FOR YOUNG PEOPLE. Montreal, n.d. 28p [OLU QMSS

Macpherson, Donald (pseud)

GO HOME, UNICORN. By Donald Macpherson [pseud]. London, Faber, 1935. 271p [BM LC NBFU

MEN ARE LIKE ANIMALS. By Donald Macpherson [pseud]. London, Faber, 1937. 321p [BM LC OTU

McTavish, R. Lorne

FOR A BETTER TO-MORROW. Ilfracombe, Devon, Stockwell, 1952. 176p

Magee, Knox, 1877–1934

MARK EVERARD. A Romance. New York, Fenno, 1901. 421p [BM LC OLU

WITH RING OF SHIELD. New York, Fenno, 1900. 363p [LC OOP

Magwood, Millie

PINE LAKE. A Story of Northern Ontario. Toronto, Briggs, 1901. 198p [BM BVaU OTMC

THE YEAR THAT FOLLOWED. (A Sequel to PINE LAKE.) Toronto, Briggs, 1907. 188p [BM NSHD OTUV

Mahler, Helen A.

EMPRESS OF BYZANTIUM. Trans. from the German original by the author with the assistance of Leona Nevler. New York, Coward-McCann, 1952. 376p

Mainer, R. Henry, 1878–

NANCY McVEIGH OF THE MONK ROAD. Toronto, Briggs, 1908. 127p [BM BVaU NSHD OTP

Mallette, Gertrude Ethel, 1887–

BRIGHT SIDE UP. Garden City, N.Y., Doubleday, 1954. 218p

CALLING DOCTOR MARCIA. New York, Doubleday, 1940. 296p [AEU NBS

CHEE-CHA-KO. New York, Doubleday, 1938. 299p [BM LC

CLEAR TO LAND. Garden City, Doubleday, 1950. 212p [LC

FLYING WING MYSTERY. By Alan Gregg [pseud]. Garden City, Doubleday, 1948.
213p [LC

FOR KEEPS. New York, Doubleday, 1936. 309p [BM LC

HIDDEN WINGS MYSTERY. By Alan Gregg [pseud]. Garden City, Doubleday, 1941.
271p [LC

INSIDE OUT. Garden City, Doubleday, 1942. 278p [BM LC OTU

INTO THE WIND. Garden City, Doubleday, 1942. 295p [NBS OTU

MYSTERY IN BLUE. Garden City, Doubleday, 1945. 217p [BM LC NBS

THE MYSTERY OF BATTY RIDGE. By Alan Gregg [pseud]. Garden City, Doubleday,
1946. 213p [LC

THE MYSTERY OF FLIGHT 24. By Alan Gregg [pseud]. Garden City, Doubleday,
1947. 215p [LC

THE MYSTERY OF THE KING TURTLE. By Alan Gregg [pseud]. Garden City,
Doubleday, 1943. 213p [LC

NO VACANCIES. Garden City, Doubleday, 1939. 311p [BM LC OTU

ONCE IS FOREVER. Garden City, Doubleday, 1946. 250p [BVaU LC OTU

PRICELESS MOMENT. Garden City, Doubleday, 1947. 214p [LC

PRIVATE PROPS. Garden City, Doubleday, 1937. 297p [AEU BM OTU

SINGLE STONES. New York, Doubleday, 1940. 296p [BM LC

SKYWINDER MYSTERY. By Alan Gregg [pseud]. Garden City, Doubleday, 1942.
279p [BM LC

UNEXPECTED SUMMER. Garden City, Doubleday, 1949. 212p [BVaU LC

WENDERLEY. Garden City, Doubleday, 1943. 250p [BM LC

WINGED MYSTERY. By Alan Gregg [pseud]. New York, Doubleday, 1940.
302p [BM LC

Manchee, Carol M. (Cassidy)

DOWNY WINGS AND SHARP EARS. By Carol Cassidy Cole [pseud]. Toronto,
Musson, 1923. 152p [BM BVaU NBFU OTP

LITTLE BIG-EARS AND THE PRINCESS. By Carol Cassidy Cole [pseud]. Toronto,
Musson, [c1926, 1944]. 132p [BVaU NBFU OTP

LITTLE WOODEN DUCK. By Carol Cassidy Cole [pseud]. Toronto, Musson, 1945.
140p [OTMC

VELVET PAWS AND SHINY EYES. By Carol Cassidy Cole [pseud]. Toronto, Musson,
1922. 152p [BM BVaU OTP

Manigault, Gabriel, 1809–1888

SAINT CECILIA. A Modern Tale from Real Life. [Anon] London, Low Marston,
1871–72. 3v [LC

Manning, Zella M.

LORDS OF THE WILDERNESS. Comp. by ——. Toronto, Ryerson, 1934. 188p
[BVaU NBFU QMSS

Mansell, Mrs. C.B.
THE POWER OF GOLD. By Everett St. Clair [pseud]. Vancouver, Artcraft, 1929. 330p [BVaU NBFU OTMC

Mantley, John, 1920–
THE SNOW BIRCH. New York, Dutton, 1958. 316p [Also pub. as WOMAN OBSESSED. Montreal, Permabooks, 1958. 265p]
THE TWENTY-SEVENTH DAY. London, M. Joseph, 1957. 271p [First pub. 1956.]

Margeson, Mabel (Jones), 1875?–1951
A TALE OF OLD ACADIA. Saint John, Barnes, 1925. 269p [BVaU NBFU OTU QMSS

Margolian, Abraham, 1917–
A PIECE OF BLUE HEAVEN. Fredericton, New Elizabethan Pub. Co., 1956. 240p [A Story of Nazi persecution of the Jews in Amsterdam, 1942–44.]

Marlyn, John, 1912–
UNDER THE RIBS OF DEATH. Toronto, McClelland, 1957. 287p

Marquis, Thomas Guthrie, 1864–1936
THE KING'S WISH. Toronto, Ryerson, 1924. 164p [BVaU NSHD OTU
MARGUERITE DE ROBERVAL. A Romance of the Days of Jacques Cartier. Toronto, Copp Clark, 1899. 250p [BM NSHD OTP QMSS

Mars, Alastair, 1915–
ARCTIC SUBMARINE. London, Elek Books, 1955. 191p
ATOMIC SUBMARINE. A Story of Tomorrow. London, Elek Books, 1957. 192p [Pub. in U.S. as FIRE IN ANGER, New York, Mill Co. & W. Morrow, 1958. 222p]
SUBMARINE AT BAY. London, Elek Books, 1956. 164p

Marsh, Edith Louise, –1960
TRILLIUM HILL. New York, Lothrop, Lee & Shepard Co., 1955. 159p

Marshall, Joyce, 1913–
LOVERS AND STRANGERS. A Novel. Philadelphia, Lippincott, 1957. 246p
PRESENTLY TOMORROW. Boston, Little Brown, 1946. 310p [BVaU LC NBFU OTU QMM

Marshall, Robin
CAMPBELL OF THE MOUNTIES. Toronto, Musson, 1937. 283p [BM OOP

Mary Rose, Sister, 1903–
NOT AT SEVENTEEN? By Rena Ray [pseud]. Montreal, Holy Cross Press, 1959. 128p

Mary St. George, Mother
ROAD'S END. By Mary Douglas [pseud]. Toronto, Ryerson, 1943. 150p [LC NBFU OTU

Mason, Mrs. E.M.
FACES THAT FOLLOW. With illus. by J.W. Bengough. Toronto, Briggs, 1898. 206p
 [BM BVaU NSHD OTMC

Max, Felix
BROKEN BONDS. A Prize Temperance Story. Toronto, 1878. 109p [Bound with
 SOCIAL HEROISM. A Canadian Prize Temperance Story. By F. Louise Morse.
 Toronto, 1878. 82p] [Antique cat. 41

Mayse, Arthur William Caswell, 1912—
THE DESPERATE SEARCH. New York, Morrow, 1952. 216p
MORGAN'S MOUNTAIN. New York, Morrow, 1960. 211p
PERILOUS PASSAGE. New York, Morrow, 1949. 247p [BM BVaU LC OTMC

Meade, Edward F., 1912—
REMEMBER ME. London, Faber, 1946. 318p [BM BVaU LC NSHD OTMC
 QMM

Meek, Gladys Clements
THE DEVIL'S PUNCH BOWL. Edmonton, Inst. of Applied Art, 1946. 221p [OTMC

Meredith, Wendy A.D.M.
"TOES UP!" SAID THE BRIGAND, AND OTHER STORIES. Vancouver, 1929. 36p
 [Written by Wendy Meredith between ages of 10 and 13.] [BVaU

Merrick, Rev. Earl Chauncey, 1905—
PACO OF THE HIGH COUNTRY (BOLIVIA). Toronto, Ryerson, 1952. 49p

Merrill, Marion, 1912—
SYD OF TAR-PAPER SHACK. Chicago, Wilcox & Follett, 1947. 259p [LC
TREASURE CAVE TRAIL. New York, Morrow, 1943. 158p [LC
THE YOUNG BILLINGS OF BUCKHORN. New York, Morrow, 1942. 71p [LC OTU

Middleton, Jesse Edgar, 1872—1960
THE CLEVER ONES. New York, Nelson, 1936. 296p [BM BVaU LC NBFU OTU
GREEN PLUSH. London, Methuen, 1932. 250p [BM NBFU OTU

Millar, Margaret (Sturm), 1915—
AN AIR THAT KILLS. New York, Random House, 1957. 247p [English ed.
 (London, Gollancz, 1957. 222p) has title: THE SOFT TALKERS.]
BEAST IN VIEW. New York, Random House, 1955. 249p
THE CANNIBAL HEART. New York, Random House, 1949. 207p [BM LC OTMC
THE DEVIL LOVES ME. Garden City, Doubleday, 1942. 304p [LC OTMC
DO EVIL IN RETURN. New York, Random House, 1950. 243p [BM LC NBFU
 OTU
EXPERIMENT IN SPRINGTIME. New York, Random House, 1947. 279p [LC
 OTMC
FIRE WILL FREEZE. New York, Random House, 1944. 225p [LC OTU

THE INVISIBLE WORM. New York, Doubleday, 1941. 273p [BM LC OTU
THE IRON GATES. New York, Random House, 1945. 241p [LC OTU
IT'S ALL IN THE FAMILY. New York, Random House, 1948. 243p [LC OTU
THE LISTENING WALLS. London, Gollancz, 1959. 236p
ROSE'S LAST SUMMER. New York, Random House, 1952. 245p
A STRANGER IN MY GRAVE. London, Gollancz, 1960. 240p
TASTE OF FEARS. A Psychological Novel. London, Hale, 1950. 224p [BM
VANISH IN AN INSTANT. New York, Random House, 1952. 245p
WALL OF EYES. New York, Random House, 1943. 243p [LC OTU
THE WEAK-EYED BAT. Garden City, Doubleday, 1942. 280p [BM LC OTU
WIVES AND LOVERS. New York, Random House, 1954. 308p

Miller, Muriel, 1908–

PETER'S ADVENTURES IN THE OUT-OF-DOORS. ... Toronto, Ryerson, 1940.
218p [AEU

Millner, George F.

THE SERGEANT OF FORT TORONTO. Toronto, Copp Clark, 1914. 370p [BM
BVaU LC NBFU OTU

Mirvish, Robert Franklin, 1921–

DUST ON THE SEA. London, Redmond, 1960. 251p
THE LONG WATCH. New York, Sloane, 1954. 343p
TEXANA. A Novel. New York, Sloane, 1954. 279p
TWO WOMEN, TWO WORLDS. New York, Sloane, 1960. 309p
WOMAN IN A ROOM. London, Redman, 1959. 287p

Mitchell, John, 1882–1951

ROBERT HARDING. A Story of Every Day Life. By Patrick Slater [pseud].
Toronto, Allen, 1938. 273p [BVaU NBFU OTMC
THE YELLOW BRIAR. A Story of the Irish on the Canadian Countryside. By Patrick
Slater [pseud]. Toronto, Allen, 1933_253p [Also: Toronto, Macmillan, 1945.
293p] [BM BVaU NBFU OTMC QMM

Mitchell, Ronald Elwy

DESIGN FOR NOVEMBER. New York, Harper, 1947. 282p [BM LC

Mitchell, Sylvia Elizabeth Fisher

PRAIRIE ADVENTURES. Regina, Author, 1958. 61p

Mitchell, William Ormond, 1914–

WHO HAS SEEN THE WIND. Toronto, Macmillan, 1947. 344p [BVaU LC NBFU
OTU QMM

Molnar, Eugene Frank, 1891–

THE SLAVE OF EA. A Sumerian Legend. Philadelphia, Dorrance, 1934. 299p [LC
OKQ

Monckton, Geoffrey F.

LOP-EARED DICK. His Book. ... Being a disjointed Account of the Trials of a genial Cowboy in a World of Widows and Wild Animals. London, Ouseley, 1913. 293p [BM

Monro, Edith

STORY OF MY LIFE. The Trials and Triumphs of Sandy the Scrapper. As Told by Himself. Vancouver, Saturday Sunset Press, 1914. 58p [BVaU

Montgomery, Lucy Maud [Mrs. Evan MacDonald], 1874–1942

ANNE OF AVONLEA. Boston, Page, 1909. 367p [BM BVaU LC NBFU OTU QMBM

ANNE OF GREEN GABLES. Boston, Page, 1908. 396p [Numerous later editions. Also dramatized as a 3-act play by Alice Chadwicke. New York, French, 1937. 139p] [BM BVaU LC NBFU OTU

ANNE OF INGLESIDE. New York, Stokes, 1939. 323p [BM BVa LC NBFU OTU

ANNE OF THE ISLAND. Boston, Page, 1915. 326p [BM BVaU LC NBFU OTU

ANNE OF WINDY POPLARS. New York, Stokes, 1936. 301p [BM BVaU LC OTU

ANNE'S HOUSE OF DREAMS. New York, Stokes, 1917. 346p [BM BVaU LC NBFU OTU

AUNT BECKY BEGAN IT. See A TANGLED WEB , below.

THE BLUE CASTLE. A Novel. Toronto, McClelland, 1926. 309p [BM BVaU LC OTU QMM

CHRONICLES OF AVONLEA. In which Anne Shirley of Green Gables and Avonlea plays some part. Boston, Page, 1912. 306p [BM BVaU LC NBFU OTMC

EMILY CLIMBS. New York, Stokes, 1925. 312p [BM BVaU LC NBFU OTU

EMILY OF NEW MOON. New York, Stokes, 1923. 351p [BM BVaU LC NSHD OTU

EMILY'S QUEST. New York, Stokes, 1927. 310p [BM BVaU LC NSHD OTMC

FURTHER CHRONICLES OF AVONLEA. Which have to do with many Personalities and Events in and about Avonlea. ... Boston, Page, 1920. 301p [First Canadian ed.: Toronto, Ryerson, 1953. 301p] [BM BVaU LC OTMC

THE GOLDEN ROAD. Boston, Page 1913. 369p [BM BVaU LC NBFU OTU

JANE OF LANTERN HILL. Toronto, McClelland, 1937. 297p [BM BVaU LC OTU

KILMENY OF THE ORCHARD. Boston, Page, 1910. 256p [BM BVaU LC OTU

MAGIC FOR MARIGOLD. Toronto, McClelland, 1929. 328p [BM BVaU LC NBFU OTMC

MISTRESS PAT. A Novel of Silver Bush. New York, Stokes, 1935. 338p [BM BVa LC OTU

PAT OF SILVER BUSH. New York, Stokes, 1933. 329p [BM BVa LC NBFU OTU

RAINBOW VALLEY. Toronto, McClelland, 1919. 341p [BM BVaU LC NBFU OTU

RILLA OF INGLESIDE. Toronto, McClelland, 1921. 370p [BM BVaU LC NBFU OTU

THE STORY GIRL. Boston, Page, 1911. 365p [BM BVaU LC NBFU OTU
A TANGLED WEB. New York, Stokes, 1931. 324p [Pub. in England under title:
AUNT BECKY BEGAN IT. London, Hodder, 1931.] [BM BVaU LC NSHD OTU

Montreuil, Mrs. Anna B., 1886—
DUMB-BELL. Boston, Christopher, 1929. 264p [LC OKQ

Moodie, Marion Elizabeth, 1867—
LEGEND OF DRYAS. N.p., 1926. 8p [OTMC

Moodie, Susanna (Strickland), 1803—1885
DOROTHY CHANCE. 1867. [BCF
FLORA LINDSAY; or, Passages in an Eventful Life. London, Bentley, 1854. 2v
[BVaU BM LC OTP
GEOFFREY MONCTON; or, The Faithless Guardian. New York, DeWitt, 1855.
362p [Cf. THE MONCKTONS. A Novel. London, 1856. 2v] [BM BVaU LC
NSHD OTMC QMM
GEORGE LEATRIM; or, The Mother's Test. Edinburgh, Hamilton, 1875. [Later ed.:
Edinburgh, Oliphant, Anderson & Ferrier, 1882. 63p] [BM OH
JOSIAH SHIRLEY, the Little Quaker. [BibC
THE LITTLE BLACK PONY AND OTHER STORIES. Philadelphia, Collins, 1850.
[AmCat BibC
THE LITTLE PRISONER; or, Passion and Patience: and, Amendment; or, Charles
Grant and his Sister. By the Authors of *Hugh Latimer* [i.e., Susanna Strickland]
and *Disobedience* [i.e., Elizabeth Strickland], *etc.* London, 1828. 144p [BM
MARK HURDLESTONE, The Gold Worshipper. London, Bentley, 1853. 2v [Also
pub. as: MARK HURDLESTONE; or, The Two Brothers. New York, DeWitt, n.d.
359p] [BM BVaU LC NBFU OKQ
MATRIMONIAL SPECULATIONS. London, Bentley, 1854. 352p [BM LC OONL
THE MONCKTONS. A Novel. London, Bentley, 1856. 2v [BM OTL
PRECEPT AND PRACTICE; or, The Vicar's Tales. [BibC
PROFESSION AND PRINCIPLE. Tales. By S. Strickland. London, Dean, 1833.
[EngCat
ROWLAND MASSINGHAM; or, I Will Be my Own Master. By S. Strickland. London,
Dean, 1837. 185p [OLU
THE SOLDIER'S ORPHAN; or, Hugh Latimer. (Something more about the Soldier's
Orphan, or, the further Adventures of Hugh Latimer.) 2pts London, Dean, 1853.
[BM
SPARTACUS. A Roman Story. [Anon] London, Newman, 1822. 131p [Variant
title listed in BibC: SPARTACUS; or, The Slave's Struggle for Freedom.] [BM
THE WORLD BEFORE THEM. A Novel. London, Bentley, 1868. 3v [BM

Moody, Irene Helen (Hawkins), —1958
DELPHINE OF THE 'EIGHTIES. London, Bale & Danielson, 1931. 252p [BM BVaU
NBFU OTMC

Moore, Arthur W.
NORMAN STANLEY'S CRUSADE; or, The Dunkin Act in Turnipham. Montreal,
Dougall, 1877. 197p [OTP

Moore, Ida Cecil
LUCKY ORPHAN. New York, Scribner, 1947. 121p [LC

Moore, Philip Hooper, 1879–1961
THE CASTLE BUCK. Hunting and Fishing Adventures with a Nova Scotia Guide.
London, Longmans, 1945. 300p [BVaU LC OTMC
SLAG AND GOLD. A Tale of the Porcupine Trail. Toronto, Allen, 1924. 314p
[BM BVaU NBFU OTMC

Moore, William Henry, 1872–1960
POLLY MASSON. A Political Novel. Toronto, Dent, 1919. 339p [BM BVaU
NSHD OTP QMSS

Moorhouse, Arthur Herbert Joseph, 1882–
EVERY MAN FOR HIMSELF. By Hopkins Moorhouse [pseud]. Toronto, Musson,
1920. 342p [BM BVaU LC NBFU OTMC
THE GAUNTLET OF ALCESTE. By Hopkins Moorhouse [pseud]. Toronto, Musson,
1921. 311p [BM BVaU LC OTMC
THE GOLDEN SCARAB. By Hopkins Moorhouse [pseud]. Toronto, Musson, 1926.
311p [BM BVaU NBFU OTMC QMM

Morgan, Grace Jones
SALVAGE ALL. New York, Croswell, 1928. 337p [BM BViPA LC OTP
TENTS OF SHEM. London, Sampson, Low, 1930. 250p [BM

Morison, John Archibald, 1867–
THE WORLD, THE CHURCH, AND THE DEVIL. Boston, Badger, 1916. 198p [LC
NSWA

Morphy, J.
NED FENTON'S PORTFOLIO. Quebec, Palmer, 1863. 141p [LC OTP QMM

Morris, Eric Cecil, 1914–
LE DERNIER VOYAGE. Un Roman de la Gaspésie. French trans. by Martine
Hébert-Duguay. Montreal, Chantecler, 1951. 255p [French version of his
A VOICE IS CALLING.]
TRESPASS AGAINST NONE. Montreal, Whitcombe & Gilmour, 1950. 317p [NBFU
OONL
A VOICE IS CALLING. Montreal, Simpson, 1945. 487p [BVaU OTU QMBM

Morrison, Dorothy, 1909–
TALES THE ESKIMOS TELL. Selected and Retold. Regina, School Aids and Text
Book Pub. Co., 1944. 60p [OTU

Morse, F. Louise

SOCIAL HEROISM. A Canadian Prize Temperance Story. Toronto, 1878. 82p
[Bound with BROKEN BONDS. A Prize Temperance Story. By Felix Max.]
[Patrick cat. 27

Morse, Harry Havelock, 1883–1918

THE ACADIAN HUNTER; or, Jean Breau, the French Brother. An Historical Romance.
Ed. by William Inglis Morse. Boston, priv. print. by W.I. Morse, 1927. 462p
[LC NSHD

Morton, Guy Eugene, 1884–1948

ASHES OF MURDER. London, Skeffington, 1935. 288p [NBFU
BLACK GOLD. Boston, Small Maynard, 1924. 310p [LC NBFU OOP
THE BLACK ROBE. New York, Minton Balch, 1927. 278p [Pub. in England as
KING OF THE WORLD, q.v.] [LC
BURLEIGH MURDERS. London, Skeffington, 1936. 288p [OTU
THE ENEMY WITHIN. Baltimore, Saulsbury, 1918. 315p [LC
THE FORBIDDEN ROAD. London, Hodder, 1928. 312p [LC OOP
KING OF THE WORLD; or, The Pommeray Case. London, Hodder, 1927. 320p
[Pub. in U.S. as THE BLACK ROBE, q.v.] [LC NBFU
MURDER. London, Skeffington, 1934. 287p [CBI
MYSTERY AT HARDACRES. London, Skeffington, 1936. 288p [OTU
MYSTERY AT HERMIT'S END. London, Skeffington, 1932. 287p [CBI
PERRIN MURDER CASE. London, Skeffington, 1930. 288p [CBI
THE RAGGED ROBIN MURDERS. New York, Greenberg, [1935?]. 310p [BVaU
RANGY PETE. Boston, Small Maynard, 1922. 409p [AEU LC NBFU OTMC
RED LADY. London, Skeffington, 1930. 288p [CBI
SCARLET THUMB-PRINT. London, Skeffington, 1932. 288p [CBI
SILVER-VOICED MURDER. London, Skeffington, 1933. 288p [CBI
WARDS OF THE AZURE HILLS. London, Hoddard, 1926. 309p [LC NBFU
ZOLA'S THIRTEEN. London, Skeffington, 1929. 288p [BVaU

Morton, James

POLSON'S PROBATION. A Story of Manitoba. Toronto, Briggs, 1897. 368p [BM
BVaU NSHD OTU

Morton, James [of Victoria, B.C.], 1870?–1967

THE SINGULAR TRAVELS OF MEDIUS MIDDLEMAN. Entries from the Journal of his
Adventures with Similus Buljo in the Lands of Obesia and Exigua. By Jay Jingle
[pseud]. New York, Vantage Press, 1952. 239p

Mountcastle, Clara H., 1837–

A MYSTERY. By Caris Sima [pseud]. Toronto, Rose, 1886. 151p [BVaU OTU

Mowat, Angus McGill, 1892–

CARRYING PLACE. Toronto, Saunders, 1944. 318p [BVaU NBFU OTU QMBM
THEN I'LL LOOK UP. Toronto, Saunders, 1938. 309p [BM BVaU LC NBFU OTU

Mowat, Farley McGill, 1921–

LOST IN THE BARRENS. Boston, Little Brown, 1956. 244p

Mowat, Grace Helen, 1875–1964

BROKEN BARRIER. ... A Romance of Staten Island and the Province of New Brunswick. ... Fredericton, University Press, 1951. 182p

Munday, Albert Henry, 1896–

CAPTAINS OF THE SKY. The Way of Life of a Military Aviator. Evanston, Ill., Row Peterson, 1942. 64p [LC

NO OTHER GODS. A Novel of Saskatchewan. Boston, Meador, 1934. 271p [LC NBFU OTMC

Munn, Henry Toke

HOME IS THE HUNTER. By Henry Toke Munn and Elizabeth Sprigge. Toronto, Macmillan, 1930. 296p [BM BVaU NBS OH

Munro, Bruce Weston, 1860–1900?

A BLUNDERING BOY. A Humorous Story. Toronto, Munro, 1887. 395p [BVaU NBFU OTU

SPLINTERS; or, A Grist of Giggles. [Anon] Toronto, Carswell, 1886. 279p [OTU

Murat, Eugene

PAPETA. A Story. Abridged and Arranged from the Diary and Private Papers of Mr. Eugene Murat. Saint John, 1867. [BCF NBB

Murdoch, Rev. Benedict Joseph, 1886–

THE MENDERS. Francestown, N.H., M. Jones Co., 1953. 259p

SOUVENIR. Lancaster, Wickersham Press, 1926. 198p [LC NBFU OTMC

SPRIGS. Cedar Rapids, Ia., Torch Press, 1927. 210p [LC NBFU

Murdoch, John A.

IN THE WOODS AND ON THE WATERS. Winnipeg, Stovel, 1896. 135p [BM BVaU OTP

Murphy, Emily Gowan (Ferguson), 1868–1933

OUR LITTLE CANADIAN COUSIN OF THE GREAT NORTHWEST. Boston, Page, 1923. 86p [LC

Murphy, Rev. William Leo, 1899–

THE GOLDEN HERITAGE. New York, Kenedy, 1929. 281p [LC OONL

THE HILL OF TRIUMPH. A Story of Jerusalem in the Time of Christ. New York, Kenedy, 1928. 322p [LC NSHD OONL

SILVER GLADE. A Novel. St. Nazianz, Wis., Soc. of the Divine Savior, 1947. 256p [LC

TRAIL'S END. A Tale of the Royal Canadian Mounted Police in the Catholic Land of Evangeline. Ozone Park, N.Y., Catholic Literary Guild, 1941. 208p [LC NBFU

WITHIN THY HEART. Halifax, Mitchell, 1953. 156p

Murray, Rev. John Clark, 1836–1917
HE THAT HAD RECEIVED THE FIVE TALENTS. London, Unwin, 1904. 446p [BM
   OTU

Murray, Kate
THE GUIDING ANGEL. Toronto, Wesleyan Book Room, 1871. 136p [OONL

Murray, Lillian (Marjoram) 1918–
GINNIE AND THE SNOW GYPSIES. London, Hutchinson, 1958. 191p
IN THE TRACK OF THE HUSKIES. Toronto, McClelland, 1960. 207p

Murray, William Waldie, 1891–1956
FIVE NINES AND WHIZZ BANGS. By the Orderly Sergeant [pseud]. Ottawa,
   Legionary Library, 1937. 244p [BVaU NBFU OTU

Musgrave, Fanny Wood
GABRIELLE AMETHYST. Toronto, Briggs, 1908. 246p [BM NSHD OTU
GYPSY. [MOR'12
A RAY OF LIGHT. [MOR'12
TRUE TO THE LAST. [MOR'12

Nablo, James Benson, 1910–
THE LONG NOVEMBER. New York, Dutton, 1946. 224p [BVaU LC OTMC

Nani, Mrs. Kathleen, 1900–
RAINBOW'S END. Ed. by Albert Nani. New York, Pageant Press, 1953. 162p

Nasmith, George Gallie, 1877–1965
SMITHS OF A BETTER QUALITY. Ottawa, National Council of Education, 1925.
   138p [Eugenics presented in fictionalized form.] [BM BVaU OTMC

Naugler, Gertrude Paist, 1912–
THE WORLD AND JULIE. New York, Scribner, 1955. 286p

Nease, Lilla Stewart (Dunlap), 1858–
IN MUSIC'S THRALL. Toronto, Briggs, 1903. 146p [BM NBFU OTMC

Neil, Stephen, 1877–1947
ALL THE KING'S MEN. Toronto, Macmillan, 1934. 332p [BVaU NBFU OTP

Nelson, Frederick
TORONTO IN 1928 A.D. Toronto, National Business Methods & Pub. Co., 1908.
   48p [BM BVaU OTU

Nelson, George Edmondson, 1902–
NORTHERN LIGHTS. A New Collection of Distinguished Writing by Canadian
   Authors. Ed. by ——. Garden City, N.Y., Doubleday, 1960. 736p

Nelson, John Bertram
FEATHERS IN THE WIND. New York, Vantage Press, 1959. 127p

Nil Desperandum (pseud)
AN EASTER LILY AND OTHER STORIES. By Nil Desperandum [pseud]. Toronto,
1898. [OONL

Niven, Frederick John, 1878–1944
ABOVE YOUR HEADS. London, Martin Secker, 1911. 300p [BM OONL
BROTHERS IN ARMS. Being the Account written by James Niven ... of Glasgow, in
the 18th Century. ... London, Collins, 1942. 255p [BM LC NBFU OONL
CINDERELLA OF SKOOKUM CREEK. London, Nash, 1916. 319p [BM BVa OONL
DEAD MEN'S BELLS. London, Martin Secker, 1912. 309p [BM BVaU OONL
ELLEN ADAIR. New York, Boni, 1925. 287p [1st ed.: London, Nash, 1913.
320p] [BM BVaU LC NBFU OONL
THE FLYING YEARS. London, Collins, 1935. 284p [BM BVaU LC OONL QMM
HANDS UP! New York, Lane, 1913. 315p [BM BVaU LC NBFU OONL
THE ISLAND PROVIDENCE. New York, Lane, 1910. 310p [BM BVaU LC OONL
JUSTICE OF THE PEACE. New York, Boni, 1923. 453p [Earlier ed.: London, Nash,
1914. 434p] [BM BVaU LC NBFU OONL
THE LADY OF THE CROSSING. Toronto, Hodder, 1919. 317p [BM BVaU LC
NBFU OONL
THE LOST CABIN MINE. London, Lane, 1908. 254p [Also: New York, Lane,
1909. 312p] [BM BVaU LC NBFU OONL
MINE INHERITANCE. New York, Macmillan, 1940. 432p [BM BVaU LC NBFU
OONL QMSS
MRS. BARRY. New York, Dutton, 1933. 256p [BM BVaU LC NBFU OONL
OLD SOLDIER. A Novel. London, Collins, 1936. 250p [BM BVaU LC NBFU
OONL
THE PAISLEY SHAWL. New York, Dodd Mead, 1931. 252p [BM BVaU NBFU
OONL
PENNY SCOT'S TREASURE. London, Collins, 1918. 306p [BM NBFU OTMC
THE PORCELAIN LADY. London, Martin Secker, 1913. 354p [BM OONL
QUEER FELLOWS. London, Lane, 1927. 251p [Same as WILD HONEY.] [BM
NBFU OONL QMM
THE RICH WIFE. London, Collins, 1932. 256p [BM BVaU LC NBFU
THE S.S. GLORY. London, Heinemann, 1915. 220p [BM BVaU LC NBFU
OONL
SAGE-BRUSH STORIES. London, Nash, 1917. 304p [BM OTMC
THE STAFF AT SIMSON'S. A Novel. London, Collins, 1937. 318p [BM BVaU LC
NBFU OTMC QMM
THE STORY OF THEIR DAYS. London, Collins, 1939. 444p [BM BVaU LC
NBFU OONL QMM
A TALE THAT IS TOLD. Toronto, Collins, 1920. 338p [BM BVaU LC NBFU
OONL

THE THREE MARYS. London, Collins, 1930. 284p [BM BVaU LC NBFU OONL
THE TRANSPLANTED. Toronto, Collins, 1944. 310p [BVaU LC NBFU OONL
TREASURE TRAIL. New York, Dodd Mead, 1923. 254p [BVaU LC NBFU
   OONL
TRIUMPH. New York, Dutton, 1934. 252p [BM BVaU LC NBFU OONL
TWO GENERATIONS. London, Nash, 1916. 358p [BM OTMC QMM
UNDER WHICH KING. London, Collins, 1943. 192p [BM BVaU LC NBFU
   OONL
WILD HONEY. New York, Dodd Mead, 1927. 251p [Same as QUEER FELLOWS.]
   [BVaU LC NBFU OONL
A WILDERNESS OF MONKEYS. New York, Lane, 1911. 283p [BM BVaU LC
   NBFU OONL QMM
THE WOLFER. New York, Dodd Mead, 1923. 314p [BVaU LC NBFU OONL

Nixon, James Leroy

A MAID OF ONTARIO. A Story of Buffalo, Toronto, and the Fenian Raid of 1866.
   Welland, Ont., Yedis Pub. Co., 1905. 348p [BM OTMC

Nixon, Marian Essley

MARTHA. A Story. London, Stockwell, [1933?]. 64p [CC

Nobile, Achilles Alexander, 1833—

AN ANONYMOUS LETTER. A Novel. Trans. from the Italian. (Fac. page: UNA
   LETTERA ANONIMA, versione italiana.) Buffalo, Baker, 1885. 217p [OTU

Noel, Mrs. John Vavasour, 1815—1878

THE ABBEY OF RATHMORE, AND OTHER TALES. Kingston, Creighton, 1859. 272p
   [Includes "Madeline Beresford, or The Infidel's Betrothed" and "Grace Raymond,
   or The Slave's Revenge."] [BVaU OTU
HILDA; or, The Merchant's Secret. [BCF
PASSION AND PRINCIPLE. [BCF

Nolting, Rev. William Carl, 1907—

OUR SALLY. A Novel. New York, Vantage Press, 1954. 175p

Norman, Dorothy, 1905—

MARJORIE'S ANTIQUE SHOP. New York, Penn, 1942. 261p [LC

Nota Bene (pseud)

TO HELL AND BACK. Winnipeg, T.H. Best, 1949. 291p [QMBM

Nursey, Walter R., 1847—1927

THE ROMANCE OF THE MERRY MAIDEN; or, How the Farm Mortgage was Lifted by
   a Jersey Beauty. Lowell, Mass., Hood, 1898. 192p [LC OTU

Oakes, Christopher

THE CANADIAN SENATOR; or, A Romance of Love and Politics. Toronto, National
   Pub. Co., 1890. 179p [BM BVaU LC NBFU OTP

Obodiac, Stanlee, 1922–
CASHMIR OF THE R.C.A.F. New York, Pageant Press, 1955. 221p

O'Brien, Agnes
WINNOWING. Toronto, Extension Print., 1935. 483p [OTMC

O'Brien, Rev. Cornelius, 1843–1906
AFTER WEARY YEARS. A Novel. Baltimore, Murphy, 1885. 433p [LC NSHD
OOU

Odle, E.V.
THE CLOCKWORK MAN. London, Heinemann, 1923. 213p [BM LC
THE HISTORY OF ALFRED RUDD. A Novel. London, Collins, 1922. 273p [BM

Ogilvy, Maud
THE KEEPER OF BIC LIGHT HOUSE. A Canadian Story of To-day. Montreal, Renouf,
1891. 138p [BVaU NBFU OTP
MARIE GOURDON. A Romance of the Lower St. Lawrence. Montreal, Lovell,
1890. 129p [BVaU NSHD OTP

Ognall, Leopold Horace, 1908–
ALIBI. By Harry Carmichael [pseud]. London, Collins, 1961. 192p
THE ARMITAGE SECRET. By Hartley Howard [pseud]. London, Collins, 1959.
256p
THE BIG SNATCH. By Hartley Howard [pseud]. London, Collins, 1958. 191p
BOWMAN AT A VENTURE. By Hartley Howard [pseud]. London, Collins, 1954.
192p
BOWMAN STRIKES AGAIN. By Hartley Howard [pseud]. London, Collins, 1958.
192p
THE BOWMAN TOUCH. By Hartley Howard [pseud]. London, Collins, 1956. 192p
THE DEAD OF THE NIGHT. By Harry Carmichael [pseud]. London, Collins, 1956.
192p
DEADLINE. By Hartley Howard [pseud]. London, Collins, 1959. 192p
DEADLY NIGHT-CAP. By Harry Carmichael [pseud]. London, Collins, 1953. 192p
DEATH OF CECILIA. By Hartley Howard [pseud]. London, Collins, 1952. 188p
DEATH COUNTS THREE. By Harry Carmichael [pseud]. London, Collins, 1954.
192p
EMERGENCY EXIT. By Harry Carmichael [pseud]. London, Collins, 1957. 192p
EXTORTION. By Hartley Howard [pseud]. London, Collins, 1960. 192p
FALL GUY. By Hartley Howard [pseud]. London, Collins, 1960. 256p
A HEARSE FOR CINDERELLA. By Hartley Howard [pseud]. London, Collins, 1956.
192p
INTO THIN AIR. By Harry Carmichael [pseud]. New York, Doubleday, 1958. 191p
JAMES KNOWLAND: DECEASED. By Harry Carmichael [pseud]. London, Collins,
1958. 192p
JUSTICE ENOUGH. By Harry Carmichael [pseud]. London, Collins, 1956. 192p

KEY TO THE MORGUE. By Hartley Howard [pseud]. London, Collins, 1957. 192p

THE LAST APPOINTMENT. By Hartley Howard [pseud]. London, Collins, 1951. 256p

THE LAST DECEPTION. By Hartley Howard [pseud]. London, Collins, 1951. 256p

THE LAST VANITY. By Hartley Howard [pseud]. London, Collins, 1951. 252p

THE LONG NIGHT. By Hartley Howard [pseud]. London, Collins, 1957. 192p

MONEY FOR MURDER. By Harry Carmichael [pseud]. London, Collins, [1955]. 192p

NOOSE FOR A LADY. By Harry Carmichael [pseud]. London, Collins, 1955. 192p

NO TARGET FOR BOWMAN. By Hartley Howard [pseud]. London, Collins, 1955. 192p

... OR BE HE DEAD. By Harry Carmichael [pseud]. London, Collins, 1959. 192p

THE OTHER SIDE OF THE DOOR. By Hartley Howard [pseud]. London, Collins, 1953. 188p

PUT OUT THAT STAR. By Harry Carmichael [pseud]. London, Collins, 1957. 192p

A QUESTION OF TIME. By Harry Carmichael [pseud]. London, Collins, 1958. 192p

REQUIEM FOR CHARLES. By Harry Carmichael [pseud]. London, Collins, 1960. 256p

SCHOOL FOR MURDER. By Harry Carmichael [pseud]. London, Collins, 1953. 192p

THE SCREAMING RABBIT. By Harry Carmichael [pseud]. New York, Simon & Schuster, 1955. 277p [First pub. under title: DEATH COUNTS THREE, q.v.]

THE SEEDS OF HATE. By Harry Carmichael [pseud]. London, Collins, 1960. 192p

SLEEP FOR THE WICKED. By Hartley Howard [pseud]. London, Collins, 1955. 192p

SLEEP, MY PRETTY ONE. By Hartley Howard [pseud]. London, Collins, 1958. 192p

STRANGLEHOLD. By Harry Carmichael [pseud]. London, Collins, 1959. 192p

THE VANISHING TRICK. By Harry Carmichael [pseud]. London, Collins, 1955. 188p

WHY KILL JOHNNY? By Harry Carmichael [pseud]. London, Collins, 1954. 191p

O'Hagan, Howard, 1902–

TAY JOHN. London, Laidlaw, 1939. 264p [Also: New York, Potter, 1960. 264p] [BM BVaU NBFU OTMC

O'Hara, Mrs. Melita L.

COAST TO COAST IN A PUDDLE JUMPER, AND OTHER STORIES. Tessier, Sask., Author, 1930. 109p [Also: Philadelphia, Dorrance, 1930.] [BVaU NBFU OONL QMSS

O'Higgins, Harvey Jerrold, 1876–1929

THE ADVENTURES OF DETECTIVE BARNEY. New York, Century, 1915. 305p [BM LC

CLARA BARRON. New York, Harper, 1922. 335p [BM BVaU LC OTMC

DON-A-DREAMS. A Story of Love and Youth. New York, Century, 1906. 412p
[BM BVaU LC OTMC

FROM THE LIFE. Imaginary Portraits of Some Distinguished Americans. New York,
Harper, 1919. 334p [BM LC NBFU OTMC

A GRAND ARMY MAN. New York, Century, 1908. 253p [BM LC OTMC

HIS MOTHER. Toronto, Charles Press, 1909. 24p [OTMC

JULIE CANE. New York, Harper, 1924. 343p [BM BVaU LC OTMC

OLD CLINKERS. A Story of the New York Fire Department. Boston, Small Maynard, 1909. 277p [LC OTU

THE SECRET SPRINGS. New York, Harper, 1920. 242p [BM LC NSHD OTU

SILENT SAM, AND OTHER STORIES OF OUR DAY. New York, Century, 1914. 390p
[BM LC OTMC

THE SMOKE-EATERS. The Story of a Fire Crew. New York, Century, 1905. 296p
[BM LC

SOME DISTINGUISHED AMERICANS. Imaginary Portraits. London, Harper, 1922.
335p [BM LC NBFU OTMC

Olson, Oscar, 1908–
MOUNTIE ON TRIAL. Toronto, Ryerson, 1953. 257p

Omond, Helen B.
DILARAM. New York, Fortuny's, 1938. 175p [OTU

O'Reilly, John A.
THE LAST SENTINEL OF CASTLE HILL. A Newfoundland Story. London, Stock,
1916. 382p [BVaU NBFU OTP QQLA

Ormsby, Ïerne
JANE OF THE CROW'S NEST. ... London, Hutchinson, 1936. 256p [BM
WILD WEST SALLY. London, Lutterworth, 1939. 222p [BM OTU

Osler, Edmund Boyd, 1919–
LIGHT IN THE WILDERNESS. Toronto, Harlequin Books, 1953. 192p

Ostenso, Martha, 1900–1963
THE DARK DAWN. New York, Dodd Mead, 1926. 294p [BM BVaU NBFU OTP
LOVE PASSED THIS WAY. New York, Dodd Mead, 1942. 217p [LC NBFU OTMC
THE MAD CAREWS. New York, Dodd Mead, 1927. 346p [BM BVaU LC NBFU
OTMC QMM
A MAN HAD TALL SONS. New York, Dodd Mead, 1958. 365p
THE MANDRAKE ROOT. New York, Dodd Mead, 1938. 304p [LC NBFU OTMC
QMM
MILK ROUTE. New York, Dodd Mead, 1948. 250p [BVaU LC NBFU OTMC
QMM
O RIVER, REMEMBER! New York, Dodd Mead, 1943. 393p [BM BVaU LC
NBFU OTU QMM

THE PASSIONATE FLIGHT. *See* WILD GEESE, below.

PROLOGUE TO LOVE. New York, Dodd Mead, 1932. 265p [BVaU NBFU LC OTMC QMM

THE STONE FIELD. New York, Dodd Mead, 1937. 310p [BVaU LC NBFU OTMC QMM

THE SUNSET TREE. New York, Dodd Mead, 1949. 255p [BM LC NBFU OTMC

THERE'S ALWAYS ANOTHER YEAR. New York, Dodd Mead, 1933. 268p [BVaU LC NBFU OTMC QMM

THE WATERS UNDER THE EARTH. New York, Dodd Mead, 1930. 319p [BM BVaU LC NBFU OTMC QMM

THE WHITE REEF. New York, Dodd Mead, 1934. 288p [BM BVaU LC NBFU OTMC QMM

WILD GEESE. Toronto, McClelland, 1925. 356p [English title: THE PASSIONATE FLIGHT. London, Hodder, 1925. 320p] [BM BVaU LC NBFU OTMC

THE YOUNG MAY MOON. New York, Dodd Mead, 1929. 301p [BM BVaU LC NBFU OTMC QMM

O'Sullivan, Francis Joseph, 1870–

THE CHRONICLES OF CROFTON. Toronto, Hunter Rose, 1926. 188p [NBFU OTP

Owen, John Spencer

TETE JAUNE CACHE. New York, Pageant Press, 1953. 223p

Oxley, James Macdonald, 1855–1907

ARCHIE OF ATHABASCA. Boston, Lothrop, 1893. 262p [Also as: ARCHIE McKENZIE, the Young Nor'-Wester. London, Religious Tract Soc., 1894; and THE YOUNG NOR'-WESTER. London, Religious Tract Soc., 1908. 256p] [BM BVaU OTMC

BAFFLING THE BLOCKADE. London, Nelson, 1896. 375p [BM OONL

BERT LLOYD'S BOYHOOD. A Story of Nova Scotia. Philadelphia, American Baptist Pub. Soc., 1889. 347p [Also: London, Hodder, 1892. 363p] [BM LC NSHD OONL

THE BOY TRAMPS; or, Across Canada. New York, Crowell, 1896. 361p [Also as: TWO BOY TRAMPS. London, Chambers, 1896. 320p] [BM BVaU LC NBFU OTMC

THE CHORE-BOY OF CAMP KIPPEWA. Philadelphia, American Baptist Pub. Soc., 1891. 144p [Also as: THE YOUNG WOODSMAN. London, Nelson, 1894.] [BM LC OONL

DIAMOND ROCK; or, On the Right Track. London, Nelson, 1893. 302p [Same as: THE GOOD SHIP GRYPHON, *q.v.*] [BM OONL

DONALBLANE OF DARIEN. Toronto, Musson, n.d. 126p [Also: London, Partridge, 1902.] [BM OONL

DONALD GRANT'S DEVELOPMENT. Philadelphia, American Baptist Pub. Soc., 1892. 256p [Also as: MAKING HIS WAY. London, Nelson, 1896.] [BM LC NSHD OONL

THE FAMILY ON WHEELS. Adapted from the French. ... New York, Crowell, 1905. 219p [LC

FERGUS MACTAVISH; or, Portage and Prairie. A Story of the Hudson's Bay Co. Philadelphia, American Baptist Pub. Soc., 1892. 344p [BM BVaU LC OONL

FIFE AND DRUM AT LOUISBOURG. Boston, Little Brown, 1899. 307p [BM BVaU LC NSHD OTMC QMSS

FROM RUNG TO RUNG. London, Kelly, 1899. 124p [BM

THE GOOD SHIP GRYPHON. Philadelphia, American Baptist Pub. Soc., 1893. 248p [Same as: DIAMOND ROCK, q.v.] [LC OTMC

THE HERO OF START POINT AND OTHER STORIES. Philadelphia, American Baptist Pub. Soc., 1896. 254p [LC

IN PATHS OF PERIL. Boy's Adventure in Nova Scotia. London, Partridge, 1903. 128p [BM BVaU

IN THE SWING OF THE SEA. Philadelphia, American Baptist Pub. Soc., 1898. 268p [BM LC NSHD

IN THE WILDS OF THE WEST COAST. New York, Nelson, 1895. 398p [BM BVaU LC NBFU OTMC

L'HASA AT LAST. Philadelphia, American Baptist Pub. Soc., 1900. 269p [BM BVaU LC OTMC

MY STRANGE RESCUE AND OTHER STORIES. London, Nelson, 1894. 368p [BM OONL

NORMAN'S NUGGET. London, Partridge, 1901. 297p [BM OTMC

NORTH OVERLAND WITH FRANKLIN. London, Religious Tract Soc., 1901. 256p [BM BVaU LC NSHD OTP

ON THE WORLD'S ROOF. Philadelphia, American Baptist Pub. Soc., 1897. 271p [1st ed.: London, Nisbet, 1896. 242p] [BM LC NSHD OTMC

STANDING THE TEST. London, Religious Tract Soc., 1898. 127p [BM

THE SPECIMEN HUNTERS. New ed. London, Religious Tract Soc., 1907. 256p [Earlier ed. at Toronto? –OOP] [BM OONL

TERRY'S TRIALS AND TRIUMPHS. London, Nelson, 1899. 186p [BM OTMC

TI-TI-PU. A Boy of Red River. Toronto, Musson, n.d. 126p [ACG BViPA NSWA OOA

UP AMONG THE ICE-FLOES. Philadelphia, American Baptist Pub. Soc., 1890. 250p [BM LC OONL

WITH ROGERS ON THE FRONTIER. A Story of '56. New York, Wessels, 1902. 253p [LC OONL

WON IN WESTERN CANADA. N.p., 1903. 39p [OTP

THE WRECKERS OF SABLE ISLAND. Philadelphia, American Baptist Pub. Soc., 1891. 108p [Also: London, Nelson, 1904. 121p] [BM BVaU LC NSHD OONL

THE YOUNG NOR'-WESTER. See ARCHIE OF ATHABASKA, above.

THE YOUNG WOODSMAN; or, Life in the Forests of Canada. London, Nelson, 1895. 156p [OLU

Pacey, Desmond, 1917–

A BOOK OF CANADIAN STORIES. Ed. by ——. Toronto, Ryerson, 1947. 295p
[2nd ed., rev. & enl., 1950. 310p. School ed., with intro. and notes by ——,
1952. xxxviii + 312p]   [BVaU NSHD OTMC QMBM

THE PICNIC AND OTHER STORIES. Toronto, Ryerson, 1958. xi + 143p

Packard, Frank Lucius, 1877–1942

THE ADVENTURES OF JIMMY DALE. Toronto, Copp Clark, 1917. 468p [BM
BVaU LC NBFU OTU QMM

THE BELOVED TRAITOR. Toronto, Copp Clark, 1915. 347p [BM BVaU LC
NBFU OTMC QMM

THE BIG SHOT. Toronto, Copp Clark, 1929. 286p [BM LC NBFU OTU QMM

BROKEN WATERS. Toronto, Copp Clark, 1925. 294p [BM BVaU LC NBFU
OTMC QMM

THE DEVIL'S MANTLE. New York, Doran, 1927. 313p [BM BVaU LC OTU
QMM

DOORS OF THE NIGHT. Toronto, Copp Clark, 1922. 298p [BM BVaU LC NBFU
OTMC QMM

THE DRAGON'S JAWS. New York, Doran, 1937. 310p [BM LC NBFU OTMC

THE FOUR STRAGGLERS. Toronto, Copp Clark, 1923. 303p [BM BVaU LC
NBFU OTMC QMM

FROM NOW ON. Toronto, Copp Clark, 1919. 346p [BM NBFU OTMC QMM

THE FURTHER ADVENTURES OF JIMMY DALE. New York, Burt, 1919. 340p [BM
BVaU OTMC

THE GOLD SKULL MURDERS. New York, Doran, 1931. 303p [BM BVaU LC
NBFU OTMC

GREATER LOVE HATH NO MAN. Toronto, Copp Clark, 1913. 294p [BM BVaU
LC NBFU OTMC QMM

THE HIDDEN DOOR. New York, Doubleday, 1933. 300p [BM BVaU LC NBFU
OTMC QMM

JIMMY DALE AND THE BLUE ENVELOPE MURDER. Toronto, Copp Clark, 1930.
290p [BM BVa LC NBFU OTMC QMM

JIMMY DALE AND THE MISSING HOUR. New York, Doubleday, 1935. 310p [BM
LC OTMC

JIMMY DALE AND THE PHANTOM CLUE. Toronto, Copp Clark, 1922. 302p [BM
BVa LC NBFU OTMC QMM

THE LOCKED BOOK. Toronto, Copp Clark, 1924. 320p [BM BVaU LC NBFU
OTMC QMM

THE MIRACLE MAN. Toronto, Copp Clark, 1914. 300p [BM BVaU LC NBFU
OTMC QMM

MORE KNAVES THAN ONE. London, Stoughton, 1938. 286p [BM LC OTU

THE NIGHT OPERATOR. Toronto, Copp Clark, 1919. 320p [BM BVaU NBFU
OTMC QMM

ON THE IRON AT BIG CLOUD. New York, Crowell, 1911. 343p [BM LC NBFU
OTMC

PAWNED. Toronto, Copp Clark, 1921. 288p [BM LC NBFU OTMC

THE PURPLE BALL. New York, Doran, 1933. 310p [BM BVaU LC NBFU OTMC

THE RED LEDGER. New York, Doran, 1926. 318p [BM BVaU LC NBFU OTMC QMM

RUNNING SPECIAL. Toronto, Copp Clark, 1925. 304p [BM BVaU LC NBFU OOP OTMC QMM

SHANGHAI JIM. Garden City, Doubleday, 1928. 374p [BM BVaU LC NBFU OTMC

THE SIN THAT WAS HIS. Toronto, Copp Clark, 1917. 374p [BM BVaU LC NBFU OTMC QMM

THE SLAVE JUNK. London, Hodder, 1927. 312p [AEU BM

TIGER CLAWS. New York, Doran, 1928. 305p [BM BVaU LC NBFU OTMC

TWO STOLEN IDOLS. New York, Burt, 1927. 314p [LC NBFU OTMC QMM

THE WHITE MOLL. Toronto, Copp Clark, 1920. 306p [BM BVaU LC NBFU OTMC QMM

THE WIRE DEVILS. Toronto, Copp Clark, 1918. 318p [BM BVaU LC NBFU OTMC QMM

Page, Mrs. Elizabeth Merwin, 1889—

THE TREE OF LIBERTY. New York, Farrar, 1939. 985p [BM BVaU LC NBFU OTU

WILDERNESS ADVENTURE. New York, Rinehart, 1946. 300p [BM LC NBFU

Page, Patricia Kathleen, 1916—

THE SUN AND THE MOON. By Judith Cape [pseud]. Toronto, Macmillan, 1944. 200p [BVaU OTU

Parker, Alice Elizabeth (Foster), 1884—

BONDS IN A FAMILY. Victoria, Hunter Rose, 1933. 212p [BVaU NBFU OTP

Parker, Ellanore J.

THE LAND LAY WAITING. ... New York, Pageant Press, 1955. 236p

Parker, Gilbert, 1862—1932

AN ADVENTURER OF THE NORTH. Being a Continuation of PIERRE AND HIS PEOPLE. London, Methuen, 1895. 392p [BM BVaU LC NBFU OTMC QMM

THE BATTLE OF THE STRONG. A Romance of Two Kingdoms. London, Methuen, 1898. 432p [BM BVaU LC NBFU OTU QMSS

BORN WITH A GOLDEN SPOON. New York, Doubleday, 1899. 277p [BM LC

CARNAC. Toronto, Copp Clark, 1922. 319p [Cf. CARNAC'S FOLLY.] [BM BVaU OTMC QMM

CARNAC'S FOLLY. Philadelphia, Lippincott, 1922. 352p [Cf. preceding title.] [LC NBFU OTMC

THE CHIEF FACTOR. A Tale of the Hudson's Bay Company. New York, Trow Directory Co., 1892. 175p [Same title, but also containing "A Ricochet." New York, Home Pub. Co., 1893. 265p] [LC OTMC

THE CHIEF FACTOR. "Good Words" Christmas Story. London, Isbister & Co., 1892. 68p [Probably same as preceding title.] [BVaU QMSS

CUMNER'S SON AND OTHER SOUTH SEA FOLK. London, Heinemann, 1910. 283p [BM BVaU LC NBFU OTMC QMSS

DONOVAN PASHA, AND SOME PEOPLE OF EGYPT. London, Heinemann, 1902. 308p [BM BVaU LC NBFU OTMC QMM

THE GOING OF THE WHITE SWAN. New York, Appleton, 1912. 55p [Reprinted from AN ADVENTURER OF THE NORTH.] [BM BVaU LC NBFU OTMC

THE HILL OF PAINS. Boston, Badger, 1899. 151p [Contains also THE CAVE OF CRYS.] [AmCat has note saying Parker denies authorship "of any book" with this title.] [BVaU LC OTMC

THE JUDGEMENT HOUSE. A Novel. Toronto, Copp Clark, 1913. 470p [BM BVaU LC NBFU OTMC QMM

A LADDER OF SWORDS. A Tale of Love, Laughter, and Tears. London, Heinemann, 1904. 286p [Later pub. under title: MICHEL AND ANGELE. New York, Scribner, 1923. 245p] [BM BVaU LC NBFU OTMC QMSS

THE LANE THAT HAD NO TURNING, and Other Associated Tales concerning the People of Pontiac. New York, Doubleday, 1900. 359p [BM BVaU LC NBFU OTP QMM

THE LIAR. Boston, Brown, 1899. 142p [BVaU LC NBFU OTMC QMM

A LOVER'S DIARY. Songs in Sequence. London, Methuen, 1894. 147p [Also pub. with EMBERS. 2v in 1. New York, Scribner, 1913.] [BM BVaU LC NBFU OTP

THE MARCH OF THE WHITE GUARD. New York, Fenno, 1901. 133p [Reprinted from TAVISTOCK TALES. By Gilbert Parker and Others. London, Isbister, 1893. 254p] [BM BVaU LC NBFU OTMC QMM

THE MONEY MASTER. Being the Curious History of Jean Jacques Barbille, his Labours, his Loves and his Ladies. New York, Harper, 1915. 359p [BM BVaU LC NBFU OTP QMM

MRS. FALCHION. A Novel. London, Methuen, 1893. 2v [New ed.: London, Methuen, 1894. 428p] [BM BVaU LC NBFU OTMC QMSS

NO DEFENCE. Toronto, Copp Clark, 1920. 347p [BM BVaU LC NBFU OTMC QMM

NORTHERN LIGHTS. Toronto, Copp Clark, 1909. 375p [BM BVaU LC NBFU OTP QMM

PIERRE AND HIS PEOPLE. Tales of the Far North. London, Methuen, 1892. 323p [BM BVaU LC NBFU OTMC QMM

THE POMP OF THE LAVILETTES. Boston, Lamson Wolffe, 1896. 191p [BM BVaU LC NBFU OTMC QMM

THE POWER AND THE GLORY. A Romance of the Great La Salle. New York,
Harper, 1925. 339p [BM BVaU LC NBFU OTP QMM

THE PROMISED LAND. A Story of David in Israel. London, Cassell, 1928. 325p
[BM BVaU LC NBFU OOP OTMC QMM

THE RIGHT OF WAY. Being the Story of Charley Steele, and Another. London,
Heinemann, 1901. 368p [BM BVaU LC NBFU OTMC QMM

A ROMANY OF THE SNOWS. Second Series of AN ADVENTURER OF THE NORTH.
Being a continuation of PIERRE AND HIS PEOPLE. New York, Stone & Kimball,
1896. 218p [Same title: Toronto, Copp Clark, 1898. 392p] [BM BVaU LC
NBFU OTP QMM

THE SEATS OF THE MIGHTY. Being the Memoirs of Captain Robert Moray, Some
Time an Officer in the Virginia Regiment, and Afterwards of Amherst's Regiment.
London, Methuen, 1896. 376p [BM BVaU LC NBFU OTMC QMSS

TARBOE. The Story of a Life. New York, Harper, 1927. 196p [BM BVaU LC
NBFU OTMC QMM

THE TRAIL OF THE SWORD. New York, Appleton, 1894. 277p [BM BVaU LC
NBFU OTP

THE TRANSLATION OF A SAVAGE. New York, Appleton, 1893. 184p [BM BVaU
LC NBFU OTP QMM

THE TRESPASSER. New York, Appleton, 1893. 275p [BM BVaU LC NBFU
OTU QMM

AN UNPARDONABLE LIAR. Chicago, Sergel, 1900. 185p [Cf. THE LIAR. Boston,
Brown, 1899. 142p] [LC

THE WEAVERS. A Tale of England and Egypt of Fifty Years Ago. New York,
Harper, 1907. 531p [BM BVaU LC NBFU OTMC QMM

WHEN VALMOND CAME TO PONTIAC. The Story of a Lost Napoleon. London,
Methuen, 1895. 312p [BM BVaU LC NBFU OTMC QMM

WILD YOUTH, AND ANOTHER. [Tale: "Jordan is a Hard Road"]. Philadelphia,
Lippincott, 1919. 290p [BM BVaU LC NSHD OTP

THE WORKS OF GILBERT PARKER. Imperial Ed. New York, Scribner, 1912-23. 23v
[BM BVaU LC NSHD OTU QMM

THE WORLD FOR SALE. New York, Harper, 1916. 405p [BM BVaU LC NBFU
OTU QMM

YOU NEVER KNOW YOUR LUCK. Being the Story of a Matrimonial Deserter. New
York, Doran, 1914. 328p [BM BVaU LC NBFU OTMC QMM

Parker, K.Y.
BEYOND THE WEST. Truro, N.S., Truro Print., n.d. 145p [OTMC

Parker, William Wilder McKinley, 1894–
FLOWING GOLD. Edmonton, Author, 1957. 60p

GREENER PRAIRIE. Edmonton, Author, 1959. 68p

SILVER FORKS. Edmonton, Author, 1955. 66p

Parks, Georgina
RUKE ANEHM. By Gabrielle [pseud]. Philadelphia, Dorrance, 1938. 139p [LC OTU

Parsons, Nell Wilson, 1898—1968
THE CURLEW CRIED. A Love Story of the Canadian Prairie. Seattle, Frank McCaffrey, 1947. 383p [AEU OTU

Parsons, Vivian (Lajeunesse)
LUCIEN. Toronto, McClelland, 1939. 383p [LC OTP QMM
NOT WITHOUT HONOR. New York, Dodd Mead, 1941. 342p [AEU LC QMBM

Partridge, Basil Gilpin, 1894—
CHAPLET OF GRACE. Philadelphia, Westminster Press, 1956. 283p
LARRY PENNINGTON. Philadelphia, Westminster Press, 1954. 273p
THE PENNINGTONS. Philadelphia, Westminster Press, 1951. 284p

Paterson, Isabel M. (Bowler)
THE FOURTH QUEEN. Toronto, Macmillan, 1926. 315p [BM BVaU LC NBFU
THE GOLDEN VANITY. New York, Morrow, 1934. 372p [BVaU LC NBFU OTMC
IF IT PROVE FAIR WEATHER. New York, Putnam, 1940. 306p [BVaU LC NBFU
THE MAGPIE'S NEST. New York, Lane, 1917. 303p [BM BVaU LC NBFU
NEVER ASK THE END. New York, Morrow, 1933. 332p [BM BVaU LC NBFU OTMC
THE ROAD OF THE GODS. New York, Boni, 1930. 264p [BVaU LC NBFU
THE SHADOW RIDERS. New York, Lane, 1916. 379p [BM BVaU LC NSHD OTMC
THE SINGING SEASON. New York, Boni, 1924. 304p [BM BVaU LC NBFU

Paterson, Maude Elizabeth, 1867—
CHILD'S GARDEN OF STORIES. Toronto, Morang, 1911. 155p [2nd rev. ed., Toronto, Macmillan, 1931. 160p] [BM

Patriarche, Valance St. Just (Berryman), 1875—
RORY OF WILLOW BEACH. London, Cassell, 1912. 195p [BM OOP
TAG; or, The Chien Boule Dog. Boston, Page, 1909. 138p [BVaU LC NBFU OTMC

Pearce, Theodocia, 1894—1925?
THE EVERLASTING BEAUTY. New York, Lawren, 1926. 281p [BVaU NSHD

Pedley, Rev. Hugh, 1852—1923
LOOKING FORWARD. The Strange Experience of the Rev. Fergus McCheyne. Toronto, Briggs, 1913. 294p [BM BVaU NSHD OTU QMSS

Pedro, Dom (pseud)
SKETCHES. By Dom Pedro [pseud]. Toronto, Rose Pub. Co., 1891. 120p [OTU
SKETCHES. Dedicated to the Veterans of '85. By Dom Pedro [pseud]. Toronto,
  Hill & Weir, n.d. 32p [AEU NBFU

Penfield, Wilder Graves, 1891–
NO OTHER GODS. Boston, Little Brown, 1954. ix + 340p
THE TORCH. Boston, Little Brown, 1960. xiv + 370p

Pennington, Richard, 1904–
PETERLEY HARVEST. The Private Diary of David Peterley now for the First Time
  printed. London, Hutchinson, 1960. 285p

Pericum, Hic (pseud)
THE JINX OF THE MINE. A Romance of the Girl Prospector. By Hic Pericum [pseud].
  Toronto, Compliments of I.H. Perigoe & Co., Stock Brokers, 1937. 16p [OPAL

Perrot, Irene
CATHEDRAL WINDOWS. Montreal, Palm Pub., 1949. 147p [UTQ
TREES GROW TALL. A Novel. Toronto, Ryerson, 1946. 250p [NBS OTU
THE TWAIN TRADITION. New York, Pageant Press, 1952. 169p

Perry, Alma (Jordan)
GENTLY SMILING JAWS. New York, Vantage Press, 1959. 118p

Perry, James Black, 1845–1936
YON TOON O' MINE. By Logan Weir [pseud]. Toronto, Ryerson, 1924. 220p
  [BVaU NBFU OTP

Perry, Martha Eugenie
THE GIRL IN THE SILK DRESS, AND OTHER STORIES. Victoria, Author, 1931.
  144p [BVaU NBFU OTMC

Peterson, Charles Walter, 1868–1944
THE FRUITS OF THE EARTH. A Story of the Canadian Prairies. Ottawa, Graphic,
  1928. 304p [BViPA NBFU OTP

Peterson, Len, 1917–
CHIPMUNK. Toronto, McClelland, 1949. 299p [BVaU NBFU OTMC

Petitt, Maud
BETH WOODBURN. A Canadian Tale. Toronto, Briggs, 1897. 158p [BM BVaU
  OTUV

Phelan, Josephine, 1905–
THE BOY WHO RAN AWAY. Toronto, Macmillan, 1954. 152p

Philip, Alex, 1882–
THE CRIMSON WEST. Toronto, Allen, 1925. 282p [BM BVaU LC NBFU OTMC

THE PAINTED CLIFF. Ottawa, Graphic, 1927. 213p [BVaU OTMC QMM

WHISPERING LEAVES. Ottawa, Graphic, 1931. 340p [BVaU NBFU OTMC

Phillipps-Wolley, Clive Oldnall, 1854–1918

THE CHICAMON STONE. London, Bell, 1900. 295p [BM BVaU OOP

GOLD, GOLD, IN CARIBOO! A Story of Adventure in British Columbia. London, Blackie, 1894. 288p [BM BVaU OTMC

MY SOLDIER'S KEEPER. London, Soc. for Prop. Christian Knowledge, 1888. [EngCat

ONE OF THE BROKEN BRIGADE. London, Smith Elder, 1897. 279p [BM BVaU OTMC

THE QUEENSBERRY CUP. London, Methuen, 1895. 313p [BM

THE REMITTANCE MAN. [BCF

SNAP. A Legend of the Lone Mountain. London, Longmans, 1890. 310p [BM BVaU OTMC

Phillips, John Arthur, 1842–1907

FROM BAD TO WORSE; HARD TO BEAT; and A TERRIBLE CHRISTMAS. Three Stories of Montreal Life. Montreal, Lovell, 1877. 277p [OTP

THE GHOST OF A DOG. A Christmas Story in Four Acts, with a Prologue and Epilogue. Ottawa, Woodburn, 1885. 155p [BVaU OTP QMBM

OUT OF THE SNOW, AND OTHER STORIES AND SKETCHES. Ottawa, Free Press, [1886?]. 172p [OTP QMSS

Pickard, Hannah Maynard (Thompson), 1812–1844

MEMOIR AND WRITINGS OF MRS. HANNAH MAYNARD PICKARD. ... By Edward Otheman. Boston, Ela, 1845. 311p [NBFU OTP

PROCRASTINATION; or, Maria Louisa Winslow. By a Lady [pseud]. Boston, King, 1840. 115p [Brown U

THE WIDOW'S JEWELS. In Two Stories. By a Lady [pseud]. Boston, Waite Pierce, 1844. 114p [NBB

Pickford, Mary, 1893–

THE DEMI-WIDOW. Indianapolis, Bobbs-Merrill, 1935. 272p [BM LC NBFU OTMC

LITTLE LIAR.——. New York, O'Brien, 1934. 22p [BM LC

STICKYFINGERS. A Story. London, Allied Artists Corporation, 1927. [BM

Pickthall, Marjorie Lowry Christie, 1883–1922

ANGELS' SHOES, AND OTHER STORIES. London, Hodder, 1923. 320p [BM BVaU NBFU OTMC QMM

BILLY'S HERO; or, The Valley of Gold. Toronto, Musson, 1908. 128p [BM BVaU NBFU OKQ

THE BRIDGE. A Story of the Great Lakes. London, Hodder, 1922. 320p [BM BVaU LC NBFU OTP QMM

DICK'S DESERTION. A Boy's Adventures in Canadian Forests. Toronto, Musson, 1905. 128p [BM BVaU NBFU OKQ

LITTLE HEARTS. London, Methuen, 1915. 309p [Other eds., 1922, 1926.] [BM BVaU NBFU OTP QMM

THE STRAIGHT ROAD. Toronto, Musson, [1906?]. 127p [BM BVaU NBFU OKQ

THE WORKER IN SANDALWOOD. New York, Everyland, 1914. 16p [Same title: Toronto, Ryerson, 1934 and 1943.] [BVaU LC NBFU OKQ

Pimm, Mrs. Ella G.
HENRY. London, Hodder, 1924. 155p [BM

Piner, Jack, 1923?–1958
FEAR NOT MY SON. A Novel. New York, Pageant Press, 1955. 264p

Pinkerton, Kathrene Sutherland (Gedney), 1887–
ADVENTURE NORTH. New York, Carrick & Evans, 1940. 268p [BM BVaU LC
A GOOD PARTNER. New York, Harcourt, 1948. 269p [LC
HIDDEN HARBOR. New York, Harcourt, 1951. 278p
THE LONG TRAVERSE. By Kathrene and Robert Pinkerton. New York, Doubleday, 1920. 249p [BM LC NBFU OTMC
PEDDLER'S CREW. New York, Harcourt, 1954. 243p [Pub. in England as ROYAL BROWNE. q.v.]
PENITENTIARY POST. By Kathrene and Robert Pinkerton. New York, Doubleday, 1920. 245p [BM BViPA LC OTMC
ROYAL BROWNE. A Novel for Older Girls and Boys. London, Bodley Head, 1955. 192p
THE SILVER STRAIN. New York, Harcourt, 1946. 263p [LC
TOMORROW ISLAND. New York, Harcourt, 1960. 217p
WINDIGO. New York, Harcourt, 1945. 223p [BViPA LC

Pitts, Herman Henry, 1858–
OUR JOSHUA AS A REPORTER. By Brother Jonathan [pseud]. Fredericton, "Reporter," 1884. 159p [NBB OONL QMM

Plenderleith, William Alexander, 1901–
CONFLICT. Toronto, Ryerson, 1950. 328p [BVaU NBFU OTMC QMBM

Plummer, Norman M.
THE GOAD. A Human Story of the Last Great West in the Early Part of the Twentieth Century. London, Stockwell, 1930. 180p [BM BVaU NBFU OTMC
THE LONG ARM. Toronto, Nelson, 1939. 275p [AEU BM NBFU

Pocklington, Mrs. Kathryn
THE MORNIN'-GLORY GIRL. By Alice M. Winlow and Kathryn Pocklington. Toronto, McClelland, 1920. 224p [BVaU NBFU

Pocock, Roger, 1865–1941
THE ARCTIC NIGHT. London, Chapman, 1896. 180p [EngCat

THE BLACKGUARD. London, Beeman, 1897. 178p [BM NSWA

THE CHARIOT OF THE SUN. A Fantasy. London, Chapman, 1910. 316p [ACG BM

THE CHEERFUL BLACKGUARD. Indianapolis, Bobbs-Merrill, 1915. 400p [Same as THE BLACKGUARD?] [LC

CURLY. A Tale of the Arizona Desert. Boston, Little Brown, 1905. 320p [Pub. in England in 1904.] [BM BVaU LC OTMC

THE DRAGON-SLAYER. London, Chapman, 1896. 414p [Also: New York, Grosset, n.d. 320p] [BM EngCat OTMC

JESSE OF CARIBOO. London, Murray, 1911. 285p [BM BVaU LC

A MAN IN THE OPEN. Indianapolis, Bobbs-Merrill, 1912. 352p [BM BVaU LC

SWORD AND DRAGON. London, Hodder, 1909. 320p [BM

THE SPLENDID BLACKGUARD. London, Murray, 1915. 342p [Same as THE BLACKGUARD (1897)? THE CHEERFUL BLACKGUARD (1915)?] [EngCat BM

THE WOLF TRAIL. Oxford, Blackwell, 1923. 309p [BM BVaU LC OTMC

Pocock, Wilfred Theodore, 1895–

THE THREE GIFTS. New York, Pageant Press, 1959. 375p

Pollock, Francis Lillie, 1876–

BITTER HONEY. Toronto, Nelson, 1935. 315p [BM BVaU LC NBFU OOP

THE FROZEN FORTUNE. New York, Macaulay, 1910. 322p [LC NBFU

THE GLACIER GATE. An Adventure Story. New York, Chelsea House, 1926. 254p [OTMC

HONEY OF DANGER. New York, Chelsea, 1927. 251p [LC

JUPITER EIGHT. Toronto, Nelson, 1936. 286p [BM BVaU OTU

NORTHERN DIAMONDS. New York, Houghton, 1917. 259p [LC NBFU

RAINBOW LANDING. New York, Chelsea House, 1926. 250p [BVaU

THE TIMBER TREASURE. New York, Century, 1923. 269p [LC NBFU

THE TREASURE TRAIL. Boston, Page, 1906. 367p [LC NBFU

WILDERNESS HONEY. New York, Century, 1917. 325p [LC

THE WOODS-RIDER. New York, Century, 1922. 384p [LC

Pope, William (fl. 1952)

PENNILESS DREAMER. New York, Pageant Press, 1952. 186p

Portlock, Rosa (Elliott), 1839–1928

THE HEAD KEEPER. Toronto, Briggs, 1898. 227p [OTU

Potter, Rev. Austin, 1842–1913

FROM WEALTH TO POVERTY; or, The Tricks of the Traffic. A Story of the Drink Curse. Toronto, Briggs, 1884. 328p [OH

Pound, Bunny

LILA AND THE WATERFALL FAIRIES. By Bunny Pound (aged 11 years). Vancouver, Brookhouse, 1922. 14p [BVaU OKQ

Prentice, James Douglas

TEDDY'S STORY. Toronto, Macmillan, 1937. 356p [BM NBFU

Preston, Anna, 1887–
THE GLORY AND THE DREAM. New York, Huebsch, 1915. 244p [LC
THE RECORD OF A SILENT LIFE. New York, Huebsch, 1912. 327p [BM LC

Preston, Margaret Mary, 1911–
AS A WHITE CANDLE. New York, Pageant Press, 1952. 250p

Preston, Sydney Herman, 1858–1931
THE ABANDONED FARMER. Toronto, Copp, 1901. 288p [BM QMM
ON COMMON GROUND. New York, Holt, 1906. 316p [BM

Price, Alfred
RAIL LIFE. A Book of Yarns. Toronto, Allen, 1925. 285p [BM BVaU NBFU
OTMC

Price, Willard De Mille, 1887–
SOUTH SEA ADVENTURE. New York, Day, 1952. x + 243p

Price-Brown, John, 1844–1938
HICKORY. A Tale of the Lakes. By Eric Bohn [pseud]. Toronto, 1904. [Pub. in
The Farming World, 1904?] [BCF T&C
HOW HARTMANN WON. A Story of Old Ontario. By Eric Bohn [pseud]. Toronto,
Morang, 1903. 269p [BM BVaU OTMC QMM
IN THE VAN; or, The Builders. By Price-Brown [pseud]. Toronto, McLeod, 1906.
352p [BM BVaU NBFU OTMC QMM
LAURA, THE UNDAUNTED. A Canadian Historical Romance. Toronto, Ryerson,
1930. 280p [BVaU OKQ OTMC QMM
THE MAC'S OF '37. A Story of the Canadian Rebellion. By Price-Brown [pseud].
Toronto, McLeod & Allen, 1910. 332p [BM BVaU NSHD OTMC QMM

Primmer, Phyllis (Griesbach), 1926–
AT THE RIVER'S TURNING. Grand Rapids, Mich., Zondervan Pub. House, 1960
[c1958]. 120p

Pringle, Rev. George Charles Fraser, 1873–1949
TILLICUMS OF THE TRAIL. Being Klondike Yarns Told to Canadian Soldiers Over-
seas by a Sourdough Padre. Toronto, McClelland, 1922. 253p [BM BVaU
NBFU OTMC

Procter, John James, 1838–1910
THE PHILOSOPHER IN THE CLEARING. Quebec, Daily Telegraph, 1897. 251p
[BM BVaU OTP QMBM

Prower, Nelson, 1856–
FREDDY BARTON'S SCHOOLDAYS. London, Ouseley, 1911. 274p [BM
REGGIE ABBOTT; or, The Adventures of a Swedish Officer. London, Rodway, 1890.
314p [BM

Raddall, Thomas Head, 1903—

AT THE TIDE'S TURN, AND OTHER STORIES. With intro. by Allan Bevan. Toronto, McClelland, 1959. ix + 178p [New Canadian Library, no. 9]

THE GOVERNOR'S LADY. Garden City, N.Y., Doubleday, 1960. 474p

HIS MAJESTY'S YANKEES. Garden City, Doubleday, 1942. 409p [BM BVaU LC NBFU OTP QMM

A MUSTER OF ARMS AND OTHER STORIES. Toronto, McClelland, 1954. 236p

THE NYMPH AND THE LAMP. A Novel. Boston, Little Brown, 1950. 376p [BM BVaU LC NBFU OTMC QMBM

THE PIED PIPER OF DIPPER CREEK AND OTHER TALES. Edinburgh, Blackwood, 1938. 318p [BM BVaU LC NBFU OTP QMM

PRIDE'S FANCY. Toronto, McClelland, 1946. 308p [BM BVaU LC NBFU OTP QMM

ROGER SUDDEN. Toronto, McClelland, 1944. 358p [BM BVaU LC NBFU OTP QMM

THE ROVER. The Story of a Canadian Privateer. Toronto, Macmillan, 1958. 156p

THE SON OF THE HAWK. Philadelphia, Winston, 1950. 247p [BM BVaU LC NBFU OTMC QMBM

TAMBOUR AND OTHER STORIES. Toronto,˙McClelland, 1945. 388p [BVaU NBFU OTP QMM

TIDEFALL. A Novel. Toronto, McClelland, 1953. 309p

THE WEDDING GIFT AND OTHER STORIES. Toronto, McClelland, 1947. 325p [BVaU NBFU OTMC QMM

THE WINGS OF NIGHT. New York, Doubleday, 1956. 319p

Rand, Rev. Silas Tertius, 1810—1889

LEGENDS OF THE MICMACS. New York, Longmans, 1894. xlvi + 452p [BM BVaU LC NBFU OTP QMM

Rankin, Rev. Duncan Joseph, 1874—1954

ON THIS ROCK. ... Ottawa, Overbrook Press, 1930. 198p [NBFU QMSS

OUR AIN FOLK AND OTHERS. Toronto, Macmillan, 1930. 208p [BVa NBFU OTU QMM

Rankin, George Cameron, 1841—1903

BORDER CANUCKS. Our Friendly Relations. Detroit, Rankin, 1890. 305p [LC

Rashleigh, George

JOHN THE FLUNKY. Designed and written as an Attempt to Assist in Impressing upon Children and Young People Generally the Reform most Necessary for the Future Greatness and Happiness of our Country. Ottawa, Woodburn, 1883. 102p [BVaU OTP

Ravenhill, Alice, 1859—1954

FOLKLORE OF THE FAR WEST. With Some Clues to Characteristics and Customs. Ed. by ——. Victoria, 1953. 87p

Ray, George Raymond, 1869–1935
KASBA (WHITE PARTRIDGE). A Story of Hudson Bay. Toronto, Briggs, 1915.
259p [BM BVaU LC NBFU OTMC QMM

Read, Elfreida (Ennock), 1920–
THE MAGIC OF LIGHT. London, Hutchinson, 1959. 127p

Reade, Mrs. Frances Lawson
ARABESQUE. By Yolande Langworthy [pseud]. New York, Lewis Copeland, 1931.
158p [LC OTP

Ready, William Bernard, 1914–
THE POOR HATER. A Novel. Chicago, Regnery, 1958. 337p

Rebbeck, Mrs. Elizabeth
HOME OF THE DRAGON. A Tonquinese Idyll. By Anna Catherina [pseud]. London,
Unwin, 1893. 222p [BM
THE STRAGGLERS. A Tale of Primal Asperities. London, Griffiths, 1910. 178p
[BM BVaU

Reed, Else Clarissa (Porter), 1887–
A MAN FORBID. New York, Morrow, 1935. 281p [BM LC NBFU OOP

Reeve, Winifred (Eaton) Babcock, 1879–
CATTLE. By Onoto Watanna [pseud]. Toronto, Hodder, 1923. 256p [Also: a
New York ed., 1924.] [BM BVaU LC NBFU OTMC
DAUGHTERS OF NIJO. A Romance of Japan. By Onoto Watanna [pseud]. New
York, Macmillan, 1904. 397p [BM BVaU LC OTMC
THE DIARY OF DELIA. Being a Veracious Chronicle of the Kitchen, with some
Sidelights on the Parlour. By Onoto Watanna [pseud]. New York, Doubleday,
1907. 229p [BM LC
THE HEART OF HYACINTH. By Onoto Watanna [pseud]. New York, Harper, 1903.
250p [BM BVaU LC OTMC
HIS ROYAL NIBS. New York, Watt, 1925. 318p [LC OTMC
THE HONORABLE MISS MOONLIGHT. By Onoto Watanna [pseud]. New York,
Harper, 1912. 174p [BM LC
A JAPANESE BLOSSOM. By Onoto Watanna [pseud]. New York, Harper, 1906.
263p [BM LC OTMC
A JAPANESE NIGHTINGALE. By Onoto Watanna [pseud]. New York, Harper, 1901.
225p [BM LC OOP
THE LOVE OF AZALEA. By Onoto Watanna [pseud]. New York, Dodd Mead, 1904.
239p [BM LC NBFU OTMC
MARION. The Story of an Artist's Model. By Herself and the Author of ME
[pseudonyms for Sara Bosse and Mrs. Reeve]. New York, Watt, 1916. 307p
[Written in collaboration with her sister, Mrs. Karl Bosse.] [LC
ME. A Book of Remembrance. [Anon] New York, Century, 1915. 356p [BM
LC OOP

MISS NUME OF JAPAN. A Japanese-American Romance. By Onoto Watanna [pseud].
New York, Rand McNally, 1899. 220p [Toronto ed., 1913.] [BVaU LC
SUNNY-SAN. By Onoto Watanna [pseud]. New York, Doran, 1922. 311p [BM
BVaU LC OTMC
TAMA. By Onoto Watanna [pseud]. New York, Harper, 1910. 243p [BM LC
OTMC
THE WOOING OF WISTARIA. By Onoto Watanna [pseud]. New York, Harper, 1902.
388p [BM BVaU LC OTMC
In addition, three other novels, not located, are listed in *Can. Bookman* for April
1922:
LEND ME YOUR TITLE.
MISS SPRING MORNING.
OTHER PEOPLE'S TROUBLES.

Regan, John Hugh
THE END OF THE FURROW. London, Hutchinson, 1927. 288p [BM LC
VALIANT HEART. A Story of a Canadian Ranch. London, Hutchinson, 1926. 312p
[BM QMM

Reid, Leslie Hartley, 1896–
CAULDRON BUBBLE. London, Gollancz, 1934. 448p [BM
THE RECTOR OF MALISEET. London, Dent, 1925. 272p [BM NBFU OTMC
SALTACRES. London, Dent, [1927?]. 370p [BM BVaU NBFU OOP QMM
TREVY, THE RIVER. London, Dent, 1928. 299p [BM NBFU OTMC QMM

Reville, Frederick Douglas, 1866–1944
A REBELLION. A Story of the Red River Uprising. Brantford, Hurley, 1912. 198p
[BM BVaU NSHD OTP QMM

Reynolds, H.T.
THE UNQUENCHED FLAX. A Story of Western Canada. London, Stockwell, [1931].
206p [AEU BM OWA

Reynolds, Helen Mary Greenwood (Campbell) Dickson, 1884–
ANGRY RIVER. By Dickson Reynolds [pseud]. Toronto, Nelson, 1951. 181p
BIG SHARK. By Dickson Reynolds [pseud]. New York, Nelson, 1948. 159p
[BViPA LC
CAPTAIN PEGGY OF THE MAMIE L. By Helen Dickson, New York, Nelson, 1943.
176p [LC OTU
CAROL OF LONG CHANCE MINE. New York, Funk & Wagnalls, 1959. 216p
CHERRIES ARE RIPE. By Dickson Reynolds [pseud]. New York, Nelson, 1950.
191p [LC OTU
DORIS OF SUNSHINE RANCH. By Helen Dickson. London, Nelson, 1948. 184p
[BM BViPA
THE FAMILY AT SUNSHINE RANCH. By Helen Dickson. London, Nelson, 1939.
204p [BM OTU

THE FIRE PATROL. By Dickson Reynolds [pseud]. New York, Nelson, 1949.
192p [BViPA LC NBFU OTMC

FORTUNE TRAIL. By Dickson Reynolds [pseud]. New York, Funk & Wagnalls,
1954. 213p

THE FUR BRIGADE. By Dickson Reynolds [pseud]. New York, Funk & Wagnalls,
1953. 207p

GOLD IN MOSQUITO CREEK. By Dickson Reynolds [pseud]. New York, Nelson,
1946. 192p [BM BViPA LC

HE WILL RETURN. By Dickson Reynolds [pseud]. Toronto, Ryerson, 1959. 256p

"KAREN PRESENTS ..." New York, Funk & Wagnalls, 1955. 218p

McBAIN'S BRIER ROSE. By Helen Dickson Reynolds. Toronto, Ryerson, 1957.
191p

MUSIC FOR MELANIE. New York, Funk & Wagnalls, 1958. 220p

MYSTERY OF THE LOGGING CAMP. By Dickson Reynolds [pseud]. New York,
Nelson, 1945. 171p [BViPA LC

PERILOUS PRAIRIE. By Dickson Reynolds [pseud]. Toronto, Ryerson, 1956. 189p

PICKUPPIES. By Helen Dickson. London, Stockwell, 1931. 23p [BM

RED BLANKET. By Dickson Reynolds [pseud]. London, Nelson, 1939. 127p
[BM BVaU OTU

SUMMER OF SURPRISE. New York, Funk & Wagnalls, 1960. 186p

WE CHASED A RAINBOW. New York, Funk & Wagnalls, 1957. 214p

YOSHIO. Japanese Boy in Canada. By Helen Dickson. London, Nelson, 1937. 111p
[BM BVaU OTU

Richardson, Evelyn May (Fox), 1902—

DESIRED HAVEN. Toronto, Ryerson, 1953. 286p

NO SMALL TEMPEST. Toronto, Ryerson, 1957. 229p [Sequel to DESIRED HAVEN.]

Richardson, John, 1796—1852

THE CANADIAN BROTHERS; or, The Prophecy Fulfilled. A Tale of the Late
American War. Montreal, Armour & Ramsay, 1840. 2v [Pub. in the U.S. as:
MATILDA MONTGOMERIE. New York, Dewitt & Davenport, 1851. 191p] [BVaU
NSHPL OTP QMM

ECARTE; or, The Salons of Paris. [Anon] London, Colburn, 1829. 3v
[Republished: New York, Dewitt, 1851. 206p; and New York, Pollard & Moss,
1888.] [BM BVaU LC NBFU OKQ

HARDSCRABBLE; or, The Fall of Chicago. A Tale of Indian Warfare. New York,
Dewitt, [1856]. 99p [In *Papers of the Bibliog. Soc. of Canada*, v5, W.F.E.
Morley argues that the date of first pub. is either 1850 or 1851. Also seen with
imprint: New York, Pollard & Moss, 1888. 113p] [LC NSWA OONL QMSS

MATILDA MONTGOMERIE; or, The Prophecy Fulfilled. ... Being a Sequel to
WACOUSTA. New York, Dewitt, 1851. 191p [See under THE CANADIAN
BROTHERS.] [BM BVa LC NSHD OTP

THE MONK KNIGHT OF ST. JOHN. A Tale of the Crusades. New York, DeWitt,
1850. 192p [BM NBFU

WACOUSTA; or, The Prophecy. A Tale of the Canadas. By the Author of ECARTE [pseud]. London, Cadell, 1832. 3v [First Am. ed.: Philadelphia, Kay & Biddle, 1833. 2v. First Can. ed.: Montreal, Lovell, 1868. 167p. Several other editions.] [BM BVaU LC NBFU OTP QMM

WAU-NAN-GEE; or, The Massacre at Chicago. A Romance. New York, Long, [1852]. 126p [BM LC NBFU OKQ

WESTBROOK; or, The Outlaw. [Diligent search discovered no copy of this work, whose title has been attributed to Richardson by H.J. Morgan in *Bibliotheca Canadensis* (1867) and, subsequently, by various others.]

Richardson, Robert Lorne, 1860–1921

THE CAMERONS OF BRUCE. Toronto, Briggs, 1906. 301p [BM BVaU NBFU OTP
COLIN OF THE NINTH CONCESSION. Toronto, Morang, 1903. 360p [BVaU NBFU OTP

Richler, Mordecai, 1931–

THE ACROBATS. A Novel. London, Deutsch, 1954. 204p [Also pub. as WICKED WE LOVE in Popular Library ed.]
THE APPRENTICESHIP OF DUDDY KRAVITZ. Don Mills, Ont., Deutsch, 1959. 319p
SON OF A SMALLER HERO. A Novel. London, Deutsch, 1955. 232p

Rickerson, Nena C.

THE BANKER'S GRANDCHILDREN. A Story. Saint John, Day, 1876. 108p [NBB

Riis, Stella Eugenie (Asling), 1877–

CROWNED AT ELIM. New York, Smith & Wilkins, 1903. 263p [LC
THE GREAT FRESH SEA. N.p., Author, 1931. 92p [OLU
STAR OVER FLUSHING. Boston, Humphries, 1939. 268p [LC

Riley, Louise, 1904–1957

THE MYSTERY HORSE. Oxford, Blackwell, 1957. 188p
ONE HAPPY MOMENT. A Novel. Toronto, Copp Clark, 1951. 212p
A SPELL AT SCOGGIN'S CROSSING. New York, Abelard-Schuman, 1960. 175p
TRAIN FOR TIGER LILY. Toronto, Macmillan, 1954. 186p

Ringwood, Gwendolyn Margaret (Pharis), 1910–

YOUNGER BROTHER. Toronto, Longmans, 1959. 213p

Ritchie, Cicero Theodore, 1914–

BLACK ANGELS. New York, Abelard-Schuman, 1959. 256p
THE WILLING MAID. London, Abelard-Schuman, 1957. 310p

Robb, Wallace Havelock, 1888–

THUNDERBIRD. [Epic of the Mohawks of the Kente.] Kingston, Abbey Dawn, 1949. 242p [BVaU OTP QMM

Robbins, Ronald Cynewulf, 1915–

BLOOD FOR BREAKFAST. New York, Pageant Press, 1955. 151p

Roberts, Charles George Douglas, 1860–1943

AROUND THE CAMPFIRE. New York, Crowell, 1896. 349p [BM BVaU LC
NBFU OTP

BABES OF THE WILD. New York, Cassell, 1912. 243p [Also pub. under title:
CHILDREN OF THE WILD. New York, Macmillan, 1913. 300p] [BM LC OTU
QMM

THE BACKWOODSMEN. New York, Macmillan, 1909. 269p [BM BVaU LC
NBFU OTU QMM

A BALKAN PRINCE. London, Everett, 1913. 248p [BM BVaU NBFU OTU

BARBARA LADD. Boston, Page, 1902. 377p [BM BVaU LC NBFU OKQ

BY THE MARSHES OF MINAS. New York, Silver Burdett, 1900. 285p [BM
BVaU LC NSHD OKQ

CHILDREN OF THE WILD. New York, Macmillan, 1913. 300p [Same as BABES
OF THE WILD, *q.v.*] [BVaU LC NSHD OTMC QMM

COCK-CROW. New York, Federal Print., 1916. 14p [Also included in THE SECRET
TRAILS.] [NBFU

THE CRUISE OF THE YACHT "DIDO." A Tale of the Tide Country. Boston, Page,
1906. 145p [A reprint of REUBE DARE'S SHAD BOAT.] [LC NBFU OTMC

EARTH'S ENIGMAS. A Book of Animal and Nature Life. Boston, Lamson Wolffe,
1896. 290p [New ed., with 3 stories added, 3 dropped: Boston, Page, 1903.
285p] [BM BVaU LC NBFU OTU QMM

EYES OF THE WILDERNESS. New York, Macmillan, 1933. 269p [BM LC NSHD
OTMC QMM

THE FEET OF THE FURTIVE. London, Ward Lock, 1912. 277p [BM BVaU LC
NBFU OTMC QMM

FOREST FOLK. Chosen and Ed. by Ethel Hume Bennett. Toronto, Ryerson, 1949.
237p [BViP OTMC

THE FORGE IN THE FOREST. Being the Narrative of the Acadian Ranger, Jean de
Mer. New York, Lamson Wolffe, 1896. 311p [BM BVaU LC NBFU OTP
QMM

FURTHER ANIMAL STORIES. London, Dent, 1935. 128p [BM

THE HAUNTER OF THE PINE GLOOM. Boston, Page, 1905. 61p [Also included in
THE KINDRED OF THE WILD.] [BVaU LC OTMC

THE HAUNTERS OF THE SILENCES. A Book of Animal Life. Boston, Page, 1907.
316p [BM BVaU LC NBFU OKQ

THE HEART OF THE ANCIENT WOOD. New York, Silver Burdett, 1900. 276p [BM
BVaU LC NBFU OTU QMM

THE HEART THAT KNOWS. Boston, Page, 1906. 378p [BM BVaU NBFU OTU
QMM

HOOF AND CLAW. London, Ward Lock, 1913. 267p [BM BVaU LC NSHD OTU
QMM

THE HOUSE IN THE WATER. A Book of Animal Life. Boston, Page, 1908. 301p
[BM BVaU LC NBFU OKQ

IN THE DEEP OF THE SNOW. New York, Crowell, 1907. 78p [Also in THE BACKWOODSMEN.] [LC NBFU OTU

IN THE MORNING OF TIME. London, Hutchinson, 1919. 319p [BM BVaU NBFU OTU QMM

JIM. The Story of a Backwoods Police Dog [And Other Stories]. New York, Macmillan, 1924. 216p [Same as THE LEDGE ON BALD FACE.] [BVaU LC NBFU OTU QMM

THE KINDRED OF THE WILD. A Book of Animal Life. Boston, Page, 1902. 374p [BM BVaU NBFU OTU QMM

THE KING OF THE MAMOZEKEL. Boston, Page, 1905. 84p [Also included in THE KINDRED OF THE WILD.] [BVaU NBFU

KINGS IN EXILE. London, Ward Lock, 1909. 306p [BM BVaU NBFU OTP

THE LAST BARRIER, AND OTHER STORIES. Intro. by Alec Lucas. Toronto, McClelland, 1958. x + 153p [New Canadian Library, no.7]

THE LEDGE ON BALD FACE. London, Ward Lock, 1918. 255p [Also pub. under title: JIM. The Story of a Backwoods Police Dog. New York, Macmillan, 1924. 216p] [BM BVaU NBFU OKQ

THE LITTLE PEOPLE OF THE SYCAMORE. Boston, Page, 1906. 58p [Also included in THE WATCHERS OF THE TRAILS.] [LC

THE LORD OF THE AIR. Boston, Page, 1905. 59p [Also included in THE KINDRED OF THE WILD.] [BVaU LC OKQ

LOVERS IN ACADIE. London, Dent, 1924. 278p [New ed. of A SISTER TO EVANGELINE, q.v.] [BM NBFU OTU QMM

MORE ANIMAL STORIES. London, Dent, 1922. 127p [BM BVaU NBFU OTU

MORE KINDRED OF THE WILD. London, Ward Lock, 1911. 264p [BM BVaU NBFU OKQ

THE MORNING OF THE SILVER FROST. New York, Federal Print., 1916. 8p [Also included in THE SECRET TRAILS.] [NBFU

NEIGHBOURS UNKNOWN. New York, Macmillan, 1911. 266p [BM BVaU LC NSHD OLU QMM

THE PRISONER OF MADEMOISELLE. A Love Story. Boston, Page, 1904. 265p [BM BVaU LC NBFU OKQ

THE RAID FROM BEAUSEJOUR, and HOW THE CARTER BOYS LIFTED THE MORTGAGE. Two Stories of Acadie. New York, Hunt & Eaton, 1894. 230p [First story later pub. under title: THE YOUNG ACADIAN; or, The Raid from Beauséjour. Boston, Page, 1907. 139p] [BVaU LC NBFU OKQ

RED FOX. The Story of his Adventurous Career. ... Boston, Page, 1905. 340p [BM BVaU NSHD OTP QMM

THE RED OXEN OF BONVAL. New York, Dodd Mead, 1908. 71p [Reprinted from: A HOUSE PARTY. An Account of the Stories Told at a Gathering of Famous American Authors. Boston, Small Maynard, 1901. 418p] [NBFU

THE RETURN TO THE TRAILS. Boston, Page, 1906. 50p [Also included in THE WATCHERS OF THE TRAILS.] [LC NBFU

REUBE DARE'S SHAD BOAT. A Tale of the Tide Country. New York, Hunt & Eaton, 1895. 145p [Later reprinted under title: THE CRUISE OF THE YACHT "DIDO." Boston, Page, 1906. 145p] [LC OLU

THE SECRET TRAILS. New York, Macmillan, 1916. 212p [BM BVaU LC NSHD OTU QMM

A SISTER TO EVANGELINE. Being the Story of Yvonne de Lamourie. Boston, Lamson Wolffe, 1898. 289p [New ed. pub. under title: LOVERS IN ACADIE. London, Dent, 1924. 278p] [BM BVaU LC NBFU OKQ

SOME ANIMAL STORIES. London, Dent, [1921]. 128p [BM NBFU

THEY WHO WALK IN THE WILD. New York, Macmillan, 1924. 212p [Pub. in England under title: THEY THAT WALK IN THE WILD. London, Dent, 1924. 290p] [BM BVaU LC NSHD OTU QMM

THIRTEEN BEARS. Chosen and Ed. by Ethel Hume Bennett. Toronto, Ryerson, 1947. 254p [BVaU OTP

THE WATCHERS OF THE CAMP-FIRE. Boston, Page, 1905. 49p [Also included in THE KINDRED OF THE WILD.] [LC OKQ

THE WATCHERS OF THE TRAILS. A Book of Animal Life. Boston, Page, 1904. 361p [BM BVaU LC NBFU OTU QMM

WISDOM OF THE WILDERNESS. Toronto, Dent, 1922. 218p [Also: New York, Macmillan, 1923. 184p] [BM BVaU LC NSHD OKQ QMM

THE YOUNG ACADIAN. Boston, Page, 1907. 139p [Same as THE RAID FROM BEAUSEJOUR.] [BVaU LC OOP QMSS

Roberts, Leslie, 1896—

WHEN THE GODS LAUGHED. Toronto, Musson, 1930. 282p [BM LC NBFU OTMC

Roberts, Theodore Goodridge, 1877—1953

BLESSINGTON'S FOLLY. London, Long, 1914. 320p [BM BVaU

BROTHERS OF PERIL. A Story of Old Newfoundland. Boston, Page, 1905. 327p [BVaU LC NBFU OKQ

CAPTAIN LOVE. Boston, Page, 1908. 282p [BVaU LC NBFU OTMC

A CAPTAIN OF RALEIGH'S. Boston, Page, 1911. 351p [LC NBFU

A CAVALIER OF VIRGINIA. Boston, Page, 1910. 313p [BVaU LC

COMRADES OF THE TRAILS. Boston, Page, 1910. 308p [BVaU LC

THE EXILED LOVER. London, Long, 1919. 320p [BM BVaU

THE FIGHTING STARKLEYS. Boston, Page, 1922. 250p [BVa LC NBFU

FLYING PLOVER. His Stories. Told him by Squat-by-the-fire. Boston, Page, 1909. 124p [LC OTU

FOREST FUGITIVES. Toronto, McClelland, 1917. 320p [BM BVaU

THE GOLDEN HIGHLANDERS; or, The Romantic Adventures of Alastair MacIver. Boston, Page, 1929. 308p [BM LC NBFU

GREEN TIMBER THOROUGHBREDS. Garden City, Garden City Pub. Co., 1924. 120p [LC

THE HARBOR MASTER. Boston, Page, 1913. 300p [Same as THE TOLL OF THE TIDES. London, Laurie, 1913. 240p] [LC NBFU

HEMMING, THE ADVENTURER. Boston, Page, 1904. 328p [BVaU LC NBFU OTMC

HONEST FOOL. London, Hodder, 1925. 319p [BM

THE HOUSE OF ISSTENS. Boston, Page, 1900. [CT CWW'49

IN THE HIGH WOODS. London, Long, 1916. 320p [BM BVaU LC NBFU

THE ISLANDS OF ADVENTURE. New York, Hodder, 1918. 312p [BM BVaU NBFU

JESS OF THE RIVER. New York, Dillingham, 1914. 329p [BM LC OTMC

LOVE ON SMOKY RIVER. London, Long, 1913. 320p [BM OTMC

THE LURE OF PIPER'S GLEN. New York, Doubleday, 1921. 120p [CWW'49

THE MASTER OF THE MOOSE HORN, and Other Backcountry Stories. London, Hodder, 1919. 315p [BM NBFU

MOONSHINE. London, Hodder, 1920. 317p [BM NBFU

MUSKET HOUSE. New York, Doubleday, 1922. 120p [CWW'49

THE OXBOW WIZARD. Garden City, Garden City Pub. Co., 1924. 121p [BVaU

PRIZE MONEY. Boston, Page, 1926. [CT

RAYTON. A Backwoods Mystery. Boston, Page, 1912. 314p [LC NBFU

THE RED FEATHERS. Boston, Page, 1907. 325p [BVaU LC NBFU OTMC

THE RED PIROGUE. A Tale of Adventure in the Canadian Wilds. Boston, Page, 1924. 272p [BVaU LC NBFU OTMC QMM

SOLDIER OF VALLEY FORGE. [Joint author, with Robert Neilson Stephens.] Boston, Page, 1911. [CBI

THE STRANGER FROM UP-ALONG. Toronto, Gundy, 1924. 188p [BM NBFU

THE TOLL OF THE TIDES. London, Laurie, 1912. 240p [Same as THE HARBOR MASTER.] [BM

TOM AKERLEY. His Adventures in the Tall Timber and at Gaspard's Clearing. Boston, Page, 1923. 283p [BVaU LC OTMC

TWO SHALL BE BORN. New York, Cassell, 1913. 319p [BVaU LC

THE WASP. New York, Dillingham, 1914. 352p [BM BVaU LC

Robertson, Rev. James, 1801?–1878

JICKLING'S EXPERIENCES. A Reminiscence of Eton Life. Ed. by J.R. Montreal, Drysdale, 1896. 45p [BM OTMC QMSS

Robertson, James D.

THE DREAM OF LIFE (Aisling Na Beatha). London, Williams & Norgate, 1934. 356p [BM LC OTP

Robertson, Margaret Murray, 1821–1897

ALLISON BAIN; or, By a Way She Knew Not. London, Hodder, 1891. 482p [See also BY A WAY SHE KNEW NOT, below.]

THE BAIRNS; or, Janet's Love and Service. A Story from Canada. By the Author of "Christie Redfern's Troubles"; "The Orphans of Glen Elder, A Story of Scottish

Life"; etc. [pseud]. London, Hodder, 1870. 581p [Another ed.: 1885.] [BM
BVaU OTP

BY A WAY SHE KNEW NOT. Story of Allison Bain. New York, Randolph, 1887.
[BM

CHRISTIE REDFERN'S TROUBLES. [Anon] London, Religious Tract Soc., 1866.
[New eds., 1886 and 1905] [BM

DAVID FLEMING'S FORGIVENESS. New York, Randolph, 1879. [Also pub. as:
By the Author of "The Bairns." London, Hodder, 1891.] [AmCat BM

EUNICE. The Story of Domestic Life in New England. New York, Randolph,
1887. [BM

FREDERICA AND HER GUARDIANS. Boston, Lothrop, 1880. [See THE PERILS OF
ORPHANHOOD, below.] [AmCat

THE INGLISES; or, How the Way Opened. New York, Randolph, 1872. [BM

JANET'S LOVE AND SERVICE. New York, Randolph, 1869. 581p [Same as
THE BAIRNS? q.v.] [AmCat NBFU

A LITTLE HOUSE IN THE HOLLOW. By the Author of "Christie Redfern's Troubles"
[pseud]. Philadelphia, Am. Sunday School Union, 1868. 237p [LC

LITTLE SERENA IN A STRANGE LAND. By the Author of "Christie Redfern's
Troubles," etc. [pseud]. London, Religious Tract Soc., 1870. [BM

THE ORPHANS OF GLEN ELDER. [Anon] London, Religious Tract Soc., 1868.
[EngCat

THE PERILS OF ORPHANHOOD; or, Frederica and Her Guardians. By the Author
of "The Bairns," "Christie Redfern's Troubles," etc. [pseud]. London, 1874.
[BM

SHENAC'S WORK AT HOME. A Story of Canadian Life. By the Author of "Christie
Redfern's Troubles" [pseud]. London, Religious Tract Soc., [1868]. 262p
[BM BVaU NBFU OTP

STEPHEN GRATTAN'S FAITH. By the Author of "Christie Redfern's Troubles"
[pseud]. Philadelphia, Am. Sunday School Union, 1867. 142p [LC OTMC

THE TWO MISS JEAN DAWSONS. New York, Randolph, 1880. 350p [BM NBFU

A YEAR AND A DAY. A Story of Canadian Life. By the Author of "Christie
Redfern's Troubles," etc. [pseud]. London, Religious Tract Soc., 1886. [BM

Robins, John Daniel, 1884–1952

LOGGING WITH PAUL BUNYAN. Ed. by Edith Fowke. Toronto, Ryerson, 1957.
xvii + 97p

Robinson, Frank Alfred, 1874–

MASTERED MEN. New York, Doran, 1922. 256p [BVaU LC OTMC

OLD CALEB AND HIS LAST CHRISTMAS. Story from Life in Rural England. Toronto,
Livingstone Press, 1941. 46p [OTP

TRAIL TALES OF WESTERN CANADA. London, Marshall, [1914]. 255p [BVaU
NBFU OTP

Rogers, Charles Gordon
THE SCRAGGVILLE BANDITS; or, The White Caps of Pepper Island, and Other
Stories. Ottawa, Woodburn, 1889. 198p [OONL

Rogers, Frank D.
FOLK-STORIES OF THE NORTHERN BORDER. Clayton, N.Y., Thousand Islands,
1897. 273p [BM LC

Rogers, Frederick
IN THE END. Being the Romance of Two Worlds. New York, Editor Pub. Co.,
1903. 229p [LC
NONSENSE. Being Certain Foolish Tales. Detroit, American Pub. Co., 1900. [BM
LC OONL

Rogers, Grace Dean (McLeod), 1865–1958
THE BREAD OF WICKEDNESS. London, Hurst & Blackett, 1925. 288p [BM
JOAN AT HALFWAY. Toronto, McClelland, 1919. 414p [BM BVaU LC NSHD
OTU
RAYMOND'S INHERITANCE. London, Harrap, 1937. 255p [BM
THE SECRET OF VAN ROYEN'S FARM, etc. London, Nelson, 1929. 94p [BM
STORIES OF THE LAND OF EVANGELINE. Boston, Lothrop, 1891. 336p [New ed.:
Toronto, McClelland, 1923. 341p] [BM BVaU LC NBFU OTU QMM

Roper, Edward
A CLAIM ON KLONDYKE. A Romance of the Arctic ElDorado. Edinburgh, Black-
wood, 1899. 312p [BM BViPA LC OTU
FRED SEAGOOD: His Travels and Triumphs, etc. London, Swan Sonnenschein,
1904. 349p [BM OTMC
ICE-BOUND; or, The Anticosti Crusoes. London, Partridge, 1902. 330p [AEU
BM NfSM OTUV

Rorke, Louise Richardson, –1949
BLACK VIC. Toronto, Nelson, 1949. 176p [BVaU OTMC
LEFTY. The Story of a Boy and a Dog. With a foreword by Marshall Saunders.
Toronto, Nelson, 1931. 165p [BVaU NBFU OOP
LEFTY'S ADVENTURE. A Tale for Children. Toronto, Nelson, 1945. 220p [BM
BVaU OTMC
SUGAR SHANTY. New York, Nelson, 1941. 314p [LC NBFU OLU

Ross, Angus, 1860–1929
MOUNT MORIAH. A Story [of the Lumber Camps]. Founded on Fact. London,
Stockwell, [1934]. 128p [OONL

Ross, Ellen Edith Alice (McGregor), –1892
A LEGEND OF THE GRAND GORDONS. Ed. by Mrs. Alexander Ross. Montreal,
Stevenson, 1873. 647p [BVaU LC NSHD OTP

THE LEGEND OF THE HOLY STONE. Ed. by Mrs. Alexander Ross. Montreal, Stevenson, 1878. 473p [BVaU LC NSHD OTP

VIOLET KEITH; or, Convent Life in Canada. An Autobiography. Montreal, Lovell, 1868. 472p [BVaU LC NBFU OTP QMM

THE WRECK OF THE "WHITE BEAR," EAST INDIAMAN. Montreal, Lovell, 1870. 2v [BVaU LC NSHD OTP QMM

Ross, (James) Sinclair, 1908–

AS FOR ME AND MY HOUSE. A Novel. New York, Reynal, 1941. 296p [Also, with intro. by Roy Daniells. Toronto, McClelland, 1957. x + 165p] [BVaU NSHD OTMC

THE WELL. Toronto, Macmillan, 1958. 256p

Rouleau, Corinne Rocheleau

LAURENTIAN HERITAGE. Ed. with foreword ... by W.F. Langford. Toronto, Longmans, 1948. 178p [BM BVaU NBFU OTP QMBM

Rowe, Lizzie

AN OLD WOMAN'S STORY. Regina, Leader Printing Co., 1886. 15p [BM MWP OOP

Rowell, Mrs. John H.

JULIA CAMPBELL; or, The Enlightenment of a Mind. Montreal, Chapleau, 1876. 86p [OOP

Roy, D. Kinmount

LINKED LIVES. London, Heath Cranton, 1913. 336p [BM

Roy, Irene

JUNETTE; or, Are Women Just to One Another? Edmonton, Douglas, 1919. 292p [BVaU OTMC

Roy, Katherine (Morris), 1907–

THE GENTLE FRAUD. Toronto, McClelland, 1959. 183p

LISE. Toronto, McClelland, 1954. 250p

Royal, Matthew J., –1900

THE ISLE OF THE VIRGINS. A Romance. Buffalo, Wenborne-Summer, 1899. 328p [LC

Ruddy, Anna Christian, 1861–

FROM TENDERFOOT TO SCOUT. New York, Doran, 1911. 297p [LC OTMC

Running, Arnold, 1918–

STAY BUT TILL TOMORROW. Toronto, Longmans, 1958. 191p

Russell, Rev. George Stanley, 1883–1957

THE MONASTERY BY THE RIVER. New York, Smith, 1930. 107p [BVaU LC NSHD OTP

Russell, Sheila (MacKay), 1920–
A LAMP IS HEAVY. Toronto, Longmans, 1950. 257p [BM BVaU NBFU OTU
THE LIVING EARTH. Toronto, Longmans, 1954. 317p

Ryland, Richard
THE COINERS OF POMPEII. Toronto, Rowsell, 1845. 136p [OTU

S., V.M.F.
PEGGY SINCLAIR'S TRIP ACROSS THE CONTINENT. By V.M.F.S. Montreal, Lovell,
   1892. 231p [NSWA OOP QMBM

Sabiston, Colin A.
ZOYA. London, Selwyn & Blount, 1933. 288p [BM OTP

Sadlier, Anna Teresa, 1854–1932
ARABELLA. St. Louis, Herder, 1907. 177p [LC
COUSIN WILHELMINA. St. Louis, Herder, 1907. 201 p [LC
ETHEL HAMILTON. New York, Sadlier, 1877. 79p [LC
GERALD DE LACEY'S DAUGHTER. New York, Kenedy, 1916. 473p [LC OTMC
HOW FRANK DID IT. THAT WORTHLESS LAD. LITTLE JOHN. Three Stories. New
   York, Wildermann, 1898. 63p [LC
THE KING'S PAGE. New York, Sadlier, 1877. 51p [LC
THE LOST JEWEL OF THE MORTIMERS. St. Louis, Herder, 1904. 258p [LC
THE MAN FROM NOWHERE. New York, Benziger, 1918. 187p [LC
MARY TRACY'S FORTUNE. New York, Benziger, 1902. 169p [LC
THE MYSTERIOUS DOORWAY. New York, Benziger, 1900. 135p [LC
THE MYSTERY OF HORNBY HALL. New York, Benziger, 1906. 214p [LC
PAULINE ARCHER. New York, Benziger, 1900. 167p [LC
PHILEAS FOX, ATTORNEY. Notre Dame, Ind., Ave Maria, 1909. 349p [LC
THE PILKINGTON HEIR. New York, Benziger, 1903. 212p [LC
THE RED INN OF SAINT LYPHAR. New York, Benziger, 1904. 179p [LC
SEVEN YEARS AND MAIR. New York, Harper, 1878. 184p [LC
SHORT STORIES. Series II. New York, Wildermann, 1900. 3v in 1. [The Catholic
   Library, v. 38, 48, 58.] [LC
THE SILENCE OF SEBASTIAN. Notre Dame, Ind., Ave Maria, 1913. 405p [LC
STORIES OF THE PROMISES AND OTHER TALES. By Mrs. M.A. Sadlier and her
   Daughter. Montreal, Sadlier, [1895?]. 247p [OONL QMSS
THE TALISMAN. New York, Benziger, 1903. 186p [LC
THE TRUE STORY OF MASTER GERARD. New York, Benziger, 1900. 321p [LC
WAYWARD WINIFRED. New York, Benziger, 1905. 220p [LC OOU
WHERE THE ROAD LED, AND OTHER STORIES. New York, Benziger, 1905. 209p
   [LC
WYVERN HALL. TEDDY'S LUCK. A CONTRAST. Three Stories. New York,
   Wildermann, 1898. 61p [LC

Sadlier, Mary Anne (Madden), 1820–1903

ALICE RIORDAN. The Blind Man's Daughter. A Tale for the Young. Boston,
   Noonan, 1854. 289p [Also: Dublin, Gill, 1884. 294p. An earlier ed.: Boston,
   Donahoe, 1851.] [BM OOU

AS GOOD AS GOLD. (Wilhelm; or, Christian Forgiveness.) Trans. from the French
   by ——. Dublin, Gill, 1890. 246p [BM

AUNT HONOR'S KEEPSAKE. A Chapter from Life. New York, Sadlier, 1866. 322p
   [LC OOU

BENJAMIN. New York, Sadlier, 1885. 249p [A trans. from the French. An
   earlier ed. in 1852?] [BM LC

BESSY CONWAY; or, The Irish Girl in America. New York, Sadlier, 1862. [AmCat

THE BLAKES AND FLANAGANS. New York, Sadlier, 1858. 391p [An earlier ed.,
   dated 1855—AmCat.] [LC QQL

THE CASTLE OF ROUSSILLON; or, Quercy in the Sixteenth Century. Trans. from the
   French by ——. Dublin, Gill, 1884. 278p [BM

CON O'REGAN; or, Emigrant Life in the New World. New York, Sadlier, 1864.
   405p [BM BVaU LC QMSS

THE CONFEDERATE CHIEFTAINS. A Tale of the Irish Rebellion of 1641. New York,
   Sadlier, 1868. 461p [An earlier ed. listed in AmCat for 1858–61.] [LC QQL

CONFESSIONS OF AN APOSTATE. New York, Sadlier, 1864. 252p [Also as:
   SIMON KERRIGAN. The Confessions of an Apostate. London, Washburne,
   1889.—EngCat.] [BM LC

THE DAUGHTER OF TYRCONNELL. A Tale of the Reign of James I. New York,
   Sadlier, 1863. 152p [BM LC

ELINOR PRESTON; or, Scenes at Home and Abroad. New York, Sadlier & Co., 1861.
   298p [BVaS

THE EXILE OF TADMOR, AND OTHER TALES. Trans. by ——. New York, Sadlier,
   1885. 144p [An earlier ed. 1866—AmCat.] [LC

THE FATE OF FATHER SHEEHY. A Tale of Tipperary Eighty Years Ago. New York,
   Sadlier, 1863. 132p [LC NfSM OOSJ

THE HEIRESS OF KILORGAN. New York, Sadlier, 1867. 420p [BM LC

THE HERMIT OF THE ROCK. A Tale of Cashel. New York, Sadlier, 1868. 492p
   [BM LC OOSJ

IDLENESS; or, The Double Lesson, and Other Tales. Trans. from the French by
   ——. New York Sadlier, 1862. [BM

THE KNOUT. A Tale of Poland. Trans. from the French by ——. Dublin, Gill,
   1884. 280p [BM QQL

THE LOST SON. An Episode of the French Revolution. New York, Sadlier, [1885].
   260p [An earlier ed., 1862—AmCat] [OOU

MacCARTHY MORE; or, The Fortunes of an Irish Chief. New York, Sadlier, 1868.
   [AmCat BM

MAUREEN DHU, THE ADMIRAL'S DAUGHTER. New York, Sadlier, 1870. 391p
   [BM LC

THE MINISTER'S WIFE, AND OTHER STORIES. New York, Wildermann, 1898. 64p
[LC

NEW LIGHTS; or, Life in Galway. New York, Sadlier, 1867. 443p [An earlier ed.:
New York, Sadlier, 1853. —Am Cat.] [LC OTMC QMSS

O'BRYNE; or, The Expatriated. New York, Wildermann, 1898. 64p [LC

OLD AND NEW; or, Taste Versus Fashion. New York, Sadlier, 1862. 486p [LC
QQL

THE OLD HOUSE BY THE BOYNE; or, Recollections of an Irish Borough. New
York, Sadlier, 1865. 375p [Also: Dublin, Gill, 1888. 320p] [BM LC OOU

THE POPE'S NIECE AND OTHER TALES. Trans. from the French by ——. New
York, Sadlier, 1862. [BM

THE RED HAND OF ULSTER; or, The Fortunes of Hugh O'Neill. Boston, Donahoe,
n.d. 344p [OTL OTMC

SHORT STORIES. Series II. New York, Wildermann, 1900. 3v in 1. [The Catholic
Library, v. 32, 42, 52.] [LC

THE SPANISH CAVALIERS. A Tale of the Moorish Wars in Spain. New York,
Sadlier, 1861. 203p [OOU

STORIES OF THE PROMISES AND OTHER TALES. By Mrs. M.A. Sadlier and her
Daughter. Montreal, Sadlier, [1895?]. 247p [OONL QMSS

TALES AND STORIES. Trans. from the French by ——. New York, Sadlier, 1866.
144p [BM OTMC

TALES OF THE OLDEN TIME. Montreal. [MOR'98

THE VENDETTA AND OTHER TALES. Trans. from the French by ——. New York,
Sadlier, 1862. [BM

WILLY BURKE; or, The Irish Orphan in America. Boston, Donahoe, 1850. 298p
[LC

THE YOUNG LADIES' READER. New York, Sadlier, [187–?]. [AmCat 1876

St. George, Mother Mary

ROAD'S END. By Mary Douglas [pseud]. Toronto, Ryerson, 1943. 150p [NBFU
OTP

Sallans, George Herbert, 1895–1960

LITTLE MAN. Toronto, Ryerson, 1942. 420p [BVaU LC NBFU OTP QMM

Salverson, Laura (Goodman), 1890–1970

BLACK LACE. Toronto, Ryerson, 1938. 255p [BM NBFU OTU

CONFESSIONS OF AN IMMIGRANT'S DAUGHTER. London, Faber, 1939. 523p
[BM BVaU LC NBFU OTP QMM

THE DARK WEAVER. Toronto, Ryerson, 1937. 415p [BM BVaU LC NBFU
OTU

THE DOVE OF EL-DJEZAIRE. ... Toronto, Ryerson, 1933. 287p [BM BVaU
NSHD OKQ

IMMORTAL ROCK. The Saga of the Kensington Stone. ... Toronto, Ryerson, 1954.
267p

LORD OF THE SILVER DRAGON. Toronto, McClelland, 1927. 343p [BVaU NBFU OTP QMM

THE VIKING HEART. New York, 1923. 326p [BM BVaU NBFU OTP

WHEN SPARROWS FALL. Toronto, Allen, 1925. 292p [BM BVaU NBFU OTMC QMM

Sanderson, Douglas, 1922—

BLONDES ARE MY TROUBLE. A Novel of Suspense. By Martin Brett [pseud].
Toronto, Popular Library, 1955 [i.e., 1956]. 174p [First pub. as THE DARKER
TRAFFIC. New York, Dodd Mead, 1954. 213p]

CRY WOLFRAM. A Novel. London, Secker & Warburg, 1959. 190p

DARK PASSIONS SUBDUE. New York, Dodd Mead, 1952. 296p

EXIT IN GREEN. By Martin Brett [pseud]. New York, Dodd Mead, 1953. 256p
[Pub. in England as MURDER CAME TUMBLING, London, Hammond, 1959. 221p]

THE FINAL RUN. A Novel. London, Secker & Warburg, 1956. 178p [Paperback ed.
(New York, Popular Library, 1957) has title: FLEE FROM TERROR, by Martin Brett
(pseud).]

HOT FREEZE. By Martin Brett [pseud]. New York, Dodd Mead, 1954. 246p

NIGHT OF THE HORNS. A Novel. London, Secker & Warburg, 1958. 189p

Sanderson, Elizabeth

THE CIRCLE OF THE YEAR. Toronto, Briggs, 1904. 46p [BM OKQ

Sands, Harold Percy, 1873—

THE DASHING SALLY DUEL AND OTHER STORIES. New York, Broadway Pub. Co.,
1905. 143p [BVaU LC OOP

Sandwell, Mrs. Helen B.

THE VALLEY OF COLOR-DAYS. Boston, Little Brown, 1924. 299p [BM LC NBFU OTMC

Sandys, Edwyn William, 1860—1909

TRAPPER "JIM." New York, Macmillan, 1903. 441p [BM BVaU LC OTMC

SPORTSMAN "JOE." New York, Macmillan, 1904. 338p [BM LC

Sanford, Mary Bourchier

THE HAPPY HARFORDS. London, Collins, 1930. 128p [BM

ISLE OF GLADNESS. London, Religious Tract Soc., 1929. 224p [BM

THE ROMANCE OF A JESUIT MISSION. Toronto, Revell, 1897. 292p [BVa LC OTU

THE TRAIL OF THE IROQUOIS. A Pioneer Romance of Canada. Toronto, Longmans,
1925. 256p [BM BVaU OTP QMM

URANIA'S TRAINING. London, Religious Tract Soc., 1925. 237p [BM

THE WANDERING TWINS. A Story of Labrador. Chicago, McClurg, 1904. 300p
[BM BVaU LC NBFU

THE YOUNG GORDONS IN CANADA. London, Religious Tract Soc., 1913. 286p [BM

Saunders, Margaret Bell, 1894–

HUBBLE-BUBBLE. By Margaret Bell [pseud]. New York, Dodd Mead, 1927. 337p
[LC QMM

Saunders, Margaret Marshall, 1861–1947

ALPATOCK. The Story of an Eskimo Dog. Boston, Page, 1906. 51p [LC

BEAUTIFUL JOE. An Autobiography. Philadelphia, American Baptist Pub. Soc.,
1894. 304p [Many later editions.] [BM BVaU LC NSHD OKQ QMM

BEAUTIFUL JOE'S PARADISE. Boston, Page, 1902. 365p [BM BVaU LC NBFU OTU

BONNIE PRINCE FETLAR. The Story of a Pony and His Friends. ... Toronto,
McClelland, 1920. 352p [LC NSHD OTU

"BOY" THE WANDERING DOG. New York, Grosset, 1916. 363p [BM OTU

CHARLES AND HIS LAMB. Philadelphia, Banes, 1895. 73p [BVaU LC NSHD
OTMC

DAISY. A Tale. Philadelphia, Banes, [189–?]. 57p [NSHD

DEFICIENT SAINTS. A Tale of Maine. Boston, Page, 1899. 431p [BM LC NBFU
OTMC

ESTHER DE WARREN. The Story of a Mid-Victorian Maiden. New York, Doran,
1927. 305p [LC NSHD OKQ QMM

FOR HIS COUNTRY; and GRANDMOTHER AND THE CROW. ... Boston, Page, 1900.
60p [LC OOP

FOR THE OTHER BOY'S SAKE, AND OTHER STORIES. Philadelphia, Banes, 1896.
374p [LC NBFU OTMC

THE GIRL FROM VERMONT. The Story of a Vacation School Teacher. Boston,
Griffith & Rowland, 1910. 248p [BVaU LC OTU

GOLDEN DICKY. The Story of a Canary and his Friends. New York, Stokes, 1919.
280p [BM BVaU LC OKQ QMM

HER SAILOR. A Love Story. Boston, Page, 1900. 321p [An enlarged ed. of MY
SPANISH SAILOR.] [LC OTU

THE HOUSE OF ARMOUR. Philadelphia, Rowland, 1897. 543p [LC NSHD OKQ

JIMMY GOLDCOAST; or, The Story of a Monkey and his Friends. Toronto, Hodder,
1923. 319p [BM BVaU LC NSHD OTU

THE KING OF THE PARK. New York, Crowell, 1897. 226p [LC NBFU OTMC

MY SPANISH SAILOR. London, Ward, 1889. 215p [Later rev. and enl. as: HER
SAILOR. Boston, Page, 1900. 321p] [BM OOP

NITA. The Story of an Irish Setter. Boston, Page, 1904. 77p [LC

PRINCESS SUKEY. The Story of a Pigeon and her Human Friends. New York,
Eaton & Mains, 1905. 336p [BVaU LC OTU

PUSSY BLACK-FACE; or, The Story of a Kitten ... Boston, Page, 1913. 311p [BM
LC OOP

ROSE À CHARLITTE. An Acadian Romance. Boston, Page, 1898. 516p [Pub. also
under title ROSE OF ACADIA.] [BM BVaU LC NBFU OTP

THE STORY OF AN ESKIMO DOG. London, Hodder, 1906. 63p [Same as
ALPATOCK? *q.v.*] [BM

THE STORY OF THE GRAVELEYS. Toronto, Briggs, 1903. 283p [BM BVaU LC
NBFU OTU

'TILDA JANE. An Orphan in Search of a Home. Boston, Page, 1901. 287p [BM
LC OKQ

'TILDA JANE'S ORPHANS. Boston, Page, 1909. 345p [NSWA SRL

THE WANDERING DOG. Adventures of a Fox-Terrier. New York, Doran, 1916.
363p [BVaU LC NBFU OTMC QMM

Savage, Mrs. William T.

MIRAMICHI. 2nd ed. Boston, Loring, 1865. 232p [Later pub. as ADELE DUBOIS.
A Story of the Lovely Miramichi Valley in New Brunswick. Boston, Loring,
1865. 232p] [BVaU LC NBFU

Savigny, Mrs. Annie Gregg, −1901

DICK NIVEN AND HIS HORSE NOBBY. Lantern Slide Lecture, etc. Toronto, 1898.
20p [BM

A HEART-SONG OF TO-DAY (Disturbed by Fire From the 'Unruly Member'). A
Novel. Toronto, Hunter Rose, 1886. 351p [BVaU OTP QMM

LION, THE MASTIFF; From Life. Toronto, Briggs, 1895. 206p [BM BVaU NBFU
OTU QMM

A ROMANCE OF TORONTO(Founded on Fact). A Novel. Toronto, Briggs, 1888.
229p [BVaU NSHD OTP

THREE WEDDING RINGS. Toronto, Rose Pub. Co., 1892. 254p [OTMC

Scaife, Arthur Hodgkin

AS IT WAS IN THE FIFTIES. By Kim Bilir [pseud]. Victoria, Province Pub. Co.,
1895. 287p [BM BVaU

GEMINI AND LESSER LIGHTS. By "Kim Bilir" [pseud]. Victoria, Province Pub. Co.,
1895. 187p [BM BVaU

THREE LETTERS OF CREDIT AND OTHER STORIES. By Kim Bilir [pseud]. Victoria,
Province Pub. Co., 1894. 123p [OTP

Scott, Duncan Campbell, 1862−1947

IN THE VILLAGE OF VIGER. Boston, Copeland Day, 1896. 135p [Also: Toronto
Ryerson, 1945. 114p First Can. ed., a complete reprint of the original.] [BVaU
LC NBFU OTP QMM

THE WITCHING OF ELSPIE. A Book of Stories. New York, Doran, 1923. 248p
[BVaU LC NBFU OTP

Scott, Rev. Frederick George, 1861−1944

ELTON HAZELWOOD. A Memoir by his Friend Harry Vane. New York, Whittaker,
1891. 146p [BM BVaU NBFU OTU QMM

Scott, Margerie (Waite)
THE DARLING ILLUSION. Toronto, McClelland, 1955. 246p
LIFE BEGINS FOR FATHER. London, Hutchinson, 1939. 255p [BM
MINE OWN CONTENT. Toronto, McClelland, 1952. 248p

Secretan, James Henry Edward, 1852–1926
OUT WEST. By Secretan. Ottawa, Esdaile Press, 1910. 206p [BM BVaU LC OTP
QMM

Sellar, Robert, 1841–1919
GLEANER TALES. [Vol. I.] Huntingdon, Que., Canadian Gleaner Office, 1886.
162p [V.2: Huntingdon, Gleaner Office, 1895. 462p] [BM BVaU NSHD
OTP QMM
HEMLOCK. A Tale of the War of 1812. Montreal, Grafton, 1890. 223p (Half-title:
Gleaner Tales. 2nd Series.) [Later ed.: Toronto, Britnell, 1918.] [BM BVaU
LC NBFU OTP QMM
MORVEN. The Highland United Empire Loyalist. Huntingdon, Que., Gleaner, 1911.
177p [BM BVaU LC NSHD OTP QMM
THE NARRATIVE OF GORDON SELLAR, who Emigrated to Canada in 1825.
Huntingdon, Que., Gleaner Book Room, 1915. 185p [Cover-title: THE TRUE
MAKERS OF CANADA.] [BM BVaU LC OTP QMM

Service, Robert William, 1874–1958
THE HOUSE OF FEAR. New York, Dodd Mead, 1927. 408p [BM BVaU LC
NBFU OTU QMM
THE MASTER OF THE MICROBE. New York, Barse, 1926. 424p [BM BVaU LC
NBFU OTU
THE POISONED PARADISE. A Romance of Monte Carlo. New York, Dodd Mead,
1922. 412p [BM BVaU LC NBFU OKQ QMM
THE PRETENDER. A Story of the Latin Quarter. New York, Dodd Mead, 1914.
349p [BM BVaU LC NBFU OTU QMM
THE ROUGHNECK. A Tale of Tahiti. New York, Barse, 1923. 448p [BM BVaU
LC NBFU OTMC QMM
THE TRAIL OF '98. A Northland Romance. Toronto, Briggs, 1911. 514p [BM
BVaU LC NBFU OKQ QMM

Servos, Launcelot Cressy
FRONTENAC AND THE MAID OF THE MIST. A Romance of Theala and Frontenac at
the Time when Frontenac ruled Canada and Ourouehati dominated over what is
now New York State. Toronto, DeGruchy, 1927. 310p [Also: Toronto,
Smithers & Bonellie, 1938.] [BVaU LC NSHD OTP QMSS

Seton, Ernest Thompson, 1860–1946
ANIMAL HEROES. New York, Scribner, 1905. 362p [BM BVaU LC NBFU OTU
BANNERTAIL. The Story of a Gray Squirrel. New York, Scribner, 1922. 265p
[BM BVaU LC NBFU OTU QMM

THE BEST OF ERNEST THOMPSON SETON. Selected by W. Kay Robinson. London, Hodder, 1949. 408p [BM LC

BILLY, AND OTHER STORIES FROM "WILD ANIMAL WAYS." London, Hodder, 1925. 128p [ACG BM NBFU OTMC

THE BIOGRAPHY OF A GRIZZLY. New York, Century, 1900. 167p [BM BVaU LC NBFU OTU QMM

THE BIOGRAPHY OF AN ARCTIC FOX. New York, Appleton-Century, 1937. 126p [LC

THE BIOGRAPHY OF A SILVER FOX. New York, Century, 1909. 209p [BM BVaU LC NBFU OTU QMM

THE BUFFALO WIND. Santa Fé, Seton Village Press, 1938. 12p [LC NBFU

CHINK ... AND OTHER STORIES FROM "LIVES OF THE HUNTED" AND "WILD ANIMALS AT HOME." London, Hodder, 1929. 128p [AEU BM OTMC

THE CUTE COYOTE, AND OTHER ANIMAL STORIES ... TAKEN FROM "WILD ANIMALS AT HOME," "WILD ANIMAL WAYS," "LIVES OF THE HUNTED." London, U. of London Press, 1930. 159p [ACG BM

ERNEST THOMPSON SETON'S TRAIL AND CAMP-FIRE STORIES. Ed. by Julia M. Seton. ... New York, Appleton-Century, 1940. 155p [BM LC

FAMOUS ANIMAL STORIES. ... Myths, Fables, Fairy Tales. Stories of Real Animals. Ed. by ——. New York, Brentano, 1932. 686p [BM LC NSHD

FOAM RAZORBACK ... AND OTHER STORIES FROM "WILD ANIMAL WAYS." London, Hodder, 1929. 128p [BM NBFU OTMC

GREAT HISTORIC ANIMALS: MAINLY ABOUT WOLVES. London, Methuen, 1937. 320p [LC QMM

JOHNNY BEAR, AND OTHER STORIES FROM "LIVES OF THE HUNTED." London, Hodder, 1925. 124p [BM BViV

JOHNNY BEAR, LOBO, AND OTHER STORIES. New York, Scribner, 1935. 162p [LC

KATUG THE SNOW CHILD. Oxford, Blackwell, 1929. 51p [BM

KRAG AND JOHNNY BEAR. New York, Scribner, 1902. 141p [Stories from his LIVES OF THE HUNTED.] [BVaU LC OLU

KRAG, THE KOOTENAY RAM, AND OTHER ANIMAL STORIES. London, U. of London Press, 1929. 176p [ACG BM

LIVES OF THE HUNTED. New York, Scribner, 1901. 360p [BM BVaU LC NBFU OTMC QMM

LOBO, RAG, AND VIXEN. New York, Scribner, 1899. 147p [Stories from WILD ANIMALS I HAVE KNOWN.] [BM LC NBFU OTU

MONARCH, THE BIG BEAR OF TALLAC. New York, Scribner, 1904. 214p [BM BVaU LC NBFU OTU

THE NATURAL HISTORY OF THE TEN COMMANDMENTS. New York, Scribner, 1907. 78p [See below: THE TEN COMMANDMENTS. ...] [BM LC NBFU QMM

OLD SILVER GRIZZLE, THE BADGER, AND OTHER STORIES FROM "WILD ANIMALS AT HOME." London, Hodder, 1925. 128p [BViV BM OTMC

THE PREACHER OF CEDAR MOUNTAIN. A Tale of the Open Country. New York, Doubleday, 1917. 426p [BM BVaU LC NBFU OTMC

RAGGYLUG. Philadelphia, Inst. for the Instruction of the Blind, 1900. 59p [Braille ed.] [LC

RAGGYLUG, AND OTHER STORIES FROM "WILD ANIMALS I HAVE KNOWN." London, Hodder, 1925. 126p [BM OTMC

RAGGYLUG, THE COTTONTAIL RABBIT AND OTHER ANIMAL STORIES. London, Nutt, 1900. 147p [AEU BM

REDRUFF. Philadelphia, Inst. for the Instruction of the Blind, 1900. 65p [Braille ed.] [LC

ROLF IN THE WOODS. New York, Doubleday, 1911. 437p [BM BVaU LC NBFU OTU QMBM

SANTANA, THE HERO DOG OF FRANCE. Los Angeles, Pheonix Press, 1945. 61p [LC

THE SLUM CAT. SNAP. THE WINNIPEG WOLF. [Three stories.] London, Constable, 1915. 135p [OTMC

THE TEN COMMANDMENTS IN THE ANIMAL WORLD. New York, Doubleday, 1923. 78p [First pub. under title: THE NATURAL HISTORY OF THE TEN COMMAND- MENTS. 1907.] [BM LC

THE THOMPSON SETON READERS. (Selected Tales from his Works.) London, Constable, 1915. 5 parts [BM

THE TRAIL OF THE SANDHILL STAG. New York, Scribner, 1899. 93p [BM BVaU LC NBFU OTP

TWO LITTLE SAVAGES. Montreal, Montreal News Co., 1903. 552p [BM BVaU LC NSHD OTMC QMM

VIXEN. Philadelphia, Inst. for the Instruction of the Blind, 1900. 45p [Braille ed.] [LC

THE WHITE REINDEER. ARNAUX. THE BOY AND THE LYNX. [Three stories.] London, Constable, 1915. 125p [OTMC

WILD ANIMALS AT HOME. Toronto, Briggs, 1913. 226p [BM BVaU LC NBFU OTU

WILD ANIMALS I HAVE KNOWN. New York, Scribner, 1898. 359p [BM BVaU LC NBFU OTU QMM

WILD ANIMAL WAYS. Garden City, Doubleday, 1916. 247p [Another ed., with 3 fewer chapters: New York, Houghton, 1916. 140p] [BM BVaU LC NBFU OTMC QMM

WOODLAND TALES. New York, Doubleday, 1921. 238p [BM BVaU LC NBFU OTMC

WOODMYTH AND FABLE. Toronto, Briggs, 1905. 181p [BM BVaU LC NBFU OTP

Seymour, Rev. James Cooke, 1839–1902

THE TEMPERANCE BATTLE-FIELD AND HOW TO GAIN THE DAY. A Book for the Young of All Ages, full of Humorous and Pathetic Stories. Toronto, Briggs, 1882. 188p [OTP

Shannon, Mary Jane, —1964
THE GOLDEN STALLION. By Lytle Shannon [pseud]. New York, Bouregy & Curl, 1952. 252p

Shapiro, Lionel Sebastian Berk, 1908—1958
THE SEALED VERDICT. New York, Doubleday, 1947. 278p [BM BVaU LC NBFU OTU QMM
THE SIXTH OF JUNE. Garden City, N.Y., Doubleday, 1955. 351p
TORCH FOR A DARK JOURNEY. Garden City, Doubleday, 1950. 273p [BM BVaU NBFU OTU

Sharman, Mrs. Lyon, 1872—
BAMBOO. Tales of the Orient-born. San Francisco, Elder, 1914. 81p [BM LC
THE HORSE THAT EDUCATED THE CHILDREN. A Christmas Story of the Canadian Prairie. Winnipeg, Franklin Press, 1912. [BM

Sharp, Edith Lambert
NKWALA. Boston, Little Brown, 1958. 125p

Shaw, Campbell
A ROMANCE OF THE ROCKIES. Toronto, Bryce, [1888]. 102p [BViPA OOP

Shaw, Marlow Alexander, 1867—1929
THE HAPPY ISLANDS. Stories and Sketches of the Georgian Bay. Toronto, McClelland, 1926. 254p [BVaU LC NBFU OTP QMM

Sheard, Virna (Stanton), 1865? —1943
BELOW THE SALT. Toronto, Ryerson, 1936. 316p [BM OTP
BY THE QUEEN'S GRACE. New York, Stokes, 1904. 316p [BM BVaU LC NBFU OKQ
FORTUNE TURNS HER WHEEL. Toronto, McClelland, 1929. 351p [NBFU OTU
THE GOLDEN APPLE TREE. Toronto, McClelland, 1920. 218p [LC NBFU OTMC
A MAID OF MANY MOODS. Toronto, Copp Clark , 1902. 177p [BVa LC OTMC
THE MAN AT LONE LAKE. London, Cassell, 1912. 309p [BVaU LC OTMC QMM
TREVELYAN'S LITTLE DAUGHTERS. Toronto, Briggs, 1898. 197p [BM BVa NBFU OKQ

Shepherd, J.C.
A FARMER'S THREE YEARS' EXPERIENCE IN MERCHANDISE. St. Thomas, Journal, 1891. 155p [OLU

Sheppard, Edmund Ernest, 1855—1924
A BAD MAN'S SWEETHEART. Toronto, Sheppard Pub. Co., 1889. 202p [OTU
DOLLY, THE YOUNG WIDDER UP TO FELDER'S. Toronto, Rose, 1886. 135p [BVaU OTU
WIDOWER JONES. A Faithful History of his "Loss" and Adventures in Search of a "Companion." A Realistic Story of Rural Life. Toronto, Sheppard Pub. Co., 1888. 197p [OTP

Sherman, Ralph S.
MOTHER NATURE STORIES. Toronto, Dent, 1924. 259p [BVaU NBFU OOP

Sherwood, Roland Harold, 1902–
STORY PARADE. Sackville, N.B., Tribune Press, 1948. 245p [NBFU OTU

Shibley, Fred. Warner, 1864–
A BUNDLE OF YARNS. Providence, R.I., Gregory, 1899. 249p [LC OTU

Shinnick, J.
THE BANKER'S DAUGHTER; or, Her First and Last Ball. A Novel. Montreal, Gazette
Print., 1891. 74p [OTP

Shipley, Nancy (Sommerville)
THE SCARLET LILY. New York, Fell, 1959. 234p

Shute, Evan Vere, 1905–
SKY PAINTER. By Vere Jameson [pseud]. London, Ont., Hunter, 1950. 94p [OTU

Silver, Barbara (pseud)
OUR YOUNG BARBARIANS; or, Letters from Oxford. ... By Barbara Silver [pseud].
London, Macmillan, 1935. 305p [BM BVaU LC NBFU OTU QMM

Sim, Mrs. R.S.
UNDER THE MAPLES. Blandford Station, Ont., Author, n.d. 98p [AEU OTU

Sime, Jessie Georgina, 1880–
CANADA CHAPS. London, Lane, 1917. 271p [BM NBFU OTMC QMSS
INEZ AND HER ANGEL. By Georgina Sime & Frank Nicholson. London, Chapman
& Hall, 1954. 141p
OUR LITTLE LIFE. A Novel of Today. New York, Stokes, 1921. 394p [BM LC
NBFU OTMC QMM
SISTER WOMAN. London, Richards, 1919. 293p [BM NBFU OTMC QMM
A TALE OF TWO WORLDS. By Georgina Sime and Frank Nicholson. London,
Chapman & Hall, 1953. 683p

Simms, Florence Mary
ETOFFE DU PAYS. Lower St. Lawrence Sketches. Toronto, Musson, [1913?]. 87p
[BM BVaU NSHD OKQ

Simon, Samuel William, 1893–
THE FUR COAT. A Humorous True Story, Eye-witnessed by the Author. Montreal,
Author, 1950. 96p [OONL

Simonds, Peter, 1906–
THE CASE OF CONSTABLE SHIELDS. By Richard Greaves [pseud]. Philadelphia,
Dorrance, 1940. 341p [LC
RED SEPULCHRE. A Story of Adventure Behind the Iron Curtain. Montreal, Adanac
Press, 1947. 391p [QMBM

Simpson, Maria
"BROTHER G.M. ROSE." A Temperance Story. Toronto, Hunter Rose, 1879. 236p
[OTU
RONALD McFARLANE. A Temperance Story. Toronto, Hunter Rose, 1878. 74p
[OTMC
ROSEVILLE SEMINARY. A Temperance Story. Toronto, Hunter Rose, 1878. 234p
[AEU OLU OTMC
THE TORONTO RINE BOYS. A Temperance Story. Toronto, Author, 1878. 62p
[OTP

Sinclair, Bertrand William, 1878–
BIG TIMBER. A Story of the Northwest. Boston, Little Brown, 1916. 321p [BM
BVaU LC OTMC
BOTH SIDES OF THE LAW. London, Wright & Brown, 1955. 156p
BURNED BRIDGES. Toronto, Briggs, 1919. 308p [BM BVaU LC NBFU OTMC
DOWN THE DARK ALLEY. Boston, Little Brown, 1936. 291p [BM BVaU LC
OTU
GUNPOWDER LIGHTNING. Boston, Little Brown, 1930. 298p [BM BVaU LC
OTMC
THE HIDDEN PLACES. Toronto, Ryerson, 1922. 318p [BM BVaU LC NBFU
OTMC
THE INVERTED PYRAMID. Boston, Little Brown, 1924. 339p [BM BVaU LC
NBFU OTMC
THE LAND OF FROZEN SUNS. New York, Dillingham, 1910. 309p [BVaU LC
OTMC
NORTH OF FIFTY-THREE. Boston, Little Brown, 1914. 345p [BM BVaU LC
NBFU OTMC
PIRATES OF THE PLAINS. London, Hodder, 1928. 318p [BM BViPA
POOR MAN'S ROCK. Boston, Little Brown, 1920. 307p [BM BVaU LC NBFU
OTMC
RAW GOLD. A Novel. New York, Dillingham, 1908. 311p [BVaU LC OTMC
ROOM FOR THE ROLLING M. London, Wright & Brown, 1954. 158p
WILD WEST. Toronto, Ryerson, 1926. 288p [BM BVaU LC OTMC

Sinclair, Coll McLean
THE DEAR OLD FARM. A Canadian Story. By Malcolm [pseud]. St. Thomas, The
Journal, 1897. 198p [BM BVaU NSHPL OTP

Sinclair, Mary R.
CHILDREN OF THE PIONEERS. Toronto, Dent, 1931. 138p [OTMC

Sirluck, Lesley (McNaught)
GUP. Toronto, Ryerson, 1946. 48p [BVa OTMC

Skelton, Mme. Henrietta
THE CHRISTMAS TREE. A Story of German Domestic Life. Cincinnati, Walden &
Stowe; New York, Phillips & Hunt, 1883. 279p [LC

GRACE MORTON. By Madame Skelton. Toronto, Irving, 1873.   212p [BVaU
OTMC
A MAN TRAP, and THE FATAL INHERITANCE. Two Temperance Tales. By Mrs. H.
Skelton. Toronto, Magurn, 1876. 152p [OTP

Skelton, James, 1880–
DOWN NORTH FOR ADVENTURE. Ilfracombe, Devon, Stockwell, 1958. 224p
HO! FOR THE LABRADOR. Ilfracombe, Devon, Stockwell, 1957. 159p

Skinner, Constance Lindsay, 1879? –1939
ANDY BREAKS TRAIL. New York, Macmillan, 1928. 199p [LC
BECKY LANDERS. Frontier Warrior. New York, Macmillan, 1928. 234p [LC
DEBBY BARNES, TRADER. New York, Macmillan, 1932. 244p [LC NBFU
"GOOD MORNING, ROSAMOND!" New York, Doubleday, 1917. 384p [BVaU LC
NBFU OTMC
THE RANCH OF THE GOLDEN FLOWERS. New York, Macmillan, 1928. 182p [LC
NBFU
RED MAN'S LUCK. New York, Coward-McCann, 1930. 251p [BVa LC NBFU
RED WILLOWS. Toronto, McClelland, 1929. 412p [BVaU LC MWU NBFU OTU
ROB ROY. The Frontier Twins. New York, Macmillan, 1934. 218p [LC
ROSELLE OF THE NORTH. New York, Macmillan, 1927. 256p [BVa LC NBFU
QMM
SILENT SCOT, FRONTIER SCOUT. New York, Macmillan, 1925. 234p [BVa LC
THE SEARCH RELENTLESS. London, Methuen, 1925. 311p [BM BViPA LC
NBFU OTMC
THE TIGER WHO WALKS ALONE. New York, Macmillan, 1927. 211p [LC NBFU
OTMC
THE WHITE LEADER. New York, Macmillan, 1926. 219p [LC NBFU

Sluman, Norma Pauline (Hardman), 1924–
BLACKFOOT CROSSING. Toronto, Ryerson, 1959. 255p

Smith, A. de Herries, 1881–
DRUMS OF THE NORTH. New York, Macaulay, 1928. 312p [BVaU LC NBFU

Smith, Donald Taylor, 1909–
CHINA COASTER. A Novel of Suspense. New York, Holt, 1953. 211p

Smith, Edgar Maurice, 1870–
ANEROESTES THE GAUL. A Fragment of the Second Punic War. Montreal, Grafton,
1898. 242p [BM NSHD OTU
THE BARONESS OF DENONVILLE. Montreal, 1900. [BCF
A DAUGHTER OF HUMANITY. A Novel. Boston, Arena, 1895. 317p [BM LC

Smith, Frank Clifford, 1865–1937
A DAUGHTER OF PATRICIANS. Toronto, Publishers Synd., 1901. 327p [BVaU OTU

A LOVER IN HOMESPUN, AND OTHER STORIES. Toronto, Briggs, 1896. 201p
  [BVaU NSHD OTU QMBM
THE TRAITOR. Toronto, Briggs, 1912. 230p [OOP

Smith, George, 1852–1930
THE AMISHMAN. By Clyde Smith [pseud]. Toronto, Briggs, 1912. 132p [BM
  BVaU OTP

Smith, George Washington, 1855–1945
THE SMILEYS. A Tale of Hardwoodlands. Windsor, N.S., Anslow, 1901. 119p
  [BVaU NBFU QMM

Smith, Jean Mitchell
SUNSHINE-SHADDER. Sketches of Ontario Life. Toronto, Briggs, 1911. 80p [BM
  BVa OTMC

Smith, Josephine
PERTH-ON-THE-TAY. A Tale of the Transplanted Highlanders. Ottawa, Mortimer,
  1901. 266p [BVaU NBFU OTP

Smith, Minnie
IS IT JUST? A Tale of British Columbia Life. Toronto, Briggs, 1911. 135p [BM
  BVaU NBFU OTU

Smith, Rev. Oswald Jeffrey, 1889–
THE ADVENTURES OF ANDY McGINNIS. Grand Rapids, Mich., Zondervan, 1945.
  67p [BM LC
OSWALD SMITH'S SHORT STORIES. Grand Rapids, Mich., Zondervan, 1943. 163p
  [BM LC NBFU

Smith, Thomas Barlow, 1839–1933
ROSE CARNEY. A Story of Ever Shifting Scenes on Land and Sea. Windsor, N.S.,
  Anslow, 1890. 204p [NSHD OOP
SERAPH ON THE SEA; or, The Career of a Highland Drummer Boy. ... Windsor, N.S.,
  Anslow, 1891. 156p [NSHD
YOUNG LION OF THE WOODS; or, A Story of Early Colonial Days. Halifax, Nova
  Scotia Print., 1889. 147p [BVaU NSHD OTP

Smythe, Albert Ernest Stafford, 1861–1947
MRS. LOTHBURY'S GOSPEL. [A Story]. [Toronto], 1920. 36p [BM NSWA
  OTU

Smythe, Carroll F.
THE VAGABOND VENDER. Toronto, Dominion Bureau of Circulation, 1929. 65p
  [OTMC QSherU

Sollows, Atlanta Sara, 1889–1954
WHITHER THOU GOEST. Toronto, Allen, 1947. 211p [NBFU

Somerville, Alexander, 1811–1885
THE LIFE OF ROGER MOWBRAY. London, 1853. [BM

Souster, Raymond, 1921–
THE WINTER OF TIME. By Raymond Holmes [pseud]. New Toronto, Export Pub.
Enterprises, 1949. 160p [Priv. info.

Spang, Edward
"COBALT," THE MASCOT OF COBALT SILVER CAMP, AND OTHER STORIES. Sudbury,
Sudbury News, 1922. 134p [BM BVaU OTP

Sparrow, Charles, 1877–
A DOOMED MANSION. Toronto, Briggs, 1905. 139p [BVaU NSHD OTMC
THE HOUSE ON THE CLIFF. Toronto, Briggs, 1909. 122p [BVaU NSHD OTMC
THE ROMANCE OF THE HOUSE OF ARNOLD; or, Ravendale Manor. Toronto, Briggs,
1913. 168p [BM BVaU NSHD
SHADOWS OF THE DEEP. Toronto, Briggs, 1903. 176p [NSHD
THE TURNING POINT. Toronto, Briggs, 1911. 137p [BM BVaU NSHD OTMC

Sparrow, Malcolm Weethie, 1862–1936
THE LADY OF CHATEAU BLANC. An Historical Romance. By Max Moineau [pseud].
Toronto, Brough, 1896. 70p [BM

Spedon, Andrew Learmont, 1831–1884
CANADIAN SUMMER EVENING TALES. Montreal, Lovell, 1866. 208p [BVaU OTP
TALES FOR CANADIAN HOMES. [The Black-sealed Letter; The Poetic Wreath.]
Montreal, Mitchell, 1872. 112p [BVaU OKQ
TALES OF THE CANADIAN FOREST. Montreal, Lovell, 1861. 221p [BVaU LC
NBFU OTP QMM

Sprague, Miss E.
AN EARNEST TRIFLER. Toronto, Belfords, 1880. 254p [OKQ

Sprigge, Elizabeth, 1900–
CASTLE IN ANDALUSIA. London, Heinemann, 1935. 343p [BM BVaU LC NBFU
OTMC
CHILDREN ALONE. London, Heinemann, 1935. 272p [BM
FAINT AMORIST. London, Knopf, 1927. 272p [BM LC NBFU
HOME IS THE HUNTER. By Henry Toke Munn and Elizabeth Sprigge. Toronto,
Macmillan, 1930. 296p [BM OTMC
THE OLD MAN DIES. A Novel. London, Heinemann, 1933. 292p [BM BVaU LC
NBFU OTMC
PONY TRACKS. New York, Scribner, 1936. 156p [BM LC NBFU OTU
THE RAVEN'S WING. London, Macmillan, 1940. 419p [BM LC NBFU OTMC
A SHADOWY THIRD. London, Knopf, 1927. 259p [BM
THE SON OF THE HOUSE. London, Collins, 1937. 315p [BM BVaU LC NBFU
OTU

TWO LOST ON DARTMOOR. London, Eyre & Spottiswoode, 1940. 172p [BM OTU

Starkey, Mrs. Allistene
THE GRAFTED TWIG. New York, Arcadia House, 1940. 320p [LC NBFU

Starr, J.R.L.
MOST THOROUGH. A Father and Son Story. Toronto, Allen, 1927. 28p [OTMC

Stavrakov, Marion
CHESTER GNOMIE. And His Friends the Elves — and the Blueberries — and the Old Grey Goose. Montreal, Palm Pub., 1950. 24p [OONL

Stead, Robert James Campbell, 1880–1959
THE BAIL JUMPER. Toronto, Briggs, 1914. 335p [BM BVaU OTMC
THE COPPER DISC. New York, Doubleday, 1931. 321p [BM BVaU LC NBFU OTMC
THE COW PUNCHER. New York, Harper, 1918. 331p [BM BVaU LC NBFU OTMC
DENNISON GRANT. A Novel of Today. Toronto, Musson, 1920. 388p [BM BVaU NBFU OTMC
GRAIN. Toronto, McClelland, 1926. 281p [BM BVaU LC NBFU OTMC QMM
THE HOMESTEADERS. A Novel of the Canadian West. Toronto, Musson, 1916. 314p [BM BVaU NBFU OTMC
NEIGHBOURS. Toronto, Hodder, 1922. 315p [BVaU NBFU OTMC QMM
THE SMOKING FLAX. Toronto, McClelland, 1924. 301p [BM BVaU LC NBFU OTMC
ZEN OF THE Y.D. A Novel of the Foothills. [A revised ed. of DENNISON GRANT.] London, Hodder, 1925. 320p [BM

Steele, Harwood Elmes Robert, 1897–
GHOSTS RETURNING. Toronto, Ryerson, 1950. 272p [BVaU NBFU OTMC QMM
"I SHALL ARISE." London, Hodder, 1926. 320p [BM BVaU NBFU QMM
THE NINTH CIRCLE. New York, Doubleday, 1928. 312p [BM BVaU LC NBFU OORD QMM
SPIRIT-OF-IRON. An Authentic Novel of the North West Mounted Police. Toronto, McClelland, 1923. 358p [BM BVaU LC NBFU OTMC
TO EFFECT AN ARREST. Adventures of the Royal Canadian Mounted Police. Toronto, Ryerson, 1947. 311p [BM BVaU LC NBFU OTU QMBM

Stefansson, Vilhjalmur, 1879–1962
KAK, THE COPPER ESKIMO. By Vilhjalmur Stefansson and Violet Irwin. ... New York, Macmillan, 1924. 253p [BM BVaU LC NBFU OTP
THE MOUNTAIN OF JADE. By Violet Irwin and ——. London, Macmillan, 1926. 236p [BM LC OTMC

Steinhouse, Herbert, 1922–

TEN YEARS AFTER. London, Bodley Head, 1958. 371p

THE TIME OF THE JUGGERNAUT. New York, Morrow, 1958. 470p [Same as TEN YEARS AFTER.]

Stephen, Alexander Maitland, 1882–1942

THE GLEAMING ARCHWAY. London, Dent, 1929. 296p [BViPA NSHD OTMC QMM

THE KINGDOM OF THE SUN. A Romance of the Far West Coast. Toronto, Dent, 1927. 285p [BM BVaU NBFU OTMC QMM

Stern, Karl, 1906–

THROUGH DOOMS OF LOVE. A Novel. New York, Farrar Straus, 1960. 433p

Stevens, Charles A.

A SAILOR BOY'S EXPERIENCE. Napanee, Ont., 1892. 107p [OLU

Stevens, George Roy, 1895–

THE REMEMBRANCE OF SHERE JEHAN. By G.R.S. Montreal, Author, 1960. 16p

Stevenson, Laura Agnes

THE LADIES' BENEVOLENT AND INDUSTRIAL SALLYMAG SOCIETY. By L.S. Charlottetown, Bremner, 1868. 131p [LC NSHD OTP

Stewart, Alexander Charles, 1867–1944

THE DISCARD. Being the Historical Remnants of a Rough Neck. ... By Professor A.C.S. [pseud]. Toronto, Hunter Rose, 1919. 265p [BVaU NBFU OTMC

Stewart, James Livingstone, 1872–1946

THE GODDESS OF MERCY. A Tale of Love and Turmoil of Modern China. New York, Revell, 1927. 351p [BM LC NBFU OTMC

GODS OF WEALTH AND WAR. A Tale of Modern China. New York, Revell, 1931. 288p [BVaU LC OKQ

THE LAUGHING BUDDHA. A Tale of Love and Adventure in Western China. New York, Revell, 1925. 347p [BM LC NBFU OKQ

Stilman, Abram, 1903–

HEALER OF ALL FLESH. A Novel. New York, Whittier Books, 1959. 441p

Stirling, Helen

A SOLDIER OF THE KING. Toronto, Oxford U. Press, 1915. 55p [OTMC

Stirling, Lilla May Elderkin, 1904–

JOCKIE. A Story of Prince Edward Island. New York, Scribner, 1951. 202p

Stobo, Rev. Edward John, 1838–1918

THE O'ERTURN O' BOTANY BAY. By Aletheia [pseud]. Philadelphia, American Baptist Pub. Soc., 1901. 270p [LC

Stockford, Lela E.
MEDICO OF THE VALLEY. By Joan Hamilton-Stockford [pseud]. Philadelphia, Dorrance, 1939. 226p [LC

Storey, Arthur George, 1915–
PRAIRIE HARVEST. Toronto, Ryerson, 1959. 210p

Stormont, Lan (pseud)
TAN MING. A Fantasy. By Lan Stormont [pseud]. New York, Exposition Press, 1955. 471p

Strange, William, 1902–
SUNSET IN EBONY. Toronto, Macmillan, 1935. 305p [BM NBFU

Stredder, Eleanor
LOST IN THE WILDS. A Canadian Story. London, Nelson, 1896. 227p [BM NBFU OTU QMBM

Stringer, Arthur John Arbuthnot, 1874–1950
ARE ALL MEN ALIKE?–THE LOST TITIAN. [See TWIN TALES . ...]
THE CITY OF PERIL. New York, Knopf, 1923. 317p [BVaU LC NBFU OTU
CHRISTINA AND I. Indianapolis, Bobbs-Merrill, 1929. 301p [BM BVaU LC NBFU OTMC
THE DARK WING. New York, Bobbs-Merrill, 1939. 311p [BM LC NBFU OTU
THE DEVASTATOR. Toronto, McClelland, 1944. 198p [BM BVaU LC NBFU OTU
THE DIAMOND THIEVES. Indianapolis, Bobbs-Merrill, 1923. 416p [BM LC NBFU OTU
THE DOOR OF DREAD. A Secret Service Romance. Indianapolis, Bobbs-Merrill, 1916. 375p [BM LC NSWA OTMC
EMPTY HANDS. Indianapolis, Bobbs-Merrill, 1924. 360p [BM BVaU LC NBFU OTU
THE GHOST PLANE. Indianapolis, Bobbs-Merrill, 1940. 304p [BM BVaU LC NBFU OTU
THE GUN-RUNNER. A Novel. New York, Dodge, 1909. 370p [Also: Toronto, McClelland, 1923. 316p] [BM BVaU LC NBFU OTU QMM
THE HAND OF PERIL. New York, Macmillan, 1915. 331p [BVaU LC NBFU OTU
HEATHER OF THE HIGH HAND. A Novel of the North. New York, Bobbs-Merrill, 1937. 291p [BM BVaU LC NBFU OTU
THE HOUSE OF INTRIGUE. Indianapolis, Bobbs-Merrill, 1918. 363p [BM LC NBFU OTU
IN BAD WITH SINBAD. Indianapolis, Bobbs-Merrill, 1926. 185p [BM BVaU LC NBFU OTU
INTRUDERS IN EDEN. A Novel. Indianapolis, Bobbs-Merrill, 1942. 308p [BM BVaU LC OTMC

A LADY QUITE LOST. A Novel. Indianapolis, Bobbs-Merrill, 1931. 303p [Pub. in *Saturday Evening Post* under title: THE SQUAW WOMAN.] [BM BVaU LC NBFU OTMC

THE LAMP IN THE VALLEY. A Novel of Alaska. New York, Bobbs-Merrill, 1938. 314p [BM BVaU LC OTU

LONELY O'MALLEY. A Story of Boy Life. Boston, Houghton, 1905. 383p [Also: Toronto, McClelland, 1924. 383p] [BM BVaU LC OTU

THE LOOM OF DESTINY. Boston, Small Maynard, 1899. 208p [BM BVaU LC NBFU OTU

MAN LOST. Indianapolis, Bobbs-Merrill, 1934. 328p [BM BVaU LC OOP

THE MAN WHO COULDN'T SLEEP. Being a Relation of the Divers Strange Adventures which befell Witter Kerfoot ... along the Highways and Byways of Manhattan. Indianapolis, Bobbs-Merrill, 1919. 351p [BM BVaU LC NBFU OTU

MANHANDLED. By Arthur Stringer and Russell Holman. ... New York, Bobbs-Merrill, 1924. 312p [BM BVaU LC OTMC

MARRIAGE BY CAPTURE. Indianapolis, Bobbs-Merrill, 1933. 316p [BM LC NBFU OTU

THE MUD LARK. Indianapolis, Bobbs-Merrill, 1932. 331p [BM LC NBFU OTU QMM

NEVER-FAIL BLAKE. New York, Burt, 1924. 302p [Originally pub. under title: THE SHADOW.] [LC NBFU OTMC

NIGHT HAWK. A Novel. New York, Burt, 1926. 307p [LC

THE OCCASIONAL OFFENDER. [MOR'12

PHANTOM WIRES. Boston, Little Brown, 1907. 295p [Another ed., 1923.] [BM BVaU LC NBFU OTU

POWER. Indianapolis, Bobbs-Merrill, 1925. 308p [BM BVaU LC NSHD OTU

THE PRAIRIE CHILD. Indianapolis, Bobbs-Merrill, 1922. 382p [BM BVaU LC NBFU OTU QMM

THE PRAIRIE MOTHER. Toronto, McClelland, 1920. 359p [BM BVaU LC NBFU OTU

THE PRAIRIE OMNIBUS. Containing Two Complete Novels ... THE PRAIRIE WIFE, THE PRAIRIE MOTHER. New York, Grosset & Dunlap, n.d. 316 + 359p [OTMC QMG

PRAIRIE STORIES. Containing THE PRAIRIE WIFE, THE PRAIRIE MOTHER, THE PRAIRIE CHILD. New York, Burt, 1936. 1057p [OLU

THE PRAIRIE WIFE. A Novel. Indianapolis, Bobbs-Merrill, 1915. 316p [BM BVaU LC NBFU OTU

THE SHADOW. New York, Century, 1913. 302p [Later pub. under title: NEVER-FAIL BLAKE.] [BM BVaU LC OTMC

THE SILVER POPPY. A Novel. New York, Appleton, 1903. 291p [Another ed., 1924.] [BM BVaU LC NBFU OTMC

STAR IN A MIST. A Novel. Indianapolis, Bobbs-Merrill, 1943. 312p [BM LC NBFU OTMC

THE STORY WITHOUT A NAME. By Arthur Stringer and Russell Holman. New York, Grosset, 1924. 316p [BM BVaU LC NBFU OTMC

THE STRANGER. Toronto, Dominion Publicity Com. Victory Loan, 1919. 16p [NSHPL OTMC

TOOLOONA. A Novel of the North. London, Methuen, 1936. 248p [BM

TWIN TALES: ARE ALL MEN ALIKE? and THE LOST TITIAN. Indianapolis, Bobbs-Merrill, 1921. 288p [BVaU LC NBFU OTU QMM

THE UNDER GROOVE. A Novel. New York, McClure, 1908. 335p [BVaU LC NBFU OTMC

WHITE HANDS. Indianapolis, Bobbs-Merrill, 1927. 302p [BM BVaU LC OTU

THE WIFE TRADERS. A Tale of the North. Indianapolis, Bobbs-Merrill, 1936. 319p [BM BVaU LC NBFU OLU

THE WINE OF LIFE. New York, Knopf, 1921. 389p [BVaU LC NBFU OTU QMM

THE WIRE TAPPERS. Boston, Little Brown, 1906. 324p [Another ed., 1922.] [BM BVaU LC NBFU OTU

THE WOLF WOMAN. A Novel. Indianapolis, Bobbs-Merrill, 1928. 331p [BM BVaU LC NBFU OTMC

THE WOMAN WHO COULDN'T DIE. Indianapolis, Bobbs-Merrill, 1929. 314p [BVaU LC NBFU OTU

Stroud, Amelia Panton

DAISY DALTON'S DECISION. Toronto, Bain, 1894. 218p [OTMC

Sullivan, Alan, 1868—1947

"AND FROM THAT DAY." Toronto, Ryerson, 1944. 195p [BVaU LC NSHD OOP OTU QMM

ANTIDOTE. By Sinclair Murray [pseud]. London, J. Murray, 1932. 332p / [BM LC

THE BIRTHMARK. London, Arnold, 1924. 319p [EngCat

BLANTYRE—ALIEN. London, Dent, 1914. 265p [BVaU NSHD OTMC

THE BROKEN MARRIAGE. By Sinclair Murray [pseud]. New York, Dutton, 1929. 319p [Also: London, Murray, 1928.] [BM LC

BROTHER BLACKFOOT. New York, Century, 1927. 300p [LC NBFU OOP

BROTHER ESKIMO. Toronto, McClelland, 1921. 249p [BVaU NBFU OTMC

THE CARIBOO ROAD. A Novel. Toronto, Nelson, 1946. 311p [BVaU NBFU OTMC QMM

COLONEL PLUCKETT. London, Ward Lock, 1932. 256p [LC NBFU

CORNISH INTERLUDE. By Sinclair Murray [pseud]. London, J. Murray, 1932. 303p [BM

THE CRUCIBLE. By Sinclair Murray [pseud]. London, Bles, 1925. 318p [BM LC NBFU

THE DAYS OF THEIR YOUTH. New York, Century, 1926. 332p [BVaU LC NBFU OTU

DOUBLE LIVES. By Sinclair Murray [pseud]. Toronto, Macmillan, 1929. 318p [Also: London, Murray, 1929. 318p] [BM NBFU

THE FUR MASTERS. London, Murray, 1938. 320p [BVaU LC NBFU OTU QMM

GOLDEN FOUNDLING. By Sinclair Murray [pseud]. Toronto, Macmillan, 1931. 338p [BM NBFU

THE GREAT DIVIDE. A Romance of the Canadian Pacific Railway. Toronto, Macmillan, 1935. 417p [BVaU LC NBFU OTU QMM

HUMAN CLAY. By Sinclair Murray [pseud] and B.V. Shann. London, J. Murray, 1926. 318p [BM OOP

IN THE BEGINNING. London, Hurst & Blackett, 1926. 280p [LC NBFU OTMC

THE INNER DOOR. New York, Century, 1917. 388p [LC NBFU OTMC

THE IRONMASTER. London, J. Murray, 1931. 345p [CBI

THE JADE GOD. London, Bles, 1924. 316p [Dramatized as 3-act play with same title by William Edwin Barry: New York, French, 1930. 77p −CBI] [BVaU LC NBFU OTMC

JOHN FRENSHAM, K.C. By Sinclair Murray [pseud]. New York, Dutton, 1928. 293p [Same title, but with B. V. Shann as jt. author: London, J. Murray, 1925. 320p −EngCat] [BM LC NBFU

A LITTLE WAY AHEAD. Toronto, Macmillan, 1930. 316p [LC NBFU OTU QMM

THE MAGIC MAKERS. London, J. Murray, 1930. 297p [NBS

MAN AT LONE TREE. London, Ward Lock, 1933. 256p [CBI

THE MONEY SPINNERS. By Sinclair Murray [pseud]. London, Low Marston, 1936. 378p [BM LC NBFU OTU

MR. ABSALOM. London, Murray, 1930. 316p [CBI

NO SECRETS ISLAND. London, Murray, 1931. 314p [CBI

THE OBSTINATE VIRGIN. London, Low Marston, 1934. 314p [BM

THE PASSING OF OUL-I-BUT AND OTHER TALES. Toronto, Dent, 1913. 302p [BVaU NSHD OTMC

QUEER PARTNERS. By Sinclair Murray [pseud]. Toronto, Macmillan, 1930. 313p [BM NBFU OOP

THE RAPIDS. Toronto, Copp Clark, 1922. 337p [BVaU LC NSHD OTU QMM

SANDS OF FORTUNE. By Sinclair Murray [pseud]. New York, Dutton, 1928. 300p [BM LC NBFU

THE SPLENDID SILENCE. New York, Dutton, 1929. 278p [LC NBFU OTMC

THE STORY OF ONE-EAR. London, Philip, 1929. 68p [CBI

THREE CAME TO VILLE MARIE. Toronto, Oxford U. Press, 1941. 391p [BVaU LC NSHD OTMC QMM

THE TRAINING OF THE SEA. London, Philip, 1929. 72p [CBI

UNDER THE NORTHERN LIGHTS. London, Dent, 1926. 218p [BVaU LC NSHD OTU QMM

THE VERDICT OF THE SEA. London, Hurst & Blackett, 1927. 288p [BVaU LC NBFU OTU

WHAT FOOLS MEN ARE! By Sinclair Murray [pseud]. London, Sampson Low, 1933. 316p [BM NBFU

WHISPERING LODGE. By Sinclair Murray [pseud]. Toronto, Ryerson, 1927. 336p [Also: London, Murray, 1927. 336p] [BM NBFU

WITH LOVE FROM RACHEL. By Sinclair Murray [pseud]. Toronto, Oxford U. Press, 1938. 312p [BM NBFU OTU

Sullivan, Archibald Beresford Dennistown, 1886–1921

THE LAUGHING BIRDS AND OTHER STORIES. Toronto, Macmillan, 1925. 283p [AEU BVaU NBFU OTMC

Sullivan, Barry Seaghan

FIBRE. London, Faber, 1945. 246p [BM LC

Sutton, Mrs. Rose

DRIFT. New York, Vantage Press, 1955. 157p

Swabey, Maurice, 1832?–1902

VOICES FROM ABEGWEET; or, The Home on the Wave. London, Nisbet, 1878. 71p [BM NSHD

Swayze, James Frederick, 1907–1967

RUN FOR YOUR LIFE! The Adventures of John Rutherfurd at Pontiac's Siege of Detroit, 1763. Toronto, Ryerson, 1960. 149p

Sweatman, Mrs. Constance Travers

HALF PRICE. Toronto, McClelland, 1927. 277p [BM BVaU LC NBFU OTMC

SINCE ADAM. A Novel. London, Hurst & Blackett, 1927. 287p [BM

TO LOVE AND TO CHERISH. Toronto, Macmillan, 1929. 342p [NBFU OTMC

YOUNG FOLK, OLD FOLK. A Novel of the Younger Set. Toronto, Allen, 1926. 304p [BM LC NBFU OTMC

Sykes, Hon. Villum (pseud.)

LETTERS TO HIS HEXCELLENT LORD CATHCART (GOV'NOR AS VOS) ... HEX-PLAININ VOT IS VOT IN CANARDEY, AS VEL AS VOT HOUGHTN'T TO BE. By the Hon. Villum Sykes [pseud], late Hinspector hof Cabs and Lisenses. Montreal, Donoghue & Mantz, 1846. 38p [OTP

Symons, Harry Lutz, 1893–

THREE SHIPS WEST. ... Toronto, Ryerson, 1949. 315p [NBFU OTMC QMBM

Taggart, William Stuart, 1859–1925

"GUILTY." Forgiven–Reclaimed; "TRUTH IS STRANGER THAN FICTION." A Canadian Story from Real Life. By Lance Bilton [pseud]. Ottawa, Crain, 1906. 305p [BM BVaU OTMC

Tait, George Edward, 1910–
THE SADDLE OF CARLOS PEREZ. Toronto, Ryerson, 1949. 87p [OONL
THE SILENT GULLS. Toronto, Ryerson, 1950. 95p [OONL

Tait, John, 1896? –1955
GRANDMA TAKES A HAND. Toronto, Ryerson, 1956. 155p

Talbot, Thomas, (fl. 1844–82)
THE GRANVILLES. An Irish Tale. London, Sampson, 1882. 3v [BM

Tapley, K.C.
TAPPINGS. By Casey Tap [pseud]. Saint John, McMillan, 1884. 58p [NBS
OONL

Tate, Frank J., 1902–
RED WILDERNESS. Toronto, Oxford U. Press, 1938. 461p [LC NBFU OTU
QMBM

Taylor, Archibald M'Alpine
JEAN GRANT. A Novel. New York, Lovell, 1890. 242p [LC

Taylor, Daphne
POMPOUS PARROT, AND OTHER WEST INDIAN TALES. Toronto, Macmillan,
1947. 114p [CC

Taylor, Miss E.A.
BEATRICE OF OLD YORK. Toronto, Musson, 1929. 214p [BVaU NBFU OKQ

Taylor, Gaie
ANASTASIA'S DAUGHTER. Toronto, Ryerson, 1955. 256p

Taylor, Gladys (Tall), 1917–
THE KING TREE. Toronto, Ryerson, 1958. 335p
PINE ROOTS. Toronto, Ryerson, 1956. 238p

Teetgen, Ada B.
A WHITE PASSION. London, Gardner, 1913. 346p [BM BVaU OOP

Tempest, Judith (pseud)
MONKSWOLD. Saint John, Author, 1903. 156p [Earlier ed., 1895 –BCF]
[BCF NBS

Templeton-Armstrong, Mrs. I.
THE OLD VICE AND THE NEW CHIVALRY. Toronto, Briggs, 1884. 178p [BVaU
OTP

Tennant, Margaret E.
THE GOLDEN CHORD. A Story of Trial and Conquest. Almonte, Ont., McLeod
& McEwen, 1899. 133p [BVaU

Tennenhaus, Hanna (Faust), 1923–
EVA. Bathurst, N.B., Aire Pub., 1959. 188p

Teskey, Adeline Margaret, –1924
ALEXANDER McBAIN, B.A. Prince in Penury. New York, Revell, 1906. 297p
   [LC OTU
CANDLELIGHT DAYS. London, Cassell, 1913. 344p [BM BVaU NSHD OTU
THE LITTLE CELESTIAL. Toronto, 1912. [DCB MOR'12
A LITTLE CHILD SHALL LEAD THEM. London, Hodder, 1911. 31p [AEU BM
   BVaS
THE VILLAGE ARTIST. New York, Revell, 1905. 216p [BM BVaU LC OTMC
WHERE THE SUGAR MAPLE GROWS. Idylls of a Canadian Village. New York,
   Fenno, 1901. 268p [BM BVaU LC NBFU OTU QMM
THE YELLOW PEARL. New York, Hodder, 1911. 208p [BM BVaU LC OTMC

Thomas, Cyrus, 1836–1908
THE FRONTIER SCHOOLMASTER. The Autobiography of a Teacher. ... Montreal,
   Lovell, 1880. 465p [BVaU OTMC QMM
THE REVEREND JOHN AND A FEW PHILANTHROPISTS. [A Novel.] Montreal,
   Lovell, 1903. 492p [BM BVaU NBFU OTMC QMM

Thomas, Lillian (Beynon), 1874–1961
NEW SECRET. Toronto, Allen, 1946. 214p [BVaU NBFU OTMC

Thomas, Martha Banning
STORMALONG GERT. New York, Green Circle Books, 1936. 318p [Pub. in
   England as: WOMAN OF THE SEA. London, Long, 1938. 254p] [LC OTU

Thompson, Dora Olive, 1895? –1934
ADELE IN SEARCH OF A HOME. London, Girl's Own Paper, 1926. 288p [BM
A DEALER IN SUNSHINE. London, Girl's Own Paper, 1926. 224p [BM
DIMPLES. London, Religious Tract Soc., 1929. 269p [BM
JOY MEREDITH. London, Religious Tract Soc., 1928. 255p [BM
KATHLEEN AND PETER. Toronto, Upper Canada Tract Soc., 1934. 271p [BM
LIZZIE ANNE. London, Girl's Own Paper, 1927. 288p [BM
NANCY-ROSE. London, Girl's Own Paper, n.d. 256p [NBS
THAT GIRL GINGER. London, Religious Tract Soc., 1931. 286p [BM

Thompson, Mrs. James C.
SKETCHES FROM LIFE. Being Tales on the Ten Commandments. Toronto,
   Hunter, 1876. 240p [OTMC

Thompson, Sheila Sonia, 1917–
LIKE A FLOWER. Toronto, Nelson, 1946. 208p [BM LC

Thompson, Thomas Phillips, 1843–1933
THE POLITICAL EXPERIENCES OF JIMUEL BRIGGS [pseud] ... AT TORONTO,
   OTTAWA AND ELSEWHERE. ... Toronto, Flint Morton, 1873. 126p [LC OTUV

Thomson, Edward William, 1849–1924

BETWEEN EARTH AND SKY, AND OTHER STRANGE STORIES OF DELIVERANCE.
Toronto, Briggs, 1897. 297p [BM BVa OTUV

OLD MAN SAVARIN, AND OTHER STORIES. Toronto, Briggs, 1895. 289p [BM
BVaU LC NBFU OTMC QMM

OLD MAN SAVARIN STORIES. Tales of Canada and Canadians. Toronto, Gundy,
1917. 344p [BM BVaU LC OTMC QMM

SMOKY DAYS. New York, Crowell, 1901. [AmCat

WALTER GIBBS, THE YOUNG BOSS; AND OTHER STORIES. A Book for Boys.
Toronto, Briggs, 1896. 361p [BM BVa OOP QMM

Thorold, William James, 1871–

NEAR THE THRONE. New York, Meyer, 1899. 289p [LC

ZEROLA OF NAZARETH. By Louie Barron [pseud]. Toronto, Musson, 1895.
160p [BM OOP

Tibbits, Ethel Caswell (Burnett), 1890–

ON TO THE SUNSET. Toronto, Ryerson, 1953. 155p

Tiller, Stanley C., 1902–

STORMSWEPT. Toronto, Ryerson, 1950. 213p [BVaU NBFU OTMC

Todd, Robert Henry, 1877–

THE SOLVER OF MYSTERIES AND OTHER STORIES. Brampton, Charters, 1930.
292p [NBFU OTMC

Tomkinson, Grace (Avard), 1890–

THE CAPE AND THE RIVER. London, Johnson, 1947. 256p [Same as HER OWN
PEOPLE, q.v.] [BM OWtU

HER OWN PEOPLE. A Novel. New York, Ives Washburn, 1945. 248p [Pub. in
England as: THE CAPE AND THE RIVER, 1947.] [BVaU LC NBFU OTMC

WELCOME WILDERNESS. New York, Ives Washburn, 1946. 289p [BM BVaU
NBFU OTU

Toronto, Ont. Writers' Club

... FICTION. Toronto, 1936. 48p [Selected from 300 mss submitted in a national
competition.] [OTP

Tovell, Ruth (Massey), 1889–

THE CRIME IN THE BOULEVARD RASPAIL. By Ruth Massey. Edinburgh, Nelson,
1932. 318p [Also as: DEATH IN THE WIND. ... New York, Nelson, 1932.] [AEU
BM CBI CC

Townley, Alice Ashworth

OPINIONS OF MARY. Toronto, Briggs, 1909. 229p [BM BVaU OTMC

Traill, Catharine Parr (Strickland), 1802–1899

ADVENTURES OF LITTLE DOWNY; THE FIELD MOUSE; and THE LITTLE PRINCESS,
or Passion and Patience. By Miss Strickland. New ed. London, Dean, 1844.

78p [Attributed to Mrs. Traill by Agnes Fitzgibbon in sketch prefaced to
Mrs. Traill's PEARLS AND PEBBLES.] [BM

AFAR IN THE FOREST; or, Pictures of Life and Scenery in the Wilds of Canada.
London, Nelson, 1869. 207p [Various editions. Also pub. under titles:
LADY MARY AND HER NURSE; LITTLE MARY AND HER NURSE; STORIES OF THE
CANADIAN FOREST —OTP] [BM BVaU OKQ

THE CANADIAN CRUSOES. A Tale of the Rice Lake Plains. Ed. by Agnes Strickland.
London, Hall, 1850. 368p [Also: Toronto, McClelland, 1923. 322p Other
editions have title: LOST IN THE BACKWOODS. London, Nelson, 1882. Etc.]
[BM BVaU NSHD OLU QMM

COT AND CRADLE STORIES. Ed. by Mary Agnes Fitzgibbon. ... Toronto, Briggs,
1895. 239p [BM BVaU LC MWU NBFU OKQ

IN THE FOREST; or, Pictures of Life and Scenery in the Woods of Canada. London,
Nelson, 1886. 188p [See AFAR IN THE FOREST.] [BVaU NBFU QMBM

LADY MARY AND HER NURSE; or, A Peep into the Canadian Forest. London,
Hall, 1856. 204p [See AFAR IN THE FOREST.] [BM OTU QMSS

LOST IN THE BACKWOODS. A Tale of the Canadian Forest. London, Nelson,
1882. 319p [See THE CANADIAN CRUSOES.] [BM BVaU NSHD QMM

PREJUDICE REPROVED; or, The History of the Negro Toy-Seller. By the Author
of the "Tell-Tale" [i.e., Agnes Strickland], "Reformation" [i.e., Catharine P.
Strickland], "Disobedience" [i.e., Elizabeth Strickland], "Early Lessons," etc.
London, Harvey and Darton, 1826. 86p [BM

REFORMATION; or, The Cousin. London, 1819. [BM

STORIES OF THE CANADIAN FOREST; or, Little Mary and her Nurse. Boston,
Crosby & Nichols, 1861. 240p [See also AFAR IN THE FOREST.] [BVaU
NBFU OTP QMM

Treleaven, Emma
PEACE AT THE LAST. Ilfracombe, Devon, Stockwell, 1958. 287p

Tremblay, Jean Jacques, 1926—
TEN CANADIAN LEGENDS. Fredericton, Brunswick Press, 1955. 32p

Trill, Matthew, 1887—
GOOD KING WENCESLAS. A Tale of Old Gods and New Inspired by the Ancient
Carol. By Hew Trill. Montreal, Ronalds, 1934. 21p [BVaU NBFU QMM
THE STRANGER WITHIN. New York, Stokes, 1935. 319p [BM LC NBFU
OTMC

Trueman, Stuart, 1911—
COUSIN ELVA. Toronto, McClelland, 1955. 224p

Tsyr, Paul
G. DWYER, K.W. A Novel. Montreal, Lovell, 1895. 250p [NSHD OTP

Tuck, Clyde Edwin
THE BALD KNOBBERS. Indianapolis, Bowen, 1910. 325p [LC
FOR LOVE OF YOU. Indianapolis, Bowen, 1909. 87p [LC

Tuckwell, Ronald Wesley, 1889–
PHIL. ACTON'S PROMISE. London, Stockwell, 1932. 95p [BM
THE WINSTONE WAY (AND OTHER STORIES OF WINSTONE SCHOOL).
Ilfracombe, Devon, Stockwell, 1960. 128p

Tupper, Kathryn (Munro)
WHISKERS IN LILACTOWN. By Kathryn Munro. Kentville, N.S., Kentville Pub.
Co., 1934. 61p [BVaU NBFU OTMC

Tyrrell, Mary Edith (Carey), 1870? –1945
FURRY AND FLUFFY. The Story My Children Loved Best. Toronto, Ryerson,
1946. 16p [OTU

Uren, Alfred Ernest, 1881–
BOB AND BILL GO FARMING. Toronto, Bob and Bill Pubs., 1935. 80p [CAR

Urtica, R. (pseud)
THE STORY OF JOHN AND JONATHAN. Ottawa, Bell, 1871. 28p [OKQ

Vaczek, Louis Charles, 1913–
THE FRIGHTENED DOVE. By Peter Hardin [pseud]. New York, Scribner, 1951.
192p
THE GOLDEN CALF. New York, Sloane, 1956. 317p
THE HIDDEN GRAVE. By Peter Hardin [pseud]. New York, Dell, 1955. 188p
RIVER AND EMPTY SEA. A Novel. Boston, Houghton, 1950. 372p [BM BVaU
LC NBFU OTMC

Van Der Mark, Christine, 1917–
IN DUE SEASON. Toronto, Oxford U. Press, 1947. 363p [BVaU LC NBFU
OTMC QMM

Van Vogt, Alfred Elton, 1912–
AWAY AND BEYOND. New York, Pellegrini, 1952. 300p
THE BOOK OF PTATH. ... ˙Reading, Pa., Fantasy Press, 1947. 227p [LC
DESTINATION: UNIVERSE! New York, Pellegrini, 1952. 295p
THE HOUSE THAT STOOD STILL. New York, Greenberg, 1950. 210p [BM LC
OONL
MASTERS OF TIME. Reading, Pa., Fantasy Press, 1950. 227p [LC NBFU OTMC
THE MIND CAGE. A Science-Fiction Novel. New York, Simon & Schuster, 1957.
190p
THE MIXED MEN. New York, Gnome Press, 1952. 223p

OUT OF THE UNKNOWN. Los Angeles, Fantasy Pub. Co., 1948. 141p [LC NBFU
SLAN. Sauk City, Wis., Arkham House, 1946. 216p [BM LC OONL
THE WEAPON MAKERS. Providence, R.I., Hadley, 1947. 224p [BM LC
THE WEAPON SHOPS OF ISHER. New York, Greenberg, 1952. 220p
THE VOYAGE OF THE SPACE BEAGLE. New York, Simon & Schuster, 1950.
   240p [Reprinted as: MISSION: INTERPLANETARY. New York, New
   American Library (Signet Books), 1952. 174p] [BM LC OONL
THE WAR AGAINST THE RULL. New York, Simon & Schuster, 1959. 244p
THE WORLD OF Ā. New York, Simon & Schuster, 1948. 246p [LC NBFU
   OTMC

Vaughan, Leslie
CHARLIE OGILBIE. A Romance of Scotland and New Brunswick. Toronto,
   Bryce, 1889. 158p [NSHD OTU

Verral, Charles Spain, 1904–
CAPTAIN OF THE ICE. New York, Crowell, 1953. 151p
THE CASE OF THE MISSING MESSAGE. New York, Golden Press, 1959. 188p
CHAMPION OF THE COURT. New York, Crowell, 1954. 192p
HIGH DANGER. New York, Sterling Pub. Co., 1955. 192p
THE KING OF THE DIAMOND. New York, Crowell, 1955. 179p
RIN TIN TIN AND THE HIDDEN TREASURE. Authorized ed. New York, Simon
   & Schuster, 1958. 28p
THE WINNING QUARTERBACK. New York, Crowell, 1960. 248p

Vial, Alexia Agnes
GRIM TRUTH. A Short Story. Montreal, Lovell, 1890. 37p [NSHD OTP QMM

Waagen, Mary Elizabeth (Hickson)
THE CALL OF GOD. By Mary Elizabeth Hickson. Montreal, Author, 1911. [CAR
MADAME JANVIER'S CHURCH. By Mary Elizabeth Hickson. Toronto, Musson,
   [1911?]. 70p [BM BVaU NBFU OTMC QMBM
THE WAYSIDE CROSS. Toronto, Musson, 1924. 136p [BVaU NBFU OTP
   QMM

Waitt, Georgina Seymour
THREE GIRLS UNDER CANVAS. Victoria, "In Black and White," 1900. 154p
   [BVaU OTMC

Wakeham, Pius Joseph, 1910–
A BOOK OF NEWFOUNDLAND STORIES. St. John's, Long Bros., 1955. 258p
ISLAND ROMANCE. St. John's, Dicks & Co., 1959. 325p
MUTINY AT MIDNIGHT. A Thrilling Adventure Story. St. John's, Long Bros., 1951.
   233p

THE ROYAL IMPOSTOR. St. John's, Dicks & Co., 1960. 398p

TWENTY NEWFOUNDLAND STORIES. St. John's, Long Bros., 1953. 322p

Walford, Austin

CONFESSION OF THE HILLS. Winnipeg, Middle West Pub. Co., 1915. 313p [BM LC OTMC

Walker, Annie Louisa (Mrs. Henry Coghill), 1836–1907

AGAINST HER WILL. A Novel. London, Tinsley, 1877. 3v [BM

A CANADIAN HEROINE. By the Author of LEAVES FROM THE BACKWOODS. London, Tinsley, 1873. 3v [OKQ

HOLLYWOOD. London, Tinsley, 1875. 3v [BM

LADY'S HOLM. A Novel. London, Tinsley, 1878. 3v [BM

TRIAL OF MARY BROOM. By Mrs. Coghill. London, Hutchinson, 1894. 149p [BM

TWO RIVAL LOVERS. A Novel. London, White, 1881. 3v [BM

Walker, David Harry, 1911–

DIGBY. A Novel. London, Collins, 1953. 254p

GEORDIE. Boston, Houghton, 1950. 209p [BM LC NBFU OTMC

HARRY BLACK. A Novel. London, Collins, 1956. 320p

THE PILLAR. Boston, Houghton, 1952. 313p [Also pub. as THE WIRE. Garden City, N.Y., Permabooks, 1953. 382p]

SANDY WAS A SOLDIER'S BOY. London, Collins, 1957. 159p

THE STORM AND THE SILENCE. Boston, Houghton, 1949. 248p [BM BVaU LC OTMC

WHERE THE HIGH WINDS BLOW. Boston, Houghton, 1960. 536p

Walker, Ella May (Jacoby), 1892–1960

FORTRESS NORTH. Toronto, Allen, 1947. 419p [2nd ed., rev.: Montreal, Renouf, 1956. xi + 423p] [BVaU NBFU OTMC QMBM

Walker, Joan (Suter)

REPENT AT LEISURE. Toronto, Ryerson,–1957. 284p

Walker, Major Benson

ON DOWN THE ROAD. Ottawa, Graphic, 1928. 253p [BVaU NBFU OTMC

SCOTTIE. The True Story of a Dog. Ottawa, Graphic, 1927. 176p [NBFU OTMC

"SKIPPER." The Story of a Dog. New York, Crowell, 1930. 238p [LC

Walker, Rev. William Wesley, 1858–1945

ALTER EGO. A Tale. Toronto, Briggs, 1907. 69p [BM BVaU NSHD OTMC QMBM

OCCIDENT AND ORIENT. A Tale. Toronto, Briggs, 1905. 113p [BM BVaU NSHD OTMC

Wallace, Rev. Archer, 1884–1958

ADVENTURES IN THE AIR. Toronto, Ryerson, 1932. 117p [BM QMSS

THE FIELD OF HONOR. Toronto, Ryerson, 1949. 157p [LC OTMC
ONE HUNDRED STORIES FOR BOYS. Nashville, Abingdon-Cokesbury, 1947. 171p
[Also: Toronto, Ryerson, 1947. 264p] [BVaU LC OTMC

Wallace, Frederick William, 1886–1958

BLUE WATER. A Tale of the Deep Sea Fishermen. Toronto, Musson, 1907. 303p
[Also: Toronto, Musson, 1935. 322p] [BM BVaU NBFU OTU
CAPTAIN SALVATION. Toronto, Musson, 1925. 397p [BM BVaU NSHD OTU
QMM
SALT SEAS AND SAILORMEN. Toronto, Hodder, 1922. 288p [BM BVaU NBFU
OKQ
THE SHACK-LOCKER. Yarns of the Deep Sea Fishing Fleets. Toronto, Hodder,
1916. 303p [BM BVaU NSHD OKQ QMM
TEA FROM CHINA, and Other Yarns of the Sea. Toronto, Musson, 1926. 326p [BM
BVaU LC NSHD OTMC QMM
THE VIKING BLOOD. A Story of Seafaring. Toronto, Musson, 1920. 407p [BM
BVaU NBFU OTU

Wallace, Rev. Michael A., −1892

WELL! WELL! A Tale Founded on Fact. New York, Sadlier, 1863. 312p [An
earlier ed.: New York, Sadlier, 1856. —AmCat] [LC OOP

Wallace, Paul Anthony Wilson, 1891–

BAPTISTE LAROCQUE. Legends of French-Canada. Toronto, Musson, 1923. 129p
[BM BVaU NSHD OTMC QMM
SELECTIONS FROM SAM SLICK (JUDGE HALIBURTON). Ed. by ——. Toronto,
Ryerson, 1923. 150p [BM BVaU OTU QMM
THE TWIST AND OTHER STORIES. Toronto, Ryerson, 1923. 167p [BM BVaU
NSHD OTP
THE WHITE ROOTS OF PEACE. [Indian Legends.] Philadelphia, U. of Penn. Press,
1946. 57p [BM BVa LC OTU QMM

Wallis, Mrs. Ella Bell

THE EXQUISITE GIFT. Ottawa, Ariston, 1930. 249p [BVaU NSHD OTP QMM

Walsh, Henry Cecil

BONHOMME. French-Canadian Stories and Sketches. Toronto, Briggs, 1899. 252p
[BM BVaU NBFU OTP QMM

Walsh, Leo P.

THE SINFUL TOWN. A Novel. New York, Exposition Press, 1948. 208p [LC

Walsh, William Emmett, 1868–

THE DOOM OF CONAIRE-MOR (CONARY THE GREAT). New York, Carrier, 1929.
346p [LC NBFU OTMC

Walshe, Elizabeth Hely, 1835? −1869

CEDAR CREEK. From the Shanty to the Settlement. [Anon] London, Religious

Tract Soc., 1863. 269p [Later eds. under titles: CEDAR CREEK. A Tale of
Canadian Life. London, R.T.S., 1902. 384p and KINGSTON'S REVENGE. ...
London, R.T.S., 1917. 320p] [BM BVaU NBFU OTMC OTU

THE FOSTER BROTHERS OF DOON. A Tale of [the Irish Rebellion of] 1798.
[Anon] London, Religious Tract Soc., 1866. [Later ed.: London, R.T.S.,
1906. 382p] [BM OTMC

GOLDEN HILLS; A Tale of the Irish Famine. By the Author of "Cedar Creek."
London, Religious Tract Soc., 1865. 272p [BM

KINGSTON'S REVENGE. ... See above under CEDAR CREEK.

THE MANUSCRIPT MAN; or, The Bible in Ireland. London, Religious Tract Soc.,
1869. [BM

WITHIN SEA WALLS; or, How the Dutch Kept the Faith. By Elizabeth H. Walshe
and George Etell Sargent. London, Religious Tract Soc., 1880. 378p [Also:
Boston, Bradley, 1881. 378p] [BM BVaU LC

UNDER THE INQUISITION. Story of the Inquisition in Italy. London, Religious
Tract Soc., 1904. 348p [BM

Walters, Harry Macdonald

WESBLOCK. The Autobiography of an Automaton. Toronto, Dent, 1914. 172p
[BM BVaU OTMC

Ward, James Edward, 1883—1958

THE WAYFARER. Leaves from a Wanderer's Log. Toronto, Macmillan, 1922. 231p
[BM BVaU LC NBFU OTMC QMM

Warman, Cy, 1855—1914

THE EXPRESS MESSENGER, and Other Tales of the Rail. New York, Scribner, 1897.
238p [BM BVa LC OTMC

FRONTIER STORIES. New York, Scribner, 1898. 246p [LC OTMC

THE LAST SPIKE, and Other Railroad Stories. New York, Scribner, 1906. 286p
[BVaU LC NBFU OTMC

SHORT RAILS. New York, Scribner, 1900. 310p [BVaU LC

SNOW ON THE HEADLIGHT. A Story of the Great Burlington Strike. New York,
Appleton, 1899. 248p [LC OTMC

TALES OF AN ENGINEER, with Rhymes of the Rail. New York, 1895. 242p
[BVaU LC OLU

WEIGA OF TEMAGAMI, and Other Indian Tales. Toronto, McLeod & Allen, 1908.
206p [BM BVaU LC NSHD OTP QMM

THE WHITE MAIL. New York, Scribner, 1899. 197p [BVa LC QMM

Warnock, Amelia Beers (Mrs. John Garvin), 1878—1956

LEGENDS OF THE ST. LAWRENCE. Retold by Katherine Hale [pseud]. Montreal,
Canadian Pacific Railway, 1926. 47p [BVaU NBFU OTMC

Warren, Mrs. Sara Evangeline Matheson

ANDY THE MILKMAN. Ilfracombe, Devon, Stockwell, 1957. 128p

Warwick, Joseph, 1892—

ANNA OF THE TROUBLED VALLEY. A Tale of Rural Life. Winnipeg, North Star
Pub. Co., [1923]. 174p [ACG

Watson, Muriel F.

FIREWEED. Toronto, Hodder, 1924. 315p [BM BVaU NBFU OTMC

Watson, Robert, 1882—1948

A BOY OF THE GREAT NORTH-WEST. Ottawa, Graphic, 1930. 259p [BVaU LC
NBFU OTMC QMSS

THE GIRL OF O.K. VALLEY. A Romance of the Okanagan. Toronto, McClelland,
1919. 297p [BVaU LC NBFU OTMC

GORDON OF THE LOST LAGOON. A Romance of the Pacific Coast. Toronto, Allen,
1924. 271p [BM BVaU LC NBFU OTP

HIGH HAZARD. A Romance of the Far Arctic. Montreal, Carrier, 1929. 346p
[BM BVaU LC NBFU OTMC QMM

ME AND PETER. Toronto, Allen, 1926. 248p [BM NBFU OTMC

MY BRAVE AND GALLANT GENTLEMAN. A Romance of British Columbia. Toronto,
McClelland, 1918. 339p [BM BVaU LC NBFU OTMC

THE SPOILERS OF THE VALLEY. New York, Doran, 1921. 395p [BM BVaU LC
NBFU OTMC

STRONGER THAN HIS SEA. Toronto, McClelland, 1920. 307p [BM BVaU LC
NBFU OTMC

WHEN CHRISTMAS CAME TO FORT GARRY. A Romance of the Early Red River
Days. Toronto, Ryerson, 1935. 35p [BVaU NBFU OTMC

Watson, Samuel James, 1837—1881

THE PEACE KILLER; or, The Massacre of Lachine. Toronto, 1870. 30p [BCF
NSWA QMSS

Watson, Mrs. Sheila, 1919—

THE DOUBLE HOOK. Toronto, McClelland, 1959. 127p

Weatherby, Hugh Wallace, 1908—

FIR FOREST FUN. Toronto, Ryerson, 1947. 132p [BVa OTMC

HOW THE FIR FOREST WAS SAVED. Victoria, British Columbia Forest Service,
1949. 54p [AEU OTMC

TALES THE TOTEMS TELL. Toronto, Macmillan, 1944, 96p [Also: Toronto,
Macmillan, 1951. x + 96p] [BVaU LC OTP

TEDDY, DAPPY AND JOE. Toronto, Ryerson, 1948. 75p [OTMC

Weaver, Emily Poynton, 1865—1943

MY LADY NELL. An English Story of the Olden Time. London, Warne, 1890. 312p
[Also: Boston, Congregational Church Pub. House, 1889. —AmCat] [BM

THE ONLY GIRL. A Tale of 1837. Toronto, Macmillan, 1925. 298p [OTP

PRINCE RUPERT'S NAME-SAKE; or, After the Restoration. Edinburgh, Oliphant,

1894. 394p [Also: Boston, Congregational Church Pub. House, 1893 —AmCat] [BM

THE RABBI'S SONS. A Story of the Days of St. Paul. London, Kelly, 1891. 270p [Also: Boston, Congregational Church Pub. House, 1891. —AmCat] [BM

THE RAINPROOF INVENTION. Boston, Congregational Sunday-School & Pub. Soc., 1897. 414p [LC

THE SEARCH FOR MOLLY MARLING. Toronto, Musson, [1903?]. 224p [BM NBFU

SOLDIERS OF LIBERTY. A Story of Wars in the Netherlands. Toronto, Briggs, 1892. 128p [BM OTU

THE TROUBLE MAN; or, The Wards of St. James. Toronto, Musson, [1911?]. 315p [BM BVaU NBFU OTMC

Weaver, Robert Leigh, 1921–

CANADIAN SHORT STORIES. Ed. by Robert Weaver and Helen James. Toronto, Oxford U. Press, 1952. 248p

CANADIAN SHORT STORIES. Selected and with an intro. by ——. London, Toronto, Oxford U. Press, 1960. xiii + 420p [Different selections from preceding title]

Webber, Franklyn Millard, 1900–

CODE OF THE RANGELAND. Edmonton, Author, 1959. 236p [mimeographed]

TWENTY PEBBLES AND OTHER STORIES. New York, Pageant Press, 1955. 89p

Webber, William Lester, 1882–

THE THUNDERBIRD "TOOTOOCH" LEGENDS. Folk Tales of the Indian Tribes of the Pacific Northwest. Seattle, Ace Print., 1936. xxi + 38p [Rev. ed., Vancouver, Author, 1952. 65p] [AEU LC OTMC

Webling, Lucy

ONE WAY STREET. A Novel. By Lucy Betty McRaye. London, Hutchinson, 1933. 286p [BM

CENTRE STAGE. By Lucy Betty McRaye. London, Hutchinson, 1938. 256p [BM

Webling, Peggy

THE AMBER MERCHANT. London, Hutchinson, 1925. 288p [BM

ANNA MARIA. London, Hutchinson, 1927. 284p [BM

ASPIDISTRA'S CAREER. London, Hutchinson, 1936. 320p [BM

BLUE JAY. New York, Reynolds, 1905. 378p [BM LC

BOUNDARY HOUSE. London, Hutchinson, 1916. 324p [BM LC OTMC

COMEDY CORNER. London, Hutchinson, 1920. 288p [BM

EDGAR CHIRRUP. New York, Putnam, 1915. 362p [BM LC OTMC

FELIX CHRISTIE. London, Methuen, 1912. 345p [BM

THE FRUITLESS ORCHARD. London, Hutchinson, 1922. 288p [BM

IN OUR STREET. London, Hutchinson, 1918. 256p [BM LC

THE LIFE OF ISOBEL ERNE. London, Hutchinson, 1922. 294p [BM OTMC

OPAL SCREENS. London, Hutchinson, 1937. 288p [BM

THE PEARL STRINGER. London, Methuen, 1913. 318p [BM
THE SCENT SHOP. London, Hutchinson, 1919. 288p [BM
A SPIRIT OF MIRTH. London, Methuen, 1910. 312p [BM LC
THE STORY OF VIRGINIA PERFECT. London, Methuen, 1909. 316p [BM
STRANGE ENCHANTMENT. London, Hutchinson, 1932. 288p [BM
VIRGINIA PERFECT. London, Methuen, 1911. 224p [*Cf.* THE STORY OF
 VIRGINIA PERFECT, 1909.] [EngCat
YOUNG LAETITIA. London, Hutchinson, 1939. 288p [BM

Weekes, Mrs. Mary Loretto, 1885–
ACADIAN BETRAYAL. Toronto, Burns & MacEachern, 1955. 301p
PAINTED ARROWS. New York, Nelson, 1941. 262p [Same title: Regina, School
 Aids & Text Book Pub. Co., 1949. 148p. — OOP] [BVa LC NBFU OTU
ROUND THE COUNCIL FIRES. Toronto, Ryerson, 1935. 113p [BVaU NBFU
 OTMC
THE SILVER PELT. London, Blackie, 1960. 174p

Wees, Frances Shelley (Johnson), 1902–
THE COUNTRY OF THE STRANGERS. Garden City, N.Y., Doubleday, 1960. 235p
DETECTIVES LTD. London, Eyre & Spottiswoode, 1933. 287p [First pub. as
 THE MAESTRO MURDERS, *q.v.*] [BM LC NBFU OOP
HONEYMOON MOUNTAIN. Philadelphia, Macrae Smith, 1934. 318p [LC OTMC
IT BEGAN IN EDEN. Philadelphia, Macrae Smith, 1936. 285p [BM LC NBFU
 OTU
THE KEYS OF MY PRISON. London, Jenkins, 1956. 190p
LOST HOUSE. Philadelphia, Macrae Smith, 1938. 285p [BM LC NBFU
THE MAESTRO MURDERS. New York, Mystery League, 1931. 286p [Pub. in
 England as DETECTIVES LTD., *q.v.*] [BM LC NBFU
MELODY UNHEARD. Philadelphia, Macrae Smith, 1950. 253p [BM LC NBFU
 OTMC
M'LORD, I AM NOT GUILTY. London, Jenkins, 1954. 192p
THE MYSTERY OF THE CREEPING MAN. Philadelphia, Macrae Smith, 1931. 330p
 [BM LC NBFU OTMC
ROMANCE ISLAND. Philadelphia, Macrae Smith, 1933. 296p [BM LC
SOMEONE CALLED MAGGIE LANE. Philadelphia, Macrae Smith, 1947. 244p [BM
 LC
A STAR FOR SUSAN. Philadelphia, Macrae Smith, 1940. 254p [BM LC OTMC
THIS NECESSARY MURDER. London, Jenkins, 1957. 190p
UNDER THE QUIET WATER. Philadelphia, Macrae Smith, 1949. 256p [BM LC
 NBFU OTMC
UNTRAVELLED WORLD. London, Eyre & Spottiswoode, 1936. 375p [BM OLU
WHERE IS JENNY NOW? London, Jenkins, 1958. 192p

Weller, Mrs. Evelyn L.
CARDINAL ROAD. Toronto, Burns & MacEachern, 1955. 254p

WINGS OF THE SPIRIT. Toronto, Musson, 1921. 244p [BM BVaU NBFU OTU QMSS

Wemyss, Prof., F.R.S.A.
THE HEATHER PRINCE; or, Scotland for Ever. Brockville, n.p., n.d. 50p [OOP

Weston, Garnett James, 1890–
CITIZENS—TO ARMS! London, Cassell, 1943. 287p [English title of THE MAN WITH THE MONOCLE.] [BM
DEAD MEN ARE DANGEROUS. New York, Stokes, 1937. 310p [BM LC NBFU OTMC
DEATH NEVER FORGETS. London, Hutchinson, 1935. 288p [BM
THE HIDDEN PORTAL. New York, Doubleday, 1946. 284p [LC NBFU OTMC
LEGACY OF FEAR. New York, Mill & Morrow, 1950. 245p [BM BViPA LC NBFU OONL
THE MAN WITH THE MONOCLE. New York, Doubleday, 1943. 245p [LC NBFU OTMC
MURDER IN HASTE. New York, Stokes, 1935. 310p [LC
MURDER ON SHADOW ISLAND. New York, Farrar & Rinehart, 1933. 309p [BM LC NBFU
POLDRATE STREET. New York, Messner, 1944. 256p [LC NBFU
THE UNDERTAKER DIES. London, Methuen, 1940. 288p [BM

Wetherald, Agnes Ethelwyn, 1857–1940
AN ALGONQUIN MAIDEN. A Romance of the Early Days of Upper Canada. By G. Mercer Adam and A. Ethelwyn Wetherald. Montreal, Lovell, 1887. 240p [BM BVaU LC NBFU OTU QMM

Wherry, Edith Margaret
JADE MOUNTAIN. London, Hutchinson, 1926. 268p [BM LC QMM
THE RED LANTERN. Being the Story of the Goddess of the Red Lantern Light. New York, Lane, 1911. 306p [BM LC OTMC QMM
THE WANDERER ON A THOUSAND HILLS. New York, Lane, 1917. 305p [BM LC QMM

White, Samuel Alexander, 1885–1956
AMBUSH. New York, Doubleday, 1920. 244p [BVa LC NBFU OTU
CALLED NORTHWEST. New York, Phoenix, 1943. 256p [LC OTU
THE CODE OF THE NORTHWEST. New York, Phoenix, 1940. 255p [BM BViPA LC NBFU OTU
EMPERY. A Story of Love and Battle in Rupert's Land. Toronto, Musson, 1913. 332p [Same as: LAW OF THE NORTH. A Story of Love and Battle in Rupert's Land. New York, Grosset, 1913. 332p] [BVaU LC NBFU OTU QMM
FLAMING FUR LANDS. Toronto, Ryerson, 1948. 153p [BVaU NBFU OTU QMBM
THE FOAMING FORE SHORE. New York, Doubleday, 1920. 248p [LC NBFU OTU

LAW OF THE NORTH. [See EMPERY, above.]

MAN SCENT. New York, Scribner, 1936. 286p [BM LC NBFU OTU

MORGAN OF THE MOUNTED. New York, Phoenix, 1939. 258p [BM LC NBFU OTU

NIGHTHAWK OF THE NORTHWEST. New York, Phoenix, 1938. 256p [BM LC OTU

NORTH OF THE BORDER. New York, Phoenix, 1940. 256p [BM LC NBFU OTU

NORTH OF THE LAW. New York, Doubleday, 1920. 250p [LC NBFU OTU

NORTH WEST CROSSING. New York, Phoenix, 1944. 256p [BM LC NBFU OTU

NORTHWEST LAW. New York, Phoenix, 1942. 256p [BViPA LC OTU

NORTHWEST PATROL. New York, Phoenix, 1943. 254p [BM LC OTU

NORTHWEST RAIDERS. New York, Phoenix, 1945. 256p [BM LC OTU

NORTHWEST WAGONS. New York, Phoenix, 1941. 254p [BM LC NBFU OTU

THE STAMPEDER. Toronto, Briggs, 1910. 275p [BM BVaU NBFU OTU

THE WILDCATTERS. A Tale of Cobalt. Toronto, Briggs, 1912. 219p [BM BVaU NBFU OTU

THE WONDERSTRANDS. Garden City, N.Y., Garden City Pub. Co., 1924. 120p [AEU BM OTU

Whitehouse, Francis Cecil, 1879–

PLAIN FOLKS. A Story of the Canadian Prairies. Ottawa, Graphic, 1926. 301p [BVaU NSHD OTP QMM

Whitell, Evelyn

THE BUILDER'S CROWN OF JEWELS. Los Angeles, Master Press, 1925. 142p [LC

A CALIFORNIA POPPY. The Story of a Child Healer. 4th ed. Los Angeles, Master Press, 1925. 33p [BViPA

CANADIAN TIM. Vancouver, Author, n.d. 101p [BViPA

EXTRAORDINARY MARY. Los Angeles, Master Mind Pub. Co., 1920. 72p [LC

THE GOLDEN AGE FAIRY TALES. Vancouver, Vancouver Bindery Ltd., 1942. 195p [BVaU

THE HEALING OF THE HAWAIIAN. A Story of the Hawaiian Islands. Los Angeles, Master Press, 1923. 155p [LC

THE LIGHT OF GAMBIER ISLAND. London, The Rally, n.d. 45p [BVaU

SHEKINAH. Los Angeles, De Vorss, 1937. 342p [LC NBSU

THE WOMAN HEALER. Los Angeles, Master Mind Pub. Co., 1920. 88p [BViPA LC

Wild, Roland Gibson, 1903–

NINE O'CLOCK GUN. London, Cassell, 1952. 223p

Wilkinson, Anne Cochran (Boyd), 1910–1961

SWANN & DAPHNE. Toronto, Oxford U. Press, 1960. 47p

Williams, Charles R., –1859?

THE RIVAL FAMILIES; or, Virtue and Vice, and THE STOLEN JEWELS; or, The Matchmaking Mamma. Cobourg, 1858. 147p [BibC

Williams, Flos (Jewell), 1893–
BROKEN GODS. Ottawa, Graphic, 1930. 304p [BVaU NBFU OTMC QMM
FOLD HOME. Toronto, Ryerson, 1950. 265p [NBFU OTMC
THE JUDGMENT OF SOLOMON. Toronto, Musson, 1925. 315p [BM BVaU LC
  NBFU OTMC
NEW FURROWS. A Story of the Alberta Foothills. Ottawa, Graphic, 1926. 303p
  [BVaU NBFU OTMC QMM

Williams, Frances de Wolfe (Fenwick)
THE ARCH-SATIRIST. Boston, Lothrop, 1910. 358p [LC NSHD OOP
A SOUL ON FIRE. New York, Lane, 1915. 316p [Pub. in England as THEODORA.
  A Soul on Fire. London, Lane, 1915.] [BM LC NSHD OOP QMM
VIKING'S REST. A Story of the Land of Evangeline. ... Toronto, Goodchild, 1924.
  301p [BM BVaU LC NSHD OTMC QMSS

Williams, Murray Edmund, 1877–1930
GOLDEN DIVIDENDS. Toronto, McClelland, 1927. 411p [BVaU NBFU OTMC
  QMM

Williamson, John, –1840
THE NARRATIVE OF A COMMUTED PENSIONER. By J.W. Montreal, Starke, 1838.
  320p [BVaU NSHD

Williamson, Owen Templeton Garrett, 1883–
MIKE MULLINS OF BOSTON CRICK. Toronto, Ryerson, 1953. xiv + 114p

Willis, Arthur Robert
NORTH OF THE YUKON. Toronto, Ryerson, 1956. 254p

Willis, T.K.
THE LETTERS OF A PRAIRIE DOG. Victoria, Colonist Print. & Pub. Co., 1945.
  65p [BViPA

Willison, Marjory (MacMurchy), –1938
THE CHILD'S HOUSE. A Comedy of Vanessa from the Age of Eight. By Marjory
  MacMurchy. Toronto, Macmillan, 1923. 242p [BM BVaU LC NBFU OTU
THE LONGEST WAY ROUND. Toronto, Macmillan, 1937. 325p [BVaU NBFU
  OTU QMBM

Willson, (Henry) Beckles, 1869–1942
DRIFT. 1894. [MOR'98
HAROLD. A Race Experiment. 1891. [MOR'98
THE LOSING OF VIREL. 1892. [MOR'98
REDEMPTION. A Novel. By Beckles Willson. New York, Putnam, 1924. 399p
  [BM LC OKQ

Wilson, Anna May
THE DAYS OF MOHAMMED. Elgin, Cook, 1897. 95p [LC
A STAR IN PRISON. A Tale of Canada. Elgin, Cook, 1898. 96p [BVaU LC OTU

Wilson, Clifford Parnell, 1902–
ADVENTURERS ALL. Tales of Forgotten Heroes in New France. Toronto,
Macmillan, 1933. 244p [BM BVaU OTMC NBFU QMBM

Wilson, Cornelius, –1909
RESCUED IN TIME. A Tale. Toronto, Briggs, 1894. 304p [OLU

Wilson, Ethel Davis (Bryant), 1890–
THE EQUATIONS OF LOVE: Tuesday and Wednesday; Lilly's story. Toronto,
Macmillan, 1952. 280p
HETTY DORVAL. Toronto, Macmillan, 1947. 116p [BM BVaU NBFU OTU
QMM
THE INNOCENT TRAVELLER. Toronto, Macmillan, 1949. 276p [BM BVaU LC
NBFU OTP
LILLY'S STORY. New York, Harper, 1952. 208p [First pub. as part of THE
EQUATIONS OF LOVE, *q.v.*]
LOVE AND SALT WATER. Toronto, Macmillan, 1956. ix + 202p
SWAMP ANGEL. Toronto, Macmillan, 1954. 215p

Wilson, Herbert Emerson, 1881–
GREED. Vancouver, Authors Agency Pub., n.d. 323p [BVaU OTU

Wilson, Lawrence Maurice, 1896–
THE CANADIAN MEMBER OF PARLIAMENT. A Satire. Montreal, Momus Press,
1958. 20p

Wilson, May
CARMICHAEL. By Anison North [pseud]. London, Ont., Weld, 1907. 338p
[Also: New York, Doubleday, 1907. 338p] [BM LC NBFU OTMC
THE FORGING OF THE PIKES. A Romance of the Upper Canadian Rebellion of
1837. By Anison North [pseud]. New York, Doran, 1920. 319p [BM BVaU
LC NBFU OTP

Wilson, Rev. Robert, 1833–1912
NEVER GIVE UP; or, Life in the Lower Provinces. ... Saint John, "Daily News,"
1878. 287p [BVaU NSHD
TRIED BUT TRUE. A Tale. By Mark Mapleton [pseud]. Saint John, "Daily News,"
1874. 293p [NSHD OOP

Winlow, Alice Maud (Dudley), 1885–
THE MORNIN'-GLORY GIRL. By Alice M. Winlow and Kathryn Pocklington.
Toronto, McClelland, 1920. 224p [BVaU NBFU OTU

Winslow, Elizabeth Bruce R.
ROSAMONDE OF MONTERRE. A Canadian Pastoral. Boston, Four Seas Co., 1923.
102p [LC NBFU

Wiseman, Adele, 1928–
THE SACRIFICE. A Novel. Toronto, Macmillan, 1956. 346p

Withrow, Rev. William Henry, 1839–1908

BARBARA HECK. A Tale of Early Methodism in America. Toronto, Methodist
  Mission Rooms, 1895. 238p [BM BVaU LC NSHD OTP

THE KING'S MESSENGER; or, Lawrence Temple's Probation. A Story of Canadian
  Life. Toronto, Methodist Book, 1879. 232p [Several later editions.] [BM
  BVaU NBFU OTP

LIFE IN A PARSONAGE; or, Lights and Shadows of the Itinerancy. London,
  Woolmer, 1885. 160p [Also: Toronto, Briggs, 1886. 214p] [BM BVaU OTP

NEVILLE TRUEMAN, THE PIONEER PREACHER. A Tale of the War of 1812.
  Toronto, Briggs, 1880. 244p [Also as: A VICTORY AND ITS COST; or, Neville
  Trueman, the Pioneer Preacher. ... London, Wesleyan Methodist Sunday School
  Union, 1893. 224p] [BM BVaU LC NBFU OTU QMM

VALERIA. A Tale of Early Christian Life in Rome. Toronto, Briggs, 1882. 243p
  [BM BVaU NBFU OTU QMM

A VICTORY AND ITS COST. ... [See under NEVILLE TRUEMAN. ...]

Wodson, Harry Milner, 1874–1952

THE LAD FELIX. A Tragedy of *Ne Temere*. By Henry Milner [pseud]. Toronto,
  Briggs, 1912. 302p [BM OTP

Wood, Edgar Allardyce, 1907–

COWBOY YARNS FOR YOUNG FOLK. By Kerry Wood [pseud]. Toronto, Copp
  Clark, 1951. 137p

THREE MILE BEND. By Kerry Wood [pseud]. Toronto, Ryerson, 1945. 170p [BVa
  LC NBFU OTU

WILD WINTER. By Kerry Wood [pseud]. Boston, Houghton Mifflin, 1954. 175p

WILLOWDALE. By Kerry Wood [pseud]. Toronto, McClelland, 1956. 216p

Wood, Esther, 1905–

BELINDA BLUE. New York, Longmans, 1940. 31p [BM LC

GREAT SWEEPING DAY. New York, Longmans, 1936. 158p [BM LC

THE HOUSE IN THE HOO. New York, Longmans, 1941. 32p [LC

PEDRO'S COCONUT SKATES. New York, Longmans, 1938. 191p [BM LC

PEPPER MOON. New York, Longmans, 1940. 32p [BM LC

SILK AND SATIN LANE. New York, Longmans, 1939. 225p [BM LC

SILVER WIDGEON. New York, Longmans, 1942. 227p [BM LC OOP

Wood, Ethel M.

SALVAGE. Victoria, Victoria Pub. Co., 1945. 54p [BViPA OTMC

Wood, Joanna E., –1919

A DAUGHTER OF WITCHES. Toronto, Gage, 1900. 342p [BM OTUV

FARDEN HA'. London, Hurst & Blackett, 1901. 340p [BM

JUDITH MOORE; or, Fashioning a Pipe. Toronto, Ontario Pub. Co., 1898. 240p
  [BM BVaU NBFU OTP QMM

THE LYNCHPIN SENSATION. [MOR'12

A MARTYR TO LOVE. New York, Town Topics, 1903. [AmCat
THE UNTEMPERED WIND. New York, Tait, 1894. 314p [LC OTU
UNTO THE THIRD GENERATION. [MOR'12
WHERE WATERS BECKON. [MOR'12

Woodley, Rev. Edward Carruthers, 1878–1955
CANADIAN LEGENDS. Montreal, Northern Electric Co., 1950. 32p [OONL
LEGENDS OF FRENCH CANADA. Toronto, Nelson, 1931. 105p [BM BVaU LC
   NBFU OTP QMM
UNTOLD TALES OF OLD QUEBEC. Toronto, Dent, 1949. 216p [BVaU NBFU
   OTP QMM

Woods, Alexandrina
LITTLE GRAY DOORS. Springfield, Mass., Bradley, 1926. 120p [LC

Wreford, Marjorie
LITTLE WILDING. Toronto, Nelson, 1948. 156p [OTMC

Wright, James Frederick Church, 1904–
ALL CLEAR, CANADA! By Jim Wright. Toronto, Copp Clark, 1944. 160p [LC
   NBFU OTP

Wrong, Edward Murray, 1889–1928
CRIME AND DETECTION. Ed. by ——. New York, Oxford U. Press, 1926. 394p
   [An anthology of stories by famous authors.] [BM LC NBFU OTU QMM

Yates, Abel
TRUTH AND FICTION. [Canada?] , 1898. 20p [BM
VIOLETS; or, Jasper Luckings. The Kanuck Landlord and California Gardiner. A
   Tragi-comedy in Four Acts. 1884. 47p [BCF OONL

Yeigh, Kate (Westlake), 1856–1906
A SPECIMEN SPINSTER. Toronto, Copp Clark, 1905. 314p [Also: Philadelphia,
   Griffith & Rowland, 1906.—-OTUV] [BM OTU

York, Eva Rose (Fitch), 1858–
CHAON ORR.Portions of his Autobiography. Belleville, Sun Print., [1896]. 113p
   [OTP
THE WHITE LETTER. A Tale of Retribution and Reward. Toronto, Briggs, 1903.
   107p [BM BVaU NSHD OTU

Young, Rev. Egerton Ryerson, 1840–1909
ALGONQUIN INDIAN TALES. Collected by ——. New York, Eaton & Mains, 1903.
   258p [BM BVaU LC OTU
THE BATTLE OF THE BEARS. ... Reminiscences of Life in the Indian Country.
   London, R. Culley, [1907?]. 318p [ACG BViPA OTUV

CHILDREN OF THE FOREST. A Story of Indian Love. New York, Revell, 1904. 282p [BM LC NBFU OOP

DUCK LAKE. New York, Eaton & Mains, 1905. 191p [BM BVaU LC NBFU OTMC

HECTOR MY DOG. His Autobiography. Boston, Wilde, 1905. 332p [BM LC OTMC

OOWIKAPUN; or, How the Gospel Reached the Nelson River Indians. London, Kelly, 1895. 162p [BM BViPA LC NBFU OTP

STORIES FROM INDIAN WIGWAMS AND NORTHERN CAMP-FIRES. Toronto, Briggs, 1893. 293p [BM BVaU LC NSHD OTU QMM

THREE BOYS IN THE WILD NORTH LAND, SUMMER. New York, Eaton & Mains, 1896. 260p [BM LC OTMC

WINTER ADVENTURES OF THREE BOYS IN THE GREAT LONE LAND. New York, Eaton & Mains, 1899. 377p [BM BVa LC OTMC

Young, Rev. Egerton Ryerson, 1869–

THE CAMP DOCTOR, AND OTHER STORIES. London, Religious Tract Soc., n.d. 320p [BM OTUV

JUST DOGS. Philadelphia, Sunday School Times Co., 1926. 151p [LC

THREE ARROWS. New York, Friendship Press, 1932. 183p [BM LC OTMC

WHEN THE BLACKFEET WENT SOUTH AND OTHER STORIES. London, Boy's Own Paper, 1936. 128p [Also: London, Lutterworth Press, 1954. 95p [BM BVaU OTMC

Young, Katherine A.

STORIES OF THE MAPLE LAND. Tales of the Early Days of Canada for Children. Toronto, Copp Clark, 1898. 120p [BM BVaU NSHD OTU

Young, Patricia Lucy, 1922–

BLACK DAHLIA GIRL. London, Ward Lock, 1958. 191p

THE DEVIL AND HIS APPLE. London, Ward Lock, 1945. 188p [BM

DOCKSIDE SYMPHONY. London, Ward Lock, 1947. 192p [BM

EAST OF BOW BELLS. London, Ward Lock, 1950. 221p [BM NBFU OPAL

FAR FLUNG SEED. London, Ward Lock, 1943. 223p [BM

FOOLS' PENCE. London, Ward Lock, 1946. 192p [BM

THE GALLANT OPPORTUNIST. London, Ward Lock, 1949. 215p [BM

GIPSIES MARSH. London, Ward Lock, 1944. 220p [BM

HALF PAST YESTERDAY. London, Ward Lock, 1959. 187p

HUNGER FOR LOVE. London, Ward Lock, 1952. 191p

IF A MAN LOVE. London, Ward Lock, 1948. 190p [BM

LONDON'S CHILD. London, Ward Lock, 1954. 189p

A MAN AND HIS COUNTRY. London, Ward Lock, 1953. 187p

NARROW STREETS. London, Ward Lock, 1942. 192p [BM

PRIDE OF PRINCES. London, Ward Lock, 1950. 192p [BM

SILENCE IS THE SINNER. London, Ward Lock, 1956. 189p

SPECIAL SHOES. London, Ward Lock, 1948. 207p [BM
A STORY THEY TELL. London, Ward Lock, 1947. 191p [BM
TOMORROW'S DREAMS. London, Ward Lock, 1952. 188p

Young, Phyllis (Brett)
PSYCHE. A Novel. Toronto, Longmans, 1959. 319p
THE TORONTONIANS. Toronto, Longmans, 1960. 319p

Young, Scott, 1918–
BOY ON DEFENSE. Toronto, McClelland, 1953. 246p
THE FLOOD. Toronto, McClelland, 1956. 222p
SCRUBS ON SKATES. Toronto, McClelland, 1952. 218p

Yule, Pamelia S. (Vining), 1825?–1897
ADA EMORY; or, The Sister's Bible. By Mrs. J.C. Yule. Philadelphia, Am. Baptist
  Pub. Co., [1876?]. [AmCat
UP HILL; or, Paul Sutherland's Progress. By Mrs. J.C. Yule. Philadelphia, Am.
  Baptist Pub. Co., 1887. 416p [LC

Zehnder, Meinrad, 1887–
ANTHONY MARTIN'S FIRST LOVE. A First Love Story of Switzerland. Toronto,
  Author, 1929. 307p [OTMC QMM
ON BROKEN CRUTCHES. A Psychological Novel. Toronto, Author, 1932. 469p
  [NBFU OTMC

Zero (pseud)
ONE MISTAKE. A Manitoban Reminiscence. By Zero [pseud]. Montreal, Canada
  Bank Note Co., 1888. 120p [BVaU OLU

DRAMA

Stage and radio plays

Aikins, Charles Carroll Colby, 1888–
THE GOD OF GODS. A Play in Three Acts. British Columbia, priv. print., 1919.
51p [BM NBFU OTU

Allan, Adam, 1757–1823
THE NEW GENTLE SHEPHERD. A Pastoral Comedy Originally Written in the Scotch
Dialect, by Allan Ramsay. Reduced to English by Lieutenant Adam Allan. To
which is annexed a Description of the Great Falls of the River Saint John. ...
London, Richardson, 1798. 75p [LC

Allan, Marguerite Martha, 1895–1942
ALL OF A SUMMER'S DAY. [DCB
SUMMER SOLSTICE. A Drama in One Act. By Martha Allan. Toronto, French, 1935.
36p [BM LC OTP
WHAT FOOLS WE MORTALS BE. [DCB

Allen, Joseph Antisell, 1814–1900
THE TRUE ROMANTIC LOVE-STORY OF COL. AND MRS. HUTCHINSON. A Drama in
Verse. London, Elliot Stock, 1883. 88p [BM BVaU OTU

Anderson, Clara (Rothwell), –1958·
.....AUNT SOPHIA SPEAKS. [Ottawa, Author, 19—?]. 24p [OH
A CHARACTER SKETCH ENTERTAINMENT, ENTITLED AFTERNOON TEA IN FRIENDLY
VILLAGE, 1862. Ottawa, J. Hope, 1912. 40p [BM OONL
A CHARACTER SKETCH ENTERTAINMENT. ... ENTITLED THE YOUNG VILLAGE
DOCTOR. Ottawa, J. Hope, 1915. 44p [BM OONL
THE JOGGSVILLE CONVENTION. A Play (for all women). Ottawa, Author, n.d. 36p
[AEU
... "LET MARY LOU DO IT." [Ottawa, 19—?]. 40p [OH
... MARRYING ANNE? [Ottawa, 19—?]. 48p [OH
"MARTHA MADE OVER." Ottawa, Pattison, 1923. 48p [AEU
THE MINISTER'S BRIDE. A Character Entertainment for Young People's Societies,
Bible Classes, and other Church Organizations. Ottawa, J. Hope, 1913. 38p
[AEU BM OONL
AN OLD-TIME LADIES' AID BUSINESS MEETING AT MOHAWK CROSS-ROADS. [A
Play]. Ottawa, J. Hope, 1912. 32p [AEU BM OONL

PLAY ENTITLED "THE YOUNG COUNTRY SCHOOLM'AM." Ottawa, J. Hope, 1920.
45p [AEU BM OTU

WANTED, A WIFE. [Ottawa, n.p., 19—?]. 41p [OH

Anderson, William E.

A ROMAN DRAMA IN FIVE ACTS ENTITLED LEO AND VENETIA. Pickering, Ont.,
Pickering Newsprint, 1895. [CAAE

Anonymous

DERMOT McMURROUGH. A Drama. [Anon] Toronto, Hunter Rose, 1882. [Bound
with THE FIREWORSHIPPERS. A Drama.] [OTP

THE FIREWORSHIPPERS. A Drama. [Anon] Toronto, 1882. [Bound with DERMOT
McMURROUGH. A Drama.] [OTP

THE LAND SWAP. A Satire. Montreal, 1875. 79p [OTP OTU

SIR JOHN AND SIR CHARLES; or, The Secrets of the Syndicate. Montreal, a
Syndicate, 1881. 8p [BVaU OTP QQL

Archibald, Edith Jessie (Mortimer), 1854–1938

THE TOKEN. A Play in Three Acts of the Old Days in Cape Breton. ... Halifax,
Royal Print., 1927. 56p [An earlier "suppressed edition" with title THE TOKEN.
A Homespun Yarn of Old Cape Breton Days in Three Tangled Skeins. [Ottawa,
Graphic], 1926. 66p is held by NSWA.] [BM NSHD OONL

Armstrong, Louis Olivier, 1874–

THE BOOK OF THE PLAY OF HIAWATHA, THE MOHAWK. ... [N.p.], 1909. 24p
[?An earlier ed.: HIAWATHA; or, Manabozho, or, Ojibway Indian Play. Montreal,
Author, 1901.] [BVaU LC

Ascher, Isidore Gordon, 1835–1914

CIRCUMSTANCES ALTER CASES. A Comedietta, in One Act. London, French, 1888.
20p [BM

LOVE, MARRIAGE AND HAPPINESS. By Isidore [pseud]. London, Digby & Long,
1894. 96p [BM

Ascher, Mrs. Isidore Gordon

PLAYS AND PROSE. London, Elliot Stock, 1929. 100p [BM

Baker, Ida Emma (Fitch), 1858–1948

DIALOGUES AND DRAMAS FOR SCHOOL AND HOME. Toronto, 1928. [Dora Hood
cat. 84

THE STORY OF CANADA. Toronto, Musson, 1927. 27p [BVaU OONL QMM

Baker, William King

GEORGE AND MARGARET FOX. London, Routledge, 1926. 118p [BM NSHD
OTU

Baxter, Arthur Beverley, 1891–1964

IT HAPPENED IN SEPTEMBER. A Play. London, Hutchinson, 1943. 120p [BM LC

Bengough, John Wilson, 1851–1923

THE BREACH OF PROMISE TRIAL BARDELL v PICKWICK. Adapted from *The Pickwick Papers* of Charles Dickens ... as presented by the Dickens Fellowship Company of Players at Toronto, May 9, 10, 15 and 28, 1907. Toronto, [Dickens Fellowship], 1907. 45p [AEU

BUNTHORNE ABROAD; or, the Lass that Loved a Pirate. Original Comic Opera in 2 Acts. Toronto, 1883. 28p [BVaU OONL

Benson, Nathaniel Anketell Michael, 1903–1966

THREE PLAYS FOR PATRIOTS. Ottawa, Graphic, 1930. 153p ["The Paths of Glory, 1812"; "The Patriot, 1837"; "The Leather Medal."] [BVaU NBFU OKQ QMM

Bicknell, Minnie Evans

RELIEF. A Play in One Act. Toronto, Macmillan, 1938. 28p [MW SRL

Bidwell, Barnabas, 1763–1833

THE MERCENARY MATCH. A Tragedy. By Barna [*sic*] Bidwell. New Haven, Meigs Bowen & Dana, [1784?] 57p [Reprinted: New York, McMurtrie, 1925. 57p] [BM LC NBFU

Birney, Earle, 1904–

TRIAL OF A CITY, and Other Verse. Toronto, Ryerson, 1952. 71p

Braden, Bernard, 1916–

THESE ENGLISH. Toronto, McClelland, 1948. 240p [OTP

Brewer, George McKenzie, 1889–

THE HOLY GRAIL. A Whitsuntide Mystery of the Quest of the Soul, Founded on Ancient Legends Derived from Various Sources. ... Montreal, Herald Press, 1933. 50p [BVaU LC OTP QMM

Brickenden, Catharine (McCormick), 1896–

A PIG IN A POKE. A Farce Comedy in Three Acts. Toronto, French, 1948. 72p [BVaU OTP

Brooke, Frances (Moore), 1724–1789

MARIAN. A Comic Opera in Two Acts. London, Longman, 1800. 31p [BM QMM

ROSINA. A Comic Opera in Two Acts. [Anon] London, Cadell, 1783. 46p [Many later editions.] [BM LC OTU QMM

THE SIEGE OF SINOPE. A Tragedy. London, Cadell, 1781. 71p [BM

VIRGINIA. A Tragedy. With Odes, Pastorals, and Translations. London, Author, 1756. 159p [BM

Broughall, George, 1861–1927

THE 90TH ON ACTIVE SERVICE; or, Campaigning in the North West. A Musical and Dramatic Burlesque in Two Acts, with an Introductory, Interlude and Final

Tableau. Written by Staff Sergeant Geo. Broughall. Songs by Major L. Buchan, Chaplain D.M. Gordon [and others]. Winnipeg, G. Bishop, 1885. 42p [Brown U NSWA

THE TEARFUL AND TRAGICAL TALE OF THE TRICKY TROUBADOUR; or, the Truant Tracked. A Topical and Tuneful Tradition Told in Travesty. A Four Act Burlesque. Winnipeg, Manitoba Free Press, 1886. 34p [BViPA

Buckskin (pseud)

THE PASSING OF THE BUFFALO. By Buckskin [pseud]. Vancouver, Selkirk, 1916. 47p [BM BVaU LC NSHD OTP SSU

Bullock-Webster, Llewelyn, 1879–

THE CURSE OF CHIRRA-POONJE. Victoria, B.C. Dramatic School, 1924. [T&C

HE PASSED THROUGH SAMARIA. A Religious Play in One Act. New York, Fitzgerald, 1932. 27p [BViP LC

REMORSE. A Play in One Act. Rock Island, Ill., Ingram, 1936. 24p [BVaU

THE SHADOW OF THE NILE. A Play in One Act. Toronto, French, 1935. 28p [BM BVaU LC OTP

Burkholder, Mabel Grace (Clare), 1881–

MR. SCROOGE ON MAIN STREET. A Pageant in 2 Scenes. Chicago, Hope Pub. Co., 1928. 16p [LC

A PAGEANT OF BETHLEHEM. In Four Scenes. Mount Hamilton, Author, 1922. 8p [BM

A PRINCE OF EGYPT. Mount Hamilton, Author, 1922. 16p [BM

THE TEN VIRGINS. In One Scene. Mount Hamilton, Author, 1922. 7p [BM

Burnette, Norman L.

ANGRY MEN. A Play in Four Episodes. By N.L. Burnette and Ella Monckton. Ottawa, Metropolitan Life Insurance Co., 1942. 42p [NSHPL

Burton, Franklin Wicher

ACHILLES. Toronto, U. of Toronto Press, 1928. 20p [The Jardine Prize for Poetry, 1927.] [BVaU NBFU OTU QMU

Buschlen, John Preston, 1888–

ASSEMBLY CALL. A Play by a Flyer's Dad. Hollywood, Murray & Gee, 1943. 102p [LC

THE PLEASURES OF THE WORLD. A Religious Comedy in Three Acts. By John Preston [pseud]. Lamoni, Ia., Herald, 1915. 64p [LC

TRUANTS. A Comedy in One Act. ... By John Preston [pseud]. Lamoni, Ia., Herald, 1915. 33p [LC

Bush, Thomas

SANTIAGO. A Drama in Five Acts. Toronto, Rollo & Adam, 1866. 55p [OTP

Cadogan, Mrs. Elda Magill, 1916–
THE INVISIBLE WORM. Durham, Ont., Durham House, 1953. 18p
THE OTHER HALF. Durham, Ont., Durham House, 1954. 23p
RISE AND SHINE. Durham, Ont., Durham Chronicle, 1952. 19p

Caldwell, James Ernest, 1862–1954
THE YELLOW BAG. A Drama [and Poems]. Ottawa, Thorburn, 1907. 74p [BM
  BVaU OTP

Callan, J.B.
A PAGEANT OF CANADIAN HISTORY. By J.B. Callan, T.C. Mulvihill, E.C. Scully.
  Toronto, French, 1938. 32p [Brown U OTP

Cameron, George Frederick, 1854–1885
LEO, THE ROYAL CADET. An entirely new and original Military Opera in Four Acts.
  Libretto by G.F. Cameron, music by Oscar F. Telgmann. Kingston, Henderson,
  [1889?]. 111p [OKQ

Campbell, Wilfred, 1858–1918
MORDRED AND HILDEBRAND. A Book of Tragedies. Ottawa, Durie, 1895. 168p
  [BVaU NBFU OTP
POETICAL TRAGEDIES. Toronto, Briggs, 1908. 316p [Contents: MORDRED;
  DAULAC; MORNING; HILDEBRAND.] [BM BVaU OTU NBFU QMM

Canadian Authors' Association. Montreal Branch
ONE-ACT PLAYS. By Canadian Authors. 19 Short Canadian Plays. Montreal, the
  Branch, 1926. 228p [BVaU NSHD OTP QMBM

Candidus, Caroli (pseud)
THE FEMALE CONSISTORY OF BROCKVILLE. A Melodrama in Three Acts.
  Brockville, Author, 1856. 60p [OTP

Card, Patricia
LIFE OF A TOY. Toronto, Author, 1940. 11p [CC

Card, Raymond William George, 1893–
GENERAL WOLFE. A One-Act Play. Toronto, Nelson, 1931. 28p [BVaU NBFU
  OTP
"ON GUARD FOR FREEDOM." An Empire Pageant. Toronto, Robinson Plays, 1940.
  7p [CC

Carleton, John Louis, 1861–1939
HILDEBRAND. A Drama in Five Acts. Saint John, Author, 1903. 74p [OTP
A MEDIEVAL HUN. A Five Act Historical Drama. Boston, Cornhill, 1921. 165p
  [AEU LC NSHD OTP
MORE SINNED AGAINST THAN SINNING. New York, DeWitt, [1882].

Carman, Bliss, 1861–1929
DAUGHTERS OF DAWN. A Lyrical Pageant or Series of Historic Scenes for Presenta-

tion with Music and Dancing. By Bliss Carman and Mary Perry King. New York, Kennerley, 1913. 118p [BVaU LC NSHD OKQ

EARTH DEITIES, AND OTHER RHYTHMIC MASQUES. By Bliss Carman and Mary Perry King. New York, Kennerley, 1914. 85p [BVa LC NSHD OKQ

Cecil-Smith, E.

EIGHT MEN SPEAK. A Political Act in Six Acts. By E. Cecil-Smith, Oscar Ryan, H. Francis, and Mildred Goldberg. Toronto, Progressive Arts, 1934. 43p [BVaU OTU

Chapman, Doris

MIDNIGHT AND CHRISTMAS EVE. Toronto, Tower Print., [1932?]. 11p [OONL

Chesnut, T. Herbert

NINA, OR A CHRISTMAS IN THE MEDITERRANEAN. A Nautical Comic Operetta in Two Acts. Written for the Harmonic Club to whom it is Respectfully Dedicated. Hamilton, Author, n.d. 23p [NSWA

Clarke, Wilfred John, 1896–1965

TWO ONE-ACT PLAYS. Entitled "St. Paul's Defence" and "A Plea of Judas." [Fredericton, Usbell, 1950.] 19p [NBFU

Coates, Carol

THE JADE HEART. New York, Junior Leagues of America, Inc., 1946. [mimeographed] [CanLit No. 48, p56

Cockings, George, –1802

THE CONQUEST OF CANADA; or, The Siege of Quebec. An Historical Tragedy of Five Acts. London, Cooke Haysell, 1766. 76p [BM LC OTP

Cohen, Maxwell Charles, 1926–

THE MEMBER FROM TROIS-RIVIERES. A One Act Play based on the Life of Ezekiel Hart—the First Jew to be elected to Public Office in Canada. Montreal, Canadian Jewish Congress, 1959. 17p [mimeographed]

Colquhoun, Kathryn E.

HIS BLONDE DILEMMA. Toronto, Robinson, 1937. 50p [mimeographed] [CC
A RUN FOR HIS MONEY. A Comedy in One Act. Toronto, Robinson, 1937. 28p [Brown U

Connor, Fredric Jarrett, 1920–

THE STATES. [Poetic Drama.] By Fredric Jarrett [pseud]. Shawbridge, Que., Hart Severance, 1949. 104p [AEU BVaU NSHD OTP

Conover, Dora Smith

THE CAT AND THE MUSHROOMS. Toronto, Robinson, 1937. 24p [mimeographed] [CC

Cooper, Douglas

WIDOWS LEARN FAST. A Farcical Comedy in Three Acts. Toronto, Robinson, 1950. 76p [AEU OTP

Corbett, Maurice William, 1900—

WOMAN CALLED "X". Franklin, Ohio, Eldridge, 1951. 95p

Cosentino, Nicholas

BIGGEST HALL IN BROOKLYN. Chicago, Dramatic Pub. Co., 1937. [CAAE

MOON OVER MULBERRY STREET. Chicago, Dramatic Pub. Co., 1936. 109p [BVaU

Coulter, John William, 1888—

DEIRDRE OF THE SORROWS. An Ancient and Noble Tale Retold by John Coulter for Music by Healey Willan. Toronto, Macmillan, 1944. 72p [BVaU NBFU OTP

THE HOUSE IN THE QUIET GLEN, and THE FAMILY PORTRAIT. [Two Dramas.] Toronto, Macmillan, 1937. 124p [BVaU NBFU OTP

... TRANSIT THROUGH FIRE. Written by John Coulter for Music by Healey Willan. Toronto, Macmillan, 1942. 8p [OTP

Cowan, John Bruce, 1882—

CANUCK. A Play in Three Acts. Vancouver, Rose, Cowan & Latta, 1931. 149p [BVaU QMM

NUMBER FIVE CHEYNE ROW. A Play in Four Acts. Vancouver, Rose, Cowan & Latta, 1950. 128p [BVaU OTP

Creighton, Anthony

EPITAPH FOR GEORGE DILLON. A Play in Three Acts. By John Osborne and Anthony Creighton. New York, Criterion Books, 1958. 94p

Crowell, Edwin, 1853—1926

CHEVROSE, THE HERMIT OF CAPE SABLE. One Act Play. Yarmouth, N.S., Yarmouth Herald, 1925. 27p [NSHD QMBM

Curzon, Mrs. Sarah Anne, 1833—1898

LAURA SECORD, THE HEROINE OF 1812, A Drama; And Other Poems. Toronto, Robinson, 1887. 215p [BM BVaU LC MWU NSHD OTP QMM

Cushing, Eliza Lanesford (Foster), 1794—

ESTHER, A Sacred Drama; with JUDITH, A Poem. Boston, Dowe, 1840. 118p [BM LC OLU

Dakin, Laurence B., 1904—

IRENEO. A Tragedy in Three Acts. Portland, Me., Falmouth Book House, 1936. 54p [BM LC NSHD

MARCO POLO. A Drama in Four Acts. Portland, Me., Falmouth Book House, 1936. 53p [Another ed., 1946.] [BM BVaU LC NSHD

PROMETHEUS, THE FIRE GIVER. A Lyrical Drama in Three Acts. Paris, Obelisk
Press, 1938. 84p [BM NSHD OTU

PYRAMUS AND THISBE. A Tragedy in Three Acts. Portland, Me., Falmouth Book
House, 1939. 38p [BM LC NSHD OTU

TANCRED: PRINCE OF SALERNO. Toronto, Dent, 1948. 58p [BM BVaU NBFU
OTU

Davidson, Ida Marion

THE ACADIAN TRAGEDY. Winnipeg, Manitoba Text Book Bureau, 1932. 28p
(Canadian History Plays) [OORD PC

ALEXANDER MACKENZIE. Winnipeg, Manitoba Text Book Bureau, 1932. 28p
(Canadian History Plays) [BViPA OORD

CANADIAN HISTORY PLAYS. Illus. by Evelyn Gowanlock. Winnipeg, Manitoba
Text Book Bureau, 1929–1932. 6v [Contents: 1 "Alexander Mackenzie";
2 "The Capture of Quebec" and "Madeline de Vercheres"; 3 "Gentlemen
Adventurers"; 4 "Lord Selkirk"; 5 "Sir Isaac Brock" and "Laura Secord";
6 "The Acadian Tragedy."] [OH

GENTLEMEN ADVENTURERS. Winnipeg, Manitoba Text Book Bureau, 1932. 36p
[ACG OORD PC

LORD SELKIRK. Winnipeg, Manitoba Text Book Bureau, 1932. 48p [BVaU OTP
PC

Davidson, True, 1901–

CANADA IN STORY AND SONG. A Pageant. Toronto, Dent, [1927]. 16p [BVaU
NBS OLU

LA CLAIRE FONTAINE. Toronto, Author, n.d. 13p [mimeographed] [OTU

Davies, Robertson, 1913–

AT MY HEART'S CORE. Toronto, Clarke Irwin, 1950. 91p [BVaU NSHD OONL

EROS AT BREAKFAST, AND OTHER PLAYS. ... Toronto, Clarke Irwin, 1949. 129p
[BVaU LC NSHD OKQ

FORTUNE MY FOE. Toronto, Clarke Irwin, 1949. 99p [BVaU NBFU OTU

A JIG FOR THE GYPSY. Toronto, Clarke Irwin, 1954. 98p

A MASQUE OF AESOP. Toronto, Clarke Irwin, 1952. 47p

OVERLAID. A Comedy. Toronto, French, 1948. 24p [BVaU OTU

SHAKESPEARE FOR YOUNG PLAYERS. A Junior Course. Toronto, Clarke Irwin,
1942. 255p [AEU NBSaM OONL

Davin, Nicholas Flood, 1843–1901

THE FAIR GRIT; or, The Advantages of Coalition. A Farce. Toronto, Belford, 1876.
35p [BM MWU NSHD OTU

De La Roche, Mazo, 1879–1961

COME TRUE. A Play. Toronto, Macmillan, 1927. 47p [BVaU NBFU OTU QMM

LOW LIFE. A Comedy in One Act. Toronto, Macmillan, 1925. 37p [BVaU NBFU
OKQ

LOW LIFE AND OTHER PLAYS. Boston, Little Brown, 1929. 109p [BVaU LC NBFU OKQ

THE RETURN OF THE EMIGRANT. Boston, Little Brown, 1929. 34p [BM BVaU LC

WHITEOAKS. A Play. Boston, Little Brown, 1936. 124p [Also: London, Fox, n.d. 68p] [BM BVaU LC OTU

Denison, Merrill, 1893–

BROTHERS IN ARMS. A Play in One Act. New York, French, 1923. 27p [BM BVaU LC NBFU OTU

HAVEN OF THE SPIRIT. A Play in One Act. New York, Dramatists Play Service, 1939. 34p [BM BVaU LC

HENRY HUDSON AND OTHER PLAYS. Six Plays for the Microphone from the Romance of Canada Series. ... Toronto, Ryerson, 1931. 183p [BVaU LC NSHD OTU

ON CHRISTMAS NIGHT. A Play in One Act. London, French, 1934. 26p [BM LC

THE PRIZE WINNER. A Comedy in One Act. New York, Appleton, 1928. 35p [BM LC OLU

THE UNHEROIC NORTH. Four Canadian Plays. Toronto, McClelland, 1923. 183p [BM BVaU NSHD OKQ

THE U.S. VS. SUSAN B. ANTHONY. A Play in One Act. New York, Dramatists Play Service, 1941. 29p [LC

Devlin, Edward Wade

ROSE LATULIPPE. A Canadian Folk-Play in One Act. Toronto, French, 1935. 32p [BM BVaU OTP

Dickie, Donalda James, 1883–

CANADIAN SCHOOL PLAYS. By D.J. Dickie and Others. Toronto, Dent, 1931. 158p [BVaU OTU

Dixon, Frederick Augustus, 1843–1919

FIFINE, THE FISHER MAID; or, The Magic Shrimps. By F.A.D. Ottawa, Woodburn, 1877. 50p [NSHPL OLU

LITTLE NOBODY. A Fairy Play. By F.A.D. Toronto, Adam & Stevenson, 1875. 37p [AEU OTUV

MAIDEN MONA THE MERMAID. A Fairy Play for Fairy People. By F.A.D. Toronto, Belford, 1877. 42p [BVaU OTP QMSS

THE MAIRE OF ST. BRIEUX. An Operetta in One Act ... for H.E. the Countess of Dufferin's Private Theatricals ... Feb. 1875. Ottawa, [1875?]. 34p [Adelphi cat. 61

A MASQUE ENTITLED "CANADA'S WELCOME." Shown Before His Excellency the Marquis of Lorne and Her Royal Highness the Princess Louise, on Feb. 24th, 1879, at the Opera House. Written by Frederick A. Dixon; composed by Arthur A. Clappe. Ottawa, Maclean Roger, 1879. 19p [BVaU MWU NSHPL OTP

PIPANDOR. A Comic Opera. Ottawa, Citizen Print., 1884. 55p [AEU OOP

YE LAST SWEET THING IN CORNERS. Being ye Faithful Drama of ye Artists' Vendetta. By F.A.D. Philadelphia, Duncan & Hall, [1880]. 66p [OONL

Doherty, Brian, 1906–

FATHER MALACHY'S MIRACLE. A Play in Three Acts. New York, Random House, 1938. 201p [Dramatization of Bruce Marshall's novel of the same title.] [BM BVaU LC OLU

Dollard, Rev. James Bernard, 1872–1946

CLONTARF. An Irish National Drama in Four Acts. Dublin, Catholic Truth Soc., 1920. 48p [Also with imprint: Toronto, 1915. See T&C] [OH

Doughty, Arthur George, 1860–1936

BONNIE PRINCE CHARLIE. ... An Original Comic Opera in Two Acts. Montreal, Desbarats, 1892. 15p [BM

Dowsett, Rev. Geoffrey Nevil

THE BETRAYAL. A Passion Play in Three Acts. New York, French, 1942. 94p [BM LC OTP

Duvar, John Hunter-, 1830–1899

DE ROBERVAL, A Drama; also THE EMIGRATION OF THE FAIRIES, and THE TRIUMPH OF CONSTANCY, A Romaunt. Saint John, McMillan, 1888. 192p [BVaU LC MWU NSHD OKQ

THE ENAMORADO. A Drama. Summerside, Graves, 1879. 120p [BVaU NSHD OTP QMM

FIN DE SIECLE. A Comedy. [MOR'98

Edgar, Mary Susanne, 1889–

THE CHRISTMAS TREE BLUEBIRD. New York, Woman's Press, 1920. 19p [BVaU

THE WAYSIDE PIPER. New York, Nat'l Board Y.W.C.A., 1915. 27p [LC NSHD

Edgerton, E. Maud

RUBY OF MELCHIOR. Toronto, Robinson, 1937. 15p [UTQ'38

Edmond, Reby

GUEST HOUSE, VERY EXCLUSIVE. A Christmas Play in One Act. New York, French, 1937. 34p [BM LC

THE SPIRIT OF THE THING. A Comedy in One Act. New York, Fitzgerald, 1934. 34p [BVaU

Fairbairn, Archibald Macdonald Duff

PLAYS OF THE PACIFIC COAST. Toronto, French, 1935. 111p [Contains: EBB-TIDE, THE WAR DRUMS OF SKEDANS, THE TRAGEDY OF TANOO, and A PACIFIC COAST TRAGEDY.] [BVaU OTU QMM

Fairbairn, Robert Edis, 1880–1951
WHEN THE KING SMILED. A Drama of the Resurrection in Four Scenes. Toronto, French, 1935. 24p [BM BVaU OTP

Farquharson, Mary Frederica (McLean)
SURE OF A FOURTH. A Satirical Comedy in One Act. Toronto, French, 1935. 27p [BM BVaU LC OTP

THEY MEET AGAIN. A Comedy in One Act. Toronto, Macmillan, 1938. 26p [BVi QMM

Ferguson, James P., 1900–
COURAGE, MR. GREENE. A Comedy. Toronto, French, 1936. 20p [BM BVaU OTU

Finch, Robert Duer Claydon, 1900–
A CENTURY HAS ROOTS. A Masque performed at Hart House Theatre to commemorate the One Hundredth Anniversary of the Foundation of University College, Toronto, 1853. Toronto, U. of Toronto Press, 1953. 28p

Fowke, Helen Shirley, 1914–
A GIFT FOR BENJAMIN. A One-Act Christmas Play for Children. Fredericton, Brunswick Press, 1960. 16p

Fraser, Donald Andrew, 1875–1948
THE POTTER'S DREAM. A Playlet for Young Folks. Denver, Eldridge Entertainment House, 1928. 9p [LC

Fraser, Hermia (Harris), 1902–
HOB'S HEAVEN. Denver, Eldridge Entertainment House, 1937. 8p [LC

Freund, Philip, 1909–
MARIO'S WELL. A One Act Comedy. New York, French, 1937. 18p [BM LC

PRINCE HAMLET. A Play. New York, Bookman Associates, 1953. 70p [BVaU

Fuller, William Henry
H.M.S. "PARLIAMENT"; or, The Lady who Loved a Government Clerk. [Anon] Ottawa, Citizen Pub. Co., 1880. 37p [BVaU OTP

THE UNSPECIFIC SCANDAL. An Original, Political, Critical and Grittical Extravaganza, performed at the great Dominion Theatre, Ottawa, in the year of grace 1873. [Anon] Ottawa, Woodburn, 1874. 19p [BVaU OOA

Gagnieur, Elizabeth
CONFLICT AND TRIUMPH. A Drama in Three Acts. Montreal, Canadian Messenger Press, 1908. 339p [QMBM

Garcia, A.E. de
CANADA, FAIR CANADA. A Modern Romantic Tragedy. Montreal, Montreal
   Shorthand Institute & Business College, 1902. 100p [BM Brown U LC

Garnier, John Hutchison, 1810? [1823?]–1898
PRINCE PEDRO. A Tragedy. Toronto, Belford, 1877. 158p [BVaU OTU QMM

Gibbon, John Murray, 1875–1952
THE MAN COMES DOWN FROM THE MOON. Musical Playlet based on "Northland
   Songs." Toronto, Thompson, 1937. 15p [OTP
THE ORDER OF GOOD CHEER. From the French version of Louvigny de Montigny.
   Canadian-historical Ballad Opera of the First Settlers in Canada. Reconstructed
   by ——. Toronto, Dent, 1929. 30p [Brown U

Goulding, Dorothy Jane, 1923–
THE MASTER CAT AND OTHER PLAYS. Toronto, Dent, 1955. 138p

Gowan, Elsie Park (Young), 1905–
BREECHES FROM BOND STREET. A Comedy in One Act. New York, S. French,
   1952. 24p
SHOP IN TOAD LANE. Edmonton, Alberta Co-operative Wholesale Assoc., 1940.
   16p [UTQ'41

Gray, James Orman
ANTICHRIST. Vancouver, Thomson, 1912. 106p [At head of title: The Plays of
   James Orman Gray, L.L.B.] [BM BVaU

Green, Harry A.V.
THE DEATH OF PIERROT. A Trivial Tragedy in One Act. Winnipeg, Community
   Players, 1923. 25p [MWU OTU

Greene, Barnet M.
"WOMAN–THE MASTERPIECE," A Play in Four Episodes; and "THE GOD-
   INTOXICATED MAN," A Play in Three Acts. Toronto, Ryerson, 1923. 148p
   [BVaU NSHD OTU QMM

Grey, Francis William, 1860–1939
FOUR PLAYS. LOVE'S PILGRIMAGE, A Passiontide Mystery in a Prologue and Three
   Acts; BISHOP AND KING, Blessed Oliver Plunkett and Charles II; THE
   BRIDEGROOM COMETH, A Morality Play in One Act; THE VALIANT WOMAN, An
   Epiphany Masque. Ottawa, Miller, 1931. [Separate pagination.] [OOP
SIXTEEN-NINETY. A Series of Historical Tableaux. Ottawa, Mortimer, 1904. 42p
   [QMM

Groves, Edith (Lelean), 1870–1931
BRITANNIA. [A Play.] Toronto, McClelland, 1917. 18p [AEU OTU
CANADA CALLS. A Timely Patriotic Play, Dedicated to the Children of Canada.
   Toronto, McClelland, 1918. 22p [BM NSWA

A CANADIAN FAIRY TALE. A Patriotic Play. By Edith Lelean. Toronto, Briggs, 1916. 31p [BM Brown U BVaU

THE KEY OF JACK CANUCK'S TREAURE-HOUSE. Toronto, Briggs, 1916. 16p [BM BVaU

THE MAKING OF CANADA'S FLAG: A Patriotic Play. Toronto, Briggs, 1916. 20p [BM BVaU NSHPL OH

A PATRIOTIC AUCTION. Toronto, McClelland, 1918. 22p [OONL

THE WAR ON THE WESTERN FRONT. A Patriotic Play. Toronto, Briggs, 1916. 23p [BM Brown U BVaU

THE WOOING OF MISS CANADA. Toronto, McClelland, 1917. 32p [BM BVaU OTP

Gustafson, Ralph Barker, 1909–

ALFRED THE GREAT. London, Joseph, 1937. 119p [BM BVa NSHD OTU QMM

Hailey, Arthur, 1920–

CLOSE-UP ON WRITING FOR TELEVISION. [Six Plays.] Garden City, N.Y., Doubleday, 1960. 307p

Hammond, George Arthur

THE CROWNING TEST. A Drama. Kingsclear, N.B., Lahstok Rustic Press, 1901. 92p [NSWA

JASSOKET AND ANEMON. A Ramble. Kingsclear, N.B., Lahstok Pub., 156p [NBFU OTP

STARBORN THE CONJURER. A Dramatic Poem. Kingsclear, N.B., 1903. [Various pagings] [NSWA

A TRIAD. Lahstok, N.B., Rural Press, 1887. 3 parts in one. [Pt. 1: The Lake of Tears, an Allegory; Various Poems. Pt. 2: On the Strand, a Fable; Golden Circle Dirges. Pt. 3: Knud Iverson, a Dramatic Sketch; Twilight Cimmerian; Autumnal Musings; The Loiterer, a Fragment.] [OTP

THE TWO OFFERINGS. A Drama. [LAMECH. A Drama.] Kingsclear, N.B., Lahstok Rural Press, 1890. [Various pagings] [NSWA

Hammond, Josephine, 1876–

EVERYWOMAN'S ROAD. A Morality of Woman, Creator, Worker, Waster, Joy-Giver, and Keeper of the Flame. New York, Kennerley, 1911. 55p [BVaU LC

Harper, John Murdoch, 1845–1919

CHAMPLAIN. A Drama in Three Acts. With an Intro. entitled "Twenty Years and After," and a Chapter on "Champlain the Explorer." Toronto, Trade Pub. Co., 1908. 296p [BM BVaU LC NSHD OKQ

Harris, Walter Eric, 1889–

SUCH HARMONY. A Play in One Act. Toronto, French, 1936. 37p [OTP

TWENTY-FIVE CENTS. Toronto, French, 1936. 32p [NSHD OTP

Harrison, Susie Frances (Riley), 1859–1935
FOUR BALLADS AND A PLAY. By "Seranus" [pseud]. N.p., 1933. 18p [OTP

Heavysege, Charles, 1816–1876
COUNT FILIPPO; or, The Unequal Marriage. A Drama in Five Acts. By The Author
of SAUL [pseud]. Montreal, Author, 1860. 153p [BM BVaU LC NBFU OKQ
SAUL. A Drama. In Three Parts. [Anon] Montreal, Rose, 1857. 315p [Second ed.,
rev.: Montreal, 1859. 328p] [Also pub. under title: SAUL: A Drama in Three
Parts. By Charles Heavysege. A new and rev. ed. Boston, Fields Osgood, 1869.
436p] [BM BVaU LC MWU NSHD OTU QMM

Henderson, J. Duff
ALVIRA alias ORCA. The Nineteenth Century Story. [Also some Poems and some
Dramas.] Toronto, Hunter Rose, 1899. 279p [BCF OTP

Hensley, Sophia Margaret (Almon), 1866–
PRINCESS MIGNON. A Musical Play in Three Acts. Founded on One of Andrew
Lang's Fairy Tales. Written by Almon Hensley. New York, Kenworth, 1900. 30p
[AEU LC

Herman, Alan, 1916–
DOUBLE IMAGE. A Play in three acts. By Roger MacDougall and Ted Allan [pseud].
Based on a story by Roy Vickers. London, French, 1957. 76p
THE MONEY MAKERS. By Ted Allan [pseud]. Trans. into Russian by V. Abramova.
Moscow, Iskusstvo, 1958. 130p [Title and text in Russian. English title from t.p.
verso. Translation of Russian Title: Mr. Finch Makes Money. First produced
Toronto, 1953. Rewritten and produced, London, 1955, under title: "The Ghost
Writers."]

Hezzelwood, Oliver, 1861–1933
POEMS. And a Play: "THE INVISIBLE URGE." Toronto, Ontario Press, 1926. 168p
[BVaU OKQ QMM

Hill, Thomas, –1860
THE PROVINCIAL ASSOCIATION. A Tragi-Comedy in Verse. Fredericton, 1845.
[NBB

Hitchins, William English, 1910–
"EVEN OUR FAITH." A Pageant depicting the Story of the Anglican Church in
Canada from Pioneer Days. Toronto, General Board of Religious Education,
[1952?]. xiii + 62p

Hoare, John Edward, 1886–
CASH AS CATCH CAN. A Comedy of Sicily in Two Scenes. London, French, 1937.
27p [BM LC

RED PLANET. By —— and John Lloyd Balderston. New York, French, 1931. 33p [PC

THE SHOEMAKERS OF SYRACUSE. A Play in One Act. London, French, 1948. 36p [BM LC

Hooke, Hilda Mary, 1898–

ONE ACT PLAYS FROM CANADIAN HISTORY. Toronto, Longmans, 1942. 157p [BVaU LC OTP

Hooper, Dora M.

WHERE THE BUFFALO ROAM. New York, French, 1940. [24p] [LC

Ingraham, Mary (Kinley), 1874–1949

ACADIA. A Play in Five Acts. Wolfville, Davidson, 1920. 19p [BVaU NBFU OTP

Irvine, William, 1885–1962

THE BRAINS WE TRUST. A Play in Three Acts. Toronto, Nelson, 1935. 48p [BVi OTP

YOU CAN'T DO THAT. A Play in Three Acts. Toronto, Nelson, 1936. 48p [OTP

Jacob, Fred, 1882–1926

ONE THIRD OF A BILL. Five Short Canadian Plays. Toronto, Macmillan, 1925. 140p [BVaU LC NSHD OTU

Jacobson, Percy Nathanial, 1886–1952

THE ACCIDENT. Rock Island, Ill., Ingram, 1937. 12p [CC

AND SENDETH RAIN. Rock Island, Ill., Ingram, 1934. [CC

NOT ONLY THE GUPPY. Rock Island, Ill., Ingram, 1934. [CC

RIDICULOUS AND SUBLIME. A Comedy in One Act. Boston, Baker, 1948. 38p [AEU

THE USUAL THREE. Comedy-Drama. Toronto, French, 1948. 20p [AEU OTP

Jones, Emrys Maldwyn, 1905–

CANADIAN SCHOOL PLAYS. Series One. Toronto, Ryerson, 1948. 201p [BVa LC OTU

Jones, James Edmund, 1866–1939

SCENES FROM DICKENS. Arranged by the Dickens Fellowship Players of Toronto. Ed. by ——. Toronto, McClelland, 1923. 335p [BVaU OTU

Joudry, Patricia, 1921–

TEACH ME HOW TO CRY. Drama in Three Acts. New York, Dramatists Play Service, 1955. 78p

Keating, James W.
THE SHRIEVALTY OF LYNDEN. A Tragedy in One Act. St. Catharines, Sherwood,
   1889. 23p [AEU OTP

Kerr, William Hastings, 1826–1888
THE KIDNAPPERS. A Tragico-Comical Melodrama in Ten Acts. [Anon] Montreal,
   [1867?]. 8p [BVaU NSWA OTU QMSS

Kirkconnell, Watson, 1895–
THE MOD AT GRAND PRE. A Nova Scotian Light Opera in Two Acts. Wolfville,
   priv. print., 1955. 35p

Knight, Mary A.
PAGEANTS AND PLAYS. Four Plays which have been Awarded Prizes by the Imperial
   Order of the Daughters of the Empire. [Three plays by Mary A. Knight; one play
   by Marguerite Letson.] Toronto, Nelson, 1935. 57p [PC

Knister, Raymond, 1900–1932
YOUTH GOES WEST. A Play in One Act. [In *Poet Lore,* 39: 582–95. Boston,
   1928.] [LC

Knowles, A. Beatrice
THE SAINT. A Play in One Act. New York, French, 1936. 32p [AEU OTP

Knox, Alexander, 1907–
OLD MASTER. A Comedy. London, Constable, 1940. 128p [BM Brown U OLU

Lambie, Alexander, 1870–
THE LADY OF LADORE. A Play-form Tale of Derwentdale. Vancouver, Author,
   1928. 220p [BM BVaU NBFU

Lane, Wilmot Burkmar, 1872–
QUEBEC. Toronto, Macmillan, 1936. 40p [NSHD OTP

Lanigan, John Alphonsus, 1854–1919
EITHNE; or, The Siege of Armagh. A Drama in Four Acts. Buffalo, Express Steam
   Print., 1872. 49p [LC

Leacock, Stephen Butler, 1869–1944
"Q". A Farce in One Act. By Stephen Leacock and Basil Macdonald Hastings. New
   York, French, 1915. 23p [BM LC

Lesperance, John Talon, 1838–1891
ONE HUNDRED YEARS AGO. An Historical Drama of the War of Independence in 4
   Acts and 20 Tableaux. [Anon] Montreal, "La Minerva" Steam Presses, 1876.
   108p [LC

Llwyd, Rev. John Plummer Derwent, 1861–1933
THE VESTAL VIRGIN. A Dramatic Poem. Halifax, 1920. 58p [BM LC OOP

Macbeth, Madge Hamilton (Lyons), 1878–1965
CURIOSITY REWARDED. A Dialogue between Gilbert Knox and the Curious Public.
Ottawa, Graphic, 1926. 12p [NBFU OTU
THE GOOSE'S SAUCE. A Comedy in One Act. Toronto, French, 1935. 20p [BM
LC OTP

McConkey, Hugh T., 1922–
TRILOGY IN A GARDEN. A Play for Voices in Three Parts. New York, Exposition,
[1955]. 58p

MacDonald, Wilson
IN SUNNY FRANCE. A Musical Comedy. Moose Jaw, 1924. 48p [OKQ

Macdonell, Amice Anna Botham
HISTORICAL PLAYS FOR CHILDREN. First Series. London, Allen, 1909. 249p [BM
LC
HISTORICAL PLAYS FOR CHILDREN. Second Series. London, Allen, 1910. 272p
[BM LC
THE NAME ON THE ROCK. A Play in Three Acts. London, Allen & Unwin, 1933.
61p [BM BViPA LC
THE SACRED FIRE. A Morality Play for the League of Nations. In One Act.
Oxford, Blackwell, 1924. 24p [BM
THE STORY OF THE ARMADA. A Play for Children. In Three Acts. London, League
of the Empire, 1908. 32p [BM

McDonnell, William, 1814–1900
MARINA, THE FISHERMAN'S DAUGHTER. An Operatic Romance in Three Acts.
Toronto, Strange & Co., 1883. 48p [OTP

MacDougall, James Brown, 1871–1950
MISS CANADA'S RECEPTION. Toronto, McClelland, 1917. 12p [OTU

McEvoy, Bernard, 1842–1932
THE SPRATTS. A Comedy in Three Acts. Montreal, Southam, 1927. 28p [BVaU

McGee, Thomas D'Arcy, 1825–1868
SEBASTIAN; or, The Roman Martyr. A Drama. New York, 1861. 52p [OOP

McIlwraith, Jean Newton, 1859–1938
PTARMIGAN. ... [Comic Opera]. Hamilton, Spectator, 1895. 27p [OTU

MacIntosh, Claire (Harris), 1882–
TWO PLAYS FOR CHILD ACTORS. (FLOWERS, for six little girls; THE TEA PARTY AT
THE SHOE.) 1934. 15p [NSHD

MacKay, Isabel Ecclestone (Macpherson), 1875–1928
GOBLIN GOLD. A Comedy Drama in Three Acts. New York, French, 1933. 89p
  [LC OTP
THE LAST CACHE. ... New York, French, 1927. 31p [BVaU
THE SECOND LIE. A Play in One Act. [In CANADIAN PLAYS FROM HART HOUSE
  THEATRE. Ed. by Vincent Massey. Toronto, Macmillan, 1926. V. 1,
  pp. 125–51.] [BVaU NBFU OTP QMM
TREASURE. A Play in One Act. New York, French, 1927. 25p [BM BVaU OTP
  QMM
TWO TOO MANY. A Comedy in Three Acts. Philadelphia, Penn. Pub. Co., 1927.
  78p [A 3-act play which won third prize of $250 from the Penn. Pub. Co., of
  Philadelphia in 1927.] [BVaU OKQ

MacKay, Louis Alexander, 1901–
THE FREEDOM OF JEAN GUICHET. A Play in Three Acts. [In CANADIAN PLAYS
  FROM HART HOUSE THEATRE. Ed. by Vincent Massey. Toronto, Macmillan,
  1927. V. 2, pp. 69–129.] [BVaU NBFU OTP QMM

Mackenzie, James Bovell, 1851–1919
THAYENDANEGEA. An Historico-Military Drama. Toronto, Briggs, 1898. 179p
  [Thayendanegea–Joseph Brant, Sachem of the Mohawks.] [BVaU NBFU OTP
  QMSS

MacKenzie, Malcolm
CANADA FOREVER; or, Home is the Roamer. Boston, Baker's Plays, 1950. 77p
  [BVaU

Maclennan, J. Munro, 1900–
SEVEN CAESARS' RANSOMS. A Dramatic Poem in 3 Acts. New York, Exposition
  Press, 1952. 149p

Macphail, Andrew, 1864–1938
THE LAND. A Play of Character. Montreal, University Magazine, 1914. 82p [BM
  QMM

Mahon, James, 1910–
THE IMAGINARY LINE. A Mystical Comedy. Toronto, Author, 1946. 56 leaves.
  [CC

Mair, Charles, 1838–1927
TECUMSEH. A Drama. Toronto, Hunter Rose, 1886. 205p [A second ed., with
  other poems: Toronto, Briggs, 1901.] [BM BVaU MWU NBFU OTP QMBM

Mary Agnes, Sister [dramatist]
THE ARCH OF SUCCESS. A Dialogue for Commencement Day. By S.M.A. Winnipeg,
  St. Mary's Academy, 1919. 11p [BM

THE BEST GIFT. (A May Festival. The Divine Guest. The Birthday of the Divine
Child. Pearls for the Missions. Uncle Jerry's Silver Jubilee. Winnipeg, Sister Mary
Agnes, 1924. 3pts. [BM

BETTER THAN GOLD. A Play for Girls. By S.M.A. Winnipeg, 1922. 27p [BM

THE EMPRESS HELENA; or, The Victory of the Cross. An Historical Drama for
Girls. By S.M.A. Winnipeg, 1920. 27p [BM

AN IRISH PRINCESS. (Also: The Step Sisters. Old Friends and New.) By S.M.A.
Winnipeg, St. Mary's Academy, 1917. 3pts. [BM

THE LAST OF THE VESTALS. (Also: At the Court of Isabella. Those Shamrocks
from Ireland. A Patriot's Daughter. Choosing a Model.) By S.M.A. Winnipeg,
1914. 177p [BM

MARY MAGDALEN, AND OTHER PLAYS. By S.M.A. Winnipeg, St. Mary's Academy,
1918. 4pts. [BM

MOTHER'S BIRTHDAY. By S.M.A. St. Boniface, Le Manitoba, 1921. 19p [BM

THE QUEEN OF SHEBA. A Biblical Drama. (Also: Christmas Guests. That
Millionaire's Daughter. A Shakespeare Pageant. Plans for The Holidays.)
By S.M.A. Winnipeg, St. Mary's Academy, 1915. 5pts. [BM

SENSE AND SENTIMENT. A School Play for Girls. By S.M.A. Winnipeg, 1920. 23p
[BM

ZUMA, THE PERUVIAN MAID; CROSS AND CHRYSANTHEMUM; SHORT PLAYS AND
RECITATIONS. [Three Pamphlets in one volume.] Winnipeg, St. Mary's Academy,
1922. 37 + 48 + 45p [BM OOP

Mason, Harold Campbell, 1895–
SMITH BROADENS OUT. A Play in Two Acts. Toronto, 1923. 30p [BM

Massey, Vincent, 1887–1967
CANADIAN PLAYS FROM HART HOUSE THEATRE. Ed. by ——. Toronto, Macmillan,
1926–27. 2v [BM BVaU NBFU OTP QMM

Maura, Sister (née Mary Power), 1881–1957
VIA VITAE. By a Sister of Charity [pseud]. London, Milford, 1923. 24p [LC

Merritt, Catharine Nina
"WHEN GEORGE III WAS KING." An Historical Drama in Three Acts. Toronto,
Rowsell & Hutchinson, 1897. 30p [BM BVaU

Middleton, Jesse Edgar, 1872–1960
PILGRIMS AND STRANGERS. A Picture in Two Lights. Toronto, Crocker, 1914.
39p [BM

Miller, Hanson Orlo, 1911–
"THIS WAS LONDON." [A Play in 3 Acts.] London, Ont., Author, 1955. 89p
[mimeographed]

Milligan, James Lewis, 1876–
JUDAS ISCARIOT. A Poetical Play. Toronto, Ryerson, 1929. 31p [NBFU OKQ

Milne, William Samuel, 1902–

THE FAILURE. One-Act Comedy. Toronto, Robinson, 1937. 24p [OTU

THE LAMPSHADE. A Guignol Piece in One Scene. Toronto, French, 1936. 19p
[BM LC OTP

Mitchell, Ronald Elwy

ANGELS AND SUCH. Comedy in One Act. New York, Dramatists Play Service,
1938. 29p [BM LC

BETTER DAYS. A Play in One Act. New York, French, 1934. 30p [BM LC

THE GOBLIN. A Welsh Comedy in One Act. New York, French, 1934. 23p [BM
LC

A HANDFUL OF SHEEP. A Comedy of North Wales, in One Act. New York, French,
1935. 24p [BM LC

HE THAT HOPS. A Play for Young Children. New York, French, 1935. 20p [BM
LC

THE HOLY DRAGON. A Play in One Act. New York, French, 1935. 22p [BM LC

A HUSBAND FOR BREAKFAST. Comedy in One Act. New York, Dramatists Play
Service, 1937. 32p [Also pub. as: A HUSBAND FOR BREAKFAST. A Comedy in
a Welsh Setting. London, French, 1937. 26p] [BM LC

THE MEDDLER IN MIRACLES. A One-Act Play. New York, French, 1936. 24p
[BM LC

NO BOOTS IN BED. A Comedy in Three Acts. New York, French, 1942. 102p [LC

PANIC OVER PORTERHOUSE. A Comedy in One Act. London, French, 1937. 30p
[BM LC

RESURRECTION EZRA. Comedy in One Act. New York, Dramatists Play Service,
1938. 35p [BM LC

A ROCKY WOOING. Comedy in One Act. New York, French, 1935. 28p [BM LC

A ROGUE IN BED. London, French, 1937. 25p [A version in Scots, by David Rorie,
pub. as: A BEDFAST PROPHET. London, French, 1937. 25p] [BM LC

LA SANDRA. A Play in One Act. New York, French, 1936. 25p′ [BM LC

THE WAY TO LONDON. A Welsh Play in One Act. New York, French, 1935. 24p
[BM LC

Moray, Elspeth

THE DREAM OF THE MONTHS. A New Year Pageant. Toronto, McClelland, 1918.
25p [BVaU NSWA

THE FESTIVAL OF THE WHEAT. A Play for the Little Folk. Toronto, McClelland,
1918. 11p [NSWA

Morrison, Frank

TZINQUAW. A Musical Dramatization of the Cowichan Indian Legend, the
Thunderbird and the Killer-Whale. In Four Scenes. Vancouver, n.p., 1950. 16p
[OONL

Mountford, George Frederick, 1890–1950

CROOKS FOR A MONTH. A Comedy in Three Acts. Chicago, Denison, 1926. 99p
  [LC
DO YOU TAKE THIS WOMAN? A One-Act Comedy. Chicago, Denison, 1929. 26p
  [LC
FRIDAY FOR LUCK. A Comedy in One Act. Chicago, Denison, 1924. 30p [LC
THE LOOSE BRICKS IN THE CHIMNEY. A One-Act Comedy. Chicago, Denison, 1935.
  33p [LC
RATS! One-Act Farce. Chicago, Denison, 1924. 30p [LC
SAY IT WITH TAFFY. A One-Act Comedy. Chicago, Denison, 1927. 29p [LC
YOU CAN'T STOP CUPID. A One-Act Comedy. Chicago, Denison, 1930. 30p [LC
YOU'RE A CUCKOO. A One-Act Comedy. Chicago, Denison, 1925. 32p [LC

Moyse, Charles Ebenezer, 1852–1924

SHAKESPEARE'S SKULL AND FALSTAFF'S NOSE. A Fancy in Three Acts. By
  Belgrave Titmarsh [pseud]. London, Stock, 1889. 80p [BM OOU QMM

Murray, David Graham, 1926–

THE LINE. Durham, Ont., Durham House, 1954. 29p

Norwood, Gilbert, 1880–1954

THE ACHARNIANS. An Abridged Acting Edition. Arranged and trans. by Gilbert
  Norwood. Oxford, Blackwell, 1911. 67p [OTU
THE MOSTELLARIA OF PLAUTUS. Trans. into English verse, and ed. for Actors.
  Manchester, U. Press, 1908. 85p [OTU

Norwood, Rev. Robert Winkworth, 1874–1932

THE MAN OF KERIOTH. New York, Doran, 1919. 138p [BVaU LC NSHD OKQ
THE WITCH OF ENDOR. A Tragedy. New York, Doran, 1916. 121p [BVaU LC
  NBFU OKQ QMM

O'Higgins, Harvey Jerrold, 1876–1929

THE DUMMY. A Detective Comedy in Four Acts. By Harvey O'Higgins and Harriet
  Ford. New York, French, 1925. 113p [LC
MR. LAZARUS. A Comedy in Four Acts. By Harvey O'Higgins and Harriet Ford.
  New York, French, 1926. 134p [LC
OLD P.Q. A Play in Three Acts. By Harvey O'Higgins and Harriet Ford. New York,
  French, 1928. 81p [LC
ON THE HIRING LINE. A Comedy in Three Acts. By Harvey O'Higgins and Harriet
  Ford. New York, French, 1923. 116p [LC
ORPHAN AGGIE. A Romantic Comedy. By Harvey O'Higgins and Harriet Ford. New
  York, French, 1927. 96p [LC

"WHEN A FELLER NEEDS A FRIEND." A Play in Three Acts. By Harvey O'Higgins and Harriet Ford. [New York], 1920. 106p [LC

O'Meara, Martin
SITTING BILL. A Comedy in One Act. Toronto, French, 1949. 30p [OTU

Osborne, Marian (Francis), 1871–1931
SAPPHO AND PHAON. A Lyrical Drama. Toronto, Macmillan, 1926. 68p [BM BVaU NBFU OTU QMM

Owens, Charles R.
TATTERED ROSES. A Play in One Act. Mimico, Ont., Epworth Press, 1928. 38p [OKQ

Pacaud, George Washington, 1879–
SOCIAL IDOLATRY. New York, French, 1920. 93p [BM LC NSHD QMBM

Palmer, George Alfred, 1869–
MADAME VERITE AT BATH. A Comedy in One Act. Toronto, French, 1935. 24p [BM BVaU LC OTP
HAIL. An Original Domestic Drama in Two Acts. Regina, Author, 1933. 39p [Brown U

Parker, Gilbert, 1862–1932
ADAPTATION OF FAUST. 1888. [MOR'12
THE VENDETTA. 1889. [MOR'12

Pearson, Harry Mitchell, 1891–1938
THE LOVE GIFT. A Religious Mystery Play in Three Acts. Toronto, Ryerson, 1923. 31p [BM OTU

Plunkett, M.W.
CAPTAIN M.W. PLUNKETT, MANAGER AND OWNER, PRESENTS "THE DUMBELLS" IN BIFF-BING-BANG. N.p., 1921. 14p [BM
THE NEW DUMBELLS PLAY, "CARRY ON." N.p., 1923. 12p [BM

Potter, Ida Elizabeth
"ANNABEL'S M.I. CLUB." A Three-Act Play. [Portage la Prairie], Author, 1931. 20p [MBC
"AT HOPPER'S CORNERS." A Two-Act Play. N.p., Author, 1927. 32p [AEU
"FARMER MAXWELL'S CITY NIECE." A Three-Act Drama. N.p., Author, 1926. 39p [AEU
"MOTHER DUNN AND HER FAMILY." A Two-Act Comedy. Portage la Prairie, Author, 1924. [CC Rhod p824
WE ARE COMING. A Five-Act Modern Drama. Portage la Prairie, Author, 1923. [CC Rhod p824

Price, Marjorie

GOD CAESAR. A Comedy in One Act. Toronto, French, 1935. 24p [BM
BVaU LC OTP

THE SIX QUEENS OF HENRY. An Historical Fantasy in One Act. Toronto,
French, 1937. 39p [BM LC OTP

Ramsay, Alexander

COERCION. A One Act Play. Toronto, French, 1935. 28p [BM LC

Reynolds, Lois

NELLIE McNABB. A One-Act Farce Comedy. Toronto, French, 1937. 26p
[BM BVaU LC OTP

SUMMER HOTEL. A Play in One Act. Chicago, Denison, 1936. 28p [BM

Richards, Stanley, 1918–

CANADA ON STAGE. A Collection of One-Act Plays. Ed. and intro. by ——.
Toronto, Clarke Irwin, 1960. xvii + 324p

Ringwood, Gwendolyn Margaret (Pharis), 1910–

THE COURTING OF MARIE JENVRIN. A Comedy of the Far North. By Gwen Pharis.
Toronto, French, 1951. 35p

DARK HARVEST. A Tragedy of the Canadian Prairies. By Gwen Pharis. With notes,
acting suggestions, and questions by G.L. Broderson. Toronto, Nelson, 1945.
143p [BVaU NBFU OTUV

LAMENT FOR HARMONICA (MAYA). Ottawa, Little Theatre, [1960]. 20p

STILL STANDS THE HOUSE. A Drama in One Act. Toronto, French, 1939. 28p
[OTU PC

Roberts, Jessie (Alexander), –1907

ENCORE! A New Book of Platform Sketches. By Jessie Alexander. Toronto,
McClelland, 1922. 312p [BM BVaU OTP

JESSIE ALEXANDER'S PLATFORM SKETCHES. Original and adapted. Toronto,
McClelland, 1916. 227p [BM BVaU OTP

SUCCESSFUL RECITATIONS. By Jessie Alexander. Toronto, McClelland, 1927.
240p [OTP

Robinson, Hazel Alberta, 1913–1955

POEMS AND A PLAY. Toronto, Ryerson, 1955. 39p [Radio play, "This
Perilous Dream," presented on the CBC, Nov. 11, 1949.]

Roddick, Amy (Redpath), –1954

THE BIRTH OF MONTREAL (A Chronicle Play), and Other Poems. Montreal,
Dougall, 1921. 174p [BM BVaU NSHD OTP QMM

IN A VENETIAN GARDEN; ST. URSULA. Two Plays. Montreal, Dougall, 1926.
119p [BVaU OTU QMM

THE SEEKERS. An Indian Mystery Play. Montreal, Dougall, 1920. 75p [BM BVaU LC NSHD OTP QMM

THARBIS. A Poetic Drama. Montreal, Dougall, 1937. 80p [BVaU LC OTP QMM

THE TOMAHAWK. A Playlet; And Other Poems. Montreal, Dougall, 1938. 76p [BVaU LC OTU QMM

Rogers, Robert, 1731–1795

PONTEACH; or, The Savages of America. A Tragedy. London, Author, 1766. 110p [New ed., with an intro. and biography of the author by Allan Nevins. Chicago, Caxton Club, 1914. 261p] [BM LC OTP QMM

Roy, James Alexander, 1884–

THE BREAKING OF THE BRIDGE. A Play in One Act. Kingston, Jackson, 1923. 19p [LC QMM

Sadlier, Mary Anne (Madden), 1820–1903

THE BABBLER. A Drama for Boys, in One Act. Adapted from the French. New York, Sadlier, 1863. 23p [AEU BM

ELDER BROTHER. New York, Sadlier, 187–? [AmCat 1876

INVISIBLE HAND. New York, Sadlier, 187–? [AmCat 1876

JULIA; or, The Gold Thimble. A Drama for Girls, In One Act. New York, Sadlier, 1861. [AmCat

THE SECRET. A Drama. London, Washbourne, 1880. 32p [An earlier ed.: New York, Sadlier, 1865. AmCat] [BM

THE TALISMAN. A Drama in Three Acts. New York, Sadlier, 1863. [AmCat BM

Scott, Duncan Campbell, 1862–1947

PIERRE. A Play in One Act. [CANADIAN PLAYS FROM HART HOUSE THEATRE. Ed. by Vincent Massey. Toronto, Macmillan, 1926. V.1, pp. 51–76.] [BM BVaU NBFU OTP QMM

Scott, Elise Aylen, 1904–

THE HOLY CROWN. By Elise Aylen. [In *The Best One-Act Plays of 1937.* Selected by J.W. Marriott. London, Harrap, 1938.] [BM

Scott, Rev. Frederick George, 1861–1944

THE KEY OF LIFE. A Mystery-Play. Quebec, Dussault, 1907. 42p [3rd ed., 1927.] [BM BVaU OTP QMM

Scribble, Sam (pseud)

DOLORSOLATIO. A Local Political Burlesque. Montreal, Lovell, 1865. 22p [OTP

NOT DEAD YET; or, The Skating Carnival. A Farce in One Act. Montreal, Lovell, 1865. 23p [OTUV

Sellar, Robert, 1841–1919
THE TRAGEDY OF WALLACE. Huntingdon, Que., Gleaner Book, 1919. 49p
[BVaU OTP

Seton, Ernest Thompson, 1860–1946
THE WILD ANIMAL PLAY FOR CHILDREN. New York, Doubleday, 1900. 79p
[BM LC NBFU OTP

Sharman, Mrs. Lyon, 1872–
A SOMERSAULT TO LOVE. A Comedy of Changing Manners in China. Toronto,
Macmillan, 1926. 48p [BVaU OTU

Sharpe, Lynch Lawdon
THE VICEROY'S DREAM; or, The Canadian Government Not "Wide Awake."
A Mono-Dramatico-Political Poem. London, Whittaker, 1838. 25p [BM LC
OTP

Ship, Reuben, 1915–
THE INVESTIGATOR. A Narrative in Dialogue. London, Sidgwick and Jackson,
1956. 118p

Sinclair, Lister Shedden, 1921–
A PLAY ON WORDS AND OTHER RADIO PLAYS. Toronto, Dent, 1948. 298p
[BVaU NBFU OTP QMM
SOCRATES. A Drama in Three Acts. Toronto, Book Society of Canada, 1957.
103p
WAYS OF MANKIND. Thirteen Dramas of Peoples of the World and How They
Live. By Lister Sinclair [and others] . Ed. with commentary by Walter
Goldschmidt. Boston, Beacon Press, 1954. 212p

Skey, Francis W.
RED RIDING-HOOD. An Operatic Interlude, in Two Acts. Quebec, 1854. 20p
[NSWA

Social Credit Board
ALICE IN BLUNDERLAND. A Humorous Sketch in One Act. Edmonton, the
Board, 1941. 12p [ACG

Stephen, Alexander Maitland, 1882–1942
CLASS-ROOM PLAYS FROM CANADIAN HISTORY. Toronto, Dent, 1929. 164p
[AE BVa NSHPL OLU

Stewart, Luke
ANDREW McMURTY, IMMIGRANT. Toronto, French, 1938. 30p [BM BVaU
LC QMBM
DAFT DANNY. A Comedy in One Act. Toronto, French, 1947. 26p [BVaU
OTP
RELEASE. Toronto, French, 1937. 28p [BM BVaU LC QMBM

Stratford, Phyllis (Coate), 1900–
BRIGHT AND GLORIOUS. Toronto, French, 1938. 32p [BM BVaU OTP
QMBM

Stringer, Arthur John Arbuthnot, 1874–1950
ALEXANDER WAS GREAT. Greek Burlesque in One Act. Toronto, French,
1937. 25p [Also included in THE CLEVEREST WOMAN IN THE WORLD. ...]
[UTQ'38
THE BLOT. A Drama. [MOR'12
THE CLEVEREST WOMAN IN THE WORLD AND OTHER ONE-ACT PLAYS. New
York, Bobbs-Merrill, 1939. 272p [BM LC OLU

Telgmann, Heinrich Bertram
AGAINST THE WORLD; or, Life in London. A Drama in Four Acts. Kingston,
British Whig Office, 1889. 50p [BM LC

Thomas, Lillian (Beynon), 1874–1961
JIM BARBER'S SPITE FENCE. A Comedy in One Act. Toronto, French, 1935.
32p [BM BVaU NBFU

Thompson, Elizabeth Jane (Sweetland), 1858–
A DOUBLE LIFE. A Drama in 5 Acts. Toronto, Hill & Weir, 1884. 38p [OOP

Thompson, John Sparrow
CADETS OF TEMPERANCE. Entertainment for the Christmas Holidays. ...
Halifax, Bowes, 1852. 25p [NSHD

Thompson, Ruth C.
BEYOND THE SKYLINE. A Play of Modern China (in Four Scenes). Toronto,
Committee on Missionary Education, United Church of Canada, 1937. 14p
[Brown U

Thorlakson, E.J.
PIONEER THEATRE SERIES. Bk. 1. MARIE HEBERT; THE KING'S GIRLS; FATHER
LACOMBE; POET OF THE PLAINS. Edmonton, Institute of Applied Art, 1936.
36p [Brown U

Tremayne, William Andrew, 1864–
THE MAN WHO WENT. A Play in Four Acts. Boston, Baker, 1918. 96p [OTP

Underhill, John
DAMON AND PYTHIAS. A Drama of Quebec Liberalism. N.p., Author, 1891.
31p [MWU NSHD QMSS

Voaden, Herman Arthur, 1903—

A BOOK OF PLAYS FOR SCHOOLS AND COMMUNITY DRAMA GROUPS IN CANADA.
Ed. by ——. Toronto, Macmillan, 1935. xviii + 316p [OTU

ON STAGE. Plays for School and Community. Ed. by ——. Toronto, Macmillan,
1945. 445p [BVaU OTP

SIX CANADIAN PLAYS. Ed. by ——. Toronto, Copp Clark, 1930. 136p [BVaU
NSHD OTP QMM

Waight, Quentin, 1894—

PRELUDE TO GLORY. [Poems and a Play.] Seattle, Superior Pub. Co., 1951.
xiv + 166p [Includes a one-act play.]

Walker, Annie Louisa (Mrs. Harry Coghill), 1836—1907

PLAYS FOR CHILDREN. London, Routledge, 1876. [BM

Ward, James Edward, 1883—1958

THE CRADLE IN THE HILLS. A Play of the Nativity. Toronto, Tyrrell, 1941. 30p
[LC OTU

... GOD'S PLENTY. A Pastoral Idyll Founded on the Book of Ruth. With Incidental
Lyrics. Toronto, Longmans, 1945. 66p [BVaU OTP

Watson, Samuel James, 1837—1881

THE LEGEND OF THE ROSES—A Poem; RAVLAN—A Drama. Toronto, Hunter Rose,
1876. 228p [BVaU NBFU OTU QMM

Waygood, John

LIKE AS TWO P'S. A Comedy in Four Acts. N.p., n.p., n.d. 24p [No title page.
Bound with Alexander Begg's PRACTICAL HANDBOOK AND GUIDE TO MANITOBA.
...] [BViPA

Williams, Minnie (Harvey)

THE ROMANCE OF CANADA. An Historical Pageant. Toronto, Ryerson, 1923. 29p
[BM OTP

Williams, Norman, 1923—

A BATTLE OF WITS. A Play in One Act. Toronto, French, 1956. 29p

WORLDS APART. Six Prize-Winning Plays. Toronto, Copp Clark, 1956. xii + 203p

Winlow, Alice Maud (Dudley), 1885—

THE BROKEN FLOWER. London, Fowler Wright, 1927. 16p [OKQ

THE MIRACLE OF ROSES. Vancouver, Chalmers, 1926. 94p [BVaU OTU QMM

Wood, W.P.

MINNIE TRAIL; or, The Woman of Wentworth. A Tragedy in Three Acts, &c. &c.
Hamilton, Evening Times, 1871. 37p [OTUV

Worth, Edward
WORTH'S BURLESQUE RITUAL. Includes Initiation of a Candidate, Opening and
   Closing Ceremony, Minutes, Orders of Business, Etc., with General Instructions,
   Written for the Purpose of Creating Amusement at Anniversaries of Secret
   Societies and for Public Entertainments. ... Kent Bridge, Ont., Author, 1896.
   19p [BM

Wren, Frances
THE EARLY HISTORY OF ST. ANDREWS AS SHOWN BY HISTORICAL TABLEAUS,
   AUGUST, 1942. [St. Andrews, N.B.? 1942?]. 12p [NBFU

Young, David Leonard, 1886–
THE LIGHT. A Play for Christmas or Easter. Boston, Baker, 1943. 29p [LC

PART II

BIOGRAPHY

Including memoirs, memorial sermons, genealogy,
autobiography, reminiscences, letters, diaries, etc.

Abraham, Dorothy E., 1894–
LONE CONE. A Journal of Life on the West Coast of Vancouver Island. 3rd ed.
Victoria, Author, [1945]. 100p [Later eds., 1946, 1952, 1961.] [AEP BVi
OTU

Acadia University.
THE ACADIA RECORD, 1838–1953. [4th ed., rev. and enl. by Watson Kirkconnell.]
Wolfville, N.S., Acadia University, 1953. 565 p
RECORDS OF THE GRADUATES OF ACADIA UNIVERSITY, 1843–1926. Arranged by
Classes. ... Wolfville, Associated Alumni, 1926. 296p [BVaU LC NSWA OTU

Adam, Graeme Mercer, 1839–1912
PROMINENT MEN OF CANADA. ... Ed. by ——. Toronto, Canadian Biographical
Pub. Co., 1892. 476p [BM BVaU LC NSHD OTP

Adams, Mrs. Mary, 1928–
I MARRIED A MONK. Toronto, Evangelical Mission, [1951?]. 67p

Adamson, Rev. William Agar, 1800–1868
LETTERS AND ADDRESSES, presented to the Rev. W. Agar Adamson, D.C.L.,
Chaplain to the ... Legislative Council of Canada. Toronto, Lovell, 1856.
24p [OTP

Aitken, Katherine (Scott), 1891–1971
MAKING YOUR LIVING IS FUN. Toronto, Longmans, 1959. 213p
NEVER A DAY SO BRIGHT. Toronto, Longmans, 1956. 249p

Albani, Emma, 1847–1930
FORTY YEARS OF SONG. London, Mills & Boon, 1911. 285p [BM LC

Alderton, Haddon,
ONE MAN'S MEAT. London, Long, 1937. 288p [BM LC

Alexander, James Edward, 1803–1885
PASSAGES IN THE LIFE OF A SOLDIER. London, Hurst & Blackett, 1857. 300p
[BM BVaU NSHD OTP

Allan, Rev. David, 1860–1940
"FROM THE LUMBER CAMP TO THE MINISTRY." The Autobiography of Rev. David
Allan. Toronto, Evangelical Pubs., 1938. 230p [OTP

Allan, Iris Constance (Sommerville), 1910–
THE BOY IN BUCKSKINS (BOYHOOD OF JOHN McDOUGALL). Edmonton, Institute of Applied Art, 1959. 160p

Allen, Grant, 1848–1899
BIOGRAPHIES OF WORKING MEN. London, Soc. Pro. Christian Knowledge, 1885. 191p [NSHD OLU
... CHARLES DARWIN. New York, Appleton, 1885. 206p [BM LC OTU
IN MEMORIAM GEORGE PAUL MACDONELL. London, Lund, 1895. 64p [BM OTU

Allen, Joseph Antisell, 1814–1900
DR. RYERSON. A Review and a Study. Toronto, 1884. 10p [LC OTP
ORANGEISM, CATHOLICISM, AND SIR FRANCIS HINCKS. Toronto, 1877. [MWU

Alline, Rev. Henry, 1748–1784
LIFE AND JOURNALS OF THE REV. MR. HENRY ALLINE. Boston, Gilbert & Dean, 1806. 180p [NSWA OOP

Allison, Leonard A., 1853–1903
THE REV. OLIVER ARNOLD. Saint John, Sun Print., 1892. 30p [LC NSHD OONL

Alward, Silas, 1842–1919
AN ORATION ON PROF. C.F. HARTT, at Acadia College, N.S. Saint John, Knodell, 1884. 11p [NSWA QMBM

Ambridge, Douglas White, 1898–
FRANK HARRIS ANSON (1859–1923) PIONEER IN THE NORTH. New York, Montreal, Newcomen Society in North America, 1952. 24p

Anahareo, 1907?–   (Chippewa Woman)
MY LIFE WITH GREY OWL. London, Davies, 1940. 230p [BM LC OTP

Anderson, Rev. Duncan, 1828–1903
SCOTTISH FOLK-LORE; or, Reminiscences of Aberdeenshire, from Pinafore to Gown. New York, Selwin Tait, 1895. 245p [BM OTP

Anderson, Rev. John, 1823–1908
REMINISCENCES AND INCIDENTS CONNECTED WITH THE LIFE ... OF THE REV. JOHN ANDERSON. Ed. by his son, the Rev. J.D. Anderson. Toronto, Briggs, 1910. 340p [BM BVaU OTU

Anderson, Patrick, 1915–
FIRST STEPS IN GREECE. London, Chatto, 1958. 211p
SEARCH ME. Autobiography–the Black Country, Canada and Spain. London, Chatto, 1957. 237p
SNAKE WINE. A Singapore Episode. London, Chatto, 1955. 288p

Anderson, Pete, 1869–

I, THAT'S ME. Escape from a German Prison and Other Adventures. Edmonton, Bradbury Print., [1920?]. 174p [AE

Anderson, William James, 1813?–1873

CANADIAN HISTORY AND BIOGRAPHY, AND PASSAGES IN THE LIVES OF A BRITISH PRINCE AND A CANADIAN SEIGNEUR, the Father of the Queen and the Hero of Chateauguay. A Paper read before the Literary and Historical Society of Quebec, December 19th, 1866. Quebec, Middleton & Dawson, 1867. 51p [BVaU LC QMSS

THE LIFE OF F.M., H.R.H. EDWARD, DUKE OF KENT. Illustrated by his Correspondence with the De Salaberry Family ... from 1791–1814. Toronto, Hunter Rose, 1870. 241p [BM BVaU LC NSWA OOU

Andrew, Frederick William, 1879–

KLINKER. A Country Doctor's Dog. Toronto, Author, 1948. 101p [BVaU OTP

Angier, Mrs. Vena

AT HOME IN THE WOODS. Living The Life of Thoreau Today. By Vena and Bradford Angier. New York, Sheridan House, 1951. 255p

Annis, Levi Edward, 1858–1933

ANNIS ANNALS, 1638–1931. Pickering, Printer's Guild, 1931. 56p [OTP

Anonymous

A BRIEF BIOGRAPHICAL SKETCH OF THE HON. ROBERT CHARLES WILKINS. Belleville, Chronicle Office, 1866. 8p [OTP

THE CANADIAN BIOGRAPHICAL DICTIONARY AND PORTRAIT GALLERY OF EMINENT AND SELF-MADE MEN. Quebec and Maritime Provinces Volume. Toronto, Am. Biographical Pub. Co., 1880. 778p [BVaU NBFU OLU

THE CANADIAN WHO'S WHO. Toronto, Musson, 1910. 243p [BVaU NSWA OTP

HEARTS OF GOLD. Being Chronicles of Heroism in Canadian History. [Toronto?], Ontario Women's Liberal Association, 1915. 30p [NSHD OLU QMU

JAMES STANLEY McLEAN. An Appreciation by a Group of his Friends. Toronto, R.C. Stone, 1957. 80p

LIFE OF RIGHT REVEREND PATRICK PHELAN, THIRD BISHOP OF KINGSTON. To Which is Added a Synopsis of the Lives of the Two First Bishops of Kingston. By the Clergyman who served Bishop Phelan's Last Mass. Kingston, Lightfoot, 1862. 46p [Haight Pt I

A MEMOIR OF THE LATE MR. WILLIAM RUTTAN. By a Friend. To Which is Prefixed a Sermon ... by the Rev. A.N. Bethune. Cobourg, Chatterton, 1837. 55p [OTP

NARRATIVE OF THE LIFE OF THE DARING MURDERER, HIGHWAYMAN AND BURGLAR, WILLIAM TOWNSEND, JUST TRIED AT THE HALDIMAND ASSIZES FOR THE MURDER OF MR. JOHN H. NELLES OF CAYUGA TOWNSHIP. ... Hamilton, Franklin Lightning Press, 1857. 14p [OTU

THE PEARL OF TROYES; or, Reminiscences of the Early Days of Ville-Marie. Revealed to us in the Heroic Life of Sister Marguerite Bourgeoys, Foundress and First Superior of the Congregation of Notre Dame. Montreal, Can. Print., 1878. 375p [NSWA OTU

PIONEER LIFE ON THE BAY OF QUINTE. Including Genealogies of old Families and Biographical Sketches of Representative Citizens. Toronto, Rolph, n.d. 1005p [BVa NSHD OTP

SKETCH OF THE LIFE OF CATHERINE BREITHAUPT, HER FAMILY AND TIMES. Berlin, Ont., 1911. [Hood cat. no. 87

Anslow, Florence
THE HALIBURTON MEMORIAL MUSEUM. Windsor, N.S., 1954. 21p

Arcand, Mrs. Anne
UNFORGETTABLE DAYS. [Quebec?], 1958. 15p

Archer, William L.
JOE ATKINSON'S TORONTO STAR. The Genius of Crooked Lane. Montreal, [194–?]. 20p [OTP

Archibald, Edith Jessie (Mortimer), 1854–1938
LIFE AND LETTERS OF SIR EDWARD MORTIMER ARCHIBALD. By his Daughter, ——. Toronto, Morang, 1924. 266p [BM BVaU LC NSHD OKQ

ONE OF THE WONDERS OF PERSONAL SUCCESS. By an Eyewitness [pseud]. N.p., n.d. 10p [OTU

Archibald, Raymond Clare, 1875–1955
CARLYLE'S FIRST LOVE, MARGARET GORDON, LADY BANNERMAN. London, Lane, 1910. 213p [BM BViP LC NSWA OLU

Ardagh, Henry Hatton, 1853–1936
LIFE OF HON. SIR JAMES ROBERT GOWAN, K.C.M.G., LL.D., SENATOR OF CANADA. By his Nephew, ——. Toronto, U. of Toronto Press, 1911. 328p [Rev. and enl. ed. of a memoir previously ed. by A.H.U. Colquhoun, *q.v.*] [BM OTP

Armstrong, Rev. John
THE LIFE AND LETTERS OF THE REV. GEORGE MORTIMER, RECTOR OF THORN-HILL. London, Aylott & Jones, 1847. 308p [BM BVaU OTP

Armstrong, Nevill Alexander Drummond, 1878?–
YUKON YESTERDAYS. Thirty Years of Adventure in the Klondike. London, Long, 1936. 287p [BM BVaU LC OTU

Arsenault, Aubin Edmond, 1870–
MEMOIRS OF THE HON. A.E. ARSENAULT, Former Premier and Retired Justice, Supreme Court of Prince Edward Island. Charlottetown, Island Guardian Pub., 1951. 188p

Ashbridge, Wellington Thomas, 1869–
THE ASHBRIDGE BOOK. Relating to Past and Present Ashbridge Families in America. Toronto, Copp Clark, 1912. 182p [LC OOP

Ashton, Harry, 1882–
MADAME LAFAYETTE. Toronto, Macmillan, 1922. 292p [BM BVaU LC NSHD OTU

Askin, John, 1739–1815
THE JOHN ASKIN PAPERS. ... Ed. by Milo M. Quaife. [Detroit], Public Library Commission, 1928, 1931. 2v [BM BVaU LC NBFU OTU

Asselstine, Kathryn Rachel
A PIONEER FAMILY. [Genealogical history.] Windsor, Ont., priv. print., 1954. 75p

Atherton, William Henry, 1867–1950
A CANADIAN EDUCATIONIST OF THE 17TH CENTURY: THE VENERABLE MARGUERITE BOURGEOYS. Montreal, Gazette, 1920. 16p [OTL
THE SAINTLY LIFE OF JEANNE MANCE. First Lay Nurse in North America. St. Louis, Mo., Catholic Hospital Assoc., 1945. 95p [OTP

Atlay, James Beresford, 1860–1912
LORD HALIBURTON. A Memoir. ... Toronto, Briggs, 1909. 296p [BM BVaU NBFU OTU

Ayscough, Florence (Wheelock), 1878–1942
FLORENCE AYSCOUGH AND AMY LOWELL: CORRESPONDENCE OF A FRIENDSHIP. Ed. by Harley Farnsworth MacNair. Chicago, U. of Chicago Press, 1945. 288p [BM BVaU LC QMM

Bagnall, F.W.
NOT MENTIONED IN DESPATCHES. By Ex-Quaker [pseud]. North Vancouver, North Shore Press, 1933. 116p [BVaU NSWA

Bailey, Jacob, 1731–1808
THE FRONTIER MISSIONARY. A Memoir of the Life of the Rev. Jacob Bailey, Missionary at Pownalborough, Maine, Cornwallis and Annapolis, N.S. Ed. by Wm. S. Bartlet. Boston, Ide & Dutton, 1853. 365p [BM BVaU NBFU OTP

Bailey, Joseph Whitman, 1865–1932
THE CURIOUS STORY OF DR. MARSHALL WITH A FEW LIGHTS ON NAPOLEON AND OTHER PERSONS OF CONSEQUENCE. Cambridge, Mass., Murray, 1930. 113p [BM LC NBFU OTU
LORING WOART BAILEY. The Story of a Man of Science. Saint John, McMillan, 1925. 141p [BM BVaU NBFU OTU

Bailey, Thomas Melville, 1912—
TRACES, PLACES AND FACES. Links Between Canada and Scotland. Hamilton, Author, 1957. 67p

Baines, Henry Edward, 1840—1866
... THE CRUISE OF THE BREEZE. N.p., n.d. 40p [OTP
IN MEMORIAM, HENRY EDWARD BAINES. [Anon] London, Hunt, [1866?]. 30p [OTP

Baird, Rev. Frank, 1870—1951
ADDRESSES AT THE CELEBRATION OF THE ONE HUNDRED AND FIFTIETH ANNI-VERSARY OF THE ARRIVAL IN NOVA SCOTIA OF REV. JAMES DRUMMOND MACGREGOR. ... Ed. by ——. Toronto, Presbyterian Pub., 1937. 310p [QMM

Baird, William Thomas, 1819—1897
SEVENTY YEARS OF NEW BRUNSWICK LIFE. Autobiographical Sketches. ... Saint John, Day, 1890. 358p [BVaU LC NSWA OTU QMM

Baker, George Harold, 1877—1916
A CANADIAN SOLDIER. [Letters ... and a Memoir by J.W. Cunliffe.] New York, priv. print., [1917?]. 83p [BVaU OOP

Baker, William King
JOHN T. DORLAND. ... Ed. and with a preface by Anne W. Richardson. London, Headley, 1898. 433p [BM BVaU OLU
A QUAKER WARRIOR. The Life of William Hobson. London, Headley, 1913. 178p [BM

Baldwin, Harold, 1888—
A FARM FOR TWO POUNDS. Being the Odyssey of an Emigrant. London, Murray, 1935. 300p [BM LC NSHD OTU QMM
"HOLDING THE LINE." Chicago, McClurg, 1918. 305p [BM LC NSHD OTU

Balfour, Rev. Charles Wilfred, 1877—
LIFE AND WORK AND MEMOIRS OF GEORGE THORNELOE, D.C.L., D.D., 1848—1935, BISHOP OF THE DIOCESE OF ALGOMA (1897—1927), METROPOLITAN OF ONTARIO AND ARCHBISHOP OF ONTARIO (1915—1926). By his son-in-law. Peterborough, Ont., Author, 1955. 112p

Ball, Ernest A.
JIMMY DAROU, THE KING OF COURAGE. Montreal, priv. print., 1938. 28p [QMBM

Ball, Geraldine F.
SOME EXTRACTS AND REMINISCENCES OF A LIFETIME. Regina, Leader, 1922. 165p [ACG SRL

Ballantyne, Mabel (Erb), 1890—
THE HISTORY OF THE BALLANTYNE FAMILY. Ed. by ——. N.p., Editor, 1952. 87p

Banfill, Bessie Jane, 1899–
LABRADOR NURSE. Toronto, Ryerson, 1952. 218p

Banks, Margaret Amelia, 1928–
EDWARD BLAKE, IRISH NATIONALIST. A Canadian Statesman in Irish Politics, 1892–1907. Toronto, U. of Toronto Press, 1957. xii + 370p

Banwell, Selwyn, 1880–
A FRONTIER JUDGE [Sir Matthew Begbie]. British Justice in the Earliest Days of Farthest West. Toronto, Rous & Mann, 1938. 30p [BVaU NSHPL OTP

Baptist Union of Western Canada
SOME BAPTIST PIONEERS. Edmonton, 1932. 64p [ACG

Bapty, Walter, 1884–
MEMOIRS. 1st print. N.p., W. Bapty, 1959. 1v (various pagings). [mimeographed]

Barbeau, Charles Marius, 1883–1969
CORNELIUS KRIEGHOFF. Pioneer Painter of North America. Toronto, Macmillan, 1934. 152p [BM BVaU LC NBFU OKQ QMM
COTE, THE WOOD CARVER. Toronto, Ryerson, 1943. 43p [BVaU NBFU OTU QMM
HENRI JULIEN. Toronto, Ryerson, 1941. 44p [BM BVaU LC NBFU OTU QMM
PAINTERS OF QUEBEC. Toronto, Ryerson, 1946. 48p [BVaU LC NSHD OTU QMM

Barclay, Charles
LETTERS FROM THE DORKING EMIGRANTS WHO WENT TO UPPER CANADA IN THE SPRING OF 1832. Edited by C. Barclay. London, J. & A. Arch, 1833. 44p [BM OTP

Barclay, Rev. John, 1812–1887
EXTRACT FROM A SERMON PREACHED IN ST. ANDREW'S CHURCH, TORONTO ... ON THE OCCASION OF THE SUDDEN DEATH OF COLONEL E.W. THOMSON, One of the Elders of the Congregation. Montreal, Lovell, 1865. 11p [OTP
A SERMON PREACHED ON THE OCCASION OF THE LAMENTED DEATH OF THE HON. ARCHIBALD McLEAN, President of Her Majesty's Court of Error and Appeal for Upper Canada. Toronto, Leader, 1865. 39p [OTP

Bar-David, Molly (Lyons), 1910–
MY PROMISED LAND. New York, Putnam, 1953. x + 307p

Barnes, Rev. Joshua Ninyon, 1830–1915
LIGHTS AND SHADOWS OF EIGHTY YEARS. An Autobiography. ... Rev. and ed. by his son, Edwin N.C. Barnes. Saint John, Barnes, 1911. 218p [NBFU OTP

Barnes, William Morris, 1850–
ROLLING HOME. When Ships were Ships and not Tin Pots. London, Cassell, 1931. 471p [BM LC NfSM

Barrass, Rev. Edward, 1821—1898
A GALLERY OF DISTINGUISHED MEN. Napanee, Author, 1870. 346p [BM BVaU
OTP
SMILES AND TEARS; or, Sketches from Real Life. ... With intro. by Rev. W.H.
Withrow. First Series. Toronto, Hunter Rose, 1879. 200p [BVaU OTP

Bartlett, Rev. Leonard, 1872—1963
"UNCLE JOE LITTLE." Life and Memoirs of Joseph Russell Little. Toronto, Briggs,
1903. 251p [BM BVaU OLU

Bartlett, Robert Abram, 1875—1946
THE LOG OF BOB BARTLETT. The True Story of Forty Years Seafaring and Ex-
ploration. New York, Putnam, 1928. 352p [Also: New York, Blue Ribbon
Books, 1932.] [BM BVaU LC QMM

Bateman, Reginald John Godfrey, 1884?—1918
REGINALD BATEMAN, TEACHER AND SOLDIER. A Memorial Volume of Selections
from his Lectures and other Writings. London, Sotheran, 1922. 147p [BVaU
OOA

Bates, Walter, 1760—1842
COMPANION FOR CARABOO. A Narrative of the Conduct and Adventures of Henry
Frederic Moon, Alias Henry Frederic More Smith ... his Unparalleled Artifices,
Impostures, Mechanical Ingenuities. ... With an Introductory Description of New
Brunswick; and a Postscript, containing Some Account of Caraboo, the late
Female Impostor, at Bristol. ... 2nd ed. London, Allman, 1817. 84p [Various
later editions, incorporating additional material under variant titles, such as: THE
MYSTERIOUS STRANGER; or, THE ADVENTURES OF HENRY MORE SMITH.
Charlottetown, Steam Press, 1855. 109p] [BM BVaU NSWA OTU
THE MYSTERIOUS STRANGER; or, The Adventures of Henry More Smith. [See
note under preceding title.]

Battell, Jud, 1867—1951
JUD BATTELL'S STORY OF THE EARLY DAYS OF THE WEST. By [i.e., as told to]
Evangeline Chapman. Moose Jaw, Bowes Publishers, 1953. 32p

Baxter, Arthur Beverley, 1891—1964
MEN, MARTYRS AND MOUNTEBANKS. Beverley Baxter's Inner Story of Person-
alities and Events Behind the War. London, Hutchinson, 1940. 286p [BM
BVaU LC OTU QMM
STRANGE STREET. London, Hutchinson, 1935. 286p [BM BVaU LC NBFU
OKQ QMM
WESTMINSTER WATCHTOWER. Toronto, Collins, 1938. 319p [BVaU NBFU OTU
QMM

Baxter, John Babington Maccaulay, 1868—
SIMON BAXTER (The First United Empire Loyalist to Settle in New Brunswick),

His Ancestry and Descendants. Saint John, New Brunswick Museum, 1943. 46p
[BVaU LC OOP

Bayne, J.N.
A BRIEF STORY OF JOHN WEIR [1840–1940] AND HIS WIFE. Regina, 1940. 42p
[OOP

Baynes, George Edgar
EDGAR G. BAYNES, PIONEER OF THE WEST, 1870–1956. Vancouver, Author, 1957.
12p

Beattie, Jessie Louise, 1896–
ALONG THE ROAD. Toronto, Ryerson, 1954. 168p
BLACK MOSES, THE REAL UNCLE TOM. Toronto, Ryerson, 1957. xiii + 215p
[Life of Josiah Henson]
JOHN CHRISTIE HOLLAND, MAN OF THE YEAR. Toronto, Ryerson, 1956. xiv +
169p

Beattie, Kim, 1900–
BROTHER, HERE'S A MAN! The Saga of Klondike Boyle. New York, Macmillan,
1940. 309p [BVa LC OTU

Begg, Alexander, 1825–1905
A SKETCH OF THE SUCCESSFUL MISSIONARY WORK OF WILLIAM DUNCAN,
amongst the Indian Tribes in Northern British Columbia from 1858–1901.
Victoria, 1901. 32p [BVa

Begg, Alexander, 1839–1897
SEVENTEEN YEARS IN THE CANADIAN NORTH-WEST. London, Spottiswoode,
1884. 35p [BM BVaU NSWA

Beland, Henri Sévérin, 1869–1935
MY THREE YEARS IN A GERMAN PRISON. Toronto, Briggs, 1919. 280p [BVaU
LC OTU

Belaney, George Stansfeld, 1888–1938
A BIOGRAPHICAL NOTE, AND A DAY AT BEAVER LODGE. By Wa-Sha-Quon-Asin
(Grey Owl) [pseud]. London, 1937. 13p [The material quoted in A DAY AT
BEAVER LODGE is selected from Grey Owl's writings and published in this form
as a souvenir of his visit to the United Kingdom in the autumn of 1937.]
[UTQ'39

Belcher, Edward, 1799–1877
THE LAST OF THE ARCTIC VOYAGES. Being a Narrative of the Expedition ... in
Search of Sir John Franklin, during the Years 1852–53–54. ... London, Reeve,
1855. 2v [BM BVaU LC NSWA OLU QMM
NARRATIVE OF A VOYAGE ROUND THE WORLD; Performed in Her Majesty's Ship
Sulphur, during the Years 1836–1842. London, Colburn, 1843. 2v [BM BVaU
LC NSHD

NARRATIVE OF THE VOYAGE OF H.M.S. SAMARANG, during the Years 1843–46; Employed Surveying the Islands of the Eastern Archipelago. Accompanied by a Brief Vocabulary of the Principal Languages. London, Reeve, 1848. 2v [BM BVaU LC NSHD

Bell Telephone Company of Canada
ALEXANDER GRAHAM BELL, SCIENTIST, TEACHER AND HUMANITARIAN WHOSE INVENTIVE GENIUS GAVE US THE TELEPHONE. Montreal, The Company, 1954. 31p [Rev. ed. First ed., 1947.]

Bell, Andrew
BRITISH-CANADIAN CENTENNIUM, 1759-1859. General James Wolfe, his Life and Death. A Lecture Delivered in ... Montreal. Montreal, Lovell, 1859. 48p [NSWA OTP

Bell, Edwin Wallace, 1908–
ISRAEL KENNY. His Children and Their Families. Ed. by Lilian M.B. Maxwell. [Vancouver], 1944. 111p [LC NBFU OTP

Bell, Frederick McKelvey, 1878–1931
THE FIRST CANADIANS IN FRANCE. The Chronicle of a Military Hospital in the War Zone. New York, Doran, 1917. 308p [LC NSWA OTU QMM

Bell, Winthrop Pickard, 1884–
BRIGADIER-GENERAL JEDIDIAH PREBLE (1707–1784) AND HIS PARTICIPATION IN NOVA SCOTIA HISTORY. Halifax, Halcraft Print., 1954. 39p

Bellamy, Herbie
A SKETCH OF THE LIFE OF HERBIE BELLAMY. Toronto, Women's Missionary Soc. of Methodist Church, 1902. 29p [Peel Supp

Bender, Louis Prosper, 1844–1917
OLD AND NEW CANADA, 1753–1844: Historic Scenes and Social Pictures; or, The Life of Joseph-François Perrault. Montreal, Dawson, 1882. 291p [BM BVaU LC MWU NSWA OTU QMM

Benson, Nathaniel Anketell Michael, 1903–1966
"IN MEMORIAM PRINCIPIS." A Memorial Tribute To My Honoured Friend The Right Honourable W.L. Mackenzie King, O.M., P.C. (1874–1950) on The First Anniversary of His Death, July 22nd, 1951. Toronto, 1951. 2 + vip
NONE OF IT CAME EASY. The Story of James Garfield Gardiner. Toronto, Burns & MacEachern, 1955. 272p

Bergmann, Werner, 1915–
DOCTORS ARE PEOPLE. By W. Berg Mann [pseud]. New York, Vantage Press 1954. 88p

Bernier, Joseph Elzéar, 1852–1934
MASTER MARINER AND ARCTIC EXPLORER. A Narrative of Sixty Years at Sea. ...
Ottawa, Le Droit, 1939. 409p [BM BVaU LC OTU QMM

Berton, Laura Beatrice (Thompson)
I MARRIED THE KLONDIKE. Boston, Toronto, Little Brown, 1954. x + 269p

Berton, Pierre Francis de Marigny, 1920–
THE ROYAL FAMILY. The Story of the British Monarchy from Victoria to
Elizabeth. Toronto, McClelland, 1954. 273p

Bertrand, Elie-Oscar, 1894–
NOTES, SOUVENIRS OF FORTY YEARS OF FAMILY LIFE, AND PUBLIC AND
POLITICAL ACTIVITIES. ... Ottawa, Author, 1955. 88p

Bethune, Rev. Alexander Neil, 1800–1879
MEMOIR OF THE RIGHT REV. JOHN STRACHAN, FIRST BISHOP OF TORONTO.
Toronto, Rowsell, 1870. 385p [BM BVaU LC NSWA OTU
A SERMON PREACHED ... ON OCCASION OF THE DEATH OF MRS. BOULTON, Wife of
George Strange Boulton, Esquire, M.P.P. Cobourg, Chatterton, 1838. 21p [OTP
A SERMON PREACHED IN THE CHURCH OF ST. GEORGE THE MARTYR, TORONTO,
ON SUNDAY, NOVEMBER 19, 1876, ON OCCASION OF THE DEATH OF THE
HONORABLE JOHN HILLYARD CAMERON. Toronto, Rowsell & Hutchinson, 1876.
16p [NSWA OTP
SERMON. By ——. Prefixed to A MEMOIR OF THE LATE MR. WILLIAM RUTTAN. By
a Friend. Cobourg, Chatterton, 1837. [OTP

Bethune, Rev. John, 1791–1872
A NARRATIVE OF THE CONNECTION OF THE REV. J. BETHUNE, D.D., WITH McGILL
COLLEGE. ... Montreal, Lovell & Gibson, 1846. 56p [OTP
A SERMON ... ON THE OCCASION OF THE DEATH OF THE LATE HON. CHIEF JUSTICE
REID. Montreal, Lovell & Gibson, 1848. 17p [BM NSHD QMM

Beurling, George F.
MALTA SPITFIRE. The Story of a Fighter Pilot. By Flying Officer F. Beurling and
Leslie Roberts. Toronto, Oxford U. Press, 1943. 235p [BM BVaU OTU QMSS

Bezanson, A. Maynard, 1878–1958
SODBUSTERS INVADE THE PEACE. Toronto, Ryerson, 1954. 209p

Bezanson, Rev. W.B.
THE ROMANCE OF RELIGION. A Sketch of the Life of Henry Alline, in the Pioneer
Days of the Maritime Provinces. Kentville, N.S., Kentville Pub. Co., 1927. 71p
[NSWA OTP

Biggar, Charles Robert Webster, 1847–1909
SIR OLIVER MOWAT. A Biographical Sketch. Toronto, Warwick & Rutter, 1905. 2v
[BM BVaU LC NSWA OTU QMM

Biggar, Emerson Bristol, 1853–1921
ANECDOTAL LIFE OF SIR JOHN MACDONALD. ... Montreal, Lovell, 1891. 332p
[BM BVaU LC NSWA OKQ QMM

Biggar, Henry Percival, 1872–1938
A COLLECTION OF DOCUMENTS RELATING TO JACQUES CARTIER AND THE SIEUR
DE ROBERVAL. Ottawa, Public Archives, 1930. 577p [BVaU NSHD OTU
QMM

Bilkey, Paul Ernest, 1878–
PERSONS, PAPERS AND THINGS. Being the Casual Recollections of a Journalist,
with some Flounderings in Philosophy. Toronto, Ryerson, 1940. 235p [BM
BVaU NBFU OTU QMM

Bingham, Helen E.
AN IRISH SAINT. The Life Story of Ann Preston ("Holy Ann"). Toronto, Briggs,
1907. 155p [BM BVaU OTU

Binnie-Clark, Georgina
WHEAT AND WOMAN. Toronto, Bell & Cockburn, 1914. 413p [BM BVaU LC
NSHD OTU

Bird, William Richard, 1891–
AND WE GO ON. Toronto, Hunter Rose, 1931. [OTU
THE TWO JACKS. The Amazing Adventures of Major Jack M. Veness and Major
Jack L. Fairweather. Philadelphia, Smith, 1954. 209p

Bishop, William Avery, 1894–1956
THE FLYING SQUAD. By Colonel William A. Bishop and Major Rothesay
Stuart-Wortley. New York, Doran, 1927. 260p [BM LC OTMC QMM
WINGED WARFARE. Hunting the Huns in the Air. London, Hodder, 1918. 301p
[BM BVaU LC NSHD OTU QMM

Black, Cyrus, 1811?–1900
HISTORICAL RECORD OF THE POSTERITY OF WILLIAM BLACK WHO SETTLED IN
THIS COUNTRY IN 1775. Brought up to the year 1885 by Cyrus Black of Amherst,
N.S. The records from 1885 to 1959 were compiled by L.W. Black of Middle
Sackville, N.B. Sackville, Tribune Press, 1959. 167p

Black, Martha Louise (Munger), 1866–1957
KLONDIKE DAYS. Whitehorse, priv. print., 1954. 38p
MY FIRST CHRISTMAS MEMORY DURING THE CHICAGO FIRE OF 1871. Whitehorse,
priv. print., 1953. 11p
MY SEVENTY YEARS. By Mrs. George Black. ... As told to Elizabeth Bailey Price. ...
London, Nelson, 1938. 317p [BM BVaU LC NSHD OTU QMM
TWO ROYAL ELIZABETHS. Whitehorse, priv. print., 1953. 16p

Blakeny, Charles Hanford, 1888–1961

THE STORY OF A BUSINESS AND ITS FOUNDERS. Moncton, N.B., priv. print., 1960. 160p [Record of the origin and development of Blakeny & Son Ltd., and Blakeny Concrete Products Ltd., 1900–60.]

Blanchard, Henry Percy, 1862–

THE ANCESTRAL McCURDYS. Their Origin and Remote History. London, Covenant, 1930. 42p [LC NSWA OOA

GENEALOGICAL RECORD & BIOGRAPHICAL SKETCHES OF THE McCURDYS OF NOVA SCOTIA. Comp. and ed. by ——. London, Covenant, 1930. xxi + 228p [BM LC NBFU

I REMEMBER. Sketches. N.p., Tribune Job Print., n.d. 58p [NSWA

Bland, Salem Goldworth, 1859–1950

JAMES HENDERSON, D.D. Toronto, McClelland, 1926. 360p [BM BVaU OTU QMM

Blauveldt, Robert Brooks, 1894–

THE BLAUVELDT FAMILY IN NOVA SCOTIA. Including all the Yarmouth County Lents and Many of the Van Nordens and Hatfields; with all these Lines Traced back to their Arrival in America in the Early 1600's. Comp. by ——. [Tusket? N.S., 1939.] 19p [BM LC NSHD

LEADERS OF NOVA SCOTIA, 1936. A "Who's Who" of the Political, Professional, Commercial and Moral Leaders of the Province. Ed. by ——. Yarmouth, Loyalist Press, 1936. 82p [BM LC OTP

Blyth, Stephen Cleveland, 1771–

THE CONVERSION OF STEPHEN CLEVELAND BLYTH, TO THE FAITH OF THE CATHOLIC, APOSTOLIC & ROMAN CHURCH. ... Montreal, Nahum Mower, 1822. 100p [OTP

Bock, William George, 1884–

THE BOOK OF SKELETONS. Saskatoon, Modern Press, 1960. 173p

Boddy, Samuel Johnson, 1826–1905

A BRIEF MEMOIR OF THE REV. SAMUEL B. ARDAGH. Toronto, Rowsell & Hutchinson, 1874. 174p [OTP

Bogart, Marshall Campbell, 1847–

SOME NOTES ON THE HISTORY OF THE BOGART FAMILY IN CANADA. With Genealogical Record of my Parents, Lewis Lazier Bogart and Elizabeth Cronk Bogart. Comp. by ——. Toronto, Briggs, 1918. 71p [LC OTP

Boggs, William Edward, 1867–1935

THE GENEALOGICAL RECORD OF THE BOGGS FAMILY, THE DESCENDANTS OF EZEKIEL BOGGS. Halifax, Royal Print., 1916. 105p [NSHD

Bompas, Charlotte Selina (Cox), 1830–1917

A HEROINE OF THE NORTH. Memoirs of Charlotte Selina Bompas (1830–1917), Wife of the First Bishop of Selkirk (Yukon). Comp. by S.A. Archer. Toronto, Macmillan, 1929. 187p [BM BVaU LC OTU QMM

Bond, George John, 1850–

SKIPPER GEORGE NETMAN. A Story of Outpost Methodism in Newfoundland. London, Woolmer, 1887. 126p [A later ed.: Toronto, 1911. 126p] [BM BVaU OTU

Bone, Peter Turner, 1859–1945

WHEN THE STEEL WENT THROUGH. Reminiscences of a Railroad Pioneer. Toronto, Macmillan, 1947. 180p [BVaU LC NSHD OTU QMM

Boniface, Father, 1880–

PIONEERING IN THE WEST. Memories of His Life and Experiences in the West with the Franciscans. Vancouver, Alverna Distributors, 1957. xiv + 277p

Borden, Robert Laird, 1854–1937

ROBERT LAIRD BORDEN: HIS MEMOIRS. Ed. and with a preface by Henry Borden, with an intro. by Arthur Meighen. Toronto, Macmillan, 1938. 2v [BM BVaU LC NSHD OTU QMM

Borthwick, Rev. John Douglas, 1832–1912

HISTORY AND BIOGRAPHICAL GAZETEER OF MONTREAL TO THE YEAR 1892. Montreal, Lovell, 1892. 531p [BVaU OTU QMM

MONTREAL, ITS HISTORY. To Which is Added Biographical Sketches. Montreal, Drysdale, 1875. 153p [BVaU LC NSWA QMM

Bossin, Hye

A SAINT IN STREET CLOTHES. Willie Frankel, His Life and Loyalties. Toronto, Newsboy's Benefit Fund, 1939. 33p [QMJ

Boulton, Charles Arkoll, 1841–1899

REMININSCENCES OF THE NORTH-WEST REBELLIONS ... and a Chapter on Canadian Social and Political Life. Toronto, Grip, 1886. 531p [BM BVaU NSWA OTP

Bourinot, Arthur Stanley, 1893–1969

EDWARD WILLIAM THOMSON (1849–1924). A Bibliography, with Notes and some Letters. Ottawa, Author, 1955. 28p

FIVE CANADIAN POETS: Duncan Campbell Scott, Archibald Lampman, William E. Marshall, Charles Sangster, George Frederick Cameron. Ottawa, Author, 1954. 26p [Rev. ed., 1956]

MORE LETTERS OF DUNCAN CAMPBELL SCOTT. ... (2nd series). Sel. and ed. by ——. (With some personal recollections by the editor.) Ottawa, Editor, 1960. 104p

SOME LETTERS OF DUNCAN CAMPBELL SCOTT, ARCHIBALD LAMPMAN & OTHERS. Ed. by ——. Ottawa, Editor, 1959. 63p

Bourinot, John George, 1837–1902
BUILDERS OF NOVA SCOTIA. Toronto, Copp Clark, 1900. 197p [BVaU LC
NSWA OTU QMM
LORD ELGIN. Toronto, Morang, 1903. 276p [BM BVaU LC NSHD OTU QMM

Boyd, John, 1864–1933
SIR GEORGE ETIENNE CARTIER, BART. His Life and Times. A Political History of
Canada from 1814 until 1873. Toronto, Macmillan, 1914. 439p [BM BVaU LC
NSHD OKQ QMM

Boyle, David, 1842–1911
NOTES ON THE LIFE OF DR. JOSEPH WORKMAN. Toronto, 1894. [DCB

Boyle, George, 1902–1956
PIONEER IN PURPLE. The Life and Work of Archbishop Neil McNeil. Montreal,
Palm Publishers, 1951. 290p
FATHER TOMPKINS OF NOVA SCOTIA. New York, Kenedy, 1953. 234p
THE POOR MAN'S PRAYER. The Story of Credit Union Beginnings. [Fictionized
biography of Alphonse Desjardins.] New York, Harper, 1951. 207p

Bradley, Mrs. Mary, 1771–
A NARRATIVE OF THE LIFE AND CHRISTIAN EXPERIENCE OF MRS. MARY BRADLEY
OF ST. JOHN, N.B. Written by herself. ... Boston, Strong & Brodhead, 1849. 374p
[BVaU NBFU OOP

Brady, Alexander, 1896–
THOMAS D'ARCY McGEE. Toronto, Macmillan, 1925. 182p [BM BVaU LC
NSHD OTU QMM

Brandis, Maxine (van Vollenhoven), 1910–
LAND FOR OUR SONS. London, Toronto, Hurst & Blackett, 1958. 195p

Brasset, Edmund Alfred, 1907–
A DOCTOR'S PILGRIMAGE. Philadelphia, Lippincott, 1951. 256p [Later ed. with
title: BACKWOODS DOCTOR. London, Transworld Pubs., 1956. 253p]

Bready, John Wesley, 1887–1953
DOCTOR BARNARDO. Physician, Pioneer, Prophet. Child Life Yesterday and To-day.
London, Allen & Unwin, 1931. 271p [BM BVaU LC NSHD OTU QMM

Breckenridge, William, 1894–
FROM VIMY TO MONS. A Historical Narrative. N.p., 1957. 251p [Autobiographical
account of the author's experiences in World War 1.] [mimeographed]

Bridgman, Rev. Wellington, 1853–1922
BREAKING PRAIRIE SOD. The Story of a Pioneer Preacher in the Eighties. With a
Discussion of the Burning Question of Today, "Shall the Alien Go?" Toronto,
Musson, 1920. 265p [OTU

Bridle, Augustus, 1869–1952
SONS OF CANADA. Short Studies of Characteristic Canadians. Toronto, Dent, 1916.
279p [BM BVaU LC NSWA OTU QMM

Brierley, James Samuel, 1858–1935
1881 AND ONWARD. Reminiscences of St. Thomas and Elgin County Half a
Century Ago. St. Thomas, Ont., Author, 1931. 47p [OLU

Britnell, John
BOOKS AND BOOKSELLERS IN ANCIENT AND MODERN TIMES. With
Autobiographical Experiences of the Past Sixty Years. Toronto, priv. print.,
1923. 32p [LC OTU

Brock, Anna Maude (Cawthra)
BROCK FAMILY RECORDS. Toronto, Stapleton, 1927. 153p [BM LC NSWA
OTU
THE CAWTHRA FAMILY. Past and Present. Notes by Henry Cawthra and Others.
Comp. by A. Maude (Cawthra) Brock, and ed. by A.H. Young. Toronto, 1924.
47p [BM OLU
THE MILLS, HOLTON, AND SMITH FAMILIES. Comp. by ——. Toronto, 1927. [BM
OTU

Brockington, Leonard Walter, 1888–
MR. MACKENZIE KING'S PUBLIC BEQUESTS. A Commentary. C.B.C. National
Network, Aug. 8, 1950. Ottawa, Estate of W.L.M. King, 1950. 7p [OONL

Brodie, Neil
TWELVE DAYS WITH THE INDIANS, MAY 14–MAY 26, 1885. ... Being his Experience
in Poundmaker's Camp during the Rebellion of 1885. Battleford, Saskatchewan
Herald, 1932. 8p [SSU

Broley, Mrs. Myrtle Jeanne
EAGLE MAN. Charles L. Broley's Field Adventures with American Eagles. New
York, Pellegrini & Cudahy, 1952. xiv + 210p

Brooks, Rev. Edward Arnold
PADRE HOLMES. Portrait of a Ministry. Ed. by ——. Toronto, Editorial Department
of the General Board of Religious Education for the Diocese of Niagara, 1958.
66p

Brown, Audrey Alexàndra, 1904–
THE LOG OF A LAME DUCK. Toronto, Macmillan, 1938. 292p [BM BVaU LC
NSHD OKQ

Brown, Margaret Adeline (Porter), 1867–
EXTRACTS FROM THE LIFE OF JOSEPH BRANT, and history of Six Nations Indians.
Brantford, Moyer, 1941. 44p [Extracts from a book not then published.] [CC

LIFE OF JOSEPH BRANT. Comprising in Part the Origin and History of the Iroquois or Six Nations Indians. N.p., n.d. 166p [OTL OLU

Brown, Rev. Robert Christopher Lundin, –1876
KLATSASSAN, AND OTHER REMINISCENCES OF MISSIONARY LIFE IN BRITISH COLUMBIA. London, S.P.C.K., 1873. 199p [BM BVaU LC NBFU

Brown, Thomas Storrow, 1803–1888
1837: MY CONNECTION WITH IT. Quebec, Renault, 1898. 38p [BM BVaU NBFU OTU QMBM

Brown, William Gordon, 1904–
TO TESTIFY ... THE GRACE OF GOD. In Memoriam Pastor W.J.H. Brown. Toronto, Author, 1935. 60p [CC

Bruce, Herbert Alexander, 1868–1963
VARIED OPERATIONS. An Autobiography. Toronto, Longmans, 1958. xiv + 366p

Bryce, Rev. George, 1844–1931
JOHN BLACK, THE APOSTLE OF THE RED RIVER. Toronto, Briggs, 1898. 158p [BM BVaU NSWA OTP
THE LIFE OF LORD SELKIRK. Coloniser of Western Canada. Toronto, Musson, 1912. 95p [BVaU LC NSHD OKQ QMM
MACKENZIE, SELKIRK, SIMPSON. Toronto, Morang, 1905. 305p [BM BVaU LC NSHD OTU QMM
SKETCH OF THE LIFE AND DISCOVERIES OF ROBERT CAMPBELL. Winnipeg, Manitoba Free Press, 1898. 18p [LC OTP

Bublitz, Mrs. Dorothea E. (Mackie), 1894–
LIFE ON THE DOTTED LINE. New York, Vantage Press, 1960. 110p

Buchanan, Arthur William Patrick, 1870–1939
THE BENCH AND BAR OF LOWER CANADA DOWN TO 1850. Montreal, Burton's, 1925. 219p [BM BVaU LC NBFU OTU QMM
THE BUCHANAN BOOK. The Life of Alexander Buchanan, Q.C., of Montreal, Followed by an Account of the Family of Buchanan. Montreal, Author, 1911. 475p [BVaU LC OTU QMM
LATER LEAVES OF THE BUCHANAN BOOK. Montreal, Garand, 1929. 482p [QMM

Buchanan, Donald William, 1908–1966
JAMES WILSON MORRICE. Toronto, Ryerson, 1937. 187p [BM BVaU LC NSHD OTU QMM

Buckingham, William, 1832–1915
THE HON. ALEXANDER MACKENZIE. His Life and Times. By William Buckingham and Hon. Geo. W. Ross. Toronto, Rose, 1892. 678p [BM BVaU LC NSWA OTU QMM

Buffalo Child Long Lance, Blood Indian Chief, −1932
LONG LANCE. London, Transworld Publishers, 1956. 236p [First pub. New York, Cosmopolitan Book Corp., 1928.]

Bull, William Perkins, 1870−1947
FROM BROCK TO CURRIE. The Military Development and Exploits of Canadians in General and of the Men of Peel in Particular, 1791−1930. (Perkins Bull Hist. Ser.) Toronto, Perkins Bull Fdn., George J. McLeod, 1935. xxiv + 772p [BM BVaU NSHD OKQ OOA

Bullock, Reginald Heber, 1828−
A MEMOIR OF THE VERY REV. WILLIAM BULLOCK, DEAN OF NOVA SCOTIA. Halifax, Morton, 1899. 42p [NSWA OTU

Bullock, Rev. William, 1797−1874
THE RULER'S DAUGHTER RAISED. A Funeral Discourse on the Occasion of the Death of Miss Bliss. Halifax, 1851. 11p [BibC

Bullock Family (Benjamin Bullock, 1792−1852). Canadian Branch.
DESCENDANTS OF BENJAMIN BULLOCK III. Lethbridge, Paramount Print., 1956. 278p

Burgess, Barry Hovey, 1888−
BURGESS GENEALOGY, KING'S COUNTY, NOVA SCOTIA. New York, Fitchett, 1941. 93p [BVaU LC NSHD OTU QMM

Burkholder, Mabel Grace (Clare), 1881−
KIT. Comp. by ——. Niagara Falls, Evening Review, 1933. 16p [Life of Kathleen Blake Coleman.] [Brown U OTU

Burnett, Rev. Andrew Ian, 1906−
THE RIGHT HONOURABLE WILLIAM LYON MACKENZIE KING. P.C., O.M., December 17th, 1874−July 22nd, 1950. Memorial Addresses Delivered at St. Andrew's Church, Ottawa ... July 26th ... July 30th, 1950. Ottawa, Laurier House, 1950. 15p [OONL

Burnham, John Hampden, 1860−1940
CANADIANS IN THE IMPERIAL NAVAL AND MILITARY SERVICE ABROAD. Toronto, Williamson, 1891. 240p [BM BVaU NSHD OTU

Burns, Rev. Robert Ferrier, 1826−1896
THE LIFE AND TIMES OF THE REV. ROBERT BURNS. Including an Unfinished Autobiography. Ed. by his Son, ——. Toronto, Campbell, 1872. 462p [BVaU LC NSHD OOP QMM

Burns, William C., 1857−1929?
SEEING THE WORLD THROUGH THE EYES OF OTHERS. Edmonton, 1929. 16p [ACG

TWENTY YEARS OF THRILLING ADVENTURES IN THE SILENT PLACES OF THE
NORTH. By W.C. Burns (blind), [with the assistance of Ruby Erwin. Edmonton,
Douglas Print., 1929?]. 72p [AEU

Burpee, Lawrence Johnstone, 1873–1946
CHARLES HEAVYSEGE. A Monograph. Ottawa, Royal Society of Canada, 1901.
42p [NSHD OLU
PATHFINDERS OF THE GREAT PLAINS. A Chronicle of La Vérendrye and his Sons.
Toronto, Glasgow Brook, 1914. 116p [BM BVaU LC NSWA OTU QMM
SANDFORD FLEMING, EMPIRE BUILDER. London, Oxford U. Press, 1915. 288p
[BM BVaU LC NSHD OTU QMM

Burris, Matthew George, 1887–1948
MY PIONEER ANCESTORS. An Account of the Burris and Dean Families of
Musquodoboit, Nova Scotia. ... [Truro, N.S.? 1950?]. 293p [OONL

Burt, Silas Wright, 1830–1912
AN ENGINEER ON THE GREAT WESTERN. A Selection from the Personal
Reminiscences of Silas Wright Burt. Ed. by A.G. Bogue and Lilian R. Benson.
London, Ont., Lawson Memorial Library, U. of Western Ontario, 1952. 35p

Burton, Charles Luther, 1876–
A SENSE OF URGENCY. Memoirs of a Canadian Merchant. Toronto, Clarke Irwin,
1952. 363p

Burton, Jean, 1905–1952
ELISABETH NEY. By Jan Fortune and Jean Burton. Toronto, Ryerson, 1943.
300p [BM BVaU LC QMM
GARIBALDI, KNIGHT OF LIBERTY. New York, Knopf, 1945. 225p [LC
HEYDAY OF A WIZARD: DANIEL HOME, THE MEDIUM. New York, Knopf, 1944.
275p [BM LC OTU QMM
KATHERINE FELTON AND HER SOCIAL WORK IN SAN FRANCISCO. Stanford U.,
Delkin, 1947. 274p [LC OTU
LYDIA PINKHAM IS HER NAME. New York, Farrar, 1949. 279p [LC OTU QMM
SIR RICHARD BURTON'S WIFE. New York, Knopf, 1941. 378p [BM BVaU LC
OTU QMM

Burwash, Rev. Nathanael, 1839–1918
EGERTON RYERSON. Toronto, Morang, 1903. 303p [Pref.: "The little work is the
product of joint labour with my ... colleague, Dr. A.H. Reynar."] [BM BVaU
LC NSWA OTU QMM
MEMORIALS OF THE LIFE OF EDWARD & LYDIA ANN JACKSON. Toronto, Rose,
1876. 86p [BVaU LC OKQ

Buschlen, John Preston, 1888–
SENOR PLUMMER. The Life and Laughter of an Old Californian. By Don Juan
[pseud]. Los Angeles, Times Mirror, 1942. 242p [BVaU LC

Butler, William Francis, 1838–1910
SIR WILLIAM BUTLER. An Autobiography. London, Constable, 1911. 476p [BM BVaU NSWA OTP QMM

Byerly, Alpheus Edward, 1894–1960
THE McCRAES OF GUELPH. Elora, Ont., Elora Express, 1932. 13p [BVaU OTP

C., A.L.O. (pseud)
THE STORY OF A DARK PLOT; or, Tyranny on the Frontier. By A.L.O.C. [pseud]. Montreal, Lovell, 1898. 197p [Also: Boston, Warren Press, 1903.] [On dismissal of Wm. W. Smith, temperance agitator, from the service of the C.P.R.] [BM BVaU OTU

Calnek, William Arthur, 1822–1892
A BRIEF MEMOIR OF THE LATE HON. JAMES WILLIAM JOHNSTON, FIRST JUDGE IN EQUITY OF NOVA SCOTIA. Saint John, Knodell, 1884. 49p [NSWA QMM

Calvert, Reuben, 1865–1940
THE STORY OF ABIGAIL BECKER, THE HEROINE OF LONG POINT. As Told by her Step-Daughter, Mrs. Henry Wheeler. Ed. by ——. Toronto, Briggs, 1899. 20p [OTP

Cameron, James Malcolm, 1913–
THE DESCENDANTS OF DONALD CAMERON, A HIGHLAND IMMIGRANT WHO SETTLED AT PITCHER'S FARM, COUNTY OF ANTIGONISH, NOVA SCOTIA, CANADA. New Glasgow, N.S., Hector Pub. Co., 1957. 73p
SHIPS AND SEAMEN OF NEW GLASGOW, NOVA SCOTIA. New Glasgow, Author, 1959. 45p

Campbell, Mrs. Dorothy de Brissac
DU BARRY. An Intimate Biography. New York, Covici Friede, 1931. 351p [BVaU LC QMM
THE INTRIGUING DUCHESS, MARIE DE ROHAN, DUCHESSE DE CHEVREUSE. New York, Covici Friede, 1930. 392p [BM LC NBFU OTP QMM

Campbell, Gray, 1912–
WE FOUND PEACE. Toronto, Ryerson, 1953. 244p

Campbell, Jessie (Buchanan)
THE PIONEER PASTOR. Some Reminiscences of the Life and Labours of the Rev. George Buchanan, M.D., First Presbyterian Minister of Beckwith, Lanark County, Upper Canada. Toronto, Author, 1900. 56p [Another ed., 1905.] [BVaU OLU

Campbell, John Lorne, 1906–
FR ALLAN McDONALD OF ERISKAY, 1859–1905, PRIEST, POET, AND FOLKLORIST. Based upon a Broadcast Talk Recorded at Antigonish, Nova Scotia, in May, 1953, and Printed to Mark the Fiftieth Anniversary of the Consecration of Eriskay Church, built by Fr. Allan. London, Oliver & Boyd, 1954. 31p

Campbell, Marjorie Elliott (Wilkins), 1901–
THE SOIL IS NOT ENOUGH. Toronto, Macmillan, 1938. 285p [Biography of her father, William Herbert Wilkins.] [BM BVaU LC OTU SSU

Campbell, Marjorie (Freeman), 1896–
HOLBROOK OF THE SAN. Toronto, Ryerson, 1953. xi + 212p

Campbell, Milton Neil, 1881–
REMINISCENCES OF PIONEER DAYS IN THE WEST. Hamilton, Author, [1960?]. 12p

Campbell, Robert, 1808–1894
TWO JOURNALS OF ROBERT CAMPBELL (CHIEF FACTOR, HUDSON'S BAY COMPANY) 1808 TO 1853. ... Seattle, 1958. 151p [Preface signed John W. Todd, Jr.] [mimeographed]

Campbell, Robert Eldon, 1871–
I WOULD DO IT AGAIN. Reminiscences of the Rockies. Toronto, Ryerson, 1959. ix + 204p

Campbell, Robert McAlpine, 1907–
WHEE! THE PEOPLE. A Collection of Election Yarns. Toronto, Nelson, 1957. 75p

Camsell, Charles, 1876–1958
SON OF THE NORTH. Toronto, Ryerson, 1954. xii + 244p

Canadian Association of Children's Librarians.
LILLIAN H. SMITH, A TRIBUTE FROM THE C.A.C.L. Ottawa, Canadian Library Association, 1952. 60p

Canadian Daily Newspaper Publishers Association.
RENOWNED EDITORS OF CANADIAN DAILY NEWSPAPERS. Toronto, Thomson Newspapers, 1957. 21p

Canadian Music Library Association.
A BIO-BIBLIOGRAPHICAL FINDING LIST OF CANADIAN MUSICIANS AND THOSE WHO HAVE CONTRIBUTED TO MUSIC IN CANADA, COMPILED BY A COMMITTEE OF THE CANADIAN MUSIC LIBRARY ASSOCIATION, 1960–61. Ottawa, Canadian Library Association, 1961. 53p [mimeographed]

Canadian Newspaper Service
REFERENCE BOOK, 1927+. Biographical Reference Data and Other General

Information for Library, Newspaper and Individual Use. Montreal, Can. Newspaper Service, 1928 +. [Title changed in 1936 to NATIONAL REFERENCE BOOK ON CANADIAN MEN AND WOMEN.]   [BVaU LC NBFU OTU QMM

Canadian Press Syndicate
ENCYCLOPEDIA OF CANADIAN BIOGRAPHY. Containing Brief Sketches and Steel Engravings of Canada's Prominent Men. Montreal, Canadian Press Syndicate, 1904–7. 3v [OTU

Canadian Publicity Co.
PIONEERS AND PROMINENT PEOPLE OF MANITOBA. Winnipeg, Bulman, 1925. 367p [BVaU OTU
PIONEERS AND PROMINENT PEOPLE OF SASKATCHEWAN. Toronto, Ryerson, 1924. 343p [BVaU
PROMINENT PEOPLE OF THE MARITIME PROVINCES. Saint John, Canadian Pub. Co., 1922. 215p [OTU
PROMINENT PEOPLE OF THE PROVINCE OF ONTARIO. Ottawa, Can. Biographies, 1925. 274p [OTU

Cannell, Kathleen Biggar (Eaton), 1891–
JAM YESTERDAY. New York, Morrow, 1945. 239p [LC OTU QMM

Careless, James Maurice Stockford, 1919–
BROWN OF THE GLOBE. Toronto, Macmillan, 1959–63. 2v

Carman, Bliss, 1861–1929
BLISS CARMAN'S SCRAP BOOK. A Table of Contents. Ed. with a postscript by Lorne Pierce. Toronto, Ryerson, [1931]. 18p [An index of a scrap book kept by Carman of his fugitive writings, 1883–1919.] [BVaU LC NSHD QMM

Carr, Emily, 1871–1945
THE BOOK OF SMALL. Toronto, Oxford U. Press, 1942. 245p [BM BVaU LC NSHD OTU
EMILY CARR: HER PAINTINGS AND SKETCHES. Toronto, Oxford U. Press, 1945. 64p [BM BVaU LC NBFU OTU
GROWING PAINS. The Autobiography of Emily Carr. Toronto, Oxford U. Press, 1946. 381p [BM BVaU LC NSHD OTU QMM
THE HEART OF A PEACOCK. Ed. by Ira Dilworth. Toronto, Oxford U. Press, 1953. 234p
THE HOUSE OF ALL SORTS. Toronto, Oxford U. Press, 1944. 222p [BM BVaU LC NSHD OTU
KLEE WYCK. Toronto, Oxford U. Press, 1941. 155p [BM BVaU LC NBFU OKQ

Carr, William James Guy, 1895–1959
BRASS HATS AND BELL-BOTTOMED TROUSERS. Unforgettable and Splendid

Feats of the Harwich Patrol. Being volume two of BY GUESS AND BY GOD.
London, Hutchinson, 1939. 272p [OTP

BY GUESS AND BY GOD. The Story of the British Submarines in the War.
Garden City, Doubleday, 1930. 310p [BM BVaU LC OTU QMM

GOOD HUNTING. Being volume three of BY GUESS AND BY GOD. London,
Hutchinson, 1940. 288p [BM OTP

HELL'S ANGELS OF THE DEEP. Toronto, Gundy, 1932. 288p [BM OTP

HIGH AND DRY. The Post-War Experiences of the Author of BY GUESS AND
BY GOD. London, Hutchinson, 1938. 253p [BM LC NBFU OTU

Carr-Harris, Bertha Hannah (Wright), 1863–1949

LIGHTS AND SHADES OF MISSION WORK; or, Leaves from a Worker's Note
Book. Being Reminiscences of Seven Years' Service at the Capital,
1885–1892. By B.H.W. [pseud]. Ottawa, Free Press, 1892. [Amtmann
cat. 145

THE WHITE CHIEF OF THE OTTAWA. Toronto, Briggs, 1903. 252p [Biography
of Philemon Wright.] [BM BVaU NBFU OTP QMM

Carrel, Frank, 1870–1940

IMPRESSIONS OF WAR. Quebec, Telegraph Print., 1919. 248p [BM OTP

Carroll, Rev. John, 1809–1884

CASE AND HIS CONTEMPORARIES; or, The Canadian Itinerants' Memorial. ...
A Biographical History of Methodism in Canada. Toronto, Rose, 1867–77.
5v [BVaU LC NSWA OKQ

"FATHER CORSON"; or, The Old Style Canadian Itinerant. Embracing the Life
and Gospel Labours of the Rev. Robert Corson. Toronto, Rose, 1879.
277p [BVaU OTP

MY BOY LIFE. Presented in a Succession of True Stories. Toronto, Briggs, 1882.
288p [BVaU LC NBFU OTP

THE STRIPLING PREACHER; or ... The Life ... of the Rev. Alexander S. Byrne.
Toronto, Green, 1852. 255p [BVaU NSWA OTP

Carroll, Peter Owen

THE LIFE AND ADVENTURES OF DETECTIVE PETER OWEN CARROLL. N.p.,
n.pub., 1923. 80p [BVaU NSWA

Carruthers, John, –1866

RETROSPECT OF THIRTY-SIX YEARS' RESIDENCE IN CANADA WEST. Hamilton,
M'Intosh, 1861. 253p [BVaU NSHD OTP QMM

Carter, J. Smyth, 1877–

DOCTOR M.W. LOCKE AND THE WILLIAMSBURG SCENE. Toronto, 1933. 138p
[BVaU LC OTP

Carter, S.M.

WHO'S WHO IN BRITISH COLUMBIA, 1930+. An Illustrated Record. ... Ed. by ——.
Victoria, Carter, 1930+. [A continuing serial.] [BVaU LC OOP

Cartwright, Rev. Conway Edward, 1837–1920

LIFE AND LETTERS OF THE LATE HON. RICHARD CARTWRIGHT. Ed. by ——.
Toronto, Belford, 1876. 145p [BVaU LC NSWA OKQ

Cartwright, George, 1739–1819

CAPTAIN CARTWRIGHT AND HIS LABRADOR JOURNAL. Ed. by Charles Wendell
Townsend. Boston, Estes, 1911. xxxiii + 385p [BM BVaU LC NSWA
OTU

Cartwright, Richard John, 1835–1912

REMINISCENCES. Toronto, Briggs, 1912. 408p [BM BVaU LC NSWA OTP

Case, Rev. William, 1780–1855

A CIRCUIT RIDER ON THE RIVER THAMES. The Diary of William Case, 20
June–26 August 1809. Ed. by John S. Moir. London, Ont., Lawson
Memorial Library, U. of Western Ontario, 1958. 22p

Casey, Rev. David A., 1886–

CAPT. THE REV. T.E. MOONEY. Kingston, Can. Register, n.d. 36p [OTU

Cashman, Anthony Walcott, 1923–

ERNEST C. MANNING. A Biographical Sketch. Edmonton, Alberta Social Credit
League, 1958. 35p

THE VICE-REGAL COWBOY. Life and Times of Alberta's J.J. Bowlen. Edmonton,
Institute of Applied Art, 1957. 200p

Chadwick, Edward Marion, 1840–1921

THE CHADWICKS OF GUELPH AND TORONTO AND THEIR COUSINS. Toronto,
Davis & Henderson, 1914. 88p [Contains also genealogy of the Bell family.]
[LC OTU

ONTARIAN FAMILIES. Genealogies of United-Empire-Loyalist and Other
Pioneer Families of Upper Canada. Toronto, Rolph Smith, 1895–98. 2v
[BM LC NSWA OTU QMM

Chalmers, John West, 1910–

FUR TRADE GOVERNOR, GEORGE SIMPSON, 1820–1860. Edmonton, Institute
of Applied Art, 1960. 190p

Charlesworth, Hector Willoughby, 1872–1945

A CYCLOPAEDIA OF CANADIAN BIOGRAPHY. In the Twentieth Century. Ed.
by ——. Toronto, Hunter Rose, 1919. 303p [BVaU LC OTU

GRENVILLE KLEISER, EXPONENT OF SELF-HELP. New York, Funk & Wagnalls,
1919. 19p [BM

Chaureth, Sophie (Berthelette), 1799—
SKETCHES OF THE LIFE, TROUBLES, AND GRIEVANCES OF A FRENCH CANADIAN
LADY. Caused Especially by Civil and Religionist Political Persecution. Written
by herself. Toronto, 1857. 32p [OTP

Chester, Rev. Eldred Augustus, 1890—
THIS I LEARNED. Toronto, Ryerson, 1957. 78p [Reminiscences of a
Methodist minister.]

Chiniquy, Rev. Charles Paschal Télesphore, 1809—1899
FIFTY YEARS IN THE CHURCH OF ROME. Chicago, Craig & Barlow, 1885.
832p [Numerous later editions.] [BM BVaU LC NSWA OTU QMBM
FORTY YEARS IN THE CHURCH OF CHRIST. Chicago, Revell, 1900. 498p
[BVaU BM LC NSWA QMSS
THE LIFE AND LABOURS OF THE REV. FATHER CHINIQUY. Glasgow, Religious
Tract Soc., 1861. 33p [BM QMSS
THE TWO CHINIQUYS: FATHER CHINIQUY VERSUS MINISTER CHINIQUY.
Montreal, True Witness, 1898. 24p [Earlier ed., 1893?] [BVaU QMSS

Chisholm, Joseph Andrew, 1863—1950
JOSEPH HOWE. A Sketch, with a Chronology. Halifax, Chronicle Print., 1909.
44p [BM NSWA QMM

Chown, Alice Amelia, 1866—1949
THE STAIRWAY. Boston, Cornhill, 1921. 340p [LC NBFU OTP

Church, Herbert E., 1868—
AN EMIGRANT IN THE CANADIAN NORTHWEST. London, Methuen, 1929. 134p
[BM BVaU OTU SSU
MAKING A START IN CANADA. Letters from Two Young Emigrants, with an
intro. by Alfred J. Church, M.A. By —— and Richard Church. London,
Seeley, 1889. 224p [BM LC NSHD OOP SSU

Chute, Rev. Arthur Crawley, 1853—1936
BIOGRAPHY OF JOHN THOMAS. N.p., Baptist Book, 1893. 58p [NSWA

Chute, Arthur Hunt, 1890—1929
THE REAL FRONT. New York, Harper, 1918. 308p [BM BVaU LC NSWA
QMM

Clark, Jeremiah Simpson, 1872—1950
RAND AND THE MICMACS. Charlottetown, Examiner, 1899. 81p [BM BVaU
NSHD OTU QMM

Clark, Mattie M.I.
THE POSITIVE SIDE OF JOHN GRAVES SIMCOE. Toronto, Forward, 1943. 121p
[OTU

Clarke, Adele

OLD MONTREAL. John Clarke—his Adventures, Friends and Family. By his daughter. Montreal, Herald, 1906. 47p [BVaU MWU OTU

Clarke, Charles, 1826–1909

SIXTY YEARS IN UPPER CANADA. With Autobiographical Recollections. Toronto, Briggs, 1908. 321p [BM BVaU NSHD OKQ

Clarke, Henry J.

A SHORT SKETCH OF THE LIFE OF THE HON. D'ARCY McGEE. Montreal, Lovell, 1868. 80p [BVaU OTU QMM

Clarke, Peter Dooyentate

ORIGIN AND TRADITIONAL HISTORY OF THE WYANDOTTS, AND SKETCHES OF OTHER INDIAN TRIBES OF NORTH AMERICA. True Traditional Stories of Tecumseh and his League in the Years 1811 and 1812. [Anon] Toronto, Hunter Rose, 1870. 158p [BVaU LC OTU

Clarke, William Fletcher, 1824–1902

"IN MEMORIAM": THE LATE REV. JOHN ROAF. Toronto, Chewett, [1863?]. 12p [OTP

Clarke, William Henry, 1902–1955

WILLIAM HENRY CLARKE, 1902–1955. A Memorial Volume, Containing Some Recent Speeches and Writing Chiefly Concerned with Publishing & Education in Canada over Thirty Years. Toronto, Clarke Irwin, 1956. xvii + 141p

Clegg, Howard

A CANUCK IN ENGLAND. Journal of a Canadian Soldier. London, Harrap, 1942. 160p [BVaU NBS OTP

Clint, Mabel Brown, 1874–1939

OUR BIT. Memories of War Service by a Nursing Sister. Montreal, Barwick, 1934. 177p [BVa NBSaM OTU QMSS

Coates, M. Helen

IN MYSTERIOUS WAYS. White Rock, B.C. [Printed by Bulman Bros., Winnipeg], 1952? 62p

Coats, Robert Hamilton, 1874–1960

SIR JAMES DOUGLAS. By Robert Hamilton Coats and R.E. Gosnell. De luxe ed. Toronto, Morang, 1908. 369p [Also: Toronto, Oxford U. Press, 1926. 386p] [BM BVaU LC NSHD OTU

Coburn, Rev. John, 1874–1954

I KEPT MY POWDER DRY. Toronto, Ryerson, 1950. 185p [BVaU NSHD OTU
GRACE, GRIT, AND GUMPTION. Toronto, Ryerson, 1952. 181p [Sequel to his I KEPT MY POWDER DRY.]

Cochrane, Charles Norris, 1889—1945
DAVID THOMPSON, THE EXPLORER. Toronto, Macmillan, 1924. 173p [BM
BVaU LC NSHD OTU

Cochrane, James Arthur, 1891—1947
LAVOISIER. London, Constable, 1931. 264p [BM LC OTU QMM

Cochrane, Rev. William, 1831—1898
THE CANADIAN ALBUM. Men of Canada; or, Success by Example. ... Brantford,
Bradley Garretson, 1891—96. 5v [BM BVaU NSWA OTP
MEMOIRS AND REMAINS OF THE REV. WALTER INGLIS, African Missionary and
Canadian Pastor. Toronto, Robinson, 1887. 325p [BVaU OTP
A QUIET AND GENTLE LIFE. In Memoriam Mary Neilson Houstoun Cochrane
[1834—1871]. Brantford, Hudson & Sutherland, 1871. 84p [OTP

Cody, Hiram Alfred, 1872—1948
AN APOSTLE OF THE NORTH. Memoirs of the Right Reverend William Carpenter
Bompas, D.D., First Bishop of Athabaska, 1874—1884, First Bishop of
Mackenzie River, 1884—1891, First Bishop of Selkirk (Yukon), 1891—1906.
Toronto, Musson, 1908. 385p [BM BVaU LC NSWA OTU
ON TRAIL AND RAPID BY DOGSLED AND CANOE. The Story of Bishop Bompas's
Life amongst the Red Indians and Eskimos. Told for Boys and Girls. Toronto,
Musson, 1911. 203p [Also later editions.] [BM BVaU LC OTUV

Colby, Charles Williams, 1867—1955
THE FIGHTING GOVERNOR. A Chronicle of Frontenac. Toronto, Glasgow
Brook, 1915. 167p [BM BVaU LC NSWA OTU
THE FOUNDER OF NEW FRANCE. A Chronicle of Champlain. Toronto,
Glasgow Brook, 1915. 158p [BM BVaU LC NSWA OTU

Colgate, William G., 1882—
ARCHIBALD LAMPMAN, A DEDICATION AND A NOTE. Toronto, priv. print.,
1957. 15p
ARTHUR HEMING. Recorder of the North. Toronto, Best, 1934. 13p [Another
ed.: Toronto, Best, 1938. 16p] [OTP
C.W. JEFFERYS. Toronto, Ryerson, 1945. 42p [BVaU NBFU OTP
TWO LETTERS OF TOM THOMSON, 1915 AND 1916. Weston, Ont., Old Rectory
Press, 1946. 15p (Printed as a Christmas message for Dr. and Mrs. A.D.A.
Mason of Toronto.) [BVaU NBFU OTP

Colley, B.W., 1852?—
REMINISCENCES. Toronto, Author, 1944. 72p [OTP

Collier, Eric, 1903—1966
THREE AGAINST THE WILDERNESS. New York, Dutton, 1959. 349p

Collins, Alice Helen (Roger),   −1955

A BIOGRAPHICAL SKETCH OF KATHERINE E. WALLIS, CANADIAN ARTIST.
Fort Erie, Review Co., 1948. 52p [OTP

PEN PICTURES ... REAL PEOPLE, SKETCH NO. I: ABRAHAM GROVES. [Walkerton,
Telescope, 1931.] 23p [OTP

PEN PICTURES ... REAL PEOPLE, SKETCH NO. II: MARION G. FERGUSON.
Walkerton, Author, [1932?]. 18p [OTP

PEN PICTURES ... REAL PEOPLE, SKETCH NO. III: SIR CHARLES BRUCE ... AND
LADY BRUCE AND THE ISLAND OF MAURITIUS. [Walkerton, Telescope,
1933.] 30p [OTP

PEN PICTURES ... REAL PEOPLE, SKETCH NO. IV: JULES TREMBLAY. [Walkerton,
Telescope, 1934.] 34p [OTP

PEN PICTURES ... REAL PEOPLE, SKETCHES NO. V, VI, VII, VIII: ELIZABETH
VEALS; PETER McARTHUR; ELLEN MARY KNOX; J.L. YULE. [Walkerton,
Herald-Times, 1935.] 50p [OTP

PEN PICTURES ... REAL PEOPLE, SKETCHES NO. IX, X: HARRY M. FIELD; "THE
GLIDDONS." London, Ont., Chapman, 1936. 77p [OTP

PEN PICTURES ... REAL PEOPLE, SKETCH NO. XI: IVY G. COVENTRY. Walkerton,
Herald-Times, 1937. 19p [OTP

PEN PICTURES ... REAL PEOPLE, SKETCH NO. XII: MARGARET MACKELLER.
Walkerton, Herald-Times, n.d. 36p [OTU

REAL PEOPLE, PEN PICTURES: AUGUSTUS STEPHEN VOGT. Sketch 12. Elora,
Express Pr., n.d. 38p [UTQ'42

Collins, Joseph Edmund, 1855−1892

CANADA'S PATRIOTIC STATESMAN. The Life and Career of the Right Honorable
Sir John A. Macdonald. Based on the work of Edmund Collins. Rev. by
G. Mercer Adams. Toronto, Rose, 1891. 613p [First pub. under title:
LIFE AND TIMES OF THE RIGHT HONORABLE SIR JOHN A. MACDONALD.
Toronto, Rose, 1883. 642p] [BM BVaU LC NSHD OTP

Collison, Rev. William Henry, 1847−1922

IN THE WAKE OF THE WAR CANOE. A Stirring Record of Forty Years'
Successful Labour, Peril & Adventure among the Savage Indian Tribes of the
Pacific Coast, and the Piratical Head-hunting Haidas of the Queen
Charlotte Islands, B.C. London, Seeley, 1915. 352p [BM BVaU LC NBFU
OKQ

Colquhoun, Arthur Hugh Urquhart, 1861−1936

THE HON. JAMES R. GOWAN, MEMBER OF CANADIAN SENATE. A Memoir. Ed.
by ——. Toronto, priv. print., 1894. 170p [BVaU NBFU OTU

PRESS, POLITICS AND PEOPLE. The Life and Letters of Sir John Willison,
Journalist and Correspondent of *The Times.* Toronto, Macmillan, 1935.
306p [BM BVaU LC NSHD OTP

Comfort, Charles Fraser, 1900–
ARTIST AT WAR. Toronto, Ryerson, 1956. xvii + 187p

Composers, Authors, and Publishers Association of Canada
TRIBUTE TO A NATION BUILDER. An Appreciation of Dr. John Murray Gibbon.
Toronto, The Association, 1946. 31p [NBFU OTP

Connolly, Rev. Thomas Louis, 1815–1876
FUNERAL ORATION ON THE LATE HON. THOMAS D'ARCY McGEE, Delivered in
the Metropolitan Church of St. Mary's, Halifax, Nova Scotia. Halifax, Compton,
1868. 24p [NSWA

Connon, John Robert, 1862–1931
FLORENCE NIGHTINGALE'S LOVER ... The Life of the Rev. John Smithurst.
[No title page.] 4p [OTU

Constance, Arthur, 1891–
THE GLAZIER. London, Laurie, 1956. 279p [Biography of H.J. Constance.]

Cook, Frederick, 1858–1943
THE CANADIAN WHO'S WHO. Ed. by ——. Toronto, 1910. [NBFU OOP

Cook, Rev. John, 1805–1892
A SERMON PREACHED ON THE OCCASION OF THE DEATH OF THE REV. ROBERT
McGILL, Minister of St. Paul's Church, Montreal. Montreal, Ramsay, 1856.
27p [NSWA OTP

Cooke, Martha Stoddard (Colby), 1865–1951
ABOVE THE POST OFFICE. Memories, Sketches and Stories. Vancouver,
priv. print., 1953. 38p

Cooney, Rev. Robert, 1800–1870
THE AUTOBIOGRAPHY OF A WESLEYAN METHODIST MISSIONARY (Formerly a
Roman Catholic). ... Montreal, Pickup, 1856. 407p [NSWA OTP QMM

Cooper, John Alexander, 1868–1956
MEN OF CANADA. ... A Portrait Gallery. ... Ed. by ——. Montreal, Can. Historical
Co., 1901–2. 296p [BVaU LC NSHD OTU QMM

Cooper, William Barrett, 1857–
LIFE AND WORK OF WILLIAM TINDALE. Toronto, Longmans, 1924. 54p
[BM BVaU LC OTUV

Copeland, Donalda Murray (McKillop), 1916–
REMEMBER, NURSE. As Told to Eugenie Louise Myles. Toronto, Ryerson,
1960. 250p

Copway, George, 1818–1863
THE LIFE, HISTORY, AND TRAVELS OF KAH-GE-GA-GAH-BOWH (GEORGE COPWAY)
... Chief of the Ojebwa Nation ... and a Missionary to his People. ... Written by

himself. Philadelphia, Harmstead, 1847. 158p (2nd ed.) [BM LC NSWA OTP QMM

THE LIFE, LETTERS AND SPEECHES OF KAH-GE-GA-GAH-BOWH, or G. Copway. ... New York, Benedict, 1850. 224p [Includes THE LIFE, HISTORY, AND TRAVELS OF KAH-GE-GA-GAH-BOWH.] [BM LC OTP

RECOLLECTIONS OF A FOREST LIFE; or, The Life and Travels of Kah-ge-ga-gah-bowh, or George Copway, Chief of the Ojibway Nation. London, Gilpin, [Preface 1850]. 248p [BM BVaU OTP

RUNNING SKETCHES OF MEN AND PLACES, IN ENGLAND, FRANCE, GERMANY, BELGIUM, AND SCOTLAND. New York, Riker, 1851. 346p [BM LC OOU

Corbett, Edward Annand, 1887–

FATHER, GOD BLESS HIM. Toronto, Ryerson, 1953. 76p [Life of Thomas C. Corbett.]

HENRY MARSHALL TORY: BELOVED CANADIAN. Toronto, Ryerson, 1954. 242p

McQUEEN OF EDMONTON. Toronto, Ryerson, 1934. 125p [BVaU OTP SSU

WE HAVE WITH US TONIGHT. Toronto, Ryerson, 1957. xviii + 222p [Autobiographical account of the author's work in adult education, 1920–51.]

Cormack, Barbara (Villy), 1903–

THE RED CROSS LADY (MARY H. CONQUEST, M.B.E.) Edmonton, Institute of Applied Art, 1960. 92p

Costain, Thomas Bertram, 1885–1965

THE CHORD OF STEEL. The Story of the Invention of the Telephone. Garden City, N.Y., Doubleday, 1960. 238p

Coventry, Ivy G.

BIOGRAPHY OF JOHN COVENTRY, M.D., 1836–1902. Toronto, Author, n.d. 8p

Cowan, Charles L.

THE TRAIL OF THE SKY PILOT. Toronto, Westminster Press, 1929. 208p [BVaU NBFU OTMC

Cowan, John Bruce, 1882–

CANADA'S GOVERNORS-GENERAL, 1867–1952. Toronto, York Pub. Co., 1952. 210p

JOHN INNES, PAINTER OF THE CANADIAN WEST. Vancouver, Rose, Cowan & Latta, 1945. 33p [BVaU OTP SSU

Cowans, David

ANECDOTES OF A LIFE ON THE OCEAN. Being a Portion of the Experiences of Twenty-seven Years' Service in many Parts of the World. Montreal, Lovell, 1871. 198p [BVaU LC NSHD OKQ

Cowie, Isaac, 1848–1917

THE COMPANY OF ADVENTURERS. A Narrative of Seven Years in the Service of the Hudson's Bay Company during 1867–1874, on the Great Buffalo Plains, with Historical and Biographical Notes and Comments. Toronto, Briggs, 1913. 515p [BM BVaU LC NBFU SSU

Cox, Corolyn
CANADIAN STRENGTH. Biographical Sketches. Toronto, Ryerson, 1946. 192p [BM BVaU LC NSHD OTU

Cox, Harold Robert Wakeford, 1907–
GREENHORNS IN BLUE PASTURES. New York, Smith & Durrell, 1945. 162p [BVaU NSHPL OTP

Cox, Ross, 1793–1853
ADVENTURES ON THE COLUMBIA RIVER. Including the Narrative of a Residence of Six Years on the Western Side of the Rocky Mountains, among various Tribes of Indians hitherto unknown; Together with a Journey across the American Continent. London, Colburn & Bentley, 1831. 2v [Also pub. as: ADVENTURES ON THE COLUMBIA RIVER. ... New York, Harper, 1832. 335p; and London, Colburn & Bentley, 1832. 2v] [BM BVaU LC NSWA OTP SSU

Coyne, James Henry, 1849–1942
RICHARD MAURICE BUCKE. A Sketch. Toronto, Saunders, 1923. 77p [BM BVaU LC OTP

Cragg, Kenneth C., 1904–1948
FATHER ON THE FARM. Toronto, Longmans, 1947. 173p [BVaU LC NBFU OKQ QMM

Craig, James Beverley, 1894–
THE CRAIGS OF GOULBOURNE AND NORTH GOWER. Kingston, Hanson & Edgar, 1929. 220p [LC OLU

Cramp, Rev. John Mockett, 1796–1881
A MEMOIR OF MADAME FELLER. With an Account of the Origin and Progress of the Grande Ligne Mission. Comp. by ——. Montreal, Grafton & Drysdale, 1876. 254p [BVaU BM LC NSWA OTU QMM
A PORTRAITURE FROM LIFE. By a Bereaved Husband [pseud]. Halifax, Christian Messenger, 1862. 18p [Haight Pt I

Cramp, Mary
THE RADIANT LIFE. A Memoir of Ruth Marion Shatford-Holmes. By Mary Cramp and Maud C. Edgar. 55p [NSHD

Cranston, James Herbert, 1880–1952
ETIENNE BRULE: IMMORTAL SCOUNDREL. Toronto, Ryerson, 1949. 144p [BM BVaU LC NSHD OTU QMM
INK ON MY FINGERS. Toronto, Ryerson, 1953. 188p

Crawley, Rev. Edmund Albern, 1799–1888

FUNERAL DISCOURSE ... JANUARY 4, 1874, ON THE DEATH OF ... JAMES W. JOHNSTON, Judge in Equity for the Province of Nova Scotia. Halifax, Bowes, 1874. 20p [NSHP

A SERMON PREACHED IN ... HALIFAX, N.S., MARCH 12, 1837 ON THE OCCASION OF THE DECEASE OF ELIZA L. TREMAIN. Halifax, English & Blackadar, 1837. 17p [NSHD

Creighton, Donald Grant, 1902–

HAROLD ADAMS INNIS. Portrait of a Scholar. Toronto, U. of Toronto Press, 1957. 146p

JOHN A. MACDONALD. The Young Politician. Toronto, Macmillan, 1952. 524p

JOHN A. MACDONALD. The Old Chieftain. Toronto, Macmillan, 1955. 630p

Creighton, William Black, 1864–1946

ROUND 'BOUT SUN-UP. Some Memories that Live. Toronto, Ryerson, 1946. 55p [BVaU LC NBFU OTP QMM

Crockett, Asa James, 1870–

GEORGE MUNRO "THE PUBLISHER." Halifax, Dalhousie U. Press, 1957. 34p

Crofton, Francis Blake, 1841–1912

HALIBURTON, THE MAN AND THE WRITER. A Study. Winslow, N.S., Anslow, 1889. 73p [BM BVaU LC NBFU OTU QMM

Crofton, Walter Cavendish, 1806?–1870

A BRIEF SKETCH OF THE LIFE OF CHARLES, BARON METCALFE ... to the Period of his Resigning the Office of Governor General of the British North American Colonies, in 1845. Originally compiled for the "British Whig." By "Uncle Ben" [pseud]. Kingston, Atheneum, 1846, 37p [OTP

Croil, James, 1821–1916

LIFE OF JAMES CROIL, MONTREAL. An Autobiography, 1821–1916. Montreal, Mitchell & Wilson, 1918. 247p [BVaU OTUV

LIFE OF THE REV. ALEX. MATHIESON. [Anon] ... With a Funeral Sermon by the Rev. John Jenkins ... and three Discourses ... by Dr. Mathieson. Montreal, Dawson, 1870. 261p [The LIFE is often attributed to the Rev. John Jenkins.] [BM BVaU NSWA OTP QMSS

Crompton, F.C.B.

GLIMPSES OF EARLY CANADIANS: LAHONTAN. Toronto, Nelson, 1925. 101p [BM BVaU LC NBFU OTU

Crosby, Rev. Thomas, 1840–1914

DAVID SALIOSALTON. Toronto, Briggs, n.d. 62p [BViPA OTP

AMONG THE AN-KO-ME-NUMS OR FLATHEAD TRIBES OF INDIANS OF THE PACIFIC
COAST. Toronto, Briggs, 1907. 243p [BM BVaU LC NSHD OTU
UP AND DOWN THE NORTH PACIFIC COAST BY CANOE AND MISSION SHIP.
Toronto, The Missionary Soc., Methodist Church, 1914. 403p [BVaU LC
NSHD OKQ

Cross, Austin Fletcher, 1898–
THE PEOPLE'S MOUTHS. Toronto, Macmillan, 1943. 171p [BVaU LC OTU
QMM

Crowe, John Congdon, 1888–
IN THE DAYS OF THE WINDJAMMERS. Toronto, Ryerson, 1959. xi + 176p

Crowell, William Arthur, 1879–
THE ROAR OF THE SEA. Dartmouth, N.S., Author, 1955. 93p

Crowfoot, Alfred Henchman, 1881–
BENJAMIN CRONYN, FIRST BISHOP OF HURON. London, Ont., Incorporated
Synod of the Diocese of Huron, 1957. 142p

Cruikshank, Ernest Alexander, 1854–1939
THE CORRESPONDENCE OF THE HONOURABLE PETER RUSSELL WITH ALLIED
DOCUMENTS Relating to his Administration of the Government of Upper
Canada. ... Coll. & ed. by E.A. Cruikshank and A.F. Hunter. Toronto,
Ontario Hist. Soc., 1932–1936. 3v [BM NBFU OTU QMM
THE LIFE OF SIR HENRY MORGAN. With an Account of the English Settlement
of the Island of Jamaica (1655–1688). Toronto, Macmillan, 1935. 448p
[BM BVaU OTU
A MEMOIR OF COLONEL THE HONOURABLE JAMES KERBY. His Life in Letters.
Welland, Hist. Soc., 1931. 349p [BM BVaU QMSS
THE POLITICAL ADVENTURES OF JOHN HENRY. The Record of an International
Imbroglio. Toronto, Macmillan, 1936. 206p [BM BVaU OTU

Cruikshank, Julia E. (Kennedy), –1921
WHIRLPOOL HEIGHTS. The Dream-House on the Niagara River. London,
Allen, 1915. 254p [BM OTL

Currelly, Charles Trick, 1876–1957
I BROUGHT THE AGES HOME. Toronto, Ryerson, 1956. xx + 312p

Currie, Arthur William, 1875–1933
SIX YEARS AT McGILL. A Review. [Montreal, McGill Univ., 1926.] 50p
[BVaU NSHD OTU QMM

Currie, Emma Augusta (Harvey), 1829–1913
THE STORY OF LAURA SECORD AND CANADIAN REMINISCENCES. Toronto,
Briggs, 1900. 195p [Same title: St. Catharines, Ont., 1913. 254p] [BM
BVaU LC NSHD OKQ

Currie, John Allister, 1868–1931
"THE RED WATCH." With the First Canadian Division in Flanders. Toronto, McClelland, 1916. 308p [BM LC NSWA OTP

Curtis, James Davis, 1868–
ST. THOMAS AND ELGIN MEDICAL MEN OF THE PAST. St. Thomas, Ont., Elgin County Pioneer Museum, 1956. 122p

Curwen, Samuel, 1715–1802
JOURNAL AND LETTERS OF THE LATE SAMUEL CURWEN. ... To which are added, Biographical Notices of Many American Loyalists and Other Eminent Persons. By George Atkinson Ward. New York, Francis & Co., 1842. 578p [Several later editions.] [BM LC NSWA OTP QMSS

Curzon, Mrs. Sarah Anne, 1833–1898
THE STORY OF LAURA SECORD, 1813. Toronto, Williamson, 1891. 15p [Also: Welland, Ont., Telegraph, 1898. 16p] [BM BVaU LC NSWA OTU

Cushing, Elmer
AN APPEAL, ADDRESSED TO A CANDID PUBLIC ... WHEREIN IS DISPLAYED THE SINGULAR HISTORY OF THE AUTHOR TOGETHER WITH THAT OF OTHER AMERICANS SETTLED IN THE PROVINCE OF LOWER CANADA. Stanstead, Author, 1826. 88p [NSWA

Cushing, James Stevenson, 1878–
GENEALOGICAL RECORD OF THE DESCENDANTS OF JOHN WALTERS AND MARY DeVAISSAILLE. Montreal, 1944. [2nd ed. Montreal, 1952. 62p]

Cushing, Lemuel
THE GENEALOGY OF THE CUSHING FAMILY. Montreal, Lovell, 1877. 117p [NSWA OTP

Cyr, Narcisse, 1823?–1894
MEMOIR OF THE REV. C.H.O. COTE, M.D. ... With a Memoir of Mrs. M.Y. Cote, and a History of the Grande Ligne Mission, Canada East. Philadelphia, Am. Baptist Pub. Soc., 1852. 144p [BM LC NSWA OTU

Dafoe, John Wesley, 1866–1944
CLIFFORD SIFTON IN RELATION TO HIS TIMES. Toronto, Macmillan, 1931. 552p [BM BVaU LC MWU NSHD OTU
LAURIER. A Study in Canadian Politics. Toronto, Allen, 1922. 182p [BM BVaU LC NSWA OKQ
SIXTY YEARS IN JOURNALISM. Text of Address delivered ... Winnipeg Press Club. ... Winnipeg, Royal Alexandra Hotel, 1943. 13p [OTU

Dale-Harris, Leslie Ruth (Howard), 1924–
A QUITE REMARKABLE FATHER. By Leslie Ruth Howard. New York, Harcourt, 1959. 307p

Daly, George Thomas, 1872–1956
MY FATHER. The Life of an Exemplary Catholic Layman. Toronto, Catholic Truth Soc., 1945. 153p [OTU

Darling, Rev. William Stewart, 1818–1886
SKETCHES OF CANADIAN LIFE. Lay and Ecclesiastical. By a Presbyter of the Diocese of Toronto [pseud]. London, Bogue, 1849. 310p [BM BVaU LC NBFU OTU

Darwin, Oliver, 1860–1961
PIONEERING WITH PIONEERS. (An Autobiography). Toronto, United Church of Canada, 1949. 151p [BVaU

Davidson, William Harold
AN ACCOUNT OF THE LIFE OF WILLIAM DAVIDSON OTHERWISE JOHN GODSMAN. Saint John, New Brunswick Museum, 1947. 60p [BVaU NBFU

Davidson, William McCartney, 1872–1942
LOUIS RIEL, 1844–1885. A Biography. Calgary, Albertan Pub. Co., 1955. 214p [Complete ed.; to replace earlier THE LIFE AND TIMES OF LOUIS RIEL. Calgary, The Albertan, 1951. 114p]

Davies, Blodwen, 1897–1966
PADDLE AND PALETTE. The Story of Thom Thomson. ... Toronto, Ryerson, 1930. 35p [BVaU OTP
A STUDY OF TOM THOMSON. A Story of a Man who Looked for Beauty and for Truth in the Wilderness. Toronto, Discus Press, 1935. 133p [BVaU LC NBFU OTU

Davies, Evan, 1881?–1959?
BEYOND THE OLD BONE TRAIL. By Evan Davies and Aled Vaughan. London, Cassell, 1960. 172p

Davies, William, 1831–1921
LETTERS OF WILLIAM DAVIES, TORONTO, 1854–1861. Ed. by William Sherwood Fox. Toronto, U. of Toronto Press, 1945. 144p [BM BVaU LC NSHD OTU QMM

Davin, Nicholas Flood, 1843–1901
THE EARL OF BEACONSFIELD. With Disraeli anecdotes never before published. Regina, Leader Co., 1890. 12p [Earlier ed.: Toronto, Belford, 1876. 42p] [LC OTU
THE SECRETARY OF THE ROYAL SOCIETY OF CANADA (J.G. Bourinot). A Literary Fraud. Ottawa, 1882. 20p [BM LC NSHD OTU

Davis, Bruce Pettit, and Davis, Carroll Langstaff
THE DAVIS FAMILY & THE LEATHER INDUSTRY, 1834–1934. Toronto, Ryerson, 1934. 145p [BM BVaU LC OTU

Davis, Herbert John, 1893–
CHARLES DOUGHTY, 1843–1926. New York, Hammer, 1945. 31p [LC OTU

Davis, Rev. John, 1803?–1875
THE PATRIARCH OF WESTERN NOVA SCOTIA. Life and Times of the Late Rev. Harris Harding, Yarmouth, N.S. Comp. by ——. With an intro. by J.W. Nutting. Charlottetown, Bremner, 1866. xxii + 271p [BVaU NSWA OTP

Dawson, Rev. Aeneas MacDonell, 1810–1894
PIUS IX, AND HIS TIME. London, Coffey, 1880. 440p [BM OTU
SERMONS. D'Arcy McGee ... etc. Ottawa, 1868. [OTU

Dawson, John William, 1820–1899
BIOGRAPHICAL SKETCH OF JAMES McGILL. N.p., n. pub., 1859. 14p [NSWA
FIFTY YEARS OF WORK IN CANADA, SCIENTIFIC AND EDUCATIONAL. Being Autobiographical Notes by Sir William Dawson. ... Ed. by Rankine Dawson. London, Ballantyne, 1901. 308p [BM BVaU LC NSHD OTU QMM
IN MEMORIAM, PETER REDPATH. Governor and Benefactor of McGill University. ... Montreal, "Witness" Print., 1894. 39p [OLU QMM

Dawson, Robert MacGregor, 1895–1958
WILLIAM LYON MACKENZIE KING. A Political Biography. Toronto, U. of Toronto Press, 1958. V. 1: 1874–1923. 500p

Day, Effie Jamieson
ANNIE ELIZABETH BRADLEY. Toronto, Women's Missionary Society of the United Church of Canada, 1936. 31p [UTQ'37

Day, Frank Parker, 1881–1950
THE AUTOBIOGRAPHY OF A FISHERMAN. Garden City, Doubleday, 1927. 202p [Also: New York, Minton Balch, 1932.] [BM BVaU NBFU OKQ QMM

Deacon, William Arthur, 1890–
PETER McARTHUR. Toronto, Ryerson, 1923. 180p [BM BVaU NSHD OTU

Deane, Richard Burton, 1848–1930
MOUNTED POLICE LIFE IN CANADA. London, Cassell, 1916. 311p [BM BVaU NBFU OTU QMM

Deans, Dorothea
C.A. FLEMING. A Biography. Owen Sound, Ont., 1953. 162p

De La Roche, Mazo, 1879—1961
RINGING THE CHANGES. An Autobiography. Toronto, Macmillan, 1957.
xvi + 304p

De Mille, James, 1833—1880
MANUSCRIPT COLLECTION. ... Letters ... Documents, Unpublished Manuscripts of
James De Mille [and other members of the De Mille family] , covering the years
1850—1881. [NSHD

Denison, George Taylor, 1839—1925
RECOLLECTIONS OF A POLICE MAGISTRATE. Toronto, Musson, 1920. 263p
[BVaU LC NSHD OTU QMM
SOLDIERING IN CANADA. Recollections and Experiences. ... Toronto, Morang,
1901. 364p [BM BVaU LC NSWA OKQ

Denison, Richard Lonton, 1910—
THE CANADIAN PIONEER DENISON FAMILY OF COUNTY YORK, ENGLAND, AND
COUNTY YORK, ONTARIO. A History, Genealogy and Biography. Toronto,
Author, 1951—52. 3v.

Denison, Septimus Julius Augustus, 1859—1937
MEMOIRS. Toronto, Best, 1927. 174p [BM OTU QMM

Dennis, William Alexander, 1903—1961
THE DENNIS GENEALOGY. An Account of the Dennis Ancestry with Supplements
on the Millers and Archibalds, Biographical and Genealogical with Portraits.
Kentville, N.S., priv. print., 1959. 38 + 4p

Denny, Cecil Edward, 1850—1928
THE LAW MARCHES WEST. Toronto, Dent, 1939. 319p [BM BVaU OLU
THE RIDERS OF THE PLAINS. A Reminiscence. ... Calgary, Herald, 1905. 223p
[BVaU OTUV QMM

Dent, John Charles, 1841—1888
THE CANADIAN PORTRAIT GALLERY. Toronto, Magurn, 1880—81. 4v [BVaU
LC NSWA OKQ QMM

Desaulniers, Abel, 1913—
IN LOVE WITH WINGS. The Story of a Barnstorming Pilot. New York, Exposition
Press, 1959. 78p

Dewar, David G.
QUEEN'S PROFILES. [Biographical Sketches of 14 Former Members of the Faculty
at Queen's University.] Kingston, Queen's University, 1951. 124p

DeWitt, Norman Wentworth, 1876—1958
IN MEMORIAM ANDREW JAMES BELL, 1856—1932. ... Toronto, Clarke Irwin, 1934.
29p [OLU

Dezell, Robert, 1866–

FIRE AND FROST. The Meadow Lea Tragedy. Toronto, Briggs, 1907. 131p [Title changed same year to: A NIGHT ON THE PRAIRIE: The Meadow Lea Tragedy. Bound with THE LIFE STORY OF FINLAY BOOTH, by Hamilton Wigle.] [BM BVaU NSHD OTU

Dick, Catharine (Bond), 1891–

TRAILS I'VE RIDDEN. An Era in the Prairie-foothill Country of Alberta. Calgary, Dick, 1946. 63p [ACG LC

Dickie, Charles Herbert, 1859–

OUT OF THE PAST. By an M.P. [pseud]. N.p., [1934?]. 128p [OOP

Dickson, Lovat, 1902–

THE ANTE-ROOM. Toronto, Macmillan, 1959. 270p

THE GREEN LEAF. A Tribute to Grey Owl. Ed. by ——. London, Lovat Dickson, 1938. 109p [ACG BM LC NBFU OTU

HALF-BREED. The Story of Grey Owl (Wa-Sha-Quon-Asin). London, Davies, 1939. 345p [BM BVaU LC OKQ

RICHARD HILLARY. London, Macmillan, 1950. 201p [BM BVaU LC

Diesel, Gladys Cynthia Rebecca (Shope), 1907–

SALUTE TO THE PAST. Edmonton, Commercial Printers, 1957. 188p

Dionne, Emil

REMINISCING. Spokane, Wash., Evergreen Press, 1952. 64p

Dixon, James Dunbar, 1819–

HISTORY OF CHARLES DIXON. One of the Early Settlers of Sackville, N.B. Comp. by ——. Rockfort, Ill., Forest City Pub. Co., 1891. 200p [BVaU LC NSWA OTU

Dodds, Edmund King, –1910

CANADIAN TURF RECOLLECTIONS AND OTHER SKETCHES. Toronto, 1909. 304p [BM BVaU OTU

Doherty, Rev. Patrick J., 1838–1872

PRINCIPAL ENGLISH WRITINGS OF THE LATE REV. P.J. DOHERTY. With a Sketch of his Life. Quebec, Huot, 1873. 237p [BVaU OTP

Dooner, Alfred James, 1865?–1949

COLONEL JOHN MacDONELL. First Speaker of the House of Assembly of Upper Canada, 1750–1809. Toronto, Extension Print., n.d. 15p [OTU

HON. ALEXANDER McDONELL (COLLACHIE). Speaker of the Legislative Assembly of Upper Canada, 1762–1842. Toronto, Author, [194–?]. 24p [OTP

RIGHT REV. EDMUND BURKE., D.D. Apostle of Upper Canada ... Vicar Apostolic of Nova Scotia. Hull, Leclerc, 1941. 17p [CC

Doran, George Henry, 1869–1956
CHRONICLES OF BARABBAS, 1884–1934 and FURTHER CHRONICLES AND COMMENT, 1952. New York, Rinehart, 1952. xiii + 446p [First ed. of CHRONICLES OF BARABBAS: New York, Harcourt Brace, 1935.]

Doughty, Arthur George, 1860–1936
A DAUGHTER OF NEW FRANCE. Being a Story of the Life and Times of Magdelaine de Verchères, 1665–1692. Ottawa, Mortimer, 1916. 166p [BM BVaU LC NBFU OTU QMM

Douglas, Alice Vibert, 1894–
THE LIFE OF ARTHUR STANLEY EDDINGTON. London, Nelson, 1956. xi + 207p

Douglas, James, 1800–1886
JOURNALS AND REMINISCENCES OF JAMES DOUGLAS, M.D. Ed. by his son. New York, priv. print., 1910. 254p [BM BVaU LC OTU

Douglas, James, 1837–1918
A MEMOIR OF THOMAS STERRY HUNT. Philadelphia, MacCalla, 1898. 61p [LC OTU QMM

Douglas, John Harvey, 1888–
CAPTURED. Sixteen Months as a Prisoner of War. Toronto, McClelland, 1918. 195p [BVaU NSHD OTP QQL

Doull, John, 1878–
REVEREND ALEXANDER McGILLIVRAY, D.D. Halifax, Author, 1938. 24p [OTU

Dow, Rev. John, 1885–
ALFRED GANDIER. Man of Vision and Achievement. Toronto, United Church Pub. House, 1951. 138p

Doyle, Sister St. Ignatius
MARGUERITE BOURGEOYS AND HER CONGREGATION. Gardenvale, Que., Garden City Press, 1941. 325p [OTU

Dressler, Marie, 1873–1934
THE EMINENT AMERICAN COMEDIENNE MARIE DRESSLER. In the Life Story of an Ugly Duckling. An Autobiographical Fragment. ... New York, McBride, 1924. 234p [BM LC
MY OWN STORY AS TOLD TO MILDRED HARRINGTON. Boston, Little Brown, 1934. 289p [BM LC OTU QMM

Drew, Andrew, 1792–1878
THE BURNING OF THE CAROLINE, AND OTHER REMINISCENCES OF 1837–38. By Rear-Admiral Drew ... and Judge [Robert Stuart] Woods. Chatham, Ont., Banner, 1896. 20p [OTP
A NARRATIVE OF THE CAPTURE AND DESTRUCTION OF THE STEAMER 'CAROLINE,'

AND HER DESCENT OVER THE FALLS OF NIAGARA. ... London, Spottiswoode, 1864. 31p [BM OKQ

Drummond, May Isobel (Harvey)

THE GRAND OLD MAN OF DUDSWELL. Being the Memoirs of the Rev. Thos. Shaw Chapman, M.A., Rector of St. Paul's Church, Marbleton. Quebec, Telegraph, 1916. 182p [BVaU OTU

Duff, Louis Blake, 1878–1959

ADDRESS ... AT A DINNER ... ON THE OCCASION OF THE UNVEILING OF A BRONZE BUST OF STEPHEN LEACOCK BY ELIZABETH WYN WOOD, Orillia Public Library, Friday, 14th Sept., 1951. Fort Erie, Review Co., 1951. 16p

AMAZING STORY OF THE WINGHAMITE SECRETARY OF LOUIS RIEL. London, Ont., Lawson Memorial Library, U. of Western Ontario, 1955. 37p [Biography of William Henry Jackson.]

BURNABY. Welland, Tribune-Telegraph, 1926. 38p [BM BVaU OKQ QMM

JANE SUSAN DUFF ... HER BOOK. Welland, Baskerville Press, 1940. 44p [OTU

MUDDIMAN, THE FIRST EDITOR. Welland, Tribune-Telegraph, 1925. 9p [OTU

Duncan, Dorothy, 1903–1957

PARTNER IN THREE WORLDS. New York, Harper, 1944. 340p [Biography of Jan Rieger (pseud). Pub. in England under title: PORTRAIT OF JAN.] [BM BVaU LC NBFU OTU QMM

Duncan, Eric, 1858–1944

FIFTY SEVEN YEARS IN THE COMOX VALLEY. Courtenay, B.C., Comox Argus Co., 1934. 61p [BVaU OTP

FROM SHETLAND TO VANCOUVER ISLAND. Recollections of Seventy-five Years. Edinburgh, Oliver & Boyd, 1937. 277p [3rd ed., enl., 1939. 303p] [BM BVaU LC OTU

Duncan, Norman, 1871–1916

DR. GRENFELL'S PARISH: THE DEEP SEA FISHERMEN. Toronto, Revell, 1905. 155p [BM BVaU LC NSWA OTU

HIGGINS, A MAN'S CHRISTIAN. New York, Harper, 1909. 116p [Biography of Francis Edmund Higgins.] [BVaU LC OKQ

Dunlop, William, 1792–1848

RECOLLECTIONS OF THE AMERICAN WAR 1812–14. Ed. with a Biographical Sketch of the Author by A.H.U. Colquhoun. Toronto, Historical Pub. Co., 1905. 112p [BM BVaU LC NSHD OTP QMM

WILLIAM "TIGER" DUNLOP, "BLACKWOODIAN BACKWOODSMAN." Essays by and about Dunlop, sel. and ed. by Carl F. Klinck. Toronto, Ryerson, 1958. xii + 185p

Durand, Charles, 1811–1905

REMINISCENCES OF CHARLES DURAND OF TORONTO, BARRISTER. Toronto,

Hunter Rose, 1897, 1899. 663p [Pub. in two forms—one in 1897 with 536p and again with added material paged continuously, 537–663.] [BM BVaU LC MWU NBFU OLU

Duval, Paul
ALFRED JOSEPH CASSON, PRESIDENT, ROYAL CANADIAN ACADEMY. Toronto, Ryerson, 1952. 64p

Earl, Lawrence, 1915–
CROCODILE FEVER. A True Story of Adventure. New York, Knopf, 1954. x + 293p

Eaton, Arthur Wentworth Hamilton, 1849–1937
THE COCHRAN-INGLIS FAMILY OF HALIFAX. Halifax, Ruggles, 1899. 18p [BM BVaU LC NSWA
THE EATON FAMILY OF NOVA SCOTIA, 1760–1929. Cambridge, Mass., Murray, 1929. 247p [BM BVaU LC NSHD OTU
THE ELMWOOD EATONS. Kentville, N.S., Advertiser, 1895. 29p [BM LC NSWA OOA
FAMILIES OF EATON–SUTHERLAND, LAYTON-HILL. New York, priv. print., 1899. 20p [BM BVaU LC NSWA
THE FAMOUS MATHER BYLES, THE NOTED BOSTON TORY PREACHER, POET, AND WIT, 1707–1788. Boston, Butterfield, 1914. 258p [BM BVaU LC NSWA OTU
GENEALOGICAL SKETCH OF THE NOVA SCOTIA EATONS. Halifax, Morning Herald, 1885. 128p [BM BVaU LC NSWA OTU
LT. COL. OTHO HAMILTON OF OLIVESTOB ... MEMBER OF THE NOVA SCOTIA COUNCIL FROM 1731–1744; HIS SONS, CAPTAIN JOHN AND LIEUTENANT-COLONEL OTHO HAMILTON 2ND, AND HIS GRANDSON, SIR RALPH HAMILTON, KT. Halifax, Ruggles, 1899. 22p [BM BVaU NSWA OTP
MEMORIAL SKETCH OF WILLIAM EATON. New York, priv. print., 1893. 16p [BVaU NSWA OTP
THE OLIVESTOB HAMILTONS. New York, Author, 1893. 32p [BM BVaU LC NSWA

Eaton, Evelyn Sybil Mary, 1902–
EVERY MONTH WAS MAY. New York, Harper, 1947. 241p [BM BVi LC OOP QMM
THE NORTH STAR IS NEARER. New York, Farrar Straus, 1949. 232p [BM BVi LC OOP QMM

Eaton, Flora McCrea, 1880–1970
MEMORY'S WALL. The Autobiography of Flora McCrea Eaton. Toronto, Clarke Irwin, 1956. xii + 214p

Eayrs, Hugh Smithurst, 1894–1940
SIR ISAAC BROCK. An Historical Monograph. Toronto, Macmillan, 1918. 108p
[Rev. ed., 1924.] [BM BVaU LC NSWA OKQ

Eby, Ezra E., 1850–
BIOGRAPHICAL HISTORY OF THE EBY FAMILY AND OF THEIR SETTLEMENT IN
AMERICA. Berlin, Ont., Hett & Alby, 1889. 144p [LC OTU

Eccles, William John, 1917–
FRONTENAC, THE COURTIER GOVERNOR. Toronto, McClelland, 1959. ix + 406p

Edgar, Helen Madeline (Boulton), –1933
DAHABEAH DAYS. An Egyptian Winter Holiday. Toronto, Ryerson, 1923. 85p
[BM BVaU OTU QMM

Edgar, Matilda (Ridout), 1844–1910
A COLONIAL GOVERNOR IN MARYLAND: HORATIO SHARPE AND HIS TIMES, 1753–
1773. London, Longmans, 1912. 311p [BM BVaU NSHD OTU QMM
GENERAL BROCK. Toronto, Morang, 1904. 322p [Also: London, Oxford U. Press,
1926. 324p] [BM BVaU LC NSWA OTU

Edwards, Charles Austin McNally, 1917–
BROOK WATSON OF BEAUSEJOUR. Toronto, Ryerson, 1957. 183p
TAYLOR STATTEN. A Biography. With a foreword by J. Alex. Edmison. Toronto,
Ryerson, 1960. xii + 161p

Ellerby, John Williams, 1862–
THE ELLERBY FAMILY TREE. Weston, Charters Pub. Co., 1935. 50p [CC

Elliott, Sophy Louisa, 1880–
OUR CANADIAN STATESMEN. Ed. by ——. Montreal, D'Arcy McGee Pub. Co.,
1958. 36p
THE WOMEN PIONEERS OF NORTH AMERICA. Gardenvale, Que., Garden City Press,
1941. 299p [BVaU OTU

Elliott, William Edmund, 1883–
POLITICS IS FUNNY. Toronto, Britannia Printers, 1951. 128p [2nd ed., Toronto,
Burns & MacEachern, 1952. 170p]

Ellis, Jean MacLachlan
FACE POWDER AND GUNPOWDER. By Jean M. Ellis with Isabel Dingman. Toronto,
Saunders, 1947. 229p [BVaU OTU QMM

Ermatinger, Edward, 1797–1876
LIFE OF COLONEL TALBOT, AND THE TALBOT SETTLEMENT. Its Rise and Progress,
with Sketches of ... Public Characters. ... St. Thomas, McLachlin, 1859. 230p
[BVaU LC NSWA OTP QMM

Estabrooks, Florence Cecilia, 1883—
THE ESTABROOKS FAMILY IN CONCORD, MASSACHUSETTS AND ON THE SAINT
JOHN RIVER, NEW BRUNSWICK, CANADA, ALSO IN HAVERHILL, MASSACHUSETTS.
Saint John, Author, 1953—1956. 2v [mimeographed].
GENEALOGY OF THE ANGLO-DUTCH ESTABROOKS FAMILY OF THE SAINT JOHN
RIVER, NEW BRUNSWICK. Rev. 1958. Saint John, Author, 1935 [i.e., 1959].
210p

Eustace, Cecil John, 1903—
A CANADIAN FOUNDRESS. The Life of Aurelie Caouette, Foundress of the
Institute of the Precious Blood. Toronto, Basilian Press, 1947. 31p [OTU

Evans, Hubert Reginald, 1892—
NORTH TO THE UNKNOWN. The Achievements and Adventures of David Thompson.
New York, Dodd Mead, 1949. 224p [BVi LC OOP

Evans, Rev. Richard C., 1861—
AUTOBIOGRAPHY OF ELDER R.C. EVANS, One of the First Presidency of the
Reorganized Church of Jesus Christ of Latter Day Saints. London, Ont.,
Advertiser, 1907. 358p [T&C
FORTY YEARS IN THE MORMON CHURCH: WHY I LEFT IT. Toronto, n.p. [pref.
1920]. [OTUV

Factor, Alexander, 1896—
OLD TIMES. Ilfracombe, Devon, Stockwell, 1956. 127p

Fairbairn, Rev. Charles Victor, 1890—
I CALL TO REMEMBRANCE. Winona Lake, Ind., Light and Life Press, 1960. 185p

Fairley, Thomas Christopher, 1919—
THE TRUE NORTH. The Story of Captain Joseph Bernier. By T.C. Fairley & Charles
E. Israel. Toronto, Macmillan, 1957. 160p

Falconer, Rev. James William, 1868—1956
JOHN GEDDIE, HERO OF THE NEW HEBRIDES. Toronto, Presbyterian Church in
Canada, 1915. 118p [NSHD OTUV QMM

Fallis, Rev. George Oliver, 1885—1952
A PADRE'S PILGRIMAGE. Toronto, Ryerson, 1953. xi + 166p

Fanning, David, 1756?—1825
THE NARRATIVE OF COL. DAVID FANNING. ... Giving an Account of his Adventures
... from 1775—1783. As Written by Himself. Ed. with intro. and notes. New
York, J. Sabin's Reprints, 1865. xxvi + 86p [First printed in 1861 in Richmond,
Va. Later re-edited by A.W. Savary and reprinted from *The Canadian Magazine*
1908.] [BVaU LC NSHPL OONL QMBM

Farmer, Jones Hughes, 1858–1928

E.W. DADSON: THE MAN AND HIS MESSAGE. Ed. by ——. Toronto, Briggs, 1902. 379p [NSWA OTU

Farnalls, Paul L.

MEMOIRS OF LIFE IN ALBERTA. N.p., [1960?] 46p

Farquharson, Mrs. James

RECOLLECTIONS OF A PIONEER MINISTER AND HIS WORK. By his Wife. N.p., 1927. 34p [MWUC

Farthing, Rev. John Cragg, 1861–1947

RECOLLECTIONS OF THE RIGHT REVEREND JOHN CRAGG FARTHING, BISHOP OF MONTREAL, 1909–1939. Toronto, Church House, 1945. 191p [BVaU OTP

Fast, Gerhard Andrew, 1853–1924

TO FIND THE DAILY BREAD. Pt. 1 written by Gerhard Andrew Fast. Pt. 2 by Jacob Fast. Saskatoon, Western Producer, 1954. 48p

Faughnan, Thomas, fl. 1835–1883

STIRRING INCIDENTS IN THE LIFE OF A BRITISH SOLDIER. An Autobiography. Toronto, Hunter Rose, 1879. 336p [Several later editions, same place and publisher, e.g., "3rd edition" in 1881, 360p, and one in 1885, "Twenty-second Thousand—Enlarged and Illustrated" 536p] [BVaU LC NSHD OTP QMBM

Fawcett, Edgar, 1847–1923

SOME REMINISCENCES OF OLD VICTORIA. Toronto, Briggs, 1912. 294p [BM BVaU NBFU OTU

Fea, Rev. Samuel, 1872–1943

IRISH NED, THE WINNIPEG NEWSY. Toronto, Briggs, 1910. 28p [BM BVaU OTU

Fenety, George Edward, 1812–1899

LIFE AND TIMES OF THE HON. JOSEPH HOWE. Saint John, Carter, 1896. 376p [BM BVaU NSWA OTP

Ferguson, George Victor, 1897–

JOHN W. DAFOE. Toronto, Ryerson, 1948. 127p [BM BVaU LC NSHD OTU QMM

Fergusson, Charles Bruce, 1911–

CHARLES FENERTY. The Life and Achievement of a Native of Sackville, Halifax County, N.S. Halifax, 1955. 15p

Ferns, Henry Stanley, 1913–

THE AGE OF MACKENZIE KING. By H.S. Ferns and B. Ostrey. V.1: The Rise of the Leader. London, Heinemann; Toronto, British Book Service, 1955. xii + 356p

Ferrie, Adam, 1777–1863
AUTOBIOGRAPHY, LATE HON. ADAM FERRIE. N.p., n.d. 36p [OTP

Fetherstonhaugh, Robert Collier, 1892–1949
CHARLES FLEETFORD SISE, 1834–1918. A Biography. Montreal, Gazette, 1944.
238p [BM BVaU OTU QMM

Firbank, Thomas, 1910–
I BOUGHT A STAR. London, Harrap, 1951. 240p [Author's military experiences.]
LOG HUT. London, Harrap, 1954. 200p

Fisher, Claude Laing
JAMES, CARDINAL McGUIGAN, ARCHBISHOP OF TORONTO. Toronto, McClelland,
1948. 133p [BVaU NBFU OTP

Fitkin, Edward
"COME ON, TEEDER!" The Story of Ted (Teeder) Kennedy, Captain of The
Toronto Maple Leafs. Toronto, Baxter Pub. Co., 1950. 141p [OONL
FOOTLOOSE IN HOCKEY. Toronto, Baxter Pub. Co., 1951. 144p
THE GASHOUSE GANG OF HOCKEY. Toronto, Baxter Pub., 1951. 144p
MAURICE RICHARD, HOCKEY'S ROCKET. Toronto, Baxter Pub., 1951. 144p
MAX BENTLEY, HOCKEY'S DIPSY-DOODLE DANDY. Toronto, Baxter Pub., 1951.
144p
TURK BRODA OF THE LEAFS. The Story of One of Hockey's Greatest Goalkeepers.
Toronto, Baxter Pub., 1950. 143p [OONL

Fitzgibbon, Mary Agnes, 1851–1915
A VETERAN OF 1812. The Life of James Fitzgibbon. Toronto, Briggs, 1894. 347p
[BM BVaU LC NSHD OTP

Fitzpatrick, Frank Joseph Emile, 1861–
SERGEANT 331: Personal Recollections of a Member of the Canadian Northwest
Mounted Police from 1879–1885. New York, Author, 1921. 126p [BVaU LC
OTU

Fleming, Rev. Archibald Lang, 1883–1953
ARCHIBALD THE ARCTIC. New York, Appleton-Century-Crofts., 1956. 399p
THE HUNTER-HOME; or, Joseph Pudlo, a Life Obedient to a Commanding Purpose.
Toronto, 1930. 43p [OLU
PERILS OF THE POLAR PACK; or, The Adventures of the Rev. E.W.T. Greenshield,
of Blacklead Island, Baffin Land. Toronto, Missionary Society of Church of
England in Canada, 1932. 175p [BM OTU

Flenley, Ralph, 1886–1969
SAMUEL DE CHAMPLAIN, FOUNDER OF NEW FRANCE. Toronto, Macmillan, 1924.
149p [BM BVaU LC NSHD OTU QMM

Fontaine, Robert Louis, 1911–1965
HELLO TO SPRINGTIME. New York, Crowell, 1955. 246p

Footner, Hulbert, 1879–1944
SAILOR OF FORTUNE. The Life and Adventures of Commodore Barney, U.S.N.
New York, Harper, 1940. 323p [LC OONL

Foran, Joseph Kearney, 1857–1931
JEANNE MANCE; or, "The Angel of the Colony," Foundress of the Hotel-Dieu
Hospital, Pioneer Nurse of North America, 1642–1673. Montreal, Herald, 1931.
192p [BVaU LC NBFU OTU QMM

Ford, Arthur Rutherford, 1880–1968
AS THE WORLD WAGS ON. The Autobiography of a Roving Editor. Toronto,
Ryerson, 1950. 228p [BVaU NBFU OTUV

Ford, Frederick Samuel Lampson, 1869–
WILLIAM DUNLOP. Toronto, Britnell, 1934. 60p [BVaU OTP

Fordyce, Alexander Dingwall, –1894
EPITOME; or, Who? What? Where? When? respecting the Family of Dingwall
Fordyce and Connexions, 1655–1884. Comp. by A.D.F. Fergus, Ont., 1884.
107p [OKQ
FAMILY RECORD OF THE NAME OF DINGWALL FORDYCE IN ABERDEENSHIRE.
Showing Descent ... both Direct and Collateral. ... Comp. by ——. Fergus, Ont.,
n. pub., 1885–88. 2v [LC OLU
THE MONUMENTAL INSCRIPTIONS IN THE CEMETERY AT BELLESIDE, FERGUS.
Fergus, Ont., Author, 1883. 80p [OTP

Forster, John Wycliffe Lowes, 1850–1938
UNDER THE STUDIO LIGHT. Leaves from a Portrait Painter's Sketch Book. Toronto,
Macmillan, 1928. 244p [BVaU LC NBFU OTU QMM

Foster, George Eulas, 1847–1931
MEMOIRS. Ed. by W.S. Wallace. Toronto, Macmillan, 1933. 291p [BVaU NBFU
OTUV

Foster, William Alexander, 1840–1888
CANADA FIRST. A Memorial of the Late William A. Foster, Q.C. With intro. by
Goldwin Smith. Toronto, Hunter Rose, 1890. 221p [BVaU LC NSWA OKQ
QMM

Fox, William Sherwood, 1878–1967
SILKEN LINES AND SILVER HOOKS. A Life-long Fisherman Recounts His Catch.
Toronto, Copp Clark, 1954. xii + 152p

Fraser, Alexander, 1860–1936
BROCK CENTENARY, 1812–1912. Account of the Celebration at Queenston Heights,

Ontario on the 12th October 1912. Ed. by ——. Toronto, Briggs, 1913. 92p
[BM BVaU LC NBFU OTU

Fraser, Rev. Donald, 1826–1892
AUTOBIOGRAPHY OF THE LATE D. FRASER. With a Selection from his Sermons.
London, Nisbet, 1892. 243p [OTUV QMM
CANADA AS I REMEMBER IT, AND AS IT IS. [London, 1876.] 33p [BVaU NSWA
LEAVES FROM A MINISTER'S PORTFOLIO. London, Nisbet, 1858. 141p [NSWA
LC OTU QMM
MARY JANE KINNAIRD. London, Nisbet, 1890. 160p [LC QMM
THOMAS CHALMERS, D.D., LL.D. New York, Armstrong, 1882. [LC OLU

Fraser, Hermia (Harris), 1902–
TALL BRIGADE. True Adventures of Tom McKay, Brigade Leader for the Early
Hudson's Bay Company. Portland, Oregon, Binfords & Mort, 1956. 294p

Fraser, Rev. Joshua, fl. 1858–1883
SHANTY, FOREST AND RIVER LIFE IN THE BACKWOODS OF CANADA. By the
author of THREE MONTHS AMONG THE MOOSE. Montreal, Lovell, 1883. 361p
[BM BVaU LC MWU OTU QMM
THREE MONTHS AMONG THE MOOSE. "A Winter's Tale" of the Northern Wilds of
Canada. By a Military Chaplain [pseud]. Montreal, Lovell, 1881. 168p [BVaU
LC NSHD OTU QMM

Fraser, Robert James, 1887–
AS OTHERS SEE US. Scots of the Seaway Valley. Beamsville, Ont., Express, 1959.
328p

Fraser, Roy, 1889–1957
HAPPY JOURNEY. Toronto, Ryerson, 1958. xiv + 124p

Fraser, Simon, 1776–1862
LETTERS AND JOURNALS, 1806–1808. Ed. with an intro. by W. Kaye Lamb.
Toronto, Macmillan, 1960. 292p

Freed, Augustus Toplady, 1835–
HANCOCK. The Life ... of Winfield Scott Hancock. Chicago, Summer, 1880. 74p
[BM LC

French, Maida (Parlow)
APPLES DON'T JUST GROW. Toronto, McClelland, 1954. 226p

Freshman, Rev. Charles, 1819–1875
THE AUTOBIOGRAPHY OF THE REV. CHARLES FRESHMAN, late Rabbi of the Jewish
Synagogue at Quebec ... at present German Wesleyan Minister at Preston, Ontario.
... Toronto, Rose, 1868. 316p [BVaU LC NSWA OTU QMM

Fry, Henry
A BIOGRAPHICAL SKETCH OF SIR N.F. BELLEAU. Quebec, Côté, 1894. 12p [QMSS

Fudger, Harris Henry

MEMOIR AND WRITINGS. Comp. by his Daughter. Toronto, priv. print., 1931.
[BVaU OTUV

Führer, Mrs. Charlotte H.

THE MYSTERIES OF MONTREAL. Being Recollections of a Female Physician.
Montreal, Lovell, 1881. 245p [BVaU LC NSWA OTU QMM

Fulford, Rev. Francis, 1803–1868

A SERMON ... AFTER THE DEATH OF H.R.H. THE PRINCE CONSORT. Montreal,
Lovell, 1862. 15p [BM OTP

Fuller, Peter, 1826–1890

PETER FULLER, HIS STEPS AND HIS LIFE, PRINCIPALLY FROM HIS OWN DIARIES.
On the Occasion of the Centennial of the Founding of Christ's Church, the
Church of England, Meaford. Sel. by F. Stanley Knight. Meaford, Ont., 1959.
34p

Fuller, Rev. Thomas Brock, 1810–1884

MEMOIR OF MR. JOHN BEATTY, who died at Port Robinson, C.W., 15th February,
1861. Toronto, Rowsell, 1861. 24p [OTU

Gaisford, John

THEATRICAL THOUGHTS. By John Gaisford ... and Conundrums, Sent to John
Gaisford. Montreal, Lovell, 1848. 75p [LC OTP

Gallishaw, John, 1890–

TRENCHING AT GALLIPOLI. Toronto, Gundy, 1916. 241p [NSHPL OTY

Galloway, Margaret Agnes

I LIVED IN PARADISE. Winnipeg, Bulman Bros., 1942. 257p [BViPA LC OLU

Galt, Ont. Knox Church

REV. DR. JOHN BAYNE, D.D., MINISTER OF KNOX CHURCH, GALT, 1835–1859.
[Galt?], 1935. 16p [OTU

Ganong, William Francis, 1864–1941

A GENEALOGY OF THE NEW BRUNSWICK BRANCH OF THE DESCENDANTS OF
THOMAS GANONG. ... Comp. by ——. Cambridge, Mass., Graves & Henry, 1893.
27p [BM LC OOP

Garland, Bessie (Ford)

THE OLD MAN'S DARLING. A Series of Character Sketches. Toronto, Author, 1881.
157p [BVaU OTP

Garrioch, Rev. Alfred Campbell, 1848–1934

A HATCHET MARK IN DUPLICATE. Toronto, Ryerson, 1929. 283p [BM BVaU
OTU SSU

Gates, William, 1815—
RECOLLECTIONS OF LIFE IN VAN DIEMAN'S LAND. Lockport, N.Y., Crandall, 1850.
231p [NBFU OTP QMM

Gaudin, Rev. Samuel D., 1861—1947?
FORTY-FOUR YEARS WITH THE NORTHERN CREES. Toronto, Mundy-Goodfellow
Print., 1942. 170p [AEU OTU

Gemmill, John Alexander, 1847—1905
THE OGILVIES OF MONTREAL WITH A GENEALOGICAL ACCOUNT OF THE
DESCENDANTS OF THEIR GRANDFATHER, ARCHIBALD OGILVIE. [Ed. by J.A.G.]
Montreal, Gazette, 1904. 98p [OTU

Ghent, Percy Parker, 1888—1952
JOHN READE AND HIS FRIENDS. Toronto, Belcher, 1925. 63p [BM BVaU NBFU
OTP
LITERARY AND HISTORIC FRAGMENTS OF CANADIAN INTEREST. Adventures in
Book and Autograph Collecting. Toronto, Belcher, 1927. 86p [BVaU NBFU
OTP

Gibbon, Mary Elizabeth, 1925—
NORTHWARD MY CALLING. By Mary E. Hope [pseud]. Toronto, Ryerson, 1954.
170p

Gibbons, Arthur
A GUEST OF THE KAISER. The Plain Story of a Lucky Soldier. Toronto, Dent,
1919. xvi + 798p [LC NSHPL OTU

Gibson, George Herbert Rae, 1881—1932
MAPLE LEAVES IN FLANDER'S FIELDS. By Herbert Rae [pseud]. Toronto, Briggs,
1916. 268p [BM BVaU OTU QMM

Gibson, Jesse
THOMAS BONE, THE SAILOR'S FRIEND. The Story of his Work on the Welland Canal.
Toronto, U.C. Tract Society, [1908?]. 158p [BVaU OTP

Gifford, Rev. William Alva, 1877—1960
JOHN WESLEY: PATRIOT AND STATESMAN. Toronto, Ryerson, 1922. 30p [BM
OTUV

Gilbert, Geoffrey, 1893—
THE ANCESTORS OF MOSES HASKELL GILBERT OF VERMONT AND MONTREAL,
1790—1843. Pt. 1. The Ancestry of his Father, Solomon Gilbert. Pt. 2. The
Ancestry of his Mother, Thankful Haskell. Gilbert Material comp. and ed. by
Geoffrey Gilbert. Nineteen "stories" on Maternal Lines by Eva L. Moffatt.
Victoria, Author, 1954. 144p [mimeographed]

GILBERTS OF NEW ENGLAND. Pt. 1. Descendants of John Gilbert of Dorchester. Comp. by George Gordon Gilbert and Geoffrey Gilbert. Pt. 2. Descendants of Matthew Gilbert of New Haven, Humphrey Gilbert of Ipswich, and William Gilbert of Boston. From the Gilbert Family Manuscript Genealogy by Homer W. Brainard and Clarence A. Torrey. ... Ed. by ——. Victoria, Author, 1959. xv + 484p

Gillespie, Alexander, 1880–1948
JOURNEY THROUGH LIFE. Biography of Alexander Gillespie, 1880–1948. Victoria, priv. print., 1954. 143p

Gillespie, Gerald Joseph, 1911–
BLUENOSE SKIPPER. Fredericton, Brunswick Press, 1955. 129p

Gillis, Elsie (McCall)
NORTH POLE BOARDING HOUSE. As Told by Elsie McCall Gillis to Eugenie Myles. Toronto, Ryerson, 1951. 206p

Gillis, James Donald, 1870–
THE CAPE BRETON GIANT. A Truthful Memoir. Montreal, Lovell, 1899. 102p [Also: Halifax, Allen, 1914 and 1919.] [BVaU NSWA OTU QMM
A LITTLE SKETCH OF MY LIFE. Halifax, Allen, n.d. 12p [NSHPL OTUV QMM
MY PALESTINE PILGRIMAGE. ... 1936 A.D. North Sydney, N.S., Herald Print., 1936. 72p [NSHD OTU QMBM

Glass, Rev. Charles Gordon
STRAY LEAVES FROM SCOTCH AND ENGLISH HISTORY. With the Life of Sir William Wallace. Montreal, Lovell, 1873. 400p [2nd ed.: Montreal, Stevenson, 1876. 399p] [BVaU NSHD OTU QMBM

Glazebrook, George Parkin de Twenebrokes, 1900–
SIR CHARLES BAGOT IN CANADA. A Study in British Colonial Government. London, Oxford U. Press, 1929. 160p [BM BVaU LC NSHD OTU
SIR EDMUND WALKER. London, Oxford U. Press, 1933. 160p [BM BVaU NBFU OTU

Godfrey, Miss L.M.
INDIRECT DOMESTIC INFLUENCE; or, Nova Scotia as it was, as it is, and as it may be. ... Combining Sketches of Provincial Character. ... By a Provincial [pseud]. Boston, Author, 1855. 64p [Enl. ed. under title: SECRET INQUISITIONS; or, Nova Scotia as it was, is, and may be. ... (Anon) Boston, French, 1856. 112p] [NSHD OTP

Godsell, Jean Walker (Turner), 1896–
I WAS NO LADY. I Followed the Call of the Wild. The Autobiography of a Fur Trader's Wife. ... Toronto, Ryerson, 1959. xiv + 212p

Godsell, Philip Henry, 1889–1961
PILOTS OF THE PURPLE TWILIGHT. The Story of Canada's Early Bush Flyers.
Toronto, Ryerson, 1955. xii + 225p

Goldbloom, Alton, 1890–
SMALL PATIENTS. The Autobiography of a Children's Doctor. Toronto, Longmans,
1959. 316p

Goldsmith, Oliver, 1794–1861
THE AUTOBIOGRAPHY OF OLIVER GOLDSMITH. Published for the First Time from
the Original Manuscript of the Author of "The Rising Village." With intro. and
notes by Rev. Wilfrid E. Myatt. ... Toronto, Ryerson, 1943. 76p [BVaU NSHD
OTP

Good, William Charles, 1876–
FARMER CITIZEN. My Fifty Years in the Canadian Farmers' Movement. Toronto,
Ryerson, 1958. xiv + 294p

Good Templar, A (pseud)
RECOLLECTIONS OF A CHECKERED LIFE. By a Good Templar [pseud]. Napanee,
Hamond, 1868. 116p [Reminiscences by member of a temperance
organization.] [Haight Pt I OLU

Goodfellow, Florence Askin (Agassiz)
MEMORIES OF PIONEER LIFE IN BRITISH COLUMBIA. Wenatchee, Wash., Author,
1945. 43p [BVaU

Goodhand, Henrietta McIntosh
FOOT PRINTS. A Memoir. Minot, N.D., Author, 1948. 134p [Pioneer days in
Ontario and Alberta.] [OTU

Goodman, Alfred Edwin, 1860–
GOODMAN, A FAMILY HISTORY. [Anon] Vancouver, Timms, 1916. 548p [BVaU

Gordon, Rev. Charles William, 1860–1937
THE LIFE OF JAMES ROBERTSON, Missionary Superintendent in the Northwest
Territories. By Charles W. Gordon (Ralph Connor). Toronto, Westminster, 1908.
403p [BM BVaU LC NSWA OTU
POSTSCRIPT TO ADVENTURE. The Autobiography of Ralph Connor. New York,
Farrar, 1938. 430p [BM BVaU LC NSHD OTU

Gordon, Rev. James D., –1872
THE LAST MARTYRS OF EROMANGA. Being a Memoir of the Rev. George N.
Gordon, and Ellen Catherine Powell, His Wife. ... Halifax, McNab & Shaffer,
1863. 294p [BVaU NSHD

Gordon, Robert Kay, 1887–
JOHN GALT. Toronto, Oxford U. Press, 1920. 121p [BM LC OTU QMM

Gordon, Wilhelmina, 1885–
DANIEL M. GORDON, HIS LIFE. Toronto, Ryerson, 1941. 313p [BM BVaU NBFU OTU QMM

Gosling, William Gilbert, 1863–1930
THE LIFE OF SIR HUMPHREY GILBERT, England's First Empire Builder. London, Constable, 1911. 304p [BM BVaU LC NBFU OTU

Gough, Thomas Bunbury
BOYISH REMINISCENCES OF HIS MAJESTY THE KING'S VISIT TO CANADA IN 1860. London, Murray, 1910. 242p [BM BVaU LC NSWA OTU QMM

Gourlay, Robert Fleming, 1778–1863
THE BANISHED BRITON AND NEPTUNIAN. ... The Life ... of Robert Gourlay, Esq., now Robert Fleming Gourlay. Boston, Dickinson, 1843–46. [Issued in 38 parts proper, and an appendage. The Toronto Public Library's holdings are incomplete.] [BVaU OLU OTP
CHRONICLES OF CANADA. Being a Record of Robert Gourlay, Esq., now Robert Fleming Gourlay, "The Banished Briton." St. Catharines, "Journal," 1842. 40p [An abridged ed. with an additional section pub.: Ingersoll, C.W., "Chronicle," 1857. 40p] [LC OTP
MR. GOURLAY'S CASE BEFORE THE LEGISLATURE, WITH HIS SPEECH. Toronto, Globe, 1858. 29p [OTP

Gouzenko, Svetlana (Gouseva)
BEFORE IGOR. Memories of my Soviet Youth. New York, Norton, 1960. 252p

Gowanlock, Mrs. Theresa, –1899
TWO MONTHS IN THE CAMP OF BIG BEAR. The Life and Adventures of Theresa Gowanlock and Theresa Delaney. Parkdale, Times Office, 1885. 136p [BVaU NSWA OTUV SSU

Gowland, John Stafford, 1898–
SMOKE OVER SIKANASKA. London, Laurie, 1955. 224p

Graham, Angus A., 1867–
THE GOLDEN GRINDSTONE. The Adventures of George M. Mitchell. Recorded by Angus Graham. Toronto, Oxford U. Press, 1935. 304p [BM BVaU LC OTU

Graham, Ellen Maud, 1876–
A CANADIAN GIRL IN SOUTH AFRICA. Toronto, Briggs, 1905. 192p [NSHD OLU

Graham, Percy Wentworth
SIR ADAM BECK. London, Carl Smith, 1925. 64p [BVaU OTU

Graham, William Creighton, 1887–1955
JOHN WESLEY AS A LETTER WRITER. ... Toronto, Ryerson, 1923. 35p [OTUV

Graham, William Roger, 1919–
ARTHUR MEIGHEN. A Biography. Toronto, Clarke Irwin, 1960–65. 3v

Grant, Douglas, 1921–1969
THE FUEL OF THE FIRE. London, Cresset, 1950. 235p [BM BVaU NBFU OTU

Grant, Rev. George Monro, 1835–1902
JOSEPH HOWE. Halifax, MacKinlay, 1904. 83p [2nd ed., incl. Howe's essay on
"The Organization of the Empire"· Halifax, MacKinlay, 1906. 110p] [BVaU
NSWA OTP QMM

Grant, Mrs. Hilda Kay, 1910–
THE SALT-BOX. By Jan Hilliard [pseud]. New York, Norton, 1951. 212p
[Reminiscences of author's girlhood in Nova Scotia.]

Grant, Kenneth James, 1839–
MY MISSIONARY MEMORIES. Halifax, Imperial, 1923. 203p [BVaU NSWA

Grant, Rev. Robert, 1824?–1900
EAST RIVER WORTHIES. ... New Glasgow, Scotia Printers, [1900?]. 66p [NSHL
OTP
LIFE AND TIMES OF GEORGE R. YOUNG. ... New Glasgow, MacKenzie, 1886. 7p
[NSHD

Grant, Robert Neil, –1909
LIFE OF REV. WILLIAM COCHRANE. Toronto, Briggs, 1899. 290p [BVaU OTU

Grant, William Lawson, 1872–1935
IN MEMORIAM, WILLIAM GEORGE McINTYRE. ... N.p., n.d. 38p [OTU
PRINCIPAL GRANT. By W.L. Grant and Frederick Hamilton. Toronto, Morang,
1904. 531p [Also as: GEORGE MONRO GRANT. Edinburgh, Jack, 1905. 531p]
[BM BVaU LC NSWA OTU QMM
THE TRIBUNE OF NOVA SCOTIA. A Chronicle of Joseph Howe. Toronto, Glasgow
Brook, 1915. 163p [BM BVaU LC NBFU OTU

Gray, Edwin Roy
IN ALL THY WAYS. Letters from a Canadian Flying Officer. ... Toronto, Oxford U.
Press, 1944. 47p [OTUV

Gray, John Morgan, 1907–
A.W. MACKENZIE, M.A., D.D., THE GROVE, LAKEFIELD. A Memoir. Toronto, Grove˙
Old Boys' Assoc., 1938. 25p [BVaU OTU

Gray, Rev. John William Dering, 1797–1868
A SERMON, UPON THE DEATH OF HIS LATE MAJESTY WILLIAM IV, and upon the
Accession of our Present Sovereign, Queen Victoria. Saint John, Chubb, 1837.
16p [LC NSWA OTP

Gray, William
MORE LETTERS FROM BILLY. By the Author of A SUNNY SUBALTERN [pseud].
Toronto, McClelland, 1917. 121p [BVaU LC OLU
A SUNNY SUBALTERN. Billy's Letters from Flanders. [Anon] Toronto, McClelland,
1916. 175p [Also under title: A CANADIAN SUBALTERN. Billy's Letters to his
Mother. London, Constable, 1917. 128p] [BM BVaU LC NSHD OLU

Green, Rev. Anson, 1801–1879
THE LIFE AND TIMES OF THE REV. ANSON GREEN, D.D. Written by himself.
Toronto, Methodist Book Room, 1877. 448p [BVaU LC NBFU OTU QMM

Green, Henry Gordon, 1912–
THE SILVER DART. The Authentic Story of the Hon. J.A.D. McCurdy, Canada's
First Pilot. Fredericton, Brunswick Press, 1959. xvi + 208p

Greene, Barnet M.
WHO'S WHO IN CANADA. ... Ed. by ——. Toronto, International Press, 1915/16.
[A continuing series. Title varies, early vols. being entitled: WHO'S WHO AND
WHY. ...] [BVaU LC MWU NSHD OTP QMM

Greene, Rev. David Leslie, 1883–
BY THE SWIFT WATERS. London, Colonial and Continental Church Society,
[1943?]. 31p [OTU SSU

Greene, Gordon Kay, 1927–
DANIEL KENT GREENE, HIS LIFE & TIMES, 1851–1921, AND PART II, THE PROGENY
OF EVAN MOLBOURNE GREENE, 1814–1960. Edmonton, Author, 1960.
151 + 157p

Grenfell, Wilfred Thomason, 1865–1940
FORTY YEARS FOR LABRADOR. Boston, Houghton, 1932. 372p [BM BVaU LC
NSHD OTU QMM
A LABRADOR DOCTOR. The Autobiography of ——. Boston, Houghton, 1919.
441p [BM BVaU LC NSHD OTU QMM
A LABRADOR DOCTOR. ... London, Hodder, 1948. 349p [An " 'amalgam' of two
previous autobiographies ... FORTY YEARS FOR LABRADOR and A LABRADOR
DOCTOR."] [BM LC QMM
THE STORY OF A LABRADOR DOCTOR. London, Hodder, n.d. 300p [BM BVaU
NSWA OTU

Grierson, Frank, 1865–
WILLIAM LYON MACKENZIE KING. A Memoir Presented for the Earnest
Consideration of All Patriotic Canadians. Ottawa, priv. print., 1952. 110p

Griesbach, William Antrobus, 1878–1945
I REMEMBER. Toronto, Ryerson, 1946. 353p [BVaU LC OTU QMM

Griffin, Frederick G., 1889–1946

MAJOR-GENERAL SIR HENRY MILL PELLATT, C.VO., D.C.L., V.D. ... Toronto, Ontario Pub. Co., 1942. 30p [LC OTP

VARIETY SHOW. Twenty Years of Watching the News Parade. Toronto, Macmillan, 1936. 359p [LC OTU

Griffin, Justin Alonzo, 1846?–

ANCESTORS AND DESCENDANTS OF RICHARD GRIFFIN OF SMITHVILLE, ONTARIO. A Pioneer Family, with a Brief Account of Some Related Griffin Families in Canada. Hamilton, Griffin & Richmond, 1924. 168p [BM LC OTU

Griffin, W.H.

THE PRINTER OF GREEN GROVE FARM. Being a Biographical Sketch of the Late Adam L. Lewis. Montreal, Author, n.d. 30p [QMM

THREE SCORE YEARS. Toronto, Griffin Agency, 1948. 51p [UTQ'50

Griffith, Margaret R.

JEAN DOW, M.D. A Beloved Physician. Toronto, United Church, n.d. 63p [OTP

Grigg, David Henry, 1883–

FROM ONE TO SEVENTY. Vancouver, Mitchell, 1955. [c1953]. 199p

Grove, Frederick Philip, 1879–1948

IN SEARCH OF MYSELF. Toronto, Macmillan, 1946. 457p [BVaU LC NSHD OTU QMM

Groves, Abraham, 1847–1935

ALL IN THE DAY'S WORK. Leaves from a Doctor's Case-Book. Toronto, Macmillan, 1934. xv + 181p [AEU BVaU OLU QMM

Gudlaugson, Magnus Gudmundur, 1880–

THREE TIMES A PIONEER. Ed. by Holmfridur Danielson. Winnipeg, Author, 1958. 104p [mimeographed].

Guernsey, Isabel Russell

FREE TRIP TO BERLIN. Toronto, Macmillan, 1943. 230p [BVaU OTU QMM

Guillet, Edwin Clarence, 1898–

PATHFINDERS OF NORTH AMERICA. By E.C. and Mary Guillet. Toronto, Macmillan, 1939. 304p [BM BVaU OTU

THIS MAN HANGED HIMSELF! A Study of the Evidence in the King *versus* Newell. ... Toronto, Ontario Pub. Co., 1943. 210p [An account of the trial of Hugh William A. Newell for the murder of his wife Sept. 29, 1940.] [BVaU NBFU OTU QMM

Gurd, Norman St. Clair, 1870–1943

THE STORY OF TECUMSEH. Toronto, Briggs, 1912. 190p [BM BVaU LC NSHD OTP

Hague, Rev. Dyson, 1857–1935
BISHOP BALDWIN. A Brief Sketch of One of Canada's Greatest Preachers and Noblest
Church Leaders. Toronto, Evangelical Pub., 1927. 63p [OTU QMM
THE LIFE AND WORK OF JOHN WYCLIFFE. 2nd ed., enl. London, Church Book
Room, 1935. 200p [1st ed. pub. 1909.] [BM BVaU LC OTU

Hahn, James Emanuel, 1892–
FOR ACTION. The Autobiography of a Canadian Industrialist. Toronto, Clarke
Irwin, 1954. xii + 305p

Haig, Kennethe Macmahon
BRAVE HARVEST. The Life Story of E. Cora Hind, LL.D. Toronto, Allen, 1945.
275p [BVaU NBFU OTP QMM
COLONEL J.B. MITCHELL, FOR WHOM A WINNIPEG SCHOOL IS NAMED. [Winnipeg,
1957?]. 32p

Haig-Brown, Roderick Langmere, 1908–
CAPTAIN OF THE DISCOVERY. The Story of Captain George Vancouver. Toronto,
Macmillan, 1956. 181p
FISHERMAN'S WINTER. New York, Morrow, 1954. 288p

Haight, Canniff, 1825–1901
COUNTRY LIFE IN CANADA FIFTY YEARS AGO. Personal Recollections and
Reminiscences of a Sexagenarian. Toronto, Hunter Rose, 1885. 303p [BM
BVaU LC MWU NSWA OKQ
A GENEALOGICAL NARRATIVE OF THE DANIEL HAIGHT FAMILY. Toronto,
Rowsell & Hutchison, 1899. 71p [LC OTP

Haliburton, Robert Grant, 1831–1901
MEN OF THE NORTH AND THEIR PLACE IN HISTORY. ... Montreal, Lovell, 1869.
12p [NSHD OTU

Haliburton Club. King's College, Windsor, N.S.
HALIBURTON. A Centenary Chaplet. With a bibliography by John Parker Anderson.
Toronto, Briggs, 1897. 116p [BM BVaU LC OTU QMM

Hallam, Lillian Gertrude (Best), –1939
THE FIRST PROTESTANT MISSIONARY IN CANADA. By Mrs. W.T. Hallam. Toronto,
Canadian Churchman, [19—?]. 14p [OTP

Halliday, William May, 1866–
POTLATCH AND TOTEM, AND THE RECOLLECTIONS OF AN INDIAN AGENT.
Toronto, Dent, 1935. 240p [BM BVaU LC OTU

Ham, George Henry, 1847–1926
THE MIRACLE MAN OF MONTREAL. [Brother André]. Toronto, Musson, 1922. 68p
[BM BVaU NSHD OTU QMM

REMINISCENCES OF A RACONTEUR, BETWEEN THE '40s AND THE '20s. Toronto, Musson, 1921. 330p [BM BVaU LC NSHD OTU

Hamer-Jackson, Celesta (Grivot de Grandcourt)
DISCOVERERS AND EXPLORERS OF NORTH AMERICA. Toronto, Nelson, 1931. 319p [BM BVaU OTP

Hamil, Frederick Coyne, 1903–
LAKE ERIE BARON. The Story of Colonel Thomas Talbot. Toronto, Macmillan, 1955. ix + 326p

Hamilton, James Cleland, 1836–1907
OSGOODE HALL. Reminiscences of the Bench and Bar. Toronto, Carswell, 1904. 196p [BM BVaU LC OTP

Hamilton, Marie Albina (Bonneau), 1878–
THESE ARE THE PRAIRIES. By Zachary MacCaulay Hamilton and Marie Albina Hamilton. Regina, School Aids & Text Book Pub. Co., 1954. [pref. 1948]. 277p

Hamilton, Ross
PROMINENT MEN OF CANADA, 1931–2. Ed. by ——. Montreal, National Pub. Co., 1932. 640p [BM BVaU LC OTU

Hammond, Melvin Ormond, 1876–1934
CANADIAN CONFEDERATION AND ITS LEADERS. New York, Doran, 1917. 333p [BM BVaU LC NSWA OTU
HORATIO WALKER: PAINTER OF THE HABITANT. N.p., n.pub., n.d. 36p [NSWA
A TRIBUTE TO SAMUEL T. WOOD. [Anon] Toronto, Author, 1917. 32p [NBFU

Hanley, Annie Harvey (Ross) Foster, 1875–
THE MOHAWK PRINCESS. Being some Account of the Life of Tekahion-wake (E. Pauline Johnson). By Mrs. W. Garland Foster. Vancouver, Lion's Gate Pub., 1931. 216p [BM BVaU LC NBFU OTP

Hanna, David Blythe, 1858–1938
TRAINS OF RECOLLECTION. Drawn from Fifty Years' Railway Service in Scotland and Canada. By D.B. Hanna, as told to Arthur Hawkes. Toronto, Macmillan, 1924. 340p [BM BVaU LC NSHD OTU

Hannay, James, 1842–1910
THE HEROINE OF ACADIA ... FRANCES MARIE JACQUELINE, WIFE OF SIEUR DE LATOUR. Saint John, Bowes, 1910. 24p [BVaU NSHD OTU
NINE YEARS A CAPTIVE; or, John Gyles' Experience among the Milicete Indians from 1689–1698. With an intro. and historical notes by ——. Saint John, "Daily Telegraph," 1875. 38p [NBB
SIR LEONARD TILLEY. [See under WILMOT & TILLEY.]

WILMOT & TILLEY. Toronto, Morang, 1907. 301p [Later pub. as: LEMUEL ALLAN WILMOT. Toronto, Oxford U. Press, 1926. 164p; and SIR LEONARD TILLEY. Toronto, Oxford U. Press, 1926. 156p [BM BVaU LC NSWA OTP QMM

Hanning-Lee, Muriel, 1927?–1957
HEAD IN THE CLOUDS. London, Hodder, 1958. 191p

Hardy, Henry Reginald, 1903–
MACKENZIE KING OF CANADA. A Biography. Toronto, Oxford U. Press, 1949. 390p [BVaU LC NBFU OLU

Hargrave, Letitia (Mactavish), 1813–1854
THE LETTERS OF LETITIA HARGRAVE. Ed. with intro. & notes by Mrs. Margaret Arnett MacLeod. Toronto, Champlain Soc., 1947. cliv + 310p [BM BVaU LC NBFU OLU

Harrington, Bernard James, 1848–1907
LIFE OF SIR WILLIAM E. LOGAN ... Chiefly Compiled from his Letters, Journals and Reports. Montreal, Dawson, 1883. 432p [BM BVaU LC NSHD OTU

Harris, John Norman, 1915–1964
KNIGHTS OF THE AIR. Canadian Aces of World War I. Toronto, Macmillan, 1958. 156p

Harris, Rev. Joseph Hemington, 1800–1881
A LETTER TO THE HON. & VEN. ARCHDEACON STRACHAN in Reply to ... his "Letter ... on the Life and Character of Bishop Hobart". ... York, [Correspondent Print.], 1833. 21p [OTP

Harris, Reginald Vanderbilt, 1881–
CATALOGUE OF PORTRAITS OF THE JUDGES OF THE SUPREME COURT OF NOVA SCOTIA. ... [Halifax? 1921?]. 111p [LC NSHD OOA
CHARLES INGLIS, Missionary, Loyalist, Bishop (1734–1816). Toronto, General Board of Religious Education, 1937. 186p [BVaU LC NBFU OTP

Harrison, Charles Yale, 1898–1954
CLARENCE DARROW. New York, Cape & Smith, 1931. 380p [BM LC OTU

Harrold, Ernest William, 1889–1945
THE DIARY OF OUR OWN PEPYS. E.W. Harrold's Record of Canadian Life. Ed. by I. Norman Smith. Toronto, Ryerson, 1947. 296p [BVaU LC NBFU OTP

Hart, Margaret Janet (McPhee), 1867–1941
OUR WEB OF LIFE. Some Account of Dougal McPhee, Pioneer to Eastern Nova Scotia, his Wife Mary McMillan, and their Family. Vancouver, 1959. 17 + 5p [mimeographed].

Hart, Rev. William Edward, 1907–
AN APPRECIATION OF JOHN HOWARD. Saint John, Author, 1959. 51p

Hartley, Rev. H.A.S.
TA TOU PRAGMA EMOU BIOU; or, Some Concerns of my Life. Amherst, 1890.
   310p [NBFU

Hartwell, George E.
GRANARY OF HEAVEN. Toronto, United Church, 1939. 228p [BVaU OTUV

Harvey, Athelstan George, 1884–1950
DOUGLAS OF THE FIR. A Biography of David Douglas, Botanist. Cambridge,
   Mass., Harvard U. Press, 1947. 290p [BM BVaU LC OOA

Harvey, Daniel Cobb, 1886–
THE CENTENARY OF EDWARD WHELAN. Lecture delivered in Strand Theatre,
   Charlottetown, P.E.I., August 9, 1926. [Charlottetown?], Irwin, 1926.
   21p [OTU
JOSEPH HOWE AND LOCAL PATRIOTISM. An Inaugural Lecture delivered on
   March 10th, 1921. Winnipeg, 1921. 28p [BVaU NSWA OKQ
LETTERS OF REV. NORMAN McLEOD, 1835–51. Ed. by ——. Halifax, Pub.
   Archives, 1939. 32p [UTQ'40
THOMAS D'ARCY McGEE. The Prophet of Canadian Nationality. A Popular
   Lecture. ... Winnipeg, U. of Manitoba, 1923. 30p [BM BVaU NSWA OKQ

Harvey, Ruth (Walker), 1900–
CURTAIN TIME. Toronto, Allen, 1949. 310p [BVaU NBFU OTU

Hassard, Albert Richard, 1873–1940
A NEW LIGHT ON LORD MACAULAY. Toronto, Rockingham Press, 1918.
   76p [BM LC NSHD OTU QMM

Hathaway, Ann, 1848–
MUSKOKA MEMORIES. Sketches from Real Life. Toronto, Briggs, 1904. 127p
   [BM OTU

Hathaway, Ernest Jackson, 1871–1930
JESSE KETCHUM AND HIS TIMES. Being a Chronicle of the Social Life and
   Public Affairs of the Capital of the Province of Upper Canada during its
   First Half Century. Toronto, McClelland, 1929. 359p [BM BVaU LC
   NSHD OLU

Hatzan, Alexander Leon, 1864–
THE TRUE STORY OF HIAWATHA, AND HISTORY OF THE SIX NATION INDIANS.
   Toronto, McClelland, 1925. 298p [BM BVaU NSHD OTU QMSS

Haultain, Theodore Arnold, 1857–1941
GOLDWIN SMITH, HIS LIFE AND OPINIONS. London, Werner Laurie, 1913.
   304p [BM BVaU LC NSWA OTU QMM

Haw, Rev. William
FIFTEEN YEARS IN CANADA. ... Edinburgh, Ziegler, 1850. 120p [BM LC
OTP

Hay, George Upham, 1843–1913
MEMORIAL SKETCH OF PROF. C.F. HARTT. Saint John, 1881. [NBB

Haydon, Andrew, 1867–1932
MACKENZIE KING AND THE LIBERAL PARTY. Toronto, Allen, 1930. 54p
[BVaU OTU

Healy, William Joseph, 1867–1950
WOMEN OF THE RED RIVER. Being a Book Written from the Recollections of
Women Surviving from the Red River Era. ... Winnipeg, Russell Lang, 1923.
261p [BM BVaU NSHD OTU QMM

Hearne, Samuel, 1745–1792
COPPERMINE JOURNEY. An Account of a Great Adventure. Selected from the
Journals of Samuel Hearne, by Farley Mowat. Toronto, McClelland, 1958.
144p

Heeney, Rev. William Bertal, 1873–1955
I WALK WITH A BISHOP [Charles James Stewart] . Toronto, Ontario Pub. Co.,
1931. 113p [BVaU OKQ
JOHN WEST AND HIS RED RIVER MISSION. Toronto, Musson, 1920. 56p
[AEU BVaU OTUV

Helwig, Mrs. Solomon
A HISTORY OF THE DIEBEL FAMILY. By Mrs. Solomon Helwig and Mrs. John
A. Helwig. Hanover, Ont., Post Press, 1936. 93p [OTU

Hemsley, Richard, 1846–1931
LOOKING BACK. Montreal, Gazette, 1930. 175p [BM BVaU OTP QMM

Henderson, Dorothy (McLaughlin), 1900–
BIOGRAPHICAL SKETCHES OF SIX HUMANITARIANS WHOSE LIVES HAVE BEEN
FOR THE GREATER GLORY. Toronto, Ryerson, 1958. 188p [Cover title:
FOR THE GREATER GLORY.]

Henderson, John
GREAT MEN OF CANADA. Toronto, Southam, 1928. 239p [BVaU NBFU
OTU
HOWARD FERGUSON. The Romance of a Personality. ... Toronto, Macmillan,
1930. 145p [BM BVaU NBFU OTP

Henderson, Mary (Gillespie), 1840–1935
MEMORIES OF MY EARLY YEARS. Montreal, Charters & Charters, 1937. 58p
[BVaU LC OTU

Henry, Lorne James, 1893–

CANADIANS. A Book of Biographies. Toronto, Longmans, 1950. 153p [BVaU NBFU OONL

Henry, Mrs. P.A.

MEMOIR OF REV. THOMAS HENRY, Christian Minister, York Pioneer, and Soldier of 1812. Toronto, Hill, 1880. 192p [BVaU NSWA OTU

Henry, Walter, 1791–1860

TRIFLES FROM MY PORT-FOLIO; or, Recollections of ... France, the East Indies ... St. Helena during the Detention and until the Death of Napoleon, and Upper and Lower Canada. By a Staff Surgeon [pseud]. Quebec, Neilson, 1839. 2v [2nd ed. with alterations, under title: EVENTS OF A MILITARY LIFE. London, Pickering, 1843. 2v] [BM BVaU LC NSHD OTU QMM

Henson, Josiah, 1789–1883

AN AUTOBIOGRAPHY OF THE REV. JOSIAH HENSON ("Uncle Tom") from 1789 to 1881. With a Preface by Mrs. Harriet Beecher Stowe ... London, Ont., Schuyler Smith, 1881. 256p [OTP

"TRUTH IS STRANGER THAN FICTION." An Autobiography of the Rev. Josiah Henson (Mrs. Harriet Beecher Stowe's "Uncle Tom"), from 1789–1879. With a preface by Mrs. Harriet Beecher Stowe ... Wendell Phillips and John G. Whittier. ... Boston, Russell, 1879. 336p [LC

TRUTH STRANGER THAN FICTION. Father Henson's Story of his Own Life. With an intro. by Mrs. H.B. Stowe. Boston, Jewett, 1858. 212p [LC OTUV

THE LIFE OF JOSIAH HENSON, Formerly a Slave, Now an Inhabitant of Canada. As Narrated by himself. Boston, Phelps, 1849. 76p [Also: Dresden, Ont., 1965.] [BM BVaU LC

UNCLE TOM'S STORY OF HIMSELF. London, 1877. [BM

Hereford, Sara Lillian (Jakes), 1887–

OUR UNITED EMPIRE LOYALIST ANCESTRY. By Sally Hereford. Ottawa, Mutual Press, 1958. 27p [Descendants of John Chester, United Empire Loyalist.]

Herklots, Rev. Hugh Gerard Gibson, 1903–

THE FIRST WINTER. A Canadian Chronicle. Toronto, Dent, 1935. 176p [BM BVaU LC NBFU OTU

Herman, Alan, 1916–

THE SCALPEL, THE SWORD. The Story of Dr. Norman Bethune. By Ted Allan [pseud] and Sydney Gordon. Boston, Little Brown, [1952]. 336p

Herrington, Walter Stevens, 1860–1947

HEROINES OF CANADIAN HISTORY. Toronto, Briggs, 1909. 78p [BM BVaU NSHD OTP

THE MARTYRS OF NEW FRANCE. Toronto, Briggs, 1909. 159p [BM BVaU OKQ QMBM

Hewitt, William Abraham, 1875—
DOWN THE STRETCH. Recollections of a Pioneer Sportsman and Journalist. Toronto, Ryerson, 1958. xi + 239p

Hickey, Rev. Raymond Myles, 1909—
THE SCARLET DAWN. Campbellton, N.B., Tribune, 1949 [i.e. 1950]. 277p [BVaU OONL

Hiemstra, Mary (Pinder), 1897—
GULLY FARM. Toronto, McClelland, 1955. 311p

Higgins, Rev. Thomas Alfred, 1823—1905
THE LIFE OF JOHN MOCKETT CRAMP, D.D., 1796—1881, Late President of Acadia College. Montreal, Drysdale, 1887. 396p [BVaU NSHD OTP

Higgins, W.H.
THE LIFE AND TIMES OF JOSEPH GOULD. ... Struggles of the Early Canadian Settlers, Settlement of Uxbridge, Sketch of the History of the County of Ontario, the Rebellion of 1837, Parliamentary Career, etc. Reminiscences of Sixty Years of Active Political and Municipal Life. Toronto, Robinson, 1887. 304p [BM BVaU OTP

Higginson, Thomas Boyd, 1912—
DESCENDANTS OF THE REVEREND THOMAS HIGGINSON. London, Research Pub. Co., 1958. 64p

Higginson, Thomas Tweed, 1828—1903
DIARIES. Ed. by Thomas Boyd Higginson. London, Ont, Research Pub. Co., 1960. 91p

Higinbotham, John David, 1864—1961
WHEN THE WEST WAS YOUNG. Historical Reminiscences. ... Toronto, Ryerson, 1933. 328p [BM BVaU NBFU OTP

Hill, Rev. Allan Massie, 1876—1943
IT HAPPENED TO ME. Toronto, Thorn Press, 1942. 111p [LC OTP

Hill, Rev. George William, 1824—1906
IN MEMORY OF ROBERT FITZGERALD UNIACKE, Rector of St. George's Halifax. ... Halifax, Blackadar, 1870. 25p [BVaU NSHD
MEMOIR OF SIR BRENTON HALLIBURTON. Late Chief Justice of the Province of Nova Scotia. ... Halifax, Bowes, 1864. 207 + 47p [Appended is: JOHN BULL AND HIS CALVES; see **Halliburton, Brenton.**] [BM BVaU LC NSWA OTP

Hill, Rev. James Edgar, 1842–1911
MEMORIAL SERVICE, JANUARY 10TH, 1897, BEING THE SUNDAY AFTER THE
FUNERAL OF SIR JOSEPH HICKSON. Montreal, Gazette, 1897. 16p [OTP

Hilts, Rev. Joseph Henry, 1819–1903
EXPERIENCES OF A BACKWOODS PREACHER; or, Facts & Incidents Culled from
Thirty Years of Ministerial Life. Toronto, Briggs, 1887. 352p [BVaU OTP

Hincks, Francis, 1807–1885
REMINISCENCES OF HIS PUBLIC LIFE. Montreal, Drysdale, 1884. 450p [BM
BVaU NSWA OTP

Hines, Rev. John, 1850–1931
THE RED INDIANS OF THE PLAINS. Thirty Years' Missionary Experience in
Saskatchewan. London, S.P.C.K., 1915. 332p [BM BVaU NSHD OTP
QMM

Hobart, John Henry, 1902–
QUAKER BY CONVINCEMENT. New York, McKay, 1951. 227p

Hobson, Richmond Pearson, 1907–
GRASS BEYOND THE MOUNTAINS. Discovering the Last Great Cattle Frontier
on the North American Continent. Philadelphia, Lippincott, 1951. 256p
NOTHING TOO GOOD FOR A COWBOY. Philadelphia, Lippincott, 1955. 252p

Hodgins, James Cobourg, 1866–1953
THE REV. DR. HENDERSON & HIS CRITICS. Toronto, Hunter, 1916. 14p
[OTU

Hodgins, John George, 1821–1912
THE REV. EGERTON RYERSON. ... Founder of the School System of Ontario.
An Historical Retrospect. ... [Toronto? 1889.] 16p [LC OTU
RYERSON MEMORIAL VOLUME. ... Toronto, Warwick, 1889. 131p [BM BVaU
NSHD OTU
SKETCH OF THE REVEREND DOCTOR RYERSON. [Toronto? 1894?] 15p
[LC OTU

Hoemberg, Elisabeth (Sims), 1909–
THY PEOPLE, MY PEOPLE. London, Dent, 1950. 314p [OONL

Holden, Mrs. John Rose
A PRIMITIVE CIVILIZATION. THE BRANT FAMILY. N.p., Wentworth Historical
Soc., [1904?]. 33p [OTU

Holliday, Charles W., 1870–
THE VALLEY OF YOUTH. Caldwell, Idaho, Caxton, 1948. 357p [BVaU LC
OOA

Holt, Miss C.E.

AN AUTOBIOGRAPHICAL SKETCH OF A TEACHER'S LIFE, Including a Residence in the Northern and Southern States, California, Cuba and Peru. By Miss Holt. Quebec, Carrel, 1875. 117p [BVaU LC OTU QMSS

SUPPLEMENT TO MISS HOLT'S "AUTOBIOGRAPHICAL SKETCH." Quebec, 1875. 11p [QMSS

Hood, Dora (Ridout), 1885–

THE SIDE DOOR. Twenty-Six Years in my Book Room. Toronto, Ryerson, 1958. ix + 238p

Hoover, Dorothy (Haines)

J.W. BEATTY. Toronto, Ryerson, 1948. 37p [BVaU LC NBFU OTP

Hopkins, Arthur George, 1869–

GO WEST YOUNG MAN, I DID. Ilfracombe, Devon, Stockwell, 1956. 286p

Hopkins, John Castell, 1864–1923

LIFE AND WORK OF THE RT. HON. SIR JOHN THOMPSON ... Prime Minister of Canada. Toronto, United Pub., 1895. 479p [BVaU LC NSWA OTP

THE LIFE OF KING EDWARD VII. With a Sketch of the Career of George, Prince of Wales, and a History of the Royal Tour of the Empire in 1901. Toronto, Scull, 1910. 472p [BVaU NBFU OOU QMM

Horan, John William, 1908–

ON THE SIDE OF THE LAW. Biography of J.D. Nicholson, Formerly Assistant Superintendent, A.P.P. Edmonton, Institute of Applied Art, 1944. 275p [BVaU LC OTP

Horner, Ralph Cecil, 1854–1921

REMINISCENCES FROM HIS OWN PEN. Also Reports of Five Typical Sermons. Brockville, Mrs. A. Horner, n.d. 213p [OTU

Horton, William

MEMOIR OF THE LATE THOMAS SCRATCHERD. A Family Record. London, Ont., 1878. 262p [BVaU OTU

Howard, John George, 1803–1890

INCIDENTS IN THE LIFE OF JOHN G. HOWARD. ... Toronto, Copp, 1885. 36p [BVaU NSWA OTU

Howard, Robert Palmer, 1823–1889

A SKETCH OF THE LIFE OF THE LATE G.W. CAMPBELL ... Late Dean of the Medical Faculty, and a Summary of the History of the Faculty ... McGill University. Montreal, Gazette, 1882. 24p [BVaU NSWA OTP

Howay, Frederic William, 1867–1943

CAPTAIN GEORGE VANCOUVER. Toronto, Ryerson, 1932. 32p [BVaU

Howe, Joseph, 1804–1873
THE HEART OF HOWE. Selections from the Letters and Speeches. Ed. by D.C.
Harvey. Toronto, Oxford U. Press, 1939. 197p [BVaU LC NSHD OTP

Howell, Henry Spencer, 1857–1912
AN ISLAND PARADISE AND REMINISCENCES OF TRAVEL. Toronto, Hart &
Riddell, 1892. 296p [2nd ed.: Toronto, 1911.] [NBFU OKQ QMSS

Howell, William Boyman, 1873–
F.J. SHEPHERD–SURGEON. His Life and Times. Toronto, Dent, 1934. 251p
[BVaU LC NBFU OTUV

Howey, Mrs. Florence R., 1856?–1936
PIONEERING ON THE C.P.R. Ed. by Mrs. George E. Mabee. Ottawa, Mutual
Press, 1938. 141p [BM BViPA OLU

Hubicz, Rev. Edward Michael, 1912–
FATHER JOE–A MANITOBAN MISSIONARY. A Biographical Account of the Life
of Father Ladislaus Joseph Kreciszewski. London, Veritas Foundation Pub.
Centre, 1959. 95p

Huestis, Rev. George Oxley, 1827–1905
HISTORICAL ITEMS AND PERSONAL REMINISCENCES OF METHODISM IN
CUMBERLAND COUNTY, NOVA SCOTIA. ... Windsor, N.S., Anslow, 1902.
20p [NSWA
MEMORIALS OF WESLEYAN MISSIONARIES AND MINISTERS, who have died
within the Bounds of the Conference of Eastern British America, since the
Introduction of Methodism into these Colonies. Halifax, Macnab, 1872.
147p [BVaU NSWA OTP

Huey, John Alexander, 1882–1954
THE WARDENS, COUNCILLORS, PARLIAMENTARY REPRESENTATIVES, JUDICIAL
OFFICERS AND COUNTY OFFICIALS OF THE COUNTY OF LAMBTON FOR 100
YEARS FROM 1849 TO 1949. Comp. by ———. [Sarnia, Lambton] County
Council, 1950. 111p [OONL

Hughes, James Laughlin, 1846–1935
THE REAL ROBERT BURNS. London, Chambers, 1922. 216p [BVa LC
NSWA OKQ QMM

Hughes, Katherine, –1925
ARCHBISHOP O'BRIEN. Ottawa, Crain, 1906. 230p [BM BVaU NSWA OTP
FATHER LACOMBE, THE BLACK-ROBE VOYAGEUR. Toronto, Briggs, 1911.
467p [Several later editions.] [BM BVaU LC NSHD OTP QMM

Hume, Blanche
THE STRICKLAND SISTERS. Toronto, Ryerson, 1928. 32p [BVaU OTU

Hunt, William Harold, 1884—

BIRTHRIGHTS. A Genealogical Record of Canadian Branches of Hunt, Scott, Ives & Farwell Families, including the Lineage of John & Robert Hunt of Fitzroy Tps., Carleton Co., Ont., Daniel Scott of Dunham Tps., Mississquoi [*sic*] Co., Que., Joseph & Joel Hall Ives of Magog Tps., Stanstead Co., Que., Gladden Farwell of Compton Tps., Stanstead Co., Que., and Allied Families. Winnipeg, McCullough's Multigraphing, 1957. 1v. (various pagings). [Also: Supplement to Scott section. Winnipeg, 1961. 11 + 4p]

Hunter, Edmund Robert, 1909—

J.E.H. MACDONALD. A Biography and Catalogue of his Work. Toronto, Ryerson, 1940. 60p [BVa NBFU OTP QMM

THOREAU MACDONALD. Toronto, Ryerson, 1942. 43p [BVaU LC OTP

Hutchinson, Rev. Gerald Middleton, 1914—

MEMORIAL BOOKLET WRITTEN ON THE OCCASION OF THE 100TH ANNIVERSARY CELEBRATIONS HONORING THE ARRIVAL OF THE REVEREND THOMAS WOOLSEY AND THE REVEREND HENRY BIRD STEINHAUER IN SEPTEMBER, 1855. N.p., 1955. 23p [Cover title: "The roots of the province; Alberta's 50 years, and 100 years of Christian service."]

Hutchison, Bruce, 1901—

THE INCREDIBLE CANADIAN. A Candid Portrait of Mackenzie King: his Works, his Times, and his Nation. Toronto, Longmans, 1952. 454p [English title: MACKENZIE KING, THE INCREDIBLE CANADIAN. London, Longmans, 1953.]

Hutton, Samuel King, 1877—

BY ESKIMO DOG-SLED AND KYAK [*sic*]. A Description of a Missionary's Experiences and Adventures in Labrador. London, Seeley Service, 1919. 219p [BVaU LC NfSM OLU

A SHEPHERD IN THE SNOW. The Life Story of Walter Perret of Labrador. London, Hodder, 1936. 285p [LC NfSM OORD

Ingraham, Mary (Kinley), 1874—1949

ROBERT BRUCE KINLEY AND HIS FAMILY. Wolfville, Acadian, 1941. 4p [NSWA

Innis, Harold Adams, 1894—1952

PETER POND, FUR TRADER AND ADVENTURER. Toronto, Irwin & Gordon, 1930. 153p [BM BVaU LC NSHD OTP

Jack, Isaac Allen, 1843—1903

BIOGRAPHICAL REVIEW. This volume contains Biographical Sketches of Leading Citizens of the Province of New Brunswick. Editorial supervision of ——. Boston, Biographical Review Pub. Co., 1900. 508p [LC NSWA QMM

Jackson, Alexander Young, 1882–
BANTING AS AN ARTIST. With a memoir by F.W.W. Hipwell. Toronto, Ryerson, 1943. 37p [BVi LC OTU QMM
A PAINTER'S COUNTRY. The Autobiography of A.Y. Jackson. Toronto, Clarke Irwin, 1958. xv + 170p

Jackson, Harold McGill, 1898–1961
JUSTUS SHERWOOD, SOLDIER, LOYALIST AND NEGOTIATOR. [Aylmer East, Que.?], Author, 1958. 59p

Jackson, William H.
LIFE AND CONFESSIONS OF SOPHIA HAMILTON, who was Tried, Condemned, and Sentenced to be Hung, at Montreal, Jan. 22, 1845. Montreal, Jackson, 1845. 32p [NSWA

James, Norman Bloomfield, 1872–1963
THE AUTOBIOGRAPHY OF A NOBODY. Toronto, Dent, 1947. 239p [AEU BVaU OTP

Jamieson, Mrs. Annie Straith
WILLIAM KING, Friend and Champion of Slaves. Toronto, Missions of Evangelism, 1925. 209p [BVaU LC NSWA OTU QMM

Jarvis, Julia, 1899–
THREE CENTURIES OF ROBINSONS. The Story of a Family. Toronto, priv. print., 1953. 170p

Jarvis, Peter Robinson, 1824–1906
MEMOIRS OF P.R. JARVIS. N.p., n.d. 133p [OOP

Jenkins, Rev. John, 1813–1898
THE FAITHFUL MINISTER. A Memorial of the Late Rev. William Squire. ... Montreal, Wesleyan Book; London, Mason, 1853. 175p [NSWA OTP

Jephson, Harriet Julia (Campbell), 1854–1930
NOTES OF A NOMAD. London, Hutchinson, 1918. 368p [BM

Job, Patrick Dalzel
THE SETTLERS. By Peter Dalzel [pseud]. London, Constable, 1957. 209p

Job, Robert Brown, 1873–
JOHN JOB'S FAMILY. A Story of his Ancestors and Successors and their Business Connections with Newfoundland and Liverpool, 1730–1953. 2nd enl. ed. St. John's, Telegram Print. Co., 1954. 144p

Johnson, Mrs. Amelia B., –1888
FROM LIFE'S SCHOOL TO THE "FATHER'S HOUSE." A Brief Memoir of Amelia, Annie, & Thomas Johnson, with Letters. Comp. and ed. by M.R.J. Toronto, Hunter Rose, 1888. 204p [BVaU LC OTUV

Johnson, Wellwood Robert, 1887–

LEGEND OF LANGLEY. An Account of the Early History of Fort Langley and
an Intimate Story of the Lives of some, but not all, of the early Pioneers of
the District of Langley. Langley, B.C., the Centennial Committee, 1958. 183p

Johnston, Blanche J. (Read), 1866–

THE LADY WITH THE OTHER LAMP! The Story of Blanche Read Johnston.
As told to Mary Morgan Dean. Toronto, McClelland, 1920. 282p [BM BVaU
THE LIFE OF JOHN READ. By Blanche J. Read. Toronto, Salvation Army Pub.
House, [19—?]. 181p [OTP

Johnston, Elizabeth (Lichtenstein), 1764–1848

RECOLLECTIONS OF A GEORGIA LOYALIST. Written in 1836. Ed. by Arthur W.
Eaton. New York, Mansfield, 1901. 224p [BM BVaU LC

Johnston, Rev. Hugh, 1840–1922

MEMORIAL OF THE LATE HON. SENATOR FERRIER, OF MONTREAL. A Sermon
... with an Account of the Funeral, and an Address by the Rev. John Potts. ...
Toronto, Briggs, 1888. 42p [OTUV
MEMORIAL OF THE LATE ROBERT WALKER. Toronto, Briggs, 1885. 10p [OTUV
A MERCHANT PRINCE. Life of Hon. Senator John Macdonald. Toronto,
Briggs, 1893. 321p [BVaU NSHD OKQ
A REVIEW OF REV. F.W. MACDONALD'S LIFE OF WILLIAM MORLEY PUNSHON. ...
Toronto, Briggs, 1888. 182p [OKQ
TOWARDS THE SUNRISE. Being Sketches of Travel in Europe and the East,
to which is added a Memorial Sketch of the Rev. William Morley Punshon.
Toronto, Briggs, 1883. 459p [BVaU OTU

Johnston, Mono (Troop)

PROPHET, PRESBYTER, AND SERVANT OF MANKIND. A Memoir of Rev. Canon
G. Osborne Troop, M.A. Comp. by Mono Troop Johnston, and ed. by Dyson
Hague. Truro, News Pub. Co., 1935. 222p [UTQ

Jones, Elizabeth, 1830–1837?

MEMOIR OF ELIZABETH JONES, a Little Indian Girl, who lived at the River-
Credit Mission, Upper Canada. [Anon] London, Mason, 1838. 34p [OTP

Jones, James Edmund, 1866–1939

DESCENDANTS OF PHILIP HENRY. New ed. Kingston, "British Whig," 1925.
32 + 68p [OTU

Jones, Rev. John Gordon, 1901–

THE FIVE LIVES OF WILLIAM CAREY. N.p., Baptist Federation of Canada,
1960. 23p

Jones, Mrs. Nancy, 1890–1959

FOR GOODNESS' SAKE. Toronto, Ryerson, 1949. 291p [BVaU LC NBFU OTP

Jones, Rev. Peter (Chippewa Chief), 1802–1856
LIFE AND JOURNALS OF KAH-KE-WA-QUON-A-BY (Rev. Peter Jones), Wesleyan
Missionary. Toronto, Green, 1860. 424p [BM BVaU LC OTP QMM

Jowett, Cecilia
NO THOUGHT FOR TOMORROW. The Story of a Northern Nurse. Toronto,
Ryerson, 1954. xii + 104p

Joyal, Rev. Erwin Carlyle, 1875–
A TERCENTENIAL [*sic*] HISTORY OF THE JOYAL FAMILY. By Rev. Erwin C.
Joyal and Rev. Eleanor Ruth Joyal. Bath, N.B., the Authors, 1960. 3 pts in
2. [mimeographed]

Kaiser, Thomas Erlin, 1863–1940
THE KAISER FAMILIES OF THE COUNTY OF YORK, ONTARIO. Oshawa, Author,
1931. 22p [OTP

Karr, Willliam John, –1938
THE HISTORY OF CANADA THROUGH BIOGRAPHY. Explorers, Soldiers & Statesmen: Canadian Pacific History. Toronto, Dent, 1929. [Several volumes of
different dates.] [BVaU LC NSHD OTU QMM

Kay, Rev. John
BIOGRAPHY OF THE REV. WILLIAM GUNDY. ... Twenty Years of Methodism
in Canada. Toronto, Campbell, 1871. 176p [BVaU OTU

Kean, Abram, 1855–1945
OLD AND YOUNG AHEAD. A Millionaire in Seals. Being the Life History of
Captain Abram Kean. ... London, Heath Cranton, 1935. 218p [BM BVaU
LC OTU

Kearley, Mark H.
A FEW HINTS AND SUGGESTIONS ABOUT EMILY CARR AND HER WORK. An
Informal Talk. ... [Victoria? Federation of Canadian Artists?], 1946. 14p
[BVaU OKQ

Kearney, Lawrence Cunningham
THE LIFE OF COLONEL ... THOMAS TALBOT. ... Chatham, Rose, 1857. 51p
[OTP

Keefer, Rev. Robert, 1871–
MEMOIRS OF THE KEEFER FAMILY. Norwood, Norwood, 1935. 30p [LC
OTU

Keene, Louis
"CRUMPS." The Plain Story of a Canadian Who Went. With a prefatory note by
General Leonard Wood. Boston, Houghton, 1917. 156p [LC NBFU OTU

Kelley, Thomas Patrick, 1910—

BAD MEN OF CANADA. A History of the Ten Most Desperate Men in Canadian Crime. N.p., Arrow Pub. Co., 1950. 158p [OONL

THE BLACK DONNELLYS. Toronto, Harlequin Books, 1954. 160p

Kells, A. Edna, 1880—

ELIZABETH McDOUGALL, PIONEER. Toronto, United Church Pub. House, 1933. 48p [AEU OTP

Kelly, Fanny (Wiggins), 1845—

NARRATIVE OF MY CAPTIVITY AMONG THE SIOUX INDIANS. With a Brief Account of General Sully's Indian Expedition of 1860, Bearing upon Events Occurring in my Captivity. Toronto, Maclear, 1872. 304p [1st ed.: Cincinnati, 1871.] [BVaU LC NBFU OTU

Kemp, Harold Stuart Miller, 1892—

NORTHERN TRADER. Toronto, Ryerson, 1956. 253p

Kemp, Vernon Alfred Miller, 1895?—

WITHOUT FEAR, FAVOUR OR AFFECTION. Thirty-five Years with the Royal Canadian Mounted Police. Toronto, Longmans, 1958. ix + 263p

Kennedy, Howard Angus, 1861—1938

FATHER LACOMBE. ... Toronto, Ryerson, 1928. 32p [BVaU OTUV QMM

LORD STRATHCONA. Toronto, Ryerson, 1928. 32p [BViP NBS OLU QMSS

Kennedy, Thomas Laird, 1878—1959

TOM KENNEDY'S STORY. As told to Ralph Hyman. Toronto, the Globe, 1960. 62p

Kennedy, William Paul McClure, 1879—1963

ARCHBISHOP PARKER. London, Pitman, 1908. 306p [LC OTU

LORD ELGIN. London, Oxford U. Press, 1926. 272p [BM BVaU LC OTU QMM

Kerby, Rev. George William, 1860—1944

THE BROKEN TRAIL. Pages from a Pastor's Experience in Western Canada. Toronto, Briggs, 1909. 189p [BVaU NSHD OKQ SSU

Kern, Hannah Aikman (Hammill), 1820—1885

DIARY. Ed. by J.H. Holbrook and M.H. Farmer. London, Ont., Lawson Memorial Library, University of Western Ontario, 1958. 29p [mimeographed]

Kerr, Donald Gordon Grady, 1913—

SIR EDMUND HEAD, A SCHOLARLY GOVERNOR. By D.G.G. Kerr with the assistance of J.A. Gibson. Toronto, U. of Toronto Press in co-operation with Mount Allison University, 1954. xi + 259p

Kerr, John Blaine
BIOGRAPHICAL DICTIONARY OF WELL-KNOWN BRITISH COLUMBIANS. With a
Historical Sketch. Vancouver, Kerr & Begg, 1890. 326p [BVi LC OOP

Kerr, Wilfred Brenton, 1896–1950
ARMS AND THE MAPLE LEAF. Memories of Canada's Corps, 1918. Seaforth, Ont.,
Huron Expositor, 1943. 90p [A continuation of "SHRIEKS AND CRASHES."]
[BM LC OTP
FROM SCOTLAND TO HURON. A History of the Kerr Family. Seaforth, Ont., Huron
Expositor, 1949. 48p [OTP
"SHRIEKS AND CRASHES." Being Memories of Canada's Corps, 1917. Toronto,
Hunter Rose, 1929. 218p [BM BVaU LC OTP

Ketcheson Family History Publication Committee
A GENEALOGICAL HISTORY THROUGH EIGHT GENERATIONS IN CANADA OF THE
KETCHESON FAMILY AND DESCENDANTS. N.p., 1958. 72p

Ketchum, Creston Donald
HIS PATH IS IN THE WATERS. New York, Prentice-Hall, 1955. 183p

Ketchum, William, 1798–1876
MEMOIR OF THE DISTINGUISHED MOHAWK INDIAN CHIEF, SACHEM, AND WARRIOR,
CAPT. JOSEPH BRANT. [Anon] Brantford, Stewart, 1872. 89p [NSWA OTU

Ketchum, Rev. William Quintard, 1818–1901
THE LIFE AND WORK OF THE MOST REVEREND JOHN MEDLEY, D.D., First Bishop
of Fredericton and Metropolitan of Canada. Saint John, McMillan, 1893. 335p
[BM BVaU LC NSWA OTU

Key, Sydney James, 1918–
JOHN CONSTABLE. His Life and Work. Toronto, Dent, 1948. 128p [BM BVa LC
OTU

Kibbe, James Allen
THE WOOD FAMILY, SACKVILLE, N.B. A Genealogy of the Line from Thomas Wood,
of Rowley, Mass., born about 1634, to Josiah Wood, of Sackville, N.B., born in
1843. Gathered and arranged by ——. Sackville, Wood, 1904. 43p [BM BVaU
LC NSHD OOP

Kidd, Henry George, 1878–
THE MEGANTIC OUTLAW. Toronto, 1948. 139p [NBFU OTP

Kilbourn, William Morley, 1926–
THE FIREBRAND. William Lyon Mackenzie and the Rebellion in Upper Canada.
Toronto, Clarke Irwin, 1956. xv + 283p

King, Rev. George Brockwell, –1956
FOND MEMORY AND THE LIGHT OF OTHER DAYS. The Old Leslie Street School,
and a Last Century Tragedy "over the Don." Toronto, priv. print. 195–. 10p

King, Herbert Baxter, 1879—
SOLOMON MUSSALLEM. A Biography. Haney, B.C., priv. print., 1955. ix + 143p

King, John, 1843—1916
McCAUL: CROFT: FORNERI. Personalities of Early University Days. Toronto,
   Macmillan, 1914. 256p [OTP

King, Rev. John Mark, 1829—1899
THE GOOD FIGHT. A Sermon Preached in the Presbyterian Church, Gould St.,
   Toronto, on August 22nd, 1869, on Occasion of the Death of the Rev. Robert
   Burns. Toronto, Adam Stevenson, 1869. 23p [NSHD OTP

King, William Cornwallis, 1845—1940
TRADER KING. As Told to Mary Weekes. Regina, School Aids and Text Book Pub.
   Co., 1949. 184p [King was one of the last of the "Wintering Partners" of the
   Hudson's Bay Co., serving 40 years in the Northwest Territories.] [BVaU OTU

King, William Lyon Mackenzie, 1874—1950
ADDRESS ... ON ... YEARS OF LEADERSHIP—AND REASONS FOR RETIREMENT AS
   LEADER OF THE PARTY ... August 6, 1948. Ottawa, National Liberal Federation,
   1948. 16p [OOL
THE MACKENZIE KING RECORD. Ed. by J.W. Pickersgill. Toronto, U. of Toronto
   Press, 1960. v. 1: 1939—1945.
THE SECRET OF HEROISM. A Memoir of Henry Albert Harper. Toronto, Revell,
   1906. 161p [Also: Toronto, Musson, 1919.] [BM BVaU LC NBFU OTU
TRIBUTE TO LATE LORD TWEEDSMUIR, GOVERNOR GENERAL OF CANADA. ...
   Ottawa, King's Printer, 1940. 6p [UTQ'41

Kingsford, Maurice Rooke, 1894—
THE LIFE, WORK AND INFLUENCE OF WILLIAM HENRY GILES KINGSTON. Toronto,
   Ryerson, 1947. 220p [BVaU NSHD OTU

Kingsford, William, 1819—1898
SIR DANIEL WILSON. N.p., 1893. 10p [Reprinted from Trans. Roy. Soc. Can.]
   [NSWA

Kingsmill, Col. William, 1794—1876
THE GREENWOOD TRAGEDY. ... The Suicide of William Greenwood. Guelph,
   "Herald," 1864. 35p [BVaU OTP

Kinton, Ada Florence, 1859—1905
JUST ONE BLUE BONNET. The Life Story of Ada Florence Kinton, Artist and
   Salvationist. Told mostly by herself with pen and pencil. Ed. by her sister Sara
   A. Randleson. Toronto, Briggs, 1907. 192p [BM OOP

Kirby, William, 1817—1906
ALFRED, LORD TENNYSON AND WILLIAM KIRBY. Unpublished Correspondence, to
   which are added some Letters from Hallam, Lord Tennyson. Ed by Lorne Pierce.
   Toronto, Macmillan, 1929. 71p [BM BVaU OTU

REMINISCENCES OF A VISIT TO QUEBEC, JULY, 1839. Niagara, Author, 1903. 16p
  [BVaU OTP

THE SERVOS FAMILY. ... [Same as: THE UNITED EMPIRE LOYALISTS OF CANADA,
  q.v.] [NSWA

SIR JAMES LE MOINE. A Family Memoir. Together with "The Knight of Spencer
  Grange." Quebec, Author, 1898. 12p

THE UNITED EMPIRE LOYALISTS OF CANADA. Illustrated by Memorials of the
  Servos Family. Toronto, Briggs, 1884. 20p [LC OOP

Kirkconnell, Watson, 1895–

A CANADIAN HEADMASTER. A Brief Biography of Thomas Allison Kirkconnell,
  1862–1934. Toronto, Clarke Irwin, 1935. 156p [BM BVaU LC NSHD OTU

Kirkwood, Kenneth Porter, 1899–

A GARDEN IN POLAND. Karachi, Process Pakistan, 1953. 34p [On Chopin.]
  [BM OTU

Klengenberg, Capt. Christian, 1869–1931

KLENGENBERG OF THE ARCTIC. An Autobiography. Ed. by Tom MacInnes.
  London, Cape, 1932. 360p [BM BVaU LC OTU QMM

Klinck, Vernon Edward, 1904–

THE KLINCK FAMILY. Leonard Klinck and Elizabeth Brown Grant, Their Parents and
  Descendants for Six Generations, Together with Notes concerning certain of the
  Early Members. Comp. and ed. by Vernon Edward Klinck, Harry Osborne Klinck,
  and Leonard Sylvanus Klinck. Stouffville, Ont., 1955. 72p [mimeographed]

Knox, Ellen Mary, 1858–1924

ELLEN MARY KNOX. A Memorial volume. [Anon] Toronto, Havergal College,
  [1925]. 107p [OLU

Knox, Olive Elsie (Robinson)

JOHN BLACK OF OLD KILDONAN. Toronto, Ryerson, 1958. 198p

LITTLE GIANT (MISS-TOP-ASHISH). The Story of Henry Kelsey. Toronto,
  Ryerson, 1951. 196p [Also: New York, Bouregy & Curl, 1954. 186p]

MRS. MINISTER. Philadelphia, Westminster Press, 1956. 190p

Kristjanson, Wilhelm, 1896–

GLIMPSES OF OXFORD. Winnipeg, Columbia Press, 1935. 68p [CC

Lambert, Richard Stanton, 1894–

ADVENTURE TO THE POLAR SEA. The Story of Sir John Franklin. ... Indianapolis,
  Bobbs-Merrill, 1950. 302p [LC OONL

FOR THE TIME IS AT HAND. An Account of the Prophecies of Henry Wentworth
  Monk of Ottawa, Friend of the Jews and Pioneer of World Peace. Toronto,
  Ryerson, 1947. 168p [BM BVaU OTU

FRANKLIN OF THE ARCTIC. A Life of Adventure. Toronto, McClelland, 1949. 354p [Also: London, Bodley Head, 1954. 354p] [BM BVaU NBFU OTU QMM

REDCOAT SAILOR. The Adventures of Sir Howard Douglas. Toronto, Macmillan, 1956. 160p

THEY WENT EXPLORING. Agincourt, Ont., Book Society of Canada, 1955. 168p

TRAILMAKER. The Story of Alexander Mackenzie. Toronto, McClelland, 1957. 160p

Lambton County, Ont.

COMMEMORATIVE BIOGRAPHICAL RECORD OF THE COUNTY OF LAMBTON. Toronto, Hill Bind. Co., 1906. 840p [OLU

Lampman, Archibald, 1861–1899

ARCHIBALD LAMPMAN'S LETTERS TO EDWARD WILLIAM THOMSON (1890-1898). Ed. with an intro., annotations, a bibliography with notes, and his "Essay on Happiness," by Arthur S. Bourinot. Ottawa, Editor, 1956. 74p

Lamontagne, Père Onésime, 1913–

ILLUSTRATED LIFE OF GOOD FATHER FREDERIC. Trois-Rivières, Editions Bon Père Frédéric, 1950. 77p [OONL

THIS IS GOOD FATHER FREDERIC. Trois-Rivières, Editions Bon Père Frédéric, 1950. 72p [OONL

Land, Robert Ernest Augustus, 1847–1927

FIFTY YEARS IN THE MALTA ORDER. Toronto, priv. print., 1928. 2v [BM LC OTU

Lande, Lawrence Montague, 1906–

CREDO and AN OPEN LETTER TO A SCIENTIST. Montreal, Author, 1950. 28p [OONL

THE 3rd DUKE OF RICHMOND. A Study in Early Canadian History. Montreal, Author, 1956. 138p

Landon, Fred, 1880–1969

AN EXILE FROM CANADA TO VAN DIEMEN'S LAND. Being the Story of Elijah Woodman transported overseas for Participation in the Upper Canada Troubles of 1837–38. Toronto, Longmans, 1960. 321p

Langton, Anne, 1804?–1893

A GENTLEWOMAN IN UPPER CANADA. The Journals of Anne Langton. Ed. by H.H. Langton. Toronto, Clarke Irwin, 1950. 249p [BVaU NBFU OTP

LANGTON RECORDS. Journals and Letters from Canada 1837–1846. [By Anne Langton and others.] Preface by Ellen Josephine Philips. Edinburgh, Clark, 1904. 369p (Printed for private circulation only.) [BM OTU

THE STORY OF OUR FAMILY. Manchester, Sowler, 1881. 204p [OTP

Langton, Hugh Hornby, 1862–1953

JAMES DOUGLAS. A Memoir. Toronto, U. of Toronto Press, 1940. 130p [BM BVaU LC OTU QMM

JAMES LOUDON AND THE UNIVERSITY OF TORONTO. Toronto, U. of Toronto Press, 1927. 32p [BVaU OTU QMM

SIR DANIEL WILSON. A Memoir. Toronto, Nelson, 1929. 250p [BM BVaU NSHD OTU

SIR JOHN CUNNINGHAM McLENNAN. A Memoir. Toronto, U. of Toronto Press, 1939. 123p [BM BVaU OTP

Langton, John, 1808–1894

EARLY DAYS IN UPPER CANADA. Letters of John Langton from the Backwoods of Upper Canada. ... Ed. by W.A. Langton. Toronto, Macmillan, 1926. 310p [BM BVaU LC NSHD OKQ QMM

Laporte, Pierre, 1921–1970

THE TRUE FACE OF DUPLESSIS. Montreal, Harvest House, 1960. 140p

Lapp, Eula (Carscallen), 1905–

A HISTORY OF ONE BRANCH OF THE CARSCALLEN FAMILY (THE DESCENDANTS OF EDWARD CARSCALLEN, U.E.L. ...) Meaford, Ont., 1956. vi + 68p [Cover title: "Seven generations of Carscallens."]

Large, William Sydney, 1916–1943

DIARY OF A CANADIAN FIGHTER PILOT. Toronto, Saunders, 1944. 64p [BVa OTU QMM

Lathern, Rev. John, 1831–1905

THE HON. JUDGE WILMOT. A Biographical Sketch. Halifax, Wesleyan Office, 1880. 133p [Rev. ed.: Toronto, Methodist Book House, 1881. 165p] [BM BVaU NSHD OKQ

Laurie, Richard Carnie, 1858–1938

REMINISCENCES OF EARLY DAYS IN BATTLEFORD AND WITH MIDDLETON'S COLUMN. ... Recollections of Incidents of Travel, Early Surveys, Poundmaker ... etc. Battleford, Saskatchewan Herald, 1935. 140p [SSU

Laurier, Wilfrid, 1841–1919

LETTERS TO MY FATHER AND MOTHER. Selected and ed. by Lucien Pacaud. Toronto, Ryerson, 1935. 148p [BM BVaU OLU

Lauriston, Victor, 1881–

POSTSCRIPT TO A POET. Off the Record Tales about Arthur Stringer. Chatham, Tiny Tree Club, 1941. 48p [BVaU OLU

Laut, Agnes Christina, 1871–1936

CADILLAC, KNIGHT ERRANT OF THE WILDERNESS, FOUNDER OF DETROIT. Indianapolis, Bobbs-Merrill, 1931. 298p [BM BVaU LC NSHD OKQ QMM

Lawrence, Joseph Wilson, 1818–1892

THE JUDGES OF NEW BRUNSWICK AND THEIR TIMES. From the Manuscript of the late Joseph Wilson Lawrence. Ed. and annotated by Alfred A. Stockton. ... Saint John, Jack, 1907. 532p [LC NSHD OOP OTU QMM

Lawrence, Sheridan, 1870–1952

SHERIDAN LAWRENCE, EMPEROR OF THE PEACE, 1870–1952. As told to his wife, Julia Lawrence. N.p., priv. print., n.d. 61p

Laws, William Black, 1811–1875

THE WRITING AND LIFE OF W.B. LAWS. Montreal, Lovell, 1895. 132p [BM LC OTUV

Lawson, John Murray, 1848–1925

YARMOUTH, PAST AND PRESENT. A Book of Reminiscences. Comp. by ——. Yarmouth, Herald, 1902. 647p [BM BVaU LC NSWA OKQ QMM

Lawson, William, 1793–1875

THE LIFE OF WILLIAM LAWSON, J.P., ONE OF THE BUILDERS OF CANADA. Written by Himself, with an intro. and notes by a grandson. Columbia, Mo., 1917. 38 + xp [OTP

Leacock, Stephen Butler, 1869–1944

BALDWIN, LAFONTAINE, HINCKS: Responsible Government. Toronto, Morang, 1907. 371p [BM BVaU LC NSWA OTP

THE BOY I LEFT BEHIND ME. Garden City, Doubleday, 1946. 184p [BM BVaU LC NSHD OKQ

MACKENZIE, BALDWIN, LAFONTAINE, HINCKS. Toronto, Oxford U. Press, 1926. 395p [An Expansion of BALDWIN, LAFONTAINE, HINCKS: Responsible Government. Toronto, Morang, 1907. 371p] [BM BVaU LC OTU QMM

MY MEMORIES AND MISERIES AS A SCHOOLMASTER. Toronto, Upper Canada College Endowment and Extension Fund, [19–?]. 15p [OTP

Leatherbarrow, Mrs. Margaret F.

GOLD IN THE GRASS. Toronto, Ryerson, 1954. 278p

Lee, Norman, 1862–1939

THE JOURNAL OF NORMAN LEE, 1898. ... The Account of a Cattle-drive from the Chilcotin Country to Teslin Lake by the Telegraph Trail. Prepared for pub. by Gordon R. Elliott. Vancouver, R. and F. Reid, 1959. x + 58p

KLONDIKE CATTLE DRIVE. The Journal of Norman Lee. Ed. by Gordon Elliott. Vancouver, Mitchell Press, 1960. xxii + 58p

Lee, Thomas Roche, 1915–

ALBERT H. ROBINSON, "THE PAINTER'S PAINTER." Montreal, priv. print., 1956. 45p

Lees, John, fl. 1764–1775

JOURNAL OF JOHN LEES, OF QUEBEC, Merchant. [Travel-diary, April–October,

1768 ... trip to New England, New York, and return.] Detroit, Speaker-Hines Press, 1911. 55p [BM BVaU LC OTU

Leggo, William, 1822–1888
THE HISTORY OF THE ADMINISTRATION OF THE RIGHT HONORABLE FREDERICK TEMPLE, Earl of Dufferin ... late Governor General of Canada. Montreal, Lovell, 1878. 901p [BM BVaU LC NSHD OTU QMM

LeMoine, James MacPherson, 1825–1912
THE HON. HENRY CALDWELL. 1904. [MOR'12
THE SWORD OF BRIGADIER-GENERAL RICHARD MONTGOMERY. ... A Memoir. Comp. by ——. Quebec, Middleton & Dawson, 1870. 36p [BVaU LC OKQ QMSS

Leonard, Elijah, 1814–1891
THE HONOURABLE ELIJAH LEONARD. A Memoir. [Anon] London, Ont., Advertiser, [1894?]. 51p [BVaU NSWA OTU

Leslie, Percy Campbell, 1871–
THE FAMILY OF LESLIE. Montreal, 1953. 14p

Le Sueur, William Dawson, 1840–1917
COUNT FRONTENAC. Toronto, Morang, 1906. 382p [BM BVaU LC NSWA OTU QMM
[LIFE OF WILLIAM LYON MACKENZIE.] N.p., n.d. 553p [No title page. "Author's proof Copy." Typewritten.] [OTU

Levine, Albert Norman, 1923–
CANADA MADE ME. London, Putnam, 1958. 277p

Lewis, Ada Maria (Leigh), –1931
THE LIFE OF JOHN TRAVERS LEWIS, D.D., First Archbishop of Ontario. By his Wife. ... Foreword by Sir Gilbert Parker. London, Skeffington, 1930. 160p [BM BVaU OTP

Lewis, Charles Edward
REVERIES OF AN OLD SMOKER. Interspersed with Reminiscences of Travel and Adventure. Toronto, Hunter Rose, 1881. 384p [BVaU OTP

Lewis, John, 1858–1935
GEORGE BROWN. Toronto, Morang, 1906. 281p [Also pub.: Toronto, Oxford U. Press, 1926.] [BM BVaU LC NSWA OTU QMM
MACKENZIE KING, THE MAN, HIS ACHIEVEMENTS. Toronto, Morang, 1925. 136p [Rev. and extended by Norman McLeod Rogers: Toronto, Nelson, 1935. 212p] [BM BVaU LC MWU NSWA OTP QMM

Lewis, Thaddeus, 1793–
AUTOBIOGRAPHY OF THADDEUS LEWIS, a Minister of the Methodist Episcopal

Church in Canada. Picton, "North American" Office, 1865. 205p [BVaU
OTP

Liedl, Charles
HUNTING WITH RIFLE AND PENCIL. Fredericton, Brunswick Press, 1955. 186p

Lighthall, William Douw, 1857–1954
LA CORNE ST. LUC. The "General of the Indians." Montreal, n.p., 1908. 8p
[NBFU OTU
THOMAS POWNALL: His Part in the Conquest of Canada. Ottawa, Hope, 1904. 5p
[BVaU NBFU

Lindsey, Charles, 1820–1908
THE LIFE AND TIMES OF WM. LYON MACKENZIE. ... Toronto, Randall, 1862. 2v
[Later ed. by G.G.S. Lindsey, with Additions, in "Makers of Canada" series:
Toronto, Morang, 1908. 542p] [BM BVaU LC NSWA OTP QMM

Linnell, J.B.
THE STORY OF A PIONEER. As Told to his Daughter-in-law, Ruth Linnell at
Summerberry, Sask., February, 1949. Grenfell, Sask., Grenfell Sun Print., 1949.
24p [BViPA SSU

Little, George E., 1906–
THE LITTLES OF GALLOWAY AND THE COUNTY OF KENT, N.B. Moncton, Author,
1956. 153p

Little, Robert H., 1859?–
REMINISCENCES OF MY PIONEERING EXPERIENCES IN TWP. 7, RANGE 12, CYPRESS
RIVER LOCALITY, DURING THE WINTER OF 1879–1880. Treherne, Man., Times
Print., 1931. 36p [MWP OTP

Livesay, John Frederick Bligh, 1875–1944
THE MAKING OF A CANADIAN. Ed. with a memoir by F.R. Livesay. Toronto,
Ryerson, 1947. 181p [BM BVa LC NSHD OTP QMM

Livingston, Helen Armina Mary, 1899–
HER NAME WAS MINA HAGER. A Short Sketch. Hamilton, Ont., Livingston United
Church, 1958. 12p [Biographical sketch of Mina Hager Livingston.]

Lloyd-Owen, Frances
GOLD NUGGET CHARLIE. A Narrative Compiled from the Notes of Charles E.
Musson. London, Harrap, 1939. 260p [BM BVaU LC MWU

Llwyd, Rev. John Plummer Derwent, 1861–1933
SON OF THUNDER. A Study of the Life and Work of John of Bethsaida, Fisher
of Men. New York, Long & Smith, 1932. 170p [BVa LC NSHD OTU

Locke, George Herbert, 1870–1937
THE QUEEN'S RANGERS. By G.H. Locke and Margaret Ray. Toronto, Public
Library, 1923. 30p [BM NBFU OKQ

Logan, Annie Robertson (Macfarlane), —1933
AN ACCOUNT OF THE EXPLORATIONS AND DISCOVERIES OF SAMUEL DE CHAM-
PLAIN, AND OF THE FOUNDING OF QUEBEC. By Mrs. J.E. Logan. Montreal,
Montreal News, 1908. 50p [OOP QMM

Logan, John Daniel, 1869–1929
LOVE'S PILGRIM ... [John Killick Bathurst]. Halifax, Allen, 1921. 22p [BM
BVaU NBFU OOP
THOMAS CHANDLER HALIBURTON. Toronto, Ryerson, 1923. 176p [BM BVaU
NSHD OTU

Long, John, fl. 1768–1791
JOHN LONG'S JOURNAL, 1768–1782. Cleveland, Clark, 1904. 329p [BVaU OTP

Longley, James Wilberforce, 1849–1922
JOSEPH HOWE. Toronto, Morang, 1904. 307p [BVaU LC NSWA OTP
SIR CHARLES TUPPER. Toronto, Morang, 1916. 304p [BVa LC NSWA OTU
QMM

Longley, Ronald Stewart, 1896–
SIR FRANCIS HINCKS. Toronto, U. of Toronto Press, 1943. 480p [BM BVaU
LC NBFU OTP

Longstaffe Family
THE HOUSE OF LONGSTAFFE, 70TH YEAR, 1888–1958. N.p., 1958. 12p [Genealogy
of the descendants of Edwin and Lottie Longstaffe of Toronto.]

Longworth, Israel
THE LIFE OF S.G.W. ARCHIBALD. Halifax, Huestis, 1881. 179p [BM BVaU LC
NSWA OKQ

Lord, Rev. George A., 1820–
A SHORT NARRATIVE OF THE LIFE AND CONVERSION OF REV. GEORGE A. LORD.
... Albany, N.Y., Author, 1847. 34p [Other eds.: N.p., 1854. 46p; Troy, N.Y.,
1855. 36p] [BM OTP

Loudon, William James, 1860–1951
A CANADIAN GEOLOGIST. Toronto, Macmillan, 1930. 257p [Life of J.B. Tyrrell.]
[BM BVaU NBFU OTP
SIR WILLIAM MULOCK. A Short Biography. Toronto, Macmillan, 1932. 384p
[BM BVaU LC OTP QMBM

Love, Christopher Charles
FREDERICK CLARK STEPHENSON, 1864–1941. Toronto, Ryerson, 1957. 36p

Lower, Arthur Reginald Marsden, 1889–
UNCONVENTIONAL VOYAGES. Toronto, Ryerson, 1953. xii + 156p

M., Mrs. E.M.

RECOLLECTIONS OF A BELOVED PASTOR. By Mrs. E.M.M. Kingston, News, 1845. 37p [An appreciation of Rev. R.D. Cartwright.] [OTU

McAleer, George, 1845–

REMINISCENT AND OTHERWISE. Life in the Eastern Townships of the Province of Quebec, Canada, Fifty Years Ago. Worcester, Mass., Goddard, 1901. 20p [BM BVaU OTU QMSS

A STUDY IN THE ORIGIN AND SIGNIFICATION OF THE SURNAME McALEER, and a Contribution to the McAleer Genealogy. Comp. by ——. Worcester, Mass., McAleer, 1909. 103p [LC

MacAlister, Alexander Wardrope Greenshields, 1876–

THE BENCH AND BAR OF THE PROVINCES OF QUEBEC, NOVA SCOTIA, AND NEW BRUNSWICK. Ed. by ——. Montreal, Lovell, 1907. 371p [BM LC OLU

McAlister, George Alexander

HIGH-SKY! The Ups and Downs of a Pinfeather Pilot. Toronto, Ryerson, 1944. 124p [BVa LC OTP

McAllister, George Clinton, 1804–1842

THE JOURNAL OF CAPTAIN GEORGE C.McALLISTER, JANUARY 1, 1831 TO JULY 27, 1833. Copied from the original note books by Mary Hill, January, 1931. Intro. and notes by Evans Hill. St. Stephen, N.B., 1958. 121p

McAllister, Ronald Nelson, 1917–

FOOTBALL STARS TODAY AND YESTERDAY. From The Canadian Sports Album [Radio Programme]. Intro. by James Vipond. Toronto, McClelland, 1950. 120p [OONL

HOCKEY STARS TODAY AND YESTERDAY. From The Canadian Sports Album [Radio Programme]. Intro. by Elmer Ferguson. Toronto, McClelland, 1950. 126p [OONL

SWIM TO GLORY. The Story of Marilyn Bell and the Lakeshore Swimming Club. Toronto, McClelland, 1954. 128p

McAra, Peter, 1862–1949

SIXTY-TWO YEARS ON THE SASKATCHEWAN PRAIRIES. [Anon] Regina, 1945. 48p [SSU

McAree, John Verner, 1876–1958

CABBAGETOWN STORE. Toronto, Ryerson, 1953. 113p

McArthur, Peter, 1866–1924

SIR WILFRID LAURIER. Toronto, Dent, 1919. 183p [BM BVaU LC NSWA OKQ

Macbeth, John Douglas

SOMEWHERE IN ENGLAND. War Letters of a Canadian Officer on Overseas Service. Toronto, Macmillan, 1941. 32p [LC OTP

Macbeth, Madge Hamilton (Lyons), 1878–1965
BOULEVARD CAREER. Toronto, Kingswood House, 1957. x + 230p
OVER MY SHOULDER. Toronto, Ryerson, 1953. 170p

MacBeth, Rev. Roderick George, 1858–1934
THE MAKING OF THE CANADIAN WEST. Being the Reminiscences of an Eyewitness.
  Toronto, Briggs, 1898. 230p [2nd ed.: Toronto, Briggs, 1905. 280p] [BM
  BVaU LC NSWA OTP QMBM
PEACE RIVER LETTERS. Vancouver, White & Bindon, 1915. 31p [BVaU LC
  MWP OKQ
RECENT CANADIAN WEST LETTERS. Historical and Descriptive. Brantford, Hurley
  Print., 1912. 52p [OLU
SIR AUGUSTUS NANTON. A Biography. Toronto, Macmillan, 1931. 130p [BVaU
  LC NSHD OTU

McCall, Delbert Thomas, 1871–
GENEALOGY AND HISTORY OF THE NORFOLK McCALL FAMILY AND ASSOCIATED
  DESCENDANTS, 1796–1946. Comp. by ——. Simcoe, Norfolk McCall Soc., 1946.
  215p [NBFU OTP

McCarthy, Pearl, 1895–
LEO SMITH. A Biographical Sketch. Toronto, U. of Toronto Press, 1956.
  ix + 53p

McCaskill, Rev. John James, 1875–
THE BUSINESS MAN AS HERO. Being a Memoir of Duncan Alexander McCaskill. ...
  1908. [MOR'12

McCharles, Aeneas, 1844–1906
BEMOCKED OF DESTINY. The Actual Struggles and Experiences of a Canadian
  Pioneer, and the Recollections of a Lifetime. Toronto, Briggs, 1908. 244p [BM
  BVaU LC NSHD OTP

McClung, Nellie Letitia (Mooney), 1873–1951
CLEARING IN THE WEST. My Own Story. Toronto, Allen, 1935. 378p [BM BVaU
  LC NBFU OTU SSU
THE STREAM RUNS FAST. My Own Story. Toronto, Allen, 1945. 316p [BVaU
  NBFU OTP QMM SSU

McCorkell, Edmund Joseph, 1891–
CAPTAIN, THE REVEREND WILLIAM LEO MURRAY ... 1890–1937, First Pastor of
  St. John the Evangelist Church, Campbell's Bay, Quebec. ... A Memoir. Ed. by
  ——. Toronto, St. Michael's College, 1939. 48p [OTP

McCourt, Edward Alexander, 1907–1972
BUCKSKIN BRIGADIER. The Story of the Alberta Field Force. Toronto, Macmillan,
  1955. 150p

McCourt, Peter
BIOGRAPHICAL SKETCH OF THE HONOURABLE EDWARD WHELAN. Together with
a Compilation of his Principal Speeches. ... Charlottetown, Author, 1888. 301p
[BVaU LC NSWA OLU

McCulley, Joseph
REFLECTIONS OF A HEADMASTER. Newmarket, Ont., Pickering College, 1938.
20p [OTU

McCulloch, John Herries, 1892–
NORTH RANGE. A Record of Hard Living and Adventure on the Colourful Northern
Rim of the British Empire. London, Chambers, 1954. 191p

McCulloch, Mercy Emma (Powell)
THAT REMINDS ME OF N.A.P. ... By M.E.M. Toronto, Ryerson, 1942. 78p
[Biography of Newton Albert Powell.] [BVaU LC OTP

McCulloch, William, 1811–1895?
LIFE OF THOMAS McCULLOCH D.D., PICTOU. ... Truro, priv. print., 1920. 218p
[BVaU NSHD OTU

McCully, Elizabeth A.
A CORN OF WHEAT; or, The Life of Rev. W.J. McKenzie of Korea. Toronto,
Westminster Co., 1903. 290p [BM BVaU NBFU

McCurdy, Rev. James Frederick, 1847–1935
LIFE AND WORK OF D.J. MACDONNELL, Minister of St. Andrew's Church, Toronto,
with a Selection of Sermons and Prayers. Toronto, Briggs, 1897. 512p [BM
BVaU NBFU OTP QMM

MacDermot, Hugh Ernest, 1888–
MAUD ABBOTT. A Memoir. Toronto, Macmillan, 1941. 264p [BVaU LC OTP
QMBM
SIR THOMAS RODDICK. His Work in Medicine and Public Life. Toronto, Macmillan,
1938. 160p [BM BVaU OTU QMBM

Macdonald, Adrian, 1889–
CANADIAN PORTRAITS. Toronto, Ryerson, 1925. 230p [BM BVaU LC NSHD
OTU

MacDonald, Rev. Alexander, 1858–1941
A BIT OF AUTOBIOGRAPHY. Victoria, Willows Press, 1920. 61p [BVaU NSHD

Macdonald, Edward Mortimer, 1865–1940
RECOLLECTIONS, POLITICAL AND PERSONAL. Toronto, Ryerson, 1938. 584p
[BM BVaU LC NBFU OTP

MacDonald, Eileen Harrison (Button)
I MARRIED AN ARTIST. By Billy Button. Toronto, Ryerson, 1951. 238p

MacDonald, Frank C.
THE KAISER'S GUEST. Garden City, N.Y., Country Life Press, 1918. 250p [LC
  BViV

Macdonald, Frederick Charles, −1936
EDWARD ASHURST WELCH, M.A., D.C.L., LL.D., OF GATESHEAD, TORONTO, WAKE-
  FIELD AND SOUTH CHURCH. A Memoir. Toronto, General Board of Religious
  Education, 1936. 93p [BM OTU

MacDonald, Hugh N., 1856−
MACDONALD AND MACKINNON FAMILIES. A Biographical Sketch. Whycomagh,
  N.S., Author, 1937. 32p [OTU

Macdonald, James, 1878−
DR. LOCKE, HEALER OF MEN. A Biography. Toronto, MacLean Pub., 1933. 83p
  [LC

Macdonald, James Simon, 1837−1914
BIOGRAPHICAL PAPERS READ BEFORE THE NOVA SCOTIA HISTORICAL SOCIETY,
  1899−1904. Halifax, McAlpine, 1905. 100p [Re: Edward Cornwallis, 1713−
  1776; Charles Lawrence, 1709−1760; Richard Bulkeley, 1717−1800.] [LC
  OOP
MEMOIR OF GOVERNOR JOHN PARR. N.p., n.pub., n.d. 38p [NSWA

Macdonald, John Alexander, 1815−1891
CORRESPONDENCE OF SIR JOHN MACDONALD. Selections from the Correspondence
  of the Right Honourable Sir John Alexander Macdonald. ... Made by his
  Literary Executor, Sir Joseph Pope. Toronto, Oxford U. Press, 1921. 502p
  [BVaU LC NBFU OTP

MacDonald, John Howard
THE HONORABLE EDWARD CORNWALLIS. A Biographical Sketch. Kentville, N.S.,
  D.A.R., 1930. 20p [NSWA

Macdonald, R.C.
SKETCHES OF HIGHLANDERS. With an Account of their Early Arrival in North
  America. ... Saint John, Chubb, 1843. 70p [BVaU NSWA OTU

MacDonald, Ranald, 1824−1894
RANALD MACDONALD. The Narrative of his Early Life under the Hudson's Bay
  Company's Regime; of his Experiences in the Pacific Whale Fishery; and of
  his Great Adventure to Japan; with a Sketch of his Later Life on the Western
  Frontier. Ed. and annotated ... by William S. Lewis and Naojiro Murakami.
  Spokane, Wash., Inland-American Print., 1923. 333p [BM BVaU NBFU OTU

Macdonald, William John, 1832−1916
A PIONEER, 1851. [Anon] N.p., n.pub., 1914. 30p [Macdonald lived on
  Vancouver Island, 1851−1916.] [BVaU OTU

Macdonell, John Alexander, 1851—1930

A SKETCH OF THE LIFE OF THE HONOURABLE AND RIGHT REVEREND ALEXANDER MACDONELL, Chaplain of the Glengarry Fencible. ... First Catholic Bishop of Upper Canada, and a Member of the Legislative Council. ... Alexandria, The Glengarrian, 1890. 86p [LC NSWA OTP QMM

Macdonell, W.J.

REMINISCENCES OF THE LATE HON. AND RIGHT REV. ALEX. MACDONELL, First Catholic Bishop of Upper Canada. ... [Anon]   Toronto, Williamson, 1888. 55p [NSHD OTU

Macdonnell, James Smellie, 1878?—

STOPPING PLACES. A Biographic Journey. Pasadena, Calif., Star-News Press, 1946. 93p [BVaU OTU

Macdougall, Rev. Archibald, 1849—1922

THE LIFE AND LETTERS OF REV. DR. ARCHIBALD MACDOUGALL. Ed. by Helen J. McLean. Hyde Park, Mass., Editor, 1933. 116p [CC

McDougall, Rev. John, 1842—1917

GEORGE MILLWARD McDOUGALL, THE PIONEER, PATRIOT, AND MISSIONARY. Toronto, Briggs, 1888. 242p [BM BVaU NSWA OTP QMSS

McDowall, Rev. James, 1826?—1864

A BRIEF MEMOIR AND SOME REMAINS OF THE LATE REV. JAMES McDOWALL. Ed. by Rev. James Cameron. Toronto, 1866. 54p [BibC

McDowell, Louise, 1872—

PAST AND PRESENT. A Canadian Musician's Reminiscences. Kirkland Lake, Ont., priv. print., 1957. xvii + 211p

McElheran, Irene Beatrice (Brock), 1879—1955

THAT'S WHAT I'M HERE FOR. Robert B. McElheran, His Days and His Ways. Toronto, Ryerson, 1955. xvii + 122p

MacEwan, Grant, 1902—

EYE OPENER BOB. The Story of Bob Edwards. Edmonton, Institute of Applied Art, 1957. 227p

FIFTY MIGHTY MEN. Saskatoon, Modern Press, 1958. 342p

JOHN WARE'S COW COUNTRY. Edmonton, Institute of Applied Art, 1960. 261p

McEwen, Thomas Alexander, 1891—

HE WROTE FOR US. The Story of Bill Bennett, Pioneer Socialist Journalist. Vancouver, Tribune Pub. Co., 1951. 159p

McGee, Thomas D'Arcy, 1825—1868

HISTORICAL SKETCHES OF O'CONNELL AND HIS FRIENDS. ... With a Glance at the Future Destiny of Ireland. 3rd ed. Boston, Donahue & Rohan, 1845. 208p [BM BVaU LC NSWA OTP QMSS

A LIFE OF THE RT. REV. EDWARD MAGINN, Coadjutor Bishop of Derry. With Selections from his Correspondence. New York, O'Shea, 1857. 306p [BM LC OTP QMSS

A MEMOIR OF THE LIFE AND CONQUEST OF ART MACMURROGH, King of Leinster, from A.D. 1377 to A.D. 1417. Dublin, Duffy, 1886. 200p [An earlier edition in 1847.] [BM LC OLU

McGibbon, Robert Davidson, 1857–1906

THOMAS D'ARCY McGEE. An Address. ... Montreal, Dawson, 1884. 19p [BVaU LC NSHPL OKQ QMBM

MacGill, Elizabeth Muriel Gregory, 1905–

MY MOTHER, THE JUDGE. A Biography of Judge Helen Gregory MacGill. By Elsie Gregory MacGill. Toronto, Ryerson, 1955. xvi + 248p

McGill University. Osler Society

W.W. FRANCIS, TRIBUTES FROM HIS FRIENDS, ON THE OCCASION OF THE THIRTY-FIFTH ANNIVERSARY OF THE OSLER SOCIETY OF McGILL UNIVERSITY. Montreal, Society, 1956. xv + 123p

McGillicuddy, Owen Ernest, 1887–1954

THE MAKING OF A PREMIER – An Outline of the Life Story of the Right Hon. W.L. Mackenzie King. ... Toronto, Musson, 1922. 91p [BM BVaU NSHD OKQ QMM

MacGillivray, C.J.

TIMOTHY HIERLIHY AND HIS TIMES. The Story of the Founder of Antigonish, N.S. Antigonish, Casket Print, 1935. 173p [NSWA· OTU

M'Gillivray, Duncan, –1808

THE JOURNAL OF DUNCAN M'GILLIVRAY OF THE NORTH-WEST COMPANY ... 1794–5. With intro., notes and appendix by A.S. Morton. Toronto, Macmillan, 1929. lxxviii + 79 + 24 + 6p [BM BVaU LC NBFU OTP QMSS

McGoey, John Heck, 1915–

NOR SCRIP NOR SHOES. Boston, Little Brown, 1958. 280p

McGregor, Daniel Arthur

MEMOIR OF D.A. McGREGOR, Late Principal of Toronto Baptist College. Toronto, The Alumni, 1891. [BVaU NSWA OTU

MacGregor, James Grierson, 1905–

BEHOLD THE SHINING MOUNTAINS. Being an Account of Anthony Henday, 1754–55, the First White Man to Enter Alberta. Edmonton, Applied Art Products, 1954. 276p
NORTH-WEST OF 16. Toronto, McClelland, 1958. 224p

MacGregor, Mary Esther (Miller), 1876–1961

THE BLACK BEARDED BARBARIAN. The Life of George Leslie Mackay of Formosa.

By Marian Keith [pseud]. New York, Missionary Education Movement, 1912.
307p [BVaU LC NBFU OTP

Machar, Agnes Maule, 1837–1927

FAITHFUL UNTO DEATH. A Memorial of John Anderson [1810–1859], Late
Janitor of Queen's College, Kingston. ... [Anon] Kingston, Creighton,
1859. 66p [OKQ

HEROES OF CANADA. Based upon "Stories of New France." Toronto, Copp
Clark, 1893. 96p [*See* STORIES OF NEW FRANCE, p. 885 below.] [OTU QMSS

Machar, Rev. John, 1796–1863

MEMORIALS OF THE LIFE AND MINISTRY OF THE REV. JOHN MACHAR, D.D.,
1796–1863. Late Minister of St. Andrew's Church, Kingston. Ed. by Members
of his Family. Toronto, Campbell, 1873. 301p [BVaU NSWA OTP

Machum, George Cecil, 1896–1958

CANADA'S V.C.'S, THE STORY OF CANADIANS WHO HAVE BEEN AWARDED THE
VICTORIA CROSS. A Centenary Memorial, 1956. Comp. by ——. Toronto,
McClelland, 1956. 208p

THE STORY OF THE "JEFF" RUSSEL MEMORIAL TROPHY. A Tribute to the
Memory of a Great Athlete and Gentleman. Ed. by ——. Montreal, [Industrial
Shops for the Deaf], 1958. 68p

McIlwraith, Jean Newton, 1859–1938

SIR FREDERICK HALDIMAND. Toronto, Morang, 1904. 356p [BM BVaU
LC NSWA OTP

MacInnis, Grace (Woodsworth), 1905–

J.S. WOODSWORTH, A MAN TO REMEMBER. Toronto, Macmillan, 1953.
xiv + 336p

McIntosh (or Mackintosh), Hugh Fraser, 1862–

FATHER LOUIS DELLA VAGNA, CAPUCHIN, Pastor of St. Mary's Church, Toronto,
1856–1857. Toronto, "Catholic Weekly Review," 1888. 22p [NSHD OTP

McIntyre, Fred, 1877–

THE TRUE LIFE STORY OF A PIONEER. Syracuse, Ind., Nonpareil Press, 1955.
240p

Mack, Harry Wilson, 1892–

THE MACK AND SINE FAMILIES. With Allied Families: Althouse, Sarles, Chard,
Rosebush, Hills, Kromenaker, Grant and others. Detroit, Mich., E.P. Mack,
1955. 74p

Mackay, Charles Angus, 1872–

MEMOIRS OF THE LIFE OF CHARLES ANGUS MACKAY. By Himself. Victoria,
Colonist, 1930. 50p [BVaU

Mackay, Miss Janet
CATHERINE OF BRAGANZA. London, Long, 1937. 315p [BM
LITTLE MADAM. A Biography of Henrietta Maria. London, Bell, 1939. 380p
[BM NBS OWtU

Mackay, Robert Walter Stuart, 1809?–1854
THE CANADA DIRECTORY. Containing the Names of the Professional and
Business Men of every description, in the Cities, Towns, and Principal Villages
of Canada ... [etc.]. Montreal, Lovell, 1851. 692p [OTU QMBM

MacKellar, Margaret, 1861–
LIFE OF AMELIA J. HARRIS. Toronto, United Church of Canada, 1937. 16p
[OTU

Mackenzie, Alexander, 1822–1892
THE LIFE AND SPEECHES OF HON. GEORGE BROWN. Toronto, Globe, 1882.
381p [BM BVaU LC NSWA OTP QMSS

MacKenzie, Donald, 1908–
FUGITIVES. An Autobiography. London, Elek Books, 1955. 206p [American
title: OCCUPATION: THIEF. Indianapolis, Bobbs-Merrill, 1955. 260p]
GENTLEMEN AT CRIME. An Autobiography. London, Elek Books, 1956.
199p [Sequel to: FUGITIVES.]

Mackenzie, John Joseph, 1865–1922
NUMBER 4 CANADIAN HOSPITAL. The Letters of Professor J.J. Mackenzie from
the Salonika Front. ... Toronto, Macmillan, 1933. 247p [BM LC OTU
QMM

Mackenzie, Kenneth Ferns, 1882–
SABOTS AND SLIPPERS. Toronto, priv. print., 1954. 131p

McKenzie, Nathaniel Murdoch William John, 1856–1943
THE MEN OF THE HUDSON'S BAY COMPANY 1670 A.D.–1920 A.D. Fort William,
Times-Journal, 1921. 214p [BM BVaU LC OTP

McKenzie, Thomas, 1830–
MY LIFE AS A SOLDIER. Saint John, McMillan, 1898. 202p [BVaU NSWA
OTP QMSS

Mackenzie, William Lyon, 1795–1861
MACKENZIE'S OWN NARRATIVE OF THE LATE REBELLION. Toronto, Palladium
Office, 1838. 23p [Same title: Toronto, Rous & Mann, 1937. 30p] [BVaU
LC NSWA OTP QMSS
THE SONS OF THE EMERALD ISLE; or, Lives of One Thousand Remarkable
Irishmen, including Memoirs of Noted Characters of Irish Parentage or
Descent. New York, Burgess Stringer, 1845. 108p [LC, OTL and OTU
copies have only 60 pages, rest missing; OTP copy has 108 pages, but is an
incomplete copy with p. 109ff missing.] [LC OTL OTP OTU

McKeown, Hugh Charles, 1841–1889

THE LIFE AND LABORS OF MOST REV. JOHN JOSEPH LYNCH, D.D. Cong., Miss.,
  First Archbishop of Toronto. Montreal & Toronto, Sadlier, 1886. 353p
  [BM BVaU LC OTP

McKinley, Mabel (Burns)

CANADIAN HEROES OF PIONEER DAYS. Toronto, Longmans, 1930. 119p
  [BM BViPA OLU

CANADIAN HEROINES OF PIONEER DAYS. New York, Longmans, 1929.
  66p [LC QMSS

FAMOUS MEN AND WOMEN OF CANADA. Toronto, Longmans, 1938. 128p
  [BM BVa OOA

Mackinnon, Rev. Clarence D., 1868–1937

A BRIEF SKETCH OF THE LIFE OF THE REVEREND JOHN FRANKLIN FORBES. ...
  Saint John, Globe, 1905. 56p [NSWA OTU

THE LIFE OF PRINCIPAL OLIVER. ... Toronto, Ryerson, 1936. 162p [BM
  BViPA LC OKQ SSU

REMINISCENCES. Toronto, Ryerson, 1938. 236p [BM LC OTP

McKinnon, John Angus, 1898–

LACHLIN McKINNON, 1865-1948. Calgary, Author, 1956. 130p

McKitrick, Thomas George, 1873–1952

ANDREW STEWART OF THE PRAIRIE HOMESTEADS. Crystal City, Man., Author,
  1950. 134p [BVaU OTU

MacLane, Mary, 1881–1929

I, MARY MacLANE. A Diary of Human Days. New York, Stokes, 1917. 317p
  [BM LC OH

MY FRIEND, ANNABEL LEE. Chicago, Stone, 1903. 262p [AEU LC OTU

THE STORY OF MARY MacLANE. By Herself. Chicago, Stone 1902. 322p [New
  ed., with added chapter, New York, Duffield, 1911. 354p] [BM LC NBFL
  OTMC

McLaurin, Rev. Colin Campbell, 1854–1941

SIXTY YEARS IN THE MINISTRY. Edmonton, Institute Press, 1937. 13p
  [OTU

MacLean, Andrew Dyas, 1896–

R.B. BENNETT, PRIME MINISTER OF CANADA. Toronto, Excelsior, 1934.
  112p [BVaU LC NBFU OTP QMBM

McLean, Charles Herbert, 1877–

PROMINENT PEOPLE OF NEW BRUNSWICK IN THE RELIGIOUS, EDUCATIONAL,
  POLITICAL, PROFESSIONAL, COMMERCIAL, AND SOCIAL ACTIVITIES. ...
  Comp. by ——. With an introductory essay by A.G. Bailey. Saint John,
  Biographical Society of Canada, 1938. 261p [BM NBFU

McLean, John, 1799–1890
NOTES OF A TWENTY-FIVE YEARS' SERVICE IN THE HUDSON'S BAY TERRITORY. London, Bentley, 1849. 2v (Also: Ed. by W.S. Wallace. Toronto, Champlain Society, 1932. xxxvi + 402p) [BVaU LC NBFU OTP QMBM

Maclean, Rev. John, 1851–1928
HENRY B. STEINHAUER, His Work among the Cree Indians of the Western Plains of Canada. Toronto, Methodist Church Pub., n.d. 51p [BVaU OTUV

JAMES EVANS, Inventor of the Syllabic System of the Cree Language. Toronto, Briggs, 1890. 208p [BM BVaU LC OTU

McDOUGALL OF ALBERTA. A Life of Rev. John McDougall, D.D., Pathfinder of Empire and Prophet of the Plains. Toronto, Ryerson, 1927. 282p [BM BVaU NBFU OTP QMM

VANGUARDS OF CANADA. Toronto, Missionary Society of the Methodist Church, 1918. 262p [Biographies of missionaries across Canada.] [BM BViPA NSWA OTP SSU

THE WARDEN OF THE PLAINS, and Other Stories of Life in the Canadian Northwest. Toronto, Briggs, 1896. 301p [BM BVaU LC MWP OKQ

WILLIAM BLACK, THE APOSTLE OF METHODISM IN THE MARITIME PROVINCES. ... Halifax, Methodist Book Room, 1907. 64p [BM BVaU NBFU OKQ

McLeish, John Alexander Buchanan, 1913–
SEPTEMBER GALE. A Study of Arthur Lismer of the Group of Seven. Toronto, Dent, 1955. xi + 212p

McLennan, John Stewart, 1853–1939
HUGH McLENNAN, 1825–1899. Montreal, Author, 1936. 100p [QMM

McLeod, Donald [of Woodstock, Ont.]
DONALD McLEOD'S GLOOMY MEMORIES IN THE HIGHLANDS OF SCOTLAND *versus* MRS. HARRIET BEECHER STOWE'S "SUNNY MEMORIES IN (ENGLAND) A FOREIGN LAND"; or, A Faithful Picture of the Extirpation of the Celtic Race from the Highlands of Scotland. Toronto, Thompson, 1857. 212p [NSHD OTU QMM

McMahon, Hugh, 1836–1911
REMINISCENCES. Toronto, 1908. 57p [OTU

MacMechan, Archibald McKellar, 1862–1933
WILLIAM GREENWOOD. N.p., n. pub., 1914. 12p [OTU

MacMillan, Don A.
ONLY THE STARS KNOW. Toronto, Dent, 1944. 138p [BVaU LC NBFU OTP QMSS

McNab, Rev. John, 1887–
FOUR CAMEOS, 1846–1946. ... Toronto, British & Foreign Bible Soc., 1946. 15p [OKQ

IN OTHER TONGUES. Tales of the Triumphs of Canadian Translators of Scripture. Toronto, Thorn Press, 1939. 141p [BVaU OTU
THEY WENT FORTH. Toronto, McClelland, 1933. 207p [Rev. ed., 1955. 240p] [Biogs. of missionaries.] [BVaU LC OTU

McNabb, John H., 1880–1954
THE HOMESTEAD DAYS OF JOHN H. AND ROBERT D. McNABB. Saskatoon, [1953?]. 24p

McNaught, Kenneth William Kirkpatrick, 1918–
A PROPHET IN POLITICS. A Biography of J.S. Woodsworth. Toronto, U. of Toronto Press, 1959. 339p

Macnaughton, John, 1858–1943
LORD STRATHCONA. London, Oxford U. Press, 1926. 391p [BM BVaU LC NSHD OTP QMM

McNeill, William Everett, 1876–
WALLACE OF QUEEN'S. [Kingston, Queen's University, 1951]. 12p

MacNutt, William Stewart, 1908–
DAYS OF LORNE. From the Private Papers of the Marquis of Lorne, 1878–1883, in the Possession of the Duke of Argyll at Inverary Castle, Scotland. Fredericton, Brunswick Press, 1955. x + 262p

Macoun, John, 1831–1920
AUTOBIOGRAPHY OF JOHN MACOUN, Canadian Explorer and Naturalist. A Memorial Volume. Ottawa, Field-Naturalists' Club, 1922. 305p [BM BVaU LC NBFU OTP

McPhail, Alexander James, 1883–1931
THE DIARY OF ALEXANDER JAMES McPHAIL. Ed. by Harold A. Innis. Toronto, U. of Toronto Press, 1940. 289p [BM BViPA LC NSHD OTP QMM

Macphail, Andrew, 1864–1938
THE MASTER'S WIFE. Montreal, Gnaedinger Print., 1939. 246p [BVaU NBFU OTP QMM
THREE PERSONS. 3rd ed. London, Murray, 1929. 346p [BM BVaU LC NSHD OTU QMM

Macpherson, Charlotte Holt (Gethings), fl. 1828–1890
OLD MEMORIES, AMUSING AND HISTORICAL. A sequel to REMINISCENCES OF OLD QUEBEC. By Mrs. Daniel Macpherson. ... Montreal, Author, 1890. 128p [BVaU LC NSWA OTP QMBM
REMINISCENCES OF OLD QUEBEC. By Mrs. Daniel Macpherson. Montreal, Lovell, 1890. 128p [BVaU LC NSWA OTP QMM

Macpherson, James Pennington, 1839–1916
LIFE OF THE RIGHT HON. SIR JOHN A. MACDONALD. ... By his Nephew. Saint
John, Earle, 1891. 2v [BVaU LC NBFU OTP QMBM

MacPherson, Stewart
THE MIKE AND I. London, Home & Van Thal, 1948. 191p [BM OOP

MacPhie, Rev. John Peter, 1854–1931
PICTONIANS AT HOME AND ABROAD. Sketches of Professional Men and Women of
Pictou County—Its History and Institutions. Boston, Pinkham, 1914. 232p
[BVaU NBFU OTU

McRae, James Archibald, 1889–
CALL ME TOMORROW. Toronto, Ryerson, 1960. 240p

McRaye, Walter Jackson, 1876–1946
PAULINE JOHNSON AND HER FRIENDS. Toronto, Ryerson, 1947. 182p [NBFU
OTP QMM
PIONEERS AND PROMINENT PEOPLE OF MANITOBA. Ed. by ——. Winnipeg, Can.
Publicity Co., [1925?]. 353p [BViV SSU
TOWN HALL TONIGHT. Toronto, Ryerson, 1929. 256p [BVaU NBFU OTP

McRobie, William Orme
FIGHTING THE FLAMES; or, Twenty-Seven Years in the Montreal Fire Brigade. ...
Montreal, "Witness" Print., 1881. 299p [BVaU NSWA OTP QMBM

MacTavish, Newton McFaul, 1875–1941
GEORGE HAM. Sketch of a Gentleman on Whom the Sun Never Sets. N.p., priv.
print., n.d. 16p [NBFU

McTavish, Rev. William Sharpe, 1858–1932
MISSIONARY PATHFINDERS. Presbyterian Laborers at Home and Abroad. Ed. by
——. Toronto, Musson, 1907. 272p [BM BVaU OOP

MacVicar, Rev. Donald Harvey, 1831–1902
IN MEMORIAM: A SERMON PREACHED ON THE OCCASION OF THE DEATH OF JOHN
REDPATH. Montreal, Lovell, 1869. 29p [NSWA

Macvicar, Helena
MARGARET SCOTT, A TRIBUTE: The Margaret Scott Nursing Mission. Winnipeg,
Stovel, 1948. 28p [UTQ'50

MacVicar, Rev. John Harvey, 1864–
LIFE AND WORK OF DONALD HARVEY MacVICAR. Toronto, Westminster Co.,
1904. 351p [BM BVaU OTP QMM

Magrath, Charles Alexander, 1860–1949
THE GALTS, FATHER AND SON, Pioneers in the Development of Southern Alberta.
Lethbridge, Herald, 1936. 64p [BM BVaU LC NSHD OTP QMBM

Malone, Richard Sankey, 1909–
MISSING FROM THE RECORD. Toronto, Collins, 1946. 227p [BM BVaU LC NSHD OTU QMBM

Manion, James Patrick, 1907–1959
A CANADIAN ERRANT. Twenty-five Years in the Canadian Foreign Service. Ed. by Guy Sylvestre. Toronto, Ryerson, 1960. ix + 196p

Manion, Robert James, 1881–1943
LIFE IS AN ADVENTURE. Toronto, Ryerson, 1936. 360p [BVaU OTP QMM
A SURGEON IN ARMS. New York, Appleton, 1918. 310p [BM NSHD OTL

Manly, Rev. John G., 1814–1908
A PULPIT ESTIMATE OF WELLINGTON. ... London, 1852. [BM

Marquis, Thomas Guthrie, 1864–1936
BROCK, THE HERO OF UPPER CANADA. Toronto, Morang, 1912. 142p [BM BVaU OOP QMBM
BUILDERS OF CANADA FROM CARTIER TO LAURIER. ... Ed. by ——. Toronto, Winston, 1903. 570p [Also pub. as: GIANTS OF THE DOMINION FROM CARTIER TO LAURIER. Philadelphia, 1905.] [BVaU LC NSWA OTP QMSS
THE WAR CHIEF OF THE OTTAWAS. A Chronicle of the Pontiac War. Toronto, Glasgow Brook, 1915. 145p [BM BVaU LC NSWA OTU

Mars, Alastair, 1915–
COURT MARTIAL. London, Muller, 1954. 223p

Marsden, Rev. Joshua, 1777–1837
GRACE DISPLAYED. An Interesting Narrative of the Life, Conversion, Christian Experience, Ministry, and Missionary Labours of ——. New York, Paul & Thomas, 1813. 240p [LC OTUV
SKETCHES OF THE EARLY LIFE OF A SAILOR, NOW A PREACHER OF THE GOSPEL. Hull, Ross, 1820. N.p. [OTUV

Marsh, D'Arcy Gilbert, 1906–
THE TRAGEDY OF HENRY THORNTON. Toronto, Macmillan, 1935. 293p [BM BVaU LC NBFU OTP QMBM

Marshall, James Stirrat, 1899–
ADVENTURE IN TWO HEMISPHERES, INCLUDING CAPTAIN VANCOUVER'S VOYAGE. By James Stirrat Marshall and Carrie Marshall. Vancouver, Talex Print., 1955. xii + 208p

Marshall, John George, 1786–1880
PERSONAL NARRATIVES. With Reflections and Remarks. ... Halifax, Chamberlain, 1866. 154p [NSHD OOP

Marsters, Joseph Dimock
GENEALOGY OF THE DIMOCK FAMILY FROM THE YEAR 1637. Windsor, N.S.,
Anslow, 1899. 44p [NSWA

Martin, Alfred Tobias John
THE REMAINS OF THE LATE T. [i.e., Tobias] MARTIN. ... With a memoir of the
author. Helston, 1831. [BM

Martin, Chester Bailey, 1882–1958
LORD SELKIRK'S WORK IN CANADA. Oxford, Clarendon, 1916. 240p [BM
BVaU LC NSHD OTP

Marty, Aletta Elise, 1866–1929
MY EDUCATIONAL CREED. Toronto, Ryerson, 1924. 52p [BM BVaU NSHD
OKQ

Marwick, Alice (Stinson), 1892–1956
THE HONOURABLE FRANK COCHRANE. A Tribute. Cochrane, Ont., Author, 1950.
22p [OONL

Mason, Rev. George
IN MEMORY OF SIR JAS. DOUGLAS. N.p., n.d. 3p [BViPA

Massey, Hart Almerrin, 1823–1896
HART ALMERRIN MASSEY. Pioneer Farmer, Farm Implement Manufacturer,
Public-Spirited Citizen, Philanthropist. ... [Anon] Toronto, priv. print.,
[1896]. 35p [OOP

Matheson, Charles Winfield, 1878–
THE THREE RICHARDS OF THE DALHOUSIE LAW SCHOOL WHO BECAME KNIGHTS
[Richard McBride, Richard Bennett, and Richard Squires]. Calgary, priv. print.,
1954. 4p

Mathieson, Rev. Alexander, 1795–1890
SERMON ON THE DEATH OF MR. ROBERT WATSON. Montreal, 1827. [BibC
A TRIBUTE OF RESPECT TO THE MEMORY OF A GOOD MAN. A Sermon on the
Death of Hugh Brodie, Esq. Montreal, 1852. 44p [BibC

Matthews, Richard F., 1832–
DIARY [January 28th, 1863 to March 17, 1899]. London, Ont., 1947. 3v [LC

Matthews, Matthew George
MATTHEWS' FAMOUS STORIES AND WORK. Windsor, Ont., Jaques & Sons, 1915.
234p [OTP

Mavor, James, 1854–1925
MY WINDOWS ON THE STREET OF THE WORLD. New York, Dutton, 1923. 2v [BM
BVaU LC NSHD OTP QMBM

Mayerhoffer, Rev. Vincent Philip, 1784–1859
TWELVE YEARS A ROMAN CATHOLIC PRIEST; or, The Autobiography of ——.
Toronto, Rowsell & Ellis, 1861. 340p [BVaU LC NSWA OTP QMM

Meilicke, Emil Julius, 1852–1934
LEAVES FROM THE LIFE OF A PIONEER. Being the Autobiography of Sometime
Senator Emil Julius Meilicke (with Editorial Notes). Vancouver, Wrigley, 1948.
163p [BVaU OTP SSU

Mellick, Henry George, 1857–1937
TIMOTHY'S BOYHOOD; or, Pioneer Country Life on Prince Edward Island. By
Timothy, a Country Boy [pseud]. Kentville, N.S., Kentville Pub. Co., 1933.
[Rhod p683

Mellor, T.C.
SKETCH OF THE LIFE OF HIS HONOUR JUDGE SAVARY DELIVERED BEFORE THE
HISTORICAL ASSOCIATION OF ANNAPOLIS ROYAL. ... Annapolis Royal,
Spectator, 1922. 41p [NSWA

Merkel, Andrew Doane, 1884–1954
LETTERS FROM THE FRONT. ... Halifax, Ross Print., [Preface 1914]. 128p
[NSHD

Merkley, E. May
OUR DOCTOR. Morrisburg, Ont., Leader Pub., 1933. 61p [On Dr. Mahlon
W. Locke.] [LC OTU

Merrick, Rev. Earl Chauncey, 1905–
JOHN BATES McLAURIN ... A Biography. Toronto, priv. print. by Mrs. J.B.
McLaurin, 1955. x + 134p

Merritt, Jedediah Prendergast, 1820–1901
BIOGRAPHY OF THE HON. W.H. MERRITT, M.P., of Lincoln, District of Niagara.
St. Catharines, Leavenworth, 1875. 429p [BM BVaU LC NSHD OTU QMSS

Methodius, Brother
REVEREND BROTHER STANISLAUS JOSEPH. Yorkton, Sask., St. Joseph's College,
1953. 30p

Middleton, Jesse Edgar, 1872–1960
NATIONAL ENCYCLOPEDIA OF CANADIAN BIOGRAPHY. Ed. by Jesse Edgar
Middleton and W. Scott Downs. Toronto, Dominion Pub., 1935. 383p [Also
in 1937. 336p] [BVaU NSHD OTU

Middleton, Samuel H., 1884–
KOOTENAI BROWN, ADVENTURER, PIONEER, PLAINSMAN, PARK WARDEN. ...
Lethbridge, Herald, 1954. 64p

Mikel, William Charles, 1867–1950
GODLOVE MIKEL (UNITED EMPIRE LOYALIST). Historical Notes Concerning

One of the Old Log Cabin Family. Trenton, Quinte Sun, 1939. 63p [BVaU OTP

Miller, John Ormsby, 1861–1936
BRIEF BIOGRAPHIES SUPPLEMENTING CANADIAN HISTORY (Heroes of the Northland). Toronto, Copp Clark, 1902. 152p [BM BVaU NSWA OTU

Miller, Linus Wilson, 1818?–1880
NOTES OF AN EXILE TO VAN DIEMEN'S LAND. Fredonia, N.Y., McKinstry, 1846. 378p [Reprinted New York, Johnson Reprint, 1968.] [BVaU LC OTP QQL

Miller, William
INCIDENTS IN THE POLITICAL CAREER OF THE LATE SIR JOHN THOMPSON NOT CONTAINED IN MR. J. CASTELL HOPKINS' BOOK. ... N.p., [1895?]. 21p [NSWA OTU

Millman, Rev. Thomas Reagh, 1905–
LIFE OF ... CHARLES JAMES STEWART, D.D., SECOND LORD BISHOP OF QUEBEC. Edinburgh, Stewart, [1948]. 12p [BM OTU
LIFE OF THE RT. REV. THE HON. CHARLES JAMES STEWART. London, Ont., Huron College, 1953. 237p
JACOB MOUNTAIN. First Lord Bishop of Quebec. Toronto, U. of Toronto Press, 1947. 310p [BM BVaU LC NBFU OTP QMM
A SKETCH OF THE LIFE AND WORK OF THE RIGHT REVEREND JACOB MOUNTAIN, D.D., FIRST LORD BISHOP OF QUEBEC. A Sermon preached on Sunday, October 31, 1943 ... on the Occasion of the 150th Anniversary of the Arrival of the Bishop. Durham, P.Q., Author, 1943. 10p [BM OTP

Mills, Stanley, 1863–
GENEALOGICAL AND HISTORICAL RECORDS OF THE MILLS AND GAGE FAMILIES, 1776–1926. ... Comp. by ——. Hamilton, Reid Press, 1926. 101p [BM BVaU LC OKQ

Milner, William Cochrane, 1846–1939
OUR LIEUTENANT GOVERNORS. Saint John, Busy East Press, 1928. 60p [BVaU NSWA OOA

Miner, Jack (John Thomas Miner), 1865–1944
JACK MINER AND THE BIRDS; and Some Things I Know about Nature. Toronto, Ryerson, 1923. 178p [BM BVaU LC NBFU OTU QMM

Moberly, Henry John, 1835–1931
WHEN FUR WAS KING. By ——. In collaboration with William Bleasdell Cameron. ... Toronto, Dent, 1929. 237p [BM BVaU LC NSHD OLU QMM

Mockridge, Rev. Charles Henry, 1844–1913
THE BISHOPS OF THE CHURCH OF ENGLAND IN CANADA AND NEWFOUNDLAND. Toronto, Brown, 1896. 380p [BM BVaU LC NBFU OLU QMM

Moffat, Eva L., —1947

THE ANCESTORS OF DANIEL FREEMAN BRITTON OF WESTMORELAND, N.H.,
AND GANANOQUE, ONT., 1808–1887. Pt. 1. The Ancestry of his Father, Daniel
Britton. Pt. 2. The Ancestry of his Mother, Sally Wood. Comp. by ——. Ed.
and correlated by Geoffrey Gilbert. Victoria, Editor, 1953. 135 + 81p
[mimeographed]

THE ANCESTORS OF NANCY MARIA MOFFATT, WIFE OF DANIEL FREEMAN
BRITTON. Pt. 1. The Ancestry of her Mother, Nancy Treadway. Pt. 2. The
Ancestry of her Father, Melvin Moffatt. Comp. by ——. Ed. and correlated
by Geoffrey Gilbert. Victoria, Editor, 1952. 159 + 69p

THE ANCESTRY OF EZRA HOLTON OF NORTHFIELD, MASS., AND SOPERTON, ONT.,
1785–1824. Twenty-eight "Stories." Comp. by ——. Ed. and correlated by
Geoffrey Gilbert. Victoria, Editor, 1953. 158p

THE ANCESTRY OF WILLIAM FORBES OF BARRE, MASS., AND MONTREAL, QUE.,
1778–1833. Thirteen "Stories." Ed. and correlated by Geoffrey Gilbert.
Victoria, Editor, 1953. 103p

Montgomery, Lucy Maud, 1874–1942

THE GREEN GABLES LETTERS, FROM L.M. MONTGOMERY TO EPHRAIM WEBER,
1905–1909. Ed. by Wilfrid Eggleston. Toronto, Ryerson, 1960. 102p

Montreal, Que. Jewish Public Library

TRIBUTE TO ISRAEL RABINOVITCH ON HIS SIXTIETH BIRTHDAY. Observed Sunday
Evening in The Library Auditorium, December 26, 1954. Montreal, 1954. 24p

Montreal, Que. Zion Church

JUBILEE SERVICES ... TO CELEBRATE THE 50TH ANNIVERSARY OF THE MINIS-
TERIAL WORK OF REV. HENRY WILKES. Montreal, The Church, 1878. 39p
[NSWA

Montreuil, Mrs. Anna B., 1886–

THREE CAME WITH GIFTS. The Story of the First Hospital, the First School, and
the First Cloister in Canada and their Heroic Founders [the Duchesse d'Aiguillon,
Madame de la Peltrie, and Mère Marie de l'Incarnation]. Toronto, Ryerson, 1955.
60p

Monture, Mrs. Ethel Brant, 1894–

FAMOUS INDIANS: Brant, Crowfoot, Oronhyatekha. Toronto, Clarke Irwin, 1960.
160p

Moodie, John Wedderburn Dunbar, 1797–1869

SCENES AND ADVENTURES AS A SOLDIER AND SETTLER DURING HALF A CENTURY.
Montreal, Lovell, 1866. 299p [BVaU LC NSWA OTP QMM

Moodie, Susanna (Strickland), 1803–1885

THE HISTORY OF MARY PRINCE, A WEST INDIAN SLAVE. [Anon] London, Maunder,
1831. [Authorship identified by C. Ballstadt in *Can. Notes & Queries*, Nov. 1971]
[BM

LIFE IN THE BACKWOODS. A Sequel to ROUGHING IT IN THE BUSH. New York, Lovell, 1887. 224p [LC OTUV QMM

LIFE IN THE CLEARING VERSUS THE BUSH. London, Bentley, 1853. 384p [Also: ed. with an intro. by Robert L. McDougall. Toronto, Macmillan, 1959. xxxiii + 298p] [BM BVaU NSHD OTP QMM

NEGRO SLAVERY DESCRIBED BY A NEGRO. Being the Narrative of Ashton Warner, a Native of St. Vincents. ... [Anon] London, Maunder, 1831. [Authorship identified by C. Ballstadt in *Can. Notes & Queries*, Nov. 1971] [National Library, Scotland

ROUGHING IT IN THE BUSH; or, Life in Canada. London, Bentley, 1852. 2v [Many later editions.] [BM BVaU LC NSHD OTP QMM

Moody, James, 1744?—1809

NARRATIVE OF HIS EXERTIONS AND SUFFERINGS IN THE CAUSE OF GOVERN-MENT SINCE THE YEAR 1776. London, Richardson & Urquhart, 1783. 64p [First pub. in 1782] [NSHP OHM

Moody, Joseph Palmer, 1919—

ARCTIC DOCTOR. An Account of Strange Adventures among the Eskimos. By Joseph P. Moody with W. de Groot van Embden. London, Odhams Press, 1955. 256p

Mooney, Daniel, 1860?—

THE TRAVELS AND PHILOSOPHY AND LIFE AND TIMES OF DANIEL MOONEY, Born in the Year 1860 on the Dublin Road between Banbridge and Drommore, County Down, Ireland. An Irish Exile. Winnipeg, Author, 1930. 442p [OTP

Moore, Rev. Arthur Henry, 1869—1938

A MINISTRY OF LOVE. A Sermon preached in All Saints Cathedral, Halifax ... at a Memorial Service to the Rev. Dr. Robert Norwood ..., Oct. 23, 1932. N.p., 1932. 13p [NSHD

Moore, Cay

SHE SKATED INTO OUR HEARTS. [Story of Barbara Ann Scott, figure skater.] Toronto, McClelland, 1948. 117p [QMBM

Moore, Irene, 1876—1947

VALIANT LA VERANRYE [*sic*! VERANDRYE]. Quebec, Proulx, 1927. 382p [BM BVaU LC NSHD OKQ

Moreton, Rev. Julian, 1825—1900

LIFE AND WORK IN NEWFOUNDLAND. Reminiscences of Thirteen Years Spent There. London, Rivingtons, 1863. 106p [BM BVaU LC NSHD OTP

Morgan, Henry James, 1842—1913

AD MULTOS ANNOS. A Tribute to Sir Charles Tupper on his Political Birthday, 1900. Toronto, Briggs, 1900. 16p [BM LC NSHD OTP QMBM

THE CANADIAN MEN AND WOMEN OF THE TIME. A Handbook of Canadian Biography. Ed. by ——. Toronto, Briggs, 1898. 1118p [2nd ed., much enl.:

Toronto, Briggs, 1912. 1218p]   [BM BVaU LC NBFU OTU QMM

IN MEMORIAM: RECOLLECTIONS OF FATHER DAWSON. ... To which are added a
Portion of a Sermon preached by the Rev. W.T. Herridge referring to Dr. Dawson's
Example and Career, and Other Tributes to his Memory. Ottawa, Paynter &
Abbott, 1895. 16p [NSHD OTP QMSS

SKETCHES OF CELEBRATED CANADIANS AND PERSONS CONNECTED WITH CANADA.
Quebec, Hunter Rose, 1862. 779p [BM BVaU LC NBFU OTP

TYPES OF CANADIAN WOMEN, and of Women who are or have been Connected
with Canada. Toronto, Briggs, 1903. v. 1. 382p [No more published.] [BM
BVaU LC NBFU OTU QMM

Morice, Rev. Adrian Gabriel, 1859–1938

FIFTY YEARS IN WESTERN CANADA. Being the Abridged Memoirs of ——.
Toronto, Ryerson, 1930. 267p [BM BVaU LC OTU

Morphy, Edward M., 1820–1905

LIFE PICTURES. A York Pioneer's Recollections of Youthful Days in the Emerald
Isle ... his Emigration and first Impressions of Canada, especially Toronto (late
York), and its Inhabitants when the City was only one Year old. Toronto,
Author, 1893. 35p [OTU QMBM

SAINTY SMITH AND "THE SCHOOL UPON THE HILL." A Reminiscence . ... Toronto,
Author, [1890?]. 16p [OTP

A YORK PIONEER LOOKING BACK, 1834–1884. ... With Amusing Incidents and
Anecdotes. ... Toronto, Press of the Budget, 1890. 32p [OLU

Morphy, J.

RECOLLECTIONS OF A VISIT TO GREAT BRITAIN AND IRELAND IN THE SUMMER
OF 1862. Quebec, Palmer, 1863. 95p [BVaU LC OTP QMM

Morris, John M., 1856–1936

A KERFOOT HISTORY, CANADIAN BRANCH. London, Ont., Watt Letter Service,
1953. 187p [mimeographed]

Morrison, Edith (Lennox)

WILLIAM TYRRELL OF WESTON. By Edith Lennox Morrison and J.E. Middleton.
Toronto, Macmillan, 1937. 152p [BVaU OTP

Morrissey, Sister Helen

ETHAN ALLEN'S DAUGHTER. Gardenvale, Que., Garden City Press, 1940. 134p
[LC OTU

Morse, William Inglis, 1874–1952

AUTOBIOGRAPHICAL RECORDS OF WILLIAM INGLIS MORSE 1874–1905. ...
Boston, McIver-Johnson, 1943. 56p [BM LC

THE DIARY OF A MUSKETEER. Boston, Sawyer, 1926. 71p [LC NSWA

EWART GLADSTONE MORSE, 1892–1935. A Memoir. Boston, Sawyer, 1940. 23p
[NSHD

GENEALOGIAE; or, Data Concerning the Families of Morse, Chipman, Phinney, Ensign and Whiting. Ed. by ——. Boston, Sawyer, 1925. 189p [BM LC NSHD OTP

PIERRE DU GUA, SIEUR DE MONTS. Records, Colonial and "Saintongeois." Collected and ed. by ——. London, Quaritch, 1939. 67p [BM LC OTP

RICORDATI, 1874–1924. By W.I.M. Boston, Sawyer, 1925. 56p [LC NSWA

Morton, Arthur Silver, 1870–1945

SIR GEORGE SIMPSON, Overseas Governor of the Hudson's Bay Company. ... Toronto, Dent, 1944. 310p [BVaU LC NBFU OTP QMM

Morton, James [of Victoria, B.C.], 1870?–1967

HONEST JOHN OLIVER. The Life Story of the Honourable John Oliver, Premier of British Columbia, 1918–1927. Toronto, Dent, 1933. 272p [BM BVaU OTP

Morton, Sarah Etter (Silver)

JOHN MORTON OF TRINIDAD. ... Journals, Letters and Papers. ... Ed. by Sarah E. Morton and Arthur S. Morton. Toronto, Westminister, 1916. 491p [NSHD OLU

THE STORY OF JOSEPH ANNAJEE. ... Halifax, Nova Scotia Print. Co., 1879. 27p [NSHD

Moser, Rev. Charles

REMINISCENCES OF THE WEST COAST OF VANCOUVER ISLAND. Comp. by ——. Victoria, Acme Press, 1926. 192p [BM BVa LC OTP

Moss, Thomas Patteson, 1915–1936

PAT MOSS: CANADIAN AND ENGLISH LETTERS, 1924–36. Toronto, U. of Toronto Press, 1940. 425p [BM BVaU LC OTP

Mountain, Armine Wale, 1823–1885

A MEMOIR OF GEORGE JEHOSHAPHAT MOUNTAIN, D.D., D.C.L., Late Bishop of Quebec. ... By his son, Armine W. Mountain. ... London, Low & Marston; Montreal, Lovell, 1866. 477p [BM BVaU LC NSHD OTP QMM

Mountain, Mrs. Armine Simcoe Henry

MEMOIRS AND LETTERS OF THE LATE COLONEL ARMINE S.H. MOUNTAIN. ... Ed. by ——. London, Longman, 1857. 319p [BM NSWA

SOME ACCOUNT OF A SOWING TIME ON THE RUGGED SHORES OF NEWFOUNDLAND. With a Memoir of the Author. London, Society for the Propagation of the Gospel, 1857. 38p [NSWA

Mountain, Rev. George Jehoshaphat, 1789–1863

A SERMON PREACHED ... 1819, AFTER ... THE DEATH OF ... THE DUKE OF RICHMOND. ... Quebec, Neilson, 1819. 17p [OTP

Mowat, Farley McGill, 1921–

THE DOG WHO WOULDN'T BE. Boston, Little Brown, 1957. 238p

Mullally, Emmet J.

A SKETCH OF THE LIFE AND TIMES OF THE RIGHT REVEREND ANGUS BERNARD

MACEACHREN, THE FIRST BISHOP OF THE DIOCESE OF CHARLOTTETOWN. ...
Montreal, [Can. Catholic Hist. Assoc.], 1947. 38p [OLU PCL QMM

Munday, Mrs. Luta
A MOUNTY'S WIFE. Being the Life Story of One Attached to the Force, but not
of it. London, Sheldon Press, 1930. 217p [BM BVaU LC NBFU OTP

Munroe, Jack
MOPPING UP! Through the Eyes of Bobbie Burns, Regimental Mascot [dog].
New York, H.K. Fly, 1918. 319p [BViP OTU

Murdoch, Rev. Benedict Joseph, 1886–
FAR AWAY PLACE. Francestown, N.H., M. Jones Co., 1952. 185p
THE RED VINEYARD. Cedar Rapids, Iowa, Torch Press, 1923. 313p [BVaU LC
NBFU OTP

Murphy, Belva Gene (Atkinson)
AT HOME WITH THE MURPHYS. Chicago, Moody Press, 1959. 127p
MOMMIE OF THE MIXING BOWL. Biography of Doris Coffin Aldrich. Chicago,
Moody Press, 1959. 192p

Murphy, George Henry, 1875–1958
WOOD, HAY AND STUBBLE. Antigonish, N.S., Casket Print., 1956. 143p

Murray, Frances Elizabeth
IN MEMORIAM: FREDERICK HERVEY JOHN BRIGSTOCKE, Archdeacon of St. John.
[Anon] Saint John, McMillan, 1899. 159p [BVaU NBFU OLU
MEMOIR OF LeBARON BOTSFORD, M.D. By his Niece. ... Saint John, McMillan,
1892. 285p [NBFU OLU

Murray, John Wilson, 1840–1906
MEMOIRS OF A GREAT DETECTIVE. Incidents in the Life of John Wilson Murray.
Ed. by Victor Speer. ... New York, Baker & Taylor, 1905. 484p [Earlier ed.:
London, Heinemann, 1904. 455p] [BM BVaU LC OTU

Nannary, Miss M.A.
MEMOIRS OF THE LIFE OF REV. E.J. DUNPHY. Saint John, Weekly Herald, 1877.
128p [OTP

Narraway, Rev. J.R.
SERMON ON THE OCCASION OF THE DEATH OF CHARLES F. ALLISON, Founder of
Mount Allison Academy. Halifax, Wesleyan Conference Steam Press, 1859.
19p [NSHD

Nasmith, George Gallie, 1877–1965
ON THE FRINGE OF THE GREAT FIGHT. Toronto, McClelland, 1917. 263p [BM
LC NBFU OTP QMM
TIMOTHY EATON. Toronto, McClelland, 1923. 312p [BM BVaU OTU

Need, Thomas, 1808–
SIX YEARS IN THE BUSH; or, Extracts from the Journal of a Settler in Upper Canada,
1832–1838. [Anon] London, Simpkin Marshall, 1838. 126p [Sometimes
attributed to Susanna Moodie.] [BM BVaU LC NSWA OTP

Needler, George Henry, 1866–1962
COLONEL ANTHONY VAN EGMOND. From Napoleon and Waterloo to Mackenzie
and Rebellion. Toronto, Burns & MacEachern, 1956. 63p
LETTERS OF ANNA JAMESON TO OTTILIE von GOETHE. Ed. by ——. London,
Oxford U. Press, 1939. 247p [BM BVaU OTU
LOUIS RIEL. The Rebellion of 1885. Toronto, Burns & MacEachern, 1957. 81p
OTANABEE PIONEERS. The Story of the Stewarts, the Stricklands, the Traills, and
the Moodies. Toronto, Burns & MacEachern, 1953. 172p

Neilson, Joseph, 1813–1888
MEMORIES OF RUFUS CHOATE. ... Boston, Houghton, 1884. 460p [BM LC QMM

Nelson, George, 1785?–
A WINTER IN THE ST. CROIX VALLEY. George Nelson's Reminiscences, 1802–03.
Ed. with an intro. and notes by Richard Bardon and Grace Lee Nute. St. Paul,
Minnesota Hist. Soc., 1948. 46p [OTP

Nelson, Hugh Spence, 1865–1946
FOUR MONTHS UNDER ARMS. A Reminiscence of Events prior to and during the
Second Riel Rebellion. Nelson, B.C., Daily News, n.d. 20p [BVaU OOA

Nesbitt, James Knight, 1908–
ALBUM OF VICTORIA OLD HOMES AND FAMILIES. Victoria, Hebden Print., 1956.
63p

New, Chester William, 1882–1960
LORD DURHAM. A Biography. Oxford, Clarendon, 1929. 612p [BM BVaU LC
NBFU OTP QMM

Newman, Peter Charles, 1929–
FLAME OF POWER. Intimate Profiles of Canada's Greatest Businessmen. Toronto,
Longmans, 1959. 263p

Newton, Rev. William, 1828–1910
TWENTY YEARS ON THE SASKATCHEWAN. London, Stock, 1897. 184p [BM
BVaU LC OTP QMBM

Nicolson, Alexander Wylie, –1903
MEMORIES OF JAMES BAIN MORROW. Toronto, Methodist Book & Pub. House.
1881. 179p [BVaU NSWA OTP

Niven, Frederick John, 1878–1944
COLOURED SPECTACLES. London, Collins, 1938. 352p [BM BVaU LC NBFU OTU
THE STORY OF ALEXANDER SELKIRK. London, Wells Gardner, 1929. 119p [BM

Norris, Armine Frank, —1918

"MAINLY FOR MOTHER." Toronto, Ryerson, 1919. 219p [OTU

Nourse, Hugh Campbell Boyd, 1892—

RECORDS OF NOURSE AND BOYD DESCENDANTS BASED ON THE FAMILY AND
    CONNECTIONS OF ALFRED T. NOURSE. Comp. by ——. Montreal, Compiler,
    1954. 43p

Nursey, Walter R., 1847—1927

THE STORY OF ISAAC BROCK, HERO, DEFENDER AND SAVIOUR OF UPPER CANADA,
    1812. Toronto, Briggs, 1908. 181p [Also: Toronto, McClelland, 1923. 238p]
    [BM BVaU LC NBFU OTU QMM

Obodiac, Stanlee, 1922—

MY EXPERIENCES AT A CANADIAN AUTHORS' CONVENTION. Saskatoon, Modern
    Press, 1958. 133p

O'Brien, Arthur Henry, 1865—

HALIBURTON ("SAM SLICK"). A Sketch and Bibliography. 2nd ed. Montreal,
    Gazette, 1909. 26p [BM BVaU NBFU OTU QMSS

O'Brien, Rev. Cornelius, 1843—1906

FUNERAL SERMON ON SIR JOHN THOMPSON. Halifax, Meagher, 1906. 23p
    [BVaU NSWA OTU QMSS

MEMOIRS OF RT. REV. EDMUND BURKE, First Vicar Apostolic of Nova Scotia.
    Ottawa, Thorburn, 1894. 154p [BM LC NBFU OTP

O'Connor, Daniel, 1796—1858

DIARY AND OTHER MEMOIRS OF DANIEL O'CONNOR ... One of the Pioneers of
    By-Town ... 1827. Ottawa, priv. print., 1901. 45p [OOP

O'Connor, John, 1824—1887

WANDERINGS OF A VAGABOND. An Autobiography. Ed. by John Morris [pseud].
    New York, Author, 1873. 492p [LC

Odle, E.V.

GREAT STORIES OF HUMAN COURAGE. Selected and edited by ——. London,
    Lane, 1933. 645p [BM MWU OHM

QUEST AND CONQUEST. An Anthology of Personal Adventures. Comp. by ——.
    Toronto, Macmillan, 1938. 231p [BM OONL QMSS

O'Donnell, John Harrison, 1844—1912

MANITOBA AS I SAW IT. From 1869 to Date. ... Toronto, Musson, 1909. 158p
    [BVaU LC NSHD OTP

O'Hagan, Howard, 1902—

WILDERNESS MEN. Garden City, N.Y., Doubleday, 1958. 263p

O'Hagan, Thomas, 1855—1939
FATHER MORICE. (On the Missionary Work of Adrian Gabriel Morice in North-West Canada.) Toronto, Ryerson, 1928. 31p [BM BViP NBSaM OTU QMSS

Oldfield, Mabel (Dimock), 1878—
WITH YOU ALWAY. The Life of a South China Missionary. Halifax, Author, 1958. 252p

Oliver, William Sandford, 1751?—1813
A COLLECTION OF PAPERS AND FACTS RELATIVE TO THE DISMISSION OF WILLIAM SANDFORD OLIVER, ESQ., FROM THE OFFICE OF SHERIFF OF THE CITY AND COUNTY OF ST. JOHN ... N.B. [Saint John?], 1791. 24p [OTP.

Olson, Oscar, 1908—
I JOINED THE MOUNTIES. New York, Pageant Press, 1956. 183p

O'Malley, James
LIFE OF JAMES O'MALLEY. Montreal, Desaulniers, 1893. 192p [BVaU NBFU OTP QMM

One of Them (pseud)
UNKNOWN SOLDIERS. By One of Them. New York, Vantage Press, 1959. 170p [Veteran's account of service with the Canadian Expeditionary Force during World War I.]

Orillia, Ont. Historical Society
A MEDONTE PIONEER AND HIS FAMOUS SON [Sir Samuel B. Steele]. Orillia, Ont., the Society, 1954. 15p

Osler, Featherstone Lake, 1805—1895
RECORDS OF THE LIVES OF ELLEN FREE PICKTON AND FEATHERSTONE LAKE OSLER. London, priv. print., 1915. 257p [OTP

Osler, William, 1849—1919
MICHAEL SERVETUS. London, Frowde, 1909. 35p [BM LC OTP
THOMAS LINACRE. Cambridge, The University Press, 1908. 64p [BM BVaU LC OTU

Ossinger, Mrs. June Eileen
LAMP IN THE WILDERNESS. By June Lydiard Spencer [pseud]. New York, Vantage Press, 1955. 135p

Ostenso, Martha, 1900—1963
AND THEY SHALL WALK. The Life Story of Sister Elizabeth Kenny. Written in Collaboration with Martha Ostenso. New York, Dodd Mead, 1943. 282p [BM BVaU OTU

Ostrander, Manly, 1874—
THE HOUSE OF OSTRANDER. ... Deseronto, Ont., 1942. 32p [LC OTP

MEMORIAL TO CAPTAIN BRADSHAW. Comp. by —— and Charles G. Crouse. Oshawa, C.G. Crouse, 1942. 31p [LC OTP

Otheman, Edward

MEMOIR AND WRITINGS OF MRS. HANNAH MAYNARD PICKARD. Late Wife of Rev. Humphrey Pickard, A.M., Principal of the Wesleyan Academy at Sackville, N.B. Boston, Ela, 1845. 311p [NSWA OTP

Ottawa, Ont. National Gallery of Canada

EMILY CARR, HER PAINTINGS AND SKETCHES. Toronto, Oxford U. Press, 1945. 64p [BM NSHD

Owen, William, 1738?–1778

THE JOURNAL OF CAPTAIN WILLIAM OWEN ... DURING HIS RESIDENCE ON CAMPOBELLO IN 1770–1771. Ed. by W.F. Ganong, Saint John, Sun Print., 1899. 27p [BVaU LC NSWA QMBM

Owen Sound, Ont. Junior Chamber of Commerce

TOM THOMSON, 1877–1917. A Tribute. Owen Sound, 1956. 12p

Page, Frank E.

HOMER WATSON, ARTIST AND MAN. Kitchener, Commercial Print., 1939. 182p [BM OTP

Paget, Rev. Edward Clarence, 1851–1927

MEMOIR OF THE HON. SIR CHARLES PAGET, G.C.H., 1778–1839. With a Short History of the Paget Family. London, Longmans, 1913. 131p [First printed: Toronto, Briggs, 1911. 100p] [BM OTP QMM

A YEAR UNDER THE SHADOW OF ST. PAUL'S. Early Undergraduate Days in Keble College, Oxford, and Other Papers. Calgary, Author, 1908. 213p [ACG BVaU

Panabaker, Frank Shirley, 1904–

REFLECTED LIGHTS. Toronto, Ryerson, 1957. xvi + 159p

Parent, Rev. Amand, 1818–1907

THE LIFE OF REV. AMAND PARENT, THE FIRST FRENCH-CANADIAN ORDAINED BY THE METHODIST CHURCH. Forty-Seven Years' Experience in the Evangelical Work in Canada. Toronto, Briggs, 1887. 235p [BM BVaU NSWA OTP QMBM

Parham, Henry James, 1870–

A NATURE LOVER IN BRITISH COLUMBIA. London, Witherby, 1938. 202p [ACG BVaU OKQ

Parker, William Frederick, 1860–1918

DANIEL McNEILL PARKER, M.D. His Ancestry and a Memoir of his Life. Toronto, Briggs, 1910. 604p [BM BVaU NSWA OOP

Parkin, George Robert, 1846–1922
EDWARD THRING, HEADMASTER OF UPPINGHAM SCHOOL. Life, Diary and
Letters. London, Macmillan, 1898. 2v [BM BVaU LC NSHD OTP QMM
SIR JOHN A. MACDONALD. Toronto, Morang, 1908. 372p [BM BVaU LC
NSWA OTP QMM

Patrick, Mary Niven (Cattanach), 1884–1954
GROWING OLD IN VICTORIA. Victoria, priv. print., 1954. 6p

Patterson, Andrew Dickson, 1854–1930
WILLIAM RICE, POET AND BOOKMAN. Biographical Sketch and Portraits.
Toronto, Author, 1904. 11p [OOP

Patterson, Frank Harris, 1891–
JOHN PATTERSON, THE FOUNDER OF PICTOU TOWN. By his Great-Grandson.
Truro, N.S., Truro Print., 1955. 110p
MARY DICKSON. By Her Great-Grandson. Truro, N.S., Truro Print., 1952. 60p
STEWART KISSLEPAUGH. Truro, N.S., Truro Print., 1953. 28p

Patterson, Rev. George, 1824–1897
A BRIEF SKETCH OF THE LIFE AND LABOURS OF THE LATE REV. JOHN KEIR, D.D.,
S.T.P. Pictou, 1859. 43p [BibC
MEMOIR OF THE REV. JAMES MACGREGOR, D.D., Missionary ... to Pictou, Nova
Scotia, 1786–1830. By his Grandson, ——. Philadelphia [etc.], Wilson
[etc.], 1859. 533p [BM BVaU NBFU OTP QMM
MEMOIRS OF THE REV. S.F. JOHNSTON, THE REV. J.W. MATHESON, AND MRS.
MARY JOHNSTON MATHESON, MISSIONARIES ON TANNA. With Selections from
their Diaries and Correspondence. Philadelphia, Martien, [1864]. 504p
[NSWA OTU
MISSIONARY LIFE AMONG THE CANNIBALS. Being the Life of the Rev. John
Geddie, First Missionary to the New Hebrides. Toronto, Campbell, 1882.
512p [NSHD OTU
SKETCH OF THE LIFE AND LABORS OF THE REV. JOHN CAMPBELL, OF ST.
MARY'S, N.S. New Glasgow, MacKenzie, 1889. 37p [NSWA

Patterson, Raymond Murray, 1898–
DANGEROUS RIVER. New York, Sloane, 1954. 314p

Pattillo, Thomas Richard, 1833–1910
MOOSE-HUNTING, SALMON-FISHING, AND OTHER SKETCHES OF SPORT. Being
the Record of Personal Experiences ... in Canada. Toronto, Briggs, 1902.
299p [BVaU LC NSWA OTP QMSS

Pearce, Bruce M., 1900–
FIRST GRAND MASTER. A Biography of William Mercer Wilson, First Grand
Master of the Grand Lodge of Canada, A.F. & A.M. Simcoe, Pearce Pub.
Co., 1932. 189p [BM OTP

Pearce, Richard

MAROONED IN THE ARCTIC. Diary of the Dominion Explorers' Expedition to the Arctic, August to December, 1929. Toronto, 1931. 71p [BVaU OTP

Pearson, Carol (Williams), 1910–

EMILY CARR AS I KNEW HER. Toronto, Clarke Irwin, 1954. x + 162p

Pearson, James Johnston, 1884–

LAY ON, MACDUFF! Dublin, priv. print., 1960. xi + 107p

Peat, Harold Reginald, 1893–1960

PRIVATE PEAT. His Own Story. Toronto, McLeod, 1917. 235p [BM BVaU LC NSHD OTU QMM

Peat, Louisa (Watson)

MRS. PRIVATE PEAT. By Herself. Indianapolis, Bobbs-Merrill, 1918. 236p [BM LC

Pedley, James Henry, 1892–1945

ONLY THIS– A War Retrospect. Ottawa, Graphic, 1927. 371p [BVaU OTU

Pedley, James William, 1856–1933

BIOGRAPHY OF LORD STRATHCONA AND MOUNT ROYAL. Toronto, Nichols, 1915. 187p [BM BVaU LC OTP QMBM

Pelley, Richard

TALES OF THE SEA. Hamilton, Time Job Print., 1926. 204p [OKQ

Pennefather, John Pyne, 1833–1913

THIRTEEN YEARS ON THE PRAIRIES. From Winnipeg to Cold Lake, Fifteen Hundred Miles. London, Kegan Paul, 1892. 127p [BVaU OTP QMSS

Pennington, Myles, 1814–1898

RAILWAYS AND OTHER WAYS. Being Reminiscences of Canal and Railway Life during a Period of Sixty-seven Years. Toronto, Williamson, 1894. 407p [BM BVaU LC NSWA OTP QMM

Penny, Arthur Guy, 1886–1963

THE SHIRT-SLEEVED GENERATION. An Account of the Life and Times of a Canadian Newspaper Man. ... Quebec, Chronicle-Telegraph, 1953. 335p

Perkins, Simeon, 1735–1812

DIARY. 1780–1789. Ed. with an intro. by D.C. Harvey, with notes by C. Bruce Fergusson. Toronto, Champlain Society, 1958. lviii + 531 + xvip

THE DIARY OF SIMEON PERKINS, 1766–1780. Ed. with intro. and notes by Harold A. Innis. Toronto, Champlain Society, 1948. 298p [BM BVaU LC NBFU OTP QMM

Perry, Rev. Charles Ebenezer, 1835–1917

THE HON. N. CLARKE WALLACE, GRAND MASTER, LOYAL ORANGE ASSOCIATION

OF BRITISH AMERICA. His Action on the "Remedial Bill" and what led up to it. With an appendix by W.W. Colpitts. N.p., 1897. 138p [BVaU NfSM OOP QMBM

Perry, James Black, 1845–1936
HAPPENINGS IN A HAPPY LIFE. An Autobiography. Kingston, Jackson Press, 1925. 125p [OKQ

Phelan, Josephine, 1905–
THE ARDENT EXILE. The Life and Times of Thos. D'Arcy McGee. Toronto, Macmillan, 1951. 317p
THE BOLD HEART. The Story of Father Lacombe. Toronto, Macmillan, 1956. 182p

Phillips, Mrs. Bluebell Stewart, 1904–
SOMETHING ALWAYS TURNED UP. Toronto, Ryerson, 1958 [i.e. 1959]. 134p

Phillipps-Wolley, Clive Oldnall, 1854–1918
SPORT IN THE CRIMEA AND CAUCASUS. London, Bentley, 1881. 370p [BVaU OTP

Pichette, J.A. Robert
A BOOK OF MOTTOES. [Gives Mottoes of Leading English-speaking New Brunswick Families.] Edmundston, N.B., "Le Madawaska," n.d. 12p

Pickering, Joseph
EMIGRATION, OR NO EMIGRATION. Being the Narrative of the Author (an English Farmer) from the Year 1824 to 1830. London, Longman Rees, 1830. 132p [3rd ed. pub. under title: INQUIRIES OF AN EMIGRANT. London, Wilson, 1832. 207p] [BM BVaU LC OOP

Pickersgill, Frank H.D., 1915–1944
THE PICKERSGILL LETTERS. Written during the Period 1934–1943. Ed. with a memoir by George H. Ford. Toronto, Ryerson, 1948. 229p [BVa LC NSHD OTU QMM

Pickford, Mary, 1893–
THE FILM LIFE OF MARY PICKFORD. London, Page & Thomas, 1914. [BM
MY STRANGE LIFE. The Intimate Life Story of a Moving Picture Actress. New York, Grosset & Dunlap, 1915. 280p [OONL
SUNSHINE AND SHADOW. Garden City, N.Y., Doubleday, 1955. 382p

Pidhainy, Semen Aleksandrovich, 1907–
ISLANDS OF DEATH. Toronto, Burns & MacEachern, 1953. 240p [Experiences in Russian prison camps.]

Pierce, Lorne Albert, 1890–1961
ALBERT DURRANT WATSON. An Appraisal. Toronto, Ryerson, 1923. 10p [BM BVaU LC NBFU OTP QMM

E. GRACE COOMBS (MRS. JAMES SHARP LAWSON), A.O.C.A., O.S.A. Toronto,
Ryerson, 1949. 32p [BM BVaU LC NSHD OTP

FIFTY YEARS OF PUBLIC SERVICE: A LIFE OF JAMES L. HUGHES. Toronto, Oxford
U. Press, 1924. 256p [BM BVaU LC NBFU OTP

IN MEMORIAM: CHARLES W. JEFFERYS, 1869–1951. N.p., 1951. 4p

MARJORIE PICKTHALL. A Book of Remembrance. Toronto, Ryerson, [1925].
217p [BM BVaU NBFU OTP QMM

MARJORIE PICKTHALL. A Memorial Address. Toronto, Ryerson, 1943. 20p
[BM BVaU LC NBFU OTP QMM

A POSTSCRIPT OF J.E.H. MACDONALD, 1873–1932. Toronto, Ryerson, 1940. 12p
[BM BVaU LC NBFU OTP QMM

THOREAU MACDONALD. Toronto, Ryerson, 1942. 8p [BM BVaU LC NBFU
OTP QMM

THREE FREDERICTON POETS: WRITERS OF THE UNIVERSITY OF NEW BRUNSWICK
AND THE NEW DOMINION. Toronto, Ryerson, 1933. 30p [BM BVaU NBFU
OTP QMM

WILLIAM KIRBY. The Portrait of a Tory Loyalist. Toronto, Macmillan, 1929. 477p
[BM BVaU LC NBFU OTP QMM

Pierce, Rev. William Henry, 1856–1948

FROM POTLATCH TO PULPIT. Being the Autobiography of the Rev. William Henry
Pierce. Ed. by Rev. J.P. Hicks. Vancouver, Vancouver Bindery, 1933. 176p
[BM BVaU LC NBFU OTP

Piers, Harry, 1870–1940

BIOGRAPHICAL REVIEW. Biographical Sketches of Leading Citizens of the Province
of Nova Scotia. Ed. by ——. Boston, Biographical Review Pub. Co., 1900.
487p [NSWA

ROBERT FIELD. Portrait Painter in Oils, Miniature, Water-Colours, and Engraver.
New York, Sherman, 1927. 202p [NSHD OTU

Piersol, Mary Cameron (Blackadar)

THE RECORDS OF THE VAN EVERY FAMILY, UNITED EMPIRE LOYALISTS, New York
State, 1653–1784, Canada, 1784–1947. Toronto, Best, 1947. 131p [OTP

Pinkerton, Kathrene Sutherland (Gedney), 1887–

BRIGHT WITH SILVER. New York, Sloane, 1947. 347p [Story of Fromm Bros.,
Inc.] [BVa LC OOP

TWO ENDS TO OUR SHOESTRING. New York, Harcourt, 1941. 362p [BM BVaU
LC OTU QMM

Pitblado, Rev. Charles Bruce, 1836–1913

ROBERT BURNS, HIS LIFE AND POETRY. An Address Delivered in Selkirk Hall,
Winnipeg, Manitoba, February 25th, 1884. Winnipeg, Isaac Pitblado, 1955.
43p

Plewman, William Rothwell, 1880–
ADAM BECK AND THE ONTARIO HYDRO. Toronto, Ryerson, 1947. 494p [BVaU
LC NSHD OTP QMM
MY DIARY OF THE GREAT WAR. Being a Current History of the World's Greatest
Struggle. Toronto, Ontario Press, 1918. 203p [OTP

Plummer, John Orme, 1894–
CANADIAN PIONEERS. History of the Plummer Family. Toronto, priv. print.,
1958. 35p

Plunkett, Albert William, 1899?–1957
AL PLUNKETT, THE FAMOUS DUMBELL. By Patrise Earle, as told by Al Plunkett.
New York, Pageant Press, 1956. 107p

Pocock, Roger, 1865–1941
CAPTAINS OF ADVENTURE. Indianapolis, Bobbs-Merrill, 1913. 376p [BViPA LC
NBSaM
CHORUS TO ADVENTURERS. Being the Later Life of Roger Pocock, ("A Frontiers-
man"). London, Lane, 1931. 304p [BM LC OTU QMM
A FRONTIERSMAN. London, Methuen, 1903. 307p [Pub. also under title:
FOLLOWING THE FRONTIER. New York, McClure, 1903. 338p] [BM BVaU
LC OLU QMM

Pollard, William Correll, 1878–
LIFE ON THE FRONTIER. A Sketch of the Parry Sound Colonists. London, Stockwell, n.d. 112p [Also pub. under title: PIONEERING IN THE PRAIRIE WEST.
2nd ed. Uxbridge, Ont., Cave, 1925; London, Stockwell, 1933. 110p]
[BM BVaU OTP QMSS

Pollett, Ronald, 1900–
PETER THE GRATE. St. John's, Guardian Associates, 1952. 64p ["An outport
character study."]

Pomeroy, Elsie May, 1886–
SIR CHARLES G.D. ROBERTS. A Biography. Toronto, Ryerson, 1943. 371p [BM
BVaU LC NBFU OTP QMM
TRIBUTES THROUGH THE YEARS. The Centenary of the Birth of Sir Charles G.D.
Roberts, January 10, 1960. Ed. by ——. Toronto, priv. print., 1959. 19p
WILLIAM SAUNDERS AND HIS FIVE SONS. The Story of The Marquis Wheat Family.
Toronto, Ryerson, 1956. xiii + 192p

Poole, Evelyn Lavina, 1907–
THE HISTORY OF THE MACFARLANES, 1831–1931. London, Ont., Middlesex,
1931. 80p [OTU

Poole, Rev. William Henry, 1820–1896
A SERMON, OCCASIONED BY THE DEATH OF EDWARD JACKSON, ESQ. Toronto,
Wesleyan, 1872. 32p [OTUV

Pope, Joseph, 1854–1926

THE DAY OF SIR JOHN MACDONALD. Toronto, Brook, 1915. 195p [BM BVaU
LC NBFU OTP QMM

JACQUES CARTIER. His Life and Voyages. Ottawa, Woodburn, 1890. 168p [BM
BVaU LC NBFU OTU QMM

MEMOIRS OF THE RIGHT HONOURABLE SIR JOHN ALEXANDER MACDONALD.
London, Arnold, 1894. 2v [Also: Toronto, Oxford U. Press, 1930. 816p]
[BM BVaU LC NBFU OTP QMM

PUBLIC SERVANT. The Memoirs of Sir Joseph Pope. Ed. and completed by Maurice
Pope. Toronto, Oxford U. Press, 1960. 312p

SIR JOHN A. MACDONALD VINDICATED. A Review of the Right Hon. Sir Richard
Cartwright's Reminiscences. Toronto, Publishers' Association, 1912. 24p [BM
BVaU NBFU OTU QMSS

Portlock, Rosa (Elliott), 1839–1928

TWENTY-FIVE YEARS OF CANADIAN LIFE. With a Study on Bible Prophecy.
Toronto, Briggs, 1901. 195p [BVaU OTP

Powell, Oscar Reginald, 1884–

SO SOON FORGOTTEN. By Dick Fairfax [pseud]. Saskatoon, Modern Press, 1955.
132p [Life on the Canadian Prairies, 1904–20.]

Pratt, Viola Leone (Whitney), 1892–

FAMOUS DOCTORS: Osler, Banting, Penfield. Toronto, Clarke Irwin, 1956.
xi + 160p

Preston, Richard Arthur, 1910–

GORGES OF PLYMOUTH FORT. A Life of Sir Ferdinando Gorges, Captain of
Plymouth Fort, Governor of New England, and Lord of the Province of Maine.
Toronto, U. of Toronto Press in cooperation with the Royal Military College
of Canada, 1953. 495p

Preston, William Thomas Rochester, 1851–1942

THE LIFE AND TIMES OF LORD STRATHCONA. Toronto, McClelland, 1914. 324p
[BM BVaU NSWA OTP QMM

MY GENERATION OF POLITICS AND POLITICIANS. Toronto, Rose, 1927. 462p
[BVaU LC NSHD OTP QMSS

Pringle, Rev. George Charles Fraser, 1873–1949

ADVENTURES IN SERVICE. Toronto, McClelland, 1929. 282p [BVaU OOP

Pringle, Jacob Farrand, 1816–1901

THE GENEALOGY OF JACOB FARRAND PRINGLE AND ... ISABELLA FRASER
PRINGLE. Cornwall, 1892. 35p [OTU

Provencher, Paul, 1902–

I LIVE IN THE WOODS. A Book of Personal Recollections and Woodland Lore.
Fredericton, Brunswick Press, 1953. 188p

Prychodko, Nicholas, 1904–
ONE OF THE FIFTEEN MILLION. Toronto, Dent, 1952. 169p [Account of prison experiences in USSR, and escape into western Europe.]

Pugsley, William Howard, 1912–
SAILOR REMEMBER. Toronto, Collins, 1948. 185p [BVa OTU QMBM
SAINTS, DEVILS, AND ORDINARY SEAMEN. Life on the Royal Canadian Navy's Lower Deck. Toronto, Collins, 1945. 241p [BM BVaU LC NBFU OLU QMM

Purkis, Leslie S.
THE FIRE KINDLERS. The Story of the Purkis Family. Hamilton, Davis-Lisson, 1939. 55p [BM OOA QMBM

Putman, John Harold, 1866–1940
EGERTON RYERSON AND EDUCATION IN UPPER CANADA. Toronto, Briggs, 1912. 270p [BM BVaU NSWA OTU QMM
FIFTY YEARS AT SCHOOL. An Educationist Looks at Life. Toronto, Clarke Irwin, 1938. 253p [BM OTU
SCHOOLMASTERS ABROAD. A 1937 Diary. Toronto, Clarke Irwin, 1937. 98p [BVaU OTU

Putnam, Ben
FIFTY YEARS OF PROGRESS. Chiefly the Story of the Pioneers of the Watson District from 1900–1910. Ed. by Ben Putnam and Others. Muenster, Sask., St. Peter's Press, 1951. 111p

Raber, Jessie (Browne), 1885?–
PIONEERING IN ALBERTA. New York, Exposition Press, 1951. 171p

Randell, Jack, 1879–
I'M ALONE. Indianapolis, Bobbs-Merrill, 1930. 317p [AEU LC NSHPL OKQ

Ransford, Henry, 1804–
DATES AND EVENTS CONNECTED WITH MY FAMILY (1667–1881). London, Ont., Library, U. of Western Ontario, 1959. 81p [mimeographed].

Rasky, Frank, 1923–
GAY CANADIAN ROGUES. Swindlers, Gold-Diggers and Spies. Toronto, Nelson, 1958. 190p

Ravenhill, Alice, 1859–1954
ALICE RAVENHILL, THE MEMOIRS OF AN EDUCATIONAL PIONEER. With a foreword by Norman MacKenzie. Toronto, Dent, 1951. 241p

Rawlinson, James H.
THROUGH ST. DUNSTAN'S TO LIGHT. Toronto, Allen, 1919. 90p [BM BVaU OTP

Raymond, Ethel T.

TECUMSEH. A Chronicle of the Last Great Leader of his People. Toronto, Glasgow Brook, 1915. 159p [BM BVaU NSWA OTU

Read, David Breakenridge, 1823–1904

THE LIEUTENANT-GOVERNORS OF UPPER CANADA AND ONTARIO, 1792–1899. Toronto, Briggs, 1900. 253p [BM BVaU LC NBFU OTP QMM

THE LIFE AND TIMES OF GEN. JOHN GRAVES SIMCOE, First Governor of Upper Canada. Toronto, Virtue, 1890. 305p [BM BVaU LC NBFU OTP QMM

THE LIFE AND TIMES OF MAJOR-GENERAL SIR ISAAC BROCK. Toronto, Briggs, 1894. 266p [BM BVaU LC NSHD OTP QMM

THE LIVES OF THE JUDGES OF UPPER CANADA AND ONTARIO FROM 1791 TO THE PRESENT TIME. Toronto, Rowsell & Hutchinson, 1888. 486p [BM BVaU LC NBFU OTP QMM

Reesor, A.D. (presumed author)

THE REESOR FAMILY IN CANADA. Genealogical and Historical Records, 1804–1950. Markham, Ont., A.D. Reesor, 1950. 160p [OONL

Remits, Ernest Lorand, 1901–

JOTTINGS FROM THE NEW AND OLD COUNTRIES. Ottawa, Progressive, 1935. 116p [OOU

Renison, Rev. Robert John, 1875–1957

ONE DAY AT A TIME. The Autobiography of Robert John Renison. Ed. by Margaret Blackstock. Toronto, Kingswood House, 1957. x + 322p

Reynolds, William Kilby, 1848–1902

THE REV. WILLIAM DONALD, D.D., OF ST. ANDREW'S CHURCH, ST. JOHN, N.B. A Sketch of his Life and Character. Mobile, Ala., Mobile Stationery Co., 1898. 84p [NSWA QMM

Richan, Sarah (Hopkins), 1871–

THE BOOK OF RICHAN ... A.D. 938 to ... 1936. Comp. and ed. by ——. Barrington & Yarmouth, N.S., Author, 1936. 39p [BM OOA

Richardson, Evelyn May (Fox), 1902–

MY OTHER ISLANDS. Toronto, Ryerson, 1960. 213p

WE KEEP A LIGHT. Toronto, Ryerson, 1945. 260p [Also, with added chapter, Toronto, Ryerson, 1961. 271p Pub. in the U.S. as: WE BOUGHT AN ISLAND. Philadelphia, Macrae Smith, 1954. 281p] [BM BVa LC NBFU OTP QMM

Richardson, John, 1796–1852

CORRESPONDENCE, Submitted to Parliament, between Major Richardson, Late Superintendent of Police on the Welland Canal, and the Hon. Dominick Daly, Provincial Secretary. Montreal, Donoghue, 1846. 62p [NSWA OTP

EIGHT YEARS IN CANADA. Embracing a Review of the Administrations of Lords

Durham and Sydenham, Sir Chas. Bagot, and Lord Metcalfe; and Including
Numerous Interesting Letters from Lord Durham, Mr. Chas. Buller, and other
well-known Public Characters. Montreal, Cunningham, 1847. 232p [BM BVaU
LC NSWA OTU QMM

THE GUARDS IN CANADA; or, The Point of Honor. Being a Sequel to Major
Richardson's EIGHT YEARS IN CANADA. Montreal, Cunningham, 1848. 54p
[BM BVaU NSWA OTP QMM

JOURNAL OF THE MOVEMENTS OF THE BRITISH LEGION. By an Officer [J.
Richardson]. London, Effingham Wilson, 1836. 262p [BM OTP

MOVEMENTS OF THE BRITISH LEGION, with Strictures on the Course of Conduct
Pursued by Lieutenant-General Evans. 2nd ed. To which is added ... a
Continuation of the Operations from the 5th of May, 1836, to the close of
March, 1837. London, Simpkin Marshall, 1837. 330p [1st ed.: London, 1836.]
[BM BVaU LC NSHD OTU QMBM

PERSONAL MEMOIRS OF MAJOR RICHARDSON ... as Connected with the Singular
Oppression of that Officer while in Spain. Montreal, Armour & Ramsay, 1838.
145p [BM BVaU LC NSWA OTU QMSS

SKETCH OF THE LATE BATTLE OF THE WIND MILL, NEAR PRESCOTT, IN NOVEMBER,
1838. Prescott, 1839. 12p [In *Papers of the Bibliog. Soc. of Canada,* v.4,
Morley says of this title: "almost certainly not" by Richardson.] [QMM

TECUMSEH AND RICHARDSON. The Story of a Trip to Walpole Island and Port
Sarnia. With an Intro. and Biographical Sketch by A.H.U. Colquhoun. Toronto,
Ontario Book Co., [1924]. 124p [The "Trip ..." was originally pub. anony-
mously in the *Literary Garland,* Jan., 1849.] [BM BVaU LC NSHD OLU
QMM

WAR OF 1812. First Series. [Brockville, Author], 1842. 182p [Reprinted from
Richardson's *The New Era or Canadian Chronicle,* v. 2, no. 1–15, Mar. 2–July
22, 1842.] (Ed. with extended biography and a full bibliography of Richardson's
work by Alexander Clark Casselman. Toronto, Historical Pub. Co., and Musson,
1902. lviii + 320p) [BM BVaU LC NSWA OTP QMM

Richey, Rev. Matthew, 1803–1883

A MEMOIR OF THE LATE REV. WILLIAM BLACK, Wesleyan Minister, Halifax, N.S.
Including an Account of the Rise and Progress of Methodism in Nova Scotia.
Halifax, Cunnabell, 1839. 370p [NBFU OTP

SERMON ON OCCASION OF THE DEATH OF THE REV. WILLIAM BENNETT, Preached
... Dec. 27, 1857. Halifax, Wesleyan, 1858. 19p [NSHD

A SERMON OCCASIONED BY THE DEATH OF THE REV. WILLIAM CROSCOMBE.
Halifax, Wesleyan, 1859. 27p [NSWA

SERMON ON THE DEATH OF THE REV. WILLIAM McDONALD, Late Wesleyan
Missionary. Halifax, 1834. 32p [NSWA

Rickard, Thomas Arthur, 1864–1953

RETROSPECT. An Autobiography. Toronto, McLeod, 1937. [BVaU OTU

Riddell, Robert Gerald, 1908–1951

CANADIAN PORTRAITS. C.B.C. Broadcasts. Ed. by ——. Toronto, Oxford U. Press, 1940. 154p [BVaU LC NSHD OTP QMM

Riddell, William Renwick, 1852–1945

JOHN RICHARDSON. Toronto, Ryerson, [1923]. 226p [BM BVaU LC NBFU OTU

THE LIFE OF JOHN GRAVES SIMCOE. Toronto, McClelland, [1926]. 492p [BM BVaU LC NSHD OTP QMM

THE LIFE OF WILLIAM DUMMER POWELL, First Judge at Detroit and Fifth Chief Justice of Upper Canada. Lansing, Michigan Historical Commission, 1924. 305p [BM BVaU LC NSHD OTP QMM

WILLIAM KIRBY. Toronto, Ryerson, 1923. 176p [BM BVaU NSWA OTU

Ridley, Hilda M., –1960

THE STORY OF L.M. MONTGOMERY. Toronto, Ryerson, 1956. xiii + 137p

Riley, Robert Thomas, 1851–1944

MEMOIRS. Winnipeg, C.S. Riley, 1947. 119p [BViPA MWU SSU

Rintoul, Rev. David

MEMOIR OF ROBERT POLLOK, A.M. Toronto, Cleland, 1845. 61p [NSWA OTU

Ritchie, Mary Christine

MAJOR-GENERAL SIR GEOFFREY TWINING. A Biographical Sketch and the Story of his East African Diaries. Montreal, Chapman, 1922. 102p [NSWA OTP QMSS

Rivard, Edmond Samuel, 1861–

NOTES ON THE LIFE OF REV. LAURENT E. RIVARD. By his son, ——. Montreal, Janes-Rondeau, 1944. 80p [OTP

Roberton, Thomas Beattie, 1879–1936

THE FIGHTING BISHOP, JOHN STRACHAN ... AND OTHER ESSAYS IN HIS TIMES. Ottawa, Graphic, 1926. 179p [BM BVaU NBFU OTU QMM

Roberts, Charles George Douglas, 1860–1943

THE CANADIAN WHO'S WHO. Ed. by Charles G.D. Roberts and Arthur L. Tunnell. Toronto, Trans-Canada Press, 1938–. [A continuing serial of irregular issue.] [BVaU NSHD OTP QMM

A STANDARD DICTIONARY OF CANADIAN BIOGRAPHY. The Canadian Who Was Who. Ed. by Charles G.D. Roberts and Arthur L. Tunnell. Toronto, Trans-Canada press, 1934–1938. 2v [No more pub.] [BM BVaU NBFU OTP QMM

Roberts, Leslie, 1896–

C.D. The Life and Times of Clarence Decatur Howe. Toronto, Clarke Irwin, 1957. 246p

MALTA SPITFIRE. The Story of a Fighter Pilot. By Flying Officer F. Beurling and Leslie Roberts. Toronto, Oxford U. Press, 1943. 235p [BM BVaU OTU QMSS

THESE BE YOUR GODS. Toronto, Musson, 1929. 319p [BVaU OTU QMM

Roberts, Lloyd, 1884–1966
THE BOOK OF ROBERTS. Toronto, Ryerson, 1923. 147p [BM BVaU NBFU OTP

Roberts, Theodore Goodridge, 1877–1953
LOYALISTS. A Compilation of Histories, Biographies, and Genealogies of United Empire Loyalists and their Descendants. Pt. 1. Toronto, Roberts, 1937–. [LC NBFU OTU

THIRTY CANADIAN V.C.'S. London, Skeffington, 1918. 96p [BM BVaU OLU

Robertson, Jessie Ewart, 1859–1888
A TEACHER'S LIFE: JESSIE E. ROBERTSON. With Extracts from her Diaries, Essays, and Letters. By her Sisters and Friends. Ed. by Robert McQueen. Hamilton, Griffin & Kidner, 1890. [OTUV

Robertson, John Kellock, 1885–1958
TAYVILLE. Toronto, Ryerson, 1932. 136p [BVaU NSHD OKQ

Robertson, John Ross, 1841–1918
THE DIARY OF MRS. JOHN GRAVES SIMCOE, Wife of the First Lieutenant-Governor of Upper Canada, 1792–6. Ed. by ——. Toronto, Briggs, 1911. 440p [BM BVaU LC NSHD OTU QMM

Robertson, William Norrie, 1855–
YUKON MEMORIES. Sourdough Tells of Chaos and Changes in the Klondike Vale. Toronto, Hunter Rose, 1930. 359p [BM BVaU NBFU OTP

Robinson, Charles Walker, 1836–1924
LIFE OF SIR JOHN BEVERLY ROBINSON, Chief Justice of Upper Canada. Toronto, Morang, 1904. 490p [BM BVaU LC NBFU OTP QMM

Robinson, Judith
TOM CULLEN OF BALTIMORE. Toronto, Oxford U. Press, 1949. 435p [BM BVaU LC NBFU OTP QMM

Robinson, Noel, 1880–
BLAZING THE TRAIL THROUGH THE ROCKIES. The Story of Walter Moberley and his Share in the Making of Vancouver. Vancouver, News-Advertiser, 1913. 118p [BVaU LC NSHD OTP QMM

Robson, Elizabeth
EARLY DAYS IN CANADA. London, Stockwell, 1939. 108p [BM OTU

Roe, Rev. Henry, 1829–1909
MEMOIR OF THE REV. ARCHIBALD CAMPBELL SCARTH. Sherbrooke, Stevens & Price, 1904. 46p [OTU

Rogers, Robert, 1731—1795
JOURNALS OF MAJOR ROBERT ROGERS ... during the Late War. London, Author, 1765. 236p [New ed. by Franklin B. Hough. Albany, Munsell, 1883. 297p] [BM LC NSHD OLU

REMINISCENCES OF THE FRENCH WAR. Containing Rogers' Expeditions with the New-England Rangers ... as published in London in 1765. To which is added an Account of the Life ... of Maj. Gen. John Stark. Concord, N.H., Luther Roby, 1831. 275p [BM BVaU LC NBFU OTP QMM

Roher, Martin, 1924—1954
DAYS OF LIVING. The Journal of Martin Roher. Ed. by Joseph Pollick. Toronto, Ryerson, 1959. xii + 145p

Rokeby-Thomas, Rev. Howard Rokeby, 1907—
CHRONICLES OF THE ROOKS AND RAVENS. [Port Stanley, Ont.?] , Author, 1951. 1v. (unpaged) [Genealogy of Thomas, Rokeby, and related families.]

Rolph, William Kirby, 1917—1953
HENRY WISE WOOD OF ALBERTA. Toronto, U. of Toronto Press, 1950. 235p [BM BVaU NSHD OTU

Romaniuk, Gus, 1902—
TAKING ROOT IN CANADA. An Autobiography. Winnipeg, Columbia Press, 1954. 283p

Rose, George MacLean, 1829-1898
A CYCLOPAEDIA OF CANADIAN BIOGRAPHY. Being Chiefly Men of the Time. Ed. by ——. Toronto, Rose, 1886—1919. 3v [Cover title: REPRESENTATIVE CANADIANS.] [BM BVaU LC NBFU OTP QMM

IN MEMORY OF THE LATE HON. WILLIAM COSTELLO KENNEDY, P.C., M.P. Toronto, Hunter Rose, 1923. [OLU

Rosewarne, Winnifred Marguerite (Grindell), 1892—
THE FAMILY HISTORY OF HENRY GRINDELL AND HIS DESCENDANTS, 1832—1956. By Winnifred & Robert Rosewarne. Ottawa, Authors, 1957. viii + 65 + 13p [mimeographed]

Ross, Alexander, 1783—1856
LETTERS OF A PIONEER, ALEXANDER ROSS. Ed. by George Bryce. Winnipeg, Manitoba Free Press, 1903. 15p [BViPA LC OTP

Ross, Alexander Milton, 1832—1897
MEMOIRS OF A REFORMER (1832—1892). Toronto, Hunter Rose, 1893. 271p [BVaU NBFU OTP

RECOLLECTIONS AND EXPERIENCES OF AN ABOLITIONIST, FROM 1855—1865. Toronto, Rowsell & Hutchinson, 1875. 224p [BM NSWA OTP

Ross, Mrs. Anna
THE MAN WITH THE BOOK; or, Memoirs of "John Ross of Brucefield." Toronto, McLean, 1897. 264p [BVaU OTP

Ross, George William, 1841–1914
GETTING INTO PARLIAMENT AND AFTER. Toronto, Briggs, 1913. 342p [BM BVaU NSWA OTU

Ross, Hugh Robert, 1870–1937
THIRTY-FIVE YEARS IN THE LIMELIGHT. Sir Rodmond P. Roblin and his Times. ... Winnipeg, Farmer's Advocate, 1936. 205p [BM BViPA OTP

Ross, J.L.W.
MEDICAL STUDENT'S LETTERS TO HIS PARENTS. By "Scugog" [pseud]. Toronto, Murray Print., 1909. 139p [OTP SSU

Ross, James K.M.
BOOTS AND SADDLES. The Story of the Fabulous Ross Stable in the Golden Days of Racing. New York, Dutton, 1956. 272p

Ross, Margaret, 1846?–1935
SIR GEORGE W. ROSS. A Biographical Sketch. Toronto, Ryerson, 1923. 195p [BM BVaU OTP

Ross, Philip Dansken, 1858–1949
RETROSPECTS OF A NEWSPAPER PERSON. Toronto, Oxford U. Press, 1931. 327p [BVaU LC NSHD OTP QMM

Ross, Victoria (Burrill), 1877–
MOMENTS MAKE A YEAR. Sackville, Tribune, [1958]. 216p [Log of Mount Allison Ladies College]

Rouse, Rev. John James, 1869–
PIONEER WORK IN CANADA, PRACTICALLY PRESENTED. Kilmarnock, Scotland, Ritchie, 1935. 181p [Autobiography.] [AEP BVaU OTU

Rowley, Owsley Robert, 1868–1949
THE HOUSE OF BISHOPS. Portraits of the Living Archbishops and Bishops of the Church of England in Canada. Comp. by ——. Montreal, Morton Phillips, 1907. 55p [BM BVaU NSWA OLU

Roy, James Alexander, 1884–
THE HEART IS HIGHLAND. Toronto, McClelland, 1947. 262p [BVaU NBFU OTP QMBM
JOSEPH HOWE. A Study in Achievement and Frustration. Toronto, Macmillan, 1935. 347p [BM BVaU LC NSHD OTP QMBM

Rundle, Edwin George, 1838–
A SOLDIER'S LIFE. Being ... Personal Reminiscences. Toronto, Briggs, 1909. 127p [BVaU BViPA LC OTU

Russell, Benjamin, 1849–1935

AUTOBIOGRAPHY OF BENJAMIN RUSSELL. Halifax, Royal, 1932. 307p [BM
  BVaU LC NSWA OTP QMM

NOVA SCOTIA BLUE BOOK AND ENCYCLOPAEDIA. Toronto, Historical Pub. Assoc.,
  1932. 127p [LC NSWA OTU

Russell, Rev. George Stanley, 1883–1957

THE ROAD BEHIND ME. Toronto, Macmillan, 1936. 287p [BM BVaU LC OTP

Rutledge, Stanley

PEN PICTURES FROM THE TRENCHES. Toronto, Briggs, 1918. 125p [BM BVaU
  OKQ

Ryder, Mrs. Huia Gwendoline, 1904–

EDWARD JOHN RUSSELL, MARINE ARTIST. With a Catalogue of the Artist's Marine
  Paintings compiled by George MacBeath. Saint John, New Brunswick Museum,
  1953. 27p

Ryerson, Rev. Adolphus Egerton, 1803–1882

CHRISTIANS ON EARTH AND IN HEAVEN ... Discourse delivered in ... Toronto ...
  October 29th, 1848, on the Occasion of the death of Mrs. Sanderson, late wife of
  the Rev. Geo. Sanderson, Ed. of the "Christian Guardian." Toronto, 1848. 34p
  [OTU

MY DEAREST SOPHIE. Letters from Egerton Ryerson to his Daughter. Ed. by C.B.
  Sissons. Toronto, Ryerson, 1955. xxxvi + 350p

"THE STORY OF MY LIFE." ... Being Reminiscences of Sixty Years' Public Service
  in Canada. Prepared under the Supervision of his Literary Trustees. ... Ed. by
  J. George Hodgins. Toronto, Briggs, 1883. 612p [BM BVaU LC NBFU OTP
  QMM

Ryerson, Geoffrey Parker

MEMOIRS OF A CANADIAN SECRETARY. Toronto, Greenleaf & Kirkland, 1928.
  42p [NBSM QMBM

Ryerson, George Ansel Sterling, 1854–1925

LOOKING BACKWARD. Toronto, Ryerson, 1924. 264p [BM BVaU NSHD OKQ

Sage, Walter Noble, 1888–1963

THE CHRONICLES OF THOMAS SPROTT. Kingston, 1916. 12p [BVaU NBFU OLU
  QMM

SIR ALEXANDER MACKENZIE AND HIS INFLUENCE ON THE HISTORY OF THE
  NORTHWEST. Kingston, Jackson, 1922. 18p [BVaU LC NBFU OLU QMM

SIR GEORGE ARTHUR AND HIS ADMINISTRATION OF UPPER CANADA. Kingston,
  Jackson, 1918. 32p [BM BVaU LC NBFU OTP QMM

SIR JAMES DOUGLAS AND BRITISH COLUMBIA. Toronto, U. of Toronto Press, 1930. 398p [BM BVaU LC OTP QMM

Sanders, Byrne Hope, 1902–

EMILY MURPHY, CRUSADER ("JANEY CANUCK"). With intro. by Nellie L. McClung. Toronto, Macmillan, 1945. 355p [BM BVaU LC NBFU OKQ QMM

FAMOUS WOMEN. Carr, Hind, Gullen, Murphy. Toronto, Clarke Irwin, 1958. ix + 145p

Sanderson, Camilla

JOHN SANDERSON THE FIRST; or, A Pioneer Preacher at Home. ... With intro. by F.W. Wallace. Toronto, Briggs, 1910. 237p [BM BVaU OTP

Sanderson, Rev. Joseph Edward, 1830–1913

MESSENGERS OF THE CHURCH. ... Pioneer Missionaries. Toronto, Briggs, 1900–01. 2v [BVaU OTP

Sandwell, Bernard Keble, 1876–1954

THE MOLSON FAMILY. With a foreword by Herbert Molson. Montreal, priv. print., 1933. 256p [BM OTU QMM

Sandys, Edwyn William, 1860–1909

SPORTING SKETCHES. New York, Macmillan, 1905. 389p [BM BVaU LC

Saskatchewan, University of

ARTHUR SILVER MORTON. Professor of History and Librarian, 1914–40. Saskatoon, the University, 1943. 23p [BM BVaU NSHD OTU

Saunders, Rev. Edward Manning, 1829–1916

THE LIFE AND LETTERS OF THE RT. HON. SIR CHARLES TUPPER. Ed. by ——. London, Cassell, 1916. 2v [BM BVaU LC NBFU OTP QMM

THE LIFE AND TIMES OF REV. JOHN WISWALL, M.A., AN EPISCOPAL UNITED EMPIRE LOYALIST. Halifax, Nova Scotia Hist. Soc., 1908. 73p [NSWA

THREE PREMIERS OF NOVA SCOTIA: THE HON. J.W. JOHNSTONE, THE HON. JOSEPH HOWE, THE HON. CHARLES TUPPER. Toronto, Briggs, 1909. 628p [BM BVaU LC NBFU OTP QMM

Savary, Alfred William, 1831–1920

ANCESTRY OF GENERAL SIR WILLIAM FENWICK WILLIAMS OF KARS. Exeter, Pollard, 1911. 15p [NSWA OTU

A GENEALOGICAL AND BIOGRAPHICAL RECORD OF THE SAVARY FAMILIES ... AND OF THE SEVERY FAMILY. ... By A.W. Savary and L.A. Savary. Boston, Collins, 1893. 266p [Supplement pub.: Boston, 1905.] [BM NSWA OTP

Scadding, Rev. Henry, 1813–1901

EXTRACTS FROM THE DIARY OF THE REV. HENRY SCADDING, 1837–1838. Toronto, 1906. 32p [LC

THE FIRST BISHOP OF TORONTO. A Review and a Study. Toronto, Chewett, 1868. 85p [Life of John Strachan, D.D.] [BVaU OTU QMM

A MEMORIAL OF THE REV. WILLIAM HONEYWOOD RIPLEY, Classical Master in Upper Canada College. Toronto, 1849. [BibC

Schofield, Mrs. Emily M.

CHARLES DEBEVER SCHOFIELD, Late Bishop of British Columbia. Victoria, Author, 1941. 69p [BVaU OTU

Schull, Joseph, 1910–

BATTLE FOR THE ROCK. The Story of Wolfe and Montcalm. Toronto, Macmillan, 1960. 158p

THE SALT–WATER MEN. Canada's Deep-Sea Sailors. Toronto, Macmillan, 1957. 144p

Schuster, Rev. Anselm, 1834?–1885

THE LIFE AND LABOURS OF REV. ANSELM SCHUSTER. Ed. by David Mitchell. Belleville, Daily Intelligencer Steam Print., 1886. 167p [OOP

Scott, Rev. Alexander Hugh, 1853–1931

TEN YEARS IN MY FIRST CHARGE. Toronto, Hart, 1891. 357p [BVaU NBFU OTP

Scott, Barbara Ann, 1928–

SKATE WITH ME. Garden City, N.Y., Doubleday, 1950. 159p [OONL

Scott, Duncan Campbell, 1862–1947

JOHN GRAVES SIMCOE. Toronto, Morang, 1905. 241p [BM BVaU LC NSHD OTP QMM

WALTER J. PHILLIPS, R.C.A. Toronto, Ryerson, 1947. 59p [BVaU LC NBFU OTP QMM

Scott, Rev. Frederick George, 1861–1944

THE GREAT WAR AS I SAW IT. Toronto, Goodchild, 1922. 328p [BM BVaU NSWA OTP QMM

Scott, Jonathan, 1744–1819

A BRIEF VIEW OF THE RELIGIOUS TENETS AND SENTIMENTS, LATELY PUBLISHED AND SPREAD IN ... "TWO MITES" ... PUBLICATIONS OF MR. HENRY ALLINE. Halifax, Howe, 1784. 334p [NSHP QMBM

Scott, Robert C.

MY CAPTAIN OLIVER. A Story of Two Missionaries on the B.C. Coast. Toronto, United Church, 1947. 200p [BVaU OTU

Scott, William Louis, 1862–1947

THE MACDONNELLS OF LEEK, COLLACHIE, AND ABERCHALDER. Ottawa, Author, 1935. 12p [OTP

Segall, Jean (Brown)
WINGS OF THE MORNING. Toronto, Macmillan, 1945. 152p [Biography of
Canadian pilot, Mark Henry Brown.] [BVa LC MWP

Sellar, Robert, 1841–1919
GEORGE BROWN AND CONFEDERATION. Huntingdon, Que., 1917. 32p [Same as
following title?] [BVaU
GEORGE BROWN, THE GLOBE, CONFEDERATION. Toronto, Britnell, 1917. 32p
[BVa OTP SSU

Service, Robert William, 1874–1958
HARPER OF HEAVEN. New York, Dodd Mead, 1948. 452p [V. 2 of Service's
autobiography. See also: PLOUGHMAN OF THE MOON.] [BM BVaU LC OTU
QMM
PLOUGHMAN OF THE MOON. An Adventure into Memory. New York, Dodd Mead,
1945. 472p [V. 1 of Service's autobiography. See also: HARPER OF HEAVEN.]
[BM BVaU LC NSHD OKQ QMM

Seton, Ernest Thompson, 1860–1946
TRAIL OF AN ARTIST-NATURALIST. The Autobiography of ——. New York,
Scribner, 1940. 412p [BM BVaU LC NBFU OTU QMM

Shand, Margaret (Clark), 1851–1943
THE SUMMIT AND BEYOND. By Margaret Clark Shand and Ora M. Shand. Caldwell,
Idaho, Caxton Printers, 1959. xix + 326p

Shanly, Walter, 1819–1899
DAYLIGHT THROUGH THE MOUNTAIN. Letters and Labours of Civil Engineers,
Walter and Francis Shanly. Ed. by Frank Norman Walker. Research by Gladys
Chantler Walker. Montreal, Engineering Institute of Canada, 1957. xiii + 442p

Shapiro, Lionel Sebastian Berk, 1908–1958
THEY LEFT THE BACK DOOR OPEN. A Chronicle of the Allied Campaign in Sicily
and Italy. Toronto, Ryerson, 1944. 191p [BM BVaU LC OTP QMM

Sharcott, Margaret (Brampton), 1928–
A PLACE OF MANY WINDS. London, Davies, 1960. 236p

Sharman, Mrs. Lyon, 1872–
SUN YAT-SEN, HIS LIFE AND ITS MEANING. A Critical Biography. New York, Day,
1934. 418p [BM BVaU LC OTU

Shatford, Rev. Allan Pearson, 1873–1935
HE ... YET SPEAKETH. Glimpses of the Life Work of Canon Allan P. Shatford. ...
With an intro. by Dr. Arthur H. Moore. Toronto, Musson, 1938. 250p [BVaU
OTU QMBM

Shaw, Bertha Mary Constance, 1880–

BORN TO GROW OLD. Timmins, Northern Stationery & Print., 1960. 163p

BROKEN THREADS. Memories of a Northern Ontario Schoolteacher. New York, Exposition Press, 1955. 153p

LAUGHTER AND TEARS. Memoirs from between the Limestone Hills and the Blue Georgian Bay, Ontario. New York, Exposition Press, 1957. 183p [Reminiscences of an Ontario schoolteacher.]

Shaw, Lloyd Ethelbert, 1878–1960

MY LIFE IN THE BRICK INDUSTRY. [Halifax?], Author, 1955. 92p

Shaw, Margaret Mason, 1904–

GEOLOGISTS AND PROSPECTORS. Toronto, Clarke Irwin, 1958. xi + 190p

HE CONQUERED DEATH. The Story of Frederick Grant Banting. Toronto, Macmillan, 1946. 111p [BVaU LC OTP QMM

Shearwood, Mary Howard (Henderson), 1869–1962

BY WATER AND THE WORD. A Transcription of the Diary of the Right Reverend J.A. Newnham ... while Plying the Waters and Ice Fields of Northern Canada in the Diocese of Moosonee. By Mrs. F.P. Shearwood. Toronto, Macmillan, 1943. 216p [BVaU LC MWP NSHPL OTP QMBM

Shenton, Mrs. M.J. (Lodge)

A BIOGRAPHICAL SKETCH OF THE LATE REV. JOB SHENTON. With Some of his Sermons and Lectures. Saint John, McMillan, 1902. 160p [NSWA

Shepherd, Francis John, 1851–1929

SIR WILLIAM OSLER, BART. Montreal, 1921. 105p [LC

REMINISCENCES OF STUDENT DAYS AND DISSECTING ROOM. Montreal, priv. print., 1919. 28p [QMM

Shepherd, Peter

WITH GLOWING HEARTS. True Stories of Canadians in the Making. Toronto, United Church of Canada, 1946. 138p [OTU

Shier, Morley, 1888?–

FIRESIDE MINING. A Compendium of Mining Stories. Vancouver, Author, 1958. 78p

Shipley, Nancy (Sommerville)

ANNA AND THE INDIANS. Toronto, Ryerson, 1955. 237p [Life of Anna, wife of Rev. Samuel Gaudin, missionary in northern Manitoba.]

FRANCES AND THE CREES. Toronto, Ryerson, 1957. ix + 181p [Life of Frances (Pickell) Stevens, wife of Dr. Fred Stevens, missionary in the Fisher River area, Manitoba. Covers the years 1897–1946.]

Shortt, Adam, 1859—1931
LORD SYDENHAM. Toronto, Morang, 1908. 367p [BM BVaU LC NSWA OTP QMM

Shulman, Milton, 1913—
HOW TO BE A CELEBRITY. [With] Caricatures by Vicky of the [London] *News Chronicle.* London, Reinhardt & Evans, 1950. 215p [OONL

Sibbald, Susan (Mein), 1783—1866
THE MEMOIRS OF SUSAN SIBBALD (1783—1812). Ed. by ... Francis Paget Hett. London, Lane, 1926. 339p [BM BVaU LC NSHD OTP QMM

Sibbald, Thomas, 1810—1890
REMINISCENCES OF A BRITISH NAVAL OFFICER. By an Old Salt [pseud]. Toronto, Bain, 1885. 124p [BM

Sifton, Clifford, 1893—
THE SIFTON FAMILY RECORD. Information that has been Collected from Miscellaneous Sources, pertaining to the Family of Charles and Rebecca Sifton, who came from County Tipperary, Ireland, to London Township, Middlesex County, in Upper Canada in 1819, and their Descendants and Espouses. Toronto, Author, 1956. 136p

Sillitoe, Violet E. (Pelly)
PIONEER DAYS IN BRITISH COLUMBIA. Reminiscences. Vancouver, Evans & Hastings, [1922?]. 32p [BVaU LC OTU QMM

Simcoe, Elizabeth Posthuma (Gwillim), 1766—1850
THE DIARY OF MRS. JOHN GRAVES SIMCOE, Wife of the First Lieutenant-Governor of ... Upper Canada, 1792—6. With Notes and a Biography by J. Ross Robertson. Toronto, Briggs, 1911. xxix + 440p [BM BVaU LC NSHD OTP QMM
A SIMCOE RELIC AMONG THE THOUSAND ISLES IN 1796. Fragment of a MS. Journal of Mrs. Simcoe. Ed. by Rev. H. Scadding. Toronto, 1896. 7p [OTP QMM

Simcoe, John Graves, 1752—1806
THE CORRESPONDENCE, WITH ALLIED DOCUMENTS RELATING TO HIS ADMINISTRATION OF UPPER CANADA. Coll. and ed. by E.A. Cruickshank. Toronto, Ontario Hist. Soc., 1923—1936. 5v [BM BVaU NSHD OTU QMM

Sime, Jessie Georgina, 1880—
BRAVE SPIRITS. By Georgina Sime and Frank Nicholson. London, priv. print., 1952. 165p

Simmons, Mervin C.
THREE TIMES AND OUT. Told by Private [Mervin C.] Simmons. Written by Nellie McClung. Toronto, Allen, 1918. 247p [BVaU LC OTU

Simms, Lewis Wesley, 1885—
A TRIBUTE TO THE MEMORY OF T.S. SIMMS, on the Occasion of the Centennial of his Birth. Saint John, Author, 1945. 49p [OTP

Sinclair, Alexander, 1818–1897
PIONEER REMINISCENCES. Toronto, Warwick & Rutter, 1898. 22p [OTP

Sinclair, Rev. Alexander Maclean, 1840–1924
CLAN GILLEAN. ... Charlottetown, Haszard & Moore, 1899. 529p [BM NSHD
THE MACKENZIES OF APPLECROSS. Charlottetown, Mackenzie, 1901. 11p [NSWA
THE SINCLAIRS OF ROSLIN, CAITHNESS, AND GOSHEN. Charlottetown, Examiner,
   1901. 44p [NSWA

Sinclair, John H., 1848–
CAPTAIN GEORGE McKENZIE. An Appreciation. Ottawa, Hope, [1920?]. 24p
   [BVaU NSWA OOP
THE LIFE OF JAMES WILLIAM CARMICHAEL, AND SOME TALES OF THE SEA.
   Halifax, Allen, [1911]. 180p [BM NSHD OTU

Sinton, Robert, 1854–1952
LOOKING BACKWARD FROM THE EIGHTIETH MILESTONE, 1935–1854. Memories
   Recalled. Regina, Paragon Business College, 1935. 102p [mimeographed] [SSU

Sissons, Charles Bruce, 1879–1965
EGERTON RYERSON. His Life and Letters. ... Toronto, Clarke Irwin, 1937–47. 2v
   [BM BVaU LC NBFU OTP QMM
LETTERS OF MARY LEWIS RYERSON FROM 1832–1942. Ed. by ——. Toronto,
   Victoria U. Library, 1948. 18p [BM NBFU OTUV

Sissons, Constance (Kerr), 1875–
JOHN KERR. Toronto, Oxford U. Press, 1946. 282p [BM BVaU LC NSHD OTP

Sisterhood of St. John The Divine, Toronto
A MEMOIR OF THE LIFE AND WORK OF HANNAH GRIER COOME, Mother-Foundress
   of the Sisterhood of St. John the Divine, Toronto, Canada. London, Oxford U.
   Press, 1933. 294p [OTP

Skelton, Isabel (Murphy)
ISAAC JOGUES. Toronto, Ryerson, 1928. 32p [BVa OTU
THE LIFE OF THOMAS D'ARCY McGEE. Gardenvale, Que., Garden City Press, 1925.
   554p [BM BVaU NSHD OTP QMM
A MAN AUSTERE. William Bell, Parson and Pioneer. Toronto, Ryerson, 1947. 337p
   [BVaU LC NBFU OTP QMM

Skelton, Oscar Douglas, 1878–1941
THE DAY OF SIR WILFRID LAURIER. A Chronicle of our own Times. Toronto,
   Glasgow Brook, 1916. 340p [BM BVaU MWU NSWA OLU QMM
LIFE AND LETTERS OF SIR WILFRID LAURIER. Toronto, Gundy, 1921. 2v [BM
   BVaU LC MWU NBFU OTP QMM
THE LIFE AND TIMES OF SIR ALEXANDER TILLOCH GALT. Toronto, Oxford U.
   Press, 1920. 586p [BM BVaU NSWA OTP QMM

Smallwood, Joseph Roberts, 1900–
COAKER OF NEWFOUNDLAND. The Man who led the Deep-sea Fishermen to
Political Power. London, Labour Pub. Co., 1927. 96p [BM OTU

Smellie, George, 1811–1896
MEMOIR OF THE REV. JOHN BAYNE, D.D., OF GALT. ... With Dr. Bayne's Essay on
Man's Responsibility for his Belief. Toronto, Campbell, 1871. 139p [BVaU
NSWA OTP

Smith, Rev. Albert Edward, 1871–1947
ALL MY LIFE. An Autobiography. Toronto, Progress Books, 1949. 224p [BVaU
NfSM OTP QMBM

Smith, George Havens, 1884–
LOUIS BLAKE DUFF, THE COMPOSITE MAN. Port Colborne, Ont., priv. print., 1959.
23p

Smith, Goldwin, 1823–1910
THE MORAL CRUSADER, WILLIAM LLOYD GARRISON. Toronto, Williamson, 1892.
190p [BM BVaU LC NSWA OTU QMM
MY MEMORY OF GLADSTONE. Toronto, Tyrrell, 1904. 87p [BM BVaU NSHD
OTU QMM
REMINISCENCES. Ed. by Arnold Haultain. New York, Macmillan, 1910. 477p [BM
BVaU LC NSHD OTU QMM

Smith, Henry Robert
A GLIMPSE OF THE PAST. Ottawa, 1912. [Matthews

Smith, Irving Norman, 1909–
J.F.B. LIVESAY. A Memory. Ottawa, Mortimer, 1944. 53p [OTP QMM

Smith, Rev. James Frazer, 1858–1948
LIFE'S WAKING PART. Toronto, Nelson, 1937. 345p [LC OTP

Smith, Nicholas
FIFTY-TWO YEARS AT THE LABRADOR FISHERY. London, Stockwell, 1936. 199p
[BVaU OTU

Smith, Rev. Oswald Jeffrey, 1889–
THE STORY OF MY LIFE. Toronto, Peoples Press, 1950. 104p [Title varies with
later eds.] [LC SRL OLH

Smith, Waldo Edward Lovel, 1901–
WHAT TIME THE TEMPEST. An Army Chaplain's Story. Toronto, Ryerson, 1953.
305p

Smith, William, 1728–1793
HISTORICAL MEMOIRS OF WILLIAM SMITH, HISTORIAN OF THE PROVINCE OF NEW
YORK, MEMBER OF THE GOVERNOR'S COUNCIL AND LAST CHIEF JUSTICE OF

THAT PROVINCE UNDER THE CROWN, CHIEF JUSTICE OF QUEBEC. Ed. with an intro., biography and notes by William H.W. Sabine. From the previously unpublished manuscript in the New York Public Library. New York, Colburn & Tegg, 1956–58. 2v

Smith, William, 1859–1932
POLITICAL LEADERS OF UPPER CANADA. Toronto, Nelson, 1931. 292p [BM BVaU NSHD OTU QMM

ROBERT GOURLAY. Kingston, Jackson, 1926. 20p [BM BVaU NBFU OLU QMM

Smith, William Edward, 1864–1944
A CANADIAN DOCTOR IN WEST CHINA. Forty Years under Three Flags. Toronto, Ryerson, 1939. 278p [BM OTU

Smyth, Eleanor Caroline (Hill), 1831–1926
AN OCTOGENARIAN'S REMINISCENCES. ... [Anon] N.p., Author, [1916]. 131p [BViPA

Snider, David William, 1859–1924
THE LIFE AND WORK OF W.K. SNIDER, GTR CONDUCTOR. Also Sermons and Lectures. Toronto, Briggs, 1898. 116p [BM OTP

Snodgrass, Rev. William, 1827–1906
THE NIGHT OF DEATH. A Sermon preached ... after the Funeral of the Hon. Peter M'Gill. Montreal, Owler, 1860. 37p [NSWA

SERMON ON THE DEATH OF HEW RAMSAY, ESQ. Montreal, Lovell, 1857. 27p [NSWA

Snow, Samuel
THE EXILE'S RETURN. Cleveland, Smead & Cowles, 1846. 32p [Autobiography of an 1837 rebel.] [QMBM

Somers, Hugh Joseph, 1902–
THE LIFE AND TIMES OF THE HON. AND RT. REV. ALEXANDER MACDONELL, First Bishop of Upper Canada, 1762–1840. Washington, Catholic Univ. of America, 1931. 232p [BVaU LC NSHD OLU

Somerville, Alexander, 1811–1885
THE AUTOBIOGRAPHY OF A WORKING MAN. By "One who has Whistled at a Plough." London, Gilpin, 1848. 511p [Later ed.: with an intro. by John Carswell. London, Turnstile Press, 1951. xxxiv + 283p] [BM BVaU LC OTU

CONSERVATIVE SCIENCE OF NATIONS. Being the First Complete Narrative of Somerville's Diligent Life in the Service of Public Safety in Britain. Montreal, Lovell, 1860. 320p [Extracted from his AUTOBIOGRAPHY.] [BM BVaU LC NSHD OTP QMM

NARRATIVE OF AN EVENTFUL LIFE. A Contribution to the Conservative Science of Nations. Hamilton, 1863. 320p [OTP

Soward, Frederic Hubert, 1899–
MOULDERS OF NATIONAL DESTINIES. London, Oxford U. Press, 1938. 203p [Rev. ed.: London, Oxford U. Press, 1939. 248p] [BM BVaU OTU QMM

Spaight, George
TRIAL OF PATRICK J. WHELAN FOR THE MURDER OF THE HON. D'ARCY McGEE. ... Ottawa, Desbarats, 1868. 88p [NSWA

Spark, Rev. Alexander, 1762–1819
A SERMON. ... By the Late Rev. Alex. Spark, D.D. on the ... Day of his Death. Also a Funeral Sermon. [With intro. signed Daniel Wilkie.] Quebec, Neilson, 1819. 26p [Contains a biographical and bibliographical note.] [LC OTP

Springett, Evelyn Cartier (Galt)
FOR MY CHILDREN'S CHILDREN. Montreal, Unity, 1937. 204p [BM BViPA LC OTU QMM

Sprott, Rev. John, 1790–1869
MEMORIALS OF THE REV. JOHN SPROTT. Ed. by his son, George W. Sprott. Edinburgh, Morton, 1906. 232p [NSWA OOP

Squair, John, 1850–1928
THE AUTOBIOGRAPHY OF A TEACHER OF FRENCH. Toronto, U. of Toronto Press, 1928. 292p [BVaU OTP

Stackhouse, Cyril, 1886–
THE CHURCHES OF ST. JOHN THE DIVINE, DERBY (1859) – YALE (1860) IN THE CROWN COLONY OF BRITISH COLUMBIA, AND THEIR FIRST RECTOR, THE REVEREND WILLIAM BURTON CRICKMER, M.A. (Oxon.). Vancouver, Archives Society of Vancouver, 1960. 32p

Stairs, William James, 1819–1906
FAMILY HISTORY: STAIRS, MORROW, including Letters, Diaries, Essays, Poems, etc. Comp. by W.J. Stairs and Mrs. S.M. Stairs. Halifax, McAlpine, 1906. 264p [BVaU LC NSHD

Stansford, Joshua
FIFTY YEARS OF MY LIFE. Ilfracombe, Devon, Stockwell, 1952. 216p [Journal of a Newfoundland Fisherman between the Years 1904 and 1950.]

Steele, Harwood Elmes Robert, 1897–
THE MARCHING CALL. Toronto, Nelson, 1955. x + 249p

Steele, Samuel Benfield, 1849–1919
FORTY YEARS IN CANADA. Reminiscences of the Great North-West. London, Jenkins, 1915. 428p [BM BVaU LC NSHD OTP QMM

Steeves, Dorothy Gretchen (Biersteker), 1895–
THE COMPASSIONATE REBEL. Ernest E. Winch and his Times. Vancouver, Evergreen Press, 1960. xi + 227p

Stephens, Hiram B.
JACQUES CARTIER AND HIS FOUR VOYAGES TO CANADA. An Essay. Toronto, Musson, 1890. 163p [BM BVaU NBFU OTP QMM

Stern, Karl, 1906–
THE PILLAR OF FIRE. [An Autobiography.] New York, Harcourt, 1951. 310p

Stevens, Gerald Francis, 1909–
FREDERICK SIMPSON COBURN, R.C.A. Toronto, Ryerson, 1958. xi + 72p
THE OLD STONE HOUSE. Toronto, Ryerson, 1954. 119p

Stevens, Muriel G.
MRS. AGNES DENNIS, C.B.E. Her Life. [Halifax, 1938.] 13p [NSWA

Stevenson, Lionel, 1902–
THE WILD IRISH GIRL. The Life of Sydney Owenson, Lady Morgan, 1766–1859. London, Chapman & Hall, 1936. 330p [BM BVaU LC OKQ QMM

Stevenson, Lloyd Grenfell, 1918–
NOBEL PRIZE WINNERS IN MEDICINE AND PHYSIOLOGY, 1901–1950. New York, Schuman, 1953. xi + 291p
SIR FREDERICK BANTING. Toronto, Ryerson, 1946. 446p [BM BVaU LC NBFU OTP QMM

Stevenson, Orlando John, 1869–1950
REMINISCENCES. N.p., n.d. 32p [OTU
THE TALKING WIRE. New York, Messner, 1947. 207p [The story of Alexander Graham Bell.] [BM BVaU LC OTU

Steward, Austin, 1794–
TWENTY-TWO YEARS A SLAVE, and Forty Years a Freeman. Rochester, N.Y., Alling, 1857. 360p [Includes a Life of the Author while in Canada, 1831–1857.] [BM LC OTP

Stewart, Frances (Browne), 1794–1872
OUR FOREST HOME. Being Extracts from the Correspondence of the Late Frances Stewart. Ed. by her daughter, E.S. Dunlop. Toronto, Presbyterian Printing, 1889. 210p [Also: Montreal, Gazette, 1902. 300 + xcip] [BVa BVaU MWU OTP QMM

Stewart, Margaret Dorothy (McCall), 1904–
ASK NO QUARTER. A Biography of Agnes Macphail. By Margaret Stewart and Doris French. Toronto, Longmans, 1959. 311p

Stokes, William Edward Herbert, 1869–1948
THE RED MAN'S RELIGION, AND FIVE TRUE TALES OF MY HAPPY CAREER. Regina, Caxton Press, 1910. 78p [BVaU MWP QMBM

Stong, Daniel Alexander, 1883–
THE STONG GENEALOGY OF CANADA AND UNITED STATES. Weston, Ont., Author, 1958. 79p

Story, Duncan Albert, 1853–
THE DeLANCEYS. A Romance of a Great Family. With Notes on those Allied Families who Remained Loyal to the British Crown during the Revolutionary War. N.p., Author, 1931. 180p [NSHD OTP

Stothers, Robert
A BIOGRAPHICAL MEMORIAL TO ROBERT HENRY COWLEY, 1859–1927. Toronto, Nelson, 1935. xix + 151p [LC OTP
A TRIBUTE OF APPRECIATION TO THE MEMORY OF THE LATE LIEUT. ROBERT ERIC GREENE, of the 38th Ottawa Battalion, C.E.F. Ottawa, 1916. 11p [OTU

Stovel, Joseph Hodder, 1880–
A MINING TRAIL, 1902–1945. N.p., [1956?]. 68p

Strachan, Rev. John, 1778–1867
A SERMON ON THE DEATH OF THE HONORABLE RICHARD CARTWRIGHT. With a short Account of his Life. Preached at Kingston on the 3rd of September, 1815. Montreal, Gray, 1816. 56p [NSWA OTP
A SERMON PREACHED AT YORK ... THIRD OF JULY, ON THE DEATH OF THE LATE LORD BISHOP OF QUEBEC [Rev. Jacob Mountain, 1749–1825]. Kingston, Macfarlane, 1826. 34p [OTP

Strang, Rev. Peter, 1856–1934
AUTOBIOGRAPHY. Regina, Author, 1933. 53p [mimeographed] [MWP SSU

Strange, Kathleen (Redman), 1896–1968
NEVER A DULL MOMENT. By Harry and Kathleen Strange. Toronto, Macmillan, 1941. 373p [BVaU OTP QMM
WITH THE WEST IN HER EYES. The Story of a Modern Pioneer. Toronto, McLeod, 1937. 292p [Later ed., 1945, with added foreword and an epilogue.] [BM BVaU LC NBFU OTP QMM

Strange, Thomas Bland, 1831–1925
GUNNER JINGO'S JUBILEE. An Autobiography. 3rd ed. London, Macqueen, 1896. 346p [BM BVaU LC NSHD OTU

Strange, William, 1902–
INTO THE BLITZ. A British Journey. Toronto, Macmillan, 1941. 266p [BVaU OTP

Strickland, Samuel, 1804–1867
TWENTY-SEVEN YEARS IN CANADA WEST; or, The Experience of an Early Settler.
By Major Strickland. Ed. by Agnes Strickland. London, Bentley, 1853. 2v [BM
BVaU LC NSWA OTP QMM

Strickland, William Thomas
ADRIFT ... ON THE BANKS IN A DORY! St. John's, Author, 1953. 15p

Stuart, Arabella Mary (pseud)
ARABELLA'S LETTERS, TOGETHER WITH THE CONTENTS OF HER SMALL DIARY,
1823–1828. Ed. by Mrs. Percy Domville. Toronto, Musson, 1927. 300p [BM
LC OTP QMBM

Stuart, Campbell, 1885–
OPPORTUNITY KNOCKS ONCE. London, Collins, 1952. 248p

Stubbs, Roy St. George, 1907–
LAWYERS AND LAYMEN OF WESTERN CANADA. Toronto, Ryerson, 1939. 197p
[BVaU LC NSHD OTP
PRAIRIE PORTRAITS. Toronto, McClelland, 1954. ix + 176p

Student Christian Movement of Canada
THIS ONE THING. A Tribute to Henry Burton Sharman, ... 1865–1953. Prepared by
a group of friends. Toronto, Student Christian Movement of Canada, 1959. 96p

Swayze, James Frederick, 1907–1967
THE FIGHTING LE MOYNES. Toronto, Ryerson, 1958. 201p
FRONTENAC AND THE IROQUOIS. The Fighting Governor of New France. Toronto,
Macmillan, 1959. 158p
TONTY OF THE IRON HAND. Toronto, Ryerson, 1957. 194p [Story of Henri de
Tonty]

Swayze, Nansi, 1936–
THE MAN HUNTERS: JENNESS, BARBEAU, WINTEMBERG. Toronto, Clarke Irwin,
1960. xi + 180p

Symonds, Rev. Herbert, 1860–1921
HERBERT SYMONDS. A Memoir. Comp. by Friends. Montreal, Renouf, 1921. 319p
[BM OTU QMSS

Symons, John, 1808–1902
THE BATTLE OF QUEENSTON HEIGHTS. Being a Narrative of the Opening of the
War of 1812, with Notices of the Life of Major-General Sir Isaac Brock. ...
Toronto, Thompson, 1859. 39p [OTP QMM

Tait, George, 1828–
AUTOBIOGRAPHY OF G. TAIT, a Deaf Mute who first gave Instructions to the Deaf
and Dumb in the City of Halifax. Halifax, Bowes, 1892. 32p [NSHD

Tait, Rev. Robert Cowie, 1884–
A LITTLE KNOWN CHAPTER IN CANADIAN HISTORY. Sherbrooke, Que., 1958. 12p
[Story of the watchmaking industry, carried on in Lennoxville, Que., in the 19th
century, by Charles and George Henry.]

Taylor, Fennings, 1817–1882
THE HON. THOS. D'ARCY McGEE. A Sketch of his Life and Death. Montreal, Lovell,
1864. 40p [New ed., rev. & enl., Montreal, Lovell, 1868. 60p] [BVaU MWU
NBFU OTU
THE LAST THREE BISHOPS APPOINTED BY THE CROWN FOR THE ANGLICAN
CHURCH OF CANADA. Montreal, Lovell, 1869. 281p [Also: Montreal, Dawson,
1870. 281p] [BM BVaU LC NSWA OLU QMM
PORTRAITS OF BRITISH AMERICANS. By W. Notman. ... With Biographical Sketches
by Fennings Taylor. Montreal, Notman, 1865–68. 3v [BM BVaU NSWA OTP
QMM

Taylor, James P., fl. 1851–1899
HOW A SCHOOLMASTER BECAME A CATHOLIC. Renfrew, Gravelle, 1889. 140p
[Rev. ed.: Lindsay, Canada Post Book Dept., 1890. 214p] [OTP OTU

Taylor, Thomas Griffith, 1880–
JOURNEYMAN TAYLOR. The Education of a Scientist. Abridged and ed. by Alasdair
Alpin MacGregor. London, Hale, 1958. 352p
WITH SCOTT. The Silver Lining. New York, Dodd Mead, 1916. 464p [BM LC
OTU QMM

Taylor, Rev. William, 1803–1876
IN MEMORIAM. REV. WILLIAM TAYLOR. Montreal, Erskine Church, 1876. 51p
[NSWA

Thompson, George S., 1848–
UP TO DATE; or, The Life of a Lumberman. Peterboro, Times Print., 1895. 126p
[BVaU MWU OTUV

Thompson, John Henry, 1853–
GENEALOGY: THOMPSON-SPAFFORD, 1630–1830; CHASE-GORDON, 1788–1930;
OSBORN-GADSBY, GADSBY-WOODCOCK. ... Comp. by ——. Thorold, Ont.,
Author, [1930?]. 120p [LC

Thompson, Samuel, 1810–1886
REMINISCENCES OF A CANADIAN PIONEER FOR THE LAST FIFTY YEARS. An Autobiography. Toronto, Hunter Rose, 1884. 392p [BM BVaU NSWA OTU QMM

Thompson, Thomas, 1832–1909
THE TWO YORKS; or, Sitting at the "King's Table." Written ... for his Golden Wedding. ... N.p., [1905?]. 36p [Deals with the Thompson family of Toronto.] [OTP

Thomson, Dale C., 1923–

ALEXANDER MACKENZIE, CLEAR GRIT. Toronto, Macmillan, 1960. 436p

Thomson, Edward William, 1849–1924

THE LETTERS OF EDWARD WILLIAM THOMSON TO ARCHIBALD LAMPMAN (1891–1897). Ed. with notes, a bibliography and other material on Thomson and Lampman by Arthur S. Bourinot. Ottawa, Editor, 1957. 49p

Thomson, Watson, –1969

PIONEER IN COMMUNITY. Henri Lasserre's contribution to the Fully Cooperative Society. Toronto, Ryerson, 1949. 123p [BVa OTP QMM

Thornhill, Mary Elizabeth, 1865–

BETWEEN FRIENDS. Toronto, Saunders, 1935. 252p [BVaU OTU QMM

Throop, Herbert David, 1899–

THROOP GENEALOGY. With Special Reference to the Throops of Grenville County, Ontario. ... Ottawa, Author, 1931. 33p [BM LC OTP

Tolboom, Wanda (Neill)

ARCTIC BRIDE. Toronto, Ryerson, 1956. x + 256p

Tollemache, Stratford Haliday Robert Louis, 1864–1937

REMINISCENCES OF THE YUKON. Toronto, Briggs, 1912. 316p [BM BVaU LC OTU

Tomkinson, Constance, 1915–

LES GIRLS. Boston, Little Brown, 1956. 274p

Toronto, Ont. Baptist College. Alumni

MEMOIR OF DANIEL ARTHUR McGREGOR, Late Principal of Toronto Baptist College. Pub. by the Alumni Association of Toronto Baptist College. Toronto, Dudley & Burns, 1891. 248p [BVaU NSWA OTP

Toronto, Ont. Ryerson School. Old Boys' Association

MEMORIAL OF SAMUEL McALLISTER, Principal of Ryerson School. ... 1877–1906. Toronto, The Association, 1907. 45p [NBFU

Toronto, University of

THE INSTALLATION OF CLAUDE THOMAS BISSELL, EIGHTH PRESIDENT, UNIVERSITY OF TORONTO, OCTOBER 1958. Toronto, U. of Toronto Press, 1958. 55p

Toronto, University of. Victoria College

IN MEMORIAM, MARGARET ADDISON, 1868–1940. Toronto, Clarke Irwin, 1941. 26p [UTQ'42

Toronto Scottish Officers' Association

COLONEL COLIN CLARKE HARBOTTLE, C.M.G., D.S.O., V.D. Ed. by H.M. Jackson. Toronto, the Association, 1958. 20p

Townsend, Rev. Arthur Herbert, 1912–
SOD-BUSTERS. New York, Vantage Press, 1957. 180p

Townshend, Charles James, 1844–1924
LIFE OF HONOURABLE ALEXANDER STEWART. N.p., n.d. 114p [NSWA

Trotter, Beecham, –1933?
A HORSEMAN AND THE WEST. Reminiscences as told to Arthur Hawkes. Toronto,
Macmillan, 1925. 304p [BM BVaU OTU

Tuck, Clyde Edwin
BIOGRAPHICAL SKETCHES OF REPRESENTATIVE CITIZENS [OF NOVA SCOTIA] AND
GENEALOGICAL RECORDS OF OLD FAMILIES. [V. 3 of David Allison's HISTORY
OF NOVA SCOTIA. Halifax, Bowen, 1916. 3v] [BVaU LC NSWA OTP

Tunnell, Arthur L.
THE CANADIAN WHO'S WHO. Ed. by Charles G.D. Roberts and Arthur L. Tunnel.
Toronto, Trans-Canada Press, 1938–. [A continuing serial of irregular issue.]
[BVaU NSHD OTP QMM
A STANDARD DICTIONARY OF CANADIAN BIOGRAPHY. ... Ed. by Charles G.D.
Roberts and Arthur L. Tunnell. Toronto, Trans-Canada Press, 1934–1938. 2v
[No more pub.] [BM BVaU NBFU OTP QMM

Tupper, Charles, 1821–1915
A LETTER TO THE RIGHT HONOURABLE THE EARL OF CARNARVAN. ... London,
Westerton, 1866. 78p [BVaU NSHD OTU
POLITICAL REMINISCENCES OF THE RIGHT HONOURABLE SIR CHARLES TUPPER.
Transcribed and ed. by the late W.A. Harkin. With a Biographical Sketch.
London, Constable, 1914. 303p [BM BVaU LC NSHD OTP
RECOLLECTIONS OF SIXTY YEARS. London, Cassell, 1914. 414p [BM BVaU
LC NSWA OTU QMM

Tupper, Charles Hibbert, 1855–1927
SUPPLEMENT TO THE LIFE AND LETTERS OF THE RT. HON. SIR CHARLES TUPPER,
BART. Toronto, Ryerson, 1926. 199p [BM BVaU NSHD OTU QMM

Tupper, Ferdinand Brock
FAMILY RECORDS. Containing Memoirs of Major-General Sir Isaac Brock, Lieut.
E.W. Tupper, and Col. William de Vic Tupper. ... Guernsey, Barbet, 1835. 218p
[BVaU NSHD OTU
THE LIFE AND CORRESPONDENCE OF MAJOR-GENERAL SIR ISAAC BROCK, K.B.
Interspersed with Notices of ... Tecumseh; and Comprising Brief Memoirs of D.
DeLisle Brock, Lieut. E.W. Tupper, R.N., and Colonel W. DeVic Tupper. Ed.
by ——. London, Simpkin Marshall, 1845. 468p [2nd ed., "considerably
enlarged," 492p] [BM BVaU NSHD OLU

Tupper, Reginald H.
VICTOR GORDON TUPPER. A Brother's Tribute. ...   London, Oxford U. Press, 1921.
66p [BM BVaU NSHD

Turnbull, John Fulton, 1894—
HISTORY OF THE TURNBULL FAMILY OF DIGBY, NOVA SCOTIA. Agincourt, Book
Society of Canada, 1960. 18 + 29p

Turney, Stephen, 1811—1847
THE REMARKABLE LIFE AND CONFESSIONS OF STEPHEN TURNEY, who was
Executed at Toronto ... 1847, for ... Murder..... Reduced to Writing by J.B.
Townsend, Police Constable. Also: The Confession of James Hamilton, who was
Executed ... for ... Murder. Toronto, Townsend, 1847. 16p [OTP

Tyre, Robert, 1908—
SADDLEBAG SURGEON. The Story of Murrough O'Brien, M.D. Toronto, Dent,
1954. 261p

Tyrrell, Mary Edith (Carey), 1870?—1945
I WAS THERE. A Book of Reminiscences. Toronto, Ryerson, 1938. 131p [BVaU
LC NSHD OTP

Underhill, Frank Hawkins, 1889—1971
JAMES SHAVER WOODSWORTH. Untypical Canadian. An Address. ... [Toronto],
Ontario Woodsworth Memorial Foundation, 1944. 34p [NBFU OTP

Unwin, Charles, 1829—1918
AUTOBIOGRAPHICAL SKETCH. Toronto, 1910. [Matthews

Urquhart, Hugh MacIntyre, 1880—1950
ARTHUR CURRIE. The Biography of a Great Canadian. Toronto, Dent, 1950.
xix + 363p [BVaU NSHD OONL

VanDusen, Rev. Conrad, 1801?—1878
THE INDIAN CHIEF. ... The Labours, Losses, Sufferings, and Oppression of
Ke-zig-ko-e-ne-ne (David Sawyer), a Chief of the Ojibbeway Indians in Canada
West. By Enemikeese [pseud]. London, Nichols, 1867. 204p [BVaU LC
NSWA OTP QMM
THE PRODIGY. A Brief Account of the Bright Career of ... Dr. G.E.A. Winans. ...
Toronto, Dredge, 1870. 171p [BVaU NSWA MWU OTP
THE SUCCESSFUL YOUNG EVANGELIST. An Account of the Brief but Brilliant
Career of Wm. Henry Winans, Wesleyan Preacher. ... Toronto, Dredge, 1870.
168p [OTP

Vaudry, Mary Olive
A SKETCH OF THE LIFE OF CAPTAIN JOHN SAVAGE, J.P., First Settler in Shefford County, 1792. Also the Early History of St. John's Church, West Shefford, Que., 1821–1921. [Toronto, 1921?] 20p [OTU QMM

Vaughan, Harold Withrow
THE LIVING CHURCH. A Book in Memory of the Life and Work of Rev. Richard Davidson, Principal of Emmanuel College, Toronto. Ed. by ——. Toronto, United Church Pub. House, 1949. 193p [OTU

Vaughan, Walter, 1865–1922
THE LIFE AND WORK OF SIR W. VAN HORNE. New York, Century, 1920. 388p [Also in "Makers of Canada" series: Toronto, 1926. vol. 10.] [BM BVaU LC NSWA OTU QMM

Verral, Charles Spain, 1904–
MIGHTY MEN OF BASEBALL. New York, Aladdin Books, 1955. 140p

Vieth, Frederick Harris Dawes, –1910
RECOLLECTIONS OF THE CRIMEAN CAMPAIGN AND THE EXPEDITION TO KINBURN IN 1855. Including also Sporting and Dramatic Incidents in Connection with Garrison Life in the Canadian Lower Provinces. Montreal, Lovell, 1907. 308p [BM BVaU LC NSHD OOP

Vining, Charles Arthur McLaren, 1897–
BIGWIGS. Canadians Wise and Otherwise. By R.T.L. (Charles Vining). Toronto, Macmillan, 1935. 149p [BM BVaU LC OTP QMM

Vonlandsburg, John G.
"THE NOBLEMAN'S SON." THE LIFE AND ADVENTURES OF DR. JOHN G. VONLANDSBURG, BARON OF WORMSTALL, HANOVER AND HESSON CASTELL. Halifax, 1845. 108p [BibC

Wade, G.V.
A WHO'S WHO IN SASKATCHEWAN. A Biographical Directory. Ed. by ——. 1st. ed. Saskatoon, Western Canada Directories, 1958 [c1956]. 275p

Wade, Mark Sweeten, 1858–1929
MACKENZIE OF CANADA. The Life and Adventures of Alexander Mackenzie. London, Blackwood, 1927. 332p [BM BVaU LC NSHD OTU QMM

Wakeham, Pius Joseph, 1910–
SISTER THACKERY. St. John's, Dicks & Co., 1956. 349p

Waldron, Malcolm Thomas, 1903–1931
SNOW MAN. John Hornby in the Barren Lands. Boston, Houghton, 1931. 292p [BM BVaU LC OTU QMM

Waldron, Samuel J.
REMINISCENCES OF MY LIFE. Ed. by Frances Ebbs-Canavan. Victoria, Author, 1938. 29p [BVa OTU

Walker, (Sergeant) Alexander, fl. 1848–1867
HOURS OFF AND ON SENTRY; or, Personal Recollections of Military Adventure in Great Britain, Portugal and Canada. Montreal, Lovell, 1859. 248p [BVaU OTP

Walker, Rev. William Wesley, 1858–1945
BY NORTHERN LAKES. Reminiscences of Life in Ontario Mission Fields. Toronto, Briggs, 1896. 168p [BM BVaU LC NSWA OTU

Wallace, Rev. Archer, 1884–1958
CANADIAN HEROES OF MISSION FIELDS OVERSEAS. Toronto, Can. Council of Missionary Educ., 1920. 88p [BM NSWA OOP
DEEDS OF DARING. New York, Harper, 1934. 97p [LC OKQ QMSS
HANDS AROUND THE WORLD. New York, Smith, 1930. 134p [LC OKQ
HEROES OF PEACE. Toronto, Musson, 1929. 133p [BM LC OTP
I BELIEVE IN PEOPLE. New York, Round Table, 1936. 210p [BM LC OKQ
IN SPITE OF ALL. Toronto, Ryerson, 1944. 137p [BVa LC OTP QMM
MEN WHO PLAYED THE GAME. New York, Smith, 1931. 127p [BM LC OKQ
MORE STORIES OF GRIT. New York, Smith, 1930. 140p [Also: Toronto, Musson, 1930.] [BM BVaU LC NSHD OKQ
MOTHERS OF FAMOUS MEN. Toronto, Musson, 1931. 112p [BM LC OKQ
OVERCOMING HANDICAPS. New York, Doran, 1927. 140p [BM LC
POOR MEN WHO MADE US RICH. Toronto, Ryerson, 1933. 130p [BM LC OKQ
THE RELIGIOUS FAITH OF GREAT MEN. New York, Round Table, 1934. 217p [LC OKQ
STORIES OF GRIT. Toronto, Musson, 1925. 133p [BM LC OKQ

Wallace, Elisabeth, 1910–
GOLDWIN SMITH, Victorian Liberal. Toronto, U. of Toronto Press, 1957. x + 297p

Wallace, Elizabeth, 1906–
THE SINGING HEART. [A Biography of Mother Mary Ward, Foundress of the Institute of the Blessed Virgin Mary.] Toronto, Dent, 1954. 96p

Wallace, Frederick William, 1886–1958
ROVING FISHERMAN. An Autobiography, Recounting Personal Experiences in the Commercial Fishing Fleets and Fish Industry of Canada and the United States, 1911-1924. Gardenvale, Que., *Canadian Fisherman,* 1955. xxi + 512p

Wallace, Rev. Isaiah, 1826–1907
AUTO-BIOGRAPHICAL SKETCH. With Reminiscences of Revival Work. Halifax, Burgoyne, [1903]. 181p [NSHD

Wallace, Paul Anthony Wilson, 1891–

CONRAD WEISER, 1696–1760. Friend of Colonist and Mohawk. Philadelphia, U. of Penn. Press, 1945. 648p [BM LC OTU QMM

Wallace, Robert Charles, 1881–1955

SOME GREAT MEN OF QUEEN'S: GRANT, WATSON, DUPUIS, CAPPON, JORDAN, SHORTT. Ed. by ——. Toronto, Ryerson, 1941. 133p [BVaU NSHD OTU

Wallace, William Stewart, 1884–1970

THE DICTIONARY OF CANADIAN BIOGRAPHY. Comp. by ——. Toronto, Macmillan, 1926. 433p [2nd ed.: Toronto, Macmillan, 1945. 2v] [BM BVaU LC NSHD OTU QMM

A DICTIONARY OF NORTH AMERICAN AUTHORS DECEASED BEFORE 1950. Comp. by ——. Toronto, Ryerson, 1951. 525p

THE KNIGHT OF DUNDURN. Toronto, Rous & Mann, 1960. 22p [About Sir Allan MacNab, 1798–1862.]

THE MASERES LETTERS, 1766, 1768. Ed. by ——. Toronto, University Library, 1919. 131p [BM BVaU NSWA OTP

THE MEMOIRS OF THE RIGHT HON. SIR GEORGE FOSTER. Toronto, Macmillan, 1933. 291p [BM BVaU LC NSHD OTU QMM

SIR JOHN MACDONALD. Toronto, Macmillan, 1924. 132p [BM BVaU LC NSHD OTU QMM

THE STORY OF LAURA SECORD. A Study in Historical Evidence. Toronto, Macmillan, 1932. 26p [BVaU LC OLU

Walsh, Leo J.

DROSS REFINED. A Biography on the Life of "Fighting" Billy Matheson, Ex-pugilist and Ex-bartender. London, Ont., Hayden Press, 1932. 212p [OLU

Walton, Jesse M.

FROM THE AUCTION BLOCK ... TO THE ROSTRUM. The Life of William Allan. Aurora, Walton, 1938. 8p [OTU

Warder, Richard C., 1901–

NORTHERN EXPOSURE. Tales of the North Country. New York, Pageant Press, 1957. 179p

Warnica, George and Phoebe

MEMOIRS OF GEORGE AND PHOEBE WARNICA, PIONEERS OF INNISFIL. Ed. by A.F. Hunter. Barrie, Examiner, 1891. 28p [OTL

Warren, Ernest Herbert Falkland, 1888?–

SEVENTY SOUTH ALBERTA YEARS. ... Autobiography of ——, ... as written by S. Evangeline Warren. Ilfracombe, Devon, Stockwell, 1960. 255p

Waterston, Margaret Elizabeth (Hillman), 1922–

PIONEERS IN AGRICULTURE: Massey, McIntosh, Saunders. Toronto, Clarke Irwin, 1957. 136p

Waterton, William Arthur, 1916—
THE QUICK AND THE DEAD. London, F. Muller, 1956. 237p

Watetch, Abel, 1883—
PAYEPOT AND HIS PEOPLE. As told to Blodwen Davies. Regina, Saskatchewan History and Folklore Soc., 1959. 66p

Watkin, Edward William, 1819—1901
ALDERMAN COBDEN OF MANCHESTER. Letters and Reminiscences of Richard Cobden. New York, Ward Lock, 1891. 218p [BM LC
CANADA AND THE STATES. Recollections, 1851 to 1886. New York, Ward Lock, 1887. 524p [BM BVaU LC NSWA OTU QMM

Watson, Albert Durrant, 1859—1926
ROBERT NORWOOD. Toronto, Ryerson, 1923. 124p [BM BVaU LC NSHD OTU

Watson, William Ritchie, 1904—
I GIVE YOU YESTERDAY. Toronto, Macmillan, 1938. 238p [BVaU OTU
MY DESIRE. Edmonton, U. of Alberta Press, 1932. 84p [AEU OTU

Watson, William Robinson, 1887—
MAURICE CULLEN, R.C.A. A Record of Struggle and Achievement. Toronto, Ryerson, 1931. 45p [QMM

Waugh, William Templeton, 1884—1932
JAMES WOLFE, MAN AND SOLDIER. Montreal, Carrier, 1928. 333p [BM BVaU LC NSWA OTU QMM

Weaver, Emily Poynton, 1865—1943
BUILDERS OF THE DOMINION. Men of the East. Toronto, Copp Clark, 1904. 116p [BM NBFU

Webling, Peggy
PEGGY. The Story of One Score Years and Ten. London, Hutchinson, 1924. 303p [BM OTL

Webster, John Clarence, 1863—1950
THE CAREER OF THE ABBE LE LOUTRE IN NOVA SCOTIA. With a Translation of his Autobiography. Shediac, priv. print., 1933. 50p [BM BVaU NBFU OTU QMM
CHARLES DES CHAMPS DE BOISHEBERT. A Canadian Soldier in Acadia. Priv. print., 1931. 38p [BM BVaU NSWA OTU QMM
CORNELIS STEENWYCK, DUTCH GOVERNOR OF ACADIE. ... Shediac, priv. print., 1929. 12p [BVaU NSWA OLU QMM
EDINBURGH MEMORIES AND ROBERT LOUIS STEVENSON. Sackville, Tribune Press, 1943. 19p [BVaU NBFU OTP QMM

THE JOURNAL OF JOSHUA WINSLOW ... 1760. Ed. by ———. Saint John, New Brunswick Museum, 1936. 40p [NBFU OTU QMBM

JOURNALS OF BEAUSEJOUR: DIARY OF JOHN THOMAS: JOURNAL OF LOUIS DE COURVILLE. Ed. by ———. Sackville, Tribune, 1937. 54p [BVaU LC NSWA OLU QMM

LIFE OF JOHN MONTRESOR. Ottawa, Royal Soc. of Canada, 1928. 31p [BVaU NBSM OKQ

THE LIFE OF JOSEPH FREDERICK WALLET DES BARRES. Shediac, priv. print., 1933. 70p [BM BVaU LC NSWA OTU QMM

SAMUEL VETCH. [First British Governor of Nova Scotia after the Conquest of 1710]. An Address. Shediac, priv. print., 1929. 23p [BM BVaU NSWA OTP

SIR BROOK WATSON. Friend of the Loyalists, first Agent of New Brunswick in London. Sackville, Mount Allison University, 1924. 25p [BM BVaU NSWA OTP QMM

THOMAS PICHON. "The Spy of Beausejour." Sackville, Tribune, 1937. 161p [BM BVaU LC NSWA OTP QMM

THOSE CROWDED YEARS, 1863–1944. Shediac, priv. print., 1944. 51p [Reminiscences.] [BVaU LC NBFU OTP

WILLIAM FRANCIS GANONG MEMORIAL. Ed. by ———. Saint John, New Brunswick Museum, 1942. 31p [BVaU LC NBFU OTU QMM

WOLFE AND THE ARTISTS. A Study of his Portraiture. Toronto, Ryerson, 1930. 74p [BM BVaU LC NSHD OTU

WOLFIANA. A Potpourri of Facts and Fantasies. Arranged by ———. Shediac, priv. print., 1927. 47p [BM BVaU LC NSWA OTU QMM

Webster, Rev. Thomas, 1809–1901

LIFE OF REV. JAMES RICHARDSON. Bishop of the Methodist Episcopal Church in Canada. Toronto, Magurn, 1876. 240p [BVaU LC OTP

Weekes, Mrs. Mary Loretto, 1885–

THE LAST BUFFALO HUNTER. As Told to her by Norbert Welsh. Toronto, Nelson, 1939. 304p [BViPA OTU QMSS

Weir, John, 1906–

BARD OF UKRAINE. An Introduction to the Life and Works of Taras Shevchenko. Toronto, National Jubilee Committee of the Association of United Ukrainian Canadians, 1951. 64p

Weir, William, 1823–1905

SIXTY YEARS IN CANADA. Montreal, Lovell, 1903. 268p [BM BVaU NSWA OTU QMM

Weldon, William S., 1883–

THE FAMILY OF WELDON IN CANADA, 1732–1952. Including their Lineage to the First Progenitor in England, in 1066 A.D. Altona, Man., D.W. Friesen, 1953. x + 125p

Wells, Clifford Almon, 1892–1917

FROM MONTREAL TO VIMY RIDGE AND BEYOND. The Correspondence of Lieut. Clifford Almon Wells B.A. of the 8th Battalion, Canadian B.E.F. Ed. by O.C.S. Wallace. Toronto, McClelland, 1917. 321p [BVaU LC NSHD OTU

Wells, Daniel

CAMP FIRES GLEAMING. New York, Outing Pub. Co., 1911. 142p [OONL

Wells, James Edward, 1836–1898

LIFE AND LABORS OF ROBERT ALEX. FYFE, D.D. Founder and ... Principal of the Canadian Literary Institute, now Woodstock College. ... Toronto, Gage, [189–?]. 466p [BVaU NSWA OTP

Welton, Rev. Daniel Morse, 1831–1904

JOHN LIGHTFOOT, THE ENGLISH HEBRAIST. An Historical Essay Presented to Obtain the Doctorate of Philosophy. Leipzig, Ackermann, 1878. 47p [BM NSWA

Weston, Thomas Chesmer, 1832–1911

REMINISCENCES AMONG THE ROCKS. In Connection with the Geological Survey of Canada. Toronto, Warwick, 1899. 328p [BM BVaU LC OTU QMM

Wheeler, Frances Ellen, 1895–

THE AWAKENING OF THE LAURENTIANS. A Fabulous Woman, Lucile Wheeler, and her Family who made the Laurentians Famous. New York, Vantage Press, 1958. 93p

Whidden, David Graham, 1857–1941

GENEALOGICAL RECORD OF THE ANTIGONISH WHIDDENS. Wolfville, n.p., 1930. 24p [NSWA OTU

Whillans, Rev. James William, 1880–1954?

FIRST IN THE WEST. The Story of Henry Kelsey, Discoverer of Canadian Prairies. Edmonton, Applied Art Products, 1955. 175p

Whitaker, Rev. George, 1810?–1882

A SERMON ... ON OCCASION OF THE DEATH OF THE REV. THOMAS SMITH KENNEDY. ... Toronto, Rowsell & Ellis, 1863. 12p [OTP

White, James Edward, 1822–

A GENEALOGICAL HISTORY OF THE DESCENDANTS OF PETER WHITE OF NEW JERSEY, FROM 1670, AND OF WILLIAM WHITE AND DEBORAH TILTON, HIS WIFE, LOYALISTS. Saint John, Barnes, 1906. 89p [BVaU LC NSHD OTU

White, Rev. William Charles, 1873–1960

CANON CODY OF ST. PAUL'S CHURCH. Toronto, Ryerson, 1953. 220p

Whiteside, William Carleton, 1900–
THE NOMADIC LIFE OF A SURGEON. Edmonton, Douglas Print., 1950. 89p [OONL

Whittaker, Rev. Charles Edward, 1864–1947
ARCTIC ESKIMO. A Record of Fifty Years' Experience & Observation among the
  Eskimo. ... London, Seeley Service, 1937. 259p [BM BVaU OTP

Wicksteed, Gustavus William, 1799–1898
IN MEMORIAM. GEORGE ETIENNE CARTIER. Ottawa, 1885. 19p [BM OOP QMBM

Wigle, Rev. Hamilton A., 1858–1934
HISTORY OF THE WIGLE FAMILY AND THEIR DESCENDANTS. ... Ed. by ——. N.p.,
  1931. 248p [OTP
THE LIFE STORY OF FINLAY BOOTH. Toronto, Briggs, 1900. 123p [Another ed.,
  bound with A NIGHT ON THE PRAIRIE. By R. Dezell. Toronto, Briggs, 1907. 55p]
  [BM BVaU NSHD OTU

Wild, Roland Gibson, 1903–
AMOR DE COSMOS. Toronto, Ryerson, 1958. xi + 146p
ARCTIC COMMAND. The Story of Smellie of the *Nascopie.* Toronto, Ryerson, 1955.
  xxii + 194p

Wilkes, Rev. Henry, 1805–1886
DEATH IN THE CITY. Address at the Funeral of the late John Easton Mills, Mayor of
  the City of Montreal. ... Montreal, Becket, 1848. 19p [BM QMM

Wilkinson, Anne Cochran (Boyd), 1910–1961
LIONS IN THE WAY. A Discursive History of the Oslers. Toronto, Macmillan, 1956.
  274p

Willinsky, Abraham Isaac, 1885–
A DOCTOR'S MEMOIRS. Toronto, Macmillan, 1960. x + 183p

Willis-O'Connor, Henry, 1886–
INSIDE GOVERNMENT HOUSE. As Told by Colonel H. Willis-O'Connor to Madge
  Macbeth. Toronto, Ryerson, 1954. xi + 163p

Willison, John Stephen, 1856–1927
REMINISCENCES, POLITICAL AND PERSONAL. Toronto, McClelland, 1919. 351p
  [BM BVaU LC NSHD OTU QMM
SIR GEORGE PARKIN. A Biography. London, Macmillan, 1929. 278p [BM BVaU
  NSHD OTP QMM
SIR WILFRID LAURIER. Toronto, Oxford U. Press, 1926. 472 + 526p [First 27
  chapters "were ... published in ... 1903."] [BM BVaU LC OTU
SIR WILFRID LAURIER AND THE LIBERAL PARTY. A Political History. Toronto,
  Morang, 1903. 2v [BM BVaU NSHD OTP QMM

Willson, David, 1778?–1866

A COLLECTION OF ITEMS OF THE LIFE OF DAVID WILLSON. From the Year 1801 to 1852. ... Newmarket, Porter, 1852. 10p [OTP

THE PRACTICAL LIFE OF THE AUTHOR, FROM THE YEAR 1801 TO 1860. Newmarket, Jackson, 1860. 80p [OTP

Willson, (Henry) Beckles, 1869–1942

FROM QUEBEC TO PICCADILLY. ... Some Anglo-Canadian Memories. ... London, Cape, 1929. 366p [BM BVaU NSHD OTP

THE LIFE AND LETTERS OF JAMES WOLFE. London, Heinemann, 1909. 522p [BM BVaU LC NSWA OTP QMM

THE LIFE OF LORD STRATHCONA & MOUNT ROYAL. ... London, Cassell, 1915. 631p [BM BVaU LC NBFU OTU QMM

LORD STRATHCONA, THE STORY OF HIS LIFE. ... London, Methuen, 1902. 288p [BM BVaU LC NSHD OTU

Wilson, Daniel, 1816–1892

THE LIFE OF JANE McCREA. With an Account of Burgoyne's Expedition in 1777. New York, Baker, 1853. 155p [OTL

REMINISCENCES OF OLD EDINBURGH. Edinburgh, Hamilton, 1878. 2v [BM BVaU LC OTU

WILLIAM NELSON. A Memoir. Edinburgh, Nelson, 1889. 254p [BM OTP

Wilson, George Earl, 1891–

THE LIFE OF ROBERT BALDWIN. A Study in the Struggle for Responsible Government. Toronto, Ryerson, 1933. 312p [BM BVaU LC NSHD OTP QMM

Wilson, Herbert Emerson, 1881–

I STOLE $16,000,000. New York, New American Library, 1956. 141p

Wilson, Rev. Robert, 1833–1912

PIETY PORTRAYED IN THE LIVES AND DEATHS OF MR. AND MRS. ISAAC BURPEE OF SHEFFIELD, N.B. Saint John, Chubb, 1870. 14p [NBB

Winnipeg Free Press

JOHN WESLEY DAFOE. Editor-in-Chief, Winnipeg Free Press, 1901–1944. Winnipeg, Free Press, 1944. 42p [OTP

Winslow, Edward, 1746–1815

WINSLOW PAPERS, A.D. 1778–1826. Ed. by Rev. W.O. Raymond. Saint John, Sun Print., 1901. 732p [BM BVaU NSWA OTP QMM

Winslow, Joshua, 1727–1801

THE JOURNAL OF JOSHUA WINSLOW. Recording his Participation in the Events of the Year 1750. Ed. with Intro. and Notes by Dr. J.C. Webster. ... Saint John, New Brunswick Museum, 1936. 40p [BM BVaU LC NSHD OTU QMM

Winter, Charles Francis, 1863–1946
LIEUTENANT-CENERAL SIR SAM HUGHES. ... Canada's War Minister, 1911–1916.
Toronto, Macmillan, 1931. 182p [BM BVaU LC NBFU OTUV

Withrow, Rev. William Henry, 1839–1908
BEACON LIGHTS OF THE REFORMATION. Toronto, Briggs, 1899. 304p [BM
NSHD OTP QMM
WORTHIES OF EARLY METHODISM. Toronto, Rose, 1878. 165p [OTP

Wood, Edgar Allardyce, 1907–
THE GREAT CHIEF. Maskepetoon, Warrior of the Crees. By Kerry Wood [pseud].
Toronto, Macmillan, 1957. 160p
THE MAP-MAKER. The Story of David Thompson. By Kerry Wood [pseud].
Toronto, Macmillan, 1955. 185p
THE QUEEN'S COWBOY. Colonel Macleod of the Mounties. By Kerry Wood [pseud].
Toronto, Macmillan, 1960. 157p
THE SANCTUARY. By Kerry Wood [pseud]. Red Deer, Alta., Author, 1952. 105p

Wood, Rev. John
MEMOIR OF HENRY WILKES. His Life and Times. Montreal, Grafton, 1887. 280p
[BM BVaU NSWA OTU QMSS

Wood, Louis Aubrey Lorne, 1883–1955
THE WAR CHIEF OF THE SIX NATIONS. A Chronicle of Joseph Brant. ... Toronto,
Glasgow Brook, 1914. 147p [BM BVaU LC NSWA OTU QMM

Wood, William Charles Henry, 1864–1947
THE FATHER OF BRITISH CANADA. A Chronicle of Carleton. Toronto, Glasgow
Brook, 1916. 239p [BM BVaU LC NSWA OTU QMM
MONTCALM. The Hero of a Lost Cause. Toronto, Morang, 1912. 154p [BM
THE PASSING OF NEW FRANCE. A Chronicle of Montcalm. ... Toronto, Glasgow
Brook, 1914. 149p [BM BVaU LC NSWA OOA QMM
THE WINNING OF CANADA. A Chronicle of Wolfe. Toronto, Glasgow Brook, 1914.
152p [BM BVaU LC NSWA OOA QMM
WOLFE. The Hero of Quebec. Toronto, Robert Glasgow, 1912. 156p [BM OOP

Woodruff, Norris Counsell, 1901–
TWELVE GENERATIONS FROM THE COLONY OF CONNECTICUT IN NEW ENGLAND
AND THE PROVINCE OF UPPER CANADA, 1636–1959. A Woodruff Genealogy.
Hamilton, Author, 1959. 101p

Woods, Robert Stuart, 1819–1906
THE CUTTING OUT OF THE CAROLINE AND OTHER REMINISCENCES OF 1837–38.
N.p., [1885?]. 8p [OTP

Woods, Walter Sainsbury, 1884–
THE MEN WHO CAME BACK. A Book of Memories. Toronto, Ryerson, 1956. 175p

Woodsworth, Rev. James, 1843–1917

THIRTY YEARS IN THE CANADIAN NORTH-WEST. Toronto, McClelland, 1917. 259p [BM BVaU LC NSHD OTU QMM

Woollacott, Arthur Philip, 1875–1958

MACKENZIE AND HIS VOYAGEURS. By Canoe to the Arctic and the Pacific, 1789–93. Toronto, Dent, 1927. 237p [BVaU NBFU OTU QMM

Worthington, Edward Dagge, 1820–1895

REMINISCENCES OF STUDENT LIFE AND PRACTICE. Sherbrooke, Walton, 1897. 119p [OTU QMSS

Wotherspoon, Mildred Faith (Cumberland)

THE STORY OF A HOME, "DUNAIN," 1857–1957. [Port Hope, Ont.?] , Author, 1958. 18p

Wright, Esther Isabell (Clark), 1895–

ALEXANDER CLARK, LOYALIST. A Contribution to the History of New Brunswick. Kentville, Kentville Pub. Co., 1940. 81p [BVaU NBFU OTU

GRANDMOTHER'S CHILD. The Life of Harriet H.R. Clark. Ottawa, Author, 1959. 110p

THE LOYALISTS OF NEW BRUNSWICK. Fredericton, Author, 1955. 365p

Wright, Frederick Keays, 1865–

GENEALOGY OF THE WRIGHT FAMILY, 1631–1950. Calgary, Albertan Printers, 1950. 28p [Revision to 1950 of his GENEALOGY OF THE WRIGHT FAMILY 1631–1930.] [OONL

Wrong, Edward Murray, 1889–1928

CHARLES BULLER AND RESPONSIBLE GOVERNMENT. Oxford, Clarendon Press, 1926. 352p [BM BVaU NSHD OLU

Wrong, George McKinnon, 1860–1948

THE EARL OF ELGIN. London, Methuen, 1905. 300p [BVaU LC NSHD OTU QMM

Wrong, Humphrey Hume, 1894–1954

SIR ALEXANDER MACKENZIE. Explorer and Fur-Trader. By Hume Wrong. Toronto, Macmillan, 1927. 171p [BM BVaU LC NBFU OTU QMM

York, Eva Rose (Fitch), 1858–

WHEN MY DREAM CAME TRUE. A Brief Autobiography in which the Author is Seen Seeking and Finding Abiding Joy. Toronto, Evangelical Pub., 1935. 62p [OTU

York County, Ont.

COMMEMORATIVE BIOGRAPHICAL RECORD OF THE COUNTY OF YORK. Toronto, Beers, 1907. 673p [BVaU

Youmans, Letitia (Creighton), 1827–1896
CAMPAIGN ECHOES. The Autobiography of Mrs. Letitia Youmans, the Pioneer of
the White Ribbon Movement in Canada. Toronto, Briggs, 1893. 311p [BM
BVaU LC OTP QMM

Young, Anna Grace Peterson, 1898–
OFF WATCH. Today and Yesterday on the Great Lakes. Toronto, Ryerson, 1957.
xviii + 156p

Young, Archibald Hope, 1863–1935
THE REVD. JOHN STUART, D.D., U.E.L., of Kingston, U.C., and his Family. A
Genealogical Study. Kingston, Whig Press, 1920. 64p [BVaU LC NSHD OLU
QMM

Young, Rev. Arminius
A METHODIST MISSIONARY IN LABRADOR. [Toronto], S. and A. Young, 1916.
180p [BM NSHD OTU

Young, Rev. Egerton Ryerson, 1840–1909
THE APOSTLE OF THE NORTH, REV. JAMES EVANS. New York, Revell, 1899. 262p
[BM BVaU LC MWU NSWA OTP
THE BATTLE OF THE BEARS, AND REMINISCENCES OF LIFE IN THE INDIAN
COUNTRY. London, Culley, 1907. 318p [BM LC OTU

Young, Rev. George, 1821–1910
MANITOBA MEMORIES ... 1868–1884. Toronto, Briggs, 1897. 364p [BM BVaU
LC NSWA OKQ

Young, James, 1835–1913
PUBLIC MEN AND PUBLIC LIFE IN CANADA. The Story of the Canadian Confederacy.
Being Recollections of Parliament and the Press. Toronto, Briggs, 1912. 2v
[Earlier ed., in one vol., in 1902.] [BM BVaU NSWA OTU QMBM

Yule, Pamelia S. (Vining), 1825?–1897
SOWING AND REAPING; or, Records of the Ellisson Family. Toronto, Briggs, 1899.
404p [Ryerson Impt

Ziegler, Olive Irene
WOODSWORTH: SOCIAL PIONEER. Toronto, Ontario Pub. Co., 1934. 202p [BVaU
OTP

ESSAYS AND SPEECHES

Addresses, personal and general essays, nature writings, monographs, sketches, lectures, etc.

Adamson, Rev. William Agar, 1800–1868

SALMON-FISHING IN CANADA. By a Resident [pseud]. Ed. by Sir James Edward Alexander. London, Longman, 1860. 350p [BVaU NSWA OKQ QMM

Alexander, William Hardy, 1878–1962

THESE TWENTY-FIVE YEARS. A Symposium by W.H. Alexander, E.K. Broadus, F.J. Lewis, and J.M. MacEachran of the University of Alberta. Toronto, Macmillan, 1933. 113p [BVaU NBFU OTP QMM

Alexander, William John, 1855–1944

THE STUDY OF LITERATURE. Inaugural Address Delivered at the Convocation of Dalhousie University ... Oct. 28, 1884. Halifax, Nova Scotia Print., [1884]. 22p [OTU

Allen, Egbert Chesley, 1882–1947

THE OUT-OF-DOORS. Toronto, Ryerson, 1932. 141p [AEU NSHP OTP QMM

Allen, Grant, 1848–1899

COLIN CLOUT'S CALENDAR. The Record of a Summer, April to October. London, Chatto, 1882. 237p [BM OTU

COUNTY AND TOWN IN ENGLAND. Together with Some Annals of Churnside. With an intro. by Frederick York Powell. London, Grant Richards, 1901. 274p [BVaU SSU

FALLING IN LOVE, WITH OTHER ESSAYS. London, Smith Elder, 1889. 356p [BM LC OTU

FLASHLIGHTS ON NATURE. London, Newnes, 1899. 312p [BM BVaU OTU

THE HAND OF GOD, AND OTHER POSTHUMOUS ESSAYS. London, Watts, 1909. 114p [BM OTU

IN NATURE'S WORKSHOP. London, Newnes, 1901. 240p [BM OLU

NATURAL INEQUALITY. London, Clarion Office, [189–?]. 20p [Reprinted from *Forecasts of the Coming Century.*] [LC

POST-PRANDIAL PHILOSOPHY. London, Chatto, 1894. 214p [BM OTU

SCIENCE IN ARCADY. London, Lawrence & Bullen, 1892. 304p [BM LC OTU

VIGNETTES FROM NATURE. London, Chatto, 1881. 229p [BM OTU

Allen, Robert Thomas, 1911–

THE GRASS IS NEVER GREENER. The Hilarious Adventures of a Family in Search of the Perfect Place to Live. Toronto, McClelland, 1956. 204p

TIME FOR EVERYTHING. New York, Crowell, 1955. 218p

Allison, Gerald Carlyle, 1907–1972
THE CORNER CUPBOARD. Winnipeg, Harlequin Books, 1958. 192p

Allison, William Talbot, 1874–1941
THE HISTORY OF JOURNALISM. A Lecture Delivered Aug. 9, 1921 to the Conference
of Western Journalists ... Winnipeg. Winnipeg, Manitoba Dept. of Agriculture,
[1921?]. 24p [OTU MWP
THIS FOR REMEMBRANCE. Comp. by Carlyle Allison. Toronto, Ryerson, 1949.
50p [BVaU LC NBFU OTP

Alward, Silas, 1842–1919
"OUR WESTERN HERITAGE." "THEN AND NOW"; or, "Thirty Years After." Lectures
delivered by ——. Saint John, Globe, 1910. 58p [BViPA NBFU

Anderson, Margaret Pauline, 1870–
SICK ROOM THOUGHTS AND GLEANINGS. 3rd ed. Saint John, "Progress" Book
and Job, 1895. 142p [1st ed., 1893.] [BVaU LC NBFU OLU QMM

Angus, Marion Isabel (Hand), 1902–1951
WOMAN UNVEILED. Vancouver, Vancouver Bindery, 1932. 95p [BVaU

Anonymous
ESSAY ON MARRIAGE. Quebec, Ruthven, 1829. 113 + 64p [NBFU OTP
EURIDICE AHOY! A Yacht Cruise on Lake Champlain in 1880. By the Author of
"One More Unfortunate." Montreal, Lovell, 1881. 66p [OTP QMSS
THE NEW PARTI NATIONAL. ... A Satire. Tracts for the Times in Canada, No. 1.
N.p., n.d. 16p [OTP QMBM

Ayscough, Florence (Wheelock), 1878–1942
A CHINESE MIRROR. Being Reflections of the Reality behind Appearance. Boston,
Houghton, 1925. 464p [BM LC OTP

Barber, Frank Louis, 1877–1945
IN MEMORIAM FRANK LOUIS BARBER, 1877–1945. [Contains two essays by
Dr. Barber, and a Memorial Address by W.T. Brown.] Toronto, Victoria Univ.,
1948. 19p [OTUV

Barber, Mrs. Mary Josephine Axford, 1913–
CHRISTMAS IN CANADA. The Early Days. From Sea to Sea. Spirit of Christmas
Past. Spirit of Christmas Present. Ed. by Mary Barber & Flora McPherson.
Toronto, Dent, 1959. 134p

Barr, Alfred Tennyson, 1890–
WHY NOT THINK IT OVER? Essays on Popular Fallacies. New York, Exposition
Press, 1954. 163p

Barrass, Rev. Edward, 1821–1898
CLASS MEETINGS. Their Origin, and Advantages. Sherbrooke, Walton, 1865. 21p
  [NSWA OTUV QMSS

Baxter, Arthur Beverley, 1891–1964
FIRST NIGHTS AND FOOTLIGHTS. London, Hutchinson, 1955. 256p
FIRST NIGHTS AND NOISES OFF. London, Hutchinson, 1949. 239p [LC NBFU
  OTP

Baylis, Samuel Mathewson, 1854–1941
ENCHANTING METIS. [Montreal], 1928. 18p [OTU QMM

Beers, William George, 1843–1900
PATRIOTIC SPEECH ... YOUNG CANADA'S REPLY TO "ANNEXATION". ... Montreal,
  n.p., 1888. 7p [BVaU OTP QMM

Belaney, George Stansfeld, 1888–1938
A BOOK OF GREY OWL. Pages from the Writing of Wa-Sha-Quon-Asin. Ed. by E.E.
  Reynolds. ... London, Davies, 1938. 324p [Same title, but with an intro. by
  Hugh Eayrs: Toronto, Macmillan, 1938. xxi+324p] [BM LC NBFU OTMC
FAREWELL TO THE CHILDREN OF THE BRITISH ISLES. By Wa-Sha-Quon-Asin
  (Grey Owl) [pseud]. London, Dickson, 1938. 12p [BM OTU
PILGRIMS OF THE WILD. By Wa-Sha-Quon-Asin (Grey Owl) [pseud]. London,
  Dickson, 1934. 282p [BM BVaU LC NBFU OTMC
TALES OF AN EMPTY CABIN. By Wa-Sha-Quon-Asin (Grey Owl) [pseud]. Toronto,
  Macmillan, 1936. 335p [BM BVaU LC NBFU OKQ

Belcher, Alexander Emerson, 1844–1926
WHAT I KNOW ABOUT COMMERCIAL TRAVELLING. Who We Are, What We Do, and
  How We Do It. Toronto, Hunter Rose, 1883. 149p [BVaU LC OTU

Bell, Charles William, 1876–1938
WHO SAID MURDER? Toronto, Macmillan, 1935. 403p [Essays on famous
  Canadian murders.] [BM BVaU OKQ QMM

Bell, Rev. Clifford Ritchie, 1905–
PURPLE VAPOURS. Sherbrooke, Page, 1927. [Also a 2nd series in 1931.]

Bender, Louis Prosper, 1844–1917
VISIONS OF OLD QUEBEC. Quebec, 1911. 23p [OTL

Bengough, John Wilson, 1851–1923
BENGOUGH'S CHALK-TALKS. A Series of Platform Addresses on Various Topics.
  Toronto, Musson, 1922. 162p [BM BVaU NSHD OKQ
THE DECLINE AND FALL OF KEEWATIN; or, The Free-trade Redskins. A Satire Illus.
  by J.W. Bengough. Toronto, "Grip" Office, 1876. 28p [BVaU NSHD OTP
THE GIN MILL PRIMER. A Book of Easy Reading Lessons for Children of All Ages,
  Especially for Boys who have Votes. Toronto, Briggs, 1898. 78p [BM BVaU
  OOP

THE PROHIBITION AESOP. A Book of Fables. Hamilton, Royal Templar Pub., n.d.
39p [BVaU OTU

THE UP-TO-DATE PRIMER. A First Book of Lessons for Little Political Economists,
in Words of One Syllable with Pictures. New York, Funk & Wagnalls, 1896. 75p
[BM BVaU LC NSWA OLU

THE WHOLE HOG BOOK. Being George's Thoro' Going Work "Protection or Free-
Trade?" Rendered into Words of One Syllable, and Illustrated with Pictures; or,
A Dry Subject Made Juicy. Boston, American Free-Trade League, 1908. 99p
[LC

THE GRIP-SACK. A Receptacle of Light Literature, Fun and Fancy. Toronto, Grip,
1882. 2v [NSHD OTU

Berton, Pierre Francis de Marigny, 1920—

ADVENTURES OF A COLUMNIST. Toronto, McClelland, 1960. 211p

JUST ADD WATER AND STIR. Being a Random Collection of Satirical Essays, Rude
Remarks, Used Anecdotes, Thumbnail Sketches, Ancient Wheezes, Old Nostalgias,
Wry Comments, Limp Doggerel, Intemperate Recipes, Vagrant Opinions and
Crude Drawings. Toronto, McClelland, 1959. 222p

Bethune, Rev. John, 1791—1872

ADDRESS. Delivered by the Principal of McGill College. Montreal, Lovell & Gibson,
1843. 14p [OTP

Bezanson, Rev. W.B.

STORIES OF ACADIA. Halifax, Nova Print., 1941. 57p (Birch Bark Series No. 4)
[Series apparently began in 1924 with a Dartmouth imprint. 44p] [BVaU OKQ
OTP

Bidwell, Barnabas, 1763—1833

THE PROMPTER. A Series of Essays on Civil and Social Duties. [Anon]. Kingston,
Thomson, 1821. 56p [OTP

Biggar, Emerson Bristol, 1853—1921

CANADA: A MEMORIAL VOLUME. General Reference Book of Canada. Ed. by ——.
Montreal, Biggar, 1889. 953p [BM BVaU OTU

Binmore, Charles J.

THE CANADIAN NATIONALITY. Montreal, Drysdale, 1888. 16p [BM OTU
QMBM

Bird, William Richard, 1891—

THE COMMUNICATION TRENCH. Amherst, N.S., Author, 1933. 336p [BVaU
NSWA OTP

THE STORY OF VIMY-RIDGE. [Arras (France), I.N.S.A.P.] , 1932. 24p [LC

THIRTEEN YEARS AFTER. Toronto, MacLean, 1932. 180p [BVaU NBFU

Bishop, Leslie Gurney, 1908–
BEES FROM THE UNDERGRADUATE BONNET. Oxford, Blackwell, 1929. 103p
[BM

Blake, Edward, 1833–1912
"A NATIONAL SENTIMENT!" Speech of Hon. Edward Blake at Aurora. Ottawa,
Perry, 1874. 107p [BVaU OTU
... SPEECHES BY HON. EDWARD BLAKE ON THE POLITICAL QUESTIONS OF THE
DAY, DELIVERED IN THE PROVINCE OF ONTARIO. ... Toronto, Hunter Rose,
1887. 424p [OLU QMU

Blake, William Hume, 1861–1924
BROWN WATERS, AND OTHER SKETCHES. Toronto, Macmillan, 1915. 264p
[Many later editions.] [BM BVaU LC NSHD OKQ
A FISHERMAN'S CREED. Toronto, Macmillan, 1923. 40p [BM BVaU
NSHD OKQ QMM
IN A FISHING COUNTRY. Toronto, Macmillan, 1922. 263p [BM BVaU LC
NSHD OKQ QMM

Bock, William George, 1884–
THE BOOK OF HUMBUG. Saskatoon, Modern Press, 1958. 132p

Bourinot, Arthur Stanley, 1893–1969
THE QUICK AND THE DEAD. Views and Reviews On Poetry. Ottawa, Author, 1955.
21p

Bourque, Romuald, 1889–
OUR CENTURY. Montreal, Editorial Associates, 1950. 157p [OONL

Bracken, John, 1883–
JOHN BRACKEN SAYS. Toronto, Oxford U. Press, 1944. 134p [BM BVaU OTU

Bready, John Wesley, 1887–1953
FAITH AND FREEDOM, THE ROOTS OF DEMOCRACY. Winona Lake, Ind., Light and
Life Press, 1952. 151p

Bridle, Augustus, 1869–1952
THE MASQUES OF OTTAWA. By "Domino" [pseud] . Toronto, Macmillan, 1921.
283p [BM BVaU LC NSHD OTU QMM
THE OLD 24TH OF MAY. Toronto, McLean, [19–?]. 8p [OTP

Broadus, Edmund Kemper, 1876–1936
SATURDAY AND SUNDAY. Toronto, Macmillan, 1935. 260p [BVaU LC NBFU
OTP

Brockington, Leonard Walter, 1888–
ADDRESS ... [at the] Opening of Mackenzie House, 82 Bond Street, Toronto,
Tuesday, May 9th, 1950. Toronto, W.L. Mackenzie Homestead Foundation,
1950. 10p [OONL

Brooke, Frances (Moore), 1724–1789
THE OLD MAID. By Mary Singleton, Spinster [pseud]. London, Millar, 1764.
304p [A bound periodical.] [BM OTU

Brooks, Anne (Sutherland)
THE ODD LITTLE SOUL. By Anne Sutherland. Guelph, Author, 1933. 62p [CC

Brown, Audrey Alexandra, 1904–
POETRY AND LIFE. An Address. Toronto, Macmillan, 1941. 10p [BVaU OTU
QMM

Bruce, Herbert Alexander, 1868–1963
FRIENDSHIP: THE KEY TO PEACE, AND OTHER ADDRESSES. Toronto, Macmillan,
1937. 364p [BM BVaU LC NBFU OTU QMM
OUR HERITAGE, AND OTHER ADDRESSES. Toronto, Macmillan, 1934. 392p
[BM BVaU LC OTU QMM

Brundle, John, 1882–
BROMESWELL DICK'S AND JOHNNY PIPER'S RAPHSODY [sic]. From the Pen of
John, a Suffolk Herd Boy. Roche's Point, Ont., Author, 1953. 30p

Bryce, Rev. George, 1844–1931
CANADIAN LOYALTY. Winnipeg, Manitoba Free Press, 1902. 20p [LC QMBM

Bryce, Peter Henderson, 1853–
THE ILLUMINATION OF JOSEPH KEELER, ESQ.; or, On to the Land. Boston,
American Journal of Public Health, 1915. 97p [BVaU NSHD OTU

Bucke, Richard Maurice, 1837–1902
COSMIC CONSCIOUSNESS. A Paper read before the American Medico-Psychological
Association ... 18 May 1894. Philadephia, The Conservator, 1894. 18p [OLU

Burgess, Rev. Edwin Harcus, 1858–
FOR CANADA AND THE OLD FLAG. Halifax, Knight, 1893. 46p [NSHD QMM

Burke, Luke
PHRENOLOGICAL ENQUIRIES. Pts. I and II. Quebec, Cowan, 1840. 40p [QMSS

Burn, William Scott, –1851
THE CONNECTION BETWEEN LITERATURE AND COMMERCE. In Two Essays read
before the Literary and Historical Society of Toronto. Toronto, Rowsell, 1845.
16p [OTP

Burpee, Lawrence Johnstone, 1873–1946
BY CANADIAN STREAMS. Toronto, Musson, 1909. 87p [BVaU OTU QMM
CANADIAN ELOQUENCE. Ed. and arranged by ——. Toronto, Musson, 1910.
112p [BVaU OTU QMM
GOOD NEIGHBOURS. Toronto, Ryerson, 1940. 30p [OTU

Buschlen, John Preston, 1888—

THE DESERT BATTALION. By Jack Preston [pseud] and Mrs. Edward G. Robinson. Hollywood, Murray & Gee, 1944. 97p [LC

THE DONKEY, THE ELEPHANT AND THE GOAT. [Great Falls, Mont., Montana Print., 1920.] 16p [LC

ROMANCE AND THE WEST. Falling Petals. By John Preston [pseud]. Boston, Cornhill, 1918. 49p [LC

Calamo, C.

A GRAB BAG; or, Junk from an Attic Storage. Winnipeg, Winnipeg Print., n.d. 32p [BVaS

PUG-NOSE; or, From the Ridiculous to the Sublime. [Winnipeg], Winnipeg Print., n.d. 190p [AEU MWU

Campbell, Rollo, 1803—1871

TWO LECTURES ON CANADA. Greenock, Mackenzie, 1857. 45p [Also: Toronto, 1857. 47p] [BM LC NSWA OTP QMM

Canadian Authors' Association. Western Ontario Branch

ADDRESSES ... AT ... ARCHIBALD LAMPMAN MEMORIAL CAIRN. ... London, Ont., The Branch, 1930. 16p [OTU

Canniff, William, 1830—1910

CANADIAN NATIONALITY. Its Growth and Development. Toronto, Hart & Rawlinson, 1875. 20p [BM OTP

Carman, Bliss, 1861—1929

ADDRESS TO THE GRADUATING CLASS 1911 OF THE UNITRINIAN SCHOOL OF PERSONAL HARMONIZING. ... New York, Tabord Press, 1911. 27p [BVaU LC NBFU OKQ

THE FRIENDSHIP OF ART. Boston, Page, 1904. 303p [BM BVaU LC NSHD OKQ

THE KINSHIP OF NATURE. Boston, Page, 1904. [Pub. 1903.] 298p [BM BVaU LC NSHD OTU QMM

THE MAKING OF PERSONALITY. By Bliss Carman [with Mary Perry King]. Boston, Page, 1908. 375p [BM BVaU LC NSHD OTU QMM

TALKS ON POETRY AND LIFE. Five Lectures Delivered before the Univeristy of Toronto, December 1925. [Transcribed and ed. by Blanche Hume.] Toronto, Ryerson, 1926. 58p [BVaU LC NBFU OTU QMM

THE POETRY OF LIFE. Boston, Page, 1905. 258p [BM BVaU LC NSHD OTUV QMM

Carr, Emily, 1871—1945

AN ADDRESS BY EMILY CARR. With an intro. by Ira Dilworth. Toronto, Oxford U. Press, 1955. ix + 13p

PAUSE, A SKETCH BOOK. Toronto, Clarke Irwin, 1953. 148p

Cash, Gwen (Goldsmid), 1891–
A MILLION MILES FROM OTTAWA. Toronto, Macmillan, 1942. 152p [BVaU LC
OTU QMM

Charlesworth, Hector Willoughby, 1872–1945
THE CANADIAN SCENE. Sketches: Political and Historical. Toronto, Macmillan,
1927. 235p [BM BVaU LC NSHD OKQ
CANDID CHRONICLES. Leaves from the Note Book of a Canadian Journalist.
Toronto, Macmillan 1925. 404p [BM BVaU LC NBFU OTU
I'M TELLING YOU. Being ... Further Candid Chronicles. Toronto, Macmillan, 1937.
344p [BVaU LC NBFU OTU
MORE CANDID CHRONICLES. Further Leaves from the Note Book of a Canadian
Journalist. Toronto, Macmillan, 1928. 429p [BM BVaU LC OKQ

Charlton, John, 1829–1910
SPEECHES AND ADDRESSES, POLITICAL, LITERARY, AND RELIGIOUS. Toronto,
Morang, 1905. 499p [BM BVaU NBFU OTU

Chisholme, David, 1796?–1842
THE LOWER-CANADA WATCHMAN. [Anon] Kingston, Macfarlane, 1829. 491p
[BVaU LC NSWA OTU

Clark, Gregory, 1892–
THE BEST OF GREGORY CLARK. Foreword by Craig Ballantyne. Toronto, Ryerson,
1959. 174p
SO WHAT? Toronto, Saunders, 1937. 252p [BVaU OTU
WHICH WE DID. Toronto, Saunders, 1936. 221p [BVaU NBFU OTU

Clarke, Andrew David, 1882–1948
ANDY CLARKE AND HIS NEIGHBOURLY NEWS. With an intro. by Greg. Clark.
Toronto, Ryerson, 1949. 158p [OTP

Coffin, William Foster, 1808–1878
QUIRKS OF DIPLOMACY. Read before the Literary & Scientific Society of Ottawa,
Jan. 22, 1874. Montreal, Lovell, 1874. 31p [BVaU LC OTU

Collier, Della
ECHOES FROM AN OLD GARDEN. New Westminster, Jackson, 1944. 104p [BVaU

Cook, Marjorie Grant
VERDUN DAYS IN PARIS. By Marjorie Grant. London, Collins, 1918. 239p [BM
QMM

Cooke, Ronald John Victor, 1913–
WRITING FOR THE TRADE JOURNALS. Windsor, Non-Fiction Press, [1949?]. 48p
[CC

Copleston, Mrs. Edward
CANADA: Why We Live in It, and Why We Like It. London, Parker & Bourn, 1861.
121p [BM BVaU LC OTP

Cordner, Rev. John, 1816–1894
THE FOUNDATIONS OF NATIONALITY. Montreal, Rose, 1856. 28p (Discourse preached in the Unitarian Church, Montreal, on the Sunday after the great railway celebration, Nov. 1856.) [BM BVaU NSWA OTU QMM

Corry, James Alexander, 1899–
CIVIL LIBERTIES IN TRYING TIMES. Fredericton, U. of New Brunswick, 1953. 16p

Coulon, Emile
POETICAL LEISURE HOURS AND TORONTONIAN DESCRIPTIONS. In French Verse and English Essays. ... Toronto, Rowsell, 1897. 39p [BM Brown U OTU

Cowan, Mary Edith
RAINBOW OF LIFE. Ottawa, Canadian Research and Editorial Institute, 1945. 52p [BVaU OKQ

Craik, Robert Henry, 1829–1906
PAPERS AND ADDRESSES. Montreal, Gazette, 1907. 222p [BVaU OTU QMM

Cramp, Rev. John Mockett, 1796–1881
LECTURES FOR THESE TIMES. London, Houlston & Stoneman, 1844. 308p [BM NSWA OTUV

Cramp, Mary
ETERNAL YOUTH: Addresses to Girls, 1913–1930. By Mary Cramp and Maud C. Edgar. Toronto, Macmillan, 1931. 262p [BM BVaU NBFU OTU

Creighton, Donald Grant, 1902–
FOUNDERS' DAY ADDRESS, UNIVERSITY OF NEW BRUNSWICK ... WRITING OF HISTORY IN CANADA. Fredericton, The University, 1945. 18p [BM NBFU OTU

Crofton, Francis Blake, 1841–1912
FOR CLOSER UNION. ... Halifax, Mackinlay, 1897. 57p [BM NSHD OTU
IS IT TOO LATE? London, Author, n.d. 20p [NSHD

Crombie, Keith
SACKCLOTH AND SPLASHES—Fragments from "The Goblin." By Keith Crombie and J.E. MacDougall. Toronto, McClelland, 1923. 256p [BM BVaU OTU

Crone, Kennedy, 1883–
THE SPIRIT OF MONTREAL (NON-ALCOHOLIC). An Analysis for Americans. Montreal, Woodward Press, 1929. 39p [QMBM

Crooks, Adam, 1827–1885
SPEECHES. Toronto, Robinson, 1879. 48p [NSWA OTU

Crowley, Cornelius Patrick Joseph, 1914–
THE HUMAN IMAGE. Twenty-six Scripts of Radio Talks as Given on CBC. Windsor, Ont., Assumption U. of Windsor Press, 1960. 88p

Cumming, Robert Dalziel, 1871–
SKOOKUM CHUCK FABLES. Bits of History through the Microscope (Some of which Appeared in the Ashcroft Journal). By Skookum Chuck [pseud]. N.p., 1915. 167p [BVaU

Currie, Arthur William, 1875–1933
THE NEW CANADIANISM. An Address delivered before the 8th Annual Conference of Heads of Canadian Universities held at Winnipeg, June 16th, 1922. [Montreal], 1922. 10p [NSWA OLU QMM

Currie, Margaret (Gill), 1843–
MARGARET CURRIE: HER BOOK. Toronto, Hunter Rose, 1924. 352p [NBFU OTP QMSS

Dafoe, John Wesley, 1866–1944
CANADA, AN AMERICAN NATION. New York, Columbia U. Press, 1935. 134p [BM BVaU NSHD OKQ QMM

Daor, Francis
SKETCHES [Reprinted from the Montreal *Herald*]. N.p., n.p., n.d. 69p [BVaU

Davidson, S.
STRAY SHOTS FROM SOLOMON. By James Acton [pseud]. Toronto, Acton Pub. Co., 1907. 160p [Same title: Toronto, Acton Pub. Co., 1929. 28p] [BM BVaU OTU

Davies, Blodwen, 1897–1966
YOUTH SPEAKS ITS MIND. Toronto, Ryerson, 1948. 232p [Survey of Canadian Youth Commission.] [BVaU LC OTU

Davies, Robertson, 1913–
THE DIARY OF SAMUEL MARCHBANKS. Toronto, Clarke Irwin, 1947. 204p [BVaU LC NBFU OTU
RENOWN AT STRATFORD. A Record of the Shakespeare Festival in Canada 1953. By Tyrone Guthrie, Robertson Davies, and Grant Macdonald. Toronto, Clarke Irwin, 1953. 127p
THE TABLE TALK OF SAMUEL MARCHBANKS. ... Toronto, Clarke Irwin, 1949. 248p [BM BVaU LC NSHD OKQ
THRICE THE BRINDED CAT HATH MEW'D. A Record of the Stratford Shakespearean Festival in Canada, 1955. By Robertson Davies, Tyrone Guthrie, Boyd Neel, and Tanya Moiseiwitsch. Toronto, Clarke Irwin, 1955. xii + 178p
TWICE HAVE THE TRUMPETS SOUNDED. A Record of the Stratford Shakespearean Festival in Canada, 1954. By Tyrone Guthrie, Robertson Davies, and Grant Macdonald. Toronto, Clarke Irwin, 1954. 192p

A VOICE FROM THE ATTIC. Toronto, McClelland, 1960. ix + 360 + xp [Pub. in England as THE PERSONAL ART, Reading to Good Purpose. London, Secker, 1961. 268p]

Davin, Nicholas Flood, 1843–1901

BRITISH VERSUS AMERICAN CIVILIZATION. A Lecture. ... Toronto, Adam Stevenson, 1873. 45p [LC NSHD OTU

CULTURE AND PRACTICAL POWER. An Address delivered at the Opening of Lansdowne College, Portage la Prairie. ... Regina, Leader Co., 1889. 16p [BM LC NSWA OOA

IRELAND AND THE EMPIRE. A Speech ... delivered before the St. Patrick's Society ... Montreal, on St. Patrick's Day 1885. Ottawa, Citizen Print., 1885. 18p [BM NSHD

STRATHCONA HORSE. Speech at Lansdowne Park, March 7th, A.D. 1900. ... Ottawa, Hope, 1900. 20p [BM NSWA OTU

Davis, Herbert John, 1893–

CHALLENGE TO THE INTELLECT. Three Addresses. Northampton, Mass., Hampshire Bookshop, 1941. 44p [LC

Dawson, John William, 1820–1899

THE CANADIAN STUDENT. N.p., n. pub., 1891. 8p [NSWA OTU

CREATIVE DEVELOPMENT AND EVOLUTION. Frome, Butler & Tanner, n.d. 36p [QMM

DUTIES OF EDUCATED YOUNG MEN IN BRITISH AMERICA. Montreal, Lovell, 1863. 24p [LC NSHD OTP

EDUCATED WOMEN. An Address. ... [N.p., priv. circ., 1889.] 14p [NSWA

Dawson, Samuel Edward, 1833–1916

THE NORTHERN KINGDOM. By a Colonist [pseud]. Montreal, Dawson, [1866?]. 18p [BM NSWA OTU QMM

A PLEA FOR LITERATURE. Presidential Address before the Royal Society. ... Montreal, Renouf, 1908. 26p [LC OTU QMM

Day, Frank Parker, 1881–1950

A GOOD CITIZEN. Sackville, Mt. Allison Univ., 1947. 134p [NSHD OLU

Deacon, William Arthur, 1890–

MY VISION OF CANADA. Toronto, Ontario Pub. Co., 1933. 309p [BM BVaU LC NSHD OTU QMM

OPEN HOUSE. Ed. by W.A. Deacon and Wilfred Reeves. Ottawa, Graphic, 1931. 319p [BM BVaU NSHD OKQ

PENS AND PIRATES. Toronto, Ryerson, 1923. 325p [BM BVaU NSHD OTP

POTEEN. A Pot-Pourri of Canadian Essays. Ottawa, Graphic, 1926. 241p [BM BVaU NSHD OKQ

SH-H-H ... HERE COMES THE CENSOR! An Address to the Ontario Library
Association, March 28, 1940. Toronto, Macmillan, 1940. 16p [OTU

Dean, J.K.

THE SAYINGS AND DOINGS OF THE SELF-STYLED ROYAL FAMILY, THE MAGRATHS,
OF MACKENZIE'S CASTLE, SPRINGFIELD. Toronto, 1844. 47p [OTP

Dehan, Aiken A.

WASHING THE HANDS. Toronto, McClelland, 1936. 37p [OTU

De La Roche, Mazo, 1879–1961

PORTRAIT OF A DOG. Boston, Little Brown, 1930. 199p [BM BVaU LC NBFU
OTU QMM

Dewart, Rev. Edward Hartley, 1828–1903

ESSAYS FOR THE TIMES. Studies of Eminent Men and Important Living Questions.
Toronto, Briggs, 1898. 198p [BM BVaU OTUV

Dezell, Robert, 1866–

"I SEZ, SEZ I." A Series of Talks to Talkers on what to say and how to say it.
Allenford, Ont., Author, 1911. 199p [LC
MOIKE SPAKES HIS MOIND. Toronto, Allen, 1937. 62p [LC

Dixon, Frederick John, 1881–1931

DIXON'S ADDRESS TO THE JURY IN DEFENCE OF FREEDOM OF SPEECH ... And
Judge Galt's Charge to the Jury in Rex v. Dixon. Winnipeg, Defence Committee,
[1920]. 126p [Peel

Dolman, Claude Ernest, 1906–

A LAYMAN VIEWS THE ARTIST. Vancouver, Art Gallery, 1946. 9p [BVaU
SCIENCE AND THE HUMANITIES. An Address. ... Vancouver, U. of British Columbia,
1950. 19p [BVaU OTU

Donovan, Rev. P.J.

DAD'S MUSINGS. A Household Philosopher's Kindly and Practical Reflections on
the Affairs of Average Citizens. ... Chicago, Meier, 1926. 123p [LC

Donovan, Peter, 1884–

IMPERFECTLY PROPER. By P. O'D. [pseud]. Toronto, McClelland, 1920. 379p
[BM BVaU NBFU OTU QMM
OVER 'ERE AND BACK HOME. Random Impressions of an Earnest Soul. By P. O'D.
[pseud]. Toronto, McClelland, 1922. 355p [Earlier ed. in paper covers:
Toronto, McClelland, 1918.] [BM BVaU NBFU OTP QMM

Douglas, Frances Mary

BRITANNIA WAIVES THE RULES. A Confidential Guide to the Customs, Manners
and Habits of the "Nation of Shopkeepers." By Frances Douglas (Who has
never been there) and Thelma Lecocq (Who has). Toronto, Dent, 1934. 112p
[BM NBFU OTU QMM

Douglas, Robert W., –1931
HOW BOOKS MAY HELP YOU. Vancouver, Burrard Pub. Co., 1914. 22p [BVaU

Duff, Louis Blake, 1878–1959
IMMORTAL MEMORY. An Address before the Burns Literary Society. Fort Erie,
Ont., Review Co., 1945. 16p [OTU
A STUDY OF VANITY. ... Welland, Ont., Author, 1952. 14p

Duggan, Joseph Jenkins, 1874–
THE UNFORGOTTEN VALLEY. Studies of Life and Character on the Welsh Border.
Toronto, Ryerson, 1926. 177p [OTP QMM

Duncan, Sara Jeannette (Mrs. Everard Cotes), 1861–1922
THE CROW'S NEST. New York, Dodd Mead, 1901. 248p [Pub. in Eng. as: ON THE
OTHER SIDE OF THE LATCH. London, Methuen, 1901. 266p] [BM BVaU LC
OTP
ON THE OTHER SIDE OF THE LATCH. [See under THE CROW'S NEST.]

Dunlop, William, 1792–1848
AN ADDRESS DELIVERED TO THE YORK MECHANICS' INSTITUTION, March, 1832.
York, Coates, 1832. 16p [OTU

Dunton, (Arnold) Davidson, 1912–
FREEDOM FOR MINDS, 1957. Fredericton, U. of New Brunswick, 1957. 12p

Eayrs, Hugh Smithurst, 1894–1940
THE BAROMETER POINTS TO CHANGE. An Address delivered to the Toronto
Branch of the Canadian Authors' Association ... 1938. Toronto, Macmillan,
1938. 27p [OKQ
IT ISN'T GOOD ENOUGH. An Address delivered to the Annual Meeting of the
Canadian Authors' Association ... 1939. Toronto, Macmillan, 1939. 16p [BViP
OKQ

Edmonds, Walter Everard, 1875–
BROAD HORIZONS. Maple Leaf Sketches from a Prairie Studio. ... Toronto, Musson,
1919. 224p [BVa LC OTP
THE CANADIAN FLAG DAY BOOK. Toronto, Longmans, 1927. 154p [BVa OKQ
IN A COLLEGE LIBRARY. Edmonton, Esdale Press, 1920. 91p [ACG BM

Eisendrath, Maurice Nathan, 1902–
THE NEVER FAILING STREAM. Toronto, Macmillan, 1939. 398p [BM BVaU LC
OTP
READING IN WAR-TIME. Toronto, Macmillan, 1941. 31p [BVaU LC OTP

Emberson, Frederick C., –1913
HOW TO BE HAPPY. Introduction to Secrets of Joy. ... Montreal, Foster Brown,
[18–?]. 64p [OTP QMSS

Empire Club of Canada, Toronto.
ADDRESSES. Toronto, T.H. Best, 1903–. xiii + 361p [A continuing annual publication since 1903. Publisher and pagination vary.] [AEU BVaU NBFU OTP

Ewart, John Skirving, 1849–1933
THE KINGDOM OF CANADA ... and Other Essays. Toronto, Morang, 1908. 370p [BM BVaU LC NSWA OKQ

Ewing, John Morton, 1889–
REFLECTIONS OF A DOMINIE. Toronto, Nelson, 1932. 96p [BVaU OTU QMM

Fairchild, George Moore, 1854–1912
CANADIAN LEAVES. History, Art, Science, Literature, Commerce. A Series of New Papers read before the Canadian Club of New York. Ed. by ——. New York, Thompson, 1887. 289p [BM BVaU LC NBFU OTU

Fairchild, Queenie, –1950
MY FRENCH CANADIAN NEIGHBOURS, AND OTHER SKETCHES. Quebec, Telegraph Print., 1916. 121p [BVaU NBFU OTU

Falconer, Robert Alexander, 1867–1943
CITIZENSHIP IN AN ENLARGING WORLD. Sackville, Mount Allison U., 1928. 85p [BM BVaU NBFU OKQ
IDEALISM IN NATIONAL CHARACTER. London, Hodder, 1920. 216p [BM BVaU NSHD OTP

Ferguson, George Victor, 1897–
THE NEWSPAPER IN A FREE SOCIETY. [Sesquicentennial lectures, 1950.] Fredericton, U. of New Brunswick, [1950]. 11p [OONL

Fewster, Ernest Philip, 1868–1947
MY GARDEN DREAMS. Ottawa, Graphic, 1926. 175p [BVaU NSHD OTU QMM

Fisher, John Wiggins, 1913–
JOHN FISHER REPORTS. An Anthology of Radio Scripts. Hamilton, Niagara Editorial Bureau, 1949. 185p [BVa OLU

Fisher, Raymond Anderson, 1900–
THE PSYCHOLOGY OF DESIRE; or, A Measure for Men. Saskatoon, Elliott Print., 1930. 158p [BVa OTP

Fitch, Adelaide P.
EAST AND WEST. Essays and Sketches. Toronto, Briggs, 1911. 198p [BM BVaU NBFU

Flenley, Ralph, 1886—1969
ESSAYS IN CANADIAN HISTORY. Presented to George McKinnon Wrong for his
Eightieth Birthday. Ed. by ——. Toronto, Macmillan, 1939. 372p [BM BVaU
LC NSHD OTU QMM

Fontaine, Robert Louis, 1911—1965
THAT'S A GOOD QUESTION. Boston, Author, 1960. x + 139p

Ford, Paul
OUR NATIONAL PIE AND WHAT IT CONTAINED. Being a Report of the Proceedings
of the Anglo-Franco-Hibernian-Scottish-Canadian-National Society ... 1876.
Montreal, Drysdale, 1877. 19p [BVaU NSWA OTU QMSS

Forster, John Wycliffe Lowes, 1850—1938
SIGHT AND INSIGHT. Foreword by Sir Robert Falconer. Toronto, Oxford U. Press,
1941. 176p [BVi OTP

Foster, George Eulas, 1847—1931
CANADIAN ADDRESSES. Ed. by Arnold Winterbotham. Toronto, Bell & Cockburn,
1914. 324p [BM BVaU LC NSHD OTU QMM
CITIZENSHIP. ... Sackville, Mount Allison Univ., 1926. 85p [BVaU NBFU OTU

Foster, William Alexander, 1840—1888
CANADA FIRST; or, Our New Nationality. An Address. Toronto, Adam-Stevenson,
1871. 36p [BVaU OTP QMBM

Fox, Marion Wathen, 1871—1956
CANADA'S NEW FLAG. Toronto, Hunter-Rose, 1917. 15p [NBFL OKQ

Fraser, John, 1820—1899
CANADIAN PEN AND INK SKETCHES. Montreal, Gazette, 1890. 391p [BM BVaU
LC NSHD OTU QMM

Fraser, William Alexander, 1859—1933
SORROW AND OLD FRIENDS. Philadelphia, Altemus, [1901]. 41p [LC

French, Sarah
A BOOK FOR THE YOUNG. Dedicated by Permission to the Hon. Mrs. Manners
Sutton. By a Lady [pseud]. Saint John, McMillan, 1856. 175p [NBFU OTU
LETTERS TO A YOUNG LADY ON LEAVING SCHOOL AND ENTERING THE WORLD.
Dedicated by Permission to Lady Head. By a Lady [pseud]. Boston, 1855.
158p [NBB

Frost, Rex Hanby, 1896—
THE PASSING SHOW. [Selections from his Radio Talks on Canada.] Toronto,
Ryerson, 1946. 121p [BVaU LC OTU

Frye, Northrop, 1912–
ADDRESS BY H. NORTHROP FRYE ON THE OCCASION OF HIS INSTALLATION AS PRINCIPAL OF VICTORIA COLLEGE, OCTOBER 21, 1959. Toronto, Clarke Irwin, 1959. 23p

Fulford, Rev. Francis, 1803–1868
FIVE OCCASIONAL LECTURES, DELIVERED IN MONTREAL. Montreal, Lovell, 1859. 118p [BM BVaU NSHD OTP

Fuller, William Henry
A DREAM OF PURE POLITICIANS. [MOR '98
FLAPDOODLE. A Political Encyclopedia and Manual for Public Men. Ed. by an ex-Minister [pseud]. Toronto, 1881. 28p [Attributed to John Wilson Bengough in NSHD.] [NSHD OTU QMSS

Gale, Samuel, 1783–1865
NERVA; or, A Collection of Papers Published in the Montreal Herald. [Anon] Montreal, Gray, 1814. 45p [LC OTP QMM

Galloway, Thomas
LECTURES. Uxbridge, 1896. [Earlier ed. in 1882?] [OLU OOP OTU

Garison, Isabel
LOOKING FORWARD. Montreal, Robinson, 1890. 227p [OOP QMSS

Garvie, William
BARNEY ROONEY'S LETTERS ON CONFEDERATION, BOTHERATION, AND POLITICAL TRANSMOGRIFICATION. Halifax, 1865. 56p [BibC
THE LIGHT AND THE SHADOWS; or, Christianity the Ideal of Our Race. A Lecture. Halifax, 1860. 38p [NSWA

Gates, Hartley Baxter
THE DOMINION OF CANADA. Its Interests, Prospects, and Policy. An Address. ... Montreal, Lovell, 1872. 34p [OTU QMM

George, Rev. James, 1801?–1870
THE RELATION BETWEEN PIETY AND INTELLECTUAL LABOR. An Address. ... Kingston, Daily News, 1855. 24p [OTP
THE VALUE OF EARNESTNESS. An Address. Kingston, Daily News, [1854?]. 16p [OTP

Gillis, James Donald, 1870–
MODERN ENGLISH. A Canadian Grammar. "Leave the Old to the Old." Halifax, Allen, 1913. 65p [NSHD OTU QMBM

Gould, Benjamin Apthorp, 1870–1937
THE GREATER TRAGEDY, AND OTHER THINGS. Toronto, Dent, 1916. 189p [BM
LC NSHD OLU
WAR THOUGHTS OF AN OPTIMIST. Toronto, Dent, 1915. 200p [BM LC OLU

Graham, Emma (Jeffers), –1922
ETCHINGS FROM A PARSONAGE VERANDA. ... Toronto, Briggs, 1895. 187p
[BVaU NSHD OTU

Graham, James E., 1904–
THE TIME OF YOUR LIFE. Toronto, George Weston Ltd., 1951. 47p

Graham, William Creighton, 1887–1955
EDUCATION AND THE NEW AGE. A Series of Addresses Delivered at United College,
Winnipeg. ... Toronto, Ryerson, 1947. 81p [BVaU LC NBFU OTU

Grenfell, Wilfred Thomason, 1865–1940
THE ATTRACTIVE WAY. Boston, Pilgrim, 1913. 59p [LC
YOURSELF AND YOUR BODY. New York, Scribner, 1924. 324p [BM LC NBFU

Grove, Frederick Philip, 1879–1948
IT NEEDS TO BE SAID. Toronto, Macmillan, 1929. 163p [BVaU NSHD OKQ
OVER PRAIRIE TRAILS. Toronto, McClelland, 1922. 231p [Also, with intro. by
Malcolm Ross. Toronto, McClelland, 1957. xiv + 146p] [BM BVaU LC
NSHD OKQ
THE TURN OF THE YEAR. Toronto, McClelland, 1923. 237p [BM BVaU LC
NSHD OTU

Hague, John, 1829–1906
CANADA FOR CANADIANS. A Royalist "Roland" for the Annexationist "Oliver."
... A Paper read before the Toronto Branch of the Imperial Federation League ...
23rd January, 1889. Toronto, Hart, 1889. 40p [NSWA OTP

Haig-Brown, Roderick Langmere, 1908–
FISHERMAN'S SPRING. Toronto, Collins, 1951. 222p
FISHERMAN'S SUMMER. Toronto, Collins, 1959. 253p
MEASURE OF THE YEAR. Toronto, Collins, 1950. 279p [Also: New York,
Morrow, 1950. 260p] [BVaU LC NBFU OTMC QMM
POOL AND RAPID. The Story of a River. Toronto, McClelland, 1932. 239p [Also:
London, Cape, 1936.] [BM BVaU LC NBFU OTU
RETURN TO THE RIVER. A Story of the Chinook Run. New York, Morrow, 1941.
259p [BM BVaU LC NBFU OTU QMM
A RIVER NEVER SLEEPS. New York, Morrow, 1946. 352p [BM BVaU LC
NBFU OTUV QMM

SILVER. The Life of an Atlantic Salmon. London, Black, 1931. 96p [BM BVaU
LC OTUV

SPRING CONGREGATION ADDRESS 1952: Power and People. Vancouver, U. of
British Columbia, 1952. 5p

THE WESTERN ANGLER. An Account of Pacific Salmon and Western Trout in
British Columbia. 2nd ed. New York, Morrow, 1947. 356p [First pub. in
limited ed.: New York, Derrydale Press, 1939. 2v] [BVaU LC NBFU OTP

Haliburton, Thomas Chandler, 1796–1865

AN ADDRESS ON THE PRESENT CONDITION, RESOURCES AND PROSPECTS OF
BRITISH NORTH AMERICA. ... London, Hurst & Blackett, 1857. 44p [Also:
Montreal, Lovell, 1857. 17p] [BM LC NSWA OKQ

THE ENGLISH IN AMERICA. By the Author of "Sam Slick, the Clockmaker". ...
London, Colburn, 1851. 2v [Subsequently re-titled RULE AND MISRULE OF
THE ENGLISH IN AMERICA: The English in America. London, Colburn, 1851. 2v]
[BM BVaU LC NSWA OKQ

A REPLY TO THE REPORT OF THE EARL OF DURHAM. By a Colonist [pseud].
London, Bentley, 1839. 91p [BM OTP

RULE AND MISRULE OF THE ENGLISH IN AMERICA. ... [See under THE ENGLISH
IN AMERICA.]

Halliburton, Brenton, 1775–1860

OBSERVATIONS ON THE IMPORTANCE OF THE NORTH AMERICAN COLONIES TO
GREAT BRITAIN. By an Old Inhabitant of British America [pseud].
Halifax, Royal Gazette, 1825. 34p [Also: London, Murray, 1831. 49p]
[BM BVaU LC NSWA OTU

Hambleton, John O. ("Jack"), 1901–1961

FISHERMAN'S PARADISE. Toronto, Longmans, 1946. 172p [BVa OTP

Hamilton, James H.

LOVE OF LEARNING. The Annual Lecture of the Mutual Improvement Union,
delivered at Hantsport, N.S., Sept. 27, 1866. ... Wolfville, Theakston, 1866.
32p [NSHD

Hansson, Gertrude Edith, 1917–

WE ARE BLIND. Winnipeg, Columbia Press, 1953. 63p

Harper, John Murdoch, 1845–1919

DOMINUS DOMI; or, The Chateau St. Louis. Quebec, Chien d'Or, 1898. 23p
[OTP

Harris, Lawren Stewart, 1885–1970

ABSTRACT PAINTING, A DISQUISITION. Toronto, Rous & Mann, 1954. 16p

Harris, Walter Eric, 1889–

ACHATES; or, The Future of Canada. Toronto, Musson, 1929. 93p [BVaU OTU
STAND TO YOUR WORK. Toronto, Musson, 1927. 269p [BVaU NSWA OTP

Harvey, Rev. Moses, 1820?–1901
WHERE ARE WE AND WHITHER TENDING? Three Lectures on the Reality and Worth of Human Progress. Boston, Doyle & Whittle, 1886. 134p [BM LC NSWA QMM

Harvey, William Earl, 1898–
THE PSYCHOLOGY OF COMPOSITION. St. Paul, Minn., Review Pub., 1927. 78p [LC

Hatheway, Warren Franklin, 1850–1923
CANADIAN NATIONALITY. The Cry of Labor, and Other Essays. Toronto, Briggs, 1906. 230p [BM BVaU LC NBFU OTP

Haultain, Theodore Arnold, 1857–1941
A CHRISTMAS CHAT. A Fragmentary Dialogue on Love and Religion. Toronto, Ellis, Moore & Bangs, 1887. 23p [OTP
HINTS FOR LOVERS. Boston, Houghton, 1909. 308p [BM LC NBFU OTU
THE MYSTERY OF GOLF. A Brief Account of Games in General, their Origine, Antiquity, and Rampancie, and of the Game ycleped Golfe in Particular &c &c. Boston, Houghton, 1908. 152p [BM NBFU OTU
OF WALKS AND WALKING TOURS. An Attempt to Find a Philosophy and a Creed. London, Werner Laurie, 1914. 230p [BM NSHD OTU QMM
TWO COUNTRY WALKS IN CANADA. Toronto, Morang, 1903. 93p [BM BVaU LC NSHD OTP

Hawkes, Arthur, 1871–1933
THE BIRTHRIGHT. A Search for the Canadian Canadian and the Larger Loyalty. Toronto, Dent, 1919. 380p [BM BVaU LC NSHD OLU

Hayes, E.H.
CANADIANS AS WE SEE 'EM. Cartoons, Penportraits, Caricatures. [Montreal? 1900?] [unpaged] [BVaU OKQ

Henderson, Dorothy (McLaughlin), 1900–
I LIVE AND MOVE. A Series of Sketches with Related Readings. New York, Philosophical Library, 1953. 104p

Hensley, Sophia Margaret (Almon), 1866–
LOVE AND THE WOMAN OF TOMORROW. By Almon Hensley [pseud]. London, Drane's, 1913. 216p [BM
WOMAN AND THE RACE. By Gordon Hart [pseud]. New York, Ariel, 1908. 280p [AmCat MOR'12

Herridge, Rev. William Thomas, 1857–1929
THE CALL OF THE WAR. Ottawa, Author, 1915. 12p [BM OTU

Heywood, Edward Percival, 1885–
WONDERS OF THE WORLD. Ilfracombe, Devon, Stockwell, 1959. 186p

Hill, Rev. Allan Massie, 1876–1943
SWEEPINGS FRAE THE CURLING RINK. Yarmouth, N.S., 1910. 162p [T&C

Hill, Philip Carteret, 1821–1894
UNITED STATES AND BRITISH PROVINCES. Contrasted from Personal Observation. ...
Halifax, Barnes, 1859. 30p [NSHD

Hill, Mrs. Vivian Wood, 1900–
CROSS ROADS PANORAMA. Toledo, Ont., Author, 1940. 55p [OTU
HOMEWARD JOURNEY. N.p., Author, [1945?]. 50p [OTU

Hill-Tout, Charles, 1858–1944
MAN AND HIS ANCESTORS, IN THE LIGHT OF ORGANIC EVOLUTION. Vancouver,
Cowan Brookhouse, 1925. 157p [BVaU OOA

Hodgins, John George, 1821–1912
AN HOSPITAL SUNDAY FOR TORONTO. A Paper. ... Toronto, Mail, 1887. 15p
[NSWA

Hodgins, Samuel Raymond Norris, 1895–
SOME CANADIAN ESSAYS. Ed. by ——. Toronto, Nelson, 1932. 239p [BM
BVaU NSHD OTU QMM

Holmes, Francis Joseph Sloan, 1908–
DUCKS ARE DIFFERENT. Caricatures and Candid Stories of your Favorite Water-
fowl. Winnipeg, Author, 1949. 38p [MWP

Hossack, Donald Calvin, 1862–1937
ILLUSTRIOUS MEN. Addresses. Toronto, Rose, 1903. 110p [BM OTP

Howe, Joseph, 1804–1873
ADDRESS DELIVERED ... at the Howe Festival, Framingham, Massachusetts,
August 31, 1871. Boston, Rockwell & Churchill, 1871. 21p [NSHD QMSS
ADDRESS DELIVERED BEFORE THE HALIFAX MECHANICS' INSTITUTE, ON THE 5th
OF NOV., 1834. Halifax, 1834. 23p [NSHD
ADDRESS DELIVERED ... before the Young Men's Christian Assoc., Ottawa,
Feb. 27, 1872. Ottawa, Taylor, 1872. [NSHD
CONFEDERATION CONSIDERED IN RELATION TO THE INTERESTS OF THE EMPIRE.
London, Stanford, 1866. 37p [BM BVaU NSWA OTP
SHAKESPEARE. Oration Delivered at the Request of the St. George's Society,
Halifax, Nova Scotia, 23rd April, 1864. Halifax, "Citizen," 1864. 25p [BM
NSHD OLU QMM
THE SPEECHES AND PUBLIC LETTERS OF THE HON. JOSEPH HOWE. Ed. by William
Annand. Boston, Jewett; Halifax, Mackinlay; Montreal, Dawson; London,
Sampson Low, 1858. 2v [Revised and augmented edition ed. by Joseph Andrew
Chisholm: Halifax, Chronicle Pub. Co., 1909. 2v] [BM BVaU LC NSHD OKQ
QMM

TRIAL FOR LIBEL, ON THE MAGISTRATES OF HALIFAX ... before the Chief
Justice and a Special Jury. ... Halifax, 1835. 102p   [NSHP

Howes, Ernest Albert, 1872–1940
WITH A GLANCE BACKWARD. Toronto, Oxford U. Press, 1939. 196p   [BVaU
NSHD OTP

Howley, Rev. Michael Francis, 1843–1914
CABOT'S VOYAGES. A Lecture. ... St. John's, Devine & O'Mara, 1897. 39p   [BM
LC NSHD QMSS

Hunt, Rev. John
REVERIES, REVIEWS, RECOLLECTIONS. Toronto, Briggs, 1887. 155p   [BVaU
NSWA OTP

Huntington, Lucius Seth, 1827–1886
INDEPENDENCE OF CANADA. ... Montreal, Herald Steam Press, 1869. 14p
[NSHD

Hutton, Maurice, 1856–1940
ALL THE RIVERS RUN INTO THE SEA. Toronto, Musson, 1928. 288p   [BM BVaU
LC NSHD OTU QMM
MANY MINDS. London, Hodder, 1927. 300p   [BM LC NSHD OKQ QMM
THE SISTERS, JEST AND EARNEST. London, Hodder, 1930. 288p   [Earlier ed.:
Toronto, Musson, 192–?]   [BM BVaU OLU QMM

Iles, George, 1852–1942
THE APPRAISAL OF LITERATURE. Speech at International Library Conference,
London, July 13–16, 1897. New York, 1897. 16p   [NSHPL OTU
BOOKS IN THE BALANCE. [Lecture delivered June 21st, 1922 to McGill Summer
Library School.] Montreal, 1922. 10p   [OTU QMM

Imrie, John, 1846–1902
THE SCOT AT HOME AND ABROAD. Toronto, Imrie & Graham, 1898. 29p   [BM
QMSS

Innis, Harold Adams, 1894–1952
A PLEA FOR TIME. Fredericton, U. of New Brunswick, 1950. 21p   [OONL

Jack, Annie L. (Hayr), 1839–1912
THE CANADIAN GARDEN. A Pocket Help for the Amateur. Toronto, Musson, 1910.
120p   [BM NSHD OTU QMG

Jephson, Harriet Julia (Campbell), 1854–1930
A CANADIAN SCRAP-BOOK. A Volume of Essays and Stories. London, Marshall
Russell, 1897. 183p   [BM OTP

Johnson, Charles Nelson, 1860–
THE HAND CLASP. Chicago, 1919. 76p [LC

Johnson, Rev. John H., 1826–
INAUGURAL ADDRESS AS PRINCIPAL OF THE BELLEVILLE SEMINARY. Hamilton,
1857. [BibC
MAN, THE ARCHITECT OF HIS OWN FORTUNE. A Lecture. Montreal, Wilson, 1862.
24p [QMSS

Johnson, Walter Seely, 1880–
ESSAYS OF NOON AND SHADOW. Montreal, Burton's Ltd., 1934. 158p [BVaU
OTU QMM

Johnston, Blanche J. (Read), 1866–
... OUR NEW CITIZENSHIP. 2nd ed. Toronto, McClelland, 1919. 64p [First ed.,
1917.] [BM OKQ

Johnston, John George, 1895–
OF THIS AND THAT. By J.G. Johnston, J.L. Charlesworth, and R.G. Everson.
Toronto, Authors, 1940. 64p [CC

Jones, Rev. Peter, Chippewa Chief (Kah-Ke-Wa-Quon-A-By), 1802–1856
THE SERMON AND SPEECHES OF THE REV. PETER JONES ... 1831. Leeds, Spink,
n.d. 24p [OTP

Jordan, Rev. William George, 1852–1939
ENGLAND REVISITED. ... Toronto, Ryerson, 1926. 71p [OTUV

Keate, Stuart, 1913–
PRESS AND PUBLIC. The Annual Canadian Club Lecture Delivered at the University
of British Columbia, December 10, 1955. Vancouver, U. of British Columbia,
1956. 18p

Keefer, Thomas Coltrin, 1821–1915
THE CANALS OF CANADA. Their Prospects and Influence. [A Prize Essay.]
Toronto, Armour, 1850. 111p [BM BVaU LC NSWA OTU QMM
"MONTREAL" AND "THE OTTAWA": Two Lectures. ... Montreal, Lovell, 1854.
73p [BM BVaU NSHP OLU QMM

Kennedy, Howard Angus, 1861–1938
ROBERT BURNS IN THE TWENTIETH CENTURY. New York, Caledonian Pub.,
1923. 23p [OTU

Kennedy, Roderick Stuart, 1889–1953
LAUGHTONES. Being a Series of Humorous and Inaccurate Biographical Sketches of
certain leading Canadian Advertising Managers as they appeared to an Observer

with insufficient Opportunity to become acquainted with his Subjects and of too
mean an Intellect to do them Justice, the whole embellished with twenty-six
portraits. ... [Anon]   Montreal, Family Herald, 1937. 63p [OTP

Kerr, Estelle Muriel, 1879–1971
THE TOWN CRIER OF GEVREY. New York, Macmillan, 1930. 129p [LC OTU

King, Amabel (Reeves), 1899–
RELICS OF A V.A.D. Toronto, Leslie Press, 1935. 21p [OTU

King, Reginald Harold
CLASSICAL MYTHOLOGY IN SONG AND STORY. Pts. I and II by Reginald Harold
   King and Neil Kenneth McKecknie. Toronto, Copp Clark, 1937, 1939. 2v [CC

King, William Lyon Mackenzie, 1874–1950
THE MESSAGE OF THE CARILLON, AND OTHER ADDRESSES. Toronto, Macmillan,
   1927. 274p [BM BVaU LC NSHD OTP
THE STRUGGLE FOR ENDURING PEACE. An Address Given at the Canadian Corps
   Reunion, Toronto, July 30th, 1938. Ottawa, King's Printer, 1938. [OTU

Kiriline, Louise (Flach) de, 1894–
THE LOGHOUSE NEST. Toronto, Saunders, 1945. 173p [BVaU OKQ

Kirkconnell, Watson, 1895–
TWILIGHT OF LIBERTY. London, Oxford U. Press, 1941. 193p [BM BVaU
   NSHD OTU

Kirkwood, Kenneth Porter, 1899–
EXCURSIONS AMONG BOOKS. Buenos Aires, Mitchell's Bookstore, 1945. 431p
   [BM LC OKQ

Kirkwood, Mossie May (Waddington), 1890–
FOR COLLEGE WOMEN ... AND MEN. Toronto, Oxford U. Press, 1938. 81p
   [BVaU OLU QMM

Knight, John Thomas Philip, 1851–1914
INCIDENTALLY. Being Some Account of Incidents in the Life of a Mere Man.
   J.K. Montreal, Westmount News, 1913. 152p [BVaU NSHD OKQ

Knox, Ellen Mary, 1858–1924
THE GIRL OF THE NEW DAY. Toronto, McClelland, 1919. 241p [BM BVaU
   NSHD OTU

Kristjansson, Adalsteinn
IN THE STARLIGHT. ... Winnipeg, Columbia Press, 1931. 255p [BM BVaU OTP
SUPERSTITION IN THE TWILIGHT. Winnipeg, Columbia Press, 1929. 47p [LC

Lamb, William Kaye, 1904–

A PLEA FOR QUALITY AND INEQUALITY. Vancouver, U. of British Columbia, 1957.
16p

Lambert, Richard Stanton, 1894–

HOME FRONT. Intimate Letters, both Grave and Gay, Telling how Great Britain
Faces the War. ... Collected and ed. by ——. Toronto, Ryerson, 1940. 123p
[LC OTU

Lanceley, Rev. John Ellis, 1848–1900

THE DEVIL OF NAMES, AND OTHER LECTURES AND SERMONS. Ed. by his Brother,
with Intro. by the Rev. Joseph Parker ... and a Biographical Sketch by the Rev.
N. Burwash. Toronto, Briggs, 1900. 284p [BM BVaU LC OKQ

Lande, Lawrence Montague, 1906–

THE LADDER. A Discourse before the St. James Literary Society. Montreal,
Author, 1958. 29p

Langton, John, 1808–1894

THE CENSUS OF 1861. A Paper Read before the Literary and Historical Society of
Quebec. Quebec, Hunter Rose, 1864. 22p [OTP

Laurier, Wilfrid, 1841–1919

LECTURE ON POLITICAL LIBERALISM. ... Quebec, Budget Steam Print., 1877.
44p [BVaU NSHD OTU

WILFRID LAURIER ON THE PLATFORM. Collection of the Principal Speeches made
in Parliament or before the People. Comp. by Ulric Barthe. ... Quebec, Turcotte
& Menard, 1890. 624p [BVaU LC NBFU OKQ

Lawson, Jessie (Kerr), 1838–1917

THE EPISTLES O' HUGH AIRLIE [pseud] . (Formerly o'Scotland, Presently
Conneckit wi' Tam Tamson's Warehoose in Toronto). Illus. by J.W. Bengough.
Toronto, Grip Print., 1888. 103p [BM NSHD OTP

Leacock, Stephen Butler, 1869–1944

ALL RIGHT, MR. ROOSEVELT (Canada and the United States). Toronto, Oxford U.
Press, 1939. 40p [BM OTU QMM

ESSAYS AND LITERARY STUDIES. London, Lane, 1916. 310p [BM BVaU LC
NSHD OKQ

GREATER CANADA. An Appeal. Let Us No Longer Be a Colony. Montreal,
Montreal News, 1907. 10p [BM NSWA OTU QMM

HOW TO WRITE. New York, Dodd Mead, 1943. 261p [BM BVaU NSHD OTU
QMM

LINCOLN FREES THE SLAVES. New York, Putnam, 1934. 178p [BM BVaU LC
NBFU OTU QMM

MY DISCOVERY OF ENGLAND. London, Lane, 1922. 219p [BM BVaU NSHD
OKQ QMM

MY DISCOVERY OF THE WEST. A Discussion of East and West in Canada. Toronto, Allen, 1937. 272p [BM BVaU LC NBFU OTU QMM

"MY OLD COLLEGE" 1843–1943. [Montreal], Author, 1943. 16p [QMM

OUR HERITAGE OF LIBERTY. Its Origin, Its Achievement, Its Crisis. A Book for War Time. New York, Dodd Mead, 1942. 86p [BM BVaU OTU QMM

THE PROPER LIMITATIONS OF STATE INTERFERENCE. Toronto, 1924. 14p [QMM

THE PURSUIT OF KNOWLEDGE. A Discussion of Freedom and Compulsion in Education. New York, Liveright, 1934. 48p [BVaU LC NBFU OTU

STEPHEN LEACOCK'S PLAN TO RELIEVE THE DEPRESSION IN 6 DAYS, TO REMOVE IT IN 6 MONTHS, TO ERADICATE IT IN 6 YEARS. Toronto, Macmillan, 1933. 18p [BVaU NBFU OTU QMM

TOO MUCH COLLEGE; or, Education Eating Up Life. With Kindred Essays in Education and Humour. New York, Dodd Mead, 1939. 255p [BM BVaU LC NSHD OKQ QMM

LeClaire, Gordon, 1905–

MORE LIFE IN LIVING. Through the Seven Miracles of Mind. N.p., Author, [1947]. 61p [BVaU

LeMoine, James MacPherson, 1825–1912

THE EXPLORATION OF JONATHAN OLDBUCK, F.R.S.Q., IN EASTERN LATITUDES. Canadian History–Legends. ... Quebec, Demers, 1889. 265p [BM BVaU LC NSHD OTU

MAPLE LEAVES. A Budget of Legendary, Historical, Critical and Sporting Intelligence. Seven Series. Quebec, Hunter Rose, 1863–1906. 7v [BM BVaU NSHD OTU QMM

THE SCOT IN NEW FRANCE. An Ethnological Study. Inaugural Address ... Literary Society of Quebec, 29th November, 1880. Montreal, Dawson Bros., 1881. 83p [BVaU NSWA OTP

Lett, William Pittman, 1819–1892

THE ANTLERED KINGS. A Lecture. Ottawa, 1884. [OOP

Lighthall, William Douw, 1857–1954

AN ACCOUNT OF THE BATTLE OF CHATEAUGUAY. Being a Lecture. Montreal, Drysdale, 1889. 32p [BM BVaU LC NSWA OTU

GOVERNANCE OF EMPIRE. ... Montreal, Author, 1910. 15p [BM NSHD OTU

Lloyd, Cecil Richard Francis, 1884–1938

MALVERN ESSAYS. Toronto, Ryerson, 1930. 51p [BVaU NBFU OTP

SUNLIGHT AND SHADOW. Toronto, Hunter Rose, 1928. 83p [BM OTP QMM

Llwyd, Rev. John Plummer Derwent, 1861–1933

THE MESSAGE OF AN INDIAN RELIC. Seattle, Lowman & Hanford, 1909. 21p [BViPA

MYSTICISM AND OTHER ESSAYS. Toronto, Macmillan, 1926. 108p [BVa NSHD OTP

Locke, Clark, 1890–
COUNTRY HOURS. Toronto, Ryerson, 1959. 105p

Locke, George Herbert, 1870–1937
BUILDERS OF THE CANADIAN COMMONWEALTH. Toronto, Ryerson, 1923. 317p [A selection of speeches by Canadian statesmen.] [BM BVaU LC NBFU OTP QMM

Lodge, Rupert Clendon, 1886–
MANITOBA ESSAYS. Ed. by ——. Toronto, Macmillan, 1937. 432p [BM BVaU NBFU OTU

Logan, John Daniel, 1869–1929
THE INN AT THE END OF THE WORLD. ... Halifax, Allen, 1923. 27p [BVaU OOP

Long, John Henry
SLIPS OF TONGUE AND PEN. Toronto, Copp Clark, 1886. 101p [OTU QMM

Loudon, William James, 1860–1951
STUDIES OF STUDENT LIFE. Toronto, Macmillan, 1923–37. 8v [BM BVaU NBFU OTU QMM

Lovegrove, F. Francis
RUMINATIONS. Toronto, Ryerson, 1923. 63p [BM BVaU LC OKQ

Low, Rev. George Jacobs, 1836–1906
A PARSON'S PONDERINGS. Toronto, Briggs, 1906. 184p [BM NSHD OTP

McAleer, George, 1845–
GATHERED WAIFLETS. Worcester, Mass., Author, 1913. 505p [LC

McAree, John Verner, 1876–1958
THE FOURTH COLUMN. Toronto, Macmillan, 1934. 332p [BVaU NBFU OTP

McArthur, Peter, 1866–1924
THE AFFABLE STRANGER. Toronto, Allen, 1920. 216p [BVaU LC NBFU OKQ
AROUND HOME. ... Toronto, Musson, 1925. 250p [BVaU LC NSHD OKQ QMSS
A CHANT OF MAMMONISM. Waterloo, Ont., Ont. Equitable Life, [1922]. 6p [NBFU OTU
FAMILIAR FIELDS. London, Dent, [1925?]. 157p [BM BVaU NSHD OTP
FRIENDLY ACRES. Toronto, Musson, 1927. 239p [BVaU NSHD OTP QMM
IN PASTURES GREEN. Toronto, Dent, 1915. 363p [Also: Toronto, Dent, 1948. 298p] [BM BVaU LC NSHD OTP

THE LAST LAW–BROTHERHOOD. Toronto, Allen, 1921. 57p [BM BVaU NSHD OKQ

THE RED COW AND HER FRIENDS. Toronto, Dent, 1919. 287p [BVaU LC NSHD OTU

TO BE TAKEN WITH SALT. Being an Essay in Teaching one's Grandmother to Suck Eggs. London, Limpus Baker, 1903. 196p [BM BVaU OTP

MacCallum, Duncan Campbell

ADDRESSES. Montreal, Desbarats, 1901. 168p [BVaU OOP QMSS

McCarroll, James, 1815–1896

LETTERS OF TERRY FINNEGAN [pseud], to the Hon. Thomas d'Arcy McGee. Volume 1. Complete in Itself. Toronto, 1863. 104p [OTP

McCarthy, Eugene

A TALE OF LAKE ST. JOHN. Comprising a Bit of History, a Quantity of Facts, and a Plentitude of Fish Stories. Montreal, Desbarats, [1903?]. 65p [BVaU OOP QMBM

McCawley, Stuart

STANDING THE GAFF. The Cape Breton Mines and Miners. N.p., n.d. 30p [NSHP

McClung, Nellie Letitia (Mooney), 1873–1951

IN TIMES LIKE THESE. Addresses. New York, Appleton, 1915. 217p [BM BVaU LC NBFU OTU

THE NEXT OF KIN. Stories of Those Who Wait and Wonder. Boston, Houghton, 1917. 256p [BVaU LC NBFU OTU

McCord, Frederick Augustus, 1856–1908

ERRORS IN CANADIAN HISTORY CULLED FROM "PRIZE ANSWERS." Montreal, Dawson, 1880. 45p [BVaU NSWA OTP QMM

McCowan, Daniel, 1882–1956

ANIMALS OF THE CANADIAN ROCKIES. Toronto, Macmillan, 1936. 302p [BM BVaU LC OTP QMM

A NATURALIST IN CANADA. Toronto, Macmillan, 1941. 284p [BM BVaU LC NBFU OTP QMSS

OUTDOORS WITH A CAMERA IN CANADA. Toronto, Macmillan, 1945. 102p [BM BVaU LC OTP QMBM

TIDEWATER TO TIMBERLINE. Toronto, Macmillan, 1951. x + 205p

McCulloch, Rev. Thomas, 1776–1843

THE NATURE AND USES OF A LIBERAL EDUCATION ILLUSTRATED. Being a Lecture Delivered at the Opening of the Pictou Academical Institution. Halifax, Holland, 1819. 24p [NSWA

McCurdy, John Alexander Douglas, 1886–
"NOVA SCOTIA" AND THE MEN WHO LIVED ON HER SOIL. New York, Montreal,
  Newcomen Society in North America, 1953. 28p

Macdonald, Angus Lewis, 1890–1954
SPEECHES. With a Biographical Note by A.T. Crerar. Toronto, Longmans, 1960.
  xxvii + 227p

Macdonald, Rev. James Alexander, 1862–1923
MEMORIES OF HALLOWE'EN. At the Annual Banquet of the Caledonian Society
  of Toronto on Hallowe'en, 1906. Toronto, 1906. 15p [OTP
THE NORTH AMERICAN IDEA. New York, Revell, 1917. 240p [BVaU LC NSWA
  OTP

Macdonald, John Alexander, 1815–1891
ADDRESS TO THE ELECTORS OF THE CITY OF KINGSTON. N.p., 1861. 153p
  [NSHD OTU

McDonnell, William, 1814–1900
OUR STRANGE GUEST. Lindsay, Wilson & Wilson, [1876?]. 14p [OTP

MacDougall, James Brown, 1871–1950
THE REAL MOTHER GOOSE. The Reality Behind the Rhyme. Toronto, Ryerson,
  1940. 57p [BVaU LC OTU QMM

McDougall, Robert Lorne, 1918–
OUR LIVING TRADITION. Second and third series. Ed. by ——. Toronto, pub. in
  association with Carleton University by U. of Toronto Press, 1959. xvi + 288p

McEvoy, Bernard, 1842–1932
WHICH WAY, CANADA? By Diogenes, B.A. [pseud]. N.p., n.d. 15p [QMSS

McGee, Thomas D'Arcy, 1825–1868
1825–D'ARCY McGEE–1925. A Collection of Speeches and Addresses. Selected ... by
  the Hon. Charles Murphy. Toronto, Macmillan, 1937. 366p [BM BVaU LC
  NBFU OTP QMM
THE POLITICAL CAUSES AND CONSEQUENCES OF THE PROTESTANT
  "REFORMATION." A Lecture. New York, Sadlier & Co., 1853. 27p [BM LC
  NSWA OTU

McGillen, Pete
OUTDOORS WITH PETE McGILLEN. Toronto, Ryerson, 1955. xii + 177p

McGillicuddy, Paul Clark, 1918–1942
BETWEEN LECTURES. Some Tips to Canadian Undergraduates–and their Enemies–
  and Friends. Toronto, Age Publications, 1939. 63p [NBFU OTP QMM

MacGregor, Rev. James, 1759—1830
A FEW REMAINS OF THE REV. JAMES MacGREGOR. Ed. by his grandson, the Rev. George Patterson. Philadelphia, Wilson, 1859. 274p [BM BVaU NSWA OTP

McGuire, James Leonard
OAT-CAKES AND SULPHUR. Brockville, Recorder Print., 1927. 81p [BVaU OTP QMSS

Machar, Agnes Maule, 1837—1927
YOUNG SOLDIER HEARTS OF FRANCE. Toronto, Musson, 1919. 300p [OTU

MacInnes, Thomas Robert Edward, 1867—1951
THE TEACHING OF THE OLD BOY. London, Dent, 1927. 227p [BM BVaU NBFU OLU

MacKay, Isabel Ecclestone (Macpherson), 1875—1928
THE TIMELESS TRAVELLERS. Toronto, Best, n.d. 16p [BVaU

Mackenzie, Alexander, 1822—1892
POLITICAL POINTS AND PENCILLINGS. Being Selections from Various Addresses Delivered by the Hon. Alex. Mackenzie. Toronto, "Grip" Office, 1878. 36p [NSHD OTP
SPEECHES DURING HIS RECENT VISIT TO SCOTLAND. With his Principal Speeches in Canada since the Session of 1875. With Sketch of his Life. Toronto, Campbell, 1876. 219p [BM BVaU NBFU OTP QMM

MacKenzie, Norman Archibald MacRae, 1894—
ADDRESS AT SPECIAL CONVOCATION OF MOUNT ALLISON UNIVERSITY, JAN. 31, 1941. Sackville, Mount Allison U., 1941. [OTU

Mackenzie, William Lyon, 1795—1861
SELECTED WRITINGS, 1824—1837. Ed. by Margaret Fairley. Toronto, Oxford U. Press, 1960. 383p

MacKinnon, John [of P.E.I.]
A SKETCH BOOK COMPRISING HISTORICAL INCIDENTS, TRADITIONAL TALES AND TRANSLATIONS. Saint John, Barnes, 1915. 213p [BM OTU

McLaren, John W.
LET'S ALL HATE TORONTO. Narration, Illustration & Exhortation. By Jack McLaren. Toronto, Kingswood House, 1956. xi + 66p

Maclean, Rev. John, 1851—1928
LONE LAND LIGHTS. First series. Toronto, Briggs, 1882. 75p [BVaU LC OTP SSU

MacLennan, Hugh, 1907—
CANADIAN UNITY AND QUEBEC. By Emile Vaillancourt, J.P. Humphrey, and Hugh MacLennan. Montreal, 1942. 16p [OTU QMM

CROSS COUNTRY. Toronto, Collins, 1949. 172p [BVaU NBFU OLU QMBM
THE FUTURE OF THE NOVEL AS AN ART FORM. Toronto, U. of Toronto Press,
[1959?]. 11p
THE PRESENT WORLD AS SEEN IN ITS LITERATURE. Fredericton, U. of New
Brunswick, 1952. 12p
SCOTCHMAN'S RETURN AND OTHER ESSAYS. Toronto, Macmillan, 1960. 279p
THIRTY & THREE. Ed. by Dorothy Duncan. Toronto, Macmillan, 1954. xi + 261p

McLennan, William, 1856–1904
LITERARY PAMPHLETS, CANADA. [No title page.] 19v in 1. [QMM

MacLeod, Margaret Marie (Furness)
"FOUR SCRIPTS." Trans-Canada-Matinée. Inspired by Childhood Memories in Prince
Edward Island. Montreal, Author, 1956. 19p [mimeographed]

McLeod, Robert Randall, 1839–1909
FURTHER STUDIES IN NATURE. Halifax, Commercial Print., 1910. 120p [NSHD
IN THE ACADIAN LAND. Nature Studies. Boston, Whidden, 1899. 166p [BM
BVaU LC OKQ NSHD

McLuhan, Herbert Marshall, 1911–
COUNTERBLAST 1954. Toronto, priv. print., [1954?]. 17p

MacMechan, Archibald McKellar, 1862–1933
THE BOOK OF ULTIMA THULE. Toronto, McClelland, 1927. 368p [BM BVaU
NSHD OKQ
THE LIFE OF A LITTLE COLLEGE, AND OTHER PAPERS. Boston, Houghton, 1914.
308p [BVaU LC NSHD OTU
THE LOG OF A HALIFAX PRIVATEER. Nova Scotia Chapbook No. 6. Halifax,
Marshall, 1921. [BVaU NBFU OTU
THE MEMORIAL TOWER. Nova Scotia Chapbook. Halifax, Marshall, 1922. 12p
[BVaU OTP
NOVA SCOTIA CHAP-BOOKS. Halifax, Marshall, 1919–192–?. 16v: 1, Three Sea
Songs. 2, The Nova Scotia-ness of Nova Scotia. 3, Storied Halifax. 4, The
Memorial Tower. 5, The Orchards of Ultima Thule. 6, The Log of a Halifax
Privateer. 7, Glamming; the Neredi's Embrace; the Two Games. 8, The Loss of
the Atalante. 9, "Nova Scarcity"; The Literature of Nova Scotia. 10, The
Pleasance; From Minas to the Wotan Line. 11, The Sky-Line; Old King's. 12,
Spring in Ultima Thule; The Potato Patch. 13, The Luck of the Grilse. 14, Twelve
Profitable Sonnets. 15, Twelve Unprofitable Sonnets. 16, Afoot in Ultima Thule.
[Files at the libraries are incomplete.] [BVaU NBFU NSHD OTP
THE NOVA SCOTIA-NESS OF NOVA SCOTIA. Nova Scotia Chap-Book No. 2.
Halifax, Allen, 1924. 12p [The numbering is irrelevant to order of publication,
since "four other" chapbooks have preceded this one.] [BVaU OTU
THE ORCHARDS OF ULTIMA THULE. Nova Scotia Chapbook. Halifax, Marshall,
1919. 13p [BVaU NBFU OKQ

THE PORTER OF BAGDAD, and other Fantasies. Toronto, Morang, 1901. 150p
   [BM NBFU NSHD OTU

MacMillan, Ernest Campbell, 1893–

SOME PROBLEMS OF THE CANADIAN COMPOSER. Charlottetown, Prince of
   Wales College, 1956. 14p

Macnaughton, John, 1858–1943

ESSAYS AND ADDRESSES. Selected by D.D. Calvin. Kingston, Queen's U., 1946.
   319p [BVaU LC NSHD OTP QMM

Macphail, Andrew, 1864–1938

ESSAYS IN FALLACY. New York, Longmans, 1910. 359p [BM BVaU LC
   NSHD OTU QMM

ESSAYS IN POLITICS. London, Longmans, 1909. 301p [BM BVaU LC NBFU
   OLU QMM

ESSAYS IN PURITANISM. Boston, Houghton, 1905. 339p [BM BVaU LC
   NBFU OTU QMBM

MacRae, Archibald Oswald, 1869–

WHAT IS THE MATTER WITH CANADA? Addresses. ... By "Politicus" [pseud].
   London, Stockwell, 1928. 96p [BM BVaU NSHD OTP

MacTavish, Newton McFaul, 1875–1941

THROWN IN. Toronto, Macmillan, 1923. 196p [BM BVaU NBFU OTP

Madison, Grant

RIVER FOR MY SIDEWALK. Toronto, Dent, 1953. 135p

Malone, Richard Sankey, 1909–

BOOKSHELF FREE PRESS. A Selection from the Winnipeg *Free Press.* V. 1,
   1955–56. Ed. by ——. Winnipeg, Winnipeg *Free Press*, 1956. 256p [No
   more published.]

Marsh, Edith Louise, –1960

BIRDS OF PEASEMARSH. Toronto, Musson, 1919. 233p [BM LC OTP
WITH THE BIRDS. Toronto, Dent, 1935. 86p [CC

Marshall, Mortimer Villiers, 1898–

AN APPLE FOR TEACHER. Wolfville, N.S., Bookstore, Acadia U., 1954. 40p

Mason, Louise, –1946

AFTER THE HONEYMOON. Toronto, McClelland, [1913]. 58p [Another ed.:
   Toronto, McClelland, 1922.] [BM CC T&C

Massey, Denton, 1900–

THE STUFF MEN ARE MADE OF. With an intro. by Rev. G. Stanley Russell.
   Toronto, Saunders, 1935. 254p [LC

Massey, Rev. Samuel, 1817–
"HOME SWEET HOME" – A Lecture ... on "Our City Homes, and How to make them Healthy and Sweet." Delivered in St. John's Church, Montreal. Montreal, [18—?]. 8p [OTP

Massey, Vincent, 1887–1967
AN ADDRESS AT HART HOUSE IN THE UNIVERSITY OF TORONTO BEFORE THE ASSOCIATION OF AMERICAN UNIVERSITY PRESSES. ... Toronto, U. of Toronto Press, 1951. 15p
GOOD NEIGHBOURHOOD, AND OTHER ADDRESSES IN THE UNITED STATES. Toronto, Macmillan, 1930. 362p [BM BVaU LC NSHD OTP QMM
THE MAKING OF A NATION. Boston, Houghton, 1928. 44p [BVaU LC NSHD OTP
ON BEING CANADIAN. Toronto, Dent, 1948. 198p [BM BVaU NBFU OTP QMM
ON BOOKS AND READING. The Address ... at the 125th Anniversary Dinner of the United Church Publishing House and the Ryerson Press ... October 19th, 1954. Toronto, Ryerson, 1954. 12p
SPEAKING OF CANADA. Addresses. Toronto, Macmillan, 1959. x + 244p
THE SWORD OF LIONHEART AND OTHER WARTIME SPEECHES. Toronto, Ryerson, 1942. 117p [BM BVaU LC NSHD OTP
UNCERTAIN SOUNDS. Sackville, N.B., Mount Allison University, 1957. 32p [On language.]

Matthews, James Skitt, 1878–
THE DEDICATION OF STANLEY PARK, 1889. [An Address. ...] Vancouver, City Archives, 1952. 16p

Matthews, Robertson, 1879–
HIS LOST CHORD. Glimpses of Man's Deepest Emotion in Restraint. Bolton, Ont., Bolton Enterprise, 1959. 48p

May, Rev. John, 1834–
ESSAYS ON EDUCATIONAL SUBJECTS. Ottawa, Woodburn, 1880. 52p [OTP

Medley, Rev. John, 1804–1892
ELEMENTARY REMARKS ON CHURCH ARCHITECTURE. Exeter, Hannaford, 1841. 40p [OTP

Meighen, Arthur, 1874–1960
"THE GREATEST ENGLISHMAN OF HISTORY" [Shakespeare]. An Address. Toronto, Gundy, 1936. 39p [Also: Fort Erie, Review Co., 1954. 43p] [BVaU NSHD OTU
OVERSEA ADDRESSES, JUNE–JULY, 1921. Toronto, Musson, 1921. 82p [BVaU NBFU OTP QMBM
UNREVISED AND UNREPENTED. Debating Speeches and Others. With a foreword

by M. Grattan O'Leary. Toronto, Clarke Irwin, 1949. 470p [BVaU NBFU OTP QMBM

Millard, Frederick Payne, 1878–
THE HARP OF LIFE. Toronto, McClelland, 1928. 287p [BVaU NBFU
NO OLDER AT NIGHT. Boston, Christopher Pub. House, 1926. 178p [LC QMM
THROUGH THE FOG. Kirksville, Mo., Journal Print., 1927. 262p [LC QMM

Miller, John Ormsby, 1861–1936
THE NEW ERA IN CANADA. Essays Dealing with the Upbuilding of the Canadian
Commonwealth. Ed. by ——. Toronto, Dent, 1917. 421p [BVaU LC
NBFU OLU QMM

Miller, Robert
THE LAW AND THE LOVE OF UNITY EXHIBITED IN THE CREATION. A Lecture.
Halifax, Barnes, 1858. 40p [NSHD
TRUE GREATNESS. A Lecture. ... Halifax, Barnes, 1859. 29p [NSHD QMM

Milliken, Lorene Frances (Ritz)
INTERLUDES. Prose Pieces. Winnipeg, Author, 1957. 62p

Miner, Jack (John Thomas Miner), 1865–1944
JACK MINER ON CURRENT TOPICS. Toronto, Ryerson, 1929. 111p [BVaU
OTP

Mines, Robert Frederick, 1925–
MY MIND WENT ALL TO PIECES. The Funniest Things that Patients have said to
their Psychiatrists. New York, Dial Press, 1958. 93p

Mitchell, John, 1880–
THE KINGDOM OF AMERICA. The Canadian Creed. Brampton, Banner & Times,
1930. 90p [BVaU LC NBFU OTUV

Mitchell, Roy, 1884–1944
THEOSOPHIC STUDY and A WHITE LOTUS DAY ADDRESS. Toronto, Blavatsky
Institute, 1953. 83p

Montgomery, Lucy Maud, 1874–1942
COURAGEOUS WOMEN. By L.M. Montgomery, Marian Keith [pseud], and
Mabel Burns McKinley. Toronto, McClelland, 1934. 203p [BVa LC NBFU
OTU

Montreal, Que. Literary Society
ESSAYS READ IN MONTREAL DURING THE WINTER OF 1880–81. Montreal,
1881. 54p [QMM

Moore, William Henry, 1872–1960
BY THEIR FRUITS. Pickering, Printers' Guild, 1949. 136p [BVaU OTP QMM

THE COMMANDMENTS OF MEN. Toronto, Printers' Guild, 1925. 197p [BM BVaU LC OTP QMSS

GREY DAYS. Pickering, Printers' Guild, 1946. 145p [BVaU OTP

PUBLIC LIFE. Pickering, priv. print., 1936. 64p [OTP QMSS

UNDERNEATH IT ALL. Pickering, Printers' Guild, 1942. 143p [BVa LC OTP QMM

WHEN THE IRON IS HOT. Pickering, Printers' Guild, 1943. 124p [BVaU LC NSHD OTP

Morgan, Henry James, 1842–1913

THE PLACE BRITISH AMERICANS HAVE WON IN HISTORY. Ottawa, Hunter Rose, 1866. 22p [BM LC NSWA OKQ

Morgan, Lorne Thompson, 1897–

THE PERMANENT WAR; or, Homo the Sap. Toronto, Workers' Educational Assoc., 1943. 64p [BVaU OTU

Morgan-Powell, Samuel, 1898–

MEMORIES THAT LIVE. Toronto, Macmillan, 1929. 282p [BM BVaU NBFU OTP QMBM

THIS CANADIAN LITERATURE. Being an Address. ... Toronto, Macmillan, 1940. 14p [LC OTP

Morse, William Inglis, 1874–1952

ECCENTRICS IN PARADISE, AND OTHER ESSAYS. Boston, Sawyer, 1926. 94p [LC

INTERLUDES FOR DUST EATERS (ANCIENT AND MODERN). With a Monologue. By W.I.M. Boston, Sawyer, 1923. 27p [LC

Muir, James, 1892?–1960

THE LAND WE LEFT. An Address to the Illinois Saint Andrew Society ... in ... Chicago ... December 3rd, 1949. Montreal, Royal Bank of Canada, n.d. 52p

SCOTLAND AND SAINT ANDREW. An Address to the North British Society ... in ... Halifax, ... November 30th, 1953. Montreal, Royal Bank of Canada, n.d. 45p

Muldrew, William Hawthorne, 1867–1904

SYLVAN ONTARIO. A Guide to our Native Trees and Shrubs. Toronto, Briggs, 1901. 67p [BM LC NBFU OTP

Murray, E.G.D.

STUDIA VARIA. Royal Society of Canada Literary and Scientific Papers. Ed. by ——. Toronto, Published for the Society by U. of Toronto Press, 1957. 127p

Murray, Mrs. Margaret L.

LITTLE TRAVELS TO WINDY RIDGE AND OTHER PLACES. ... Vancouver, Lillooet Pubs., 1944. 150p [BViPA OTU

Neatby, Hilda Marion Ada, 1904—
THE DEBT OF OUR REASON. Toronto, Clarke Irwin, 1954. 23p
A TEMPERATE DISPUTE. Toronto, Clarke Irwin, 1954. 97p

Newton, Frances (pseud)
LIGHT LIKE THE SUN. By Frances Newton [pseud]. New York, Dodd Mead,
   1937. 25p [On cremation.] [OTU

Nicholson, Byron, 1857—1916
IN OLD QUEBEC, AND OTHER SKETCHES. Quebec, Commercial Print., 1908.
   162p [BVaU LC NSHD OLU QMM

Nicol, Eric Patrick, 1919—
GIRDLE ME A GLOBE. Toronto, Ryerson, 1957. xii + 134p
A HISTORY OF CANADA. [Cover title: An Uninhibited History of Canada.]
   Montreal, D. Hackett, 1959. 1v. [unpaged]
IN DARKEST DOMESTICA. Toronto, Ryerson, 1959. xi + 113p
THE ROVING I. Toronto, Ryerson, 1950. 134p [BVaU NBFU OTP
SENSE AND NONSENSE. Toronto, Ryerson, 1947. 148p [BVaU NBFU
   OTU QMBM
SHALL WE JOIN THE LADIES? Toronto, Ryerson, 1955. xi + 156p
TWICE OVER LIGHTLY. Toronto, Ryerson, 1953. 137p [BVaU NBFU OTUV

Nobile, Achilles Alexander, 1833—
HERE AND THERE THROUGH THE HISTORY OF ITALY. A Lecture. ... Followed
   by MANZONI AND RATTAZZI, An Address. ... Toronto, Williams, 1884.
   37p [Bound with his MISCELLANEOUS POEMS, Translated. ...] [BVaU LC
   OTU QMBM

Norwood, Gilbert, 1880—1954
SPOKEN IN JEST. Toronto, Macmillan, 1938. 209p [BM BVaU LC NBFU
   OTU QMM
THE WOODEN MAN AND OTHER STORIES AND ESSAYS. New York, Macmillan,
   1926. 240p [BM LC OTU

Odlum, Edward, 1850—1935
WHO ARE THE JAPANESE? London, Covenant, [1932?]. 31p [LC

O'Hagan, Thomas, 1855—1939
CANADIAN ESSAYS, CRITICAL AND HISTORICAL. Toronto, Briggs, 1901. 222p
   [BM BVaU LC NBFU OTP
CHATS BY THE FIRESIDE. A Study in Life, Art and Literature. Somerset, Ohio,
   Rosary Press, [Pref. 1911]. 150p [LC OTP
ESSAYS, LITERARY, CRITICAL, AND HISTORICAL. Toronto, Briggs, 1909.
   112p [BM BVaU LC NSHD OTP

ESSAYS ON CATHOLIC LIFE. Baltimore, Murphy, 1916. 166p [LC OKQ

INTIMACIES IN CANADIAN LIFE AND LETTERS. Ottawa, Graphic, 1927. 94p
  [BVaU LC NBFU OTP

SPAIN AND HER DAUGHTERS. Toronto, Hunter Rose, 1931. 123p [BVaU
  LC NSHD OTP

WITH STAFF AND SCRIP. Toronto, Ryerson, 1924. 156p [BVaU NBFU OTP

O'Higgins, Harvey Jerrold, 1876–1929

THE AMERICAN MIND IN ACTION. By Harvey O'Higgins and Edward H. Reede.
  New York, Harper, 1924. 336p [LC

O'Loughlin, A.J., –1884?

MAN, A MATERIAL, MENTAL AND SPIRITUAL BEING. A Lecture Delivered in ...
  Kingston, C.W., Jan. 6th, 1860. Kingston, Creighton, 1860. 66p [OTP

O'Malley, Rev. Andrew, 1863–1921

ESSAYS AND LECTURES. Barrie, Gazette, [1916?]. 189p [BVaU LC OLU

O'Neill, Rev. Arthur Barry, 1858–

CLERICAL COLLOQUIES. Essays. Notre Dame, Ind., University Press, 1916.
  270p [LC OOSU

PRIESTLY PRACTICE. Familiar Essays on Clerical Topics. 2nd ed. Notre Dame,
  Ind., University Press, 1914. 249p [LC OOU

Osler, William, 1849–1919

AEQUANIMITAS. OTHER ESSAYS TO MEDICAL STUDENTS. ... London, Lewis,
  1904. 398p [Various later editions.] [BM BVaU LC NBFU OTU

AN ALABAMA STUDENT, AND OTHER BIOGRAPHICAL ESSAYS. New York,
  Oxford U. Press, 1908. 334p [BM BVaU LC NBFU OTU QMM

COUNSELS AND IDEALS. Selections. ... Oxford, Clarendon Press, 1905. 292p
  [Various other eds.] [BM BVaU LC OTU

THE OLD HUMANITIES AND THE NEW SCIENCE. London, Murray, 1919. 32p
  [Also: Boston, Houghton, 1920.] [BM BVaU LC OTU QMM

SCIENCE AND WAR. An Address. Oxford, Clarendon Press, 1915. 39p [BM
  OTU

SELECTED WRITINGS. 12 July 1849 to 20 December 1919. ... London, Oxford
  U. Press, 1951. 278p [Editor's note, by A.W. Franklin.]

SIR WILLIAM OSLER. Aphorisms from his Bedside Teachings and Writings. ...
  Collected by R.B. Bean; ed. by W.B. Bean. New York, Schuman, 1950.
  159p [LC OTU QMM

THE STUDENT LIFE. The Philosophy of Sir William Osler. Ed. by Richard E.
  Verney. Toronto, Macmillan, 1957. xiii + 214p

THE STUDENT LIFE AND OTHER ESSAYS. With an Intro. by H.H. Bashford.
  London, Constable, 1928. 36 + 145p [BM BVa LC OTU QMM

A WAY OF LIFE. An Address Delivered to Yale Students Sunday Evening,
  April 20, 1913. London, Constable, 1913. 62p [Also: New York, Hoeber,
  1937.] [BM BVaU NBFU OTU QMM

Parker, Gilbert, 1862–1932

THE UNITED STATES AND THIS WAR. A Word in Season. Speech delivered ... to the Pilgrim's Society ... London, on the 15th April, 1915, on the Occasion of the Fiftieth Anniversary of the Death of Abraham Lincoln. London, Darling & Son, 1915. 10p [BM LC OTP

Penfield, Wilder Graves, 1891–

THE LIBERAL ARTS IN CANADA. Charlottetown, Prince of Wales College, 1958. 11p

Peterson, William, 1856–1921

CANADIAN ESSAYS AND ADDRESSES. London, Longmans, 1915. 373p [BM BVaU LC NSHD OTP QMM

Phelps, Arthur Leonard, 1887–1970

CANADIAN WRITERS. Toronto, McClelland, 1951. 119p

COMMUNITY AND CULTURE. The Founders' Day Address at the University of New Brunswick. Fredericton, U. of New Brunswick, 1947. 17p [BVaU NBFU OTP

THIS CANADA. Toronto, CBC Pub. Branch, 1940. 63p [LC NBFU OOA

THESE UNITED STATES. Toronto, CBC Pub. Branch, 1941. 60p [LC OTU

Pierce, Lorne Albert, 1890–1961

THE ARMOURY IN OUR HALLS. Toronto, Ryerson, 1941. 19p [BM BVaU LC NBFU OTP QMM

THE BELOVED COMMUNITY. Toronto, Ryerson, 1924. 72p [Ryerson Impt.

A CANADIAN NATION. Toronto, Ryerson, 1960. 42p

A CANADIAN PEOPLE. Toronto, Ryerson, 1945. 84p [BVaU LC NBFU OTP QMM

THE CANADA BOOK OF PROSE AND VERSE. Ed. by Lorne Pierce and Dora Whitefield (Mrs. Hugh S. Eayrs). Toronto, Ryerson, 1932. 3v [BVaU NBFU OLU

CHRISTIANITY AND CULTURE IN OUR TIME. Toronto, Ryerson, 1947. 12p [BVaU LC NBFU OTP

AN EDITOR'S CREED. Toronto, Ryerson, 1960. 14p

NEW HISTORY FOR OLD. Discussions on Aims and Methods in Writing and Teaching History. Toronto, Ryerson, 1931. 72p [BVaU NBFU OKQ

ON PUBLISHERS AND PUBLISHING. Toronto, Ryerson, 1951. 19p

"PRIME MINISTERS TO THE BOOK." Toronto, Ryerson, 1944. 11p [BM BVaU LC NBFU OTP QMM

Poole, Rev. William Henry, 1820–1896

THE ODD MAN AND HIS ODDITIES. Detroit, Detroit Pub. Co., 1891. 143p [LC OLU

Pyper, Charles B.

ONE THING AFTER ANOTHER. Toronto, Dent, 1948. 262p [BVaU OTP

Pyramus (pseud)
GEIKIE VERSUS ELIOTT; or, The King's Canvas Bag. Halifax, 1852. 8p [NSHP

Quebec Literary and Historical Society
TRANSACTIONS. ... 1829—. [A continuing serial.] [NSHP OTU

Queen's Quarterly, Editors of
HOW CAN UNIVERSITIES BEST BENEFIT THE PROFESSION OF JOURNALISM AS A
MEANS OF MOULDING AND ELEVATING PUBLIC OPINION? A Collection of
Essays. Ed. by the editors of Queen's Quarterly. Kingston, Queen's University,
1903. 300p [BVaU NSHD OKQ

Reid, D. Clifford
HORIZONS OF THOUGHT. Seattle, Lowman & Hanford, 1935. 249p [BVaU LC

Richey, Rev. Matthew, 1803—1883
AN ADDRESS AT THE INAUGURATION OF THE YOUNG MEN'S CHRISTIAN
ASSOCIATION. Halifax, Bowes, 1854. 26p [NSHD

Ridley, Hilda M., —1960
THE POST-WAR WOMAN. Intro. by W.D. Calvert. Toronto, Ryerson, 1941.
39p [OTP QMM

Rintoul, Rev. David
TWO LECTURES ON RHETORIC. Toronto, Scobie, 1844. 48p [OLU

Robb, Wallace Havelock, 1888—
INDIAN LORE OF THE BAY OF QUINTE. Kingston, Author, 1952. 12p

Robbins, John Everett, 1903—
CANADA BETWEEN COVERS. An Address to the Rotary Club of Ottawa,
January 7, and to the Rotary Club of Ottawa West, February 12th, 1957.
Ottawa, Author, 1957. 10p
THE IDEA OF AN ENCYCLOPEDIA DEFINED AND ILLUSTRATED. An Address to
the Newman Club of Ottawa ... March 24, 1957. Ottawa, Author, 1957. 9p

Robbins, William, 1909—
HUMANISTIC VALUES IN ENGLISH LITERATURE. Five Radio Talks as heard on
CBC University of the Air. Toronto, Canadian Broadcasting Corporation,
1960. 56p

Roberton, Thomas Beattie, 1879—1936
A SECOND HELPING OF NEWSPAPER PIECES. By "T.B.R." Toronto, Macmillan,
1937. 157p [BVaU NBFU OTP
T.B.R. Newspaper Pieces. Toronto, Macmillan, 1936. 142p [BM BVaU LC
NSHD OTU

Roberts, Leslie, 1896–
WE MUST BE FREE. Reflections of a Democrat. Toronto, Macmillan, 1939.
248p [BM BVaU OTP QMM

Robertson, John Charles, 1864–1956
MIXED COMPANY. Toronto, Dent, 1939. 200p [BM BVa LC NSHD OTP

Robertson, John Ross, 1841–1918
TALKS WITH CRAFTSMEN, AND PENCILLINGS BY THE WAYSIDE. Toronto,
Hunter Rose, 1890. 191p [BM NSHD OTU

Robins, John Daniel, 1884–1952
COTTAGE CHEESE. Toronto, Collins, 1951. 232p
THE INCOMPLETE ANGLERS. Toronto, Collins, 1943. 229p [BVaU LC
NBFU OTP QMM

Roe, Rev. Henry, 1829–1909
ADVANTAGES AND MEANS OF KEEPING UP HABITS OF READING AMONG THE
CLERGY. A Paper read before the Clergy assembled in Lennoxville ... 6th July,
1864. Montreal, Lovell, 1864. 23p [NSWA OTP

Ross, Alexander Milton, 1832–1897
LETTERS ON CANADIAN INDEPENDENCE. Toronto, 1865. 11p [OTP

Ross, Rev. Ebenezer E.
THE MANLINESS OF PIETY. A Lecture. ... Halifax, Wesleyan, 1860. 24p [NSHD

Ross, Malcolm Mackenzie, 1911–
OUR SENSE OF IDENTITY. A Book of Canadian Essays. Ed. by ——. Toronto,
Ryerson, 1954. xvi + 348p

Ruark, Fletcher, 1880–1952
SKETCHES FROM LIFE. Windsor, Ont., Curtis, 1942. 94p [BVaU OTP QMM

Ryder, Kenneth Walter, 1904–
DEAR PATRICIA. Letters written to Patricia Ryder by her Father when she was in
Ottawa. N.p., priv. print., 1957. 18p

Ryerson, Rev. Adolphus Egerton, 1803–1882
CIVIL GOVERNMENT, THE LATE CONSPIRACY. A Discourse delivered in Kingston,
U.C., December 31, 1837. Toronto, Conference Office, 1838. 20p [BVaU
OTP
LETTERS ... TO THE HON. AND REVEREND DOCTOR STRACHAN. ... Kingston,
Herald Office, 1828. 42p [OTP

Salter, Frederick Millet, 1895–1962
"THIS BANK AND SHOAL OF TIME." An Address to the Annual Assembly of Victoria
College, Victoria, B.C., October 18, 1957. Victoria, Daily Colonist, 1957. 8p

Sandwell, Bernard Keble, 1876–1954
THE DIVERSIONS OF DUCHESSTOWN AND OTHER ESSAYS. With an intro. by
  Robertson Davies. Toronto, Dent, 1955. xii + 84p
THE GODS IN TWILIGHT. Vancouver, U. of British Columbia, 1948. 18p
  [BVaU LC OTP QMM
THE PRIVACITY AGENT AND OTHER MODEST PROPOSALS. Toronto, Dent, 1928.
  223p [BM BVaU LC NBFU OTU QMM
WESTING. Montreal, priv. print., 1918. 31p [BVa OKQ

Saunders, Margaret Marshall, 1861–1947
MY PETS. Real Happenings in my Aviary. Philadelphia, Griffith & Rowland,
  1908. 283p [Also: Toronto, Ryerson, 1935. 256p] [BM LC NBFU OLU

Saxe, Mary Sollace, 1868–1942
OUR LITTLE QUEBEC COUSIN. Boston, Page, 1919. 122p [BVaU LC QMSS

Scadding, Rev. Henry, 1813–1901
THE EASTERN ORIEL OPENED. An Address on the Laying of the Foundation
  Stone of the University of Toronto. Toronto, 1842. 11p [BibC
THE MAPLE LEAF AS AN EMBLEM OF CANADA. Toronto, Boyle, 1891. 6p
  [NSWA OTU
THE PRESIDENT'S VALEDICTORY ADDRESS, DELIVERED BEFORE THE ATHENAEUM
  OF TORONTO. Toronto, 1846. 12p [BibC

Schrag, Alexander Andrew, 1907–
MORTGAGE MANOR. By Lex Schrag. Aided and abetted by Jim Reidford.
  Toronto, Ryerson, 1955. xix + 156p

Scott, Duncan Campbell, 1862–1947
THE ADMINISTRATION OF INDIAN AFFAIRS IN CANADA. ... Prepared for the
  Fourth Bi-Annual Conference of the Institute of Pacific Relations ... October
  18 – November 3, 1931. Toronto, Canadian Institute of International
  Affairs, 1931. 27p [BM BVaU NBFU OKQ

Scott, Jack
FROM OUR TOWN. Toronto, McClelland, 1959. 224p

Sedgewick, Rev. Robert
AMUSEMENTS FOR YOUTH. A Lecture. Halifax, Barnes, 1858. 29p [NSHD
THE PROPER SPHERE AND INFLUENCE OF WOMAN IN CHRISTIAN SOCIETY. A
  Lecture. Halifax, Barnes, 1856. 47p [BM NSWA

Service, Robert William, 1874–1958
WHY NOT GROW YOUNG? or, Living for Longevity. New York, Barse, 1928.
  266p [BM BVaU LC OLU

Seton, Ernest Thompson, 1860–1946
ANIMAL TRACKS AND HUNTER SIGNS. Garden City, N.Y., Doubleday, 1958. 160p

... ANIMALS, Selected from "LIFE-HISTORIES OF NORTHERN ANIMALS." New York, Doubleday, 1926. 299p [BVa LC OTU

ANIMALS WORTH KNOWING. Selected from "LIFE-HISTORIES OF NORTHERN ANIMALS." New York, Doubleday, 1934. 299p [LC

THE GOSPEL OF THE REDMAN. An Indian Bible. Comp. by Ernest Thompson Seton and Julia M. Seton. Garden City, Doubleday, 1936. 121p [BM BVa LC NBFU OTP

LIFE-HISTORIES OF NORTHERN ANIMALS. An Account of the Mammals of Manitoba. New York, Scribner, 1909. 2v [BM BVaU LC OTP QMM

LIVES OF GAME ANIMALS. New York, Doubleday, 1925–28. 4v [BM BVaU NBFU OTP QMM

MAINLY ABOUT WOLVES. London, Methuen, 1937. 319p [ACG BM OWtU

THE WAR DANCE AND THE FIRE-FLY DANCE. New York, Doubleday, 1910. 10p [LC

Shatford, Rev. Allan Pearson, 1873–1935

THE INNOCENTS. A Christmas Study. Montreal, Lovell, 1912. 58p [QMSS

Sigbjornsson, Mrs. Rannveig Kristin G., 1880–

PEBBLES ON THE BEACH. Treherne, Man., Treherne Times, 1936. 17p [OTU

Simcoe, John Graves, 1752–1806

LETTER TO SIR JOSEPH BANKS ... 1792. ... To which is Added Five Official Speeches, delivered ... in [Upper Canada]. With a prefatory notice by Rev. Dr. Scadding. Toronto, Copp Clark, 1892. 18p [OLU

Sime, Jessie Georgina, 1880–

THE LAND OF DREAMS. Toronto, Macmillan, 1940. 273p [BM OOU QMM

ORPHEUS IN QUEBEC. London, Allen & Unwin, 1942. 47p [BM BVaU NBFU OTU QMM

Smith, Arthur James Marshall, 1902–

UNIVERSITY OF NEW BRUNSWICK, FOUNDERS' DAY ADDRESS. With Opening Remarks by D.L. MacLaren ... 1946. Fredericton, University, 1946. 19p [OKQ QMM

Smith, Goldwin, 1823–1910

DOES THE BIBLE SANCTION AMERICAN SLAVERY? Cambridge, Sever & Francis, 1863. 107p [BM BVaU LC NBFU OTU QMM

THE EARLY DAYS OF CORNELL. Ithaca, priv. print., 1904. 25p [OTU

THE EMPIRE. A Series of Letters Published in "The Daily News," 1862, 1863. Oxford, 1863. 306p [BM BVaU NBFU OTU QMM

ESSAYS ON QUESTIONS OF THE DAY, POLITICAL AND SOCIAL. New York, Macmillan, 1893. 360p [BM BVaU LC NSHD OTU QMM

FALSE HOPES; or, Fallacies, Socialistic and Semi-Socialistic, Briefly Answered. ... New York, Lovell, 1883. 69p [BM NBFU

THE FOUNDATION OF THE AMERICAN COLONIES. ... Oxford, 1861. [BM NBFU

KEEPING CHRISTMAS. Toronto, Robinson, 1888. 12p [BVaU LC NBFU OTU

LECTURES AND ESSAYS. Toronto, Hunter Rose, 1881. 336p [BM BVaU LC
NSHD OKQ QMM

LECTURES ON MODERN HISTORY. Delivered in Oxford, 1859—61. Oxford, Parker,
1861. [2nd ed.: 1865. 190p] [BM NSWA OTU QMM

LOYALTY. An Address ... before the Young Men's Liberal Club, Toronto, on
Feb. 2, 1891. Toronto, Hunter Rose, 1891. 20p [OTU

LOYALTY, ARISTOCRACY AND JINGOISM. Three Lectures. ... Toronto, Hunter
Rose, 1891. 96p [BM BVaU LC NBFU OTU

ON SOME SUPPOSED CONSEQUENCES OF THE DOCTRINE OF HISTORICAL PRO-
GRESS. ... Oxford, Parker, 1861. 47p [BM NBFU

OXFORD AND HER COLLEGES. London, Macmillan, 1894. 99p [Also: New York,
1895. 170p] [BM BVaU NBFU OTU QMM

THE POLITICAL DESTINY OF CANADA. With a Reply by Sir Francis Hincks. ...
Toronto, Willing & Williamson, 1878. 197p [NSHD has: Toronto, Belford, 1877.
32p Without Hincks' REPLY?] [BM BVaU NSWA OTU QMM

PROGRESS OR REVOLUTION? A Letter to a Labour Friend. Toronto, Tyrrell, 1906.
30p [NBFU OTU

A SELECTION FROM GOLDWIN SMITH'S CORRESPONDENCE ... BETWEEN THE YEARS
1846 AND 1910. Ed. by Arnold Haultain. ... London, Laurie, [1913?]. 540p
[BM BVaU LC NSHD OTU QMM

THE STUDY OF HISTORY. Two Lectures. London, Oxford U. Press, 1859. 35p
[BM BVaU NBFU

Smith, Irving Norman, 1909—

A REPORTER REPORTS. Toronto, Ryerson, 1954. x + 145p

Smith, Sidney Earle, 1897—1959

UNITY OF KNOWLEDGE: THE SCIENCES AND THE HUMANITIES. An Address before
the Royal Canadian Institute, February 23, 1952. Toronto, U. of Toronto
Press, 1952. 12p

Smith, Thomas Barlow, 1839—1933

BACKWARD GLANCES. Halifax, Bowes, 1898. 254p [BM BVaU NSWA OTP
QMM

NOVA SCOTIA. Trial and Relief. Windsor, "Hants," 1929. 42p [BM QMBM

Smith, Rev. William Wye, 1827—1917

VETULIA; or, Going to the Bottom of Things. Toronto, Dudley & Burns, 1891.
78p [OTP

Smythe, Carroll F.

SMILE, STRIVE, STICK. Success Boiled Down to Three Words. Toronto, L.R. Steel
Service Corp., [1921]. 32p [OTP

Sommerville, Rev. William, 1800–1878
SOUTHERN SLAVERY NOT FOUNDED ON SCRIPTURE WARRANT. A Lecture.
Saint John, Barnes, 1864. 27p [NSWA

Spark, Rev. Alexander, 1762–1819
AN ORATION AT THE DEDICATION OF FREE-MASON'S HALL, QUEBEC, CANADA.
Quebec, Brown, 1790. 16p [BM QMSS

Sproat, Gilbert Malcolm, 1832–1913
CANADA AND THE EMPIRE. ... London, n.p., 1873. 35p [BM NSWA OTU

Stead, Robert James Campbell, 1880–1959
THE MAPLE'S PRAISE OF FRANKLIN DELANO ROOSEVELT, 1882–1945. Canadian
Tributes. By Robert J.C. Stead, Dorothy Dumbrille, Nathaniel A. Benson.
Ottawa, Tower Books, 1945. 18p [OTU
WORDS. Winnipeg, Public Press, 1945. 21p [UTQ

Stefansson, Vilhjalmur, 1879–1962
ADVENTURES IN ERROR. Toronto, McLeod, 1936. 299p [BVaU OTP

Stevenson, Orlando John, 1869–1950
THE STUDY OF LITERATURE. Toronto, Morang, 1904. 31p [BM OTU
THROUGH THE YEARS. Toronto, Ryerson, 1952. 45p

Stewart, Herbert Leslie, 1882–1953
FROM A LIBRARY WINDOW. Reflections of a Radio Commentator. Toronto,
Macmillan, 1940. 323p [BM BVaU LC NSHD OTP
OBITER SCRIPTA. Halifax, 1914–1936. 3v [Essays on many different subjects
collected by their author, from the various magazines in which they were
published, and bound together.] [NSHD

Stirling, John Bertram, 1888–
THE FIRST HUNDRED YEARS. Fredericton, U. of New Brunswick, 1954. 13p

Strachan, Rev. John, 1778–1867
THE JOHN STRACHAN LETTER BOOK: 1812–1834. Ed. by George W. Spragge.
Toronto, Ontario Hist. Soc., 1946. 279p [BM BVaU LC NBFU OTP QMM
A LETTER FROM THE HON. AND VENERABLE DR. STRACHAN, U.C., TO DR. LEE, D.D.
Kingston, Herald, 1829. 19p [OTU

Sullivan, Alan, 1868–1947
I BELIEVE THAT ——. Toronto, Tyrrell, 1912. 59p [BM BVaU OTP

Sykes, Frederick Henry, 1863–1918
MEMORIALS. Address at the Celebration of the Twenty-fifth Anniversary of the
Bill Memorial Library, Groton, Conn., October 15th, 1913. Groton, Bill Mem.
Lib. Assoc., 1913. 20p [BM OTU

Symons, Harry Lutz, 1893–
THE BORED MEETING. Toronto, Ryerson, 1951. 121p

FRIENDSHIP. Toronto, Macmillan, 1943. 265p [BVaU OTU QMM
OJIBWAY MELODY. Stories of Georgian Bay. Toronto, Best, 1946. 294p
  [BVaU NBFU OTP QMBM
THE ORANGE BELT SPECIAL. Toronto, Nelson, 1956. xii + 210p

Thomas, Robert Brockholes
SHORT SPECULATIVE ESSAYS. Charlottetown, 1882. 91p [BM OLU

Thompson, Drew [Andrew Ruthven], 1894–
HYSTERIC HISTORIES. Ottawa, le Droit, 1941. 64p [OOP

Thompson, John Sparrow David, 1844–1894
THE EXECUTION OF LOUIS RIEL. Speech ... Delivered March 22, 1886. N.p., n.p.,
  [1886?]. 31p [BViPA NSWA OTP

Thomson, Watson, –1969
"I ACCUSE." Winnipeg, Contemporary Pub., 1943. 32p [OTU

Tocque, Rev. Philip, 1814–1899
KALEIDOSCOPE ECHOES. Being Historical, Philosophical, Scientific, and Theological
  Sketches from the Miscellaneous Writings. ... Ed. by his daughter, Annie S.W.
  Tocque. Toronto, Hunter, 1895. 300p [BVaU OTP

Todd, Henry Cook, –1862
ITEMS (IN LIFE OF AN USHER) ON TRAVEL, ANECDOTE, AND POPULAR ERRORS.
  By One in Retirement [pseud]. Montreal, 1850. 266p [Also: Quebec, 1855.
  306p] [LC OLU OTP

Toronto, Ont. National Club
MAPLE LEAVES. Being the Papers read before the National Club ... during the Winter
  1890–1891. Toronto, the Club, [1891?]. 136p [NSHD OTU

Toronto Arts & Letters Club
YEAR BOOK OF CANADIAN ART. Literature, Architecture, Music, Painting,
  Sculpture. Toronto, Dent, [1913]. V. 1. [No more pub.] [BM NBS OTU QMG

Tory, James Cranswick, 1862–
ADDRESSES. ... Ottawa, Mortimer, 1932. 291p [NSHD

Traill, Catharine Parr (Strickland), 1802–1899
CANADIAN WILD FLOWERS. Painted and Lithographed by Agnes Fitz Gibbon, with
  Botanical Descriptions by C.P. Traill. ... Montreal, Lovell, 1868. 86p [Several
  later editions.] [BM BVaU LC OLU
PEARLS AND PEBBLES; or, Notes of an Old Naturalist. With Biographical Sketch
  by Mary Agnes Fitz Gibbon. Toronto, Briggs, 1894. 241p [BM BVaU MWU
  NSHD OTP QMM

STUDIES OF PLANT LIFE IN CANADA; or, Gleanings from Forest, Lake and Plain. By Mrs. C.P. Trail. ... Illus. ... by Mrs. Chamblin. Ottawa, Woodburn, 1885. 288p [New and rev. ed., 1906.] [BM BVaU LC NSHD OTU

Twain, Mathew (pseud)
THE CRAZY QUILT SERIES. V. 1, No. 1. A Compendium of Wit, Humor and Pathos. By Mathew Twain [pseud]. Toronto, 1888. [BVaU

Voorhis, Ernest, 1859–1933
WINTER IN CANADA. [Ottawa, 1926?]. 14p [NBFU OKQ

Wallace, Rev. Archer, 1884–1958
THE FAITH OF MORN. New York, Round Table, 1940. 150p [LC OTU
THE SILVER LINING. New York, Round Table, 1937. 94p [BVaU LC

Wallace, Robert Charles, 1881–1955
THEN AND NOW. Founder's Day Address, University of New Brunswick. Fredericton, the University, 1950. 15p [BM BVaU OKQ

Ward, Norman, 1918–
MICE IN THE BEER. Toronto, Longmans, 1960. xii + 206p

Warman, Cy, 1855–1914
THE WHITE ELEPHANT. Montreal, Canada Pub., 1905. 33p [QMBM

Watson, Albert Durrant, 1859–1926
THE SOVEREIGNTY OF IDEALS. ... Westwood, Mass., Ariel Press, 1903. 38p [LC OKQ
THREE COMRADES OF JESUS. Toronto, Ryerson, 1919. 73p [BM BVaU NSWA OKQ

Watson, John, 1847–1939
EDUCATION AND LIFE. An Address delivered at the Opening of the 32nd Session of Queen's University. Kingston, Alma Mater Society, n.d. 20p [Amtmann cat. 145

Watson, Robert, 1882–1948
HOW TO WRITE, BY THOSE WHO CAN. ... Comp. by ——. Ottawa, Graphic, [1928?]. 16p [OTP

Watson, William Ritchie, 1904–
... AND ALL YOUR BEAUTY. Toronto, Macmillan, 1948. 385p [BVaU NBFU OTP

Webber, Rev. George, 1838–1907
LECTURES AND SERMONS. London, Ont., Advertiser Print., 1883. 219p [OTU

Webber, William Lester, 1882–
THE ORIGINAL THUNDER BIRD STICK GAME. Vancouver, Author, 1939. 14p
  [BViPA

Webling, Peggy
GUESTS OF THE HEART. London, Baines & Scarsbrook, 1917. 65p [BM BVaU

Webster, John Clarence, 1863–1950
THE CLASSICS OF ACADIA. Ottawa, "Progressive," 1933. 8p [QMBM
PRESENT DAY ASPECTS OF CANADIAN NATIONALISM. [An Address delivered at
  Mt. Allison University ... November 15, 1922.] N.p., 1922. 19p [OTP

Weekes, Mrs. Mary Loretto, 1885–
THE WHEATLAND. Regina, Western Printers, 1937. 29p [BVaU LC NBFU OTU

Wells, Kenneth McNeill, 1905–
BY JUMPING CAT BRIDGE. London, Heinemann; Toronto, British Book Service,
  1956. 268p
BY MOONSTONE CREEK. Toronto, Dent, 1949. 280p [BVaU NBFU OTP
THE OWL PEN. Toronto, Dent, 1947. 289p [BVaU NBFU OTP QMM
UP MEDONTE WAY. Toronto, Dent, 1951. 247p

Welton, Rev. Daniel Morse, 1831–1904
THE IMITATIVE FACULTY, ITS USE AND ABUSE. A Lecture. Halifax, Christian
  Messenger, 1858. 27p [NSHP

West, Bruce, 1912–
A CHANGE OF PACE. Toronto, U. of Toronto Press, 1956. x + 158p

West, Paul Noden, 1930–
THE GROWTH OF THE NOVEL. Eight Radio Talks as heard on CBC University of the
  Air. Toronto, Canadian Broadcasting Corporation, 1959. 84p

Whelan, Edward, 1824–1867
BIOGRAPHICAL SKETCH OF THE HONOURABLE EDWARD WHELAN TOGETHER WITH
  A COMPILATION OF HIS PRINCIPAL SPEECHES. By Peter McCourt. Charlottetown,
  Author, 1888. 301p [BVaU LC NSWA OLU

White, Thomas, 1830–1888
OUR GREAT WEST. A Lecture. ... Montreal, Dawson, 1873. 32p [BM LC OTP

Whitton, Charlotte Elizabeth, 1896–
THE DECAY OF DEMOCRACY. Charlottetown, Prince of Wales College, 1955. 19p

Wilkes, Rev. Henry, 1805–1886
LECTURE ON FREEDOM OF MIND ... And Speech of His Excellency the Right
  Hon. the Earl of Elgin & Kincardine delivered before the Mercantile Library
  Association of Montreal. ... Montreal, Potts, 1848. 27p [OTP

Williams, Mrs. Mary Elizabeth, 1877–
IT SEEMS TO ME. New York, Vantage Press, 1960. 195p

Williamson, Owen Templeton Garrett, 1883–
CIVVY STREET. Red Light or Green? Toronto Ryerson, 1945. 28p [OTP

Willison, John Stephen, 1856–1927
PARTNERS IN PEACE. The Dominion, The Empire, and The Republic. Addresses.
... Toronto, Warwick & Rutter, 1923. 94p [BM BVaU NSHD OTU

Willison, Marjory (MacMurchy), –1938
THE KING'S CROWNING. Toronto, Briggs, 1911. 12p [OTU

Wills, Harold Arthur, 1907–
FIRST PERSON PLURAL. Being Editorials for these Troubled Times; a Golden
Jubilee Collection of Editorials. Cochrane, Northland Post, 1960. xii + 276p

Wilson, Clifford Parnell, 1902–
NORTHERN TREASURY. Selections from the *Beaver*. Ed. by ––––. Edinburgh,
Toronto, Nelson, 1955. 238p

Wilson, Daniel, 1816–1892
PIPES AND TOBACCO. An Ethnographic Sketch. Toronto, Lovell & Gibson, 1857.
52p [BM LC QMM

Wilson, Rev. Robert, 1833–1912
THE TOBACCO NUISANCE. Saint John, McMillan, 1890. 18p [NSWA

Winson, J.W.
OPEN AIR JOTTINGS. Being Notes on Nature ... in British Columbia. By Wildwood
[pseud]. Vancouver, Murphy & Chapman, 1937. 23p [BVaU
WEATHER AND WINGS. Nature Essays. Toronto, Nelson, 1932. 172p [BVaU
WILDWOOD TRAILS. Vancouver, Chapman & Warich, 1946. 203p [BVaU OTU

Wodson, Harry Milner, 1874–1952
THE JUSTICE SHOP. Toronto, Sovereign Press, 1931. 119p [BVaU OKQ
PRIVATE WARWICK. Musings of a Canuck in Khaki. Toronto, Sovereign Press,
1915. 96p [BM OTU
THE WHIRLPOOL. Scenes from Toronto Police Court. Toronto, priv. print., 1917.
208p [BM BVaU OTP

Wood, Edgar Allardyce, 1907–
ROBBING THE ROOST. The Marquis of Roostburg Rules governing the Ancient
and Dishonorable Sport. Red Deer, priv. print., n.d. 8p [ACG

Wood, Samuel Thomas, 1860–1917
RAMBLES OF A CANADIAN NATURALIST. Toronto, Dent, 1916. 247p [BVaU LC
NSHD OTU QMM

Woodcock, George, 1912–
ANARCHY OR CHAOS. London, Freedom Press, 1944. 124p [BM LC
RAILWAYS AND SOCIETY. London, Freedom Press, 1943. 31p [BM LC
THE WRITER AND POLITICS. London, Porcupine, 1948. 248p [BM BVaU LC

Woodsworth, Rev. James Shaver, 1874–1942
HOURS THAT STAND APART. Ottawa, Mutual Press, 1927. 40p [OTU
LABOR'S CASE IN PARLIAMENT. A Summary and Compilation of the Speeches of
    J.S. Woodsworth, M.P. in the Canadian House of Commons, 1921–1928. Ottawa,
    Canadian Brotherhood of Railroad Employees, 1929. 92p [OTP
TOWARDS SOCIALISM. Selections from the Writings of J.S. Woodsworth. Ed. by
    Edith Fowke. Toronto, Ontario Woodsworth Memorial Foundation, 1948.
    48p [NBFU OTP

Young, Archibald Hope, 1863–1935
TRINITY COLLEGE. A Causerie, delivered ... March 14th, 1925. [Toronto, 1925.]
    19p [BM OTP
UPPER CANADA COLLEGE, TORONTO, 1829–1929. Toronto, [1929?]. 12p
    [BM NBFU OTP QMM

Young, George Paxton, 1819–1889
FREEDOM AND NECESSITY. A Lecture delivered in Knox College ... 1870.
    Toronto, Adam & Stevenson, 1870. 19p [OTP

Yule, James Colton, 1839–1876
RECORDS OF A VANISHED LIFE. Lectures, Addresses, etc., of James Colton Yule
    ... late professor of New Testament Interpretation. ... in the Canadian Literary
    Institute. A Memoir by his Wife. Toronto, Baptist Pub. Co., 1876. 174p
    [NBFU OKQ

LOCAL HISTORY AND DESCRIPTION

Historical studies and recent descriptions of communities, provinces, regions

Abraham, Dorothy E., 1894–
ROMANTIC VANCOUVER ISLAND. Victoria, Yesterday and Today. Victoria, Acme, 1947. 118p [2nd ed., 1949; 3rd ed., 1956.] [BVaU OOA

Acton, Ont. Free Press
ACTON'S EARLY DAYS. Recollections of "the Old Man" as Published in the Acton Free Press. Acton, Free Press, 1939. 285p [BVaU OTU

Adam, Graeme Mercer, 1839–1912
THE CANADIAN NORTH-WEST ... from the Early Days of the Fur-Trade to the Era of the Railway and the Settler. Toronto, etc., Rose, etc., 1885. 408p [BM BVaU LC NBFU OTP QMBM
ILLUSTRATED QUEBEC ... Under French and English Occupancy. Ed. by ——. Montreal, McConniff, 1891. 90p [BVaU LC NSWA OTP
MUSKOKA ILLUSTRATED. With Descriptive Narrative of the Picturesque Region. Toronto, Bryce, 1888. 20p [OLU
TORONTO, OLD AND NEW: ... Historical, Descriptive and Pictorial ... to mark the Hundredth Anniversary of the Passing of the Constitutional Act of 1791 ... with Some Sketches of the Men who have made or are making the Provincial Capital. By G. Mercer Adam and the Rev. Henry Scadding. Toronto, Mail, 1891. 212p [BVaU LC NSWA OTP

Adanac, Sask., Jubilee Association
THE STORY OF ADANAC. Adanac, Sask., 1955. 48p

Affleck, Edward Lloyd, 1924–
STERNWHEELERS, SANDBARS, AND SWITCHBACKS. A Chronicle of Steam Transportation in Southeastern British Columbia. Vancouver, 1958. 65p [mimeographed]

Aitken, Martha Alice (Duff), 1882–
THE BOOK OF TURNBERRY, 1857–1957. N.p., 1957. 59p

Akins, Thomas Beamish, 1809–1891
HISTORY OF HALIFAX CITY. Halifax, Nova Scotia Hist. Soc., 1895. 272p [BM NSWA OTP QMM •
PRIZE ESSAY ON THE HISTORY OF THE SETTLEMENT OF HALIFAX. Halifax, English & Blackadar, 1847. 62p [NSHD

SELECTIONS FROM THE PUBLIC DOCUMENTS OF ... NOVA SCOTIA. Ed. by ——.
Halifax, Annand, 1869. 755p [Papers relating to Acadian and English settlement, 1714–61.] [BM BVaU NSWA OTP

Alexander, James Edward, 1803–1885
THE BURNING OF THE ST. LOUIS THEATRE, QUEBEC. Quebec, 1846. 8p [LC OTP

Alexander, Mary H.T. (Strachan)
OLD FORT PRINCE OF WALES. Toronto, Ryerson, 1930. 30p [BVaU OTU

Allison, David, 1836–1924
HISTORY OF NOVA SCOTIA. By David Allison [and Clyde Edwin Tuck]. Halifax, Bowen, 1916. 3v [V. 3, by C.E. Tuck, is subtitled: BIOGRAPHICAL SKETCHES OF REPRESENTATIVE CITIZENS AND GENEALOGICAL RECORDS OF THE OLD FAMILIES.] [BVaU LC NSWA OTP

Alloway, Mary H. (Wilson), 1848–1919
FAMOUS FIRESIDES OF FRENCH CANADA. Montreal, Lovell, 1899. 217p [BM BVaU LC NSWA OTU QMM

Almon, Albert, 1873–
LOUISBOURG. The Dream City of America. Truro, News Pub. Co., 1934. 85p [NSHD OTP QMBM
ROCHEFORT POINT. A Silent City in Louisbourg. Glace Bay, Macdonald, 1940. 44p [LC NSHP QMM

Ames, Herbert Brown, 1863–1954
"THE CITY BELOW THE HILL." A Sociological Study of a Portion of the City of Montreal. Montreal, Bishop, 1897. 72p [BVaU OTP

Anderson, Mrs. Aili Sophia, 1906–
HISTORY OF SOINTULA. Sointula, B.C., Sointula Centennial Committee, 1958. 16p

Anderson, Carr
KEMPTVILLE, PAST AND PRESENT. Kemptville, 1903. [OOP

Anderson, Rev. David, 1814–1885
NOTES OF THE FLOOD AT THE RED RIVER, 1852. By the Bishop of Rupert's Land. London, Hatchard, 1852. 124p [BM BVaU LC NSWA OTP

Anderson, William James, 1813?–1873
THE LOWER ST. LAWRENCE. Its Scenery, Navigation, and Commerce, forming a Complete Tourist's Guide. Quebec, "Morning Chronicle," 1872. 49p [NSHPL OLU QMBM

Andrew, Frederick William, 1879–
THE STORY OF SUMMERLAND. Penticton, Herald, 1945. 55p [BVaU

Aneroid, Sask. High School

HISTORY OF ANEROID. Aneroid, Sask., 1955. 13 + 3p

Angus, Alexander David, 1911–1941

OLD QUEBEC IN THE DAYS BEFORE OUR DAY. Montreal, Carrier, 1949. 232p
[BVaU NBFU OTP

Annapolis Royal, N.S. 350th Anniversary Celebration Committee

WELCOME TO ANNAPOLIS ROYAL'S 350TH ANNIVERSARY. Annapolis Royal, 1955.
88p

Anonymous

A DESCRIPTION OF PRINCE EDWARD ISLAND ... AND A FEW CURSORY OBSERVA-
TIONS RESPECTING THE CLIMATE, NATURAL PRODUCTIONS, AND ADVANTAGES
OF ITS SITUATION IN REGARD TO AGRICULTURE AND COMMERCE. By a Person
Many Years Resident There. London, Ashey, n.d. 22p [Describes P.E.I. in
1795.] [OTU QMU

GLIMPSES IN AND ABOUT HALIFAX ... ITS PICTURESQUE BEAUTIES AND ATTRACT-
IVE SURROUNDINGS ILLUSTRATED AND DESCRIBED. [Halifax], Howard, n.d.
[c1900?]. 79p [NSHPL OTU

AN INTERESTING ACCOUNT ... OF THE CELEBRATED HORDE OF ROBBERS KNOWN
AS THE MARKHAM GANG. Toronto, 1846. 24p [OTP

THE PONOKA BOOK. Published as a Tribute to the Pioneers who Opened up the
District and to Commemorate the Town's Fiftieth Anniversary, 1904–1954.
Ponoka, Alta., 1954. 93p

Anspach, Rev. Lewis Amadeus

A HISTORY OF THE ISLAND OF NEWFOUNDLAND. London, Author, 1819. xxviii
+ 512p [BM BVaU LC NSWA OLU

Archer, John Hall, 1914–

HISTORIC SASKATOON [1882–1947]. A Concise Illustrated History of Saskatoon.
Comp. by John H. Archer and Joseph C. Bates. Saskatoon, Junior Chamber of
Commerce, 1948. 63p [BVaU NSHD OTU

Armstrong, Edith Vernette (Akeley), 1905–

A WHEATLAND HERITAGE. Eston, Sask., Board of Trade, 1956. 275p [History
of the Rural Municipality of Snipe Lake No. 259, Saskatchewan, 1906–1916.]

Arrell, Alex H.

A SHORT HISTORY OF CALEDONIA. Ed. by ——. Caledonia, Ont., Sachem Print.,
1950. 131p [OONL

Assiniboia, Sask. Golden Jubilee Committee

GOLDEN MEMORIES. Assiniboia, Sask., 1955. 88p [A history of the Assiniboia
district.]

Atherton, William Henry, 1867–1950
MONTREAL, 1535–1914. Montreal, Clarke, 1914. 3v [BM LC NSHD OTP

Babbitt, George W.
FREDERICTON IN THE EIGHTIES, WITH GLIMPSES OF SAINT JOHN, MONCTON, AND
ST. ANDREWS. N.p., [1954?]. 20p

Bagg, Stanley Clark, 1820–
ANTIQUITIES AND LEGENDS OF DURHAM. A Lecture. Montreal, Rose, 1866. 21p
[BM BVaU LC NSWA QMM

Baird, Rev. Frank, 1870–1951
HISTORY OF THE PARISH OF STANLEY AND ITS FAMOUS FAIR. Fredericton,
McMurray Book, 1950. 159p [OONL

Baker, Edna
PRAIRIE PLACE NAMES. Toronto, Ryerson, 1928. 28p [NBFU OTU SSU

Baldwin, Mrs. Alice Murray Sharples, 1906–
METIS, WEE SCOTLAND OF THE GASPE. N.p., 1960. 64p [History of Métis Beach,
Que.]

Barbeau, Charles Marius, 1883–1969
THE KINGDOM OF SAGUENAY. Toronto, Macmillan, 1936. 167p [BM BVaU LC
NBFU OTU QMM
QUEBEC, WHERE ANCIENT FRANCE LINGERS. Toronto, Macmillan, 1936. 173p
[BM BVaU NSHD OTU QMBM

Barnes, Clarence James, 1884–
SEVENTY YEARS IN SOUTHWESTERN MANITOBA. Medora, Man., 1954. 48p

Barnwell, Alta. Church Of Jesus Christ Of Latter Day Saints
BARNWELL HISTORY. Comp. by Barnwell Relief Society. Ann Arbor, Mich.,
Edwards Bros., 1952. 10 + 401 + 28p [History of the Relief Society founded
in 1842 and of the village of Barnwell.]

Barschel, J.F. Paul, 1875–
A HISTORY OF CANORA AND DISTRICT. Canora, Sask., Canora Golden Jubilee
Committee, 1960. 189p

Bates, Jane Eliza (Woolf), 1873–1951
FOUNDING OF CARDSTON AND VICINITY. Pioneer Problems. By Jane E. Woolf
Bates. Comp. by Zina Woolf Hickman. Salt Lake City, Utah, W.L. Woolf, 1960.
214p [On Mormon settlement in Alberta.]

Bates, Walter, 1760–1842
KINGSTON AND THE LOYALISTS OF THE "SPRING FLEET" OF A.D. 1783. ... To

which is Appended a Diary written by Sarah Frost on her Voyage to St. John, N.B., with the Loyalists of 1783. Ed. with notes by W.O. Raymond. Saint John, Barnes, 1889. 30p [LC NSWA OTP QMM

Beavan, Mrs. F.

SKETCHES AND TALES ILLUSTRATIVE OF LIFE IN THE BACKWOODS OF NEW BRUNSWICK. ... London, Routledge, 1845. 142p [Photostat copy /negative/; bound as PIONEER LIFE IN NEW BRUNSWICK.] [NBFU

Bédard, Rev. Roméo

HISTORY, MONTMARTRE, SASK., 1893–1953. [Trans. by Sister Marie Helena]. Montmartre, Sask., 1953. 97p [mimeographed]

Bedore, Bernard Vance, 1923–

THE BROAD VALLEY OF THE OTTAWA. Comp. by ——. Arnprior, Ont., Ottawa Valley Pub., 1957. 70p

Begg, Alexander, 1825–1905

HISTORY OF BRITISH COLUMBIA. ... Toronto, Briggs, 1894. 568p [BM BVaU LC MWU NSWA OTU QMM

Begg, Alexander, 1839–1897

THE CREATION OF MANITOBA; or, A History of the Red River Troubles. Toronto, Hovey, 1871. 408p [BM BVaU LC NSHD OKQ

THE GREAT CANADIAN NORTH WEST. Its Past History, Present Condition, and Glorious Prospects. Montreal, Lovell, 1881. 135p [BM BVaU LC NSWA OTU QMM

HISTORY OF THE NORTH-WEST. Toronto, Hunter Rose, 1894–95. 3v [BM BVaU LC NBFU OKQ QMM

RED RIVER JOURNAL AND OTHER PAPERS RELATIVE TO THE RED RIVER RESIS-TANCE OF 1869–1870. Ed. with an intro. by W.L. Morton. Toronto, Champlain Society, 1956. xxiii + 636 + xvip

TEN YEARS IN WINNIPEG. A Narration of the Principal Events in the History of the City of Winnipeg from ... 1870 to ... 1879. By Alexander Begg and Walter R. Nursey. Winnipeg, Times, 1879. 226p [BM BVaU LC NSWA OTU QMM

Bell, Charles Napier, 1854–1936

... OLD FORTS OF WINNIPEG (1738–1927). Winnipeg, Dawson Richardson, 1927. 39p [BVaU NSHD

THE SELKIRK SETTLEMENT AND THE SETTLERS. A Concise History of the Red River Country from its Discovery, Including Information Extracted from Original Documents lately discovered, and Notes Obtained from Selkirk Settlement Colonists. Winnipeg, "Commercial," 1887. 44p [BVaU OTU QMM

SOME HISTORICAL NAMES AND PLACES OF THE CANADIAN NORTH-WEST. Winnipeg, Manitoba Free Press, 1885. 8p [LC OTP

... SOME RED RIVER SETTLEMENT HISTORY. ... Winnipeg, Call, 1887. 8p [LC OTP

Bell, Fannie Chandler
A HISTORY OF OLD SHEDIAC, NEW BRUNSWICK. Moncton, National Print., 1937. 63p [NBFU OTP

Belsham, Alice Ada (Carroll), 1922–
HISTORY OF FORT FRASER. Comp. by Alice Belsham and J. Philip Myers. Fort Fraser, B.C., Author, 1958. 11p

Belyea, Myrtle
HISTORY OF NEREPIS, N.B. N.p., 1924. 10p [NBFU

Berry, Gerald Lloyd, 1915–
THE WHOOP-UP TRAIL (ALBERTA-MONTANA RELATIONSHIPS). Edmonton, Applied Art Products, 1953. 143p

Berry, James P., 1867–1953
CLOVER BAR IN THE MAKING, 1881–1931. [Edmonton?], 1931. 32p [ACG

Berton, Pierre Francis de Marigny, 1920–
THE GOLDEN TRAIL. The Story of the Klondike Rush. Toronto, Macmillan, 1954. 147p
KLONDIKE. The Life and Death of the Last Great Gold Rush. Toronto, McClelland, 1958. viii + 457 + xixp [American ed. (New York, Knopf, 1958) has title: KLONDIKE FEVER. The Life and Death of the Last Great Gold Rush.]

Bertrand, Joseph Placide, 1881–
HIGHWAY OF DESTINY. An Epic Story of Canadian Development. New York, Vantage Press, 1959. 301p [History of northwestern Ontario.]
PORT ARTHUR CENTENNIAL, 1857–1957, JULY 27 TO AUGUST 3. Official Programme. Ed. by J.P. Bertrand and A. Phillips. Port Arthur, Ont., City Clerk's Office, 1957. 84p

Bezanson, A. Maynard, 1878–1958
THE PEACE RIVER TRAIL. [Anon] Edmonton, Journal Co., 1907. 73p [AEP BM

Bible, George Potter, 1858–
AN HISTORICAL SKETCH OF THE ACADIANS, Their Deportation and Wanderings, together with an Historical Basis for Longfellow's poem Evangeline; with Extracts from the Original Documents Bearing upon the Subject, and Illustrations of Scenes in and around Grand Pré and Annapolis, Nova Scotia, "the Land of Evangeline." Philadelphia, Ferris & Leach, 1906. 205p [BM BVaU LC OTU

Bienfait, Sask. High School. Student Council
HISTORY OF BIENFAIT. Bienfait, Sask., 1955. 34p [mimeographed]

Biggar, Charles L.
A TALE OF EARLY DAYS ON LUNDY'S LANE. Niagara Falls, Niagara Pub., 1947.
10p [OOA

Bill, Fred Alexander
LIFE ON THE RED RIVER OF THE NORTH, 1857 TO 1887. Being the History of
Navigation on the Red River. ... Life on the River Town of Fargo and Moorhead,
by J.W. Riggs. Baltimore, Wirth, 1947. 122p [BVaU MWP

Bird, William Richard, 1891–
A CENTURY AT CHIGNECTO, THE KEY TO OLD ACADIA. Toronto, Ryerson, 1928.
245p [BVaU LC NSWA OKQ
DONE AT GRAND PRE. Toronto, Ryerson, 1955. xii + 179p
HISTORIC NOVA SCOTIA. Prepared by ——. Halifax, Govt. of N.S., [194–?].
114p [BVaU LC NBFU OTP

Black, Norman Fergus, 1876–1964
HISTORY OF SASKATCHEWAN AND THE OLD NORTH WEST. Regina, North West
Historical Co., 1913. 605p [BVaU NBFU OTU QMM

Blaine Lake, Sask. School
OUR HISTORICAL BLAINE LAKE. Blaine Lake, Sask., 1957. 27 + 6p [mimeo-
graphed]

Blakeley, Phyllis Ruth, 1922–
GLIMPSES OF HALIFAX, 1867–1900. Halifax, Public Archives of N.S., 1949. 216p
[BM NSHD OLU

Blanchard, Kathleen Helen (Barrett), 1872–
THE GOSSAMER THREAD. A True Story of Bishop Grisdale, and the Legend of
Qu'Appelle. N.p., n.d. 13p [OTU

Blue, John, 1875–1945
ALBERTA, PAST AND PRESENT. Chicago, Pioneer Hist. Pub. Co., 1924. 3v
[BVaU

Bohrson, S.D. No. 1644, Sask. School
50TH ANNIVERSARY OF BOHRSON SCHOOL DISTRICT NO. 1644, 1906–1956.
Hanley, Sask., 1956. 31p

Boissevan, Man. Jubilee Book Committee
BECKONING HILLS. Boissevan, 1956. 260p

Bompas, Charlotte Selina (Cox), 1830–1917
OWINDIA. A True Tale of the Mackenzie River Indians, North-west America.
[signed C.S.B.] London, Wells Gardner, 1886. 60p [BM OTP

Borthwick, Rev. John Douglas, 1832–1912
FROM DARKNESS TO LIGHT. History of the Eight Prisons which have been, or

are now, in Montreal, 1760–1907. Montreal, Gazette, 1907. 142p [BVaU LC OTU QMM

HISTORY AND BIOGRAPHICAL GAZETEER OF MONTREAL TO THE YEAR 1892. Montreal, Lovell, 1892. 531p [BVaU OOP QMM

HISTORY OF MONTREAL, INCLUDING THE STREETS OF MONTREAL. Their Origin and History. Montreal, Gallagher, 1897. 288p [BM BVaU LC NSWA OTU QMM

HISTORY OF THE MONTREAL PRISON, FROM A.D. 1784 TO A.D. 1886. ... Montreal, Periard, 1886. 270p [BM BVaU LC NSWA OTU QMM

MONTREAL, ITS HISTORY. To Which is added Biographical Sketches. Montreal, Drysdale, 1875. 153p [BVaU LC NSWA OTU QMM

Bosworth, Newton, 1776?–1848

HOCHELAGA DEPICTA. The Early History and Present State of ... Montreal. Ed. by ——. Montreal, Greig, 1839. 284p [Also: Toronto, Congdon & Britnell, 1901]. [BM BVaU LC NSWA OKQ QMM

HOCHELAGA DEPICTA; or, A New Picture of Montreal. ... Ed. by ——. Montreal, Mackay, 1846. 27 + 284p [New ed.] [BVaU LC NBFU OTP QMM

Bothwell, Jessie (Robson), 1884–

A HEALTH TO REGINA. N.p., 1927. 20p [ACG OTU

"PIONEERS! O PIONEERS!" Regina, 1955. 92p

Botsford, David Patterson, 1898–

AMHERSTBURG'S PLACE IN AMERICAN HISTORY. ... Amherstburg, Amherstburg Echo, 1959. 16p

Bourinot, John George, 1837–1902

HISTORICAL AND DESCRIPTIVE ACCOUNT OF THE ISLAND OF CAPE BRETON, and of its Memorials of the French Régime. ... Montreal, Brown, 1892. 183p [BM BVaU LC NSWA OTU QMM

MEMORIES OF DUNDURN AND BURLINGTON HEIGHTS. An Address delivered at Hamilton, Ontario. ... With Historical Notes. Toronto, Copp Clark, 1900. 32p [OTP

Bowen, Noel Hill, –1872

AN HISTORICAL SKETCH OF THE ISLE OF ORLEANS. Quebec, "Mercury," 1860. 40p [BVaU LC OTP QMM

Boyle, David, 1842–1911

THE TOWNSHIP OF SCARBORO 1796–1896. Ed. by ——. Toronto, Briggs, 1896. 302p [BM BVaU LC OTU

Boylen, John Chancellor

YORK TOWNSHIP, AN HISTORICAL SUMMARY [1850–1954]. Toronto, Municipal Corporation of the Township of York and Board of Education of the Township of York, 1954. 131p

Bramley-Moore, Alwyn, 1877–1916

CANADA AND HER COLONIES; or, Home Rule for Alberta. London, Stewart, 1911. 185p [BVaU NBFU OTU SSU

Brebner, John Bartlet, 1895–1957

THE NEUTRAL YANKEES OF NOVA SCOTIA. ... New York, Columbia U. Press, 1937. 388p [BM BVaU LC NSHD OTU QMM

NEW ENGLAND'S OUTPOST. Acadia before the Conquest of Canada. New York, Columbia U. Press, 1927. 293p [BM BVaU LC NSWA OTU QMM

Bredenbury, Sask. High School

HISTORY OF BREDENBURY, 1883–1955. Bredenbury, Sask., 1955. 26p [mimeographed]

Bremner, Archibald, 1849–1901

CITY OF LONDON, ONTARIO, CANADA. The Pioneer Period and the London of To-day. [Anon] London, London Print. & Lith., 1897. 136p [BM BVaU OTP

Bremner, Benjamin, 1851–1938

AN ISLAND SCRAP BOOK ... Sequel to MEMORIES OF LONG AGO. ... Charlottetown, Irwin, 1932. 161p [BM BVaU OTU QMM

MEMORIES OF LONG AGO ... Charlottetown in the Past. Charlottetown, Irwin, 1930. 96p [BVaU OTP

TALES OF ABEGWEIT [Prince Edward Island] . Containing Historical, Biographical and Humorous Sketches. ... With an Appendix of Place-names in Prince Edward Island, with their Origins or Meanings. Charlottetown, Irwin, 1936. 132p [BM LC NBSaM OTU

Brewster, Winfield, 1879–

THE FLOODGATE. Random Writings of Our Ain Folk. Hespeler, Ont., priv. print., 1952. 44p

HESPELER YARNS. Odds and Ends about the Textile Trade at Hespeler, and Some of the People who were Concerned therewith. Hespeler, Ont., Author, 1953. 46p

J. HESPELER, NEW HOPE, C.W. Hespeler, Ont., T. & T. Press, 1951. 34p

Brighton, Ont. Centennial Book Committee

CENTENNIAL OF THE INCORPORATION OF THE VILLAGE OF BRIGHTON, 1859–1959. Brighton, 1959. 90p

Britton, Freeman

SOUVENIR OF GANANOQUE AND THOUSAND ISLANDS. With short Sketch of First Owners, Early Settlement and Other Historical Notes of the Town. Gananoque, Ont., 1901. 80p [OOA

Broadview, Sask. School
THE GOOD OLD DAYS OF BROADVIEW. Ed. by Mavis Anderson, Assistant ed., Orville Fitzgerald. Broadview, Sask., 1955. 46p

Brome County, Que. Historical Society
INDEX OF BOOKS AND PAMPHLETS ... CONCERNING THE EARLY HISTORY AND SETTLERS IN THE EASTERN TOWNSHIPS. Knowlton, Que., the Society, 1949. 83p [BVaU OLU

Brown, George Stayley
YARMOUTH, NOVA SCOTIA. A Sequel to Campbell's HISTORY. Boston, Rand Avery, 1888. 524p [BVaU LC NSWA OTU QMSS

Brown, Harrison, 1893—
ADMIRALS, ADVENTURERS AND ABLE SEAMEN. Forgotten Stories about Places on our British Columbia Coast and how they got their Names. Vancouver, Keystone Press, 1954. 30p

Brown, Lewis, 1858—1930
A HISTORY OF SIMCOE, 1829—1929. ... Simcoe, Pearce, 1929. 108p [LC OTP

Brown, Mrs. O.E.A.
SETTLERS OF THE PLAINS. By O.E.A. Brown, assisted by C. Finnen. [Gilbert Plains, Man.?] , 1953. 15 + 188p

Brown, Richard
A HISTORY OF THE ISLAND OF CAPE BRETON. With some Account of the Discovery and Settlement of Canada, Nova Scotia, and Newfoundland. London, Sampson Low, 1869. 464p [BM BVaU LC NSWA OTU

Brown, Rev. Robert Christopher Lundin, —1876
BRITISH COLUMBIA. An Essay. New Westminster, Royal Engineer Press, 1863. 64 + xxxiiip [BVaU LC OTP

Brown, Thomas J.
PLACE NAMES OF THE PROVINCE OF NOVA SCOTIA. Halifax, Royal Print., 1922. 158p [BVaU LC NSWA OTU

Brown, Thomas Storrow, 1803—1888
MONTREAL FIFTY YEARS AGO. [Montreal, 1868.] 11p [QMM

Brown, Wallace William, 1923—
HISTORY OF PORT MELLON, 1908—1958. By W.W. Brown and J.B. Stewart. Port Mellon, B.C., Port Mellon Community Association, 1959. 36p

Browne, Rev. Patrick William, 1864—1937
WHERE THE FISHERS GO. The Story of Labrador. Toronto, Musson, 1909. 370p [BM BVaU LC NSHD OTU

Brownlee, Sask. Jubilee Committee
BROWNLEE DISTRICT, 1905–1955. Comp. and printed by the Citizens of the
Community of Brownlee, Saskatchewan, on the Occasion of the Celebration of
Saskatchewan's Jubilee Year – 1955. Brownlee, Sask., 1955. 84p
[mimeographed]

Bryce, Rev. George, 1844–1931
CANADIAN PAMPHLETS. (37 items in 1.) Winnipeg, Manitoba Free Press,
1875–1909. [Contains many essays separately published.] [OTP
A HISTORY OF MANITOBA. Toronto, Canadian History Co., 1906. 693p [BVaU
OTUV
MANITOBA: ITS INFANCY, GROWTH, AND PRESENT CONDITION. London, Low
Marston, 1882. 367p [BM BVaU LC NSWA OTU QMM
THE ROMANTIC SETTLEMENT OF LORD SELKIRK'S COLONISTS. (The Pioneers of
Manitoba). Toronto, Musson, 1909. 328p [BM BVaU LC MWU NSHD OKQ
QMM
... "SEVEN OAKS." An Account of the Affair of Seven Oaks. ... Winnipeg, Manitoba
Free Press, [1891?]. 38p [OTP
WILLIAM SILVERING'S SURRENDER. A Story of Western Experiences. ... [Anon]
Winnipeg, Winnipeg Forestry Assoc., 1901. 96p [NBFU OKQ QMSS

Bryce, Marion (Samuel), 1839–1920
EARLY RED RIVER CULTURE. By Mrs. George Bryce. Winnipeg, Manitoba Free
Press, 1901. 16p [OTP QMM SSU

Buckaway, Mrs. Catherine Margaret, 1919–
THE PRAIRIE ROSE STORY. 50th Anniversary. Jansen, Sask., 1960. 43p

Bugeia, Julia H.S.
IN OLD MISSISQUOI. With History and Reminiscences of Stanbridge Academy. By
Julia H.S. Bugeia and Theodora Cornell Moore. Montreal, Lovell, 1910. 211p
[BVaU OTU

Bull, William Perkins, 1870–1947
FROM THE BOYNE TO BRAMPTON; or, John the Orangeman at Home and Abroad.
Toronto, Perkins Bull Foundation, 1936. 326p [BM BVaU LC OTP
FROM OXFORD TO ONTARIO. A History of the Downsview Community. Toronto,
Perkins Bull Foundation, 1941. 310p [BM OKQ
THE PERKINS BULL COLLECTIONS. Historical Paintings by Canadian Artists
illustrating Pioneers and Pioneering in the County of Peel. Brampton, Author,
1934. 144p [BM BVaU NSHD OKQ QMM

Bullock, Mrs. Ellen Guthrie
PIONEERS OF THE PIPESTONE. Brandon, Sun. Pub. Co., 1929. 63p [MWP

Burge, Thomas Ashlee, 1922–
"THIS IS SALTSPRING." 2nd ed. Ganges, B.C., The Spotlight, 1953. 32p

Burkholder, Mabel Grace (Clare), 1881—
BARTON ON THE MOUNTAIN. A Short History of that Part of Barton Township
which is Situated on the Mountain above the City of Hamilton, from Days of
Early Settlement to the Openings [*sic*] Years of the Twentieth Century.
[Hamilton?], Author, 1956. 48p
THE STORY OF HAMILTON. Hamilton, Davis-Lisson, 1938. 183p [LC OTU QMM

Burns, Rev. Robert Ferrier, 1826—1896
OUR MODERN BABYLON. A Discourse Delivered in Fort Massey Church, Halifax,
N.S. on ... the Sabbath succeeding the "Chiniquy Riot." ... With an appendix.
Halifax, Nova Scotia Print., 1876. 22p [NSHD

Burns, William M., 1863—1943
A HISTORY AND STORY OF BOTSFORD [N.B.]. Sackville, Tribune Print., 1933.
106p [Reprinted 1962.] [NBSaM

Burrows, Charles Acton, 1853—1948
THE ANNALS OF THE TOWN OF GUELPH, 1827—1877. Comp. under the direction
of ——. Guelph, Herald, 1877. 170p [BVaU LC NSWA OTU QMM

Burt, Alfred LeRoy, 1888—
THE OLD PROVINCE OF QUEBEC. Toronto, Ryerson, 1933. 551p [BM BVaU LC
NBFU OTU QMM
THE ROMANCE OF THE PRAIRIE PROVINCES. Toronto, Gage, 1931. 262p [BM
BVaU LC OTU

Byerly, Alpheus Edward, 1894—1960
THE BEGINNING OF THINGS IN WELLINGTON AND WATERLOO COUNTIES, WITH
PARTICULAR REFERENCE TO GUELPH, GALT AND KITCHENER. Guelph, Guelph
Pub. Co., 1935. 106p [BM OTU
FERGUS, OR THE FERGUSSON-WEBSTER SETTLEMENT. ... Elora, Ont., Elora
Express, 1932—34. 372p [BM BVaU OTP
THE HISTORY OF LOWER NICHOL. Fergus, News, 1930. 16p [OTU

Byrnes, Harold
PIONEER DAYS AT CECIL LAKE [B.C.]. By Slim Byrnes. N.p., 1959. 64p

Byrnes, John Maclay
THE PATHS TO YESTERDAY. Memories of Old St. John's, Newfoundland, including
a number of typical Newfoundland poems, each from the gifted pen of a Terra
Novian. Boston, Meador, 1931. 235p [BVaU LC OTU

Calgary, Alta.
CALGARY, ALBERTA, "THE CITY WITH EVERYTHING UNDER THE SUN." Calgary,
1951. 100p

Calkin, John Burgess, 1829–1918
THE GEOGRAPHY AND HISTORY OF NOVA SCOTIA. Halifax, MacKinlay, 1859. 102p [Several later editions.] [BVaU NSWA OTP QMM

Calnek, William Arthur, 1822–1892
HISTORY OF THE COUNTY OF ANNAPOLIS. ... With Memoirs of its Representatives in the Provincial Parliament, and Biographical and Genealogical Sketches of its Early English Settlers and their Families. ... Ed. and completed by A.W. Savary. Toronto, Briggs, 1897. 660p [BM BVaU LC NSWA OTU QMM

Calverley, Eva
AND SO ... NINETTE, 1879–1919. Comp. by ——. Ninette, Man., [1958?]. 113p

Calvin, Delano Dexter, 1881–1948
A SAGA OF THE ST. LAWRENCE. Timber and Shipping through Three Generations. Toronto, Ryerson, 1945. 176p [BVaU LC NSHD OTU QMM

Cameron, William Bleasdell, 1862–1951
THE WAR TRAIL OF BIG BEAR. Being the Story of the Connection of Big Bear and other Cree Indian Chiefs and their Followers with the Canadian North-west Rebellion of 1885. ... Toronto, Ryerson, 1926. 256p [4th ed., rev., pub. under title: BLOOD RED THE SUN. ... Calgary, Kenway, 1950. 225p] [BM BVaU LC NBFU OTU QMM

Campbell, Alice A. (Hallonquist), 1892–
MILK RIVER COUNTRY. Lethbridge, Alta., Herald, 1959. 439p

Campbell, Clarence Thomas, 1843–1922
PIONEER DAYS IN LONDON. Some Account of Men and Things in London before it became a City. London, Ont., Advertiser Print., 1921. 128p [BVaU LC NSHD OTP

THE SETTLEMENT OF LONDON, ONT. N.p., [1911?]. 51p [OLU

Campbell, Duncan, 1819?–1886
HISTORY OF PRINCE EDWARD ISLAND. Charlottetown, Bremner, 1875. 224p [BM BVaU LC NSWA OTU QMM

NOVA SCOTIA. Its Historical, Mercantile and Industrial Relations. Montreal, Lovell, 1873. 548p [BM BVaU LC NSWA OTU QMM

Campbell, George Graham, 1904–
THE HISTORY OF NOVA SCOTIA. Toronto, Ryerson, 1948. 288p [BVaU LC NSHD OTU QMM

Campbell, Isabelle, 1896–
A HIBBERT REVIEW, COUNTY OF PERTH. Seaforth, Ont., Huron Expositor, 1953. 109p

A HIBBERT REVIEW (Part Two). Including the Lots Contained in Concessions I to VII, inclusive. Seaforth, Ont., Huron Expositor, 1959. 1v [unpaged]

THE STORY OF HIBBERT TOWNSHIP, COUNTY OF PERTH. Seaforth, Ont., Huron Expositor, 1952. 66p

Campbell, Rev. John Roy, 1841—1926
AN ANSWER TO SOME STRICTURES IN BROWN'S SEQUEL TO CAMPBELL'S "HISTORY OF YARMOUTH. ..." Halifax, McMillan, 1889. 18p [NSWA
A HISTORY OF THE COUNTY OF YARMOUTH, N.S. Saint John, McMillan 1876. 200p [See also: YARMOUTH, NOVA SCOTIA. A Sequel to Campbell's HISTORY. By George S. Brown. ... Boston, Rand Avery, 1888.] [BViP LC NSWA OTP QMSS

Campbell, Marjorie Elliott (Wilkins), 1901—
THE SASKATCHEWAN. ... New York, Rinehart, 1950. 400p [BVaU LC NSHD OKQ QMM

Campbell, Marjorie (Freeman), 1896—
NIAGARA, HINGE OF THE GOLDEN ARC. Toronto, Ryerson, 1958. xviii + 356p

Campbell, Mrs. Sara L.
BROOKE TOWNSHIP HISTORY, 1833—1933. Alvinston, Ont., Brooke Women's Institute, 1936. 171p [LC OTP

Camrose Canadian, The
THE GOLDEN TRAIL. Ed. by the staff of the Camrose *Canadian.* Camrose, Alta., Lions Club, 1955. 136p [A history of Camrose and area.]

Camrose Historical Society
EARLY HISTORY OF CAMROSE, ALBERTA, AND DISTRICT. [Camrose?], the Society, 1947. 36p [ACG SSU

Cando, Sask. School
THE STORY OF CANDO AND COMMUNITY. Cando, Sask., Cando School Students Council, 1955. 2v [mimeographed]

Canniff, William, 1830—1910
HISTORY OF THE PROVINCE OF ONTARIO. ... Toronto, Hovey, 1872. xxxi + 670p [BVaU LC NSWA OTU
HISTORY OF THE SETTLEMENT OF UPPER CANADA. With Special Reference to the Bay of Quinte. Toronto, Dudley & Burns, 1869. xxxi + 671p [BM BVaU LC NSWA OTU QMM

Canso, N.S.
HISTORIC CANSO. N.p., n.p., 1928. 63p [NSWA

Cantelon, Robert Alvin
EDMONTON, CROSSROADS OF THE WORLD. A Brief View of the City's Development, and its Place in the Post-war World. Edmonton, Civic Enterprises, 1944. 80p [BVa OTP

Capp, Edward Henry, 1871–

THE STORY OF BAW-A-TING. Being the Annals of Sault Sainte Marie. Sault Sainte Marie, 1907. 261p [An earlier ed., 1904.] [BVaU LC OTP

Carberry Agricultural Society. Carberry Plains Anniversary Book Committee

THE CARBERRY PLAINS. 75 Years of Progress. Carberry, Man., the Committee, 1959. 160p

Card, Brigham Young, 1914–

THE CANADIAN PRAIRIE PROVINCES FROM 1870 to 1950. A Sociological Introduction. Toronto, Dent, 1960. xi + 46p

Carlson, William E.

HISTORY OF EMERSON, FEATURING HISTORICAL SKETCHES OF SURROUNDING DISTRICTS. Emerson, Man., Journal, 1950. 80p [OTP

Carlyle, Sask. School

CARLYLE. Carlyle, Sask., 1955. 38p [mimeographed]

Carnochan, Janet, 1839–1926

HISTORY OF NIAGARA (in part). Toronto, Briggs, 1914. 333p [BM BVaU LC OTU QMM

INSCRIPTIONS AND GRAVES IN THE NIAGARA PENINSULA. Niagara, Ont., The Times, [1902?]. 72p [2nd ed.: with Additions and Corrections. Welland, The Tribune, 1910. 126p] [See also Niagara Hist. Soc. reprint with additions and corrections: Niagara-on-the-Lake, The Society, 1931. 147p] [BM LC OTP

NIAGARA ONE HUNDRED YEARS AGO. The Ancient Capital and its Vicinity. Welland, Ont., Tribune, 1892. 35p [BVaU LC NSWA OTU QMM

Carrel, Frank, 1870–1940

GUIDE TO THE CITY OF QUEBEC. ... Quebec, Carrel, 1899. 154p [Earlier ed., 1896. Many later editions, gradually lengthening; 45th ed. entitled: CARREL'S ILLUSTRATED GUIDE & MAP OF QUEBEC. ... Quebec, Chronicle-Telegraph, 1937. 213p] [BVaU LC OTP

THE QUEBEC TERCENTENARY COMMEMORATIVE HISTORY. Comp. and ed. by Frank Carrel and Louis Feiczewicz. ... Quebec, Daily Telegraph, 1908. 178p [BM LC NBFU OTP

Carter, Dyson, 1910–

SEA OF DESTINY. The Story of Hudson Bay — our Undefended Back Door. New York, Greenberg, 1940. 236p [ACU BM LC NfSG OONL

Carter, J. Smyth, 1877–

THE STORY OF DUNDAS ... from 1784 to 1904. Iroquois, Ont., St. Lawrence News, 1905. 463p [BVaU LC NSHD OTU QMM

Cartwright, George, 1739–1819
A JOURNAL OF TRANSACTIONS AND EVENTS, DURING A RESIDENCE OF NEARLY
SIXTEEN YEARS ON THE COAST OF LABRADOR. Containing many interesting
Particulars, both of the Country and its Inhabitants, not hitherto Known. ...
Newark, Allin & Ridge, 1792. 3v [A later ed., Saint John, 1882.] [ACG
NBFU OTP QMBM

Cartwright, Man. Citizens
MEMORIES ALONG THE BADGER. Seventy Five Years of our History, 1885–1960.
A Story of the Village of Cartwright, Manitoba. Steinbach, Man., Derksen
Printers, 1960. 147p [Prepared by P.A. Watts and others.]

Cashman, Anthony Walcott, 1923–
THE EDMONTON STORY. The Life and Times of Edmonton, Alberta. Edmonton,
Institute of Applied Art, 1956. 279p
MORE EDMONTON STORIES. The Life and Times of Edmonton, Alberta.
Edmonton, Institute of Applied Art, 1958. 261p

Cebryk, M. Alex
THE PROGRESS OF FISKE. Fiske, Sask., 1955. 28p [mimeographed]

Chalmers, John West, 1910–
RED RIVER ADVENTURE. The Story of the Selkirk Settlers. Toronto, Macmillan,
1956. 158p

Channell, Leonard Stewart, 1868–
HISTORY OF COMPTON COUNTY AND SKETCHES OF THE EASTERN TOWNSHIPS,
DISTRICT OF ST. FRANCIS, AND SHERBROOKE COUNTY. Comp. by ——.
Including Biography of the Late Hon. John Henry Pope, by Hon. C.H.
Mackintosh. Cookshire, Que., L.S. Channell, 1896. 289p [BM BVaU LC
OTP

Charles, Evelyn
THE HISTORY OF MULDREW LAKE [MUSKOKA]. A Record of By-gone Days
in and around the Lake, from the Archives of the Muldrew Lake Cottagers'
Club. Ed. by ——. Toronto, the Club, 1953. 15p [mimeographed]

Charlottetown, P.E.I. Centennial Committee
THE CHARLOTTETOWN CENTENNIAL, 1855–1955. Official Souvenir Booklet.
Charlottetown, [1955?]. 101p

Chase, Reta, 1940–
A HISTORY OF BURFORD. Burford, Ont., Advance, 1960. 39p

Chiel, Rabbi Arthur Abraham, 1920–
JEWISH EXPERIENCES IN EARLY MANITOBA. Winnipeg, Manitoba Jewish
Publications, 1955. xiii + 125p

Chisholm, Joseph Andrew, 1863–1950

THE HALIFAX MEMORIAL TOWER. Halifax, Canadian Club, 1913. 76p [BM
LC NSWA OTU QMM SSU

Chittick, Hattie

HANTSPORT, THE SMALLEST TOWN. Hantsport, N.S., Women's Institute, 1940.
46p [Rev. ed., 1954, with title: HANTSPORT ON AVON.] [NSWA

Christie, James R., 1877–

THE STORY OF OKANAGAN FALLS. By Jas. R. Christie and Isabel Christie
MacNaughton. Okanagan Falls, B.C., Centennial Committee, 1958. 44p

Christie, Robert, 1788–1856

A HISTORY OF THE LATE PROVINCE OF LOWER CANADA, Parliamentary and
Political, from the Commencement to the Close of its Existence as a Separate
Province ... 1791 ... 1841. ... Quebec, Cary, 1848–55. 6v [BM BVaU
LC NSWA OTP QMM

Clark, Andrew Hill, 1911–

THREE CENTURIES AND THE ISLAND. A Historical Geography of Settlement and
Agriculture in Prince Edward Island, Canada. Toronto, U. of Toronto Press,
1959. xiii + 287p

Clarke, George Frederick, 1883–

EXPULSION OF THE ACADIANS. The True Story (Documented). Fredericton,
Brunswick Press, 1955. 31p

TOO SMALL A WORLD. The Story of Acadia. Fredericton, Brunswick Press,
1958. 423p

Clarke, Gwendoline Pattie (Fitz-Gordon), 1893–

HALTON'S PAGES OF THE PAST. Acton, Ont., Dills Print., 1955. 191p [History
of Halton County, Ont.]

Clarke, W.W.

CLARKE'S HISTORY OF THE EARLIEST RAILWAYS IN NOVA SCOTIA. Windsor,
N.S., Hants Journal Press, [1925?]. 63p [Cover title.] [BVaU NBFU OTU

Clay, Charles, 1906–

THE LEASIDE STORY. Leaside, Ont., the Council, 1958. 64p

Cleasby, Henry Standley, 1868–

THE NICOLA VALLEY IN REVIEW. Merritt, B.C., Herald, 1958. V. 1.

Cleveland, Rev. Edward, 1804–1886

A SKETCH OF THE EARLY SETTLEMENT AND HISTORY OF SHIPTON, CANADA
EAST. Canada East, "Richmond County Advocate," 1858. 78p [BM LC
NSWA OTP QMM

Clingan, Ruth Mary Ida (Thompson), 1874–

THE VIRDEN STORY. Virden, Man., 1957. 13 + 264p

Cochrane, James Arthur, 1891–1947
THE STORY OF NEWFOUNDLAND. Boston, Ginn, 1938. 256p [Rev. ed.: Toronto, Ginn, 1949. 288p] [BVaU LC NSWA OTU QMM

Cohoon, William Albert, 1886–
JUBILEE REMINISCENCES AND HISTORY OF THE MACRORIE AND BRATTON DISTRICT, WITH BIOGRAPHIES OF THE PEOPLE. London, Ont., Middlesex Print., 1956. 103p [2nd ed., 1957. 120p]

Colborne, Ont. Centennial Committee
COLBORNE CENTENNIAL, JUNE 27 – JULY 1ST, 1959. Colborne, Ont., 1959. 93p [Editor: D. Peebles.]

Colborne Township, Ont. Centenary Celebration Committee
ONE HUNDRED YEARS OF MUNICIPAL GOVERNMENT IN THE TOWNSHIP OF COLBORNE, 1850–1950. With Contributed Articles on the Evolution of Educational, Agricultural, Industrial and other Activities in the Township Centennial Celebration and Reunion, June 30, 1950, at Benmiller. Goderich, Ont., 1950. 26p [OONL

Coleman, John T.
HISTORY OF THE EARLY SETTLEMENT OF BOWMANVILLE AND VICINITY. Bowmanville, West Durham Print., 1875. 43p [BVaU OTP

Coleman, MacDonald, 1919–
THE FACE OF YESTERDAY. The Story of Brandon, Manitoba. Brandon, Junior Chamber of Commerce, 1957. 106p

Coleman, Alta. Board of Trade
COLEMAN'S 50TH ANNIVERSARY BOOKLET. Coleman, Alta., [1953?]. 70p

Collier, Herbert B.
REMEMBER WHEN? History of the Viking District. Edmonton, Commercial Print., [1937?]. 72p [AEU

Collins, Rev. Donald St. Clair, 1922–
"THIS WAY, HOMESTEADER." By Rev. Don Collins and Margaret Dunham. Carnduff, Sask., Carnduff Jubilee Committee, 1955. 25p [History of Carnduff, 1905–55.]

Colonsay, Sask. High School
COLONSAY MEMOIRS, 1905–1955. Colonsay, 1955. 56p [mimeographed]

Community Clubs of Alexis Creek, B.C., and Other Districts
HISTORY AND LEGENDS OF THE CHILCOTIN. Williams Lake, B.C., Cariboo Press, 1958. 48p

Complin, Margaret (Robertson) –1951
WINGED MOCCASINS TO WINGED WORDS. Regina, Western Print., 1937. 23p [On Northwest Territories.] [OTP SSU

Connon, John Robert, 1862–1931
"ELORA." Elora, Ont., Elora Express & Fergus News-Record, 1930. 207p
  [BVaU OTP

Conquest, Sask. Homemakers' Club. Pioneer History Committee
THIS CONQUEST OF OURS, 1905–1948. Conquest, the Club, [1949]. 51p
  [UTQ'51

Consolidated Mining and Smelting Company of Canada Limited
TRAIL'S GOLDEN JUBILEE OLD TIMERS, 1901–1951. Trail, B.C., 1952. 38p

Cook, John Thomas
NIPAWIN. Moose Jaw, Quality Press, 1946. 51p [SSU

Coombs, Albert Ernest, 1871–1957
CITY OF ST. CATHARINES. Historical Facts. St. Catharines, The Standard, 1947.
  52p [OTU
HISTORY OF THE NIAGARA PENINSULA AND THE NEW WELLAND CANAL.
  Toronto, Historical Publishers, 1930. 428p [BM OTU

Coombs, William Gordon, 1884–
FROM OX TEAM TO COMBINE. Local History of Buckland District from 1907
  to 1955. Buckland, Sask., Homemakers' Club, 1955. 34p [mimeographed]

Cooney, Rev. Robert, 1800–1870
A COMPENDIOUS HISTORY OF THE NORTHERN PART OF ... NEW BRUNSWICK,
  AND OF THE DISTRICT OF GASPE, IN LOWER CANADA. Halifax, Howe, 1832.
  288p [BM BVaU LC MWU NSHD OTP

Cooper, Charles William, 1819?–1893
FRONTENAC, LENNOX & ADDINGTON. Prize Essay. Kingston, Creighton, 1856.
  105p [LC NSWA OTP

Cooper, John Irwin, 1905–
THE HISTORY OF THE MONTREAL HUNT 1826–1953. Montreal, Montreal Hunt,
  1953. 18 + 131 + 43p
MONTREAL. THE STORY OF THREE HUNDRED YEARS. Montreal, Lamirande,
  1942. 133p [BM BVaU LC OTU QMM

Cope, Leila M. (Sutton)
A HISTORY OF THE VILLAGE OF PORT CARLING. Bracebridge, Ont., Herald-
  Gazette Press, 1956. 87p

Corbitt, Harry Wellington, 1889–
THE HISTORY OF KALEDEN. Kaleden, B.C., Centenial Committee, 1958.
  61p

Corey, Rowland H., 1864?–
HISTORICAL SKETCH OF THE FIRST SETTLERS OF NEW CANAAN. [Sussex,
  N.B.?], priv. print., 1946. 30p [NBFU

Cornell, John A., 1841—
THE PIONEERS OF BEVERLEY. A Series of Sketches. ... With Supplementary
Articles on the Municipal History ... Educational Matters ... Agricultural
Society [by other hands]. Dundas, Somerville, 1889. 186p [BVaU OTU

Corner, Raymond Westley, 1894—
GLENMORE, THE APPLE VALLEY. Kelowna, B.C., Glenmore Centennial Committee,
1958. 57p

Cornwall, Ont. Old Boys' Reunion
CORNWALL AND THE UNITED COUNTIES OF STORMONT, DUNDAS AND GLEN-
GARRY. Souvenir of the Old Boys' Reunion ... [1906]. Cornwall, The
Freeholder, 1906. 171p [OTP

Cotton, William Lawson, 1848—1928
CHAPTERS IN OUR ISLAND STORY. Rev. and repub. by request. Charlottetown,
Irwin Print., 1927. 162p [BVaU NBFU OTP

Coutts, Mrs. Marjorie Ellen, 1914—
DAWSON CREEK, PAST AND PRESENT. An Historical Sketch. Ed. by ——.
Dawson Creek, B.C., Dawson Creek Historical Society, 1958. 115p

Cowan, Hugh, 1870—1943
THE DETROIT RIVER DISTRICT. Toronto, Algonquin Hist. Soc., 1929. 319p
[BVaU OTP
GOLD AND SILVER JUBILEE, Sault Ste. Marie, Ont. N.p., 1938. 32p [Anon]
[OTP

Coward, Mrs. Elizabeth Ruggles, 1887—1959
BRIDGETOWN, NOVA SCOTIA. Its History to 1900. Bridgetown, N.S., Author,
1955. 253p

Cowie, Isaac, 1848—1917
THE WESTERN PLAINS OF CANADA REDISCOVERED. [Winnipeg], 1903. 40p
[ACG

Coyne, James Henry, 1849—1942
THE COUNTRY OF THE NEUTRALS (as far as comprised in the County of Elgin)
from Champlain to Talbot. St. Thomas, Times Print., 1895. 44p [LC OTU

Craick, William Arnot, 1880—1969
PORT HOPE. Historical Sketches. Port Hope, Williamson Press, 1901. 138p
[BM BVaU OTU

Craig, John Roderick, 1837—
RANCHING WITH LORDS AND COMMONS; or, Twenty Years on the Range.
Being a Record of Actual Facts and Conditions Relating to the Cattle Industry
of the North-west Territories of Canada. Toronto, Briggs, 1903. 293p
[BM BVaU LC OTU SSU

Craig, Martha
THE GARDEN OF CANADA. Burlington, Oakville ano District. Toronto, Briggs,
1902. 96p [Ryerson Impt

Cranston, James Herbert, 1880–1952
HURONIA. The Cradle of Ontario's History. 3rd ed. Midland, Huronia Historic
Sites, 1951. 80p [First ed., 1949. 24p] [OLU OTP

Crerar, Thomas Alexander, 1876–
SILVER CREEK DISTRICT IN THE EARLY DAYS. Winnipeg, priv. print., 1955.
15p

Croil, James, 1821–1916
DUNDAS; or, A Sketch of Canadian History, and More Particularly of the
County of Dundas. ... Montreal, Dawson, 1861. 352p [BM BVaU LC
NSWA OTU QMM

Crosskill, William Hay, 1861–
PRINCE EDWARD ISLAND, GARDEN PROVINCE OF CANADA. Its History, Interests,
and Resources. ... Charlottetown, Murley & Garnhum, 1899. 79p [Later
rev. and enl. eds. in 1904 and 1906.] [BVaU LC NSWA OTP QQL

Crowell, Edwin, 1853–1926
A HISTORY OF BARRINGTON TOWNSHIP AND VICINITY, SHELBURNE COUNTY,
NOVA SCOTIA, 1604–1870. With a Biographical and Genealogical Appendix.
Yarmouth, Author, 1923. 603p [BM BVaU LC NSWA OTU QMM

Crown Zellerbach Canada Limited. Richmond Division
A HISTORY OF THE MUNICIPALITY OF RICHMOND. Richmond, B.C., 1958.
28p

Cruickshank, Frederick David
HISTORY OF WESTON. By F.D. Cruickshank and J. Nason. Weston, Ont., Times
& Guide, 1937. 162p [BVaU OTP

Cruikshank, Ernest Alexander, 1854–1939
A CENTURY OF MUNICIPAL HISTORY, 1792–1892. Comp. from the Municipal
Records of the County of Welland. Welland, Tribune Print., 1892–93.
2v in 1. [OTP
COLLECTION OF CONTEMPORARY LETTERS AND DOCUMENTS, JANUARY TO
JULY, 1813. Ed. by ——. Niagara-on-the-Lake, Niagara Hist. Soc., 1939.
87p [UTQ'41
THE FIGHT IN THE BEECHWOODS. A Study in Canadian History. Welland,
Sawle, 1895. 32p [BM BVaU NSHD OTU
HISTORICAL AND DESCRIPTIVE SKETCH OF THE COUNTY OF WELLAND, 1792–
1841. Welland, County Council, 1886. [OTU
THE SETTLEMENT OF THE UNITED EMPIRE LOYALISTS ON THE UPPER ST.

LAWRENCE AND BAY OF QUINTE IN 1784. A Documentary Record, Transcribed and ed. by ——. Toronto, Ontario Hist. Soc., 1934. 188p [BM LC NBFU OTU QMM

THE STORY OF BUTLER'S RANGERS AND THE SETTLEMENT OF NIAGARA. Welland, Tribune Print., 1893. 114p [BM BVaU NSWA OTU

TEN YEARS OF THE COLONY OF NIAGARA, 1780–1790. Welland, Tribune Print:, 1908. 50p [BVaU

Cumberland, Frederic Barlow, 1846–1913

A CENTURY OF SAIL AND STEAM ON THE NIAGARA. Toronto, Musson, 1913. 198p [BM BVaU LC OTU QMM

THE NORTHERN LAKES OF CANADA. ... A Guide. ... Toronto, Hunter Rose, 1886. 198p [BVaU OTP

Cumberland, Robert William, 1895–

THE UNITED EMPIRE LOYALIST SETTLEMENTS BETWEEN KINGSTON AND ADOLPHUSTOWN. Kingston, Jackson Press, 1923. 24p [BVaU NBFU OKQ

Cumberland, W.G.E.

A BRIEF HISTORY OF ALLISTON, FROM THE FOUNDING OF THE FIRST SETTLE-MENT BY WILLIAM FLETCHER UNTIL YEAR OF CENTENNIAL, 1947. ... Comp. by ——. Alliston, Ont., City Clerk, 1947. 128p [BViP OLU

Currie, Mary Olive, 1909–

SO MUCH TO REMEMBER AND TO LOOK FORWARD TO ... STRASBOURG, SASKATCHEWAN, 1905–1955. Strasbourg, Sask., Strasbourg and Community Booster Club, 1955. 20p

Dahlman, Laura Rose (Thorn), 1895–

TWELVE MILE LAKE HISTORY. By Mrs. Laura Dahlman and Mrs. George Cristo. Twelve Mile Lake, Sask., Authors, 1955. 10p [mimeographed]

Dartmouth, N.S. Bicentennial Committee

OFFICIAL BICENTENNIAL PROGRAM AND GUIDE BOOK OF DARTMOUTH, N.S. Halifax, Scott Publications, 1950. 95p [OONL

Davies, Blodwen, 1897–1966

OTTAWA. Portrait of a Capital. Toronto, McGraw-Hill, 1954. 185p

QUEBEC, PORTRAIT OF A PROVINCE. New York, Greenberg, 1951. xiii + 258p

THE STORIED STREETS OF QUEBEC. Montreal, Carrier, 1929. 94p [BVaU LC NBFU OTU QMM

STORIED YORK. Toronto Old and New. Toronto, Ryerson, 1931. 127p [NBFU OTU

Dawson, Carl Addington, 1887–

PIONEERING IN THE PRAIRIE PROVINCES: THE SOCIAL SIDE OF THE SETTLEMENT

PROCESS. By C.A. Dawson and Eva R. Younge. Toronto, Macmillan, 1940. 338p [BM BVaU LC NSHD OTU QMM SSU

THE SETTLEMENT OF THE PEACE RIVER COUNTRY. A Study of a Pioneer Area. Toronto, Macmillan, 1934. 284p [BM BVaU LC NSHD OTU QMM SSU

Dawson, Samuel Edward, 1833–1916

HANDBOOK TO THE CITY OF MONTREAL. With Carnival Supplement. [Anon] [Montreal, Dawson Bros., 1884.] 23 + 143p [NSHPL OLU QMBM

THE SAINT LAWRENCE BASIN. London, Lawrence & Bullen, 1905. 451p [BM BVaU LC NSWA OTU

Day, Catherine Matilda (Townsend), 1815–1899

HISTORY OF THE EASTERN TOWNSHIPS, PROVINCE OF QUEBEC. ... Montreal, Lovell, 1869. 475p [BM BVaU NSWA OTU QMM

PIONEERS OF THE EASTERN TOWNSHIPS. ... Montreal, Lovell, 1863. 171p [BM BVaU LC NSWA OTU QMM

Day, Frank, 1887?–

HERE AND THERE IN ERAMOSA. An Historical Sketch of the Early Years and of the People and Events Contributing to the Growth and Development of the Township. Rockwood, Ont., 1953. 199p

DeGarthe, William Edward, 1907–

THIS IS PEGGY'S COVE, NOVA SCOTIA, CANADA. Halifax, Author, 1956. 35p

Deloraine, Man. Deloraine and District Chamber of Commerce

DELORAINE, MANITOBA, 1880–1955. [A History.] 75th Anniversary Celebration, Sunday, June 19th to Thursday, June 23rd. Deloraine, Man., 1955. 74p

Denison, George Taylor, 1839–1925

THE FENIAN RAID ON FORT ERIE. Toronto, Rollo & Adam, 1866. 92p [BVaU OTU

Denton, Vernon Llewellyn, 1881–1944

THE FAR WEST COAST. Toronto, Dent, 1924. 297p [BM BVaU NSHD OTU

DesBarres, Joseph Frederic Wallet, 1722–1824

LETTERS TO LORD —— on A Caveat against Emigration to America, with the state of the Island of Cape Breton ... 1784 to the present. ... London, Bensley, 1804. 228p [A CAVEAT AGAINST EMIGRATION TO AMERICA, by William Smith, Chief Justice of Cape Breton, was pub. in London in 1803.] [LC

Des Brisay, Mather Byles, 1828–1896

HISTORY OF THE COUNTY OF LUNENBURG. Halifax, Bowes, 1870. 264p [2nd ed.: Toronto, Briggs, 1895. 585p] [BM BVaU LC NSHD OTU

Devine, Rev. Edward James, 1860–1927
HISTORIC CAUGHNAWAGA. Montreal, Messenger Press, 1922. 443p [BVaU
OTU QMM

OLD FORT STE. MARIE: HOME OF THE CANADIAN MARTYRS 1639–1649.
Toronto, Canadian Messenger, 1925. 52p [Earlier ed., Toronto, 1915.
58p] [NBFU OLU QMM

Devine, Patrick Kevin, 1859–1950
YE OLDE ST. JOHN'S, 1750–1939. St. John's, Robinson, 1939. 175p [LC
NSHD OTU

Devore, Roy William, 1891–
THE HISTORY OF WALTERDALE. Edmonton, Author, 1956. 17p

Dimock, Celia C. (Gillis),   –1959
CHILDREN OF THE SHEILING. Sydney, N.S., Lynk Print., n.d. 98p [NSHP
ISLE ROYALE: "THE FRONT DOOR OF CANADA." Halifax, Allen, 1929. 81p
[2nd ed., 1946.] [AEU NSHL OKQ

Doane, Frank Augustus, 1862–1950
OLD TIMES IN BARRINGTON. Truro, Truro Pub. Co., 1948. 95p [NSHD QMM

Dobbin, Francis Hincks, 1850–1923
OUR OLD HOME TOWN. Toronto, Dent, 1943. 246p [About Peterborough,
Ont.] [BM BVaU LC OTU

Doe, Ernest
HISTORY OF SALMON ARM, 1885–1912. Comp. by ——. Salmon Arm, B.C.,
Salmon Arm Observer, 1947. 83p [BVaU OTP
SALMON ARM. A Basic History ... to 1912. Comp. by ——. Salmon Arm,
B.C., 1939. 64p [BVaU

Donohoe, E.F.
KITCHENER CENTENNIAL, 1854–1954. Ed. by ——. Kitchener, Ont., Kitchener -
Waterloo Record, 1954. 108p

Dooner, Alfred James, 1865?–1949
CATHOLIC PIONEERS IN UPPER CANADA. Toronto, Macmillan, 1947. 251p
[BVaU LC OTP

Dorian, Charles Edward, 1881–
THE FIRST 75 YEARS. A Headline History of Sudbury, Canada. Ilfracombe,
Devon, Stockwell, 1959. xi + 300p

Doughty, Arthur George, 1860–1936
THE ACADIAN EXILES. A Chronicle of the Land of Evangeline. Toronto,
Glasgow Brook, 1916. 178p [BM BVaU LC NSHD OTU QMM
THE CRADLE OF NEW FRANCE. A Story of the City Founded by Champlain.
Montreal, Cambridge Corp., 1908. 314p [BM BVaU LC NSWA OTU QMM

THE FORTRESS OF QUEBEC, 1608–1903. Quebec, Dussault & Proulx, 1904.
126p [BM LC NSWA

THE KING'S BOOK OF QUEBEC. Comp. by A.G. Doughty and W.C.H. Wood.
Ottawa, Mortimer, 1911. 2v [Memorial of tercentenary celebrations of 1908.]
[BM NBFU OTU

QUEBEC OF YESTER-YEAR. Toronto, Nelson, 1932. 198p [BM BVaU LC
NSHD OTU QMM

QUEBEC UNDER TWO FLAGS. A Brief History of the City. ... By A.G. Doughty
and N.E. Dionne. Quebec, Quebec News, 1903. 424p [BM BVaU NSWA
OTU QMM

THE SIEGE OF QUEBEC AND THE BATTLE OF THE PLAINS OF ABRAHAM. [In
collab. with G.W. Parmelee.] Quebec, Dussault & Proulx, 1901–2. 6v
[BM BVaU NBFU OTU

Douglas, Mrs. Helen Frances, 1898–

GOLDEN KERNELS OF GRANUM. The Story of the Early Settlers of Granum.
Granum, Alta., Author, n.d. 79p

Douglas, James, 1837–1918

OLD FRANCE IN THE NEW WORLD. Quebec in the Seventeenth Century. Cleveland,
Burrows, 1905. 597p [BM BVaU NSHD OTU

Douglas, Robert, 1881–1930

PLACE-NAMES OF PRINCE EDWARD ISLAND, WITH MEANINGS. Comp. by ——.
Ottawa, King's Printer, 1925. 55p [BM BVaU OLU OONL

Downs, Arthur George, 1924–

QUESNEL, BRITISH COLUMBIA. Quesnel, B.C., Cariboo Digest, 1954. 30p

WAGON ROAD NORTH. The Story of the Cariboo Gold Rush in Historical
Photos. Quesnel, B.C., Northwest Digest, 1960. 76p

Drake, Earl Gordon, 1928–

REGINA, THE QUEEN CITY. Toronto, McClelland, 1955. ix + 260p

Draper, William George, –1868

HISTORY OF THE CITY OF KINGSTON. Kingston, Creighton, 1862. 28p [OTP

Driver, Sask. School

HISTORY OF DRIVER S.D. NO. 811 AND VICINITY. Driver, Sask., 1955. 1v
(unpaged) [mimeographed]

Drouin, Lucien Henri, 1919–

HISTORY OF ST. PAUL. Histoire de Saint-Paul. 1909–1959. By L.H. Drouin and
others. St. Paul, Alta., St. Paul Journal, 1960. 232p [Text partly in English,
partly in French.]

Drury, Ernest Charles, 1878–

ALL FOR A BEAVER HAT. A History of Early Simcoe County. Toronto, Ryerson,
1959. xvi + 160p

THE STORY OF SIMCOE COUNTY, LAND OF HOLIDAY AND HISTORY. Barrie,
  Ont., County Council of Simcoe, 1955. 28p

Duff, Louis Blake, 1878–1959
CROWLAND. Welland, Baskerville, 1928. 60p [BM BVaU NBFU OTU QMM

Dumbrille, Dorothy, 1898–
BRAGGART IN MY STEP. More Stories of Glengarry. Toronto, Ryerson, 1956.
  ix + 173p
UP AND DOWN THE GLENS. The Story of Glengarry. Toronto, Ryerson, 1954.
  139p

Duncan, Mrs. Frances Imogene, 1926–
THE SAYWARD-KELSEY BAY SAGA. Courtenay, B.C., Argus Pub. Co., 1958.
  51p

Dundas County, Ont.
HISTORY OF THE COUNTY OF DUNDAS FROM 1784 TO 1904. Iroquois, 1905.
  [BVaU NBFU OOP

Dundurn, Sask. School
DUNDURN. The Village and District of Dundurn Throughout the Years. Dundurn,
  Sask., 1955. 89p [mimeographed]

Dunham, Bertha Mabel, 1881–1957
GRAND RIVER. Toronto, McClelland, 1945. 299p [BVaU NBFU OKQ QMM

Dunn, Charles William, 1915–
HIGHLAND SETTLER. A Portrait of the Scottish Gael in Nova Scotia. Toronto,
  U. of Toronto Press, 1953. 179p

Duquette, Rev. Carson W., 1913–
GENTLE PEOPLE. Gatineau Story. Ottawa, 1955. 72 + 78p [History of the town
  of Gatineau, Que. Text in English and French.]

Earle, Emily Mae (Waite), 1882–
FOOTPRINTS IN NEW BRUNSWICK. An Historical Account of Victoria County,
  New Brunswick. Perth, N.B., 1959. 175p

Earle, Evelyn Purvis
LEEDS THE LOVELY. Toronto, Ryerson, 1951. 174p

Eastern Irrigation District, Brooks, Alta.
THE HISTORY OF THE EASTERN IRRIGATION DISTRICT. 25th Anniversary,
  May 1st, 1960. Brooks, Alta., the District, 1960. 64p

Eaton, Arthur Wentworth Hamilton, 1849–1937
THE HISTORY OF KING'S COUNTY, NOVA SCOTIA. Giving a Sketch of the French

and their Expulsion and a History of the New England Planters ... 1604–1910. Salem, Mass., Salem Press, 1910. 898p [BM BVaU LC NSWA OTU QMSS

Eaton, Mrs. Grace Elvira, 1905–

GREEN HILL. The Story of a Prairie Community and its Pioneers. By Grace E. Eaton and Lloyd L. Vallée. Carlyle, Sask., Authors, 1955. [unpaged]

Eatonia, Sask. School

AS FAR AS I REMEMBER. Comp. and pub. by Eatonia School staff and pupils. Eatonia, Sask., The Enterprise, 1955. 8p

Eby, Ezra E., 1850–

A BIOGRAPHICAL HISTORY OF WATERLOO TOWNSHIP AND OTHER TOWNSHIPS OF THE COUNTY. Being a History of the Early Settlers and their Descendants &c. Berlin, Ont., n.p., 1895–96. 2v [OTU

Edgar, Matilda (Ridout), 1844–1910

TEN YEARS OF UPPER CANADA IN PEACE AND WAR, 1805–1815. Being the Ridout Letters. With annotations by ——. (Appendix: THE NARRATIVE OF THE CAPTIVITY AMONG THE SHAWANESE INDIANS, IN 1788, OF THOS. RIDOUT.) Toronto, Briggs, 1890. 389p [BM BVaU LC NSHD OTP

Edmonds, Walter Everard, 1875–

EDMONTON, PAST AND PRESENT. Edmonton, Douglas, 1943. 32p [BVaU OTP SSU

Edstrom, Mrs. Sylvia, 1914–

MEMOIRS OF THE EDBERG PIONEERS. Comp. by Sylvia Edstrom and Florence Lundstrom. Edberg, Alta., 1956. 121p

Edwards, Joseph Plimsoll, 1857–1930

LOUISBOURG. An Historical Sketch. ... Halifax, Nova Scotia Print., 1895. 62p [BM NSWA OTU QMM

Elder, Annie Edna (Vallis), 1882–

HISTORY OF NEW JERUSALEM [in Queen's County, N.B.]. Fredericton, priv. print., 1953. 97p

Elliott, George B.

WINNIPEG AS IT IS IN 1874; and as it was in 1860. ... Ottawa, Free Press Office, 1875. 36p [ACG NSHPL OTP QMSS

Elliott, Gordon Raymond, 1920–

QUESNEL. Commercial Centre of the Cariboo Gold Rush. Quesnel, B.C., Cariboo Historical Society, 1958. 190p

Elstow, Sask. High School

SOD SHACK TO ATOMIC AGE. Elstow-Clavet. Elstow, Sask., 1955. 36p [mimeographed]

Emigrant Lady (pseud)
LETTERS FROM MUSKOKA. By an Emigrant Lady [pseud]. London, Bentley, 1878.
xii + 289p [BM LC OTU

England, Robert, 1894–
THE COLONIZATION OF WESTERN CANADA. A Study of Contemporary Land
Settlement (1896–1934). London, King, 1936. 341p [BM BVaU LC OTU
QMM

English, Leo Edward Francis, 1887–
OUTLINE OF NEWFOUNDLAND HISTORY. London, Toronto, Nelson, [1929]. 109p
[2nd ed., rev., with title: NEWFOUNDLAND PAST AND PRESENT. Toronto, Nelson,
1949. 128p] [BM NfSM OTP

Entremont, H. Leander d', 1862–
THE BARONNIE DE POMBCOUP AND THE ACADIANS. Yarmouth, Herald-Telegram,
1931. 192p [BM BVaU NSWA OTU
THE FORTS OF CAPE SABLE OF THE SEVENTEENTH CENTURY. Centre East Pubnico,
N.S., Davis, 1938. 106p [LC NBFU OTU

Ermatinger, Charles Oakes Zaccheus, 1851–1921
RECORD OF THE CELEBRATION OF THE CENTENARY OF THE TALBOT SETTLEMENT
... 1903. St. Thomas, Elgin Historical and Scientific Institute, 1910. 72p [OLU
OTU
THE TALBOT REGIME; or, The First Half Century of the Talbot Settlement. St.
Thomas, Municipal World, 1904. 393p [BM BVaU LC NBFU OTU QMM

Essex County, Ont.
COMMEMORATIVE BIOGRAPHICAL RECORD OF THE COUNTY OF ESSEX. ... Toronto,
Beers, 1905. 676p [OLU

Essex County, Ont. Tourist Association
ESSEX COUNTY SKETCHES. Windsor, Ont., Herald Press, 1947. 50p [OTU

Evans, Len
THE COPELAND STORY, 1905–1955. By Len Evans and others. Wynyard, Sask.,
Wynyard Advance, 1955. 15p

Ewart, John Skirving, 1849–1933
THE MANITOBA SCHOOL QUESTION. An Historical Account of the Red River
Outbreak in 1869 and 1870. ... Toronto, Copp Clark, 1894. 401p [BM BVaU
LC NSHD OTU

Fahrni, Margaret (Morton)
THIRD CROSSING. A History of the First Quarter Century of the Town and District
of Gladstone in the Province of Manitoba. By Margaret Morton Fahrni and William
Lewis Morton. Winnipeg, Advocate Press, 1946. 118p [BVaU LC QMM SSU

Fairchild, George Moore, 1854–1912

FROM MY QUEBEC SCRAP BOOK. Quebec, Carrel, 1907. 316p [BM BVaU OTU QMM

GLEANINGS FROM QUEBEC. Quebec, Carrel, 1908. 216p [BM BVaU LC OTU

A HISTORY OF THE QUEBEC WINTER CARNIVAL. Quebec, Carrel, 1894. 140p [BM BVa OTU

JOURNAL OF AN AMERICAN PRISONER AT FORT MALDEN AND QUEBEC IN THE WAR OF 1812. Ed. by ——. Quebec, Carrel, 1909. 32p [BVaU OTU

A SHORT ACCOUNT OF YE QUEBEC WINTER CARNIVAL HOLDEN IN 1894. Quebec, Daily Telegraph, 1894. [BVaU

Farewell, John Edwin Chandler, 1840–1923

COUNTY OF ONTARIO. Short Notes as to the Early Settlement and Progress of the County, and Brief References to the Pioneers and some Ontario County Men who have taken a Prominent Part in Provincial and Dominion Affairs. Whitby, Gazette-Chronicle, 1907. 318p [BVaU OTU

Farm Women's Union of Alberta. Beddington Local

THE NOSE CREEK STORY FROM 1792. Prepared and Written by Members of the Community. Calgary, 1960. 156p [History of the district between Calgary and Airdrie, Alta.]

Farmer, Samuel, 1871–1948

ON THE SHORES OF THE SCUGOG. Rev. and enl. ed. Port Perry, Ont., Port Perry Star, 1934. 256p [First pub. in 1913.] [OTP

Farquharson, Donald Robert

TALES AND MEMOIRS OF CROMAR AND CANADA. Chatham, Planet, [1930?]. 215p [BVaU NBFU OLU

Ferrier, Alexander David, 1813–1890

REMINISCENCES OF CANADA AND THE EARLY DAYS OF FERGUS. Being Three Lectures delivered ... in 1864 and 1865. Fergus, Ont., News-Record, 1923. 47p [First pub. in 1866.] [BVaU OTP

Fife Lake, Sask. School

FIFE LAKE, A LOCAL HISTORY. Saskatchewan Jubilee, 1955. Fife Lake, 1956. 10p [mimeographed]

Finch Township, Ont. Teachers

PIONEER HISTORY OF FINCH TOWNSHIP. Comp. by the teachers of Finch Township. Finch, Ont., 1957. 47p [mimeographed]

Findlay, J.W.M.

THE PEMBROKE CENTENNIAL SOUVENIR BOOK. ... Commemorating the Centennial of Pembroke's Incorporation as a Village in 1858. ... Ed. by ——. Pembroke, Ont., Pembroke Observer, 1958. 156p

Finn, T.D.

CENTENARY OF OTTAWA, 1854–1954. "The Capital Chosen by a Queen." Ed. by ——. Ottawa, 1954. 76p

Fisher, Peter, 1782–1848

HISTORY OF NEW BRUNSWICK ... As Originally Published in 1825. Saint John, New Brunswick Historical Soc., 1921. 133p [1st ed. under title: SKETCHES OF NEW BRUNSWICK. Containing an Account of the First Settlement of the Province. By an Inhabitant of the Province [pseud]. Saint John, Chubb & Sears, 1825. 108p] [BM BVaU NSWA OLU

NOTITIA OF NEW-BRUNSWICK, FOR 1836, AND EXTENDING INTO 1837. ... By an Inhabitant. Saint John, Chubb, 1838. 134p [NSWA OTP

SKETCHES OF NEW BRUNSWICK. ... [See under HISTORY OF NEW BRUNSWICK].

Fitzgerald, James Edward, 1818–1896

AN EXAMINATION OF THE CHARTER AND PROCEEDINGS OF THE HUDSON'S BAY COMPANY, WITH REFERENCE TO ... VANCOUVER'S ISLAND. London, Saunders, 1849. 293p [BM BVaU OTU

Fleming, John, 1786?–1832

POLITICAL ANNALS OF LOWER CANADA. Being a Review of the Political and Legislative History ... under the Act of the Imperial Parliament ... Which Established a House of Assembly and Legislative Council. Showing the Defects. ... By a British Settler [pseud]. Montreal, Herald & Gazette, 1828. lxxviii + 180p [Covers period 1759–1811, and ends with the words: "End of the first part." No more published.] [BM BVaU LC NSWA OTP QMM

Fleming, Sandford, 1827–1915

MEMORIAL OF THE PEOPLE OF RED RIVER ... ON THE COLONIZATION ... AND THE ESTABLISHMENT OF A GREAT TERRITORIAL ROAD ... TO BRITISH COLUMBIA. Quebec, Hunter Rose, 1863. 57p [BViPA

Fonthill, Ont. Women's Institute

HISTORY OF THE VILLAGE OF FONTHILL. Welland, the Institute, 1944. 51p [OTU

Forest, Ont. Centennial Committee

FOREST AND DISTRICT CENTENNIAL 1859–1959. Forest, 1959. 195p

Fort Erie, Ont. Times-Review

FORT ERIE CENTENNIAL, 1857–1957. Fort Erie, Review Co., 1957. 56p

GOLDEN JUBILEE SUPPLEMENT, July 18, 1945. Fort Erie, Times Review, 1945. 48p [OTU

Fox, William Sherwood, 1878–1967

THE BRUCE BECKONS. The Story of Lake Huron's Great Peninsula. Toronto, U. of Toronto Press, 1952. xviii + 235p

'T AIN'T RUNNIN' NO MORE. The Story of Grand Bend, the Pinery and the Old

River Bed. ... London, Ont., Holmes, 1946. 55p [BVaU LC NBFU OKQ
'T AIN'T RUNNIN' NO MORE—TWENTY YEARS AFTER. The Story of Grand Bend, the Pinery and the Watershed of the Aux Sables River. London, Ont., Oxford Book Shop, 1958. xii + 89p

Frame, Archibald
SELMAH IN 1853. A Paper read before the Presbyterian Social in Selmah, N.S. Halifax, Herald Print., 1894. 18p [NSHP OKQ

Frame, Elizabeth, 1820–1913
A LIST OF MICMAC NAMES OF PLACES, RIVERS, ETC., IN NOVA SCOTIA. Comp. by ——. Cambridge, Wilson, 1892. 12p [BM LC NSWA OTU

Fraser, Alexander, 1860–1936
A HISTORY OF ONTARIO. Toronto, Canada Hist. Co., 1907. 2v [BVaU LC OTU QMM
THE LAST LAIRD OF MACNAB. An Episode in the Settlement of MacNab Township, Upper Canada. Toronto, Imrie Graham, 1899. 218p [BVaU LC OTP
TORONTO, HISTORICAL, DESCRIPTIVE AND PICTORIAL. Toronto, Waverley Press, 1901. 46p [BM BVaU OTU

Fraser, George B.
MORRIS, MANITOBA, GROWTH AND PROGRESS. With Personal Sketches. Morris, Herald Print., 1882. 31p [Peel

Fraser, George Johnston, 1872–
THE STORY OF OSOYOOS, SEPTEMBER 1811 TO DECEMBER 1952. Penticton, B.C., Penticton Herald, 1952. 212p

Fraser, John, 1820–1899
HISTORIC CANADIAN GROUND. The LaSalle Homestead of 1666 and Other Old Landmarks of French Canada. ... Montreal, Witness, 1892. 30p [BM BVaU LC NSHD OTU QMM

Fraser, L.R., 1873?–
HISTORY OF MUSKOKA. Bracebridge, Ont., Thomas, 1946. 152p [BVaU OTP

Fredericton, N.B. City Council
FREDERICTON'S 100 YEARS: Then and Now. Fredericton, the Council, 1948. 267p [NBFU OTU

Frith, B.M.
A SHORT HISTORY OF THE WAKOW DISTRICT. Wakow, Recorder, 1932. 60p [SSU

Fryer, Charles Edmund, 1876–
A HISTORY OF QUEBEC, ITS RESOURCES AND ITS PEOPLE. By Benjamin Sulte ... C.E. Fryer ... L.O. David. Montreal & Toronto, Canada History Co., 1908. 2v [BM LC OLU

Gabriel, Theresa
VERNON, BRITISH COLUMBIA. A Brief History. Vernon, Centennial Committee, 1958. 63p

Gaetz, Annie Louise (Siddall), 1881–
THE PARK COUNTRY. A History of Red Deer and District. Red Deer, Alta., Author, 1948. 173p [Rev. ed., 1960.] [AEU BVaU OTU
TRAILS OF YESTERDAY. Folk Lore of the Red Deer District. Red Deer, Alta., Author, 1952. 99p

Gaetz, Rev. Leonard, 1841–1907
REPORT OF SIX YEARS' EXPERIENCE OF A FARMER IN THE RED DEER DISTRICT. Ottawa, Dawson, 1892. 31p [OTU SSU

Gale, George Gordon, 1857–1940
HISTORIC TALES OF OLD QUEBEC. Quebec, Telegraph, 1920. 245p [Rev. and enl.: 1923. 344p] [BM BVaU LC NSHD OTU QMM
QUEBEC 'TWIXT OLD AND NEW. Quebec, Telegraph, 1915. 296p [BM BVaU LC NBFU OTU

Gallagher, Edward L.
HISTORY OF OLD KINGSTON AND REXTON. Sussex, N.B., Maritime, 1948. 51p [NBFU OTU QMM

Galloway, Hazel Frances (Dempsey), 1921–
A HISTORY OF THE CEDAR, BRIGHT, CRANBERRY AND OYSTER DISTRICTS ON VANCOUVER ISLAND, B.C. Comp. by Mrs. Allan Galloway and Robert Strachan. Ladysmith, B.C., Cedar Centennial Committee, 1958. 26p [mimeographed]

Ganong, William Francis, 1864–1941
THE HISTORY OF CARAQUET & POKEMOUCHE. Rev. and Enl. from the Author's MS. Notes. Ed. by Susan Brittain Ganong. Saint John, New Brunswick Museum, 1948. 62p [OTU
THE HISTORY OF MISCOU AND SHIPPEGAN. Rev. and Enl. from the Author's MS. Notes. Ed. by Susan Brittain Ganong. Saint John, New Brunswick Museum, 1946. 92p [BVaU NSWA OTU
A MONOGRAPH OF HISTORIC SITES IN THE PROVINCE OF NEW BRUNSWICK. Ottawa, Hope, 1899. 357p [BVaU OLU
STE. CROIX (DOUCHET) ISLAND. Ed. by Susan Brittain Ganong. Saint John, 1945. 125p [LC NSWA OKQ

Gardiner, Herbert Fairbairn, 1849–1924
NOTHING BUT NAMES. ... Toronto, Morang, 1899. 561p [BVaU NSHD OTP

Garratt, Alfred Webster, 1871–
HISTORY OF MILESTONE, 1893–1910. Milestone, Sask., Author, 1948. 129p [BVaU OOA SSU

Garrett, Anne (Evans)

THE BOWEN ISLAND STORY. Bowen Island, B.C., 1957. 16p

Garrett, Rev. John C.

... HISTORIC BUILDINGS; THE CENTENNIAL – AN OLD CANADIAN FORT. Welland, Tribune, 1911. 57p [LC OLU

Garrioch, Rev. Alfred Campbell, 1848–1934

THE CORRECTION LINE. Winnipeg, Stovel, 1933. 414p [BM BVaU OTU

FIRST FURROWS. A History of the Early Settlement of the Red River Country, including that of Portage la Prairie. Winnipeg, Stovel, 1923. 336p [BM BVaU LC OTU SSU

Gayton, Albert, 1840–1923

KEMPTVILLE, YARMOUTH COUNTY, NOVA SCOTIA. An Historical Sketch. Yarmouth, Vickery, 1911. 19p [NSWA OOA

Gellatly, Dorothy (Hewlett)

A BIT OF OKANAGAN HISTORY. Kelowna, Kelowna Print., 1932. 80p [Rev. Centennial ed., Kelowna, Orchard City Press, 1958. 133p] [BVaU OTU

Gerein, Rev. Frank

HISTORY OF ODESSA. To Commemorate the 50th Anniversary of the Advent of Odessa's First Settlers and the 40th Anniversary of the Founding of Holy Family Parish, Odessa, Saskatchewan. ... Regina, Western Printers, 1954. 68p

Gershaw, Frederick William, 1883–

MEDICINE HAT. Sidelights on Early Days in Medicine Hat and Vicinity. N.p., [1950?]. 66p [OOP

"MEDICINE HAT." Early Days in Southern Alberta. N.p., [1954?]. 70p [Same as preceding title?]

RANCHING IN SOUTHERN ALBERTA. [Medicine Hat, Modern Press], n.d. 24p [OTU

"THE SHORT GRASS AREA." A Brief History of Southern Alberta. N.p., [1956?]. 123p

Ghent, Percy Parker, 1888–1952

YULETIDE IN LITTLE YORK. Sleigh Ride through the Quaint Town that Became the City of Toronto. Toronto, Bond, 1937. 11p [OTU

Ghost Pine Community Group

MEMOIRS OF THE GHOST PINE HOMESTEADERS. Three Hills, Alta., Capital Printers, 1954. 196p

Gibbon, John Murray, 1875–1952

TIME AND TIDE IN THE ATLANTIC PROVINCES. By John Murray Gibbon and Leo Cox. Sackville, N.B., Enamel and Heating Products Ltd., 1952, 46p

OUR OLD MONTREAL. Toronto, McClelland, 1947. 266p [BVaU LC QMM

Gilbert, George, 1867?–1957
BATHURST, 1891–1951. Bathurst, N.B., n.d. 18p

Gilpin, John Bernard, 1810–1892
SABLE ISLAND. Its Past History, Present Appearance, Natural History, Etc.
Halifax, Wesleyan Conference, 1858. 34p [Bound with a lecture by Joseph
Darby and a poem by Joseph Howe.] [LC NSWA OTP QMM

Gilroy, Marion
LOYALISTS AND LAND SETTLEMENT IN NOVA SCOTIA. Comp. by ——. Halifax,
Nova Scotia Archives, 1937. 154p [BM BVaU NSHD OLU QMBM

Given, Robert A.
THE STORY OF ETOBICOKE. Etobicoke, Ont., 1950. 76p [OONL

Glover, Terrot Reaveley, 1869–1943
A CORNER OF EMPIRE, THE OLD ONTARIO STRAND. By T.R. Glover and D.D.
Calvin. Toronto, Macmillan, 1937. 178p [BVaU NBFU OKQ QMM

Gogo, Jean Louise, 1901–
LIGHTS ON THE ST. LAWRENCE. An Anthology. Ed. by ——. Toronto, Ryerson,
1958. 303p

Golden, B.C. Centennial Committee. Historical Branch
GOLDEN MEMORIES OF THE TOWN WHERE THE TURBULENT KICKING HORSE
MEETS THE MIGHTY COLUMBIA. Golden, B.C., the Committee, 1958. 91p
[mimeographed]

Goodchild, Frederick Henry, 1892–1955
BRITISH COLUMBIA. Its History, People and Industry. London, Allen & Unwin,
1951. 219p

Goodfellow, John Christie, 1890–
THE STORY OF SIMILKAMEEN. Princeton, B.C., Similkameen Spotlight, 1958.
V. 1.
TOTEM POLES IN STANLEY PARK. Vancouver, Art Historical and Scientific
Assn., 1924. 44p [BM BVaU LC OTU

Goodyear, Hedley John, 1886–1918
NEWFOUNDLAND AND ITS POLITICAL AND COMMERCIAL RELATION TO CANADA.
Toronto, U. of Toronto Press, [1913]. 48p [NfSM OTUV

Gordon, George Lawson, 1853–1919
RIVER JOHN, ITS PASTORS AND PEOPLE. New Glasgow, N.S., Author, 1911.
152p [BVaU NSWA OTP

Gordon, William Austin, 1885–
LAKE ERIE'S ISLE OF ROMANCE. Port Dover, Ont., Author, 1934. 56p [OTU

Gosling, William Gilbert, 1863–1930

LABRADOR. Its Discovery, Exploration and Development. London, Rivers, 1910. 574p [BM BVaU LC NSWA OKQ QMU

Gosnell, R. Edward, 1860–1931

A HISTORY: BRITISH COLUMBIA. [Victoria?], Hill Binding Co., 1906. 783p [BVaU OOP

LAND OF THE OKANAGAN, BRITISH COLUMBIA. Vancouver, Daily Telegram, [1891?]. 48p [OOA

Gourlay, John Lowry, 1821–1904

HISTORY OF THE OTTAWA VALLEY. A Collection of Facts, Events and Reminiscences for over half a Century. Ottawa, 1896. 288p [BM BVaU LC MWU NSWA OTU QMM

Gow, John Milne, 1844–1898

CAPE BRETON ILLUSTRATED. Historic, Picturesque and Descriptive. ... Toronto, Briggs, 1893. 423p [BM BVaU LC NSWA OTU QMM

Graham, Audrey, 1912–

HISTORIC ST. JOHN'S AT YORK MILLS, 1816–43. Comp. by ——. Toronto, Hendrick-Jewell, 1935. 61p [BVaU OTP

Graham, Clara

FUR AND GOLD IN THE KOOTENAYS. Vancouver, Wrigley, 1945. 206p [BVaU NBFU OTP

Graham, Janet (Pollock), 1880–

THE WATER HIGHWAY OF ARGENTEUIL AND ITS CENTENNIAL ANNIVERSARY. Lachute, Que., Watchman, 1933. 16p [OTP

Graham, Myrtle E., 1892–

DALRYMPLE ON THE LAKE, 1855–1955. By Myrtle Graham, Grace Deverell, and Margaret Stewart. Sebright, Ont., 1956. 47p

Grant, Rev. George Monro, 1835–1902

THE EASTERNMOST RIDGE OF THE CONTINENT. Historical and Descriptive Sketch of the Scenery and Life in New Brunswick, Nova Scotia, and Prince Edward Island. Ed. by ——. Chicago, Belford, 1899. 216p [BVaU LC NBFU OLU QMBM

FRENCH CANADIAN LIFE AND CHARACTER. With Historical and Descriptive Sketches of the Scenery and Life in Quebec, Montreal, Ottawa, and Surrounding Country. Ed. by ——. Chicago, Belford, 1899. 249p [BVaU LC OTP

Grant, Rev. Robert, 1824?–1900

EAST RIVER SKETCHES: HISTORICAL AND BIOGRAPHICAL. New Glasgow, MacKenzie, 1895. 92p [NSWA OTU

Grant, Robert W.
THE HUMBOLDT STORY, 1903–1953. A Brief History of the Town of Humboldt,
   its Pioneers and Development. Humboldt, Sask., Board of Trade, 1954. 65p

Gray, Clayton, 1918–
THE MONTREAL STORY. Montreal, Whitcombe & Gilmour, 1949. 84p [OONL

Greeley, Hugh Payne, 1884–
WORK AND PLAY IN THE GRENFELL MISSION. ... By Hugh Payne Greeley and
   Floretta Elmore Greeley. With an intro. by Dr. Wilfred T. Grenfell. Toronto,
   Revell, 1920. 192p [BVaU LC OTU

Green, Ernest, 1882–1947
LINCOLN AT BAY. A Sketch of 1814. Welland, Tribune-Telegraph, 1923.
   78p [BVaU LC NSHD OTU QMM
SOME GRAVES IN LUNDY'S LANE. Niagara, Historical Soc., 1912. 82p [LC
   OTP

Green, George, –1955
HISTORY OF BURNABY AND VICINITY. ... North Vancouver, Author, 1947.
   233p [BVaU LC OTU

Greening, Roy M., 1925–
THE KNOTTY SERPENT. A Tale of Ogopogo. Kelowna, B.C., Author, 1957.
   17p

Greenwood, Rev. Walter R.
HISTORY OF FREEPORT, N.S., 1784–1934. Freeport, Davis, 1934. 46p [LC
   NSWA OOA

Greig, Emma (Danard), 1889–
THE SWAN RIVER VALLEY, 1898–1958. Comp. by ——. N.p., 1958. 80p

Griffin, Harold John Michael, 1912–
BRITISH COLUMBIA. The People's Early Story. Vancouver, Tribune Pub., 1958.
   95p

Guardian Associates Ltd.
GRAND FALLS, BOTWOOD, BISHOP'S FALLS, BADGER, MILLERTOWN, TERRA NOVA,
   NEWFOUNDLAND. Paper and Pulpwood Towns of the Interior. Montreal,
   1951. 48p [Story by Ewart Young.]
ST. JOHN'S NEWFOUNDLAND. The Oldest City in North America, Capital of
   Canada's Newest Province. Montreal, St. John's Publicity Committee of the
   Newfoundland Board of Trade, 1950. 64p [OONL

Guillet, Edwin Clarence, 1898–
COBOURG, 1798–1948. ... Oshawa, Goodfellow, 1948. 259p [BVaU OTP
THE COBOURG CONSPIRACY. An Account of a Little-Known Episode in the

disturbed Times which followed the Rebellion of 1837. ... Toronto, 1949. 27p [OTP

EARLY LIFE IN UPPER CANADA. Toronto, Ontario Pub. Co., 1933. 782p [BM BVaU LC NBFU OTP QMM

THE LIVES AND TIMES OF THE PATRIOTS. An Account of the Rebellion in Upper Canada, 1837–1838, and the Patriot Agitation in the United States, 1837–1842. Toronto, Nelson, 1938. 304p [BM BVaU LC NBFU OTU QMM

PIONEER LIFE IN THE COUNTY OF YORK. Toronto, Hess-Trade Typesetting Co., 1946. 166p [OTU

TORONTO FROM TRADING POST TO GREAT CITY. Toronto, Ontario Pub. Co., 1934. 495p [BM BVaU LC NSHD OKQ

THE VALLEY OF THE TRENT. Ed. by ——. Toronto, Champlain Society for the Government of Ontario, 1957. lviii + 474p

Gunn, Donald, 1797–1878

HISTORY OF MANITOBA. From the Earliest Settlement till 1835. Ottawa, Maclean, 1880. 482p [BM BVaU LC NSWA OTU QMM

Gunn, John J., 1861–1907

ECHOES OF THE RED. A Reprint of Some of the Early Writings of the Author depicting Pioneer Days in the Red River Settlements. ... Toronto, Macmillan, 1930. 246p [BM BVaU LC OTU

Hafford, Sask. District History Committee

SKETCHES OF HAFFORD AND DISTRICT. Hafford, Sask., 1955. 9p

Hahn, Josephine Elizabeth

HOME OF MY YOUTH, HANOVER. Hanover, Ont., Author, 1947. 298p [OTP

Haig-Brown, Roderick Langmere, 1908–

THE FARTHEST SHORES. Toronto, Longmans Green, 1960. ix + 127p [Radio dramatizations of the exploration of British Columbia, produced over the CBC national network during 1958.]

Haliburton, Robert Grant, 1831–1901

THE PAST AND FUTURE OF NOVA SCOTIA. An Address on the 113th Anniversary of the Settlement of that Province. Halifax, 1862. 27p [BM NSWA

Haliburton, Thomas Chandler, 1796–1865

AN HISTORICAL AND STATISTICAL ACCOUNT OF NOVA SCOTIA. ... Halifax, Howe, 1829. 2v [BM BVaU LC NSWA OTU QMM

Hall, Mrs. Mary Georgina Caroline

A LADY'S LIFE ON A FARM IN MANITOBA. By Mrs. Cecil Hall. London, Allen, 1884. 171p [BVaU OTP

Hallam, Lillian Gertrude (Best), —1939
WHEN YOU ARE IN HALIFAX. Sketches of Life in the First English Settlement
in Canada. By Mrs. W.T. Hallam. Toronto, Church Book Room, 1937. 83p
[BVaU LC NSHD OTP

Halliwell, Mrs. Gladys M., 1892—
THREE SCORE AND TEN, 1886—1956. A Story of the Swedish settlement of
Stockholm and District. By Gladys M. Halliwell and M. Zetta D. Persson.
Yorkton, Sask., Redeemer's Voice Press, 1959. 192p

Hambley, Rev. George Henry, 1896—
HISTORICAL RECORDS AND ACCOUNTS OF THE EARLY PIONEERS OF THE
DISTRICT OF SWAN LAKE, MANITOBA, FROM ITS EARLY SETTLEMENT, 1873—1950.
N.p., 1952. 280p [Jacket title: PIONEERS, OH! PIONEERS.]
TRAILS OF THE PIONEERS. Records, Accounts, Historical Studies, Data, Reports,
Letters of the Section of Manitoba, Canada, Lying Southwest of Winnipeg
in the Red River Valley and Centered on the Town of Roland, Manitoba.
Altona, Man., D.W. Friesen, 1956. xiii + 295p

Hamil, Frederick Coyne, 1903—
THE VALLEY OF THE LOWER THAMES, 1640 TO 1850. Toronto, U. of Toronto
Press, 1951. xi + 390p

Hamilton, Basil G.
THE LEGEND OF WINDERMERE. 2nd ed. Invermere, B.C., Author, 1921. 12p
[BViPA OONM
NAMING OF COLUMBIA RIVER AND THE PROVINCE OF BRITISH COLUMBIA.
[Cranbrook, B.C.], Cranbrook Courier, [1921]. 16p [BVaU OORD

Hamilton, James Herbert, 1879—
WESTERN SHORES. Narratives of the Pacific Coast. By Captain Kettle [pseud].
Vancouver, Progress, 1932. 218p [BM BVaU NBFU OTU

Hamilton, Reuben, 1888—
MOUNT PLEASANT EARLY DAYS. Memories of Reuben Hamilton, Pioneer, 1890.
Vancouver, City Archives, 1957. 64p

Hamilton, Ont. Spectator
HAMILTON SPECTATOR, 100th ANNIVERSARY, 1846—1946. Reflections of a
Hundred Years. Hamilton, Spectator, 1946. 84p [OTU
WENTWORTH LANDMARKS. [Collected from the Columns of the Hamilton
Spectator.] Hamilton, Spectator, n.d. 147p [OOP

Hamlyn, Rupert Gladstone, 1887—
BOWMANVILLE. A Retrospect by Rupert G. Hamlyn, Elsie Carruthers Lunney,
and David R. Morrison. Bowmanville, Ont., Centennial Committee, 1958.
10 + 80p

Hannay, James, 1842–1910

THE HISTORY OF ACADIA. From its First Discovery to its Surrender to England, by the Treaty of Paris. Saint John, McMillan, 1879. 440p [BM BVaU LC NBFU OKQ QMU

HISTORY OF NEW BRUNSWICK. Saint John, Bowes, 1909. 2v [BM BVaU LC NSWA OTU

LIFE AND TIMES OF SIR LEONARD TILLEY. Being a Political History of New Brunswick, for the past Seventy Years. Saint John, 1897. 400p [BM BVaU NSHD OTU

THE STORY OF ACADIA. Kentville, Dominion Atlantic Railway, [19—?]. 128p [An abridgement of THE HISTORY OF ACADIA.] [BVaU NSHD OLU

Hanley, Sask. High School

HANLEY. The Story of the Town and District. Prepared by the pupils of Hanley High School, Saskatchewan, 1954–1955, Jubilee year. Hanley, Sask., 1955. 134p [mimeographed]

Hanson, Mrs. Sarah Foss

HOMESTEADING AT CLAVET, SASKATCHEWAN. Clavet, Sask., Homemakers' Club, 1956. 24p

Hargrave, Joseph James, 1841–1894

RED RIVER. Montreal, Lovell, 1871. 506p [BM BVaU LC NSWA OTP SSU

Harker, Douglas Edward, 1911–

THE CITY AND THE STORE. Vancouver, Woodward Stores, 1958. 29p

Harkness, John Graham, 1865–1948

STORMONT, DUNDAS, AND GLENGARRY. A History, 1784–1945. Morrisburg, Author, 1946. 601p [BVaU NSWA OTU

Harnett, Legh

TWO LECTURES ON BRITISH COLUMBIA. Victoria, Higgins & Long, 1868. 50p [BVaU NSHP

Harper, J. Russell

THE EARLY HISTORY OF HALDIMAND COUNTY. Caledonia, Ont., Grand River Sachem, 1950. 78p [OKQ

PORTLAND POINT, CROSSROADS OF NEW BRUNSWICK HISTORY. Preliminary Report of the 1955 Excavation. Saint John, New Brunswick Museum, 1956. 51p

Harper, John Murdoch, 1845–1919

THE HISTORY OF NEW BRUNSWICK AND THE OTHER MARITIME PROVINCES. Saint John, McMillan, 1876. 158p [BVaU NSWA OOA

THE MONTGOMERY SIEGE. Quebec, Michaels, [1908?]. 102p [Quebec City siege, 1775–76.] [BVaU LC NBFU OOP

... THEN AND NOW: THE EARLIEST BEGINNINGS OF CANADA: THE SILLERY
  MISSION. Toronto, Trade Pub. Co., [1908?]. 26 + 104 + 27p [BVaU OTP

Harris, Edward William, 1832–1925
RECOLLECTIONS OF LONG POINT. Toronto, Warwick, 1918. 48p [OTU

Harris, Reginald Vanderbilt, 1881–
THE OAK ISLAND MYSTERY. Toronto, Ryerson, 1958. xii + 211p [Refers to
  buried treasure on Oak Island, N.S.]

Harris, Rev. William Richard, 1847–1923
TADOUSSAC AND ITS INDIAN CHAPEL, 1617–1920. N.p., n.d. 66p [OTU

Hart, George Edward
THE STORY OF OLD ABEGWEIT. A Sketch of Prince Edward Island History. ...
  [Charlottetown, 1936?]. 79p [NBFU OKQ PCPW

Hart, Gerald Ephraim, 1849–1936
THE FALL OF NEW FRANCE, 1755–1760. Montreal, Drysdale, 1888. 175p [BM
  BVaU LC NSWA OTP

Harvey, Arthur, 1834–1905
A STATISTICAL ACCOUNT OF BRITISH COLUMBIA. Ottawa, Desbarats, 1867.
  41p [BVaU LC NSHP OTU

Harvey, Daniel Cobb, 1886–
THE FRENCH REGIME IN PRINCE EDWARD ISLAND. New Haven, Yale U. Press,
  1926. 265p [BM BVaU LC NSHD OTU QMBM
HOLLAND'S DESCRIPTION OF CAPE BRETON ISLAND AND OTHER DOCUMENTS.
  Comp. by ——. Halifax, Pub. Archives, 1935. 168p [BVaU NSHD OLU
LOYALISTS AND LAND SETTLEMENT IN NOVA SCOTIA. A list comp. under the
  direction of ——. Halifax, Pub. Archives, 1937. 154p [BVa

Harvey, Rev. Moses, 1820–1901
NEWFOUNDLAND. Its History, its Present Condition and its Prospects. By
  Joseph Hatton and M. Harvey. Boston, Doyle & Whittle, 1883. 431p [BM
  BVaU LC NBFU OTU
NEWFOUNDLAND AT THE BEGINNING OF THE TWENTIETH CENTURY. A Treatise
  of History and Development. ... New York, South, 1902. 118p [BVaU
  NSHD OTP
NEWFOUNDLAND IN 1897. Being Queen Victoria's Diamond Jubilee. London,
  Low Marston, 1897. 203p [BM BVaU NSWA OTU
NEWFOUNDLAND IN 1900. St. John's, Garland, 1900. 196p [BVaU LC
  NSHD OLU
A SHORT HISTORY OF NEWFOUNDLAND. England's Oldest Colony. London,
  Chapman Hall, 1883. 489p [BM BVaU LC NSHD OLU

Harvie, Fred W.
TOWN OF THOROLD CENTENNIAL, 1850–1950. Ed. by ——. Thorold, Ont., the Town, 1950. 128p [OONL

Hathaway, Ernest Jackson, 1871–1930
THE STORY OF THE OLD FORT AT TORONTO. Toronto, Macmillan, 1934. 35p [BVaU NBFU OTP

Hatheway, Calvin L., 1796–1866
THE HISTORY OF NEW BRUNSWICK, FROM ITS FIRST SETTLEMENT. Fredericton, Phillips, 1846. 81p [BM BVaU LC NSHD OTP QMM

Haultain, Theodore Arnold, 1857–1941
A HISTORY OF RIEL'S SECOND REBELLION AND HOW IT WAS QUELLED. Toronto, Grip, 1885. 44p [BVaU LC NSWA OLU

Hawarden, Sask. Bethlehem Scandinavian Lutheran Church. Ladies' Aid
A SHORT HISTORY OF BETHLEHEM COMMUNITY, HAWARDEN, SASK., 1902–1955. Comp. by Marion Pederson. Hawarden, Sask., Mrs. O.N. Pederson, 1955. 16p

Hawarden, Sask. Homemakers' Club
THE HISTORY OF HAWARDEN AND COMMUNITY. Saskatoon, Midwest Litho Ltd., 1950. 32p [SSU

Hawkes, John, 1851–1931
THE STORY OF SASKATCHEWAN AND ITS PEOPLE. Chicago, Clarke, 1924. 3v [BVaU OTP SSU

Hawkins, Alfred, 1802?–1854
HAWKINS'S PICTURE OF QUEBEC. With Historical Recollections. Quebec, Neilson & Cowan, 1834. 477p [BM BVaU LC NSWA OTU QMM

Hawthorn, Harry Bertram, 1910–
THE INDIANS OF BRITISH COLUMBIA. A Study of Contemporary Social Adjustment. By H.B. Hawthorn, C.S. Belshaw and S.M. Jamieson. Toronto, U. of Toronto Press and U. of British Columbia, 1958. ix + 499p

Haydon, Andrew, 1867–1932
PIONEER SKETCHES IN THE DISTRICT OF BATHURST. V. 1. Toronto, Ryerson, 1925. 291p [BM BVaU LC NSHD OTU QMM

Hayes, Catherine E. (Simpson), 1852–1943
THE LEGEND OF THE WEST. Victoria, Author, 1908. [Unpaged.] [BViPA OOP

Healey, Elizabeth, 1912–
HISTORY OF ALERT BAY AND DISTRICT. Comp. by ——. Alert Bay, B.C., Centennial Committee, 1958. 101p

Healy, William Joseph, 1867–1950
WINNIPEG'S EARLY DAYS. A Short Historical Sketch. ... Winnipeg, Stovel, 1927.
59p [BVaU OTP QMM

Heartwell, Joseph Woolsey, 1882–
PIONEER DAYS – SASKATCHEWAN, IN TOWNSHIP 30, RANGE 15, WEST OF THE 3RD
MER. A Comedy of Errors, 1905–1909. Meadow Lake, Sask., 1955. (Unpaged.)
[Early history of the Rosetown District, Saskatchewan.] [mimeographed]

Heeney, Rev. William Bertal, 1873–1955
THE FOUNDING OF RUPERT'S LAND AND ITS FIRST BISHOP. Winnipeg, McIntyre
Print., 1929. 33p [Peel

Hendrie, Lilian Margaret, 1870–1952
EARLY DAYS IN MONTREAL, AND RAMBLES IN THE NEIGHBOURHOOD. Montreal,
Mercury, 1932. 70p [BVaU LC OTU QMM

Henry, Lorne James, 1893–
PIONEER DAYS IN ONTARIO. By Lorne J. Henry and Gilbert Paterson. Toronto,
Ryerson, 1938. 234p [BM OTU QMM

Hepburn, Agnes Marion, 1881–
HISTORICAL SKETCH OF THE VILLAGE OF PORT STANLEY. Comp. by ——. Port
Stanley, Ont., Women's Institute, 1952. 54p

Herbert, Sask. School
THESE GOLDEN YEARS. Herbert, Sask., 1955. 50p

Herbin, John Frederic, 1860–1923
GRAND-PRE. A Sketch of the Acadian Occupation. ... A Guide to Tourists. Toronto,
Briggs, 1898. 127p [Other editions under title: THE HISTORY OF GRAND-PRE. ...
E.g., 3rd ed.: Toronto, Briggs, 1907. 171p] [BM BVaU LC NSWA OLU QMM
THE HISTORY OF GRAND-PRE. [See under GRAND-PRE.]
THE LAND OF EVANGELINE. The Authentic Story of her Country and her People.
Toronto, Musson, 1921. 84p [BVaU NSHD OTU QMBM

Herrington, Walter Stevens, 1860–1947
THE EVOLUTION OF THE PRAIRIE PROVINCES. Toronto, Briggs, 1911. 144p [BM
BVaU OTP SSU
HISTORY OF THE COUNTY OF LENNOX AND ADDINGTON. Toronto, Macmillan,
1913. 427p [BM BVaU LC NSHD OLU

Hett, Francis Paget, 1878–
GEORGINA. A Type Study of Early Settlement and Church Buildings in Upper
Canada. Toronto, Macmillan, 1939. 128p [BM LC OLU

Hewitt, Grace Henderson
EARLY DAYS IN SIMCOE COUNTY. Orillia, Women's Canadian Club, [1927?]. 20p
[BVa OTP QMM

High River Pioneers' And Old Timers' Association

LEAVES FROM THE MEDICINE TREE. A History of the Area influenced by the Tree, and Biographies of Pioneers and Old Timers who came under its Spell prior to 1900. Lethbridge, Alta., Herald, 1960. 529p

Hill, Rev. Allan Massie, 1876–1943

SOME CHAPTERS IN THE HISTORY OF DIGBY COUNTY. Halifax, McAlpine, 1901. 115p [NSWA

Hill, Rev. George William, 1824–1906

NOVA-SCOTIA AND NOVA-SCOTIANS. ... Halifax, Bowes, 1858. 49p [BVaU LC NSHD OTP

Hill, Hamnett Pinhey, 1876–1942

ROBERT RANDALL AND THE LE BRETON FLATS. An Account of the Early Legal and Political Controversies respecting the Ownership of a large Portion of the Present City of Ottawa. Ottawa, Hope, 1919. 62p [BM BVaU LC NSHD OTP

Hill, Hazel A.E.

TALES OF THE ALBERNI VALLEY. Edmonton, Hamly Press, 1952. 48p

Hill, Robert Brown, 1843–1900

MANITOBA: HISTORY OF ITS EARLY SETTLEMENT, DEVELOPMENT, AND RESOURCES. Toronto, Briggs, 1890. 764p [BM BVaU NSWA OTP SSU

Hind, Henry Youle, 1823–1908

HISTORICAL GLEANINGS. No. 1–11. [Windsor, N.S.? 189–?] 48p [BM LC NSWA OTU

MANITOBA AND THE NORTH-WEST FRAUDS. ... Windsor, Ont., Knowles, 1883. 40p [BM NSWA

SKETCH OF THE OLD PARISH BURYING GROUND OF WINDSOR, NOVA SCOTIA. With an Appeal for its Protection. ... Windsor, N.S., Anslow, 1889. 99p [BM LC NSWA OTP QMM

Hiscock, Eric Dixon Cave, 1911–

NEWFOUNDLAND'S FIRST FIFTY YEARS. Ilfracombe, Devon, Stockwell, 1957. 46p

Hislop, Mary

THE STREETS OF WINNIPEG. Winnipeg, Taylor, 1912. 46p [BM SSU

Historical Society of Alberta

THE EARLY WEST. Ed. by H.A. Dempsey. Edmonton, the Society, 1957. 36p

Historical Society of the City and County of Peterborough

PETERBOROUGH, A TENTATIVE GUIDE. Peterborough, Ont., [1955?]. 12p

Hodgins, John George, 1821–1912

THE CITY OF TORONTO. [Anon] Toronto, Campbell, 1860. 63p [NSWA QMM

Hoffer, Clara (Schwartz)
LAND OF HOPE. By Clara Hoffer and F.H. Kahan. Saskatoon, Modern Press, 1960. 157p [On life of Jewish pioneers in southeastern Saskatchewan.]

Hoig, David Scott
REMINISCENCES AND RECOLLECTIONS. An Interesting Pen Picture of Early Days, Characters, and Events in Oshawa. Oshawa, Mundy-Goodfellow Print., 1933. 227p [BVaU OTP

Holley, George Washington, 1810–1897
NIAGARA. Its History and Geology, Incidents and Poetry. ... Toronto, Hunter Rose, 1872. 165p [Later ed.: THE FALLS OF NIAGARA AND OTHER FAMOUS CATARACTS. London, Hodder & Stoughton, 1882. xv + 185p] [BVaU OHM OLU

Holman, Carrie Ellen, 1877–
OUR ISLAND STORY. Broadcasts given over CFCY Charlottetown. ... Sackville, N.B., Tribune Press, 1949. 119p [5th ed., 1963.] [NBFU OTP

Hope, Ethel Penman, –1958
EARLY SETTLEMENT OF MEECH LAKE. [Ottawa, Author, 1957?] 10p [mimeographed]

Hope, William
SCRAPS FROM CANADA TO OLD COUNTRY FRIENDS. By a Hamiltonian [pseud]. Hamilton, Times, 1877. 62p [OTL

Hopkins, John Castell, 1864–1923
FRENCH CANADA AND THE ST. LAWRENCE. Historic, Picturesque and Descriptive. Toronto, Bell, 1913. 431p [BM BVaU LC NSHD OOA

Horan, John William, 1908–
"WEST, NOR'WEST." A History of Alberta. Edmonton, Northgate Books, 1945. 184p [BM BVaU LC OOA SSU

Horsey, Edwin Ernest, 1870–
KINGSTON, A CENTURY AGO. Kingston, Kingston Historical Society, 1938. 37p [BVaU NBFU OTP

Hotson, Zella May, 1893–
THE EARLY DAYS OF INNERKIP DISTRICT. Innerkip, Ont., Author, 1952. 176p

Howay, Frederic William, 1867–1943
BRITISH COLUMBIA AND THE UNITED STATES. The North Pacific Slope from Fur Trade to Aviation. By F.W. Howay, W.N. Sage, and H.F. Angus. Ed. by H.F. Angus. Toronto, Ryerson, 1942. 408p [BM BVaU NSHD OTP QMSS
BRITISH COLUMBIA, THE MAKING OF A PROVINCE. Toronto, Ryerson, 1928. 289p [BM BVaU LC NSHD OTU QMM

BUILDERS OF THE WEST. A Book of Heroes. Ed. by ——. Toronto, Ryerson, 1929. 251p [BM BVaU LC NSHD OTP

THE DIXON-MEARES CONTROVERSY. Containing Remarks on the Voyages of John Meares, by George Dixon; An Answer to Mr. George Dixon, by John Meares, and further remarks. ... Ed. by ——. Toronto, Ryerson, 1929. 156p [BVaU LC NBFU OKQ QMBM

... THE EARLY HISTORY OF THE FRASER RIVER MINES. Victoria, Banfield, 1926. 126p [BM BVaU LC OKQ

THE OVERLAND JOURNEY OF THE ARGONAUTS OF 1862. Ottawa, Royal Society, 1920. 55p [BVaU OTP

THE WORK OF THE ROYAL ENGINEERS IN BRITISH COLUMBIA, 1858–1863. Victoria, Wolfenden, 1910. 17p [BVaU LC OKQ

Hubbard, Benjamin F., 1798–

FORESTS AND CLEARINGS. The History of Stanstead County, Province of Quebec, with Sketches of more than Five Hundred Families. The whole revised, abridged and pub. with additions and illus. by John Lawrence. Montreal, Lovell Print. and Pub. Co., 1874. [Reprinted by Page-Sangster Print. Co., 1963, viii + 367p]

Hudson Bay, Sask. High School

THE HUDSON BAY STORY. Hudson Bay, Sask., 1955. 62p [mimeographed]

Hultgren, Peter, 1885–

A BRIEF HISTORY OF MIDALE AND DISTRICT, 1903–1953. Midale, Sask., Board of Trade, 1953. 31p

Hunter, Andrew Frederick, 1863–1940

A HISTORY OF SIMCOE COUNTY. Barrie, County Council, 1909. 2v [BM BVaU LC NSHD OTU QMM

LAKE SIMCOE AND ITS ENVIRONS. Barrie, Examiner, 1893. 44p [BVaU OTP

Hutchison, Bruce, 1901–

THE FRASER. New York, Rinehart, 1950. 368p [BVaU NSHD OTU QMM

Hutton, Samuel King, 1877–

AMONG THE ESKIMOS OF LABRADOR. A Record of Five Years Close Intercourse with the Eskimo Tribes of Labrador. Toronto, Musson, 1912. 343p [BVaU LC NSHPL OTUV QMBM

AN ESKIMO VILLAGE. London, S.P.C.K., 1929. 156p [An abridgement of AMONG THE ESKIMOS.] [ACG LC NSHPL OTP

Huxtable, Thompson Russell, 1875–1959

DOWN MEMORIES LANE. Shelburne, Ont., Free Press, 1959. 80p [Stories of early days in Ontario, especially around Horning's Mills.]

Imrie, John Mills, 1883–1942

PEACE RIVER. An Empire in the Making. Edmonton, Journal, 1930. 32p [BVa

Innes, John, 1864–1941
... THE EPIC OF WESTERN CANADA. ... Vancouver, Gehrke's, 1928. 15p [BViPA

Innisfil, Ont. Book Committee
HISTORICAL REVIEW. A Record of 100 Years of Progress ... 1850–1950. Innisfil, Township Council, 1951. 184p [Same as following title?]

Innisfil Township, Ont.
INNISFIL TOWNSHIP CENTENNIAL, 1850–1950. N.p., 1950. 185p [BVaU OTU

Instow, Sask. School
PIONEER DAYS IN THE INSTOW COMMUNITY. Instow, Sask., 1955. 35p [mimeographed]

Inwood, Ont. Women's Institute
INWOOD VILLAGE HISTORY, 1873–1947. Inwood, Women's Institute, 1947. 69p [Also, 1948. 80p] [OLU OTU

Jack, David Russell, 1864–1913
CENTENNIAL PRIZE ESSAY ON THE HISTORY OF THE CITY AND COUNTY OF ST. JOHN. Saint John, McMillan, 1883. 178p [BVaU LC NSHD OTU QMM

Jackes, Lyman Bruce, 1889–1958
TALES OF NORTH TORONTO. Toronto, North Toronto Business Men's Assoc., 1948. 28p [BVaU OTU
TALES OF NORTH TORONTO. V. 2. Toronto, Canadian Historical Press, 1952. 64p

Jackson, Mary (Percy), 1904–
ON THE LAST FRONTIER. Pioneering in the Peace River Block. Letters. ... London, Sheldon Press, 1933. 118p [BM BVaU OTU SSU

James, Charles Canniff, 1863–1916
EARLY HISTORY OF THE TOWN OF AMHERSTBURG. Amherstburg, Ont., Echo Print. Co., 1902. 23p [BVaU LC NSWA OTU QMM

James, Rev. Thomas Henry, 1871–1931
NEWFOUNDLAND: Its Resources and Discovery, and Settlements of John Guy at Cuper's Cove, Conception Bay. St. John's, Evening Telegram, 1910. 20p [NBSaM

James, William T., 1861–
TORONTO, AS IT WAS AND IS. A Graphic Historical Sketch. Toronto, James, 1903. 32p [BVaU OTU

Jamieson, Heber Carss, 1879–1962
EARLY MEDICINE IN ALBERTA. The First 75 Years. Edmonton, C.M.A. (Alta. Div.), 1947. 214p [AEU BViPA QMM

Jefferson, Robert, 1856–

FIFTY YEARS ON THE SASKATCHEWAN. Being a History of the Cree Indian
Domestic Life and the Difficulties which led to ... Conflict of 1885 in the
Battleford Locality. ... Battleford, N.W. Hist. Soc., 1929. 160p [BM BViPA
OTU SSU

Jeffery, Ranald Angus, 1880–

MACNAB. Foleyet, Ont., Macnab Hist. Assoc., 1946. 27p [OOA

Jelly, William, 1865–

PROCEEDINGS OF THE JOHNSTOWN DISTRICT COUNCIL, 1842–1849. Comp. by
——. Brockville, Farrow, 1929. 100p [OTU

Johnson, Henry Smith

NORFOLK COUNTY. An Illustrated Review. ... Simcoe, Ont., Norfolk Chamber of
Commerce, Norfolk County Council and Simcoe Town Council, 1939. 40p
[OTU

Johnson, Kate (Bailey), 1885–

PIONEER DAYS OF NAKUSP AND THE ARROW LAKES. Comp. by ——. "1892,
Nakusp Diamond Jubilee, 1952." Nakusp, B.C., Author, 1951. 146p [Rev.
ed., 1964. 240p]

Johnson, Patricia Mary, 1913–

A SHORT HISTORY OF NANAIMO. Nanaimo, B.C., Centennial Committee, 1958.
55p

Johnston, Charles Murray, 1926–

THE HEAD OF THE LAKE. A History of Wentworth County. Hamilton, Wentworth
County Council, 1958. 345p

Johnston, John George, 1895–

FROM A HUNDREDWEIGHT OF PI. ... Fort Erie, Review Co., 1933. 28p [History
of newspaper.] [OKQ

Johnston, William, 1840–1917

HISTORY OF THE COUNTY OF PERTH FROM 1825 TO 1902. Stratford, Ont.,
O'Beirne, 1903. 565p [BVaU LC NSHD OTU
THE PIONEERS OF BLANSHARD, with a Historical Sketch of the Township.
Toronto, Briggs, 1899. 278p [BVaU LC NSHD OTU

Jones, George Poole

WINDSOR [N.S.]. Its History, Points of Interest, and Representative Business Men.
Windsor, N.S., Anslow, 1893. 52p [NSWA OOA

Jones, Harold Saunders, 1880–

HISTORY AND REMINISCENCES OF EASTEND AND DISTRICT. By H.S. Jones and
others. Eastend, Sask., Author, 1955. 35p

Jones, James Edmund, 1866–1939
PIONEER CRIMES AND PUNISHMENTS IN TORONTO AND THE HOME DISTRICT. ...
Toronto, Morang, 1924. 195p [BM BVaU LC NSWA OLU QMM

Jones, Reg.
THE SASKATCHEWAN STORY. Powell River, Powell River News, 1949. 30p [OKQ

Jordon, John A., 1843–1917
THE GROSSE-ISLE TRAGEDY AND THE MONUMENT TO THE IRISH FEVER VICTIMS,
1847. Quebec, Telegraph Print., 1909. 136p [OOP

Jost, Arthur Cranswick, 1875–1958
GUYSBOROUGH SKETCHES AND ESSAYS. Guysborough, N.S., Jost, 1950. 414p
[LC NSHL OTU QMM

Jury, William Wilfrid, 1898–
CLEARVILLE PREHISTORIC VILLAGE SITE IN ORFORD TOWNSHIP, KENT COUNTY,
ONTARIO. London, Ont., 1941. [Unpaged.] [LC
CRAWFORD PREHISTORIC VILLAGE SITE. ... London, Ont., U. of Western Ontario,
1948. 18p [LC OTP
FAIRFIELD ON THE THAMES. Report of Excavations made on the Site of the
Early Mission Village. London, Ont., 1945. 35p [LC OTP
SAINTE-MARIE AMONG THE HURONS. ... Toronto, Oxford U. Press, 1954. xiii +
128p

Kaiser, Thomas Erlin, 1863–1940
HISTORIC SKETCHES OF OSHAWA. Oshawa, Reformer Print., 1921. 216p [BVaU
OTU

Kalamalka Women's Institute
TWEEDSMUIR HISTORY OF OYAMA, BRITISH COLUMBIA. Oyama, B.C., 1951. 38p
[mimeographed]

Kamloops, B.C. Centenary Celebration, 1912
THE DAYS OF OLD AND DAYS OF GOLD. Victoria, King's Printer, 1912. 15p
[BVaU OTU

Kamloops, B.C. High School. Junior Historical Club
KAMLOOPS, 1812–1937. A History. Kamloops, the Club, 1937. 107p [BVaU OTU

Kaslo, B.C. Historical Committee
HISTORY OF KASLO. Kaslo Diamond Jubilee, 1893–1953. Kaslo, 1953. 64p

Kelly, Leroy Victor, 1880–1956
THE RANGE MEN. The Story of the Ranchers and Indians of Alberta. Toronto,
Briggs, 1913. 468p [AEU BM BVaU NBFU OKQ

Kelly, Orval Edgar, 1903–

IN THE BEGINNING. The Story from the Early Days in and around Presqu'Ile
Point and Brighton, Ontario. Brighton, Ensign Print., 1942. 28p [LC OTP

Kelsey, Vera, 1891?–1961

RED RIVER RUNS NORTH. Toronto, Musson, 1951. xviii + 297p

Kemptville, Ont. Centennial Committee

HISTORICAL REVIEW OF KEMPTVILLE AND DISTRICT ON THE OCCASION OF THE
100TH ANNIVERSARY OF THE INCORPORATION OF THE VILLAGE OF KEMPT-
VILLE, JUNE 30TH TO JULY 6TH, INCLUSIVE, 1857–1957. Kemptville, Ont.,
1957. 158p

Kendrick, Mary Fletcher

DOWN THE ROAD TO YESTERDAY. A History of Springfield, Annapolis County,
Nova Scotia. Bridgewater, Macpherson, 1941. 141p [NSWA OOP

Kennedy, Charles E., 1888–

CRAIK'S GOLDEN JUBILEE STORY. Craik, Sask., Craik Agricultural Society, 1955.
58 + 28 + 28p

Kennedy, David, 1828–1903

INCIDENTS OF PIONEER DAYS AT GUELPH, AND THE COUNTY OF BRUCE. Toronto,
Author, 1903. 135p [BM OTU

Kennedy, Fred

THE CALGARY STAMPEDE STORY. Calgary, T.E. Thonger, 1952. 236p

Kennedy, Howard Angus, 1861–1938

THE BOOK OF THE WEST. The Story of Western Canada, its Birth and Early
Adventures, and its Present Ways. Toronto, Ryerson, 1925. 205p [BM
BVaU LC NSHD OTU QMM SSU

Kenney, James Francis, 1884–1946

THE FOUNDING OF CHURCHILL. Being the Journal of Captain James Knight,
Governor-in-chief in Hudson Bay from the 14th of July to the 13th of September,
1717. Ed. with an historical intro. and notes by ——. Toronto, Dent, 1932.
213p [BM BVaU OTU SSU

Kent County, Ont.

COMMEMORATIVE BIOGRAPHICAL RECORD OF THE COUNTY OF KENT. Toronto,
Beers, 1904. 874p [OLU

Kent Historical Society (Chatham, Ont.)

KENTIANA. The Story of the Settlement and Development of the County of Kent.
Summarized from the Published Records of the Society. [Chatham, Ont.],
the Society, 1939. 105p [OTU QMM

PAPERS AND ADDRESSES. Chatham, Ont., the Society, 1914–. [A continuing
serial.] [BVaU LC OTP

Kenton, Man. History Committee
FROM CRADLE TO COMBINE. Kenton, 1881–1956. Elkhorn, Man., Woodworth
Times, 1956. 91p

Kernighan, Thomas
DUFFERIN AND CARMAN, MANITOBA. Being Recollections of an Eyewitness.
Vancouver, Author, 1923. 74p [MWP

Kerr, Wilfred Brenton, 1896–1950
THE MARITIME PROVINCES OF BRITISH NORTH AMERICA AND THE AMERICAN
REVOLUTION. Sackville, N.B., Busy East Press, 1941. 172p [BVaU LC NBFU
OTU QMM

Kerrisdale Courier
THE KERRISDALE STORY. Vancouver, 1955. 85p

Kerrobert, Sask. High School
HISTORY OF KERROBERT. Kerrobert, Sask., 1955. 64p [mimeographed]

Ketchum, Thomas Carleton Lee, 1862?–1927
A SHORT HISTORY OF CARLETON COUNTY, NEW BRUNSWICK. Woodstock, N.B.,
Sentinel Pub., 1922. 86p [BM BVaU LC NBFU OTP

Keys, David Reid, 1856–1939
TORONTO, AN HISTORICAL AND DESCRIPTIVE SKETCH. Toronto, 1913. 33p
[OTP

Kidd, Mrs. Margaret Isabel, 1891–1951
THIS WAS THEIR LIFE. A Story of the Pioneers of Fairmede and Adjacent
Districts. Kindersley, Sask., 1955. 84p

Killaly, Sask. High School
50 YEARS OF PROGRESS OF THE COMMUNITY OF KILLALY. Prepared by the
Principal, Jack H. Hanowski, and students of the Killaly High School. Killaly,
Sask., 1955. 12p

Killarney, Man. Women's Institute
STORIES OF PIONEER DAYS AT KILLARNEY. Killarney, Man., Women's Institute,
1930. 47p [BVaU MWP OTU

Kindersley, Sask.
THE TOWN OF KINDERSLEY. 50 Years of Progress, 1910–1960. Kindersley, Sask.,
M. Arikado, 1960. 100p

King, John, 1843–1916
THE OTHER SIDE OF THE "STORY": BEING SOME REVIEWS OF MR. J.C. DENT'S
FIRST VOLUME OF "THE STORY OF THE UPPER CANADIAN REBELLION," and
the Letters in the Mackenzie-Rolph Controversy; Also a Critique, hitherto
unpublished, on "The New Story." [Anon] Toronto, Murray, 1886. 150p
[BVaU NSWA OTP

Kingston, Ont. Kingston Historical Society
HISTORIC KINGSTON. Being the Transactions of the Kingston Historical Society. No. 1, 1951/52. Kingston, Ont., the Society, 1952. [A continuing serial.]

Kingsville, Ont. Centennial Committee, Historical Section
KINGSVILLE THROUGH THE YEARS 1783–1952. Kingsville, Lakeshore Publishers, 1952. 105p

Kinney, J.E.
THE PORT OF YARMOUTH AND ITS DEVELOPMENT. Yarmouth, Herald, 1931. 14p [NSWA

Kirby, William, 1817–1906
ANNALS OF NIAGARA. Welland, Tribune, 1896. 269p [Also: Toronto, Macmillan, 1927. 329p] [BVaU LC NSHD OKQ

Kirkconnell, Watson, 1895–
KAPUSKASING. An Historical Sketch. Kingston, Jackson Press, 1921. 15p [BM BVaU LC NSWA OTUV QMM
VICTORIA COUNTY CENTENNIAL HISTORY. Lindsay, Ont., Watchman-Warder Press, 1921. 261p [BM BVa NSHD OTP

Kitchener-Waterloo Record
KITCHENER'S FIRST 100 YEARS, 1854–1954. Kitchener, Ont., 1954. 40p

Kittson, Arthur
THE SAGA OF SHERBROOKE STREET YESTERDAY AND TO-DAY. A Pictorial Record of Montreal's Most Colourful Thoroughfare from 1853 to 1949. Montmagny, Que., Marquis, 1949. 47p [BVaU OTU

Kitwanga, B.C. Superior School
GITWANGAG 1858 TO KITWANGA 1958. Kitwanga, B.C., the School, 1958. 33p [mimeographed]

Knight, Fulton Stanley, 1883–
THIS IS MEAFORD, 1875–1956. A Little Sketch of the Origin of our Names, Saint Vincent – Meaford, the Background of these Names, and a Short History of John Jervis, Admiral of the Fleet. ... Meaford, Ont., Author, 1956. 35p

Lacadena, Sask. Women's Association
HISTORY OF THE LACADENA COMMUNITY. Comp. by Mrs. Jean Minogue. Lacadena, Sask., 1955. 15p [mimeographed]

Lagace, Anita
HOW GRAND FALLS GREW. Grand Falls, N.B., Author, 1945. 77p [NBFU OTU QMBM

Landon, Fred, 1880–1969

UP THE PROOF LINE. The Story of a Rural Community. By Fred Landon and Orlo Miller. London, Ont., D.B. Weldon, 1955. 85p [History of the Proof Line Road and London Township.]

TRIAL AND PUNISHMENT OF THE PATRIOTS, captured at Windsor in December, 1838. London, Ont., Author, 1934. 8p [NSHD OTU

WESTERN ONTARIO AND THE AMERICAN FRONTIER. Toronto, Ryerson, 1941. 305p [BM BVaU LC NSHD OTU QMM

Landstrom, Oscar, 1871–

PIONEER HOMESTEAD STORIES, FROM 1868 TO PRESENT TIME. Govan, Sask., Western Printers, 1942. 32p [SSU

Lane, Myrtle Eliza (Mack)

LAND OF SHINING MOUNTAINS. British Columbia in Legend and Story. By Myrtle E. Lane, Margaret G. Steer and Mary Carr Wright. Toronto, Dent, 1957. 354p

Langrish, William

PIONEER DAYS IN THE OXBOW AND GLEN EWEN DISTRICTS. Containing Histories written by William Langrish, Ambrose Dowkes and Edith Campbell. Oxbow, Sask., Herald, 1955. 38p

Lanigan, Sask. Jubilee Committee

LANIGAN, 1905–1955. A Brief History of the Town and District, Written in Conjunction with Saskatchewan's Golden Jubilee. Lanigan, Sask., 1955. 68p

Large, Richard Geddes, 1901–

THE SKEENA, RIVER OF DESTINY. Vancouver, Mitchell Press, 1957. ix + 180p

Laurie, William, 1856–1927

THE BATTLE RIVER VALLEY. ... The Advantages of the country drained by the Battle and Saskatchewan Rivers as a Field for Settlement. Battleford, P.G. Laurie, 1883. 104p [SSU

Lauriston, Victor, 1881–

LAMBTON'S HUNDRED YEARS, 1849–1949. Sarnia, Haines Frontier Print., 1949. 335p [OLU

ROMANTIC KENT. More than Three Centuries of History, 1626–1952. Chatham, Ont., Shepherd Print., 1952. 784p [Cover title: THE STORY OF A COUNTY.]

Laut, Agnes Christina, 1871–1936

THE CARIBOO TRAIL. A Chronicle of the Gold-fields of British Columbia. Toronto, Glasgow Brook, 1916. 116p [BM BVaU LC NSHD OTU QMM

PIONEERS OF THE PACIFIC COAST. A Chronicle of Sea Rovers and Fur Hunters. Toronto, Glasgow Brook, 1915. 139p [BM BVaU LC NSWA OTU

Lawrence, Joseph Collins, 1918–

THE SOUTH-WEST COAST OF VANCOUVER ISLAND. From Metchosin to Bamfield, including Sooke, Otter, River Jordan and Port Renfrew. Sooke, B.C., Women's Institute, 1959. 73p [Cover title: A BRIEF HISTORY OF SOOKE DISTRICT.]

Lawrence, Joseph Wilson, 1818–1892
1783–1883. FOOT-PRINTS; or, Incidents in Early History of New Brunswick. Saint John, McMillan, 1883. 108p [BVaU LC NSWA OKQ QMM

Lawson, John Murray, 1848–1925
RECORD OF THE SHIPPING OF YARMOUTH, N.S. Containing a List of Vessels owned in the County of Yarmouth since its Settlement in 1761 ... ; also List of Vessels Lost ... and other Information in Reference to the Mercantile Marine. ... Comp. by ——. Yarmouth, 1876. 258p [LC NSHD OOP

Lawson, Mary Jane (Katzmann), 1828–1890
HISTORY OF THE TOWNSHIPS OF DARTMOUTH, PRESTON, AND LAWRENCETOWN, HALIFAX COUNTY, N.S. (Akins Historical Prize Essay.) By Mrs. William Lawson (Mary Jane Katzmann). Ed. by Harry Piers. Halifax, Morton, 1893. 260p [BVaU LC NSWA OTU

Lawton, John Thomas, 1860–1961
OLD KING'S COVE. [By J.T. Lawton and P.K. Devine.] [St. John's?], 1944. 106p [NfSM

Lay, Gregory S., 1865?–
MEMORIES OF EARLY DAYS ON ST. JOSEPH'S ISLAND. The Garden of Algoma and Tourists' Paradise. Kirkland Lake, Ont., Sutherland Print., 1951. 20p

Leavitt, Thaddeus W.H., 1844?–1909
HISTORY OF LEEDS AND GRENVILLE, ONTARIO, FROM 1749 TO 1879. With ... Biographical Sketches of some of its Prominent Men and Pioneers. Brockville, Recorder Press, 1879. 200p [BVaU LC NSWA OTU

Legget, Robert Ferguson, 1904–
RIDEAU WATERWAY. Toronto, U. of Toronto Press, 1955. xiv + 249p

LeMessurier, Henry William, 1848–1931
LECTURE: "ANCIENT ST. JOHN'S." [St. John's], Herald Print., [1915?]. 20p [NfSM
A LECTURE ON PLACENTIA. ... [St. John's, Total Abstinence Society, 1910.] 34p [NBSM

LeMoine, James MacPherson, 1825–1912
CHATEAU-BIGOT: HISTORY AND ROMANCE. Historical Sketch of the Ruins of the French Chateau ... with all the Romantic Memories which Attach to it. By the Author of MAPLE LEAVES [pseud]. Quebec, 1874. 21p [BVaU OKQ QMM
THE CHRONICLES OF THE ST. LAWRENCE. Montreal, Dawson, 1878. 380p [BM BVaU LC NSWA OTU

GLIMPSES OF QUEBEC DURING THE LAST TEN YEARS OF FRENCH DOMINATION IN
CANADA, 1749–1759. With Observations on the Past and on the Present.
Quebec, Morning Chronicle, 1879. 42p [NSWA OTU QMSS

HISTORICAL NOTES ON QUEBEC AND ITS ENVIRONS. ... Drive to Indian Lorette.
Indian Lorette. Tahourenche, the Huron Chief. The St. Louis and the Ste. Foy
roads. Château Bigot. Laval University, Picture Gallery. ... 2nd ed. Quebec,
Darveau, 1887. 59p [LC OTU

HISTORICAL NOTES ON QUEBEC AND ITS ENVIRONS. Montreal to Quebec by
Steamer—Round Town—Quebec to Jacques Cartier Monument—Quebec to
Montmorency Falls—Drive to Indian Lorette—Indian Lorette. ... 5th ed.
Quebec, Darveau, 1890. 152p [BM LC OLU QMSS

ORIGIN OF THE FESTIVAL OF SAINT-JEAN-BAPTISTE. QUEBEC, ITS GATES AND
ENVIRONS. ... Quebec, Morning Chronicle, 1880. 94p [BM NSWA

THE PORT OF QUEBEC, ITS ANNALS, 1535–1900. Quebec, Chronicle Print.,
1901. 95p [BM BVaU OKQ QMM

QUEBEC PAST AND PRESENT ... 1608–1876. Quebec, Coté, 1876. 466p [BM
BVaU NSWA OTU

QUEEN'S BIRTHDAY, 1880. QUEBEC, ITS GATES AND ENVIRONS: Something about
the Streets, Lanes and Early History of the Ancient Capital. Quebec, Morning
Chronicle, 1880. 94p [*Cf. above:* ORIGIN OF THE FESTIVAL. ...] [BM BVaU
OTU QMM

ST LOUIS STREET AND ITS STORIED PAST. A Christmas Sketch Specially Printed.
Quebec, Morning Chronicle, 1891. 19p [BVaU LC OOP

Lethbridge, Alta. Booklet Committee
LETHBRIDGE. Alberta's Golden Jubilee. Lethbridge, 1955. 68p

Lett, William Pittman, 1819–1892
THE CITY OF OTTAWA AND ITS SURROUNDINGS. Ottawa, Woodburn, 1884. 22p
[BM NSWA

RECOLLECTIONS OF BYTOWN AND ITS OLD INHABITANTS. Ottawa, "Citizen"
Print., 1874. 95p [BVaU OTU QMM

Levy, Herman David
A HISTORY OF SHERWOOD IN THE COUNTY OF LUNENBURG. Truro, N.S., Truro
Print., 1953. 98p

Lewis, Ella N.
EARLY MEDICAL MEN OF ELGIN COUNTY. St. Thomas, Sutherland, 1931. 60p
[OLU QMM

EAST ELGIN PLACE NAMES. St. Thomas, Elgin Hist. Soc., 1935. 25p [LC OTP

SIDELIGHTS ON THE TALBOT SETTLEMENT. St. Thomas, Elgin Hist. Soc., 1938.
28p [CC

Lewis, Jennie (Raycraft), 1899–
BIRR AND BEYOND. Comp. by —— *et al.* [London, Ont.?] , Birr Women's Institute,
1958. 176p [History of North London Township, Ont., and district.]

Liberty, Sask. Book Committee (Jubilee)
FIFTY YEARS OF LIBERTY, 1904–1955. Liberty, Sask., 1955. 112p

Lincoln County, Ont. Council
LINCOLN COUNTY, 1856–1956. St. Catharines, Ont., the Council, 1956. 152p

Lindsay, Frederick William, 1903–
THE CARIBOO STORY, PUBLISHED IN B.C.'S CENTENNIAL YEAR. Quesnel, B.C., Quesnel Advertiser, 1958. 52p

Lizars, Kathleen Macfarlane, –1931
THE VALLEY OF THE HUMBER, 1615–1913. Toronto, Briggs, 1913. 170p [BM BVaU LC NBFU OTP

Long, Harold Gordon, 1888–
FORT MACLEOD. The Story of the North West Mounted Police, 1874–1904, Royal North West Mounted Police, 1904–1920, Royal Canadian Mounted Police, 1920 to Present Time. Ed. by ——. Fort Macleod, Alta., Fort Macleod Historical Association, 1958. 96p

Longstaff, Frederick Victor, 1879–1961
ESQUIMALT NAVAL BASE. A History of its Work and its Defences. Victoria, Victoria Book & Stationery, 1941. 189p [BM BVaU OTU

Loreburn, Sask. School
HISTORY OF LOREBURN, 1905–1955. Loreburn, Sask., 1955. 21p [mimeographed]

Lorimer, John G., 1807–1897
HISTORY OF ISLANDS AND ISLETS IN THE BAY OF FUNDY, CHARLOTTE COUNTY, NEW BRUNSWICK. ... St. Stephens, N.B., Saint Croix Courier, 1876. 132p [LC NBSM OTP QMBM

Low, David, 1913–
KINGSTON, ONTARIO, CANADA. Kingston, Whig-Standard, 1960. 60p [Calendar, with sketches and historical outline.]
ST. THOMAS, ONTARIO, CANADA, A CENTRE OF INFLUENCE IN ELGIN COUNTY. St. Thomas, Times-Journal, 1960. 71p

Lucas, Frederick C.
AN HISTORICAL SOUVENIR DIARY OF THE CITY OF WINNIPEG. ... Comp. and ed. by ——. Winnipeg, Cartwright & Lucas, 1923. 240p [BM BVaU LC SSU

Ludditt, Alfred William, 1907–
GOLD IN THE CARIBOO. Vancouver, Evergreen Press, 1958. 40p

Lugrin, Charles Henry, 1846–1917
VANCOUVER ISLAND AND RAILWAY DEVELOPMENT. Victoria, Colonist, 1909. 37p [BViPA LC OTU

Lugrin, Nellie de Bertrand, 1874–

THE PIONEER WOMEN OF VANCOUVER ISLAND, 1843–1866. Written by N. de Bertrand Lugrin [Mrs. Charles Henry Shaw]. Ed. by John Hosie. Victoria, Women's Can. Club of Victoria, 1928. 312p [BM BVaU NBFU OKQ

Lundar, Man.

LUNDAR DIAMOND JUBILEE, 1887–1947. Winnipeg, Viking, 1948. 175p [BVa OTP

Lynch-Staunton, Mrs. Emma, 1885–1949

A HISTORY OF THE EARLY DAYS OF PINCHER CREEK, OF THE DISTRICT AND OF THE SOUTHERN MOUNTAINS. ... Lethbridge, Herald Print., 1926. 56p [SSU

Lyons, Chester Peter, 1915–

MILESTONES ON VANCOUVER ISLAND. The Story of this "Island to the West," its Past, and its Present. Vancouver, priv. print., 1958. 314p

MacBeath, George Boyd, 1924–

CHAMPLAIN AND THE ST. JOHN, 1604–1954. Ed. by —— et al. Saint John, New Brunswick Historical Society, 1954. 80p

THE STORY OF THE RESTIGOUCHE. Covering the Indian, French, and English Periods of the Restigouche Area. Saint John, New Brunswick Museum, 1954. 25p

MacBeth, Malcolm, 1868–

MORNINGTON AND ITS PIONEERS. Milverton, Ont., Milverton "Sun," 1933. 96p [OTU

MacBeth, Rev. Roderick George, 1858–1934

THE ROMANCE OF WESTERN CANADA. Toronto, Briggs, 1918. 309p [BM BVaU LC NSHD OTP QMSS

THE SELKIRK SETTLERS IN REAL LIFE. Toronto, Briggs, 1897. 119p [BM BVaU LC NSHD OTP QMSS

McCague, John Joseph E., 1899–

A CENTURY OF PROGRESS. The Centennial Review of the Township of Essa, 1850–1950. Ed. by ——. Thornton, Ont., the Township, 1950. [unpaged] [OTU

McCall, Ralph Lewis, 1925–

THE ACME STORY, 1910–1960. Acme, Alta., 1960. 5 + 43p

McColl, Hugh

SOME SKETCHES OF THE EARLY HIGHLAND PIONEERS OF THE COUNTY OF MIDDLESEX. Strathroy, Ont., Gaelic Society of Toronto, 1904. 58p [OTP

McCowan, Daniel, 1882—1956
UPLAND TRAILS. Toronto, Macmillan, 1955. xiv + 158p

MacDermot, Hugh Ernest, 1888—
A HISTORY OF THE MONTREAL GENERAL HOSPITAL. Montreal, the Hospital, 1950.
135p [BVaU NBFU
HISTORY OF SCHOOL OF NURSING OF MONTREAL GENERAL HOSPITAL. Montreal,
Alumnae Assoc., the Hospital, 1940. 125p [BVaU

MacDonald, Rev. Alexander, 1858—1941
THE BRITISH COLUMBIA ORPHANS' FRIEND HISTORICAL NUMBER. ... Victoria,
Press Pub. Co., 1913. 208p [BVaU

McDonald, Archibald, 1790—1853
NARRATIVE RESPECTING THE DESTRUCTION OF THE EARL OF SELKIRK'S SETTLE-
MENT UPON RED RIVER, IN THE YEAR 1815. London, Brettell, 1816. 14p
[BViPA OTP
REPLY TO THE LETTER ADDRESSED TO THE EARL OF SELKIRK BY JOHN
STRACHAN ... concerning the Settlement on Red River. Montreal, Gray, 1816.
50p [Reprinted from Montreal "Herald." Bound with two others.] [QMM

Macdonald, Charles Ochiltree, 1870—
THE LAST SIEGE OF LOUISBURG. London, Cassell, [1907?]. 176p [BVaU LC
NSWA OTP QMM

MacDonald, D., 1855—
CAPE NORTH AND VICINITY. Pioneer Families, History and Chronicles. ... [Port
Hastings, N.S.], Author, 1933. 160 + xivp [NBFU

MacDonald, George Heath
EDMONTON. Fort, House, Factory. Edmonton, Douglas Print., 1959. 236p
FORT AUGUSTUS—EDMONTON. Northwest Trails and Traffic. Edmonton, Douglas
Print., 1954. 255p

Macdonell, Alexander Greenfield, —1835
A NARRATIVE OF TRANSACTIONS IN THE RED RIVER COUNTRY. From the
Commencement of the Operations of the Earl of Selkirk till the Summer of the
Year 1816. London, Macmillan, 1819. 85p [BM BVaU LC OTU

Macdonell, John Alexander, 1851—1930
SKETCHES ILLUSTRATING THE EARLY SETTLEMENT AND HISTORY OF GLENGARRY
IN CANADA. ... Montreal, Foster Brown, 1893. 337p [BM BVaU LC NSWA
OTP QMSS

Macdougall, A.W.
BLACK RIVER AND ITS FIRST SETTLERS. Comp. by Louise Manny. [Chatham,
N.B.?], 1935. 56p [NBFU

McDougall, Rev. John, 1842–1917
FOREST, LAKE, AND PRAIRIE. Twenty Years of Frontier Life in Western Canada–
1842–1862. Toronto, Briggs, 1895. 267p [BM BVaU LC NBFU OTU QMSS
IN THE DAYS OF THE RED RIVER REBELLION. Life and Adventure in the Far West
of Canada (1868–1872). Toronto, Briggs, 1903. 303p [BM BVaU OTP
ON WESTERN TRAILS IN THE EARLY SEVENTIES. Frontier Life in the Canadian
Northwest. Toronto, Briggs, 1911. 279p [BM BVaU LC OKQ
PATHFINDING ON PLAIN AND PRAIRIE. Stirring Scenes of Life in the Canadian
North-west. Toronto, Briggs, 1898. 277p [BM BVaU LC OKQ
SADDLE, SLED AND SNOWSHOE. Pioneering on the Saskatchewan in the Sixties.
Toronto, Briggs, 1896. 282p [BM BVaU LC OTP

MacDougall, John L.
HISTORY OF INVERNESS COUNTY, NOVA SCOTIA. Truro, News Pub. Co., 1922.
690p [LC NBFU OTP

McEvoy, John Millar, 1864–1935
THE ONTARIO TOWNSHIP. ... Toronto, Warwick, 1889. 42p [BM NSHP OTP

MacEwan, Grant, 1902–
CALGARY CAVALCADE FROM FORT TO FORTUNE. Edmonton, Institute of Applied
Art, 1958. x + 246p

Macfie, Charles Maitland, 1872–
APPIN, ONTARIO, 1847–1947. A Century's Story of the Growth of a Village and
Community from the Primeval Forest to the Privileged Condition of Today.
Appin, Ont., Women's Institute, 1947. 35p [OOA
EKFRID TOWNSHIP, 1821–1949. Appin, Ont., Author, 1949. 48p [OOA

Macfie, Matthew
VANCOUVER ISLAND AND BRITISH COLUMBIA, THEIR HISTORY, RESOURCES, AND
PROSPECTS. London, Longmans, 1865. xxi + 574p [BVa NBSM OONL QMSS

MacGregor, James Grierson, 1905–
BLANKETS AND BEADS. A History of the Saskatchewan River. Edmonton, Institute
of Applied Art, 1949. 278p [BVaU OTP
THE LAND OF TWELVE-FOOT DAVIS. A History of the Peace River Country.
Edmonton, Applied Arts Products, 1952. 395p

MacGregor, John, 1797–1857
HISTORICAL AND DESCRIPTIVE SKETCHES OF THE MARITIME COLONIES OF
BRITISH AMERICA. London, Longman etc., 1828. 266p [LC NSWA OTP

Machar, Agnes Maule, 1837–1927
THE STORY OF OLD KINGSTON. Toronto, Musson, 1908. 291p [BM BVaU LC
NSWA OTU

MacInnes, Alexander P., 1868–
CHRONICLES OF THE CARIBOO. Dunlevy's Discovery of Gold on the Horsefly. Lillooet, B.C., Lillooet Pub., 1938. 27p [BVaU

MacInnes, Charles Malcolm, 1891–
IN THE SHADOW OF THE ROCKIES. London, Rivingtons, 1930. 347p [A history of the development of ranching in southern Alberta.] [BM BVaU LC NBFU OTU SSU

McIntosh, Donald J.
FORT ST. JAMES, PAST AND PRESENT. Vancouver, 1933. 22p [BVaU

Mack, Hazel L. (Spencer), 1903–
HISTORICAL HIGHLIGHTS OF WELLINGTON COUNTY. [Rockwood, Ont.?], Author, 1955. 44p
HISTORY OF EDEN MILLS AND VICINITY. Rockwood, Ont., Eden Crest and Eden Mills Women's Institutes, 1954. 56p

Mackay, Corday
HELMCKEN HOUSE, HISTORIC MUSEUM, VICTORIA, BRITISH COLUMBIA. Victoria, n.p., n.d. 20p

MacKay, Elsie Annie Myrtle, 1905–
SELKIRK'S 75th ANNIVERSARY. Ed. by ——. Selkirk, Man., 75th Anniversary Committee, 1957. 80p
THE STONE FORT, LOWER FORT GARRY. Selkirk, Man., the Author, 1960. 28p

McKay, Kenneth W.
THE COURT HOUSES OF A CENTURY. A Brief Historical Sketch of the Court Houses of the London District, the County of Middlesex and County of Elgin. Comp. by ——. St. Thomas, Ont., Times Print., 1901. 26p [LC OOP

MacKay, Rev. William Alexander, 1842–1905
PIONEER LIFE IN ZORRA. Toronto, Briggs, 1899. 400p [BM BVaU LC OTP QMBM
ZORRA BOYS AT HOME AND ABROAD; or, How to Succeed. Toronto, Briggs, 1900. 228p [2nd ed. under title: SUCCESS ILLUSTRATED BY EXAMPLE, 1901.] [BM BVaU NSHD OTP QMBM

McKelvie, Bruce Alistair, 1889–1960
EARLY HISTORY OF THE PROVINCE OF BRITISH COLUMBIA. London, Dent, 1926. 118p [BVaU OOA
FORT LANGLEY, OUTPOST OF EMPIRE. Vancouver, "Daily Province," 1947. 98p [BM BVaU LC NBFU OTP
HBC IN B.C. Winnipeg, Hudson's Bay Company, 1958. 26p
MAQUINNA THE MAGNIFICENT. Vancouver, "Daily Province," 1946. 65p [BVaU OTP QMBM

PAGEANT OF B.C. Glimpses into the Romantic Development of Canada's Far
Western Province. Toronto, Nelson, 1955. 263p

TALES OF CONFLICT. Vancouver, "Daily Province," 1949. 99p [BVaU OTP

McKenzie, Ina Campbell, 1897–

BRADFORD, 1857–1957. One Hundred Years in Picture and Story. Comp. and arr.
by Ina and Stewart McKenzie. Bradford, Ont., 1957. 128p

MacKinnon, Donald Alexander, 1863–

PAST AND PRESENT OF PRINCE EDWARD ISLAND. ... A Concise Review of its Early
Settlement, Development and Present Condition. By the ... Authors of the
Province. ... Ed. by D.A. MacKinnon ... and A.B. Warburton ... [with] Life
Sketches of Representative Men and Families. ... Charlottetown, Bowen, 1906.
731p [NSHD

Mackinnon, Frank, 1919–

THE GOVERNMENT OF PRINCE EDWARD ISLAND. Toronto, U. of Toronto Press,
1951. 385p

MacKinnon, Ian F., 1898–

SETTLEMENTS AND CHURCHES IN NOVA SCOTIA, 1749–1776. Montreal, Walker,
1930. 111p [BM BVaU NBFU OTP

MacKinnon, J.G.

OLD SYDNEY. Sketches of the Town and its People in Days Gone By. Sydney, N.S.,
Don MacKinnon, 1918. 143p [BVaU NSWA OOP

MacKinnon, James N., 1871–1946

MOOSOMIN AND ITS PIONEERS. Including Humorous Incidents and Up-to-date
Sketches. Moosomin, World-Spectator, 1937. 67p [SSU

A SHORT HISTORY OF THE PIONEER SCOTCH SETTLERS OF ST. ANDREWS, SASK.
Regina, Courier, 1921. 30p [SRL

McKitrick, Thomas George, 1873–1952

CORNER STONES OF EMPIRE. The Settlement of Crystal City and District in the
Rock Lake Country. Crystal City, Man., Courier Pub. Co., [194–?]. 201p [BVa
MWP

Macklin, Sask. Home and School Association

A SHORT HISTORY OF MACKLIN AND COMMUNITY, ON THE OCCASION OF
SASKATCHEWAN'S GOLDEN JUBILEE YEAR. Macklin, Sask., 1955. 32p
[mimeographed]

MacLaren, George

THE PICTOU BOOK. Stories of Our Past. New Glasgow, Hector Pub., 1955. 267p

McLaren, J.L.

STORIES OF THE DANFORTH. A Collection of Familiar Stories of the Danforth

District. Comp. by ——, from many reliable sources. Toronto, n.p., 1921. 21p
[BM OTP

McLennan, John Stewart, 1853–1939

LOUISBOURG, FROM ITS FOUNDATIONS TO ITS FALL, 1713–1758. Toronto,
Macmillan, 1918. 454p [2nd ed.: Sydney, N.S., Fortress Press, 1957. 330p]
[BVaU LC NBFU OTU QMSS

McLennan, Mary Louise, 1879–1938

A HISTORY OF THE NORTH EASTHOPE PIONEERS, COUNTY OF PERTH, CANADA,
FROM PERTHSHIRE, SCOTLAND. With an Intro. by Donald Scott. [Stratford,
Ont.?], Author, 1937. 185p [BM OOA

McLeod, Donald, 1779–1879

A BRIEF REVIEW OF THE SETTLEMENT OF UPPER CANADA BY THE U.E. LOYALISTS
AND SCOTCH HIGHLANDERS IN 1783, AND OF THE GRIEVANCES WHICH
COMPELLED THE CANADAS TO HAVE RECOURSE TO ARMS IN DEFENCE OF THEIR
RIGHTS AND LIBERTIES IN ... 1837 AND 1838. ... Cleveland, Penniman, 1841.
292p [BVaU LC NSWA OTP QMBM

McLeod, Margaret (Arnett), 1877–1966

BELLS OF RED RIVER. Winnipeg, Stovel, 1938. 41p [BVaU NSWA OTP QMBM
LOWER FORT GARRY. Winnipeg, priv. print., 1957. 12p

MacLeod, N.W.

PICTURESQUE CARDSTON AND ENVIRONMENTS. A Story of Colonization and
Progress in Southern Alberta. Cardston, Author, 1900. 116p [Reprinted as
souvenir for Cardston Golden Jubilee, June 28–July 3, 1937.] [AEP

McLeod, Robert Randall, 1839–1909

MARKLAND OR NOVA SCOTIA. Its History, Natural Resources, etc. [Berwick, N.S.],
Markland Pub. Co., 1903. 603p [BM BVaU LC NBFU OTP QMM

MacMartin, Belle D.

VERNON YESTERDAY AND TO-DAY. By Belle D. MacMartin and Beatrice R.
Porteous. Vernon, Ont., Women's Institute, 1950. 24p [OONL

MacMechan, Archibald McKellar, 1862–1933

OLD PROVINCE TALES. ... Toronto, McClelland, 1924. 345p [BM BVaU LC
NSHD OKQ
ORIGINAL MINUTES OF HIS MAJESTY'S COUNCIL AT ANNAPOLIS ROYAL, 1720–1739.
Ed. by ——. Halifax, McAlpine Pub. Co., 1908. 408p [BM NSHD OTP QMSS
PROVINCE HOUSE. Halifax, Author, 1927. 8p [BVaU OKQ
RED SNOW ON GRAND PRE. Toronto, McClelland, 1931. 224p [BM BVaU LC
NBFU OTU
SAGAS OF THE SEA. Toronto, Dent, 1924. 156p [BM BVaU LC NSHD OKQ
STORIED HALIFAX. (Nova Scotia Chapbook). Halifax, Allen, 1922. 17p [BVaU
OTP

TALES OF THE SEA. Foreword by T.H. Raddall. Toronto, McClelland, 1947. 230p [NBFU OTP QMBM

THERE GO THE SHIPS. Toronto, McClelland, 1928. 293p [BM BVaU NBFU OTP

McMeekan, John Murray

A SHORT HISTORY OF YELLOWKNIFE. Toronto, Cooper, 1944. 4p [CC

McMorran, Gordon Alexander, 1885—

THE SOURIS PLAINS. From Pemmican to Wheat, 1881—1956. Commemorating the 75th Anniversary of Souris and District, July 1956. Ed. by ——. Souris, Man., Souris Plaindealer, 1956. 68p

McMurray, Thomas, 1831—

THE FREE GRANT LANDS OF CANADA, from Practical Experience of Bush Farming in the Free Grant Lands of Muskoka and Parry Sound. Bracebridge, Northern Advocate, 1871. 146p [OTUV

MacNeil, Neil, 1891—

THE HIGHLAND HEART IN NOVA SCOTIA. New York, Scribner, 1948. 199p [Also: Toronto, Saunders, 1958.] [BVaU LC NBFU OTP QMM

McNeill, Leishman, 1896—

TALES OF THE OLD TOWN. Calgary, 1875—1950. Calgary, Herald, 1951. 92p [Reprint of articles published in *The Herald* during Calgary's 75th anniversary celebrations, 1950.]

MacNutt, William Stewart, 1908—

NEW BRUNSWICK AND ITS PEOPLE. The Biography of a Canadian Province. Ed. by A.W. Trueman. Fredericton, New Brunswick Travel Bureau, 1952. 46p

MacQueen, Malcolm Alexander, 1878—1960

HEBRIDEAN PIONEERS. Winnipeg, Henderson Directories, 1957. 104p [An account of emigrants to Belfast, P.E.I.]

SKYE PIONEERS AND "THE ISLAND." Winnipeg, Stovel, 1929. 162p [BM BVaU LC NSHD OLU QMBM

MacRae, Archibald Oswald, 1869—

HISTORY OF THE PROVINCE OF ALBERTA. Calgary, Western Canada History Co., 1912. 2v [BVaU LC NSHD OTP QMSS

MacVicar, William Mortimer, 1851—1928

A SHORT HISTORY OF ANNAPOLIS ROYAL ... 1604 to 1854. Toronto, Copp Clark, 1897. 127p [BM BVaU LC NSWA OTP QMM

Macwatt, Daniel Fraser, 1853—1920

SHORT SKETCHES, WITH PHOTOGRAPHS, OF WARDENS, PARLIAMENTARY REPRESENTATIVES, JUDICIAL OFFICERS AND COUNTY OFFICIALS OF THE COUNTY OF LAMBTON FROM 1852—1917. Sarnia, County Council, 1917. 55p [OTU

McWilliams, Margaret (Stovel), 1875–1952
MANITOBA MILESTONES. Toronto, Dent, 1928. 249p [BM BVaU LC NSHD OTP QMBM

Maidstone, Sask. Jubilee Committee
BETWEEN THE RIVERS ... MAIDSTONE, SASKATCHEWAN, 1905–1955. Maidstone, Sask., 1955. 88p

Main Centre, Sask. School
GREEN GRASS TO GOLDEN GRAIN, MAIN CENTRE. Main Centre, Sask., 1955. 18p [mimeographed]

Major, Frederick William, 1874–
MANITOULIN, THE ISLE OF THE OTTAWAS. Being a Handbook of Historical and other Information on the Grand Manitoulin Island. Gore Bay, Ont., Recorder Press, 1934. 84p [OTP

Manning, Mrs. Mary Ethel, 1919–
A VILLAGE LIBRARY. The Story of the Streetsville Library, 1854–1959. Comp. by Mrs. Mary Manning and Rev. T.D. Jones. Streetsville, Ont., W.G. Tolton, 1959. 24p

Manny, Louise, 1890–1971
SHIPS OF MIRAMICHI. A History of Shipbuilding on the Miramichi River, N.B., 1773–1919. Saint John, New Brunswick Museum, 1960. 84p

Manotick, Ont. Centennial Committee
MANOTICK'S CENTENNIAL YEAR SOUVENIR BOOK, 1859–1959. Containing the Manotick Story ... also Historical Reports of each of Manotick's Churches and of the various Social and Fraternal Orders and Associations. ... Manotick, the Committee, 1959. 75p

Mantario, Sask. Homemakers' Club
FROM OXEN TO AIRPLANE: MANTARIO, 1908–1950. Comp. by C. Evans Sargent. [Saskatoon, Midwest Litho Co., 1950.] 91p [Cf. title listed under Shipley, Mrs. R.L., below.] [SRL SSU

Markham Township, Ont. Historical Committee
HISTORICAL SKETCH OF MARKHAM TOWNSHIP, 1793–1950. Centennial Celebration of Municipal Government, 1850–1950. Unionville, Ont., the Township, 1950. 106p [OTU

Marsh, Edith Louise, –1960
A HISTORY OF THE COUNTY OF GREY. ... Owen Sound, Fleming, 1931. 487p [BVaU OTP
WHERE THE BUFFALO ROAMED. The Story of Western Canada Told for the Young. ... Toronto, Briggs, 1908. 242p [Also: Toronto, Macmillan, 1923. 257p] [BM BVaU LC NSHD OLU

Marshall, John George, 1786–1880
BRIEF HISTORY OF PUBLIC PROCEEDINGS & EVENTS ... during the Earliest Years of the Present Century. ... Halifax, "Wesleyan," [1878?]. 69p [NSWA OTL

Martin, Chester Bailey, 1882–1958
RED RIVER SETTLEMENT. Papers in the Canadian Archives Relating to the Pioneers. Sel. and ed. by ——. Ottawa, the Archives, 1910. 27p [BM BVaU NSHD OOC QMSS

Martin, John Patrick, 1886–
THE STORY OF DARTMOUTH. Dartmouth, N.S., priv. print., 1957. 550p

Marwick, Alice (Stinson), 1892–1956
NORTHLAND POST. The Story of the Town of Cochrane. Cochrane, Author, 1950. 342p [BM BVaU OTU

Mary Theodore, Sister, 1856–1951
PIONEER NUNS OF BRITISH COLUMBIA. Sisters of St. Ann. Victoria, Colonist, 1931. 146p [BVaU

Mason, Douglas H.C.
MUSKOKA. The First Islanders. Bracebridge, Ont., Herald-Gazette, 1957. 30p

Masters, Donald Campbell Charles, 1908–
THE RISE OF TORONTO, 1850–1890. Toronto, U. of Toronto Press, 1947. 239p [BVaU LC OTP QMM
THE WINNIPEG GENERAL STRIKE. Toronto, U. of Toronto Press, 1950. 159p [BM BVaU NBFU OTP

Masterton, Mrs. I.V.
HISTORY OF EMERSON, FEATURING HISTORICAL SKETCHES OF SURROUNDING DISTRICTS. Ed. by —— and W.E. Carlson. Emerson, Man., W.E. Carlson, 1953. 80p

Mather, Barry, 1909–
NEW WESTMINSTER, THE ROYAL CITY. By Barry Mather and Margaret McDonald. Vancouver, Dent and the Corporation of the City of New Westminster, 1958. xxvii + 192p

Mathews, Hazel (Chisholm)
OAKVILLE AND THE SIXTEEN. The History of an Ontario Port. Toronto, U. of Toronto Press, 1953. xxv + 521p

Maurice, Varney, 1879–
FIFTY YEARS IN THE PEACE RIVER COUNTRY, and the Story of the Alaska Highway. High Prairie, Alta., 1947. 143p [AEU

Maxwell, Lilian Mary (Beckwith), 1877–1956
HOW NEW BRUNSWICK GREW. Sackville, Tribune Press, 1943. 95p [LC NBFU
OTP
THE OLD GRAVE-YARD, FREDERICTON, NEW BRUNSWICK, EPITAPHS. ... Ed. by ——.
Sackville, Busy East Press, [1938?]. 139p [BVaU OTP
AN OUTLINE OF THE HISTORY OF CENTRAL NEW BRUNSWICK TO THE TIME OF
CONFEDERATION. Sackville, Tribune Press, 1937. 183p [BM BVaU LC NBFU
OTP QMM

Maymont, Sask. Golden Jubilee Committee
THE STORY OF MAYMONT. Maymont, Sask., 1955. 50p

Meldrum, Frances Muriel (Tanner), 1909–
KITIMAT: THE FIRST FIVE YEARS. Kitimat, B.C., Corporation of the District of
Kitimat, 1959. 40p

Melfort, Sask. Board of Trade
MELFORT, SASKATCHEWAN, CANADA, THE HEART OF THE CARROT RIVER VALLEY.
Melfort, Sask., 1952. 20p

Melville, Sask. Board of Trade
MELVILLE, THE WEST'S WONDER TOWN. Melville, Canadian Office, 1910. 44p
[SSU

Melville, Sask. High School
THE MELVILLE STORY. [Freda Lawrence, history editor.] Melville, Sask., 1955.
57p [mimeographed]

Mendham, Sask. School
MENDHAM AFTER FIFTY YEARS. Mendham, Sask., 1955. 16p

Meredith, Mrs. Alden G.
MARY'S ROSEDALE AND GOSSIP OF "LITTLE YORK." Ottawa, Graphic, 1928.
280p [BVaU NBFU OTP QMSS

Merkel, Andrew Doane, 1884–1954
SCHOONER BLUENOSE. Toronto, Ryerson, 1948. 70p [BVaU LC NSHD OTP
QMM

Merritt, Jedediah Prendergast, 1820–1901
CANADA SEVENTY YEARS AGO; or, Prince Edward's Visit to Niagara. ... 3rd ed.
St. Catharines, 1860. 13p [OTP

Metcalfe, Joseph Henry, 1870–1938
THE TREAD OF THE PIONEERS. Under the Distinguished Patronage of the
Government of the Province of Manitoba, the Corporation of the City of Portage
la Prairie, the Council of the Rural Municipality of Portage la Prairie. Ed. by ——.
Toronto, Portage la Prairie & District Old Timers' Association, 1932. 305p
[BVaU OTP

Metzler, Norbert
ILLUSTRATED HALIFAX, ITS CIVIL, MILITARY, AND NAVAL HISTORY. With a Brief
  Sketch of Acadian Annals. Montreal, McConniff, 1891. 80p [NSWA OTP QMM

Middleton, Jesse Edgar, 1872—1960
THE MUNICIPALITY OF TORONTO. A History. Toronto, Dominion Pub., 1923. 3v
  [BM BVaU LC OTP
THE PROVINCE OF ONTARIO—A History—1615-1927. By Jesse Edgar Middleton
  ... and Fred Landon. ... Toronto, Dominion Pub., 1927—28. 5v [BVaU LC
  NBFU OLU QMM
TORONTO'S 100 YEARS. Toronto, Centennial Committee, 1934. 228p [BM BVaU
  LC OTP QMM

Mikel, William Charles, 1867—1950
CITY OF BELLEVILLE HISTORY. Comp. by ——. Picton, Ont., Gazette Pub., 1943.
  322p [BVaU LC OTP QMM
SOME BAY OF QUINTE REMINISCENCES. An Address before the U.E.L. Association
  at Toronto ... April 27th, 1922. Belleville, Cherry Press, [193—?]. 24p [OTP

Milestone, Sask. School
MILESTONE HISTORY. Saskatchewan Golden Jubilee. Milestone, Sask., 1955. 37p

Miller, Hanson Orlo, 1911—
A CENTURY OF WESTERN ONTARIO. The Story of London, "The Free Press," and
  Western Ontario, 1849—1949. Toronto, Ryerson, 1949. 289p [OLU QMM

Miller, Maud (Henderson), 1866—
HISTORY OF UPPER WOODSTOCK. Saint John, Globe Print., 1940. 165p [BViP
  LC NBFU OTP

Miller, Thomas, 1803—
HISTORICAL AND GENEALOGICAL RECORD OF THE FIRST SETTLERS OF
  COLCHESTER COUNTY, DOWN TO THE PRESENT TIME. ... Halifax, MacKinlay,
  1873. 400p [BVaU LC NSHD OTU

Mills, Edward Robert Rufus, 1886—
THE STORY OF STONY MOUNTAIN AND DISTRICT. Winnipeg, De Montfort Press,
  1960. 140p

Mills, Stanley, 1863—
LAKE MEDAD AND WATERDOWN. Hamilton, Author, 1937. 114p [OKQ

Milner, William Cochrane, 1846—1939
THE BASIN OF MINAS AND ITS EARLY SETTLERS. N.p., [193—?]. 132p [BVaU
  NSWA OTP QMM
EARLY HISTORY OF DORCHESTER AND OTHER PARTS OF NEW BRUNSWICK. N.p.,
  1932. 32p [Earlier ed., 1915.] [BVaU NSWA OLU

HISTORY OF SACKVILLE, NEW BRUNSWICK. Sackville, Tribune, 1934. 185p
  [BVaU LC NBFU OTP QMM
RECORDS OF CHIGNECTO. N.p., Nova Scotia Hist. Soc., 1916. 86p [BVaU NSWA
  OONL
SAINT JOHN IN THE FORTIES. N.p., Daily Telegraph, 1923. 23p [NSWA OONL

Minden, Ont. Centennial Planning Board
MINDEN CENTENNIAL, 1859-1959. Minden, Ont., 1959. 100p

Minnedosa, Man. 75th Anniversary History Section
A HISTORY OF MINNEDOSA AND SURROUNDING DISTRICTS. Minnedosa, Man.,
  1958. 1v [unpaged]

Minter, Roy Seymour, 1916–
A YUKON POT POURRI. Vancouver, priv. print., 1958. 24p

Mitchell, John, 1882–1951
THE SETTLEMENT OF YORK COUNTY. Toronto, Municipal Corporation of the
  County of York, 1952. 114p

Moffatt, Charles W.
INTRODUCING SACKVILLE, N.B. ... Comp. by ——. Sackville, Tribune, 1946. 89p
  [BVaU LC NBSM OTP

Moir, George Thomson, 1871–
SINNERS AND SAINTS. A True Story of Early [Railroad] Days in the Farthest West.
  By an Old Timer, Written and Told by Himself. Victoria, Wooding, 1948. 165p
  [mimeographed] [BVaU OTU

Monk, Harry Albert Jervis, 1913–
A HISTORY OF COQUITLAM AND FRASER MILLS, 1858-1958. By H.A.J. Monk and
  John Stewart. New Westminster, B.C., District of Coquitlam–Fraser Mills
  Centennial Commission, 1958. 76p

Monro, Alexander, 1813–1896
NEW BRUNSWICK. With a Brief Outline of Nova Scotia, and Prince Edward Island. ...
  Halifax, Nugent, 1855. 384p [BM BVaU LC NBFU OTP QMM

Montreal, Que. Tercentenary Commission
MONTREAL–SOREL, 1642-1942. Montreal's Pageant of Progress and its Nation
  Builders. ... Montreal, Bull Dog, 1942. 44p [OTU QMM

Moore, Rev. Arthur Henry, 1869–1938
THE VALLEY OF THE RICHELIEU. An Historical Study. St. John, Que., Smith,
  1929. 46p [NSHD OTU QMM

Moose Jaw, Sask. Golden Jubilee Committee
GOLDEN JUBILEE, 1903-1953. Moose Jaw, the Committee, 1953. 50p

More, James F.
THE HISTORY OF QUEENS COUNTY, N.S. ... Halifax, Nova Scotia Print., 1873.
250p [BM BVaU LC NSWA OTU QMU

Morgan, Joan Elson, 1917–
CASTLE OF QUEBEC. Toronto, Dent, 1949. 186p [BVa NBFU OTU

Morice, Rev. Adrian Gabriel, 1859–1938
A CRITICAL HISTORY OF THE RED RIVER INSURRECTION, after Official Documents
and Non-Catholic Sources. Winnipeg, Canadian Publishers, 1935. 375p [BM
BVaU LC NBFU OTP QMBM
THE HISTORY OF THE NORTHERN INTERIOR OF BRITISH COLUMBIA, FORMERLY
NEW CALEDONIA [1660–1880]. Toronto, Briggs, 1904. 349p [BM BVaU
LC NSWA OTP QMSS

Mornington Township, Ont. Centennial Committee
MORNINGTON CENTENNIAL AND MILVERTON OLD BOYS & GIRLS REUNION,
AUGUST 2 TO AUGUST 5. Souvenir Booklet and Programme. Milverton, Ont.,
1957. 108p

Morris, Rev. M.
THE PROPOSED RAILWAY ACROSS NEWFOUNDLAND. A Lecture. ... St. John's,
Nfld., "Public Ledger" Office, 1875. 46p [LC

Morrison, Clifford Jennings, 1906–
DO YOU REMEMBER? The First Fifty Years in the Spalding District. Prepared by
C.J. Morrison from information secured by Mrs. Matt. Dircks. Spalding,
Sask., Jubilee Committee, 1955. 19p

Morrison, Mrs. Elsie C.
CALGARY, 1875–1950. A Souvenir of Calgary's Seventy-Fifth Anniversary.
Ed. by Elsie C. Morrison and P.N.R. Morrison. Calgary, Calgary Pub. Co., 1950.
247p [OONL

Morrison, Neil Farquharson, 1896–
GARDEN GATEWAY TO CANADA. One Hundred Years of Windsor and Essex
County, 1854–1954. Toronto, Ryerson, 1954. ix + 344p

Morrow, James William, 1869–1932
EARLY HISTORY OF THE MEDICINE HAT COUNTRY. Medicine Hat, News, 1923.
65p [OTU SSU

Morrow, Robert A.H.
STORY OF THE SPRINGHILL DISASTER. Comprising a Full and Authentic Account
of the Great Coal Mining Explosion at Springhill Mines, Nova Scotia, February
21st, 1891, including a History of Springhill and its Collieries. ... 2nd ed. Saint
John, Morrow, 1891. 311p [BVaU LC NSWA OTU

Morse, John Jesse, 1906–

KAMLOOPS, THE INLAND CAPITAL. A Condensed History. Kamloops, B.C., Kamloops Museum Association for the Kamloops Centennial Committee, 1957. 40p

Morse, William Inglis, 1874–1952

ACADIENSIA NOVA (1598–1779). ... New and Unpublished Documents and Other Data Relating to Acadia. Collected and ed. by ——. London, Quaritch, 1935. 2v [BM BVaU LC NSWA OTP

GRAVESTONES OF ACADIE, AND OTHER ESSAYS ON LOCAL HISTORY. London, Smith, 1929. 110p [BM BVaU LC NBFU OTP QMM

THE LAND OF THE NEW ADVENTURE (THE GEORGIAN ERA IN NOVA SCOTIA). London, Quaritch, 1932. 158p [BM BVaU LC NSWA OLU QMBM

LOCAL HISTORY OF PARADISE, ANNAPOLIS COUNTY, NOVA SCOTIA (1684–1936). Boston, Sawyer, 1937. 65p [Supplement–to 1938: Boston, Sawyer, 1938. 79p] [BM LC NSHD OTP QMM

Morton, Arthur Silver, 1870–1945

HISTORY OF PRAIRIE SETTLEMENT. Toronto, Macmillan, 1938. 571p [BM BVaU LC NBFU OTP QMM

A HISTORY OF THE CANADIAN WEST TO 1870–71. Being a History of Rupert's Land (the Hudson's Bay Company's Territory) and of the North-west Territory (including the Pacific Slope). Toronto, Nelson, 1939. 987p [BM BVaU LC NBFU OTP QMM

Morton, William Lewis, 1908–

MANITOBA. A History. Toronto, U. of Toronto Press, 1957. xii + 519p

Mowat, Grace Helen, 1875–1964

THE DIVERTING HISTORY OF A LOYALIST TOWN. St. Andrew's, N.B., Charlotte County Cottage Craft, 1932. 140p [2nd ed., Fredericton, Brunswick Press, 1953. 152p] [BVaU LC NBFU OTP

THE HOUSE THAT HURRICANE JACK BUILT. Fredericton, Brunswick Press, 1954. 14p [History of the Bayside area of New Brunswick and of the house built there by John Mowat.]

Muir, Robert Cuthbertson, 1856–1935

THE EARLY POLITICAL AND MILITARY HISTORY OF BURFORD, ONT. Quebec, Imprimerie Commerciale, 1913. 371p [OTP QMSS

Mulholland, A.H.R.

NEARLY HALF A CENTURY. London, Ont., Lawson Memorial Library, U. of Western Ontario, 1945. 7 leaves [OTU

Mullane, George, 1850–1938

FOOTPRINTS AROUND AND ABOUT BEDFORD BASIN, a District Brimful of Romantic Associations. Some Interesting Facts about its Early History. Halifax, [19—?]. 46p [BVaU OTP

MONOGRAPH OF ST. PAUL'S CEMETERY. ... Halifax, Burgoyne, 1902. 24p
[NSHD

Mullins, Janet Elizabeth
LIVERPOOL PRIVATEERING, 1756–1815. Comp. by ——. Liverpool, N.S.,
Queen's County Hist. Soc., 1936. 68p [NBSaM QMG
SOME LIVERPOOL CHRONICLES. ... Liverpool, N.S., Advance, 1941. 297p
[NSHPL

Mullock, Rev. John Thomas, 1807–1869
TWO LECTURES ON NEWFOUNDLAND DELIVERED AT ST. BONAVENTURE'S
COLLEGE. ... New York, Mullaly, 1860. 60p [BM OONL QMSS

Mulvany, Charles Pelham, 1835–1885
THE HISTORY OF THE COUNTY OF BRANT. ... By C. Pelham Mulvany and others.
Toronto, Warner Beers, 1883. 689p [OLU
HISTORY OF THE COUNTY OF PETERBOROUGH, ONTARIO. [By C. Pelham
Mulvany and others.] Toronto, Robinson, 1884. 783p [OTU
THE HISTORY OF THE NORTH-WEST REBELLION OF 1885. Toronto, Hovey,
1885. 424p [BM BVaU LC NSHD OTP QMM
HISTORY OF TORONTO AND COUNTY OF YORK, ONTARIO. By C. Pelham
Mulvany, G.M. Adam, and others. Toronto, Robinson, 1885. 2v [BM NSWA
OTU
TORONTO, PAST AND PRESENT. Toronto, Caiger, 1884. 320p [BM BVaU
LC NSWA OTP QMSS

Munday, Walter Alfred Don, 1890–1950
THE UNKNOWN MOUNTAIN. By Don Munday. London, Hodder, 1948. 268p
[Mount Waddington, B.C.] [BM BVaU OTP

Murdoch, Beamish, 1800–1876
A HISTORY OF NOVA SCOTIA, OR ACADIE. Halifax, Barnes, 1865–67. 3v [BM
BVaU LC NBFU OTP QMM

Murphy, James, 1867–1931
A CENTURY OF EVENTS IN NEWFOUNDLAND. St. John's, Author, 1924. 28p
[NfSG
ENGLAND'S OLDEST POSSESSION, THE COLONY OF NEWFOUNDLAND. A useful
Compilation of Events in her History. ... St. John's, Author, 1924. 42p [NfSM
MURPHY'S OLD SEALING DAYS. St. John's, Murphy, 1916. 46p [NfSM
THE MUSTY PAST. Incidents of Newfoundland History for 73 Years. St. John's,
Barnes, 1906. 28p [NfSG

Murphy, John Michael, 1915–
THE LONDONDERRY HEIRS. A Story of the Settlement of the Townships of
Truro, Onslow, and Londonderry. Truro, N.S., Author, 1960. 133p ["Pub.
on the Occasion of Truro's Bicentenary Celebrations, 1960."]

Namao, Alta. United Farm Women of Alberta, Local No. 61
A CAMEO OF THE WEST. Story of the Pioneers of the Sturgeon River District, 1879–1900. Edmonton, Commercial Print., 1936. 54p [AEP

Naramata, B.C. Centennial Committee
NARAMATA IN RETROSPECT. Namarata, B.C., the Committee, 1958. 15p [mimeographed]

Nase, Edith Rowena
WESTFIELD [N.B.]. An Historical Sketch. N.p., Author, [1925?]. 88p [NBSM OTP

Neal, Frederick
THE TOWNSHIP OF SANDWICH, PAST AND PRESENT. An Interesting History of the Canadian Frontier along the Detroit River. Ed. by ——. Windsor, Ont., Record Print., 1909. 232p [BM BVaU LC NBFU OTU

Neal, May
A SOUVENIR OF REGINA, "QUEEN CITY OF THE PLAINS." Ed. by ——. Regina, Western Printers, 1954. 132p

Neatby, Leslie Hamilton, 1902–
IN QUEST OF THE NORTH WEST PASSAGE. Toronto, Longmans, 1958. 194p
THE LINK BETWEEN THE OCEANS. Toronto, Longmans, 1960. 139p [On the search for Sir John Franklin's Expedition.]

Neilburg, Sask. Jubilee Committee
A GLANCE BACK, 1955 TO 1905. By Mrs. Jennie Johnson and others. Neilburg, Sask., 1955. 119p [History of Neilburg.]

Nelson, Denys, 1876–1929
FORT LANGLEY, 1827–1927. A Century of Settlement in the Valley of the Lower Fraser River. Vancouver, Evans & Hastings, 1927. 31p [BM BVaU LC OTP

New Brunswick Historical Society
COLLECTIONS. Saint John, Daily Telegraph, Barnes, 1894–. [A continuing serial.] [BM BVaU NSHD OTP QMSS
LOYALIST SOUVENIR. One Hundred and Fiftieth Anniversary of the Landing of the Loyalists in the Province of New Brunswick, 1783–1933. Saint John, the Society, 1933. 31p [BVaU LC NSHD OLU
LOYALIST'S CENTENNIAL SOUVENIR. ... Saint John, McMillan, 1887. 183p [BVaU NBFU OOA

New Liskeard, Ont. St. Paul's United Church
NEW LISKEARD THEN AND NOW. New Liskeard, Ont., [1950?]. 128p [Editor: D.K. Kitchen.] [OONL

Newmarket, Ont.
PINE ORCHARD HISTORY, 1800–1936. [Newmarket], Newmarket Era, 1936. 22p [OTU

Niagara Historical Society
PUBLICATIONS. ... Niagara, the Society, 1896–. [A continuing serial.] [BVaU
LC OTP

Nicholls, Mrs. Margaret Alexandria, 1915–
A HISTORY OF NANOOSE BAY. Nanoose Bay, B.C., Nanoose Centennial Committee,
1958. 54p [mimeographed]

Nickle, Carl Olof, 1914–
THE VALLEY OF WONDERS. The Story of Turner Valley. Calgary, Oil Bulletin,
1942. 40p [CC

Nicolls, John Pethybridge, 1870–
REAL ESTATE VALUES IN VANCOUVER. A Reminiscence. Vancouver, City
Archives, 1954. 39p

Norcross, Elizabeth Blanche, 1920–
THE WARM LAND. Duncan, B.C., Author, 1959. xi + 112p [History of the
Cowichan Valley, B.C.]

Nordra S.D. No. 1947, Sask. School
A BRIEF HISTORY OF THE NORDRA DISTRICT. Wynyard, Sask., 1954. 16p

Norris, Frederick Corbett, 1880–
THEN AND NOW. A Condensed History of Turtle Mountain Municipality and the
Town of Killarney, marking their 75th and 50th Anniversaries, July 11th to
14th, 1957. Comp. and ed. by —— et al. Killarney, Man., Killarney Guide,
1957. 125p

Norrish, Joshua
THE EARLY HISTORY OF NASAGIWEYA. Guelph, Hough, 1889. 99p [Reprinted
in: NASSAGAWEYA CENTENNIAL, 1850–1950; an Historical Volume of
Nassagaweya Township in Halton County ... including the Early History of
Nassagaweya as Written by the Late Joshua Norrish, an Early Settler. Acton,
Ont., Free Press, [1950?]. 90p] [OOA

North Battleford, Sask. Golden Jubilee Committee
SKYLINE ... THE PANORAMIC PATTERN OF A CITY. North Battleford's Golden
Jubilee Story. Editor and Historic Committee Chairman: C. Irwin McIntosh.
North Battleford, McIntosh Pub. Co., 1955. 84p

Nottawasaga, Ont. Centennial Celebration
NOTTAWASAGA. The Outburst of the Iroquois. Nottawasaga, Historical
Committee, 1934. 122p [OTP

Nova Scotia Historical Society
COLLECTIONS. Halifax, Morning Herald, 1879–. [A continuing serial.] [BM
BVaU NSHD OTP

Noyes, John Powell, 1842–1923

THE CANADIAN LOYALISTS AND EARLY SETTLERS IN THE DISTRICT OF BEDFORD. St. John, Que., the News, 1900. 20p [BVaU LC NSWA OTP QMM

SKETCHES OF SOME EARLY SHEFFORD PIONEERS. [Anon] Montreal, Gazette, 1905. 126p [BVaU OLU

Oak Bay, B.C. Municipal Council. Anniversary Committee

THE CORPORATION OF THE DISTRICT OF OAK BAY. Golden Jubilee, 1906–1956: Fifty Years of Growth. Oak Bay, the Council, 1956. 28p

Oblates of Mary Immaculate. St. Joseph's Colony, Sask.

RIPENING HARVEST. The Story of St. Joseph's Colony, 1905–1955. Denzil, Sask., 1955. 44p

Ogema, Sask. School

OGEMA'S HISTORY. Ogema, Sask., 1955. 23p [mimeographed]

Ogilvie, William, 1846–1912

EARLY DAYS ON THE YUKON. The Story of its Gold Finds. Ottawa, Thorburn Abbott, 1913. 306p [BM BVaU LC NSWA OTU QMM

Okanagan Historical Society. Penticton Branch

HISTORICAL SOUVENIR OF PENTICTION, B.C., 1908–1958. ... Penticton, City of Penticton, 1958. 164p

O'Leary, A.E.

RAMBLES THRO' MEMORY LANE WITH CHARACTERS I KNEW. [Richibucto, N.B.], Author, 1937. 109p [AEU NBSM OTP

Oliver, Edmund Henry, 1882–1935

THE CANADIAN NORTHWEST. Its Early Development and Legislative Records, Minutes of the Councils of the Red River Colony. Ed. by ——. Ottawa, Government Print. Bureau, 1914–15. 2v [BM BVaU NSHD OTP

O'Neill, William John, 1882–

STEAMBOAT DAYS ON THE SKEENA RIVER, BRITISH COLUMBIA. Ed. by Stan Rough. Kitimat, B.C., Northern Sentinel, 1960. 35p

TIME AND PLACE: STORIES OF NORTHERN BRITISH COLUMBIA. Stories of the West Coast, Skeena River, Bulkley Valley, Douglas Channel, and the old and new Kitimat. By Wiggs O'Neill [and others]. Prince Rupert, priv. print., 1958. 53p

WHITEWATER MEN OF THE SKEENA. Ed. by Stan Rough. Kitimat, B.C., 1960. 28p

Ontario Centennial Committee, 1892

CENTENNIAL OF THE PROVINCE OF UPPER CANADA, 1792–1892. ... [Toronto?], Arbuthnot & Adamson, 1893. 33p [NSHD OLU

Ontario Historical Society
PAPERS AND RECORDS. ... Toronto, Briggs, 1899–. [A continuing serial.] [BM
BVaU NSHD OTU

Ormsby, Margaret Anchoretta, 1909–
BRITISH COLUMBIA. A History. Toronto, Macmillan, 1958. x + 558p

Owen, Egbert Americus, –1908
PIONEER SKETCHES OF LONG POINT SETTLEMENT; or, Norfolk's Foundation
Builders and their Family Genealogies. Toronto, Briggs, 1898. 578p [BVaU
LC NBFU OTP

Owen, William, 1738?–1778
NARRATIVE OF AMERICAN VOYAGES AND TRAVELS, AND SETTLEMENT OF THE
ISLAND OF CAMPOBELLO ... 1766–71. Ed. by V.H. Paltsits. New York, Public
Library, 1942. 169p [BM NBFU OTP

Oxner, Mrs. Effie G., 1874–
HISTORY OF CHESTER BASIN, 1760–1951. Comp. by Effie Oxner, Olive Turner and
Jean Countway. Chester Basin, N.S., 1952. 12p

Page, Frank E.
THE STORY OF SMITHVILLE. Welland, Tribune-Telegraph, 1923. 90p [BM
BVaU LC OTP

Pain, Sidney Albert, 1896–
THREE MILES OF GOLD. The Story of Kirkland Lake. Toronto, Ryerson, 1960.
109p

Pambrun, Sask. Intermediate School
THE HISTORY OF PAMBRUN AND ITS COMMUNITY. Comp. by Mrs. E. Mumby
and her pupils of Pambrun Intermediate School. Pambrun, Sask., 1957. 31p

Parker, Gilbert, 1862–1932
OLD QUEBEC, THE FORTRESS OF NEW FRANCE. By Gilbert Parker and Claude
G. Bryan. New York, Macmillan, 1903. 486p [BM BVaU LC NBFU OTP
QMM

Parkinson, Hazel (McDonald), 1898–
THE MERE LIVING. A Biography of the Hartney District. Altona, Man., D.W.
Friesen, 1957. 301p

Paterson, Gilbert Clarence, 1887–
LAND SETTLEMENT IN UPPER CANADA 1783–1840. Toronto, James, 1921.
278p [BVaU OLU QMM

Patterson, Frank Harris, 1891–
ACADIAN TATAMAGOUCHE AND FORT FRANKLIN. Truro, N.S., Truro Print.,
1947. 84p [NSWA OTP

A HISTORY OF TATAMAGOUCHE, NOVA SCOTIA. Halifax, Royal Print., 1917. 143p [BVaU NSWA OTP QMM

Patterson, Rev. George, 1824–1897

A HISTORY OF THE COUNTY OF PICTOU. Montreal, Dawson, 1877. 471p [Reprinted: Pictou, "Advocate," 1916. 296p] [BVaU NSWA OTP QMM

SABLE ISLAND. Its History and Phenomena. Montreal, Drysdale; Halifax, Knight, 1894. 49p [BM BVaU LC NSWA OTU

Patterson, George Geddie, 1864–1951

MORE STUDIES IN NOVA SCOTIAN HISTORY. Halifax, Imperial, 1941. 180p [BVaU NSWA OTP QMBM

STUDIES IN NOVA SCOTIAN HISTORY. Halifax, Imperial, 1940. 125p [BVaU NSWA OTP

Payzant, Harry Young, 1881–1953

"PEOPLE." A Story of the People of Nova Scotia. Truro, N.S., News Pub. Co., 1935. 369p [BM BVaU LC NBFU OTU

Pearce, F.M.

EARLY DAYS IN WATERFORD. Waterford, Ont., Author, 1941. 20p [OTP

Pearson, John, 1900–

LAND OF THE PEACE ARCH. Cloverdale, B.C., Surrey Centennial Committee, 1958. xii + 159p [History of the Municipal District of Surrey, B.C.]

Pearson, William Henry, 1831–1920

RECOLLECTIONS AND RECORDS OF TORONTO OF OLD. With References to Brantford, Kingston and Other ... Towns. Toronto, Briggs, 1914. 372p [BVaU LC OTP

Pedley, Rev. Charles, 1821–1872

THE HISTORY OF NEWFOUNDLAND, FROM THE EARLIEST TIMES TO THE YEAR 1860. London, Longmans, 1863. 531p [BM BVaU LC NSWA OTP QMM

Peel, Bruce Braden, 1916–

THE SASKATOON STORY, 1882–1952. By Bruce Peel and Eric Knowles. Saskatoon, M.A. East, 1952. 86p

Pellerin, Mrs. Maude Gage, 1884–

THE STORY OF HATLEY. Hatley, Que., Author, 1951. 84p

Perkins, Charlotte Isabella

THE OLDEST HOUSES ALONG ST. GEORGE STREET, ANNAPOLIS ROYAL, N.S. Saint John, Barnes, 1925. 41p [BM NSWA

THE ROMANCE OF OLD ANNAPOLIS ROYAL, N.S. Annapolis Royal, Author, 1935. 101p [Rev. ed., 1954. 121p] [BVaU NBFU OTP

Perlin, Albert B., 1901–
THE STORY OF NEWFOUNDLAND. Comprising a new Outline of the Island's
History from 1497 to 1958. ... St. John's, Dicks & Co., 1959. 248p

Petty, Thomas, 1890–
ECHOES OF THE QU'APPELLE LAKES DISTRICT. A Guide to Some Historic Sites,
Trails and Scenes of the Qu'Appelle Lakes District. Indian Head, Sask., Author,
1955. 55p

Pick, Harry, 1881–
NEXT YEAR. A Semi-Historical Account of the Exploitations of the Far-Famed
Barr Colonists ... led by an Unscrupulous Church of England Parson ... in the
Early Years of the Twentieth Century. Toronto, Ryerson, 1928. 254p [BM
BVaU OTU

Piers, Harry, 1870–1940
A CHRONOLOGICAL TABLE OF DARTMOUTH, PRESTON, AND LAWRENCETOWN,
COUNTY OF HALIFAX, N.S. Halifax, n.p., 1894. 12p [NSWA
THE EVOLUTION OF THE HALIFAX FORTRESS, 1749–1928. ... Ed. by ——.
Halifax, Public Archives of Nova Scotia, 1947. 155p [BM BVaU LC NSHD
OTP
MASTER GOLDSMITHS AND SILVERSMITHS OF NOVA SCOTIA. Halifax, Antiquarian
Club, 1948. 161p [BVaU NSHD OTU

Pilot Mound, Man. Reunion Committee
REUNION, PILOT MOUND 50, DISTRICT 75, JULY 1954. Pilot Mound, Man., 1954.
64p [50th Anniversary of the ... Village and 75th of the ... district.]

Pincher Creek, Alta. Old Timers Association
PINCHER CREEK OLD TIMERS SOUVENIR ALBUM, 1878–1958. Pincher Creek,
Alta., the Association, 1958. 69p

Piper, William Samuel, 1863–
THE EAGLE OF THUNDER CAPE. Toronto, Warwick & Rutter, 1926. 301p
[BVaU OONL QMBM

Pirie, Alexander Fraser, 1849–1903
PICTURESQUE DUNDAS. Dundas, Ont., A.F. Pirie, 1896. 192p [DCB attributes
this title to A.F. Pirie, but OLU attributes it to "Charles N. Pirie and W.A.
Davidson" as co-compilers.] [DCB OLU

Plato, Sask. Golden Jubilee Committee
PLATO, SASKATCHEWAN, 1905–1955. Plato, Sask., 1955. 16p

Pollard, James B.
HISTORICAL SKETCH OF THE EASTERN REGIONS OF NEW FRANCE ... ALSO PRINCE
EDWARD ISLAND: Military and Civil. ... Charlottetown, Coombs, 1898.
235p [BVaU LC NSWA OTU QMSS

Ponteix S.D. 2369, Sask. School

PONTEIX, 1955. Ponteix, Sask., 1955. 24p [mimeographed]

Poole, Edmund Duval

ANNALS OF YARMOUTH AND BARRINGTON (NOVA SCOTIA) IN THE REVOLU-TIONARY WAR. Comp. by ——, from Original Manuscripts, etc., contained in the Office of the Secretary of the Commonwealth, State House, Boston, Mass. Yarmouth, Lawson, 1899. 133p [LC NSWA OTU

Poole, Thomas Wesley, 1831?–1905

A SKETCH OF THE EARLY SETTLEMENT AND SUBSEQUENT PROGRESS OF THE TOWN OF PETERBOROUGH, AND OF EACH TOWNSHIP IN THE COUNTY OF PETERBOROUGH. Peterborough, Review Office, 1867. 220p [A reprint of this work, with additional material bringing the history down to 1941, was published by the Centennial Committee of the Peterborough County Council: Peterborough, Peterborough Print., 1941. 220 + 44 + 72p] [BVaU LC NSWA OTP QMM

Porcupine, Ont. Golden Anniversary Committee

SOUVENIR BOOKLET CELEBRATING THE GOLDEN ANNIVERSARY OF THE PORCUPINE GOLD RUSH, JULY 1–5, 1959. [Porcupine, Committee, 1959.] 100p

Porter, Lancelot, 1882–

BURTON, BRITISH COLUMBIA: "Our Days Before Yesterday," as told by Bob Hewatson [pseud] to Mrs. H.D. McCormack. Burton, B.C., Burton Centennial Committee, 1958. 31p

Powell River News

BRITISH COLUMBIA CENTENNIAL, 1858–1958. Westview, B.C., 1958. 56p

Powers, John Weston, 1852–1905

THE HISTORY OF REGINA. Its Foundation and Growth. ... Regina, Leader Co., 1887. 93p [OOA SSU

Powley, Mrs. Ellen Frances Gladys, 1884–

EARLY DAYS OF WINFIELD, B.C. Comp. by ——. Winfield, B.C., Women's Institute, 1957. 30p

Prentice, Wilbur Miller, 1908–

RANDOM STORIES FROM GEORGIAN BAY. Toronto, Author, 1958. 16p [mimeographed]

Preston, Richard Arthur, 1910–

KINGSTON BEFORE THE WAR OF 1812. A Collection of Documents. Ed. by ——. Toronto, Champlain Society for the Government of Ontario, U. of Toronto Press, 1959. cxvi + 428p

ROYAL FORT FRONTENAC. Texts selected and translated from the French by

Richard A. Preston. Ed. with intro. and notes by Leopold Lamontagne.
Toronto, Champlain Society for the Government of Ontario, U. of Toronto
Press, 1958. xxx + 503p

Price, Bertha Maud (Weston), 1872–1955
GLIMPSES INTO THE PAST. Sherbrooke, Que., Daily Record, 1955. 152p [Refers
to the Eastern Townships of Quebec.]

Prince Albert, Sask. Schools
SASKATCHEWAN GOLDEN JUBILEE PROGRAM, PRINCE ALBERT SCHOOLS, MAY
25, 1955. Prince Albert, 1955. 16p [mimeographed. Chiefly a history of
Prince Albert.]

Prince Edward Island Historical Society
HISTORIC HIGHLIGHTS OF PRINCE EDWARD ISLAND. Charlottetown, the Society,
1955. 127p [Also: 1956. 98p]

Pringle, Jacob Farrand, 1816–1901
LUNENBURGH; or, THE OLD EASTERN DISTRICT. Its Settlement and Early
Progress, with Personal Recollections of the Town of Cornwall, from 1824. ...
Cornwall, Standard, 1890. 424p [BVaU LC NSHD OTP QMM

Pritchard, John, 1777–1856
GLIMPSES OF THE PAST IN THE RED RIVER SETTLEMENT. From Letters ...
1805–1836. Notes by Rev. Dr. Bryce. Middlechurch, Man., Rupert's Land
Indian Industrial School Press, 1892. 23p [BViPA OTP
NARRATIVES OF JOHN PRITCHARD, PIERRE CHRYSOLOGUE PAMBRUN, AND
FREDERICK DAMIEN HEURTER, Respecting the Aggressions of the North-west
Company, against the Earl of Selkirk's Settlement upon Red River. London,
Murray, 1819. 91p [BM BViPA LC OTP QMM

Prowse, Daniel Woodley, 1834–1914
EPISODES IN OUR EARLY HISTORY. ... St. John's, Nfld., "Morning Chronicle,"
1878. 29p [NSHD QMBM
A HISTORY OF NEWFOUNDLAND. ... With a prefatory note by Edmund Gosse.
London, Macmillan, 1895. 742p [2nd ed., rev. and corrected: London,
Eyre, 1896. 634p] [BM BVaU NSWA OTP QMM

Prowse, George Robert Farrar, 1860–
EXPLORATION OF THE GULF OF ST. LAWRENCE, 1499–1525. Winnipeg, Author,
1933. 32p [BM BVaU NSWA OTU

Pubnico, N.S. Tricentennial Committee
TRICENTENAIRE DE PUBNICO – PUBNICO'S TERCENTENARY, 1651–1951. Album-
Souvenir, Souvenir Booklet, August 21–25, 1951. Pubnico, N.S., 1951. 64p

Pumphrey, Ronald
STRANGE FACTS ABOUT NEWFOUNDLAND. By Ron Pumphrey and L.E.F.
English. St. John's, Guardian Associates, 1952. 44p

Puslinch, Ont. Historical Committee

ANNALS OF PUSLINCH, 1850–1950. Acton, Ont., Free Press, 1950. 120p [OONL

Quebec, Que.

REPORT OF THE COMMISSIONERS APPOINTED TO INQUIRE INTO THE CONDUCT OF THE POLICE AUTHORITIES ON THE OCCASION OF THE RIOT AT CHALMERS' CHURCH ON THE 6th OF JUNE, 1853. ... Quebec, Campbell, 1854. 127p [QMM

REPORT OF THE STATE TRIALS before a General Court Martial held in Montreal in 1838–9. Exhibiting a Complete History of the late Rebellion in Lower Canada. Montreal, Armour & Ramsay, 1839. 2v [OTU QMM

Quene Yip

VANCOUVER CHINATOWN. Specially Prepared for the Vancouver Golden Jubilee 1886–1936. ... Vancouver, Pacific Printers, 1936. 48p [BViPA

Quill Lake, Sask. School

QUILL LAKE HISTORY. A Tribute to the Community and its Builders. Editors, Mrs. B. McBeath and V. Gabriel. Quill Lake, 1955. 47p [mimeographed]

Raddall, Thomas Head, 1903–

HALIFAX, WARDEN OF THE NORTH. ... Toronto, McClelland, 1948. 348p [BM BVaU LC NBFU OTP QMM

Rand, Rev. Silas Tertius, 1810–1889

A SHORT STATEMENT OF FACTS RELATING TO THE HISTORY, MANNERS, CUSTOMS, LANGUAGE, AND LITERATURE OF THE MICMAC TRIBE OF INDIANS IN NOVA SCOTIA AND P.E. ISLAND. Halifax, Bowes, 1850. 40p [BM NSWA OTP QMM

Randall, Mrs. Evelina Belle, 1889–

HEALING WATERS. History of Harrison Hot Springs and Port Douglas Area. Harrison Hot Springs, B.C., Author, 1958. 34p

Rankin, Rev. Duncan Joseph, 1874–1954

A HISTORY OF THE COUNTY OF ANTIGONISH, NOVA SCOTIA. Toronto, Macmillan, 1929. 390p [BVaU LC NBFU OKQ QMM

Rannie, William Fraser, 1915–

CAVE SPRINGS FARM. Fact and Fancy about one of the Historic Places of the Niagara Peninsula. 2nd ed. Beamsville, Ont., Beamsville Express, 1960. 35p [1st ed., 1952]

Ravenhill, Alice, 1859–1954

A CORNER STONE OF CANADIAN CULTURE. An Outline of the Arts and Crafts of the Indian Tribes of British Columbia. Victoria, Banfield, 1944. 103p [BVaU OTP QMM

FOLKLORE OF THE FAR WEST. With Some Clues to Characteristics and Customs. Victoria, n.p., 1953. 87p

THE NATIVE TRIBES OF BRITISH COLUMBIA. Victoria, Banfield, 1938. 142p [BM BVaU LC OTP QMBM

Raymond, Rev. William Odber, 1853–1923

GLIMPSES OF THE PAST. History of the River St. John, 1604–1784. Saint John, 1905. 375p [Later pub. under title: THE RIVER ST. JOHN. Its Physical Features, Legends and History from 1604 to 1784. Saint John, Bowes, 1910. 552p Cf. also same title: Sackville, N.B., Tribune Press, 1943. 280p] [BM BVaU LC NBFU OTP QMM

Ream, Rev. Peter Tennant, 1925–

THE FORT ON THE SASKATCHEWAN. A History of Fort Saskatchewan. ... Edmonton, Douglas Print. Co., 1957. 155p [With APPENDIX, 1962. 18p]

Reeves, Helena K.

IN THE SHADOW OF THE SLEEPING GIANT. An Historical Sketch of Port Arthur, Ontario. Port Arthur, Chamber of Commerce, 1947. 24p [OOA

Regan, John William, 1873–1945

DARTMOUTH, NOVA SCOTIA: "The Great Harbour." ... By John Quinpool [pseud]. Halifax, 1942. 24p [LC NSHP OTP

FIRST THINGS IN ACADIA, "THE BIRTHPLACE OF A CONTINENT." ... By John Quinpool [pseud]. Halifax, First Things Pub., 1936. 304p [BM BVaU LC NSWA OTP QMM

HALIFAX, NOVA SCOTIA: "The Great Harbour." ... By John Quinpool [pseud]. Halifax, 1941. 24p [LC NSHP OTP

SKETCHES AND TRADITIONS OF THE NORTHWEST ARM. Halifax, McAlpine, 1908. 191p [BM BVaU LC NSWA OTP QMM

Reid, William, 1880–

MEMORIES OF PIONEER DAYS AT PILOT MOUND. [Anon] Pilot Mound, "Sentinel" Print., 1930. 54p [MWP OTP

Renown, Sask. High School

RENOWN, OUR STORY. By Students of Grades XI and XII and Teachers of Renown High School. Renown, Sask., 1955. 84 + 12p [mimeographed]

Revenue, Sask. High School

REVENUE REMEMBERS, 1905–1955. Revenue, Sask., 1955. 47p [mimeographed]

Reville, Frederick Douglas, 1866–1944

HISTORY OF THE COUNTY OF BRANT. Brantford, Hurley, 1920. 2v [BM BVaU OTP QMM

Reynolds, William Kilby, 1848–1902

... OLD TIME TRAGEDIES. Celebrated Cases before the Courts in St. John, N.B. ... Saint John, "Progress" Electric Print., 1895. 104p [BVaU NSHD

Rich, E.E.

MOOSE FORT JOURNALS 1783–85. Ed. by ——, assisted by A.M. Johnson. London, Hudson's Bay Record Society, 1954. xxx + 392p

Richardson, Burton Taylor, 1906–

TORONTO '59. One Hundred and Twenty Fifth Anniversary. Ed. by ——. Toronto, City Council, 1959. 168p

Rickard, Thomas Arthur, 1864–1953

HISTORIC BACKGROUNDS OF BRITISH COLUMBIA. Vancouver, Wrigley, 1948. 358p [BVaU NBFU OTP QMM

Ricker, Jackson

HISTORICAL SKETCHES OF GLENWOOD AND THE ARGYLES, YARMOUTH COUNTY, NOVA SCOTIA. ... Truro, Truro Print., 1941. 134p [NSHD

Riddell, Walter, 1814–1904

HISTORICAL SKETCH OF THE TOWNSHIP OF HAMILTON. Cobourg, 1897. [OOP

Riddell, William Renwick, 1852–1945

OLD PROVINCE TALES. Upper Canada. Toronto, Brook, 1920. 280p [LC NSHD OTP QMM

UPPER CANADA SKETCHES. Incidents in the Early Times of the Province. Toronto, Carswell, 1922. 156p [BVaU LC OTP

Rimbey, Alta. History Committee

HISTORY OF RIMBEY, ALBERTA. 50 Years of Progress. Rimbey, Alta., 1952. 60p

Ritchie, Mrs. Mary Houston, –1961

A TOWNSHIP ON THE LAKE: BEAVERTON AND THORAH, 1820–1952. Beaverton, Ont., [1952?]. 78p

Roberts, Leslie, 1896–

THE MACKENZIE. New York, Rinehart, 1949. 276p [BVaU LC NBFU OTP QMM

NORANDA. Toronto, Clarke Irwin, 1956. xiii + 223p

Robertson, John Ross, 1841–1918

LANDMARKS OF TORONTO. A Collection of Historical Sketches of the Old Town of York from 1792 until 1833, and of Toronto from 1834 to 1908. Toronto, Author, 1894–1914. 6v [BM BVaU LC NSWA OTU QMM

OLD TORONTO. A Selection of Excerpts from LANDMARKS OF TORONTO. Ed. by E.C. Kyte. Toronto, Macmillan, 1954. xi + 346p

Robertson, Norman, 1845–1936

THE HISTORY OF THE COUNTY OF BRUCE. Toronto, Briggs, 1906. 560p [BM BVaU LC NSHD OTU QMSS

Robinson, Leigh Burpee
ESQUIMALT. "Place of Shoaling Waters." Victoria, Quality Press, 1947. 126p
[BVaU NSHD OTP QMBM

Robinson, Noel, 1880–
HISTORY OF THE ART, HISTORICAL AND SCIENTIFIC ASSOCIATION. Vancouver's
First Cultural Association. Vancouver, the Association, 1944. 20p [BM BVaU
OTP

Robinson, Percy James, 1873–1953
TORONTO DURING THE FRENCH REGIME ... 1615–1793. Toronto, Ryerson, 1933.
254p [BM BVaU LC NBFU OTP QMM

Robinson, Ross, 1904–
DELISLE AND DISTRICT IN REVIEW. Delisle, Sask., 1955. 32p

Robsart, Sask. Jubilee Committee
ROBSART PIONEERS REVIEW THE YEARS. Robsart, Sask., 1956. 115p

Roche Percée, Sask. School
HISTORY OF ROCHE PERCEE, SASKATCHEWAN. Roche Percée, Sask., 1955. 14p

Rockwood-Woodlands Historical Society
ROCKWOOD ECHOES: 90 YEARS OF PROGRESS, 1870–1960. A History of the Men
and Women who Pioneered the Rockwood Municipality. Stonewall, Man., the
Society, 1960. 375p

Roger, Charles, 1819–1878
OTTAWA PAST AND PRESENT. ... Ottawa, Times Pub. Co., 1871. 124p [BM BVaU
OOP
QUEBEC: AS IT WAS, AND AS IT IS. ... 5th ed. Quebec, Author, 1867. 138p
[Earlier editions (1857, 1860, etc.) appeared under the name of Willis Russell,
but were probably written by Roger.] [BVaU NSWA OTP QMBM
STADACONA DEPICTA; or, Quebec and its Environs. ... Ed. by ——. Quebec,
Carey, 1857. 198p [BM OTP QMBM

Rogers, Grace Dean (McLeod), 1865–1958
LOUISBURG. Toronto, Ryerson, 1928. 32p [BViP NSWA OTU QMSS
PIONEER MISSIONARIES IN THE ATLANTIC PROVINCES. 1930. Toronto, Ryerson,
1930. 64p [NSWA OTU

Rogers, Mrs. Mary A.
THE STORY OF SCOTSGUARD AND VICINITY. By Mrs. Rogers and Mrs. J. Fortney.
Scotsguard, Sask., Jubilee Committee, 1955. 20p

Rome, David
THE FIRST TWO YEARS. A Record of the Jewish Pioneers on Canada's Pacific
Coast, 1858–1860. Montreal, Caiserman, 1942. 120p [BVaU OTP QMM

Ross, Alan Henderson, 1874–
REMINISCENCES OF NORTH SYDENHAM. A Retrospective Sketch of the Villages of Leith and Annan, Grey County, Ontario. By A.H.R. Owen Sound, Richardson, Bond & Wright, 1924. 256p [BVaU LC OTP

Ross, Alexander, 1783–1856
THE RED RIVER SETTLEMENT. ... London, Smith Elder, 1856. 416p [BM BVaU LC NSWA OTP QMM

Ross, Alexander Herbert Douglas, –1950
OTTAWA, PAST AND PRESENT. Toronto, Musson, 1927. 224p [BM BVaU LC NSHD OTP QMM

Ross, Daniel Keith, 1874–
THE PIONEERS AND CHURCHES. The Pioneers and Families of Big Brook and West Branch E.R. and Surrounding Sections, including Lorne, Glengarry, Elgin, Centerdale, Hopewell, Marshdale, Foxbrook. New Glasgow, N.S., Hector Pub. Co., 1957. 239p

Rossland, B.C. Centennial Committee
THE GOLDEN CITY CENTENNIAL AND FALL FAIR PROGRAMME. ... Rossland, B.C., the Committee, 1958. 27p

Round Hill, Alta.
GOLDEN JUBILEE, ROUND HILL, ALBERTA, 1905–1955. N.p., 1955. 16p

Roy, James Alexander, 1884–
KINGSTON, THE KING'S TOWN. Toronto, McClelland, 1952. 364p

Runnalls, Rev. Frank E.
A HISTORY OF PRINCE GEORGE. Prince George, B.C., Author, 1946. 197p [BVaU LC NBFU OTP QMBM

Russell, Ralph Clifford
THE CARLTON TRAIL. The Broad Highway into the Saskatchewan Country from the Red River Settlement, 1840–1880. Saskatoon, Saskatchewan Golden Jubilee Committee, 1955. 102p

Russell, Willis, 1814–1887
QUEBEC: AS IT WAS, AND AS IT IS. ... [See under **Roger, Charles.**]

Rutland, B.C. Centennial Committee
HISTORY OF THE DISTRICT OF RUTLAND, BRITISH COLUMBIA, 1858–1958. Kelowna, B.C., Orchard City Press, 1958. 127p

Ryan, Timothy Joseph, 1918–
VOICES OF THE PAST. A History of Melfort and District. Melfort, Sask., Melfort and District Golden Jubilee Committee, 1955. 138p

St. Andrews, N.B.
ST. ANDREWS, NEW BRUNSWICK, ON PASSAMAQUODY BAY. N.p., n.p., n.d. 45p
[NSWA

St. Barbe, Charles, −1929
FIRST HISTORY OF NELSON, B.C. With Sketches of Some of its Prominent
Citizens. ... N.p., Rohrabacher, n.d. 24p [BViPA

St. Basile, N.B. Madawaska Centennial Exhibition
MADAWASKA 1859−1959, ST. BASILE, N.B., 4−7 SEPT. [St. Basile, Centennial
Exhibition, 1959.] 80p

St. John, William Charles
CATECHISM OF THE HISTORY OF NEWFOUNDLAND. ... Rev. ed. Boston, Rand,
1855. 72p [First ed., 1835.] [LC NfSG OTP

Saint John, N.B.
OLD TIME TRAGEDIES [in Saint John]. Saint John, 1895. [OOP
ST. JOHN, N.B., CITY OF THE LOYALISTS. N.p., n.p., n.d. 40p [NSWA

Sandham, Alfred, 1838−1910
VILLE-MARIE; or, Sketches of Montreal, Past and Present. Montreal, Bishop, 1870.
393p [BM BVaU LC NSWA OTU QMSS

Santha, Rev. Paul, 1890−
THREE GENERATIONS, 1901−1957. The Hungarian Colony at Stockholm,
Saskatchewan, Canada. Stockholm, Sask., Author, 1959. 94p [Includes the
history of St. Elizabeth's Parish.]

Saskatoon, Sask. Historical Association
NARRATIVES OF SASKATOON, 1882−1912. By Men of the City. Saskatoon,
University Book-store, 1927. [BVaU OTU

Savary, Alfred William, 1831−1920
SUPPLEMENT TO THE HISTORY OF THE COUNTY OF ANNAPOLIS [by W.A.
Calnek]. ... Toronto, Briggs, 1913. 142p [BVaU LC NSWA OTU

Sawden, Stephen, 1867−
HISTORY OF DUFFERIN COUNTY. Orangeville, Ont., Orangeville Banner, 1952.
182p

Sawdon, Herbert H.
THE WOODBRIDGE [ONT.] STORY. N.p., [1960?]. 177p

Sawle, George Robert Tregerthen, 1877−
HOMETOWN. Historical Sketches of Persons & Spicy Incidents from the late Years
of the Nineteenth Century and the early Decades of the Twentieth. Welland,
Author, 1959. 92p

Scadding, Rev. Henry, 1813–1901

EARLY NOTICES OF TORONTO. Toronto, Chewett, 1865. 26p [BM LC OTP

HISTORY OF THE OLD FRENCH FORT AT TORONTO. Toronto, Copp Clark, 1887. 48p [BVaU LC NSWA OTP QMM

TORONTO OF OLD. Collections and Recollections Illustrative of the Early Settlement and Social Life of the Capital of Ontario. Toronto, Adam & Stevenson, 1873. 594p [BM BVaU LC NBFU OKQ QMM

TORONTO, PAST AND PRESENT. Historical and Descriptive. A Memorial Volume for the Semi-Centennial of 1884. By the Rev. Henry Scadding and John Charles Dent. Toronto, Hunter Rose, 1884. 330p [BM BVaU LC NSWA OTP

TORONTO'S FIRST GERM (FORT TORONTO). ... Toronto, "Guardian" Office, 1878. 12p [BM OTP

Schofield, Frank Howard, 1859–1929

THE STORY OF MANITOBA. Winnipeg, Clarke, 1913. 3v [BVaU LC OTP

Scholefield, Ethelbert Olaf Stuart, 1875–1919

BRITISH COLUMBIA. From the Earliest Times to the Present. By E.O.S. Scholefield and F.W. Howay. Vancouver, Clarke, 1913. 39p [A prospectus of their proposed four-volume history.] [BVaU QMM

BRITISH COLUMBIA FROM THE EARLIEST TIMES TO THE PRESENT. By E.O.S. Scholefield and F.W. Howay. Vancouver, Clarke, 1914. 4v [BM BVaU LC NBFU OTP QMM

A HISTORY OF BRITISH COLUMBIA. Part One, being a Survey of Events from the Earliest Times down to the Union of the Crown Colony of British Columbia with the Dominion of Canada. By E.O.S. Scholefield. Part Two, being a History ... since Confederation. ... By R.E. Gosnell. Vancouver, B.C. Hist. Assoc., 1913. 436p [BVaU OTP QMM

Scott, Bertha Isabel, 1881–1946

SPRINGHILL. A Hilltop in Cumberland. Springhill, N.S., n.p., 1926. 119p [BViP NSHD

Scott, Duncan Campbell, 1862–1947

NOTES ON THE MEETING PLACE OF THE FIRST PARLIAMENT OF UPPER CANADA AND THE EARLY BUILDINGS AT NIAGARA. Ottawa, Royal Society, 1913. 15p [NSWA

Scott, H. Percy, 1856–1937

HISTORIC DATA OF FORT EDWARD. ... Windsor, N.S., Tribune Pub., [1926]. 16p [Caption title: HISTORIC WINDSOR.] [NSHL

Scott, James, 1916–

HURON COUNTY IN PIONEER TIMES. Seaforth, Ont., Huron County Historical Committee, 1954. 87p

Scott, Richard William, 1825–1913
THE CHOICE OF THE CAPITAL. Ottawa, Mortimer, 1907. 44p [LC OOA
RECOLLECTIONS OF BYTOWN. Some Incidents in the History of Ottawa. Ottawa,
Mortimer Press, [1911]. 31p [BVaU NSWA OTP QMM

Seaman, Holly Skiff, 1884?–1952
MANITOBA LANDMARKS AND RED LETTER DAYS, 1610 TO 1920. Winnipeg, n.p.,
1920. 92p [BM BVaU NSHD OTP QMBM

Seary, Edgar Ronald, 1908–
TOPONYMY OF THE ISLAND OF NEWFOUNDLAND. St. John's, Memorial University,
1959. [mimeographed]

Seary, Victor Perrin, 1903–
THE ROMANCE OF THE MARITIME PROVINCES. Toronto, Gage, 1931. 243p [BVaU
LC NSHD OLU QMBM

Sederberg, Mrs. Lilian Margaret, 1926–
THE SERPENT'S TAIL. Malakwa, B.C., Centennial Committee, 1958. 15p [History
of Eagle Valley, B.C.]

Sellar, Robert, 1841–1919
THE HISTORY OF THE COUNTY OF HUNTINGDON [Quebec] AND OF THE SEIG-
NORIES OF CHATEAUGAY AND BEAUHARNOIS. From their First Settlement to
the Year 1838. Huntingdon, Que., Canadian Gleaner, 1888. 584p [BVaU
LC NSWA OTP QMM
LETTERS RELATIVE TO THE RIGHTS AND PRESENT POSITION OF THE QUEBEC
MINORITY. [Huntingdon, Que.], "Gleaner," 1890. 145p [BVaU OTP
THE TRAGEDY OF QUEBEC: THE EXPULSION OF ITS PROTESTANT FARMERS.
Huntingdon, Que., "Gleaner," 1907. 120p [Several later editions.] [BM BVaU
LC NBFU OTP QMM
THE U.S. CAMPAIGN OF 1813 TO CAPTURE MONTREAL. ... Huntingdon, Que.,
"Gleaner," 1913. 33p [BM OTU

Semmens, Rev. John, 1850–1921
THE FIELD AND THE WORK. Sketches of Missionary Life in the Far North. Toronto,
Methodist Book Room, 1884. 199p [BVaU OTP

Shaunavon, Sask. Public School
SHAUNAVON, TOWN AND COMMUNITY. Comp. by the pupils of the Shaunavon
Public and High Schools. Shaunavon, Sask., 1955. 32p

Shenston, Thomas Strahan, 1822–1895
THE OXFORD GAZETTEER. ... History of the County of Oxford. Hamilton,
Chatterton & Helliwell, 1852. 216p [BVaU LC NSWA OTP
TELANGOO MISSION SCRAP BOOK. Brantford, Expositor Book & Job Print., 1888.
251p [OLU

Shepherd, Francis John, 1851–1929
ORIGIN AND HISTORY OF THE MONTREAL GENERAL HOSPITAL. Montreal,
Gazette Print., n.d. 47p [OTU

Sherk, Michael Gonder, 1862?–1927
PEN PICTURES OF EARLY PIONEER LIFE IN UPPER CANADA. By a "Canuck" (of
the Fifth Generation). Toronto, Briggs, 1905. 280p [BVaU NSWA OTP

Sherwood, Roland Harold, 1902–
OUT OF THE PAST. Vignettes of Historical Significance in Pictou County.
Pictou, N.S., Coastal Publishers, 1954. 120p
PICTOU PARADE. Sackville, N.B., Tribune Press, 1945. 114p [NBFU OTU

Shibley, Fred. Warner, 1864–
ASPINWALL ISLAND. New York, Author, 1916. 167p [OTL

Shipley, Mrs. R.L.
FROM OXEN TO AIRPLANE. Mantario, 1908–1950. Ed. by ——. Mantario, Sask.,
Homemakers' Club, 1950. 104p [Cf. title listed under Mantario, Sask., above.]
[OONL

Shoal Lake, Man. Anniversary Committee
BRIDGING THE YEARS ... SHOAL LAKE AND DISTRICT. Municipality, 1884–1959,
Village, 1904–1959. Brandon, 1959. 31p

Shufelt, Harry Ball, 1896–
ALONG THE OLD ROADS. Reflections, Recollections, Romance of Eastern Townships History. Knowlton, Que., 1956. 48p

Simpson, Jenny Russell
GUIDE TO THE BYTOWN AND OTTAWA HISTORICAL MUSEUM. Comp. and ed. by
the Curator, ——. Ottawa, the Museum, 1929. 31p [LC

Simpson, John Garbutt, 1889–
THE STORY OF DUMMER THROUGH THE YEARS. Dummer, Sask., Dummer Ladies'
Community Club, 1955. 20p

Sioux Lookout, Ont. Junior Chamber of Commerce
SIOUX LOOKOUT, A PROGRESSIVE NORTHWESTERN ONTARIO COMMUNITY.
Sioux Lookout, 1953. 19p

Smallfield, W.E.
THE STORY OF RENFREW. From the Coming of the First Settlers about 1820. ...
By W.E. Smallfield and Rev. Robert Campbell. V.1. Renfrew, Smallfield, 1919.
[BM NSHD OTU

Smith, Alexander William, 1911–
IN THOSE DAYS. A History of North Hastings and of South Nipissing, by the People
Who Live it. Ed. by ——. Bancroft, Ont., the Editor, 1956. 56p [mimeographed]

Smith, Donald Alexander, 1905–
AT THE FORKS OF THE GRAND. 20 Historical Essays on Paris, Ontario. By Donald A. Smith, with one essay by John P. Pickell. Paris, Ont., Centennial Committee, 1956. 302p

Smith, Joseph Henry, 1839–1917
HISTORICAL SKETCH OF THE COUNTY OF WENTWORTH. Hamilton, County Council, 1897. 140p [OTU

Smith, Stanley K.
THE DRAMA OF A CITY. The Story of Stricken Halifax. New York, Weir, 1918. 178p [OTP
HEART THROBS OF THE HALIFAX HORROR. Halifax, Weir, 1918. 120p [On the Halifax explosion] [OTU

Smith, William Loe, 1855–1945
THE PIONEERS OF OLD ONTARIO. Toronto, Morang, 1923. 343p [BM BVaU NSHD OTP QMM

Smith, Rev. William Wye, 1827–1917
GAZETTEER OF THE COUNTY OF GREY FOR 1865–6. Owen Sound, 1865. 332p [OTU

Smitheram, Henry Arthur, 1918–
KNOW THY NEIGHBOUR. Merritt, B.C., Author, 1953. 11p [On Indians of The Nicola Valley, B.C.]

Smiths Falls, Ont.
75 YEARS OF PROGRESS, 1882–1957, TOWN OF SMITHS FALLS, INCORPORATED APRIL 25TH, 1882, 75TH BIRTHDAY CELEBRATION, THURSDAY, APRIL 25TH, 1957. Comp. by Mrs. W.A. Graham. Smiths Falls, Record-News Press, 1957. 4p

Smyth, Fred J.
TALES OF THE KOOTENAYS. Cranbrook, B.C., Courier, 1938. 200p [2nd ed., 1942] [BM BVaU LC OTP

Somerville, Alexander, 1811–1885
NARRATIVE OF THE FENIAN INVASION. Hamilton, Author, 1866. 128p [BM LC OTP

Sonningdale, Sask. Spartan High School
THE SONNINGDALE STORY. Sonningdale, Sask., 1955. 22p [mimeographed]

Southampton, Ont. Centennial Committee
SOUTHAMPTON CENTENNIAL. Stories of the Past, 1858–1958. Southampton, Ont., 1958. 28p [Prepared by J.F. Morton.]

South Dumfries, Ont. Centennial Committee
THE TOWNSHIP OF SOUTH DUMFRIES CENTENNIAL, 1852–1952. South Dumfries, Ont., 1952. 43 + 4p

Sparling, Mrs. Reita Bambridge
REMINISCENCES OF THE ROSSBURN PIONEERS. Rossburn, Man., Women's
Institute, 1951. 131p

Spinks, William Ward, 1851–1937
TALES OF THE BRITISH COLUMBIA FRONTIER. Toronto, Ryerson, 1933. 134p
[BM BVaU LC NSHD OTU QMM

Springfield, P.E.I. Women's Institute
SPRINGFIELD, 1828–1953. Springfield, P.E.I., 1954. 122p [mimeographed]

Squair, John, 1850–1928
THE TOWNSHIPS OF DARLINGTON AND CLARKE ... ONTARIO. ... Toronto, U. of
Toronto Press, 1927. 609p [BVaU LC NSHD OTP QMM

Squamish, B.C. Centennial Committee
A CENTENNIAL COMMENTARY UPON THE EARLY DAYS OF SQUAMISH, BRITISH
COLUMBIA. Squamish, B.C., the Committee, 1958. 32p

Stanley, George Francis Gilman, 1907–
THE BIRTH OF WESTERN CANADA. A History of the Riel Rebellion. London,
Longmans, 1936. xiv + 475p [Reprinted: Toronto, U. of Toronto Press, 1960.]
[BViP NSHPL OTP QMSS
A SHORT HISTORY OF KINGSTON AS A MILITARY AND NAVAL CENTRE. Kingston,
Royal Military College, 1950. 37p [Rev. ed., with Richard A. Preston, 1951.
39p] [OONL

Star City, Sask. Jubilee Editorial Committee
STAR CITY ... PIONEER DAYS TO JUBILEE YEAR. Star City, Sask., Star City and
District Board of Trade, 1955. 201p

Starratt, Mrs. David, 1842?–
HISTORY OF FALKLAND RIDGE, ANNAPOLIS COUNTY, NOVA SCOTIA. Ed. by Mary
F. Kendrick. N.p. n.p., 1923. 12p [NSWA

Steen, Ragna, –1962
PIONEER DAYS IN BARDO, ALBERTA. Including Sketches of Early Surrounding
Settlements. By Ragna Steen and Magda Hendrickson. Winnipeg, Dahl, 1944.
228p [SSU

Steeves, Helen Isabelle (Harper), 1873–
THE STORY OF MONCTON'S FIRST STORE AND STORE-KEEPER. Life around "the
Bend" a Century Ago. Saint John, McMillan, 1924. 178p [BM BVaU LC
NBFU OTP QMM

Stephen, Irene Simmons (Phelan), 1902–
WINGED CANOES AT NOOTKA AND OTHER STORIES OF THE EVERGREEN COAST.
Toronto, Dent, 1955. x + 227p

Stevens, Arthur Herbert, 1880–
CLIMAX BEFORE AND AFTER. Comp. by ——. Climax, Sask., Board of Trade,
   1955. 12p

Stevenson, Douglas Andrew, 1888–
A HISTORY OF THE FONTHILL PUBLIC LIBRARY. Prepared in Celebration of the One
   Hundredth Anniversary of its Opening—on Feb. 2, 1853. Fonthill, Ont.,
   Library Board, 1953. 25p

Stewart, David Alexander, 1874–1937
GLIMPSES AT MANITOBA HISTORY. An Address. Winnipeg, n.p., 1932. 15p
   [BViPA NSWA OTU

Stewart, George, 1848–1906
THE STORY OF THE GREAT FIRE IN ST. JOHN, N.B. JUNE 20, 1877. Toronto, Belford,
   1877. 272p [BVaU LC NBFU OTP

Stewart, Herbert Leslie, 1882–1953
THE IRISH IN NOVA SCOTIA. Annals of the Charitable Irish Society of Halifax
   (1786–1836). Kentville, N.S., Kentville Pub. Co., 1949. 199p [NSHD OTP
   QMM

Stewart, McLeod, 1847–1926
THE FIRST HALF CENTURY OF OTTAWA. Ottawa, Esdale, 1910. 84p [BM BVaU
   LC OTU QMM

Stewart, William James, 1889–
FROM WIGWAM TO SKYSCRAPER. Toronto, Centennial Office, 1934. [CC

Stewart Valley, Sask. School
CLIMBING THE STAIRS AT STEWART VALLEY. Stewart Valley, 1955. 28p
   [mimeographed. A history of Stewart Valley.]

Stewiacke, N.S.
CELEBRATION OF THE 100TH ANNIVERSARY ... Held on October 6, 1880.
   Truro, Guardian, 1880. 64p [Also accounts of later celebrations pub. in
   subsequent years.] [BVaU NSHP

Stone, Harry A.
A SHORT HISTORY OF CAULFEILD VILLAGE. Vancouver, Wrigley, [1940?]. 25p
   [BVaU OOA

Stone, Sask. Jubilee Committee
THE STORY OF THE STONE COMMUNITY. Stone, 1956. 12p

Stout, Clarence H., 1887–
FROM FRONTIER DAYS IN LEDUC AND DISTRICT. Ed. by ——. Leduc, Alta., 1957.
   184p

Strachan, Rev. John, 1778–1867
A LETTER to the ... Earl of Selkirk, on his Settlement at the Red River. ... London, Longman, Hurst, Rees, Orme & Brown, 1816. 76p [LC NSWA OTP

Stratford Police Association
STRATFORD TOURIST GUIDE. Old Boys Reunion and Centennial Celebration, 1853–1953. [Stratford, Ont., 1953?] 72p

Stretton, R.W.
DUNNVILLE, ONTARIO, CENTENNIAL YEAR 1950. 100 Years of Progress. Ed. by ——. Dunnville, Centennial Book Committee, 1950. 112p [OONL

Summerland, B.C. Board of Trade
SUMMERLAND GOLDEN JUBILEE, 1906–1956. Summerland, 1956. 28p

Sussex Emigrants
EMIGRATION: Letters from Sussex Emigrants ... 1832 ... for Upper Canada. Petworth, Phillips; London, Longman, 1833. 103 + 16p (Intro. signed: T. Sockett, Petworth.) [BM OTP
LETTERS FROM SUSSEX EMIGRANTS... to Upper Canada. Chichester, Mason, 1837. 10p [OTP

Sutherland, George, 1830–1893
A MANUAL OF THE GEOGRAPHY AND NATURAL AND CIVIL HISTORY OF PRINCE EDWARD ISLAND. Charlottetown, Ross, 1861. 164p [BM BVaU NSWA OTP

Sutherland, James
SUTHERLAND'S CITY OF HAMILTON AND COUNTY OF WENTWORTH DIRECTORY, for 1867–8. Published Annually. Comp. by ——. Ottawa, Hunter Rose; Hamilton, Eastwood, [Preface 1867]. xxxii + 454p [OTP

Sutton Township, Que.
SESQUICENTENNIAL OF SUTTON, 1802–1952. Sutton, Que., n.p., 1952. 69p

Swainson, J.L.
OUR ANCESTORS ARRIVE IN MANITOBA. Early Settlers of Fort Ellice, Birtle, Russell, Seeburn, Rossburn and Surrounding Districts; also Winnipeg as it was at the Turn of the Century. Winnipeg, De Montfort Press, [1958?]. 70p

Swallow, Harry Sparling, 1884–
FROM OX-TRAILS TO HIGHWAYS IN 60 YEARS. Yorkton District. Yorkton, Sask., Author, 1955. 111p

Swarthmore, Sask. Jubilee Association
GOLDEN THREADS. The Tapestry of Swarthmore. Swarthmore, 1955. 48p

Swift Current, Sask. Collegiate Institute
EVER ONWARD. The Story of the Frontier City. Pub. by the Grade XI and XII students. Swift Current, 1955. 20p [mimeographed]

GOLDEN WAVES. Comp. by the grade ten students. Ed. by Colleen Dand and others. Swift Current, 1955. 46p [mimeographed]

Swift Current, Sask. Local Council of Women
GOLDEN FURROWS. [An Historical Chronicle of Swift Current.] Swift Current, 1954. 55p

Sydney, N.S. Junior Chamber of Commerce
CAPE BRETON TOURIST GUIDE. 1957. Sydney, 1957. 80p

Sylvester, Alfred
SKETCHES OF TORONTO. ... Toronto, Holiwell, 1858. 120p [OTP

Taber, Alta. Booklet Committee
GOLDEN JUBILEE, COMMEMORATING FIFTY YEARS OF PICTURE HISTORY OF TABER, ALBERTA, 1905–1955. Taber, 1955. 204p

Tait, Robert Holland
NEWFOUNDLAND. A Summary of the History and Development of Britain's oldest Colony from 1497 to 1939. [Harrington Park, N.J., Harrington Press, 1939.] 260p [BM LC NfSG OKQ

Taylor, Andrew Winton, 1907–
OUR YESTERDAYS. A History of the Township of North Dumfries, Ontario, Canada. 1816–1952. Galt, Ont., Author, 1952. 128p

Taylor, Conyngham Crawford, 1823–1898
... TORONTO "CALLED BACK," FROM 1897 TO 1847. Toronto, Briggs, 1887. 398p [Several other editions, with various dates.] [BM BVaU LC NBFU OKQ

Taylor, Rev. Ernest Manly, 1848–1941
HISTORY OF BROME COUNTY, QUEBEC, FROM THE DATE OF GRANTS OF LAND THEREIN TO THE PRESENT TIME. With Records of Some Early Families. Montreal, Lovell, 1908–1937. 2v [BM BVaU LC OLU QMM

Taylor, Gordon de Rupe, 1923–
DELTA'S CENTURY OF PROGRESS. Cloverdale, B.C., Kerfoot-Holmes Print., 1958. 96p

Taylor, Henry Edwin, 1889–
POWELL RIVER'S FIRST 50 YEARS. Comp. by ——. Westview, B.C., Powell River News, 1960. 1v [unpaged]

Templin, Hugh Charles, 1896–
A BRIEF HISTORY OF WELLINGTON COUNTY. Fergus, Ont., News-Record, 1946. 28p [OTU
FERGUS, AND THE REBELLION OF 1837. N.p., 1937. 14p [OTU

FERGUS, THE STORY OF A LITTLE TOWN. Fergus, Ont., News-Record, 1933. 311p
[BVaU OTU

Tennant, Joseph Francis, 1848–

ROUGH TIMES, 1870–1920. ... A Souvenir of the 50th Anniversary of the Red River
Expedition and the Formation of the Province of Manitoba. [Winnipeg?], 1920.
271p [AE BViPA OTP SSU

Texada Island, B.C. Centennial Committee

TEXADA. Vananda, B.C., the Committee, 1960. xii + 51p

Thomas, Cyrus, 1836–1908

CONTRIBUTIONS TO THE HISTORY OF THE EASTERN TOWNSHIPS. Montreal,
Lovell, 1866. 376p [BVaU LC MWU NSWA OTP QMM

HISTORY OF THE COUNTIES OF ARGENTEUIL, QUE. AND PRESCOTT, ONT., FROM
THE EARLIEST SETTLEMENT TO THE PRESENT. Montreal, Lovell, 1896. 665p
[OTP QMM

THE HISTORY OF SHEFFORD. Civil, Ecclesiastical, Biographical and Statistical.
Montreal, Lovell, 1877. 143p [NSWA OTP QMM

Thomas, Lewis Gwynne, 1914–

THE LIBERAL PARTY IN ALBERTA. A History of Politics in the Province of Alberta,
1905–1921. Toronto, U. of Toronto Press, 1959. xii + 230p

Thompson, John Henry, 1853–

JUBILEE HISTORY OF THOROLD TOWNSHIP AND TOWN FROM THE TIME OF THE
REDMAN TO THE PRESENT. Thorold, Ont., Thorold Post, 1897–98. 212 + 77p
[BM OTU

THIRTY-FIVE YEARS LATER. Supplement to the Jubilee History of Thorold, 1897
to 1932. [Anon] Thorold, Ont., Thorold Post, 1932. 80p [OTU

Thompson, Muriel Lillian, 1898–

NEW HOPE ON THE PRAIRIES. A History of Stoughton, Heward, Forget, Handsworth
Districts. Weyburn, Sask., Weyburn Review, 1956. 99p

Thompson, Robert, 1816–

A BRIEF SKETCH OF THE EARLY HISTORY OF GUELPH. Guelph, Mercury Steam
Print., 1877. [Reprinted as AN EARLY VIEW OF GUELPH. Ed. by Hugh Douglass.
London, Ont., U. of Western Ontario Library, 1958. 19p] [OTP

Thomson, Thomas Muir, 1894–

HAMILTON CITY SKETCHES. Ed. by ——. Hamilton, Board of Education, 1954.
62p

Tisdale, Sask. Composite School

FIFTY YEARS ALONG THE DOGHIDE. A History of the Development of Tisdale and
District. Tisdale, 1955. 51p

Tombs, Guy, 1877–
THE HARBOUR OF MONTREAL. An Address given ... before the St. James Literary
Society of Montreal. Montreal, 1932. 56p [OTP QMM

Toronto, Ont. United Empire Loyalist Centennial Committee
THE CENTENNIAL OF THE SETTLEMENT OF UPPER CANADA BY UNITED EMPIRE
LOYALISTS, 1784–1884. The Celebration at Adolphustown, Toronto and Niagara.
With an Appendix containing a Copy of the U.E. List Preserved in the Crown
Lands Department at Toronto. ... Toronto, Rose Pub. Co., 1885. 334p [BVaU
Brown U OTU

Townshend, Charles James, 1844–1924
HISTORY OF THE COURT OF CHANCERY IN NOVA SCOTIA. Toronto, Carswell,
1900. 98p [BVaU LC NSWA

Toye, William, 1926–
THE ST. LAWRENCE. Toronto, Oxford U. Press, 1959. 296p

Trail, B.C. Board of Trade
TRAIL, B.C. A Brief Story of the History and Development of the Most Important
Industrial Center in Interior of British Columbia. Trail, Board of Trade, 1931.
52p [OTP

Trail, B.C. Golden Jubilee Society
TRAIL, B.C. A Half Century, 1901–1951. Trail, the Society, [1951?]. 48p

Tramping Lake, Sask. School
50 GOLDEN YEARS. Tramping Lake, 1905–1955. Tramping Lake, 1955. 41p
[mimeographed]

Traquair, Ramsay, 1874–
THE OLD ARCHITECTURE OF QUEBEC. A Study of the Buildings Erected in New
France from the Earliest Explorers to the Middle of the Nineteenth century.
Toronto, Macmillan, 1947. 324p [BVaU NSHD OLU QMM
THE OLD SILVER OF QUEBEC. ... Toronto, Macmillan, 1940. 169p [BM BVaU
NSHD OTU QMM

Trueman, Howard Thompson, 1837–1908
THE CHIGNECTO ISTHMUS AND ITS FIRST SETTLERS. Toronto, Briggs, 1902. 268p
[BVaU LC NSWA OTU
EARLY AGRICULTURE IN THE ATLANTIC PROVINCES. ... Moncton, "Times" Print.,
1907. 131p [NSHD OTU

Tuck, Clyde Edwin
HISTORY OF NOVA SCOTIA. V.3 Biographical Sketches. ... [For full entry, see under
Allison, David, in Local History.]

Tuck, Esme (Gardner), 1887–
A BRIEF HISTORY OF POUCE COUPE VILLAGE AND DISTRICT, BRITISH COLUMBIA,
CANADA. Pouce Coupé, B.C., Women's Institute, 1954. 28p

Tucker, Rev. William Bowman, 1859–1934
THE CAMDEN COLONY; or, The Seed of the Righteous. A Story of the United
Empire Loyalists. ... Montreal, Lovell, 1908. 216p [2nd ed. under title: THE
ROMANCE OF THE PALATINE MILLERS. ...] [BM BVaU NSHD OTU QMM
THE ROMANCE OF THE PALATINE MILLERS. A Tale of Palatine Irish-Americans and
United Empire Loyalists. Montreal, Southam Press, 1929. 369p [2nd ed., rev.
and enl., of THE CAMDEN COLONY. ...] [BM BVaU OTUV

Turner, Adam, 1852–1944
SOME RAMBLING HISTORICAL NOTES AND REMINISCENCES OF THE EARLY DAYS
IN SASKATOON. ... Saskatoon, Modern Press, 1932. 27p [BVaU

Tutt, Nellie (Hereron), 1895–
THE HISTORY OF ELLISON DISTRICT, 1858–1958. Comp. by Mrs. D. Tutt. Kelowna,
B.C., Ellison Centennial Committee, 1959. 116p

Tyrrell, Joseph Burr, 1858–1957
DOCUMENTS RELATING TO THE EARLY HISTORY OF HUDSON BAY. Ed. by ——.
Toronto, Champlain Society, 1931. 419p [BM BVaU NSHD OTP

Upton, Primrose (Walker), 1915–
THE HISTORY OF OKANAGAN MISSION. A Centennial Retrospect. Okanagan
Mission, B.C., Centennial Committee, 1958. 81p

Ure, George P.,   –1860
THE HAND-BOOK OF TORONTO. By a Member of the Press [pseud]. Toronto, Lovell
& Gibson, 1858. 272p [OTP QMM

Uttley, William Velores, 1865–1944
A HISTORY OF KITCHENER, ONTARIO. Kitchener, Chronicle, 1937. 433p [BVaU
LC OKQ

Val Marie, Sask. High School
VAL-ECHO. A History of Val Marie. By the Teachers and Pupils of Val Marie High
School. Val Marie, "Val-Echo," 1955. 61p [mimeographed]

Vallance, James Dunlop, 1903–
UNTRODDEN WAYS. Victoria, Hebden Print., 1958. 150p [History of British
Columbia.]

Van Cortlandt, Gertrude
RECORDS OF THE RISE AND PROGRESS OF THE CITY OF OTTAWA. Ottawa, Citizen. 1858. 23p [LC OTP QMM

Vancouver Exhibition Association
VANCOUVER EXHIBITION ASSOCIATION 1886–1936. Fifty Years of Progress. Vancouver, The Assoc., 1936. 47p [OTP

Vernon, Rev. Charles William, 1871–1934
CAPE BRETON, CANADA, AT THE BEGINNING OF THE TWENTIETH CENTURY. Toronto, Nation Pub. Co., 1903. 337p [BVaU LC NSWA OTU QMM

Vibank, Sask. Elsas High School
VIBANK. Vibank, 1955. 52p [mimeographed]

Virgin, Victor Ernest, 1892–
HISTORY OF NORTH AND SOUTH SAANICH PIONEERS AND DISTRICT. Victoria, Saanich Pioneer Soc., 1959. 79p

Viscount, Sask. Golden Jubilee Committee
THE VISCOUNT STORY. Viscount, 1955. 64p

Waddington, Alfred Penderill, 1801–1872
THE FRASER MINES VINDICATED; or, The History of Four Months. Victoria, P. De Garro, 1858. 49p [Reprinted: Vancouver, Private Press of Robert R. Reid, 1949. With an intro. by W.K. Lamb. xv + 95p] [BVaU OTP QMM
THE NECESSITY OF REFORM. A Tract for the Times. Addressed to the Colonists of Vancouver Island. By One of the People [pseud]. Victoria, British Colonist Office, 1859. 15p [BVaU NSWA OOA

Wade, Lennie D.
HISTORIC GLIMPSES OF PICTURESQUE BEAR RIVER, NOVA SCOTIA. [Digby, Courier Press, 1907?]. 34p [NSHL

Wade, Mark Sweeten, 1858–1929
THE FOUNDING OF KAMLOOPS. A Story of 100 Years Ago. Kamloops, Inland Sentinel, [1912]. 15p [BVaU LC OTU
THE THOMPSON COUNTRY. Being Notes on the History of Southern British Columbia, and particularly the City of Kamloops. Kamloops, Inland Sentinel, 1907. 136p [BVaU LC NSHD OTU

Wade, Robert William Gorman, 1884–
EARLY HISTORY OF HOWICK TOWNSHIP IN HURON COUNTY. Gorrie, Ont., priv. print., 1952. 64p

Walbran, John Thomas, 1848–1913

BRITISH COLUMBIA COAST NAMES, 1592–1906. Ottawa, Govt. Print. Bureau, 1909. 546p [BVaU LC NBFU OTU QMM

Waldie, Jean Hall, 1916–

THE COUNTY OF BRANT. Centennial Sketches. Brantford, Brant County Council, 1952. 51p

Wales, Benjamin Nathaniel, 1851–

MEMORIES OF OLD ST. ANDREWS AND HISTORICAL SKETCHES OF THE SEIGNIORY OF ARGENTEUIL. Lachute, Watchman Press, 1934. 135p [BVaU OTU QMM

Walkem, William Wymond, 1850–1919

STORIES OF EARLY BRITISH COLUMBIA. Vancouver, News-Advertiser, 1914. 287p [BVaU LC NBFU

Walker, Harry James William, 1892–

THE OTTAWA STORY THROUGH 150 YEARS. Ottawa, Ottawa Journal, 1953. 94p
RENFREW AND ITS FAIR THROUGH 100 YEARS. Renfrew, Ont., South Renfrew Agricultural Society, [1953]. 104p

Wallace, Frederick William, 1886–1958

THE ROMANCE OF A GREAT PORT. The Story of St. John, N.B. Saint John, Barnes, 1935. 64p [BViP LC NSWA OTU QMSS

Wallace, James Nevin, 1871–1941

THE WINTERING PARTNERS ON PEACE RIVER. From the Earliest Records to the Union in 1821. With a Summary of the Dunvegan Journal, 1806. ... Ottawa, Thorburn & Abbott, 1929. 139p [BM BViPA LC NBFU OTP

Walter, Margaret (Shaw)

EARLY DAYS AMONG THE GULF ISLANDS OF B.C. Victoria, Diggon-Hibben, 1946. 68p [2nd ed., Victoria, Hebden Print. Co., [1959?]. 67p] [BVaU LC OTP

Walton, Avis Carroll, 1911–

ABOUT VICTORIA AND VANCOUVER ISLAND. Ed. by ——. [2nd ed.] Victoria, New Neighbour Services, 1958. 212p

Walton, Jesse M.

THE STORY OF KETTLEBY. Aurora, Ont., Banner Press, [1939?]. 28p [NBFU OTP

Warburton, Alexander Bannerman, 1852–1929

A HISTORY OF PRINCE EDWARD ISLAND FROM ITS DISCOVERY IN 1534 UNTIL THE DEPARTURE OF LIEUTENANT-GOVERNOR READY IN A.D. 1831. Saint John, Barnes, 1923. 494p [BM BVaU LC NSWA OTU QMM
PRINCE EDWARD ISLAND. A Historical Sketch. Charlottetown, 1906. 59p [NSHD

Ward, Edmund, 1787–1853
AN ACCOUNT OF THE RIVER ST. JOHN, WITH ITS TRIBUTARY RIVERS AND LAKES.
Fredericton, Sentinel, 1841. 96p [LC NSHD OTU

Warman, Sask. School
WARMAN'S 50 YEARS OF PROGRESS. From Ox-cart to Airplane. Warman, 1955.
20p [mimeographed]

Warnock, Amelia Beers, 1878–1956
TORONTO. Romance of a Great City. By Katherine Hale [pseud]. Toronto,
Cassell, 1956. 262p

Warnock, Robert
A SKETCH OF THE COUNTY OF HALTON, CANADA WEST. Toronto, Leader
Steam-Press, 1862. 56p [OTP

Waterford and Townsend, Ont. Old Timers
OLD TIMERS' REUNION, WATERFORD AND TOWNSEND [1878–1960]. Waterford,
Ont., 1960. 92p

Waterloo, Ont. Centennial Advertising Committee
WATERLOO 1857–1957. Centennial Band and Folk Festival ... Souvenir Programme.
Waterloo, the Committee, 1957. 98p

Waterloo, Ont. Trust and Savings Company
A GUIDE TO PLEASANT PLACES AND JOURNEYS OF HISTORIC INTEREST WITHIN
THE COUNTY OF WATERLOO. Waterloo, Ont., the Company, 1956. 46p

Watson, Omar Kern, 1869–
MEMORIES OF THE OLD HOME TOWN–RIDGETOWN, 1930. Comp. by ——.
Ridgetown, Dominion, 1930. 71p [OTP

Watson, Robert, 1882–1948
FAMOUS FORTS OF MANITOBA. Winnipeg, Dept. of Education, 1929. 29p
[BVa
LOWER FORT GARRY. A History of the Stone Fort. Winnipeg, Hudson's Bay Co.,
1928. 69p [BVaU LC NSHD OTU

Weaver, Emily Poynton, 1865–1943
OLD QUEBEC, THE CITY OF CHAMPLAIN. Illus. by Annie E. Weaver. Toronto,
Briggs, 1907. 60p [BVaU OTP QMM
THE STORY OF THE COUNTIES OF ONTARIO. Toronto, Bell & Cockburn, 1913.
318p [BVaU OTU QMM

Weber, Manasseh, 1872–1957
SUCH WAS LIFE. Calgary, 1956. 72p [Rhymed history of Didsbury, Alta.]

Webster, Mrs. Deborah
THE THOMSON HOUSE, CHARLOTTE LANE, SHELBURNE, NOVA SCOTIA. ... Rev. ed.
Shelburne, Historical Society, 1955. 11p [First ed. 1949.]

Webster, John Clarence, 1863–1950

ACADIA AT THE END OF THE SEVENTEENTH CENTURY. Letters, Journals and Memoirs of Joseph Robineau de Villebon, Commandant in Acadia, 1690–1700. Saint John, New Brunswick Museum, 1934. 232p [BVaU LC NSWA OLU QMM

THE BUILDING OF FORT LAWRENCE IN CHIGNECTO. ... Ed. by ———. Saint John, New Brunswick Museum, 1941. 23p [BVaU LC NSWA OTP QMBM

THE FORTS OF CHIGNECTO. A Study of the Eighteenth Century Conflict between France and Great Britain in Acadia. ... Shediac, N.B., Author, 1930. 142p [BM BVaU NBFU OTU QMM

AN HISTORICAL GUIDE TO NEW BRUNSWICK. Fredericton, New Brunswick Tourist Assoc., 1928. 106p [Rev. eds. 1930, 1936, 1938, 1942, 1944.] [BM BVaU LC NSWA OTU QMM

HISTORY IN A GOVERNMENT HOUSE. [Halifax?], 1926. 16p [NSWA OTU

A HISTORY OF SHEDIAC, NEW BRUNSWICK. Shediac, N.B., priv. print., 1928. 22p [Reprinted by the New Brunswick Museum, 1953.] [BM BVaU LC NSWA OLU QMM

THE RECAPTURE OF ST. JOHN'S, NEWFOUNDLAND, IN 1762, AS DESCRIBED IN THE JOURNAL OF LT.-COL. WILLIAM AMHERST. Ed. by ———. Shediac, N.B., Author, 1928. [BM NBFU OLU

SOME EPISODES IN THE RELATION BETWEEN THE MARITIME PROVINCES AND THE AMERICAN ATLANTIC STATES. N.p., [1927?]. 20p [BM NSHD OTP QMM

Weir, Rev. F.G.

SCUGOG AND ITS ENVIRONS. Port Perry, Ont., Star Print., 1927. 143p [BVaU OTU

Welland, Ont. Centennial Committee

SOUVENIR BOOKLET. Welland, Ont., 1958. 83p [Cover title: "Welland Centennial, 1858–1958."]

Wellington County, Ont. Centennial Committee

CENTENNIAL, 1854–1954, THE COUNTY OF WELLINGTON. Fergus, Ont., 1954. 28p

Wells, Catherine Boott (Gannett), 1838–1911

CAMPOBELLO. An Historical Sketch. By Kate Gannett Wells. [Boston, 1893]. 47p [LC NSWA OTU QMM

Wells, William Benjamin, 1809–1881

CANADIANA. Containing Sketches of Upper Canada, and the Crisis in its Political Affairs. ... London, Reynell, 1837. 2 Parts: 84p and 85–202p [BVaU LC OTP

Wessel, Mrs. H.

SAGA OF WESTWOLD. By Mrs. H. Wessel, Mrs. L. Jones and Mrs. L. Ness. Westwold, B.C., Women's Institute, 1954. 12p

Wetherell, Margaret Hubner (Smith), –1933
JUBILEE HISTORY OF THOROLD TOWNSHIP. ... Thorold, Ont., Post Print., 1897.
212p [Another ed., 1933.] [OTU

Wetmore, Ralph W.
HISTORICAL MEMOIRS OF CLIFTON, N.B. Saint John, Day, 1912. 32p [NBSM
OTU

Wetton, Cecilia (Chidlow), 1893–
HISTORIC BATTLEFORD. Through the Years, 1875–1955. Battleford, Sask.,
Board of Trade Jubilee Committee, 1955. 72p
THE PROMISED LAND. The Story of the Barr Colonists. Lloydminster, Sask.,
Times, 1953. 73p

Weyburn, Sask. Golden Jubilee Committee
PIONEER DAYS OF WEYBURN. Weyburn, 1955. 40p

Whidden, David Graham, 1857–1941
THE HISTORY OF THE TOWN OF ANTIGONISH. Wolfville, 1934. 209p [BVaU
LC NSWA OTU QMM

Whitby, Ont. Centennial Committee
WHITBY, ONTARIO, CANADA, THE TOWN OF OPPORTUNITY, RESIDENTIAL,
INDUSTRIAL. Ed. by Charles H. Chaytor. Whitby, 1955. 68p

White, G.A.
HALIFAX AND ITS BUSINESS. An Historical Sketch and Description of the City.
Halifax, Nova Scotia Print., 1876. 173p [NSHD OLU

White, James, 1863–1928
PLACE-NAMES IN GEORGIAN BAY. Toronto, Ontario Hist. Soc., 1913. 81p
[BVaU LC
PLACE NAMES [IN] QUEBEC, THE THOUSAND ISLANDS, AND NORTHERN CANADA.
Ottawa, [Govt. Print. Bureau?], 1910. 302p [BVa NBFU OTU QMM
PLACE-NAMES IN THE THOUSAND ISLANDS, ST. LAWRENCE RIVER. Ottawa, Govt.
Print. Bureau, 1910. 7p [BM BVaU LC OOA QMM

White, Walter Sydney, 1909–
PAGES FROM THE HISTORY OF SOREL, 1642–1958. Sorel, Que., Author, n.d.
175p

Whittaker, Lance H.
ROSSLAND, THE GOLDEN CITY. Ed. by ——. Rossland, Rossland Miner, 1949.
[BVaU OTP

Whitton, Charlotte Elizabeth, 1896–
A HUNDRED YEARS A-FELLIN'. Some Passages from the Timber Saga of the
Ottawa in the Century ... 1842–1942. Comp. by ——. Ottawa, Runge Press,
1943. 172p [BVaU OKQ

"I BELONG ON THE OTTAWA." A Few Odd Jottings for the Casual Visitor taken from the Notebooks of Her Worship, the Mayor of Ottawa, and reproduced herewith from Articles appearing in the Ottawa Citizen in 1950–51. Ottawa, 1952. 12p

Wilkes, Rev. Frederick Alfred, 1919–
THEY ROSE FROM THE DUST. Saskatoon, Modern Press, 1958. 249p [An account of pioneer days in south central Saskatchewan.]

Wilkie, Sask. Jubilee Committee
DISTRICT OF WILKIE, SASKATCHEWAN. Ed. and comp. by W.A. Hook and others. Wilkie, Historical Section of the Jubilee Committee, 1955. 45p

Wilkinson, Douglas, 1919–
LAND OF THE LONG DAY. Toronto, Clarke Irwin, 1955. 261p [Account of a year spent on Baffin Island.]

Williamson, Owen Templeton Garrett, 1883–
THE NORTHLAND. The Romance of Northern Ontario. Toronto, Ryerson, 1946. 110p [BVaU LC OTP QMM

Willoughby, J.
THE LAND OF THE MAYFLOWER; or, The Past and Present of Nova Scotia. Halifax, Barnes, 1860. 64p [NSWA OTP

Willson, (Henry) Beckles, 1869–1942
NOVA SCOTIA. The Province That has been Passed By. London, Constable, 1911. 256p [BM BVaU LC NSWA OTU QMM
QUEBEC. The Laurentian Province. Toronto, Bell & Cockburn, 1912. 271p [BM BVaU LC NSHD OLU QMM
THE TENTH ISLAND. Being some Account of Newfoundland, its People, its Politics, its Problems, and its Peculiarities. London, Richards, 1897. 208p [Rev. ed.: THE TRUTH ABOUT NEWFOUNDLAND. ... London, Richards, 1901. 228p] [BM BVaU LC NSWA OLU QMM

Wilson, Andrew
A HISTORY OF OLD BYTOWN AND VICINITY, NOW THE CITY OF OTTAWA. ... Ottawa, "News," 1876. 89p [NSWA OTU

Wilson, Ann MacLean
HISTORY OF "BLANSHARD IN REVIEW," 1951. Comp. by ——. Blanshard Township, Ont., Historical Committee, 1951. 111p

Wilson, Isaiah Woodworth, 1848–1928
A GEOGRAPHY AND HISTORY OF THE COUNTY OF DIGBY, NOVA SCOTIA. Halifax, Holloway, 1900. 471p [BVaU LC NSWA OTU

Wilson, Lawrence Maurice, 1896–
THIS WAS MONTREAL IN 1814, 1815, 1816 AND 1817. (Life in Canada's Metropolis as

culled Verbatim from the Editorial, News and Advertising Columns of *The Montreal Herald*.) Comp. by ——. Montreal, priv. print., 1960. 205p

Wilton Rural Municipality No. 472, Sask.
RURAL MUNICIPALITY OF WILTON, NO. 472, MARSHALL, SASKATCHEWAN, 1905–1955. ... Marshall, 1955. 36p

Wingfield, Alexander Hamilton, 1898–
THE HAMILTON CENTENNIAL, 1846–1946. Ed. by ——. [Hamilton], Hamilton Centennial Committee, 1946. 122p [LC OOA

Winkler, Man. Burwalde School District
DIAMOND JUBILEE YEAR BOOK OF THE BURWALDE SCHOOL AT WINKLER, MANITOBA, 1888–1948. [Winkler?], 1948. 48p [SSU

Winnipeg Daily Tribune
CITY OF WINNIPEG. ... A General Historical, Statistical, and Descriptive Review. Winnipeg, Daily Tribune, 1891. 26p [NSWA OLU

Wintemberg, William John, 1876–1941
FOLK-LORE OF WATERLOO COUNTY, ONTARIO. Ottawa, King's Printer, 1950. 68p [BM BVaU OLU

Winter, James Spearman, 1845–1911
FRENCH TREATY RIGHTS IN NEWFOUNDLAND. The Case for the Colony stated by the People's Delegates, Sir J.S. Winter ... P.J. Scott ... and A.B. Morine. London, King, 1890. 130p [BM BVaU OTP

Women's Institute. Canada. Arundel Women's Institute, Que.
ARUNDEL, QUEBEC, CANADA, 1856–1954. Arundel, Que., the Institute, 1954. 35p

Women's Institute. Canada. Bancroft Women's Institute, Alta.
THE HERITAGE OF BANCROFT. Calgary, the Institute, [1961?]. 276p

Women's Institute. Canada. Bessborough Women's Institute, B.C.
THE BESSBOROUGH DISTRICT. Comp. June 1958, in Recognition of the British Columbia Centennial. Bessborough, the Institute, 1958. 19p [mimeographed]

Women's Institute. Canada. Bounty Homemakers' Club, Sask.
BOUNTY. Bounty, Sask., the Club, 1956. 331p [History of the Bounty District, Sask.]

Women's Institute. Canada. Burnham Homemakers' Club, Sask.
50 YEARS ALONG THE CUTBANK. Comp. by Mrs. Edna B. Linklater. Burnham, Sask., the Club, 1955. 16p

Women's Institute. Canada. Crapaud Women's Institute, P.E.I.
HISTORY OF CRAPAUD, PRINCE EDWARD ISLAND. Crapaud, the Institute, 1958. 129p

Women's Institute. Canada. Fruitvale Women's Institute, B.C.
HISTORY OF BEAVER VALLEY & PEND d'OREILLE DISTRICTS. Fruitvale, B.C., the Institute, 1958. 16p

Women's Institute. Canada. Great Village Women's Institute, N.S.
GREAT VILLAGE HISTORY. Commemorating the 40th Anniversary of Great Village Women's Institute, 1920–1960. ... Great Village, N.S., the Institute, 1960. 155p

Women's Institute. Canada. Hamiota Women's Institute, Man.
A HISTORY OF HAMIOTA VILLAGE AND MUNICIPALITY, 1879–1956. Hamiota, Man., the Institute, [1956?]. 1v [unpaged].

Women's Institute. Canada. Jonesville Homemakers' Club, Sask.
A HISTORY OF BEECHY, SASK. AND DISTRICT. Beechy, the Club, 1955. 66p

Women's Institute. Canada. Louisbourg Women's Institute, N.S.
LOUISBOURG, 1758–1958. Louisbourg, the Institute, 1958. 89p

Women's Institute. Canada. Port Clyde Women's Institute, N.S.
HISTORY OF PORT CLYDE. Shelburne, N.S., 1954. 82p

Women's Institute. Canada. Tregarva Homemakers' Club, Sask.
THIS IS TREGARVA. Tregarva, the Club, 1956. 39p

Wood, Louis Aubrey Lorne, 1883–1955
THE RED RIVER COLONY. A Chronicle of the Beginnings of Manitoba. Toronto, Glasgow Brook, 1915. 152p [BM BVaU LC NSWA OTU QMM

Wood, William Charles Henry, 1864–1947
THE GREAT FORTRESS. A Chronicle of Louisbourg 1720–1760. ... Toronto, Glasgow Brook, 1915. 144p [BM BVaU LC NSWA OTU QMSS
IN THE HEART OF OLD CANADA. Toronto, Briggs, 1913. 310p [BVaU LC NSHD OTP
THE STORIED PROVINCE OF QUEBEC, PAST AND PRESENT. Ed. by ——. Toronto, Dominion, 1931–32. 5v [BM BVaU LC NBFU OOA QMM
UNIQUE QUEBEC. A Vade-Mecum. Quebec, Lit. & Hist. Society of Quebec, 1924. 109p [BM BVaU LC NSWA OTP QMM

Wood, William Robertson, 1874–1947
PAST YEARS IN PICKERING. Sketches of the History of the Community. Toronto, Briggs, 1911. 316p [BVaU LC NSHD OTU

Wood River, Sask. Old Timers' Association. Historical Committee
PIONEER DAYS IN WOOD RIVER DISTRICT. Comp. by Historical Committee, Wood River Old Timers' Association, and George Douglas. Ed. by Allan R. Turner. Saskatoon, the Association, 1960. 116p

Woodley, Rev. Edward Carruthers, 1878–1955

CANADA'S ROMANTIC HERITAGE. The Story of New France. Toronto, Dent, 1940. 288p [BM BVaU OTP

OLD QUEBEC. Trails and Homes. Toronto, Ryerson, 1946. 137p [BVaU LC OTP QMM

THE PROVINCE OF QUEBEC THROUGH FOUR CENTURIES. ... Toronto, Gage, 1944. 230p [LC OTP

Woodrow, James

SAINT JOHN: PAST AND FUTURE. Readings in Congregational Church. ... Saint John, "Globe" Press, 1882. 24p [NBSaM

Woods, John Jex, 1895–

THE AGASSIZ-HARRISON VALLEY. History and Development. 2nd ed. Sidney, B.C., pub. for the Kent Centennial Committee by the Peninsula Print. Co., 1958. 113p

HISTORY AND DEVELOPMENT OF AGASSIZ-HARRISON VALLEY. Agassiz, Agassiz-Harrison Advance, 1941. 68p [BVaU OTU

Woods, Robert Stuart, 1819–1906

HARRISON HALL AND ITS ASSOCIATIONS; or, A History of the Municipal, Judicial, and Educational Interests of the Western Peninsula. ... Chatham, Ont., Planet, 1896. 150p [Early history of Kent County, etc.] [BVaU NSHD OLU QMM

Woods, William Carson, 1860–1902

THE ISLE OF THE MASSACRE. [Adapted from the French of the late J.C. Taché.] Toronto, Publishers Synd., 1901. 98p [BVaU NBFU OTU

Worden, Marquis Dufferin

THE STORY OF VANSCOY COMMUNITY. Vanscoy, Sask., Ladies Service Club, 1955. 23p

Wright, Arthur Walker, 1855–1944

MEMORIES OF MOUNT FOREST AND SURROUNDING TOWNSHIPS, Minto, Arthur, West Luther, Normanby, Egremont, Proton. ... Ed. by ——. Mount Forest, Ont., the Confederate, [1928?]. 202p [OTP

NOW AND THEN: PIONEER JOURNALISM IN THE COUNTY OF WELLINGTON. Prepared for the Ontario Historical Society. N.p., n.d. 25p [OTU

PIONEER DAYS IN NICHOL ... FERGUS, ELORA AND SALEM TOWNSHIPS. Ed. by ——. Mount Forest, Ont., Editor, 1924. 132p [2nd ed., enl.: 1933. 313p] [BM BVaU LC OKQ

SKETCHES OF THE EARLY DAYS OF FERGUS AND VICINITY. Comp. by ——. Mount Forest, Ont., n.d. 128p [OOA

Wright, Esther Isabell (Clark), 1895–

BLOMIDON ROSE. Toronto, Ryerson, 1957. 206p [Account of Cape Blomidon and the Annapolis Valley, Nova Scotia.]

THE MIRAMICHI. A Study of the New Brunswick River and of the People who
Settled along it. Sackville, Tribune Press, 1944. 79p [LC NSWA OLU QMM
THE PETITCODIAC. A Study of the New Brunswick River and the People who
Settled along it. Sackville, Tribune Press, 1945. 72p [BVaU NSWA OTP QMM
THE SAINT JOHN RIVER. Toronto, McClelland, 1949. 254p [NSWA OTP QMM

Wright, James Frederick Church, 1904–

SASKATCHEWAN, THE HISTORY OF A PROVINCE. Toronto, McClelland, 1955.
xi + 292p

Wright, Norman Ernest

IN VIEW OF THE TURTLE HILL. A Survey of the History of Southwestern Manitoba
to 1900. Deloraine, Man., Times Pub. Co., 1951. 146p

Yarmouth, N.S. Town Council

YARMOUTH'S 175TH ANNIVERSARY, 1936. ... [Kentville, Kentville Pub., 1936].
94p [BViP NSHL OTP

Youmans, Harriet Phelps

GRIMSBY PARK, HISTORICAL AND DESCRIPTIVE. Toronto, Briggs, 1900. 75p
[BM OTU

Young, Archibald Hope, 1863–1935

THE PARISH REGISTER OF KINGSTON, UPPER CANADA, 1785–1811. Ed. with Notes
and intro. by ——. Kingston, "British Whig," 1921. 207p [BM BVaU NSHD
OTU QMSS

Young, Cecil J.

OAKVILLE'S 100 YEARS, 1857–1957. [N.p., Author, 1957?] 48p

Young, Ewart, 1913–

CORNER BROOK, NEWFOUNDLAND, 1923–1948. 25 Years of Progress. [Corner
Brook, Western Pub., 1948?]. 64p [NfSG OOA
ST. JOHN'S, NEWFOUNDLAND, CAPITAL OF CANADA'S NEWEST PROVINCE.
[Montreal, Guardian Associates, 1949.] 64p ["3rd printing": St. John's,
Guardian Ltd., 1955.] [NfSM OOA
THIS IS NEWFOUNDLAND. Ed. by ——. With a Prologue by E.J. Pratt. ... Toronto,
Ryerson, 1949. 104p [BVaU LC NSHD OLU QMM

Young, George Renny, 1802–1853

... THE "ESCHEAT QUESTION" IN THE ISLAND OF PRINCE EDWARD ISLAND.
Together with the Causes of the Late Agitation. ... London, Swale, 1838. 72p
[BM OTP

Young, James, 1835–1913

REMINISCENCES OF THE EARLY HISTORY OF GALT AND THE SETTLEMENT OF
DUMFRIES. Toronto, Hunter Rose, 1880. 272p [BM BVaU LC NSWA OTU

Young, William Frederick Hackett, 1898–
HISTORICAL DIRECTORY, CHIPPAWA CENTENNIAL–ANNIVERSARY, 1850–1950. "The Romance of a Village." Comp. by ——. Chippawa, Ont., F.H. Young, Associates, 1950. 32p [OONL

Zelma, Sask. Homemakers' Club
THE COMMUNITY OF ZELMA, 1904–1949. Saskatoon, Saskatoon Printers, 1949. 26p [ACG BVa OOP SRL

Zurich, Ont. Historical Committee
A CENTURY OF PROGRESS, ZURICH 1856–1956. Zurich, 1956. 64p

RELIGION AND MORALITY

Sermons, denominational history, histories of local churches, doctrine, controversy, homiletics, etc.

Adams, Frank Dawson, 1859–1942
A HISTORY OF CHRIST CHURCH CATHEDRAL, MONTREAL. Montreal, Burton's Ltd., 1941. 226p [BVaU LC OTP

Adams, Robert Chamblet, 1839–
EVOLUTION: A SUMMARY OF EVIDENCE. A Lecture. ... New York, Putnam, 1883. 44p [BM LC
GOOD WITHOUT GOD. New York, Eckler, 1902. 113p [LC
PIONEER PITH. The Gist of Lectures on Rationalism. New York, Truth Seeker Co., [1889]. 99p [OLU QMSS
TRAVELS IN FAITH FROM TRADITION TO REASON. New York, Putnam, 1884. 238p [BM LC

Adamson, Rev. William Agar, 1800–1868
THINGS TO BE REMEMBERED. A Sermon. Montreal, Armour & Ramsay, 1846. 29p [NSWA QMSS

Aitken, Everett Melville, 1899–
A WORLD IN WAITING. Toronto, Ryerson, 1952. 87p

Aiton, Grace
HISTORY OF ST. PAUL'S UNITED CHURCH, SUSSEX, N.B. Sussex, The Church, 1949. 51p [OTU

Akins, Thomas Beamish, 1809–1891
A SKETCH OF THE RISE AND PROGRESS OF THE CHURCH OF ENGLAND IN THE BRITISH NORTH AMERICAN PROVINCES. Halifax, Cunnabell, 1849. 151p [NSWA OTP QMM

Alexander, William Hardy, 1878–1962
COLLEGE AND RELIGION. Talks to College Students. Boston, Badger, 1920. 107p [LC OOCC

Allan, William, 1885–1939
CROWDED WAYS. A Second Series of Meditations Broadcast from ... CFRB, Toronto. Toronto, Nelson, 1935. 147p [BM BViP OTU
MEMORIES OF BLINKBONNIE. A Second Book of Musings. Toronto, Nelson, 1939. 117p [BVaU NBFU OTU

MUSINGS. Toronto, Nelson, 1937. 125p [OTU
THE QUIET PLACE. Toronto, Nelson, 1933. 127p [NBFU OTU

Allen, Grant, 1848–1899
THE EVOLUTION OF THE IDEA OF GOD. New York, Holt, 1897. 447p [Rev. and
abridged by Franklin P. Richards. London, Watts, 1903.] [BM BVaU LC
NSHD OTU
THE EVOLUTIONIST AT LARGE. New York, Fitzgerald, 1881. 50p [Same title:
London, Chatto, 1881. 215p] [BM LC OTU
THE NEW HEDONISM. New York, Tucker, 1900. 30p [LC

Alley, Herbert Ruttan, 1892–
THINKING OF ROME? Think Twice! Toronto, United Church Pub. House, 1958.
68p

Alline, Rev. Henry, 1748–1784
THE ANTI-TRADITIONALIST. [Halifax, Anthony Henry, 1783.] 70p [Tremaine
A GOSPEL CALL TO SINNERS. A Sermon. Newburyport, Blunt & March, 1795.
35p [NSWA
A SERMON ON A DAY OF THANKSGIVING PREACHED AT LIVERPOOL. Halifax,
Henry, 1782. 40p [LC
A SERMON PREACHED ON THE 19TH OF FEB. 1783, AT FORT MIDWAY. Halifax,
Henry, 1783. 44p [NSHP
A SERMON PREACHED TO, AND AT THE REQUEST OF, A RELIGIOUS SOCIETY OF
YOUNG MEN ... IN LIVERPOOL. Halifax, Henry, 1782. 36p [NSWA
TWO MITES ON SOME OF THE MOST IMPORTANT AND MUCH DISPUTED POINTS
OF DIVINITY. Halifax, Henry, 1781. 342p [Reprinted as TWO MITES CAST INTO
THE OFFERING. ... By Henry Alline. ... With some amendments by Benjamin
Randle. Dover, N.H., 1804. 250p] [NSHD

Anderson, Rev. Arthur Edward Oswald
SAINT PETER'S, CARLINGTON, OTTAWA, 1921–1951. Ottawa, Author, 1951. 12p

Anderson, Rev. David, 1814–1885
BRITAIN'S ANSWER TO THE NATIONS. A Missionary Sermon. London, Hatchard,
1857. 36p [BM BViPA OTP
CHILDREN INSTEAD OF FATHERS. ... London, Hatchard, 1854. 32p [BM
BViPA OTP
CHRISTIAN PRIVILEGE AND DUTY. A Sermon preached in St. John's Cathedral,
Red River Settlement ... May 10th, 1868. ... Winnipeg, Nor'Western Office,
1868. 11p [OOA
THE CIRCLE OF LIGHT; or, The Conjuror's Confession. London, Hatchard, 1857.
16p [BM
FAITHFUL AND FRUITFUL. Two Sermons. ... Bristol, Chillcott, 1872. 38p [BM
THE GOSPEL IN THE REGIONS BEYOND. ... London, Hatchard, 1874. 16p [BM
OTP

THE HEART GIVEN TO GOD AND THE WORK. ... London, Hatchard, 1857. 24p [BM
   BViPA OTP
PAPAMAS; or, The Chief's Address. London, Hatchard, 1857. 16p [BM
THE SEAL OF APOSTLESHIP. London, Hatchard, 1851. 31p [BM MWP OTP
THE TRUTH AND THE CONSCIENCE. ... London, Hatchard, 1861. 35p [BM OTP
TWO SERMONS PREACHED IN ST. JAMES' MEMORIAL CHURCH, CLIFTON. ...
   London, Hamilton Adams, 1876. 31p [BM
THE WINNER OF SOULS. ... London, Hatchard, 1856. 32p [BM OTP
THE WORDS OF THE WISE. ... London, R.T.S., 1857. 30p [BM

Anglican Church of Canada. Dioceses. Nova Scotia
TWO HUNDRED AND FIFTY YEARS YOUNG. Our Diocesan Story, 1710–1960.
   Halifax, 1960. 168p

Angwin, J.G.
METHODISM IN CAPE BRETON, 1789–1914. A Retrospect. ... Sydney Mines, 1914.
   65p [BVaU NSHD OLU

Anonymous
THE EPISCOPAL CONTROVERSY. Being a Series of Letters written by the Respec-
   tive Friends of the Ven. Archdeacon Bethune and Dr. Cronyn, the two
   Candidates for the Bishopric of the Western Diocese. London, Ont., Free Press,
   1857. 79p [OTU
EPISCOPAL TESTIMONIES AGAINST DOCTRINES ADVOCATED IN THE "TRACTS FOR
   THE TIMES" PUBLISHED AT OXFORD. Kingston, The Times, 1844. 32p [OTU
THE JUDGMENTS OF THE CANADIAN BISHOPS, on ... Trinity College in Relation to
   the Theological Teaching of the College. Toronto, Rowsell & Ellis, 1863. 24p
   [OTU
REMARKS ON A PAMPHLET ENTITLED "POPERY CONDEMNED BY SCRIPTURE AND
   THE FATHERS." Halifax, Howe, 1809. 403p [NSWA
A VOICE FROM THE WILDERNESS OF CANADA. Addressed to All in General, and
   Presbyterians in Particular. Toronto, Globe Print., 1870. 234p [BVaU OTP

Armitage, Rev. William James, 1860–1929
THE CHURCH YEAR STUDIES FOR THE SUNDAYS, SACRED SEASONS AND SAINTS'
   DAYS OF THE CHRISTIAN YEAR. Oxford, Frowde, 1908. 229p [BM NSWA
THE CITIES OF REFUGE. Pictures of Gospel Principles, Gospel Promises, and
   Gospel Privileges. London, Marshall, 1908., 88p [BM NSWA OLU
THE FRUIT OF THE SPIRIT. London, Marshall, 1909. 104p [First pub. 1907.]
   [BM LC NSWA
THE SOLDIERS OF THE KING. ... London, Marshall, n.d. 135p [BM NSWA
THE STORY OF THE CANADIAN REVISION OF THE PRAYER BOOK. Cambridge,
   Eng., Cambridge U. Press, 1922. 442p [BM BVaU LC NSWA OTU QMM

Armstrong, Mrs. Allan
WAWEIG UNITED CHURCH THROUGH THE YEARS, 1848–1948. Waweig, N.B.,
   The Church, 1949. 36p [OTU

Armstrong, Rev. Maurice Whitman, 1905–1968
THE GREAT AWAKENING IN NOVA SCOTIA, 1776–1809. Hartford, Conn., Am.
Soc. of Church History, 1947. 141p [AEU LC NBSM OTU
THE PRESBYTERIAN ENTERPRISE. Sources of American Presbyterian History.
Ed. by Maurice W. Armstrong, Lefferts A. Loetscher and Charles A. Anderson.
Philadelphia, Westminster Press, 1956. 336p

Atkinson, Rev. Abraham Fuller, 1803?–1866
THE LEADING DOCTRINES OF THE GOSPEL. Montreal, Armour & Ramsay, 1836.
24p [NSWA OTP

Austin, Rev. Benjamin Fish, 1850–1932
GLIMPSES OF THE UNSEEN. Toronto, Bradley-Garretson, 1898. 504p [BM
THE GOSPEL TO THE POOR VERSUS PEW RENTS. Toronto, Briggs, 1884. 110p
[OTP
THE JESUITS. Their Origin, History, Aims, Principles, Immoral Teaching. London,
Ont., Advertiser, 1889. 40p [BVaU NSWA OTU QMSS
THE METHODIST EPISCOPAL PULPIT. A Volume of Sermons by the Members of the
Niagara and Bay of Quinte Conferences. ... V. 1. Toronto, Hunter, 1879. 315p
[OTU
POPULAR SINS. A Series of Sermons against the Sins of the Times. Toronto,
Hunter Rose, 1880. 115p [OTUV
WHAT CONVERTED ME TO SPIRITUALISM. Toronto, Austin, 1901. 205p [BM

Aylmer, Que. United Church
LIVING STONES IN A SPIRITUAL HOME. The History of Aylmer United Church,
1828–1956. Aylmer, 1956. 16p

Bagnall, Lucy A. (Lowe)
AT THE SIXTIETH MILESTONE. The Story of the First Baptist Church, Calgary,
Alberta, 1888–1948. Calgary, First Baptist Church, 1948. 81p [AC

Bagnall, Rev. Walter E.
ST. JOHN'S CHURCH, PRESTON, ONTARIO. Forty Five Years. Toronto, Livingstone,
1935. 30p [OTU

Baker, Ida Emma (Fitch), 1858–1948
HOW THEY FOUND JESUS. Toronto, Mundy, n.d. 121p [OTU

Baldwin, Rev. Maurice Scollard, 1836–1904
A BREAK IN THE OCEAN CABLE. 3rd ed., rev. Montreal, 1880. [BM OOP
A LIFE IN A LOOK. Montreal, Dawson, 1879. 113p [Also: Toronto, Briggs, n.d.
104p] [BM BVaU NSWA OLU

Ballantyne, Murray, 1909–
ALL OR NOTHING. New York, Sheed & Ward, 1956. 216p

Banner, Ont. United Church

CENTENNIAL, 1857–1957, BANNER UNITED CHURCH. Banner, [1957?]. 34p

Bannister, J.A.

A CENTENNIAL HISTORY OF GRACE UNITED CHURCH, PORT DOVER, ONTARIO, 1847–1947. Port Dover, Author, 1947. 24p [OTP

Barber, Frank Louis, 1877–1945

THE PHILOSOPHY OF JOHN WESLEY. Toronto, Ryerson, 1923. 19p [BM OTUV

Barclay, Rev. John, 1812–1887

THRONE ESTABLISHED BY RIGHTEOUSNESS. ... A Discourse preached ... on ... the Anniversary of the Birthday of ... Queen Victoria. Toronto, Lovell & Gibson, 1863. 24p [NSHD OTU

THE TIMES OF OLD AND THEIR HAPPY MEMORIES. A Discourse ... preached on the Occasion of the ... Tricentenary of the Scottish Reformation. Toronto, Leader, 1861. 46p [NSWA QMSS

Barnhill, William Perley, 1897–

THE FIRST UNITED BAPTIST CHURCH, LANCASTER, NEW BRUNSWICK. Historical Record [1881–1956]. Comp. by ——. Ed. by W. Gordon Ross and Stanley C. Ross. Lancaster, N.B., the Church, 1956. 18 + 22 + 9p [mimeographed]

Barrett, F.

A BRIEF HISTORY OF METHODISM IN WINDSOR, NOVA SCOTIA ... 1782–1925. Windsor, N.S., Hants Journal Press, 1925. 62p [NSWA

Barrowclough, Edna I. (Hill), 1902–

THE STORY OF WESLEYVILLE UNITED CHURCH AND ITS PEOPLE. Port Hope, Ont., the Author, 1960. 45p

Bates, Walter, 1760–1842

A SERIOUS CONFERENCE ... ON THE SUBJECT OF RELIGIOUS WORSHIP. Saint John, Durant, 1826. 80p [OTU

Bayer, Charles Walter, 1893–

CHRIST CHURCH, DARTMOUTH, NOVA SCOTIA, 1817 TO 1959. Dartmouth, the Church, 1960. 165p

Bayne, Rev. John, 1806–1859

IS MAN RESPONSIBLE FOR HIS BELIEF? Galt, Ainslie, 1851. 32p [Also included in George Smellie's MEMOIR OF ... JOHN BAYNE, q.v.] [BVaU NSWA OTP

WAS THE RECENT DISRUPTION OF THE SYNOD IN CANADA, IN CONNECTION WITH THE CHURCH OF SCOTLAND, CALLED FOR? An Address to the Presbyterians of Canada. ... [Anon] Galt, Ainslie, 1846. 83p [OTU

Beadle, The Venerable (pseud)

A SEASONABLE SHOVE TO THE MEMBERS OF THE ANGLICAN CHURCH IN THE DIOCESE OF QUEBEC. Quebec, Middleton, 1858. 30p [NSWA

Beattie, Rev. Francis Robert, 1848–1906
APOLOGETICS; or, THE RATIONAL VINDICATION OF CHRISTIANITY. Richmond,
Va., Presbyterian Committee of Publications, 1903. 605p [LC OTU
EXAMINATION OF THE UTILITARIAN THEORY OF MORALS. Brantford, Sutherland,
1885. 222p [OTU QMM
THE HIGHER CRITICISM. Modern Critical Theories as to the Origin and Contents
of the Literature and Religion found in the Holy Scriptures. Toronto, Briggs,
1888. 56p [OLU
THE PRESBYTERIAN STANDARDS. An Exposition of the Westminster Confession of
Faith and Catechisms. Richmond, Va., Presbyterian Committee of Publications,
1896. [OTUV

Beaubien, Père Irénée, 1916–
TOWARDS CHRISTIAN UNITY IN CANADA. A Catholic Approach. Montreal, Palm
Publisher [sic], 1956. 184p

Beaven, Rev. James, 1801–1875
"ASK FOR THE OLD PATHS." Cobourg, Diocesan Press, 1844. 19p [NSWA OTP
ELEMENTS OF NATURAL THEOLOGY. London, Rivington, 1850. 240p [OTP
S. IRENAEUS, BISHOP OF LYONS. The Doctrine, Discipline, Practices, and History
of the Church, and the Tenets and Practices of the Gnostic Heretics, During the
Second Century. London, Rivington, 1841. xxviii + 334p [LC
"THAT THEY ALL MAY BE ONE." Toronto, Rowsell & Ellis, 1859. 16p [NSWA
OTP

Beck, Lily Adams (Moresby), –1931
THE LIFE OF THE BUDDHA. London, Collins, 1939. 287p [BM LC QMSS
THE SPLENDOUR OF ASIA. The Story and Teaching of the Buddha. New York,
Dodd Mead, 1926. 269p [Repub. as THE LIFE OF THE BUDDHA. With an intro. by
George F. Maine. London, Collins, 1959. xxxix + 256p] [BM BVaU LC
NSHD OONL QMM
THE STORY OF ORIENTAL PHILOSOPHY. New York, Cosmopolitan Book, 1928.
429p [BM BVaU LC NBFU OTU QMM
THE WAY OF POWER. Studies in the Occult. New York, Cosmopolitan Book, 1928.
285p [BM LC QMM

Bellamy, Lora (Davis), 1855–1937
PIONEER DAYS OF THE FIRST BAPTIST CHURCH IN NORTHERN ALBERTA. Edmonton, 1925. 15p [History of First Baptist Church in Edmonton.] [AE

Bennett, Rev. James, 1817–1901
THE WISDOM OF THE KING; or, Studies in Ecclesiastes. Edinburgh, Oliphant, 1870.
426p [EngCat NBB

Bentley, Mrs. Verna Bessie, 1904–
ST. BARNABAS' CHURCH, Fiftieth Anniversary, 1885–1935. By Mrs. O.C. Bentley.
Toronto, The Church, 1935. 15p [OTP

Bentom, Rev. Clark

A STATEMENT OF FACTS AND LAW. Relative to the Prosecution of the Rev. Clark Bentom, Protestant Missionary from the London Missionary Society, for the Assumption of the Office of a Dissenting Minister of the Gospel in Quebec, by the King's Attorney General of Lower Canada. Troy, N.Y., Penniman, 1804. 32p [BM LC OTP

TALEBEARING A GREAT SIN. A Sermon preached Lord's Day, February 22, 1801. ... Quebec, Neilson, 1801. 31p [OTP

Berry, Rev. William George, 1903—

THIS INCREDIBLE THING—EVANGELISM. Toronto, Ryerson, 1959. ix + 32p

Bethune, Rev. Alexander Neil, 1800—1879

THE CHURCH OF THE LIVING GOD. A Sermon preached ... in St. Peter's Church, Cobourg. Toronto, Rowsell, 1864. 12p [NSWA OTP

THE CLERGY RESERVE QUESTION IN CANADA. London, Clay, 1853. 24p [BM BVaU OTU QMM

FOUR SERMONS ON THE HOLY SACRAMENT OF THE LORD'S SUPPER. Toronto, Plees, 1852. 52p [OTUV

LECTURES, EXPOSITORY AND PRACTICAL, ON THE LITURGY OF THE CHURCH OF ENGLAND. Toronto, Rowsell, 1862. 170p [BM BVaU NSWA OLU QMBM

LECTURES UPON HISTORICAL PORTIONS OF THE OLD TESTAMENT. New York, Stanford, 1857. 213p [OLU

NATIONAL JUDGMENTS PROVOKED BY NATIONAL SINS. Cobourg, Chatterton, 1838. 24p [BM

A SERMON PREACHED IN ST. PETER'S CHURCH, COBOURG, U.C., on ... the day appointed for a general thanksgiving to Almighty God for having removed the heavy judgments with which these provinces have recently been afflicted. Cobourg, Chatterton, 1833. 22p [OTP

SERMONS ON THE LITURGY OF THE CHURCH OF ENGLAND. York, Stanton, 1829. 76p [OTP

THOUGHTS UPON THE LAWFULNESS AND EXPEDIENCY OF CHURCH ESTABLISH-MENTS ... in a Letter to C.A. Hagerman. Cobourg, Chatterton, 1836. 32p [OTP

Bethune, Rev. John, 1791—1872

BAPTIST MISREPRESENTATION ON BAPTISM, WITH AN EXPOSURE OF THE SYSTEM-ATIC POLICY OF BAPTIST CHURCH PUBLICATIONS OF MISQUOTATIONS &C. Toronto, Presbyterian Print. House, 1876. 176p [BVaU OTU

A SERMON PREACHED AT BROCKVILLE, U.C., on the 18th of June, 1816, being a Day of General Thanksgiving. Montreal, Gray, 1816. 25p [OKQ

A SERMON PREACHED IN CHRIST'S CHURCH, MONTREAL, on Friday, the 4th May, 1832. Being the Day Appointed for a Public Fast, Occasioned by the Apprehension of being Visited by the Pestilence which is Scourging the Nations of Europe. Montreal, Bull, 1832. 19p [QMM

A SERMON PREACHED ON WEDNESDAY, FEBRUARY 6, 1833. Being the Day appointed ... for a General Thanksgiving to Almighty God for having Removed the Heavy Judgment of the Pestilence. Montreal, Armour, 1833. 16p [QMM

Bettridge, Rev. William Craddock, 1791–1879
A BRIEF HISTORY OF THE CHURCH IN UPPER CANADA. ... London, Painter, 1838. 143p [BM BVaU LC NSWA OOP QMM

Bezanson, Rev. W.B.
FUEL FOR MISSIONS. Kentville, Kentville Pub. Co., 1934. 60p [OTP

Bill, Rev. Ingraham E., 1805–1891
FIFTY YEARS WITH THE BAPTIST MINISTERS AND CHURCHES OF THE MARITIME PROVINCES OF CANADA. Saint John, Barnes, 1880. 778p [BM BVaU NSHD OTU

Black, William G.
THE CHURCH AND SOCIAL PROBLEMS. Brantford, Ont., Baptist Federation of Canada, 1959. 48p

Bland, Salem Goldworth, 1859–1950
THE NEW CHRISTIANITY; or, The Religion of the New Age. Toronto, McClelland, 1920. 168p [BM BVaU OTUV

Blewett, George John, 1873–1912
THE CHRISTIAN VIEW OF THE WORLD. Nathaniel William Taylor Lectures for 1910–1911, Delivered before the Divinity School of Yale University. New Haven, Yale U. Press, 1912. 344p [BM BVaU LC OTU
THE STUDY OF NATURE AND THE VISION OF GOD. With Other Essays in Philosophy. Toronto, Briggs, 1907. 358p [BM BVaU' LC OTU QMM

Bompas, Rev. William Carpenter, 1834–1906
DIOCESE OF MACKENZIE RIVER. London, S.P.C.K., 1888. 108p [BM BVaU NSWA OLU
NORTHERN LIGHTS ON THE BIBLE. Drawn from a Bishop's Experience during Twenty-Five Years in the Great Northwest. London, Nisbet, 1893. 211p [BM BVaU OKQ

Boniface, Father, 1880–
THE HISTORY OF SAINT FRANCIS PARISH, VANCOUVER. Vancouver, 1959. xii + 174p

Bonis, Rev. Robert Raynes, 1906–
THE STORY OF ST. MARGARET'S CHURCH, WEST HILL, AND THE PARISH OF SCARBOROUGH, 1833–1953. West Hill, St. Margaret's Church, 1953. 19p

Borland, Rev. John, 1809–1888
AN APPEAL TO THE MONTREAL CONFERENCE AND METHODIST CHURCH

GENERALLY FROM A CHARGE BY REV. WILLIAM SCOTT. Montreal, "Witness,"
1883. 40p [NSWA OTP

DIALOGUES BETWEEN TWO METHODISTS. ... Toronto, Author, 1856. 46p [OTP

LETTERS TO A MEMBER OF THE WESLYAN METHODIST CHURCH. Montreal,
"Witness," 1873. 43p [NSWA

OBSERVATIONS ON THE MORAL AGENCY OF MAN ... in which the Obliquity of
Universalism is Exhibited. ... Sherbrooke, Walton, 1848. 161p [NSWA OTP

Borthwick, Rev. John Douglas, 1832—1912

HISTORY OF THE DIOCESE OF MONTREAL, 1850–1910. Montreal, Lovell, 1910.
230p [BVaU LC OTU

Bovell, James, 1817—1880

DEFENCE OF DOCTRINAL STATEMENTS. Addressed to the Right Rev. the Lord
Bishop of Toronto, the Right Rev. the Lord Bishop of Huron, and the Corporation of Trinity College. ... Toronto, Rowsell & Ellis, 1860. 60p [OTP

LETTERS, Addressed to the Rev. Mr. Fletcher and Others, Framers of a Series of
Resolutions on "Ritual." Toronto, Hill, 1867. 64p [OTP

OUTLINES OF NATURAL THEOLOGY FOR THE USE OF THE CANADIAN STUDENT. ...
Toronto, Rowsell & Ellis, 1859. 649p [NSHD OTP

PASSING THOUGHTS ON MAN'S RELATION TO GOD AND ON GOD'S RELATION
TO MAN. Toronto, Rowsell & Ellis, 1862. 427p [OTP

PREPARATION FOR THE CHRISTIAN SACRIFICE; OR, HOLY COMMUNION. Toronto,
Rowsell, 1859. 294p [OTTC

THE WORLD AT THE ADVENT OF THE LORD JESUS. Toronto, Chewett, 1868. 412p
[OTU QMM

Brady, Buckskin

STORIES AND SERMONS BY BUCKSKIN BRADY, THE COWBOY EVANGELIST.
Toronto, Briggs, 1905. 135p [BM LC

Braeside, Ont. Braeside United Church

HISTORY OF THE BRAESIDE UNITED CHURCH, FORMERLY THE BRAESIDE
PRESBYTERIAN CHURCH, 1885–1952. Braeside, the Church, 1952. 23p

Brandon, Horace G.

THE THREE LAST BATTLES. A Prophetic Preview of the Last Three Struggles of a
Dying World Order, Covered up in Symbolic Terms as "Wind," "Earthquake"
and "Fire." Comp. from the Scriptures and arranged by ——. Vancouver,
Ireland & Allan Ltd., n.d. xiii + 209p

Bready, John Wesley, 1887—1953

THIS FREEDOM–WHENCE? With an intro. by Rutherford L. Decker. 12th print.,
rev. Winona Lake, Indiana, Light and Life Press, 1950. xviii + 365p
[Abridgment and revision of his ENGLAND: BEFORE AND AFTER WESLEY.
London, Hodder, 1938.] [OONL

Breckenridge, Rev. James, —1879
PREDESTINATION. A Sermon. Toronto, Presbyterian Print., 1876. 50p [BVaU

Brewing, Rev. Willard, 1881—
FAITH FOR THESE TIMES. London, Collins, 1945. 159p [BVaU OTP

Brice, Edward, 1879—
THE HISTORY OF THE WORLD A.D. 1960 TO A.D. 2000. Edmonton, Author, 1960.
  249p [On history and Biblical prophecy.]

Brigstocke, Rev. Frederick Hervey John, 1841—1899
HISTORY OF TRINITY CHURCH, SAINT JOHN, NEW BRUNSWICK, 1791—1891. Comp.
  and ed. by ——. Saint John, McMillan, 1892. 202p [BVaU NSHD OOA

Broadus, Eleanor (Hammond)
A BOOK OF THE CHRIST CHILD. New York, Appleton, 1910. 158p [BM LC

Brooker, Bertram, 1888—1955
ELIJAH. With illustrated drawings. New York, Rudge, 1930. 26p [LC OTUV

Brosnan, Rev. Michael, 1894?—1943
PIONEER HISTORY OF ST. GEORGE'S DIOCESE, NEWFOUNDLAND. [Toronto, Western
  Pub. Co., 1948.] 172p [NBFL OOA

Broughall, James Samuel, 1866—
OUTLINE OF THE HISTORY OF GRACE CHURCH-ON-THE-HILL, TORONTO 1911—1932.
  Toronto, Author, 1932. 19p [OTU

Brown, Rev. Andrew, —1834
THE PERILS OF THE TIME, AND THE PURPOSES FOR WHICH THEY ARE APPOINTED.
  A Sermon. ... Halifax, Howe & M'Kinstry, 1795. 40p [NSHD

Brown, Arnold, 1913—
WHAT HATH GOD WROUGHT? The History of the Salvation Army in Canada.
  Toronto, Salvation Army Print. and Pub. House, 1952. 130p [2nd ed., 1957]

Brown, Rev. John Willoughby, 1857—1940
AN HISTORICAL SKETCH OF THE EARLY SETTLEMENT OF NEW CANAAN [N.B.]
  AND THE HISTORIES OF THE NEW CANAAN, HAVELOCK, AND ALBERT BAPTIST
  CHURCHES. N.p., [1905?]. 39p [NSWA

Brown, Rev. Robert Christopher Lundin, —1876
THE LIFE OF PEACE. London, Masters, 1876. 160p [BM

Bryce, Rev. George, 1844—1931
THE PRESBYTERIAN CHURCH IN CANADA, AND THE CANADIAN NORTH-WEST.
  Toronto, British American Presbyterian Office, 1875. 21p [LC NSWA OTUV

Bryden, Rev. Walter Williamson, 1883—1952
SEPARATED UNTO THE GOSPEL. Toronto, Burns & MacEachern, 1956. xiv + 218p

Brymner, Douglas, 1823–1902
ENDOWMENTS OF THE CHURCH OF SCOTLAND IN CANADA. Toronto, Hunter, 1883.
42p [OTU QMBM
FAULTS AND FAILURES OF THE LATE PRESBYTERIAN UNION IN CANADA. London,
Ont., Free Press, 1879. 43p [OTU

Bucke, Richard Maurice, 1837–1902
MAN'S MORAL NATURE. An Essay. New York, Putnam, 1879. 200p [BM BVaU
LC OTU QMM
THE MORAL NATURE AND THE GREAT SYMPATHETIC. Utica, Roberts, 1878. 27p
[OTP

Buffett, Rev. Frederick M.
THE STORY OF THE CHURCH [OF ENGLAND] IN NEWFOUNDLAND. Toronto,
General Board of Religious Education, [1939]. 96p [NfSM OLU

Bull, William Perkins, 1870–1947
FROM MACDONELL TO McGUIGAN. The History of the Growth of the Roman
Catholic Church in Upper Canada. Toronto, Perkins Bull Fdn, 1939. 501p
[BM LC OKQ
FROM STRACHAN TO OWEN. How the Church of England was Planted and Tended in
British North America. Toronto, Perkins Bull Fdn, 1938. 495p [BVaU LC
NBFU OKQ
SPADUNK; or, From Paganism to Davenport United. Toronto, Perkins Bull Fdn,
1935. 467p [BM BVaU LC OLU

Bullock, Rev. William, 1797–1874
THE BAPTISTS ANSWERED. The Doctrine of Infant Baptism as Taught in the
Scripture, and Practiced in the Church. Boston, Clapp, 1843. 18p [NSHP
A WARNING TO ICE-HUNTERS. A Sermon on the Profanation of the Sabbath,
Preached ... previous to the Departure of the Vessels Engaged in the Seal
Fishery, 1832. [Anon] St. John's, Ryan & Withers, [1832]. 15p [OTP

Burgess, Rev. Edwin Harcus, 1858–
AT THE PLACE WHICH IS CALLED CALVARY. New York, Randolph, 1890.
[NSWA
LOYALTY. New York, Randolph, [1892]. 54p [LC

Burke, Rev. Edmund, 1753–1820
CONTINUATION OF THE FIRST PRINCIPLES OF CHRISTIANITY. Halifax, Howe,
1810. 451p [NSWA QMSS
LETTER OF INSTRUCTION TO THE CATHOLIC MISSIONARIES OF NOVA-SCOTIA.
Halifax, Gay, 1804. 58p [NSWA OTP
REMARKS ON A PAMPHLET ENTITLED POPERY CONDEMNED BY SCRIPTURE AND
THE FATHERS. [See McCulloch, Thomas.] Halifax, Howe, 1809. 403p
[BM NSWA OTP

REMARKS ON THE REV. MR. STANSER'S EXAMINATION OF THE REV. MR. BURKE'S LETTER OF INSTRUCTION TO THE C.M. OF NOVA-SCOTIA, Together with a Reply to the Rev. Mr. Cochran's Fifth and Last Letter to Mr. B. ... also a Short Review of his Former Letters and the Replies which were made. Halifax, Gay, 1805. 2v [BM NSHD OTP

A TREATISE ON THE FIRST PRINCIPLES OF CHRISTIANITY. Halifax, Howe, 1808–10. 2v [BM BVaU NSWA OTP

Burkholder, Lewis J., 1875–

A BRIEF HISTORY OF THE MENNONITES IN ONTARIO. [Toronto, Livingstone], 1935. 358p [BM BVaU LC OLU

Burnett, Rev. Andrew Ian, 1906–

LORD OF ALL LIFE. Toronto, Clarke Irwin, 1952. xi + 205p

Burnfield, Rev. George

VOICES FROM THE ORIENT; or, The Testimony of the Monuments ... and of the Customs and Traditions of the People in the Orient to the Veracity of the Sacred Record. 2nd ed. Toronto, Robinson, 1884. 491p [LC OTU

Burns, Rev. George, 1790–1876

LECTURES AND SERMONS. Saint John, Reynolds, 1820. 400p [NSWA OTP

A VIEW OF THE PRINCIPLES AND FORMS OF THE CHURCH OF SCOTLAND AS BY LAW ESTABLISHED. Saint John, 1817. 32p [NBB

Burns, Rev. Robert Ferrier, 1826–1896

THE PRESBYTERIAN CHURCH IN CANADA. Her Principles, Position and Prospects. A Lecture. Halifax, Nova Scotia Print., 1876. 29p [NSHD

Burwash, Rev. Nathanael, 1839–1918

INDUCTIVE STUDIES IN THEOLOGY. Including the Doctrines of Sin and the Atonement. Toronto, Briggs, 1896. 87p [OTU

MANUAL OF CHRISTIAN THEOLOGY ON THE INDUCTIVE METHOD. London, Marshall, 1900. 2v [BM BVaU OTU

THE RELATION OF CHILDREN TO THE FALL, THE ATONEMENT, AND THE CHURCH. Toronto, Briggs, 1882. 31p [OTU

WESLEY'S DOCTRINAL STANDARDS. Pt. I. The Sermons. With introduction, analysis, and notes. Toronto, Briggs, 1881. xxvii + 523p [Several later editions.] [OTU Ryerson Impt

Burwell, Rev. Adam Hood, 1790–1849

DOCTRINE OF THE HOLY SPIRIT. ... Toronto, Coates, 1835. 124p [BM OTP

ON THE PHILOSOPHY OF HUMAN PERFECTION AND HAPPINESS. Montreal, Lovell & Gibson, 1849. 29p [BM

A VOICE OF WARNING AND INSTRUCTION CONCERNING THE SIGNS OF THE TIMES. Kingston, Herald, 1835. 225p [OLU

Butchart, Reuben, 1863–1963

THE DISCIPLES OF CHRIST IN CANADA SINCE 1830. Toronto, Churches of Christ, Canada Pub., 1949. 674p [NBFU OTU QMM

OLD EVERTON AND THE PIONEER MOVEMENT AMONGST THE DISCIPLES OF CHRIST IN ERAMOSA TOWNSHIP, UPPER CANADA, FROM 1830. Everton, Ont., Church of Christ (Disciples), 1941. 58p [OTP

A PRIMER OF DISCIPLE HISTORY IN CANADA. Toronto, College of the Churches of Christ in Canada, 1942. 17p [OTP

Byerly, Alpheus Edward, 1894–1960

ONE HUNDRED YEARS AT KNOX PRESBYTERIAN CHURCH, GUELPH, ONTARIO, 1844–1944. Guelph, Author, 1944. 56p [OTP

ONE HUNDRED YEARS OF NASSAGAWEYA PRESBYTERIAN CHURCH, 1836–1936, Guelph, Author, 1936. 24p [OTU

Cahill, Rev. Joseph Allison, 1847–1914

SANCTIFICATION INSTANTANEOUS AND COMPLETE IN THIS LIFE IS UNSCRIPTURAL. Saint John, Barnes, 1885. 58p [NBB

Caird, George Bradford, 1917–

PRINCIPALITIES AND POWERS. A Study in Pauline Theology. Oxford, Clarendon, 1956. xi + 106p

Caldwell, William, 1863–1942

THE IDEA OF CREATION. Its Origin and its Value. Fort Worth, Keystone, 1909. 48p [LC QMM

Cameron, Agnes Deans, 1863–1912

A BRIEF HISTORY OF GROVE PRESBYTERIAN CHURCH, FROM ITS INCEPTION TO THE PRESENT DATE. Comp. by ———. Halifax, 1892. 14p [NSWA

Cameron, Frank

BOTANY CHURCH. Record and Memories of Botany Presbyterian Church and its Successor, St. John's United Church, 1858–1941. Howard, Ont., Author, 1941. 37p [OTU

Cameron, Viola Mary

GOD'S PLAN AND MAN'S DESTINY. With a pref. by Cornelius Van Til. Truro, N.S., Author, 1952. 164p

Cameron, Rev. William A., 1882–1956

THE CLINIC OF A CLERIC. Toronto, McClelland, 1931. 249p [OTU

THE GIFT OF GOD, AND OTHER SERMONS. Toronto, McClelland, [1925]. 230p [BM BVaU OTU QMM

JESUS AND THE RISING GENERATION. Toronto, McClelland, 1932. 228p [OTP

NO ROOM IN THE INN. A Christmas Sermon and Prayer. Toronto, McClelland, 1926. 43p [BVaU OTP

NOT BY EASTERN WINDOWS ONLY. Messages from Modern Prophets. Toronto, McClelland, 1929. 244p [BM BVaU NSHD OLU

THE POTTER'S WHEEL. Toronto, McClelland, 1927. 255p [BVaU NSWA OTUV QMM

RAINBOWS THROUGH THE RAIN. Yorkminster Sermons. Toronto, McClelland, 1938. 239p [LC OTP

SONGS OF THE AGES. Toronto, McClelland, 1934. 201p [LC OTP

Campbell, Rev. John, 1840–1904

A CONCISE HISTORY OF FRENCH-CANADIAN PROTESTANTISM. Montreal, Board of French Evangelization of the Presbyterian Church in Canada, 1896. 32p [OTP

THE GREAT ELECTION. Montreal, Lovell, 1894. 30p [QMSS

NEW LIGHT ON THE OLD PRAYER. Toronto, Briggs, 1895. 28p [OTP

PROTEST AGAINST THE DECISION OF THE PRESBYTERY OF MONTREAL AND APPEAL TO THE SYNOD OF MONTREAL AND OTTAWA. N.p., 1894. 25p [OTU

Campbell, Norman

HISTORY OF WESLEY UNITED CHURCH, PEMBROKE, ONTARIO, 1835–1935. Comp. by ——. Pembroke, Standard-Observer Print. Co., 1935. 66p [OTU QMM

Campbell, Rev. Robert, 1835–1921

HISTORY OF THE SCOTCH PRESBYTERIAN CHURCH, ST. GABRIEL STREET, MONT- REAL. Montreal, Drysdale, 1887. 807p [BVaU NSWA OTU QMM

THE PRETENSIONS EXPOSED OF MESSRS. BURNET & CO., TO BE "THE PRESBY- TERIAN CHURCH OF CANADA IN CONNEXION WITH THE CHURCH OF SCOTLAND." Montreal, Drysdale, 1878. 34p [NSWA QMM

THE RELATIONS OF THE CHRISTIAN CHURCHES TO ONE ANOTHER; and Problems Growing out of them, Especially in Canada. Toronto, Briggs, 1913. 337p [BM BVaU OTU

ON THE UNION OF PRESBYTERIANS IN CANADA. Prize Essay. Montreal, Grafton, 1871. 55p [NSWA

Canadian Layman, A (pseud)

"ESSAYS AND REVIEWS" CONSIDERED. Toronto, Chewett, 1862. 50p [NSWA OTP

Carman, Albert, 1833–1917

THE GUIDING EYE; or, The Holy Spirit's Guidance of the Believer. Toronto, Briggs, 1889. 221p [OTP

THE SUPERNATURAL. Toronto, Haynes Press, n.d. 20p [OONL

Carman, Albert Richardson, 1865–1939

THE ETHICS OF IMPERIALISM. An Enquiry whether Christian Ethics and Imperialism are Antagonistic. Boston, Turner, 1905. 177p [BM BVaU OTU

Carmichael, Rev. James, 1835–1908

CHURCH YEAR. A Series of Sermons for the Sacred Seasons. Montreal, 1893. 353p [BVaU QMM

DESIGN AND DARWINISM. Toronto, Hunter, 1880. 50p [NSWA

THE ERRORS OF THE PLYMOUTH BRETHREN. Montreal, Montreal Press & Pub. Co., 1869. 43p [Also: Montreal, Drysdale, 1888. 23p] [NSWA QMSS

HOW TWO DOCUMENTS MAY BE FOUND IN ONE. A Monograph in Connection with the Higher Criticism. Montreal, Gazette Print., 1895. 22p [BM NSWA QMSS

IS THERE A GOD FOR MAN TO KNOW? Toronto, Church of England, 1900. 113p [BM LC OTU

ORGANIC UNION OF CANADIAN CHURCHES. Montreal, Dawson, 1887. 88p [LC NSWA OTU QMM

WHY SOME FAIRLY INTELLIGENT PERSONS DO NOT ENDORSE THE HYPOTHESIS OF EVOLUTION. A Plea for Divine Intention in Creation. Montreal, Gazette Print., 1898. 48p [NSWA OTP

Carnochan, Janet, 1839–1926

ANNIVERSARY OF ST. ANDREW'S CHURCH, NIAGARA. Welland, Tribune, 1911. 13p [OTU

CENTENNIAL ST. ANDREW'S, NIAGARA, 1794–1894. Toronto, Briggs, 1895. 70p [BVaU LC OTP QMBM

CENTENNIAL, ST. MARK'S [EPISCOPAL] CHURCH, NIAGARA, 1792–1892. Toronto, Bain, 1892. 56p [LC OTP

ST. ANDREW'S, NIAGARA, 1794–1894. Toronto, Briggs, 1895. 31p [OTU

TWO FRONTIER CHURCHES. Niagara, 1890. 20p [OTU

Carr-Harris, Bertha Hannah (Wright), 1863–1949

THE HIEROGLYPHICS OF THE HEAVENS; or, The Enigma of the Ages. Toronto, Armac Press, 1933. 3v in 1. [OTP

Carrington, Rev. Philip, 1892–

ACCORDING TO MARK. A Running Commentary on the Oldest Gospel. Cambridge, Eng., U. Press, 1960. xi + 384p

THE EARLY CHRISTIAN CHURCH. Cambridge, Eng., U. Press, 1957. 2v

OUR LORD AND SAVIOUR. His Life and Teachings. Greenwich, Conn., Seabury Press, 1959. 138p

THE PRIMITIVE CHRISTIAN CALENDAR. A Study in The Making of the Marcan Gospel. Cambridge, Eng., U. Press, 1952. V. 1

THE STORY OF THE CHRIST. Toronto, General Board of Religious Education of the Anglican Church of Canada, 1956. 157p

Carroll, Rev. John, 1809–1884

THE BESIEGERS' PRAYER; or, A Christian Nation's Appeal to the God of Battles, for Success in the Righteous War. Toronto, Guardian, 1855. 25p [OTP

THE "EXPOSITION" EXPOUNDED, DEFENDED, AND SUPPLEMENTED. Toronto, Methodist Book, 1881. 159p [LC OTU

PAST AND PRESENT; or, A Description of ... Canadian Methodism for the Last
Forty Years. By a Spectator of the Scenes [pseud]. Toronto, Dredge, 1860.
331p [NSWA OTP QMM

Carry, Rev. John, 1824—1891
SERMONS, DOCTRINAL, DEVOTIONAL AND PRACTICAL. Quebec, Lovell, 1860.
202p [NSWA OTU QMM

Carter, Rev. Alexander, 1909—
ANSWERS FROM FATHER CARTER'S QUESTION BOX. Montreal, Palm Publishers,
1953. xv + 227p

Carter, Rev. Gerald Emmett, 1912—
PSYCHOLOGY AND THE CROSS. Milwaukee, Bruce Pub., 1959. xvi + 135p

Cartwright, Robert David, 1804—1843
THE FIRST AND LAST WORDS OF A PASTOR TO HIS PEOPLE. [Anon] Kingston,
Watson, 1843. 23p [OTP

Case, Rev. William, 1780—1855
JUBILEE SERMON. Toronto, Sanderson, 1855. 64p [OTU

Casey, Maurice
THE PARISH OF ST. PATRICK OF OTTAWA AND WHAT LED TO IT. An Historical
Sketch. [Anon] Ottawa, Mortimer, 1900. 103p [OOU

Caven, Rev. William, 1830—1904
CHRIST'S TEACHING CONCERNING THE LAST THINGS, AND OTHER PAPERS. [With
a biog. sketch of the Author, by James A. Macdonald.] London, Hodder, 1908.
xxxii + 328p [BM BVaU OTU
THE TESTIMONY OF CHRIST TO THE OLD TESTAMENT. Toronto, Haynes, n.d.
35p [OTU

Celebrated Astronomer, A (pseud)
PORTRAIT OF A PUSEYITE. Taken in the Moon by a Celebrated Astronomer
[pseud]. Halifax, Kirk, 1846. 24p [NSWA

Central Canada Baptist Conference
GOLDEN JUBILEE OF THE CENTRAL CANADA BAPTIST CONFERENCE. A Commemoration of Fifty Years, 1907—1957. Saskatoon, Gospel Press, [1957?]. 57p

Chalmers, Rev. Randolph Carleton, 1908—
CHALLENGE AND RESPONSE. Modern Ideas and Religion. Ed. by R.C. Chalmers
and John A. Irving. Toronto, Ryerson, 1959. 130p
A GOSPEL TO PROCLAIM. Toronto, Ryerson, 1960. x + 118p
THE LIGHT AND THE FLAME. Modern Knowledge and Religion. Ed. by R.C.
Chalmers and John A. Irving. Toronto, Ryerson, 1956. xii + 143p
THE PROTESTANT SPIRIT. Toronto, Ryerson, 1955. 90p

Champion, Thomas Edward, 1842–1910

THE ANGLICAN CHURCH IN CANADA. Toronto, Hunter Rose, 1898. 19p
[OTP

THE METHODIST CHURCHES OF TORONTO. With Biographical Sketches of many of
the Clergy and Laity. Toronto, Rose, 1899. 388p [BM OTP

Cheetham, William

CHRISTIANITY REVIEWED. Brockville, Recorder Print., 1896. 296p [BM OTP

Chiniquy, Rev. Charles Paschal Télesphore, 1809–1899

THE CHURCH OF ROME IS THE ENEMY OF THE HOLY VIRGIN AND OF JESUS
CHRIST. Trans. by Fannie Macpherson. Stratford, Maddocks, 1866. 59p
[NSHD OTP

PAPAL IDOLATRY. An Exposure of the Dogma of Transubstantiation and
Mariolatry. Chicago, Craig Press, 1889. 58p [BM NSWA QMSS

THE PERVERSION OF DR. NEWMAN TO THE CHURCH OF ROME. In the Light of
His Own Explanations, Common Sense, and the Word of God. 3rd ed.
Montreal, Witness Print., 1896. 40p [BM

PRESIDENT LINCOLN'S ASSASSINATION. Traced Directly to the Doors of Rome.
Cincinnati, Mercer, [1894?]. 46p [LC

THE PRIEST, THE WOMAN, AND THE CONFESSIONAL. London, Gibson, 1874.
192p [Also: Montreal, Grafton, 1875. 184p. Several other later eds.] [BM
BVaU NSWA OLU QMSS

Chown, Rev. Samuel Dwight, 1853–1933

SOME CAUSES OF THE DECLINE OF THE EARLIER TYPICAL EVANGELISM. Toronto,
Ryerson, 1930. 50p [OTUV

THE STORY OF CHURCH UNION IN CANADA. Toronto, Ryerson, 1930. 156p [BM
BVaU LC OTP

Church of England in Canada. Huron Diocese

HURON DIOCESE. A Jubilee Memorial. The Story of the Church [of England] and
First Fifty Years of the Diocese of Huron, 1857–1907. London, Ont., London
Print., [1907]. 122p [OLU

Church of England in Canada. Niagara Diocese

THE HISTORY OF THE DIOCESE OF NIAGARA TO 1950. Hamilton, Synod of Niagara,
1950. 98p [OONL

Churchill, Rev. Charles, fl. 1837–1879

MEMORIALS OF MISSIONARY LIFE, IN NOVA SCOTIA. London, Mason; Hamilton,
Adams; Nottingham, Dearden, 1845. 206p [BM LC NSWA OTP

Chute, Rev. Arthur Crawley, 1853–1936

THE RELIGIOUS LIFE OF ACADIA. With Chapters on its Earlier History by W.B.
Boggs. Wolfville, [Acadia U.], 1933. 249p [BVaU NBFU QMM

Clark, Rev. Howard Hewlett, 1903—
THE CHRISTIAN LIFE ACCORDING TO THE PRAYER BOOK. Toronto, Anglican
Church of Canada, 1956. 165p

Clark, John Artemas, 1878—
THE HISTORY OF FIRST BAPTIST CHURCH, CHARLOTTETOWN. Written on the
Occasion of the Opening of the new Church Edifice, Sunday, May 17, 1959.
Charlottetown, the Church, 1959. 24p

Clark, Samuel Delbert, 1910—
CHURCH AND SECT IN CANADA. Toronto, U. of Toronto Press, 1948. 458p
[BM BVaU LC NSHD OTU QMM

Clark, Rev. William Robinson, 1829—1912
THE ANGLICAN REFORMATION. New York, Christian Literature Co., 1897.
482p [BM LC OTP
THE PARACLETE. A Series of Discourses on the Person and Work of the Holy
Spirit. Toronto, Morang, 1900. 236p [BM LC OTP
PASCAL AND THE PORT ROYALISTS. Edinburgh, Clark, 1902. 235p [BM LC
OTP
THE SUFFERINGS OF CHRIST, THEIR ORIGIN, NATURE AND RESULTS. Mission
Sermons. Detroit, Young Men's Assoc. of Grace Church, 1889. 32p [LC
WITNESSES TO CHRIST. A Contribution to Christian Apologetics. Chicago,
McClurg, 1888. 300p [BM OTU

Clarke, Kathleen Margaret (Cunningham), 1905—
LETTERS TO MY HEAVENLY FATHER. Grand Rapids, Mich., Zondervan Pub.
House, 1960. 115p

Clarke, William Fletcher, 1824—1902
CANADIAN BICENTENARY PAPERS. No. I. The History of Nonconformity in
England in 1662. By W.F. Clarke. No. II. The Reasons for Nonconformity in
Canada in 1862. By Rev. F.H. Marling. Toronto, Chewett, 1862. 69p [OTP

Clayton, Hazel Maud (Snow), 1900—
HISTORY OF THE SMITHS COVE UNITED BAPTIST CHURCH. Smiths Cove, N.S.,
Author, 1957. 17p [mimeographed]

Cleaver, Solomon, 1855—1939
THE AGES ASK. ... Toronto, Mundy-Goodfellow, [1934]. 36p [BVaU OTU
AND CHRISTMAS CAME TO THE DESERT. Toronto, Mundy-Goodfellow, [1936].
29p [NBFU OTU
THE HOUSE THAT LOVE BUILT. Toronto, Mundy-Goodfellow, 1937. 32p [OTU
LIFE'S GREAT ADVENTURE, PRAYER. Toronto, Ryerson, 1931. 163p [LC OTUV
AND WE ARE THE SHEEP. Toronto, Mundy-Goodfellow, 1933. 29p [OTU

Cliffe, Albert Edward, 1892–

LESSONS IN LIVING. Practical Faith in Practice. Montreal, Author, 1949. [2nd ed., rev. and enl., London, Hodder, 1952. 152p]

Clifford, Rev. Paul Rowntree, 1913–

THE PASTORAL CALLING. London, Carey Kingsgate Press, 1959. xiii + 162p

Cochrane, Rev. William, 1831–1898

THE CHURCH AND THE COMMONWEALTH. Discussions and Orations on Questions of the Day, Practical, Biographical, Educational and Doctrinal, Written during a Twenty Years' Ministry. Brantford, Bradley Garretson, 1887. 560p [NSWA OTP

FUTURE PUNISHMENT; or, Does Death End Probation?–with Illustrative Notes from the Writings of Eminent British & American Theologians–Illus. by the celebrated French artist, Gustav Doré. Brantford, Bradley, 1886. 528p [BVaU NSWA OTU

THE HEAVENLY VISION; AND OTHER SERMONS (1863–73). ... Toronto, Adam, 1874. 367p [NSWA OTU

Coffey, John F.

THE CITY AND DIOCESE OF LONDON, ONTARIO. An Historical Sketch. ... London, Catholic Register, 1885. 78p [OLU QMBM

Cogswell, Rev. William, 1810–1847

FOUR SERMONS PREACHED ... DURING THE SEASON OF ADVENT, A.D. 1840. Halifax, Gossip & Coade, 1841. 75p [NSHD

SERMONS, CHIEFLY UPON CHAP. XVII OF ST. JOHN'S GOSPEL. ... London, Hatchard, 1839. 497p [BM NSHD

SERMONS, PREACHED IN THE PARISH CHURCH OF ST. PAUL, HALIFAX, N.S., chiefly during the year 1845. London, Nisbet, 1847. 505p [BM NSHD

SEVEN LECTURES OF THE ACTS OF THE APOSTLES, delivered in the Parish Church of St. Paul, Halifax, N.S. during the Season of Lent, A.D. 1837. Halifax, Ward, 1837. 174p [BM NSHD

Coleman, Rev. Michael Edward, 1902–

THE CROSS, THE EUCHARIST AND YOU. Toronto, Anglican Church of Canada, [1959?]. 166p

Collingwood, Ont. All Saints' Church

ONE HUNDRED YEARS OF HISTORY OF ALL SAINTS' CHURCH IN THE TOWN OF COLLINGWOOD, 1855–1955. N.p., 1955. 32p

Colquette, Richard Daniel, 1881–

ONE HUNDRED YEARS AT ST. MARK'S, UNITED CHURCH OF CANADA (FORMERLY FAIRVILLE METHODIST CHURCH) 1859–1959. Comp. by ——. Lancaster, N.B. the Church, 1959. 80p

Cook, Rev. John, 1805–1892
SERMONS PREACHED IN ST. ANDREW'S CHURCH, QUEBEC. Montreal, Dawson, 1888.
354p [NSHD OTUV QMM

Cookstown, Ont. Methodist Church
ONE HUNDRED YEARS OF METHODISM IN COOKSTOWN, 1825–1925. Cookstown,
Methodist Church, 1925. [OTU

Cooney, Rev. Robert, 1800–1870
THE GLORY OF THE GOD OF ISRAEL. Halifax, Novascotian, 1836. 34p [OTP
THE JUDGMENT SEAT OF CHRIST. A Sermon. Halifax, Cunnabell, 1838. 23p
[NSHD OTP
THE LORD IS ON OUR SIDE. ... First Anniversary of the Battle [at Odelltown].
Montreal, Campbell & Becket, 1840. 40p [NSWA OTP

Cooper, John Irwin, 1905–
THE BLESSED COMMUNION. The Origins and History of the Diocese of Montreal,
1760–1960. Montreal, the Diocese, 1960. 266p

Cordner, Rev. John, 1816–1894
A BRIEF STATEMENT OF REASONS FOR DECLINING TO RECEIVE THE DOCTRINE OF
THE TRINITY. Boston, Crosby & Nichols, 1846. 35p [BM
CHRIST, THE SON OF GOD. A Discourse in Review of the Rev. Dr. Wilkes' Sermon
entitled "Who is Christ?" ... Montreal, Potts, 1851. 28p [OTP QMSS
THE CHRISTIAN IDEA OF SACRIFICE. Montreal, Rose, 1858. 29p [BM OTU
IS PROTESTANTISM A FAILURE? The Question Considered in Five Lectures. Also
a Discourse on Christian Monotheism. Montreal, Lovell, 1869. 96p [OTP
QMU
A PASTORAL LETTER TO THE CHRISTIAN CONGREGATION ASSEMBLING FOR
WORSHIP AND EDIFICATION IN THE UNITARIAN CHURCH, MONTREAL. Montreal,
Rose, 1853. 15p [OTL
THE PHILOSOPHIC ORIGIN AND HISTORIC PROGRESS OF THE DOCTRINE OF THE
TRINITY. A Lecture delivered in the Unitarian Church, Montreal ... 1851.
Montreal, Becket, 1851. 22p [Same title: Boston, Crosby & Nichols, [1849?].
34p] [BM OTP
RIGHTEOUSNESS EXALTETH A NATION. A Discourse Concerning the Relation of
Morality to National Well-being. ... Montreal, Rose, 1860. 19p [NSWA OTUV
TWENTY-FIVE SERMONS. A Memorial of 25 Years' Ministry. Montreal, Lovell,
1868. 395p [NSWA OTP

Cormican, Leo Alphonsus, 1902–
INVITATION TO LOVE. Ottawa, Association of Mary Immaculate, 1954. 170p

Cornell, John A., 1841–
THE FIRST CHURCH OF BEVERLEY. A History and a Memorial. Toronto,
McClelland, 1921. 124p [BVaU OTU

Cornish, George Henry, 1834–1912

CYCLOPAEDIA OF METHODISM IN CANADA. Toronto, Methodist Pub. House, 1881–1903. 2v [BM BVaU NSWA MWU OTU

HAND-BOOK OF CANADIAN METHODISM. Being [a List] of all the Ministers and Preachers ... [of] Canadian Methodism. Toronto, Wesleyan Print., 1867. 238p [Later expanded as CYCLOPAEDIA OF METHODISM IN CANADA, *q.v.*] [BVaU LC NSWA OTP

Cornwall, Ont. St. Columban's Church

AN HISTORICAL SKETCH OF ST. COLUMBAN'S PARISH ... Commemorative of the Opening of the New Church, June, 1896. Cornwall, Standard Print., 1896. 36p [OTP

Cornwallis, N.S. St. John's Church

HISTORICAL SKETCH ... 1760–1910. Halifax, Macnab, [1910?]. 16p [NSWA

Coster, Rev. Frederick

THE "COMPANION TO THE PRAYER BOOK" DEFENDED AGAINST UNFOUNDED OBJECTIONS OF THE REV. J.W.D. GRAY. Saint John, 1851. [NBB

Coster, Rev. George, 1794–1859

A SERMON PREACHED IN CHRIST CHURCH, FREDERICTON. Saint John, Avery, 1842. 16p [OTU

Cowan, Hugh, 1870–1943

THE GREAT DRAMA OF HUMAN LIFE. ... Toronto, Religious Progress Assoc., 1937. 128p [NBFU OTU

Cragg, Edward, 1904–

PROTESTANT FAITH AND LIFE. Toronto, Ryerson, 1958. 58p

Craig, H.A.

ST. STEPHEN'S CHURCH, WESTMOUNT, ONE-HUNDRETH ANNIVERSARY, 1848–1948. [Anon] Westmount, The Church, 1948. 36p [OTP

Cramp, Rev. John Mockett, 1796–1881

BAPTIST HISTORY ... TO THE CLOSE OF THE 18TH CENTURY. London, Stock, 1868. 559p [BM LC NSHD OTU

CASE OF THE BAPTISTS, STATED AND EXPLAINED. ... Halifax, "Christian Messenger," 1873. 16p [NSHD

CATECHISM OF CHRISTIAN BAPTISM. ... Halifax, "Christian Messenger," 1866. 90p [NSHD

THE CENTENARY OF THE BAPTISTS IN NOVA SCOTIA. Halifax, "Christian Messenger," 1860. 30p [NSHD OTP

"FUTURE" OF THE BAPTISTS AND THEIR DUTY TO PREPARE FOR IT. A Lecture delivered at Wolfville, N.S. Halifax, Naylor, 1852. 28p [NSHD

THE GREAT EJECTMENT OF 1662. A Lecture. ... Halifax, "Christian Messenger," 1862. 40p [NSHD

LETTERS ON CHURCH RATES. Addressed to the Rev. J.E.N. Molesworth, M.A. of Canterbury. London, Wightman, 1837. 36p [BM NSHD

THE LAMB OF GOD. London, Yates, 1871. 201p [BM NSWA

PAUL AND CHRIST. A Portraiture and an Argument. London, Yates & Alexander, 1873. 198p [BM NSHD QMM

SCRIPTURE AND TRADITION. A Reply to Mr. Maturin's Letter on "The Claims of the Catholic Church." Halifax, "Christian Messenger," 1859. 64p [NSHD

THE SECOND COMING OF OUR LORD. An Essay. Halifax, "Christian Messenger," 1879. 19p [NSHD

SUCCESSION OF MARTYRS. A Sermon. ... Halifax, "Christian Messenger," 1859. 15p [NSHD

A TEXTBOOK OF POPERY. Comprising a Brief History of the Council of Trent. ... London, Holdsworth & Ball, 1831. 439p [Two later editions.] [BM NSHD OTU QMM

WHAT WILL BECOME OF THE WICKED? An Address. Halifax, "Christian Messenger." 1860. 24p [NSHP

Crawford, Alexander Wellington, 1866–1933

GERMANY'S MORAL DOWNFALL. The Tragedy of Academic Materialism. New York, Abingdon, 1919. 217p [LC OTUV QMM

Crawford, John

DEBATE ON THE POINTS OF DIFFERENCE IN FAITH AND PRACTICE BETWEEN THE TWO RELIGIOUS BODIES KNOWN AS THE DISCIPLES OF CHRIST AND THE REGULAR BAPTISTS. Held in Springfield, Elgin County, Ont. ... (Debaters: John Crawford and J.S. Sweeny). Toronto, Sheppard, 1875. 295p [OTU

Crawford, John White, 1883–

A HISTORICAL SKETCH OF GRACE PRESBYTERIAN CHURCH, CALGARY, ALBERTA. Calgary, David Print., 1935. 28p [OTU

Crawley, Rev. Edmund Albern, 1799–1888

TREATISE ON BAPTISM. ... Containing a Reply to Mr. Elder's Letters on Infant Baptism, and a solemn Appeal in Favor of a Spiritual Church. Halifax, Spike, 1835. 199p [NSHD OTUV

Creedy, Frederick, 1883–

THE NEXT STEP IN CIVILIZATION, A STAR TO STEER BY. Toronto, Ryerson, 1955. 217p

Creighton, William Black, 1864–1946

ALL IN THE DAY'S WORK. Brief Essays for Busy People. Toronto, Ryerson, 1923. 409p [BM NSHD OTP

LIFE IS LIKE THAT. Toronto, Ryerson, 1945. 254p [LC OTP

Creswicke, May (Spry), 1870–

THE HISTORY OF TRINITY CHURCH, BARRIE, ONTARIO, CANADA, 1835–1935. Comp. by Mrs. A.E.H. Creswicke. Barrie, 1935. 60p [OTP

Cridge, Edward, 1817–1913

SKETCH OF THE RISE AND PROGRESS OF METLAHKATLAH, IN THE DIOCESE OF BRITISH COLUMBIA. London, Church Missionary Soc., 1868. 16p [OTUV

Croil, James, 1821–1916

THE GENESIS OF CHURCHES IN THE UNITED STATES OF AMERICA, IN NEWFOUNDLAND AND THE DOMINION OF CANADA. Montreal, Foster Brown, 1907. 307p [BM BVaU LC NSWA OTU QMM

A HISTORICAL AND STATISTICAL REPORT OF THE PRESBYTERIAN CHURCH OF CANADA, in Connection with the Church of Scotland, for the year 1866. Montreal, Lovell, 1867. 172p [OTP

THE MISSIONARY PROBLEM. Containing a History of Protestant Missions. ... Toronto, Briggs, 1883. 224p [NSHD OTP

Cronin, Kay

CROSS IN THE WILDERNESS. Vancouver, Mitchell Press, 1960. xxiii + 255p [History of the pioneer Oblate Fathers of British Columbia.]

Cronyn, Rev. Benjamin, 1802–1871

THE BISHOP OF HURON'S OBJECTIONS TO THE THEOLOGICAL TEACHING OF TRINITY COLLEGE, WITH THE PROVOST'S REPLY. Toronto, Rowsell & Ellis, 1862. 84p [BM NSHP OTP

THE GOSPEL IN CANADA: AND ITS RELATION TO HURON COLLEGE. In Addresses by the Lord Bishop of Huron; ... Bishop of Ohio; ... Assistant Bishop of Ohio. ... With an intro. by the Rev. T.R. Birks. London, Hunt, [1865?]. 112p [OTP

Dalby, George E.

HISTORICAL MEMORANDUM, COLLEGE STREET PRESBYTERIAN CHURCH, TORONTO ... 1872–1917. Comp. by ——. Toronto, College Press, 1918. 34p [OTP

Daly, George Thomas, 1872–1956

CATHOLIC PROBLEMS IN WESTERN CANADA. Toronto, Macmillan, 1921. 352p [BM BVaU NBS OONL QMSS

Dartmouth, N.S. Christ Church

THE STORY OF CHRIST CHURCH ... SPECIALLY WRITTEN FOR THE CENTENNIAL CELEBRATION. ... Halifax, Weekes, 1917. 219p [BVaU NSWA

Dartmouth, N.S. Grace United Church

THE ONE HUNDREDTH ANNIVERSARY, GRACE UNITED CHURCH, 1853–1953. Dartmouth, the Church, 1953. 25p [mimeographed]

Davenport, Rev. John M.
MESSIAH (GOD INCARNATE), NOT MESSIAH'S MOTHER, THE "BRUISER OF THE SERPENT'S HEAD." Saint John, McMillan, 1891. 168p [NBB
PAPAL INFALLIBILITY. "Catholic's" Replies to "Cleophas." Saint John, McMillan, 1885. 106p [NBB

Davies, Trevor Hughes, 1871—
THE INNER CIRCLE. Studies in the Associates of Jesus. New York, Doran, 1924. 315p [BM LC OKQ

Davis, Rev. E.A.
COMMEMORATIVE REVIEW OF THE METHODIST, PRESBYTERIAN, AND CONGREGATIONAL CHURCHES IN BRITISH COLUMBIA. ... Comp. and pub. by Joseph Lee. Ed. by ——. Vancouver, Lee, 1925. xxxii + 380p [BVaU OTU

Davis, Rev. John, 1803?—1875
CIRCUMCISION AND BAPTISM. ... Charlottetown, Author, 1867. 24p [NSWA

Davison, Rev. William Holmes, 1884—
HE SHALL SPEAK PEACE. A Good Friday Devotion for the Three Hours Watch by the Cross. Toronto, Church of England in Canada, 1952. 54p

Dawson, Rev. Aeneas MacDonell, 1810—1894
SKETCH OF THE PARISH OF ST. MARY, ALMONTE, ONT. Almonte, 1885. [OOP

Dawson, John William, 1820—1899
ARCHAIA; or, Studies of the Cosmogony and Natural History of the Hebrew Scriptures. ... Montreal, Dawson, 1860. 406p [BM BVaU NSHD OTU
EDEN LOST AND WON. Studies of the early History and final Destiny of Man as taught in Nature and Revelation. London, Hodder, 1895. 226p [BM BVaU LC OTUV
EPISCOPAL ELECTIONS ANCIENT AND MODERN. A Study in Ecclesiastical Polity. ... Montreal, Dawson, 1877. 53p [NSHD
HISTORICAL DELUGE, IN ITS RELATION TO SCIENTIFIC DISCOVERY AND TO PRESENT QUESTIONS. New York, Revell, 1895. 56p [BM LC OTU QMBM
THE MEETING-PLACE OF GEOLOGY AND HISTORY. London, Religious Tract Soc., 1895. 223p [Also: New York, Revell, [1894].] [BM LC NSHD OTU
MODERN IDEAS OF EVOLUTION AS RELATED TO REVELATION AND SCIENCE. London, Religious Tract Soc., 1890. 240p [BM NSWA OTP QMM
MODERN SCIENCE IN BIBLE LANDS. Montreal, Dawson, 1888. 606p [BM LC NSWA OTU QMM
NATURE AND THE BIBLE. A Course of Lectures delivered in New York ... on the Morse Foundation of the Union Theological Seminary. New York, Carter, 1875. 257p [BM LC NSWA OTUV QMM
THE ORIGIN OF THE WORLD, ACCORDING TO REVELATION AND SCIENCE. Montreal, Dawson, 1877. 438p [BM BVaU NSWA OTU

POINTS OF CONTACT BETWEEN REVELATION AND NATURAL SCIENCE. London, Religious Tract Soc., [1885] . 64p [BM NSWA

THE TESTIMONY OF THE HOLY SCRIPTURES RESPECTING WINE AND STRONG DRINK. Pictou, Macdonald, 1858. 46p [3rd ed., rev.: Montreal, Grafton, 1898. 52p] [LC NSHD OTP QMM

Dawson, William Bell, 1854–

THE BIBLE CONFIRMED BY SCIENCE. London, Marshall, 1936. 159p [BM OTU

EVOLUTION CONTRASTED WITH SCRIPTURE'S TRUTH. Chicago, Bible Institute, 1926. 63p [LC

De Blois, Stephen William, 1827–1884

HISTORICAL SKETCH OF THE FIRST HORTON BAPTIST CHURCH, WOLFVILLE, for the period of one hundred years, from A.D. 1778 to A.D. 1878. Halifax, Messenger, 1879. 29p [NSHD

Delafosse, Frederick Montague, 1860–1950

CENTENARY HISTORY, ST. JOHN'S CHURCH, PETERBOROUGH, [1827–1927]. ... Peterborough, Review Press, 1927. 97p [OTP

Devine, Rev. Edward James, 1860–1927

THE CANADIAN MARTYRS. The Story of the ... Death of Eight Missionaries at the Hands of the Iroquois, 1642–1649. 2nd ed. Montreal, Canadian Messenger, 1923. 168p [3rd ed. under title: THE JESUIT MARTYRS. ...] [BVaU OOA QMBM

Dewart, Rev. Edward Hartley, 1828–1903

THE BIBLE UNDER HIGH CRITICISM. A Review of Current Evolutionary Theories about the Old Testament. Toronto, Briggs, 1900. 214p [BM NSWA OTUV

BRIEF OUTLINE OF CHRISTIAN DOCTRINE: Designed for Senior Epworth Leagues and all Bible Students. Toronto, Briggs, 1898. 67p [BM NBSaM OTUV

BROKEN REEDS; or, The Heresies of the Plymouth Brethren, shown to be Contrary to Reason and Scripture. Toronto, Wesleyan, 1869. 34p [OTP

HIGH CHURCH PRETENSIONS DISPROVED; or, Methodism and the Church of England. Toronto, Methodist Book Room, 1877. 59p [NSWA OTUV

JESUS THE MESSIAH IN PROPHECY AND FULFILMENT. A Review and Refutation of the Negative Theory of Messianic Prophecy. Toronto, Briggs, 1890. 256p [BVaU LC NSWA OTP

LIVING EPISTLES; or, Christ's Witnesses in the World, &c. &c. Toronto, Christian Guardian, 1878. 288p [OTUV

MODERN CRITICISM AND THE TEACHING OF THE OLD TESTAMENT. A brief Review of the Theories Advocated in Professor George Adam Smith's Yale Lectures. Toronto, Briggs, 1902. 32p [BM

Dezell, Robert, 1866–

LOST TRACK OF A DAY. A Stricture on Seventh Day Teaching and Sabbath Desecration. ... Owen Sound, Rutherford, 1899. 108p [BM OTUV

Dickinson, Rev. Clarence Heber, 1899—
SEVEN DAYS & THE SEVEN WORDS. Toronto, Ryerson, 1952. 54p

Dickson, James A.R., 1839—1915
"EBENEZER": A HISTORY OF THE CENTRAL PRESBYTERIAN CHURCH, GALT, ONTARIO. With Brief Sketches of Some of its Members. ... Toronto, Briggs, 1904. 394p [BM OTUV

Dorland, Arthur Garratt, 1887—
A HISTORY OF THE SOCIETY OF FRIENDS (QUAKERS) IN CANADA. Toronto, Macmillan, 1927. 343p [BM BVaU LC NSHD OTU QMM

Dougall, Lily, 1858—1923
ABSENTE REO. By the Author of "Pro Christo et Ecclesia" [pseud]. London, Macmillan, 1910. 357p [LC OTU QMM
THE CHRISTIAN DOCTRINE OF HEALTH. A Handbook on the Relation of Bodily to Spiritual and Moral Health. London, Macmillan, 1916. 197p [Also: New York, Macmillan, 1923. 181p] [BM LC OTU
CHRISTUS FUTURUS. By the Author of "Pro Christo et Ecclesia" [pseud]. London, Macmillan, 1907. 404p [Pub. in the U.S. under title: THE CHRIST THAT IS TO BE.] [BVaU LC OTU QMM
GOD'S WAY WITH MAN. ... With intro. and biog. note by Canon B.H. Streeter. London, Student Christian Movement, 1924. 123p [BM BVaU LC OTU
THE LORD OF THOUGHT. A Study of the Problems which Confronted Jesus. ... By Lily Dougall and Cyril W. Emmet. London, Student Christian Movement, 1922. 324p [BM BVaU LC OTUV
THE PRACTICE OF CHRISTIANITY. By the Author of "Pro Christo et Ecclesia" [pseud]. London, Macmillan, 1913. 291p [BM LC OTU QMM
PRO CHRISTO ET ECCLESIA. ... [Anon] London, Macmillan, 1900. 191p [Rev. ed.: 1910.] [BM BVaU LC QMM
VOLUNTAS DEI. By the Author of "Pro Christo et Ecclesia" [pseud]. London, Macmillan, 1912. 276p [QMM

Dowe, Marjorie Jean (Pierce), 1922—
144TH ANNIVERSARY, 1810—1954, THE CLEMENTSVALE UNITED BAPTIST CHURCH, CLEMENTSVALE, N.S. Clementsvale, the Church, 1954. 10p

Downer, Alfred Wallace
NOTTAWASAGA ANGLICAN CHURCHES, ONTARIO, HISTORICAL SKETCHES. Christ Church, Batteau, 1865—1935; Church of the Redeemer, Duntroon, 1875—1935; St. Paul's Church, Singhampton, 1875—1935. Comp. by ——. N.p., 1935. 58p [OTP

Driscoll, Frederick, 1834—1907
SKETCH OF THE CANADIAN MINISTRY. Montreal, 1866. 130p [NSWA OTP QMM

Duckworth, Rev. Henry Thomas Forbes, 1868–1927
THE CHURCH OF THE HOLY SEPULCHRE. Toronto, Hodder, 1922. 299p [BM BVaU OTU QMM

Duff, Louis Blake, 1878–1959
HUNDREDTH ANNIVERSARY OF TRINITY CHURCH, CHIPPEWA. The Story of the Centennial Ceremonies and the History of the Church the Past Century, 1820–1920. Welland, Tribune, [1920?]. 20p [OTU

Du Moulin, John Philip, 1836–1911
THE ETERNAL LAW. Toronto, Musson, 1903. 191p [The Slocum Lectures, 1901.] [BM LC OLU

Duncan, Jessie
MANNA FROM HEAVEN. N.p., n.d. 102p [BVaU OH
WINDOWS TOWARDS HEAVEN. N.p., n.d. 95p [OH OTUV

Duncan, B.C. St. John's Church
ANNALS OF AN UNIMPORTANT PARISH. Notes on the History of St. John's Church, Duncan, British Columbia, 1905–1956. Duncan, B.C., 1956. 17p [mimeographed]

Dunham, Bertha Mabel, 1881–1957
SO GREAT A HERITAGE. Historical Narrative of Trinity United Church [Kitchener, Ont.], 1841–1941. Ed. by ———. Kitchener, Cober Print., 1941. 70p [OTU

Eaton, Arthur Wentworth Hamilton, 1849–1937
THE CHURCH OF ENGLAND IN NOVA SCOTIA AND THE TORY CLERGY OF THE REVOLUTION. New York, Whittaker, 1891. 320p [BM BVaU LC NSHD OTU
THE HEART OF THE CREEDS: HISTORICAL RELIGION IN THE LIGHT OF MODERN THOUGHT. New York, Putnam, 1888. 200p [LC NSHD

Eaton, Rev. Charles Aubrey, 1868–1953
FOR TROUBLED HEARTS. Toronto, Poole, 1899. 130p [BM NSWA OTU
THE OLD EVANGEL AND THE NEW EVANGELISM. Chicago, Revell, 1901. 162p [BVaU LC NSWA OTU

Eby, Charles Samuel, 1845–1925
CHRISTIANITY AND HUMANITY. A Course of Lectures. ... Yokohama, Meiklejohn, 1883. 296p [BVaU LC OTP
METHODISM AND THE MISSIONARY PROBLEM. Toronto, Briggs, 1886. 66p [OTUV

Edmonton, Alta. McDougall United Church
DIAMOND JUBILEE, 1871–1931. Edmonton, 1931. 24p [AE

Elder, William, 1784–1848
INFANT SPRINKLING, Weighed in the Balance of the Sanctuary, and found wanting. In Five Letters addressed to the Rev. George Jackson. ... Halifax, Author, 1823. 56p [NSHD

Emberson, Frederick C., –1913
ARE WE IMMORTAL? Montreal, n.d. 108p [NSWA QMM

Embury, Jean Thompson (MacMillan)
HISTORY OF THE DIOCESE OF QU'APPELLE. Regina, the Diocese, 1959. 72p

Esquesing, Ont. Churchill United Church
CHURCHILL UNITED CHURCH 1838–1938. Acton, Free Press, 1938. 22p [OTU

Estabrooks, Robert Ernest, 1873–
THE HISTORY OF THE UNITED BAPTIST CHURCH AT MIDDLE SACKVILLE, 1763–1953. N.p., 1953. 15p

Eustace, Cecil John, 1903–
HOUSE OF BREAD. A Catholic Journey. Toronto, Longmans, 1943. 159p [BM BVaU LC OTP
AN INFINITY OF QUESTIONS. A Study of the Religion of Art, and of the Art of Religion in the Lives of Five Women. ... London, Dobson, 1946. 170p [BM LC OTU
MIND AND MYSTERY. A Catholic Explanation. Toronto, Longmans, 1937. 314p [BM OTU QMSS
ROMEWARDS. London, Washbourne & Bogan, 1933. 329p [BM LC OWA

Evans, Rev. Richard C., 1861–
SERMONS. London, Ont., Advertiser, 1912. 420p [BVaU OTU

Eylands, Valdimar Jonsson, 1901–
LUTHERANS IN CANADA. Winnipeg, Icelandic Evangelical Lutheran Synod, 1945. 326p [BVaU OTP

Fackenheim, Rabbi Emil Ludwig, 1916–
PATHS TO JEWISH BELIEF. A Systematic Introduction. New York, Behrman House, 1960. 157p

Fairbairn, Robert Edis, 1880–1951
APOSTATE CHRISTENDOM. London, Ken-Pax Pub. Co., n.d. 92p [BVi OTUV
AN APPEAL TO REALITY. New York, Abingdon Press, 1927. 192p [LC OTUV

Fairweather, Rev. Eugene Rathbone, 1920–
EPISCOPACY AND REUNION. By E.R. Fairweather and R.F. Hettlinger. Toronto, General Board of Religious Education of the Church of England in Canada, 1952. ix + 118p

Falconer, Rev. James William, 1868–1956

FROM APOSTLE TO PRIEST. A Study of Early Church Organization. ... Edinburgh, Clark, 1900. 292p [NSHD OTUV

THE PASSION ACCORDING TO ST. JOHN. Toronto, United Church Pub. House, 1944. 43p [LC OTU

THE THREE CROSSES. London, Hodder, 1907. 101p [NSHD OTUV

Falconer, Robert Alexander, 1867–1943

THE HEART OF THE NEW TESTAMENT. Toronto, United Church Pub. House, 1943. 46p [LC OTP

THE IDEA OF IMMORTALITY AND WESTERN CIVILIZATION. Cambridge, Mass., Harvard U. Press, 1930. 61p [BM LC OTU

THE PASTORAL EPISTLES. Introduction, Translation and Notes. Oxford, Clarendon, 1937. 164p [BVaU LC OTP

THE TRUTH OF THE APOSTOLIC GOSPEL. New York, Int'l Committee of Y.M.C.A., 1904. 148p [LC NSWA OTP

Farmer, Mary Harrington, 1905–

THE CHURCH OF THE ASCENSION, HAMILTON. A Short History, 1850–1950. Hamilton, Kinder Print. Co., 1950. 83p [OTU

Farmer, Thomas Devey Jermyn

A HISTORY OF THE PARISH OF ST. JOHN'S CHURCH, ANCASTER. With many Biographical Sketches. Guelph, Gummer Press, 1924. 304p [BVaU OTU

Farncomb, Dora, 1863–1938

THE VISION OF HIS FACE. London, Ont., Weld Co., 1909. 224p [BM LC OTUV

Fee, Norman, 1889–

KNOX PRESBYTERIAN CHURCH CENTENARY. A History of the Congregation. Ottawa, Mortimer, 1944. 78p [OTP

Ferguson, James

THE HISTORY OF ST. ANDREW'S CHURCH, BARRIE, ONTARIO, 1849–1949. Barrie, Presb. Church in Canada, 1949. 44p [UTQ'51

Ferres, James, 1905–

THE FIRST FIFTY YEARS, 1907–1957. Toronto, Anglican Church of St. Michael and All Angels, 1957. 65p

Ferrier, Rev. Andrew, –1861

CHRIST WOUNDED IN THE HOUSE OF HIS FRIENDS. A Brief Review of Proceedings in Different Courts of the Presbyterian Church of Canada. 2nd ed. Brantford, Herald, 1851. 52p [NSHD OTP

THE TOWER OF BABEL; or, Confusion in Language on Points Connected with the Question of Civil Establishments of Religion. Hamilton, Gazette, 1849. 93p [BVaU

Fischer, William Joseph, 1879–1921
THE YEARS BETWEEN. Techny, Ill., Soc. of the Divine Word, 1912. 242p [CBI MOR'12

Fitch, Ernest Robert, 1878–1935
THE BAPTISTS OF CANADA. A History of their Progress and Achievement. Ed. by E.R.F. Toronto, Standard, 1911. 304p [NSWA OTUV

Fitzgerald, Doris Marion (Chapman), 1898–
A CHRONICLE OF THE PARISH OF TRINITY CHURCH, THORNHILL, 1830–1955. Ed. by S.A.R. Wood. [Thornhill, Ont.?], 1955. 32p

Fitzroy Harbour, Ont. St. Andrew's Church
ST. ANDREW'S KIRK, 1858–1958. Fitzroy Harbour, Ont., the Church, 1958. 8p [mimeographed]

Fitzwilliam, William
THE QUODDY HERMIT; or, Conversations at Fairfield on Religion and Superstition. Boston, Dickinson, 1841. 194p [NSHD

Fleming, Rev. Archibald Lang, 1883–1953
ALL SAINTS CATHEDRAL, AKLAVIK. N.p., [1939?] 20p [OTU
A BOOK OF REMEMBRANCE; or, The History of St. John's Church. Saint John, Barnes, 1925. 416p [BM BVaU NSWA OTP
DWELLERS IN ARCTIC NIGHT. Toronto, Missionary Soc. of Church of England in Canada, 1928. 176p [BM BVaU NSWA OTU
FOR US: MEDITATIONS ON THE SEVEN WORDS FROM THE CROSS. London, Marshall, [1924]. 80p [BM NSWA

Folyard, Rev. W.
A THEOLOGICAL AND UNIVERSAL HISTORY. Describing Heaven, Earth and Hell in Panoramic Order. Saint John, Barnes, 1867. 64p [NBB

Foran, Joseph Kearney, 1857–1931
BLOSSOMS OF THE PAST, 1857–1931. Montreal, Gazette, 1935. 205p [BVaU LC NSHD OTU QMM
THE SPIRIT OF THE AGE; or, Faith and Infidelity. An Essay. Montreal, Sadlier, 1885. 184p [OTP

Forbes, Elmer Vincent, 1890–
THE STORY OF ONE HUNDRED AND FIFTY YEARS IN ST. JAMES UNITED CHURCH, ANTIGONISH, NOVA SCOTIA, 1804–1954. Antigonish, N.S., 1954. 13p [mimeographed]

Forbes, George
THE HISTORY OF ST. PETER'S PARISH (OBLATE FATHERS), NEW WESTMINSTER, B.C., 1860–1960. New Westminster, Author, 1960. 48p

Forbes, Jean (Gordon), 1880–

WIDE WINDOWS. The Story of the Woman's Missionary Society of the United Church of Canada. Toronto, United Church, 1951. 208p

Ford, Rev. John Alexander

HISTORICAL SKETCH OF THE EAST POINT BAPTIST CHURCH, P.E.I. Centennial 1833–1933. With Biographical Sketches and Account of Early Settlement. By —— and Rev. Henry George Mellick. [Kentville, N.S., Kentville Pub., 1933.] 83p [NSWA

Ford, Thomas G.

SHORT HISTORY OF ST. PAUL'S, HARBOR GRACE, PARISH (1764–1935) AND CHURCH (1835–1935). [Harbour Grace, Nfld.], Standard Print., 1935. 88p [NfSM

Forsyth, Alexander E.

REMINISCENCES OF ... THE EARLY FORMATION OF THE METHODIST CHURCH IN EASTERN ONTARIO. Cornwall, Standard, 1907. 56p [OKQ

Fortin, Rev. Octave, 1842–1927

SIXTY YEARS AND AFTER. An Historical Sketch of Holy Trinity Parish, Winnipeg. Written for the most part by the late Venerable Archdeacon Fortin. Also an Outline of Present Day Activities and Possible Future Developments, by Rev. C. Carruthers. Winnipeg, Dawson Richardson, 1928. 138p [MWP OTUV

Foulds, Elsie G.

FARRINGDON CHURCH. Its History and Background from 1833 to 1951 and the Church today. Comp. by Elsie G. Foulds and Helen M. Kippax. [Brantford, the Church], 1951. 36p

Fox, Charles James

AN HISTORICAL SKETCH OF THE PARISH OF WILMOT, 1828–1913, Diocese of Huron, Ontario. [Anon] New Hamburg, n.p., [1913]. 71p [OTU

Fox, William Sherwood, 1878–1967

A CENTURY OF SERVICE. A History of the Talbot Street Baptist Church, 1845–1945. London, Ont., Talbot Street Baptist Church, 1945. 103p [OTP

SAINT IGNACE, CANADIAN ALTAR OF MARTYRDOM. By William Sherwood Fox, with the collaboration of Wilfrid Jury. Toronto, McClelland, 1949. 175p [BVaU NBFU OTP

Franchetti, Rev. Nicolo, 1879–

A CHURCHMAN'S POCKET DICTIONARY. Toronto, General Board of Religious Education. 1959. 114p

Frankel, Rabbi Israel, 1909–
PESHAT (PLAIN EXEGESIS) IN TALMUDIC AND MIDRASHIC LITERATURE. Toronto, La Salle Press, 1956. 211p

Fraser, James MacDonell, 1882–
ST. MUNGO'S CENTENNIAL, 1836–1936. The Story of One Hundred Years at Cushing–within the Church of Scotland, the Presbyterian Church in Canada and the United Church of Canada. Cushing, Que., St. Mungo's Church, 1937. 72p [OTP

Fraser, Lennox
THE PRODIGAL FATHER. [A Sermon] Montreal, Author, 1929. [OTP QMM

Fraser, Rev. Thomas
SERMONS. Montreal, Lovell, 1867. 229p [NSHPL OTP

Fredericton, N.B. Christ Church Cathedral
CHRIST CHURCH CATHEDRAL, FREDERICTON, N.B. Fredericton, the Cathedral, 1955. 26p

Fredericton, N.B. Methodist Church
FIFTY YEARS IN THE FREDERICTON METHODIST CHURCH, and an Account in Detail of Semi-Centennial Jubilee Exercises in December, 1902. Fredericton, Herald, 1902. 74p [NSWA

Fredericton, N.B. St. Paul's Church
A CENTURY OF SERVICE. The History of St. Paul's Church, Fredericton, 1832–1932. Fredericton, [1932?]. 99p [NBFU

Freeman, John Dolliver, 1864–1943
CONCERNING THE CHRIST. New York, Armstrong, 1908. 241p [BM LC NSWA OTUV
THE EDGE OF THE AGE. London, Hodder, 1917. 288p [BM OTU NSWA
LIFE ON THE UPLANDS. An Interpretation of the Twenty-Third Psalm. Toronto, Briggs, 1906. 127p [Also: New York, Armstrong, 1907. 139p] [BM BVaU LC NSWA OTU QMM

Frerichs, Natalie H.M., 1887–
HISTORY OF TRINITY CHURCH, OTTAWA, 1876–1956. Ottawa, Trinity Church, 1956. 20p [mimeographed]

Freshman, Rev. Charles, 1819–1875
THE PENTATEUCH. Its Genuineness and Authenticity Proved and Defended against ... Bishop Colenso. Toronto, Green, 1864. 140p [OTP

Frith, Rowley Campbell, 1897–
FIRST BAPTIST CHURCH, OTTAWA, 1857–1957. By Rowley Frith and others. Ottawa, the Church, 1957. 47p

Fulford, Rev. Francis, 1803—1868

THE CONTROVERSY BETWEEN THE LORD BISHOP OF MONTREAL AND THE
VEN. ARCHDEACON HELLMUTH. London, Taylor, 1863. 16 + 26 + 75p
[Mostly replies to Fulford.] [BM OTP

SERMONS, ADDRESSES AND STATISTICS OF THE DIOCESE OF MONTREAL.
Montreal, Dawson, 1865. 308p [BM NSWA OTU QMM

Fyfe, Rev. Robert Alexander, 1816—1878

BAPTIST SENTIMENTS CONFIRMED BY THE AUTHORITY OF THE MOST LEARNED
PEDOBAPTISTS. Toronto, Globe, 1856. 28p [NSWA OTU

SUGGESTIONS TO CANADIAN BAPTIST CHURCHES, PASTORS, AND DEACONS.
Toronto, Canadian Baptist, 1866. 43p [OLU

Galbraith, J.F.

THE MENNONITES IN MANITOBA, 1875—1900. A Review of their Coming, their
Progress and their Present Prosperity. Morden, Man., Chronicle, 1900. 48p
[LC OTP

Gandier, Alfred, 1861—1932

THE DOCTRINAL BASIS OF UNION AND ITS RELATION TO THE HISTORIC CREEDS.
Toronto, Ryerson, 1926. 50p [OTUV

THE SON OF MAN COMING IN HIS KINGDOM. A Study of the Apocalyptic
Element in the Teaching of Jesus. New York, Doran, 1922. 154p [BVaU
LC OTUV

Ganges, Salt Spring Island, B.C. St. Mark's Church

ST. MARK'S CHURCH, PARISH OF SALT SPRING ISLAND. Ganges, B.C., 1952. 12p

Gant, Mrs. Sophia, 1891—

BLESSINGS GALORE. Proven Treasures of Wisdom. New York, Pageant Press,
1959. 84p

Garland, Rev. Peter Bernard, 1923—

THE DEFINITION OF SACRAMENT ACCORDING TO SAINT THOMAS. Ottawa,
U. of Ottawa Press, 1959. x + 115p

Garstin, Lawrence Hamilton, 1918—

EACH AGE IS A DREAM. A Study in Ideologies. Toronto, Ryerson, 1953.
xi + 143p

Gaynor, Rev. William Cleophas, 1855—

PAPAL INFALLIBILITY. Letters of "Cleophas." Saint John, McMillan, 1885.
104p [NSHD

Geddes, Rev. John Gamble, 1811—1891

THE MINISTERIAL CHARACTER. A Sermon. Toronto, Rowsell, 1857. 18p
[NSWA OTP

Gedye, Frank William, 1881–
AN HISTORICAL SKETCH OF THE PARISH OF BROME. Granby, Que., Simms
  Print., 1952. 48p

Geikie, John Cunningham, 1824–1906
THE ENGLISH REFORMATION. How It Came About, and Why We Should Uphold
  It. New York, Appleton, 1879. 512p [BM LC OTUV QMM
HOURS WITH THE BIBLE; or, The Scriptures in the Light of Modern Knowledge.
  An entirely new ed., rev. throughout and largely rewritten. ... New York,
  Pott, 1893. 6v [Earlier ed.: London, Partridge, 1881.] [BM BVaU LC
  OTUV
THE LIFE AND WORDS OF CHRIST. New York, Appleton, 1879. 2v [BM BVaU
  LC OTU
OLD TESTAMENT CHARACTERS. New York, Pott, 1888. 484p [BM LC

George, Rev. James, 1801?–1870
CHRIST CRUCIFIED. A Sermon. ... Toronto, Coates, 1837. 27p [OTP
THE DUTIES OF SUBJECTS TO THEIR RULERS. With a Special View to the
  Present Times. A Sermon. Toronto, Coates, 1838. 32p [NSWA OTP
THOUGHTS ON HIGH THEMES. Being a Collection of Sermons. Toronto,
  Campbell, 1874. 262p [OTU

Gifford, Rev. William Alva, 1877–1960
THE SEEKERS. A Mirror for Orthodoxy. London, Skeffington, 1955. 256p
  [First pub. Boston, Beacon Press, 1954, under title: *The Seekers: Why Christian
  Orthodoxy is Obsolete.*]
THE STORY OF THE FAITH. A Survey of Christian History for the Undogmatic.
  New York, Macmillan, 1946. 622p [BM BVaU LC NBFU OTP

Gillies, Rev. Archibald C., 1834–1887
POPERY DISSECTED. Its Absurd, Inhuman, Unscriptural, Idolatrous and Anti-
  christian Assumptions, Principles and Practices Exposed from its own Standard
  Works. ... Pictou, Harris, 1874. 83p [NSHD OTP

Gilmour, Rev. George Peel, 1900–
THE MEMOIRS CALLED GOSPELS. Toronto, Clarke Irwin, 1959. x + 299p

Glanford, Ont. St. Paul's Church
ST. PAUL'S CHURCH, (ANGLICAN), GLANFORD, ONTARIO. 100th Anniversary,
  July 1st, 1951. Glanford, Ont., 1951. 11p

Glover, George Henry Wilson, 1881–
HISTORY OF THE UNITED CHURCH OF CANADA, NORTH AND SOUTH SAANICH
  AREAS. Saanichton, B.C., Author, 1956. 35p

Glover, Terrot Reaveley, 1869–1943
DEMOCRACY AND RELIGION. Sackville, Mount Allison Univ., 1932. 108p [BVaU
  NSHD OTU

Goodspeed, Rev. Calvin, 1842–1912

BAPTISM VERSUS RANTISM. ... A Reply to the Misstatements and Fallacies of Rev. W.A. McKay. Woodstock, "Times" Office, 1880. 46p [NSHD OTU

THE MESSIAH'S SECOND ADVENT. A Study in Eschatology. Toronto, Briggs, 1900. 288p [BM OTUV

PECULIAR PRINCIPLES OF THE BAPTISTS. ... Toronto, Dudley & Burns, 1876. 43p [NSHD OTU

Gordon, Rev. Charles William, 1860–1937

THE ANGEL AND THE STAR. By Ralph Connor [pseud]. Toronto, Westminster, 1908. 24p [BM BVaU LC OTU

CHRISTIAN HOPE. By Ralph Connor [pseud]. London, Hodder, 1912. 31p [BM SSU

THE DAWN BY GALILEE. A Story of the Christ. By Ralph Connor [pseud]. London, Hodder, 1909. 30p [BM BVaU LC NBFU OTU

A FIGHT FOR FREEDOM. By Ralph Connor [pseud]. Toronto, McClelland, 1917. 13p [BM

THE RECALL OF LOVE. A Message of Hope. By Ralph Connor [pseud]. London, Hodder, 1910. 23p [BM BVaU LC OTU

Graham, Rev. Hugh, 1758–1829

THE RELATION AND RELATIVE DUTIES OF PASTOR AND PEOPLE, ILLUSTRATED IN TWO SERMONS. Halifax, 1799. [BibC

SERMONS AND ADDRESSES. Halifax, 1799. [DCB

Graham, William Creighton, 1887–1955

THE MEANING OF THE CROSS. Toronto, Ryerson, 1923. 100p [BVaU OKQ

Grant, Rev. George Monro, 1835–1902

REFORMERS OF THE NINETEENTH CENTURY. Halifax, Bowes, 1867. 32p [NSWA

THE RELIGIONS OF THE WORLD. New York, Revell, [1894?]. 137p [Also: London, Black, 1911. 137p] [BM BVaU OTP QMM

Grant, Rev. John Webster, 1919–

THE SHIP UNDER THE CROSS. Toronto, Ryerson, 1960. 106p

WORLD CHURCH. Achievement or Hope? Toronto, United Church Pub. House, 1956. 51p

Gray, Rev. Archibald

SERMON, PREACHED ON 10TH AUGUST 1804: The Day Appointed, by Government, for a General Fast. ... Halifax, Howe, 1804. 38p [NSHD

Gray, Rev. John William Dering, 1797–1868

A BRIEF VIEW OF THE SCRIPTURAL AUTHORITY AND HISTORICAL EVIDENCE OF INFANT BAPTISM. Halifax, Cunnabell, 1837. 308p [NSWA OTUV

A LETTER TO MEMBERS OF THE CHURCH OF ENGLAND IN REPLY TO A LETTER FROM EDWARD MATURIN. ... Saint John, McMillan, 1859. 124p [NSHP OTUV

A REPLY TO THE REV. F. COSTER'S DEFENCE OF THE "COMPANION TO THE PRAYER BOOK." ... Saint John, McMillan, 1849. 48p [NSHP

A REPLY TO THE STATEMENT OF THE REV. MR. WIGGINS. Saint John, McMillan, 1851. 48p [NSHP OTP

A SERMON PREACHED AT TRINITY CHURCH IN THE PARISH OF SAINT JOHN, N.B., AND DESIGNED TO RECOMMEND THE PRINCIPLES OF THE LOYALISTS OF 1783. Saint John, Macmillan, 1857. 15p [OTU

Greene, Rev. David Leslie, 1883–

AN HISTORICAL SKETCH, CHRIST CHURCH, THE PAS, MANITOBA. N.p., 1931. 24p [OORD SSU

Gregg, William, 1817–1909

HISTORY OF THE PRESBYTERIAN CHURCH IN THE DOMINION OF CANADA. From the Earliest Times to 1834. Toronto, Presbyterian Print., 1885. 646p [BVaU LC NSWA OTU QMM

SHORT HISTORY OF THE PRESBYTERIAN CHURCH IN THE DOMINION OF CANADA FROM THE EARLIEST TO THE PRESENT TIME. Toronto, Robinson, 1892. 248p [BVaU LC NBFU OTP

Grenfell, Wilfred Thomason, 1865–1940

THE ADVENTURE OF LIFE. Being the William Belden Noble Lectures for 1911. Boston, Houghton, 1912. 157p [BM BVaU LC OLU QMM

THE FISHERMEN'S SAINT. New York, Scribner, 1930. 56p [BM LC OTUV

A LABRADOR LOGBOOK. Boston, Little Brown, 1938. 372p [Another ed., London, Hodder, 1939.] [BM BVaU LC OTUV

A MAN'S FAITH. Boston, Pilgrim, 1908. 48p [New ed., 1926. 87p] [BM LC OTU QMM

A MAN'S HELPERS. Boston, Pilgrim, 1910. 76p [LC

ON IMMORTALITY. Boston, Pilgrim, 1912. 35p [BM LC

THE PRIZE OF LIFE. Boston, Pilgrim, 1914. 32p [LC

RELIGION IN EVERYDAY LIFE. Chicago, American Library Assoc., 1926. 30p [BVa LC

WHAT CAN JESUS CHRIST DO WITH ME. Boston, Pilgrim, 1912. 26p [LC

WHAT CHRIST MEANS TO ME. Boston, Houghton, 1927. 81p [Another ed., London, Hodder, 1926.] [BM BVaU LC OTU QMM

WHAT LIFE MEANS TO ME. Boston, Pilgrim, 1910. 32p [BM LC OLU

WHAT THE CHURCH MEANS TO ME. A Frank Confession and a Friendly Estimate by an Insider. Boston, Pilgrim, 1911. 36p [BVa LC

WHAT WILL YOU DO WITH JESUS CHRIST. Boston, Pilgrim, 1910. 30p [LC

Griffith, Rev. Arthur Leonard, 1920–

THE ROMAN LETTER TODAY. Toronto, Ryerson, 1959. 77p

Guelph, Ont. St. George's Church
HISTORY OF ST. GEORGE'S PARISH, GUELPH, ONT., 1832–1932. Guelph, Gummer,
1932. 91p [OTU

Gunn, Rev. William Thomas, 1867–1930
HIS DOMINION. ... Toronto, Canadian Council of the Missionary Education
Movement, 1917. 269p [BM BVaU NSHD OTP
HOMELY HOMILIES. New York, Smith, 1930. 147p [LC OTUV

Hague, Rev. Dyson, 1857–1935
THE CHURCH OF ENGLAND BEFORE THE REFORMATION. With an Introductory
Note by H.C. Moule. London, Thynne, 1897. 399p [BM OTU
THE CHURCH OF ENGLAND, THE CENTRE OF UNITY. ... Halifax, Morton, 1892.
86p [NSHD
THE HIGHER CRITICISM. Toronto, Evangelical Pub., 1923. 36p [OTP
THE PROTESTANTISM OF THE PRAYER BOOK. ... Toronto, Bryant, 1890. 171p
[BM NSHD OTUV
THROUGH THE PRAYER BOOK. An Exposition of its Teaching and Language,
the Origins and Contents of its Services; with Special Reference to the more
Recent Features of the Canadian Prayer Book. London, Longmans, 1932.
399p [BM BVaU LC OTU
ST. ANDREW'S WORK. ... Halifax, Halloway, n.d. 86p [NSWA
THE STORY OF THE ENGLISH PRAYER BOOK, its Origin and Developments. With
Special Chapters on the Scottish, Irish, American, and Canadian Prayer Books.
London, Longmans, 1926. 279p [BM BVa LC OTU QMM
WHO ARE THE HIGHER CRITICS? Priv. pub., 1910. 36p [OTU

Haig, Kennethe Macmahon
WHAT MEAN THESE STONES. Story of Old Kildonan Church. Winnipeg, the Church,
1951. 33p

Hall, Samuel
SCIENCE AND THEOLOGY. ... The Creator and the Created. ... Hamilton, Author,
1875. 60p [Haight Pt I

Hall, Rev. William Lashley, −1947
THE CONTINUITY OF REVELATION. Toronto, Briggs, 1908. 197p [BM BVaU
OTUV

Hallam, William Thomas Thompson, 1878–1956
THE VICTORY OF FAITH. A Study in Christian Missions. Toronto, Church of
England in Canada, 1952. 94p

Hamilton, Kenneth Morrison, 1917–
THE PROTESTANT WAY. London, Epworth Press, 1956. 264p

Hamilton, Margaret Lillian, 1909—
IS SURVIVAL A FACT? Winnipeg, Free Press, 1957. 35p

Hamilton, Ont. Westdale United Church
ANNIVERSARY SERVICES, 25 YEARS, 1930—1955. Hamilton, the Church, 1955. 18p

Harding, J.A.
DEBATE ON BAPTISM, EMBRACING MODE AND SUBJECTS. Between Elder J.A.
Harding, and Rev. T.L. Wilkinson. Held in Meaford, Ont., Commencing
December 15th, 1884 ... stenographically reported. Toronto, Briggs, 1886. 406p
[OKQ

Harman, H.M.
THE STORY OF THE CHURCH OF ST. GEORGE THE MARTYR [ANGLICAN] OF
TORONTO [1845—1945].Comp. by H.M. Harman and W.G. Upshall. Toronto,
Rous & Mann, 1945. 52p [OOA

Harris, John
THE BIBLE READ BY THE LIGHT OF IDEAL SCIENCE. By Kuklos (J.H.) [pseud].
Montreal, 1874. 26p [BM QMM
THE LIFE OF THE REV. FRANCIS METHERALL AND THE HISTORY OF THE BIBLE
CHRISTIAN CHURCH IN PRINCE EDWARD ISLAND. London, Bible Christian
Book, 1883. n.p. [NSWA OTUV

Harris, Rev. Joseph Hemington, 1800—1881
A SERMON ... IN AID OF THE SUNDAY SCHOOL SOCIETY. ... York, Stanton,
[1833?]. 23p [OTP

Harris, Reginald Vanderbilt, 1881—
THE CHURCH OF SAINT PAUL IN HALIFAX, NOVA SCOTIA, 1749—1949. Toronto,
Ryerson, 1949. 310p [BVaU NSHD OTP QMM

Harris, Rev. William Richard, 1847—1923
THE CATHOLIC CHURCH IN THE NIAGARA PENINSULA, 1626—1895. Toronto,
Briggs, 1895. 352p [BM BVaU LC NSHD OTU
THE CROSS-BEARERS OF THE SAGUENAY. Toronto, Dent, 1920. 202p [BVaU
LC NBFU OOA
ESSAYS IN OCCULTISM, SPIRITISM, AND DEMONOLOGY. Toronto, McClelland,
1919. 181p [BM LC NSHD OOU
HISTORY OF THE EARLY MISSIONS IN WESTERN CANADA. Toronto, Hunter Rose,
1893. 339p [BVaU LC NBFU OTP
PIONEERS OF THE CROSS IN CANADA. Toronto, McClelland, 1912. 240p [A
3rd ed.: Toronto, 1930.] [BVaU LC NSWA OLU

Hart, Lewis Alexander, 1847—
A JEWISH REPLY TO CHRISTIAN EVANGELISTS. New York, Bloch, 1906. 239p
[BM LC QMM

Hart, Walter T., 1868–1948

SIXTY-THREE YEARS OF UNINTERRUPTED SERVICE: FORT ROUGE METHODIST
   CHURCH, 1883–1925; ... CRESCENT-FORT ROUGE UNITED CHURCH, 1935–1945:
   Historical Sketch. Winnipeg, Bishop Print., 1947. 91p [OTU

Hartley, Rev. G.A.

IMMORTALITY VERSUS ANNIHILATION. Saint John, Barnes, 1867. 53p [NBB

Harvey, Rev. Moses, 1820–1901

LECTURES ON EGYPT AND ITS MONUMENTS, AS ILLUSTRATIVE OF SCRIPTURE. ...
   St. John's, McConnan, 1857. 95p [NSHD

LECTURES ON THE HARMONY OF SCIENCE AND REVELATION. ... Halifax, Barnes,
   1856. 104p [NSHD

Hawkins, Ernest, 1802–1868

ANNALS OF THE DIOCESE OF FREDERICTON. London, S.P.C.K., 1847. 74p [BM
   BVaU NSWA OTU QMM

ANNALS OF THE DIOCESE OF QUEBEC. London, S.P.C.K., 1848–1849. 2v [BM
   BVaU NSWA OTU QMM

ANNALS OF THE DIOCESE OF TORONTO. London, S.P.C.K., 1848. 246p [BVaU
   NSWA OTP

DOCUMENTS RELATIVE TO THE ERECTION AND ENDOWMENT OF ADDITIONAL
   BISHOPRICS IN THE COLONIES. ... Ed. by ——. London, Rivington, etc., 1844.
   xxxi + 62p [BM OTP

HISTORICAL NOTICES OF THE MISSIONS OF THE CHURCH OF ENGLAND IN THE
   NORTH AMERICAN COLONIES. ... London, Fellowes, 1845. 447p [BM NSWA
   OTU QMM

Heeney, Rev. William Bertal, 1873–1955

CENTENARY ADDRESSES & SERMONS. Collected & Arranged. ... The Rupert's
   Land Celebration Held in Winnipeg, October 10th to 17th, 1920. N.p.,
   n.pub., n.d. 127p [BViPA SSU

EVOLUTION AND RELIGION. Winnipeg, Laymen of St. Luke's, [1927?]. 76p
   [OKQ

LEADERS OF THE CANADIAN CHURCH. Ed. by ——. Toronto, Musson, 1918.
   319p [2nd series, 1920; 3rd series, 1943.] [BM BVaU LC NSWA OKQ QMM

SECRET OF POWER. Addresses on the Holy Spirit. Toronto, Ryerson, 1944. 38p
   [BVi OTP

WHAT OUR CHURCH STANDS FOR. The Anglican Church in Canadian Life. By
   William Bertal Heeney [and others]. Toronto, McClelland, 1932. 292p [BVa
   OTP

Hendel, Charles William, 1890–

CIVILIZATION AND RELIGION. An Argument about Values in Human Life. The
   Rockwell Lectures on Religion at the Rice Institute. ... New Haven, Yale U.
   Press, 1948. 78p [BM BVi LC NBFU QMM

Henderson, George A.

EARLY SAINT JOHN METHODISM AND HISTORY OF CENTENARY METHODIST
CHURCH, SAINT JOHN, N.B. A Jubilee Souvenir. Ed. by ———. Saint John, Day,
1890. 176p [NBFU

Hendy, Rev. Albert Edward, 1905–

ST. PAUL'S CHURCH, NANAIMO, B.C. A Brief History since its Foundation, 1859–
1952. Nanaimo, St. Paul's Church, 1953. 36p

Herklots, Rev. Hugh Gerard Gibson, 1903–

AMSTERDAM 1948. An Account of the First Assembly of the World Council of
Churches. London, S.C.M. Press, 1948. 88p [BM LC NSHD

THESE DENOMINATIONS. An Informal Introduction. ... London, S.C.M. Press,
1946. 143p [BM NSHD OTUV

THE EPISTLE OF ST. PAUL TO THE PHILIPPIANS. A Devotional Commentary.
London, Lutterworth, 1946. n.p. [BM OTUV

A FRESH APPROACH TO THE NEW TESTAMENT. London, S.C.M. Press, 1950.
n.p. [BM BVaU OTUV

HOW THE CHURCHES ARE UNITING. London, S.P.C.K., 1943. 29p [BM LC

PILGRIMAGE TO AMSTERDAM. By H.G.G. Herklots and Henry Smith Leiper.
New York, Morehouse-Gorham, 1947. 90p [BM LC

PIONEER DAYS IN THE WESTERN CHURCH. N.p., 1933. 24p [NSWA OKQ

Herridge, Rev. William Thomas, 1857–1929

THE COIGN OF VANTAGE. New York, Revell, 1908. 160p [BM QMM

THE ORBIT OF LIFE. Studies in Human Experience. New York, Revell, 1906.
147p [BM NSHD OKQ

Herzer, John E.

HOMESTEADING FOR GOD. The Story of the Lutheran Church (Missouri Synod)
in Alberta and British Columbia. Edmonton, Commercial Print., [1946?]. 70p
[ACG

Hezzelwood, Oliver, 1861–1933

TRINITY WAR BOOK. ... A Partial Description of Various War Efforts Participated
in by the People of the Trinity Methodist Church, Toronto, Containing One
Hundred New Stories from the War Front. ... Toronto, Trinity Methodist
Church, 1921. 368p [BM BVa OTU

Hill, Rev. George William, 1824–1906

LETTER TO THE PARISHIONERS OF ST. PAUL'S, HALIFAX. Halifax, Macnab &
Shaffer, 1866. 48p [BM NSHD

RECORDS OF THE CHURCH OF ENGLAND IN RAWDON FROM ITS ORIGIN UNTIL
THE PRESENT DATE. Halifax, Bowes, 1858. 28p [NSHP

RECORDS OF THE CHURCH OF ENGLAND IN NEWPORT, FROM ITS ORIGIN UNTIL
THE PRESENT DATE. Halifax, Bowes, 1858. 22p [NSHP

REVIEW OF THE RISE AND PROGRESS OF THE CHURCH OF ENGLAND IN NOVA
SCOTIA. Halifax, King's College Alumni, 1858. 33p [NSWA

Hill, Hamnett Pinhey, 1876–1942

HISTORY OF CHRIST CHURCH CATHEDRAL, OTTAWA, 1832–1932. Ottawa, Runge
Press, 1932. 122p [OTP

Hill, Rev. James Edgar, 1842–1911

QUEEN CHARITY, AND OTHER SERMONS. Montreal, 1890. 415p [BVaU OTUV
QMM

Hill, Philip Carteret, 1821–1894

DRIFTING AWAY. London, Bemrose, 1885. 46p [BM NSHD

Hirschfelder, Jacob Maier, 1819–1902

BIBLICAL EXPOSITOR AND PEOPLE'S COMMENTARY. 2v Vol 1, Introduction.
History of Hebrew Literature. Vol 2, Commentary on Genesis. Toronto,
Rowsell, 1882–5. [OTU

THE CREATION. Being Two Lectures on the Mosaic Account. ... Toronto,
Rowsell, 1874. 75p [NSHP

THE SCRIPTURES DEFENDED. Being a Reply to Bishop Colenso's Book on the
Pentateuch and the Book of Joshua. Toronto, Rowsell, 1863. 215p [OTP

Hodgins, John George, 1821–1912

HISTORICAL SKETCH OF THE DIOCESE OF TORONTO, 1839–1889. By J.G. Hodgins
and Henry Scadding. N.p., n.d. 28p [OTU

Hofer, Peter, 1885–

THE HUTTERIAN BRETHREN AND THEIR BELIEFS. Starbuck, Man., Hutterian
Brethren of Manitoba, 1955. 48p

Hominuke, J.

A CENTENARY OF UKRAINIAN BAPTISTS. A Century of Struggle and Martyrdom
for the "Faith once delivered to the Saints." Winnipeg, Ukrainian Evangelical-
Baptist Alliance, 1952. 32p

Hopewell, N.S. Union (Presbyterian) Church

HISTORY OF HOPEWELL UNION (PRESBYTERIAN) CHURCH [Pictou, N.S.] N.p.,
n.p., 1921. 23p [NSWA

Hopper, Jane (Agar), –1922

OLD-TIME PRIMITIVE METHODISM IN CANADA (1829–1884). By Mrs. R.P. Hopper.
Toronto, Briggs, 1904. 336p [BM BVaU LC NBFU OKQ

Hopper, John Elisha Peck, 1841–1895

ECCE AGNUS DEI. A Reply to ECCE HOMO. Saint John, "Christian Visitor,"
1879. [NBB

1492–1892; or, Four Hundred Years of Progress. Halifax, "Herald," 1894. [NBB
RECOGNITION OF FRIENDS IN HEAVEN. Saint John, "Progress," 1894. 100p
[NBB

Hordern, Rev. William Edward, 1920–
THE CASE FOR A NEW REFORMATION THEOLOGY. Philadelphia, Westminster
Press, 1959. 176p
CHRISTIANITY, COMMUNISM, AND HISTORY. Nashville, Tenn., Abingdon Press,
1954. 174p

Horner, Ralph Cecil, 1854–1921
ORIGINAL AND INBRED SIN. Ottawa, Crain, 1896. 148p [BM OLU
PENTECOST. Toronto, Briggs, 1891. 143p [Ryerson Impt

Hoskin, Mary
HISTORY OF ST. BASIL'S PARISH, ST. JOSEPH ST., TORONTO. Toronto, Catholic
Register, 1912. 172p [OTU

Hotson, Zella May, 1893–
PIONEER BAPTIST WORK IN OXFORD COUNTY. Woodstock, Commercial, 1939.
52p [OTP

Howley, Rev. Michael Francis, 1843–1914
ECCLESIASTICAL HISTORY OF NEWFOUNDLAND. Boston, Doyle & Whittle, 1888.
426p [BM BVaU LC NSWA OOA

Howse, Rev. Ernest Marshall, 1902–
THE LAW AND THE PROPHETS. A Series of Sermons on the Making of the Old
Testament. Toronto, Ryerson, 1947. 69p [LC OTU
THE LIVELY ORACLES. London, Allen & Unwin; Toronto, Nelson, 1956. 224p
OUR PROPHETIC HERITAGE. Toronto, Ryerson, 1945. 66p [LC NSHD OTP

Hubicz, Rev. Edward Michael, 1912–
THE HISTORY OF OUR LADY OF THE LAKE CHURCH, WINNIPEG BEACH, MANITOBA,
1911 TO 1956. An Historical Study of the Founding of a Church and of its
Development over a Period of Forty-Five Years. Winnipeg, 1956. 49p

Huestis, Rev. Charles Herbert, 1863–1951
SUNDAY IN THE MAKING. A Historical & Critical Study of the Sabbath Principle
in Inheritance and Development. New York, Abingdon Press, 1929. 256p [LC
OTUV

Hughes, James Laughlin, 1846–1935
SKETCHES OF THE SHARON TEMPLE AND OF ITS FOUNDER, DAVID WILLSON.
Toronto, Federal Print., [1918?]. 16p [OTU

Humbert, Stephen, 1768?–1849
THE RISE AND PROGRESS OF METHODISM, IN THE PROVINCE OF NEW BRUNSWICK
... UNTIL ... 1805. Saint John, Durant, 1836. 43p [NBB

Humphrey, W.H.
THE SABBATH. A Moral and Positive Institution. Being Two Sermons. ... Halifax, "Christian Messenger," 1860. 32p [NSHD

Hunter, Alexander Jardine, 1868—1940
A FRIENDLY ADVENTURE. The Story of the United Church Mission among New Canadians at Teulon, Manitoba. Toronto, United Church, 1929. 145p [BViPA MWP OTUV

Hunter, James Hogg, 1890—
THE BOW IN THE CLOUD. Toronto, Evangelical Pub., 1948. 154p [CC
THE GREAT DECEPTION. Toronto, Evangelical Pub., 1945. 126p [CC
THINE IS THE KINGDOM. Toronto, Evangelical Pub., 1951. 288p

Hunter, Rev. William John, 1835—1911
THE PLEASURE DANCE IN ITS RELATION TO RELIGION AND MORALITY. A Sermon Preached in the Bloor Street Methodist Church. ... Toronto, Methodist Book, 1881. 26p [OTUV

Huntsman, Archibald Gowanlock, 1883—
LIFE AND THE UNIVERSE. Toronto, Distributed by U. of Toronto Press Book Dept., [c1959]. x + 112p

Hutchinson, Rev. Daniel Falloon
AN ASTRONOMICAL PHILOSOPHY; or, The Study of the Heavens Made Easy. Kingston, Author, 1855. 146p [OTUV
THE GOOD OLD WAY. A Discourse on the Nature, Importance and Subjects of Christian Baptism. ... Halifax, Macnab & Shaffer, 1864. 40p [NSHD OTP

Hutchison, Rev. Harry, 1923—
THE CHURCH AND SPIRITUAL HEALING. Foreword by the Very Rev. Geo. Johnstone Jeffrey. London, Rider, 1955. 164p
A FAITH TO LIVE BY. Natick, Mass., Wilde Co., 1959. 92p

Hutton, Samuel King, 1877—
BY PATIENCE AND THE WORD. The Story of the Moravian Missions. London, Hodder, 1935. 252p [LC OTUV NSHPL

Inglis, Rev. Charles, 1734—1816
A VINDICATION OF THE BISHOP OF LANDAFF'S SERMON FROM THE GROSS MIS-REPRESENTATIONS, AND ABUSIVE REFLECTIONS CONTAINED IN MR. WILLIAM LIVINGSTON'S LETTER TO HIS LORDSHIP. ... By a Lover of Truth and Decency [pseud]. New York, Holt, 1768. 82p [LC

Inglis, Rev. David, 1825—1877
RIGHTEOUSNESS EXALTETH A NATION. ... Hamilton, "Spectator," 1866. 14p [NSWA OTP

SYSTEMATIC THEOLOGY IN ITS RELATION TO MODERN THOUGHT. A Lecture
delivered at Knox College. Toronto, Adam, 1870. 23p [NSWA

Inglis, Rev. John, 1777–1850
THE JUDGEMENT SEAT OF CHRIST. A Sermon. ... Halifax, Royal Gazette, [1835?].
20p [BM LC

Ingraham, Mary (Kinley), 1874–1949
SEVENTY-FIVE YEARS. Historical Sketch of the United Baptist Women's Missionary
Union. Kentville, N.S. [1947?]. 68p [NBFL

Innes, Rev. Thomas Christie, 1909–
BATTLE-TESTED RELIGION. New York, American Tract Soc., 1944. 191p [LC
CHRISTIAN AND SOLDIER. Toronto, Nelson, 1939. 12p [OTU
LOVE'S BLEEDING HEART. Radio and Other Messages. Toronto, Thorn Press,
1942. 142p [LC

Irving, Rev. George Clerk, –1866
PARISH, SCHOOL, AND COLLEGE SERMONS. [With a memoir of the author's life
by the Rev. George Whitaker.] Montreal, Lovell, 1867. 236p [BVaU NSWA
OLU QMSS

Irwin, William Andrew, 1884–
THE OLD TESTAMENT. Keystone of Human Culture. New York, Schuman, 1952.
293p

Ivison, Ernest Hauber Stuart, 1906–
THE BAPTISTS IN UPPER AND LOWER CANADA BEFORE 1820. By Stuart Ivison and
Fred Rosser. Toronto, U. of Toronto Press, 1956. 193p

Jack, David Russell, 1864–1913
HISTORY OF SAINT ANDREW'S CHURCH, SAINT JOHN, N.B. Saint John, Barnes, 1913.
407p [BVaU NBFU OTP QMM

Jackson, Alan Bart, 1894–
FOR CHRISTIANS ONLY. Simcoe, Ont., 1959. ix + 107p

Jackson, Rev. William
THE PORTRAIT OF THE REV. THOMAS TAYLOR; or, The Hypocrite Unmasked.
Halifax, Blackadar, 1835. 27p [NSWA
MAN OF SORROWS; or, The Providence of God Displayed. ... Balt, Wooddy, 1834.
339p [NSHD

Jackson, William, 1840–1915
IMMORTALITY VERSUS ANNIHILATION. An Inquiry Concerning the Nature and
Destiny of the Human Soul. Montreal, Grafton, 1872. 252p [OTP

Jacob, Rev. Edwin, 1795?–1868
SERMONS. Intended for the Propagation of the Gospel. Fredericton, Simpson, 1835. 164p [BM NSWA

James, Percy
A HISTORY OF ST. MARY'S CHURCH, OAK BAY, VICTORIA, B.C. Victoria, Parker Buckle, n.d. 28p [BViPA

Jameson, John
FROM WENTWORTH MISSION TO ST. ANDREWS CHURCH, 1856–1935. Hamilton, Modern Printery, 1935. 68p [OTU

Jamieson, Mrs. R.E. and Smith, W.H.
THE FIRST TEN YEARS. A Brief History of Shaughnessy Heights United Church up to November 30, 1937. [Anon] Vancouver, The Church, 1938. 15p [BViPA OTU

Janzen, Jacob H.
TALES FROM MENNONITE HISTORY. Waterloo, Ont., Author, 1945. 96p [OTP

Jaques, G.E.
CHRONICLES OF THE ST. JAMES ST. METHODIST CHURCH, MONTREAL. Toronto, Briggs, 1888. 116p [BVaU OTU

Jarvis, Thomas Stinson, 1854–1926
THE ASCENT OF LIFE; or, The Psychic Laws and Forces in Nature. Boston, Arena, 1894. 120p [LC
THE PRICE OF PEACE. Los Angeles, Rowny Press, 1921. 126p [LC

Jefferson, Rev. Robert, 1881–
FAITH OF OUR FATHERS. The Story of the Diocese of Ottawa. About the Building of the Diocese by the Right Reverend Robert Jefferson and about the People and their Churches by Leonard L. Johnson. Ottawa, Anglican Book Society, 1957. 230p

Jelfs, George Frederick
COMMENTARIES ON SIN. Boston, Sherman French, 1910. 105p [LC
MAN'S NATURAL, MORAL AND SOCIAL DUTIES. Words of Wisdom and Good Counsel, Selected ... from the Writings and Sayings of Eminent Authors, Ancient and Modern. Ed. by ——. Hamilton, Cloke's Bookstore, 1925. 227p [OTU
THE TRUE OBJECT OF LIFE. Hamilton, Spectator, 1906. 215p [BM OTU

Jenkins, Rev. John, 1813–1898
A PROTESTANT'S APPEAL TO THE DOUAY BIBLE, and Other Roman Catholic Standards, in Support of the Doctrines of the Reformation. Montreal, Wesleyan Book, 1853. 424p [LC OTP QMM

Jennings, Rev. John, 1814–1876
REASON OR REVELATION; or, The Religion, Philosophy of the Ancient Heathen,

Contrasted with Christianity and its Legitimate Consequences. ... Toronto, Cleland, 1852. 48p [NSHD OTUV
SAY NO. Toronto, 1865. 59p [BibC

Johnston, Rev. Angus Anthony, 1897–
A HISTORY OF THE CATHOLIC CHURCH IN EASTERN NOVA SCOTIA. V. 1: 1611–1827. Antigonish, St. Francis Xavier U. Press, 1960. 555p

Johnston, Rev. Hugh, 1840–1922
BEYOND DEATH. New York, Eaton & Mains, 1903. 330p [LC

Johnston, Robert, 1862–
PRESBYTERIAN WORSHIP. Its Spirit, Method and History. Toronto, Publishers' Syndicate, 1901. 163p [OTP

Johnstone, Rev. Robert Cuthbert, 1857–1934
THE STORY OF THE CHURCH OF ENGLAND IN RUPERTSLAND. Winnipeg, Bulman, 1920. 46p [OTUV SSU

Jordan, Alfred McKay
THE BOOK OF THE ONE LAW. Vancouver, Sun Job Presses, 1918. 171p [BM BVaU OOP

Jordan, Rev. Louis Henry, 1855–1923
COMPARATIVE RELIGION. Its Adjuncts and Allies. London, Milford, 1915. xxxii + 574p [BM BVaU LC NSHD OTP
COMPARATIVE RELIGION. Its Genesis and Growth. Edinburgh, Clark, 1905. 668p [BM LC NSHD OTU
COMPARATIVE RELIGION. Its Method and Scope. A Paper read in part at the Third International Congress of the History of Religions, Oxford, Sept. 17, 1908. Oxford, Frowde, 1908. 20p [BM NSHD OKQ
COMPARATIVE RELIGION. Its Origin and Outlook. A Lecture. London, Milford, 1913. 16p [BM NSHD OLU
COMPARATIVE RELIGION. Its Range and Limitations. A Lecture. Oxford, Milford, 1916. 15p [BM NSHD OKQ
COMPARATIVE RELIGION. A Survey of Its Recent Literature. ... Reprinted from the *Review of Theology and Religion.* 2 pts. Edinburgh, Schulze, 1906. [2nd ed., 1910. 72p Another edition, "revised and augmented": London, Milford, 1920. 160p] [BM BVaU LC NSHD OTP

Jordan, Mabel Ellen (Tremlett), 1908–
THE McDOUGALL MEMORIAL UNITED CHURCH, MORLEY, ALBERTA, THE CHURCH OF THE MOUNTAIN STONEYS. A Souvenir Booklet. Calgary, the Church, 1957. 8p

Jordan, Rev. William George, 1852–1939
ANCIENT HEBREW STORIES AND THEIR MODERN INTERPRETATION. London, Hodder, 1922. 344p [BM LC OKQ QMM

BIBLICAL CRITICISM AND MODERN THOUGHT; or, The Place of the Old Testament Documents in the Life of To-day. Edinburgh, Clark, 1909. 322p [BM BVaU OKQ

THE BOOK OF JOB. Its Substance and Spirit. New York, Macmillan, 1929. 193p [BVa LC OOSU

THE CHALLENGE OF THE BOOK; or, The Modern Interpretation of the Old Testament. Kingston, Jackson Press, 1921. [BVaU OTL

COMMENTARY ON THE BOOK OF DEUTERONOMY. New York, Macmillan, 1911. 263p [BVaU OKQ

HISTORY AND REVELATION. The Individuality of Israel. London, Clarke, 1926. 287p [BM BVaU OKQ

PROPHETIC IDEAS AND IDEALS. A Series of Short Studies in the Prophetic Literature of the Hebrew People. Chicago, Revell, 1902. 363p [BM BVaU OKQ QMM

RELIGION IN SONG; or, Studies in the Psalter. London, Clarke, 1918. 275p [BM BVaU OTU

THE RELIGION OF ISRAEL. Kingston, n.p., 1919. 54p [OTU

THE SONG AND THE SOIL; or, The Missionary Idea in the Old Testament. New York, Scribner, 1913. 141p [Another ed., Edinburgh, Clark, 1912.] [BM BVaU OKQ

SONGS OF SERVICE AND SACRIFICE. A Study of *Isaiah* xl–lv. London, Clarke, 1924. 188p [BM BVaU OKQ

Jose, Rev. Murray Burkholder, 1913–

MEDITATIONS AT THE LORD'S TABLE. Toronto, Ryerson, 1959. 66p

K., J. (Cobourg author)

THE CHURCH AND THE WESLEYANS. By J.K. Cobourg, Chatterton, 1838. 16p [OTP

Kaufman, Carolyn Reesor, 1883–

HISTORIC CHURCHES OF ALBERTA AND THE CANADIAN NORTH WEST. Edmonton, Author, 1958. 80p

Kaulbach, J.A.

THE HISTORY OF THE PARISH OF ST. JOHN'S, TRURO, COLCHESTER, NOVA SCOTIA. ... Ed. by W.P. Robertson. [Truro?,1913]. 117p [BVaU NSWA

Kelly, Rev. Edward, 1875–1937

THE STORY OF ST. PAUL'S PARISH, TORONTO. ... Commemorating the Centenary of the First Parish Church in the Archdiocese of Toronto. Comp. and Ed. by ——. Toronto, priv. print., 1922. 329p [BVaU OTP

Kelwood, Man. Knox United Church
A SHORT HISTORICAL SKETCH OF CHURCH WORK IN THE KELWOOD FIELD, UP TO
  AND AFTER UNION, COMPILED AND PRINTED TO MARK THE OCCASION OF THE
  50TH ANNIVERSARY OF THE BUILDING OF KNOX CHURCH, KELWOOD. Gladstone,
  Man., 1955. 12p

Kennedy, Henry Dawson, 1869–1925
MISUNDERSTOOD. Toronto, Briggs, 1903. 105p [BM OTU

Kenner, Henry, 1832–1916
POPULAR AMUSEMENTS. The Duty of the Officers and Members of the Methodist
  Church in Relation Thereto. An Essay. ... Toronto, Briggs, 1882. 15p [OTAr

Kent, Herbert Harold
AN ARCHITECT PREACHES. London, Independent Press, 1957. 205p [Sermons.]

Ker, Rev. Robert, 1843–
ST. GEORGE'S PARISH CHURCH, ST. CATHARINES. Jubilee Celebration and Historic
  and Centenary Review. Ed. by ——. St. Catharines, Star Print., [1892?]. 186p
  [BVaU LC NSWA OTU QMM

Kerr, Rev. Alexander Enoch, 1898–
IN THE LAST ANALYSIS. Toronto, Ryerson, 1958. 98p [Sermons and addresses.]
PREFACE TO CHRISTMAS. Toronto, Ryerson, 1951. 104p

Kerr, Hugh Thomson, 1909–
MYSTERY AND MEANING IN THE CHRISTIAN FAITH. Toronto, Ryerson, 1958. 51p

Kilpatrick, Thomas Buchanan, 1858–1930
NEW TESTAMENT EVANGELISM. ... London, Hodder, 1911. 313p [LC OTUV
OUR COMMON FAITH. With a Brief History of the Church Union Movement in
  Canada, by K.H. Cousland. Toronto, Ryerson, 1928. 216p [BVaU LC OTUV
  QMM

King, Basil, 1859–1928
THE ABOLISHING OF DEATH. New York, Cosmopolitan, 1919. 197p [LC OTUV
ABRAHAM'S BOSOM. London, Harper, 1918. 53p [BVaU LC OTMC
ADVENTURES IN RELIGION. Garden City, Doubleday, 1929. 252p [BM LC
THE BIBLE AND COMMON SENSE. London, Harper, 1924. 168p [LC NSHD
THE CONQUEST OF FEAR. Garden City, Doubleday,. 1921. 270p [BM BVaU
  LC NSWA OTU QMM
THE DISCOVERY OF GOD. Toronto, Copp Clark, 1923. 265p [BM BVaU NSWA
  OTP
FAITH AND SUCCESS. Garden City, Doubleday, 1925. 266p [BM LC NSHD
  OTU
THE SEVEN TORCHES OF CHARACTER. Garden City, Doubleday, 1929. 260p [BM
  LC

Kingsbridge, Ont. St. Joseph's Parish
HISTORY OF ST. JOSEPH'S PARISH, KINGSBRIDGE, ONTARIO. Kingsbridge, the
Church, 1938. 40p [OTU

Kingston, Rev. George Frederick, 1889–1950
THE FOUNDATIONS OF FAITH. Toronto, Ryerson, 1928. 75p [NSWA OTU

Kirkwall, Ont. Kirkwall Church
KIRKWALL CHURCH AND COMMUNITY, 1833–1933. Kirkwall, The Church, 1933.
120p [OTU

Kirkwood, Mossie May (Waddington), 1890–
DUTY AND HAPPINESS IN A CHANGED WORLD. Toronto, Macmillan, 1933. 207p
[BM BVaU LC OTU QMM

Kittson, Rev. Henry, 1848–1925
CHURCH HISTORY FROM THE ARCHIVES. A Study. Kingston, Jackson, [1912?].
39p [BM NSWA OTP QMSS

Kromminga, Rev. John H., 1918–
IN THE MIRROR. An Appraisal of the Christian Reformed Church. Hamilton,
Guardian Pub. Co., 1957. 178p

Krumpelmann, Rev. Cosmas W.
IN THIS SIGN THEY CONQUERED. Being the Centenary of the Grey Nuns of
St. Boniface, 1844–1944. Muenster, Sask., St. Peter's Press, 1944. 33p
[MWP

Kulbeck, Gloria Grace
WHAT GOD HATH WROUGHT. A History of the Pentecostal Assemblies of Canada.
Ed. by Walter E. McAlister and George R. Upton. Toronto, Pentecostal
Assemblies of Canada, 1958. 364p

Lahey, Mrs. Vivian Gwendolyn Davis, 1893–
THE WOMAN'S ASSOCIATION OF LUNDY'S LANE UNITED CHURCH, 1858–1958.
Niagara Falls, Ont., the Church, 1958. 6p

Lanceley, Rev. John Ellis, 1848–1900
THE DOMESTIC SANCTUARY; or, The Importance of Family Religion. Hamilton,
Spectator Print., 1878. 132p [LC OLU
THE VIRGIN MARY AND OTHER SERMONS, Preached in the New Richmond
Methodist Church, McCaul Street, Toronto. ... Toronto, Briggs, 1891. 301p
[OTP

Lande, Lawrence Montague, 1906–
TOWARD THE QUIET MIND. A Guide to Self-Discovery through the Study of the
Book of Job. Toronto, McClelland, 1954. 101p

Landon, Fred, 1880–1969
A HISTORY OF THE FIRST HUNDRED YEARS OF THE FIRST UNITED CHURCH, LON-
DON, ONTARIO ... 1832–1932. London, Ont., 1932. 59p [LC OTP

Langford, Rev. Norman Frederick, 1914–
BARRIERS TO BELIEF. Philadelphia, Westminster Press, 1958. 96p
THE TWO-EDGED SWORD: SERMONS. Philadelphia, Westminster Press, 1945.
194p [BVaU

Langtry, Rev. John, 1834–1906
CATHOLIC VERSUS ROMAN; or, Some of the Fundamental Points of Difference
between the Catholic Church and the Roman Church. In Ten Lectures,
delivered in St. Luke's Church, Toronto, in 1885. Toronto, Hunter Rose, 1886.
225p [BVaU NSWA OTP
COME HOME. An Appeal on Behalf of Reunion. Toronto, Church of England Pub.
Co., 1900. 399p [BM BVaU OOU
HISTORY OF THE CHURCH IN EASTERN CANADA AND NEWFOUNDLAND. London,
S.P.C.K., 1892. 256p [BM BVaU NBFU OTP
A STRUGGLE FOR LIFE. Higher Criticism Criticized. Toronto, Briggs, 1905. 328p
[BM OTP

Lanton, Rev. Henry, 1809?–1888
LECTURES ON THE SECOND ADVENT OF CHRIST. Montreal, Wilson, 1855. 452p
[BVaU NSWA OTU

Lappin, Rev. Maitland M.
BAPTISTS IN THE PROTESTANT TRADITION. Toronto, Ryerson, 1947. 112p
[BVaU OTU

Lathern, Rev. John, 1831–1905
BAPTISMA. A Three-fold Testimony. Water-baptism, Spirit-baptism, and the Baptism
of Fire. ... Charlottetown, Haszard, 1877. 72p [NSHD
BAPTISMA. The Mode and Subjects of Christian Baptism. Halifax, Pickard, 1879.
265p [NSHD OTU

Law, Rev. Robert, 1860–1919
THE EMOTIONS OF JESUS. Edinburgh, Clark, 1915. 155p [BM OTU
THE GRAND ADVENTURE, AND OTHER SERMONS. New York, Hodder, 1916. 219p
[LC NBFU OLU
THE HOPE OF OUR CALLING. Toronto, McClelland, 1918. 185p [T&C
OPTIMISM AND OTHER SERMONS. Toronto, McClelland, 1919. 203p [BM OTU
THE TESTS OF LIFE. A Study of the First Epistle of St. John. 2nd ed. Edinburgh,
Clark, 1909. 422p [BM BVaU LC OTU QMM

Lawson, James Reid, 1820–1891
THE MILLENIUM. A Discourse. Saint John, Barnes, 1864. 24p [NSHD

Laycock, Samuel Ralph, 1891–1971

PASTORAL COUNSELLING FOR MENTAL HEALTH. Toronto, Ryerson, 1958
x + 94p

Leach, Rev. William Turnbull, 1805–1886

AN ADDRESS ON RECHABITISM, Delivered [to] ... the Independent Order of
Rechabites ... 18th July, 1845. Montreal, Brother J.C. Becket, 1845. 12p
[Sermon to a secret society which promoted temperance.] [OTP

A DISCOURSE DELIVERED IN ST. ANDREW'S CHURCH, TORONTO, ON THE FOUR-
TEENTH DAY OF DECEMBER, 1838. Being a Day of Public Fasting and Humiliation.
... Toronto, "British Colonist," 1839. 16p [OTP

DISCOURSE ON THE NATURE AND DUTIES OF THE MILITARY PROFESSION. ...
Toronto, Scobie, 1840. 19p [OTU

Leard, George Artemas, 1908–

HISTORIC BEDEQUE, THE LOYALISTS AT WORK AND WORSHIP IN PRINCE EDWARD
ISLAND. A History of Bedeque United Church. Bedeque, P.E.I., Bedeque United
Church, 1948. 172p [NBFU OTP

SUMMERSIDE SAINTS AND SINNERS. A History of Trinity United Church, Summerside, P.E.I. Summerside, the Church, 1958. 62p

Lee, George Herbert, 1854–1905

AN HISTORICAL SKETCH OF THE FIRST FIFTY YEARS OF THE CHURCH OF ENGLAND
IN THE PROVINCE OF NEW BRUNSWICK, 1783–1833. Saint John, Sun Pub. Co.,
1880. 141p [BVaU NSWA OTU

Legal, Emile Joseph, 1849–1920

SHORT SKETCHES OF THE HISTORY OF THE CATHOLIC CHURCHES AND MISSIONS
IN CENTRAL ALBERTA. Comp. by ——. Winnipeg, West Canada Pub. Co., 1914.
174p [AEU BVaU OTP QMBM

Legge, Rev. Arthur Ernest Edgar, 1889–

THE ANGLICAN CHURCH IN THREE RIVERS, QUEBEC, 1768–1956. Russell, Ont.,
Author, 1956. xv + 191p

Leith, Ont. United Church

THE EARLY HISTORY OF LEITH UNITED CHURCH. Leith, The Church, 1942. 17p
[OTP

Lench, Rev. Charles, 1860–1931

AN ACCOUNT OF THE RISE AND PROGRESS OF METHODISM ON THE GRAND BANK
AND FORTUNE CIRCUITS FROM 1816 TO 1916. ... [St. John's, Barnes], 1916. 80p
[NfSM

THE STORY OF METHODISM IN BONAVISTA, AND THE SETTLEMENTS VISITED BY
THE EARLY PREACHERS. ... [Bonavista, Nfld.], Author, 1919. 206p [NfSM
OTU

LeSage, Rev. J.L.

ST. PATRICK'S CHURCH CENTENNIAL, 1855–1955. Comp. by ——. Ottawa, the
Church, 1955. 44p

Leslie, Rev. Charles Whitney, 1905—
NO GRAVEN IMAGES. The Contemporary Relevance of the Ten Commandments.
Toronto, Ryerson, 1954. xx + 88p

Le Sueur, William Dawson, 1840—1917
A DEFENCE OF MODERN THOUGHT. In Reply to a Recent Pamphlet, by the Bishop
of Ontario on "Agnosticism." Toronto, Hunter Rose, 1884. 40p [NSWA OTP
EVOLUTION AND THE POSITIVE ASPECTS OF MODERN THOUGHT. In Reply to the
Bishop of Ontario's Second Lecture on Agnosticism. Ottawa, Woodburn, 1884.
43p [BM QMSS

Levy, George Edward, 1902—
THE BAPTISTS OF THE MARITIME PROVINCES, 1753—1946. Saint John, Barnes-
Hopkins, 1946. 336p [LC NBFU OTP

Levy, Herman David
A HISTORY OF FIRST BAPTIST CHURCH, TRURO, N.S. Truro, the Church, 1958.
51p [A centennial history.]

Lewis, Fred
LO, THE LIGHT SHINETH, AND MAKETH CLEAR THE DARKNESS. Winnipeg, Author,
1943. 94p [OTP

Lewis, Rev. John Travers, 1825—1901
AGNOSTICISM. ... Kingston, Author, 1883. 32p [NSHD OTU

Lightbourn, Alexander Harvey, 1890—
SAINT JUDE'S CHURCH, OAKVILLE, 1842—1957. An Historical Sketch. Rev. ed.
Oakville, Ont., St. Jude's Church, 1957. 31p [First pub. in 1953.]

Lindeman, Harold Roy, 1931—
A HISTORY OF ZION EVANGELICAL LUTHERAN CHURCH, SHERWOOD, ONTARIO,
1806—1956. ... Comp. by ——. Sherwood, Ont., Author, 1956. [mimeographed]

Lindsey, Charles, 1820—1908
THE CLERGY RESERVES. ... By Charles Lindsay [*sic*]. Toronto, North American
Press, 1851. 59p [NSWA OTP

Line, Rev. John, 1885—
THE DOCTRINE OF THE CHRISTIAN MINISTRY. London, Lutterworth Press, 1959.
190p

Linscott, Rev. Thomas S., 1846—1919
THE HEART OF CHRISTIANITY. Philadelphia, Bradley-Garretson, 1906—7. 2v
[BM LC

Lockhart, Rev. Wilfred Cornett, 1906—
BETHLEHEM. The Meaning and Significance of Christmas for our Day. Toronto,
United Church Pub. House, 1955. 53p

IN SUCH AN AGE. Younger Voices in the Canadian Church. Ed. by ——. Toronto, McClelland, 1951. xxiii + 215p

Lodge, Rupert Clendon, 1886–
APPLIED PHILOSOPHY. London, Routledge and Paul, 1951. xi + 243p [American ed. (Boston, Beacon Press) has title: APPLYING PHILOSOPHY.]

London, Ont. First United Church
A HISTORY OF THE FIRST HUNDRED YEARS OF THE FIRST UNITED CHURCH, LONDON, ONTARIO (Formerly the First Presbyterian Church), 1832–1932. London, the Church, 1932. 59p [OLU

Longley, James Wilberforce, 1849–1922
LOVE. Toronto, Copp Clark, 1898. 158p [BM BVaU NSWA OLU QMBM

Longley, Ronald Stewart, 1896–
THE WOLFVILLE UNITED BAPTIST CHURCH. Wolfville, N.S., the Church, 1953. 87p

Longstaff, Frederick Victor, 1879–1961
CHRIST CHURCH CATHEDRAL, VICTORIA, B.C. A Short History. Victoria, Author, 1951. 23p

Low, Rev. George Jacobs, 1836–1906
THE FIRST MIRACLE OF CHRIST AND PROHIBITION. A Sermon preached in St. Peter's Church, Brockville ... 1886. Toronto, Robinson, 1886. 14p [NSWA OTP QMBM
THE OLD FAITH AND THE NEW PHILOSOPHY. ... With an intro. by Principal Grant. Toronto, Briggs, 1900. 160p [BM NSWA OTU

Lowe, John, 1899–1960
SAINT PETER. New York, Oxford U. Press, 1956. 65p

Lumsden, James
THE SKIPPER PARSON ON THE BAYS AND BARRENS OF NEWFOUNDLAND. ... Toronto, Briggs, 1906. 212p [Earlier eds., London, Kelly, 1905; New York, Eaton, 1905.] [BM BVaU NSWA OTU

Lunenburg, N.S. Methodist Church
HISTORY OF A CENTURY. ... Lunenburg, The Church, 1914. 28p [NSWA

Luxton, Rev. George Nasmith, 1901–
THE OLD PARISH CHURCH OF ST. CATHARINES. Historical Sermons. ... With the Book of Remembrance of St. George's Church. St. Catharines, The Church, 1935. 34p [OTU
THE BUILDING OF OLD ST. GEORGE'S, 1835–1840. St. Catharines, The Church, [1937?]. 16p [OTP

Lyall, Rev. William, 1811–1890
INTELLECT, THE EMOTIONS AND THE MORAL NATURE. Edinburgh, Constable,
1855. 627p [BM BVaU NSHD OTU QMM
THE PHILOSOPHY OF THOUGHT. A Lecture delivered at the Opening of the Free
Church College, Halifax, N.S., Session 1852–3. Halifax, Barnes, 1853. 15p
[NSWA OTU
STRICTURES ON THE IDEA OF POWER. Edinburgh, Johnstone, 1842. 52p [OTU

Lynch-Staunton, Betty (Frankish), 1895–
A SHORT HISTORY OF THE CHURCH OF ST. JOHN THE EVANGELIST, PINCHER
CREEK, ALBERTA. Pincher Creek, the Church, 1954. 12p

M., H.R.
ST. PETER'S SANCTUARY GUILD. A Brief History of the Parish of St. Peter's Church,
Brockville, Ontario. By H.R.M. Brockville, The Guild, 1927. [OTU

M., W.
THE RELATIVE THEORY. Is or Is Not the Bible Infallible? and THE CRITIC
CRITICISED COMBINED; or, Truth Vindicated & Error Confounded. Toronto,
1859. 56p [Preface signed: W.M.] [OTP

McBeth, Margaret Elliot
THE STORY OF KILDONAN PRESBYTERIAN CHURCH, 1851–1951. Commemorating
the Coming of Dr. John Black and the Organization of the Congregation.
Winnipeg, Kildonan Presbyterian Church, 1951. 16p

MacBeth, Rev. Roderick George, 1858–1934
THE BURNING BUSH AND CANADA. Toronto, Upper Canada Tract Soc., 1925.
160p [Also: Vancouver, Cowan Brookhouse, 1925.] [BVaU OKQ
OUR TASK IN CANADA. [Home Missions, Presbyterian Church.] Toronto,
Westminster, 1912. 146p [BVaU LC OTU

McCall, Oswald Walter Samuel, 1885–
THE HAND OF GOD. 4th ed. New York, Harper, 1939. 158p [BM BVa
THE USES OF LITERATURE IN THE PULPIT. London, Harper, 1932. 127p [BM
BVa LC OTUV

McCann, Rev. Leonard Albert, 1908–
THE DOCTRINE OF THE VOID. The Doctrine of the Void as Propounded by St. John
of the Cross in his Major Prose Works and as Viewed in the Light of Thomistic
Principles. Toronto, Basilian Press, 1955. 146p

McCaskill, Kenneth
THE CENTENARY: KNOX PRESBYTERIAN CHURCH, McDONALD'S CORNERS,
ONTARIO ... 1845–1945. Lanark, Ont., Era Press, 1945. 62p [OKQ

McCaul, Rev. John, 1807–1887

EMIGRATION TO A BETTER COUNTRY. A Sermon preached ... Toronto ... 1842. Toronto, Rowsell, 1842. 15p [OTP

"LOVE OF GOD AND OUR NEIGHBOUR." A Sermon preached ... March 17, 1840. Toronto, Rowsell, 1840. 18p [NSWA OTP

McCausland, Rev. John George Alban Patrick

THE CHURCH OF YOUR CHOICE. The Faith, Position and Practice of the Religious Bodies in Canada. Bracebridge, Ont., Society of St. John the Evangelist, 1954. 73p

THE CHURCH'S ANSWERS. Bracebridge, Ont., Society of Saint John the Evangelist, 1950. 107p [Reprinted, 1951, 1952, 1954.] [OONL

A PRIMER OF CHRISTIAN TRUTH. Bracebridge, Ont., Society of St. John the Evangelist, 1955. 114p

MacClung, Burt Ward

HISTORY OF THE DEVIL. Regina, 1913. 188p [BM

McCreary, Man. Knox United Church

FIFTY YEARS IN OUR CHURCH, 1905–1955. Gladstone, Man., 1955. 9p

McCulloch, Rev. Thomas, 1776–1843

CALVINISM, THE DOCTRINE OF THE SCRIPTURES. Glasgow, Collins, [1849]. 270p [NSHD OTU

MEMORIAL FROM THE COMMITTEE OF MISSIONS OF THE PRESBYTERIAN CHURCH OF NOVA SCOTIA TO THE GLASGOW SOCIETY FOR PROMOTING THE RELIGIOUS INTERESTS OF THE SCOTTISH SETTLERS IN BRITISH NORTH AMERICA. With Observations on the Constitution of that Society. ... Edinburgh, Oliver & Boyd, 1826. 75p [NSHD

POPERY CONDEMNED BY SCRIPTURE AND THE FATHERS. Being a Refutation of the Principal Popish Doctrines and Assertions maintained in the Remarks on the Rev. Mr. Stanser's Examination of the Rev. Mr. Burke's Letter of Instruction to the Catholic Missionaries of Nova Scoita. ... Edinburgh, Pillans, 1808. 385p [Also as: POPERY AGAIN CONDEMNED. ... Edinburgh, Neill, 1810. 429p [NSHD OTP

THE PROSPERITY OF THE CHURCH IN TROUBLOUS TIMES. A Sermon preached ... Feb. 25, 1814. New Glasgow, Mackenzie, 1882. 18p [NSHP

A REVIEW OF THE SUPPLEMENT TO THE FIRST ANNUAL REPORT OF THE SOCIETY FOR PROMOTING THE RELIGIOUS INTERESTS OF SCOTTISH SETTLERS IN BRITISH NORTH AMERICA. In a Series of Letters to the Rev. Robert Burns. ... Glasgow, Young, 1828. 50p [OTP

WORDS OF PEACE. Being an Address delivered to the Congregation of Halifax ... in Consequence of some Congregational Disputes. ... Halifax, Ward, 1817. 16p [NSHD

McCulloch, William, 1811–1895?
EXISTING CHURCH THOUGHT AND ACTIVITY IN RELATION TO REVEALED
CHARACTER AND OBJECTS. A Sermon preached before the Synod of the
Presbyterian Church of the Lower Provinces of British North America, June
24th, 1868. ... Halifax, Barnes, 1869. 18p [NSHD OTUV

McCurdy, Rev. James Frederick, 1847–1935
HISTORY, PROPHECY AND THE MONUMENTS; or, Israel and the Nations. London,
Macmillan, 1897–1901. 3v [BM BVaU LC NBFU OTU QMM

MacDermot, Hugh Ernest, 1888–
CHRIST CHURCH CATHEDRAL. A Century in Retrospect. Montreal, Christ
Church Cathedral, 1959. 63p

MacDonald, Rev. Alexander, 1858–1941
THE MERCIES OF THE SACRED HEART. Twelve Sermons for the First Fridays.
New York, Wagner, 1904. 56p [LC
THE SACRAMENTS. A Course of Seven Sermons. New York, Wagner, 1906.
82p [LC
THE SYMBOL IN SERMONS. A Series of Twenty-five Short Sermons on the
Articles of the Creed. New York, Christian Press Assoc., 1903. 214p [OOU
THE SYMBOL OF THE APOSTLES. A Vindication of the Apostolic Authorship of
the Creed on the Lines of Catholic Tradition. New York, Christian Press
Assoc., 1903. 377p [NSHD OOU

Macdonald, Donald Bruce, 1872–
SUNDAY EVENINGS AT ST. ANDREW'S COLLEGE. Sermons in the College Chapel.
Toronto, McClelland, 1946. 256p [CC

McDonald, Donald Gordon, 1843–1931
BIBLE BAPTISMA AND ITS QUALIFICATIONS – VERSUS REV. J. LATHERN'S
"BAPTISMA." ... Charlottetown, Coombe, 1878. 200p [NSHD

McDonald, Rev. Donald, 1783–1867
THE PLAN OF SALVATION. Charlottetown, Bremner, 1874. 211p [NSWA
THE SUBJECTS OF THE MILLENIUM. Traced in their Downward Progress from
their Ancestry through the Pre-Millennial Dispensations. Charlottetown,
Haszard, 1849. 417p [NSWA
TREATISE ON THE HOLY ORDINANCE OF BAPTISM. Containing Scriptural Views
of the Baptism of John: A Defence of the Doctrine of Infant Baptism. ...
Charlottetown, Haszard & Moore, 1898. 264p [First pub. in 1845?] [NSHD

Macdonald, Malcolm Campbell, 1898–
FROM LAKES TO NORTHERN LIGHTS. [Toronto], United Church Committee on
Missionary Education, [1951]. xii + 202p

Macdonnell, Rev. George, 1812?–1871
AID TO SACRAMENTAL COMMUNION. Montreal, Lovell, 1864. 211p [OKQ OLU

BOOK OF DEVOTIONS AND SERMONS. Montreal, Armour, 1851. 362p [NSWA

McDowall, Rev. Robert, 1769?–1841
DISCOURSES. Albany, Webster & Skinner, 1806. 123p [OTU
A SERMON ON THE NATURE OF JUSTIFICATION. ... York, U.C., 1805. [DCB

MacFarlane, Rev. Duncan Herbert, 1898–
PASSPORT TO PARADISE. [Sermons.] New York, Vantage Press, 1959. 106p

MacGeorge, Rev. Robert Jackson, 1811?–1884
THE PERFECT LAW OF LIBERTY. ... Toronto, The Church Office, 1846. 12p
[S&T

McGill, Rev. Robert, 1798–1856
DISCOURSES PREACHED ON VARIOUS OCCASIONS IN THE COURSE OF MINISTERIAL
DUTY. Montreal, Ramsay, 1853. 338p [BVaU LC NSWA OTP QMM

Macgillivray, Rev. John M., 1883–1966
ST. ANDREW'S PRESBYTERIAN CHURCH, SARNIA, ONTARIO ... 1841–1941. Sarnia,
the Church, 1941. 63p [OLU

MacGregor, Mary Esther (Miller), 1876–1961
GLAD DAYS IN GALILEE. A Story of the Boyhood of Jesus. By Marian Keith
[pseud]. Toronto, McClelland, 1935. 141p [OTMC

McGregor, Rev. P.G.
GALILEO AND THE COPERNICAN SYSTEM. How Treated by Rome. A Lecture,
delivered February 7, 1867, in St. Andrew's Hall, Antigonish. ... Halifax,
Compton, 1867. 34p [NSHD
PROVIDENCE IN REFERENCE TO NATIONS. A Lecture delivered before the Halifax
YMCA, April 6, 1858. ... Halifax, Barnes, 1858. 31p [NSHD

Machar, Rev. John, 1796–1863
A PASTOR'S LAST WORDS TO HIS PEOPLE. Kingston, Creighton, 1863. 12p [OTUV

McIntosh, William Donald, 1881–
ONE HUNDRED YEARS IN THE ZORRA CHURCH [Knox United, Embro]. Toronto,
Ryerson, 1930. 192p [BVaU OTP

Mackay, Rev. Alexander Bisset, 1842–1901
GOSPEL OF THE REV. B. FAY MILLS TESTED BY SCRIPTURE. ... Montreal, Morton
Phillips, 1894. 23p [NSHD
THE TRUE GNOSTICS. A Sermon preached in Crescent Street Presbyterian Church,
Montreal. Montreal, Drysdale, 1880. 13p [OTP

Mackay, Rev. W.P.
ABUNDANT GRACE. Selected Addresses. Toronto, Briggs, 1885. 232p [OKQ
GRACE AND TRUTH UNDER TWELVE DIFFERENT ASPECTS. Saint John, Barnes,
1881. 235p [NSWA

THE SEEKING SAVIOUR AND OTHER BIBLE THEMES. Toronto, Briggs, n.d., 247p
  [NSWA

MacKay, Rev. William Alexander, 1842–1905
IMMERSION PROVED TO BE NOT A SCRIPTURAL MODE OF BAPTISM BUT A ROMISH
  INVENTION; and Immersionists shewn to be disregarding Divine Authority in
  refusing Baptism to the Infant Children of Believers. Toronto, Briggs, n.d.
  130p [3rd ed., 1881.] [NSHD OTU QMSS

McKellar, Rev. Hugh, 1841–1934?
PRESBYTERIAN PIONEER MINISTERS. Presbyterian Pioneer Missionaries in
  Manitoba, Saskatchewan, Alberta and British Columbia. Toronto, Murray
  Print., 1924. 249p [BM BVaU OTP SSU

MacKenzie, Archibald J.
HISTORY OF CHRISTMAS ISLAND PARISH. ... [Christmas Island, N.S.?], 1926.
  167p [NSHP OTU

McKenzie, Rev. Donald
AN EXPOSITION OF OLD TESTAMENT SACRIFICES. Toronto, Briggs, 1900. 368p
  [NSWA

McKenzie, Rev. William Patrick, 1861–1942
CHRISTIAN SCIENCE. God's Lovingkindness Proved to Men. A Lecture. Boston,
  Christian Science Pub., 1914. 32p [LC

MacKinnon, John Y., 1886–1951
THE PROTESTANT DOCTRINE OF REVELATION. ... Toronto, Ryerson, 1946.
  117p [BVaU LC OTP
WHAT PROTESTANTS BELIEVE AND WHY. Toronto, United Church Pub. House,
  1944. 41p [LC OTP

MacKinnon, Murdoch Archibald, 1871–1954
THE CHORUS OF LIFE. Toronto, Ryerson, 1930. 267p [BVa LC OTU
THE IMPRISONED SPLENDOUR. London, Allenson, 1922. 159p [BM

McKinnon, Rev. William Charles, –1862
DIVINE SOVEREIGNTY. A Sermon ... preached at Elmsdale, April 14th, 1861. ...
  Halifax, Conference Job Print., 1861. 19p [NSHD
PAPACY: THE SACRIFICE OF THE MASS – Third Lecture delivered before the
  Protestant Alliance of Nova Scotia ... Jan. 11th, 1859. ... Halifax, Wesleyan
  Conference Steam Press, 1859. 28p [NSHD

Maclaren, William
LITERATURE AND DOGMA. An Inaugural Lecture ... on the Occasion of his
  Induction as Professor of Systematic Theology in Knox College. Toronto,
  Willing & Williamson, 1873. 24p [OTUV

THE ROMISH DOCTRINE OF THE RULE OF FAITH EXAMINED. A Lecture. With an appendix in which certain statements of Rev. Father Damen and Rev. Dr. O'Connor are considered. Ottawa, Henderson, [1872?]. 40p [OTUV

McLaurin, Rev. Colin Campbell, 1854–1941

MY OLD HOME CHURCH IN RURAL ONTARIO. Edmonton, Institute Press, 1937. 134p [OTP

PIONEERING IN WESTERN CANADA. A Story of the Baptists. Calgary, Author, 1939. 401p [BVaU LC OTP QMM SSU

Maclean, Alexander, 1822–1916

THE STORY OF THE KIRK IN NOVA SCOTIA. Pictou, Pictou Advocate, 1911. 102p [BVaU NSWA OTP

McLean, Alexander, 1827–1864

THE MORE PRIESTS THE MORE CRIME; or, The Challengers Defeated. Being a Series of Letters ... in Reply to the Challenge of the Catholic Citizen and Montreal True Witness. By a Protestant [pseud]. [OTP QMBM

MacLean, Rev. Donald Alexander, 1886–

CATHOLIC SCHOOLS IN WESTERN CANADA. Their Legal Status. ... Toronto, Extension Print., 1923. 162p [BM LC OTUV

Maclean, Rev. John Brown

THE SECRET OF THE STREAM. London, Allenson, 1907. 187p [BM NSHD OTU

McLelland, Rev. Joseph Cumming, 1925–

THE OTHER SIX DAYS. The Christian Meaning of Work and Property. Toronto, Burns & MacEachern, 1959. x + 121p

MacLennan, Rev. David Alexander, 1903–

JOYOUS ADVENTURE. Sermons for the Christian Year. Toronto, Clarke Irwin, 1952. 192p

A PREACHER'S PRIMER. Toronto, Clarke Irwin, 1950. 113p [OONL

RESOURCES FOR SERMON PREPARATION. Philadelphia, Westminster Press, 1957. 239p

THE STORY OF OUR CHURCH. A Little Guide for Visitors to Timothy Eaton Memorial Church. Toronto, United Church Pub., 1947. 31p [Ryerson Impt

McLeod, Rev. Alexander W.

THE METHODIST MINISTRY DEFENDED. ... Halifax, Cunnabell, 1839. 107p [NSHP

METHODIST MINISTRY FURTHER DEFENDED ... in ... Letters ... to the Rev. Charles J. Shreve. ... Pictou, Stiles, 1840. 228p [NSHD

UNIVERSALISM IN ITS MODERN AND ANCIENT FORM BROUGHT TO THE TEST AND SHOWN TO BE UNSCRIPTURAL. Halifax, Cunnabell, 1837. 163p [NSWA OTUV

MacLeod, Rev. John M., 1825–
HISTORY OF PRESBYTERIANISM ON PRINCE EDWARD ISLAND. Chicago, Winona
  Pub. Co., 1904. 279p [BVaU LC NSWA OTP QMBM

McMillan, Donald
HISTORY OF PRESBYTERIANISM IN CAPE BRETON. With brief Memorial Sketches
  of the Lives of Rev. Hugh McLeod, D.D., Rev. Matthew Wilson, Rev. Alexander
  Farquharson, and Other Pioneer Ministers. ... 3rd ed. Inverness, Inverness News,
  1905. 73p [NSWA

Macmillan, Rev. John C., 1862–1926
THE EARLY HISTORY OF THE CATHOLIC CHURCH IN PRINCE EDWARD ISLAND.
  Quebec, Evénement Print., 1905. 304p [OTP QMBM
THE HISTORY OF THE CATHOLIC CHURCH IN PRINCE EDWARD ISLAND, from 1835
  to 1891. Quebec, Evénement Print., 1913. 486p [BVaU LC OTU

Macmillan, John Walker, 1868–1932
HAPPINESS AND GOODWILL, and Other Essays on Christian Living. Toronto,
  McClelland, 1922. 154p [BVaU LC NSWA

McMullen, John Mercier, 1820–1907
THE SUPREMACY OF THE BIBLE, and its Relations to Speculative Science,
  Remote Ancient History, and the Higher Criticism. Toronto, Briggs, 1905.
  479p [LC OTU QMM

McNab, Rev. John, 1887–
OUR HERITAGE AND OUR FAITH: "Our Priceless Heritage," by John McNab,
  and "The Essence of Our Faith," by F. Scott Mackenzie. Toronto, 75th
  Anniversary Committee, Presbyterian Church in Canada, 1950. 127p [OTP

McNaughton, Rev. Duncan
LAURA CLARENCE. A Treatise on Baptism. Toronto, Robinson, 1882. 148p
  [AEU OTUV

MacNeill, Rev. John James, 1874–1937
MANY MANSIONS. Sermons on the Future Life. Toronto, McClelland, 1926.
  224p [BVaU OTP QMM
WORLD POWER: THE EMPIRE OF CHRIST. Toronto, McClelland, 1914. 203p
  [BVaU NSWA OTU

McNeill, Rev. John Thomas, 1885–
BOOKS OF FAITH AND POWER. New York, Harper, 1947. 183p [BM BVaU LC
  OTP
THE HISTORY AND CHARACTER OF CALVINISM. New York, Oxford U. Press,
  1954. x + 466p
A HISTORY OF THE CURE OF SOULS. New York, Harper, 1951. xii + 371p

MODERN CHRISTIAN MOVEMENTS. Philadelphia, Westminster Press, 1954.
197p

THE PRESBYTERIAN CHURCH IN CANADA, 1875–1925. Toronto, General Board,
Presbyterian Church in Canada, 1925. 276p [BM BVaU LC NBFU OTP
QMM

Macphail, Andrew, 1864–1938
THE BIBLE IN SCOTLAND. London, Murray, 1931. 130p [BM OTU QMM

Macphail, John Goodwill, 1877–
ST. ANDREW'S CHURCH, OTTAWA. The First Hundred Years, 1828–1928.
Ottawa, Dadson-Merrill Press, 1931. 169p [BVaU OTP

McTavish, Rev. William Sharpe, 1858–1932
REAPERS IN MANY FIELDS. A Survey of Canadian Presbyterian Missions. Toronto,
1904. 285p [BM BVaU OTU QMM

Maddox, David Crisp
FOR GOD AND PEACE. Ottawa, Author, 1937. 62p [OTU

Maine, Star Floyd, 1893–
EARLY METHODISM IN UPPER CANADA. Chicago, U. of Chicago, 1934. 120p
[Earlier ed., 1932.] [LC OLU QMM

Maloney, John James
ROME IN CANADA. Vancouver, Columbia Protestant, 1935. 167p [OTP

Manly, Rev. John G., 1814–1908
ECCLESIOGRAPHY; or, The Biblical Church Analytically Delineated. London,
Partridge & Oakey, 1852. 389p [BM LC OLU

THE NATURE, ORIGIN, PROGRESS, PRESENT STATE AND CHARACTER OF
WESLEYAN METHODISM. A Sermon preached at Picton ... 25th October, 1839. ...
Kingston, Author, 1840. 76p [NSHD OTP

THE RELIGION OF LIFE; or, Christ and Nicodemus. Toronto, Christian Guardian
Office, 1875. 155p [OTP

Mann, James
THE VICTORIOUS KING. An Allegory. ... Richmond Hill, James Mann, Printer,
1878. [Amtmann cat. 145

Mann, Rev. William Edward, 1918–
SECT, CULT, AND CHURCH IN ALBERTA. Toronto, U. of Toronto Press, 1955.
xiii + 166p

Marling, Rev. Francis Henry, 1825–
QUARTER-CENTURY MEMORIAL, 1849–1874: Bond Street Congregational Church,
Toronto. Comp. by ——. Toronto, Dudley & Burns, 1874. 56p [OTP

Marquis, Thomas Guthrie, 1864–1936

THE JESUIT MISSIONS. A Chronicle of the Cross in the Wilderness. Toronto, Glasgow Brook, 1916. 152p [BM BVaU LC NSHD OTU

Marshall, John

HISTORY OF EBENEZER CHURCH, NASSAGAWEGA, COMPILED FOR THE OCCASION OF CENTENNIAL CELEBRATION OF THE FIRST CHURCH BUILDING, 1832. [Acton, Ont., Free Press, 1932.] 22p [OTU OH

Marshall, John George, 1786–1880

ANSWER TO DOCTRINAL AND HISTORICAL ERRORS IN ARCHBISHOP CONNOLLY'S RECENT LECTURES. Halifax, MacNab, 1872. 38p [NSHD

ANSWERS TO "ESSAYS AND REVIEWS." Halifax, n.p., 1862. 224p [BM BVaU NSWA

BIBLE TRUTH VERSUS "OPPOSITIONS OF SCIENCE, FALSELY SO CALLED." Being an Answer to ... Professor Alexr. McKnight ... on Creation. Halifax, MacNab, 1876. 24p [NSHP

DOCTRINAL ERRORS in a Pamphlet by G.W. Olver ... Tested and Condemned by Scripture and Wesleyan Methodism. ... [Halifax?], n.d. 30p [NSHD

ERRORS AND FALLACIES in a Pamphlet Entitled "Catholicity and Methodism," Exposed and Refuted. ... Halifax, Nova Scotia Print., 1877. 56p [NSHD

ERRORS REVIEWED AND FALLACIES EXPOSED. Being a Protestant Answer to E. Maturin's Catholic Claims. Halifax, Wesleyan Conference Steam Press, 1859. 71p [NSWA QMSS

EXPOSURE AND REFUTATION of Unscriptural Opinions on the Lord's Second Coming. ... Halifax, "Wesleyan," n.d. 31p [NSHD

FICTIONS AND ERRORS, in a Book on "The Origin of the World According to Revelation and Science" by J.W. Dawson, Exposed and Condemned on the Authority of Divine Revelation. Halifax, Methodist Book Room, 1877. 82p [NSWA

FULL REVIEW AND EXPOSURE OF BISHOP COLENSO'S ERRORS ... in his ... "The Pentateuch and Book of Joshua Critically Examined". ... London, Freeman, 1863–64. 2pts. [NSHD

FULL REVIEW OF THE LATE LECTURE BY REV. G.M. GRANT ON THE REFORMERS OF THE NINETEENTH CENTURY, SHOWING ITS UNSCRIPTURAL AND ERRONEOUS CHARACTER. Halifax, Chamberlain, 1867. 32p [NSHD

ON SCRIPTURAL CONVERSION. The Modern Style of Preaching and the State of the Churches. Halifax, MacNab, 1871. 32p [NSWA QMSS

A PROTESTANT'S ANSWER TO PART I OF MR. EDMUND MATURIN'S "DEFENCE OF THE CLAIMS OF THE CATHOLIC CHURCH." Halifax, Bowes, 1859. 72p [NSHD QMSS

REVIEW AND REFUTATION OF LECTURES BY PROFESSOR J.M. HIRSCHFELDER ON CREATION. Halifax, MacNab, 1874. 34p [NSHP

SCRIPTURAL ANSWER TO A PAMPHLET BY A. SUTHERLAND ON THE MORAL STATUS

OF CHILDREN AND THEIR RELATION TO CHRIST AND HIS CHURCH. Halifax,
Nova Scotia Print., 1877. 23p [NSHD OTUV
SCRIPTURE TESTIMONIES TO DOCTRINES AND DUTIES OF CHRISTIANITY. ...
Carefully compiled. ... Halifax, MacNab, 1873. 216p [NSHP
SERMONS ON SOME OF THE PRINCIPAL DOCTRINES AND DUTIES OF
CHRISTIANITY. ... Halifax, Cunnabell, 1862. 296p [NSHD
TESTIMONY OF THE BIBLE CONCERNING EVERLASTING PUNISHMENT. Halifax,
Wesleyan Book, 1878. 35p [QMSS
TESTIMONY OF THE SCRIPTURES TO THEIR DIVINE INSPIRATION. London, Burns,
1865. 48p [NSHP
A TREATISE ON THE DIVINE GOODNESS AND JUSTICE, AS REVEALED IN THE HOLY
SCRIPTURES. Halifax, MacNab, 1875. 36p [NSWA QMSS

Mary Agnes, Sister, (historian) 1875–
THE CONGREGATION OF THE SISTERS OF ST. JOSEPH: LE PUY, LYONS, ST. LOUIS,
TORONTO. Toronto, St. Joseph's Convent, 1951. xvii + 225p

Mary Murphy, Sister
ST. BONIFACE HEROINES OF MERCY. Commemorating the Centenary of the
Grey Nuns of St. Boniface, 1844–1944. Muenster, Sask., St. Peter's Press,
1944. 20p [MWP

Mason, Gershom William, 1878–
THE LEGISLATIVE STRUGGLE FOR CHURCH UNION. Toronto, Ryerson, 1956.
162p

Massey, Rev. Samuel, 1817–
HISTORICAL SKETCHES OF THE PROTESTANT CHURCHES AND MINISTERS OF
MONTREAL. Montreal, Witness Print., 1885. 8p [QMBM

Mathieson, Rev. Alexander, 1795–1870
THE MORAL AND RELIGIOUS INFLUENCES OF AUTUMN. A Sermon in Three
Parts. Montreal, Starke, 1849. 72p [NSHD OTUV

Matthews, Rev. Walter McNeill, 1885–
TWO CENTURIES OF CHRISTIAN WITNESS IN TRURO, N.S. First United Church,
1760–1960. Truro, the Church, 1960. 85p

Maura, Sister, 1881–1957
THE SISTERS OF CHARITY, HALIFAX. Toronto, Ryerson, 1956. xxvi + 269p

Maxwell, Leslie Earl, 1895–
CROWDED TO CHRIST. Grand Rapids, Mich., Eerdmans Pub. Co., 1950. 354p
[OONL

May, Rev. Edward Geoffrey, 1869–1953
A HUNDRED YEARS OF CHRIST CHURCH, ST. ANDREW, P.Q. An Historical Sketch
of the Pioneer Church of the Ottawa Valley. ... St. John, Que., Smith, 1919.
71p [BVaU OLU

Mayes, Rev. Percival
THE STORY OF THE HISTORIC CHURCH OF ALL SAINTS, NIAGARA FALLS, ONTARIO.
Niagara Falls, the Church, 1951. 16p

Meacham, Albert Gallatin
A COMPENDIOUS HISTORY OF THE RISE AND PROGRESS OF THE METHODIST
CHURCH, BOTH IN EUROPE AND AMERICA. ... Hallowell, Ont., Wilson, 1832.
503p [BVaU NBFU OTP

Meagher, Nicholas Hogan, 1842–1932
THE RELIGIOUS WARFARE IN NOVA SCOTIA, 1855–1860. ... Joseph Howe's
Part in it and the Attitude of Catholics. ... Halifax, [1927?]. 193p [BVaU
NSWA OTP QMM

Medicine Hat, Alta. Westminster Presbyterian Church
AN HISTORICAL SKETCH OF WESTMINSTER PRESBYTERIAN CHURCH, MEDICINE
HAT, ALBERTA, 1914–1921. Medicine Hat, 1921. 19p [MWUC

Medley, Rev. John, 1804–1892
THE EPISCOPAL FORM OF CHURCH GOVERNMENT. ... Saint John, Avery, 1845.
46p [BM NSHD
FOUR CHARGES TO THE CLERGY OF THE DIOCESE. By John, Lord Bishop of
Fredericton, at his Triennial Visitations, holden in Christ Church Cathedral,
Fredericton, 1853, 1856, 1859, 1862. With Notes upon New Brunswick.
Oxford, Hammans, 1863. [BM NBFU
SERMONS. Published at the Request of Many of his late Parishioners. Exeter,
Hannaford, 1845. 467p [BM NBFU OTP

Mellish, Rev. Henry Frederick, 1828–1899
NO POPERY; or, a Defence of the Book of Common Prayer. The False Charges of
the so-called Reformed Episcopal Church Examined and fully Refuted.
Caledonia, Sawle, 1878. 215p [OTP

Melville, Sask. All Saints' Anglican Church
ALL SAINTS' ANGLICAN CHURCH, MELVILLE, SASKATCHEWAN, GOLDEN JUBILEE,
1909–1959. Melville, the Church, 1959. 24p

Mercer, William Henry Edgar, 1883–
CENTENNIAL SOUVENIR, THE UNITED CHURCH OF CANADA, TWILLINGATE,
NEWFOUNDLAND. A Century of Methodism in Twillingate and Notre Dame
Bay ... 1831–1931. Twillingate, Sun Office, [1933]. 163p [NfSM OONL

Methodist Church of Canada
CENTENARY OF METHODISM IN EASTERN BRITISH AMERICA, 1782–1882. ...
Halifax, Huestis, [1882]. 123p [NSHD
CENTENNIAL OF CANADIAN METHODISM. ... Published by the Direction of the
General Conference. Toronto, Briggs, 1891. 339p [BVaU OTU

Mildmay, Rev. Aubrey Neville St. John, 1865–

LAUREATES OF THE CROSS. Six Sermons. With an Intro. by W.J. Knox-Little.
  London, Elliot Stock, 1896. 91p [BM

Miller, Rev. Harry Baxter

ST. PATRICK'S CHURCH, ANGLICAN, HUDSON BAY, SASKATCHEWAN, CANADA.
  Golden Jubilee, 1903–1953. Hudson Bay, Sask., [1953?]. 49p

Millman, Rev. Thomas Reagh, 1905–

A HISTORY OF THE PARISH OF NEW LONDON, PRINCE EDWARD ISLAND. With
  Notes on the Larger Life of the Parish and Community during the First
  Three Quarters of the Nineteenth Century. Toronto, 1959. 71p
A SHORT HISTORY OF THE PARISH OF DUNHAM, QUEBEC. Granby, Que., Granby
  Print., 1946. 66p [BM OTP QMBM
THE STORY OF ST. GEORGE'S CHURCH, GRAFTON. Cobourg, Cobourg World,
  1935. 30p [OTU

Milton, Ont. St. Paul's United Church

ST. PAUL'S UNITED CHURCH, MILTON, ONTARIO, 1852–1952. Comp. by Mima
  Alma Hume *et al.* Milton, Historical Committee, 1952. 34p

Mitchell, Roy, 1884–1944

THEOSOPHY IN ACTION. Toronto, Blavatsky Institute, 1951. 86p
THROUGH TEMPLE DOORS. Studies in Occult Masonry. Toronto, Blavatsky
  Institute, 1950. 157p [OONL

Moir, John Sargent, 1926–

CHURCH AND STATE IN CANADA WEST. Three Studies in the Relation of
  Denominationalism and Nationalism, 1841–1867. Toronto, U. of Toronto
  Press, 1959. xv + 223p

Mollison, John

"WHAT IS MAN?–(THAT THOU ART MINDFUL OF HIM)." Summerside, P.E.I.,
  Journal Pub., 1932. 251p [BM NSWA

Moncton, N.B. First United Baptist Church

FIRST MONCTON UNITED BAPTIST CHURCH, 1828–1928. Centennial Services and
  Church History. Moncton, the Church, 1928. 20p [NSWA

Montreal, Que. Calvary Church

MANUAL OF CALVARY CHURCH AND REPORTS FOR THE YEAR 1884. Montreal,
  "Witness," 1885. 72p [QMBM

Montreal, Que. Erskine Church

SERMONS AND ADDRESSES DELIVERED AT JUBILEE. Montreal, Bentley, 1883.
  65p [NSWA

Moore, Rev. Arthur Henry, 1869–1938

HISTORY OF THE GOLDEN RULE LODGE (1803–1903), STANSTEAD, QUE. Toronto, Briggs, 1905. 219p [BM

Moore, Rev. William, 1838–1915

HISTORY OF BANK STREET PRESBYTERIAN CHURCH, OTTAWA, 1865–1911. [Ottawa, 1911.] 90p [OLU

A LECTURE DELIVERED ... IN THE BANK STREET PRESBYTERIAN CHURCH, Sunday, 31st December. Subject: "Is the Church of Rome Infallible?" Ottawa, Taylor [1871?]. 15p [OTP QMSS

REPORT ON THE CONDITION AND WORKING OF THE PRINCE ALBERT PRESBYTERIAN MISSION TO THE INDIANS ON THE SASKATCHEWAN. ... Ottawa, Woodburn, 1873. 52p [NSWA OKQ

Moreton, Rev. Julian, 1825–1900

A LETTER TO THE REV. H. BAILEY, IN REPLY TO RECENT STRICTURES UPON MISSIONARY SOCIETIES AND MISSIONARIES. London, Oxford U. Press, 1864. [BM

Morice, Rev. Adrian Gabriel, 1859–1938

THE CATHOLIC CHURCH IN THE CANADIAN NORTHWEST. Winnipeg, Author, 1936. 86p [BVaU OTU

HISTORY OF THE CATHOLIC CHURCH IN WESTERN CANADA, FROM LAKE SUPERIOR TO THE PACIFIC (1659–1895). Toronto, Musson, 1910. 2v [BVaU LC NSHD OTU

Morley, Rev. Frank Selkirk, 1904–

PERSONAL PEACE AND POWER. Calgary, Albertan Pub. Co., 1956. 109p

A WAY OF LIFE. Calgary, Author, 1958. 36p

WHY A PRESBYTERIAN CHURCH. Calgary, Author, 1955. 40p

Morrison, Rev. George W., 1909?–1950

COUNTRY PARSON. Ed. by William H. Cranston. Toronto, Ryerson, 1953. xi + 140p

Morrison, Rev. John, 1857–1924

THE CENTRAL METHODIST CHURCH, 1832–1919. Sarnia, the Church, 1919. 60p [OLU

Morrow, Ernest Lloyd, 1884–1951

CHURCH UNION IN CANADA. Its History, Motives, Doctrines and Government. Toronto, Allen, 1923. 450p [BVaU NBFU OTP QMM

Morton, Arthur Silver, 1870–1945

THE WAY TO UNION. Being a Study of the Principles of the Foundation and of the Historic Development of the Christian Church as bearing on the Proposed

Union of the Presbyterian, Methodist and Congregational Churches in Canada. ... Toronto, Briggs, 1912. 284p [BM BVaU NSHD OLU

Mott, Henry
JUBILEE HISTORY OF TRINITY CHURCH, MONTREAL 1840–1890. Comp. by ——. Montreal, Lovell, 1890. 64p [NSWA OOP

Mountain, Rev. George Jehoshaphat, 1789–1863
CANADIAN CHURCH DESTITUTION. Reprint of the Report made by the Right Rev. the Lord Bishop of Montreal, to the Right Hon. the Earl of Durham ... 1838. Hexham, Hatchard, n.d. 12p [OTP
A CIRCULAR LETTER FROM THE BISHOP OF MONTREAL, to the Clergy of his Diocese, on Church Vestments. London, Rivington, 1845. 39p [BM OTP
CIRCUMSTANCES PREVENTING COALITION WITH THE COLONIAL CHURCH & SCHOOL SOCIETY. Quebec, Mercury Office, 1859. 16p [OTP
THE DUTY OF THE CHRISTIAN MINISTER IN FOLLOWING CHRIST. New York, Church Depository, 1854. 32p [OTP
A FAST-DAY SERMON. Quebec, Mercury Office, 1857. 20p [OTP
THE FOUNDATION AND CONSTITUTION OF THE CHRISTIAN MINISTRY. Quebec, Neilson & Cowan, 1826. 39p [NSWA OTP QMSS
THE HOUSE OF THE LORD GOD. Two Sermons. Fredericton, Simpson, 1853. 24p [NSHD OTP
A LETTER TO MR. S.C. BLYTH, Occasioned by the Recent Publication of the Narrative of his Conversion to the Romish Faith. In 4 parts. By a Catholic Christian [pseud]. Montreal, Mower, 1822. 288p [BM OTP QMSS
A LETTER TO THE PRESIDENT OF THE ST. GEORGE'S SOCIETY OF QUEBEC, in Relation to the Choral Service of the Church of England. Quebec, Mercury Office, 1857. 8p [OTP
THE LOVE OF COUNTRY, Considered upon Christian Principles, with a Special Application to the Case of Englishmen. ... Quebec, Kemble, 1844. 17p [OTP QMSS
A PASTORAL LETTER ... UPON THE QUESTION OF AFFORDING THE USE OF CHURCHES AND CHAPELS OF THE CHURCH OF ENGLAND, FOR THE PURPOSES OF DISSENTING WORSHIP. Quebec, Cary, 1845. 18p [BM NSWA QMBM
A SERMON ON THE EDUCATION OF THE POOR ... Diffusing the Gospel, and ... Family Religion. ... Quebec, Neilson, 1822. 28p [OTP
SERMONS. London, Bell & Daldy; Cambridge, Deighton Bell, 1865. 262p [BM BVaU NSWA OTP QMBM
THE SOLDIER'S THANKSGIVING. A Sermon. Quebec, Cary, 1843. 16p [OTP
THE SPIRITUAL IMPROVEMENT of the Annual Observances of the Church. ... Quebec, Lovell & Lamoureux, 1855. 24p [OTP
THOUGHTS ON "ANNEXATION," in Connection with the Duty and the Interest of Members of the Church of England. Quebec, Cary, 1849. 28p [BVaU OTP QMM

A VALEDICTORY SERMON, Preached ... Fredericton ... 1817. Fredericton, Lugrin, 1817. 15p [OTP

Mowat, Oliver, 1820–1903
CHRISTIANITY AND ITS INFLUENCE. An Address. ... Toronto, Hunter Rose, 1898. 26p [OTU
CHRISTIANITY AND SOME OF ITS EVIDENCES POPULARLY STATED. Toronto, Williamson, 1890. 90p [2nd ed. rev. and enl.: Toronto, Briggs, 1901. 121p] [BVaU NSHD OTP

Mowatt, Rev. Andrew Joseph, 1838–1911
WORDS OF LIFE. ... Fredericton, Reporter Office, 1890. 352p [NSHD

Muckleston, William Jeffryes, 1849–
ROMAN METHODS OF CONTROVERSY, as Exemplified by the "Catholic Truth Society." A Lecture. ... Ottawa, Paynter & Abbott, 1893. 36p [NSHD OTU

Mulock, John A., –1897
METHODISM UNMASKED. In a Review of "A Vindication of the Methodist Church" (so called) "in a Pastoral Address" by Benjamin Nankevill, Wesleyan Minister. Carleton Place, Ont., Smith & Oswell, 1850. 54p [OTP

Murdoch, Rev. Benedict Joseph, 1886–
ALONE WITH THEE. Readings for the Holy Hour. Milwaukee, Bruce, 1934. 173p [LC NBFU OOSU

Murphy, Rev. James J.
FATHER MURPHY'S REPLY TO THE "WITNESS" CORRESPONDENCE EVOKED BY HIS DEFENCE OF PAPAL INFALLIBILITY. A Lecture delivered October 18th, 1875. Montreal, Sadlier, 1875. 30p [QMSS

Murphy, Rev. William Leo, 1899–
THE COBBLE STONES OF GALILEE. St. Nazianz, Wis., Society of the Divine Savior, 1946. 136p [LC

Murray, Rev. John, 1843–1935
THE HISTORY OF THE PRESBYTERIAN CHURCH IN CAPE BRETON. Truro, N.S., News Pub. Co., 1921. 282p [BVaU NBFU OTP
SCOTSBURN CONGREGATION, PICTOU COUNTY, NOVA SCOTIA. Its History, Professional Men. ... Truro, News Pub. Co., 1925. 161p [ACU NSHD OTP

Murray, Mrs. Margaret L.
ST. MARY'S OF LILLOOET. [Lillooet, B.C., 1935.] 8p [BViPA

Mussen, Joseph M.
THE CHURCH OF ST. MARK, A.D. 1792, NIAGARA-ON-THE-LAKE, ONTARIO, CANADA. Niagara-on-the-Lake, Author, 1934. 40p [OTU

Nankevill, Benjamin, 1799–1856

LETTERS TO THE REV. J.A. MULOCK. ... A Reply to Certain Charges against the Methodists. ... Carleton Place, Poole, 1850. 142p [NBFU OTP

Neal, Lucille Alethea (Schoonover), 1916–

LIKE A TREE PLANTED. New York, Pageant Press, 1955. 133p

New, Chester William, 1882–1960

CENTENARY HISTORY OF JAMES STREET BAPTIST CHURCH. By —— and George P. Gilmour. Hamilton, the Church, 1944. 78p [OLU

Newnham, Miss Sophie

THE BABES IN THE WOOD. Montreal, Lovell, 1895. 24p [NSWA OOA SSU

Nichols, John W.

A CENTURY OF METHODISM IN ST. JOHN'S NEWFOUNDLAND, 1815–1915. Ed. by ——. [St. John's], Dicks & Co., [1915]. 36p [NfSM

Nichols, Thomas E.

THE HISTORY OF THE DIOCESE OF NIAGARA TO 1950 A.D. Ed. by ——. Hamilton, Niagara Synod, 1950. 98p [NSHD OTU

Nicol, John Lennox

THROUGH THE YEARS WITH KNOX. Celebrating Sixty-five Years of Service as a Pastoral Charge, 1885–1950, and the Fiftieth Anniversary of the Opening of the First Knox Church, 1900–1950. Comp. by ——. Saskatoon, the Church, 1950. 60p [OONL SSU

Noel, Beatrice Maxine (Thistle)

THE STORY OF ONE HUNDRED YEARS AND A CHURCH, 1859–1959. ... Southampton, Ont., St. Paul's Anglican Church, 1959. 31p

Norman, Rev. Richard Whitmore, 1829–1906

CONSIDERATIONS ON THE REVISED EDITION OF THE NEW TESTAMENT. ... Montreal, Gazette, 1881. 55p [NSHD

THE IMPORTANCE OF RELIGIOUS RESERVE AND THE TEACHING OF THE CHURCH OF ENGLAND UPON CONFESSION AND ABSOLUTION. Three Sermons. Montreal, Lovell, 1873. 38p [NSWA QMSS

Norwood, Rev. Robert Winkworth, 1874–1932

HIS GLORIOUS BODY. New York, Scribner, 1930. 229p [BM LC NSHD

INCREASING CHRISTHOOD. New York, Scribner, 1932. 332p [BM LC

THE MAN WHO DARED TO BE GOD. A Story of Jesus. New York, Scribner, 1929. 324p [BM LC NSHD

PAUL TO TIMOTHY. An Epistle. N.p., [1914?]. 8p [NSHD

THE STEEP ASCENT. Noontide Meditations. ... New York, Scribner, 1928. 197p [BM NSHD

Nunn, Norman Alfred, 1900–
THE GREAT CHURCH OF ST. PAUL'S, TORONTO, CANADA. Toronto, the Church,
1954. x + 42p

O'Brien, Rev. Cornelius, 1843–1906
PHILOSOPHY OF THE BIBLE VINDICATED. Charlottetown, Bremner, 1876. 291p
[BM NSHD OTP

O'Byrne, Michael Cyprian
UPON THIS ROCK. A Life-Chronicle of the Last Century of Christian Civilization.
Toronto, Ellis, 1889. 434p [OONL

Odlum, Edward, 1850–1935
GOD'S COVENANT – MAN: BRITISH ISRAEL. Toronto, Briggs, 1916. 296p
[BM BVaU

O'Donnell, A.M.
A BRIEF HISTORY AND SOUVENIR BOOKLET OF KNOX PRESBYTERIAN CHURCH,
TRAIL, B.C., 1896–1921. Trail, Trail News, 1921. 19p [BViPA

O'Hara, Margaret, 1855–
LEAF OF THE LOTUS. Toronto, Poole, 1931. 188p [BVaU OTP

O'Higgins, Harvey Jerrold, 1876–1929
THE BEAST. A Story of Denver. By Judge Ben B. Lindsey and Harvey J. O'Higgins.
Boston, Doubleday, 1910. 340p [LC OTU

O'Leary, James M.
HISTORY OF THE IRISH CATHOLICS OF QUEBEC. Saint Patrick's Church to the
Death of Rev. P. McMahon. Quebec, Daily Telegraph, 1895. 48p [QMSS

Oliver, Mrs. Althea Pearleen, 1917–
A BRIEF HISTORY OF THE COLORED BAPTISTS OF NOVA SCOTIA, 1782–1953.
In Commemoration of Centennial Celebrations of the African United Baptist
Association of Nova Scotia. Halifax, African United Baptist Assoc. of N.S.,
1953. 84p

Oliver, Edmund Henry, 1882–1935
HIS DOMINION OF CANADA. A Study in the Background, Development and
Challenge of the Missions of the United Church of Canada. Toronto, Ryerson,
1932. 304p [BVaU OTU
THE SOCIAL ACHIEVEMENTS OF THE CHRISTIAN CHURCH. Toronto, Board of
Evangelism and Social Service of the United Church of Canada, 1930. 192p
[BVaU LC
TRACTS FOR DIFFICULT TIMES. By Edmund S. [!] Oliver. New York, Round
Table Press, 1933. 212p [LC OLU

THE WINNING OF THE FRONTIER. Toronto, United Church Pub. House, 1930. 271p ["A study in the religious history of Canada."] [BM BVaU LC NSWA OTU

O'Neill, Rev. Arthur Barry, 1858–
SACERDOTAL SAFEGUARDS. Notre Dame, Ind., U. Press, 1918. 304p [LC NBFU

Orillia, Ont. St. James's Parish
FIRST HUNDRED YEARS. Story of St. James's Parish, Orillia. Orillia, Packet-Times Press, 1941. [UTQ'42

Osborne, William Frederick, 1873–1950
THE FAITH OF A LAYMAN. Toronto, Cassell, 1910. 238p [BM BVaU LC NSWA

Osler, William, 1849–1919
MAN'S REDEMPTION OF MAN. A Lay Sermon. London, Constable, 1910. 60p [Also: New York, Hoebner, 1913. 63p] [BM BVaU OTP QMM
SCIENCE AND IMMORTALITY. Boston, Houghton, 1904. 54p [BVaU LC NBFU QMM

O'Sullivan, Dennis Ambrose, 1848–1892
ESSAYS ON THE CHURCH IN CANADA. With an intro. by His Grace, the Archbishop of Toronto. Toronto, Catholic Truth Soc., 1890. 134p [BVaU NSWA OTP

Ottawa, Ont. Congregation Adath Jeshurun
CONGREGATION ADATH JESHURUN COMMEMORATES ... THE SIXTIETH ANNI-VERSARY OF THE FOUNDING OF OUR SYNAGOGUE. Ed. by Herman S. Roodman. Ottawa, 1952. 24p

Ottawa, Ont. Congregation Beth Shalom
DEDICATION BETH SHALOM SYNAGOGUE, 1957. ... Ed. by Herman S. Roodman. Ottawa, the Synagogue, 1957. 32p

Ottawa, Ont. St. Andrew's Church
ST. ANDREW'S CHURCH, OTTAWA. The First Hundred Years, 1828–1928. Ottawa, Dadson-Merrill, 1931. 169p [BVaU

Owen, Rev. Derwyn Randulph Grier, 1914–
BODY AND SOUL. A Study on the Christian View of Man. Philadelphia, Westminster Press, 1956. 239p
SCIENTISM, MAN, AND RELIGION. Philadelphia, Westminster Press, 1952. 208p

Owen, Epenetus, 1815–
STRUCK BY LIGHTNING. ... With Incidents, Experiences, and Anecdotes for Old and Young. New ed. Otterville, Ont., A. Sims, [1891]. 190p [OONL

Page, Mrs. Elizabeth Merwin, 1889–
IN CAMP AND TEPEE. An Indian Mission Story. New York, Revell, 1915.
  245p [LC

Park, Mary Olga (Bracewell), 1891–
BETWEEN TIME AND ETERNITY. New York, Vantage Press, 1960. 105p

Parker, Rev. Stuart Crawford, 1888–1950
THE BOOK OF ST. ANDREW'S. A Short History of St. Andrew's Presbyterian
  Church, Toronto. Toronto, St. Andrew's Church, 1930. 142p [BVaU OTP
THE CHURCH AND RECONSTRUCTION. (An Address). London, Scott, 1919.
  56p [BM
THE GUEST CHAMBER. Toronto, Thorn Press, 1938. 125p [OTU
JESUS ASKS A QUESTION. Toronto, Thorn Press, 1937. 126p [OTU
LITTLE TALES OF JESUS. Toronto, Presbyterian Pub., 1935. 133p [OTU
YET NOT CONSUMED. A Short Account of the History and Antecedents of the
  Presbyterian Church in Canada. Toronto, Thorn Press, 1947. 204p [OTP

Parsons, Henry M.
BIOGRAPHICAL SKETCHES AND REVIEW. First Presbyterian Church in Toronto
  and Knox Church, 1820–1890. [Anon] Toronto, Timms, 1890. 46p
  [Haight Pt I

Paterson, Rev. James J., 1870–1928
ST. ANDREW'S CHURCH, SARNIA, 1843–1918. Sarnia, the Church, 1918. 69p
  [OLU

Patrick, Rev. William, 1852–1911
JAMES, THE LORD'S BROTHER. Edinburgh, Clark, 1906. 369p [BM BVaU LC
  OTU

Patstone, Arthur Job, 1881–
A SHORT HISTORY OF ST. PAUL'S CHURCH, NEWMARKET, ONTARIO. Toronto,
  Church of England, 1934. 16p [OTP

Patterson, Rev. George, 1824–1897
DOCTRINE OF THE TRINITY UNDERLYING THE REVELATION OF REDEMPTION.
  Edinburgh, Oliphant, 1870. 244p [BM BVaU NSHD OLU
HEATHEN WORLD. Its Need of the Gospel. Toronto, Briggs, 1884. 293p
  [NSHD OTU
"IT IS WELL." Two Sermons preached in Salem Church, Green Hill, on Sabbath,
  6th August, 1854 ... on the Occasion of the Death of his Only Child. ...
  Halifax, Bowes, 1854. 27p [NSHD
PRESENT TRUTH. A Sermon. Halifax, Barnes, 1858. 22p [NSHD

Peake, Frank Alexander, 1913–
HEROES OF THE CHURCH IN BRITISH COLUMBIA. Special Missionary Lessons,

Epiphany, 1958. Vancouver, Diocese of New Westminister, Board of Religious Education, 1957. 67p

Pearson, Rev. Leslie Trayer Holt, 1906–
THE MEMOIRS OF A CATHEDRAL. A Century of Christian Activity, 1859–1959. New Westminster, Holy Trinity Cathedral, 1959. 71p

Pelton, Sandford H.
HISTORICAL SKETCH OF SAINT JOHN'S PRESBYTERIAN CHURCH, YARMOUTH, NOVA SCOTIA, 1840–1915. Yarmouth, Herald, 1915. 43p [Amtmann

Penner, Rev. Archie, 1917–
THE CHRISTIAN, THE STATE, AND THE NEW TESTAMENT. Altona, Man., D.W. Friesen, 1959. 128p

Petrolia, Ont. Christ Church Booklet Committee
CHRIST CHURCH, PETROLIA, ONT., 1866–1959. [Petrolia, Ont., 1959?]. 70p

Phelps, Edward
A HISTORY OF BLACKWELL UNITED CHURCH AND BLACKWELL COMMUNITY. Blackwell, Ont., the Church, 1958. 54p

Pickel, Weldon U.
1891–1951 DIAMOND JUBILEE. History of the First Baptist Church, Regina, Sask. Comp. by ——. Regina, the Church, 1951. 16p [mimeographed]

Pickford, Mary, 1893–
MY RENDEZVOUS WITH LIFE. New York, Kinsey, 1935. 37p [LC
WHY NOT LOOK BEYOND? London, Methuen, 1936. 39p [BM
WHY NOT TRY GOD? New York, Kinsey, 1934. 35p [BM LC NSHPL

Pidgeon, Rev. George Campbell, 1872–1971
THE COMMUNION OF SAINTS. Toronto, Ryerson, 1935. 63p [OTUV
THE INDWELLING CHRIST. New York, Oxford U. Press, 1948. 208p [BVaU LC OTP QMM
THE UNITED CHURCH OF CANADA. The Story of the Union. Toronto, Ryerson, 1950. 107p [BVaU LC NBFU OTP
THE VICARIOUS LIFE. Toronto, Oxford U. Press, 1945. 187p [BM BVaU LC OTP
THE WAY OF SALVATION. Toronto, Clarke Irwin, 1954. 98p

Pierce, Lorne Albert, 1890–1961
THE CHRONICLE OF A CENTURY, 1829–1929. The Record of One Hundred Years of Progress in the Publishing Concerns of the Methodist, Presbyterian, and Congregational Churches in Canada. Ed. by ——. Toronto, United Church Pub. House, 1929. 271p [BVaU OTP
IN CONFERENCE WITH THE BEST MINDS. Toronto, Ryerson, 1927. 272p [LC NSWA OTP QMM

METHODISM AND THE NEW CATHOLICISM. Toronto, Ryerson, 1923. 70p
[Probably same as following title.] [Ryerson Impt

PRIMITIVE METHODISM AND THE NEW CATHOLICISM. Toronto, Methodist
Book, 1923. 70p [BVaU NBFU OKQ

Pilot Mound, Man. United Church
70TH ANNIVERSARY, PILOT MOUND UNITED CHURCH, 1888–1958. Pilot Mound,
Man., the Church, 1958. 46p [mimeographed]

Platt, Mrs. Harriet Louise
THE STORY OF THE YEARS. A History of the Women's Missionary Society of
the Methodist Church, Canada, from 1881 to 1906. V. 1: Canada. V. 2: Beyond
Seas. V. 3: Canada, 1906–1916. By Elizabeth S. Strachan. Toronto, Briggs,
1908, 1909, 1917. 155p, 148p, 338p [BM BVaU OTP

Playter, Rev. George Frederick, 1811–1866
THE HISTORY OF METHODISM IN CANADA. With an Account of the Rise and
Progress of the Work of God among the Canadian Indian Tribes, and Occasional
Notices of the Civil Affairs of the Province. Toronto, Green, 1862. 414p
[BVaU NBFU OTP QMM

Plewman, Harold Ernest, 1879–
THE STORY OF RYERSON UNITED CHURCH ... 50TH ANNIVERSARY. Hamilton,
the Church, 1958. 28p

Pond, Douglas Daaman, 1915–
ONE HUNDREDTH ANNIVERSARY, 1857–1957, UNITED BAPTIST CHURCH,
MARYSVILLE, NEW BRUNSWICK. By D.D. Pond and G.W. Crandlemire.
Marysville, the Church, 1957. 32p

Poole, Rev. Aquila James, 1908–
CENTENARY FESTIVAL, 1860–1960 ... A BRIEF HISTORY OF THE PARISH. Comp.
by ——. Ottawa, 1960. 26p [On St. John's Anglican Church, Richmond,
Ont.]

Poole, Rev. William Henry, 1820–1896
ANGLO–ISRAEL; or, The Saxon Race Proved to be the Lost Tribes of Israel.
In nine lectures. Intro. by the Rev. W.H. Withrow. Toronto, Briggs, 1889.
686p [BM BVaU LC NBFU OTP QMM

Pope, Joseph, 1854–1926
TRADITIONS. Ottawa, Durie, 1891. 20p [NSHD

Pope, Rev. William Robert, 1923–
TRIUMPH OF THE SPIRIT. Toronto, Ryerson, 1960. 62p

Port Dalhousie, Ont. St. Andrew's United Church
CENTENNIAL, 1852–1952. Port Dalhousie, Ont., the Church, 1952. 24p

Port Hope, Ont. Methodist Church
HISTORICAL SKETCH OF METHODISM IN CANADA AND PORT HOPE. Port Hope, Commercial Press, 1925. 39p [OTP

Porter, Jane
THE CHRISTIAN'S WEDDING RING. Containing Five Letters written by a Lady [pseud]. With the Sincere Desire of Sowing the Seeds of Union in the Christian Church. [Anon] Montreal, Lovell, 1874. 287p [9 pts in one, paginated separately.] [OTP QMSS

Porter, Rev. William Henry, 1840–1928
SERMON ON BAPTISM AND THE LORD'S SUPPER. With Things that Baptists DO NOT Believe, and Things that they DO Believe. Brantford, Daily Expositor, 1876. 32p [NSHD
SMOOTH STONES FROM RUNNING BROOKS. A Sermon on Baptism and the Lord's Supper. Brantford, Daily Expositor, 1876. 32p [OTUV

Pounder, Roy Mason, 1883–
ARTIST, THINKER, AND SAINT. Toronto, Ryerson, 1936. 225p [BVaU OTU

Powell, Mrs. R. Janet (Pettit), 1886–
THE HISTORY OF ST. ANDREW'S CHURCH, GRIMSBY, ONTARIO, 1794–1944. By Mrs. R.J. Powell and Harriet Walsh. Grimsby, the Church, 1944. 36p [OTU

Pratt, Edwin John, 1883–1964
STUDIES IN PAULINE ESCHATOLOGY, AND ITS BACKGROUND. Toronto, Briggs, 1917. 203p [BVaU MWU OTUV

Pratt, Viola Leone (Whitney), 1892–
ONE FAMILY. Toronto, United Church, 1937. 96p [CC

Presbyterian Church in Canada
HISTORIC SKETCHES OF THE PIONEER WORK AND THE MISSIONARY, EDUCA-TIONAL, AND BENEVOLENT AGENCIES OF THE PRESBYTERIAN CHURCH IN CANADA. Ed. by a Committee. Toronto, Murray Print., 1903. 128p [BVaU LC MWU OTU

Presbyterian Church in Canada. Hymn Book Committee
OUR HYMN WRITERS. ... Biographical Notices. ... Toronto, Campbell, 1880. 40p [NSHD OTU

Prince, Rev. Samuel Henry, 1883–1960
THE DYKES OF CIVILIZATION. Toronto, Anglican Church of Canada, 1958. 144p

Pringle, Rev. George Charles Fraser, 1873–1949
ABOARD "THE SKY PILOT" ON THE PACIFIC. N.p., Board of Home Missions, Presbyterian Church in Canada, 1923. 16p [BViPA

IN GREAT WATERS. The Story of the United Church Marine Missions. Toronto, Ryerson, 1928. 178p [BVaU OTP QMM

Proudfoot, Rev. John James Aitchison, 1821–1903
SYSTEMATIC HOMILETICS. Ed. by Rev. J.A. Turnbull and Rev. A.J. MacGillivray. Chicago, Revell, 1903. 320p [LC

Prower, Nelson, 1856–
THEOLOGY AND MORALITY. Montreal, Gazette Print., n.d. 60p [QMBM

Prowse, Daniel Woodley, 1834–1914
HISTORY OF THE CHURCHES IN NEWFOUNDLAND. London, 1895. 56p [A supp. to his HISTORY OF NEWFOUNDLAND.] [NBFU OTU QMM

Putnam, Ada MacLeod
THE SELKIRK SETTLERS AND THE CHURCH THEY BUILT AT BELFAST [P.E.I.]. Toronto, Presbyterian Pubs., 1939. 57p [NBFU OTP QMM

Pyper, James
ANIMADVERSIONS UPON THE REV. JOHN ROAF'S TWO SERMONS ON BAPTISM. Toronto, Carter & Thomas, 1851. 37p [NSWA

Quigley, Richard Francis, –1918
IPSE, IPSA; IPSE, IPSA, IPSUM; WHICH? (Latin Various Readings, Genesis iii.15). Controversial Letters ... in Vindication of the Position Assigned by the Catholic Church to the Ever-Blessed Mother of the World's Redeemer. ... In Reply to the Right Reverend Dr. Kingdon and John M. Davenport. New York, Pustet, 1890. 471p [BM BVaU NBFU OTP QMSS

Radford, Ruth, 1898–
MAYBE. An Allegory. Bowen Island, B.C., priv. print., 1954. 16p

Rae, James Penman, 1924–
THOUGHTS [Book 1]. Embodying a Doctrine of Influences. Perth, Ont., Author, 1955. 15p
THOUGHTS. Book 2. Perth, Ont., Author, 1956. 65p

Rand, Jennie Elizabeth (Magee), 1912–
HISTORICAL SKETCH OF CHURCH OF ST. JOHN, 1810–1960, AND THE PARISH OF CORNWALLIS, NOVA SCOTIA, 1760–1960. N.p., 1960. 22p

Rand, Rev. Silas Tertius, 1810–1889
A HISTORICAL SKETCH OF THE NOVA SCOTIA BAPTIST ASSOCIATION. Charlotte-town, Haszard, 1849. 31p [NSHD

Rankin, A.
JESUITS' ESTATES IN CANADA. Montreal, Becket, 1850. 134p [BM OTU

Reid, William Stanford, 1913–
THE CHURCH OF SCOTLAND IN LOWER CANADA. Toronto, Presbyterian Pub.,
1936. 190p [BM BVaU LC OTU QMM

Renison, Rev. Robert John, 1875–1957
FOR SUCH A TIME AS THIS. Toronto, McClelland, 1947. 368p [BVaU LC
OTP
WEDNESDAY MORNING. Toronto, McClelland, 1944. 275p [BVaU LC OTP

Reynar, Rev. Alfred Henry, 1840–1921
EBENEZER. Address on Methodism. Toronto, Briggs, 1900. 16p [OTU

Reynolds, Rev. Arthur Guy, 1909–
THE EARLY HISTORY OF LEITH UNITED CHURCH. Owen Sound, 1942. 20p
[OTU
THE MEANS OF GRACE. Toronto, United Church Pub. House, 1952. 56p
WHAT'S THE DIFFERENCE? Protestant and Roman Catholic Beliefs Compared.
Toronto, United Church Pub. House, 1954. 64p

Reynolds, Henry Dunbar, 1820–1864
THE NIAGARA CHURCH CASE. ... Toronto, Maclear, 1857. 113p [OTP

Richey, Rev. Matthew, 1803–1883
A PLAIN STATEMENT of Facts, Connected with the Union and Separation of
the British Canadian Conferences. By J. Stinson and M. Richey. Toronto,
Stanton, 1840. 56p [OTU QMSS
SERMONS DELIVERED ON VARIOUS OCCASIONS. Toronto, Ryerson, 1840.
280p [NSWA OTP
TWO LETTERS Addressed to the Editor of the "Church," Exposing the Intolerant
Bigotry of that Journal. ... Toronto, Rogers Thompson, 1843. 18p [OTP

Riddell, John Henry, 1863–1952
METHODISM IN THE MIDDLE WEST. Toronto, Ryerson, 1946. 371p [BVaU
LC OTP

Riddell, Walter, 1814–1904
DIARY OF VOYAGE FROM SCOTLAND TO CANADA IN 1833, and Story of St.
Andrew's Presbyterian Church, Cobourg, Ontario. With Occasional Notes by the
Honourable William Renwick Riddell. Toronto, Associated Printers, 1932.
32p [NSHD OTP QMM

Riddell, Walter Alexander, 1881–
THE RISE OF ECCLESIASTICAL CONTROL IN QUEBEC. New York, Columbia
U. Press, 1916. 195p [LC NBFU

Ritchie, David Lakie, 1864–1951

THE GENIUS OF CONGREGATIONALISM. ... Toronto, Ryerson, 1926. 36p
[OTUV

THE GOSPEL AS THE POWER OF GOD. Montreal, 1927. 10p [OKQ

Ritchie, Eliza, 1850–1933

THE PROBLEM OF PERSONALITY. ... Ithaca, Andrus & Church, 1889. 42p
[LC NSHD

Roaf, Rev. John, 1801–1862

LECTURES ON THE MILLENIUM. Toronto, 1844. 173p [BVaU NSWA OTP

RELIGIOUS LIBERTY. Being a Letter to the Editor of the "Palladium," upon the
Thanksgiving Proclamation of ... Sir F.B. Head, and a Second to the Editors
of the "Patriot," "Christian Guardian," & "Commercial Herald". ... Toronto,
Palladium Office, 1838. 8p [BM OTP

TWO SERMONS ON BAPTISM. ... Toronto, Carter & Thomas, 1850. 31p [BM
NSWA OTP

Roberts, Rev. Richard, 1874–1945

THE CHRISTIAN GOD. New York, Macmillan, 1929. 154p [BM BVaU OTP

THE CONTEMPORARY CHRIST. New York, Macmillan, 1938. 148p [BM OTU

FOR GOD AND FREEDOM. Sackville, Mount Allison U., 1945. 45p [BVaU LC
NBFU OTU QMM

THE GOSPEL AT CORINTH. New York, Macmillan, 1924. 173p [BM QMM

THE RED CAP ON THE CROSS. London, Hedley Bros., 1918. 127p [BM OTP

THE RENASCENCE OF FAITH. New York, Cassell, 1912. 308p [BM LC

THE SPIRIT OF GOD AND THE FAITH OF TODAY. New York, Willett Clark Colby,
1930. 185p [BVaU LC

THAT STRANGE MAN UPON HIS CROSS. New York, Abingdon, 1934. 139p
[BVaU LC QMM

THE UNTRIED DOOR. An Attempt to Discover the Mind of Jesus for Today.
New York, Women's Press, 1921. 174p [LC

WHAT'S BEST WORTH SAYING. New York, Doran, 1922. 131p [LC

Robertson, Rev. Hugh John, 1868–1952

THE STORY OF KNOX CHURCH, WINNIPEG. Seventy-five Years, 1872–1947.
Winnipeg, the Church, [1947?]. 48p [MWP

Robertson, Rev. James, 1801?–1878

HISTORY OF THE MISSION OF THE SECESSION CHURCH TO NOVA SCOTIA AND
PRINCE EDWARD ISLAND, FROM ITS COMMENCEMENT IN 1765. Edinburgh,
Johnstone, 1847. 292p [NSWA OTP QMSS

A TREATISE ON INFANT BAPTISM. Shewing the Scriptural Grounds and
Historical Evidence. ... Halifax, "The Novascotian" Office, 1836. xxiv + 291p
[NBFU OTP

Robinson, Frank Alfred, 1874–
RELIGIOUS REVIVAL AND SOCIAL BETTERMENT. Boston, Gorham, 1918. 54p
  [LC

Robson, Alexander Ritchie
WEST OF THE WEST. A Sketch of Early Mission Days in North-Western Canada.
  Toronto, Musson, n.d. 136p [AEU OTU

Robson, Rev. Ebenezer, 1835–1915
HOW METHODISM CAME TO BRITISH COLUMBIA. Toronto, Methodist, 1905.
  31p [BViPA OKQ

Roddan, Rev. Andrew, –1948
THE CHRIST OF THE WIRELESS WAY. Vancouver, Clarke & Stuart, 1932. 216p
  [BVaU NSWA
THE CHURCH IN THE MODERN CITY. The Story of Three Score Years of
  Practical Christian Service, 1885–1945, First United Church, Vancouver, B.C.
  Vancouver, Dunsmuir Print., n.d. 61p [BVaU

Roe, Rev. Henry, 1829–1909
BICENTENARY SERMONS. Two Sermons on the History and Scriptural Authority
  of the Book of Common Prayer. Montreal, Lovell, 1862. [NSWA
THE CONTINUITY OF THE CHURCH OF ENGLAND AND THE PAPAL ENCYCLICAL
  APOSTOLIC CURAE. Quebec, n.pub., 1897. 87p [NSWA
FAREWELL SERMON PREACHED IN ST. STEPHEN'S, OR 2ND INVERNESS CHURCH,
  MEGANTIC, ON THE 22ND OCTOBER, 1854. Montreal, Lovell, 1854. 40p [OTP
PURGATORY, TRANSUBSTANTIATION, AND THE MASS. Three Sermons. ... 2nd ed.
  Montreal, Lovell, 1863. 111p [NSWA OLU
STORY OF THE FIRST HUNDRED YEARS OF THE DIOCESE OF QUEBEC. Quebec,
  "Morning Chronicle," 1893. 63p [BVaU NSWA OTP

Rokeby-Thomas, Rev. Howard Rokeby, 1907–
CHURCH IN THE VALLEY. Port Stanley, Ont., Christ Church, 1949. 96p [OLU

Roman Collar (pseud)
THE PARSON HITS BACK. Toronto, Thorn Press, 1937. 126p [CC

Rose, Albert, 1917–
A PEOPLE AND ITS FAITH. Essays on Jews and Reform Judaism in a Changing
  Canada. Ed. by ——. Toronto, U. of Toronto Press, 1959. xiv + 204p

Rosenberg, Rabbi Stuart E., 1922–
MAN IS FREE. Sermons and Addresses. New York, Bloch Pub. Co., 1957.
  xii + 155p
THE ROAD TO CONFIDENCE. Toronto, Copp Clark, 1959. ix + 166p
A TIME TO SPEAK, OF MAN, FAITH AND SOCIETY. New York, Bloch Pub. Co.,
  1960. 181p

Ross, Mrs. Anna
THE NEW COVENANT. A Lost Secret. ... Toronto, Briggs, 1901. 193p [BM
NSWA OTU

Ross, Rev. Duncan, 1770?–1834
BAPTISM CONSIDERED IN ITS SUBJECTS AND MODE. In Three Letters to the Rev.
William Elder. Pictou, Weir Durham, 1825. 78p [NSHD
STRICTURES ON A PUBLICATION ENTITLED "BELIEVER IMMERSION." Pictou, Weir
Durham, 1828. 38p [NSHD OTP

Ross, Rev. John Jacob, 1871–
BREAKING THE SEALS. A Spiritual and Devotional Study of All the Symbols in the
Central Chapters of the Book of Revelation. New York, Revell, 1924. 221p
[LC
DANIEL'S HALF-WEEK NOW CLOSING. New York, 1922. 115p [LC
THE KINGDOM IN MYSTERY. New York, 1920. 379p [LC
OUR GLORIOUS HOPE. New York, Revell, 1922. 160p [LC
PEARLS FROM PATMOS. New York, Revell, 1923. 231p [LC
THINKING THROUGH THE NEW TESTAMENT. New York, Revell, 1921. 254p [LC

Roth, Rev. D. Luther
ACADIE AND THE ACADIANS. Philadelphia, Lutheran Pub. Soc., 1890. 427p
[Concerns the Lutheran Church in Nova Scotia] [BVaU LC NBFU OTP
QMBM
OUR SCHOOLMASTER. A Series of Lectures on the Commandments. Halifax,
Nova Scotia Print., 1880. xv + 136p [NSHPL

Rowley, Owsley Robert, 1868–1949
THE ANGLICAN EPISCOPATE OF CANADA AND NEWFOUNDLAND. Milwaukee,
Morehouse, 1928. 280p [BM BVaU NSWA OTP QMM

Roy, Rev. James, 1834–1922
BAPTISM AND SALVATION. Montreal, Rivard, 1882. 46p [OTP
CATHOLICITY AND METHODISM; or, The Relation of John Wesley to Modern
Thought. Montreal, Burland-Desbarats, 1877. 109p [BM NSWA OTP QMSS
HOW TO INTERPRET OUR BIBLE. New York, Broadway, 1911. 119p [LC NSHD
QMM

Royal Oak, Vancouver Island, B.C. St. Michael and All Angels' Church
ST. MICHAEL AND ALL ANGELS' CHURCH, WEST SAANICH ROAD, ROYAL OAK,
VANCOUVER ISLAND, BRITISH COLUMBIA, 1883 TO 1953. Victoria, n.p., 1953.
20p

Royle, Rev. Edward Cecil, 1912–
AN HISTORICAL STUDY OF THE ANGLICAN PARISH OF VAUDREUIL. Hudson
Heights, Que., Author, 1952. 76p [mimeographed]

THE HISTORY OF THE ANGLICAN PARISH OF VAUDREUIL. [2nd ed. rev. and enl.] Hudson Heights, Que., Author, 1955. 221p

Russell, Francis W.
HISTORY OF ST. MARY'S CATHEDRAL PARISH, WINNIPEG, MANITOBA. Diamond Jubilee Edition. Winnipeg, 1936. 95p [MWP

Russell, Rev. George Stanley, 1883–1957
THE CHURCH IN THE MODERN WORLD. Toronto, Allen, 1931. 179p [BVaU LC NSHD OTP
THE FACE OF GOD. New York, Harper, 1935. 114p [BM

Ryerson, Rev. Adolphus Egerton, 1803–1882
CANADIAN METHODISM, ITS EPOCHS AND CHARACTERISTICS. ... Toronto, Briggs, 1882. 440p [BVaU NBFU OTP
CLAIMS OF THE CHURCHMEN AND DISSENTERS OF UPPER CANADA. Brought to the Test in a Controversy between Several Members of the Church of England and a Methodist Preacher. [Anon] Kingston, Herald Office, 1828. 232p [OTP QMSS
THE CLERGY RESERVE QUESTION AS A MATTER OF HISTORY, A QUESTION OF LAW AND A SUBJECT OF LEGISLATION. In a Series of Letters to the Hon. W.H. Draper. Toronto, Lawrence, 1839. 156p [BM BVaU OTP QMSS
SCRIPTURAL RIGHTS OF THE MEMBERS OF CHRIST'S VISIBLE CHURCH; or, Correspondence Containing the Reasons of Dr. Ryerson's Resignation of Office in the Wesleyan Methodist Church. Toronto, Brewer McPhail, 1854. [BM NSWA OTP
WESLEYAN METHODISM IN UPPER CANADA. A Sermon. ... Toronto, Conference Office, 1837. 27p [BVaU NSWA OTP

Sackville, N.B. St. Paul's Church
100TH ANNIVERSARY, ST. PAUL'S CHURCH, SACKVILLE, N.B. Sackville, the Church, 1958. 24p

Sadlier, Mary Anne (Madden), 1820–1903
PURGATORY: DOCTRINAL, HISTORICAL AND POETICAL. New York, Sadlier, 1886. 500p [LC OWA QQL

Saint John, N.B. Exmouth Street United Church. Historical Committee
ONE HUNDREDTH ANNIVERSARY, EXMOUTH STREET UNITED CHURCH, 1857–1957. Saint John, the Church, 1957. 36p

Saint John, N.B. St. Andrew's Kirk. Historical Committee
ST. ANDREW'S KIRK, SAINT JOHN, N.B., THE UNITED CHURCH OF CANADA. One Hundred and Seventy-fifth Anniversary, May 18th, 1784–May 18th, 1959. Saint John, the Church, 1959. 113p

Saint John, N.B. St. Paul's Church
ST. PAUL'S CHURCH, SAINT JOHN, NEW BRUNSWICK, ESTABLISHED MAY 1ST, 1856. Saint John, N.B., the Church, 1958. 8p

Saint John, N.B. West Side Kirk of the United Church of Canada
THE WEST SIDE KIRK OF THE UNITED CHURCH OF CANADA. A Century of Service, 1857–1957. Ed. by Gerald Keith. Saint John, the Church, 1957. 101p

St. Laurent, Charles F. (pseud)
LANGUAGE AND NATIONALITY IN THE LIGHT OF REVELATION AND HISTORY. Montreal, Author, 1896. 104p [OTP

St. Mary's, Ont. Knox Presbyterian Church
AN HISTORICAL SKETCH OF KNOX PRESBYTERIAN CHURCH, ST. MARY'S, ONTARIO, MAY 6TH, 1956. A Souvenir of the Golden Jubilee, 1906–1956. St. Mary's, the Church, 1956. 8p

St. Paul, Mother M.
FROM DESENZANO TO "THE PINES." A Sketch of the History of the Ursulines of Ontario. ... Toronto, Macmillan, 1941. 387p [OLU QMBM

Salter, Walter Frederick, 1884–
TRUTH AS I SEE IT. Haliburton, Ont., Author, [1959?]. 14 + 129p

Sanderson, Rev. Joseph Edward, 1830–1913
THE FIRST CENTURY OF METHODISM IN CANADA. Toronto, Briggs, 1908–1910. 2v [BVaU NSWA OTP

Sangster, James Lewis, 1891–
75 YEARS OF SERVICE. A History of Olivet Baptist Church, 1878–1953. New Westminster, Olivet Board of Management, 1953. 77p

Saskatoon, Sask. Grace United Church
GRACE UNITED CHURCH, SASKATOON, 1886–1951. Saskatoon, the Church, 1951. 32p

Saskatoon, Sask. Third Avenue United Church
GOLDEN JUBILEE OF THIRD AVENUE UNITED CHURCH, SASKATOON, SASKATCHEWAN, 50TH ANNIVERSARY. A Record of Service and Achievement down through the years, 1901–1951. Saskatoon, the Church, 1951. 32p

Saunders, Rev. Edward Manning, 1829–1916
HISTORY OF THE BAPTISTS OF THE MARITIME PROVINCES. Halifax, Burgoyne, 1902. 520p [BVaU NBFU OTP
A SKETCH OF THE ORIGIN AND HISTORY OF THE GRANVILLE STREET BAPTIST CHURCH. Halifax, Christian Messenger, 1877. 78p [NSHD

Saunders, Henry Scholey, 1864–1951
THE HIGHER CONSCIOUSNESS. A Little Introduction to Dr. Richard Maurice Bucke's "Cosmic Consciousness." Toronto, Author, 1924. 47p [OTP

Savary, Alfred William, 1831–1920
FRENCH AND ANGLICAN CHURCHES AT ANNAPOLIS ROYAL. ... Annapolis Royal, Spectator, 1910. 15p [NSWA

Scadding, Rev. Henry, 1813–1901
CHRISTIAN PANTHEISM. An Address. ... Toronto, Rollo, 1865. 11p [NSWA OTU
JUBILEE OF THE DIOCESE OF TORONTO. 1839 to 1889. ... By Henry Scadding and J.G. Hodgins. Toronto, Rowsell & Hutchinson, 1890. 235p [BVaU NSWA OTU

Schrepfer, Luke
PIONEER MONKS IN NOVA SCOTIA. Tracadie, N.S., St. Augustine's Monastery, 1947. 228p [BVaU

Scollard, Robert Joseph L., 1908–
BASILIAN FATHERS. A Short Account of History, Life and Works of Congregation of Priests of St. Basil. Toronto, Basilian Press, 1940. 32p [OTU

Scott, Charles Sumner, 1858–
CHRIST CHURCH CATHEDRAL, HAMILTON, 1835–1935. Hamilton, Davis-Lisson, 1935. 88p [OTP

Scott, Rev. Frederick George, 1861–1944
THE EMPIRE AND THE COLOURS OF THE FLAG; A Sermon Addressed to the Canadian Volunteers for the War. London, Christian Knowledge Society, 1900. 8p [BM

Scott, Mary Jane, 1894–
MY ADVENTURES WITH GOD. Toronto, Nelson, 1956. 139p

Scott, Rev. Robert Balgarnie Young, 1899–
THE ORIGINAL LANGUAGE OF THE APOCALYPSE. Toronto, U. of Toronto Press, 1928. 25p [BM LC OTU
THE RELEVANCE OF THE PROPHETS. New York, Macmillan, 1944. 237p [BVaU LC OTP
TOWARDS THE CHRISTIAN REVOLUTION. Ed. by R.B.Y. Scott and Gregory Vlastos. Chicago, Willett Clark, 1936. 254p [BM BVaU LC OTP QMM

Scott, William Louis, 1862–1947
EASTERN CATHOLICS. With Special Reference to the Ruthenians in Canada. Toronto, Catholic Truth Soc., 1923. 47p [OTP

Scrimger, Rev. John, 1849–
JESUIT MORALS. On the Errors in the Moral Teaching of the Jesuits. Montreal, Drysdale, 1890. 89p [OTP QMM

Sedgewick, Rev. Robert
HOLY AND HAPPY CHURCH THE ABODE OF THE GOD OF LOVE. A Sermon. Aberdeen, Smith, 1849. 36p [NSHD

THE PAPACY: THE IDOLATRY OF ROME. A Lecture. Halifax, Wesleyan, 1859. 59p
[NSHP

WINE OF THE KINGDOM; or, Fellowship with Christ. Dundee, Middleton, 1846.
155p [BM NSHD

Seely, Rev. Ralph Arthur, 1930–
APPALLING APOSTASY. Central Bedeque, P.E.I., Author, 1955. 39p

Sellar, Robert, 1841–1919
THE PAPAL MENACE. Canada is Threatened with Papal rather than French
Domination. Toronto, Sentinel Pub. Co., [1912?]. 46p [BVaU OTP

Semmens, Rev. John, 1850–1921
THE HANDBOOK TO SCRIPTURE TRUTHS. Toronto, Methodist Mission Rooms,
1893. 46p [LC

Seymour, Rev. James Cooke, 1839–1902
CHRIST THE APOCALYPSE. New York, Eaton & Mains, 1902. 350p [LC
THE RIVER OF LIFE. An Exposition of Ezekiel's Vision. Toronto, Wesleyan, 1869.
169p [Ryerson Impt
VOICES FROM THE THRONE; or, God's Call to Faith and Obedience. Toronto,
Methodist Book, 1881. 153p [OTP

Shatford, Rev. Allan Pearson, 1873–1935
SIX MARKS OF A CHRISTIAN. Philadelphia, Winston, 1925. 122p [LC
SIX ROLES OF A CHRISTIAN. Toronto, McClelland, 1928. [CC
THE YEAR OF JUBILEE. A Brief Sketch of Fifty Years' Work in the Church of
St. James the Apostle, Montreal, 1864–1914. Montreal, Lovell, 1914. 68p
[BVaU NSWA OLU QMSS

Shaw, Gordon, 1893–
THE ROAD TO REALITY. New York, Pageant Press, 1952. xiii + 121p

Shaw, John Arthur, 1862–
SOME FEATURES OF THE FAITH. A Popular Discussion of Certain Cardinal Points
of Christian Doctrine. Milwaukee, Young Churchman, 1902. 306p [LC OTU

Shaw, Rev. John Mackintosh, 1879–
THE BELIEF IN THE HOLY SPIRIT. Stirling, Drummond Tract Depot, n.d. 16p
[OTU
CHRISTIAN DOCTRINE. A One-Volume Outline of Christian Belief. London,
Lutterworth Press, 1953. 378p
THE CHRISTIAN GOSPEL OF THE FATHERHOOD OF GOD. London, Hodder, 1925.
191p [BM BVaU LC NSHD
LIFE AFTER DEATH. The Christian View of the Future Life. Toronto, Ryerson,
1945. 110p [BVa LC OTP

THE RESURRECTION OF CHRIST. Edinburgh, Clark, 1920. 215p [BM BVaU LC NSWA QMM

THE WONDER OF THE CHRISTIAN GOSPEL. Toronto, Ryerson, 1959. 143p

Shaw, Robert
EXISTENCE AND DEITY. Illustrated and Explained. In Two Parts. Montreal, Author, 1872. 900p [OONL QMBM

Shaw, Rev. Robert Elwell, 1910–
HISTORICAL SKETCH, 1831–1956, DISCIPLES OF CHRIST, NORTH STREET CHRISTIAN CHURCH, HALIFAX, N.S. Halifax, the Church, [1956?]. 22p

Shaw, Rev. William Isaac, 1841–1911
DIGEST OF THE DOCTRINAL STANDARDS OF THE METHODIST CHURCH. Toronto, Briggs, 1895. 141p [BM OTU

Shaw, William John, 1886–
ST. ANDREW'S–ST. PAUL'S, 1857–1957. Hamilton, St. Paul's Church, 1957. 57p
ST. PAUL'S CHURCH (PRESBYTERIAN), HAMILTON. A Century of Service. Hamilton, Author, 1933. 93p [OTP

Shenston, Thomas Strahan, 1822–1895
GLEANINGS. By T.S.S. Guelph, Hough, 1893. 176p [OTP
A JUBILEE REVIEW OF THE FIRST BAPTIST CHURCH, BRANTFORD, 1833 TO 1884. ... Toronto, Bingham & Webber, 1890. 203p [OTP

Sheppard, Edmund Ernest, 1855–1924
THE THINKING UNIVERSE. Reason as Applied to the Manifestations of the Infinite. Los Angeles, Author's Co., 1915. 347p [BM LC OTU

Sheraton, Rev. James Peterson, 1841–1906
CHRISTIAN SCIENCE. N.p., 1891. 44p [NSWA OTU
THE HIGHER CRITICISM. Toronto, 1904. 69p [OTP QMM
THE INSPIRATION AND AUTHORITY OF THE HOLY SCRIPTURES. Toronto, Bryant, 1893. 58p [OTU
OUR LORD'S TEACHING CONCERNING HIMSELF. N.p., 1904. 55p [OTU

Sherbrooke, Que. Plymouth United Church
PLYMOUTH CHURCH, PAST AND PRESENT. A Brief History of Plymouth United Church. ... [1835–1955]. Sherbrooke, the Church, 1956. ix + 65p

Shields, Thomas Todhunter, 1873–1955
"OTHER LITTLE SHIPS" FREIGHTED WITH COMFORT. Toronto, Hunter Rose, 1935. 261p [BM

Sidey, John James
THE CENTENNIAL OF THE BEDEQUE BAPTIST CHURCH, P.E.I. "Overcoming"; or,

"The Victory of the Gospel". ... A Scenic Pageant, showing the early History of the Bedeques and the Founding of the Baptist Church. [Bedeque?] , 1926. [59] p [NSWA

Sigsworth, John Wilkins, 1915—
THE BATTLE WAS THE LORD'S. A History of the Free Methodist Church in Canada. Oshawa, Sage Publishers, 1960. 301p

Silcox, Rev. Claris Edwin, 1888—1961
CATHOLICS, JEWS AND PROTESTANTS. A Study in Relationships in the United States and Canada. By Claris Edwin Silcox and Galen M. Fisher. New York, Harper, 1934. 369p [BM BVaU LC OTP QMM
CHURCH UNION IN CANADA. New York, Inst. of Social and Religious Research, 1933. 493p [BM BVaU LC NSHD OTP
THE CONSECRATION OF POWER AND INTELLIGENCE. Toronto, Ryerson, 1945. 22p [BVaU OTU
AN EPISTLE TO THE HEBREWS. By John Cournos and C.E. Silcox. Toronto, Ryerson, 1938. 32p [OTU QMM
"FROM WAR TO PEACE." Sermons Preached in Newport, R.I., during the Great War. Newport, Milne Print., 1919. n.p. [OTU
PHYSICIANS, HUMAN AND DIVINE. A Sermon. Fairfield, Conn., 1922. 17p [OTU
PROTESTANT-CATHOLIC RELATIONS IN CANADA. Toronto, United Church Pub., 1938. 32p [BVaU OTU
THE RELATION OF CHURCH AND STATE. A Sermon. N.p., 1921. 18p [OTU
THE WAR AND RELIGION. Toronto, Macmillan, 1941. 30p [BVaU OTU

Sims, Rev. Albert
REMARKABLE NARRATIVES; or, Records of Powerful Revivals, Striking Providences, Wonderful Religious Experiences, Tragic Death-bed Scenes and Other Authentic Incidents. ... Kingston, Author, 1896. 352p [Another ed.: Pittsburgh, Hague, 1902. 352p] [BM BVaU LC

Sinclair, Rev. Alexander Maclean, 1840—1924
LETTERS ON THE ANGLO-ISRAEL FOLLY. Truro, McConnell, 1880. 41p [NSWA

Sinclair, John D., 1874—1947
WESTMINSTER CHURCH, THE UNITED CHURCH OF CANADA, WINNIPEG, FORTY-FIFTH YEAR. Souvenir of the Silver Jubilee of the present Church Building. Winnipeg, 1937. 101p [MWP

Sisters of St. Ann. St. Ann's Academy
THE SISTERS OF ST. ANN IN BRITISH COLUMBIA, YUKON, AND ALASKA, 1858—1958. Victoria, St. Ann's Academy, 1958. 100p

Sisters of St. Ann. Saint Joseph Province
CENTENNIAL ANNIVERSARY OF THE ARRIVAL OF THE PIONEER NUNS IN VICTORIA, B.C., JUNE 5, 1858—JUNE 5, 1958. Victoria, 1958. 63p

Sleigh, William Willcocks, 1796–

THE CHRISTIAN'S DEFENSIVE DICTIONARY. Philadelphia, Biddle, 1837. 437p
[BM LC

AN EXPOSURE OF MARIA MONK'S PRETENDED ABDUCTION. Philadelphia,
Collins, 1837. 36p [OTP

Slight, Rev. Benjamin, 1798?–1858

THE APOCALYPSE EXPLAINED. In Two Series of Discourses on the Entire Book of
the Revelation of St. John. Montreal, Miller, 1855. 516p [BM LC OTP

Smart, Rev. James Dick, 1906–

THE RECOVERY OF HUMANITY. Philadelphia, Westminster Press, 1953. 157p

Smith, Goldwin, 1823–1910

DOES THE BIBLE SANCTION AMERICAN SLAVERY? Oxford & London, Henry
& Parker, 1863. 107p [AEU NBFU OKQ

THE FOUNDER OF CHRISTENDOM. Boston, American Unitarian Assoc., 1903.
44p [BM BVaU LC NBFU OTP QMM

GUESSES AT THE RIDDLE OF EXISTENCE, AND OTHER ESSAYS ON KINDRED SUB-
JECTS. New York, Macmillan, 1897. 244p [BM BVaU LC NBFU OTU QMM

IN QUEST OF LIGHT. New York, Macmillan, 1906. 177p [BVaU LC NSHD
OLU QMM

KEEPING CHRISTMAS. Toronto, Robinson, 1888. 12p [MWU NBFU OKQ

LINES OF RELIGIOUS ENQUIRY. Toronto, Copp Clark, 1897. 21p [AEU BM
NBFU OTU

NO REFUGE BUT IN TRUTH. Toronto, Tyrrell, 1909. 93p [BM BVaU NBFU
OKQ QMM

RATIONAL RELIGION, AND THE RATIONALISTIC OBJECTIONS OF THE BAMPTON
LECTURES FOR 1858. Oxford, Wheeler, 1861. 146p [BM BVaU LC NBFU
OTU QMM

Smith, Rev. Oswald Jeffrey, 1889–

BACK TO PENTECOST. New York, Christian Alliance, 1926. 124p [LC

THE BAPTISM WITH THE HOLY SPIRIT. New York, Christian Alliance, 1925. 54p
[LC

CAN ORGANIZED RELIGION SURVIVE? Toronto, Tabernacle Pub., 1932. 299p
[OWtL

THE CLOUDS ARE LIFTING. London, Marshall, Morgan & Scott, 1939. 96p
[BM BVaU

THE DAWN IS BREAKING. London, Marshall, Morgan & Scott, [19——]. 96p
[BM BVaU

THE DAY OF SALVATION. London, Marshall, Morgan & Scott, 1955. 127p

THE ENDUEMENT OF POWER. London, Marshall, Morgan & Scott, [19——]. 119p
[BM BVaU OLU

FROM DEATH TO LIFE. New York, Christian Alliance, 1925. 128p [LC

THE GREAT PHYSICIAN. New York, Christian Alliance, 1927. 128p [LC

IS THE ANTICHRIST AT HAND?–WHAT OF MUSSOLINI. New York, Christian
Alliance, 1927. 128p [LC

THE LORD IS CALLING. London, Marshall, Morgan & Scott, [19—]. 95p [BM
BVaU

THE MAN GOD USES. New York, Christian Alliance, 1925. 133p [BM BVaU LC

THE MAN IN THE WELL. Chicago, Bible Inst., 1934. 31p [LC

THE PASSION FOR SOULS. London, Marshall, Morgan & Scott, 1950. 128p [BM

PROPHECY–WHAT LIES AHEAD? London, Marshall, Morgan & Scott, 1943. 190p
[BM LC

THE REVIVAL WE NEED. New York, Christian Alliance, 1925. 125p [BM LC

THE SALVATION OF GOD. 2nd ed. London, Marshall, Morgan & Scott, 1937. 128p
[BM BVaU

THE SPIRIT IS WORKING. London, Marshall, Morgan & Scott, [19—]. 120p
[BM BVaU

THE SPIRIT-FILLED LIFE. New York, Christian Alliance, 1926. 126p [LC

WHEN ANTICHRIST REIGNS. New York, Christian Alliance, 1927. 148p [LC

THE WORK GOD BLESSES. London, Marshall, Morgan & Scott, [19—]. 128p
[BM BVaU

Smith, Thomas Watson, 1836–1902

HISTORY OF THE METHODIST CHURCH WITHIN THE TERRITORIES EMBRACED IN
THE LATE CONFERENCE OF EASTERN BRITISH AMERICA. Including Nova Scotia,
New Brunswick, Prince Edward Island, and Bermuda. Halifax, Methodist Book
Room, 1877–1890. 2v [BVaU LC NBFU OTP

Smith, Rev. William Wye, 1827–1917

THE PRINT OF HIS SHOE; or, Following Christ. Boston, Congregational Sunday-
school, 1887. 160p [OTP

Smyth, Rev. John Paterson, 1852–1932

THE BIBLE IN THE MAKING, IN THE LIGHT OF MODERN RESEARCH. Toronto, 1914.
219p [BVaU QMM

GOD AND THE WAR. New York, Hodder, 1915. 190p [BM LC NSHD QMM

GOD, CONSCIENCE AND THE BIBLE. New York, Pott, 1924. 164p [BM LC

THE GOSPEL OF THE HEREAFTER. New York, Revell, 1910. 224p [BM BVaU LC
NSHD OTU QMM

HOW GOD INSPIRED THE BIBLE. Dublin, Eason, 1892. 222p [Also: New York,
Pott, 1918.] [BM LC

HOW WE GOT OUR BIBLE. An Answer to Questions Suggested by the New Revision.
London, Bagster, 1885. 127p [Several later editions.] [BM BVaU LC OLU
QMM

MARRIAGE AND ROMANCE, WITH OTHER STUDIES. New York, Revell, 1930. 160p
[BM LC

MYSELF, AND OTHER PROBLEMS. New York, Revell, 1927. 194p [BM LC
THE OLD DOCUMENTS AND THE NEW BIBLE. London, Bagster, 1890. 216p [BM
  BVaU QMM
ON THE RIM OF THE WORLD. New York, Revell, 1922. 83p [BM LC NSHD OTU
A PEOPLE'S LIFE OF CHRIST. Toronto, Musson, 1920. 505p [BM BVaU LC
  QMM
THE PREACHER AND HIS SERMON. London, Nisbet, 1907. 124p [Also: New York,
  Doran, 1922. 143p] [BM BVaU LC QMM
SOCIAL SERVICE IDEALS. London, Sands, 1900. 152p [BM LC
THE STORY OF ST. PAUL'S LIFE AND LETTERS. New York, Pott, 1917. 223p
  [New ed.: Toronto, Musson, 1924.] [BM BVaU LC OTU QMM

Smythe, Albert Ernest Stafford, 1861–1947
AFTER FORTY-EIGHT YEARS. Some Reflections on Theosophy in Canada, 1922–
  1923. Toronto, Author, 1923. 29p [NSWA OKQ

Snodgrass, Rev. William, 1827–1906
THE TWO BUILDERS; or, The Conclusion of the Matter. Montreal, Lovell, 1863.
  23p [NSWA

Sommerville, Rev. William, 1800–1878
ANTIPEDOBAPTISM. A Letter to the Rev. John Pryor, A.M. Halifax, Cunnabell,
  1838. 53p [NSWA
BAPTISMAL IMMERSION NOT OF GOD. Arguments Pro and Con. Saint John,
  McKillop, 1876. 77p [NSWA
A DISSERTATION ON THE NATURE AND ADMINISTRATION OF THE ORDINANCE OF
  BAPTISM. Part 1. Halifax, Nova Scotian Office, 1845. 57p [Also: Paisley,
  Gardner, 1866. 319p] [NSHD NSWA
THE EXCLUSIVE CLAIMS OF DAVID'S PSALMS. Saint John, Barnes, 1855. 189p
  [NSHD NSWA
THE SOCIAL POSITION OF REFORMED PRESBYTERIANS OR CAMERONIANS. London-
  derry, MacPherson, 1869. 38p [NSWA

Sovereign, Rev. Arthur Henry, 1881–
A TREE GROWS IN VERNON. The History of All Saints' Parish, Vernon, B.C. The
  Diamond Jubilee, 1893–1953. Vernon, B.C., Author, 1955. 36p

Spark, Rev. Alexander, 1762–1819
THE CONNEXION BETWEEN THE CIVIL AND RELIGIOUS STATE OF SOCIETY. Quebec, Neilson, 1811. 28p [BVaU OTP

Speight-Humberstone, Clara E., 1862–
SPIRITISM: THE HIDDEN SECRET IN EINSTEIN'S THEORY OF RELATIVITY.
  Kitchener, Ont., Commercial, 1922. 232p [BM LC

Spencer, Rev. James, 1812–1863
SERMONS. Toronto, Green, 1864. 391p [LC OTP

Spetz, Rev. Theobald, 1850–1921
THE CATHOLIC CHURCH IN WATERLOO COUNTY. [Toronto], Catholic Register
& Extension, 1916. 262p [OTU QMSS

Spiritus (pseud)
BRIGHTER SPHERES. By Spiritus [pseud]. Dictated through the Mediumship of
Annie F.S. With an intro. by E.J.C. Montreal, Lovell, 1890. 221p [BVaU LC
OLU

Squires, Susan Katherine (Dayton), 1869–1951
ONE HUNDRED YEARS IN LEMUEL ALLAN WILMOT'S CHURCH, WITH A BRIEF
SKETCH OF THE EARLIER DAYS OF METHODISM IN CENTRAL NEW BRUNSWICK.
Fredericton, Wilmot United Church, 1952. 44p

Stafford, Rev. Ezra Adams, 1839–1891
THE GUIDING HAND; or, Some Phases of the Religious Life of the Day. Toronto,
Briggs, 1887. 189p [OTP
THE NEED OF MINSTRELSY, AND OTHER SERMONS. Memorial Volume of the late
Rev. E.A. Stafford. ... Toronto, Briggs, 1892. 317p [OTP

Starr, Rev. George Lothrop, 1872–1925
OLD ST. GEORGE'S. Being the Story of a Church and its Ministers in an Historic
Centre of Upper Canada. Kingston, Uglow, 1913. 86p [BM BVaU OTU

Stauffer, Rev. Byron H., 1870–1922
THE BATTLE NOBODY SAW AND OTHER SERMONS. Toronto, Ryerson, 1919. 200p
[OTUV
YOUR MOTHER'S APRON STRINGS, AND OTHER TALKS TO YOUNG MEN. Toronto,
Briggs, 1910. 224p [BM BVaU OTUV

Steele, Rev. David Allan, 1838–1931
A HISTORY OF THE AMHERST BAPTIST CHURCH. To which is appended Historical
Notes of the Town of Amherst. Amherst, N.S., Black, 1895. 44p [NSHD

Steiner, Florence B., 1877–1946
ONE HUNDRED YEARS OF SERVICE. 1845–1945, FIRST UNITARIAN CHURCH,
TORONTO. Toronto, the Church, 1945. 32p [OTP

Stephens, William A., 1809–1891
PAPAL INFALLIBILITY. As seen in the Light of Catholicism, stated and defended
by the Rev. M.J. Ferguson ... and as seen in the Light of Revelation, examined
and exhibited by William A. Stephens. Owen Sound, 1871. 69p [BM

Stephenson, Annie Devina (Swinton)
ONE HUNDRED YEARS OF CANADIAN METHODIST MISSIONS, 1824–1924. By Mrs.
Frederick G. Stephenson. Toronto, Missionary Society of the Methodist Church,
1925. 265p [BVaU OKQ

THAT THEY MAY BE ONE. An Introduction to the Study of the Work of the Board of Home Missions of the United Church of Canada. ... By Mrs. Frederick G. Stephenson and Sara Vance. Toronto, Board of Home Missions, 1929. 222p [BVaU NBSaM OTUV

Stern, Rabbi Harry Joshua, 1897–

MARTYRDOM AND MIRACLE. A Collection of Addresses. New York, Bloch Pub. Co., 1950. 246p [OONL

Stevens, Rev. Lorenzo Graham

A REVIEW OF THE FIRST HALF CENTURY'S HISTORY OF ST. LUKE'S CHURCH, PORTLAND, ST. JOHN, N.B. Ed. by ——. Saint John, McMillan, 1889. 198p [BVaU NSWA OLU

Stewart, Alexander, –1840

TWO ESSAYS. The First, on the Gospel; the Second, on the Kingdom of Christ: and a Sermon on Baptism, with an Appendix Containing Remarks on Late Publications. York, U.C., W.L. Mackenzie, [1827?]. 96p [NSWA OTP

Stewart, Rev. Charles James, 1775–1837

TWO SERMONS ON FAMILY PRAYER. Montreal, Mower, 1814. 394p [LC NSWA OTP QMM

Stewart, Herbert Leslie, 1882–1953

A CENTURY OF ANGLO-CATHOLICISM. Toronto, Dent, 1929. 404p [BM BVaU LC NSHD

MODERNISM, PAST AND PRESENT. London, Murray, 1932. 369p [BM LC NSHD OTU

Stewart, James Livingstone, 1872–1946

CHINESE CULTURE AND CHRISTIANITY. New York, Revell, 1926. 316p [BM LC OTP QMM

Stewart, Robert, 1853–

ST. ANDREW'S CHURCH (PRESBYTERIAN), QUEBEC. Quebec, Chronicle-Telegraph, 1928. 91p [OTP QMM

Stewart, Rev. Thomas Millon, 1855–1923

TOWARD THE SUNRISING AND OTHER SERMONS. With a Biographical Sketch by George S. Carson. Toronto, McClelland, 1923. 219p [BVaU NSHD OTP

Stimson, Rev. Elam Rush, 1825?–1888

HISTORY OF THE SEPARATION OF CHURCH AND STATE IN CANADA. Ed. by ——. Toronto, 1887. 201p [BM BVaU LC NBFU OTP QMM

Stobo, Rev. Edward John, 1867–1922

THE GLORY OF HIS ROBE. Meditations for the Quiet Hour. New York, Doran, 1922. 269p [LC NSWA

Storrs, Monica

THE NORTH PEACE RIVER PARISH, DIOCESE OF CALEDONIA. A Brief History. By Monica Storrs *et al.* Fort St. John, B.C., Alaska Highway News, 1954. 22p

Stothers, Isaac Flexman, 1891–

INVASION BY SADDLEBAG AND BUCKBOARD. Tisdale, Sask., [1959?]. 58p
 [History of the Methodist and Presbyterian Church in the Carrot River Valley, Sask., now St. Paul's United Church, Tisdale.]   [mimeographed]

Stott, William

THE STORY OF ST. ANDREW'S UNITED CHURCH, NORTH VANCOUVER, 1865–1937. Vancouver, North Shore Press, 1937. 34p [BVaU OTU

Strachan, Rev. John, 1778–1867

THE CHRISTIAN RELIGION, RECOMMENDED IN A LETTER TO HIS PUPILS. Montreal, Mower, 1807. 32p [NSWA OTP QMM

THE CLERGY RESERVES. A Letter from the Bishop of Toronto to the Hon. A. N. Morin. Toronto, Thompson, 1854. 27p [BVaU OTP

THE CLERGY RESERVES. A Letter from the Lord Bishop of Toronto to the Duke of Newcastle, Her Majesty's Secretary for the Colonies. Toronto, "Churchman" Office, 1853. 27p [OTP

A LETTER TO THE CONGREGATION OF ST. JAMES' CHURCH, YORK, U. CANADA, OCCASIONED BY THE HON. JOHN ELMSLEY'S PUBLICATION OF THE BP. OF STRASBOURG'S OBSERVATIONS ON THE 6TH CHAPTER OF ST. JOHN'S GOSPEL. York, Stanton, 1834. 96p [BVaU NSWA OTU

A LETTER TO THE RIGHT HONORABLE THOMAS FRANKLAND LEWIS, M.P. [on Clergy Reserves]. York, Stanton, 1830. 112p [OTP

LETTERS TO THE HONORABLE WILLIAM MORRIS. Being Strictures on the Correspondence of that Gentleman with the Colonial Office, as a Delegate from the Presbyterian Body in Canada. Cobourg, Chatterton, 1838. 57p [OTP

OBSERVATIONS on the Provision made for the Maintenance of a Protestant Clergy, in the Provinces of Upper and Lower Canada. ... London, Gilbert, 1827. 44p [BVaU OTP

THE POOR MAN'S PRESERVATIVE AGAINST POPERY. ... Toronto, Bull, 1834. 54p [BM BVaU NSWA OTU

THE REPORT OF THE BISHOP OF TORONTO TO THE MOST HON. THE DUKE OF NEWCASTLE ON THE SUBJECT OF THE COLONIAL CHURCH. Toronto, Plees, 1853. 26p [QMM

SECULAR STATE OF THE CHURCH, IN THE DIOCESE OF TORONTO. Toronto, Diocesan Press, [1849?]. 40 + xixp [OTP QMM

A SPEECH, OF THE VENERABLE JOHN STRACHAN ... IN THE LEGISLATIVE COUNCIL ... SIXTH MARCH, 1828, ON THE SUBJECT OF THE CLERGY RESERVES. York, Stanton, [1828?]. 43p [OTP

Straith, Rev. John, 1826–1885
THE FIDELITY OF THE BIBLE. Being a Review of Colenso's Writings against the Pentateuch and Book of Joshua. Ingersoll, Ont., 1864. 64p [BibC

Strang, Rev. Peter, 1856–1934
HISTORY OF MISSIONS IN SOUTHERN SASKATCHEWAN. Regina, Author, 1929. 277p [BVaU OTU SRL

Stratford, Ont. Avonton Presbyterian Church. Historical Committee
CENTENNIAL, AVONTON PRESBYTERIAN CHURCH, 1857–1957. Stratford, Ont., the Committee, 1957. 28p

Stratford, Ont. Central United Church
CENTENNIAL HISTORY 1845–1945. Stratford, the Church, 1945. 96p [OOA

Stuart, Rev. Henry Coleridge, 1844–1909
THE CHURCH OF ENGLAND IN CANADA, 1759–1793. ... Montreal, Lovell, 1893. 117p [BVaU LC MWU NBFU OTP QMM

Sutherland, Rev. Alexander, 1833–1910
THE KINGDOM OF GOD, AND PROBLEMS OF TO-DAY. Toronto, Briggs, 1898. 240p [OTU
METHODISM IN CANADA. Its Work and its Story. London, Kelly, 1903. 350p [BM BVaU LC NBFU OTP
THE METHODIST CHURCH AND MISSIONS IN CANADA AND NEWFOUNDLAND. A Brief Account of the Methodist Church in Canada. What it is and what it has done. Toronto, Methodist Church Pub., 1906. 316p [BVaU OTU

Sutherland, Donald
THE CREATION; with its Glorious Prospect. Halifax, McAlpine, 1901. 32p [BM

Symonds, Rev. Herbert, 1860–1921
THE ANGLICAN CHURCH AND THE DOCTRINE OF APOSTOLIC SUCCESSION. Montreal, Renouf, 1907. 53p [QMM
THE BROAD CHURCH. A Sermon. ... Montreal, Witness Press, 1907. 14p [BVaU OTUV QMSS
LECTURES ON CHRISTIAN UNITY. Toronto, Briggs, 1899. 174p [OKQ
A SPIRITUAL FORWARD MOVEMENT. An Open Letter to Rev. Dr. Fraser. Montreal, Crites, n.d. 25p [BM OTU

Tait, James, 1829–1899
MIND IN MATTER. A Short Argument on Theism. London, Griffin, [1884]. 219p [BM

Talling, Rev. Marshall P., 1857–1921
COMMUNION WITH GOD. Extempore Prayer, its Principles, Preparation and Practice. New York, Revell, 1902. 302p [Pub. in England as: EXTEMPORE PRAYER. ...] [BM LC OTU
INTER-COMMUNION WITH GOD. New York, Revell, 1905. 206p [BM LC OTU
THE SCIENCE OF SPIRITUAL LIFE. New York, Revell, 1912. 320p [BM BVaU LC

Tara, Ont. Knox Presbyterian Church
HISTORICAL SKETCH ... READ AT THE TIME OF THE 75th ANNIVERSARY IN JUNE 1933. Tara, Leader Print., 1935. 20p [OTU

Taylor, Andrew Winton, 1907–
BANNERS UNFURLED. The History of First United Church, Galt, Canada, 1824–1949. Galt, Author, 1949. 60p [BVaU

Taylor, Rev. Thomas
THE BAPTIST COMMENTATOR REVIEWED. Two Letters to the Rev. William Jackson on Christian Baptism. ... Halifax, Cunnabell, 1835. 137p [NSWA

Taylor, Rev. William, 1803–1876
A DISCOURSE DELIVERED BEFORE THE LOYAL MONTREAL LODGE ... OF THE I.O.O.F., at their First Anniversary, Nov. 7, 1843. Montreal, Becket, 1843. 32p [QMSS
HINTS ON THE PROPER EMPLOYMENT OF HUMAN LIFE. Montreal, Campbell & Becket, 1838. 131p [BM BVaU NSWA OTP QMM

Templeton, Charles Bradley, 1915–
EVANGELISM FOR TOMORROW. New York, Harper, 1957. ix + 175p
LIFE LOOKS UP. [Sermons.] New York, Harper, 1955. 192p

Templin, Hugh Charles, 1896–
MELVILLE CHURCH, FERGUS. A History of the Congregation from 1845 to 1945. Written by Hugh Templin, John M. Imlah. ... Fergus, Ont., News-Record, 1945. 52p [OTP

Ten Broeke, Rev. James, 1859–1937
A CONSTRUCTIVE BASIS FOR THEOLOGY. London, Macmillan, 1914. 400p [BM BVaU OTU
THE MORAL LIFE AND RELIGION. A Study of Moral and Religious Personality. New York, Macmillan, 1922. 244p [BM OTP

Therrien, Eugene Alphonse, 1895–1941
BAPTIST WORK IN FRENCH CANADA. Toronto, Grande Ligne Mission, n.d. 126p [Same title: Toronto, Grande Ligne Mission, [1954]. 67p] [NSWA OTU

Thirkell, Rev. Frederick William, 1930–
THE FIRST TWO HUNDRED YEARS. The Story of the Parish of Newport and Walton. Newport, N.S., 1959. xviii + 107p

Thomas, Rev. Benjamin Daniel, 1843–1917
THE SECRET OF THE DIVINE SILENCE AND OTHER SERMONS. Toronto, Briggs, 1903. 241p [BVaU NSWA OTP

Thompson, Rev. John, 1834–1903
JESUS MY SAVIOUR. Being Brought Nigh by his Blood. New York, Revell, 1895. 121p [LC
THE LAMBS IN THE FOLD. New York, 1893. [DCB

Thompson, John S.T.
SCRIPTURE SKETCHES. Halifax, 1829. 280p [BibC

Thomson, Donald Walter, 1906–
THESE SIXTY YEARS, 1892–1952: THE STORY OF PARKDALE UNITED CHURCH, OTTAWA, AND ITS FOUNDING CONGREGATIONS. A Diamond Jubilee Record of Christian Service and Achievement in Canada's Capital. Ed. by ——. Ottawa, The Church, 1952. 31p

Thomson, Rev. James Sutherland, 1892–
THE HOPE OF THE GOSPEL. ... Toronto, Ryerson, 1955. 187p

Tobin, Patrick Gerald
OUR PARISH, PASTORS, PRIESTS. Diamond Jubilee of Our Lady of Mercy Church, Sarnia, Ontario. Petrolia, Advertiser-Topic, 1938. 82p [OLU

Tombs, Guy, 1877–
ONE HUNDRED YEARS OF ERSKINE CHURCH, MONTREAL, 1833–1933. United Church of Canada. Montreal, the Church, 1934. 122p [OOA

Toombs, Rev. Herbert Wesley, 1870–1934
MORMONISM. [Toronto?], Board of Home Missions, Presbyterian Church in Canada, [1916?]. 50p [OTP SSU

Toronto, Ont. Church of the Epiphany
GOLDEN JUBILEE, 1887–1937. Historical Review. Toronto, U. of Toronto Press, 1937. 32p [OTU

Toronto, Ont. Church of St. John The Baptist, Norway
THE STORY OF 100 YEARS OF THE CHURCH OF ST. JOHN THE BAPTIST, NORWAY. Toronto, the Church, 1950. 53p [OONL

Toronto, Ont. Kew Beach United Church
75TH ANNIVERSARY, 1882–1957. Toronto, the Church, 1957. 32p

Toronto, Ont. Rhodes Avenue United Church. 50th Anniversary Year Committee
RHODES AVENUE UNITED CHURCH. 50 Years of Blessing and Christian Witness, 1906–1956. Toronto, the Church, 1956. 8p

Toronto, Ont. St. Clement's Church
ST. CLEMENT'S CHURCH [Anglican]. A History of the Church, 1891–1941. Toronto, the Church, 1941. 16p [OTP

Toronto, University of. Trinity College
THE BISHOP OF HURON'S OBJECTIONS TO THE THEOLOGICAL TEACHING OF TRINITY COLLEGE. With the Provost's Reply. Toronto, Rowsell & Ellis, 1862. 84p [BM OTP
STRICTURES ON THE TWO LETTERS OF PROVOST WHITAKER. In Answer to Charges Brought by the Lord Bishop of Huron against the Teaching of Trinity College. By a Presbyter [pseud]. London, Ont., Evans, 1861. 96p [OTP

Toronto Theosophical Society
THEOSOPHY, AN ATTITUDE TOWARD LIFE; and Other Essays. Toronto, Toronto Theosophical Soc., 1944. 110p [OTP

Townley, Rev. Adam, 1808–1887
TEN LETTERS ON THE CHURCH AND CHURCH ESTABLISHMENTS. By an Anglo-Canadian [pseud]. Toronto, Commercial Herald Office, 1839. 79p [LC NSWA OTP

Tracy, G. Frederick, 1862–1951
BROKEN LIGHTS. Toronto, U. of Toronto Press, 1935. 140p [BVaU LC OTP

Trewhella, Ethel Willson
THE YONGE STREET QUAKERS. The Story of "The Friends" in the Early Days of York County, Ontario. Aurora, Walton, 1937. 15p [OTP

Trinier, Rev. Harold Urban, 1912–
A CENTURY OF SERVICE. Story of *The Canadian Baptist*, 1854–1954. Toronto, Board of Publication of the Baptist Convention of Ontario & Quebec, 1958. x + 149p

Trotter, Thomas, 1781?–1855
LETTERS ON THE MEANING OF BAPTIZED IN THE NEW TESTAMENT. In Reply to the Views of the Rev. Chas. Tupper. ... Pictou, "Eastern Chronicle," 1848. 76p [NSHD

Tucker, Rev. Lewis Norman, 1852–
FROM SEA TO SEA. The Dominion. 2nd ed. Toronto, Prayer and Study Union of the M.S.C.C., [1911?]. 181p [BVaU NSWA OTP
WESTERN CANADA. Toronto, Musson, [1907]. 164p (Handbooks of English Church Expansion.) [BM BVaU LC NSWA OTU QMSS

Tucker, Sarah, —1859?

THE BRIER AND MYRTLE;or, Heathenism and Christianity Illustrated in the History of Mary. London, 1851. [BM

THE RAINBOW IN THE NORTH. A Short Account of the First Establishment of Christianity in Rupert's Land. London, Nisbet, 1851. 222p [Several later editions.] [BM BVaU LC NSWA OLU QMM

Tupper, Rev. Charles, 1794—1881

BAPTIST PRINCIPLES VINDICATED. In Reply to the Rev. J.W.D. Gray's Work on Baptism. Halifax, Christian Messenger, 1844. 190p [NSHP

Turney, William Charles, 1885—

CHURCH OR SECT. Some Answers to Current Errors. Winnipeg, Author, [1956?]. 16p

Turnley, Francis Ronald, 1895?—1948

THE ALPHABET OF WISDOM. Introducing Planetarianism. Vancouver, Author, 1928. 175p [mimeographed] [BVaU BViPA

United Church of Canada. Woman's Missionary Society

THE HISTORY OF THE WOMAN'S MISSIONARY SOCIETY IN ALBERTA, THE UNITED CHURCH OF CANADA. ... Calgary, the Society, 1951. 86p

Upton, Primrose (Walker), 1915—

A HISTORY OF ST. ANDREW'S CHURCH, FEBRUARY 19TH, 1911 TO FEBRUARY 19TH, 1961. ... Okanagan Mission, B.C., the Church, 1961. 17p

Ursuline Community

GLIMPSES OF THE MONASTERY. A Brief Sketch of the History of the Ursulines during 200 years, 1639—1759. By a Member of the Community. Quebec, Darveau, 1875. 2v [2nd ed.: Brought up to 1839. Quebec, 1897.] [OTU OOP

Vancouver, B.C. Chinese United Church

A HUNDRED YEARS OF CHRISTIAN CHINESE WORK IN BRITISH COLUMBIA, 1859—1959. Vancouver, the Church, 1959. 12p

Vancouver, B.C. Schara Tzedeck Synagogue

5oTH ANNIVERSARY YEAR BOOK, SCHARA TZEDECK SYNAGOGUE. ... Vancouver, the Synagogue, [1957?]. 72p

Vanderburgh, Marjorie Kathleen (Hillman), 1899—

THE HISTORY OF SUMMERLAND BAPTIST CHURCH, 1905—1955. West Summerland, B.C., the Church, 1955. 31p

Vernon, Rev. Charles William, 1871–1934

BICENTENARY SKETCHES AND EARLY DAYS OF THE CHURCH IN NOVA SCOTIA. With ... a Chapter on King's College, by Rev. Canon Vroom. Halifax, Chronicle Print., 1910. 259p [BM BVaU NSWA OTP

THE OLD CHURCH IN THE NEW DOMINION. The Story of the Anglican Church in Canada. London, S.P.C.K., 1929. 214p [BM BVaU NSWA OLU

THE STORY OF CHRIST CHURCH, DARTMOUTH. A Hundred Years and More in the Life of a Nova Scotian Parish. Halifax, Weeks Pub. Co., 1917. 219p [BVaU NSHD

Vial, Frank Gifford, 1872–

THREE MEASURES OF MEAL. A Study in Religion. London, Oxford U. Press, 1923. 342p [BM LC NSHD OTU QMM

Viets, Rev. Roger, 1738–1811

ON CENSORIOUSNESS AND EVIL SPEAKING. Oct. 26, 1788. A Sermon. Digby, N.S. [NSHP

A SERMON, ON THE DUTY OF ATTENDING THE PUBLIC WORSHIP OF GOD. Preached at Digby in Nova-Scotia, April 19th, 1789. Hartford, Conn., Hudson & Goodwin, 1789. 43p [Book includes two other sermons.] [LC NSHP

A SERMON, PREACHED AT SISSABOO, NOW CALLED WEYMOUTH, IN NOVA-SCOTIA, ON THE 15TH OCTOBER, 1797. Saint John, Author, 1799. 15p [Tremaine

Voaden, Thomas

CHRISTIANITY AND SOCIALISM. A Lecture. ... Toronto, Briggs, 1913. 75p [NBFU OTUV

CHRIST'S COMING AGAIN. An Exposition of His Teachings on that Subject and a Refutation of Pre-Millenial Views. Toronto, McClelland, 1918. xxiv + 279p [OHM

Vokey, Rev. Edward Philip, 1933–

THE 175TH ANNIVERSARY HISTORY OF THE PARISH OF CHRIST CHURCH, SOREL, QUE. Sorel, the Church, 1959. 70p

Vroom, Rev. Fenwick Williams, 1856–1944

AN INTRODUCTION TO THE PRAYER BOOK. New York, Macmillan, 1930. 230p [Also: London, S.P.C.K., 1953.] [BM BVaU LC

Waddilove, Rev. William James Darley, 1785?–1859

CANADIAN CHURCH ROBBERY. Newcastle-upon-Tyne, Hernaman, 1840. 38p [Re: Clergy reserves.] [BM OTP

THE STEWART MISSIONS. ... The Spiritual Destitution of the Emigrants Settled in the Remote Parts of Upper Canada. To which is Prefixed a Brief Memoir of the Late Hon. & Rt. Rev. Chas. James Stewart, Lord Bishop of Quebec. Ed. by ——. London, Hatchard, 1838. 252p [BM BVaU NSWA OTP QMM

Walker, Rev. Algernon Stanley, 1890–1953
THOUGHTS FOR THE TIMES. Toronto, Dent, 1955. ix + 118p

Walker, Millidge
AN HISTORICAL ADDRESS ... ON THE ONE HUNDREDTH ANNIVERSARY OF ST.
PAUL'S PARISH, HAMPTON, N.B. Saint John, Barnes, 1910. 18p [NBSM

Walker, Rev. William Wesley, 1858–1945
SABRE THRUSTS AT FREE-THOUGHT; or, A Defence of Divine Inspiration. Toronto,
Briggs, 1898. 136p [BM NSWA OTUV

Wallace, Rev. Archer, 1884–1958
THE AUTOGRAPH OF GOD. Toronto, Ryerson, 1952. 150p
BLAZING NEW TRAILS. Toronto, Musson, 1928. 149p [BM BVaU LC OTP
IN GRATEFUL REMEMBRANCE. Toronto, Ryerson, 1955. 128p
LEAVES OF HEALING. London, Harper, 1942. 168p [BVa LC OTP
STARS IN THE SKY. Toronto, Ryerson, 1938. 147p [LC OTU

Wallace, Francis Huston, 1851–1930
THE INTERPRETATION OF THE APOCALYPSE. Toronto, Briggs, 1903. 39p [OTU
WITNESSES FOR CHRIST; or, A Sketch of the History of Preaching. Lectures
delivered under the Auspices of the Theological Union of Victoria University.
Cobourg, Briggs, 1885. 155p [OOP

Wallace, Robert Charles, 1881–1955
RELIGION, SCIENCE AND THE MODERN WORLD. Toronto, Ryerson, 1952. 66p

Wallace, Rev. William George, 1858–1949
A HALF CENTURY OF SERVICE ... 1882–1932. Toronto, Halliday, 1932. 64p
[History of Deer Park United Church, Toronto.] [OTU
THESE FORTY YEARS–AND AFTER. Toronto, Rous, 1927. 101p [History of
Bloor Street United Church, Toronto.] [OTU

Walsh, Henry Horace, 1899–
THE CHRISTIAN CHURCH IN CANADA. Toronto, Ryerson, 1956. ix + 355p

Walton, Jesse M.
LOYALIST QUAKER SETTLEMENT, PENNFIELD, N.B., 1783. Aurora, Ont., Author,
1941. [UTQ'42

Ward, James Edward, 1883–1958
THE MASTER ON THE MOUNT. Toronto, Longmans, 1943. 137p [BVaU LC OTP
THE WINDOW OF LIFE. Toronto, Macmillan, 1925. [CC

Ward, John William George, 1879–
CAMEOS FROM CALVARY. New York, Doran, 1924. 263p [LC NSWA OTW
THE MASTER AND THE TWELVE. New York, Doran, 1924. 255p [BViPA NSHPL
OTU QMBM

Ware, Francis B.
HISTORY OF CRONYN MEMORIAL CHURCH, LONDON, ONT., 1873–1949. London, the Church, 1949. 329p [OTU

Warner, Rev. David Victor, 1879–
THE CHURCH AND MODERN SOCIALISM. An Essay. Truro, News, 1909. 47p [BM NSWA

Warner, Howard Willard, 1908–
AND JACOB CALLED THE NAME OF THAT PLACE BETHEL. The History of Bethel United Church, South Augusta, Ontario, 1878–1948. Ottawa, Author, 1948. 171p [OTU

Waters, Frederick William, 1889–
PROTESTANTISM–A BAPTIST INTERPRETATION. A Treatise from the Pens and Discussion of a Number of Ministers of the Baptist Convention of Ontario and Quebec, re-cast and re-written. Toronto, Baptist Convention of Ontario and Quebec, 1958. 67p

Watson, Albert Durrant, 1859–1926
BIRTH THROUGH DEATH. The Ethics of the Twentieth Plane. A Revelation received through the Psychic Consciousness of Louis Benjamin. Toronto, McClelland, 1920. 374p [NSWA QMM
MEDIUMS AND MYSTICS. A Study in Spiritual Laws and Psychic Forces. By A.D. Watson and Margaret Lawrence. Toronto, Ryerson Press, 1923. 62p [BM NSWA OTUV
THE SOVEREIGNTY OF CHARACTER. Lessons from the Life of Jesus. ... Toronto, Briggs, 1903. 301p [BM OTU
THE TWENTIETH PLANE. A Psychic Revelation. Toronto, McClelland, 1918. 241p [BM BVaU LC NSHD OKQ

Watt, John Robert, 1919–
LET NOT YOUR HEART BE TROUBLED. Comfort for the Bereaved. New York, Nashville, Abingdon Press, 1957. 125p

Weaver, Emily Poynton, 1865–1943
SISTERS OF ST. BONIFACE. Toronto, Ryerson, [1930]. 32p [ACG OTUV

Webber, Rev. George, 1838–1907
THE PULPIT THE AGE NEEDS. Toronto, Briggs, 1886. 198p [OTUV

Webling, Peggy
SAINTS AND THEIR STORIES. London, Nisbet, 1919. 311p [BM BVaU LC

Webster, Rev. Thomas, 1809–1901
HISTORY OF THE METHODIST EPISCOPAL CHURCH IN CANADA. Hamilton, Christian Advocate, 1870. 424p [BVaU LC OTP QMM

THE UNION CONSIDERED, AND THE METHODIST EPISCOPAL CHURCH IN CANADA DEFENDED. Belleville, Victoria Chronicle Office, 1842. 100p [OTP

Welton, Rev. Daniel Morse, 1831–1904
CHRISTIAN BAPTISM. A Sermon in Reply to Rev. Dr. Richey's two Sermons on the same Subject. Also Strictures on Rev. Mr. Annand's Lectures on the Mode of Baptism. ... Halifax, Christian Messenger, 1870. 77p [NSHD

Wentworth, Ont. Baptist Church
BRIEF SKETCH FOR THE HISTORY OF THE WENTWORTH BAPTIST CHURCH OF HAMILTON. N.p., n.p., 1924. 43p [NSWA

Westgate, Rev. Harrison Palmer, 1878–
ST. JOHN'S CHURCH, SANDWICH, WINDSOR, ONTARIO, 1802–1952. The Beginnings of the Anglican Church in the Western District. Windsor, Author, 1952. 85p

Weyburn, Sask. Calvary Baptist Church
CALVARY BAPTIST CHURCH OF WEYBURN, SASKATCHEWAN, JUBILEE, 1905–1956. Weyburn, the Church, 1956. 40p [mimeographed]

Whitaker, Rev. George, 1810?–1882
SERMONS PREACHED IN TORONTO, FOR THE MOST PART IN THE CHAPEL OF TRINITY COLLEGE. London, Rivingtons, 1882. 323p [BM OTP
TWO LETTERS TO THE LORD BISHOP OF TORONTO. In Reply to Charges Brought by the Lord Bishop of Huron against the Theological Teaching of Trinity College. ... Toronto, Rowsell & Ellis, 1860. 96p [BM OTP

White, Rev. George Robert, 1854–1910
SPARKS FOR YOUR TINDER. Montreal, Drysdale, 1893. 200p [NSWA QMSS

Whitell, Evelyn
LOVINGLY IN THE HANDS OF THE FATHER. Kansas City, Unity School of Christianity, 1931. 125p [LC
THE MOTHERHOOD OF MAN. Vancouver, Author, n.d. 242p [BViPA
THE TWENTY-THIRD PSALM IN SILENCE. Los Angeles, Master Press, 1926. 61p [LC

Wiggins, Ezekiel Stone, 1839–1910
THE ARCHITECTURE OF THE HEAVENS. ... In Opposition to the Views of Dr. Colenso. Montreal, Lovell, 1864. 304p [BVaU LC NSWA OLU
UNIVERSALISM UNFOUNDED. Being a Complete Analysis and Refutation of the System. Napanee, Henry, 1867. 331p [NSWA OTP

Wild, Rev. Joseph, 1834–1908
CANADA AND THE JESUITS. Being a Series of Six Sermons. Toronto, "Canadian Advance," [1889?]. 79p [BVaU NBFU OTP
TALKS FOR THE TIMES. Toronto, Selby, 1886. 345p [OTP

Wilkes, Rev. Henry, 1805–1886
THE BRIGHT AND MORNING STAR AND OTHER SERMONS. London, 1889. 336p
  [BVaU QMM

Wilkie, Rev. Duncan, 1906–
THIS SUNDAY EVENING. [Collection of Brief Sermons for Broadcast.] Saskatoon,
  priv. print., 1951. 68p

Wilkinson, Grace Marjorie (Floyd), 1908–
THE LIVING BRANCH. Meditations on Spiritual Growth. Toronto, Ryerson, 1960.
  88p

Williams, Helen Ernestine
THREE CHURCHES. St. Paul's, 1843–1892–1941. Knowlton, Que., St. Paul's
  Church, 1941. 50p [QMM

Williamstown, Ont. St. Andrew's Presbyterian Church
REPORT OF THE CENTENARY CELEBRATIONS OF ST. ANDREW'S PRESBYTERIAN
  CHURCH, WILLIAMSTOWN ... 1912. Cornwall, Standard, 1916. 100p [OTU

Willis, Rev. Michael, 1799–1879
DEATH MADE TRIBUTARY TO THE GLORY OF GOD. A Sermon preached in Gould
  Street Presbyterian Church, Toronto ... on Occasion of the Death of Rev. Dr.
  Burns. Toronto, Adam & Stevenson, 1869. 36p [NSWA OTP
WALKING WITH GOD, AND ITS HAPPY ISSUE. A Sermon on the Death of his
  Father, with Extracts from his Diary. Glasgow, 1827. [BibC

Willson, David, 1778?–1866
THE CHILDREN OF PEACE. Newmarket, Jackson, 1866. 80p [OTU
THE IMPRESSIONS OF THE MIND. To Which are added some Remarks on Church and
  State Discipline, and The Acting Principles of Life. Toronto, Lawrence, 1835.
  358p [BM LC OTP QMM
LETTERS TO THE JEWS. Toronto, Coates, 1835. 71p [BM LC OTP
MYSTERIES OF THE MIND; or, Operations of Grace. By David Wilson [sic].
  Toronto, Leader & Patriot, 1858. 85p [OTP
THE RIGHTS OF CHRIST, ACCORDING TO THE PRINCIPLES AND DOCTRINES OF THE
  CHILDREN OF PEACE. Philadelphia, Author, 1815. 59p [OTP
SELECTIONS FROM THE WRITINGS AND SERMONS OF DAVID WILLSON. Ed. by
  J.L. Hughes. Toronto, Federal Print., n.d. 16p [BVaU OTU

Willson, (Henry) Beckles, 1869–1942
OCCULTISM AND COMMON-SENSE. London, Laurie, [1908]. 290p [BM LC
  OTL

Wilson, Rev. Alexander James, 1884–
THE CHRISTIAN AND PEACE. Toronto, United Church Pub. House, 1953. 68p

Wilson, Rev. Robert, 1833–1912
JUDEA AND THE JEWS. ... Saint John, Day, 1861. 48p [NBB

THE PAPAL SUPREMACY EXAMINED. ...   Halifax, Wesleyan Conference Steam Press, 1859. 37p [NSWA QMSS

Wilson, Rev. William, 1800?–1870
NEWFOUNDLAND AND ITS MISSIONARIES. Cambridge, Mass., Dakin & Metcalf, 1866. 448p [BVaU LC NSWA OTU QMM

Windschiegl, Rev. Peter, 1879–
FIFTY GOLDEN YEARS, 1903–1953. A Brief History of the Order of St. Benedict in the Abbacy Nullius of St. Peter, Muenster, Saskatchewan. Muenster, Sask., St. Peter's Abbey, 1954. 223p

Winnipeg (Archdiocese). Immaculate Conception Parish
SOUVENIR PROGRAMME. 70th Anniversary, 1883–1953, Immaculate Conception Parish, Winnipeg, Manitoba. Winnipeg, the Church, 1953. 16p

Winnipeg, Man. St. John's Cathedral
OUR HERITAGE, COMMEMORATING THE 25TH ANNIVERSARY OF THE PRESENT (THE THIRD) ST. JOHN'S CATHEDRAL, 1926–1951, AND THE 131ST ANNIVERSARY OF THE FOUNDING AND THE BIRTH-PLACE OF ST. JOHN'S MISSION CHURCH, THE MOTHER CHURCH OF THE CHURCH OF ENGLAND IN WESTERN CANADA, 1820–1951. Winnipeg, the Cathedral, 1951. 104p

Wishart, Rev. William Thomas,   –1853
THE DECALOGUE. The Best System of Ethics. Halifax, Bowes, 1842. 100p [NSWA
A SERIES OF OUTLINES; or, Theological Essays on Various Subjects connected with Christian Doctrine and Practice. ... Saint John, Nelson, 1846. 447p [BVaU NBFU OLU
SIX DISQUISITIONS ON DOCTRINAL AND PRACTICAL THEOLOGY. Saint John, McMillan, 1853. 246p [BVaU NSWA OTP
A SYSTEM OF TEMPORAL RETRIBUTION. Vindicated by Various Considerations, Drawn from Scripture and Observation. Halifax, MacKinlay, 1841. 70p [NSWA

Withrow, Rev. William Henry, 1839–1908
THE CATACOMBS OF ROME, AND THEIR TESTIMONY RELATIVE TO PRIMITIVE CHRISTIANITY. New York, Nelson & Phillips, 1874. 560p [Other eds. in 1888 and 1901.] [BM BVaU LC NSHD OTU
MAKERS OF METHODISM. New York, Eaton & Mains, 1898. 310p [BM BVaU LC OTU
RELIGIOUS PROGRESS IN THE CENTURY. London, Linscott, 1900. xxii + 468p [BM BVaU LC NSWA OTP
THE ROMANCE OF MISSIONS. Toronto, Rose, 1879. 152p [OTU

Wix, Rev. Edward, 1802–1866
A RETROSPECT OF THE OPERATIONS OF THE SOCIETY FOR THE PROPAGATION

OF THE GOSPEL IN NORTH AMERICA. A Sermon preached ... at St. John's Church, Newfoundland. St. John's, M'Coubrey, 1833. 22p [BM OTP

Wolsey, William Franklin, 1903–
THE MORE ABUNDANT LIFE. Vancouver, B.C., Canadian Temple of the More Abundant Life, 1952. 103p

Wood, William Charles Henry, 1864–1947
AN URSULINE EPIC. Ottawa, 1908. 59p [OTU

Woodley, Rev. Edward Carruthers, 1878–1955
THE BIBLE IN CANADA. The Story of the British and Foreign Bible Society of Canada. Toronto, Dent, 1953. 320p

Woodley, Elsie Caroline, 1909–
WITH ONE VOICE. Messages from the Bible and Literature. Toronto, 1947. [QMM

Woodworth, Hugh MacCallum, 1906–
SANITY, UNHEARD OF. Victoria, Sumas Pub. Co., 1958. 109p

Working Man, A (pseud)
A REPLY TO THE REV. FATHER GRAHAM'S LECTURE ON MODERN INFIDELITY. By a Working Man [pseud]. Montreal, Cosmopolitan, 1881. 38p [NSWA

Workman, Rev. George Coulson, 1848–1936
ARMAGEDDON; or, The World Movement. Toronto, Briggs, 1917. 68p [BM OTU
ATONEMENT. New York, Revell, 1911. 237p [BM LC
DIVINE HEALING; or, True Science vs. Christian Science and Faith-Cure. Toronto, Ryerson, 1923. 63p [BM BVaU NSWA
IS JESUS COMING AGAIN? Toronto, Ryerson, 1922. 37p [OTUV
JESUS THE MAN, AND CHRIST THE SPIRIT. New York, Macmillan, 1928. 343p [BM BVa LC OTP
MESSIANIC PROPHECY VINDICATED; or, An Explanation and Defence of the Ethical Theory. Toronto, Briggs, 1899. 83p [NSWA OKQ
THE OLD TESTAMENT VINDICATED AS CHRISTIANITY'S FOUNDATION-STONE. With an intro. by Nathanael Burwash. Toronto, Briggs, 1897. 153p [BM NSWA OTU
THE SERVANT OF JEHOVAH. New York, Longmans, 1907. 250p [BM BVaU LC OKQ

Wright, Henry Wilkes, 1878–
FAITH JUSTIFIED BY PROGRESS. New York, Scribner, 1916. 287p [LC
THE MORAL STANDARDS OF DEMOCRACY. New York, Appleton, 1925. 309p [LC QMM
THE RELIGIOUS RESPONSE. New York, Harper, 1929. 256p [LC OTU
SELF-REALISATION. An Outline of Ethics. New York, Holt, 1913. 429p [LC OTU

Young, Rev. Arminius

ONE HUNDRED YEARS OF MISSION WORK IN THE WILDS OF LABRADOR. London,
Stockwell, [1931]. 98p [BM LC NfSM OLU QMBM

Young, George Paxton, 1819–1889

THE ETHICS OF FREEDOM. Notes selected, trans. and arranged by his pupil,
J.G. Hume. Toronto, U. of Toronto Press, 1911. 76p [BVaU OTU

MISCELLANEOUS DISCOURSES AND EXPOSITIONS OF SCRIPTURE. Edinburgh,
Johnstone, 1854. 348p [BM NSHD OTU

Young, Mildred J.

THE ANGLICAN CHURCH OF CANADA, SAINT JAMES' CHURCH, SUTTON WEST,
ONTARIO ... CENTENNIAL, 1857–1957. N.p., [1957?]. 16p

Young, Rev. William Harold, 1892–

GREAT CANADIAN PREACHING. Ed. by ———. New York, Doran, 1925. 297p
[BVa LC NSHD

WHY ARE WE PROTESTANTS? Toronto, United Church Pub. House, [19—?]. 16p
[LC

Zavitz, Charles Ambrose, 1863–1942

SPIRITUAL LIFE. Personal Thoughts. London, Ont., Talbot, 1932. 30p [NBFU
OTU QMM

Zehnder, Meinrad, 1887–

UNIVERSE AND REALITY; or, Proportion of Spirit and Letter. Toronto, Author,
1929. xxxii + 736p [BVaU NSHD OTP QMM

SOCIAL HISTORY

Customs, social movements, racial groups,
communications, organizations, professions, etc.

Abbott, Maude Elizabeth Seymour, 1869–1940
HISTORY OF MEDICINE IN THE PROVINCE OF QUEBEC. Montreal, McGill U., 1931.
97p [Pub. also with imprint date 1932, as No. 63 of McGill University Publications
Series viii (Medicine).] [BM BVaU LC OTP

Allen, Joseph Antisell, 1814–1900
A REPLY TO THE SPEECH OF THE HON. EDWARD BLAKE AGAINST THE ORANGE
INCORPORATION BILL. Kingston, 1884. 52p [OTP

Angus, Henry Forbes, 1891–
CANADA AND HER GREAT NEIGHBOUR. Sociological Surveys of Opinions and
Attitudes concerning the United States. ... Ed. by ——. Toronto, Ryerson,
1938. 451p [BM BVaU LC NSHD OTP

Anonymous
ORONHYATEKHA. History of the Independent Order of Foresters. Toronto, Hunter
Rose, 1894. 862p [BVa OTP QMU

Armstrong, Charles Harold Algeo, 1888–
THE HONOURABLE SOCIETY OF OSGOODE HALL. With an Appendix on the History
and Architecture of the Fabric by E.R. Arthur. Toronto, Clarke Irwin, 1952.
60p

Armstrong, George Henry, 1858–1938
THE ORIGIN AND MEANING OF PLACE NAMES IN CANADA. Toronto, Macmillan,
1930. 312p [BM BVaU LC NSHD OKQ

Armstrong, Rinaldo William
THE SALT OF THE EARTH. A Study in Rural Life and Social Progress. Ottawa,
Graphic, 1930. 233p [BM BVaU NBFU OTU

Baby, William Lewis, 1812–1897
SOUVENIRS OF THE PAST. The Customs and Habits of the Pioneers of Canada.
Windsor, Ont., 1896. 266p [BVaU LC NSWA OKQ

Bailey, Alfred Goldsworthy, 1905–
THE CONFLICT OF EUROPEAN AND EASTERN ALGONKIAN CULTURES, 1504–1700.
A Study in Canadian Civilization. Sackville, Tribune, 1937. 206p [BVaU
NSHD OTP

Barbeau, Charles Marius, 1883–1969

INDIAN DAYS IN THE CANADIAN ROCKIES. ... Toronto, Macmillan, 1923. 208p
[BM BVaU LC NSHD OKQ QMM

TOTEM POLES. Ottawa, King's Printer, 1950. 2v [BVaU NSHD OTU QMM

TOTEM POLES OF THE GITKSAN, UPPER SKEENA RIVER, BRITISH COLUMBIA. ...
Ottawa, King's Printer, 1929. 275p [BM BVaU NBFU OTUV

The Barrie Examiner

SPECIAL CENTENNIAL SOUVENIR ED. FOR OLD HOME WEEK, AUG. 1–9, 1953.
Barrie, Ont., 1953. 100p

Bass, Charles, 1803–1863

LECTURES ON CANADA. Its Present Position ... Its Onward Progress ... Its Future
Destiny. Hamilton, Spectator, 1863. 45p [OTP QMM

Bayard, William

HISTORY OF THE GENERAL PUBLIC HOSPITAL IN THE CITY OF ST. JOHN, N.B. ...
Saint John, 1896. 47p [NSWA

Beaton, Allan

LAUGH WITH AL BEATON. Cartoons from *The Province.* The Best of Beaton for
1956. Vancouver, Vancouver Province, [1957?]. 62p

Bellasis, Margaret

"RISE, CANADIANS!" [Story of the Rebellion of 1837 in Upper Canada.] Montreal,
Palm Publishers, 1955. xv + 271p

Belliveau, John Edward, 1913–

THE COFFIN MURDER CASE. Toronto, Kingswood House, 1956. 154p

Bengough, John Wilson, 1851–1923

A CARICATURE HISTORY OF CANADIAN POLITICS. Events from the Union of 1841,
as Illustrated by Cartoons from "Grip," and Various Other Sources. Toronto,
Grip, 1886. 2v [BM BVaU LC NSWA OKQ QMM

CARTOONS OF THE CAMPAIGN. Dominion of Canada General Election, 1900.
Toronto, Poole, [1900?]. 22 plates [BVaU NBFU OTP

THE GRIP CARTOONS: Vols. I and II, May 1873 to May 1874. ... Toronto, Rogers
& Larminie, 1875. 110p [BVaU NSHD OTP

Benson, George Frederick, 1864–1953

HISTORICAL RECORD OF THE EDWARDSBURG & CANADA STARCH COMPANIES.
Montreal, Canada Starch Co., 1950. 233p [OONL

Biggar, Henry Percival, 1872–1938

THE EARLY TRADING COMPANIES OF NEW FRANCE. ... Toronto, U. of Toronto
Library, 1901. 308p [BVaU NSHD OTU

Blake, Edward, 1833–1912
THE ORANGE ASSOCIATION UNMASKED. ... Speech in the House of Commons,
March 17, 1884. ... Montreal, Post Print., 1884. 24p [OTP

Blue, John, 1875–1945
THE JUBILEE OF CONFEDERATION, 1867–1917. Manitoba, Government, 1917.
34p [OTL

Book Publishers' Association, Toronto
SUBMISSION TO THE ROYAL COMMISSION ON PATENTS, COPYRIGHTS, TRADE
MARKS AND INDUSTRIAL DESIGNS FROM THE BOOK PUBLISHERS' ASSOCIATION.
Toronto, 1955. 32p [mimeographed]

Borden, Robert Laird, 1854–1937
CANADA IN THE COMMONWEALTH. From Conflict to Co-operation. ... Oxford,
Clarendon Press, 1929. 144p [BM BVaU NSWA OTU
THE WAR AND THE FUTURE. Being a Narrative Compiled from Speeches Delivered
at Various Periods of the War in Canada, the United States, and Great Britain.
... London, Hodder, 1917. 164p [BM BVaU LC NSWA OTU QMM

Brady, Alexander, 1896–
DEMOCRACY IN THE DOMINIONS. A Comparative Study in Institutions. Toronto,
U. of Toronto Press, 1947. 475p [2nd ed., 1952. 604p] [BM BVaU NSHD
OTP

Brebner, John Bartlet, 1895–1957
THE MINGLING OF THE CANADIAN AND AMERICAN PEOPLES. V. I: Historical.
By Marcus Lee Hansen [1892–1938]. Completed and Prepared for Publication
by John Bartlet Brebner. Toronto, Ryerson, 1940. 274p [BVaU LC NBFU
OTU
NORTH ATLANTIC TRIANGLE. The Interplay of Canada, the United States and
Great Britain. New Haven, Yale U. Press; Toronto, Ryerson, 1945. 385p
[BVaU LC NSHD OTU QMM
PAUL MASCARENE OF ANNAPOLIS ROYAL. N.p., n.d. 16p [OTU

Brennan, Joseph Fletcher
A GENERAL HISTORY OF FREEMASONRY, BASED UPON ANCIENT DOCUMENTS.
Trans. and Comp. from the Masonic Histories of Emmanuel Rebold. And,
Added thereto, a History of Freemasonry in the Maritime Provinces and British
North America ... 1737 to ... 1841, by J. Fletcher Brennan. Cincinnati,
American Masonic Pub. Co., 1875. 442p [LC NBFU OLU

Brown, Evelyn Marjorie, 1911–
EDUCATING EVE. Montreal, Palm Publishers, 1957. xvi + 186p [Account of the
Quebec Family Institutes.]

Brown, George, 1818–1880
THE AMERICAN WAR AND SLAVERY. Speech ... at ... the Anti-Slavery Society.
[N.p., 1863?] 11p [BM OTP

Brown, George Williams, 1894–1963
CANADIAN DEMOCRACY IN ACTION. Toronto, Dent, 1945. [Rev. ed., 1951;
new ed., 1952. 136p] [BVaU NBFU OONL QMBM

Brown, Paola
ADDRESS ... ON SLAVERY. Hamilton, Author, 1851. 64p [OTP

Brown, Peter, 1784–1863
THE FAME AND GLORY OF ENGLAND VINDICATED. Being an Answer to THE
GLORY AND SHAME OF ENGLAND [By C. Edwards Lester]. ... By Libertas
[pseud]. New York, Wiley & Putnam, 1842. 306p [BM LC OTU QMM

Brown, Thomas Storrow, 1803–1888
A HISTORY OF THE GRAND TRUNK RAILWAY OF CANADA. ... Quebec, Author,
1864. 54p [OTP QMM

Bryce, Rev. George, 1844–1931
REMARKABLE HISTORY OF HUDSON'S BAY COMPANY. Toronto, Briggs, 1900.
501p [BM BVaU LC NSWA OTU QMM
A SHORT HISTORY OF THE CANADIAN PEOPLE. London, Low Marston, 1887.
528p [Rev. ed.: Toronto, Briggs, 1914. 621p] [BM BVaU NSHD OTU

Buck, Timothy, 1892?–
1917–1957, FORTY YEARS OF GREAT CHANGE. Canada and the Great Russian
Revolution. Toronto, Progress Books, 1957. 44p
OUR FIGHT FOR CANADA. Selected Writings (1923–1959). Toronto, Progress
Books, 1959. 407p
THIRTY YEARS, 1922–1952. The Story of the Communist Movement in Canada.
Toronto, Progress Books, 1952. 224p

Bull, William Perkins, 1870–1947
FROM MEDICINE MAN TO MEDICAL MAN. A Record of a Century and a Half of
Progress in Health and Sanitation as Exemplified by Developments in Peel.
Toronto, Perkins Bull Foundation, 1934. 457p [BM OTU
FROM RATTLESNAKE HUNT TO HOCKEY. The History of Sports in Canada and of
the Sportsmen of Peel, 1798–1934. Toronto, Perkins Bull Foundation, 1934.
564p [BM BVaU OKQ

Burnet, Jean Robertson, 1920–
NEXT-YEAR COUNTRY. A Study of Rural Social Organization in Alberta. Toronto,
U. of Toronto Press, 1951. xv + 188p

Burpee, Lawrence Johnstone, 1873–1946
CANADIAN LIFE IN TOWN AND COUNTRY. By Henry J. Morgan and Lawrence J.
Burpee. London, Newnes, 1905. 267p [BM OTU QMSS

THE DISCOVERY OF CANADA. Sackville, 1927. 68p [Same title: Ottawa, Graphic, 1930. 96p Also: Toronto, Macmillan, 1944. 280p] [BM BVaU LC NSWA OTU QMM

Calkin, John Burgess, 1829–1918
OLD TIME CUSTOMS, MEMORIES AND TRADITIONS AND OTHER ESSAYS. Halifax, Mackinlay, 1918. 188p [BVaU LC NSHD OKQ

Cameron, Stewart,
NO MATTER HOW THIN YOU SLICE IT. 63 Cartoons. Calgary, Herald, [1938?]. 64p [BVaU OOA

Campbell, Marjorie Elliott (Wilkins), 1901–
THE NORTH WEST COMPANY. Toronto, Macmillan, 1957. xiv + 295p
THE NOR'WESTERS. The Fight for the Fur Trade. Toronto Macmillan, 1954. 176p

Campbell, Wilfred, 1858–1918
REPORT ON MANUSCRIPT LISTS IN THE ARCHIVES RELATING TO THE UNITED EMPIRE LOYALISTS, WITH REFERENCE TO OTHER SOURCES. [Ottawa], Archives Branch, 1909. 30p [NSWA OTP
THE SCOTSMAN IN CANADA. By Wilfred Campbell and George Bryce. London, Sampson Low, [1911]. 2v [Campbell wrote V. 1 on eastern Canada; Bryce wrote V. 2 on western Canada.] [BM BVaU MWU NSHD OTP QMM

Canadian Association of University Teachers
THE UNIVERSITY TEACHER AND THE CRISIS OF HIGHER EDUCATION IN CANADA. A Brief Presented to the Royal Commission on Canada's Economic Prospects, at Ottawa, Ontario, on March 9, 1956. Saskatoon, the Association, 1956. 41p

Canadian Broadcasting Corporation
FIVE YEARS OF ACHIEVEMENT, 1936–1941. NO. 7: MUSIC. Toronto, The Corporation, 1941. 13p [BM OLU
FIVE YEARS OF ACHIEVEMENT, 1936–1941. NO. 8: DRAMA AND FEATURES. Toronto, The Corporation, 1941. 13p [BM OLU

Canniff, William, 1830–1910
THE MEDICAL PROFESSION IN UPPER CANADA 1783–1850. ... Toronto, Briggs, 1894. 688p [BM BVaU LC NSWA OTP QMM

Card, Raymond
THE ONTARIO ASSOCIATION OF ARCHITECTS, 1890–1950. [Toronto], U. of Toronto Press, 1960. 45p

Carry, Rev. John, 1824–1891
AN EXPOSURE OF THE MISCHIEVOUS PERVERSIONS OF HOLY SCRIPTURE IN THE NATIONAL TEMPERANCE SOCIETY'S PUBLICATIONS. Addressed to Men of Sense and Candour. Toronto, Rowsell & Hutchison, 1885. 81p [LC NSWA OTP

Case, George, 1821–
OUR CONSTITUTIONAL RIGHTS VINDICATED; or, An Argument for the Legal
Prescription of the Traffic in Alcoholic Beverages. In Six Letters to the Hon.
Francis Hincks. Toronto, Bentley, 1854. 22p [OTP

Chadwick, Edward Marion, 1840–1921
THE PEOPLE OF THE LONGHOUSE [i.e. the Iroquois Indians]. Toronto, Church of
England Publishing House, 1897. 166p [BM BVaU NBFU OTP

Chafe, James Warren, 1900–
EARLY LIFE IN CANADA. Toronto, Ryerson, 1943. 135p (Guidebook Series
in Social Studies.) [BM LC

Chambers, Ernest John, 1862–1925
THE ROYAL NORTH-WEST MOUNTED POLICE. A Corps History. Montreal, Mortimer,
1906. 160p [BM BVaU LC OTU

Chevrier, Lionel, 1903–
THE ST. LAWRENCE SEAWAY. Toronto, Macmillan, 1959. x + 174p

Christie, Robert, 1788–1856
THE MILITARY AND NAVAL OPERATIONS IN THE CANADAS DURING THE LATE WAR
WITH THE UNITED STATES. Including also the Political History of Lower-Canada
during the Administrations of Sir James Henry Craig and Sir George Prevost. ...
Quebec, 1818. 235p New York, Oran & Mott, 1818. 235p [BM LC NSWA
QMM

Clark, C.S.
OF TORONTO THE GOOD. A Social Study. The Queen City of Canada as It Is.
Montreal, Toronto Pub. Co., 1898. 210p [BVaU

Clark, Samuel Delbert, 1910–
MOVEMENTS OF POLITICAL PROTEST IN CANADA, 1640–1840. Toronto, U. of
Toronto Press, 1959. 518p
THE SOCIAL DEVELOPMENT OF CANADA. An Introductory Study with Select
Documents. Toronto, U. of Toronto Press, 1942. 484p [BM BVaU NSHD
OTU QMSS

Cleverdon, Catherine Lyle
THE WOMAN SUFFRAGE MOVEMENT IN CANADA. Toronto, U. of Toronto Press,
1950. 324p [OONL

Clint, Mabel Brown, 1874–1939
IMPERIAL ANNIVERSARY BOOK. Comp. by Harold Saxon [pseud]. Toronto,
Briggs, 1909. 306p [BM OTP

Coffin, William Foster, 1808–1878
1812: THE WAR AND ITS MORAL. A Canadian Chronicle. Montreal, Lovell,
1864. 296p [BM BVaU LC NSWA OTU

Colby, Charles William, 1867–1955
CANADIAN TYPES OF THE OLD REGIME, 1608–1698. New York, Holt, 1908. 366p
[BM BVaU LC NSHD OTU QMM

Collard, Edgar Andrew, 1911–
CANADIAN YESTERDAYS. Toronto, Longmans, 1955. 327p
A TRADITION LIVES. The Story of *The Gazette*, Montreal, Founded June 3, 1778.
Ed. by ——. Montreal Gazette Print., 1953. 56p

Collins, John Alton, 1917–
CARTOONS, 1955–1959. With an intro. by Edgar Andrew Collard. Montreal,
Montreal Gazette, 1960. 1v [unpaged]

Conant, Thomas, 1842–1905
LIFE IN CANADA. Toronto, Briggs, 1903. 290p [BM BVaU LC NBFU OTU
UPPER CANADA SKETCHES. Toronto, Briggs, 1898. 243p [BVaU BM LC
NBFU OTP

Cooper, Francis Collier
IN THE CANADIAN BUSH. London, Heath Cranton, 1914. 90p [BM LC OOP

Copeland, John Morison, 1878–
THE TRAIL OF THE SWINGING LANTERNS. A Racy, Railroading Review of
Transportation Matters, Methods and Men. Comp. by ——. Toronto,
Addison & Mainprice, 1918. 149p [BVaU LC OTP

Copway, George, 1818–1863
THE TRADITIONAL HISTORY AND CHARACTERISTIC SKETCHES OF THE OJIBWAY
NATION. London, Black, 1850. 298p [BM LC OTP QMSS

Corbett, Edward Annand, 1887–
BLACKFOOT TRAILS. Toronto, Macmillan, 1934. 139p [On history and legends
of Blackfoot Indians.] [BM BVaU OTP SSU

Costain, Thomas Bertram, 1885–1965
THE WHITE AND THE GOLD. The French Regime in Canada. Toronto, Doubleday,
1954. xii + 482p

Coughlin, William Garnet, 1912–
HERBIE [War cartoons]. By Bing Coughlin. Text by J.D.M. [J. Douglas MacFarlane].
Toronto, Nelson, [1946]. 192p [3rd ed., 1959.] [BVa NSHPL OTMC QQL
THIS ARMY. A Portfolio of Cartoons Drawn on the Italian Battle Front. Especially
for *The Maple Leaf,* Canadian Army Newspaper. By Bing Coughlin. Rome, Italy,
No. 2 Canadian Public Relations Group, 1945. 63p [OKR SRL

Cowan, Helen I.
BRITISH EMIGRATION TO BRITISH NORTH AMERICA. Rev. and enl. ed. Toronto,
U. of Toronto Press, 1961. xi + 321p [First ed.: Toronto, U. of Toronto
Library, 1928.]

Cragg, Robert Cecil, 1905–

CANADIAN DEMOCRACY AND THE ECONOMIC SETTLEMENT. Toronto, Ryerson, [1947]. 262p [BVaU LC NBFU OTU QMM

Craick, William Arnot, 1880–1969

HALLOWE'EN PRANKS IN CANADA. 1911. 11p [BM

Cramp, Mary

RETROSPECTS. A History of the Formation and Progress of the Women's Aid Societies of the Maritime Provinces. ... Halifax, Holloway Bros., 1892. 49p [NSHD

Creighton, Donald Grant, 1902–

THE COMMERCIAL EMPIRE OF THE ST. LAWRENCE (1760–1850). Toronto, Ryerson, 1937. 441p [Reprinted as: THE EMPIRE OF THE ST. LAWRENCE. Toronto, Macmillan, 1956. 441p] [BM BVaU NSHD OTU

Creighton, Helen, 1899–

BLUENOSE GHOSTS. Toronto, Ryerson, 1957. xiii + 280p

Cross, Harold Clark, 1889–

ONE HUNDRED YEARS OF SERVICE WITH YOUTH. The Story of the Montreal YMCA. Montreal, Metropolitan YMCA Montreal, 1951. 367 + xiiip

Croteau, John Tougas, 1910–

CRADLED IN THE WAVES. The Story of a People's Co-Operative Achievement in Economic Betterment on Prince Edward Island, Canada. Toronto, Ryerson, 1951. 149p

Cumberland, Frederic Barlow, 1846–1913

THE STORY OF THE UNION JACK. How it grew and what it is, particularly in its Connection with the History of Canada. Toronto, Briggs, 1897. 231p [Several later editions under title: THE HISTORY OF THE UNION JACK. ...] [BM BVaU LC OTU QMBM

Cumberland, Robert William, 1895–

PIONEER PROBLEMS IN UPPER CANADA. Kingston, Jackson, 1923. 19p [BVaU NSWA OTUV

Dafoe, John Wesley, 1866–1944

THE VOICE OF DAFOE. A Selection of Editorials on Collective Security, 1931–1944. ... Ed. by W.L. Morton. Toronto, Macmillan, 1945. 293p [BVaU NSHD OLU

D'Albertanson, Leonard

THE STORY OF ALBERTA DIVISION, CANADIAN WEEKLY NEWSPAPERS ASSOCIATION. Comp. by —— et al. Wainwright, Alta., the Association, [1955?]. 110p

Dale, Archibald, 1882–1962

THE DOO DADS IN THE WONDERLAND OF DOO. Winnipeg, 1919. 96p [BM

FIVE YEARS OF R.B. BENNETT. ... [Cartoons]. Winnipeg, Free Press, 1935. 84p
[MWU OTP

THE LEFT AND THE RIGHT. ... [Cartoons]. Winnipeg, Free Press, 1945. 63p [ACG
SRL

$25.00 A MONTH. Adventures in Aberhartia with Arch Dale and the Winnipeg Free
Press. Winnipeg, Free Press, 1938. 60p [Cartoons about Social Credit.] [BViPA
OTU

Davidson, Gordon A.

THE UKRAINIANS IN CANADA. A Study in Canadian Immigration. [Montreal, 1947.]
23p [BVaU NBSaM OTU QMU

Davidson, Gordon Charles, 1884–1922

THE NORTH WEST COMPANY. Berkeley, U. of California Press, 1918. 349p [BVaU
NBFU OTU QMM

Davin, Nicholas Flood, 1843–1901

THE IRISHMAN IN CANADA. Toronto, Maclear, 1877. 692p [BM BVaU LC
NSWA OKQ

Davis, Robert, 1798?–1838

THE CANADIAN FARMER'S TRAVELS IN THE UNITED STATES OF AMERICA. ...
Remarks ... on the Arbitrary Colonial Policy Practiced in Canada. Buffalo,
Steele's Press, 1837. 107p [OTP

Dawson, Carl Addington, 1887–

GROUP SETTLEMENT: ETHNIC COMMUNITIES IN WESTERN CANADA. Toronto,
Macmillan, 1936. xx + 395p [BM BVaU LC NSHD OTP QMU

Dawson, Samuel Edward, 1833–1916

COPYRIGHT IN BOOKS. An Inquiry into its Origin, and an Account of its Present
State in Canada. ... Montreal, Dawson, 1882. 40p [BM LC NSWA OTU QMM

Denison, Merrill, 1893–

ADVANCING AMERICA. The Drama of Transportation and Communication. New
York, Dodd Mead, 1936. 303p [BM BVaU OTY QMSS

THE BARLEY AND THE STREAM. The Molson Story, A Footnote to Canadian
History. Toronto, McClelland, 1955. xiv + 398p

HARVEST TRIUMPHANT. The Story of Massey-Harris. Toronto, McClelland, 1948.
351p [BM BVaU NBFU OTU

THIS IS SIMPSON'S. A Story of Canadian Achievement told in Celebration of the
75th Anniversary of One of her Great Institutions. Toronto, Simpson's, 1947.
18p [OTU

Dent, John Charles, 1841–1888

THE LAST FORTY YEARS: CANADA SINCE THE UNION OF 1841. Toronto, Virtue, 1881. 2v [BM BVaU NSWA OKQ

THE STORY OF THE UPPER CANADIAN REBELLION. Toronto, Robinson, 1885. 2v [BM BVaU NSWA OTU

Douglas, William

FREEMASONRY IN MANITOBA, 1884–1925. Winnipeg, Grand Lodge of Manitoba, A.F. & A.M., 1925. 6p [OTU SSU

THE HOUSE OF SHEA. The Story of a Pioneer Industry. Winnipeg, Bulman Bros., 1947. 109p [History of a Winnipeg brewery.] [OTU SSU

Duff, Louis Blake, 1878–1959

THE COUNTY KERCHIEF. Toronto, Ryerson, 1949. 224p [Accounts of death by hanging.] [OTP

Eastman, Samuel Mack, 1882–

CHURCH AND STATE IN EARLY CANADA. Edinburgh, Constable, 1915. 301p [BVaU LC NSHD OTP

Edgar, James David, 1841–1899

CANADA AND ITS CAPITAL. With Sketches of Political and Social Life at Ottawa. Toronto, Morang, 1898. 217p [BM BVaU MWU NSWA OTU

Edwards, Nina Lorraine, 1914–

THE STORY OF THE FIRST CANADIAN CLUB. Told on the Occasion of its Diamond Jubilee, 1893–1953. Hamilton, Canadian Club of Hamilton, 1953. 32p

Eggleston, Wilfrid, 1901–

SCIENTISTS AT WAR. Toronto, Oxford U. Press, 1950. x + 291p [OONL

Ellis, Frank Henry

CANADA'S FLYING HERITAGE. Toronto, U. of Toronto Press, 1954. xiv + 388p

England, Robert, 1894–

THE CENTRAL EUROPEAN IMMIGRANT IN CANADA. Toronto, Macmillan, 1929. 238p [BM BVaU LC NBFU OTU QMM

TWENTY MILLION WORLD WAR VETERANS. Toronto, Oxford U. Press, 1950. 227p [BM BVaU LC NBFU OTU

Ermatinger, Edward, 1797–1876

THE HUDSON'S BAY TERRITORIES. A Series of Letters on this Important Question. Toronto, Maclear, 1858. 32p [LC OTP QMM SSU

Estimauville, Robert Anne d', Chevalier de Beaumouchel, 1754–1831

CURSORY VIEW OF THE LOCAL, SOCIAL, MORAL, AND POLITICAL STATE OF THE COLONY OF LOWER CANADA. Quebec, Cary, 1829. 57p [BM QMBM

Falconer, Robert Alexander, 1867–1943
THE GERMAN TRAGEDY AND ITS MEANING FOR CANADA. Toronto, U. of Toronto
Press, 1915. 90p [BM BVaU LC NSHD OTU
THE UNITED STATES AS A NEIGHBOUR. From a Canadian Point of View. Cambridge,
Mass., U. Press, 1925. 259p [BM BVaU LC NSWA OTU

Farmer, Thomas William Devey, 1910–
HISTORY OF THE ROYAL CANADIAN HUMANE ASSOCIATION. Hamilton, Royal
Canadian Humane Association, 1952. 11p

Farrar, Frederick Sleigh, –1955
ARCTIC ASSIGNMENT. The Story of the St. Roch. Ed. by Barrett Bonnezen.
Toronto, Macmillan, 1955. 180p

Fergusson, Charles Bruce, 1911–
A CENTURY OF SERVICE TO THE PUBLIC, 1850–1950.
Halifax, Nova Scotia Savings, Loan and Building Society, 1950. 40p [NSHP

Ferrie, Adam, 1777–1863
LETTER TO THE RIGHT HON. EARL GREY ... IN RELATION TO EMIGRATION TO
CANADA DURING ... 1847. Montreal, "Pilot," 1847. 16p [BM NSWA OTP
QMM

Fidler, Rev. Isaac, 1795–1864
OBSERVATIONS ON PROFESSIONS, LITERATURE, MANNERS, AND EMIGRATION, IN
THE UNITED STATES AND CANADA ... IN 1832. London, Whittaker, 1833. 434p
[BM BVaU LC NSWA OTP QMM

Fitzgerald, James
A PLAN OF SETTLEMENT & COLONIZATION. Adapted to all the British North
American Provinces. Contained in a Series of Letters ... to a Friend in Ireland.
Toronto, Judd, 1850. 63p [OOA

Fitzgibbon, Mary Agnès (Bernard), 1862–1933
THE CANADIAN DOUKHOBOR SETTLEMENTS. A Series of Letters ... Reprinted by
Permission from "The Globe," Toronto. By Lally Bernard [pseud]. Toronto,
Briggs, 1899. 68p [BM BVaU OTU QMSS

Fitzpatrick, Alfred, 1862–1936
HANDBOOK FOR NEW CANADIANS. Toronto, Ryerson, 1910. 327p [BM NSWA
OTU QMM

Flatt, W.D.
THE TRAIL OF LOVE. An Appreciation of Canadian Pioneers and Pioneer Life.
Toronto, Briggs, 1916. 263p [BM BVaU OTP

Fleming, John, 1786?–1832
SOME CONSIDERATIONS ON THIS QUESTION: WHETHER THE BRITISH GOVERNMENT

ACTED WISELY IN GRANTING TO CANADA HER PRESENT CONSTITUTION? ... By a British Settler [pseud]. Montreal, Brown, 1810. 26p [NSWA OTP QMM

Fleming, Sandford, 1827–1915

THE INTERCOLONIAL. A Historical Sketch of the Inception, Location, Construction and Completion of the Line of Railway Uniting the Inland and Atlantic Provinces of the Dominions. Montreal, Dawson, 1876. 268p [BM BVaU NSWA OTU

Fortier, Loftus Morton

THE BOOK OF REMEMBRANCE OF THE HISTORICAL ASSOCIATION OF ANNAPOLIS ROYAL, A.D. 1921. Ed. by ——. Toronto, U. of Toronto Press, 1921. 96p [OORD QMSS

CHAMPLAIN'S ORDER OF GOOD CHEER AND SOME BRIEF NOTES RELATING TO ITS FOUNDER. Toronto, Nelson, 1928. 28p [BVaU NSHPL OTP QMBM

Fosdick, Lucian John, 1849–

THE FRENCH BLOOD IN AMERICA. New York, Revell, 1906. 448p [BM LC OTU

Foster, George Eulas, 1847–1931

CANADIAN PROHIBITIONISTS' HAND BOOK. Montreal, "Witness," 1884. 116p [NSWA

Foster, Mrs. Margaret Helen, 1896–

THE FIRST FIFTY YEARS. A History of the University Women's Club of Toronto, 1903–1953. Toronto, the Club, 1953. 50p

Fraser, Alexander, 1860–1936

THE CLAN FRASER IN CANADA. Souvenir of the First Annual Gathering. Toronto, Mail Print., 1895. 112p [BM OTP

RECORDS OF THE EARLY COURTS OF JUSTICE OF UPPER CANADA. Toronto, Wilgress, 1918. 478p [LC OLU

French, Donald Graham, 1873–1945

FAMOUS CANADIAN STORIES. Re-told for Boys and Girls. ... Ed. by ——. New and enl. ed. Toronto, McClelland, 1931. 470p [First pub., 1923.] [BM BVaU LC QMM

MORE FAMOUS CANADIAN STORIES. Retold for Boys and Girls. Toronto, McClelland, 1926. 363p [BVa OTUV QMM

Friedmann, Wolfgang Gaston, 1907–

GERMAN IMMIGRATION INTO CANADA. Toronto, Ryerson, 1952. 63p

Galt, Alexander Tilloch, 1817–1893

CHURCH AND STATE. Montreal, Dawson, 1876. 41p [BM BVaU NSWA OTU QMM

Geikie, John Cunningham, 1824–1906

GEORGE STANLEY; or, LIFE IN THE WOODS. A Boy's Narrative of the Adventures of a Settler's Family in Canada. Ed. by ——. London, Routledge, 1864. 408p [Also pub. under titles: LIFE IN THE WOODS. A true story of the Canadian bush. London, Strahan, 1873. 405p; and ADVENTURES IN CANADA; or, Life in the Woods. Philadelphia, Porter, [1882?]. 408p]. [BM BVaU LC OTP QMM

Gibbon, John Murray, 1875—1952
CANADIAN MOSAIC. The Making of a Northern Nation. Toronto, McClelland, 1938. 455p [BM BVaU NBFU OKQ QMM

THE NEW CANADIAN LOYALISTS. Toronto, Macmillan, 1941. 39p [BVaU LC OKQ

NEW COLOUR FOR THE CANADIAN MOSAIC. The Displaced Person. Toronto, McClelland, 1951. 30p

THE ROMANCE OF THE CANADIAN CANOE. Toronto, Ryerson, 1951. 145p

SCOTS IN CANADA. A History of the Settlement of the Dominion from the Earliest Days to the Present Time. London, Kegan Paul, 1911. 162p [BM BVaU NSHD OTU QMM

STEEL OF EMPIRE. The Romantic History of the Canadian Pacific Railway, the Northwest Passage of Today. Toronto, McClelland, 1935. 423p [BM BVaU NSHD OTU QMM

THREE CENTURIES OF CANADIAN NURSING. By J. Murray Gibbon and Mary S. Mathewson. Toronto, Macmillan, 1947. 505p [BVaU LC NBFU OTU

THE VICTORIAN ORDER OF NURSES FOR CANADA. Fiftieth Anniversary, 1897— 1947. Montreal, Southam, 1947. 124p [BVaU OTU

Gillis, Duncan Hugh, 1918—
DEMOCRACY IN THE CANADAS, 1759—1867. Toronto, Oxford U. Press, 1951. x + 217p

Glazebrook, George Parkin de Twenebrokes, 1900—
A HISTORY OF TRANSPORTATION IN CANADA. Toronto, Ryerson, 1938. 475p [BM BVaU LC NSHD OTU

Godsell, Philip Henry, 1889—1961
THEY GOT THEIR MAN. On Patrol with the North West Mounted. London, Hale, 1941. 287p [Earlier ed.: Toronto, Ryerson, 1939.] [BM BVa LC OLU

THE VANISHING FRONTIER. A Saga of Traders, Mounties and Men of the last North West. London, Hale, 1939. 285p [BM BVaU LC OTU QMM

Gordon, Rev. James D., —1872
HALIFAX. Its Sins and Sorrows. Halifax, 1862. 41p [BibC

Gosnell, R. Edward, 1860—1931
THE STORY OF CONFEDERATION. With a Postscript on the Quebec Situation. Victoria, Colonist, 1918. 156p [BM BVaU LC NSHD OTU

Gourlay, Robert Fleming, 1778—1863
ADDRESS TO THE JURY, AT KINGSTON ASSIZES, IN THE CASE OF THE KING V. ROBERT GOURLAY, FOR LIBEL. Kingston, Gazette, 1818. 24p [OTP

AN APPEAL TO ... THE BRITISH NATION. By Robert Gourlay. ... Now, and for the
last Two Years, Imprisoned without fair Examination or Trial. London,
Sherwood etc., 1826. xc + 196p [BM LC OTP

CANADA, AND CORN-LAWS; or, NO CORN-LAWS, NO CANADA. By Robert Gourlay,
Esq., now Robert Fleming Gourlay. Edinburgh, Wood, 1852. 12p [OTP

EMIGRATION AND SETTLEMENT ON WILD LAND. By Rob. Gourlay, Esq., now
Robert Fleming Gourlay. Cupar-Fife, Fife Herald, 1849. 20p [OTP

Gowans, Alan Wilbert, 1923–

LOOKING AT ARCHITECTURE IN CANADA. Toronto, Oxford U. Press, 1958. 232p

Graham, John Hamilton, 1826–1900?

OUTLINES OF THE HISTORY OF FREEMASONRY IN THE PROVINCE OF QUEBEC.
Montreal, Lovell, 1892. 645p [BM BVaU LC NSHD OTU QMM

Gray, Elma Edith (Lawson)

WILDERNESS CHRISTIANS. The Moravian Mission to the Delaware Indians. By ——,
in collaboration with Leslie Robb Gray. Toronto, Macmillan, 1956. xi + 354p

Green, Gavin Hamilton, 1862–

THE OLD LOG HOUSE AND BYGONE DAYS IN OUR VILLAGES. Goderich, Signal-Star,
1948. 203p [BVaU OLU

THE OLD LOG SCHOOL AND HURON OLD BOYS IN PIONEER DAYS. Goderich,
Signal-Star, 1939. 217p [BM BVaU LC OLU

Greenough, William Parker

CANADIAN FOLK-LIFE AND FOLK-LORE. New York, Richmond, 1897. 199p
[BVaU LC NSWA OTUV

Griffin, Selwyn Powell

OPEN SECRETS. Off the Beaten Track in Canada's Story. With Illustrations by T.G.
Greene. Toronto, Macmillan, 1929. 328p [BM BVaU LC NBFU OTU

Griffin, Watson, 1860–1952

PROVINCES AND THE STATES: WHY CANADA DOES NOT WANT ANNEXATION. ...
Toronto, Moore, 1884. 85p [BVaU NSHD OTU

Guillet, Edwin Clarence, 1898–

THE GREAT MIGRATION. The Atlantic Crossing by Sailing Ship since 1770.
Toronto, Nelson, 1937. 284p [Reissued, with a supplement, 1962.] [BM BVaU LC
NBFU OTU QMM

PIONEER ARTS AND CRAFTS. Toronto, Ontario Pub. Co., 1940. 102p [New ed. of
sec. 5 of EARLY LIFE IN UPPER CANADA.] [BVaU LC OTP

PIONEER INNS AND TAVERNS. Toronto, the Author, 1954–62. 5v [Vols. 2-4
have imprint: Toronto, Ontario Pub. Co.]

PIONEER TRAVEL. Toronto, Ontario Pub. Co., 1939. 176p [New ed. of sec. 4 of
EARLY LIFE IN UPPER CANADA.] [OTU

Haight, Canniff, 1825–1901
BEFORE THE COMING OF THE LOYALISTS. Toronto, Haight & Co., 1897. 23p
[BVaU LC NSWA OTP
COMING OF THE LOYALISTS. Toronto, Haight and Co., 1899. 20p [BVaU LC
NSWA OTP

Hallam, Lillian Gertrude (Best), –1939
SLAVE DAYS IN CANADA. By Mrs. W.T. Hallam. Toronto, Canadian Churchman,
1919. 15p [OTUV QMBM

Hamil, Frederick Coyne, 1903–
WHEN BEAVER WAS KING. Ed. by Joe L. Norris. Detroit, Wayne U. Press, 1951.
20p

Hamilton, James Cleland, 1836–1907
JOHN BROWN IN CANADA. A Monograph. [Toronto? 1894?] 21p [BM LC OTP
THE PANIS. An Historical Outline of Canadian Indian Slavery in the Eighteenth
Century. Toronto, Arbuthnot, 1897. 27p [LC OTP

Hamilton, Pierce Stevens, 1826–1893
BRITISH AMERICAN UNION. A Review of Hon. Joseph Howe's Essay, Entitled
CONFEDERATION CONSIDERED IN RELATION TO THE INTERESTS OF THE EMPIRE.
Halifax, Grant, 1866. 25p [NSHD OTP
UNION OF THE COLONIES OF BRITISH NORTH AMERICA. Being Three Papers upon
this Subject, Originally Published between the Years 1854 and 1861. ... Montreal,
Lovell, 1864. 103p [NSHD OTU

Hamilton Association for the Advancement of Literature, Science, and Art
100TH ANNIVERSARY, 1857–1957. Hamilton, the Association, 1958. 78p

Hannay, James, 1842–1910
HISTORY OF THE WAR OF 1812. Saint John, Bowes, 1901. 410p [Also: Toronto,
Morang, 1905. 372p; Pub. in England as: HOW CANADA WAS HELD FOR THE
EMPIRE. ... London, Jack, 1905. 372p] [BM BVaU LC NSWA OTP QMBM
HOW CANADA WAS HELD FOR THE EMPIRE. [See preceding title.]

Hardy, William George, 1896–
FROM SEA UNTO SEA. Canada – 1850–1910: the Road to Nationhood. Garden
City, N.Y., Doubleday, 1960. 528p

Harper, John Murdock, 1845–1919
THE GREATEST EVENT IN CANADIAN HISTORY: THE BATTLE OF THE PLAINS.
Toronto, Musson, 1909. 269p [BM BVaU NSHD OTU QMBM

Harris, Edward William, 1832–1925
... HISTORY AND HISTORIETTES: The United Empire Loyalists. Toronto, Briggs,
1897. 18p [BVaU NSWA OTP

Harris, Martha Douglas, 1854–1933

HISTORY AND FOLKLORE OF THE COWICHAN INDIANS. By M.D.H. Victoria, Colonist Print., 1901. 89p [BVaU LC OKQ

Hart, Arthur Daniel

THE JEW IN CANADA. A Complete Record of Canadian Jewry from the Days of the French Regime to the Present Time. Comp. and ed. by ——. Toronto, Canadian Jewish Pub., 1926. 575p [BM BVaU LC OTU

Harvey, Daniel Cobb, 1886–

THE COLONIZATION OF CANADA. Toronto, Clarke Irwin, 1936. 154p [BM BVaU NSHD OTU

Hassard, Albert Richard, 1873–1940

FAMOUS CANADIAN TRIALS. Toronto, Carswell, 1924. 246p [BM BVaU OTU

NOT GUILTY AND OTHER TRIALS. Toronto, Lee-Collins, 1926. 352p [BM BVaU LC OTU

Hathaway, Ernest Jackson, 1871–1930

THE STORY OF THE HURONS. Toronto, Ontario Hist. Soc., 1915. 27p [BVaU LC OTU QMM

Heagerty, John Joseph, 1879–1946

FOUR CENTURIES OF MEDICAL HISTORY IN CANADA. ... Toronto, Macmillan, 1928. 2v [BM BVaU LC NBFU OTU

THE ROMANCE OF MEDICINE IN CANADA. Toronto, Ryerson, 1940. 113p [BVaU LC NSHD OTU

Heriot, George, 1766–1844

THE HISTORY OF CANADA FROM ITS FIRST DISCOVERY. Comprehending an Account of the Original Settlement of the Colony of Louisiana. London, Longman & Rees, 1804. 616p [BVaU LC QMM

Herridge, Rev. William Thomas, 1857–1929

FRENCH AND ENGLISH IN CANADA AND ACROSS THE SEA. A Sermon. Ottawa, Canadian Print., 1917. 11p [OTU

Herrington, Walter Stevens, 1860–1947

THE HISTORY OF THE GRAND LODGE OF CANADA IN ... ONTARIO, 1855–1930. Hamilton, Duncan, 1930. 354p [BVaU OTU

PIONEER LIFE AMONG THE LOYALISTS IN UPPER CANADA. Toronto, Macmillan, 1915. 107p [BM BVaU LC NSHD OLU

THE WAR WORK OF THE COUNTY OF LENNOX AND ADDINGTON. ... Napanee, Beaver Press, 1922. 278p [BVa MW NBFU OTU QMBM

Hewitt, Foster William, 1902–

"HE SHOOTS, HE SCORES!" Toronto, Allen, 1949. 145p [OTU

HELLO CANADA, AND HOCKEY FANS IN THE UNITED STATES. Toronto, Allen, 1950. 143p [BVaU OONL

Hill-Tout, Charles, 1858–1944
BRITISH NORTH AMERICA: 1. The Far West, the Home of the Salish and Déné. London, Constable, 1907. 263p [BVaU LC OLU
... NOTES ON THE COSMOGONY AND HISTORY OF THE SQUAMISH INDIANS OF BRITISH COLUMBIA. Ottawa, Durie, 1897. 90p [BVaU LC

Hincks, Francis, 1807–1885
REPLY TO THE SPEECH OF THE HON. JOSEPH HOWE ... ON THE UNION OF THE NORTH AMERICAN PROVINCES. ... London, Ridgway, 1855. 43p [BM OTP

Hodgins, J. Herbert
WOMEN AT WAR. Comp. by —— et al. Montreal, Maclean, 1943. 190p [AEU MWP OTU SSU

Hodgins, John George, 1821–1912
THE GEOGRAPHY AND HISTORY OF BRITISH AMERICA, AND OF THE OTHER COLONIES. ... To which is added a Sketch of the various Indian Tribes of Canada, with Brief Biographical Notices of Eminent Persons connected with the History of Canada. Toronto, Maclear, 1857. 128p [BM BViPA LC NSHD OTP QMM
IRISHMEN IN CANADA. Their Union not Inconsistent with the Development of Canadian National Feeling. Toronto, Lovell, 1875. 24p [BM OTP

Hopkins, John Castell, 1864–1923
CANADA: AN ENCYCLOPEDIA OF THE COUNTRY. By a Corps of Eminent Writers and Specialists. Ed. by ——. Toronto, Linscott, 1898–1900. 6v [BM BVaU LC NSWA OLU
HISTORICAL SKETCH OF A GREAT NEWSPAPER. Montreal, Star Pub. Co., 1910. 16p [OTU
PROGRESS OF CANADA IN THE NINETEENTH CENTURY. Toronto, Progress of Canada Pub. Co., 1900. 538p [BM BVi NSWA OTP

Horetsky, Charles G., 1840–1900
SOME STARTLING FACTS RELATING TO THE CANADIAN PACIFIC RAILWAY AND THE NORTH-WEST LANDS, ALSO A BRIEF DISCUSSION REGARDING THE ROUTE, THE WESTERN TERMINUS, AND THE LANDS AVAILABLE FOR SETTLEMENT. Ottawa, "Free Press," 1880. 76p [BVaU LC NSWA OTP

Howard, Rev. Allen Leslie, 1875?–
7000 FACTS ABOUT TEMPERANCE. ... Toronto, Briggs, 1908. 120p [BM OTP

Howard, Clifford S.
CANADIAN BANKS AND BANK-NOTES. A Record. Toronto, Author, 1951. 48p

Hughes, James Laughlin, 1846–1935
EQUAL SUFFRAGE. Toronto, Briggs, 1895. 53p [NSHD OTP

Hunter, Arthur Thomas, 1872–1949
CHRONICLE OF ALCOHOLIC BEVERAGES IN THE NORTHWEST TERRITORIES AND SASKATCHEWAN. Regina, Commercial Print., [1946?]. 32p [SRL

Hunter, Rev. William John, 1835–1911

MANHOOD WRECKED AND RESCUED. ... Toronto, Briggs, 1894. 241p [BVaU OTU

Hutchison, Bruce, 1901–

CANADA, TOMORROW'S GIANT. Toronto, Longmans, 1957. 325p

THE STRUGGLE FOR THE BORDER. Toronto, Longmans, 1955. x + 500p

WINDS OF CHANCE. Montreal, Northern Electric Co., 1951. 31p

Inglis, Rev. Charles, 1734–1816

THE LETTERS OF PAPINIAN: In Which the Conduct, Present State and Prospects of
   the American Congress are Examined. ... New York, Gaine, 1779. 130p [LC

PLAIN TRUTH ... Containing Remarks on a Late Pamphlet, entitled "Common
   Sense. ..." By Candidus [pseud]. London, Almon, 1776. 47p (2nd ed.) [Long
   attributed to Charles Inglis; also to Wm. Smith and others. See S&T.] [BM LC
   OTP

THE TRUE INTEREST OF AMERICA IMPARTIALLY STATED. In certain Strictures on
   a Pamphlet intitled "Common Sense." By an American [pseud]. Philadelphia,
   Humphreys, 1776. 71p [BM LC

Innes, John, 1864–1941

FROM TRAIL TO RAIL. The Epic of Transportation ... told in Twenty-One Oil
   Paintings. [Vancouver, Gehrke's, 1930.] 19p [BViPA

Innis, Harold Adams, 1894–1952

BIAS OF COMMUNICATION. Toronto, U. of Toronto Press, 1951. 226p

CHANGING CONCEPTS OF TIME. Toronto, U. of Toronto Press, 1952. 142p
   [Includes THE STRATEGY OF CULTURE, *q.v.*]

THE COD FISHERIES. The History of an International Economy. New Haven, Yale
   U. Press, 1940. 520p [Rev. ed., 1954.] [BM BVaU LC NBFU OTU

EMPIRE AND COMMUNICATIONS. ... Oxford, Clarendon, 1950. 230p [BM BVaU
   NSHD OTU

THE FUR TRADE IN CANADA. An Introduction to Canadian Economic History. Rev.
   ed. Toronto, U. of Toronto Press, 1956. xi + 463p [First pub.: New Haven,
   Conn., Yale U. Press, 1930.]

A HISTORY OF THE CANADIAN PACIFIC RAILWAY. Toronto, McClelland, 1923.
   365p [BM BVaU NSHD OLU

THE PRESS: A NEGLECTED FACTOR IN THE HISTORY OF THE TWENTIETH CENTURY.
   London, Oxford U. Press, 1949. 48p [BM LC NBFU OTU

THE STRATEGY OF CULTURE. Toronto, U. of Toronto Press, 1952. 45p

Innis, Mary E. (Quayle), 1899–

UNFOLD THE YEARS. A History of the Young Women's Christian Association in
   Canada. Toronto, McClelland, 1949. 243p [BVaU OTP QMM

Irving, John Allan, 1903–
THE SOCIAL CREDIT MOVEMENT IN ALBERTA. Toronto, U. of Toronto Press, 1959.
xi + 369p

Jack, Isaac Allen, 1843–1903
HISTORY OF ST. ANDREW'S SOCIETY OF ST. JOHN, N.B., CANADA, 1798–1903.
Saint John, McMillan, 1903. 260p [BVaU NSWA OTP

Jackes, Lyman Bruce, 1889–1958
HOW CANADA GOT ITS FIRST POSTAGE STAMPS. Toronto, Author, 1948. 16p [CC

Jackson, Louis
OUR CAUGHNAWAGAS IN EGYPT. A Narrative of what was seen and accomplished
by the Contingent of North American Indian Voyageurs who led the British Boat
Expedition for the Relief of Khartoum. Montreal, Drysdale, 1885. 35p [BM
OTU

Jamieson, Rev. William Henry, 1849–
THE NATION AND THE SABBATH. Toronto, Briggs, 1901. 148p [OTUV

Jefferys, Charles William, 1869–1951
CANADA'S PAST IN PICTURES. Written and illus. by ——. Toronto, Ryerson, 1934.
131p [BVaU OKQ
DRAMATIC EPISODES IN CANADA'S STORY. Written and illus. by ——. Toronto,
Hunter Rose, 1930. 74p [BVaU NSHD OKQ
PICTURE GALLERY OF CANADIAN HISTORY. Illustrations drawn and collected by
C.W. Jeffreys, assisted by T.W. McLean. Toronto, Ryerson, 1942–50. 3v [BM
BVaU NSHD OTU

Johns, Ethel, 1881–
THE WINNIPEG GENERAL HOSPITAL SCHOOL OF NURSING, 1887–1953. [Winnipeg?],
1957. 85p

Jones, Charles Hugh LePailleur, 1876–
THE MARKLAND SAGAS. With a Discussion of their Relation to Nova Scotia. By
C.H.L. Jones and T.H. Raddall. Montreal, Gazette, 1934. 118p [BVa NSHD
OOA QMM
THE SAGA OF THE ROVER. By C.H.L. Jones, Thomas H. Raddall, Thomas W.
Hayhurst. Halifax, Royal Print. & Litho. Ltd., [1932?]. 92p [OTU

Jones, Cyril Meredith, 1904–
INDIAN, PSEUDO-INDIAN PLACE NAMES IN THE CANADIAN WEST. Winnipeg,
Ukrainian Free Academy of Sciences, 1956. 19p

Jones, James Edmund, 1866–1939
CAMPING AND CANOEING. What to Take, How to Travel, How to Cook, Where to
Go. Toronto, Briggs, 1903. 154p [BM OTU

Jones, Rev. Peter, Chippewa Chief (Kah-Ke-Wa-Quon-A-By), 1802–1856
HISTORY OF THE OJEBWAY INDIANS. With Especial Reference to their Conversion
to Christianity. [Includes a brief memoir of the writer.] London, Bennett,
[1861?]. 278p [BM BVaU LC NSWA OTP QMM

Kaiser, Thomas Erlin, 1863–1940
A HISTORY OF THE MEDICAL PROFESSION OF THE COUNTY OF ONTARIO. Ed.
by ——. Oshawa, County Medical Assoc., 1934. 126p [OTP

Kallmann, Helmut, 1922–
A HISTORY OF MUSIC IN CANADA, 1534–1914. Toronto, U. of Toronto Press, 1960.
xiv + 311p

Kaye, Vladimir Julian, 1896–
PARTICIPATION OF UKRAINIANS IN THE POLITICAL LIFE OF CANADA. Ottawa,
Author, 1957. 24p

Keenleyside, Hugh Llewellyn, 1898–
CANADA AND THE UNITED STATES. Some Aspects of their Historical Relations.
Rev. and enl. ed. By H. Ll. Keenleyside and G.S. Brown. Intro. by W.P.M.
Kennedy. New York, Knopf, 1952. 406p [1st ed., 1929.] [BM BVaU NSHD
OTU QMM

Keen, George, 1869?–1953
THE BIRTH OF A MOVEMENT. Reminiscences of a Co-Operator. [Toronto,
Co-Operative Union of Ontario, 1950.] 62p [OONL

Keil, Doris Amelia Parkin, 1900–
CHATHAM'S THIRTEEN PUBLIC LIBRARIES FROM 1839–1903. ... Chatham, Ont.,
Public Library, 1953. 16p

Kelly, John Hall, 1879–1941
THE POSITION OF THE SETTLER IN THE PROVINCE OF QUEBEC. N.p., [1906]. 59p
[QMSS

Kennedy, Cecil Howard, 1910–
THE KINGSTON GENERAL HOSPITAL. A Summary of its Growth, 1835–1954.
Kingston, Ont., the Hospital, 1955. 35p [mimeographed]

Kennedy, Howard Angus, 1861–1938
NEW CANADA AND THE NEW CANADIANS. Toronto, Musson, 1907. 264p [BM
BVaU LC NSHD OKQ QMM

Kenney, James Francis, 1884–1946
A BRITISH REPORT ON CANADA, 1711. Toronto, U. of Toronto Press, 1920. 54p
[BM OTU

Kerr, Donald Gordon Grady, 1913–
A HISTORICAL ATLAS OF CANADA. Ed. by ——. Toronto, Nelson, 1960. ix + 120p

Ketchum, Thomas Carleton Lee, 1862?–1927
HIGH SPOTS IN CANADIAN HISTORY. Saint John, Globe, 1926. 123p [LC NBFU OTP

King, John, 1843–1916
A DECADE IN THE HISTORY OF NEWSPAPER LIBEL. A Paper read at the Annual Meeting of the Canadian Press Association ... Ottawa, March 6-7, 1892. Woodstock, Sentinel-Review, 1892. 50p [OKQ OTU

King, William Lyon Mackenzie, 1874–1950
THE BRIDGE-BUILDERS. Address at Dedication of Thousand Islands International Bridge at Ivy Lea, Ont., Aug. 18th, 1938. Ottawa, King's Printer, 1938. 9p [OTU
CANADA AND THE FIGHT FOR FREEDOM. Toronto, Macmillan, 1944. 326p [BM BVaU NBFU OTU QMM
CANADA AND THE WAR. Victory: Reconstruction and Peace. A Series of Addresses. ... Ottawa, 1945. 142p [BVaU NSHD OTU
CANADA AT BRITAIN'S SIDE. Toronto, Macmillan, 1941. 332p [BM BVaU NBFU OTU QMSS

Kingsford, William, 1819–1898
THE CANADIAN CANALS. Their History and Cost, with an Inquiry into the Policy to Advance the Well-Being of the Province. Toronto, Rollo & Adam, 1865. 191p [BM BVaU LC NSHD OTU QMM
A CANADIAN POLITICAL COIN. A Monograph. ... Ottawa, Perry, 1874. 24p [BM BVaU NSHD OTU

Kirby, William, 1817–1906
COUNTER MANIFESTO TO THE ANNEXATIONISTS OF MONTREAL. By Britannicus [pseud]. Niagara, Davidson, 1849. 16p [OTP

Kirkconnell, Watson, 1895–
CANADIANS ALL. A Primer of Canadian National Unity. Ottawa, Director Public Information, 1941. 42p [LC OLU

Lancefield, Richard Thomas, 1854–1911
NOTES ON COPYRIGHT ... Domestic and International. Hamilton, Canadian Literary Bureau, 1896. 92p [2nd ed., 1897. 108p] [BM LC OTP QMM

Large, Richard Geddes, 1901–
SOOGWILIS. A Collection of Kwakiutl Indian Designs and Legends. Toronto, Ryerson, 1951. 77 + 10p

Larmour, Robert, 1841–
CANADA'S OPPORTUNITY. A Review of Butler's GREAT LONE LAND in its Relation

to Present Day Conditions and Future Prospects. Toronto, Briggs, 1907. 32p [BVaU LC OTU

Laut, Agnes Christina, 1871–1936

THE 'ADVENTURERS OF ENGLAND' ON HUDSON BAY. A Chronicle of the Fur Trade in the North. Toronto, Glasgow Brook, 1914. 133p [BVaU LC NSWA OTU QMM

CANADA AT THE CROSS ROADS. Toronto, Macmillan, 1921. 279p [BVaU NSHD OKQ

THE CONQUEST OF THE GREAT NORTHWEST. Being the Story of the Adventurers of England known as the Hudson's Bay Company. New York, Outing Pub., 1908. 2v [BVaU LC NSWA OTU

THE FUR TRADE OF AMERICA. New York, Macmillan, 1921. 341p [BVaU NBFU

THE STORY OF THE TRAPPER. Toronto, Briggs, 1902. 284p [BVaU NSWA OTU

Leacock, Stephen Butler, 1869–1944

BACK TO PROSPERITY. The Great Opportunity of the Empire Conference. ... New York, Macmillan, 1932. 108p [BM BVaU LC NSHD OTU

CANADA: THE FOUNDATIONS OF ITS FUTURE. Montreal, Distillers Corp. Ltd., 1941. 257p [BM BVaU NSHD OKQ

CANADA AND THE SEA. Montreal, Beatty, 1944. 63p [OTU QMSS

ECONOMIC PROSPERITY IN THE BRITISH EMPIRE. ... Toronto, Macmillan, 1930. 245p [BM BVaU NSHD OTU

THE UNSOLVED RIDDLE OF SOCIAL JUSTICE. New York, Lane, 1920. 152p [BM BVaU LC NSHD OKQ

WHILE THERE IS TIME. The Case against Social Catastrophe. Toronto, McClelland, 1945. 136p [BVaU OTU QMM

Lebourdais, Donat Marc, 1887–

CANADA'S CENTURY. ... Toronto, Methuen, 1951. 214p

SUDBURY BASIN. The Story of Nickel. Toronto, Ryerson, 1953. xiv + 210p

Lewis, Ada Maria (Leigh), –1931

HOMELESS IN PARIS. The Founding of the "Ada Leigh" Homes. London, S.P.C.K., 1920. 147p [BM QMM

Lighthall, William Douw, 1857–1954

CANADA, A MODERN NATION. Montreal, Witness, 1904. 78p [LC NSHD OTU QMSS

Lillie, Rev. Adam, 1803–1869

CANADA, ITS GROWTH AND PROSPECTS. ... Brockville, Wylie, 1852. 60p [Also: Toronto, Bentley, 1852. 47p] [BM BVaU LC NSWA OTP

Lindal, Walter Jacobson, 1887–

THE SASKATCHEWAN ICELANDERS, A STRAND OF THE CANADIAN FABRIC. Winnipeg, Columbia Press, 1955. 363p

Lindsey, Charles, 1820–1908
ROME IN CANADA. The Ultramontane Struggle for Supremacy over the Civil
Authority. Toronto, Lovell, 1877. 398p [BM BVaU NBFU OKQ QMM

Linton, John James Edmonstoune, 1804–1869
THE LIFE OF A BACKWOODSMAN; or, Particulars of the Emigrant's Situation in ...
Canada. By a Settler, at Stratford [pseud]. London, Marchant Singer and Smith,
1843. 31p [OTP
[STATEMENTS FROM SETTLERS ON THE CANADA COMPANY LAND IN THE HURON
DISTRICT.] London, Marchant Singer and Smith, [1842?]. 30p [No title page;
information from colophon.] [OTP

Livesay, John Frederick Bligh, 1875–1944
THE CANADIAN PRESS, ITS BIRTH AND DEVELOPMENT. Quebec, Chronicle-
Telegraph, 1939. 19p [OTU

Lizars, Robina, –1918
HUMOURS OF '37. Grave, Gay and Grim. Rebellion Times in the Canadas. By Robina
and Kathleen M. Lizars. Toronto, Briggs, 1897. 370p [BM BVaU NBFU OTP
IN THE DAYS OF THE CANADA COMPANY. The Story of the Settlement of the Huron
Tract and a View of the Social Life of the Period. 1825–1850. By Robina and
Kathleen M. Lizars. Toronto, Briggs, 1896. 494p [BM BVaU LC NSWA OTP
QMM

Locke, George Herbert, 1870–1937
WHEN CANADA WAS NEW FRANCE. Toronto, Dent, 1919. 154p [BM BVaU LC
NBFU OTP

Logan, John Daniel, 1869–1929
DEMOCRACY, EDUCATION AND THE NEW DISPENSATION. A Constructive Essay on
Social Theory. ... Toronto, Briggs, 1908. 20p [NSWA OKQ

Long, John Robert, 1874–1937
CANADIAN POLITICS. With Speeches by the Leaders of Reform and Progress in
Canadian Politics and Government. St. Catharines, "Journal," 1903. 260p
[BVaU LC OTP QMSS

Longstreth, Thomas Morris, 1900–
THE FORCE CARRIES ON. The Sequel to THE SCARLET FORCE. Toronto, Macmillan,
1954. ix + 182p
THE SCARLET FORCE. The Making of the Mounted Police. Toronto, Macmillan,
1953. ix + 182p

Low, Rev. George Jacobs, 1836–1906
PAPERS ON PROHIBITION. New York, United States Brewers' Assoc., 1887. 79p
[LC QMBM

Lower, Arthur Reginald Marsden, 1889–

CANADA, NATION AND NEIGHBOUR. ... Toronto, Ryerson, 1952. 202p

CANADIANS IN THE MAKING. A Social History of Canada. Toronto, Longmans, 1958. xxiv + 475p

COLONY TO NATION. A History of Canada. Toronto, Longmans, 1946. 600p [BM BVaU NSHD OTU

SETTLEMENT AND THE FOREST FRONTIER IN EASTERN CANADA. ... With SETTLEMENT AND THE MINING FRONTIER. By H.A. Innis. Toronto, Macmillan, 1936. 424p [BM BVaU NBFU OTU QMM

THIS MOST FAMOUS STREAM. The Liberal Democratic Way of Life. Toronto, Ryerson, 1954. xii + 193p

Loyal Orange Association of British America. Committee on Orange History

HISTORY OF THE ORANGE ASSOCIATION IN THE DOMINION OF CANADA. No. 1. One Man's Loyalty. By Rev. Walter McCleary. Toronto, the Committee, 1953. 95p

Lucas, Rev. Daniel Vannorman, 1834–1911

TWINS. A Reply to the Anti-Scott Act Address of Mrs. Goldwin Smith at St. Catharines, Ont. ... Montreal, Witness, 1885. 28p [NSHD

Lumsden, James

THROUGH CANADA IN HARVEST TIME. A Study of Life and Labour in the Golden West. London, Unwin, 1903. 363p [BM BVaU NSHD OTU

Lyle-Smythe, Alan, 1914–

THE SHAKESPEARE FESTIVAL, A SHORT HISTORY OF THE INITIAL FIVE YEARS OF CANADA'S FIRST SHAKESPEARE FESTIVAL, 1949–1954. By Alan Caillou [pseud], Arnold M. Walter, and Frank Chappell. Toronto, Ryerson, 1954. 48p

Lysenko, Vera

MEN IN SHEEPSKIN COATS. A Study in Assimilation. Toronto, Ryerson, 1947. 312p [BVaU LC NBFU OTU QMM

Macauley, John

LETTERS TO MY HOMELESS ORPHANS AND TO THE PEOPLE OF CANADA. ["Revealing bigotry, perfidy, perjury, prosecution & plunder of orphans !! and judicial jugglery and ministerial delinquency in the County of Ottawa, P.Q." —— from cover.] Ottawa, n.p., 1879. 66p [BVaU OTP

Macbeth, Madge Hamilton (Lyons), 1878–1965

THE LADY STANLEY INSTITUTE FOR TRAINED NURSES. [A History.] Ottawa, Lady Stanley Institute Alumnae Association, 1959. 101p

MacBeth, Rev. Roderick George, 1858–1934

POLICING THE PLAINS. Being the Real-Life Record of the famous North-West

Mounted Police. New York, Hodder, 1921. 320p [Rev. and enl. ed.: Toronto, Musson, 1931. 352p] [BM BVaU LC NSWA OTP QMBM

ROMANCE OF THE CANADIAN PACIFIC RAILWAY. ... Toronto, Ryerson, 1924. 263p [BM BVaU NSHD OTU

McConnell, Newton, 1877?–1940

VANITY FAIR. A Portfolio of Caricatures. Preface by J.E. Middleton. Toronto, Johnston, 1912. 334p [BM BVaU OTU

McCord, Frederick Augustus, 1856–1908

HAND-BOOK OF CANADIAN DATES. Ed. by ——. Montreal, Dawson, 1888. 102p [BM BVaU LC NBFU OTP QMM

MacCormack, John Patrick, 1895–1958

CANADA: AMERICA'S PROBLEM. New York, Viking, 1940. 287p [BVaU OLU

McCrea, Frances (Morden), 1880–

HISTORY IN WOOD. The McCrea Models. Toronto, Royal Ontario Museum, 1957. 63p

McCrimmon, Abraham Lincoln, 1865–1935

THE WOMAN MOVEMENT. Philadelphia, Griffith, 1915. 254p [LC NSWA

McCully, Jonathan, 1809–1877

BRITISH AMERICA. Arguments against a Union of the Provinces Reviewed, with Further Reasons for Confederation. London, Algar, 1867. 32p [BM NSWA OTP QMSS

MacDermot, Hugh Ernest, 1888–

HISTORY OF THE CANADIAN MEDICAL ASSOCIATION, 1867–1921. Toronto, Murray, 1935. 209p [V.2, covering 1920–1956. Toronto, Murray, 1958. 153p] [BM BVaU OTP QMBM

A HISTORY OF THE MONTREAL GENERAL HOSPITAL. Montreal, the Hospital, 1950. 135p [OONL

Macdonald, Helen Grace, 1888–

CANADIAN PUBLIC OPINION ON THE AMERICAN CIVIL WAR. New York, Columbia U., 1926. 237p [BM BVaU LC NSWA OTP QMSS

Macdonald, Rev. James Alexander, 1862–1923

DEMOCRACY AND THE NATIONS. A Canadian View. ... New York, Doran, 1915. 244p [BM BVaU NSHD OLU

Macdonald, James Simon, 1837–1914

ANNALS OF THE NORTH BRITISH SOCIETY OF HALIFAX ... FROM ITS FOUNDATION, IN 1768 TO ... 1868. Comp. by ——. Halifax, "Citizen" Steam Print., 1868. 288p [AEU NSHP OKQ

MacDonald, John Alexander, 1846–1922

TROUBLOUS TIMES IN CANADA. A History of the Fenian Raids of 1866 and 1870. Toronto, Johnston, 1910. 255p [BVaU LC NSWA OTP QMSS

Macdonald, Thoreau, 1901–

A FEW OF THE OLD GATES AT THORNHILL AND SOME NEARBY FARMS. Toronto, Woodchuck Press, 1933. [OTU

SOME TOOLS OF THE PIONEERS. Drawn by Thoreau Macdonald. Thornhill, Woodchuck Press, 1936. 14p [OTP

A SPECIMEN BOOK OF CUTS USED BY THE WOODCHUCK PRESS. Drawn by Thoreau Macdonald. Toronto, Ryerson, 1946. 21p [LC NBFU OTP

McDougall, Rev. John, 1842–1917

RURAL LIFE IN CANADA. Its Trends and Tasks. By John MacDougall [sic]. ... Toronto, Westminster, 1913. 248p [BM BVaU LC NSHD OTP QMM

MacEwan, Grant, 1902–

AGRICULTURE ON PARADE. The Story of the Fairs and Exhibitions of Western Canada. Toronto, Nelson, 1950. 200p [BVaU OTP SSU

THE SODBUSTERS. Toronto, Nelson, 1948. 240p [BVaU OTP SSU

McGee, Thomas D'Arcy, 1825–1868

THE CROWN AND THE CONFEDERATION. Three Letters to the Hon. John Alexander McDonald. ... By a Backwoodsman [pseud]. Montreal, Lovell, 1864. 36p [NSWA OTP QMBM

EMIGRATION AND COLONIZATION IN CANADA. A Speech Delivered in the House of Assembly, Quebec, 25th April, 1862. Quebec, Hunter, 1862. 25p [NSWA

A HISTORY OF THE IRISH SETTLERS IN NORTH AMERICA. From the Earliest Period to the Census of 1850. Boston, "American Celt," 1851. 180p [5th ed.: Boston, Donahoe, 1852. 240p] [BM BVaU LC NSWA OTP QMBM

THE IRISH POSITION IN BRITISH AND IN REPUBLICAN NORTH AMERICA. A Letter to the Editors of the Irish Press. ... Montreal, Longmoore, 1866. 45p [BVaU LC MWU NSHD OTP QMM

SPEECHES AND ADDRESSES CHIEFLY ON THE SUBJECT OF BRITISH AMERICAN UNION. London, Chapman & Hall, 1865. 308p [BM BVaU LC NSWA OTP QMSS

TWO SPEECHES ON THE UNION OF THE PROVINCES. Quebec, Hunter Rose, 1865. 34p [BVaU NSWA OTP QMM

McGill, Rev. Robert, 1798–1856

THE LOVE OF COUNTRY. A Discourse preached at St. Andrew's Church, Niagara, on Tuesday, the 6th February, 1838. (A Day appointed for Public Thanksgiving, on Account of our Deliverance from the Miseries of the Late Insurrection.) Niagara, Sewell, 1838. 22p [BVaU NSWA OTP QMBM

Machar, Agnes Maule, 1837–1927

STORIES OF THE BRITISH EMPIRE FOR YOUNG FOLKS AND BUSY FOLKS. ... Series

I and II. London, Elliot Stock; Toronto, Briggs, 1913. 2v in 1 [OTUM

STORIES OF NEW FRANCE. Being Tales of Adventure and Heroism from the early History of Canada. In two series. First series by Agnes Maule Machar; Second Series by Thomas G. Marquis. Boston, Lothrop, 1890. 313p [BM BVaU LC NSHD OTU QMM

McInnes, Graham Campbell, 1912–

A SHORT HISTORY OF CANADIAN ART. Toronto, Macmillan, 1939. 125p [Rev. and enl. ed. pub. under title: CANADIAN ART. Toronto, Macmillan, 1950. 140p] [BM BVaU LC NSHD OTP QMM

MacInnes, Thomas Robert Edward, 1867–1951

ORIENTAL OCCUPATION OF BRITISH COLUMBIA. Vancouver, Sun. Pub. Co., 1927. 170p [BVaU LC NBFU OTP

MacKay, Douglas, 1900–1938

THE HONOURABLE COMPANY. A History of the Hudson's Bay Company. ... Indianapolis, Bobbs-Merrill, 1936. 396p [Rev. ed.: Toronto, McClelland, 1949. 397p] [BM BVaU LC NBFU OTP QMM

Mackenzie, Alexander, 1822–1892

ADDRESS ... TO THE TORONTO WORKINGMEN ON THE "NATIONAL POLICY." ... Toronto, Globe, 1878. 32p [NSHD OTU

Mackenzie, James Bovell, 1851–1919

TREATISE ON THE SIX-NATION INDIANS. ... Toronto, Guardian, 1882. 63p [Also as: THE SIX-NATION INDIANS IN CANADA [1896].] [BVaU NSHD OLU

Mackenzie, William Lyon, 1795–1861

AN ALMANAC OF INDEPENDENCE & FREEDOM FOR THE YEAR 1860. Containing a Plea for the Relief of the Inhabitants of Canada from a State of Colonial Vassalage or Irresponsible Rule. ... Toronto, Author, 1860. 62p [OTP

THE LEGISLATIVE BLACK LIST OF UPPER CANADA; or, Official Corruption and Hypocrisy Unmasked. York, Colonial Advocate, 1828. 39p [BVaU OTP

A NEW ALMANAC FOR THE CANADIAN TRUE BLUES. With which is Incorporated the Constitutional Reformer's Text Book, for the Millenial and Prophetical Year of the Grand General Election for Upper Canada and Total and Everlasting Downfall of Toryism in the British Empire. By Patrick Swift [pseud]. 2nd ed. York, Baxter, [1833?]. 23p [OTP

"POOR RICHARD"; or, The Yorkshire Almanac. ... By Patrick Swift [pseud]. York, Mackenzie, [1931?]. 16p (Continued annually.) [OTP

THE SEVENTH REPORT FROM THE SELECT COMMITTEE OF THE HOUSE OF ASSEMBLY OF UPPER CANADA ON GRIEVANCES ... W.L. Mackenzie, esq., chairman. Toronto, Reynolds, 1835. 470p [NSWA OOA

SKETCHES OF CANADA AND THE UNITED STATES. London, Effingham Wilson, 1833. 504p [BM BVaU LC OTP QMSS

Maclean, Rev. John, 1851–1928

CANADIAN SAVAGE FOLK. The Native Tribes of Canada. Toronto, Briggs, 1896. 641p [BM BVaU LC NSHD OTU

THE INDIANS, THEIR MANNERS AND CUSTOMS. London, Kelly, 1889. 351p [BVa LC OKQ

McLoughlin, John, 1784–1857

LETTERS OF DR. JOHN McLOUGHLIN, written at Fort Vancouver 1829–1832. Ed. by B.B. Barker. Portland, Ore., Binfords & Mort, 1948. 376p [BVaU LC NBFU OTP QMM

THE LETTERS OF JOHN McLOUGHLIN ... FROM FORT VANCOUVER TO THE GOVERNOR AND COMMITTEE. ... Ed. by E.E. Rich. With intro. by W. Kaye Lamb. Toronto, Champlain Society, 1941–44. 3v [BM BVaU LC NBFU OTP

Macmillan Company of Canada

A CANADIAN PUBLISHING HOUSE. Toronto, Macmillan, 1923. [BVaU OTU

McPhedran, Marie (Green), 1904–

CARGOES ON THE GREAT LAKES. Toronto, Macmillan, 1952. 226p

Macpherson, Crawford Brough

DEMOCRACY IN ALBERTA. The Theory and Practice of a Quasi-Party System. Toronto, U. of Toronto Press, 1953 [i.e., 1954]. xii + 258p

Macpherson, Duncan Ian, 1924–

TORONTO DAILY STAR CARTOONS. Toronto, Toronto Star, 1959. 1v [unpaged]

MacPherson, Mrs. Lydia Eliza, 1883–

HISTORICAL SKETCH OF THE WOMAN'S CHRISTIAN TEMPERANCE UNION OF BRITISH COLUMBIA, COMMEMORATING SEVENTY YEARS OF SERVICE, 1883–1953. Vancouver, n.p., 1953. 11p

McWilliams, Margaret (Stovel), 1875–1952

THIS NEW CANADA. London, Dent, 1948. 328p [BM BVa LC NBFU OTP QMM

Mair, John, 1798–1877

NEPHALEIA; or, Total Abstinence from Intoxicating Liquors in Man's Normal State of Health. The Doctrine of the Bible in a Series of Letters with Addenda, to Edward C. Delavan. New York, Sheldon, 1861. 302p [LC OTP

Marquis, Thomas Guthrie, 1864–1936

STORIES FROM CANADIAN HISTORY. Toronto, Copp Clark, 1936. 157p [Earlier ed.: Toronto, Copp Clark, 1893.] [BVaU LC OTU

Marshall, John George, 1786–1880

THE CANADIAN DOMINION TESTED BY THE EVIDENCE OF SCRIPTURE AND HISTORY. ... Halifax, Strong, 1868. 39p [NSHD QMSS

THE JUSTICE OF THE PEACE, AND COUNTY AND TOWNSHIP OFFICERS FOR NOVA SCOTIA. Halifax, Gossip & Coade, 1837–45. 646p [BVaU NSHPL OTP QMML

Martin, Chester Bailey, 1882–1958
FOUNDATIONS OF CANADIAN NATIONHOOD. Toronto, U. of Toronto Press, 1955. xx + 554p

Martin, Horace Tassie, 1859–1905?
CASTOROLOGIA; or, the History and Traditions of the Canadian Beaver. Montreal, Drysdale, 1892. 238p [BM BVaU LC OTU

Mavor, James, 1854–1925
NOTES ON APPRECIATION OF ART AND ON ART IN ONTARIO. With Remarks on the Exhibition of the Ontario Society of Artists, 1898. Toronto, Morang, 1898. 28p [OTP

Merriken, Ellenor Ranghild (Olsen), 1899–
THE NOSE HILLS COUNTRY. Federalsburg, Md., 1960. 133p [Autobiography of pioneer life in Alberta.]

Mewburn, John, 1788–1864
A LETTER TO MR. STICKNEY, OF HOLDERNESS, ON EMIGRATION TO CANADA. Darlington, Coates & Farmer, 1833. 12p [BM NSWA OTP

Meyers, Leonard William, 1917–
TWENTY-THREE SKIDOO. Toronto, Kingswood House, 1958. x + 227p

Miller, Hanson Orlo, 1911–
RAIDERS OF THE MOHAWK. The Story of Butler's Rangers. Toronto, Macmillan, 1954. ix + 182p

Miller, John James, 1860–1950
EARLY HISTORY OF THE VANCOUVER EXHIBITION ASSOCIATION. ... Vancouver, City Archives, 1953. 46p

Mitchell, Rosslyn Brough, 1880–
MEDICINE IN MANITOBA. The Story of its Beginnings. Winnipeg, 1955. 141p

Moberly, Walter, 1832–1915
THE EARLY HISTORY OF THE CANADIAN PACIFIC ROAD. Vancouver, 1909. 15p [BM BVaU LC NSWA OTU

Monro, Alexander, 1813–1896
ANNEXATION; or, Union with the United States is the Manifest Destiny of British North America. Saint John, Barnes, 1868. 52p [LC
THE UNITED STATES AND THE DOMINION OF CANADA. Their Future. Saint John, Barnes, 1879. 192p [BVaU LC NBFU OTU

Montague, Sydney Robert
RIDERS IN SCARLET. The Way of Life of the Mounties. Evanston, Ill., Row Peterson, 1941. 64p [BVa LC OOA

Montgomery, George Hugh Alexander, 1874–1951
MISSISSQUOI BAY. (Philipsburg, Que.) Granby, Que., Granby Pub., 1950. 132p
  [OTU

Montreal, Que. Pen and Pencil Club
THE PEN AND PENCIL CLUB, 1890–1959. Montreal, the Club, 1959. 15p

Montreal, Que. Shakespeare Dramatic and Literary Club
ANNUAL REPORT, for the year 1844. Montreal, 1845. 11p [QMM

Moore, Gordon, 1922–
AROUND OUR TOWN. Montreal, Whitcombe & Gilmour, 1948. 131p [OTP

Moore, William Henry, 1872–1960
THE CLASH. A Study in Nationalities. Toronto, Dent, 1918. 356p [BM BVaU
  LC NBFU OTP QMM
THE IRRESPONSIBLE FIVE. A New Family Compact. Toronto, McClelland, 1917.
  67p [BM BVaU OTP QMSS

Moorhouse, Arthur Herbert Joseph, 1882–
DEEP FURROWS. Which Tells of Pioneer Trails along which the Farmers of Western
  Canada fought their way to Great Achievements in Co-operation. By Hopkins
  Moorhouse [pseud]. Toronto, McLeod, 1918. 229p [BM BVaU LC NSWA
  OOA QMM

Morgan, Henry James, 1842–1913
CANADIAN LIFE IN TOWN & COUNTRY. By Henry J. Morgan and Lawrence J.
  Burpee. ... London, Newnes, 1905. 266p [BM BVaU LC OTP
DOMINION ANNUAL REGISTER AND REVIEW, 1878–1886. Ed. by ——. Montreal,
  Dawson, 1879–1887. 7v [BM BVaU NBFU OTU

Morris, Alexander, 1826–1889
CANADA AND HER RESOURCES. [A Prize Essay.] Montreal, Lovell, 1855. 156p
  [2nd ed.: Montreal, Dawson, 1855. 119p] [BM BVaU LC NSWA OTP
NOVA BRITANNIA; or, British North America, its Extent and Future. A Lecture.
  Montreal, Lovell, 1858. 67p [BM BVaU LC NSWA OTP QMM
NOVA BRITANNIA; or, Our New Canadian Dominion Foreshadowed. Being a Series
  of Lectures. Toronto, Hunter Rose, 1884. 187p [BM BVaU LC NBFU OTP
  QMM

Morton, William Lewis, 1908–
THE PROGRESSIVE PARTY IN CANADA. Toronto, U. of Toronto Press, 1950. 331p
  [OONL

Mountain, Rev. George Jehoshaphat, 1789–1863
A RETROSPECT OF THE SUMMER AND AUTUMN OF 1832. ... Quebec, Cary, 1833.
  33p [Appendix, on facts of a recent plague.] [BM OTP QMSS

Munro, Robert Ross, 1913–
GAUNTLET TO OVERLORD. The Story of the Canadian Army. Toronto, Macmillan, 1945. 477p [BM BVaU LC OTP QMM

Munro, William F.
THE BACKWOODS' LIFE. Toronto, Hunter Rose, 1869. 79p [Republished as: THE BACKWOODS' LIFE. An Interesting Story of Pioneer Days in Melancthon Township. Shelburne, Free Press Office, 1910. 59p] [BVaU LC NSHD OTP QMSS

Murphy, Emily Gowan (Ferguson), 1868–1933
THE BLACK CANDLE. Toronto, Allen, 1922. 405p [Re: Drug traffic.] [BM BVaU LC NSWA OTP QMM

Murphy, Herbert H., 1881–
ROYAL JUBILEE HOSPITAL, VICTORIA, B.C., 1858–1958. ... Victoria, Hebden Print., 1958. 160p

Murray, N.
THE EXPERIENCE OF AN OLD COUNTRY PEDLER AMONG THE MONTREAL SERVANT GIRLS AND THEIR MISTRESSES. Ottawa, Gov't., 1891. 16p [NSWA

Murray, Norman, 1853–
THE CELTIC TRAGEDY. British Races, Languages and Religions–the Anglo-Saxon Myth and Orange Fanaticism. Montreal, Murray, 1919–21. [OTU

Nasmith, George Gallie, 1877–1965
CANADA'S SONS AND GREAT BRITAIN IN THE WORLD WAR. Toronto, Winston, 1919. 607p [BM BVaU NSHD OTP

National Council of Women of Canada
WOMEN OF CANADA, THEIR LIFE AND WORK. Comp. by ——. N.p., the Council, 1900. 422p [BVaU NSWA OTP QMM

Newman, Fred C.
THE FIRST FIFTY YEARS. A Brief History of the St. James Literary Society. ... Montreal, the Society, 1948. 22p [OTP

Newspaper Cartoonists' Association of Manitoba
MANITOBANS AS WE SEE 'EM, 1908 and 1909. Winnipeg, the Association, 1909. 227 plates. [Cartoons of prominent Manitobans.] [BVaU SSU

Nichols, Thomas E.
THESE WERE THE THIRTIES. By T.E. Nichols. With Cartoons by the Late Ivan Glassco. Hamilton, Spectator, 1949. 102p [BViV OH

Nicholson, Anna Mary
100 YEARS OF MEDICINE, 1849–1949. Ed. by ——. Saskatoon, Modern Press, 1949. 44p [About women pioneers in medicine.] [SSU

Nicholson, Byron, 1857–1916
THE FRENCH-CANADIAN. A Sketch of his More Prominent Characteristics. Toronto, Bryant Press, 1902. 132p [BM BVaU OKQ QMM

Norris, Leonard Matheson, 1913–
THE BEST OF NORRIS, AS SELECTED BY HIMSELF. Toronto, McClelland, 1955. 123p
NORRIS CARTOONS IN THE VANCOUVER SUN. His World and You're in it. Vancouver, Sun. Pub. Co., 1952. 100p [An annual publication. Title varies.]

North Renfrew, Ont. Agricultural Society. Centennial Committee
CENTENNIAL, NORTH RENFREW AGRICULTURAL SOCIETY, 1857–1957. Pembroke, Ont., the Society, 1957. 134p [Comp. by Mrs. Carl Price.]

O'Connor, John, 1824–1887
LETTERS OF JOHN O'CONNOR, ESQ., M.P., ON FENIANISM. Toronto, Rose, 1870. 17p [QMBM

Ord, Lewis Redman, 1856–1942
REMINISCENCES OF A BUNGLE. By One of the Bunglers [pseud]. Toronto, Grip Print., 1887. 66p [On Riel Rebellion.] [OOA

Ottawa, Ont. National Gallery of Canada
THE MASSEY COLLECTION OF ENGLISH PAINTING. Ottawa, 1946. 30p [BM BVaU LC
CATALOGUE OF PAINTINGS, DRAWINGS, ETCHINGS AND SCULPTURE. Ottawa, Government Print. Bureau, 1912. 152p [LC

Paget, Amelia Anne (McLean), 1867–1922
THE PEOPLE OF THE PLAINS. Ed. with intro. by D.C. Scott. Toronto, Briggs, 1909. 199p [On North American Indians.] [BVaU LC‑ NBFU OTP

Paluk, William, 1914–
CANADIAN COSSACKS. Essays, Articles, and Stories on Ukrainian-Canadian Life. Winnipeg, Canadian Ukrainian Rev., 1943. 129p [MWP OTP

Parker, Gilbert, 1862–1932
THE WORLD IN THE CRUCIBLE. An Account of the Origin and Conduct of the Great War. London, Murray, 1915. 432p [BM BVaU LC OTU

Parkin, George Robert, 1846–1922
IMPERIAL FEDERATION. The Problem of Imperial Unity. London, Macmillan, 1892. 314p [BM BVaU LC NBFU OONL QMSS

Paterson, Isabel M. (Bowler)
THE GOD OF THE MACHINE. New York, Putnam, 1943. 292p [BVaU OTU QMSS

Peat, Louisa (Watson)
GRANDMA DID IT THIS WAY. New York, Holt, 1950. 247p [BVa LC

Phillips, Alan, 1916–
THE LIVING LEGEND. The Story of the Royal Canadian Mounted Police. Winnipeg,
  Harlequin Books, 1960. 192p [Earlier eds.: Boston, Little Brown; London,
  Cassell, 1957.]

Pierce, Lorne Albert, 1890–1961
THE HOUSE OF RYERSON, 1829–1954. Toronto, Ryerson, 1954. ix + 52p
MASTER BUILDERS. Toronto, Ryerson, 1937. 45p [On Masonic order.]
  [BVaU OKQ
TOWARD THE BONNE ENTENTE. Toronto, Ryerson, 1929. 43p [BVaU NBFU
  OTU QMM

Poole, Rev. William Henry, 1820–1896
TOBACCO, SMOKING, CHEWING, SNUFFING. A Lecture. Brockville, Wylie, 1866.
  30p [OTP

Powell, Robert Wynyard, 1856–1935
THE DOCTOR IN CANADA. His Whereabouts and the Laws which Govern him. A
  Ready Book of Reference. Montreal, Gazette, 1890. 342p [BVaU NSWA
  OTP QMSS

Quebec Literary and Historical Society
THE CENTENARY VOLUME, 1824–1924. Quebec, Evénement, 1924. 196p [BVaU
  QMM

Racey, Arthur George, 1870–1942
CANADIAN MEN OF AFFAIRS IN CARTOON. Illus. by A.G. Racey. Montreal,
  Southam Press, 1922. 129p [OTU
THE ENGLISHMAN IN CANADA. [Cartoons.] Montreal, Montreal News Co., 1902.
  22p [BM OLU

Raddall, Thomas Head, 1903–
THE PATH OF DESTINY. Canada from the British Conquest to Home Rule:
  1763–1850. Toronto, Doubleday, 1957. x + 468p

Ramsey, Bruce, 1924–
A HISTORY OF THE GERMAN-CANADIANS IN BRITISH COLUMBIA. Winnipeg,
  National Publishers, 1958. 69p

Rattray, William Jordan, 1835–1883

THE SCOT IN BRITISH NORTH AMERICA. Toronto, Maclear, 1880–84. 4v [BM
BVaU LC NBFU OTP QMM

Raymond, Rev. William Odber, 1853–1923

THE UNITED EMPIRE LOYALISTS. Saint Stephen, N.B., St. Croix Pub. Co., 1893.
46p [NSHD OTP QMM

Read, David Breakenridge, 1823–1904

THE CANADIAN REBELLION OF 1837. Toronto, Robinson, 1896. 372p [BM
BVaU NBFU OTP QMM

Reaman, George Elmore, 1889–

THE TRAIL OF THE BLACK WALNUT. Toronto, McClelland, 1957. xx + 256p
[A study of the Pennsylvania Germans and related ethnic groups who migrated
to Ontario during the American Revolution.]

Rhinewine, Abraham, 1887–1932

LOOKING BACK A CENTURY ON THE CENTENNIAL OF JEWISH POLITICAL
EQUALITY IN CANADA. Rev. and enl. by Isidore Goldstick. Toronto, Kraft,
1932. 148p [BM BVaU LC NSHD OTP QMM

Richardson, Evelyn May (Fox), 1902–

THE WRECKWOOD CHAIR. Sagas of the Sea told in Wood. Comp. for the
Shelburne Historical Society. Shelburne, N.S., the Society, 1957. 51p

Rickard, Thomas Arthur, 1864–1953

THE ROMANCE OF MINING. Toronto, Macmillan, 1944. 450p [BVaU LC
NBFU OTP QMM

Riddell, William Renwick, 1852–1945

THE BAR AND THE COURTS OF THE PROVINCE OF UPPER CANADA OR ONTARIO.
Toronto, Macmillan, 1928. 251p [LC OTU

THE LEGAL PROFESSION IN UPPER CANADA IN ITS EARLY PERIODS. Toronto,
Law Society, 1916. 194p [BVaU NSWA OTU ⁻

SOME EARLY LEGISLATION AND LEGISLATORS IN UPPER CANADA. Toronto,
Carswell, 1913. 39p [OTU QMM

Roberts, Charles George Douglas, 1860–1943

CANADA IN FLANDERS. With a Preface by Lord Beaverbrook. V. 3. London,
Hodder, 1918. 144p [BM BVaU NBFU OTU QMSS

THE CANADIANS OF OLD. By Philippe Aubert de Gaspé. Trans. by Charles
G.D. Roberts. New York, Appleton, 1890. 287p [New ed. under title:
CAMERON OF LOCHIEL. Boston, Page, 1905. 287p] [BVaU LC OTU

A HISTORY OF CANADA, for High Schools and Academies. Boston, Lamson
Wolffe, 1897. 493p [BM BVaU LC NSWA OTU

Roberts, Leslie, 1896–
CANADA: THE GOLDEN HINGE. Toronto, Clarke Irwin, 1952. 288p

Robertson, John Ross, 1841–1918
THE HISTORY OF FREEMASONRY IN CANADA, FROM ITS INTRODUCTION IN
1749. ... Toronto, Hunter Rose, 1899. 2v [BM BVaU NSWA OTU
HISTORY OF THE KNIGHTS TEMPLARS OF CANADA, FROM THE FOUNDATION ...
IN A.D. 1800 TO THE PRESENT TIME. ... Toronto, Hunter Rose, 1890. 401p
[BM BViP OLU
LANDMARKS OF CANADA. What Art has done for Canadian History. A Guide to
the J. Ross Robertson Collection in the Public Reference Library, Toronto.
Toronto, Author, 1917. 566p [BVaU NSHD OOP QMSS

Robinson, William Gordon, 1918–
TALES OF KITAMAAT. A Selection of Legends, Folk Stories and Customs of the
Haisla People, a Branch of the Kwakiutl Indian Language-Group who live on
the West Coast of British Columbia. Kitimat, B.C., 1956. 46p

Roddan, Rev. Andrew, –1948
CANADA'S UNTOUCHABLES. The Story of the Man without a Home. Vancouver,
Clarke & Stewart, 1932. 111p [BVaU
GOD IN THE JUNGLES. The Story of the Man without a Home. Vancouver, 1931.
64p [BVaU OKQ

Roger, Charles, 1819–1878
THE RISE OF CANADA FROM BARBARISM TO WEALTH AND CIVILIZATION.
Quebec, Sinclair, 1856. V. 1 [History to 1824.] 412p [No more published.]
[BM BVaU NSWA OLU QMM

Rohold, Rev. Sabetti B.
THE JEWS IN CANADA. 2nd ed. N.p., Home Missions, 1913. 24p [NSWA

Rome, David
CANADIAN JEWS IN WORLD WAR II. Pt. 1, Decorations; Pt. 2, Casualties. Ed.
by ——. Montreal, Canadian Jewish Congress, 1947–8. 2v in 1. [BM NBFU
OLU QMM

Rosenberg, Louis, 1893–
CANADA'S JEWS. A Social and Economic Study. ... Montreal, Canadian Jewish
Congress, 1939. 418p [BM BVaU LC NSHD OTU
CHRONOLOGY OF CANADIAN JEWISH HISTORY. Montreal, National Bicentenary
Committee, Canadian Jewish Congress, 1959. 24p
A STUDY OF THE GROWTH AND CHANGES IN THE DISTRIBUTION OF THE JEWISH
POPULATION OF MONTREAL 1851–1951. Montreal, Bureau of Social and
Economic Research, Canadian Jewish Congress, 1955. 51p

Ross, Murray George, 1911–
THE Y.M.C.A. IN CANADA. The Chronicle of a Century. Toronto, Ryerson, 1951.
xvii + 517p

Ross, William
EARLY HISTORY OF FREEMASONRY IN NOVA SCOTIA. Halifax, Chronicle, 1910.
32p [NSWA

Rosser, Frederick Thomas
THE WELSH SETTLEMENT IN UPPER CANADA. London, Ont., Lawson Memorial
Library, U. of Western Ontario, 1954. 150p

Roy, James Alexander, 1884–
THE SCOT AND CANADA. Toronto, McClelland, 1947. 117p [BVaU NSHD
OTP QMM

Roy, Mgr. Maurice, 1905–
THE PARISH AND DEMOCRACY IN FRENCH CANADA. Toronto, U. of Toronto
Press, 1950. 37p [OONL

Ryan, Alonzo
CARICATURE POLITIQUE AU CANADA. Free Lance Political Caricature in
Canada. Introductions by Lucien Lasalle and H.M. Williams. Montreal,
Chapman, 1904. 112p [NSWA OTP QMSS

Ryerson, Rev. Adolphus Egerton, 1803–1882
DR. RYERSON'S LETTERS IN REPLY TO THE ATTACKS OF THE HON. GEORGE
BROWN. Toronto, Lovell & Gibson; and Caverhill, 1859. 110p [BM BVaU
LC NSWA OTP
THE HON. R.B. SULLIVAN'S ATTACKS UPON SIR CHARLES METCALFE, REFUTED BY
EGERTON RYERSON. ... Being a Reply to the Letters of "Legion" [pseud].
Toronto, British Colonist, 1844. 63p [LC OTP
THE LOYALISTS OF AMERICA AND THEIR TIMES. From 1620 to 1816. Toronto,
Briggs, 1880. 2v [BM BVaU NBFU OTP QMM
SIR CHARLES METCALFE DEFENDED AGAINST THE ATTACKS OF HIS LATE
COUNSELLORS. Toronto, British Colonist, 1844. [Probably same as THE HON.
R.B. SULLIVAN'S ATTACKS. ..., above.] [BVaU

Ryerson, George Ansel Sterling, 1854–1925
THE AFTERMATH OF A REVOLUTION. Being the Inaugural Address as President of
the United Empire Loyalist Association ... Nov. 12, 1896. Toronto, Briggs,
1896. 16p [OTU

Sack, Benjamin Gutelius, 1889–1967
HISTORY OF THE JEWS IN CANADA, FROM THE EARLIEST BEGINNINGS TO THE

PRESENT DAY. Montreal, Canadian Jewish Congress, 1945—. [V. 1: FROM THE FRENCH REGIME TO THE END OF THE NINETEENTH CENTURY. 273p] [BM BVaU LC NSHD OTU

Safarian, Albert Edward, 1924—
THE CANADIAN ECONOMY IN THE GREAT DEPRESSION. Toronto, U. of Toronto Press, 1959. xii + 185p

Sandham, Alfred, 1838—1910
COINS, TOKENS AND MEDALS OF THE DOMINION OF CANADA. Montreal, Rose, 1869. 72p [BM BVaU LC NSWA OTU
HISTORY OF THE MONTREAL YOUNG MEN'S CHRISTIAN ASSOCIATION. ... Montreal, 1873. 120p [QMM

Sandwell, Bernard Keble, 1876—1954
THE CANADIAN PEOPLES. London, Oxford U. Press, 1941. 128p [BVaU LC MWU NSHD OTP QMM

Saskatoon Star-Phoenix
50TH ANNIVERSARY OF THE SASKATOON STAR-PHOENIX, 1902—1952. 70th Anniversary of the City of Saskatoon, 1882—1952. Saskatoon, 1952. 104p

Scadding, Rev. Henry, 1813—1901
CANADA IN SCULPTURE. A Paper Read before the Canadian Institute. ... Toronto, Copp, 1887. 12p [BVaU NSWA OTU

Schull, Joseph, 1910—
THE FAR DISTANT SHIPS. An Official Account of Canadian Naval Operations in the Second World War. Ottawa, King's Printer, 1950. 515p [BVaU NSHD OTP QMM

Sclater, William, 1906—
HAIDA. With an intro. by Rt. Hon. A.V. Alexander. Toronto, Oxford U. Press, 1946. 221p [An account of the destroyer "Haida."] [BM BVaU LC NSHD OTP QMM

Scott, Francis Reginald, 1899—
CANADA AND THE UNITED STATES. Boston, World Peace Foundation, 1941. 80p [BVaU NBFU OTU
CANADA TO-DAY. A Study of her National Interests and National Policy. London, Oxford U. Press, 1938. 184p [BM BVaU LC NBFU OTU
MAKE THIS *your* CANADA. A Review of C.C.F. History and Policy. By D. Lewis and F. Scott. With a foreword by M.J. Coldwell. Toronto, Central Canada Pub. Co., 1943. 223p [BVaU NBFU OLU QMM

Scott, H. Percy, 1856—1937
THE NEW SLAVERY. Toronto, Briggs, 1914. 190p [BM NSWA OTU QMM

Scott, Rev. William, 1812?–1891

THE TEETOTALER'S HAND-BOOK. In Four Parts. Being a Compilation of Valuable Information for the Use of all Classes. Toronto, Dredge, 1860. 408p [OKQ

Seaborn, Edwin, 1872–1951

THE MARCH OF MEDICINE IN WESTERN ONTARIO. Toronto, Ryerson, 1944. 386p [BVaU LC OTP QMM

Secretan, James Henry Edward, 1852–1926

CANADA'S GREAT HIGHWAY. From the First Stake to the Last Spike. London, Lane, 1924. 252p [BM BVaU NBFU OTU QMM

Shannon, James A.

HARD TIMES IN ONTARIO. A Pretty Story Certainly. ... Kingston, Daily News, 1872. 36p [NSHD

Shortt, Adam, 1859–1931

CANADA AND ITS PROVINCES. A History of the Canadian People and their Institutions. Ed. by Adam Shortt and Arthur G. Doughty. Toronto, Constable, 1913–17. 23v [BM BVaU LC NSWA OTU QMM

LIFE OF THE SETTLER IN WESTERN CANADA BEFORE THE WAR OF 1812. Kingston, Jackson, 1914. 18p [BM BVaU LC NSWA OTP QMM

Simonds, Peter, 1906–

MAPLE LEAF UP–MAPLE LEAF DOWN. The Story of Canadians in the Second World War. Toronto, Saunders, [1947]. 356p [BM BVaU OTP QMM

Simpkins, James Nathaniel, 1910–

JASPER. New York, Rinehart; Toronto, Burns & MacEachern, 1960. 1v [unpaged] [Cartoons, mainly previously published in *Maclean's* magazine.]

Simpson, John, 1788–1873

ESSAY ON MODERN REFORMERS. ... Kingston, Miles, 1818. 19p [Attack on the Reform Party, with a letter to Robert Gourlay.] [OTP

Simpson, Maria

SAYINGS AND DOINGS OF NOTED TEMPERANCE ADVOCATES. Toronto, Hunter Rose, 1879. 170p [OTP

Skelton, Isabel (Murphy)

THE BACKWOODSWOMAN. A Chronicle of Pioneer Home Life in Upper and Lower Canada. Toronto, Ryerson, 1924. 261p [BM BVaU LC NSHD OKQ QMM

Skelton, Oscar Douglas, 1878–1941

THE RAILWAY BUILDERS. Toronto, Glasgow Brook, 1916. 254p [BM BVaU NSWA OTU

Skinner, Constance Lindsay, 1879?–1939
ADVENTURERS OF OREGON. A Chronicle of the Fur Trade. New Haven, Yale
U. Press, 1920. 290p [BM BVaU LC NSHD OTU
BEAVER KINGS AND CABINS. New York, Macmillan, 1933. 272p [BM BVaU
LC NBFU OTU QMM

Slight, Rev. Benjamin, 1798?–1858
INDIAN RESEARCHES; or, Facts concerning the North American Indians. Montreal,
Miller, 1844. 179p [BM LC NSWA OTP QMM

Smith, Goldwin, 1823–1910
CANADA AND THE CANADIAN QUESTION. Toronto, Hunter Rose, 1891. 325p
[Also: 1892. 346p] [BM BVaU NSHD OKQ QMM

Smith, William, 1769–1847
HISTORY OF CANADA, FROM ITS FIRST DISCOVERY, TO THE YEAR 1791. Quebec,
Neilson, 1815. 2v [BM BVaU LC NBFU OTP QMM

Smith, William, 1859–1932
THE EVOLUTION OF GOVERNMENT IN CANADA. Montreal, Gazette, 1928. 273p
[BM BVaU NSHD OTU QMM
FIRST DAYS OF BRITISH RULE IN CANADA. Kingston, Jackson, 1922. 18p [BM
BVaU NBFU OKQ
THE HISTORY OF THE POST OFFICE IN BRITISH NORTH AMERICA, 1639–1870.
Cambridge, U. Press, 1920. 356p [BM BVaU LC NSHD OTU QMM

Smith, William George, 1872–1943
BUILDING THE NATION. A Study of some Problems Concerning the Churches'
Relation to the Immigrants. Toronto, Canadian Council of the Missionary
Education Movement, 1922. 202p [BM BVaU NSWA OKQ
A STUDY IN CANADIAN IMMIGRATION. Toronto, Ryerson, 1920. 406p [BM
BVaU LC NSWA OKQ

Smith, William Peter (pseud?)
THE VICTORIA DIAMOND JUBILEE HISTORY OF CANADA. By William Peter
Smith, Esq., M.A., F.R.C.S. [and others]. ... Toronto, Rose, 1897. 174p
[NSHPL OTP

Snider, Charles Henry Jeremiah, 1879–1971
THE GLORIOUS "SHANNON'S" OLD BLUE DUSTER, AND OTHER FADED FLAGS OF
FADELESS FAME. Toronto, McClelland, 1923. 430p [BM BVaU LC NBFU
OTU
THE GRIFFON. Toronto, Rous & Mann Press, 1956. 23p [About La Salle's
Griffon, first ship on the Great Lakes.]
IN THE WAKE OF THE EIGHTEENTWELVERS. Toronto, Bell & Cockburn, 1913.
291p [Later eds. under title: STORY OF THE "NANCY" AND OTHER EIGHTEEN-
TWELVERS.] [BM BVaU LC NSHD OTU

LEAVES FROM THE WAR LOG OF THE "NANCY," EIGHTEEN HUNDRED AND THIRTEEN. Ed. by ——. Toronto, Rous & Mann, 1936. [LC

STORY OF THE "NANCY" AND OTHER EIGHTEENTWELVERS. Toronto, McClelland, 1926. 334p [BM BVaU LC NSHD OTU

TARRY BREEKS AND VELVET GARTERS. Sail on the Great Lakes of America, in War, Discovery, and the Fur Trade, under the Fleur-de-lys. Toronto, Ryerson, 1958. xvii + 148p

UNDER THE RED JACK. Privateers of the Maritime Provinces of Canada in the War of 1812. ... London, Hopkinson, 1928. 268p [BM BVaU LC NSHD NBFU

Spence, Ruth Elizabeth, 1890–

PROHIBITION IN CANADA. A Memorial to Francis Stephens Spence. Toronto, Dominion Alliance, 1919. 624p [BM BVaU NSWA OTP

Spendlove, Francis St. George, 1897–1962

THE FACE OF EARLY CANADA. Pictures of Canada which have Helped to Make History. Toronto, Ryerson, 1958. xxi + 162p

Stacey, Charles Perry, 1906–

CANADA AND THE BRITISH ARMY, 1846–1871. ... New York, Longmans, 1936. 287p [BM BVaU LC NSHD OTU

THE CANADIAN ARMY, 1939–1945. An Official Historical Summary. Ottawa, King's Printer, 1948. 354p [BM BVaU LC NSHD OTU

Stanley, George Francis Gilman, 1907–

CANADA'S SOLDIERS, 1604–1954. The Military History of an Unmilitary People. Toronto, Macmillan, 1954. 401p [BVaU NBFU OTP QMBM

Stearns, Anna (Seidner), 1904–

NEW CANADIANS OF SLAVIC ORIGIN. A Problem in Creative Reorientation. Winnipeg, Montreal, Ukrainian Free Academy of Sciences, 1960. 144p

Steele, Harwood Elmes Robert, 1897–

THE CANADIANS IN FRANCE, 1915–1918. Toronto, Copp Clark, 1920. 364p [BM NSHD OTU QMM

Stephenson, Harry Edward, 1874–1940

THE STORY OF ADVERTISING IN CANADA. A Chronicle of Fifty Years. By H.E. Stephenson and Carlton McNaught. Toronto, Ryerson, 1940. 364p [BVaU LC NBFU OTU

Stevens, Gerald Francis, 1909–

THE CANADIAN COLLECTOR. Glass, Pottery, Furniture, Firearms, of the Nineteenth Century. Toronto, Ryerson, 1957. xvii + 100p

Stewart, George, 1848–1906

CANADA UNDER THE ADMINISTRATION OF THE EARL OF DUFFERIN. Toronto, Rose-Belford, 1878. 696p [BM BVaU NSWA OKQ QMM

Strachan, Rev. John, 1778–1867
OBSERVATIONS ON THE HISTORY AND RECENT PROCEEDINGS OF THE CANADA
COMPANY. Addresses in Four Letters to Frederick Widder. ... N.p., 1845. 54p
[OLU
PASTORAL LETTER ... on the Subject of the Cholera. Toronto, Diocesan Press,
1848. 14p [OTP

Sullivan, Robert Baldwin, 1802–1853
ADDRESS ON EMIGRATION AND COLONIZATION. ... Toronto, Brown's Print.,
1847. 41p [OTP
LETTERS ON RESPONSIBLE GOVERNMENT. By Legion [pseud]. Toronto, Examiner,
1844. 216p [OTP QMM

Sutherland, Rev. Alexander, 1833–1910
ERRING THROUGH WINE. A Discourse delivered in the Richmond Street Church,
Toronto ... December 18, 1870. Toronto, Burnett, 1871. 16p [OTP

Symons, Harry Lutz, 1893–
FENCES. Toronto, Ryerson, 1958. x + 155p

Talbot, Mrs. Marjorie, 1882–
OLD LEGENDS AND CUSTOMS OF THE BRITISH COLUMBIA COAST INDIANS.
New Westminster, Author, 1952. 8p

Talman, James John, 1904–
LOYALIST NARRATIVES FROM UPPER CANADA. Ed. by ——. Toronto, Champlain
Society, 1946. 411p [BM BVaU LC NSHD OTU QMM

Taylor, Henry, fl. 1819–1860
ON THE PRESENT CONDITION OF UNITED CANADA. ... Montreal, Author, [1843?].
104p [Same title: London, Ont., Sutherland, 1849. 168p — OOP] [BVaU
NBFU OTP

Taylor, Thomas Griffith, 1880–
CANADA. A Study of Cool Continental Environments and their Effect on British
and French Settlement. Toronto, Saunders, 1947. 542p [Rev. ed., 1950.]
[BVaU LC NSHD OTU QMM
ENVIRONMENT, RACE, AND MIGRATION. ... Toronto, U. of Toronto Press, 1937.
483p [Special reference to Canada and Australia.] [BVaU LC NSHD OTU
QMM

Taylor, Rev. William, 1803–1876
A TESTIMONY AGAINST DUELLING. A Sermon. ... Montreal, Campbell &
Becket, 1838. 32p [QMM

Textor, Lucy Elizabeth
A COLONY OF EMIGRES IN CANADA, 1798–1816. Toronto, U. of Toronto
  Library, 1905. 86p [BM BVaU LC NSWA OTU

Thomson, Donald Walter, 1906–
THE FOUNDATION AND THE MAN. By Walter Dawson [pseud]. Toronto, priv.
  print., 1959. 23p [History of the Canadian Writers' Foundation founded by
  Dr. Pelham Edgar.]

Timar, Leslie Joseph, 1899–
A SHORT HISTORY OF THE HUNGARIAN PEOPLE IN CANADA. Toronto, Across
  Canada Press, 1957. 19p

Toronto, Ont. Public Library
RECORDING TORONTO. A Catalogue of Selected Pictures of early Buildings and
  Street Scenes in the Town of York and the City of Toronto from the John
  Ross Robertson Historical Collection and other Picture Collections of the
  Toronto Public Libraries. Comp. by Elspeth Smith. Toronto, the Library,
  1960. 36p

Toronto Arts & Letters Club
FIFTY YEARS, 1908–1958. Toronto, the Club, 1958. 8p

Toronto Literary Association
TORONTO LITERARY ASSOCIATION. Laws of the Toronto Literary Association,
  Instituted 7th July, 1853. Toronto, Leader Office, 1856. 16p [OTP

Toronto Transportation Commission
PICTURE STORY. Public Transportation in Toronto. Toronto, the Commission,
  1950. 30p [OONL

Tory, Henry Marshall, 1864–1947
A HISTORY OF SCIENCE IN CANADA. By Frank Dawson Adams *et al.* Ed. by ——.
  Toronto, Ryerson, 1939. 152p [BM BVaU NBFU OTU QMSS

Townsley, Benjamin Franklin, 1890–1939
MINE-FINDERS. The History and Romance of Canadian Mineral Discoveries.
  Toronto, Sat. Night Press, 1935. 246p [BM BVaU LC OTU QMM

Tremaine, Marie
CANADIAN BOOK OF PRINTING. How Printing Came to Canada and the Story
  of the Graphic Arts. Told Mainly in Pictures. Ed. by ——. Toronto, Public
  Libraries, 1940. 130p [BVaU LC NSHD OLU
EARLY PRINTING IN CANADA. Toronto, Golden Dog Press, 1934. 13p [BVaU
  NSWA OTP QMM

Trotter, Rev. Thomas, 1853–1918
LIFE PICTURES FROM RUM'S GALLERY; or, Sketches written from Personal

Knowledge of Persons who have been ruined through Liquor. Toronto, Briggs, 1886. 364p [BVaU OTP

Tucker, Gilbert Norman, 1898–1955
THE NAVAL SERVICE OF CANADA. Its Official History. Ottawa, King's Printer, 1952. 2v

Tupper, Rev. Charles, 1794–1881
PROHIBITION AND ANTI-PROHIBITION. Being a Series of Letters ... in Favor of Prohibition, and Replies to the Same, by John Bent. ... Saint John, Barnes, 1856. 40p [NSHP QMSS

Turek, Victor, 1910–
THE POLISH PAST IN CANADA. Contributions to the History of the Poles in Canada and of the Polish Canadian Relations. Ed. by ——. Toronto, Polish Alliance Press, 1960. 138p

Turner, John Peter, 1879–1948
THE NORTH-WEST MOUNTED POLICE, 1873–1893. ... Ottawa, King's Printer, 1950. 2v [BM BVaU LC NSHD OTU

U.E.L. Centennial Committee
THE CENTENNIAL OF THE SETTLEMENT OF UPPER CANADA BY THE UNITED EMPIRE LOYALISTS, 1784–1884. The Celebrations at Adolphustown, Toronto, and Niagara, with an Appendix containing a Copy of the U.E.L. List, Preserved in the Crown Lands Department at Toronto. Toronto, Rose, 1885. 334p [BVaU LC OTU

Ure, George P., –1860
THE MAINE LAW ILLUSTRATED. Being the Result of an Investigation made in the Maine Law States. By A. Farewell and G.P. Ure. Toronto, Can. Prohibitory Liquor Law League, 1855. 94p [OTU QMM

Vancouver, B.C. Community Arts Survey Committee
"THE ARTS AND OUR TOWN." Vancouver, Keystone Press, 1946. 201p [BVaU

Vlassis, George Demetrios, 1897–
THE GREEKS IN CANADA. 2nd ed. Ottawa, LeClerc Printers, 1953. 364p [1st ed., 1942.]

Voorhis, Ernest, 1859–1933
HISTORIC FORTS AND TRADING POSTS OF THE FRENCH REGIME AND OF THE ENGLISH FUR TRADING COMPANIES. Ottawa, Dept. of the Interior, 1930. 188p [BM BVaU NSHD OTP

Walker, Annie
FIFTY YEARS OF ACHIEVEMENT: ... 50th Anniversary of the Founding of the
Women's Institute of Ontario. Toronto, Federated Women's Insts. of Ont.,
1948. 163p [OTU

Walker, Frank Norman, 1892–
FOUR WHISTLES TO WOOD-UP! Stories of the Northern Railway of Canada.
Toronto, Upper Canada Railway Society, 1953. 64p

Wallace, Frederick William, 1886–1958
IN THE WAKE OF THE WIND SHIPS. Notes, Records, and Biographies. Toronto,
Musson, 1927. 282p [BM BVaU NSWA OTU
WOODEN SHIPS AND IRON MEN. The Story of the Square-rigged Merchant
Marine of British North America. ... Toronto, Hodder, 1923. 337p [BM
BVaU NSHD OTU QMM

Wallace, William Stewart, 1884–1970
THE FAMILY COMPACT. A Chronicle of the Rebellion in Upper Canada. Toronto,
Glasgow Brook, 1915. 172p [BVaU LC NSWA OTU QMM
THE GROWTH OF CANADIAN NATIONAL FEELING. Toronto, Macmillan, 1927.
85p [BVaU LC NSHD OTU QMBM
MURDERS AND MYSTERIES. A Canadian Series. Toronto, Macmillan, 1931.
333p [BVaU LC NBFU OTU QMM
THE PEDLARS FROM QUEBEC AND OTHER PAPERS ON THE NOR'WESTERS.
Toronto, Ryerson, 1954. xii + 101p
THE ROYAL CANADIAN INSTITUTE CENTENNIAL VOLUME, 1849–1949. Toronto,
The Institute, 1949. 232p [BVaU OTU
A SKETCH OF THE HISTORY OF THE CHAMPLAIN SOCIETY. Toronto, The Society,
1937. 8p [Rev. ed., 1957. 15p] [BVaU LC NBFU OTU
THE UNITED EMPIRE LOYALISTS. A Chronicle of the Great Migration. ... Toronto,
Glasgow Brook, 1914. 148p [BVaU LC NSWA OOU QMM

Warnock, Amelia Beers (Mrs. John Garvin), 1878–1956
CANADA'S PEACE TOWER AND MEMORIAL CHAMBER. ... Toronto, Mundy-
Goodfellow, 1935. 29p [BVaU OKQ

Warwick Bros. and Rutter, Ltd.
THE STORY OF THE BUSINESS, 1848–1923. As Told, Printed, and Published on
its 75th Anniversary. Toronto, Warwick & Rutter, 1923. 97p [OTU

Watson, Samuel James, 1837–1881
THE POWERS OF CANADIAN PARLIAMENTS. ... Toronto, Robinson, 1880. 160p
[BVaU NSHD OTU

Weaver, Emily Poynton, 1865–1943
CANADA AND THE BRITISH IMMIGRANT. London, Religious Tract Soc., 1914.
312p [BM BVaU LC OTP

Webster, John Clarence, 1863–1950
THE DISTRESSED MARITIMES. A Study of Educational and Cultural Conditions in Canada. Toronto, Ryerson, 1926. 46p [BM BVaU NSWA OTP QMM

Wetherell, James Elgin, 1851–1940
THREE CENTURIES OF CANADIAN STORIES FROM JOHN CABOT TO JOHN FRANKLIN. Toronto, Musson, 1928. [BM OTU

Whelan, Edward, 1824–1867
THE UNION OF THE BRITISH PROVINCES. A Brief Account of the Several Conferences held in the Maritime Provinces and in Canada, in September and October, 1864. Together with a Report of the Speeches delivered by the Delegates. ... Charlottetown, Haszard, 1865. 231p [BM BVaU NSWA OTU QMSS

White, Thomas, 1830–1888
NEWSPAPERS, THEIR DEVELOPMENT IN THE PROVINCE OF QUEBEC. A Lecture. ... Montreal, 1883. 15p [OTP QMM

White, William, 1830–1912
THE ANNALS OF CANADA. [Pt. 1, 1492–1760; pt. 2, 1763–1814.] Comp. by —— Toronto, Adam & Stevenson, 1875–8. 138p [Issued as supplement to *Canadian Monthly & National Revue.*] [BVaU LC OOA

Whitton, Charlotte Elizabeth, 1896–
THE DAWN OF AMPLER LIFE. ... Contains Summaries of Marsh, Heagerty and Beveridge Reports. Toronto, Macmillan, 1943. 154p [BVaU NSHD OTU
GOD'S GOOD TIDE. Toronto, Ryerson, 1941. 20p [BVaU OTU

Wightman, Rev. Frederick Arnold, 1860–1939
OUR CANADIAN HERITAGE. Its Resources and Possibilities. Toronto, Briggs, 1905. 287p [BM BVaU NBFU OKQ

Wilder, H.E.
THE 100TH ANNIVERSARY OF JEWISH EMANCIPATION IN CANADA (1832–1932) AND THE 50TH ANNIVERSARY OF THE JEW IN THE WEST. Winnipeg, Israelite Daily Press, 1932. 60 + 60p [Text in English and Hebrew] [OTU

Williams, Helen Ernestine
SPINNING WHEELS AND HOMESPUN. Toronto, McClelland, 1923. 314p [BM BVaU LC NSHD OTU QMM

Willison, John Stephen, 1856–1927
THE NEW CANADA. A Survey of the Conditions and Problems of the Dominion. By the Canadian Correspondent of "The Times." London, The Times, 1912. 118p [NBFU OTP

Willison, Marjory (MacMurchy), —1938

THE WOMAN–BLESS HER. Not as Amiable a Book as it Sounds. ... Toronto, Gundy, 1916. 155p [BVaU LC NSHD OTU

WOMEN OF TODAY AND TOMORROW. Toronto, Reconstruction Assoc., 1919 [CAR

Willson, (Henry) Beckles, 1869–1942

THE GREAT COMPANY. A History of the Honourable Company of Merchants-Adventurers trading into Hudson's Bay. With an intro. by Lord Strathcona. Toronto, Copp Clark, 1899. 541p [BM BVaU LC NSWA OTU QMM

IN THE YPRES SALIENT. ... London, Simpkin Marshall, 1916. 80p [BM BVaU NSHD OTU

YOUTH BE DAMNED! Being a Protest and an Exhortation. London, Laurie, 1938. 214p [OTU

Withrow, Oswald Charles Joseph, 1878–1946

THE ROMANCE OF THE CANADIAN NATIONAL EXHIBITION. Toronto, Saunders, 1936. 157p [OTU

SHACKLING THE TRANSGRESSOR. An Indictment of the Canadian Penal System. ... Toronto, Nelson, 1933. 229p [BVaU LC NSHD OTP

Withrow, Rev. William Henry, 1839–1908

THE BIBLE AND THE TEMPERANCE QUESTION. Toronto, Rose, 1876. 29p [OTUV

INTEMPERANCE. Its Evils and their Remedies. Napanee, Can. Temperance Union, 1869. 58p [OTP

Wood, A.C.

OLD DAYS ON THE FARM. Toronto, McClelland, 1918. 255p [BVaU OKQ

Wood, Louis Aubrey Lorne, 1883–1955

A HISTORY OF FARMERS' MOVEMENTS IN CANADA. Toronto, Ryerson, 1924. 372p [BM BVaU LC NSHD OTU QMM

Wood, William Charles Henry, 1864–1947

ALL AFLOAT. A Chronicle of Craft and Waterways. Toronto, Glasgow Brook, 1914. 199p [BM BVaU LC NSWA OTP

Woodsworth, Rev. James Shaver, 1874–1942

ON THE WATERFRONT. With the Workers on the Docks at Vancouver. Some Observations and Experiences. Ottawa, Montreal Print., [1918?]. 31p [BVaU OTU

STRANGERS WITHIN OUR GATES; or, Coming Canadians. Toronto, Missionary Society of the Methodist Church, 1909. 356p [BM BVaU LC NSWA OTP QMM

Wright, James Frederick Church, 1904–

SLAVA BOHU. The Story of the Doukhobors. New York, Farrar & Rinehart, 1940. 438p [BM BVaU LC NBFU OLU QMM

Wrong, Dennis Hume, 1923–
AMERICAN AND CANADIAN VIEWPOINTS. Prepared for the Canada–United States
Committee on Education. Washington, D.C., American Council on Education,
1955. 62p [A comparison of national values.]

Wrong, George McKinnon, 1860–1948
CANADA AND THE AMERICAN REVOLUTION. The Disruption of the First British
Empire. Toronto, Macmillan, 1935. 497p [BM BVaU NSHD OTU QMM
A CANADIAN MANOR AND ITS SEIGNEURS, 1761–1860. Toronto, Macmillan,
1908. 295p [An account of Murray Bay, Quebec, and the Nairne Family. ...]
[BM BVaU LC NSHD OTU QMM
CHRONICLES OF CANADA. Ed. by G.M. Wrong and H.H. Langton. Toronto,
Glasgow Brook, 1914–16. 32v [BM BVaU LC NBFU OTU QMM
THE CONQUEST OF NEW FRANCE. A Chronicle of the Colonial Wars. New Haven,
Yale U. Press, 1918. 246p [BM BVaU LC NSHD OTU
THE UNITED STATES AND CANADA. A Political Study. New York, Abingdon Press,
1921. 191p [BM BVaU LC NBFU OTU

York, Eva Rose (Fitch), 1858–
FEATHERS WITH YELLOW GOLD. Ed. by Ray Palmer Baker and Eva Rose York.
Toronto, Evangelical Pub., 1920. 235p [OTU

Young, James, 1835–1913
OUR NATIONAL FUTURE. Being Four Letters ... in Opposition to Commercial
Union ... and Imperial Federation. ... Galt, Collie & McGiverin, 1887. 19p
[OTP

Young, Katherine A.
EARLY DAYS IN THE MAPLE LAND. Stories for Children of Stirring Deeds under
Three Flags. New York, Pott & Co., 1901. 120p [OONL

Yuzyk, Paul, 1913–
THE UKRAINIANS IN MANITOBA. A Social History. Toronto, U. of Toronto Press,
1953. xv + 232p

SCHOLARSHIP

Studies and criticism in literature and the other humanities

Abell, Walter Halsey, 1897—1956

REPRESENTATION AND FORM. A Study of Aesthetic Values in Representational Art. New York, Scribner, 1936. 172p [BM BVaU NBFU OTU

Adair, Mary

SHORT STORY STUDIES, IN SHORT STORY CLASSICS. ... Boston, Badger, 1930. 344p [LC OTP

Adams, Sinclair MacLardy, 1891—

SOPHOCLES THE PLAYWRIGHT. Toronto, U. of Toronto Press, 1957. 182p

Alexander, Henry, 1893—

THE STORY OF OUR LANGUAGE. Toronto, Nelson, 1940. 242p [Earlier ed.: Garden City, N.Y., Doubleday, 1926.] [BVaU LC NSHD OTU

Alexander, William Hardy, 1878—1962

THE AMIABLE TYRANNY OF PEISISTRATUS; or, The Future of Classical Studies. Edmonton, U. of Alberta Press, 1931. 20p [OTU

AUREA MEDIOCRITAS. An Address ... on the ... Two Thousandth Anniversary of the Birth of Horace. Edmonton, U. of Alberta Press, 1935. 17p [BM BVaU OTP

NOTES AND EMENDATIONS TO THE XII DIALOGES OF L. ANNAEUS SENECA. Edmonton, U. of Alberta Press, 1934. 33p [BM NSHD OLU QMM

NOTES AND EMENDATIONS TO THE EPISTULAE MORALES OF L. ANNAEUS SENECA. Edmonton, U. of Alberta Press, 1932. 15p [BM LC OTP

PENTASYLLABIC ENDINGS IN THE LATIN HEXAMETER WITH PARTICULAR REFERENCE TO THE VERSE OF LUCRETIUS. N.p., 1900. 32p [OTU

PUBLIUS VERGILIUS MARO, THE POET OF A LAND AND OF A RACE. Bimillenary Celebration Lecture given at the University of Alberta. N.p., 1930. 21p [OTU

SENECA'S DIALOGI. Los Angeles, U. of California Press, 1943—45. 3v [BM BVaU LC

SENECA'S EPISTULAE MORALES. The Text Emended and Explained. Berkeley, U. of California Press, 1940. [BM BVaU LC NSHD OTU

SENECA'S NATURALES QUAESTIONES. Berkeley, U. of California Press, 1948. 332p [BM BVaU LC OLU

SOME TEXTUAL CRITICISMS ON THE EIGHTH BOOK OF THE DE VITA CAESARUM OF SUETONIUS. Berkeley, U. of California Press, 1908. 33p [BM BVaU LC OLU

Alexander, William John, 1855–1944
AN INTRODUCTION TO THE POETRY OF ROBERT BROWNING. Boston, Ginn, 1899.
212p [BM BVaU LC NSHD OTU
THE STUDY OF LITERATURE. Inaugural Lecture Delivered in the Convocation
Hall, October 12th, 1889. Toronto, Rowsell & Hutchinson, 1889. 34p [OTP

Allen, Grant, 1848–1899
THE COLOUR SENSE: ITS ORIGIN AND DEVELOPMENT. An Essay in Comparative
Psychology. London, Trubner, 1879. 282p [BM OTU
EVOLUTION IN ITALIAN ART. London, Richards, 1908. 368p [BM OTU
FORCE AND ENERGY. A Theory of Dynamics. London, Longmans, 1888. 161p
[BM OTU
THE MISCELLANEOUS AND POSTHUMOUS WORKS OF H.T. BUCKLE. Abridged ed.
Ed. by ——. London, Longmans, 1885. 2v [BM OTU
THE NATURAL HISTORY OF SELBORNE. By Gilbert White. Ed. with notes by ——.
London, Lane, 1899. 568p [BM BVaU
PHYSIOLOGICAL AESTHETICS. London, King, 1877. 283p [BM OTU

Allison, William Talbot, 1874–1941
BLAZING A NEW TRAIL. [Anon] Toronto, Musson, 1920. [On Canadian authors.]
BOLSHEVISM IN ENGLISH LITERATURE . An Inaugural Lecture. Winnipeg, U. of
Manitoba, 1921. 21p [OTUV

Anderson, Fulton Henry, 1895–1968
THE ARGUMENT OF PLATO. Toronto, Dent, 1934. 216p [BM BVaU LC NSHD
OTP
THE INFLUENCE OF CONTEMPORARY SCIENCE ON LOCKE'S METHOD AND RESULTS.
Toronto, University Library, 1923. 31p [BVaU LC NSWA OTU
THE PHILOSOPHY OF FRANCIS BACON. Chicago, U. of Chicago Press, 1948. 312p
[BM BVaU LC NSHD OTP

Anstensen, Ansten, 1899–
THE PROVERB IN IBSEN. Proverbial Sayings and Citations as Elements in His
Style. New York, Columbia U. Press, 1936. 255p [BM LC OTU QMM

Ashton, Harry, 1882–
THE FRENCH NOVEL. London, Benn, 1928. 80p [BM BVaU OTU
MOLIERE. London, Routledge, 1930. 263p [BM BVaU LC NSHD OTU
A PREFACE TO MOLIERE. Toronto, Longmans, 1927. 177p [BM BVaU LC
OTU

Ayscough, Florence (Wheelock), 1878–1942
TU FU. The Autobiography of a Chinese Poet, A.D. 712–770. Arranged from his
Poems. Boston, Houghton, 1928. 450p [BM BVaU NSHD OTU

Bagnani, Gilbert
ARBITER OF ELEGANCE. A Study of the Life and Works of C. Petronius. Toronto,
U. of Toronto Press, 1954. xi + 91p

Baker, Ray Palmer, 1883–
A HISTORY OF ENGLISH-CANADIAN LITERATURE TO THE CONFEDERATION.
Cambridge, Harvard U. Press, 1920. 200p [BM BVaU LC NSHD OTU

Barker, Arthur Edward, 1911–
MILTON AND THE PURITAN DILEMMA, 1641–1660. Toronto, U. of Toronto Press,
1942. xxiv + 440p [Reprinted, 1955.] [BM BVaU NSHD OTP

Barnes, Duane Clayton, 1905–
WORDLORE. New York, Dutton, 1948. 135p [BViP LC

Baylis, Samuel Mathewson, 1854–1941
"SHAKE-SPEARE." An Enquiry. Paper read before the St. James Literary Society,
Montreal. Toronto, Briggs, 1910. 32p [BM OTP

Beaugrand, Honoré, 1849–1906
NEW STUDIES OF CANADIAN FOLK LORE. Montreal, Renouf, 1904. 130p [BVaU
LC NBFU OTUV

Beck, Lily Adams (Moresby), –1931
THE GHOST PLAYS OF JAPAN. New York, Japan Society, 1933. 35p [BVaU
LC OTU

Bedford-Jones, Henry James O'Brien, 1887–1949
THE GRADUATE FICTIONEER. Denver, Col., Author & Journalist Pub. Co., 1932.
126p [LC
THIS FICTION BUSINESS. New York, Covici Friede, 1929. 178p [First pub. as:
THE FICTION BUSINESS. Evansville, Ind., 1922. 72p] [BVaU LC

Bell, Andrew James, 1856–1932
THE LATIN DUAL AND POETIC DICTION. London, Oxford U. Press, 1923. 468p
[BM LC NBFU OTU

Bell, Inglis Freeman, 1917–
THE ENGLISH NOVEL, 1578–1956. A Checklist of Twentieth-Century Criticisms.
By Inglis F. Bell and Donald Baird. Denver, A. Swallow, 1959 [c1958].
xii + 169p

Bender, Louis Prosper, 1844–1917
LITERARY SHEAVES; or, La Littérature au Canada Français. The Drama, History,
Romance, Poetry, Lectures, Sketches, &c. Montreal, Dawson, 1881. 215p [BM
BVaU LC NBFU OTU QMM

Berlis, Rudolph John
CITY UNDER SIEGE. Montreal, Author, 1940. 8p [CC

Birch, Thomas Albany, 1897–
THE ENGLISH MIND AS REFLECTED IN LITERATURE. Montreal, Renouf Pub. Co., 1956. xi + 332p

Bissell, Claude Thomas, 1916–
OUR LIVING TRADITION. Seven Canadians. Ed. by ——. Toronto, Published in association with Carleton University by U. of Toronto Press, 1957. x + 149p [Public lectures given at Carleton University, Ottawa, 1957.]

Black, Norman Fergus, 1876–1964
ENGLISH FOR THE NON ENGLISH. Regina, Regina Book Shop, 1913. 211p [BM OTU

Blanchard, Kathleen Helen (Barrett), 1872–
STORIES OF BEAUTIFUL HYMNS. Grand Rapids, Mich., Zondervan, 1942. 117p [BVa LC
STORIES OF FAVORITE HYMNS. Grand Rapids, Mich., Zondervan, 1941. 118p [BVa LC
STORIES OF POPULAR HYMNS. Grand Rapids, Mich., Zondervan, 1939. 142p [BVa LC OTUV
STORIES OF WONDERFUL HYMNS. Grand Rapids, Mich., Zondervan, 1947. 109p [BVa

Borneman, Ernst Wilhelm Julius, 1915–
A CRITIC LOOKS AT JAZZ. London, Jazz Music Books, 1946. 53p [LC

Bossin, Hye
STARS OF DAVID. Toronto, Jewish Standard, 1956. 39p [Account of the Jewish contribution to the theatre in Toronto.]

Bourinot, Arthur Stanley, 1893–1969
AT THE MERMAID INN. By A. Lampman, W.W. Campbell, Duncan C. Scott. Being Selections from Essays on Life and Literature which appeared in the Toronto Globe, 1892–1893. Ed., annotated, and selected by ——. Ottawa, Bourinot, 1958. 96p

Bourinot, John George, 1837–1902
THE INTELLECTUAL DEVELOPMENT OF THE CANADIAN PEOPLE. An Historical Review. Toronto, Hunter Rose, 1881. 128p [BM BVaU LC MWU NSHD OTU QMM
OUR INTELLECTUAL STRENGTH AND WEAKNESS. A Short Historical and Critical Review of Literature, Art and Education in Canada. Montreal, Brown, 1893. 99p [BM BVaU LC NSHD OTU QMM

Brebner, John Bartlet, 1895–1957
SCHOLARSHIP FOR CANADA. The Function of Graduate Studies. Ottawa, Social Science Research Council, 1945. 90p [BVaU LC NSHD OTU QMM

Brennan, Joseph Fletcher

A POPULAR ILLUSTRATED HISTORY OF THE FINE ARTS OF PAINTING AND SCULPTURE FROM THE EARLIEST AGES TO THE PRESENT. Cincinnati, Franklin Type, 1884. 320p [LC

Brett, George Sidney, 1879–1944

THE GOVERNMENT OF MAN. An Introduction to Ethics and Politics. London, Bell, 1920. 318p [BM BVaU LC OLU

THE HISTORY OF PSYCHOLOGY, ANCIENT AND PATRISTIC. London, Allen, 1912–21. 3v [Abridged ed. in one vol., 1953.] [BM BVaU LC NBFU OTU

THE PHILOSOPHY OF GASSENDI. London, Macmillan, 1908. 310p [BM BVaU LC OTU

PSYCHOLOGY, ANCIENT AND MODERN. New York, Longmans, 1928. 164p [BM BVaU LC NSHD OTU QMM

Bridle, Augustus, 1869–1952

THE STORY OF THE CLUB. Toronto, Arts and Letters Club, 1945. 83p [NBFU OTP

Broadus, Edmund Kemper, 1876–1936

BOOKS AND IDEALS. An Anthology Selected and Arranged by ——. London, Oxford U. Press, 1921. 212p [BM LC QMM

THE LAUREATESHIP. A Study of the Office of Poet Laureate in England with Some Account of the Poets. Oxford, Clarendon Press, 1921. 239p [BM LC NSHD OTU QMM

THE STORY OF ENGLISH LITERATURE. New York, Macmillan, 1931. 624p [Rev. ed.: Toronto, Macmillan, 1936. 818p] [BM BVaU LC OTU QMM

Brown, Edward Killoran, 1905–1951

EDITH WHARTON. Paris, Didier, 1938. 11p [OTU

EDITH WHARTON, ETUDE CRITIQUE. Paris, Droz, 1935. 348p [BM OTU

MATTHEW ARNOLD. A Study in Conflict. Toronto, Ryerson, 1948. 223p [BM BVaU NSHD OTU QMM

ON CANADIAN POETRY. Toronto, Ryerson, 1943. 157p [Rev. and enl. ed.: Toronto, Ryerson, 1944. 172p] [BM BVaU LC NSHD OTU QMM

REPRESENTATIVE ESSAYS OF MATTHEW ARNOLD. Ed. by ——. Toronto, Macmillan, 1936. 240p [BVaU OTU

RHYTHM IN THE NOVEL. Toronto, U. of Toronto Press, 1950. 118p [BM BVaU NSHD OTU QMM

STUDIES IN THE TEXT OF MATTHEW ARNOLD'S PROSE WORKS. Paris, André, 1935. 139p [BM LC OTU

WILLA CATHER. A Critical Biography. ... Completed by Leon Edel. New York, Knopf, 1953. 351p

VICTORIAN POETRY. Ed. by ——. New York, Ronald, 1942. 912p [BVaU LC NBFU OTU

Bryce, Rev. George, 1844–1931

A POET'S MESSAGE. [Winnipeg? 1909?] 15p [On David, the Psalmist] [LC OTU

Buchanan, Donald William, 1908–1966
CANADIAN PAINTERS. From Paul Kane to the Group of Seven. Ed. by ——.
  Oxford, Phaidon, 1945. 25p (87 plates.) [BM BVaU LC NSHD OTU QMM
EDUCATIONAL AND CULTURAL FILMS IN CANADA. A Survey of the Situation,
  together with Recommendations, &c. Ottawa, n.p., 1936. 23p [BVaU OTU
THE GROWTH OF CANADIAN PAINTING. Toronto, Collins, 1950. 112p [BM BVaU
  NSHD OTU

Buchanan, Milton Alexander, 1878–1952
THE CHRONOLOGY OF LOPE DE VEGA'S PLAYS. Toronto, University Library, 1922.
  25p [BM BVaU LC OTU QMM
SPANISH POETRY OF THE GOLDEN AGE. Ed. by ——. Toronto, U. of Toronto
  Press, 1942. 149p [2nd ed. 1947.] [BVaU LC NSHD OTU QMM

Bucke, Richard Maurice, 1837–1902
COSMIC CONSCIOUSNESS. A Study in the Evolution of the Human Mind.
  Philadelphia, Innes, 1901. 318p [Many later editions.] [BM BVaU LC OTU
  QMM
IN RE WALT WHITMAN. Edited by his Literary Executors, H.L. Traubel, R.M.
  Bucke, T.B. Larned. Philadelphia, McKay, 1893. 452p [LC OLU QMM
WALT WHITMAN. Philadelphia, McKay, 1883. 236p [BM BVaU LC OTU QMM
THE WOUND DRESSER. Letters written to his [Walt Whitman's] Mother from the
  Hospitals in Washington during the Civil War. Ed. by ——. With an intro. by
  Oscar Cargill. New York, Bodley Press, 1949. 200p [Earlier ed.: Boston, Small
  Maynard, 1897.] [BM BVaU LC

Buckley, Jerome Hamilton, 1917–
THE VICTORIAN TEMPER. A Study in Literary Culture. Cambridge, Mass.,
  Harvard U. Press, 1951. viii + 282p

Buckley, Joan
THE TECHNIQUE OF POETRY. Hints on Verse-Writing. Vancouver, Clarke &
  Stuart, 1944. 63p [BVaU OKQ

Burpee, Lawrence Johnstone, 1873–1946
CANADIAN NOVELS AND NOVELISTS. N.p., [1901]. 28p [BVaU OTP
A LITTLE BOOK OF CANADIAN ESSAYS. Toronto, Musson, 1909. 87p [BVaU LC
  NBFU OKQ QMM

Burrell, Martin, 1858–1938
BETWIXT HEAVEN AND CHARING CROSS. Toronto, Macmillan, 1928. 328p [BM
  BVaU LC NSHD OTU QMM
CRUMBS ARE ALSO BREAD. Toronto, Macmillan, 1934. 340p [BM BVaU LC
  NSHD OTU QMM

Burton, Alice Elizabeth, 1908–
THE ELIZABETHANS AT HOME. London, Secker & Warburg, 1958. 276p

Caldwell, William, 1863–1942

PRAGMATISM AND IDEALISM. London, Black, 1913. 268p [BM BVaU LC NBFU OTU QMM

SCHOPENHAUER'S SYSTEM IN ITS PHILOSOPHICAL SIGNIFICANCE. Edinburgh, Blackwood, 1896. 538p [BM BVaU OTU QMM

Campbell, Colin D.

THE NATURE OF LITERATURE. (1) The Definition. Regina, Leader Pub. Co., 1926. 19p [OKQ

WHAT IS ART? Regina, Commercial Printers, 1934. 15p [OKQ

Campbell, Rev. John, 1840–1904

THE HITTITES. Their Inscriptions and History. Toronto, Williamson, 1890. 2v [BM BVaU OTU

Campbell-McInnes, James, 1874–

THE MUSIC OF LANGUAGE. London, Harris, 1939. 92p [BVaU LC OTU

Canada. Royal Commission on National Development in the Arts, Letters and Sciences, 1949–1951

REPORT. Ottawa, King's Printer, 1951. xxi + 517p [Vincent Massey, Chairman.]

ROYAL COMMISSION STUDIES. A Selection of Essays. Ottawa, King's Printer, 1951. 430p

Canadian Broadcasting Corporation

CANADIAN LITERATURE TO-DAY. Series of broadcasts sponsored by CBC. Toronto, U. of Toronto Press, 1938. 70p [Contributors: E.K. Brown, P. Child, W.E. Collin, F.P. Grove, W. Kirkconnell, J.F. Macdonald, E. McInnis, A.L. Phelps, W. Tyrrell.] [BM BVaU LC OTU

Canadian Press Association

A HISTORY OF CANADIAN JOURNALISM IN THE SEVERAL PORTIONS OF THE DOMINION. With a Sketch of the Canadian Press Association 1859–1908. Ed. by a Committee of the Association. Toronto, Murray Print., 1908. 242p [The sequel, V. 2, was authored by William Arnot Craick, *q.v.*] [BVaU LC NBFU OTU

Cappon, James, 1854–1939

BLISS CARMAN AND THE LITERARY CURRENTS AND INFLUENCES OF HIS TIME. Toronto, Ryerson, 1930. 340p [BM BVaU LC NSHD OTU QMM

CHARLES G.D. ROBERTS. Toronto, Ryerson, [1925]. 148p [BM BVaU NSHD OTU

ROBERTS AND THE INFLUENCES OF HIS TIME. Toronto, Briggs, 1905. 88p [Studies in Canadian Poetry, No. 1.] [NSHD OTP QMM

VICTOR HUGO. Edinburgh, Blackwood, 1885. 394p [BM LC OLU

WHAT CLASSICAL EDUCATION MEANS. Kingston, Jackson, n.d. 13p [OTU

Carman, Bliss, 1861–1929

JAMES WHITCOMB RILEY. An Essay by Bliss Carman, and Some Letters to him from James Whitcomb Riley [August 30, 1898–October 12, 1915]. ... New York, priv. print. for George D. Smith, [1917]. [Reprinted: Metuchen, N.J., Heartman, 1925–1926. 86p] [BM BVaU LC NSHD OKQ

Carter, Alfred Edward, 1914–

THE IDEA OF DECADENCE IN FRENCH LITERATURE, 1830–1900. Toronto, U. of Toronto Press, 1958. ix + 154p

Chittick, Victor Lovitt Oakes, 1882–

THOMAS CHANDLER HALIBURTON ("Sam Slick"). A Study in Provincial Toryism. New York, Columbia U. Press, 1924. 695p [BM BVaU LC NSHD OTU

Clark, Alexander Frederick Bruce, 1884–

BOILEAU AND THE FRENCH CLASSICAL CRITICS IN ENGLAND (1660–1830). Paris, Champion, 1925. 534p [BM BVaU LC NSHD OTU

JEAN RACINE. Cambridge, Harvard U. Press, 1939. 354p [BM BVaU LC NSHD OTU

Clarke, George Herbert, 1873–1953

THE ESSAYS OR COUNSELS CIVIL AND MORAL OF FRANCIS BACON. Ed. with intro. and notes by ——. New York, Macmillan, 1905. 318p [BM LC

SELECTED POEMS OF PERCY BYSSHE SHELLEY. Ed. with intro. and notes by ——. Boston, Houghton, 1907. 266p [BM LC OTU

SOME REMINISCENCES AND EARLY LETTERS OF SIDNEY LANIER. Macon, Ga., Burke, 1907. 27p [BM LC NSWA

Coburn, Kathleen Hazel, 1905–

INQUIRING SPIRIT. A New Presentation of Coleridge from His Published and Unpublished Prose Writings. Ed. by ——. London, Routledge, 1951. 454p

NOTEBOOKS OF SAMUEL TAYLOR COLERIDGE. New York, Pantheon Books; London, Routledge–Paul, 1957–. Ed. by ——. [V. 1 in two parts, text and notes, 1794–1804, pub. in 1957; other volumes to follow.]

THE PHILOSOPHICAL LECTURES OF SAMUEL TAYLOR COLERIDGE, HITHERTO UN-PUBLISHED. Ed. by ——. London, Pilot Press, 1949. 480p [BM BVaU LC NBFU OTU

Cochrane, Charles Norris, 1889–1945

CHRISTIANITY AND CLASSICAL CULTURE. A Study of Thought and Action from Augustus to Augustine. Oxford, Clarendon Press, 1940. 523p [BM BVaU LC NSHD OTU

THUCYDIDES AND THE SCIENCE OF HISTORY. London, Oxford U. Press, 1929. 180p [BM BVaU LC NSHD OTU

Colgate, William G., 1882–

CANADIAN ART. Its Origin and Development. Toronto, Ryerson, 1943. 278p [BM BVaU NSHD OTU QMM

Collin, William Edwin, 1893—

CLOCKMAKER OF SOULS. A Study of Paul-Jean Toulet. New York, Kendall, 1933.
203p [BM LC OLU QMSS

THE WHITE SAVANNAHS. Toronto, Macmillan, 1936. 288p [On Canadian poets.]
[BM BVaU LC NSHD OKQ

Connor, Carl Yoder, 1890—

ARCHIBALD LAMPMAN, CANADIAN POET OF NATURE. New York & Montreal,
Carrier, 1929. 210p [BM BVaU LC NSWA OTU QMM

Corrigan, Beatrice Marion, 1903—

CURIOUS ANNALS. New Documents Relating to Browning's Roman Murder Story.
Translated, edited, and with an intro. by ——. Toronto, U. of Toronto Press,
1956. 142p

Coulter, John William, 1888—

RADIO DRAMA IS NOT THEATRE. By John Coulter and Ivor Lewis. Toronto,
Macmillan, 1937. 10p [OTP

Coventry, George, 1793—1870

A CRITICAL ENQUIRY REGARDING THE REAL AUTHOR OF THE LETTERS OF JUNIUS.
Proving them to have been Written by Lord Viscount Sackville. London, Phillips,
1825. 382p [BM BVaU LC OTU QMM

Cragg, Rev. Gerald Robertson, 1908—

FROM PURITANISM TO THE AGE OF REASON. A Study of Changes in Religious
Thought within the Church of England. 1660 to 1700. Cambridge, Eng.,
U. Press, 1950. 247p [OONL

PURITANISM IN THE PERIOD OF THE GREAT PERSECUTION, 1660—1688.
Cambridge, Eng., University Press, 1957. ix + 325p

Craick, William Arnot, 1880—1969

A HISTORY OF CANADIAN JOURNALISM. V. 2: Last Years of the Canadian Press
Association, with a Continuing Record of the Canadian Daily Newspaper Pub-
lishers Association, 1919—1959. Toronto, Ont. Pub. Co., [1959]. 311p [Sequel
to A HISTORY OF CANADIAN JOURNALISM IN THE SEVERAL PORTIONS OF THE
DOMINION, WITH A SKETCH OF THE CANADIAN PRESS ASSOCIATION, 1859—1908.
By the Canadian Press Association. Toronto, Murray Print., 1908. 242p]

Crawford, Alexander Wellington, 1866—1933

THE GENIUS OF KEATS. An Interpretation. London, Stockwell, 1932. 202p [BM
LC OTU

HAMLET, AN IDEAL PRINCE, AND OTHER ESSAYS IN SHAKESPEARIAN INTERPRE-
TATION. ... Boston, Badger, 1916. 317p [BM BVaU LC OTU

THE PHILOSOPHY OF F.H. JACOBI. ... New York, Macmillan, 1905. 90p [BM LC
OTU

Creighton, Helen, 1899–
FOLKLORE OF LUNENBURG COUNTY, NOVA SCOTIA. Ottawa, King's Printer, 1950.
163p [BM BVaU LC NSHD OTP

Cridge, Edward, 1817–1913
AS IT WAS IN THE BEGINNING; or, The Historic Principle Applied to the Mosaic
Scriptures. Chicago, Revell, 1900. 121p [BVaU LC

Dalton, Annie Charlotte (Armitage), 1865–1938
THE FUTURE OF OUR POETRY. Vancouver, priv. print., 1931. 16p [BVaU

Daniells, Roy, 1902–
THOMAS TRAHERNE, A SERIOUS AND PATHETIC CONTEMPLATION OF MERCIES OF
GOD, IN SEVERAL MOST DEVOUT AND SUBLIME THANKSGIVINGS FOR THE SAME.
Ed. by ——. Toronto, U. of Toronto Press, 1941. 127p [BM BVaU OTU

Davies, Blodwen, 1897–1966
PLANETARY DEMOCRACY. An Introduction to Scientific Humanism and Applied
Semantics. By Oliver L. Reiser and Blodwen Davies. New York, Creative Age,
1944. 242p [OTU QMM

Davies, Robertson, 1913–
SHAKESPEARE'S BOY ACTORS. London, Dent, 1939. 208p [Also: New York,
Russell, 1964.] [BM BVaU OTU

Davies, Trevor Hughes, 1871–
SPIRITUAL VOICES IN MODERN LITERATURE. Toronto, Ryerson, 1919. 312p
[BM BVaU LC OTU QMM
TO LIVE IN CHRIST. London, Oxford U. Press, 1938. 250p [Lectures on
Augustine, Dante, Kingsley, Osler, etc.] [LC OTU

Davis, Herbert John, 1893–
NINETEENTH CENTURY STUDIES. Collected and ed. by ——. Ithaca, Cornell U.
Press, 1940. 303p [BM BVaU LC OTU
THE PROSE WORKS OF JONATHAN SWIFT. Ed. by ——. Oxford, Shakespeare Head
Press, 1939–62. 14v [BM BVaU LC OTU
THE SATIRE OF JONATHAN SWIFT. New York, Macmillan, 1947. 109p [BM
BVaU LC NSHD OTU QMM
STELLA. A Gentlewoman of the Eighteenth Century. New York, Macmillan, 1942.
103p [BM BVaU LC NSHD OTU QMM

Dawson, Robert MacGregor, 1927–
PLACE NAMES IN NOVA SCOTIA. A Paper Read before the Linguistic Circle of
Manitoba and North Dakota on May 16th, 1959. Winnipeg, Ukrainian Free
Academy of Science, 1960. 16p

Dawson, Samuel Edward, 1833–1916

THE PROSE WRITERS OF CANADA. An Address Delivered before the Teachers of the City and District of Montreal, Renouf, 1901. 39p [BVaU LC NSHD OTU QMM

A STUDY WITH CRITICAL AND EXPLANATORY NOTES OF ALFRED TENNYSON'S POEM "THE PRINCESS." Montreal, Dawson, 1882. 120p [BM BVaU LC NSHD OTU

Deacon, William Arthur, 1890–

THE FOUR JAMESES. Ottawa, Graphic, 1927. 224p [Rev. ed., Toronto, Ryerson, 1953. 210p] [BVaU NSHD OTU QMM

De Mille, Alban Bertram, 1873–

AMERICAN POETRY. Edited with Intro., Notes, Questions, and Biographical Sketches. Boston, Allyn & Bacon, 1923. 339p [BVa

LITERATURE IN THE CENTURY. (The Nineteenth Century Series. V. 2.) Philadelphia, Bradley Garretson, 1903. 548p [Earlier ed.: London, Linscott, 1900.] [BM BVaU LC NSHD OTP

De Mille, James, 1833–1880

THE ELEMENTS OF RHETORIC. New York, Harper, 1878. 564p [BVaU LC NSHD OTU QMM

de Pauley, Rev. William Cecil, 1893–

THE CANDLE OF THE LORD. Studies in the Cambridge Platonists. New York, Macmillan, 1937. 248p [BM BVaU LC OTU

Devine, Patrick Kevin, 1859–1950

DEVINE'S FOLK LORE OF NEWFOUNDLAND IN OLD WORDS, PHRASES AND EX-PRESSIONS, THEIR ORIGIN AND MEANING. St. John's, Robinson, 1937. 80p [NSHD OTU

DeWitt, Norman Wentworth, 1876–1958

THE DIDO EPISODE IN THE AENEID OF VIRGIL. ... Toronto, Briggs, 1907. 78p [LC OTU QMM

EPICURUS AND HIS PHILOSOPHY. Minneapolis, U. of Minnesota Press, 1954. 388p

ST. PAUL AND EPICURUS. Toronto, Ryerson, 1954. 201p

VIRGIL'S BIOGRAPHIA LITTERARIA. Toronto, Victoria College Press, 1923. 192p [BM BVaU LC NSHD OTU

Doughty, Arthur George, 1860–1936

THE CANADIAN ARCHIVES AND ITS ACTIVITIES. Ottawa, Acland, 1924. 88p [BM BVaU LC NSWA OTU QMM

Dray, William Herbert, 1921–

LAWS AND EXPLANATION IN HISTORY. London, Oxford U. Press, 1957. 174p

Dudek, Louis, 1918–
LITERATURE AND THE PRESS. A History of Printing, Printed Media, and their Relation to Literature. Toronto, Ryerson, 1960. 238p

Duncan, Alastair Robert Campbell, 1915–
PRACTICAL REASON AND MORALITY. A Study of Immanuel Kant's Foundations for the Metaphysics of Morals. London, Nelson, 1957. xviii + 182p

Duvar, John Hunter–, 1830–1899
THE STONE, BRONZE AND IRON AGES. A Popular Treatise on Early Archaeology. London, Swan Sonnenschein, 1892. 285p [BM LC

Edgar, Oscar Pelham, 1871–1948
ACROSS MY PATH. Ed. by Northrop Frye. Toronto, Ryerson, 1952. 167p
THE ART OF THE NOVEL FROM 1700 TO THE PRESENT TIME. New York, Macmillan, 1933. 493p [BM BVaU LC NSHD OTU
COLERIDGE AND WORDSWORTH. Select Poems. With intro. and notes. Ed. by ——. Toronto, Morang, 1902. 244p [BM OTUV
HENRY JAMES, MAN AND AUTHOR. Boston, Houghton, 1927. 351p [Earlier ed.: London, Richards, 1925.] [BM BVaU LC NSHD OTU
A STUDY OF SHELLEY, WITH SPECIAL REFERENCE TO HIS NATURE POETRY. Toronto, Briggs, 1899. 155p [BM LC NBFU

Eggleston, Wilfrid, 1901–
THE FRONTIER & CANADIAN LETTERS. Toronto, Ryerson, 1957. ix + 164p

Engel, Srul Morris von, 1931–
THE PROBLEM OF TRAGEDY. Fredericton, Brunswick Press, 1960. 81p

Fairley, Barker, 1887–
CHARLES M. DOUGHTY. A Critical Study. London. Cape, 1927. 256p [BM BVaU LC NSHD OTU QMM
GOETHE AS REVEALED IN HIS POETRY. London, Dent, 1932. 210p [BM BVaU LC NSHD OTU QMM
GOETHE'S "FAUST." Six Essays. Oxford, Clarendon, 1953. 132p
HEINRICH HEINE, AN INTERPRETATION. Oxford, Clarendon, 1954. 176p
SELECTED POEMS OF JOHANN WOLFGANG VON GOETHE. Ed. by ——. New York, Rinehart, 1955. xxvii + 221p [First pub. London, Heinemann, 1954.]
A STUDY OF GOETHE. Oxford, Clarendon, 1947. 280p [BM BVaU LC NSHD OTU QMM

Fairweather, Rev. Eugene Rathbone, 1920–
A SCHOLASTIC MISCELLANY. Anselm to Ockham. Ed. by ——. London, SCM Press, 1956. 457p

Ferguson, Rev. George Dalrymple, 1829–1926

LECTURES ON THE HISTORY OF THE MIDDLE AGES. Kingston, Uglow, 1904. 634p
[BM LC OTU QMM

Fitzgerald, Rev. D.

A LECTURE ON THE REFORMATION. Charlottetown, Haszard, 1859. 94p [NSHP

Flenley, Ralph, 1886–1969

A HISTORY OF MONTREAL, 1640–1672. From the French of François Dollier de
Casson. Trans. and ed. with a life of the author. London, Dent, 1928. 384p [BM
BVaU OTU

Ford, George Harry, 1914–

KEATS AND THE VICTORIANS. A Study of his Influence and Rise to Fame, 1821–
1895. New Haven, Yale U. Press, 1944. 200p [BM BVaU LC NBFU OTU
QMM

Fox, William Sherwood, 1878–1967

GREEK AND ROMAN MYTHOLOGY. Boston, Marshall Jones, 1916. lxii + 354p
[Later ed., 1928. 402p] [BM BVa LC NSHD OLU QMM
GREEK INSCRIPTIONS IN THE ROYAL ONTARIO MUSEUM. London, Ont., 1917.
14p [OTU

French, Donald Graham, 1873–1945

THE APPEAL OF POETRY. Toronto, McClelland, 1923. 137p [BM BVaU NSHD
OKQ
THE CANADIAN WRITERS' NOTE BOOK. Toronto, Writers' Studio, 1932. 73p [OTU
POINTS ABOUT POETRY. Ridgewood, N.J., Editor Co., 1910. 85p [BVaU LC OTP

Freshman, Rev. Charles, 1819–1875

THE JEWS AND THE ISRAELITES. Their Religion, Philosophy, Traditions and
Literature. Toronto, Dredge, 1870. 456p [NSHD OTU QMM

Freund, Philip, 1909–

HOW TO BECOME A LITERARY CRITIC. New York, Beechhurst, 1947. 200p
[BVaU LC QMM

Frye, Northrop, 1912–

ANATOMY OF CRITICISM. Four Essays. Princeton, N.J., Princeton U. Press, 1957.
x + 383p
FEARFUL SYMMETRY. A Study of William Blake. Princeton, N.J., Princeton U.
Press, 1947. 462p [BM BVaU LC NSHD OTU QMM
SOUND AND POETRY. Ed. with an intro. by ——. New York, Columbia U. Press,
1957. xxvii + 156p

Geikie, John Cunningham, 1824–1906

RALPH WALDO EMERSON: HIS WRITINGS AND OPINIONS. A Lecture. Toronto,
Geikie, 1859. 28p [NSWA OTP

George, Rev. James, 1801?–1870
A BRIEF INQUIRY INTO THE CAUSES OF THE POETIC ELEMENT IN THE SCOTTISH
MIND. A Lecture. ... Kingston, Creighton, 1857. 60p [NSWA OLU

Gibbon, John Murray, 1875–1952
THE MAGIC OF MELODY. London, Dent, [1933]. 128p [BVaU OKQ QMM
MELODY AND THE LYRIC, FROM CHAUCER TO THE CAVALIERS. London, Dent,
[1930]. 204p [BVaU NBFU OTU QMM

Glazebrook, George Parkin de Twenebrokes, 1900–
THE HARGRAVE CORRESPONDENCE, 1821–1843. Ed. by ——. Toronto,
Champlain Society, 1938. 472p [BM BVaU LC NSHD OTU

Gordon, Robert Kay, 1887–
ANGLO-SAXON POETRY. Selected and trans. by ——. London, Dent, 1927.
367p [BM BVaU LC NBFU OTU
THE STORY OF TROILUS. As Told by Benoit de Saint-Maure, Giovanni Boccaccio
(translated into English prose), Geoffrey Chaucer, and Robert Henryson. Trans.
and intro. by ——. London, Dent, 1934. 388p [BM BVaU LC NBFU OTU
QMM

Goudge, Thomas Anderson, 1910–
THE THOUGHTS OF C.S. PEIRCE. Toronto, U. of Toronto Press, 1950. 360p [BM
BVaU LC NBFU OTU

Graff, Willem Laurens, 1890–
LANGUAGE AND LANGUAGES. An Introduction to Linguistics. New York,
Appleton, 1932. 487p [BM BVaU OTU
RAINER MARIA RILKE. Creative Anguish of a Modern Poet. Princeton, N.J.,
Princeton U. Press, 1956. x + 353p

Grafstein, Melech W.
ISAAC LEIBUSH PERETZ. Published in Commemoration of his 100th Birthday.
Ed. by ——. London, Ont., Jewish Observer, [1951?] 55 + 57p

Graham, Franklin Thomas, 1869–
HISTRIONIC MONTREAL. Annals of the Montreal Stage, with Biographical and
Critical Notices of the Plays and Players of a Century. 2nd ed. Montreal,
Lovell, 1902. 303p [BVaU OTU

Graham, William Creighton, 1887–1955
THE PROPHETS AND ISRAEL'S CULTURE. Chicago, U. of Chicago Press, 1934. 117p
[BM BVaU LC NBFU OTU

Grant, Douglas, 1921–1969
JAMES THOMSON, POET OF "THE SEASONS." London, Cresset, 1951. 308p

Grant, George Parkin, 1918–
PHILOSOPHY IN THE MASS AGE. Toronto, Copp Clark, 1959. ix + 117p

Grant, Rev. Robert, 1824?–1900
ROBERT BURNS: VINDICATED. Halifax, Nova Scotia Print., 1883. 15p [NSWA

Grant, William Lawson, 1872–1935
A PURITAN AT THE COURT OF LOUIS XIV. Kingston, Jackson, 1913. 17p [BVaU
   LC NBFU OTUV QMM

Greene, Donald Johnson, 1916–
THE POLITICS OF SAMUEL JOHNSON. New Haven, Yale U. Press, 1960. xix + 354p

Greenshields, Edward Black, 1850–
LANDSCAPE PAINTING AND MODERN DUTCH ARTISTS. Toronto, Copp Clark, 1906.
   229p [BVaU LC NSHD OTU QMM
SUBJECTIVE VIEW OF LANDSCAPE PAINTING. With Special Reference to J.H.
   Weissenbruch and Illustrations from Works of His in Canada. Montreal, Desbarats,
   1904. 58p [QMM

Griffin, Arthur Kent, 1893–
ARISTOTLE'S PSYCHOLOGY OF CONDUCT. London, Williams & Norgate, 1932.
   186p [Ph.D. Thesis, U. of Toronto.] [BVaU LC NSHD OTU

Griffin, Frederick, 1798–1879
JUNIUS DISCOVERED. Boston, Little Brown, 1854. 310p [An attempt to identify
   Junius with Thomas Pownall, 1722–1805.] [BM LC NSHD OLU QMM

Groom, Bernard, 1892–
THE DICTION OF POETRY FROM SPENSER TO BRIDGES. Toronto, U. of Toronto
   Press, in association with McMaster University, 1955. 284p

Grube, Georges Maximilien Antoine, 1899–
THE DRAMA OF EURIPIDES. London, Methuen, [1941]. 456p [BM BVaU LC
   NSHD OTU QMM
PLATO'S THOUGHT. London, Methuen, 1935. 320p [Reprinted, 1958.] [BM
   BVaU LC NSHD OTU QMM

Guillet, Edwin Clarence, 1898–
EARLY CANADIAN LITERATURE. Literary Pioneers of the Old Newcastle District.
   Toronto, 1942. 2v [Letters re Stricklands, Traills, Moodies, etc.] [OTP

Guthrie, Norman Gregor, 1877–1929
THE POETRY OF ARCHIBALD LAMPMAN. Toronto, Musson, 1927. 58p [BVaU
   MWU NBFU OTP

Hall, Fernau
AN ANATOMY OF BALLET. London, Melrose, 1953. 470p

Hamilton, Robert Morris, 1912–
CANADIAN QUOTATIONS AND PHRASES, LITERARY AND HISTORICAL. Comp.
by ——. Toronto, McClelland, 1952. 272p

Hammond, Melvin Ormond, 1876–1934
PAINTING AND SCULPTURE IN CANADA. Toronto, Ryerson, 1930. 72p [BVaU
LC NSHD OTU QMM

Harper, John Murdoch, 1845–1919
THE ORIGIN AND DEVELOPMENT OF THE GREEK DRAMA. Quebec, "Morning
Chronicle," 1883. 35p [OTU

Harris, John
A REVIEW OF MACAULAY'S TEACHING ON THE RELATIONSHIP OF THEOLOGY TO
THE SCIENCE OF GOVERNMENT. ... By Kuklos (J.H.) [pseud] . Montreal, 1874.
2v [BM OLU QMM

Harris, Rev. William Richard, 1847–1923
THE CATHOLIC ATMOSPHERE OF SHAKESPEARE'S DRAMAS. Toronto, "The Rainbow" (Loretto Abbey), [1917?]. 13p [OTU

Hartley, Rev. H.A.S.
CLASSICAL TRANSLATIONS. ... Saint John, McMillan, 1889. 134p [NSHD

Harvey, Rev. Moses, 1820–1901
LECTURES, LITERARY AND BIOGRAPHICAL. Edinburgh, Elliot, 1864. 512p [LC
NSHD
THOUGHTS ON THE POETRY AND LITERATURE OF THE BIBLE. St. John's,
McConnan, 1853. 28p [NSWA

Hemlow, Joyce, 1906–
THE HISTORY OF FANNY BURNEY. Oxford, Clarendon, 1958. xvi + 528p

Hendel, Charles William, 1890–
JEAN-JACQUES ROUSSEAU, MORALIST. London, Oxford U. Press, 1934. 2v [BM
BVaU LC NSHD OTU QMM
STUDIES IN THE PHILOSOPHY OF DAVID HUME. Princeton, Princeton U. Press,
1925. 420p [BM BVaU LC NBFU OTU QMM

Heuser, Alan, 1926–
THE SHAPING VISION OF GERARD MANLEY HOPKINS. London, Toronto, Oxford
U. Press, 1958. 128p

Hines, Rev. Bede, 1918–
THE SOCIAL WORLD OF ALDOUS HUXLEY. Montreal, Author, 1954. 104p

Hirschfelder, Jacob Maier, 1819–1902
AN ESSAY ON THE SPIRIT AND CHARACTERISTICS OF HEBREW POETRY. [Toronto?
1855?] 37p [OTP

Hoare, John Edward, 1886–

THE PSYCHOLOGY OF PLAYWRITING. New York, Dramatists Play Service, 1949. 211p [BM BVaU

Hopkins, John Castell, 1864–1923

LIFE AND WORK OF MR. GLADSTONE. Toronto, Bradley-Garretson, 1895. 498p [BVaU NBFU OTP QMU

Housser, Frederick Broughton, 1889–1936

A CANADIAN ART MOVEMENT. The Story of the Group of Seven. Toronto, Macmillan, 1926. 221p [BM BVaU NSHD OTU QMM

Howay, Frederick William, 1867–1943

PRESIDENTIAL ADDRESS: THE EARLY LITERATURE OF THE NORTHWEST COAST. Ottawa, Royal Society, 1924. 31p [BVaU OTP

Howse, Rev. Ernest Marshall, 1902–

SPIRITUAL VALUES IN SHAKESPEARE. New York, Abingdon Press, 1955. 158p

Hubbard, Robert Hamilton, 1916–

AN ANTHOLOGY OF CANADIAN ART. Ed. by ——. Toronto, Oxford U. Press, 1960. 187p

EUROPEAN PAINTINGS IN CANADIAN COLLECTIONS. Earlier Schools, edited with an Essay on Picture Collecting in Canada. Toronto, Oxford U. Press, 1956. xxv + 154p

Hughes, James Laughlin, 1846–1935

DICKENS AS AN EDUCATOR. New York, Appleton, 1901. 319p [BM BVaU LC NBFU OTP QMM

Hurst, George Leopold, 1868–

THE LITERARY BACKGROUND OF THE NEW TESTAMENT. New York, Macmillan, 1928. 163p [BM BVa OTU

AN OUTLINE OF THE HISTORY OF CHRISTIAN LITERATURE. New York, Macmillan, 1926. 547p [BM OTP QMM

SACRED LITERATURE. London, Dent, 1905. 152p [BM NSHD

Hutchinson, Rev. Daniel Falloon

A CLASS BOOK ON RHETORIC, WHEREIN ARE EXHIBITED THE GRACES AND STYLE OF ENGLISH COMPOSITION AND PUBLIC ORATORY. Belleville, Bowell & Moore, 1850. 103p [BM LC NSHD OTP

Hutton, Maurice, 1856–1940

THE GREEK POINT OF VIEW. London, Hodder, 1925. 207p [BM BVaU LC NSHD OKQ QMM

Irving, John Allan, 1903–

PHILOSOPHY IN CANADA. A Symposium. Ed. by ——. Toronto, U. of Toronto
Press, 1952. 48p

SCIENCE AND VALUES. Explorations in Philosophy and the Social Sciences.
Toronto, Ryerson, 1952. xi + 148p

Irving, William Henry, 1891–

THE PROVIDENCE OF WIT IN THE ENGLISH LETTER WRITERS. Durham, N.C., Duke
U. Press, 1955. 382p

James, Charles Canniff, 1863–1916

A TENNYSON PILGRIMAGE, and TENNYSON THE IMPERIALIST. Toronto, 1910. 22p
[LC OTP

Jefferys, Charles William, 1869–1951

SAM SLICK IN PICTURES. The Best of the Humour of Thomas Chandler Haliburton.
Ed. by Lorne Pierce. Toronto, Ryerson, 1956. xx + 204p

Jetter, Marianne Rose (Weiss), 1911–

THE "ISLAND MOTIF" IN PROSE WORKS OF ERNST WIECHERT. Vancouver,
Continental Book Centre, 1957. 96p

Johnson, Allison Heartz, 1910–

WHITEHEAD'S PHILOSOPHY OF CIVILIZATION. Boston, Beacon Press, 1958.
xi + 211p

WHITEHEAD'S THEORY OF REALITY. Boston, Beacon Press, 1952. xiii + 262p

THE WIT AND WISDOM OF ALBERT WHITEHEAD. Ed. by ——. Boston, Beacon
Press, 1947. 102p [LC NBFU

THE WIT AND WISDOM OF JOHN DEWEY. Ed. by ——. Boston, Beacon Press, 1949.
111p [LC OTU

Johnstone, John Keith, 1923–

THE BLOOMSBURY GROUP. A Study of E.M. Forster, Lytton Strachey, Virginia
Woolf, and their Circle. London, Secker & Warburg, 1954. x + 383p

Jordan, Rev. William George, 1852–1939

VOLTAIRE, THE CRUSADER. Toronto, Ryerson, 1930. 64p [OTU

Kennedy, Roderick Stuart, 1889–1953

BIBLIOGRAPHY OF G.A. HENTY & HENTYANA. By R.S. Kennedy & B.J. Farmer.
London, B.J. Farmer, 1956. 93p [mimeographed]

Kenner, William Hugh, 1923—
DUBLIN'S JOYCE. London, Chatto & Windus, 1955. xi + 372p
GNOMON. Essays on Contemporary Literature. New York, McDowell Obolensky, 1958. 300p
WYNDHAM LEWIS. London, Methuen, 1954. xv + 169p

King, Rev. John Mark, 1829—1899
A CRITICAL STUDY OF "IN MEMORIAM." Toronto, Morang, 1898. 253p [BVaU OTP

King, Thomas Davies, 1819—1884
BACON VERSUS SHAKESPEARE. A Plea for the Defendant. Montreal, Lovell, 1875. 187p [BVaU OTP
LECTURE OF "SHAKESPEARE AND HIS MORAL INFLUENCES." Montreal, Salter, 1859. [OOC
SHALL WE OPEN SHAKESPEARE'S GRAVE? NO. A Reply ... to ... J. Parker Norris. ... Montreal, Robinson, 1884. 30p [BM BVaU OTP

King, William Lyon Mackenzie, 1874—1950
INDUSTRY AND HUMANITY. A Study in the Principles underlying Industrial Reconstruction. Toronto, Allen, 1918. 567p [BM BVaU NSHD OTP QMBM

Kirkconnell, Watson, 1895—
THE CELESTIAL CYCLE. The Theme of Paradise Lost in World Literature, with Translations of the Major Analogues. Toronto, U. of Toronto Press, 1952. 701p
THE EUROPEAN HERITAGE. A Synopsis of European Cultural Achievement. Toronto, Dent, 1930. 184p [BM BVaU LC NSHD OTP
THE HUMANITIES IN CANADA. By Watson Kirkconnell and A.S.P. Woodhouse. Ottawa, Humanities Research Council, 1947. 287p [BM BVaU LC NSHD OKQ QMM

Kirkwood, Kenneth Porter, 1899—
ARNOLD J. TOYNBEE, PHILOSOPHER OF HISTORY. An Address Given at the British Council, Karachi, March 29, 1953. Karachi, priv. print., 1953. 30p
DID SHAKESPEARE VISIT DENMARK? Karachi, Process Pakistan, 1953. 74p
A GARDEN IN POLAND. [On Chopin] Karachi, priv. print., 1953. 34p
THE IMMORTAL MEMORY OF ROBERT BURNS. Ottawa, priv. print., 1958. 7 + 68p
MAUD. An Essay on Tennyson's Poem. Ottawa, Le Droit, 1951. 216p
OPHELIA OF ELSINORE. Ottawa, priv. print., 1958. 162p
RENAISSANCE IN JAPAN. A Cultural Survey of the Seventeenth Century. Tokyo, Meiji Press, 1938. 414p [BM BVaU OTU QMM
UNFAMILIAR LAFCADIO HEARN. Tokyo, Hokuseido Press, 1936, 97p [LC QMM

Kirkwood, Mossie May (Waddington), 1890—
THE DEVELOPMENT OF BRITISH THOUGHT FROM 1820 TO 1890. With Special Reference to German Influences. By Mossie May Waddington. Toronto, Dent, 1919. 194p [BM BVaU LC OTP

Klinck, Carl Frederick, 1908–

EDWIN J. PRATT, THE MAN AND HIS POETRY. By Henry W. Wells and Carl F. Klinck. Toronto, Ryerson, 1947. 197p [BVaU LC NBFU OTU QMM

WILFRED CAMPBELL. A Study in Late Provincial Victorianism. Toronto, Ryerson, 1942. 289p [BM BVaU LC MWU NSHD OTU QMM

Lacey, Alexander, 1887–

PIXERECOURT AND THE FRENCH ROMANTIC DRAMA. Toronto, U. of Toronto Press, 1928. 88p [BM BVaU LC OTP

Lambert, Richard Stanton, 1894–

THE ADVENTURE OF CANADIAN PAINTING. Toronto, McClelland, 1947. 226p [BVaU NBFU OTU QMM

THE FORTUNATE TRAVELLER. A Short History of Touring and Travel for Pleasure. London, Melrose, 1950. 242p [OONL

PICTURES FOR LASTING PLEASURE, BY SIX CANADIAN ARTISTS. Toronto, Laing Galleries, 1943. 23p [BVa

Lande, Lawrence Montague, 1906–

OLD LAMPS AGLOW. An Appreciation of Early Canadian Poetry. Montreal, Author, 1957. xiv + 329p

Lapp, John Clarke, 1917–

ASPECTS OF RACINIAN TRAGEDY. Toronto, U. of Toronto Press, 1955. x + 195p

Lathern, Rev. John, 1831–1905

INSTITUTE LECTURES: Cromwell, Cobden, Havelock and the English Reformers. Saint John, McMillan, 1871. 106p [NBFU OOP

Lauriston, Victor, 1881–

ARTHUR STRINGER, SON OF THE NORTH. Biography and Anthology. Toronto, Ryerson, 1941. 178p [BM BVaU LC NSHD OTU QMM

Lavell, Cecil Fairfield, 1872–1948

A BIOGRAPHY OF THE GREEK PEOPLE. Boston, Houghton, 1934. 297p [BM BVa LC NSHD OTU QMM

THE EVOLUTION OF GREEK MORAL EDUCATION. ... Kingston, Jackson Press, 1911. 97p [LC

Lawrence, Margaret Isabel

THE SCHOOL OF FEMININITY. A Book for and about Women as they are Interpreted through Feminine Writers of Yesterday and Today. Toronto, Nelson, 1936. 382p [Pub. in England as: WE WRITE AS WOMEN. London, Joseph, 1937. 314p] [BM BVa OLU QMM

Leacock, Stephen Butler, 1869–1944

CHARLES DICKENS, HIS LIFE AND WORK. London, Davies, 1933. 275p [BM BVaU LC NSHD OTU

ELEMENTS OF POLITICAL SCIENCE. ... Boston, Houghton, 1906. 417p [Several
later eds.] [BM BVaU NSHD OTU

THE GREATEST PAGES OF AMERICAN HUMOR. Selected and discussed by ——.
Garden City, Doubleday, 1916. 293p [BM BVaU LC OTU QMM

THE GREATEST PAGES OF CHARLES DICKENS. A Biographical Reader and a
Chronological Selection from the Works of Dickens. With a Commentary on
his Life and Art. Garden City, Doubleday, 1934. 233p [QMM

HUMOUR AND HUMANITY. An Introduction to the Study of Humour. London,
Butterworth, 1937. 254p [BM BVaU LC NBFU OTU QMM

HUMOR, ITS THEORY AND TECHNIQUE. With Examples and Samples: A Book of
Discovery. Toronto, Dodd Mead, 1935. 268p [BM BVaU OTU QMM

LAHONTAN'S VOYAGES. Ed. with intro. and notes by ——. Ottawa, Graphic,
1932. 348p [BM BVaU NBFU QMM

MARK TWAIN. London, Davies, 1932. 167p [BM BVaU LC OTU QMM

LeRossignol, James Edward, 1866–

THE ETHICAL PHILOSOPHY OF SAMUEL CLARKE. Leipzig, 1892. 98p [Dissertation
for Ph.D. degree at Leipzig.] [OLU QMM

Leroy, Albert

THE FORMS OF VALUE. The Extension of Hedonistic Axiology. Toronto, Oxford
U. Press, 1950. 352p

Lewis, Jay, 1881–1947

OTHER MEN'S MINDS. The Critical Writings of Jay Lewis. New York, Putnam,
1948. 172p [LC

Lighthall, William Douw, 1857–1954

THE COSMIC ASPECT OF THE OUTER CONSCIOUSNESS. Montreal, Author, 1924.
16p [BVaU OKQ QMM

THE PERSON OF EVOLUTION; THE OUTER CONSCIOUSNESS; THE OUTER KNOW-
LEDGE; THE DIRECTIVE POWER. Studies of Instinct as Contributions to a
Philosophy of Evolution. Montreal, Kennedy, 1930. 216p [Enlarged ed.:
Toronto, Macmillan, 1933. 246p] [BM BVaU NSWA OTP QMM

A PHILOSOPHY OF PURPOSE. Montreal, Author, 1920. 15p [OTU

SKETCH OF NEW UTILITARIANISM, INCLUDING A CRITICISM OF THE ORDINARY
ARGUMENT FROM DESIGN AND OTHER MATTER. Montreal, Witness, 1887.
40p [BM QMM

SPIRITUALIZED HAPPINESS-THEORY; OR, NEW UTILITARIANISM. A Lecture before
the Farmington School of Philosophy. Montreal, Witness, 1890. 22p [BM
NSWA OTU

SUPERPERSONALISM. The Outer Consciousness, a Biological Entity. ... Montreal,
Witness, 1926. 115p [BM BVaU NSHD OKQ QMM

THE TELEOLOGY OF THE OUTER CONSCIOUSNESS. Montreal, Author, 1924.
13p [BVaU OTU

Lodge, Rupert Clendon, 1886–

THE GREAT THINKERS. London, Routledge, 1949. 310p [BM LC NSHD OTU QMM

AN INTRODUCTION TO MODERN LOGIC. Minneapolis, Perine Book Co., 1920. 361p [BM BVaU LC QMM

THE MEANING AND FUNCTION OF SIMPLE MODES IN THE PHILOSOPHY OF JOHN LOCKE. Minneapolis, U. of Minnesota, 1918. 86p [BM BVaU LC NSHD OTU QMM

PHILOSOPHY OF EDUCATION. London, Harper, 1937. 328p [BM BVaU LC NBFU OOSU QMM

THE PHILOSOPHY OF PLATO. London, Routledge-Paul, 1956. ix + 347p

PLATO'S THEORY OF ART. London, Routledge-Paul, 1953. 316p

PLATO'S THEORY OF EDUCATION. ... London, Kegan Paul, 1947. 322p [BM BVaU LC NSHD OTP QMM

PLATO'S THEORY OF ETHICS. The Moral Criterion, and the Highest Good. London, Kegan Paul, 1928. 558p [BM BVaU LC NBFU OLU QMM

THE QUESTIONING MIND. A Survey of Philosophical Tendencies. London, Dent, 1937. 311p [BM LC OTP

Logan, John Daniel, 1869–1929

AESTHETIC CRITICISM IN CANADA. Its Aims, Methods and Status. ... Toronto, McClelland, 1917. 29p [BM NBFU OTP

DALHOUSIE UNIVERSITY AND CANADIAN LITERATURE. Being the History of an Attempt to have Canadian Literature included in the Curriculum of Dalhousie University. With a Criticism and a Justification. Halifax, Author, 1922. 24p [BVaU NBFU OTP

HIGHWAYS OF CANADIAN LITERATURE. A Synoptic Introduction to the Literary History of Canada (English) from 1760 to 1924. By J.D. Logan and Donald G. French. Toronto, McClelland, 1924. 418p [BM BVaU LC NBFU OTP

A LITERARY CHAMELEON. A New Estimate of Mr. H.L. Mencken. Milwaukee, Author, 1926. 26p [LC NBFU OTP

MARJORIE PICKTHALL. Her Poetic Genius and Art. Halifax, Allen, 1922. 44p [BM BVaU NSHD OTP

THE RELIGIOUS FUNCTIONS OF COMEDY. 1907. [NBFU

SCOTT AND HALIBURTON. An Essay in the Psychology of Creative Satiric Humor. Halifax, Allen, 1921. 22p [BM BVaU NBFU OTP

Lomer, Gerhard Richard, 1882–1970

STEPHEN LEACOCK. A Check-List and Index of his Writings. Ottawa, National Library, 1954. 153p

Long, Marcus, –1968

THE SPIRIT OF PHILOSOPHY. Toronto, U. of Toronto Press, 1953. 306p

Luckyj, George Stephen Nestor, 1919–

LITERARY POLITICS IN THE SOVIET UKRAINE, 1917–1934. New York, Columbia U. Press, 1956. x + 323p

McAleer, George, 1845—
A STUDY IN THE ETYMOLOGY OF THE INDIAN PLACE NAME MISSISQUOI.
Worcester, Blanchard Press, 1906. 104p [BM BVaU OLU

McArthur, Peter, 1866—1924
STEPHEN LEACOCK. Toronto, Ryerson, 1923. 176p [BM LC NSHD OTU

MacCallum, Reid, 1897—1949
IMITATION & DESIGN AND OTHER ESSAYS. Ed. by William Blissett. Toronto, U. of
Toronto Press, 1953. xvii + 209p
TIME LOST AND REGAINED. The Theme of Eliot's Four Quartets. Toronto, priv.
print., [1949?]. 26p [BVaU OTP

McCaul, Rev. John, 1807—1887
BRITANNO-ROMAN INSCRIPTIONS, WITH CRITICAL NOTES. Toronto, Rowsell, 1863.
290p [OTU
CHRISTIAN EPITAPHS OF THE FIRST SIX CENTURIES. Toronto, Chewett, 1869. 72p
[OTP
THE METERS OF THE GREEK TRAGEDIES EXPLAINED AND ILLUSTRATED. Dublin,
Milliken, 1828. 115p [OTP

McCourt, Edward Alexander, 1907—1972
THE CANADIAN WEST IN FICTION. Toronto, Ryerson, 1949. 131p [BVaU NBFU
OTU QMBM

Macdonald, Daniel Joseph, 1881—
THE RADICALISM OF SHELLEY AND ITS SOURCES. Washington, Catholic Education
Press, 1912. 143p [BM BVaU LC NSHD OTU

Macdonald, John Ford, 1878—
WILLIAM HENRY DRUMMOND. Toronto, Ryerson, [1923?]. 132p [BM BVaU LC
NSHD OTU QMBM

MacDonald, John Harry
MARJORIE PICKTHALL. Sunny Brae, N.S., 1927. 109p [An M.A. thesis.] [NSHD

Macdonald, Thoreau, 1901—
THE GROUP OF SEVEN. Toronto, Ryerson, 1944. 34p [3rd ed., 1952.] [BVaU
LC NSHD OTP QMM

MacDonald, Wilbert Lorne, 1879—
BEGINNINGS OF THE ENGLISH ESSAY. Toronto, U. of Toronto Library, 1914. 122p
[BM BVaU LC OTP QMM
POPE AND HIS CRITICS. A Study in Eighteenth Century Personalities. London, Dent,
1951. 340p

McGee, Thomas D'Arcy, 1825—1868
GALLERY OF IRISH WRITERS. The Irish Writers of the Seventeenth Century.
Dublin, 1846. [BM OLU

MacGillivray, James Robertson
KEATS. A Bibliography and Reference Guide, with an Essay on Keats' Reputation. Toronto, U. of Toronto Press, 1949. 210p [BM BVaU LC NBFU OTP QMM

McGregor, Patrick, 1816–1882
A SYSTEM OF LOGIC, COMPRISING A DISCUSSION OF THE VARIOUS MEANS OF ACQUIRING AND RETAINING KNOWLEDGE AND AVOIDING ERROR. New York, 1862. 469p [NBFU

McIlwraith, Jean Newton, 1859–1938
A BOOK ABOUT LONGFELLOW. London, Nelson, 1900. 165p [BM OTP
A BOOK ABOUT SHAKESPEARE. London, Nelson, 1898. 222p [BM OLU

MacKay, Louis Alexander, 1901–
THE WRATH OF HOMER. Toronto, U. of Toronto Press, 1948. 131p [BVaU LC NSHD OTP QMM

Macklem, Michael
THE ANATOMY OF THE WORLD. Relations between Natural and Moral Law from Donne to Pope. Minneapolis, U. of Minnesota Press, 1958. 189p

MacLean, Kenneth
AGRARIAN AGE. A Background for Wordsworth. New Haven, Yale U. Press, 1950. 103p [BM BVaU LC NSHD OTUV
JOHN LOCKE AND ENGLISH LITERATURE OF THE EIGHTEENTH CENTURY. New Haven, Yale U. Press, 1936. 176p [BM BVaU OTU· QMM

McLelland, Rev. Joseph Cumming, 1925–
THE VISIBLE WORDS OF GOD. An Exposition of the Sacramental Theology of Peter Martyr Vermigli, A.D. 1500–1562. Edinburgh, Oliver & Boyd, 1957. ix + 291p

MacLennan, Hugh, 1907–
OXYRHYNCHUS. An Economic and Social Study. Princeton, Princeton U., 1935. 93p [LC OTU

McLuhan, (Herbert) Marshall, 1911–
THE MECHANICAL BRIDE. Folklore of Industrial Man. New York, Vanguard Press, 1951. 157p

MacLure, Millar, 1917–
THE PAUL'S CROSS SERMONS, 1534–1642. Toronto, U. of Toronto Press, 1958. 261p

MacMechan, Archibald McKellar, 1862–1933
HEAD-WATERS OF CANADIAN LITERATURE. Toronto, McClelland, 1924. 247p [BM BVaU LC NSHD OTP
THE CENTENARY OF HALIBURTON'S "NOVA-SCOTIA." Halifax, Author, 1930. 15p [BVaU NSHD OTP QMM

CONCERNING THE OLDEST ENGLISH LITERATURE. Halifax, Bowes, 1889. 22p
[OTU
THE RELATION OF HANS SACHS TO THE DECAMERON, AS SHOWN IN AN
EXAMINATION OF THE THIRTEEN SHROVETIDE PLAYS DRAWN FROM THAT
SOURCE. Halifax, Nova Scotia Print., 1889. 81p [BM NSHD OTU
VERGIL. [An Appreciation.] N.p., 1897. 25p [OTU

MacMurchy, Archibald, 1832–1912
HANDBOOK OF CANADIAN LITERATURE (ENGLISH). Toronto, Briggs, 1906. 236p
[BM BVaU LC NBFU OTP QMBM

McRae, Douglas George Wallis, 1908–
THE ARTS AND CRAFTS OF CANADA. Toronto, Macmillan, 1944. 80p [BM BVaU
LC OTP QMM

MacTavish, Newton McFaul, 1875–1941
ARS LONGA. Toronto, Ontario Pub. Co., 1938. 236p [BVaU LC OTP
THE FINE ARTS IN CANADA. Toronto, Macmillan, 1925. 181p [BM BVaU LC
NSHD OTP QMM

Mahon, Rev. Alexander Wylie, 1853–1930
CANADIAN HYMNS AND HYMN WRITERS. Saint John, Globe, 1908. 56p [BVaU
LC NBFU OTP QMBM

Marquis, Thomas Guthrie, 1864–1936
ENGLISH-CANADIAN LITERATURE. Toronto, Glasgow Brook, 1913. 103p [BM
BVaU NBFU OTP QMM

Martin, Burns, 1895–
ALLAN RAMSAY. A Study of his Life and Works. Cambridge, Mass., Harvard U.
Press, 1931. 203p [BVaU NBFU OTY

Masta, Henry Lorne, 1853–
ABENAKI INDIAN LEGENDS, GRAMMAR, AND PLACE NAMES. Victoriaville, Que.,
La Voix des Bois-Francs, 1932. 110p [BViV NBSM OTP QMBM

Maura, Sister (née Mary Power), 1881–1957
SHAKESPEARE'S CATHOLICISM. Cambridge, Riverside Press, 1924. 171p [BVaU
LC NBFU QMM

Medley, Rev. John, 1804–1892
THE BOOK OF JOB. Trans. from the Hebrew Text, with an Intro., a Summary of each
Chapter, and Brief Notes in Explanation of Obscure Passages. ... Saint John,
McMillan, 1879. 149p [NBFU OLU

Meek, Theophile James, 1881–
HEBREW ORIGINS. The Haskell Lectures for 1933–34, the Graduate School of
Theology, Oberlin College. New York, Harper, 1936. 220p [Rev. ed., Toronto,
U. of Toronto Press, 1951. 246p] [BM BVaU LC NSHD OTP

Meikle, W.
THE CANADIAN NEWSPAPER DIRECTORY. Containing a Complete List of all the Newspapers in Canada, the Circulation of each, and all Information in Reference thereto. Toronto, Blackburn's City Steam Press, 1858. 60p [OTU

Michener, Norah Eveline (Willis), 1902–
MARITAIN ON THE NATURE OF MAN IN A CHRISTIAN DEMOCRACY. Hull, Editions "L'Eclair," 1955. xiii + 149p

Middleton, Jesse Edgar, 1872–1960
THE FIRST CANADIAN CHRISTMAS CAROL. Toronto, Rous, 1927. 15p [OTU

Miller, Muriel, 1908–
BLISS CARMAN. A Portrait. Toronto, Ryerson, 1935. 136p [BVaU LC NBFU OTP QMM
G.A. REID, CANADIAN ARTIST. Toronto, Ryerson, 1946. 230p [BM LC NBFU OTP QMBM
HOMER WATSON, THE MAN OF DOON. Toronto, Ryerson, 1938. 164p [LC OTP QMM

Mitchell, Roy, 1884–1944
CREATIVE THEATRE. New York, Day, 1929. 256p [BM BVaU LC OTP QMM
THE SCHOOL-THEATRE. A Handbook of Theory and Practice. Toronto, Nat. Council of Education, 1925. 104p [BM BVaU LC OTP QMM
SHAKESPEARE FOR COMMUNITY PLAYERS. Toronto, Dent, 1919. 142p [BM BVa LC OTP QMM

Mitchell, Thomas H., 1865–1945
THE DRAMA OF LIFE. A Series of Reflections on Shakespeare's "Seven Ages." Toronto, Allen, 1922. 183p [BM BVaU LC OTU

Moore, William Francis, 1851–1935
INDIAN PLACE NAMES IN ONTARIO. Toronto, Macmillan, 1930. 48p [BVaU OLU QMM

Morgan, Henry James, 1842–1913
BIBLIOTHECA CANADENSIS; or, A Manual of Canadian Literature. Ottawa, Desbarats, 1867. 411p [BM BVaU LC NBFU OTP

Morris, Edmund Montague, 1871–1913
ART IN CANADA: The Early Painters. [Toronto, 1911?] 40p [BM LC OTP QMBM

Morrison, A.H.
THE ART GALLERY OF THE ENGLISH LANGUAGE. Toronto, Williamson, 1886. 282p [BM NSWA OKQ

Morse, William Inglis, 1874–1952

BLISS CARMAN. Bibliography, Letters, Fugitive Verses, and Other Data. Windham, Conn., Hawthorne House, 1941. 86p [BM BVaU LC NSHD OKQ

Moyse, Charles Ebenezer, 1852–1924

DRAMATIC ART OF SHAKESPEARE. With Special Reference to "A Midsummer Night's Dream." Montreal, 1879. 34p [NSHPL QMM

POETRY AS A FINE ART. A University Lecture delivered in McGill College, Montreal. Montreal, "Witness," 1882. 30p [Also: London, 1883. 79p] [BM BVaU OTP QMM

Muddiman, Bernard

THE MEN OF THE NINETIES. London, Danielson, 1920. 145p [BM BVaU LC OTU

Munn, Allan Macgregor, 1920–

FREE-WILL AND DETERMINISM. Toronto,, U. of Toronto Press, 1960. 218p

Murphy, George Henry, 1875–1958

SHAKESPEARE AND THE ORDINARY MAN. Toronto, Ryerson, 1939. 41p [BM LC NBFU OTU

Murray, Rev. John Clark, 1836–1917

THE BALLADS AND SONGS OF SCOTLAND. In View of their Influence on the Character of the People. London, Macmillan, 1874. 205p [BM LC NSHD OTP QMM

A HANDBOOK OF PSYCHOLOGY. London, Gardner, 1885. 422p [Also: Boston, DeWolfe Fiske, 1897.] [BVaU NSHD QMM

A HANDBOOK OF CHRISTIAN ETHICS. Edinburgh, Clark, 1908. 328p [BM LC OLU QMM

AN INTRODUCTION TO ETHICS. Boston, De Wolfe Fiske, 1891. 407p [BM LC NSHD QMM

OUTLINE OF SIR WILLIAM HAMILTON'S PHILOSOPHY. ... Boston, Gould & Lincoln, 1870. 257p [BM BVaU LC NBFU

Murray, John Tucker

ENGLISH DRAMATIC COMPANIES, 1558–1642. London, Constable, 1910. 2v [BM BVaU LC NSHD OTP QMM

Mustard, Wilfred Pirt, 1864–1932

CLASSICAL ECHOES IN TENNYSON. New York, Macmillan, 1904. 164p [BM LC NSHD OTU QMM

TENNYSON AND VIRGIL. Baltimore, Author, 1899. 11p [OTU

Needler, George Henry, 1866–1962

GOETHE AND SCOTT. Toronto, Oxford U. Press, 1950. 140p [BM BVaU NBFU OTP

JOHN GALT'S DRAMAS. A Brief Review. Toronto, U. of Toronto Press, 1945. 39p [BM LC OTP

THE LONE SHIELING. Origin and Authorship of the Blackwood "Canadian Boat-Song." Toronto, U. of Toronto Press, 1941. 109p [BM BVaU LC NBFU OTP QMM

MOORE AND HIS CANADIAN BOAT SONG. Toronto, Ryerson, 1950. 14p [NSHD OTP

RICHARD COEUR DE LION IN LITERATURE. Leipzig, Fock, 1890. 75p [BM BVaU OTU

Neville, Kenneth Percival Rutherford, 1876–

THE CASE CONSTRUCTION AFTER THE COMPARATIVE IN LATIN. Ithaca, N.Y., Cornell U., 1901. 86p [Also in Cornell Studies in Classical Philology, XV.] [BM LC NSHD OTU

Nichols, Mark Edgar, 1873–1961

(CP) THE STORY OF THE CANADIAN PRESS. Toronto, Ryerson, 1948. 327p [BM BVaU LC OTU QMM

Norwood, Gilbert, 1880–1954

THE ART OF TERENCE. Oxford, Blackwell, 1923. 156p [BM BVaU LC NSHD OTU QMM

ESSAYS ON EURIPIDEAN DRAMA. Berkeley, U. of California Press; London, Cambridge U. Press; Toronto, U. of Toronto Press, 1954. 197p

EURIPIDES AND SHAW WITH OTHER ESSAYS. Boston, Luce, 1921. 226p [BM BVaU LC NBFU OTU QMM

GREEK COMEDY. London, Methuen, 1931. 413p [BM BVaU LC NBFU OTP QMM

GREEK TRAGEDY. London, Methuen, 1920. 394p [4th ed., 1948] [BM BVaU LC NSHD OOU QMM

PINDAR. Berkeley, U. of California Press, 1945. 302p [BM BVaU LC NBFU OTU QMM

PLAUTUS AND TERENCE. New York, Longmans, 1932. 212p [BM BVaU LC NBFU OTU QMM

THE RIDDLE OF "THE BACCHAE." The Last Stage of Euripides' Religious Views. Manchester, U. Press, 1908. 188p [BM LC NSHD OTU

THE WRITERS OF GREECE. London, Oxford U. Press, 1925. 142p [BM BVa LC NSHD OTU QMM

O'Donnell, J. Reginald, 1907–

NINE MEDIAEVAL THINKERS. A Collection of Hitherto Unedited Texts. Ed. by ——. Toronto, Pontifical Institute of Mediaeval Studies, 1955. xi + 382p

O'Hagan, Thomas, 1855–1939

THE GENESIS OF CHRISTIAN ART. New York, Macmillan, 1926. 170p [BM LC OTP

STUDIES IN POETRY: CRITICAL. Boston, Marlier & Callanan, 1900. 114p [BM LC

WHAT SHAKESPEARE IS NOT. Toronto, Hunter Rose, 1936. 115p [LC OTU QMM

O'Higgins, Harvey Jerrold, 1876–1929

ALIAS WALT WHITMAN. Newark, N.J., Carteret, 1930. 49p [LC

Osborne, William Frederick, 1873–1950

THE GENIUS OF SHAKESPEARE, AND OTHER ESSAYS. Toronto, Briggs, 1908. 149p [BM BVaU NSHD OKQ

Osler, William, 1849–1919

JOHN KEATS, THE APOTHECARY POET. Baltimore, Friedenwald, 1896. 18p [LC

Owen, Eric Trevor, 1882–1948

THE HARMONY OF AESCHYLUS. Toronto, Clarke Irwin, 1952. 130p

THE STORY OF THE ILIAD. As Told in the Iliad. Toronto, Clarke Irwin, 1946. 248p [BM BVaU LC MWU NBFU OTU

Pacey, Desmond, 1917–

CREATIVE WRITING IN CANADA. A Short History of English-Canadian Literature. Toronto, Ryerson, 1952. 220p [2nd ed., rev. & enl., 1961. 314p]

FREDERICK PHILIP GROVE. Toronto, Ryerson, 1945. 150p [BVaU LC NBFU OTP

TEN CANADIAN POETS. A Group of Biographical and Critical Essays. Toronto, Ryerson, 1958. ix + 350p

Patterson, Rev. George, 1824–1897

NOTES ON THE DIALECT OF THE PEOPLE OF NEWFOUNDLAND. [Montreal? 1894.] 19p [NSWA QMM

NOTES ON THE FOLK-LORE OF NEWFOUNDLAND. [No title page.]   6p [NSWA QMM

NEWFOUNDLAND FOLK-LORE AND DIALECT. Boston, American Folk-Lore Society, 1895. 40p [OTP

Peardon, Thomas Preston, 1899–

THE TRANSITION IN ENGLISH HISTORICAL WRITING 1760–1830. New York, Columbia U. Press, 1933. 341p [BM BVaU LC NBFU QMM

Percival, Walter Pilling, 1885–1966

LEADING CANADIAN POETS. Ed. by ——. Toronto, Ryerson, 1948. 271p [BVaU LC NBFU OTP QMM

Peter, John Desmond, 1921–

COMPLAINT AND SATIRE IN EARLY ENGLISH LITERATURE. Oxford, Clarendon, 1956. 323p

A CRITIQUE OF PARADISE LOST. New York, Columbia U. Press, 1960. ix + 172p

Peterson, William, 1856–1921

COLLATIONS FROM THE CODEX CLUNIACENSIS S. HOLKHAMICUS. A Ninth Century Manuscript of Cicero. With Hitherto Unpublished Scholia, and a History of the Codex. Oxford, Clarendon, 1901. 62 + 14p [BM LC QMM

Pierce, Lorne Albert, 1890–1961

ALFRED, LORD TENNYSON AND WILLIAM KIRBY. Unpublished Correspondence, to which are added Some Letters from Hallam, Lord Tennyson. Toronto, Macmillan, 1929. 71p [BM BVaU OTP QMSS

BLISS CARMAN'S SCRAP-BOOK. A Table of Contents. Ed. with a postscript by ——. Toronto, Ryerson, 1931. 19p [An index to Carman's scrapbook of his fugitive verse, 1883–1921.] [BM BVaU LC NBFU OTP QMM

ENGLISH CANADIAN LITERATURE, 1882–1932. Ottawa, 1932. 8p [BVaU NBFU OTP QMM

THE HOUSE OF RYERSON. Toronto, Ryerson, 1954. 52p

AN OUTLINE OF CANADIAN LITERATURE (French and English). Toronto, Ryerson, 1927. 251p [BM BVaU LC NSHD OTU QMM

UNEXPLORED FIELDS OF CANADIAN LITERATURE. Toronto, Ryerson, 1932. 32p [BVaU NBFU OTP QMM

Pomeroy, Elsie May, 1886–

G.B. LANCASTER: 1873–1945. A Canadian Tribune. Toronto, priv. print., 1948. 16p [NBFU OTP

Porter, Harry Culverwell

REFORMATION AND REACTION IN TUDOR CAMBRIDGE. Cambridge, Eng., University Press, 1958. x + 461p

Priestley, Francis Ethelbert Louis, 1905–

WILLIAM GODWIN'S ENQUIRY CONCERNING POLITICAL JUSTICE AND ITS INFLUENCE ON MORALS AND HAPPINESS. Photographic facsimile of the 3rd ed., corrected and ed. with variant readings, and with a critical intro. and notes by ——. Toronto, U. of Toronto Press, 1946. 3v [BM BVaU LC OTU

Raftis, James Ambrose, 1922–

THE ESTATES OF RAMSEY ABBEY. A Study in Economic Growth and Organization. Toronto, Pontifical Institute of Mediaeval Studies, 1957. xvii + 341p

Rand, Rev. Silas Tertius, 1810–1889

DICTIONARY OF THE LANGUAGE OF THE MICMAC INDIANS, who Reside in N.S.,

N.B., P.E.I., Cape Breton and Newfoundland. Halifax, Nova Scotia Print., 1888.
286p [BM BVaU LC NBFU OTU QMM
A FIRST READING BOOK IN THE MICMAC LANGUAGE. Halifax, Nova Scotia Print.,
1875. 108p [BM NSHD OTU
MICMAC PLACE NAMES IN THE MARITIME PROVINCES AND GASPE PENINSULA ...
1852 ... 1890. Ottawa, Surveyor's Office, 1919. 116p [BVaU LC OTU

Rashley, Richard Ernest, 1909 –
POETRY IN CANADA, THE FIRST THREE STEPS. Toronto, Ryerson, 1958. xvii +
166p

Raymond, Rev. William Odber, 1853–1923
SELECTIONS FROM SWINBURNE. Ed. by William Odber Raymond. New York,
Harcourt, 1925. 392p [OTU

Raymond, William Odber, 1880–
THE INFINITE MOMENT AND OTHER ESSAYS IN ROBERT BROWNING. Toronto, U.
of Toronto Press, 1950. 249p [BM BVa NBFU OTP QMM

Rhodenizer, Vernon Blair, 1886–1968
AT THE SIGN OF THE HAND AND PEN. Nova-Scotian Authors. N.p., Canadian
Authors' Association., Nova Scotia Branch, 1948. 43p [BVaU NSWA OTP
A HANDBOOK OF CANADIAN LITERATURE. Ottawa, Graphic, 1930. 295p [Also:
Toronto, Nelson, 1932. 295p] [BM BVaU LC NBFU OTP QMM

Ridington, John, 1868–1945
LIBRARIES IN CANADA. A Study of Library Conditions and Needs. By the
Commission of Enquiry, John Ridington, Chairman, Mary J.L. Black, George H.
Locke. Toronto, Ryerson, 1933. 153p [BVaU LC NBFU OTU
THE POETRY OF THE WAR. An Address delivered before the Pacific Northwest
Library Association ... Portland, Oregon. ... Vancouver, priv. print., 1917. 40p
[BVaU LC

Robbins, William, 1909 –
THE ETHICAL IDEALISM OF MATTHEW ARNOLD. A Study of the Nature and Sources
of his Moral and Religious Ideas. Toronto, U. of Toronto Press, 1959. xi + 259p

Roberts, Charles George Douglas, 1860–1943
ALASTOR AND ADONAIS. By Percy Bysshe Shelley. Ed. with an Essay on "The
Pastoral Elegy" by ——. Boston, Silver Burdett, 1902. 108p [LC

Roberts, Rev. Richard, 1874–1945
THE PREACHER AS MAN OF LETTERS. London, Dent, 1931. 216p [BM BVaU
OTP
THAT ONE FACE. Studies of the Place of Jesus in the Minds of Poets and Prophets.
New York, Association Press, 1919. 199p [BVaU LC OLU

Robertson, John Charles, 1864–1956

THE GORGIANIC FIGURES IN EARLY GREEK PROSE. Baltimore, Friedenwald, 1893.
41p [BM OTU

THE STORY OF GREECE AND ROME, THEIR GROWTH AND THEIR LEGACY TO OUR
WESTERN WORLD. By J.C. Robertson and H.G. Robertson. London, Dent, 1928.
352p [BM BVaU OTU QMM

Robertson, Percy, 1874–

CONTEMPORARY AUTHORS OF FORMER TIMES. A Chart and an Index. Comp.
by ——. Toronto, [1944?]. [BM OTP QMM

Robins, John Daniel, 1884–1952

A BOOK OF CANADIAN HUMOUR. Ed. by J.D. Robins and Margaret V. Ray.
Toronto, Ryerson, 1951. 308p

Robson, Albert Henry, 1882–1939

A.Y. JACKSON. Toronto, Ryerson, 1938. 32p [BVaU LC NBFU OTP QMBM

CANADIAN LANDSCAPE PAINTERS. Toronto, Ryerson, 1932. 227p [BM BVaU
LC NBFU OTP, QMM

CLARENCE A. GAGNON, R.C.A., LL.D. Toronto, Ryerson, 1938. 32p [BVaU LC
NBFU OTP QMBM

CORNELIUS KRIEGHOFF. Toronto, Ryerson, 1937. 32p [BVaU NBFU OTP
QMM

J.E.H. MACDONALD. Toronto, Ryerson, 1937. 32p [BVaU LC NBFU OTP QMM

PAUL KANE. Toronto, Ryerson, 1938. 32p [BVaU LC NBFU OTP QMBM

TOM THOMSON. Toronto, Ryerson, 1937. 32p [BVaU LC OTP QMM

Ross, Malcolm Mackenzie, 1911–

THE ARTS IN CANADA. Stock-taking at Mid-Century. ... Ed. by ——. Toronto,
Macmillan, 1958. 176p

MILTON'S ROYALISM. A Study of the Conflict of Symbol and Idea in the Poems.
Ithaca, Cornell U. Press, 1943. 152p [BM BVaU NSHD OTU

POETRY & DOGMA. The Transfiguration of Eucharistic Symbols in Seventeenth
Century English Poetry. New Brunswick, N.J., Rutgers U. Press, 1954. xii + 256p

Ross, Philip Dansken, 1858–1949

CANADIAN POETS AND THE SHORT WORD. Ottawa, Author, 1938. 23p [OTU

SHORT WORD IN ENGLISH POETRY. Ottawa, Author, 1937. [UTQ

Rothstein, Samuel, 1921–

THE DEVELOPMENT OF REFERENCE SERVICES THROUGH ACADEMIC TRADITIONS,
PUBLIC LIBRARY PRACTICE, AND SPECIAL LIBRARIANSHIP. Chicago, Association
of College and Reference Libraries, 1955. ix + 124p

Roy, Rev. James, 1834–1922

LAW IN LANGUAGE. A Thesis. Montreal, Witness, 1883. 23p [NSWA

Roy, James Alexander, 1884–

COWPER AND HIS POETRY. London, Harrap, 1914. 181p [BM LC OTU

IS THERE A SCOTTISH LITERATURE? Kingston, Queen's University, 1945. 16p [LC OTP

JAMES MATTHEW BARRIE. An Appreciation. London, Jarrolds, 1937. 255p [BM BVa LC NSHD OTP QMM

Salmon, Edward Togo, 1905–

A HISTORY OF THE ROMAN WORLD FROM 30 B.C. TO A.D. 138. 3rd ed. London, Methuen, 1957. xiii + 365p [First pub. 1944. 2nd ed. rev. 1950.]

Salter, Frederick Millet, 1895–1962

MEDIAEVAL DRAMA IN CHESTER. Toronto, U. of Toronto press, 1955. xi + 138p

Sandilands, John

WESTERN CANADIAN DICTIONARY AND PHRASE BOOKS. Explaining in Plain English ... the Meaning of the Most Popular Canadianisms, Colloquialisms, and Slang. ... 2nd ed. Winnipeg, Telegram, 1912. 30p [BM BVaU LC OTU

Sandwell, Bernard Keble, 1876–1954

THE MUSICAL RED BOOK OF MONTREAL. A Record of Music in Montreal from 1895 to 1907. Ed. by ——. Montreal, 1907. 229p [QMM

Saunders, Henry Scholey, 1864–1951

ILLUSTRATIONS TO WALT WHITMAN'S LEAVES OF GRASS. Toronto, Author, n.d. 122p [Edition limited to 10 copies.] [LC

AN INTRODUCTION TO WALT WHITMAN. Toronto, Author, 1934. 25p [LC OTP QMM

PARODIES ON WALT WHITMAN. Comp. by ——. New York, American Library Service, 1923. 171p [LC OTU

PORTRAIT GALLERY OF WHITMAN WRITERS. With Quotations. Comp. by ——. Toronto, Author, 1927. 122p [Ten copies made.] [LC

WHITMAN MUSIC. Comp. by ——. Toronto, Saunders, 1940. 16p [Typewritten.] [LC

WHITMAN PORTRAITS. With Notes. Comp. by ——. Toronto, Author, 1922. 73p [Nine copies made.] [LC

WHITMAN PORTRAITS. With Notes. Comp. by ——. Toronto, Author, 1923. 114p [Contains over 500 mounted photographs with typewritten descriptions. Four copies made.] [LC

Scadding, Rev. Henry, 1813–1901

FIRST GAZETTEER OF UPPER CANADA. Toronto, Copp, 1876. 23p [OTU

SHAKESPEARE, THE SEER, THE INTERPRETER. Address delivered before the St. George's Society ... April 23, 1864. Toronto, Copp Clark, 1864. 88p [OTP

SOME CANADIAN NOMS-DE-PLUME IDENTIFIED. Toronto, Copp Clark, 1877. 57p
[LC NSWA OTP

SOME LAPSED NAMES IN CANADIAN LOCAL NOMENCLATURE. 1897. [OTU

Sedgewick, Garnett Gladwin, 1882–1949

OF IRONY, ESPECIALLY IN DRAMA. Toronto, U. of Toronto Press, 1935. 100p
[Also: Toronto, U. of Toronto Press, 1948. 127p [BM BVaU LC NSHD OTP
QMM

Shaw, James Eustace, 1876–1962

ESSAYS ON THE VITA NUOVA. Princeton, U. Press, 1929. 236p [BM BVaU LC
OTU

GUIDO CAVALCANTI'S THEORY OF LOVE. ... Toronto, U. of Toronto Press, 1949.
228p [BM LC OTP

THE LADY "PHILOSOPHY" IN THE CONVIVIO. Cambridge, Mass., Dante Society,
1938. 29p [BM LC OTU

Shea, Albert A.

CULTURE IN CANADA. A Study of the Findings of the Royal Commission on
National Development in the Arts, Letters and Sciences, (1949-1951). Ed. by ——
Toronto, CORE Pub., 1952. 65p

Shoolman, Regina Lenore, 1909–

THE ENJOYMENT OF ART IN AMERICA. A Survey of the Permanent Collections of
Painting, Sculpture, Ceramics & Decorative Arts in American and Canadian
Museums. By Regina Shoolman and Charles E. Slatkin. Philadelphia, Lippincott,
1942. 792p [LC OTP QMM

SIX CENTURIES OF FRENCH MASTER DRAWINGS IN AMERICA. By Regina Shoolman
and Charles E. Slatkin. New York, Oxford U. Press, 1950. 256p [LC OTP

THE STORY OF ART. The Lives and Times of the Great Masters. By Regina Shoolman
and Charles Slatkin. New York, Halcyon, 1940. 332p [LC QMM

Sime, Jessie Georgina, 1880–

THOMAS HARDY OF THE WESSEX NOVELS. An Essay and Biographical Note.
Montreal, Carrier, 1928. 58p [BVaU NBFU OTU QMSS

Sinden, Margaret Jane, 1915–

GERHART HAUPTMANN. The Prose Plays. Toronto, U. of Toronto Press, 1957.
238p

Slater, Rev. Robert Henry Lawson, 1896–

PARADOX AND NIRVANA. A Study of Religious Ultimates, with Special Reference
to Burmese Buddhism. Chicago, U. of Chicago Press, 1951. 145p

Smith, Arthur James Marshall, 1902–

THE POETRY OF ROBERT BRIDGES. Montreal, Burton's, n.d. 15p [QMM

Smith, Goldwin, 1823–1910

THE ALLUSIONS IN "LOTHAIR." N.p., n.d. 4p [OTU

COWPER. New York, Harper, 1880. 128p [Same title: New York, Acme Library, 1880. Series 2. 363p] [BM BVaU LC NBFU OTU QMM

THE FEDERALIST. Collection of Essays by Alexander Hamilton, John Jay, and James Madison. With a special intro. by ———. New York, Colonial Press, 1901. 488p [OTU

LIFE OF COWPER. New York, Lovell, 1884. 82p [Same title: Toronto, Copp Clark, 1894. 166p] [LC NSWA OTU

LIFE OF JANE AUSTEN. London, Scott, 1890. 195p [BM BVaU LC NBFU OKQ QMM

QUAENAM FUERIT MULIERUM APUD VETERES GRAECOS CONDITIO? [Inquiry into the Status of Woman in Ancient Greece.] Oxford, Macpherson, 1846. 32p [OTU

SHAKESPEARE, THE MAN. An Attempt to find Traces of the Dramatist's Character in his Drama. Toronto, Morang, 1899. 60p [BM BVaU LC MWU NBFU OTP QMM

SPECIMENS OF GREEK TRAGEDY. Trans. by ———. New York, Macmillan, 1893. 2v [BM NBFU

Smith, Grant F.O., 1877–1949

THE MAN ROBERT BURNS. Toronto, Ryerson, 1940. 396p [BM BVaU LC NBFU OTU

ROBERT BURNS, 1759–1796. Comp. by ———. Toronto, 1936. 47p [MWP OTU

Smith, Marion (Bodwell), 1912–

MARLOWE'S IMAGERY AND THE MARLOWE CANON. Philadelphia, 1940. 213p [BVaU LC QMM

Smith, Wilfred Cantwell, 1916–

ISLAM IN MODERN HISTORY. Princeton, N.J., Princeton U. Press, 1957. ix + 317p

Sprigge, Elizabeth, 1900–

THE STRANGE LIFE OF AUGUST STRINDBERG. London, Hamilton, 1949. 246p [BM BVaU NBFU OTP

Sproat, Gilbert Malcolm, 1832–1913

SIR WALTER SCOTT AS A POET. Edinburgh, Montreal, 1871. [BM

Sprott, Samuel Ernest

MILTON'S ART OF PROSODY. Oxford, Blackwell, 1953. xi + 147p

Stanley, Carleton Wellesley, 1886–1971

MATTHEW ARNOLD. Toronto, U. of Toronto Press, 1938. 163p [BM BVaU LC NSHD OTP QMM

ROOTS OF THE TREE. Toronto, Oxford U. Press, 1936. 107p [BM LC NBFU OTP QMM

Stern, Karl, 1906–
THE THIRD REVOLUTION. A Study of Psychiatry and Religion. New York, Harcourt, 1954. xii + 306p

Stevenson, Lionel, 1902–
APPRAISALS OF CANADIAN LITERATURE. Toronto, Macmillan, 1926. 272p [BM BVaU LC NBFU OTP QMM
DARWIN AMONG THE POETS. Chicago, U. Press, 1932. 357p [BM BVaU LC NBFU OTU
DR. QUICKSILVER. The Life of Charles Lever. London, Chapman & Hall, 1939. 308p [BM BVaU LC OTP QMM
THE ENGLISH NOVEL. A Panorama. Boston, Houghton, 1960. 539p
THE ORDEAL OF GEORGE MEREDITH. New York, Scribner, 1953. 368p
THE SHOWMAN OF VANITY FAIR. The Life of William Makepeace Thackeray. New York, Scribner, 1947. 405p [BM BVaU LC NBFU OTP QMM

Stevenson, Orlando John, 1869–1950
A PEOPLE'S BEST. Toronto, Musson, 1927. 266p [BVaU NBFU OTU QMBM

Stewart, Alexander Charles, 1867–1944
THE POETICAL REVIEW. A Brief Notice of Canadian Poets and Poetry. Toronto, Anderson, 1896. 24p [OTP

Stewart, George, 1848–1906
ESSAYS FROM REVIEWS. First series: Quebec, Dawson, 1892. 171p [Second series: Quebec, Dawson, 1893. 159p] [BM BVaU NSHD OTP QMM
EVENINGS IN THE LIBRARY. Bits of Gossip about Books and those who Write them. Saint John, Morrow, 1878. 254p [BVaU LC NBFU OTP QMM
THE GENIUS AND LIFE-WORK OF LONGFELLOW. A Paper read before the Literary and Historical Society of Quebec. Quebec, Chronicle, 1883. 26p [NSWA
LECTURE ON ALCOTT. Delivered before the Literary and Historical Society of Quebec. Quebec, Chronicle, 1880. 27p [NSWA
THOREAU. The Hermit of Walden. Quebec, Morning Chronicle, 1882. 30p [NSHD OTP

Stewart, Herbert Leslie, 1882–1953
ANATOLE FRANCE, THE PARISIAN. Toronto, Dodd Mead, 1927. 394p [BVaU LC NSHD OTP QMM
NIETZSCHE AND THE IDEALS OF MODERN GERMANY. London, Arnold, 1915. 235p [BVaU LC NSHD OTU QMM
QUESTIONS OF THE DAY IN PHILOSOPHY AND PSYCHOLOGY. London, Arnold, 1912. 284p [BVaU LC NSHD OTU QMM

WINGED WORDS. Sir Winston Churchill as Writer and Speaker. Toronto, Ryerson, 1953. 114p

Stewart, James McGregor, 1889–1955

RUDYARD KIPLING. A Bibliographical Catalogue. Ed. by A.W. Yeats. Toronto, Dalhousie U. Press and U. of Toronto Press, 1959. xv + 673p

Stockelbach, Mrs. Lavonia Ruth

THE BIRDS OF SHAKESPEARE. London, Batsford, 1954. xiv + 94p

Stone, Rev. James Samuel, 1852–

RICHARD HOOKER. A Sketch of his Life, Writings, and Times. Toronto, Hunter, 1882. 48p [NSWA OTU

THOMAS CRANMER, ARCHBISHOP AND MARTYR. An Essay. Toronto, Hunter, 1882. 83p [NSWA OTP

Story, George Morley, 1927–

A NEWFOUNDLAND DIALECT DICTIONARY. A Survey of the Problems. St. John's, Memorial University, 1956. 14p

Stratton, Thomas, 1816–1886

THE AFFINITY BETWEEN THE HEBREW LANGUAGE AND THE CELTIC. 2nd ed., 1870. [3rd ed., Edinburgh, 1872.] [BM OLU

ILLUSTRATIONS OF THE AFFINITY OF THE LATIN LANGUAGE TO THE GAELIC OR CELTIC OF SCOTLAND. Toronto, Scobie, 1840. 26p [BM OTP

ILLUSTRATIONS OF THE AFFINITY OF THE LATIN LANGUAGE TO THE GAELIC OR CELTIC OF SCOTLAND AND TO THE LANGUAGE SPOKEN IN THE COUNTRY OF GLENGARRY, UPPER CANADA. Kingston, 1839. 91p [Manuscript.] [BM QMM

PROOFS OF THE CELTIC ORIGIN OF A GREAT PART OF THE GREEK LANGUAGE. Kingston, Chronicle & Gazette Office, 1840. 8p [BM OTP

Stringer, Arthur John Arbuthnot, 1874–1950

RED WINE OF YOUTH. A Life of Rupert Brooke. Indianapolis, Bobbs-Merrill, 1948. 287p [BVa LC NBFU OTU QMM

A STUDY IN KING LEAR. [MOR'12

Sutherland, John, 1919–1956

THE POETRY OF E.J. PRATT. A New Interpretation. Toronto, Ryerson, 1956. 109p

Sykes, Frederick Henry, 1863–1918

FRENCH ELEMENTS IN MIDDLE ENGLISH. Oxford, Hart, 1899. 64p [BM LC OTP QMM

POEMS OF ALFRED TENNYSON AND ROBERT BROWNING. With intro. and notes by ——. Toronto, Gage, 1907. 224p [BM OTU

SYLLABUS OF A COURSE OF SIX LECTURES ON ENGLISH WRITERS OF THE
PRESENT ERA: Carlyle, Newman, Kingsley, Ruskin, Matthew Arnold, Kipling.
Philadelphia, American Soc. for Extension of University Teaching, 1899.
35p [OTU
SYLLABUS OF A COLLEGIATE COURSE OF THIRTY LECTURES ON SHAKESPEARE.
New York, Teachers' College, Columbia U., 1903. 31p [LC

Talbot, Thomas, fl. 1844–1882

GREECE AND THE GREEKS; or, A Historic Sketch of Attic Life and Manners.
London, Sampson Low, etc., 1881. 334p [BM OTP
THE HEBREWS AT HOME; or, An Historical Sketch ... of the Ancient Hebrews.
Montreat, Lovell, 1874. 270p [BM

Tardivel, Jules Paul, 1857–1905

BORROWED AND STOLEN FEATHERS; or, A Glance through Mr. J.M. Lemoine's
latest work, THE CHRONICLES OF THE ST. LAWRENCE. Quebec, "Le Canadien,"
1878. 33p [BVaU LC NSWA OTP QMM

Taylor, Henry, fl. 1819–1860

AN ATTEMPT TO FORM A SYSTEM OF THE CREATION OF OUR GLOBE, OF THE
PLANETS, AND THE SUN OF OUR SYSTEM. ... Toronto, Coates, 1836. 119p
[2nd ed. rev. and enl.: Quebec, Cowan, 1840. 136p] [3rd ed. rev. and enl.:
Montreal, Becket, 1842. 156p] [9th ed. rev. and enl.: Quebec, Bureau &
Marcotte, 1854. 213p] [Haight quotes from preface: "The original manuscript
of this work was composed between the years 1819 and 1825."] [BM NSWA
OOA QMM
CLASSIC ART. An Exponent of Religious Sentiment. A Lecture delivered ...
Belleville, Ont., June 21st, 1875. New York, Great American Print., 1875.
28p [NSWA

Taylor, Rev. William Edington, 1877–

THE ETHICAL AND RELIGIOUS THEORIES OF BISHOP BUTLER. Toronto, Bryant,
1903. 79p [BM BVaU OTU

Thomas, Clara Eileen (McCandless), 1919–

CANADIAN NOVELISTS, 1920–1945. Toronto, Longmans, 1946. 141p [BM
BVaU LC NBFU OTU QMM

Thompson, Claude Willett

HUMANISM IN ACTION. Toronto, Pitman, 1950. 275p [BVaU OTU
WILLIAM WOOD, CANADIAN HISTORIAN AND AUTHOR: BIBLIOGRAPHY. Forty
Years of Study and Writing, 1896–1936. Montreal, n.p., 1939. 12p [OTU

Todd, Henry Cook, –1862

A MANUAL OF ORTHOEPY. With Numerous Notes upon the Origin and Abuse of

Words. 4th ed. with large additions and corrections. [Anon] York, Office of the Guardian, 1833. 104p [First pub. in London, 1832.] [BM OTP QMM

Toronto, Ont. Public Libraries
CANADIAN PERIODICAL INDEX, 1931–. Toronto, Public Libraries, 1931–. [A continuing serial, which suspended publication 1933–37.] [BM BVaU LC NSHD OTP QMM

Toronto, University of. University College
STUDIES IN ENGLISH. By Members of University College. Collected by ... Malcolm W. Wallace. Toronto, U. of Toronto Press, 1931. 254p [BVaU NBFU OTU

Tovell, Ruth (Massey), 1889–
FLEMISH ARTISTS OF THE VALOIS COURTS. ... Toronto, U. of Toronto Press, 1950. 157p [BM BVaU LC OTP

Tracy, Clarence, 1908–
THE ARTIFICIAL BASTARD. A Biography of Richard Savage. Toronto, pub. in co-operation with the U. of Saskatchewan by U. of Toronto Press, 1953. xvii + 164p

Turnbull, Jane Mason, 1896–
ESSENTIAL TRAITS OF FRENCH-CANADIAN POETRY. Toronto, Macmillan, 1938. 225p [An abstract was pub. at the U. of Chicago, 1937. 27p] [BM BVaU LC NSHD OTU

Ullman, Solomon Baruch, 1908–
CULTURE AND JUDAISM. Selected Essays. Toronto, Lieberman's Jewish Book Centre, 1956. 184p

Vickery, Mrs. Olga Westland, 1925–
THE NOVELS OF WILLIAM FAULKNER. A Critical Interpretation. Baton Rouge, Louisiana State U. Press, 1959. x + 269p
WILLIAM FAULKNER. Three Decades of Criticism. Ed. with an intro. and bibliography by Frederick J. Hoffman and Olga W. Vickery. New ed. East Lansing, Michigan State U. Press, 1960. xi + 428p [First ed. 1951.]

Wallace, Malcolm William, 1873–1960
ENGLISH CHARACTER AND THE ENGLISH LITERARY TRADITION. Toronto, U. of Toronto Press, 1952. viii + 78p
THE LIFE OF SIR PHILIP SIDNEY. Cambridge, U. Press, 1915. 428p [BM BVaU LC NBFU OTP QMM

Walter, Hermann, 1863–1952

HEINRICH HEINE. A Critical Examination of the Poet and his Works. London, Dent, 1930. 322p [MWU NSHPL OTY

MOSES MENDELSSOHN, CRITIC AND PHILOSOPHER. New York, Bloch, 1930. 220p [MWU OLU NSHPL

Warnock, Amelia Beers (Mrs. John Garvin), 1878–1956

ISABELLA VALANCY CRAWFORD. By Katherine Hale [pseud]. Toronto, Ryerson, 1923. 125p [BM BVaU NSHD OTU

Watson, John, 1847–1939

CHRISTIANITY AND IDEALISM. New York, Macmillan, 1897. xxxvii + 292p [BM BVaU LC NSHD OTU QMM

COMTE, MILL, AND SPENCER. New York, Macmillan, 1895. 302p [BM BVaU NSHD OTU QMM

HEDONISTIC THEORIES FROM ARISTIPPUS TO SPENCER. New York, Macmillan, 1895. 248p [BM BVaU LC NSHD OTP QMM

THE INTERPRETATION OF RELIGIOUS EXPERIENCE. Glasgow, Maclehose, 1912. 2v [BM BVaU LC OTP

KANT AND HIS ENGLISH CRITICS. A Comparison of Critical and Empirical Philosophy. Glasgow, Maclehose, 1881. 402p [BM BVaU LC NSHD OTP QMM

AN OUTLINE OF PHILOSOPHY. With Notes Historical and Critical. ... New York, Macmillan, 1898. 489p [2nd ed. of COMTE, MILL, AND SPENCER.] [BM BVaU LC NSHD OTP QMM

THE PHILOSOPHICAL BASIS OF RELIGION. A Series of Lectures. Glasgow, Maclehose, 1907. 485p [BM BVaUᵀ LC NSHD OTP QMM

THE PHILOSOPHY OF KANT EXPLAINED. Glasgow, Maclehose, 1908. 515p [BM BVaU LC NBFU OTP

THE RELATION OF PHILOSOPHY TO SCIENCE. An Inaugural Lecture ... Queen's University, Kingston ... October 16th, 1872. Kingston, Bailie, 1872. 37p [OTP

SCHELLING'S TRANSCENDENTAL IDEALISM. Chicago, Griggs, 1882. 251p [BM LC NSHD OTU QMM

THE STATE IN PEACE AND WAR. Toronto, Macmillan, 1919. 296p [BM NBFU OLU QMM

Webling, Peggy

A SKETCH OF JOHN RUSKIN. London, Baines & Scarsbrook, 1916. 29p [BM BVaU

West, Paul Noden, 1930–

BYRON AND THE SPOILER'S ART. London, Chatto & Windus, 1960. 155p

THE FOSSILS OF PIETY. Literary Humanism in Decline. ... New York, Vantage Press, 1959. 85p

Wetmore, Jessie Helen Louise

SENECA'S CONCEPTION OF THE STOIC SAGE AS SHOWN IN HIS PROSE WORKS.
Edmonton, U. of Alberta Press, 1936. 66p [BM BVaU OTU

Whalley, George, 1915–

COLERIDGE AND SARA HUTCHINSON AND THE ASRA POEMS. Toronto, U. of
Toronto Press, 1955. xxi + 188p

THE POETIC PROCESS. An Essay in Poetics. London, Routledge, 1953. 256p

Wharton, Lewis, 1885–

FRANCOIS VILLON. Blackguard and Immortal. Vancouver, Seymour Press, 1931.
29p [BM BVaU LC OOP QMSS

White, Mary E., 1908–

STUDIES IN HONOUR OF GILBERT NORWOOD. Ed. by ——. Toronto, U. of
Toronto Press, 1952. xvii + 278p

Wiles, Roy McKeen, 1903–

SERIAL PUBLICATION IN ENGLAND BEFORE 1750. Cambridge, Eng., U. Press,
1957. xv + 391p

Williams, Cecil

THE FOUNDATIONS OF INTELLIGENCE. New York, Comet Press Books, 1953.
126p

Wilson, Daniel, 1816–1892

CALIBAN, THE MISSING LINK. London, Macmillan, 1873. 274p [BM BVaU LC
NSHD OTP QMM

CHATTERTON. A Biographical Study. London, Macmillan, 1869. 328p [BM LC
OTU QMM

THE LOST ATLANTIS, AND OTHER ETHNOGRAPHIC STUDIES. Edinburgh, Douglas,
1892. 411p [BM BVaU LC OTU

MEMORIALS OF EDINBURGH IN THE OLDEN TIME. Edinburgh, 1848. 2v [Several
later editions.] [BM LC OTU

OLIVER CROMWELL AND THE PROTECTORATE. London, Nelson, 1848. 304p
[BM OLU

REMINISCENCES OF OLD EDINBURGH. Edinburgh, Douglas, 1898. [Same as
MEMORIALS OF EDINBURGH ... ?] [BVaU

Wilson, Harold Sowerby, 1904–

ON THE DESIGN OF SHAKESPEARIAN TRAGEDY. Toronto, U. of Toronto Press,
1957. 256p

Wilson, Harry Langford, 1867–1913

THE METAPHOR IN THE EPIC POEMS OF PUBLIUS PAPINIUS STATIUS. Baltimore,
Murphy, 1898. 30p [BM LC QMM

Wilson, Milton Thomas, 1923–
SHELLEY'S LATER POETRY. A Study of his Prophetic Imagination. New York,
Columbia U. Press, 1959. 332p

Wilson, Neil Leslie, 1922–
THE CONCEPT OF LANGUAGE. Toronto, U. of Toronto Press, 1959. 153p

Wilson, Richard Albert, 1874–1949
THE MIRACULOUS BIRTH OF LANGUAGE. Preface by George Bernard Shaw.
London, Dent, 1946. 196p [First pub. in 1937 under title: THE BIRTH OF
LANGUAGE.] [BM BVaU OTP QMM

Winspear, Alban Dewes, 1899–
THE GENESIS OF PLATO'S THOUGHT. [2nd ed., rev.] New York, S.A. Russell,
1956. 390p [First pub., New York, Dryden Press, 1940.]

Wood, Louis Aubrey Lorne, 1883–1955
THE FORM AND ORIGIN OF MILTON'S ANTITRINITARIAN CONCEPTION. Inaugural
Dissertation. London, Ont., Advertiser, 1911. 96p [BM NSHD OTP QMM

Woodcock, George, 1912–
THE ANARCHIST PRINCE. A Biographical Study of Peter Kropotkin. By George
Woodcock and Ivan Avakumovic. New York, Boardman, 1950. 463p [BVaU
LC NSHD OTU
BRITISH POETRY TO-DAY. An Address. ... Vancouver, U. of British Columbia, 1950.
15p [BVaU LC NBFU OTU
THE INCOMPARABLE APHRA. London, Boardman, 1948. 248p [Biography of
Aphra Behn.] [BM BVaU LC OTU
LETTERS OF CHARLES LAMB. Selected, with intro. and notes by ——. London,
Grey Walls Press, 1950. 227p [OTU
THE PARADOX OF OSCAR WILDE. New York, Macmillan, 1949. 250p [BM
BVaU LC NSHD OTU
PIERRE-JOSEPH PROUDHON. A Biography. New York, Macmillan, 1956. 291p
WILLIAM GODWIN. A Biographical Study. London, Porcupine, 1946. 266p [BM
BVaU LC NSHD OTU

Woodhouse, Arthur Sutherland Pigott, 1895–1964
MILTON THE POET. Vancouver, U. of British Columbia, Dent, 1955. 30p
PURITANISM AND LIBERTY. Being the Army Debates (1647–9) ... with
Supplementary Documents. Selected and ed. with an intro. by ——. London,
Dent, 1938. 100 + 506p [2nd ed.: Chicago, U. of Chicago Press, 1951.]
[BM BVaU NBFU OTP QMM

Woodhouse, Hugh Frederick
THE DOCTRINE OF THE CHURCH IN ANGLICAN THEOLOGY, 1547–1603. New
York, Macmillan, 1954. 223p

Woodworth, Hugh MacCallum, 1906–

THE NATURE AND TECHNIQUE OF UNDERSTANDING. Some Fundamentals of Semantics. Victoria, Author, 1949. 142p [BVaU OTU

Yarrill, Eric Herbert, 1914–

BROWNING'S "ROMAN MURDER STORY" AS RECORDED IN A HITHERTO UNKNOWN ITALIAN CONTEMPORARY MS. Trans. by ——. With intro. by W.O. Raymond. Waco, Texas, Baylor U., 1939. 47p [BVaU OTU

Young, George Renny, 1802–1853

ON COLONIAL LITERATURE, SCIENCE AND EDUCATION. Written with a View of Improving the Literary, Educational, and Public Institutions of British North America. In Three Volumes. Halifax, Crosskill, 1842. 363p [Apparently only v. 1 ever appeared, although the publication of v. 2 was promised "in June next," and its table of contents was included in v. 1 as an addendum.] [NBFU NSHD OLU OTP

TRAVEL AND DESCRIPTION

Emigrant handbooks, early descriptions of Canada both general and local, travel journals, reports by Canadians of experiences and travel in Canada

Abbott, Rev. Joseph, 1789–1863
MEMORANDA OF A SETTLER IN LOWER CANADA; or, The Emigrant to North America. Being a Compendium of Useful Practical Hints. ... By an Emigrant Farmer [pseud]. Montreal, Lovell, 1842. 80p [2nd and 3rd eds. pub. under title: THE EMIGRANT TO NORTH AMERICA, from Memoranda of a Settler. ... Montreal, Lovell, 1843. 116p; Edinburgh, Blackwood, 1844. 120p] [BM LC NSWA OTP

Alexander, James Edward, 1803–1885
L'ACADIE; or, Seven Years' Explorations in British America. London, Colburn, 1849. 2v [BM BVaU NSHD OTP
TRANSATLANTIC SKETCHES ... in North and South America, and the West Indies. London, Bentley, 1833. 2v [BM BVaU LC NSHD OTP

Anderson, Alexander Caulfield, 1814–1884
THE DOMINION AT THE WEST. A Brief Description of ... British Columbia, its Climate and Resources. The Government Prize Essay, 1872. Victoria, Wolfenden, 1872. 112p [BVaU LC NSWA
NOTES ON NORTH-WESTERN AMERICA. Montreal, Mitchell & Wilson, 1876. 22p [BM BVaU LC OTP

Anderson, Rev. David, 1814–1885
THE NET IN THE BAY; or, Journal of a Visit to Moose and Albany. By the Bishop of Rupert's Land. London, Hatchard, 1854. 276p [BM BVaU LC NSWA OTP

Anderson, William James, 1813?–1873
THE VALLEY OF THE CHAUDIERE. Its Scenery and Gold Fields. Quebec, Morning Chronicle, 1872. 38p [OOA

Anonymous
THE FACE OF CANADA. Toronto, Clarke Irwin, 1959. x + 229p
LETTERS FROM CANADA WITH NUMEROUS ILLUSTRATIONS. Quebec, Morning Chronicle, 1862. 56p [Same title: London, Algar, 1863. 83p] [BVaU NSHP OTU QMSS
LETTERS FROM NOVA SCOTIA AND NEW BRUNSWICK ILLUSTRATIVE OF THEIR MORAL, RELIGIOUS, AND PHYSICAL CIRCUMSTANCES DURING THE YEARS 1826, 1827, AND 1828. Edinburgh, Waugh & Innes, 1829. 201p [LC NSHD OTU
NOTES OF OUR TRIP ACROSS BRITISH COLUMBIA. Hamilton, Spectator Print., 1889. 34p [OTU

Armstrong, Nevill Alexander Drummond, 1878?–
AFTER BIG GAME IN THE UPPER YUKON. London, Long, 1937. 287p [BM BVaU LC OLU

Atkinson, Rev. William Christopher
THE EMIGRANT'S GUIDE TO NEW BRUNSWICK. Berwick-upon-Tweed, Warder's Office, 1842. 124p [Title change: A HISTORICAL AND STATISTICAL ACCOUNT OF NEW BRUNSWICK. Edinburgh, Anderson and Bryce, 1844. 3rd ed. improved and corrected. 284p] [BVaU QMM

Bailey, Joseph Whitman, 1865–1932
THE ST. JOHN RIVER IN MAINE, QUEBEC, AND NEW BRUNSWICK. Cambridge, Riverside Press, 1894. 178p [LC NSWA OTU

Baillie, Thomas, 1797?–1863
AN ACCOUNT OF THE PROVINCE OF NEW BRUNSWICK ... with Advice to Emigrants. London, Rivington, 1832. 134p [BM BVaU NSWA OTP

Baker, Everett
TRAILS AND TRACES OF RUPERT'S LAND AND THE NORTH-WEST TERRITORIES AS SEEN FROM 1940–1955. Shaunavon, Sask., 1955. 40p

Barbeau, Charles Marius, 1883–1969
I HAVE SEEN QUEBEC. Toronto, Macmillan, 1957. 1v [unpaged]
PATHFINDERS IN THE NORTH PACIFIC. Toronto, Ryerson, 1958. 235p

Barclay, Isabel
WORLDS WITHOUT END. Explorations from 2000 Years B.C. to To-day. New York, Doubleday, 1956. 352p [Later pub. in three separate vols.: V.1: THE EARLY EXPLORERS. London, Dobson, 1957. 154p; V.2: THE GREAT AGE OF DISCOVERY. London, Dobson, 1958. 168p; V.3: FILLING IN THE MAP. London, Dobson, [1959. 191p]

Barker, Bertram
NORTH OF '53. London, Methuen, 1934. 242p [BM BViPA LC OTU

Barnes, H.H.
JOURNAL OF A TRIP TO MANITOBA AND BACK, JUNE AND JULY 1878. Halifax, Doley, 1879. 22p [NSHP

Bartlett, Robert Abram, 1875–1946
THE LAST VOYAGE OF THE KARLUK. Flagship of Vilhjalmar Stefansson's Canadian Arctic Expedition of 1913–16. As Related by her Master, Robert A. Bartlett, and here set down by Ralph T. Hale. Boston, Small Maynard, 1916. 329p [Title changed to: NORTHWARD HO! THE LAST VOYAGE OF THE KARLUK. Boston, Small Maynard, 1919. 329p] [BM BVaU LC NBFU OTU QMM
SAILS OVER ICE. New York, Scribner, 1934. 301p [BM BVa LC

Baskine, Mrs. Gertrude
HITCH-HIKING THE ALASKA HIGHWAY. Toronto, Macmillan, 1944. 317p [BM
LC OTU QMM

Beaven, Rev. James, 1801–1875
RECREATIONS OF A LONG VACATION; or, A Visit to Indian Missions in Upper
Canada. Toronto, Rowsell, 1846. 196p [BM BVaU LC NSWA OKQ QMM

Bedford-Jones, Henry James O'Brien, 1887–1949
THE MYTH WAWATAM; or, Alex. Henry Refuted [and] ... Remarks upon ... Fort
Michillimackinac, All of Which is Herein Written & Publish'd from the Notes of
Henry McConnell, Gent. Santa Barbara, Author, 1917. 21p [LC

Belaney, George Stansfeld, 1888–1938
THE MEN OF THE LAST FRONTIER. By Grey Owl [pseud]. Toronto, Macmillan,
1932. 253p [BM BVaU LC NBFU OKQ

Bell, Charles Napier, 1854–1936
THE JOURNAL OF HENRY KELSEY (1691–1692), the First White Man to Reach the
Saskatchewan River from Hudson Bay. ... Winnipeg, Dawson Richardson, 1928.
43p [BVaU LC NSHD OLU
TANGWEERA, LIFE AND ADVENTURES AMONG GENTLE SAVAGES. London, Arnold,
1899. 318p [BM OTP

Bell, Rev. William, 1780–1857
HINTS TO EMIGRANTS. In a Series of Letters from Upper Canada. Edinburgh,
Waugh & Innes, 1824. 236p [BVaU LC NSWA OTP

Bennett, Rev. James, 1817–1901
DOWN EAST: WHERE TO GO; WHAT TO DO; HOW TO DO IT. Saint John, Chubb,
1872. 114p [NBB

Bernier, Joseph Elzéar, 1852–1934
REPORT ON THE DOMINION OF CANADA GOVERNMENT EXPEDITION TO THE
ARCTIC ISLANDS AND HUDSON STRAIT ON BOARD THE D.G.S. "ARCTIC,"
1906–1907. Ottawa, Gov't. Print. Bureau, 1910. 529p [BM BVaU NSWA OTU
QMM

Berton, Pierre Francis de Marigny, 1920–
THE MYSTERIOUS NORTH. New York, Knopf, 1956. 345 + xivp

Bickersteth, John Burgon, 1888–
THE LAND OF OPEN DOORS. Being Letters from Western Canada. London,
Gardner & Darton, 1914. xxiv + 265p [BM BVaU LC NBFU OTU

Bigsby, John Jeremiah, 1792–1881
THE SHOE AND CANOE; or, Pictures of Travel in the Canadas. ... London, Chapman
& Hall, 1850. 2v [BM BVaU LC NSWA OTU QMM

Binnie-Clark, Georgina

A SUMMER ON THE CANADIAN PRAIRIE. London, Arnold, 1910. 311p [BM BVaU LC OLU

Bird, William Richard, 1891–

OFF-TRAIL IN NOVA SCOTIA. Toronto, Ryerson, 1956. xiv + 314p

THESE ARE THE MARITIMES. Toronto, Ryerson, 1959. 333p

THIS IS NOVA SCOTIA. Toronto, Ryerson, 1950. 299p [BVaU LC NBFU OTP QMM

Blakeny, Charles Hanford, 1888–1961

"BITS AND PIECES." Rambling through Britain, France, Italy and Switzerland. [Moncton?], Author, 1954. 115p

"FRAGMENTS." Impressions of Holland, Belgium, Germany, Austria, Luxembourg, France, Italy, Scotland and England. [Moncton?], Author, 1956. 121p

Bonnycastle, Richard Henry, 1791–1847

CANADA AND THE CANADIANS IN 1846. London, Colburn, 1846. 2v [BM BVaU LC NSWA OTP

CANADA, AS IT WAS, IS, AND MAY BE. London, Colburn, 1852. 2v [A continuation of THE CANADAS IN 1841 and CANADA AND THE CANADIANS IN 1846.] [BM BVaU LC NSWA OTP QMM

THE CANADAS IN 1841. London, Colburn, 1841. 2v [Also pub. under title: THE CANADAS IN 1851 (!)] [BM BVaU LC NBFU OTP QMM

NEWFOUNDLAND, IN 1842. ... London, Colburn, 1842. 2v [BM BVaU NSWA OTU QMM

Borthwick, Rev. John Douglas, 1832–1912

... THE TOURIST'S PLEASURE BOOK; or, The Water Falls of Canada, its Lakes and Rivers. Montreal, Lovell, 1874. 28p [LC QMSS

Boulton, D'Arcy, 1759–1834

SKETCH OF ... UPPER CANADA. London, Rickaby, 1805. 99p [Also: Toronto, Baxter Pub. Co., 1961. 11 + 91p] [BM BVaU LC NSWA OTP QMM

Boulton, Henry John, 1790–1870

A SHORT SKETCH OF ... UPPER CANADA. ... London, Murray, 1826. 60p [BM OTP

Bramble, Charles A.

KLONDIKE. A Manual for Goldseekers. New York, Fenno, 1897. 313p [BVaU LC

LAND OF THE LOBSTICK. The Log of a Canoe Journey in The Pas District of Northern Manitoba. Winnipeg, Manitoba Publicity Commissioner, 1920. 20p [BVaU MWP OTU

Brown, James, 1790–1870

... NEW BRUNSWICK, AS A HOME FOR EMIGRANTS. ... Saint John, Barnes, 1860. 21p [BM NSWA OTP

Brown, James Bryce
VIEWS OF CANADA AND THE COLONISTS. ... By a Four Years' Resident [pseud].
Edinburgh, Black, 1844. 266p [2nd ed., enlarged: Edinburgh, Black, 1851.
xxxii + 468p] [BM BVaU LC NSWA OTU QMM

Bryce, Rev. George, 1844—1931
HOLIDAY RAMBLES BETWEEN WINNIPEG AND VICTORIA. Winnipeg, 1888. 87p
[MWU NSWA OLU

Brydone, James Marr
NARRATIVE OF A VOYAGE with a Party of Emigrants from Sussex, in 1834 ... to
Montreal, thence up the river Ottawa and through the Rideau Canal, to Toronto,
Upper Canada, and afterwards to Hamilton. London, Wilson, 1834. 66p [LC
OOP

Buchanan, Alexander Carlisle, 1786—1840
EMIGRATION PRACTICALLY CONSIDERED. London, Colburn, 1828. 148p [BM
OTP

Buchanan, Alexander Carlisle, 1808—1868
CANADA, 1863, FOR THE INFORMATION OF IMMIGRANTS. Quebec, Duquet, 1863.
49p [OTP
CANADA, FOR THE INFORMATION OF INTENDING EMIGRANTS. Quebec, Blackburn,
1864. 74p [OTP

Burpee, Lawrence Johnstone, 1873—1946
AMONG THE CANADIAN ALPS. New York, Lane, 1914. 239p [BM BVaU LC
NSHD OTU QMM
JUNGLING IN JASPER. Ottawa, Graphic, 1929. 200p [BM BVaU LC NSHD OTU
QMM
ON THE OLD ATHABASKA TRAIL. Toronto, Ryerson, [Pref., 1926]. 259p [BM
BVaU LC NSWA OTU QMM
THE SEARCH FOR THE WESTERN SEA. The Story of the Exploration of North-
Western America. New and rev. ed. Toronto, Macmillan, 1935. 2v [Earlier ed.:
Toronto, Musson, 1908. 651p] [BM BVaU NSHD OKQ QMM
SCOUTS OF EMPIRE. The Story of the Discovery of the Great North-West. Toronto,
Musson, 1912. 104p [BVaU QMM

Burrows, Charles Acton, 1853—1948
NORTH WESTERN CANADA. A Practical Guide to the Illimitable Fertile Regions of
Manitoba and the North West Territories. Winnipeg, Donaldson, 1880. 87p
[NSHP OTU

Burtis, William Richard M., 1818—1882
NEW BRUNSWICK, AS A HOME FOR EMIGRANTS. Saint John, Barnes, 1860. 50p
[NSWA OTP

Butler, William Francis, 1838–1910

FAR OUT. Rovings Re-told. London, Isbister, 1880. xx + 386p [BVaU OOU MWP

THE GREAT LONE LAND. A Narrative of Travel and Adventure in the North-West. London, Sampson Low, 1872. 388p [BM BVaU NSWA OTU QMM

THE WILD NORTH LAND. Being the Story of a Winter Journey, with Dogs, Across Northern North America. London, Sampson, 1873. 358p [Numerous other editions.] [BM BVaU LC NSWA OTU QMM

Call, Frank Oliver, 1878–1956

THE SPELL OF ACADIA. Boston, Page, 1930. 427p [BM BVaU LC NSHD OTU

THE SPELL OF FRENCH CANADA. Boston, Page, 1926. 372p [BM BVaU LC NSWA OTU QMM

Cameron, Agnes Deans, 1863–1912

THE NEW NORTH. A Woman's Journey through Canada to the Arctic. New York, Appleton, 1910. 398p [BM BVaU LC NSHD OTU QMM

Cameron, Alexander Alfred, 1912–

PRAIRIE PROGRESS. By Alex. A. Cameron and Leo Thordarson. Toronto, Dent, 1954. ix + 241p

Campbell, Mrs. Isabella, 1830–1887

MRS. CAMPBELL AND HER FRIEND AT THE FAIR. Montreal, 1901. [Dionne

ROUGH AND SMOOTH; or, Ho! for an Australian Gold Field. By Mrs. A. Campbell. Quebec, Hunter Rose, 1865. 138p [NSWA OTP QMSS

Campbell, Marjorie Elliott (Wilkins), 1901–

ONTARIO. Toronto, Ryerson, 1953. 219p

Campbell, Wilfred, 1858–1918

THE BEAUTY, HISTORY, ROMANCE AND MYSTERY OF THE CANADIAN LAKE REGION. Toronto, Musson, 1910. 191p [New and enl. ed.: Toronto, Musson, 1914. 215p Also various other editions.] [BM BVaU LC NBFU OTU

CANADA. Painted by T. Mower Martin. Described by Wilfred Campbell. London, Black, 1907. 272p [BM BVaU LC NSWA OKQ

Carmichael, Rev. James, 1835–1908

A HOLIDAY TRIP, MONTREAL TO VICTORIA AND RETURN, VIA THE CANADIAN PACIFIC RAILWAY, MIDSUMMER, 1888. [Anon] [Montreal? 1888?] 32p [OTP

Carnegie, Robert Kenneth, 1884–1951

AND THE PEOPLE CHEERED. Ottawa, Legionary Library, 1940. 176p [BM BViP NBFU OTP

Carrel, Frank, 1870–1940

CANADA'S WEST AND FARTHER WEST. Toronto, Musson, 1911. 258p [BM BVaU LC NSWA OKQ

THREE WEEKS OUT WEST. Quebec, Telegraph Print., 1919. 40p [QMBM

Carter, James, 1831–1925

IN THE WAKE OF THE SETTING SUN. London, Hurst & Blackett, 1908. [NfSG OKQ QMU

SIX MONTHS IN EUROPE AND THE ORIENT. Descriptive Letters. ... Montreal, Witness Press, 1906. 502p [AEU OTP NfSG

Cartwright, George, 1739–1819

A JOURNAL OF ... SIXTEEN YEARS ON THE COAST OF LABRADOR. ... Newark, Allin & Ridge, 1792. 3v [BM BVaU LC NSWA OTP

Cash, Gwen (Goldsmid), 1891–

I LIKE BRITISH COLUMBIA. Toronto, Macmillan, 1938. 192p [BM BVaU LC OTU

Cassap, Rev. William Henry, 1874–1949

WINNIPEG TO LONDON VIA HUDSON BAY. London, S.P.C.K., 1936. 48p [BVaU OLU

Chambers, Edward Thomas Davies, 1852–1931

THE ANGLER'S GUIDE TO EASTERN CANADA. Quebec, "Morning Chronicle," 1898. 114p [BM OTP

THE GUIDE TO QUEBEC. Quebec, Morning Chronicle, 1895. 129p [BM LC OTP

QUEBEC, LAKE ST. JOHN AND THE SAGUENAY. N.p., n.pub., 1902. 62p [NSWA

Chambers, Ernest John, 1862–1925

THE BOOK OF MONTREAL. A Souvenir of Canada's Commercial Metropolis. Montreal, Book of Montreal Co., 1903. 257p [BM OTP QMM

Champion, Helen Jean, 1910–1968

OVER ON THE ISLAND [Prince Edward Island]. Toronto, Ryerson, 1939. 262p [BVaU LC NSHD OTP

Champlain, Samuel de, 1567?–1635

VOYAGES OF SAMUEL DE CHAMPLAIN. Trans. by Charles Pomeroy Otis. Memoir by the Rev. Edmund F. Slafter. Boston, Prince Society, 1878–82. 3v [BM BVaU LC NSHD OTP

THE WORKS OF SAMUEL DE CHAMPLAIN. ...Ed. by H.P. Biggar. Toronto, Champlain Society, 1922–36. 6v [Translation.] [BM BVaU LC NSHD OTP

Charland, Gustave-Marquis

FACTS AND FANCIES. By Gustave-Marquis Charland and Dorothy Lovell Charland. Sherbrooke, Tribune, 1943. 404p [Bk.I (Travels) ... by G.M.C.; Bk.II (Poetry and Prose) by D.L.C.] [BVaU LC OTU QMM

Christie, Alexander James, 1787–1843
THE EMIGRANT'S ASSISTANT; or, Remarks on the Agricultural Interest of the
Canadas. ... Montreal, Mower, 1821. 2v [NSHD OTP QMBM

Clarke, George Frederick, 1883–
SIX SALMON RIVERS AND ANOTHER. London, Jenkins; Fredericton, Brunswick
Press, 1960. 190p

Coccola, Rev. Raymond de, 1912–
AYORAMA. By Raymond de Coccola and Paul King. Toronto, Oxford U. Press,
1955. 316p [Eskimo life as seen by a missionary.]

Cochrane, John Crawford, 1878–
TRAILS AND TALES OF THE NORTH LAND. Toronto, Committee on Young
People's Missionary Education, 1934. 162p [BVaU NBFU OTU

Coleman, Kathleen Blake (Watkins), 1864–1915
TO LONDON FOR THE JUBILEE. By Kit [pseud]. Toronto, Morang, 1897. 154p
[BM BVaU OTP

Colmer, Joseph Grose, 1856–1937
ACROSS THE CANADIAN PRAIRIES. A Two Months' Holiday in the Dominion.
London, European Mail, 1896. 85p [BM OLU SSU

Comeau, Napoleon Alexander, 1848–1923
LIFE AND SPORT ON THE NORTH SHORE OF THE LOWER ST. LAWRENCE AND
GULF. ... Quebec, Telegraph, 1909. 440p [2nd ed., 1923; 3rd ed., 1954.]
[BM BVaU LC NBFU OTU

Cormack, William Epps, 1796–1868
NARRATIVE OF A JOURNEY ACROSS THE ISLAND OF NEWFOUNDLAND. ...
St. John's, Morning Chronicle, 1873. 99p [Earlier ed., 1856; also London,
Longmans, 1928.] [BM BVaU NSWA OTU

Craig, Gerald Marquis, 1916–
EARLY TRAVELLERS IN THE CANADAS, 1791–1867. Ed. by ——. Toronto,
Macmillan, 1955. xxxvi + 300p

Croskill, John H., 1810–1855
COMPREHENSIVE OUTLINE OF THE GEOGRAPHY AND HISTORY OF NOVA SCOTIA.
By John Crosskill [sic]. Halifax, Author, 1838. 76p [Another ed., Halifax,
Crosskill & Co., 1842. 96p] [NSWA

Cross, Austin Fletcher, 1898–
CROSS ROADS. Montreal, Southam Press, 1936. 301p [BM BVaU LC OTU
SNOBS AND SPIRES. Toronto, Ryerson, 1937. 342p [BVaU QMM OTU

Crosskill, Herbert
NOVA SCOTIA. Its Climate, Resources, and Advantages. ... 2nd ed. Halifax,
Annand, 1874. 92p [BM LC OTU

Cumming, Robert Dalziel, 1871–

SAILING ON TO ICELAND; and ACROSS CANADA BY RAIL. Ashcroft, B.C., Ashcroft
Journal, 1937. 130p (Two works bound together.) [Also: London, Mitre Press,
1938. 79p] [BM BVaU OKQ

Cuppage, Edith M. (Reade)

HERE AND THERE ON VANCOUVER ISLAND. Victoria, Buckle, n.d. 28p
[BViPA OKQ

ISLAND TRAILS. Highways and Byways on Vancouver Island. Victoria, Buckle,
1945. 36p [BViPA

Daly, Thomas Mayne, 1852–1911

DESCRIPTION OF THE PROVINCE OF MANITOBA. Ottawa, King's Printer, 1893.
365p [OTL

Davenport, Mrs. N.

JOURNAL OF A FOURTEEN DAYS' RIDE THROUGH THE BUSH FROM QUEBEC TO
LAKE ST. JOHN. Quebec, Daily Mercury, 1872. 35p [BM BVaU OOP

Davies, Blodwen, 1897–1966

THE CHARM OF OTTAWA. Toronto, McClelland, 1932. 250p [BVaU OTP

GASPE, LAND OF HISTORY AND ROMANCE. New York, Greenberg, 1949. 233p
[BVaU LC OTU QMM

QUEBEC. Portrait of a Province. Toronto, Heinemann, 1951. 258p

ROMANTIC QUEBEC. New York, Dodd Mead, 1932. 213p [BVaU LC NBFU
OKQ

SAGUENAY "SAGINAWA," THE RIVER OF DEEP WATERS. Toronto, McClelland,
1930. 204p [BVaU LC OTU QMM

Davin, Nicholas Flood, 1843–1901

HOMES FOR THE MILLIONS. The Great Canadian North-West. Its Resources Fully
Described. Ottawa, Queen's Printer, 1891. 108p [OOA

Dawson, Rev. Aeneas MacDonell, 1810–1894

THE NORTH-WEST TERRITORIES AND BRITISH COLUMBIA. Ottawa, Mitchell, 1881.
232p [BM BVaU LC NSWA OLU

Dawson, Carl Addington, 1887–

THE NEW NORTHWEST. Ed. by ——. Toronto, U. of Toronto Press, 1947. 341p
[BM BVaU LC NSHD OTU

Dawson, Samuel Edward, 1833–1916

DISCOVERY OF AMERICA BY JOHN CABOT IN 1497 ... and the Voyages of the Cabots.
... Ottawa, Hope, 1896. 30p [BVaU NSHD OTU

HANDBOOK FOR THE DOMINION OF CANADA. ... Montreal, Dawson, 1884. 335p
[BM BVaU NSHD NBFU OTU QMM

Day, James Wentworth, 1899—
NEWFOUNDLAND, THE FORTRESS ISLE. Fredericton, pub. for the Govt. of Newfoundland by Brunswick Press, 1960. 65p

De La Roche, Mazo, 1879—1961
QUEBEC. Historic Seaport. Garden City, Doubleday, 1944. 212p [BM BVaU NBFU OKQ QMM

Delaute, Joseph François, 1909—
THE VOYAGEURS. Canoe Trip Diary, Hayes River, 1956. Ottawa, Author, 1957. 48p

Denis, Keith, 1909—
CANOE TRAILS THROUGH QUETICO. Toronto, Quetico Foundation, 1959. ix + 84p

Denison, Grace Elizabeth (Sandys), —1914
A HAPPY HOLIDAY. Toronto, 1890. 229p [AEU OLU

Denison, Merrill, 1893—
KLONDIKE MIKE. An Alaskan Odyssey. New York, Morrow, 1943. 393p [BM BVaU LC NBFU OTU QMM

Dennis, Clara
CAPE BRETON OVER. Toronto, Ryerson, 1942. 342p [BVaU LC NSHD OTU QMM
DOWN IN NOVA SCOTIA, MY OWN, MY NATIVE LAND. Toronto, Ryerson, 1934. 410p [BM BVaU LC NSHD OTU QMM
MORE ABOUT NOVA SCOTIA, MY OWN, MY NATIVE LAND. Toronto, Ryerson, 1937. 412p [BM BVaU LC NSWA OTU

Devine, Rev. Edward James, 1860—1927
ACROSS WIDEST AMERICA: NEWFOUNDLAND TO ALASKA. ... Montreal, Canadian Messenger, 1905. 307p [BVaU NBFU OTU QMM

Doane, Frank Augustus, 1862—1950
NOVA SCOTIA SKETCHES. Truro, Truro Pub. Co., 1949. 121p [BVaU NSHD OTUV

Douglas, David, 1798—1834
JOURNAL KEPT BY DAVID DOUGLAS DURING HIS TRAVELS IN NORTH AMERICA 1823—1827. ... London, Wesley, 1914. 364p [BM BVaU LC NSHD OTP

Douglas, George Mellis
LANDS FORLORN. A Story of an Expedition to Hearne's Coppermine River. ... New York, Putnam, 1914. 285p [BM BVaU LC NBFU OTU

Duncan, Dorothy, 1903—1957
BLUENOSE. A Portrait of Nova Scotia. New York, Harper, 1942. 273p [BVaU LC NSHD OTU QMSS

HERE'S TO CANADA! New York, Harper, 1941. 334p [BM BVaU LC NSHD OTU QMM

Duncan, John Morison, 1795?–1825

TRAVELS THROUGH PART OF THE UNITED STATES AND CANADA IN 1818 AND 1819. Glasgow [etc.], U. Press [etc.], 1823. 2v [BM BVaU LC NSWA OTP QMM

Duncan, Norman, 1871–1916

AUSTRALIAN BYWAYS. The Narrative of a Sentimental Traveller. New York, Harper, 1915. 293p [BM BVaU LC NBFU

GOING DOWN FROM JERUSALEM. The Narrative of a Sentimental Traveller. New York, Harper, 1909. 210p [BM BVaU LC OLU

Duncan, Sara Jeannette (Mrs. Everard Cotes), 1861–1922

A SOCIAL DEPARTURE. How Orthodocia and I Went round the World by Ourselves. London, Chatto & Windus, 1890. 417p [BM BVaU LC NSHD OTMC

Dunlop, William, 1792–1848

STATISTICAL SKETCHES OF UPPER CANADA, for the Use of Emigrants. By a Backwoodsman [pseud]. London, Murray, 1832. 120p [BM BVaU LC OTP

Edgar, James

NEW BRUNSWICK, AS A HOME FOR EMIGRANTS. ... Prize Essay. Saint John, Barnes, 1860. 37p [BM BVaU NSWA OTP

Edwards, Ralph, 1877?–

TRAIL TO THE CHARMED LAND. [Banff and the Rockies.] Saskatoon, H.R. Larson, 1950. 135p [OONL

Ellis, John Valentine, 1835–1913

NEW BRUNSWICK, AS A HOME FOR EMIGRANTS. ... First Prize Essay. ... Saint John, Barnes, 1860. 60p [BVaU NBFU OTP

Emberson, Alfred J.

ALL ABOUT VICTORIA. Victoria, Victoria Pub. Co., 1916. 104p [BM BVaU OTU

Emmerson, John

BRITISH COLUMBIA AND VANCOUVER ISLAND. Voyages, Travels & Adventures. Durham, Eng., Ainsley, 1865. 154p [BViPA LC OOP

Englebert, Reginald, 1911–

THIS IS OTTAWA. Toronto, Garden City Press Co-op., 1950. 64p [OONL
THIS IS TORONTO. Toronto, Garden City Press Co-op., 1950. 88p [OONL
THIS IS VANCOUVER ISLAND. Victoria, Diggon-Hibben, 1948. 88p [BVaU

Evans, Francis A., –1832

THE EMIGRANT'S DIRECTORY AND GUIDE to Obtain Lands and Effect a Settlement in the Canadas. Dublin [etc.], Curry [etc.], 1833. 180p [BM BVaU LC NSWA OTP QMM

Fairchild, George Moore, 1854–1912
ROD AND CANOE, RIFLE AND SNOWSHOE IN QUEBEC'S ADIRONDACKS. Quebec, Carrel, 1896. 207p [BM BVaU NSWA LC OTU QMM

Finnie, Richard, 1906–
CANADA MOVES NORTH. New York, Macmillan, 1942. 227p [Rev. ed.: Toronto, Macmillan, 1948. 239p] [BM BVaU LC NSHD OTU QMM
LURE OF THE NORTH. Philadelphia, McKay, 1940. 227p [BVaU LC OTU QMM

Fisher, John Wiggins, 1913–
CANADA. As Seen by the Camera of Yousuf Karsh and described in Words by John Fisher. Toronto, Allen, 1960. 165p

Fitzgibbon, Mary Agnes, 1851–1915
A TRIP TO MANITOBA; or, Roughing it on the Line. Toronto, Rose-Belford, 1880. 267p [BM BVaU LC NSWA OKQ SSU

Fleming, Sandford, 1827–1915
ENGLAND AND CANADA. A Summer Tour between Old and New Westminster. ... London, Low Marston, 1884. 449p [BM BVaU NSWA OTU QMM

Footner, Hulbert, 1879–1944
NEW RIVERS OF THE NORTH. A Yarn of Two Amateur Explorers of the Head Waters of the Fraser, Peace River, the Hay River, Alexandra Falls. New York, Doran, 1912. 281p [BM BVaU LC OTU QMM

Forster, Victor Wadham, 1909–
VANCOUVER THROUGH THE EYES OF A HOBO. By V.W.F. Vancouver, McCormick Press, 1934. 63p [OTP

Fraser, William, 1808–1892
THE EMIGRANT'S GUIDE; or, Sketches of Canada. ... By a Scotch Minister [pseud]. Thirty-six Years Resident in Canada, from 1831–1867. Glasgow, Porteous Bros., 1867. 72p [OTP

Futcher, Winnifred M. (Hall)
THE GREAT NORTH ROAD TO THE CARIBOO. Ed. by ——. Vancouver, Wrigley, 1938. 113p [BVaU LC NBFU OTU QMM

Galbraith, J.F.
A SKETCH OF BOTH SIDES OF MANITOBA. By Jeff Gee [pseud]. Nelsonville, Man., Manitoba Mountaineer Book & Job Print., 1881. 143p [OTU

Galloway, Christian F.J.
THE CALL OF THE WEST. Letters from British Columbia. New York, Stokes, 1916. 328p [BM BVaU LC NBFU OTP

Gesner, Abraham, 1797–1864
NEW BRUNSWICK. With Notes for Emigrants. London, Simmonds, 1847. 388p [BM BVaU LC NSWA OTP QMSS

Gilbert, Alexander Glen, 1840–1913
FROM MONTREAL TO THE MARITIME PROVINCES AND BACK. Montreal, Montreal Print. & Pub. Co., 1867. 63p [Also a facsimile ed., with an intro. by Douglas Lochhead. Toronto, Bibliographical Society of Canada, 1967.] [NSHL OOP QMBM

Gislason, Ingvar
PRAIRIE PANORAMA. A Brief Study of the Prairie Provinces. Calgary, Western Canada Institute, 1948. 196p [BVa LC OTU

Glass, Chester, −1921
THE WORLD: ROUND IT AND OVER IT. Being Letters. ... Toronto, Rose Belford, 1881. 528p [BM LC OTU QMM

Godsell, Philip Henry, 1889–1961
ARCTIC TRADER. The Account of Twenty Years with the Hudson's Bay Company. New York, Putnam, 1934. 329p [BM BVaU LC NBFU OTU QMM
RED HUNTERS OF THE SNOWS. An Account of Thirty Years' Experience with the Primitive Indian and Eskimo Tribes of the Canadian North-West and Arctic Coast. ... Toronto, Ryerson, 1938. 324p [BM BVaU LC OTU
THE ROMANCE OF THE ALASKA HIGHWAY. Toronto, Ryerson, 1944. 235p [BVaU LC OTU QMM

Goldie, John, 1793–1886
DIARY OF A JOURNEY THROUGH UPPER CANADA AND SOME OF THE NEW ENGLAND STATES, 1819. Toronto, Tyrrell, 1897. 56p [BVaU OKQ

Gomery, Percy, 1881–1960
HOT AND COLD LAID ON. Burrowing in Britain. By Percy and Bernadette Gomery. Toronto, Ryerson, 1946. 288p [BVaU LC OTU QMM
A MOTOR SCAMPER 'CROSS CANADA. ... Toronto, Ryerson, 1922. 208p [BM BVaU NBFU OTU QMM

Gordon, Rev. Daniel Miner, 1845–1925
MOUNTAIN AND PRAIRIE. A Journey from Victoria to Winnipeg, via Peace River Pass. Montreal, Dawson, 1880. 310p [BM BVaU LC NSWA OTU

Gourlay, Robert Fleming, 1778–1863
STATISTICAL ACCOUNT OF UPPER CANADA. ... London, Simpkin & Marshall, 1822. 2v [BM BVaU LC NBFU OTP

Gowland, John Stafford, 1898–
RETURN TO CANADA. London, Laurie, 1957. 199p
SIKANASKA TRAIL. London, Laurie, 1956. 207p

Grant, Rev. George Monro, 1835–1902
ARTISTIC QUEBEC DESCRIBED BY PEN AND PENCIL. Ed. by ——. Toronto, Belden,
   1888. 141p [OKQ
OCEAN TO OCEAN. Sandford Fleming's Expedition through Canada in 1872. ...
   Toronto, Campbell, 1873. 371p [Various later editions, enl. and rev. Imprint
   varies.] [BM BVaU LC NSWA OTU QMM
OUR PICTURESQUE NORTHERN NEIGHBOUR. Ed. by ——. Chicago, Belford, 1899.
   280p [BVaU NSWA OTP QMBM
PICTURESQUE CANADA. The Country as it was and is. Ed. by ——. Toronto,
   Belden, 1882. 2v [BM BVaU NSWA OTU QMM
PICTURESQUE SPOTS OF THE NORTH. Ed. by ——. Chicago, Belford, 1899. 205p
   [OLU

Gray, Hugh
LETTERS FROM CANADA, WRITTEN ... IN ... 1806, 1807, AND 1808, SHEWING THE
   PRESENT STATE OF CANADA ... THE COMMERCIAL IMPORTANCE OF NOVA-SCOTIA,
   NEW BRUNSWICK, AND CAPE BRETON. ... London, Longmans, 1809. 406p [BM
   BVaU NBS OTP QMG

Greenhill, Ralph Ackland, 1924–
THE FACE OF TORONTO. Toronto, Oxford U. Press, 1960. 22 + 58p

Grenfell, Wilfred Thomason, 1865–1940
ADRIFT ON AN ICE-PAN. New York, Houghton, 1909. 68p [BM BVaU LC NSHD
   OTU
LABRADOR LOOKS AT THE ORIENT. Notes of Travel in the Near and the Far East.
   Boston, Houghton, 1923. 297p [BM BVaU OTU QMM
LABRADOR, THE COUNTRY AND THE PEOPLE. By Wilfred T. Grenfell ... and Others.
   New York, Macmillan, 1909. 497p [BVaU LC NSHD OTU QMM
LABRADOR'S FIGHT FOR ECONOMIC FREEDOM. London, Benn, 1929. 36p [BM
   OTU
THE ROMANCE OF LABRADOR. New York, Macmillan, 1934. 329p [BM BVaU
   LC NSHD OTU QMM
VIKINGS OF TO-DAY; or, Life and Medical Work among the Fishermen of Labrador.
   London, Marshall, 1895. 240p [BM BVaU LC MWU NSWA OLU
A VOYAGE ON A PAN OF ICE. Boston, Ellis, 1908. 14p [LC OTU

Hadfield, Joseph, 1759–1851
AN ENGLISHMAN IN AMERICA, 1785. Being the Diary of ——. Ed. by Douglas S.
   Robertson. Toronto, Hunter Rose, 1933. 232p [BM BVaU LC NBFU OTP

Haight, Canniff, 1825–1901

HERE AND THERE IN THE HOME LAND. England, Scotland and Ireland, as seen by a Canadian. Toronto, Briggs, 1895. 616p [Later pub. as: A UNITED EMPIRE LOYALIST IN GREAT BRITAIN: Here & There in the Home Land. ... With a Biographical Introduction. ... Toronto, Briggs, 1904. 616p] [BM BVaU LC NBFU OTP

A UNITED EMPIRE LOYALIST IN GREAT BRITAIN. [See under HERE AND THERE IN THE HOME LAND.]

Haliburton, Thomas Chandler, 1796–1865

THE AMERICANS AT HOME; or, Byeways, Backwoods, and Prairies. Ed. by the Author of "Sam Slick". ... London, Hurst & Blackett, 1854. 3v [BM BVaU LC NSHD OTU QMM

A GENERAL DESCRIPTION OF NOVA SCOTIA. ... [Anon] Halifax, Royal Acadian School, 1823. 200p [Also: Halifax, Belcher, 1825. Occasionally this work is attributed to Clement Belcher or Walter Bromley.] [BM BVaU LC NSWA OTP

Hambleton, John O. ("Jack"), 1901–1961

HUNTER'S HOLIDAYS. Toronto, Longmans, 1947. 207p [BVaU LC OTP

Hamilton, James Cleland, 1836–1907

THE GEORGIAN BAY. An Account of its Position, Inhabitants, Mineral Interests, Fish, Timber and other Resources. Toronto, Carswell, 1893. 170p [BM BVaU LC NSWA OTU

THE PRAIRIE PROVINCE. Sketches of Travel from Lake Ontario to Lake Winnipeg, and an Account of the Geographical Position, Climate, Civil Institutions, Inhabitants, Productions and Resources of the Red River Valley. ... Toronto, Belford, 1876. 259p [BM BVaU LC NSWA OTU

Hamilton, John R.

NEW BRUNSWICK AND ITS SCENERY. A Tourists' and Anglers' Guide to the Province. ... Saint John, M'Millan, 1874. 157p [BVaU NSHD OTP QMBM

OUR ROYAL GUESTS. A Souvenir of the Visits of the Duke and Duchess of Cornwall and York and other members of the Royal Family to St. John and the Province of New Brunswick, Canada. Saint John, Hamilton, [1902]. 100p [LC NSWA

ST. JOHN AND THE PROVINCE OF NEW BRUNSWICK. A Handbook. 3rd ed. Saint John, Hamilton, 1884. 120p [BM BVaU LC NSHD OTP

Hamilton, Pierce Stevens, 1826–1893

NOVA-SCOTIA CONSIDERED AS A FIELD FOR EMIGRATION. London, Weale, 1858. 91p [BM LC NSWA OTU QMM

Hammond, Melvin Ormond, 1876–1934

CANADIAN FOOTPRINTS. A Study in Foregrounds and Backgrounds. Toronto, Macmillan, 1926. 305p [BM BVaU LC NSWA OLU

Hardy, Campbell, 1831–1919

FOREST LIFE IN ACADIE. Sketches of Sport and Natural History in the Lower
Provinces of the Canadian Dominion. London, Chapman & Hall, 1869. 371p
[BM BVaU LC NSWA OTU

SPORTING ADVENTURES IN THE NEW WORLD; or, Days and Nights of Moose-
Hunting in the Pine Forests of Acadia. London, Hurst & Blackett, 1855. 2v
[BM BVaU LC NSHD OTU

Harmon, Daniel Williams, 1778–1845

A JOURNAL OF VOYAGES AND TRAVELS IN THE INTERIOUR OF NORTH AMERICA ...
from Montreal nearly to the Pacific Ocean. ... Andover, Flagg & Gould, 1820.
xxiv + 432p [Also: Toronto, Morang, 1904. 382p; and: Toronto, Courier, 1911.
382p] [BM BVaU NSWA OTU QMSS

SIXTEEN YEARS IN THE INDIAN COUNTRY. The Journal of Daniel Williams Harmon,
1800–1816. Ed. with an intro. by W. Kaye Lamb. Toronto, Macmillan, 1957.
xxviii + 277p

Harrington, Evelyn (Davis), 1911–

MANITOBA ROUNDABOUT. Toronto, Ryerson, 1951. xii + 237p

Harrington, Michael Francis, 1916–

SEA STORIES FROM NEWFOUNDLAND. Toronto, Ryerson, 1958. xi + 172p

Harrington, Richard Walter, 1911–

BRITISH COLUMBIA IN PICTURES. Text by Lyn Harrington. Toronto, Nelson, 1958.
1v [unpaged]

THE FACE OF THE ARCTIC. A Cameraman's Story in Words and Pictures of Five
Journeys into the Far North. New York, Schuman, 1952. xii + 369p

NORTHERN EXPOSURES. Canada's Backwoods and Barrens Pictured in Monochrome
and Color. Text and arrangement by Clifford Wilson. New York, Schuman;
Toronto, Nelson, 1953. 119p

Hart-McHarg, William F.R., 1869–1915

FROM QUEBEC TO PRETORIA, with the Royal Canadian Regiment. Toronto, Briggs,
1902. 276p [BVaU NBFU OKQ

Harvey, Daniel Cobb, 1886–

JOURNEYS TO THE ISLAND OF ST. JOHN OR PRINCE EDWARD ISLAND, 1775–1832.
Ed. by ——. Toronto, Macmillan, 1955. 213p

Harvey, Rev. Moses, 1820–1901

ACROSS NEWFOUNDLAND WITH THE GOVERNOR. A Visit to our Mining Region; and
This Newfoundland of Ours. Being a Series of Papers on the Natural Resources
and Future Prospects of the Colony. St. John's, "Morning Chronicle," 1879.
122p [LC NSWA OOA

NEWFOUNDLAND AS IT IS IN 1894. A Hand-Book and Tourist's Guide. St. John's,
Withers, 1894. 298p [BVaU LC NSHD OTP QMU

Hearne, Samuel, 1745–1792

JOURNALS OF SAMUEL HEARNE AND PHILIP TURNOR. Ed. with intro. by J.B. Tyrrell. Toronto, Champlain Society, 1934. xviii + 611 + xiip [BM BVaU LC NSHD OTP QMM

A JOURNEY FROM PRINCE OF WALES' FORT IN HUDSON'S BAY, TO THE NORTHERN OCEAN ... IN THE YEARS 1769, 1770, 1771, & 1772. London, Strahan & Cadell, 1795. xliv + 458p [New ed., with intro. and notes by J.B. Tyrrell: Toronto, Champlain Society, 1911. xv + 437 + viip. Also ed. with intro. by Richard Glover. Toronto, Macmillan, 1958. lxxii + 301p] [BM BVaU LC NSWA OKQ

Heming, Arthur Henry Howard, 1870–1940

THE DRAMA OF THE FORESTS. Romance and Adventure. Garden City, Doubleday, 1921. 324p [BVaU LC NBFU OKQ

Henry, Alexander, 1739–1824

TRAVELS AND ADVENTURES IN CANADA and the Indian Territories, between the Years 1760 and 1776. ... New York, Riley, 1809. 330p [New ed. with notes by James Bain: Toronto, Morang, 1901. xxxv + 41 + 347p] [BM BVaU LC NSWA OTP

Henry, Alexander, –1814

HENRY'S JOURNAL, Covering Adventures and Experiences in the Fur Trade on the Red River, 1799–1801. Ed. by Charles N. Bell. Winnipeg, Manitoba Free Press, 1888–89. 2v [BVaU LC OTP

NEW LIGHT ON THE EARLY HISTORY OF THE GREATER NORTHWEST. THE MANU-SCRIPT JOURNALS OF ALEXANDER HENRY ... AND OF DAVID THOMPSON ... 1799–1814. Ed. by Elliott Coues. New York, Harper, 1897. 3v [Edited and condensed from the MS copy in the Library of Parliament, Ottawa, made by George Coventry, Montreal, 1824.] [BM BVaU LC NBFU OTP QMM

Henry, George

THE EMIGRANT'S GUIDE, OR CANADA AS IT IS. ... Quebec, Gray, [1834?]. xxiv + 173p [NSWA OTU

Heriot, George, 1766–1844

TRAVELS THROUGH THE CANADAS. ... London, Phillips, 1807. 602p [BM BVaU LC NSWA OTU

Herring, Frances Elizabeth (Clarke), 1851–1916

AMONG THE PEOPLE OF BRITISH COLUMBIA, Red, White, Yellow and Brown. London, Unwin, 1903. 299p [BM BVaU LC NBFU OOA

CANADIAN CAMP LIFE. London, Unwin, 1900. 247p [BM BVaU LC NSHD

IN THE PATHLESS WEST WITH SOLDIERS, PIONEERS, MINERS AND SAVAGES. London, Unwin, 1904. 240p [BM BVaU LC NBFU OTP

Hill, S.S.

THE EMIGRANT'S INTRODUCTION TO AN ACQUAINTANCE WITH THE BRITISH

AMERICAN COLONIES, AND THE PRESENT CONDITION AND PROSPECTS OF THE
COLONISTS. London, Parbury, 1837. 324p [BM OTP

A SHORT ACCOUNT OF PRINCE EDWARD ISLAND. ... By the Author of "The
Emigrant's Introduction. ..." [pseud]. London, Madden, 1839. 90p [BVaU
LC NSWA OTP QMM

Hind, Ella Cora, 1861–1942

MY TRAVELS AND FINDINGS. Toronto, Macmillan, 1939. 185p [OTU QMBM

Hind, Henry Youle, 1823–1908

THE CANOE ROUTE BETWEEN FORT WILLIAM, LAKE SUPERIOR, AND FORT GARRY,
RED RIVER. ... 1857. Toronto, Derbishire & Desbarats, 1858. 16p [BM GTP
SSU

EXPLORATIONS IN THE INTERIOR OF THE LABRADOR PENINSULA. London,
Longmans, 1863. 2v [BM BVaU LC NSWA OLU

LAKE SUPERIOR AND THE RED RIVER SETTLEMENT. Presented to ... Parliament by
Command of Her Majesty. London, Eyre & Spottiswoode, 1859. 163p [BM OTP

NARRATIVE OF THE CANADIAN RED RIVER EXPLORING EXPEDITION OF 1857, and
of the Assinniboine [sic] and Saskatchewan Exploring Expedition of 1858.
London, Longmans, 1860. 2v [BM BVaU LC NSWA OLU

NORTH-WEST TERRITORY. ... Assiniboine and Saskatchewan Exploring Expedition.
... Toronto, Lovell, 1859. 201p [With supplementary volume: PHOTOGRAPHS
ACCOMPANYING A REPORT ON THE ASSINIBOINE AND SASKATCHEWAN
EXPLORING EXPEDITION. N.p., n.d.] [BM BVaU LC NSWA OTP QMM

A SKETCH OF AN OVERLAND ROUTE TO BRITISH COLUMBIA. Toronto, Chewett,
1862. 129p [BVaU NSWA OLU

Hinton, Arthur Cherry

THE YUKON. By A. Cherry Hinton in Collaboration with Philip H. Godsell.
Toronto, Ryerson, 1954. xiv + 184p

Hodgins, Samuel Raymond Norris, 1895–

SO THIS IS QUEBEC! By Norris Hodgins. St. Anne de Bellevue, Author, 1926. 29p
[BVaU QMSS

Hollingsworth, S.

THE PRESENT STATE OF NOVA SCOTIA. ... [Anon] 2nd ed., enl. Edinburgh,
Creech, 1787. 221p [1st ed. in 1786. 157p] [BM BVaU NSWA OKQ QMM

Hooper, John, 1791–1869

THE ADVANTAGES OF EMIGRATING TO THE BRITISH COLONIES OF NEW
BRUNSWICK, NOVA SCOTIA, ETC. By a Resident of St. John [pseud]. London,
Wilson, 1832. 71p [BM EngCat NBB

Horetsky, Charles G., 1840–1900

CANADA ON THE PACIFIC. Being an Account of a Journey from Edmonton to the
Pacific by the Peace River Valley; and of a Winter Voyage Along the Western

Coast of the Dominion. ... Montreal, Dawson, 1874. 244p [BVaU LC NSWA OTU QMM

Howard, Hilda (Glynn), 1887–

THE GLAMOUR OF BRITISH COLUMBIA. By H. Glynn-Ward [pseud]. Toronto, Macmillan, 1926. 238p [BVaU LC NBFU OTU

Howard, W.H.

GLIMPSES IN AND ABOUT HALIFAX. ... [Halifax], W.H. Howard, [1897?]. 80p [NSHD

Howay, Frederic William, 1867–1943

VOYAGES OF THE "COLUMBIA" TO THE NORTHWEST COAST 1787–1790 AND 1790–1793. Ed. by ——. Boston, Massachusetts Historical Society, 1941. 518p [BM BVaU LC NBFU OTP

Hunter, George, 1921–

CANADA IN COLOUR. By George Hunter and Leslie Roberts. Toronto, Clarke Irwin, 1959. 88p

Hunter, William S.

EASTERN TOWNSHIPS SCENERY. Stanstead, Hunter, 1860. 35p [BM BVaU NSWA OTL

HUNTER'S PANORAMIC GUIDE FROM NIAGARA FALLS TO QUEBEC. Montreal, Dawson; Boston, Jewitt, 1857. 66p [Later ed., Montreal, Hunter & Pickup, 1860. 66p] [BM BVaU LC OLU

OTTAWA SCENERY. Ottawa, Hunter, 1855. 16p [BVaU LC NSWA OTU

Hutchison, Bruce, 1901–

THE UNKNOWN COUNTRY. Canada and her People. New York, Coward McCann, 1942. 386p [Toronto, Longmans, 1943. 326p] [BM BVaU LC NSHD OKQ QMM

Innis, Mary E. (Quayle), 1899–1972

TRAVELLERS WEST. Toronto, Clarke Irwin, 1956. ix + 339p

Jackson, Alexander Young, 1882–

THE FAR NORTH. A Book of Drawings ... with an Intro. by Dr. F.G. Banting, and Descriptive Notes by the Artist. Toronto, Rous & Mann, [1928?]. 8p 17 plates. [BVaU NSHD OKQ

Jacobs, Rev. Peter, 1808–1858

JOURNAL OF THE REVEREND PETER JACOBS. ... From Rice Lake to the Hudson's Bay Territory ... 1852. ... Toronto, Green, 1853. 32p [2nd ed.: Boston, Rand,

1853. 55p; 3rd ed.: New York, Author, 1858. 96p] [BM BViPA LC NSWA
OTP

Jarvis, Thomas Stinson, 1854–1926

LETTERS FROM EAST LONGITUDES. Sketches of Travel in Egypt, the Holy Land,
Greece, and Cities of the Levant. Toronto, James Capmbell, 1875. 267p [AEU
OTP

Johnston, Lukin

BEYOND THE ROCKIES. Three Thousand Miles by Trail and Canoe through
Little-known British Columbia. Toronto, Dent, 1929. 212p [BM BVaU LC
OLU

Johnstone, Walter

LETTERS, DESCRIPTIVE OF PRINCE EDWARD ISLAND. Dumfries, Swan, 1822. 72p
[BM OTP

TRAVELS IN PRINCE EDWARD ISLAND ... in ... 1820–21. Edinburgh [etc.], Brown
[etc.], 1823. 132p [BM BVaU LC NSWA OTP

Judson, William Lee, 1842–1928

A TOUR OF THE THAMES. Written and Illustrated with A. Faber's B.B. By Professor
Blot [pseud]. London, Ont., Advertiser, 1881. 140p [Cover title:
KUHLEBORN.] [OLU

Kane, Paul, 1810–1871

WANDERINGS OF AN ARTIST AMONG THE INDIANS OF NORTH AMERICA. From
Canada to Vancouver's Island and Oregon, through the Hudson's Bay Company's
Territory and Back Again. London, Longman, Brown, etc., 1859. 455p [Also:
Toronto, Radisson Society, 1925. 329p] [BM BVaU LC NSWA OTU SSU

Kavanagh, Martin, 1895–

ASSINIBOINE BASIN. A Social Study of the Discovery, Exploration, and
Settlement of Manitoba. Winnipeg, Public Press, 1946. 282p [BVaU LC NSHD
OTU QMBM

Kelsey, Henry, 1670?–1724?

THE KELSEY PAPERS. With an intro. by Arthur G. Doughty ... & Chester Martin. ...
Ottawa, Acland, 1929. lxxxiii + 128p [BVaU LC NBFU OTP QMBM

Kennedy, Ida Mara

TOURING QUEBEC AND THE MARITIMES. Toronto, Armac Press, 1929. 112p
[OTU

Kingsford, William, 1819–1898

IMPRESSIONS OF THE WEST AND SOUTH DURING A SIX WEEKS' HOLIDAY. [Anon]
Toronto, Armour, 1858. 83p ["These letters first appeared in a Toronto
newspaper" –Preface.] [BM LC NSWA OTU

Kitto, Franklin Hugo, 1880–
MAXWELLTON DISTRICT, NOVA SCOTIA. A new Area for Settlement in an old
settled Province. Ottawa, Dept. of the Interior, 1924. 44p [NSHP OONL
QMSS

Knott, Leonard Lewis, 1905–
HIGHWAYS OF HISTORY. Montreal, Northern Electric Co., 1954. 28p

Kristjansson, Adalsteinn
IN THE WEST. Santa Barbara, Schauer Print., 1935. 3v [BVa LC

Ladue, Joseph
KLONDYKE FACTS. Being a Complete Guide Book to the Gold Regions of the Great
Canadian Northwest Territories and Alaska. Montreal, Lovell, 1897. 205p [BM
BVaU LC NSWA OTU
KLONDYKE NUGGETS. Being a Brief Description of the Famous Gold Regions of
the Great Canadian Northwest and Alaska. Montreal, Lovell, 1897. 92p [BM
BVaU OTU

Landon, Fred, 1880–1969
LAKE HURON. ... Indianapolis, Bobbs-Merrill, 1944. 398p [BM BVaU LC OKQ
QMM

Lanphier, Rev. Charles B.
OUR TRIP TO ROME. Toronto, Catholic Truth Society of Canada, 1953. 207p

Large, Richard Geddes, 1901–
PRINCE RUPERT, A GATEWAY TO ALASKA. Vancouver, Mitchell Press, 1960. 210p

Lauder, Mrs. Maria Elise Turner
EVERGREEN LEAVES. Being Notes from my Travel Book. By Toofie [pseud].
Toronto, Belford, 1877. 384p [Same as following title.] [OTU
EVERGREEN LEAVES; or, "Toofie" in Europe. Toronto, Rose, 1884. 384p [NBFU
OTP

Laut, Agnes Christina, 1871–1936
THE CONQUEST OF OUR WESTERN EMPIRE. New York, McBride, 1927. 363p
[BVaU LC OTU
PATHFINDERS OF THE WEST. Being the Thrilling Story of the Adventures of the
Men who Discovered the great Northwest. New York, Macmillan, 1904. 380p
[BVaU LC NSWA OTU
VIKINGS OF THE PACIFIC. The Adventures of the Explorers who came from the
West, Eastward. Toronto, Macmillan, 1905. 349p [BVaU OTU

Lawson, Jessie Isabel, 1879–1961
THIS IS NEW BRUNSWICK. By Jessie I. Lawson and Jean MacCallum Sweet. Toronto,
Ryerson, 1951. 202p

Lawson, John
LETTERS ON PRINCE EDWARD ISLAND. Charlottetown, Haszard, 1851. 76p [NSHP

Leacock, Stephen Butler, 1869–1944
ADVENTURERS OF THE FAR NORTH. A Chronicle of the Frozen Seas. Toronto, Glasgow Brook, 1914. 152p [BM BVaU LC NSWA OTU QMM
THE DAWN OF CANADIAN HISTORY. A Chronicle of Aboriginal Canada and the Coming of the White Man. Toronto, Glasgow Brook, 1914. 112p [BM BVaU LC NSWA OTU
THE MARINER OF ST. MALO. A Chronicle of the Voyages of Jacques Cartier. Toronto, Glasgow Brook, 1914. 125p [BM BVaU LC NSHD OTU
MONTREAL: SEAPORT AND CITY. Garden City, Doubleday, 1942. 340p [BM BVaU LC NSHD OTU QMM

Lebourdais, Donat Marc, 1887–
NORTHWARD ON THE NEW FRONTIER. Ottawa, Graphic, 1931. 311p [BM BVaU LC OTU

Leechman, John Douglas, 1890–
ESKIMO SUMMER. Toronto, Ryerson, 1945. 247p [BM BVaU LC NBFU OTP
INDIAN SUMMER. Toronto, Ryerson, 1949. 182p [BVaU LC NBFU OTU QMM

LeMoine, James MacPherson, 1825–1912
HISTORICAL AND SPORTING NOTES ON QUEBEC AND ITS ENVIRONS. ... Quebec, Demers, 1889. 133p [1st ed.: Montreal, Burland, 1879. 30p] [BM BVaU OTU QMM
PICTURESQUE QUEBEC. A Sequel to QUEBEC PAST AND PRESENT. [See above p.701]. Montreal, Dawson, 1882. 535p [BM BVaU NSHD OKQ QMM
THE TOURIST'S NOTE-BOOK. By Cosmopolite [pseud]. 2nd ed. Quebec, Garant, 1876. 64p [BVaU NSHP OOA QMSS

Liddell, Kenneth Eric, 1912–
ALBERTA REVISITED. Toronto, Ryerson, 1960. xiv + 234p
THIS IS ALBERTA. Toronto, Ryerson, 1952. 190p
THIS IS BRITISH COLUMBIA. Toronto, Ryerson, 1958. xiv + 250p

Lighthall, William Douw, 1857–1954
MONTREAL AFTER 250 YEARS. Montreal, Grafton, 1892. 149p [Also pub. under title: SIGHTS AND SHRINES OF MONTREAL. Montreal, Grafton, 1907. 180p] [BM BVaU LC NSWA OTU QMBM

Lillie, Rev. Adam, 1803–1869
CANADA. Physical, Economic and Social. Toronto, Maclear, 1855. 294p [BM BVaU LC NSHD OLU

Littlehales, Edward Baker, —1825

JOURNAL ... of an Exploratory Tour ... Niagara to Detroit, made in ... 1793 by ... Lieut.-Gov. Simcoe. With intro. and notes by Henry Scadding. Toronto, Copp Clark, 1889. 23p [OTP

Livesay, John Frederick Bligh, 1875—1944

PEGGY'S COVE. Toronto, Ryerson, 1944. 100p [BVaU LC NBFU OTP

Lofthouse, Rev. Joseph, 1855—1933

A THOUSAND MILES FROM A POST OFFICE; or, Twenty Years' Life and Travel in the Hudson's Bay Regions. Toronto, Macmillan, 1922. 183p [BM BVaU LC OTP

Long, John, fl. 1768—1791

VOYAGES AND TRAVELS OF AN INDIAN INTERPRETER AND TRADER. London, Author, 1791. 295p [BM BVaU LC NSWA OTP

Low, Albert Peter, 1861—1942

REPORT ON EXPLORATIONS IN THE LABRADOR PENINSULA ... IN 1892—93—94—95. Ottawa, Queen's Printer, 1896. 387p [BM BVaU LC NBSM OKQ

Lucas, Rev. Daniel Vannorman, 1834—1911

ALL ABOUT CANADA. Montreal, Witness, 1883. 72p [BViPA OTP
CANAAN AND CANADA. Toronto, Briggs, 1904. 247p [BVaU LC OTP

Lugrin, Charles Henry, 1846—1917

NEW BRUNSWICK (CANADA): its Resources, Progress and Advantages. Fredericton, Gov't. of New Brunswick, 1886. 191p [BM BVaU LC NBFU OTU
YUKON GOLD FIELDS. ... Victoria, Colonist, 1897. 32p [BVaU LC QMM

Lugrin, Nellie de Bertrand, 1874—

A HANDBOOK OF VANCOUVER ISLAND. Victoria, Buckle, [19—?]. 51p [BM BViP OTP

Lyons, Chester Peter, 1915—

MILESTONES ON THE MIGHTY FRASER. Toronto, Dent, 1950. xxxvi + 157p [Also: Vancouver, Evergreen Press, 1957. xv + 215p] [OONL

McAlpine, Thomas H.

McALPINE'S ILLUSTRATED TOURISTS' AND TRAVELLERS' GUIDE. ... NOVA SCOTIA, NEW BRUNSWICK AND PRINCE EDWARD ISLAND. Saint John, Sun Print., 1897. 692p [BM OTP

Macaulay, R.H.H.

TRADING INTO HUDSON'S BAY. A Narrative of the Visit of Patrick Ashley Cooper. ... Winnipeg, Hudson's Bay Co., 1934. 108p [BM BVaU LC OTU

Macbeth, Madge Hamilton (Lyons), 1878–1965
OVER THE GANGPLANK TO SPAIN. Ottawa, Graphic, 1931. 359p [BVaU
  OTUV QQL

McCormick, James Hanna
LLOYDMINSTER; or, 5000 Miles with the Barr Colonists. London, Drane's,
  [1924?]. 254p [BM BVaU OTP SSU

McDiarmid, Margaret Agnes (Galloway)
I LIVED IN PARADISE. Winnipeg, Bulman, 1943. 257p [OTP

MacDonald, Rev. Alexander, 1858–1941
STRAY LEAVES; or, Traces of Travel. New York, Christian Press Assoc., 1914.
  171p [BViPA OOU

McDonald, Archibald, 1790–1853
PEACE RIVER: A CANOE VOYAGE FROM HUDSON'S BAY TO THE PACIFIC BY THE
  LATE SIR GEORGE SIMPSON ... IN 1828; Journal of the Late Chief Factor,
  Archibald McDonald ... who Accompanied him. Ed. with Notes by Malcolm
  McLeod. Ottawa, Durie, 1872. 119p [BVaU LC NSWA OTP QMM

Macdonald, Rev. James Alexander, 1862–1923
WHAT A NEWSPAPERMAN SAW IN BRITAIN. Toronto, the Globe, 1909. 30p
  [NBFU OTU

Macdonald, Rev. Peter McLaren
LETTERS FROM THE CANADIAN WEST. Truro, N.S., Chronicle, 1903. 55p
  [BVaU NSWA OKQ SSU

MacDonald, Wilson Pugsley, 1880–1967
ON MY OWN IN MOSCOW. Toronto, Northern Book House, 1958. 37p

MacDougall, James Brown, 1871–1950
TWO THOUSAND MILES OF GOLD. From Val d'Or to Yellowknife. Toronto,
  McClelland, 1946. 234p [BVa OTU

McDougall, Margaret (Dixon), 1826–1898
THE LETTERS OF "NORAH" [pseud] ON HER TOUR THROUGH IRELAND. Being a
  series of Letters to the Montreal "Witness" as Special Correspondent to Ireland.
  Montreal, Pub. by Public Subscription, 1882. 303p [OTP QMSS

McEachren, Duncan McNab, 1841–1924
A TRIP TO BOW RIVER. Montreal, n.pub., [1888?]. 23p [NSWA

McEvoy, Bernard, 1842–1932
FROM THE GREAT LAKES TO THE WIDE WEST. Impressions of a Tour between
  Toronto and the Pacific. Toronto, Briggs, 1902. 288p [BM BVaU LC OTP
  QMBM

MacEwan, Grant, 1902–
BETWEEN THE RED AND THE ROCKIES. Toronto, U. of Toronto Press, 1952. 300p

McGrath, Patrick Thomas, 1868–1929
NEWFOUNDLAND IN 1911. ... London, Whitehead, Morris & Co., 1911. 271p [BM
   BVaU NSHD OTU QMM

Mackay, Robert Walter Stuart, 1809?–1854
THE STRANGER'S GUIDE TO ... CANADA. ... Montreal, Bryson, 1854. 168p [OTP
   QMM
THE STRANGER'S GUIDE TO THE ISLAND AND CITY OF MONTREAL. Montreal,
   Lovell & Gibson, 1848. 46p [OOC QMBM

McKenna, James Andrew Joseph, 1862–1919
THE HUDSON BAY ROUTE. A Compilation of Facts with Conclusions. Ottawa,
   Dept. of Interior, 1907. 54p [BVaU OLU QMBM SSU

Mackenzie, Alexander, 1764–1820
VOYAGES FROM MONTREAL ... through the Continent of North America, to the
   Frozen and Pacific Oceans; in the Years 1789 and 1793. With a Preliminary
   Account of ... the Fur Trade. ... London, Cadell, etc., 1801. cxxxii + 412p
   [Many later editions.] [BM BVaU LC NSWA OTP QMM

Mackenzie, John, 1895–
ONTARIO IN YOUR CAR. By John and Marjorie Mackenzie. Toronto, Clarke
   Irwin, 1950. xvii + 291p [OONL
QUEBEC IN YOUR CAR. By John and Marjorie Mackenzie. Toronto, Clarke Irwin,
   1952. xii + 302p

MacKinnon, John [of P.E.I.]
TRAVELS IN BRITAIN, FRANCE, PRUSSIA, SWITZERLAND, ITALY, BELGIUM AND
   HOLLAND. ... Summerside, P.E.I., Schurman & Taylor, [189–?]. [NSHD

Maclean's Magazine
CANADA. Portrait of a Country. Sel. and ed. by Leslie F. Hannon. Toronto,
   McClelland, 1960. 248p

MacLennan, Kenneth John, 1878–
NOVA SCOTIA. Her Rivers, Lakes, and History. New York, Vantage Press, 1956.
   88p

McNaughton, Margaret (Peebles)
OVERLAND TO CARIBOO. An Eventful Journey of Canadian Pioneers to the
   Gold-Fields of British Columbia in 1862. ... Toronto, Briggs, 1896. 176p [BM
   BVaU LC NBFU OTU QMM

Macoun, John, 1831–1920
MANITOBA AND THE GREAT NORTH WEST. An Encyclopaedia of Information in

Regard to the Great North West. ... Guelph, World Pub. Co., 1882. 687p [BM BVaU NSWA OTP QMM

MacVicar, Nell

TALES AND TRAILS OF WESTERN CANADA. By —— and Irene Craig. Regina, School Aids & Text Book Pub. Co., 1947. 144p [BVaU SSU

McVicar, Robert

LETTERS ON EMIGRATION from the British Isles, and the Settlement of the Waste Lands in the Province of Canada. Hamilton, Hewson, 1853. 118p [BVaU LC OTP QMBM

MacWhirter, Margaret Grant, —1940

TREASURE TROVE IN GASPE AND THE BAIE DES CHALEURS. 3rd ed. Quebec, Telegraph Print., 1919. 217p [BM BVaU NBFU OTP QMBM

Magrath, Thomas William, 1769—1851

AUTHENTIC LETTERS FROM UPPER CANADA. With an Account of Canadian Field Sports. Ed. by the Rev. T. Radcliff. Dublin [etc.], Curry [etc.], 1833. 334p [Reprinted: Toronto, Macmillan, 1953. xxiv + 207p] [BVaU LC NSWA OTP QMM

Mair, Charles, 1838—1927

THROUGH THE MACKENZIE BASIN. A Narrative of the Athabasca and Peace River Treaty Expedition of 1899. Toronto, Briggs, 1908. 494p [BM BVaU LC NBFU OTP QMBM

Manitoba. Travel and Publicity Bureau

MANITOBA GUIDE BOOK. Winnipeg, King's Printer, 1951. 207p

Manning, Ella Wallace (Jackson), 1910—

IGLOO FOR THE NIGHT. By Mrs. Tom Manning. London, Hodder, 1943. 232p [Canadian ed.: Toronto, U. of Toronto Press, 1946. 234p] [BM BVaU NSHD OTP QMM

A SUMMER ON HUDSON BAY. London, Hodder, 1949. 223p [BM BVa LC NBFU OTP QMM

Marsden, Rev. Joshua, 1777—1837

THE NARRATIVE OF A MISSION TO NOVA SCOTIA, NEW BRUNSWICK, AND THE SOMERS ISLANDS; with a Tour to Lake Ontario. To which is added, THE MISSION, An Original Poem. ... Plymouth-Dock, Johns, 1816. 289p [2nd ed., 1827.] [BM BVaU LC NSWA OTP QMSS

Maxwell, Lilian Mary (Beckwith), 1877—1956

'ROUND NEW BRUNSWICK ROADS. Toronto, Ryerson, 1951. 191p

Menzies, George, 1796?—1847

ALBUM OF THE TABLE ROCK, NIAGARA FALLS. ... Ed. by ——. Niagara, Chronicle Office, 1846. 79p [LC

Middleton, Jesse Edgar, 1872–1960
CANADIAN LANDSCAPE. As Pictured by F.H. Brigden. ... Biographical Notes by
J.E. Middleton. Toronto, Ryerson, 1944. 111p [BM BVaU LC OTP QMM
THE ROMANCE OF ONTARIO. Toronto, Gage, 1931. 267p [BM BVaU LC OLU

Mitchell, Peter, 1824–1899
THE WEST AND NORTHWEST. Notes of a Holiday Trip. Reliable Information for
Immigrants. Montreal, 1880. 63p [BM OTP QMM SSU

Montague, Sydney Robert
I LIVED WITH THE ESKIMOS. New York, McBride, 1939. 222p [BM BVaU LC
NORTH TO ADVENTURE. New York, McBride, 1939. 284p [BM BVaU LC
OTU QMM

Moodie, John Wedderburn Dunbar, 1797–1869
TEN YEARS IN SOUTH AFRICA. London, Bentley, 1835. 2v [BM LC

Moon, Robert James, 1925–
I FOUND CANADA ABROAD. Toronto, Ryerson, 1957. xx + 156p
THIS IS SASKATCHEWAN. Toronto, Ryerson, 1953. 242p

Moore, Philip Hooper, 1879–1961
WITH GUN AND ROD IN CANADA. London, Cape, 1922. 260p [BM BVaU
LC NSHD OKQ

Moorsom, William Scarth, 1804–1863
LETTERS FROM NOVA SCOTIA. Comprising Sketches of a Young Country.
London, Colburn & Bentley, 1830. 371p [BM BVaU LC NSWA OTP QMM

Morgan, Henry James, 1842–1913
THE TOUR OF H.R.H. THE PRINCE OF WALES THROUGH BRITISH AMERICA AND THE
UNITED STATES. By A British Canadian [pseud]. Montreal, Lovell, 1860. 271p
[BM BVaU LC NBFU OLU

Morris, Alexander, 1826–1889
THE HUDSON'S BAY AND PACIFIC TERRITORIES. A Lecture. ... Montreal, Lovell,
1859. 57p [BM BVaU NSWA OTP QMSS

Morton, Arthur Silver, 1870–1945
UNDER WESTERN SKIES. Being a Series of Pen-Pictures of the Canadian West in
Early Fur Trade Times. Toronto, Nelson, 1937. 232p [BM BVaU LC
NBFU OTP QMM

Mountain, Rev. George Jehoshaphat, 1789–1863
JOURNAL OF THE BISHOP OF MONTREAL DURING A VISIT TO THE CHURCH
MISSIONARY SOCIETY'S N.W. AMERICA MISSION. London, Seeley, 1845. 236p
[2nd ed.: London, Seeley, 1849. 1xxxix + 166p] [BM BVaU LC NSWA
OTP QMM

VISIT TO THE GASPE COAST, 1824. Quebec, King's Printer, 1941–42. 44p [NSHD OOA QMSS

Mowat, Farley McGill, 1921–
THE DESPERATE PEOPLE. Boston, Little Brown, 1959. xii + 305p [Refers to the Ihalmiut Eskimos: Sequel to PEOPLE OF THE DEER.]
ORDEAL BY ICE. Ed. by ——. Toronto, McClelland, 1960. 364p
PEOPLE OF THE DEER. London, Joseph, 1952. 316p [Also: Boston, Little Brown, 1952. 344p; reprinted, 1958. 320p] [Account of two years spent with the Ihalmiut, an almost extinct Eskimo tribe of the Keewatin District.]

Mullock, Rev. John Thomas, 1807–1869
LECTURES ON NEWFOUNDLAND. St. John's, Patriot Office, 1860. 37p [LC
TWO LECTURES ON NEWFOUNDLAND. New York, Mullaly, 1860. 60p [BM QMSS

Munn, Henry Toke
PRAIRIE TRAILS AND ARCTIC BY-WAYS. London, Hurst & Blackett, 1932. 288p [BM BVaU LC NBFU OTP QMM
TALES OF THE ESKIMO. Being Impressions of a ... People. London, Chambers, 1925. 196p [BM BVaU LC NBFU OLU QMM

Munro, William F.
THE BACKWOODS OF ONTARIO, AND THE PRAIRIES OF THE NORTH WEST. London, Simpkin Marshall, 1881. 127p [BM OTP
EMIGRATION MADE EASY; or, How to Settle on the Prairie. ... Glasgow, Macrone, 1883. 10p [BViPA NSWA

Murphy, Emily Gowan (Ferguson), 1868–1933
THE IMPRESSIONS OF JANEY CANUCK ABROAD. Toronto, 1902. 186p [BM OTP
JANEY CANUCK IN THE WEST. London, Cassell, 1910. 305p [Also: London, Dent, 1919. 223p] [BM BVaU OKQ
OPEN TRAILS. By "Janey Canuck" [pseud]. London, Cassell, 1912. 291p [BM BVaU LC NBFU OTP
SEEDS OF PINE. By Janey Canuck [pseud]. London, Hodder, 1914. 307p [Also: Toronto, Musson, 1922. 301p] [BM BVaU LC NBFU OTP

Neilson, Joseph, 1813–1888
OBSERVATIONS UPON EMIGRATION TO UPPER CANADA. [Prize Essay.] Kingston, Chronicle & Gazette, 1837. 74p [OTP

Newcombe, Charles Frederic, 1851–
THE FIRST CIRCUMNAVIGATION OF VANCOUVER'S ISLAND. Victoria, Cullin, 1914. 69p [BM BVaU LC OTU

Niven, Frederick John, 1878–1944
CANADA WEST. London, Dent, 1929. 188p [BM BVaU LC NSHD OONL
COLOUR IN THE CANADIAN ROCKIES. By Walter J. Phillips and Frederick Niven.
Toronto, Nelson, 1937. 125p [BM BVaU NSHPL SRL
GO NORTH, WHERE THE WORLD IS YOUNG. Alaska ... Atlin, Land of Reflections
and Moods. ... N.p., n.d. 38p [BVaU QMBM

O'Brien, Godfrey S.
THE TOURIST'S GUIDE TO QUEBEC. Quebec, Hunter Rose, 1864. 70p [OTP

Ogilvie, William, 1846–1912
THE KLONDIKE OFFICIAL GUIDE. Toronto, Hunter Rose, 1898. 152p [BVaU LC
NSWA OTP
LECTURE ON THE KLONDIKE MINING DISTRICT. Victoria, Wolfenden, 1897. 14p
[BVaU OTU
LECTURE ON THE YUKON GOLD FIELDS (CANADA) DELIVERED AT VICTORIA, B.C.
Rev., amplified, and authorized by the Lecturer. Victoria, Colonist Press, 1897.
32p [OTU QMM
THE YUKON TERRITORY. The Narrative of W.H. Dall ... 1866–1868. The Narrative
of an Exploration made in 1887 ... by George M. Dawson. Extracts from the
Report of an Exploration made in 1896–1897 by Wm. Ogilvie. London, Downey,
1898. 438p [OTU QMSS

O'Gorman, P.T.
MAGNIFICENT ONTARIO. Ilfracombe, Devon, Stockwell, 1952. 175p

Onraet, Anthony (Tony)
SIXTY BELOW. With an intro. by Dr. Thomas Wood. Toronto, Cape, 1944. 192p
[Also pub. as: DOWN NORTH. London, Cape, 1944. 157p] [BM BVa LC
NBFU OTP QMBM

Oppenheimer, David, 1834–1897
VANCOUVER CITY. Its Progress and Industries, With Practical Hints for Capitalists
and Intending Settlers. Vancouver, 1889. 64p [NSWA OOA

Orford, Mrs. Mena
JOURNEY NORTH. Toronto, McClelland, 1957. 190p [Experiences among the
Eskimos of Baffin Island.]

Ottawa Publicity Department
INDUSTRIAL AND PICTURESQUE OTTAWA, THE CAPITAL OF THE DOMINION OF
CANADA. Ottawa, Crain, 1905. 40p [LC
OTTAWA, CANADA, THE GREAT CHEAP POWER CITY. ... Ottawa, Esdale, 1912.
48p [LC OTU
OTTAWA, CANADA'S CAPITAL. Ottawa, City Council, [1904?]. 49p [LC

Outram, James, 1864–1925

IN THE HEART OF THE CANADIAN ROCKIES. London, Macmillan, 1905. 466p
[BVaU LC NSHD OTU

Outram, Joseph, 1803–1885

A HANDBOOK OF INFORMATION FOR THE EMIGRANTS TO NOVA SCOTIA. Halifax,
1864. 36p [BM

NOVA SCOTIA. Its Condition and Resources. Edinburgh, Blackwood, 1850. 35p
[BM

Page, Mrs. Elizabeth Merwin, 1889–

WAGONS WEST. A Story of the Oregon Trail. New York, Farrar, 1930. 361p
[Narrative based on letters of Henry Page.] [BViPA LC

WILD HORSES AND GOLD. From Wyoming to the Yukon. New York, Farrar, 1932.
362p [Narrative based on a diary kept by "Kansas Gilbert."] [BM BVaU LC
OTU

Palliser, John, 1807–1887

EXPLORATION. ... The Journals ... Relative to the Exploration, by Captain Palliser
... between the Western Shore of Lake Superior and the Pacific Ocean during the
Years 1857, 1858, 1859, and 1860. London, Eyre & Spottiswoode, 1863. 325p
[BVaU NSWA OTP

THE SOLITARY HUNTER; or, Sporting Adventures in the Prairies. London,
Routledge, 1856. 234p [BM BViPA LC OOC

SOLITARY RAMBLES AND ADVENTURES OF A HUNTER IN THE PRAIRIES. London,
Murray, 1853. 326p [BM BVaU LC MWU OTP QMM

Panton, James Hoyes, 1847–1898

RAMBLES IN THE NORTH-WEST, ACROSS THE PRAIRIES, AND IN THE PASSES OF THE
ROCKY MOUNTAINS. Guelph, Mercury Steam Print., 1885. 20p [BVa NSWA
OTP

Parker, Gilbert, 1862–1932

ROUND THE COMPASS IN AUSTRALIA. London, Hutchinson, 1892. 447p [Another
ed. pub. in Melbourne.] [BM BVaU OTP

Parkin, George Robert, 1846–1922

THE GREAT DOMINION. Studies of Canada. London, Macmillan, 1895. 251p [BM
BVaU NBFU OTP QMM

Peat, Louisa (Watson)

CANADA, NEW WORLD POWER. Toronto, McLeod, 1945. 293p [BVaU LC OTP
QMM

Percival, Walter Pilling, 1885–1966

THE LURE OF MONTREAL. Toronto, Ryerson, 1945. 240p [BVaU LC OTU QMM

THE LURE OF QUEBEC. Toronto, Ryerson, 1941. 216p [Also later eds.] [BM
BVaU LC OTP QMM

Phillipps-Wolley, Clive Oldnall, 1854–1918
SAVAGE SWANETIA. London, Bentley, 1883. 2v [BM BViP OTU
A SPORTSMAN'S EDEN. London, Bentley, 1888. 261p [BM BVaU OTU QMBM
TROTTINGS OF A TENDERFOOT; or, A Visit to the Columbian Fiords and Spitz-
bergen. London, Bentley, 1884. 252p [BM BVaU NSWA OTP

Phillips, Walter J.
COLOUR IN THE CANADIAN ROCKIES. By Walter J. Phillips and Frederick Niven.
Toronto, Nelson, 1937. 125p [BM BVaU NSHPL SRL

Pike, Warburton Mayer, 1861–1915
THE BARREN GROUND OF NORTHERN CANADA. New York, Macmillan, 1892. 300p
[Also: New York, Dutton, 1917. 334p] [BM BVaU LC NSWA OTP QMM
THROUGH THE SUBARCTIC FOREST. New York, Arnold, 1896. 295p [BM BVaU
LC OTU QMM

Pinkerton, Kathrene Sutherland (Gedney), 1887–
FARTHER NORTH. New York, Harcourt, 1944. 181p [BM BVaU LC
FOX ISLAND. New York, Harcourt, 1942. 195p [BM BVaU LC OOP
THREE'S A CREW. New York, Carrick & Evans, 1940. 316p [BM BVa LC NSHD
OTU QMM
WILDERNESS WIFE. New York, Carrick & Evans, 1939. 327p [BM BVaU LC
NSHD QMM

Pocock, Roger, 1865–1941
TALES OF WESTERN LIFE, LAKE SUPERIOR, AND THE CANADIAN PRAIRIE.
Ottawa, Mitchell, 1888. 164p [BM BViPA OTU

Porter, Jane
A SIX WEEKS' TOUR IN WESTERN CANADA. By a Lady [pseud]. Montreal, Lovell,
1865. 40p [OTP

Potvin, Damase, 1881–
THE SAGUENAY TRIP. Montreal, Canada Steamship Lines, [195–?]. 124 + xiip

Price, Bertha Maud (Weston), 1872–1955
THE TRAIL OF THE BROAD HIGHWAY. [With] Pen and Ink Sketches by Maude
Gage Pellerin. Sherbrooke, Que., Authors, 1929. 121p [OONL QMBM

Prowse, Daniel Woodley, 1834–1914
THE NEWFOUNDLAND GUIDE-BOOK, 1905. Ed. by ——. London, Bradbury & Agnew,
1905. 182p [BM LC NBFU OTU QMM

Pyke, Magnus, 1909–
GO WEST, YOUNG MAN, GO WEST. Ottawa, Graphic, 1930. 303p [BVaU NBFU
OOP

Reid, Edgar Cameron, 1902—
FAST FLOWS THE FRASER. New York, Comet Press, 1958. 45p

Reid, J.H. Stewart, 1909—1963
MOUNTAINS, MEN AND RIVERS. British Columbia in Legend and Story. Toronto, Ryerson, 1954. x + 229p

Reynolds, Helen Mary Greenwood (Campbell) Dickson, 1884—
UP CANADA WAY. By Helen Dickson [pseud]. Boston, Heath, 1942. 64p [LC

Reynolds, William Kilby, 1848—1902
PLEASANT PLACES BY THE SHORE AND IN THE FORESTS OF QUEBEC AND THE MARITIME PROVINCES. ... [Anon] Toronto, Dixon, [1882?]. 65p [NBFU OTP QMSS

Rickard, Thomas Arthur, 1864—1953
JOURNEYS OF OBSERVATION. San Francisco, Dewey, 1907. 130p [LC
THROUGH THE YUKON AND ALASKA. San Francisco, Mining and Scientific Press, 1909. 392p [BVaU LC OTP

Roberts, Charles George Douglas, 1860—1943
THE CANADIAN GUIDE-BOOK. The Tourist's and Sportsman's Guide to Eastern Canada and Newfoundland. ... New York, Appleton, 1891. 270p [Several later eds. with slight change in sub-title.] [BM BVaU NSWA OTU QMM
DISCOVERIES AND EXPLORATIONS IN THE CENTURY. ... (Nineteenth Century Series). Philadelphia, Linscott, 1904. 529p [BM BVaU LC NSHD
THE LAND OF EVANGELINE AND THE GATEWAYS THITHER. ... With Many Illustrations and Appendices for Sportsman and Tourist. Kentville, Dominion Atlantic Railway Co., [1894?]. 92p [BM BVaU NSWA OKQ QMBM

Roberts, Leslie, 1896—
HOME FROM THE COLD WARS. Boston, Beacon Press, 1948. 224p [BVaU LC OTP
SO THIS IS OTTAWA. Toronto, Macmillan, 1933. 222p [BM BVaU OTP QMM

Robertson, Douglas Sinclair, 1877—
TO THE ARCTIC WITH THE MOUNTIES. Toronto, Macmillan, 1934. 309p [BVaU NBFU OTU QMM

Robinson, Frank Alfred, 1874—
FRIENDLY LETTERS FROM F.A.R. AWAY. Toronto, Mundy-Goodfellow, 1937. 172p [OTU
GUEST ROOMS ENJOYED AND ENDURED IN THE KING'S SERVICE. Toronto, Missions of Biblical Education, 1933. 256p [BViPA NBSaM OLU

Robinson, Judith
AS WE CAME BY. Toronto, Dent, 1951. 160p

Roger, Charles, 1819–1878
GLIMPSES OF LONDON, AND ATLANTIC EXPERIENCES ... IN THE WINTER OF 1872–73.
Ottawa, Robertson Roger, 1873. 47p [BM QMSS

Rogers, Robert, 1731–1795
A CONCISE ACCOUNT OF NORTH AMERICA. London, Millan, 1765. 264p [Also:
Dublin, Milliken, 1769. 264p] [BM BVaU LC NSWA OTP QMM

Roper, Edward
BY TRACK AND TRAIL. A Journey through Canada. With Numerous Original
Sketches by the Author. London, Allen, 1891. 455p [BM BVaU LC NBFU
OTU

Rose, Rev. A.W.H.
THE EMIGRANT CHURCHMAN IN CANADA; or, Canada in 1849. Pictures of Canadian
Life by a Pioneer of the Wilderness. Ed. by the Rev. Henry Christmas. London,
Bentley, 1849. 2v [Also issued as CANADA IN 1849.] [BVaU NBFU OTP
QMSS

Ross, Alexander, 1783–1856
ADVENTURES OF THE FIRST SETTLERS ON THE OREGON OR COLUMBIA RIVER.
Being a Narrative of the Expedition Fitted out by John Jacob Astor. ... London,
Smith Elder, 1849. 352p [Also: Cleveland, Ohio, Clark, 1904. 332p] [BM BVaU
NBFU OTP QMM
THE FUR HUNTERS OF THE FAR WEST. ... London, Smith Elder, 1855. 2v
[Also: Chicago, Donnelly, 1924, and Norman, U. of Oklahoma Press, 1956.]
[BM BVaU LC NSHD OTP QMM

Ross, Rev. William Wilson, 1838–1884
10,000 MILES BY LAND AND SEA. Toronto, Campbell, 1876. 284p [BM BVaU
LC OTP

Rowlands, John James, 1892–
CACHE LAKE COUNTRY. Life in the North Woods. New York, Norton, 1947.
272p [BM BVaU LC OTP QMM

Ryerson, Rev. John, 1800–1878
HUDSON'S BAY; or, A Missionary Tour. ... Toronto, Sanderson, 1855. xxiv + 190p
[BM BVaU NSWA OTP QMM

St. John, Frederick Edward Molyneux, 1838–1904
THE SEA OF MOUNTAINS. An Account of Lord Dufferin's Tour through British
Columbia in 1876. London, Hurst & Blackett, 1877. 2v [BM BVaU OTP

Schaffer, Mary Townsend (Sharples), 1861–1939
OLD INDIAN TRAILS OF THE CANADIAN ROCKIES. Incidents of Camp and Trail
Life. Toronto, Briggs, 1911. 364p [BM BVaU NBFU OTU

Schrag, Alexander Andrew, 1907–

CRATER COUNTRY. By Lex Schrag. Toronto, Ryerson, 1958 [i.e., 1959]. ix + 169p

Scott, H.G.

FROM STORM TO STORM. Vancouver, Sun Pub. Co., 1947. 242p [BVaU OLU QMBM

Scott, H. Percy, 1856–1937

SEEING CANADA AND THE SOUTH. Toronto, Briggs, 1911. 137p [BM BVaU NSWA OTU QMBM

Secretan, James Henry Edward, 1852–1926

TO THE KLONDYKE AND BACK. A Journey down the Yukon from its Source to its Mouth. ... With Hints to Intending Prospectors. London, Hurst & Blackett, 1898. 260p [BM BVaU OTP QMM

Seton, Ernest Thompson, 1860–1946

THE ARCTIC PRAIRIES. A Canoe Journey of 2,000 Miles in Search of the Caribou. Being the Account of a Voyage to the Region north of Aylmer Lake. ... New York, Scribner, 1911. 415p [BM BVaU LC NBFU OKQ QMM

Sharcott, Margaret (Brampton), 1928–

TROLLER'S HOLIDAY. London, Davies, 1957. 221p [Account of a voyage around Vancouver Island.]

Sibbald, Thomas, 1810–1890

A FEW DAYS IN THE UNITED STATES AND CANADA, With Some Hints to Settlers. [Anon] London, 1846. 48p [BM

Silver, Arthur Peters, 1851–1908

FARM-COTTAGE, CAMP AND CANOE IN MARITIME CANADA; or, The Call of Nova Scotia to the Emigrant and Sportsman. Toronto, Musson, 1908. 249p [BM BVaU LC NSWA OKQ QMM

THROUGH MIRAMICHI WITH ROD AND RIFLE; or, A Birch-bark Canoe Trip in Northern New Brunswick. Halifax, Holloway, 1890. 30p [OOP

Sime, Jessie Georgina, 1880–

IN A CANADIAN SHACK. London, Dickson, 1937. 241p [BM BVaU LC NSHD OTP QMM

Simpson, George, 1787–1860

CALIFORNIA. ... From Sir George Simpson's OVERLAND JOURNEY ROUND THE WORLD. ... By John T. Hughes. Cincinnati, James, 1848. 105p [LC

FUR TRADE AND EMPIRE. George Simpson's Journal. Ed. by Frederick Merk. Cambridge, Harvard U. Press, 1931. xxxvi + 370p [BM BVaU LC NSHD OTP QMM

JOURNAL OF OCCURRENCES IN THE ATHABASCA DEPARTMENT ... 1820 AND 1821, AND REPORT. Ed. by E.E. Rich, with a foreword by Lord Tweedsmuir and an

intro. by Chester Martin. Toronto, Champlain Soc., 1938. lix + 498p [BM
BVaU LC NBFU OTP

NARRATIVE OF A JOURNEY ROUND THE WORLD, DURING THE YEARS 1841 AND
1842. London, Colburn, 1847. 2v [BM BVaU LC NBFU OTP QMM

NARRATIVE OF A VOYAGE TO CALIFORNIA PORTS IN 1841–42. ... From the
NARRATIVE OF A VOYAGE ROUND THE WORLD. ... San Francisco, Russell,
1930. 232p [BViPA LC

AN OVERLAND JOURNEY ROUND THE WORLD, DURING THE YEARS 1841 AND 1842.
Philadelphia, Lee & Blanchard, 1847. 272p [BViPA LC OTP QMM

PART OF DISPATCH FROM GEORGE SIMPSON, ESQR., GOVERNOR OF RUPERTS LAND,
TO THE GOVERNOR AND COMMITTEE OF THE HUDSON'S BAY COMPANY ... 1829.
Ed. by E.E. Rich, with an intro. by W.S. Wallace. Toronto, Champlain Society,
1947. 277p [BM BVaU LC NBFU OTP QMM

Sinclair, Gordon Allan, 1900–

BRIGHT PATHS TO ADVENTURE. Toronto, McClelland, 1945. 280p [BVaU NBFU
OTP

FOOT-LOOSE IN INDIA. New York, Farrar, 1933. 312p [BM BVaU LC OTU QMM

CANNIBAL QUEST. Toronto, Doubleday, 1933. 300p [BM BVaU LC NBFU OTU

KHYBER CARAVAN. Toronto, Oxford U. Press, 1936. 316p [BM LC OTU

LOOSE AMONG THE DEVILS. A Voyage from Devil's Island. Toronto, Doubleday,
1935. 276p [BM BVa LC NBFU OTU

SIGNPOSTS TO ADVENTURE. Toronto, McClelland, 1947. 369p [BVa OOP

Sleigh, Burrows Willcocks Arthur, 1821–1869

PINE FORESTS AND HACMATACK CLEARINGS; or, Travel, Life and Adventure in
the British North American Provinces. London, Bentley, 1853. 408p [BM
BVaU LC NBFU OTP QMM

Smallwood, Joseph Roberts, 1900–

THE BOOK OF NEWFOUNDLAND. Ed. by ——. St. John's, Newfoundland Book
Pub., 1937. 2v [BM BVaU LC NSHD OTP QMM

THE NEW NEWFOUNDLAND. An Account of the Revolutionary Developments which
are Transforming Britain's Oldest Colony from "The Cinderella of the Empire"
into one of the Great Small Nations of the World. New York, Macmillan, 1931.
277p [BM BVaU LC NBFU OTU QMM

Smith, Goldwin, 1823–1910

A TRIP TO ENGLAND. Toronto, Robinson, 1888. 61p [Same title: New York,
Macmillan, 1892. 136p] [BM BVaU LC NBFU OKQ QMM

Smith, Thomas Barlow, 1839–1933

LITTLE MAYFLOWER LAND. Halifax, Bowes, 1900. 80p [LC NSHD OTP QMM

Smith, William Henry, fl. 1846–1873

CANADA. ... A Historical, Geographical, Geological and Statistical Account of
Canada West. Toronto, Maclear, 1851. 2v [BM BVaU LC NSWA OTP QMM

SMITH'S CANADIAN GAZETTEER. Comprising Statistical and General Information
... of ... Canada West. Toronto, Rowsell, 1846. 285p [BM BVaU LC NSWA
OTP QMM

Somerville, Alexander, 1811–1885

CANADA, A BATTLE FIELD. (TRAVELS IN CANADA AND THE FRONTIER UNITED
STATES). Hamilton, 1862. 64p [BM OTP QMM
THE WHISTLER AT THE PLOUGH. Manchester, Ainsworth, 1852. 632p [BM LC
OTP

Spedon, Andrew Learmont, 1831–1884

RAMBLES AMONG THE BLUE-NOSES; or, Reminiscences of a Tour through New
Brunswick and Nova Scotia ... 1862. Montreal, Lovell, 1863. 229p [BVaU LC
NBFU OTP QMM
SKETCHES OF A TOUR FROM CANADA TO PARIS, by way of the British Isles, during
the Summer of 1867. Montreal, Lovell, 1868. 238p [BM BVaU NSWA OLU

Spragge, Ellen Elizabeth (Cameron), 1854–1932

FROM ONTARIO TO THE PACIFIC BY THE C.P.R. By Mrs. Arthur Spragge. Toronto,
Robinson, 1887. 188p [BM BVaU LC NSWA OTU QMSS

Springer, John S.

FOREST LIFE AND FOREST TREES. Winter Camp-life among the Loggers, and Wildwood Adventure. New York, Harper, 1851. 259p [BM BVaU LC OTP

Sproat, Gilbert Malcolm, 1832–1913

DESCRIPTION OF KOOTENAY DISTRICT. Victoria, Wolfenden, 1884. 30p [LC
SCENES AND STUDIES OF SAVAGE LIFE. London, Smith Elder, 1868. 317p [BM
BVaU LC OTP

Steele, Harwood Elmes Robert, 1897–

POLICING THE ARCTIC. ... Toronto, Ryerson, 1936. 390p [BM BVaU LC OTP
QMM

Stefansson, Vilhjalmur, 1879–1962

THE ADVENTURE OF WRANGEL ISLAND. New York, Macmillan, 1925. 424p [BM
BVaU LC NSHD OTP QMM
THE ARCTIC IN FACT AND FABLE. New York, Foreign Policy Assoc., 1945. 96p
[BVaU LC OTP
THE FRIENDLY ARCTIC. Five Years in Polar Regions. New York, Macmillan, 1921.
xxxi + 784p [BM BVaU LC NBFU OTP QMM
GREAT ADVENTURES AND EXPLORATIONS. Ed. by ——. New York, Dial Press,
1947. 788p [BVaU LC NBFU OTP QMM
GREENLAND. Garden City, Doubleday, 1942. 338p [BM BVaU LC NSHD OTP
QMM

HUNTERS OF THE GREAT NORTH. New York, Harcourt, 1922. 301p [BM BVaU LC OKQ QMM

ICELAND: FIRST AMERICAN REPUBLIC. New York, Doubleday, 1939. 275p [BM BVaU OTU

MY LIFE WITH THE ESKIMO. New York, Macmillan, 1913. 538p [New and abridged ed.: New York, Macmillan, 1927.] [BM BVaU LC NSHD OTP QMM

THE NORTHWARD COURSE OF EMPIRE. New York, Harcourt, 1922. 274p [BM BVaU LC NSHD OTU

NORTHWEST TO FORTUNE. The Search of Western Man for a Commercially Practical Route to the Far East. New York, Duell Sloan, 1958. xix + 356p

NOT BY BREAD ALONE. New York, Macmillan, 1946. 339p [BVaU OTU QMM

THE SHAMAN'S REVENGE. By Violet Irwin, based on the Arctic Diaries of Vilhjalmur Stefansson. New York, Macmillan, 1925. 286p [LC OTMC

THREE VOYAGES OF MARTIN FROBISHER. In Search of a Passage to Cathay and India by the North-West, A.D. 1576–8. London, Argonaut Press, 1938. 2v [NBFU OTU

ULTIMA THULE. Further Mysteries of the Arctic. New York, Macmillan, 1940. 383p [BM BVaU LC NSHD OTP QMM

UNSOLVED MYSTERIES OF THE ARCTIC. ... With an intro. by Stephen Leacock telling how this Book Came to be Written. New York, Macmillan, 1939. 381p [BM LC OTU

Stewart, Rev. Charles James, 1775–1837

THE EASTERN TOWNSHIPS IN THE PROVINCE OF LOWER CANADA. Montreal, Mower, 1815. 18p [BVaU NSWA OTP

REPORT OF A MISSIONARY JOURNEY ... THROUGH UPPER CANADA IN 1820. Ed. by James J. Talman. London, Ont., University of Western Ontario, 1942. 18p [BVaU LC OTP OTU QMM

A SHORT VIEW OF THE PRESENT STATE OF THE EASTERN TOWNSHIPS IN THE PROVINCE OF LOWER CANADA. Montreal, Hatchard, 1815. 20p [BM BVaU NSWA QMM

Stewart, Elihu, 1844–1935

DOWN THE MACKENZIE AND UP THE YUKON IN 1906. New York, Lane, 1913. 270p [BM BVaU LC NBFU OTP QMM

Stewart, John, 1758?–1834

AN ACCOUNT OF PRINCE EDWARD ISLAND. London, Winchester, 1806. 304p ˙ [BM BVaU NSHD OTP QMM

Strachan, Rev. John, 1778–1867

A JOURNAL OF VISITATION TO THE WESTERN PORTION OF HIS DIOCESE ... 1842. 3rd ed. London, Soc. for the Propagation of the Gospel, 1846. 64p [LC OTP QMM

REMARKS ON EMIGRATION FROM THE UNITED KINGDOM. London, Murray, 1827. 96p [BM OTP

Stuart, Charles, 1783–1865
THE EMIGRANT'S GUIDE TO UPPER CANADA; or, Sketches of the Present State of that Province. London, Longmans, 1820. 335p [BM BVaU NSHD OTP QMBM

Stuck, Rev. Hudson, 1863–1920
TEN THOUSAND MILES WITH A DOG SLED. A Narrative of Winter Travel in Interior Alaska. New York, Scribner, 1914. 420p [BM BVaU LC OTP QMM
VOYAGES ON THE YUKON AND ITS TRIBUTARIES. New York, Scribner, 1917. 397p [BM BVaU LC OTP QMM
A WINTER CIRCUIT OF OUR ARCTIC COAST. A Narrative of a Journey with Dog-Sleds around the entire Arctic Coast of Alaska. New York, Scribner, 1920. 360p [BM BVaU LC OTP

Sullivan, Alan, 1868–1947
THE CYCLE OF THE NORTH. London, Dent, 1938. 180p [BM QMM

Sutherland, Rev. Alexander, 1833–1910
A SUMMER IN PRAIRIE LAND. Notes of a Tour through the North-West Territory. Toronto, Methodist Pub. House, 1881. 198p [BVaU LC NSWA OTU

Sutherland, John Campbell, 1860–1936
THE PROVINCE OF QUEBEC. Geographical and Social Studies. Montreal, Renouf, 1922. 157p [2nd rev. ed.: Toronto, Nelson, 1931. 126p] [BM BVaU LC NSWA OTP QMM
THE ROMANCE OF QUEBEC. Toronto, Gage, 1934. 246p [BM OLU

Talbot, Edward Allen, 1801–1839
FIVE YEARS' RESIDENCE IN THE CANADAS. ... London, Longmans, 1824. 2v [BM BVaU LC NSHD OTP QMM

Talbot, Thomas, fl. 1844–1882
NEWFOUNDLAND; or, a Letter Addressed to a Friend in Ireland ... with an Especial View to Emigration. London, Sampson, 1882. 67p [NSHP

Taylor, Henry, fl. 1819–1860
JOURNAL OF A TOUR FROM MONTREAL ... to the Eastern Townships. Quebec, Cowan, 1840. 84p [OTP

Thompson, David, 1770–1857
DAVID THOMPSON'S NARRATIVE OF HIS EXPLORATIONS IN WESTERN AMERICA 1784–1812. Ed. by J.B. Tyrrell. Toronto, Champlain Society, 1916. xcviii + 582p [BM BVaU LC NSHD OTU QMM

JOURNALS RELATING TO MONTANA AND ADJACENT REGIONS, 1808–1812. Ed. by
M. Catherine White. Missoula, Montana U. Press, 1950. 345p [BVaU OTU

NEW LIGHT ON THE EARLY HISTORY OF THE GREATER NORTHWEST. The Manu-
script Journals of Alexander Henry ... and of David Thompson ... 1799–1814.
Ed. by Elliott Coues. New York, Harper, 1897. 3v [BM BVaU NBFU OTU
QMM

Till, William, –1860

NEW BRUNSWICK, AS A HOME FOR EMIGRANTS. ... Saint John, Barnes, 1860. 25p
[OTP

Tobe, John H., 1907–

HUNZA. Adventures in a Land of Paradise. Toronto, McLeod, 1960. 646p

Tocque, Rev. Philip, 1814–1899

NEWFOUNDLAND: AS IT WAS, AND AS IT IS IN 1877. Toronto, Magurn, 1878. 511p
[BM BVaU LC NSHD OTP QMM

A PEEP AT UNCLE SAM'S FARM, WORKSHOP, FISHERIES, &c. Boston, Pierce, 1851.
229p [LC NSWA OKQ

WANDERING THOUGHTS; or, Solitary hours. London, Richardson, 1846. 387p
[BVaU NSHP OTP

Todd, Henry Cook, –1862

NOTES UPON CANADA AND THE UNITED STATES, from 1832 to 1840. ... By a
Traveller [pseud]. Toronto, Rogers & Thompson, 1840. 184p [Same main
title: ... in the year 1835. By a Traveller. Toronto, Coates, 1835. 95p —BVaU]
[BM LC OOA QMM

Tolboom, Wanda (Neill)

PEOPLE OF THE SNOW. Eskimos of Arctic Canada. New York, Coward-McCann,
1956. 96p

Tolfrey, Frederic

THE SPORTSMAN IN CANADA. London, Newby, 1845. 2v [BM LC NSWA OTU

Traill, Catharine Parr (Strickland), 1802–1899

THE BACKWOODS OF CANADA. Being Letters from the Wife of an Emigrant Officer.
Illustrative of the Domestic Economy of British America. London, Knight, 1836.
352p [Various editions. Editions of 1846 and 1849 precede above title with
CANADA AND THE OREGON, and add to subtitle: "To which is Appended an
Account of the Country of the Oregon."] [BM BVaU LC NSWA OTP QMM

CANADA AND THE OREGON. ... [See preceding title.]

THE CANADIAN EMIGRANT HOUSEKEEPER'S GUIDE. Toronto, Lovell & Gibson,
1862. 150p [Much the same as THE FEMALE EMIGRANT'S GUIDE.] [NSHD OTP

THE CANADIAN SETTLER'S GUIDE. Toronto, Old Countryman Office, 1855.
13 + 218 + 40p [Numerous editions. Also pub. under title: THE FEMALE
EMIGRANT'S GUIDE.] [BM BVaU LC NSWA OTP QMM

THE FEMALE EMIGRANT'S GUIDE, and Hints on Canadian Housekeeping. Toronto, Maclear, 1854. xi + 218 + 40p [Later editions pub. as: THE CANADIAN SETTLER'S GUIDE.] [BM BVaU OTU

Tranter, Mrs. Gladdis Joy, 1902–

LINK TO THE NORTH. London, Hodder, 1946. 255p [BM BVaU LC OTP QMM

PLOWING THE ARCTIC. Being an Account of the Voyage of the R.C.M.P. "St. Roch." Toronto, Longmans, 1945. 316p [BM BVaU LC NSHD OTP QMM

Trow, James, 1825–1892

MANITOBA AND NORTH WEST TERRITORIES. Letters. ... Ottawa, Dept. of Agriculture, 1878. 100p [BM BViPA LC OTP

A TRIP TO MANITOBA. Quebec, Marcotte, 1875. 86p [BVaU LC OTP

Tyre, Robert, 1908–

ALONG THE HIGHWAY. [Travel Tales ... from the Log of Galloping Gus, a Roving Reporter in Saskatchewan.] Regina, School Aids and Text Book Pub. Co., 1950. 124p [OONL

Tyrrell, James Williams, 1863–1945

ACROSS THE SUB-ARCTICS OF CANADA. Toronto, Briggs, 1897. 280p [BM BVaU LC NSWA OOA

Umfreville, Edward, fl. 1771–1790

NIPIGON TO WINNIPEG. Canoe Voyage ... in 1784. Ed. by R. Douglas. With Extracts from the Writings of other Early Travellers through the Region. Ottawa, Douglas, 1929. 65p [BM BVaU OTU

THE PRESENT STATE OF HUDSON'S BAY. ... London, Stalker, 1790. 226p [Also ed. with intro. and notes by W. Stewart Wallace. Toronto, Ryerson, 1954. xv + 122p] [BM BVaU LC NSWA OTP QMM

Vancouver, George, 1757–1798

A VOYAGE OF DISCOVERY TO THE NORTH PACIFIC OCEAN, AND ROUND THE WORLD. ... London, Robinson, 1798. 3v [BM BVaU NSWA OTP QMM

Waddington, Alfred Penderill, 1801–1872

OVERLAND ROUTE THROUGH BRITISH NORTH AMERICA. London, Longmans, 1868. 48p [BM BViPA LC OOA QMM

Wade, Mark Sweeten, 1858–1929

THE OVERLANDERS OF '62. Ed. by John Hosie. Victoria, Banfield, 1931. 174p [BM BVaU LC NSHD OTP QMM

Walker, Gertrude E.
ROMANTIC WINNIPEG. Winnipeg, Farmer's Advocate Press, 1937. 48p [2nd ed.: 1938. 68p] [OTU

Wallace, Frederick William, 1886–1958
UNDER SAIL IN THE LAST OF THE CLIPPERS. Glasgow, Brown, 1936. 251p [BM OTU

Wallace, William Stewart, 1884–1970
BY STAR AND COMPASS. Tales of the Explorers of Canada. Toronto, Oxford U. Press, 1922. 190p [BM BVaU LC NSHD OTU QMM

Walsh, William Emmett, 1868–
THE SOUTH OF FRANCE. Boston, Four Seas, 1928. 175p [LC QMM

Warman, Cy, 1855–1914
AT THE RAINBOW'S TIP. N.p., [1908?]. 15p [Issued by the General Passenger Department, Grand Trunk Railway. A description of the Prince Rupert area, B.C.] [NSHD

Warnock, Amelia Beers, 1878–1956
CANADIAN CITIES OF ROMANCE. By Katherine Hale [pseud]. Enl. ed. Toronto, McClelland, 1933. 240p [BM BVaU NSHD OTP
CANADIAN HOUSES OF ROMANCE. By Katherine Hale [pseud]. Toronto, Macmillan, 1926. 213p [BM BVaU NSHD OKQ
HISTORIC HOUSES OF CANADA. By Katherine Hale [pseud]. Toronto, Ryerson, 1952. 152p [An enl. and completely rev. ed. of the author's CANADIAN HOUSES OF ROMANCE, q.v.]
THE ROMANCE OF CANADIAN CITIES. Toronto, McClelland, 1922. 191p [Subsequently enl. and re-titled CANADIAN CITIES OF ROMANCE, q.v.] [OTU
THIS IS ONTARIO! By Katherine Hale [pseud]. Toronto, Ryerson, 1937. 241p [Rev. ed.: 1946. 246p] [BVaU OTU

Watkin, Edward William, 1819–1901
A TRIP TO THE UNITED STATES AND CANADA. In a Series of Letters. London, Smith, 1852. 149p [BM NSWA OTP

Watt, Gertrude Balmer (Hogg), 1879–1963
TOWN AND TRAIL. Edmonton, New Pub. Co., 1908. 85p [AEU BVaU LC OTU
A WOMAN IN THE WEST. Edmonton, News Pub. Co., 1907. 52p [MWP OTU

Watt, Madge Robertson
THE SOUTHMOST DISTRICTS, VANCOUVER ISLAND. Colwood, Metchosin, Sooke. Victoria, Colonist, 1910. 64p [BVaU

Weir, Arthur, 1864–1902
A CANUCK DOWN SOUTH. Montreal, Lovell, 1898. 182p [BVaU LC OTU

Wells, Kenneth McNeill, 1905–
CRUISING THE NORTH CHANNEL. Toronto, Kingswood House, 1960. xv + 232p
[Guide to the channel north of Manitoulin Island.]
CRUISING THE TRENT-SEVERN WATERWAY. Toronto, Kingswood House, 1959.
120p
THE HERITAGE OF CANADA IN COLOUR. London, Batsford, 1960. 64p

Westbury, George H.
MISADVENTURES OF A WORKING HOBO IN CANADA. London, Routledge, 1930.
172p [BM BVaU LC NBFU OTU

Wetherell, James Elgin, 1851–1940
FIELDS OF FAME IN ENGLAND AND SCOTLAND. Toronto, Macmillan, 1915. 171p
[BM NSHD OTU QMM
OVER THE SEA. A Summer Trip to Britain. Strathroy, Ont., Evans, 1892. 120p
[NSWA OTU
STRANGE CORNERS OF THE WORLD. New York, Nelson, 1927. 244p [LC OTU
QMM

Whishaw, Lorna (Hall)
AS FAR AS YOU'LL TAKE ME. New York, Dodd Mead, 1958. 216p [Account of a
hitchhiking trip from Edmonton to Alaska.]

Wife of a British Officer ... , The
HENRY; or, The Juvenile Traveller. ... By the Wife of a British Officer, Resident in
Canada [pseud]. London, Simpkin Marshall, 1836. 136p [BM OOA

Wilcox, Elmer Naman, 1908–
GRAND MANAN, NEW BRUNSWICK, CANADA. Ed. by E.N. Wilcox and L.K. Ingersoll.
3rd ed. Grand Manan, Board of Trade, 1959. 40p

Willison, Marjory (MacMurchy), –1938
VICTORIA, B.C., CITY OF ENCHANTMENT IN CANADA'S EVERGREEN PLAYGROUND.
Victoria, Empress Hotel, 1933. 31p [BVaU OTU

Wilson, Clifford Parnell, 1902–
THE NEW NORTH IN PICTURES. Ed. by ——. Toronto, Ryerson, 1947. 223p
[BViPA LC OTP QMM
NORTH OF 55°. Canada from the 55th Parallel to the Pole. Ed. by ——. Toronto,
Ryerson, 1954. 190p
PAGEANT OF THE NORTH. A Photographic Adventure into Canada's Northland.
Ed. by ——. Toronto, Ryerson, 1957. 175p

Withrow, Rev. William Henry, 1839–1908
A CANADIAN IN EUROPE. Being Sketches of Travel in France, Switzerland,
Germany, Holland, and Belgium, Great Britain, and Ireland. Toronto, Briggs,
1881. 376p [BVaU NBFU OTU QMM

CHINA AND ITS PEOPLE. Toronto, Briggs, 1894. 304p [OTP
OUR OWN COUNTRY. Canada, Scenic and Descriptive. Toronto, Briggs, 1889. 608p
[BM BVaU LC MWU NSWA OTU

Wix, Rev. Edward, 1802–1866
SIX MONTHS OF A NEWFOUNDLAND MISSIONARY'S JOURNAL. London, Smith
Elder, 1836. 264p [BM BVaU LC NSWA OTU QMM

Woodcock, George, 1912–
RAVENS AND PROPHETS. An Account of Journeys in British Columbia, Alberta,
and Southern Alaska. London, Wingate, 1952. 244p
TO THE CITY OF THE DEAD. An Account of Travels in Mexico. London, Faber
& Faber, 1957. 271p

Work, John, 1792–1861
FUR BRIGADE TO THE BONAVENTURA. John Work's California Expedition,
1832–1833, for the Hudson's Bay Company. Ed. by Alice Bay Maloney. ...
San Francisco, California Historical Soc., 1945. xxii + 112p [BVaU NBFU LC
THE JOURNAL OF JOHN WORK ... during his Expedition from Vancouver to the
Flatheads and Blackfeet of the Pacific Northwest. Ed., and with an Account of
the Fur Trade in the Northwest, and Life of Work by William S. Lewis and
Paul C. Phillips. Cleveland, Ohio, Clark, 1923. 209p [BM BVaU LC NBFU
OKQ
THE JOURNAL OF JOHN WORK, January to October, 1835. ... Ed. by Henry
Drummond Dee. Victoria, Banfield, 1945. 98p [BVaU LC OOA

Wright, Esther Isabell (Clark), 1895–
FUNDY PARK 1950. N.p., Author, 1950. 8p [OONL

Yeigh, Frank, 1861–1935
THROUGH THE HEART OF CANADA. Toronto, Frowde, 1910. 319p [BM BVaU
LC NSWA OTU

Young, Rev. Egerton Ryerson, 1840–1909
BY CANOE AND DOG TRAIN AMONG THE CREE AND SALTEAUX INDIANS. Toronto,
Briggs, 1890. 267p [BM BVaU LC NSWA OTU QMM
INDIAN LIFE IN THE GREAT NORTHWEST. London, Partridge, 1901. 126p [BM
BVaU LC OTU QMSS
MY DOGS IN THE NORTHLAND. New York, Revell, 1902. 285p [BM BVaU LC
NSHD OTU
ON THE INDIAN TRAIL. Stories of Missionary Work among the Cree and Salteaux
Indians. New York, Revell, 1897. 214p [BM BVaU LC NSHD OTU QMBM

INDEXES

INDEX OF ANONYMOUS TITLES

(The dates in parentheses are dates of publication. Cross-references are to the General Index which follows.)

ADDRESS TO THE LIEGE MEN OF EVERY BRITISH COLONY, AN (1822) 8
ADOPTED DAUGHTER, THE; or, The Trials of Sabra (1858) 238
ANDY O'HARA; or, The Child of Promise (1861). *See* De Mille, James
ANNAPOLIS-ROYAL [Poem] (1788). *See* Viets, Rev. Roger
ANONYMOUS POEMS (1889). *See* Black, Hibbert Crane

BEAUTIES OF BELLEVILLE, THE (n.d.). *See* Breeze, James T.
BIOGRAPHICAL SKETCHES AND REVIEW. First Presbyterian Church in Toronto and
    Knox Church, 1820–1890. (1890) *See* Parsons, Henry M.
BLAZING A NEW TRAIL (1920). *See* Allison, William Talbot
BRIEF BIOGRAPHICAL SKETCH OF THE HON. ROBERT CHARLES WILKINS, A (1866)
    457

CANADA. A Descriptive Poem, written at Quebec, 1805 ... (1806). *See* Bayley,
    Cornwall
CANADA. A Satire. By One of her Sons (18–?) 8
CANADIAN BIOGRAPHICAL DICTIONARY AND PORTRAIT GALLERY OF EMINENT
    AND SELF-MADE MEN, THE. Quebec and Maritime Provinces Volume (1880) 457
CANADIAN CANTICLES [A Collection of 127 Poems] (1912?) 8
CANADIAN NAVY, THE (n.d.). *See* Bowen, Minnie Hallowell
CANADIAN SUBALTERN, A (1917) [a later ed. of A SUNNY SUBALTERN]. *See* Gray,
    William
CANADIAN TEMPERANCE MINSTREL, THE. Being a Collection of Hymns, Songs,
    and Poetry ... (1842) 8
CANADIAN WHO'S WHO, THE (1910) 457
CARLETON ELECTION, THE; or, The Tale of a Bytown Ram. An Epic Poem ... (1832) 8
CEDAR CREEK. A Tale of Canadian Life (1902) [a later ed. of the following title]
CEDAR CREEK. From the Shanty to the Settlement (1863). *See* Walshe, Elizabeth Hely
CHARIVARI, THE; or, Canadian Poetics. A Tale after the Manner of Beppo (1824).
    See Adams, Levi
CHRISTIAN'S WEDDING RING, THE. Containing Five Letters ... (1874). *See* Porter, Jane
CHRISTIE REDFERN'S TROUBLES (1866, etc.). *See* Robertson, Margaret Murray
CLAIMS OF THE CHURCHMEN & DISSENTERS OF UPPER CANADA ... (1828). *See*
    Ryerson, Adolphus Egerton
CITY OF LONDON, ONTARIO, CANADA. The Pioneer Period and the London of To-day
    (1897). *See* Bremner, Archibald
CITY OF TORONTO, THE (1860). *See* Hodgins, John George

GOLD AND SILVER JUBILEE, Sault Ste Marie, Ont. (1938). *See* Cowan, Hugh

GOODMAN. A Family History (1916). *See* Goodman, Alfred Edwin

HANDBOOK TO THE CITY OF MONTREAL. With Carnival Supplement (1884). *See*
Dawson, Samuel Edward

HART ALMERRIN MASSEY. Pioneer Farmer, Farm Implement Manufacturer ... (1896).
See Massey, Hart Almerrin

HEARTS OF GOLD. Being Chronicles of Heroism in Canadian History (1915) 457

HELENA'S HOUSEHOLD. A Tale of Rome in the First Century (1867, etc.). *See*
De Mille, James

HELEN'S POEMS (1944). *See* Moore, Helen

HISTORICAL SKETCH OF THE PARISH OF WILMOT, 1828–1913 ... (1913). *See*
Fox, Charles James

H.M.S. "PARLIAMENT"; or, The Lady who Loved a Government Clerk (1880). *See*
Fuller, William Henry

HOLIDAY TRIP, MONTREAL TO VICTORIA AND RETURN, A (1888?). *See*
Carmichael, Rev. James

HONOURABLE ELIJAH LEONARD, THE. A Memoir (1894?). *See* Leonard, Elijah

HOURS OF CHILDHOOD, AND OTHER POEMS (1820). *See* Bowman, Ariel

HOUSE OF THE GALLERY. ... Official Correspondence ... relative to the Construction
of the Imperial, Lunar, Grand, Mid-Air, Lunatic Government Railway ... (1875) 238

HUNTED OUTLAW, THE; or, Donald Morrison the Canadian Rob Roy (1889) 238

HUNTING ADVENTURES IN UTOPIA (1880) 8

HYMNS FOR SPECIAL SERVICES (1868) 8

IMPRESSIONS OF THE WEST AND SOUTH DURING A SIX WEEKS' HOLIDAY (1858). *See*
Kingsford, William

IN MEMORIAM: FREDERICK HERVEY JOHN BRIGSTOCKE ... (1899). *See* Murray,
Frances Elizabeth

IN MEMORIAM: HENRY EDWARD BAINES, 1840–1866 (1866?). *See* Baines, Henry Edward

INDIRECT DOMESTIC INFLUENCE; or, Nova Scotia as it was, as it is, and as it may be
... (1855). *See* Godfrey, L.M.

INNER SHRINE, THE. A Novel of Today (1909). *See* King, Basil

INTERESTING ACCOUNT ... OF THE CELEBRATED HORDE OF ROBBERS KNOWN AS
THE MARKHAM GANG, AN (1846) 650

JAMES STANLEY McLEAN. An Appreciation by a Group of his Friends (1957) 457

JOHN WHEELER'S TWO UNCLES; or, Launching into Life (1860?). *See* De Mille, James

JOHNNY CRAPAUD. A Legend of Bygone Days ... (1851) 8

JUDGEMENTS OF THE CANADIAN BISHOPS ON ... TRINITY COLLEGE ... , THE (1863) 756

KHAN'S BOOK OF VERSE, THE (1925). *See* Kernighan, Robert Kirkland

KIDNAPPERS, THE. A Tragico-Comical Melodrama in Ten Acts (1867?). *See* Kerr,
William Hastings

GENERAL INDEX OF NAMES, INITIALS AND PSEUDONYMS

Harrington, Richard Walter (1911–) 964
Harris, Bertha Carr. *See* Carr-Harris, Bertha Hannah (Wright)
Harris, Mrs. C.W. *See* Harris, Mrs. Carrie Jenkins
Harris, Mrs. Carrie Jenkins (–1903) 307
Harris, Christie Lucy (Irwin) (1907–) 308
Harris, Edward William (1832–1925) 687, 873
Harris, Eric. *See* Harris, Walter Eric
Harris, John 791, 921
Harris, John Norman (1915–1964) 512
Harris, Rev. Joseph Hemington (1800–1881) 512, 791
Harris, Lawren Stewart (1885–1970) 86, 617
Harris, Martha Douglas (1854–1933) 874
Harris, Reginald Vanderbilt (1881–) 512, 687, 791
Harris, Robert (1849–1919) 86
Harris, Walter Eric (1889–) 436, 617
Harris, William Critchlow 86
Harris, Rev. William Richard (1847–1923) 687, 791, 921
Harrison, Charles Yale (1898–1954) 308, 512
Harrison, Edna Kent 86
Harrison, Elizabeth 86
Harrison, Stanley Gordon (1889–) 86
Harrison, Susie Frances (Riley) (1859–1935) 86, 308, 437
Harrold, Ernest William (1889–1945) 512
Harshaw, Augusta F. 86
Hart, Adolphus Mordecai (1813–1879) 308
Hart, Arthur Daniel 874
Hart, George Edward 687
Hart, Gerald Ephraim (1849–1936) 678
Hart, Gordon (pseud). *See* Hensley, Sophia Margaret (Almon)
Hart, Julia Catherine (Beckwith) (1796–1867) 308
Hart, Lewis Alexander (1847–) 791
Hart, Margaret Janet (McPhee) (1867–1941) 512
Hart, Percy William Edward (1870–) 308
Hart, Rev. William Edward (1907–) 513
Hart, Walter T. (1868–1948) 792
Hart-McHarg, William F.R. (1869–1915) 964
Hartley, Rev. G.A. 792
Hartley, Rev. H.A.S. 513, 921
Hartwell, George E. 513
Harvey, Arthur (1834–1905) 687
Harvey, Athelstan George (1884–1950) 513
Harvey, Daniel Cobb (1886–) 513, 687, 874, 964. *See also* Howe, Joseph

Harvey, Emeline Daggett 87, 308
Harvey, Rev. Moses (1820–1901) 618, 687, 792, 921, 964
Harvey, Peggy (1884–) 87
Harvey, Ruth (Walker) (1900–) 513
Harvey, William Earl (1898–) 87, 308, 618
Harvie, Fred W. 688
Haskins, James (1805–1845) 87
Hassard, Albert Richard (1873–1940) 513, 874
Hathaway, Ann (1848–) 513
Hathaway, Ernest Jackson (1871–1930) 513, 688, 874
Hatheway, Calvin L. (1796–1866) 688
Hatheway, Warren Franklin (1850–1923) 87, 224, 618
Hatt, Daniel Elisha (1869–1942) 87
Hatzan, Alexander Leon (1864–) 87, 513
Haughton, William 87
Haultain, Theodore Arnold (1857–1941) 87, 513, 618, 688
Haverson, James Percival (1880–) 87
Haw, Rev. William 514
Hawarden, Sask. Bethlehem Scandinavian Lutheran Church. Ladies' Aid 688
Hawarden, Sask. Homemakers' Club 688
Haweis, Lionel Thomas Joy (1870–1942) 88
Hawkes, Arthur (1871–1933) 618. *See also* Hanna, David Blythe and Trotter, Beecham
Hawkes, John (1851–1931) 688
Hawkins, Alfred (1802?–1854) 688
Hawkins, Ernest (1802–1868) 792
Hawley, William Fitz (1804–1855) 88
Hawthorn, Harry Bertram (1910–) 688
Hawthorne, Marx (pseud). *See* Greenwood, A.E.
Hay, George Upham (1843–1913) 514
Haydon, Andrew (1867–1932) 514, 688
Hayes, Catherine E. (Simpson) (1852–1943) 88, 224, 309, 688
Hayes, E.H. 618
Hayes, J. Finley (pseud). *See* Hayes, John Francis (1904–)
Hayes, John Francis (1904–) 309
Hayes, Kate E. *See* Hayes, Catherine E. (Simpson)
Hayhurst, Thomas W. *See* Jones, Charles Hugh L.
Hayman, Robert (1579?–1631?) 88
Haynes, James 88
Haynes, Laura E. (Nixon) (1876–) 88
Hayward, Mrs. Caroline 88
Hazel, Emily (1882–1955) 88

Low, Albert Peter (1861–1942) 971
Low, David (1913–   ) 702
Low, Rev. George Jacobs (1836–1906)
625, 806, 881
Low, May (Austin) (1863–   ) 118, 330
Low, Mildred (–1963) 119
Lowe, John (1899–1960) 806
Lower, Arthur Reginald Marsden (1889–   )
533, 882
Lowrey, David 119
Lowrey, Harold C. (1886–   ) 330
Lowry, Malcolm (1909–1957) 330
Lowry-Calder, Sarah Isabell 119
Lowther, Armstrong John (1880–1948)
119
Loyal Janet (pseud). See Jack, Annie L. (Hayr)
Loyal Orange Association of British America.
Committee on Orange History 882
Lucas, Rev. Daniel Vannorman (1834–1911)
882, 971
Lucas, Frederick C. 702
Luckyj, George Stephen Nestor (1919–   )
927
Ludditt, Alfred William (1907–   ) 702
Lugrin, Charles Henry (1846–1917) 702,
971
Lugrin, Nellie de Bertrand (1874–   ) 703,
971
Lumsden, James 806, 882
Lund, Charles Edward (1850–   ) 119
Lund, Captain T. 330
Lundar, Man. 703
Lunenburg, N.S. Methodist Church 806
Luxton, Rev. George Nasmith (1901–   ) 806
Luxton, Mary Clendinning O'Donnell
(Martin) (1879–   ) 119
Lyall, Rev. William (1811–1890) 807
Lyle-Smythe, Alan (1914–   ) 330, 882,
Lynch, Norman C. 119
Lynch-Staunton, Betty (Frankish) (1895–   )
807
Lynch-Staunton, Mrs. Emma (1885–1949) 703
Lyons, Chester Peter (1915–   ) 703, 971
Lysenko, Vera 330, 882
Lytle, Mrs. W.J.A. 119

M., A. 119
M., A.L.O. (pseud). See Frank, Mrs. M.J.
M., A.M. See Machar, Agnes Maule
M., Mrs. E.M. 534
M., F. 119
M., F.R. See Moore, Francis
M., H.R. 807
M., J. See Marsden, Rev. Joshua
M., M.E. See McCulloch, Mrs. Mercy E.
M., Miss R.E. See Leprohon, Rosanna
Eleanor (Mullins)

M., W. 807
M., W.I. See Morse, William Inglis
M., W.M. See MacKeracher, William Mackay
Mabee, Mrs. George E. See Howey, Mrs.
Florence R.
McAleer, George (1845–   ) 534, 625,
928
MacAlister, Alexander Wardrope Greenshields
(1876–   ) 534
McAlister, George Alexander 534
McAlister, Lottie (Plewes) (1865–   ) 331
McAllister, George Clinton (1804–1842) 534
McAllister, Ronald Nelson (1917–   ) 534
McAlpine, Mrs. Jennie 331
McAlpine, Thomas H.. 971
McAra, Peter (1862–1949) 534
McAree, John Verner (1876–1958) 534,
625
McArthur, Peter (1866–1924) 119, 331,
534, 625, 928
Macaulay, R.H.H. 971
Macauley, John 882
MacBeath, George Boyd (1924–   ) 703
Macbeth, John Douglas 534
Macbeth, Madge Hamilton (Lyons) (1878–
1965) 331, 440, 535, 882, 972
MacBeth, Malcolm (1868–   ) 703
McBeth, Margaret Elliot 807
MacBeth, Rev. Roderick George (1858–
1934) 535, 703, 807, 882
MacBride, Morrison Mann (1877–1938)
119
McBride, Robert 119
MacCabe, Cameron (pseud). See Borne-
mann, Ernst Wilhelm Julius
McCaffrey, Mary Ann Agnes. See Mary
Francis of Jesus, Sister
McCague, John Joseph E. (1899–   ) 703
McCaig, Donald (1832–1905) 120
McCall, Delbert Thomas (1871–   ) 535
McCall, Oswald Walter Samuel (1885–   )
120, 807
McCall. Ralph Lewis (1925–   ) 703
MacCallum, Duncan Campbell 626
McCallum, John 120
MacCallum, Reid (1897–1949) 928
McCann, Rev. Leonard Albert (1908–   ) 807
McCarroll, James (1815–1896) 120, 331,
626
McCarthy, Eugene 626
McCarthy, Pearl (1895–   ) 535
McCaskill, Rev. John James (1875–   ) 535
McCaskill, Kenneth 807
McCaughey, Lloyd 331
McCaul, Rev. John (1807–1887) 808,
928